Contents

OFFICIAL
1992 NCAA®
FOOTBALL

NATIONAL COLLEGIATE ATHLETIC ASSOCIATION

[ISSN 0735-5475]

THE NATIONAL COLLEGIATE ATHLETIC ASSOCIATION
6201 College Boulevard
Overland Park, Kansas 66211-2422
913/339-1906
July 1992

Compiled By: Richard M. Campbell, *Assistant Statistics Coordinator;* John D. Painter, *Assistant Statistics Coordinator;* Sean W. Straziscar, *Assistant Statistics Coordinator;* James M. Van Valkenburg, *Director of Statistics.*

Edited By: J. Gregory Summers, *Assistant Director of Publishing.*

Designed By: Victor M. Royal, *Director of Graphics.*

Cover Photography By: *Young Company, Kansas City, Missouri.*

DIVISION I-A RECORDS

San Diego State running back Marshall Faulk had one of the most remarkable freshman seasons ever in 1991. He led Division I-A in both scoring (15.6 points per game) and rushing (158.8 yards per game),

Under a three-division reorganization plan adopted by the special NCAA Convention of August 1973, teams classified major-college in football on August 1, 1973, were placed in Division I. College-division teams were divided into Division II and Division III. At the NCAA Convention of January 1978, Division I was divided into Division I-A and Division I-AA for football only.

From 1937, when official national statistics rankings began, through 1969, individual rankings were by totals. Beginning in 1970, most season individual rankings were by per-game averages. In total offense, rushing and scoring, it is yards or points per game; in receiving, catches per game and yards per game; in interceptions, catches per game; and in punt and kickoff returns, yards per return. Punting always has been by average, and all team rankings have been per game. Beginning in 1979, passers were rated in all divisions on Efficiency Rating Points, which are derived from a formula that compares passers to the national averages for 14 seasons of two-platoon Division I football starting with the 1965 season. One hundred points equals the 14-year averages for all players in Division I. Those averages break down to 6.29 yards per attempt, 47.14 percent completions, 3.97 percent touchdown passes and 6.54 percent interceptions. The formula assumes that touchdowns are as good as interceptions are bad; therefore, these two figures offset each other for the average player. To determine **Efficiency Rating Points**, multiply a passer's yards per attempt by 8.4, add his completion percentage, add his touchdown percentage times 3.3, then subtract his interception percentage times two.

Passers must have a minimum of 15 attempts per game to determine rating points because fewer attempts could allow a player to win the championship with fewer than 100 attempts in a season. A passer must play in at least 75 percent of his team's games to qualify for the rankings (e.g., a player on a team with a nine-game season could qualify by playing in seven games; thus, a passer with 105 attempts could qualify for the national rankings).

All individual and team records and rankings include regular-season games only. Career records of other players who played in both Division I and Divisions II or III—such as Grambling's Doug Williams—will be found where they played the majority of their career. Williams played three of his four seasons in Division II; thus, his career records are in the Division II section.

Statistics in some team categories were not tabulated until the advent of the computerized statistics program in 1966. The records listed in those categories begin with the 1966 season and are so indicated.

In 1954, the regular-season schedule was limited to a maximum of 10 games, and in 1970, to a limit of 11 games, excluding postseason competition.

A player whose career includes statistics for parts of five seasons (or an active player who will have five seasons) because he was granted an additional season of competition for reasons of hardship (Bylaw 14.2.5) or a freshman redshirt (Bylaw 14.2.1) are denoted by [$].

Collegiate Records

Collegiate records—individual and team, game, season, and career—are determined by comparing the Division I-A record with the Divisions I-AA, II and III records in comparable categories. The only exceptions are collegiate career records held by players who played half of their careers in each division (such as Dennis Shaw of San Diego State, Howard Stevens of Louisville and Randolph-Macon, and Tom Ehrhardt of LIU-C. W. Post and Rhode Island). For individual collegiate career leaders, see page 263.

COLLEGE FOOTBALL'S FIRST GAME

November 6, 1869

It all started on a cold day. There was, in fact, a threat of snow in the air that November day when a team of 25 and some faithful followers boarded a train in Princeton for New Brunswick, New Jersey. There, starting at 3 o'clock after a leisurely dinner, some billiards and some girl-watching, Rutgers and Princeton played the first game of intercollegiate football. At that point, the history of football began.

The football that was played that day, on a field where the Rutgers gymnasium now stands, bore no resemblance to the football of today. It was, essentially, soccer. There were 25 men on a side. There was no running with the ball, or throwing it. It had to be kicked or headed. Scoring was done by kicking the ball through the opponent's goal and, according to the rules, "goals must be eight paces," presumably eight yards between two posts stuck in the ground. After each goal (or game, as it was called), the teams changed sides. Time was not important, except in the case of darkness. A game was decided by the number of goals kicked. In this case, the one kicking six first was the winner. The field was 120 yards long and 75 yards wide, a vacant lot with a wooden fence on one side across from the old Rutgers campus.

Accounts of this game are rather hazy, as might be expected. The best is from the Rutgers *Targum,* the student paper, and it speaks, somewhat dramatically, of "grim men, silently stripping" before the kickoff. What they stripped to it doesn't say, but it wasn't much. The players simply took off their hats, coats and vests, and they were ready. No uniforms. The only color was provided by scarlet turbans the Rutgers boys wore on their heads.

As was frequently the case in those days, teams had their own rules. William S. Gummere, the Princeton captain later to become chief justice of the New Jersey Supreme Court, acceded to Rutgers captain William Leggett, and the game was played under Rutgers rules. This was one of the few juridical mistakes Mr. Gummere ever made. Rutgers won the game, 6 goals to 4, after Princeton had overcome an early deficit to draw even at 4-all.

However, another game was played later that month at Princeton, this one under Princeton rules, which permitted free kicks if anyone caught the ball on the fly or the first bounce. Unaccustomed to this sort of business, Rutgers was shut out, 8-0.

Account by Len Elliott, sports editor, The Newark News, 1939-1968, as printed in One Hundred Years of Princeton Football 1869-1969, William C. Stryker ('50), editor. Reprinted from the 1991 Princeton University football media guide.

INDIVIDUAL RECORDS

TOTAL OFFENSE
(Rushing Plus Passing)

Most Plays

Quarter
35—Mike Romo, Southern Methodist vs. Rice, Nov. 10, 1990 (4th; 31 passes, 4 rushes); Chris Rowland, Washington vs. California, Oct. 6, 1973 (4th; 31 passes, 4 rushes)

Half
53—Matt Vogler, Texas Christian vs. Houston, Nov. 3, 1990 (2nd; 47 passes, 6 rushes)

Game
94—Matt Vogler, Texas Christian vs. Houston, Nov. 3, 1990 (696 yards)

Season
704—David Klingler, Houston, 1990 (5,221 yards)

2 Yrs
1,294—David Klingler, Houston, 1990-91 (8,447 yards)

3 Yrs
1,548—Ty Detmer, Brigham Young, 1988-91 (13,456 yards)

Career
(4 yrs.) 1,795—Ty Detmer, Brigham Young, 1988-91 (14,665 yards)

Most Plays Per Game

Season
64.0—David Klingler, Houston, 1990 (704 in 11)

2 Yrs
61.6—David Klingler, Houston, 1990-91 (1,294 in 21)

Career
48.5—Doug Gaynor, Long Beach St., 1984-85 (1,067 in 22)

Most Plays by a Freshman

Game
76—Sandy Schwab, Northwestern vs. Michigan, Oct. 23, 1982 (431 yards)

Season
504—Sandy Schwab, Northwestern, 1982 (2,555 yards)
Also holds per-game record at 45.8 (504 in 11)

Most Yards Gained

Quarter
340—Andre Ware, Houston vs. Southern Methodist, Oct. 21, 1989 (2nd)

Half
510—Andre Ware, Houston vs. Southern Methodist, Oct. 21, 1989 (1st)

Game
732—David Klingler, Houston vs. Arizona St., Dec. 2, 1990 (716 passing, 16 rushing)

Season
5,221—David Klingler, Houston, 1990 (81 rushing, 5,140 passing)

2 Yrs
9,455—Ty Detmer, Brigham Young, 1989-90 (-293 rushing, 9,748 passing)

3 Yrs
10,664—Ty Detmer, Brigham Young, 1988-90 (-336 rushing, 11,000 passing)

Career
(4 yrs.) 14,665—Ty Detmer, Brigham Young, 1988-91 (-366 rushing, 15,031 passing)

Most Yards Gained Per Game

Season
474.6—David Klingler, Houston, 1990 (5,221 in 11)

2 Yrs
402.2—David Klingler, Houston, 1990-91 (8,447 in 21)

Career
318.8—Ty Detmer, Brigham Young, 1988-91 (14,665 in 46)

Most Yards Gained, First Two Seasons
6,710—Doug Gaynor, Long Beach St., 1984-85
Also holds per-game record at 305.0

Most Seasons Gaining 4,000 Yards or More
3—Ty Detmer, Brigham Young, 1989-91

Most Seasons Gaining 3,000 Yards or More
3—Ty Detmer, Brigham Young, 1989-91

Most Seasons Gaining 2,500 Yards or More
3—Ty Detmer, Brigham Young, 1989-91; Shawn Moore, Virginia, 1988-90; Erik Wilhelm, Oregon St., 1986-88; Brian McClure, Bowling Green, 1983-85; Randall Cunningham, Nevada-Las Vegas, 1982-84; Doug Flutie, Boston College, 1982-84; John Elway, Stanford, 1980-82

Most Yards Gained by a Freshman

Game
458—Bob Hoernschemeyer, Indiana vs. Nebraska, Oct. 9, 1943 (37 plays)

Season
2,975—Todd Ellis, South Caro., 1986 (436 plays)
Also holds per-game record at 270.5

Most Yards Gained by a Sophomore

Game
625—Scott Mitchell, Utah vs. Air Force, Oct. 15, 1988 (631 passing, -6 rushing)

Season
4,433—Ty Detmer, Brigham Young, 1989 (12 games, 497 plays)
Per-game record—390.8, Scott Mitchell, Utah, 1988

Most Yards Gained in First Game of Career
483—Billy Stevens, UTEP vs. North Texas, Sept. 18, 1965

Most Yards Gained, Two, Three and Four Consecutive Games

2 Games
1,310—David Klingler, Houston, 1990 (578 vs. Eastern Wash., Nov. 17; 732 vs. Arizona St., Dec. 2)

3 Games
1,651—David Klingler, Houston, 1990 (341 vs. Texas, Nov. 10; 578 vs. Eastern Wash., Nov. 17; 732 vs. Arizona St., Dec. 2)

4 Games
2,276—David Klingler, Houston, 1990 (625 vs. Texas Christian, Nov. 3; 341 vs. Texas, Nov. 10; 578 vs. Eastern Wash., Nov. 17; 732 vs. Arizona St., Dec. 2)

8

Most Games Gaining 300 Yards or More
Season
12—Ty Detmer, Brigham Young, 1990
Career
33—Ty Detmer, Brigham Young, 1988-91

Most Consecutive Games Gaining 300 Yards or More
Season
12—Ty Detmer, Brigham Young, 1990
Career
19—Ty Detmer, Brigham Young, 1989-90

Most Games Gaining 400 Yards or More
Season
9—David Klingler, Houston, 1990
Career
13—Ty Detmer, Brigham Young, 1988-91

Most Consecutive Games Gaining 400 Yards or More
Season
5—Ty Detmer, Brigham Young, 1990
Also holds career record at 5

Most Yards Gained Against One Opponent
Career
1,483—Ty Detmer, Brigham Young vs. San Diego St., 1988-91

Most Yards Gained Per Game Against One Opponent
Career
(Min. 3 games) 383.7—Gary Schofield, Wake Forest vs. Maryland, 1981-83 (1,151 yards)
(Min. 4 games) 370.8—Ty Detmer, Brigham Young vs. San Diego St., 1988-91 (1,483 yards)

Most Yards Gained by Two Opposing Players
Game
1,321—Matt Vogler, Texas Christian (696) & David Klingler, Houston (625), Nov. 3, 1990

Gaining 1,000 Yards Rushing and 1,000 Yards Passing
Season
Michael Carter (QB), Hawaii, 1991 (1,092 rushing, 1,172 passing); Brian Mitchell (QB), Southwestern La., 1989 (1,311 rushing, 1,966 passing); Dee Dowis (QB), Air Force, 1989 (1,286 rushing, 1,285 passing); Darian Hagan (QB), Colorado, 1989 (1,004 rushing, 1,002 passing); Bart Weiss (QB), Air Force, 1985 (1,032 rushing, 1,449 passing); Reggie Collier (QB), Southern Miss., 1981 (1,005 rushing, 1,004 passing); Johnny Bright (HB), Drake, 1950 (1,232 rushing, 1,168 passing)

A Quarterback Gaining 2,000 Yards Rushing and 4,000 Yards Passing
Career
Major Harris, West Va., 1987-89 (2,030 rushing, 4,834 passing); Brian Mitchell, Southwestern La., 1986-89 (3,335 rushing, 5,447 passing); Rickey Foggie, Minnesota, 1984-87 (2,038 rushing, 4,903 passing); John Bond, Mississippi St., 1980-83 (2,280 rushing, 4,621 passing); Prince McJunkins, Wichita St., 1979-82 (2,047 rushing, 4,544 passing)

A Quarterback Gaining 300 Yards Passing and 100 Yards Rushing
Game
Donald Douglas, Houston vs. Southern Methodist, Oct. 19, 1991 (319 passing, 103 rushing)

A Quarterback Gaining 200 Yards Rushing and 200 Yards Passing
Game
Brian Mitchell, Southwestern La. vs. Colorado St., Nov. 21, 1987 (271 rushing, 205 passing); Steve Gage, Tulsa vs. New Mexico, Nov. 8, 1986 (212 rushing, 209 passing); Reds Bagnell, Pennsylvania vs. Dartmouth, Oct. 14, 1950 (214 rushing, 276 passing)

Teams Having a 3,000-Yard Passer, 1,000-Yard Rusher and 1,000-Yard Receiver in the Same Year
4—Pacific (Cal.), 1991 (Troy Kopp [3,767 passer], Aaron Turner [1,604 receiver] and Ryan Benjamin [1,581 rusher]); Houston, 1989 (Andre Ware [4,699 passer], Manny Hazard [1,689 receiver] and Chuck Weatherspoon [1,146 rusher]); Colorado St., 1983 (Terry Nugent [3,319 passer], Jeff Champine [1,002 receiver] and Steve Bartalo [1,113 rusher]); Southern Methodist, 1968 (Chuck Hixson [3,103 passer], Jerry LeVias [1,131 receiver] and Mike Richardson [1,034 rusher])

Highest Average Gain Per Play
Game
(Min. 37-48 plays) 12.76—Mike Perez, San Jose St. vs. Pacific (Cal.), Oct. 25, 1986 (42 for 536)
(Min. 63 plays) 9.92—David Klingler, Houston vs. Texas Christian, Nov. 3, 1990 (63 for 625)
Season
(Min. 3,000 yards) 8.92—Ty Detmer, Brigham Young, 1989 (497 for 4,433)
Career
(Min. 7,500 yards) 8.17—Ty Detmer, Brigham Young, 1988-91 (1,795 for 14,665)

Most Touchdowns Responsible For (TDs Scored and Passed For)
Game
11—David Klingler, Houston vs. Eastern Wash., Nov. 17, 1990 (passed for 11)
Season
55—David Klingler, Houston, 1990 (scored 1, passed for 54)
2 Yrs
85—David Klingler, Houston, 1990-91 (scored 2, passed for 83)
3 Yrs
122—Ty Detmer, Brigham Young, 1989-91 (scored 14, passed for 108)
Career
135—Ty Detmer, Brigham Young, 1988-91 (scored 14, passed for 121)

Most Touchdowns Responsible For Per Game
Season
5.0—David Klingler, Houston, 1990 (55 in 11)
2 Yrs
4.05—David Klingler, Houston, 1990-91 (85 in 21)
3 Yrs
3.39—Ty Detmer, Brigham Young, 1989-91 (122 in 36)
Career
2.93—Ty Detmer, Brigham Young, 1988-91 (135 in 46)
Collegiate record—3.60, Dennis Shaw, San Diego St., 1968-69 (72 in 20)

Most Points Responsible For (Points Scored and Passed For)

Game
66—David Klingler, Houston vs. Eastern Wash., Nov. 17, 1990 (passed for 11 TDs)

Season
334—David Klingler, Houston, 1990 (scored 1 TD, passed for 54 TDs, accounted for 2 two-point conversions)

2 Yrs
514—David Klingler, Houston, 1990-91 (scored 2 TDs, passed for 83 TDs, accounted for 2 two-point conversions)

3 Yrs
582—Ty Detmer, Brigham Young, 1988-90 (scored 10 TDs, passed for 86 TDs, accounted for 3 two-point conversions)

Career
820—Ty Detmer, Brigham Young, 1988-91 (scored 14 TDs, passed for 121 TDs, accounted for 5 two-point conversions)

Most Points Responsible For Per Game

Season
30.4—David Klingler, Houston, 1990 (334 in 11)

2 Yrs
22.8—Jim McMahon, Brigham Young, 1980-81 (502 in 22)

3 Yrs
17.1—Ty Detmer, Brigham Young, 1988-90 (582 in 34)

Career
17.8—Ty Detmer, Brigham Young, 1988-91 (820 in 46)
Collegiate record—21.6, Dennis Shaw, San Diego St., 1968-69 (432 in 20)

Scoring 200 Points and Passing for 200 Points

Career
Rick Leach, Michigan, 1975-78 (scored 204, passed for 270)

RUSHING

Most Rushes

Quarter
20—Kent Kitzmann, Minnesota vs. Illinois, Nov. 12, 1977 (3rd); Steve Owens, Oklahoma vs. Oklahoma St., Nov. 29, 1969 (3rd); O. J. Simpson, Southern Cal vs. Oregon St., Nov. 16, 1968 (4th)

Half
34—Tony Sands, Kansas vs. Missouri, Nov. 23, 1991 (2nd, 240 yards)

Game
58—Tony Sands, Kansas vs. Missouri, Nov. 23, 1991 (396 yards)

Season
403—Marcus Allen, Southern Cal, 1981 (2,342 yards)

2 Yrs
757—Marcus Allen, Southern Cal, 1980-81 (3,905 yards)

Career
(3 yrs.) 994—Herschel Walker, Georgia, 1980-82 (5,259 yards)
(4 yrs.) 1,215—Steve Bartalo, Colorado St., 1983-86 (4,813 yards)

Most Rushes Per Game

Season
39.6—Ed Marinaro, Cornell, 1971 (356 in 9)

2 Yrs
36.0—Marcus Allen, Southern Cal, 1980-81 (757 in 21)

Career
34.0—Ed Marinaro, Cornell, 1969-71 (918 in 27)

Most Rushes by a Freshman

Game
45—James McDougal, Wake Forest vs. Clemson, Oct. 9, 1976 (249 yards)

Season
292—Steve Bartalo, Colorado St., 1983 (1,113 yards)

Most Rushes Per Game by a Freshman

Season
29.2—Steve Bartalo, Colorado St., 1983 (292 in 10)

Most Consecutive Rushes by Same Player

Game
16—William Howard, Tennessee vs. Mississippi, Nov. 15, 1986 (during two possessions)

Most Rushes in Two Consecutive Games

Season
102—Lorenzo White, Michigan St., 1985 (53 vs. Purdue, Oct. 26; 49 vs. Minnesota, Nov. 2)

Most Yards Gained

Quarter
214—Andre Herrera, Southern Ill. vs. Northern Ill., Oct. 23, 1976 (1st, 17 rushes)

Half
287—Stacey Robinson, Northern Ill. vs. Fresno St., Oct. 6, 1990 (1st; 114 in first quarter, 173 in second quarter; 20 rushes)

Game
396—Tony Sands, Kansas vs. Missouri, Nov. 23, 1991 (58 rushes) (240 yards on 34 carries, second half)

Season
2,628—Barry Sanders, Oklahoma St., 1988 (344 rushes, 11 games)

2 Yrs
3,905—Marcus Allen, Southern Cal, 1980-81 (757 rushes)

Career
(3 yrs.) 5,259—Herschel Walker, Georgia, 1980-82 (994 rushes)
(4 yrs.) 6,082—Tony Dorsett, Pittsburgh, 1973-76 (1,074 rushes)

Most Yards Gained Per Game

Season
238.9—Barry Sanders, Oklahoma St., 1988 (2,628 in 11)

2 Yrs
186.0—Marcus Allen, Southern Cal, 1980-81 (3,905 in 21)

Career
174.6—Ed Marinaro, Cornell, 1969-71 (4,715 in 27)

Most Yards Gained by a Freshman

Game
386—Marshall Faulk, San Diego St. vs. Pacific (Cal.), Sept. 14, 1991 (37 rushes)

Season
1,616—Herschel Walker, Georgia, 1980 (274 rushes)
Per-game record—158.8, Marshall Faulk, San Diego St., 1991 (1,429 in 9)

3 Games
1,798—David Klingler, Houston, 1990-91 (572 vs. Eastern Wash., Nov. 17, 1990; 716 vs. Arizona St., Dec. 2, 1990; 510 vs. Louisiana Tech, Aug. 31, 1991)
4 Games
2,150—David Klingler, Houston, 1990 (563 vs. Texas Christian, Nov. 3; 299 vs. Texas, Nov. 10; 572 vs. Eastern Wash., Nov. 17; 716 vs. Arizona St., Dec. 2)

Most Games Gaining 200 Yards or More
Season
12—Ty Detmer, Brigham Young, 1990, 1989; Robbie Bosco, Brigham Young, 1985, 1984
Career
38—Ty Detmer, Brigham Young, 1988-91

Most Consecutive Games Gaining 200 Yards or More
Season
12—Ty Detmer, Brigham Young, 1990, 1989; Robbie Bosco, Brigham Young, 1984
Career
27—Ty Detmer, Brigham Young (from Sept. 2, 1989, to Sept. 21, 1991)

Most Games Gaining 300 Yards or More
Season
12—Ty Detmer, Brigham Young, 1989, 1990
Career
33—Ty Detmer, Brigham Young, 1988-91

Most Consecutive Games Gaining 300 Yards or More
Season
12—Ty Detmer, Brigham Young, 1990, 1989
Career
24—Ty Detmer, Brigham Young (from Sept. 2, 1989, to Dec. 1, 1990)

Most Games Gaining 400 Yards or More
Season
9—David Klingler, Houston, 1990
Career
12—Ty Detmer, Brigham Young, 1988-90

Most Yards Gained by Two Opposing Players
Game
1,253—Matt Vogler, Texas Christian (690) & David Klingler, Houston (563), Nov. 3, 1990

Two Players, Same Team, Each Passing for 250 Yards or More
Game
Andre Ware (517) & David Klingler (254), Houston vs. Southern Methodist, Oct. 21, 1989; Steve Cottrell (311) & John Elway (270), Stanford vs. Arizona St., Oct. 24, 1981

Most Yards Gained in an Opening Game of a Season
511—Scott Mitchell, Utah vs. Idaho St., Sept. 10, 1988

Most Yards Gained Against One Opponent
Career
1,495—Ty Detmer, Brigham Young vs. New Mexico, 1988-91

Most Yards Gained Per Game Against One Opponent
Career
(Min. 3 games) 410.7—Gary Schofield, Wake Forest vs. Maryland, 1981-83 (1,232 yards)
Career
(Min. 4 games) 373.8—Ty Detmer, Brigham Young vs. New Mexico, 1988-91 (1,495 yards)

Most Yards Gained Per Attempt
Game
(Min. 40 atts.) 13.93—Marc Wilson, Brigham Young vs. Utah, Nov. 5, 1977 (41 for 571)
(Min. 60 atts.) 10.52—Scott Mitchell, Utah vs. Air Force, Oct. 15, 1988 (60 for 631)
Season
(Min. 412 atts.) 11.07—Ty Detmer, Brigham Young, 1989 (412 for 4,560)
Career
(Min. 1,000 atts.) 9.82—Ty Detmer, Brigham Young, 1988-91 (1,530 for 15,031)

Most Yards Gained Per Completion
Game
(Min. 22 comps.) 22.8—Marc Wilson, Brigham Young vs. Utah, Nov. 5, 1977 (26 for 571)
Also holds record for all players who completed from 22 to 41 passes
(Min. 42 comps.) 15.7—Matt Vogler, Texas Christian vs. Houston, Nov. 3, 1990 (44 for 690)
Season
(Min. 109-204 comps.) 18.2—Doug Williams, Grambling, 1977 (181 for 3,286)
(Min. 205 comps.) 17.2—Ty Detmer, Brigham Young, 1989 (265 for 4,560)
Career
(Min. 275 comps.) 17.2—Danny White, Arizona St., 1971-73 (345 for 5,932)
(Min. 400 comps.) 15.7—Shawn Moore, Virginia, 1987-90 (421 for 6,629)

Most Touchdown Passes
Quarter
6—David Klingler, Houston vs. Louisiana Tech, Aug. 31, 1991 (2nd)
Half
7—Dennis Shaw, San Diego St. vs. New Mexico St., Nov. 15, 1969 (1st)
Game
11—David Klingler, Houston vs. Eastern Wash., Nov. 17, 1990
Season
54—David Klingler, Houston, 1990 (11 games)
2 Yrs
83—David Klingler, Houston, 1990-91
Also holds per-game record at 3.95 (83 in 21)
3 Yrs
108—Ty Detmer, Brigham Young, 1989-91
Career
121—Ty Detmer, Brigham Young, 1988-91

Most Touchdown Passes Per Game
Season
4.91—David Klingler, Houston, 1990 (54 in 11)
Career
2.84—David Klingler, Houston, 1988-91 (91 in 32)
Collegiate record—2.90, Dennis Shaw, San Diego St., 1968-69 (58 in 20)

Highest Percentage of Passes for Touchdowns
Season
(Min. 175 atts.) 11.6%—Dennis Shaw, San Diego St., 1969 (39 of 335)
(Min. 375 atts.) 10.6%—Jim McMahon, Brigham Young, 1980 (47 of 445)
Career
(Min. 400 atts.) 9.74%—Rick Leach, Michigan, 1975-78 (45 of 462)
(Min. 500 atts.) 9.09%—Danny White, Arizona St., 1971-73 (59 of 649)

**Most Consecutive Games Throwing
a Touchdown Pass**
Career
35—Ty Detmer, Brigham Young (from Sept. 7,
1989, to Nov. 23, 1991)

**Most Consecutive Passes Completed
for Touchdowns**
Game
6—Brooks Dawson, UTEP vs. New Mexico,
Oct. 28, 1967 (first six completions of the
game)

**Most Touchdown Passes in First Game of
a Career**
5—John Reaves, Florida vs. Houston, Sept. 20,
1969

Most Touchdown Passes by a Freshman
Game
6—Bob Hoernschemeyer, Indiana vs. Nebraska, Oct. 9, 1943
Season
20—Todd Ellis, South Caro., 1986

**Most Touchdown Passes in Freshman
and Sophomore Seasons**
45—Ty Detmer, Brigham Young, 1988 (13) &
1989 (32)

**Most Touchdown Passes at Conclusion
of Junior Year**
86—Ty Detmer, Brigham Young, 1988 (13),
1989 (32) & 1990 (41)

**Most Touchdown Passes, Same Passer
and Receiver**
Season
19—Elvis Grbac to Desmond Howard, Michigan, 1991; Andre Ware to Manny Hazard,
Houston, 1989
Career
30—Elvis Grbac to Desmond Howard, Michigan, 1989-91; Steve Ramsey to Ron Shanklin,
North Texas, 1967-69

**Most Passes Attempted Without
a Touchdown Pass**
Season
266—Stu Rayburn, Kent, 1984 (completed
125)

Fewest Times Sacked Attempting to Pass
Season
(Min. 300 atts.) 4—Steve Walsh, Miami (Fla.),
1988, in 390 attempts. Last 4 games of the
season: Tulsa, 1 for -8 yards; Louisiana St., 1
for -2; Arkansas, 1 for -12; Brigham Young, 1
for -9.

RECEIVING

Most Passes Caught
Game
22—Jay Miller, Brigham Young vs. New Mexico,
Nov. 3, 1973 (263 yards)
Season
142—Manny Hazard, Houston, 1989 (1,689
yards)
Career
(2 yrs.) 220—Manny Hazard, Houston, 1989-90
(2,635 yards)
(3 yrs.) 261—Howard Twilley, Tulsa, 1963-65
(3,343 yards)
(4 yrs.) 263—Terance Mathis, New Mexico,
1985-87, 89 (4,254 yards)

Most Passes Caught Per Game
Season
13.4—Howard Twilley, Tulsa, 1965 (134 in 10)
Career
10.5—Manny Hazard, Houston, 1989-90 (220
in 21)

**Most Passes Caught by Two Players,
Same Team**
Season
212—Howard Twilley (134) & Neal Sweeney
(78), Tulsa, 1965 (2,662 yards, 24 TDs)
Career
453—Mark Templeton (262) & Charles Lockett
(191), Long Beach St., 1983-86 (4,871 yards,
30 TDs)

Most Passes Caught in Consecutive Games
38—Manny Hazard, Houston, 1989 (19 vs.
Texas Christian, Nov. 4; 19 vs. Texas, Nov. 11)

Most Consecutive Games Catching a Pass
Career
44—Gary Williams, Ohio St., 1979-82 (every
game)

Most Passes Caught by a Tight End
Game
17—Jon Harvey, Northwestern vs. Michigan,
Oct. 23, 1982 (208 yards); Emilio Vallez, New
Mexico vs. UTEP, Oct. 27, 1967 (257 yards)

Season
73—Dennis Smith, Utah, 1989 (1,089 yards)
Career
181—Kelly Blackwell, Texas Christian, 1988-91
(2,155 yards)

Most Passes Caught Per Game by a Tight End
Season
6.36—Chuck Scott, Vanderbilt, 1983 (70 in 11);
Mark Dowdell, Bowling Green, 1983 (70 in
11)
Career
5.39—Gordon Hudson, Brigham Young, 1980-
83 (178 in 33)

Most Passes Caught by a Running Back
Game
18—Mark Templeton, Long Beach St. vs. Utah
St., Nov. 1, 1986 (173 yards)
Season
99—Mark Templeton, Long Beach St., 1986
(688 yards)
Career
262—Mark Templeton, Long Beach St., 1983-
86 (1,969 yards)

Most Passes Caught by a Freshman
Game
18—Richard Woodley (WR), Texas Christian
vs. Texas Tech, Nov. 10, 1990 (180 yards)
Season
61—Jason Wolf, Southern Methodist, 1989
(676 yards)
Also holds per-game record at 5.55

**Catching at Least 50 Passes and Gaining
at Least 1,000 Yards Rushing**
Season
By 10 players. Most recent: Ryan Benjamin,
Pacific (Cal.), 1991 (51 catches and 1,581
yards rushing)
Darrin Nelson, Stanford, holds record for most
seasons at 3 (1977-78, 81)

Catching at Least 60 Passes and Gaining at Least 1,000 Yards Rushing

Johnny Johnson, San Jose St., 1988 (61 catches and 1,219 yards rushing); Brad Muster, Stanford, 1986 (61 catches and 1,053 yards rushing); Darrin Nelson, Stanford, 1981 (67 catches and 1,014 yards rushing)

Most Yards Gained

Game
349—Chuck Hughes, UTEP vs. North Texas, Sept. 18, 1965 (caught 10)
Season
1,779—Howard Twilley, Tulsa, 1965 (caught 134)
Career
4,254—Terance Mathis, New Mexico, 1985-87, 89 (caught 263)

Most Yards Gained Per Game

Season
177.9—Howard Twilley, Tulsa, 1965 (1,779 in 10)
Career
128.6—Howard Twilley, Tulsa, 1963-65 (3,343 in 26)

Most Yards Gained by a Tight End

Game
259—Gordon Hudson, Brigham Young vs. Utah, Nov. 21, 1981 (caught 13)
Season
1,156—Chris Smith, Brigham Young, 1990 (caught 68)
Career
2,484—Gordon Hudson, Brigham Young, 1980-83 (caught 178)

Most Yards Gained Per Game by a Tight End

Season
102.0—Mike Moore, Grambling, 1977 (1,122 in 11)
Career
75.3—Gordon Hudson, Brigham Young, 1980-83 (2,484 in 33)

Most Yards Gained by a Freshman

Game
243—Darnay Scott, San Diego St. vs. Brigham Young, Nov. 16, 1991 (caught 8)
Season
870—Cormac Carney, Air Force, 1978 (caught 57)
Also holds per-game record at 79.1

Most Games Gaining 100 Yards or More

Season
11—Aaron Turner, Pacific (Cal.), 1991
Also holds consecutive record at 11
Career
18—Ron Sellers, Florida St., 1966-68 (in 30 games played)

Most Games Gaining 200 Yards or More

Season
5—Howard Twilley, Tulsa, 1965
Also holds consecutive record at 3

Most Yards Gained by Two Players, Same Team

Game
640—Rick Eber (322) & Harry Wood (318), Tulsa vs. Idaho St., Oct. 7, 1967 (caught 33, 6 TDs)
Season
2,662—Howard Twilley (1,779) & Neal Sweeney (883), Tulsa, 1965

Two Players, Same Team, Each Gaining 1,000 yards

Andy Boyce (1,241; 79 catches) & Chris Smith (1,156; 68 catches), Brigham Young, 1990; Patrick Rowe (1,392; 71 catches) & Dennis Arey (1,118; 68 catches), San Diego St., 1990; Jason Phillips (1,443; 108 catches) & James Dixon (1,103; 102 catches), Houston, 1988

Two Players, Same Team, Ranked No. 1 & No. 2 in Final Receiving Rankings

Season
Jason Phillips (No. 1, 9.8 catches per game) & James Dixon (No. 2, 9.3 catches per game), Houston, 1988

Three Players, Same Team, Each Catching 60 Passes or More

Patrick Rowe (71), Dennis Arey (68) & Jimmy Raye (62), San Diego St., 1990

Highest Average Gain Per Reception

Game
(Min. 3) 72.7—Terry Gallaher, East Caro. vs. Appalachian St., Sept. 13, 1975 (3 for 218; 82, 77, 59 yards)
(Min. 5) 52.6—Alex Wright, Auburn vs. Pacific (Cal.), Sept. 9, 1989 (5 for 263; 78, 60, 41, 73, 11 yards)
(Min. 10) 34.9—Chuck Hughes, UTEP vs. North Texas, Sept. 18, 1965 (10 for 349)
Season
(Min. 30-49) 27.9—Elmo Wright, Houston, 1968 (43 for 1,198)
(Min. 50) 24.4—Henry Ellard, Fresno St., 1982 (62 for 1,510)
Career
(Min. 75) 25.7—Wesley Walker, California, 1973-76 (86 for 2,206)
(Min. 105) 22.0—Herman Moore, Virginia, 1988-90 (114 for 2,504)

Duke's Clarkston Hines set a Division I-A record with 38 touchdown receptions from 1986 through 1989.

Highest Average Gain Per Reception by a Tight End
Season
(Min. 30) 22.6—Jay Novacek, Wyoming, 1984 (33 for 745)
Career
(Min. 75) 19.2—Clay Brown, Brigham Young, 1978-80 (88 for 1,691)

Most Touchdown Passes Caught
Game
6—Tim Delaney, San Diego St. vs. New Mexico St., Nov. 15, 1969 (16 receptions)
Season
22—Manny Hazard, Houston, 1989 (142 receptions)
Per-game record—2.25, Tom Reynolds, San Diego St., 1969 (18 in 8)
Career
38—Clarkston Hines, Duke, 1986-89 (189 receptions)

Most Games Catching a Touchdown Pass
Season
10—Desmond Howard, Michigan, 1991; Aaron Turner, Pacific (Cal.), 1991; Herman Moore, Virginia, 1990; Manny Hazard, Houston, 1989
Career
26—Terance Mathis, New Mexico, 1985-87, 89 (caught a total of 36 in 44 games)

Most Consecutive Games Catching a Touchdown Pass
Season
10—Desmond Howard, Michigan, 1991
Career
12—Desmond Howard, Michigan (last two games of 1990 and first 10 games of 1991); Aaron Turner, Pacific (Cal.) (last three games of 1990 and first nine games of 1991)

Most Touchdown Passes Caught by a Tight End
Season
18—Dennis Smith, Utah, 1989 (73 receptions)
Career
24—Dennis Smith, Utah, 1987-89 (156 receptions); Dave Young, Purdue, 1977-80 (172 receptions)

Highest Percentage of Passes Caught for Touchdowns
Season
(Min. 10 TDs) 58.8%—Kevin Williams, Southern Cal, 1978 (10 of 17)
Career
(Min. 20 TDs) 35.3%—Kevin Williams, Southern Cal, 1977-80 (24 of 68)
Also holds record for touchdown frequency: 1 TD every 2.83 catches

Highest Average Yards Per Touchdown Pass
Season
(Min. 10) 56.1—Elmo Wright, Houston, 1968 (11 for 617 yards; 87, 50, 75, 2, 80, 79, 13, 67, 61, 43, 60 yards)

Most Touchdown Passes Caught, 50 Yards or More
Season
8—Henry Ellard, Fresno St., 1982 (68, 51, 80, 61, 67, 72, 80, 72 yards); Elmo Wright, Houston, 1968 (87, 50, 75, 80, 79, 67, 61, 60 yards)

Most Consecutive Passes Caught for Touchdowns
6—Carlos Carson, Louisiana St., 1977 (5 vs. Rice, Sept. 24, 1 vs. Florida, Oct. 1; first receptions of his career)

Most Touchdown Passes Caught by a Freshman
Season
10—Dwight Collins, Pittsburgh, 1980

PUNTING

Most Punts
Game
36—Charlie Calhoun, Texas Tech vs. Centenary, Nov. 11, 1939 (1,318 yards; 20 were returned, 8 went out of bounds, 6 were downed, 1 was blocked [blocked kicks counted against the punter until 1955] and 1 went into the end zone for a touchback. Thirty-three of the punts occurred on first down during a heavy downpour in the game played at Shreveport, Louisiana)
Season
101—Jim Bailey, Va. Military, 1969 (3,507 yards)
Career
(3 yrs.) 276—Jim Bailey, Va. Military, 1969-71 (10,127 yards)
(4 yrs.) 320—Cameron Young, Texas Christian, 1976-79 (12,947 yards)

Highest Average Per Punt
Game
(Min. 5) 60.4—Lee Johnson, Brigham Young vs. Wyoming, Oct. 8, 1983 (5 for 302; 53, 44, 63, 62, 80 yards)
(Min. 10) 53.6—Jim Benien, Oklahoma St. vs. Colorado, Nov. 13, 1971 (10 for 536)
Season
(Min. 40) 49.8—Reggie Roby, Iowa, 1981 (44 for 2,193)
(Min. 50) 48.2—Ricky Anderson, Vanderbilt, 1984 (58 for 2,793)
(Min. 75) 45.8—Bucky Scribner, Kansas, 1982 (76 for 3,478)

Career
(Min. 150) 45.6—Reggie Roby, Iowa, 1979-82 (172 for 7,849)
(Min. 200) 44.7—Ray Guy, Southern Miss., 1970-72 (200 for 8,934)
(Min. 250) 44.3—Bill Smith, Mississippi, 1983-86 (254 for 11,260)

Highest Average Per Punt by a Freshman
Season
(Min. 40) 47.0—Tom Tupa, Ohio St., 1984 (41 for 1,927)

Most Yards on Punts
Game
1,318—Charlie Calhoun, Texas Tech vs. Centenary, Nov. 11, 1939 (36 punts)
Season
4,138—Johnny Pingel, Michigan St., 1938 (99 punts)
Career
12,947—Cameron Young, Texas Christian, 1976-79 (320 punts)

Most Games With a 40-Yard Average or More
Career
(Min. 4 punts) 36—Bill Smith, Mississippi, 1983-86 (punted in 44 games)

Most Punts, 50 Yards or More
Season
31—Chuck Ramsey, Wake Forest, 1973 (87 punts); Marv Bateman, Utah, 1971 (68 punts)

first 25 in 1982, ending with last attempt vs. Washington St., Nov. 20)

Most Games Kicking a Field Goal
Career
40—Gary Gussman, Miami (Ohio), 1984-87 (in 44 games played)

Most Consecutive Games Kicking a Field Goal
19—Gary Gussman, Miami (Ohio), 1986-87; Larry Roach, Oklahoma St., 1983-84

Most Field Goals Made, 60 Yards or More
Game
2—Tony Franklin, Texas A&M vs. Baylor, Oct. 16, 1976 (65 & 64 yards)
Season
3—Russell Erxleben, Texas, 1977 (67 vs. Rice, Oct. 1; 64 vs. Baylor, Oct. 16; 60 vs. Texas Tech, Oct. 29) (4 attempts)
Career
3—Russell Erxleben, Texas, 1975-78 (see Season Record above)

Most Field Goals Attempted, 60 Yards or More
Season
5—Tony Franklin, Texas A&M, 1976 (2 made)
Career
11—Tony Franklin, Texas A&M, 1975-78 (2 made)

Most Field Goals Made, 50 Yards or More
Game
3—Sergio Lopez-Chavero, Wichita St. vs. Drake, Oct. 27, 1984 (54, 54, 51 yards); Jerry DePoyster, Wyoming vs. Utah, Oct. 8, 1966 (54, 54, 52 yards)
Season
8—Fuad Reveiz, Tennessee, 1982 (10 attempts)
Career
20—Jason Hanson, Washington St., 1988-91 (35 attempts)

Most Field Goals Attempted, 50 Yards or More
Season
17—Jerry DePoyster, Wyoming, 1966 (5 made)
Career
38—Tony Franklin, Texas A&M, 1975-78 (16 made)

Highest Percentage of Field Goals Made, 50 Yards or More
Season
(Min. 10 atts.) 80.0%—Fuad Reveiz, Tennessee, 1982 (8 of 10)
Career
(Min. 15 atts.) 60.9%—Max Zendejas, Arizona, 1982-85 (14 of 23)

Most Field Goals Made, 40 Yards or More
Game
5—Alan Smith, Texas A&M vs. Arkansas St., Sept. 17, 1983 (44, 45, 42, 59, 57 yards)
Season
14—Chris Jacke, UTEP, 1988 (16 attempts)
Career
39—Jason Hanson, Washington St., 1988-91 (66 attempts) (19 of 31, 40-49 yards; 20 of 35, 50 or more yards)

Most Field Goals Attempted, 40 Yards or More
Season
25—Jerry DePoyster, Wyoming, 1966 (6 made)
Career
66—Jason Hanson, Washington St., 1988-91 (39 made)

Highest Percentage of Field Goals Made, 40 Yards or More
Season
(Min. 10) 90.9%—John Carney, Notre Dame, 1984 (10 of 11)
Career
(Min. 20) 69.4%—John Lee, UCLA, 1982-85 (25 of 36)

Highest Percentage of Field Goals Made, 40-49 Yards
Season
(Min. 10) 100%—John Carney, Notre Dame, 1984 (10 of 10)
Career
(Min. 15) 82.6%—Jeff Jaeger, Washington, 1983-86 (19 of 23)

Most Consecutive Field Goals Made, 40-49 Yards
Career
12—John Carney, Notre Dame, 1984-85

Highest Percentage of Field Goals Made, Under 40 Yards
Season
(Min. 16) 100%—Philip Doyle, Alabama, 1989 (19 of 19); Scott Slater, Texas A&M, 1986 (16 of 16); Bobby Raymond, Florida, 1984 (18 of 18); John Lee, UCLA, 1984 (16 of 16); Randy Pratt, California, 1983 (16 of 16); Paul Woodside, West Va., 1982 (23 of 23)
Career
(Min. 30) 97.0%—Bobby Raymond, Florida, 1983-84 (32 of 33)
(Min. 40) 96.4%—John Lee, UCLA, 1982-85 (54 of 56)

Longest Average Distance Field Goals Made
Game
(Min. 4) 49.5—Jeff Heath, East Caro. vs. Texas-Arlington, Nov. 6, 1982 (58, 53, 42, 45 yards)
Season
(Min. 10) 50.9—Jason Hanson, Washington St., 1991 (10 made)
Career
(Min. 25) 42.4—Russell Erxleben, Texas, 1975-78 (49 made)

Longest Average Distance Field Goals Attempted
Season
(Min. 20 atts.) 51.2—Jason Hanson, Washington St., 1991 (22 attempts)
Career
(Min. 40 atts.) 44.7—Russell Erxleben, Texas, 1975-78 (78 attempts)

Most Times Kicking Two Field Goals in a Game
Season
7—John Ivanic, Northern Ill., 1987; Derek Schmidt, Florida St., 1987; Rex Robinson, Georgia, 1980 (consecutive games)
Career
17—Kevin Butler, Georgia, 1981-84

Most Times Kicking Two or More Field Goals in a Game
Season
10—Paul Woodside, West Va., 1982
Career
27—Kevin Butler, Georgia, 1981-84

Most Times Kicking Three Field Goals in a Game
Season
4—By eight players. Most recent: Chris Jacke, UTEP, 1988

Career
9—Max Zendejas, Arizona, 1982-85; Lee Pistor, Arizona, 1974-77

Most Times Kicking Three or More Field Goals in a Game
Season
6—Luis Zendejas, Arizona St., 1983
Career
13—Luis Zendejas, Arizona St., 1981-84

Most Times Kicking Four Field Goals in a Game
Season
4—Matt Bahr, Penn St., 1978
Career
6—John Lee, UCLA, 1982-85
Also holds career record for most times kicking four or more field goals in a game at 8

Longest Field Goal Made
67—Joe Williams, Wichita St. vs. Southern Ill., Oct. 21, 1978; Steve Little, Arkansas vs. Texas, Oct. 15, 1977; Russell Erxleben, Texas vs. Rice, Oct. 1, 1977

Longest Indoor Field Goal Made
57—Juan Carrillo, Cal St. Fullerton vs. Northern Ariz., Oct. 15, 1977

Longest Field Goal Made Without Use of a Kicking Tee
62—Jason Hanson, Washington St. vs. Nevada-Las Vegas, Sept. 28, 1991

Longest Field Goal Made by a Freshman
59—Barry Childers, Marshall vs. Western Caro., Oct. 25, 1980; Tony Franklin, Texas A&M vs. Rice, Nov. 15, 1975

Longest Field Goal Made on First Attempt of a Career
61—Ralf Mojsiejenko, Michigan St. vs. Illinois, Sept. 11, 1982

Most Field Goals Made in First Game of a Career
5—Jose Oceguera, Long Beach St. vs. Kansas St., Sept. 3, 1983 (5 attempts); Nathan Ritter, North Caro. St. vs. East Caro., Sept. 9, 1978 (6 attempts); Joe Liljenquist, Brigham Young vs. Colorado St., Sept. 20, 1969 (6 attempts)

Most Games in Which Field Goal(s) Provided the Winning Margin
Season
6—Henrik Mike-Mayer, Drake, 1981
Career
10—Jeff Ward, Texas, 1983-86; John Lee, UCLA, 1982-85; Dan Miller, Miami (Fla.), 1978-81

TEAM RECORDS

SINGLE GAME—OFFENSE
TOTAL OFFENSE

Most Plays
112—Montana vs. Montana St., Nov. 1, 1952 (475 yards)

Most Plays, Both Teams
196—San Diego St. (99) & North Texas (97), Dec. 4, 1971 (851 yards)

Fewest Plays
12—Texas Tech vs. Centenary, Nov. 11, 1939 (10 rushes, 2 passes, -1 yard)

Fewest Plays, Both Teams
33—Texas Tech (12) & Centenary (21), Nov. 11, 1939 (28 rushes, 5 passes, 30 yards)

Most Yards Gained
1,021—Houston vs. Southern Methodist, Oct. 21, 1989 (250 rushing, 771 passing, 86 plays)

Most Yards Gained, Both Teams
1,563—Houston (827) & Texas Christian (736), Nov. 3, 1990 (187 plays)

Fewest Yards Gained
Minus 47—Syracuse vs. Penn St., Oct. 18, 1947 (-107 rushing, gained 60 passing, 49 plays)

Fewest Yards Gained, Both Teams
30—Texas Tech (-1) & Centenary (31), Nov. 11, 1939 (33 plays)

Most Yards Gained by a Losing Team
736—Texas Christian vs. Houston, Nov. 3, 1990 (lost 35-56)

Both Teams Gaining 600 Yards or More
In 12 games. Most recent: Brigham Young (767) & San Diego St. (695), Nov. 16, 1991 (168 plays); Houston (684) & Texas Tech (636), Nov. 30, 1991 (182 plays); San Jose St. (616) & Pacific (Cal.) (603), Oct. 19, 1991 (157 plays)

Fewest Yards Gained by a Winning Team
22—Citadel vs. Davidson, Nov. 23, 1946 (won 21-13)

Highest Average Gain Per Play
(Min. 75 plays) 11.9—Houston vs. Southern Methodist, Oct. 21, 1989 (86 for 1,021)

Most Touchdowns Scored by Rushing and Passing
15—Wyoming vs. Northern Colo., Nov. 5, 1949 (9 rushing, 6 passing)

RUSHING

Most Rushes
99—Missouri vs. Colorado, Oct. 12, 1968 (421 yards)

Most Rushes, Both Teams
141—Colgate (82) & Bucknell (59), Nov. 6, 1971 (440 yards)

Fewest Rushes
5—Houston vs. Texas Tech, Nov. 25, 1989 (36 yards)

Fewest Rushes, Both Teams
28—Texas Tech (10) & Centenary (18), Nov. 11, 1939 (23 yards)

Most Yards Gained
768—Oklahoma vs. Kansas St., Oct. 15, 1988 (72 rushes)

Most Yards Gained, Both Teams
1,039—Lenoir-Rhyne (837) & Davidson (202), Oct. 11, 1975 (111 rushes)

Fewest Yards Gained, Both Teams
Minus 24—San Jose St. (-102) & UTEP (78), Oct. 22, 1966 (75 rushes)

Most Yards Gained, Both Teams, Major-College Opponents
956—Oklahoma (711) & Kansas St. (245), Oct. 23, 1971 (111 rushes)

Most Yards Gained Without Loss
677—Nebraska vs. New Mexico St., Sept. 18, 1982 (78 rushes)

Most Yards Gained by a Losing Team
525—Air Force vs. New Mexico, Nov. 2, 1991 (70 rushes, lost 32-34)

Highest Average Gain Per Rush (Min. 50 Rushes)
11.9—Alabama vs. Virginia Tech, Oct. 27, 1973 (63 for 748)

Most Players on One Team Each Gaining 100 Yards or More
4—Army vs. Montana, Nov. 17, 1984 (Doug Black 183, Nate Sassaman 155, Clarence Jones 130, Jarvis Hollingsworth 124); Alabama vs. Virginia Tech, Oct. 27, 1973 (Jimmy Taylor 142, Wilbur Jackson 138, Calvin Culliver 127, Richard Todd 102); Texas vs. Southern Methodist, Nov. 1, 1969 (Jim Bertelsen 137, Steve Worster 137, James Street 121, Ted Koy 111); Arizona St. vs. Arizona, Nov. 10, 1951 (Bob Tarwater 140, Harley Cooper 123, Duane Morrison 118, Buzz Walker 113)

Most Touchdowns Scored by Rushing
12—UTEP vs. New Mexico St., Nov. 25, 1948

PASSING

Most Passes Attempted
81—Houston vs. Southern Methodist, Oct. 20, 1990 (completed 53)

Most Passes Attempted, Both Teams
135—Texas Christian (79) & Houston (56), Nov. 3, 1990 (completed 81)

Fewest Passes Attempted
0—By many teams. Most recent: Oklahoma vs. Colorado, Nov. 15, 1986

Fewest Passes Attempted, Both Teams
1—Michigan St. (0) & Maryland (1), Oct. 20, 1944 (not completed)

Most Passes Attempted Without a Completion
18—West Va. vs. Temple, Oct. 18, 1946

Most Passes Attempted Without Interception
72—Houston vs. Texas Christian, Nov. 4, 1989 (completed 47)

Most Passes Attempted Without Interception, Both Teams
114—Illinois (67) & Purdue (47), Oct. 12, 1985 (completed 67)

Most Consecutive Passes Attempted Without a Rushing Play
32—North Caro. St. vs. Duke, Nov. 11, 1989 (3rd & 4th quarters, completed 16)

Most Passes Completed
53—Houston vs. Southern Methodist, Oct. 20, 1990 (attempted 81)

Most Passes Completed, Both Teams
81—Texas Christian (44) & Houston (37), Nov. 3, 1990 (attempted 135)

Best Perfect Game (1.000 Pct.)
11 of 11—North Caro. vs. William & Mary, Oct. 5, 1991; Air Force vs. Northwestern, Sept. 17, 1988; Oregon St. vs. UCLA, Oct. 2, 1971; Southern Cal vs. Washington, Oct. 9, 1965

Highest Percentage of Passes Completed
(Min. 15 comps.) 95.0%—Mississippi vs. Tulane, Nov. 6, 1982 (19 of 20)
(Min. 25 comps.) 92.6%—UCLA vs. Washington, Oct. 29, 1983 (25 of 27)
(Min. 35 comps.) 81.1%—California vs. Florida, Sept. 13, 1980 (43 of 53)

Highest Percentage of Passes Completed, Both Teams
(Min. 40 comps.) 84.6%—UCLA & Washington, Oct. 29, 1983 (44 of 52)

Most Passes Had Intercepted
10—California vs. UCLA, Oct. 21, 1978 (52 attempts); Detroit Mercy vs. Oklahoma St., Nov. 28, 1942

Most Yards Gained
771—Houston vs. Southern Methodist, Oct. 21, 1989 (completed 40 of 61)

Most Yards Gained, Both Teams
1,253—Texas Christian (690) & Houston (563), Nov. 3, 1990 (135 attempts)

Fewest Yards Gained, Both Teams
Minus 13—North Caro. (-7 on 1 of 3 attempts) & Pennsylvania (-6 on 2 of 12 attempts), Nov. 13, 1943

Most Yards Gained Per Attempt
(Min. 30 atts.) 14.6—Arizona St. vs. Stanford, Oct. 24, 1981 (35 for 511)
(Min. 40 atts.) 15.9—UTEP vs. North Texas, Sept. 18, 1965 (40 for 634)

Most Yards Gained Per Completion
(Min. 15 comps.) 31.9—UTEP vs. New Mexico, Oct. 28, 1967 (16 for 510)
(Min. 25 comps.) 25.4—UTEP vs. North Texas, Sept. 18, 1965 (25 for 634)

Most Touchdown Passes
11—Houston vs. Eastern Wash., Nov. 17, 1990

Most Touchdown Passes, Major-College Opponents
10—Houston vs. Southern Methodist, Oct. 21, 1989; San Diego St. vs. New Mexico St., Nov. 15, 1969

Most Touchdown Passes, Both Teams
14—Houston (11) & Eastern Wash. (3), Nov. 17, 1990

Most Touchdown Passes, Both Teams, Major-College Opponents
13—San Diego St. (10) & New Mexico St. (3), Nov. 15, 1969

PUNTING

Most Punts
    39—Texas Tech vs. Centenary, Nov. 11, 1939 (1,377 yards)
    38—Centenary vs. Texas Tech, Nov. 11, 1939 (1,248 yards)

Most Punts, Both Teams
    77—Texas Tech (39) & Centenary (38), Nov. 11, 1939 (2,625 yards) (The game was played in a heavy downpour in Shreveport, Louisiana. Forty-two punts were returned, 19 went out of bounds, 10 were downed, 1 went into the end zone for a touchback, 4 were blocked and 1 was fair caught. Sixty-seven punts [34 by Texas Tech and 33 by Centenary] occurred on first-down plays, including 22 consecutively in the third and fourth quarters. The game was a scoreless tie.)

Fewest Punts
    0—By many teams. Most recent: Nebraska vs. Colorado St., Sept. 14, 1991 (won 71-14)

Fewest Punts by a Losing Team
    0—By many teams; 2 teams in 1989. Most recent: Iowa St. vs. Oklahoma, Oct. 21, 1989 (lost 40-43)

Highest Average Per Punt (Min. 5 Punts)
    60.4—Brigham Young vs. Wyoming, Oct. 8, 1983 (5 for 302)

Highest Average Per Punt (Min. 10 Punts)
    53.6—Oklahoma St. vs. Colorado, Nov. 13, 1971 (10 for 536)

Highest Average Per Punt, Both Teams (Min. 10 Punts)
    55.3—Brigham Young & Wyoming, Oct. 8, 1983 (11 for 608)

Most Opponents' Punts Blocked By
    4—Michigan vs. Ohio St., Nov. 25, 1950; Southern Methodist vs. Texas-Arlington, Sept. 30, 1944

PUNT RETURNS

Most Punt Returns
    22—Texas Tech vs. Centenary, Nov. 11, 1939 (112 yards)

Most Punt Returns, Both Teams
    42—Texas Tech (22) & Centenary (20), Nov. 11, 1939 (233 yards)

Most Yards on Punt Returns
    319—Texas A&M vs. North Texas, Sept. 21, 1946 (10 returns)

Highest Average Gain Per Return (Min. 5 Returns)
    44.2—Denver vs. Colorado Col., Sept. 17, 1954 (6 for 265)

Most Touchdowns Scored on Punt Returns
    3—Holy Cross vs. Brown, Sept. 21, 1974; Louisiana St. vs. Mississippi, Dec. 5, 1970; Wichita St. vs. Northern St. (S.D.), Oct. 22, 1949; Wisconsin vs. Iowa, Nov. 8, 1947

KICKOFF RETURNS

Most Kickoff Returns
    14—Arizona St. vs. Nevada, Oct. 12, 1946 (290 yards)

Most Yards on Kickoff Returns
    295—Cincinnati vs. Memphis St., Oct. 30, 1971 (8 returns)

Highest Average Gain Per Return (Min. 6 Returns)
    46.2—Southern Cal vs. Washington St., Nov. 7, 1970 (6 for 277)

Most Touchdowns Scored on Kickoff Returns
    2—By many teams. Most recent: Brigham Young vs. Air Force, Nov. 11, 1989; Notre Dame vs. Michigan, Sept. 16, 1989; New Mexico St. vs. Drake, Oct. 15, 1983 (consecutive returns)

Touchdowns Scored on Back-to-Back Kickoff Returns, Both Teams
    2—By many teams. Most recent: Wisconsin & Northern Ill., Sept. 14, 1985

TOTAL KICK RETURNS

(Combined Punt and Kickoff Returns)

Most Yards on Kick Returns
    376—Florida St. vs. Virginia Tech, Nov. 16, 1974 (9 returns)

Highest Average Gain Per Return (Min. 7 Returns)
    41.8—Florida St. vs. Virginia Tech, Nov. 16, 1974 (9 for 376)

SCORING

Most Points Scored
    103—Wyoming vs. Northern Colo. (0), Nov. 5, 1949 (15 TDs, 13 PATs)

Most Points Scored Against a Major-College Opponent
    100—Houston vs. Tulsa (6), Nov. 23, 1968 (14 TDs, 13 PATs, 1 FG)

Most Points Scored, Both Teams
    124—Oklahoma (82) & Colorado (42), Oct. 4, 1980

Most Points Scored by a Losing Team
    51—San Diego St. vs. Wyoming (52), Oct. 6, 1990

Most Points, Both Teams in a Tie Game
    104—Brigham Young (52) & San Diego St. (52), Nov. 16, 1991

Most Points Scored in One Quarter
    49—Fresno St. vs. New Mexico, Oct. 5, 1991 (2nd quarter); Davidson vs. Furman, Sept. 27, 1969 (2nd quarter); Houston vs. Tulsa, Nov. 23, 1968 (4th quarter)

Most Points Scored in One Half
76—Houston vs. Tulsa, Nov. 23, 1968 (2nd half)

Most Touchdowns Scored
15—Wyoming vs. Northern Colo., Nov. 5, 1949 (9 rushing, 6 passing)

Most Touchdowns Scored, Both Teams
18—Oklahoma (12) & Colorado (6), Oct. 4, 1980

Most Extra Points Made by Kicking
13—Fresno St. vs. New Mexico, Oct. 5, 1991 (attempted 13); Houston vs. Tulsa, Nov. 23, 1968 (attempted 14); Wyoming vs. Northern Colo., Nov. 5, 1949 (attempted 15)

Most Two-Point Attempts Scored
7—Pacific (Cal.) vs. San Diego St., Nov. 22, 1958 (attempted 9)

Most Defensive Extra-Point Attempts
2—Northern Ill. vs. Akron, Nov. 3, 1990 (2 interception returns); Rice vs. Notre Dame, Nov. 5, 1988 (2 kick returns; 1 scored)

Most Defensive Extra-Point Attempts Scored
1—By 18 teams. Most recent: Ohio St. vs. Iowa, Nov. 2, 1991 (kick return); Colorado vs. Nebraska, Nov. 2, 1991 (kick return)

Most Field Goals Made
7—Nebraska vs. Missouri, Oct. 19, 1985 (attempted 7); Western Mich. vs. Marshall, Sept. 29, 1984 (attempted 9)

Most Field Goals Made, Both Teams
9—Southwestern La. (5) & Central Mich. (4), Sept. 9, 1989 (attempted 11)

Most Field Goals Attempted
9—Western Mich. vs. Marshall, Sept. 29, 1984 (made 7)

Most Field Goals Attempted, Both Teams
12—Clemson (6) & Georgia (6), Sept. 17, 1983 (made 6)

Most Field Goals Missed
7—Louisiana St. vs. Florida, Nov. 25, 1972 (attempted 8)

FIRST DOWNS

Most First Downs
44—Nebraska vs. Utah St., Sept. 7, 1991 (33 rush, 10 pass, 1 penalty)

Most First Downs, Both Teams
72—New Mexico (37) & San Diego St. (35), Sept. 27, 1986

Fewest First Downs by a Winning Team
0—Michigan vs. Ohio St., Nov. 25, 1950 (won

9-3); North Caro. St. vs. Virginia, Sept. 30, 1944 (won 13-0)

Most First Downs by Rushing
36—Nebraska vs. New Mexico St., Sept. 18, 1982

Most First Downs by Passing
30—Brigham Young vs. Colorado St., Nov. 7, 1981; Tulsa vs. Idaho St., Oct. 7, 1967

FUMBLES

Most Fumbles
17—Wichita St. vs. Florida St., Sept. 20, 1969 (lost 10)

Most Fumbles, Both Teams
27—Wichita St. (17) & Florida St. (10), Sept. 20, 1969 (lost 17)

Most Fumbles Lost
10—Wichita St. vs. Florida St., Sept. 20, 1969 (17 fumbles)

Most Fumbles Lost, Both Teams
17—Wichita St. (10) & Florida St. (7), Sept. 20, 1969 (27 fumbles)

Most Fumbles Lost in a Quarter
5—San Diego St. vs. California, Sept. 18, 1982 (1st quarter); East Caro. vs. Southwestern La., Sept. 13, 1980 (3rd quarter on 5 consecutive possessions)

PENALTIES

Most Penalties Against
24—San Jose St. vs. Fresno St., Oct. 4, 1986 (199 yards)

Most Penalties, Both Teams
36—San Jose St. (24) & Fresno St. (12), Oct. 4, 1986 (317 yards)

Fewest Penalties, Both Teams
0—Most recent: Army & Navy, Dec. 6, 1986

Most Yards Penalized
238—Arizona St. vs. UTEP, Nov. 11, 1961 (13 penalties)

Most Yards Penalized, Both Teams
421—Grambling (16 for 216 yards) & Texas Southern (17 for 205 yards), Oct. 29, 1977

TURNOVERS

(Number of Times Losing the Ball on Interceptions and Fumbles)

Most Turnovers Lost
13—Georgia vs. Georgia Tech, Dec. 1, 1951 (8 interceptions, 5 fumbles)

Most Turnovers, Both Teams
20—Wichita St. (12) & Florida St. (8), Sept. 20, 1969 (17 fumbles, 3 interceptions)

Most Total Plays Without a Turnover (Rushes, Passes, All Runbacks)
110—Baylor vs. Rice, Nov. 13, 1976; California vs. San Jose St., Oct. 5, 1968 (also did not fumble)

Division I-A Team Records

Most Total Plays Without a Turnover, Both Teams
184—Arkansas (93) & Texas A&M (91), Nov. 2, 1968

Most Total Plays Without a Turnover or a Fumble, Both Teams
158—Stanford (88) & Oregon (70), Nov. 2, 1957

Most Turnovers by a Winning Team
11—Purdue vs. Illinois, Oct. 2, 1943 (9 fumbles, 2 interceptions; won 40-21)

Most Passes Had Intercepted by a Winning Team
7—Pittsburgh vs. Army, Nov. 15, 1980 (54 attempts; won 45-7)

Most Fumbles Lost by a Winning Team
9—Arizona St. vs. Utah, Oct. 14, 1972 (10 fumbles; won 59-48); Purdue vs. Illinois, Oct. 2, 1943 (10 fumbles; won 40-21)

SINGLE GAME—DEFENSE
TOTAL DEFENSE

Fewest Plays Allowed
12—Centenary vs. Texas Tech, Nov. 11, 1939 (10 rushes, 2 passes; -1 yard)

Fewest Yards Allowed
Minus 47—Penn St. vs. Syracuse, Oct. 18, 1947 (-107 rushing, 60 passing; 49 plays)

Most Yards Allowed
1,021—Southern Methodist vs. Houston, Oct. 21, 1989 (250 rushing, 771 passing)

RUSHING DEFENSE

Fewest Rushes Allowed
5—Texas Tech vs. Houston, Nov. 25, 1989 (36 yards)

Fewest Rushing Yards Allowed
Minus 109—Toledo vs. Northern Ill., Nov. 11, 1967 (33 rushes)

PASS DEFENSE

Fewest Attempts Allowed
0—By many teams. Most recent: Colorado vs. Oklahoma, Nov. 15, 1986

Fewest Completions Allowed
0—By many teams. Most recent: Air Force vs. Army, Nov. 10, 1990 (2 attempts)

Lowest Completion Percentage Allowed (Min. 10 Atts.)
.000—Temple vs. West Va., Oct. 18, 1946 (0 of 18 attempts)

Fewest Yards Allowed
Minus 16—Va. Military vs. Richmond, Oct. 5, 1957 (2 completions)

Most Passes Intercepted By
11—Brown vs. Rhode Island, Oct. 8, 1949 (136 yards)

Most Passes Intercepted By Against a Major-College Opponent
10—UCLA vs. California, Oct. 21, 1978; Oklahoma St. vs. Detroit Mercy, Nov. 28, 1942

Most Yards on Interception Returns
240—Kentucky vs. Mississippi, Oct. 1, 1949 (6 returns)

Most Touchdowns on Interception Returns
4—Houston vs. Texas, Nov. 7, 1987 (198 yards; 3 TDs in the fourth quarter)

FIRST DOWNS

Fewest First Downs Allowed
0—By many teams. Most recent: North Caro. St. vs. Western Caro., Sept. 1, 1990

OPPONENTS' KICKS BLOCKED

Most Opponents' Punts Blocked
3—Purdue vs. Northwestern, Nov. 11, 1989 (11 attempts)

Most Opponents' Punts Blocked, One Quarter
3—Purdue vs. Northwestern, Nov. 11, 1989 (4 attempts)

TURNOVERS GAINED
(Number of Times Gaining the Ball on Interceptions and Fumbles)

Most Turnovers Gained
13—Georgia Tech vs. Georgia, Dec. 1, 1951 (8 interceptions, 5 fumbles)

Most Consecutive Opponents' Series Resulting in Turnovers
7—Florida vs. Florida St., Oct. 7, 1972 (3 interceptions, 4 fumbles lost; first seven series of the game)

DEFENSIVE EXTRA POINTS

Most Defensive Extra Points Scored Against
1—By many teams. Most recent: Iowa vs. Ohio St., Nov. 2, 1991 (kick return); Nebraska vs. Colorado, Nov. 2, 1991 (kick return)

Most Defensive Extra-Point Attempts Against
2—Akron vs. Northern Ill., Nov. 3, 1990 (2 interception returns); Notre Dame vs. Rice, Nov. 5, 1988 (2 blocked kick returns, 1 scored)

SEASON—OFFENSE

TOTAL OFFENSE

Most Yards Gained Per Game
624.9—Houston, 1989 (6,874 in 11)

Most Yards Gained
6,874—Houston, 1989 (11 games)

Highest Average Gain Per Play
7.61—Brigham Young, 1989 (852 for 6,485)

Gaining 300 Yards or More Per Game Rushing and 200 Yards or More Per Game Passing
Arizona St., 1973 (310.2 rushing, 255.3 passing); Houston, 1968 (361.7 rushing, 200.3 passing)

Most Plays Per Game
92.4—Notre Dame, 1970 (924 in 10)

Most Touchdowns Rushing and Passing
84—Nebraska, 1983
Also holds per-game record at 7.0

RUSHING

Most Yards Gained Per Game
472.4—Oklahoma, 1971 (5,196 in 11)

Highest Average Gain Per Rush
7.64—Army, 1945 (424 for 3,238)

Highest Average Gain Per Rush (Min. 500 Rushes)
6.83—Oklahoma, 1971 (761 for 5,196)

Most Rushes Per Game
73.9—Oklahoma, 1974 (813 in 11)

Most Touchdowns Rushing Per Game
5.1—Texas, 1970, 1969; Oklahoma, 1956 (each 51 in 10)

PASSING

Most Yards Gained Per Game
511.3—Houston, 1989 (5,624 in 11)

Most Yards Gained
5,624—Houston, 1989 (11 games)

Highest Average Gain Per Attempt
(Min. 225 atts.) 10.07—Syracuse, 1987 (250 for 2,518)
(Min. 350 atts.) 10.93—Brigham Young, 1989 (433 for 4,732)

Highest Average Gain Per Completion
(Min. 100 comps.) 19.1—Houston, 1968 (105 for 2,003)
(Min. 175 comps.) 18.0—Grambling, 1977 (187 for 3,360)
(Min. 225 comps.) 16.96—Brigham Young, 1989 (279 for 4,732)

Most Passes Attempted Per Game
63.1—Houston, 1989 (694 in 11)

Most Passes Completed Per Game
39.4—Houston, 1989 (434 in 11)

Highest Percentage Completed
(Min. 150 atts.) 70.8%—Long Beach St., 1985 (323 of 456)

Lowest Percentage Had Intercepted
(Min. 300 atts.) 1.13%—Georgia, 1991 (4 of 355)
(Min. 400 atts.) 1.65%—San Diego St., 1990 (8 of 485)

Most Touchdown Passes Per Game
5.0—Houston, 1989 (55 in 11)

Most Touchdown Passes
55—Houston, 1989 (11 games)

Fewest Touchdown Passes
0—By 5 teams since 1975. Most recent: Air Force, 1990 (11 games, 90 attempts)

Highest Passing Efficiency Rating Points
(Min. 150 atts.) 174.45—Brigham Young, 1989 (433 attempts, 279 completions, 15 interceptions, 4,732 yards, 33 TD passes)

A Team With a 3,000-Yard Passer, 1,000-Yard Receiver and 1,000-Yard Rusher
Houston, 1989 (Andre Ware 4,699 passing, Manny Hazard 1,689 receiving, Chuck Weatherspoon 1,146 rushing); Colorado St., 1983 (Terry Nugent 3,319 passing, Jeff Champine 1,002 receiving, Steve Bartalo 1,113 rushing); Southern Methodist, 1968 (Chuck Hixson 3,103 passing, Jerry LeVias 1,131 receiving, Mike Richardson 1,034 rushing)

A Team With Two 1,000-Yard Receivers
San Diego St., 1990 (Patrick Rowe, 1,392 & Dennis Arey, 1,118); Brigham Young, 1990 (Andy Boyce, 1,241 & Chris Smith, 1,156); Houston, 1988 (Jason Phillips, 1,444 & James Dixon, 1,103)

A Team With the No. 1 & No. 2 Receivers
Houston, 1988 (Jason Phillips, No. 1, 9.82 catches per game & James Dixon, No. 2, 9.27 catches per game)

Most 100-Yard Receiving Games in a Season, One Team
19—San Diego St., 1990 (Patrick Rowe 9, Dennis Arey 8 & Jimmy Raye 2)

PUNTING

Most Punts Per Game
13.9—Tennessee, 1937 (139 in 10)

Fewest Punts Per Game
2.0—Nevada, 1948 (18 in 9)

Highest Punting Average
50.6—Brigham Young, 1983 (24 for 1,215 yards)

Highest Punting Average (Min. 40 Punts)
47.6—Vanderbilt, 1984 (59 for 2,810)

Highest Net Punting Average
45.0—Brigham Young, 1983 (24 for 1,215 yards, 134 yards in punts returned)

Highest Net Punting Average (Min. 40 Punts)
44.4—Colorado St., 1976 (72 for 3,323, 123 yards in punts returned)

PUNT RETURNS

Most Punt Returns Per Game
6.9—Texas A&M, 1943 (69 in 10)

Fewest Punt Returns Per Game
0.55—Iowa, 1971 (6 in 11)

Most Punt-Return Yards Per Game
114.5—Colgate, 1941 (916 in 8)

Highest Average Gain Per Return
(Min. 15 rets.) 25.2—Arizona St., 1952 (18 for 454 yards)
(Min. 30 rets.) 22.4—Oklahoma, 1948 (43 for 963)

Most Touchdowns Scored on Punt Returns (From 1966)
7—Southern Miss., 1987 (on 46 returns)

KICKOFF RETURNS

Most Kickoff Returns Per Game
7.3—Cal St. Fullerton, 1990 (80 in 11)

Fewest Kickoff Returns Per Game
0.7—Boston College, 1939 (7 in 10)

Most Kickoff-Return Yards Per Game
134.7—Virginia Tech, 1973 (1,482 in 11)

Highest Average Gain Per Return
(Min. 25 rets.) 29.5—Maryland, 1975 (26 for 768)
(Min. 35 rets.) 27.5—Rice, 1973 (39 for 1,074)

Most Touchdowns Scored on Kickoff Returns (From 1966)
4—Dayton, 1974 (on 44 returns)

SCORING

Most Points Per Game
56.0—Army, 1944 (504 in 9)

Most Points Scored
624—Nebraska, 1983 (12 games)

Highest Scoring Margin
52.1—Army, 1944 (scored 504 points for 56.0 average and allowed 35 points for 3.9 average in 9 games)

Most Points Scored, Two Consecutive Games
177—Houston, 1968 (77-3 vs. Idaho, Nov. 16, and 100-6 vs. Tulsa, Nov. 23)

Most Touchdowns Per Game
8.22—Army, 1944 (74 in 9)

Most Touchdowns
89—Nebraska, 1983 (12 games)

Most Extra Points Made by Kicking
77—Nebraska, 1983 (77 in 12, attempted 85) Also holds per-game record at 6.4

Most Consecutive Extra Points Made by Kicking
67—Oklahoma St., 1988 (attempted 67)

Most Two-Point Attempts Made Per Game
2.22—Rutgers, 1958 (20 in 9, attempted 31)

Most Defensive Extra-Point Attempts
3—Rice, 1988 (1 vs. Southwestern La., Sept. 24, blocked kick return; 2 vs. Notre Dame, Nov. 5, 2 blocked kick returns, 1 scored)

Most Defensive Extra-Point Attempts Scored
1—By 18 teams. Most recent: Ohio St. vs. Iowa, Nov. 2, 1991 (kick return); Colorado vs. Nebraska, Nov. 2, 1991 (kick return)

Most Field Goals Per Game
2.64—UCLA, 1984 (29 in 11)

FIRST DOWNS

Most First Downs Per Game
30.9—Brigham Young, 1983 (340 in 11)

Most Rushing First Downs Per Game
21.4—Oklahoma, 1974 (235 in 11)

Most Passing First Downs Per Game
19.8—Brigham Young, 1990 (237 in 12)

FUMBLES

Most Fumbles
68—Texas Southern, 1977 (lost 39)

Most Fumbles Lost
39—Texas Southern, 1977 (fumbled 68 times)

Fewest Own Fumbles Lost
2—Dayton, 1968; UCLA, 1952; Tulsa, 1942; Washington, 1941

Most Consecutive Fumbles Lost
14—Oklahoma, 1983 (during 5 games, Oct. 8-Nov. 5)

PENALTIES

Most Penalties Per Game
12.9—Grambling, 1977 (142 in 11, 1,476 yards)

Most Yards Penalized Per Game
134.2—Grambling, 1977 (1,476 in 11, 142 penalties)

TURNOVERS (GIVEAWAYS)
(Passes Had Intercepted and Fumbles Lost)

Fewest Turnovers
8—Miami (Ohio), 1966 (4 interceptions, 4 fumbles lost)

Most Turnovers
61—Tulsa, 1976 (24 interceptions, 37 fumbles lost); North Texas, 1971 (33 interceptions, 28 fumbles lost)

Fewest Turnovers Per Game
0.80—Miami (Ohio), 1966 (8 in 10 games)

Most Turnovers Per Game
6.1—Mississippi St., 1949 (55 in 9 games; 25 interceptions, 30 fumbles lost)

SEASON—DEFENSE
TOTAL DEFENSE

Fewest Yards Allowed Per Game
69.9—Santa Clara, 1937 (559 in 8)

Fewest Rushing and Passing Touchdowns Allowed Per Game
0.0—Tennessee, 1939; Duke, 1938

Lowest Average Yards Allowed Per Play
1.71—Texas A&M, 1939 (447 for 763)

Lowest Average Yards Allowed Per Play (Min. 600 Plays)
2.51—Nebraska, 1967 (627 for 1,576)

Lowest Average Yards Allowed Per Play (Min. 700 Plays)
2.69—Toledo, 1971 (734 for 1,795)

Most Yards Allowed Per Game
536.0—Kansas, 1988 (5,896 in 11)

RUSHING DEFENSE

Fewest Yards Allowed Per Game
17.0—Penn St., 1947 (153 in 9)

Most Yards Lost by Opponents Per Game
70.1—Wyoming, 1968 (701 in 10, 458 rushes)

Lowest Average Yards Allowed Per Rush
0.64—Penn St., 1947 (240 for 153)

Lowest Average Yards Allowed Per Rush (Min. 400 Rushes)
1.26—North Texas, 1966 (408 for 513)

Lowest Average Yards Allowed Per Rush (Min. 500 Rushes)
2.06—Nebraska, 1971 (500 for 1,031)

PASS DEFENSE

Fewest Yards Allowed Per Game
13.1—Penn St., 1938 (105 in 8)

Fewest Yards Allowed Per Attempt
(Min. 200 atts.) 3.41—Toledo, 1970 (251 for 856)
(Min. 300 atts.) 3.78—Notre Dame, 1967 (306 for 1,158)

Fewest Yards Allowed Per Completion
(Min. 100 comps.) 9.36—Oklahoma, 1986 (128 for 1,198)
(Min. 150 comps.) 9.56—Miami (Fla.), 1983 (176 for 1,683)

Lowest Completion Percentage Allowed
(Min. 150 atts.) 31.1%—Virginia, 1952 (50 of 161)
(Min. 200 atts.) 33.3%—Notre Dame, 1967 (102 of 306)

Fewest Touchdowns Allowed by Passing
0—By many teams. Most recent: Louisiana St. & North Texas, 1959

Lowest Pass Efficiency Defensive Rating (From 1990)
77.37—Texas, 1991 (304 attempts, 115 completions, 15 interceptions, 1,513 yards, 7 TDs)

Most Passes Intercepted By Per Game
4.13—Pennsylvania, 1940 (33 in 8)

Highest Percentage Intercepted By
(Min. 150 atts.) 17.9%—Army, 1944 (36 of 201)
(Min. 200 atts.) 17.2%—Hardin-Simmons, 1951 (37 of 215)

Most Yards Gained on Interception Returns
782—Tennessee, 1971 (25 interceptions)

Most Interception Yards Per Game
72.5—Texas, 1943 (580 in 8)

Highest Average Per Interception Return
(Min. 10 ints.) 36.3—Oregon St., 1959 (12 for 436)
(Min. 15 ints.) 31.3—Tennessee, 1971 (25 for 782)

Most Touchdowns on Interception Returns
7—Tennessee, 1971 (25 interceptions; 287 pass attempts against)

PUNTING

Most Opponents' Punts Blocked By
11—Arkansas St., 1975 (11 games, 95 punts against)

PUNT RETURNS

Fewest Returns Allowed
5—Notre Dame, 1968 (52 yards)

Fewest Yards Allowed
2—Miami (Fla.), 1989 (12 returns)

Lowest Average Yards Allowed Per Punt Return
0.17—Miami (Fla.), 1989 (12 for 2 yards)

KICKOFF RETURNS

Lowest Average Yards Allowed Per Kickoff Return
8.35—Richmond, 1951 (23 for 192 yards)

SCORING

Fewest Points Allowed Per Game
0.0—Tennessee, 1939 (10 games); Duke, 1938 (9 games)

Most Points Allowed and Points Allowed Per Game
544 and 49.5—UTEP, 1973 (11 games)

Most Defensive Extra-Point Attempts Against
2—Notre Dame, 1988 (2 kick returns, 1 scored); Southwestern La., 1988 (2 kick returns, none scored)

FUMBLES

Most Opponents' Fumbles Recovered
36—Brigham Young, 1977; North Texas, 1972

TURNOVERS (TAKEAWAYS)
(Opponents' Passes Intercepted and Fumbles Recovered)

Most Opponents' Turnovers
57—Tennessee, 1970 (36 interceptions, 21 fumbles lost)

Most Opponents' Turnovers Per Game
5.44—UCLA, 1954 (49 in 9); UCLA, 1952 (49 in 9); Pennsylvania, 1950 (49 in 9); Wyoming, 1950 (49 in 9)

Highest Margin of Turnovers Per Game Over Opponents
4.0—UCLA, 1952 (36 in 9; 13 giveaways vs. 49 takeaways)
Also holds total-margin record at 36

Highest Margin of Turnovers Per Game by Opponents
3.1—Southern Miss., 1969 (31 in 10; 45 giveaways vs. 14 takeaways)

CONSECUTIVE RECORDS

Most Consecutive Victories
47—Oklahoma, 1953-57

Most Consecutive Games Without Defeat
48—Oklahoma, 1953-57 (1 tie)

Most Consecutive Losses
34—Northwestern, from Sept. 22, 1979, vs. Syracuse through Sept. 18, 1982, vs. Miami (Ohio)
Ended with 31-6 victory over Northern Ill., Sept. 25, 1982

Most Consecutive Games Without a Victory on the Road
46—Northwestern (including one tie), from Nov. 23, 1974, through Oct. 30, 1982

Most Consecutive Games Without a Tie
287—Miami (Fla.) (current), from Nov. 11, 1966

Most Consecutive Games Without Being Shut Out
240—UCLA (current), from Oct. 2, 1971

Most Consecutive Shutouts (Regular Season)
17—Tennessee, from Nov. 5, 1938, through Oct. 12, 1940

Most Consecutive Quarters Opponents Held Scoreless (Regular Season)
71—Tennessee, from 2nd quarter vs. Louisiana St., Oct. 29, 1938, to 2nd quarter vs. Alabama, Oct. 19, 1940

Most Consecutive Victories at Home
57—Alabama (at Tuscaloosa), from Oct. 26, 1963, through Oct. 23, 1982

Most Consecutive Winning Seasons
30—Nebraska (current), from 1962

Most Consecutive Non-Losing Seasons
49—Penn St., 1939-1987

Most Consecutive Non-Winning Seasons
28—Rice (current), from 1964

Most Consecutive Seasons Winning Nine or More Games
23—Nebraska (current), from 1969

Most Consecutive Games Scoring on a Pass
37—Brigham Young, from Nov. 31, 1981, through Sept. 7, 1985

Most Consecutive Games Passing for 200 Yards or More
64 — Brigham Young, from Sept. 13, 1980, through Oct. 19, 1985

Most Consecutive Games Scored On
203 — Tulane (current), from Dec. 29, 1973

Most Consecutive Extra Points Made
262 — Syracuse, from Nov. 18, 1978, to Sept. 9, 1989. (By the following kickers: Dave Jacobs, last PAT of 1978; Gary Anderson, 72 from 1979 through 1981; Russ Carpentieri, 17 in 1982; Don McAulay, 62 from 1983 through 1985; Tim Vesling, 71 in 1986 and 1987; Kevin Greene, 37 in 1988; John Biskup, 2 in 1989.)

ADDITIONAL RECORDS

Highest-Scoring Tie Game
52-52 — Brigham Young & San Diego St., Nov. 16, 1991

Most Tie Games in a Season
4 — Central Mich., 1991 (11 games); UCLA, 1939 (10 games); Temple, 1937 (9 games)

Most Scoreless Tie Games in a Season
4 — Temple, 1937 (9 games)

Most Consecutive Scoreless Tie Games
2 — Alabama, 1954 vs. Georgia, Oct. 30 & vs. Tulane, Nov. 6; Georgia Tech, 1938 vs. Florida, Nov. 19 & vs. Georgia, Nov. 26

Last Scoreless Tie Game
Nov. 19, 1983 — Oregon & Oregon St.

Most Points Overcome to Win a Game (Between Division I-A Teams)
31 — Ohio St. (41), Minnesota (37), Oct. 28, 1989 (trailed 0-31 with 4:29 remaining in 2nd quarter); Maryland (42), Miami (Fla.) (40), Nov. 10, 1984 (trailed 0-31 with 12:35 remaining in 3rd quarter)

Most Points Scored in Fourth Quarter to Win a Game
28 — Washington St. (49) vs. Stanford (42), Oct. 20, 1984 (trailed 14-42 with 5:38 remaining in third quarter and scored 35 consecutive points)

Most Points Scored in a Brief Period of Time
41 in 2:55 of possession time during six drives — Nebraska vs. Colorado, Oct. 15, 1983 (6 TDs, 5 PATs in 3rd quarter. Drives occurred during 9:10 of total playing time in the period)
21 in 1:24 of total playing time — San Jose St. (42) vs. Fresno St. (7), Nov. 17, 1990 (3 TDs, 3 PATs in second quarter; 1:17 of possession time on two drives and one intercepted pass returned for a TD)

Most Improved Won-Lost Record
8 games — Purdue, 1943 (9-0) from 1942 (1-8); Stanford, 1940 (10-0, including a bowl win) from 1939 (1-7-1)

Most Improved Won-Lost Record Following Winless Season
7 games — Florida, 1980 (8-4-0, including a bowl win) from 1979 (0-10-1)

ANNUAL CHAMPIONS, ALL-TIME LEADERS

TOTAL OFFENSE

Career Yards Per Game

Player, Team	Years	Games	Plays	Yards	TDR‡	Yd. PG
Ty Detmer, Brigham Young	1988-91	46	*1,795	*14,665	*135	*318.8
Mike Perez, San Jose St.	1986-87	20	875	6,182	37	309.1
Doug Gaynor, Long Beach St.	1984-85	22	1,067	6,710	45	305.0
Tony Eason, Illinois	1981-82	22	1,016	6,589	43	299.5
David Klingler, Houston	1988-91	32	1,431	9,327	93	291.5
Steve Young, Brigham Young	1981-83	31	1,177	8,817	74	284.4
Doug Flutie, Boston College	1981-84	42	1,558	11,317	74	269.5
Brent Snyder, Utah St.	1987-88	22	1,040	5,916	43	268.9
Larry Egger, Utah	1985-86	22	903	5,651	42	256.9
Jim Plunkett, Stanford	1968-70	31	1,174	7,887	62	254.4
Randall Cunningham, Nev.-Las Vegas	1982-84	33	1,330	8,224	67	249.2
Erik Wilhelm, Oregon St.	1985-88	37	1,689	9,062	55	244.9
Todd Dillon, Long Beach St.	1982-83	23	1,031	5,588	38	243.0
Bernie Kosar, Miami (Fla.)	1983-84	23	847	5,585	48	242.8
Jack Trudeau, Illinois	1981, 83-85	34	1,318	8,096	56	238.1
Chuck Hixson, Southern Methodist	1968-70	29	1,358	6,884	50	237.4
Robbie Bosco, Brigham Young	1983-85	35	1,159	8,299	72	237.1
Dan McGwire, Iowa/San Diego St.	1986-87, 89-90	32	1,067	7,557	50	236.2
Johnny Bright, Drake	1949-51	25	825	5,903	64	236.1
Brian McClure, Bowling Green	1982-85	42	1,630	9,774	67	232.7
Marc Wilson, Brigham Young	1977-79	33	1,183	7,602	68	230.4
Todd Santos, San Diego St.	1984-87	46	1,722	10,513	71	228.5
Pat Sullivan, Auburn	1969-71	30	970	6,844	71	228.1
John Reaves, Florida	1969-71	32	1,258	7,283	58	227.6
Steve Ramsey, North Texas	1967-69	29	1,132	6,568	71	226.5

Player, Team	Years	Games	Plays	Yards	TDR‡	Yd. PG
Steve Clarkson, San Jose St.............	1979-82	31	1,124	6,995	68	225.6
Gifford Nielsen, Brigham Young	1975-77	24	871	5,391	58	224.6
Jay Venuto, Wake Forest................	1979-80	22	923	4,893	39	222.4
Jim McMahon, Brigham Young	1977-78, 80-81	44	1,325	9,723	94	221.0
Mike Hohensee, Minnesota	1981-82	22	850	4,859	38	220.9

Record. ‡ *Touchdowns-responsible-for are player's TDs scored and passed for.*

Season Yards Per Game

Player, Team	Year	Games	Plays	Yards	TDR‡	Yd. PG
David Klingler, Houston	†1990	11	*704	*5,221	*55	*474.6
Andre Ware, Houston	†1989	11	628	4,661	49	423.7
Ty Detmer, Brigham Young	1990	12	635	5,022	45	418.5
Steve Young, Brigham Young	†1983	11	531	4,346	41	395.1
Scott Mitchell, Utah	†1988	11	589	4,299	29	390.8
Jim McMahon, Brigham Young	†1980	12	540	4,627	53	385.6
Ty Detmer, Brigham Young	1989	12	497	4,433	38	369.4
Troy Kopp, Pacific (Cal.)	1990	9	485	3,276	32	364.0
Jim McMahon, Brigham Young	†1981	10	487	3,458	30	345.8
Anthony Dilweg, Duke	1988	11	539	3,713	26	337.6
Bill Anderson, Tulsa............................	†1965	10	580	3,343	35	334.3
Ty Detmer, Brigham Young	†1991	12	478	4,001	39	333.4
Dan McGwire, San Diego St..................	1990	11	484	3,664	28	333.1
Mike Perez, San Jose St......................	†1986	9	425	2,969	14	329.9
Robbie Bosco, Brigham Young	†1984	12	543	3,932	35	327.7
Doug Flutie, Boston College	1984	11	448	3,603	30	327.5
Jim Everett, Purdue	†1985	11	518	3,589	24	326.3
Todd Dillon, Long Beach St.	†1982	11	585	3,587	23	326.1
Marc Wilson, Brigham Young	†1979	11	488	3,580	32	325.5

Record. † *National champion.* ‡ *Touchdowns-responsible-for are player's TDs scored and passed for.*

Career Yards

Player, Team	Years	Plays	Yards Rush	Yards Pass	Total	Avg.
Ty Detmer, Brigham Young	1988-91	*1,795	-366	*15,031	*14,665	#8.17
Doug Flutie, Boston College	1981-84	1,558	738	10,579	11,317	7.26
Todd Santos, San Diego St.	1984-87	1,722	-912	11,425	10,513	6.11
Kevin Sweeney, Fresno St.	$1982-86	1,700	-371	10,623	10,252	6.03
Brian McClure, Bowling Green	1982-85	1,630	-506	10,280	9,774	6.00
Jim McMahon, Brigham Young	1977-78, 80-81	1,325	187	9,536	9,723	7.34
Terrence Jones, Tulane	1985-88	1,620	1,761	7,684	9,445	5.83
David Klingler, Houston	1988-91	1,431	-103	9,430	9,327	6.52
T. J. Rubley, Tulsa	1987-89, 91	1,541	-244	9,324	9,080	5.89
John Elway, Stanford	1979-82	1,505	-279	9,349	9,070	6.03
Erik Wilhelm, Oregon St.	1985-88	1,689	-331	9,393	9,062	5.37
Ben Bennett, Duke..........................	1980-83	1,582	-553	9,614	9,061	5.73
Chuck Long, Iowa	$1981-85	1,410	-176	9,210	9,034	6.41
Todd Ellis, South Caro.	1986-89	1,517	-497	9,519	9,022	5.95
Tom Hodson, Louisiana St.	1986-89	1,307	-177	9,115	8,938	6.84
Scott Mitchell, Utah	1987-89	1,306	-145	8,981	8,836	6.77
Steve Young, Brigham Young	1981-83	1,177	1,084	7,733	8,817	7.49
Brian Mitchell, Southwestern La..........	1986-89	1,521	3,335	5,447	8,782	5.77
Jeremy Leach, New Mexico...............	1988-91	1,695	-762	9,382	8,620	5.09
Mark Herrmann, Purdue	1977-80	1,354	-744	9,188	8,444	6.24
Robbie Bosco, Brigham Young	1983-85	1,158	-101	8,400	8,299	7.17
Troy Taylor, California.....................	1986-89	1,490	110	8,126	8,236	5.53
Randall Cunningham, Nev.-Las Vegas	1982-84	1,330	204	8,020	8,224	6.18
Steve Slayden, Duke	1984-87	1,546	125	8,004	8,129	5.26
Jack Trudeau, Illinois	1981, 83-85	1,318	-50	8,146	8,096	6.14
Mark Barsotti, Fresno St...................	1988-91	1,192	768	7,321	8,089	6.79
Gene Swick, Toledo........................	1972-75	1,579	807	7,267	8,074	5.11
Andre Ware, Houston	1987-89	1,194	-144	8,202	8,058	6.75
Joe Adams, Tennessee St.	1977-80	1,256	-677	8,649	7,972	6.35
Rodney Peete, Southern Cal	1985-88	1,226	309	7,640	7,949	6.48
Shawn Moore, Virginia	1987-90	1,177	1,268	6,629	7,897	6.71
Jim Plunkett, Stanford	1968-70	1,174	343	7,544	7,887	6.72
Art Schlichter, Ohio St.....................	1978-81	1,316	1,285	6,584	7,869	5.98
Mike Gundy, Oklahoma St.	1986-89	1,275	-248	8,072	7,824	6.14
John Holman, Northeast La.	1979-82	1,376	-25	7,827	7,802	5.67

Player, Team	Years	Plays	Yards Rush	Yards Pass	Total	Avg.
Jack Thompson, Washington St.	1975-78	1,345	-120	7,818	7,698	5.72
Dan Marino, Pittsburgh	1979-82	1,185	-270	7,905	7,635	6.44
Brett Favre, Southern Miss.	1987-90	1,362	-89	7,695	7,606	5.58
Marc Wilson, Brigham Young	1977-79	1,183	-35	7,637	7,602	6.43
Dan McGwire, Iowa/San Diego St.	1986-87, 89-90	1,067	-607	8,164	7,557	7.08
John Paye, Stanford	1983-86	1,442	-131	7,669	7,538	5.23
Scott Campbell, Purdue...................	1980-83	1,305	-110	7,636	7,526	5.77
Bill Musgrave, Oregon	1987-90	1,177	-186	7,631	7,445	6.33
Tom Corontzos, Wyoming	1988-91	1,303	-203	7,601	7,398	5.68
Tom Tunnicliffe, Arizona	1980-83	1,253	-282	7,618	7,336	5.85
John Reaves, Florida.....................	1969-71	1,258	-266	7,549	7,283	5.79
Jeff Graham, Long Beach St.	1985-88	1,374	-817	8,063	7,246	5.27

* *Record.*   \$ *See page 6 for explanation.*   ¢ *Active player.*   # *Record for minimum of 6,500 yards.*

Career Yards Record Progression
(Record Yards—Player, Team, Seasons Played)

3,481—Davey O'Brien, Texas Christian, 1936-38; **3,882**—Paul Christman, Missouri, 1938-40; **4,602**—Frank Sinkwich, Georgia, 1940-42; **4,627**—Bob Fenimore, Oklahoma St., 1943-46; **4,871**—Charlie Justice, North Caro., 1946-49; **5,903**—Johnny Bright, Drake, 1949-51; **6,354**—Virgil Carter, Brigham Young, 1964-66; **6,568**—Steve Ramsey, North Texas, 1967-69; **7,887**—Jim Plunkett, Stanford, 1968-70; **8,074**—Gene Swick, Toledo, 1972-75; **8,444**—Mark Herrmann, Purdue, 1977-80; **9,723**—Jim McMahon, Brigham Young, 1977-78, 80-81; **11,317**—Doug Flutie, Boston College, 1981-84; **14,665**—Ty Detmer, Brigham Young, 1988-91.

Season Yards

Player, Team	Year	Games	Plays	Yards Rush	Yards Pass	Total	Avg.
David Klingler, Houston	†1990	11	*704	81	5,140	*5,221	7.42
Ty Detmer, Brigham Young	1990	12	635	-106	*5,188	5,022	7.91
Andre Ware, Houston	†1989	11	628	-38	4,699	4,661	7.42
Jim McMahon, Brigham Young	†1980	12	540	56	4,571	4,627	8.57
Ty Detmer, Brigham Young	1989	12	497	-127	4,560	4,433	@8.92
Steve Young, Brigham Young	†1983	11	531	444	3,902	4,346	8.18
Scott Mitchell, Utah	†1988	11	589	-23	4,322	4,299	7.30
Robbie Bosco, Brigham Young	1985	13	578	-132	4,273	4,141	7.16
Ty Detmer, Brigham Young	†1991	12	478	-30	4,031	4,001	8.37
Robbie Bosco, Brigham Young	†1984	12	543	57	3,875	3,932	7.24
Anthony Dilweg, Duke	1988	11	539	-111	3,824	3,713	6.89
Todd Santos, San Diego St.	†1987	12	562	-244	3,932	3,688	6.56
Troy Kopp, Pacific (Cal.)	1991	12	496	-81	3,767	3,686	7.43
Dan McGwire, San Diego St..............	1990	11	484	-169	3,833	3,664	7.57
Doug Flutie, Boston College	1984	11	448	149	3,454	3,603	8.04
Jim Everett, Purdue	†1985	11	518	-62	3,651	3,589	6.93
Todd Dillon, Long Beach St.	†1982	11	585	70	3,517	3,587	6.13
Marc Wilson, Brigham Young	†1979	11	488	-140	3,720	3,580	7.34
Sam King, Nevada-Las Vegas	1981	12	507	-216	3,778	3,562	7.03
Matt Kofler, San Diego St.................	1981	11	594	191	3,337	3,528	5.94
Steve Young, Brigham Young	1982	11	481	407	3,100	3,507	7.29
Doug Gaynor, Long Beach St.	1985	12	589	-96	3,563	3,467	5.89
Jim McMahon, Brigham Young	1981	10	487	-97	3,555	3,458	7.10
Dan McGwire, San Diego St...............	1989	12	504	-228	3,651	3,423	6.79
Bernie Kosar, Miami (Fla.)...............	1984	12	468	-230	3,642	3,412	7.29

* *Record.*   † *National champion.*   @ *Record for minimum of 3,000 yards.*

Single-Game Yards

Yds.	Rush	Pass	Player, Team (Opponent)	Date
732	16	716	David Klingler, Houston (Arizona St.)............................Dec. 2, 1990	
696	6	690	Matt Vogler, Texas Christian (Houston)...........................Nov. 3, 1990	
625	62	563	David Klingler, Houston (Texas Christian) ....Nov. 3, 1990	
625	-6	631	Scott Mitchell, Utah (Air Force)................................Oct. 15, 1988	
603	4	599	Ty Detmer, Brigham Young (San Diego St.) ....Nov. 16, 1991	
601	37	564	Troy Kopp, Pacific, Cal. (New Mexico St.).....................Oct. 20, 1990	
599	86	513	Virgil Carter, Brigham Young (UTEP)...........................Nov. 5, 1966	
594	-28	622	Jeremy Leach, New Mexico (Utah) ....Nov. 11, 1989	
585	-36	621	Dave Wilson, Illinois (Ohio St.)..................................Nov. 8, 1980	
582	11	571	Marc Wilson, Brigham Young (Utah) ....Nov. 5, 1977	
578	6	572	David Klingler, Houston (Eastern Wash.) ....Nov. 17, 1990	
562	25	537	Ty Detmer, Brigham Young (Washington St.) ....Sept. 7, 1989	
552	-13	565	Jim McMahon, Brigham Young (Utah)...........................Nov. 21, 1981	
548	12	536	Dave Telford, Fresno St. (Pacific, Cal.)..........................Oct. 24, 1987	
540	-45	585	Robbie Bosco, Brigham Young (New Mexico)...................Oct. 19, 1985	

Yds.	Rush	Pass	Player, Team (Opponent)	Date
540	104	436	Archie Manning, Mississippi (Alabama)	Oct. 4, 1969
539	1	538	Jim McMahon, Brigham Young (Colorado St.)	Nov. 7, 1981
537	2	535	Shane Montgomery, North Caro. St. (Duke)	Nov. 11, 1989
537	-24	561	Tony Adams, Utah St. (Utah)	Nov. 11, 1972
536	28	508	Mike Perez, San Jose St. (Pacific, Cal.)	Oct. 25, 1986
532	0	532	Jeff Van Raaphorst, Arizona St. (Florida St.)	Nov. 3, 1984
531	13	518	Jeff Graham, Long Beach St. (Hawaii)	Oct. 29, 1988
528	-40	568	David Lowery, San Diego St. (Brigham Young)	Nov. 16, 1991
528	-2	530	Dan McGwire, San Diego St. (New Mexico)	Nov. 17, 1990
527	17	510	David Klingler, Houston (Louisiana Tech)	Aug. 31, 1991
525	-29	554	Greg Cook, Cincinnati (Ohio)	Nov. 16, 1968
524	118	406	Ned James, New Mexico (Wyoming)	Nov. 1, 1986
521	-39	560	Ty Detmer, Brigham Young (Utah St.)	Nov. 24, 1990
521	57	464	Whit Taylor, Vanderbilt (Tennessee)	Nov. 28, 1981
519	-14	533	David Klingler, Houston (Texas Tech)	Nov. 30, 1991
517	45	472	Doug Flutie, Boston College (Miami, Fla.)	Nov. 23, 1984
517	73	444	Matt Kofler, San Diego St. (Iowa St.)	Oct. 10, 1981
516	-42	558	Chuck Hartlieb, Iowa (Indiana)	Oct. 29, 1988
516	31	485	Jim McMahon, Brigham Young (Utah St.)	Oct. 18, 1980
516	-11	527	Don Strock, Virginia Tech (Houston)	Oct. 7, 1972
513	2	511	Scott Mitchell, Utah (Idaho St.)	Sept. 10, 1988
512	-22	534	Paul Justin, Arizona St. (Washington St.)	Oct. 28, 1989
512	-14	526	Joe Theismann, Notre Dame (Southern Cal)	Nov. 28, 1970

Annual Champions

				Yards		
Year	Player, Team	Class	Plays	Rush	Pass	Total
1937	Byron "Whizzer" White, Colorado	Sr.	224	1,121	475	1,596
1938	Davey O'Brien, Texas Christian	Sr.	291	390	1,457	1,847
1939	Kenny Washington, UCLA	Sr.	259	811	559	1,370
1940	Johnny Knolla, Creighton	Sr.	298	813	607	1,420
1941	Bud Schwenk, Washington (Mo.)	Sr.	354	471	1,457	1,928
1942	Frank Sinkwich, Georgia	Sr.	341	795	1,392	2,187
1943	Bob Hoernschemeyer, Indiana	Fr.	355	515	1,133	1,648
1944	Bob Fenimore, Oklahoma St.	So.	241	897	861	1,758
1945	Bob Fenimore, Oklahoma St.	Jr.	203	1,048	593	1,641
1946	Travis Tidwell, Auburn	Fr.	339	772	943	1,715
1947	Fred Enke, Arizona	So.	329	535	1,406	1,941
1948	Stan Heath, Nevada	Sr.	233	-13	2,005	1,992
1949	Johnny Bright, Drake	So.	275	975	975	1,950
1950	Johnny Bright, Drake	Jr.	320	1,232	1,168	2,400
1951	Dick Kazmaier, Princeton	Sr.	272	861	966	1,827
1952	Ted Marchibroda, Detroit Mercy	Sr.	305	176	1,637	1,813
1953	Paul Larson, California	Jr.	262	141	1,431	1,572
1954	George Shaw, Oregon	Sr.	276	178	1,358	1,536
1955	George Welsh, Navy	Sr.	203	29	1,319	1,348
1956	John Brodie, Stanford	Sr.	295	9	1,633	1,642
1957	Bob Newman, Washington St.	Jr.	263	53	1,391	1,444
1958	Dick Bass, Pacific (Cal.)	Jr.	218	1,361	79	1,440
1959	Dick Norman, Stanford	Jr.	319	55	1,963	2,018
1960	Bill Kilmer, UCLA	Sr.	292	803	1,086	1,889
1961	Dave Hoppmann, Iowa St.	Jr.	320	920	718	1,638
1962	Terry Baker, Oregon St.	Sr.	318	538	1,738	2,276
1963	George Mira, Miami (Fla.)	Sr.	394	163	2,155	2,318
1964	Jerry Rhome, Tulsa	Sr.	470	258	2,870	3,128
1965	Bill Anderson, Tulsa	Sr.	580	-121	3,464	3,343
1966	Virgil Carter, Brigham Young	Sr.	388	363	2,182	2,545
1967	Sal Olivas, New Mexico St.	Sr.	368	-41	2,225	2,184
1968	Greg Cook, Cincinnati	Sr.	507	-62	3,272	3,210
1969	Dennis Shaw, San Diego St.	Sr.	388	12	3,185	3,197

Beginning in 1970, ranked on per-game (instead of total) yards

					Yards			
Year	Player, Team	Class	Games	Plays	Rush	Pass	Total	Avg.
1970	Pat Sullivan, Auburn	Jr.	10	333	270	2,586	2,856	285.6
1971	Gary Huff, Florida St.	Jr.	11	386	-83	2,736	2,653	241.2
1972	Don Strock, Virginia Tech	Sr.	11	480	-73	3,243	3,170	288.2
1973	Jesse Freitas, San Diego St.	Sr.	11	410	-92	2,993	2,901	263.7
1974	Steve Joachim, Temple	Sr.	10	331	277	1,950	2,227	222.7
1975	Gene Swick, Toledo	Sr.	11	490	219	2,487	2,706	246.0
1976	Tommy Kramer, Rice	Sr.	11	562	-45	3,317	3,272	297.5

1992 NCAA FOOTBALL

Year	Player, Team	Class	Games	Plays	Yards Rush	Pass	Total	Avg.
1977	Doug Williams, Grambling	Sr.	11	377	-57	3,286	3,229	293.5
1978	Mike Ford, Southern Methodist	So.	11	459	-50	3,007	2,957	268.8
1979	Marc Wilson, Brigham Young	Sr.	11	488	-140	3,720	3,580	325.5
1980	Jim McMahon, Brigham Young	Jr.	12	540	56	4,571	4,627	385.6
1981	Jim McMahon, Brigham Young	Sr.	10	487	-97	3,555	3,458	345.8
1982	Todd Dillon, Long Beach St.	Jr.	11	585	70	3,517	3,587	326.1
1983	Steve Young, Brigham Young	Sr.	11	531	444	3,902	4,346	395.1
1984	Robbie Bosco, Brigham Young	Jr.	12	543	57	3,875	3,932	327.7
1985	Jim Everett, Purdue	Sr.	11	518	-62	3,651	3,589	326.3
1986	Mike Perez, San Jose St.	Jr.	9	425	35	2,934	2,969	329.9
1987	Todd Santos, San Diego St.	Sr.	12	562	-244	3,932	3,688	307.3
1988	Scott Mitchell, Utah	So.	11	589	-23	4,322	4,299	390.8
1989	Andre Ware, Houston	Jr.	11	628	-38	4,699	4,661	423.7
1990	David Klingler, Houston	Jr.	11	*704	81	5,140	*5,221	*474.6
1991	Ty Detmer, Brigham Young	Sr.	12	478	-30	4,031	4,001	333.4

* Record.

RUSHING
Career Yards Per Game

Player, Team	Years	Games	Plays	Yards	TD	Yd. PG
Ed Marinaro, Cornell	1969-71	27	918	4,715	50	*174.6
O. J. Simpson, Southern Cal	1967-68	19	621	3,124	33	164.4
Herschel Walker, Georgia	1980-82	33	994	5,259	49	159.4
Tony Dorsett, Pittsburgh	1973-76	43	1,074	*6,082	55	141.4
Mike Rozier, Nebraska	1981-83	35	668	4,780	49	136.6
Howard Stevens, Louisville...............	§1971-72	20	509	2,723	25	136.2
Jerome Persell, Western Mich.	1976-78	31	842	4,190	39	135.2
Rudy Mobley, Hardin-Simmons	1942,46	19	414	2,543	32	133.8
Vaughn Dunbar, Indiana	1990-91	22	565	2,842	24	129.2
Steve Owens, Oklahoma	1967-69	30	905	3,867	56	128.9
Charles White, Southern Cal	1976-79	44	1,023	5,598	46	127.2
Johnny Bright, Drake	1949-51	25	513	3,134	39	125.4
Woody Green, Arizona St.	1971-73	30	601	3,754	33	125.1
Archie Griffin, Ohio St.	1972-75	42	845	5,177	25	123.3
Anthony Thompson, Indiana.............	1986-89	41	1,089	4,965	*64	121.1
Mark Kellar, Northern Ill.	1971-73	31	743	3,745	32	120.8
Paul Gipson, Houston....................	1966-68	23	447	2,769	25	120.4
John Cappelletti, Penn St.	‡1972-73	22	519	2,639	29	120.0
Steve Bartalo, Colorado St.	1983-86	41	*1,215	4,813	46	117.4
Louie Giammona, Utah St.	1973-75	30	756	3,499	21	116.6
Paul Palmer, Temple	1983-86	42	948	4,895	39	116.5
Bill Marek, Wisconsin	1972-75	32	719	3,709	44	115.9
Darren Lewis, Texas A&M................	1987-90	44	909	5,012	44	113.9
Dick Jauron, Yale	1970-72	26	515	2,947	27	113.3
Bo Jackson, Auburn	1982-85	38	650	4,303	43	113.2
Joe Morris, Syracuse.....................	1978-81	38	813	4,299	25	113.1
Eugene "Mercury" Morris, West Tex. St...	1966-68	30	541	3,388	34	112.9

* Record. § Competed two years in Division I-A and two years in Division II (Randolph-Macon, 1968-69). Four-year totals: 5,297 yards, 139.4 average. ‡ Defensive back in 1971.

Season Yards Per Game

Player, Team	Year	Games	Plays	Yards	TD	Yd. PG
Barry Sanders, Oklahoma St.	†1988	11	344	*2,628	*37	*232.1
Marcus Allen, Southern Cal	†1981	11	*403	2,342	22	212.9
Ed Marinaro, Cornell	†1971	9	356	1,881	24	209.0
Charles White, Southern Cal	†1979	10	293	1,803	18	180.3
Mike Rozier, Nebraska	†1983	12	275	2,148	29	179.0
Tony Dorsett, Pittsburgh	†1976	11	338	1,948	21	177.1
Ollie Matson, San Francisco	†1951	9	245	1,566	20	174.0
Lorenzo White, Michigan St.	†1985	11	386	1,908	17	173.5
Herschel Walker, Georgia	1981	11	385	1,891	18	171.9
O. J. Simpson, Southern Cal	†1968	10	355	1,709	22	170.9
Ernest Anderson, Oklahoma St..........	†1982	11	353	1,877	8	170.6
Ricky Bell, Southern Cal	†1975	11	357	1,875	13	170.5

* Record. † National champion.

Career Yards

Player, Team	Years	Plays	Yards	Avg.	Long
Tony Dorsett, Pittsburgh	1973-76	1,074	*6,082	5.66	73
Charles White, Southern Cal	1976-79	1,023	5,598	5.47	79
Herschel Walker, Georgia	1980-82	994	5,259	5.29	76
Archie Griffin, Ohio St.	1972-75	845	5,177	††6.13	75
Darren Lewis, Texas A&M	1987-90	909	5,012	5.51	84
Anthony Thompson, Indiana	1986-89	1,089	4,965	4.56	52
George Rogers, South Caro.	1977-80	902	4,958	5.50	80
Paul Palmer, Temple	1983-86	948	4,895	5.16	78
Steve Bartalo, Colorado St.	1983-86	*1,215	4,813	3.96	39
Mike Rozier, Nebraska	1981-83	668	4,780	#7.16	93
Ed Marinaro, Cornell	1969-71	918	4,715	5.14	79
Marcus Allen, Southern Cal	1978-81	893	4,682	5.24	45
Ted Brown, North Caro. St.	1975-78	860	4,602	5.35	95
Thurman Thomas, Oklahoma St.	1984-87	898	4,595	5.12	66
Terry Miller, Oklahoma St.	1974-77	847	4,582	5.41	81
Darrell Thompson, Minnesota	1986-89	911	4,518	4.96	98
Lorenzo White, Michigan St.	1984-87	991	4,513	4.55	73
Eric Dickerson, Southern Methodist	1979-82	790	4,450	5.63	80
Earl Campbell, Texas	1974-77	765	4,443	5.81	‡‡83
Amos Lawrence, North Caro.	1977-80	881	4,391	4.98	62
Bo Jackson, Auburn	1982-85	650	4,303	6.62	80
Joe Morris, Syracuse	1978-81	813	4,299	5.29	75
Reggie Taylor, Cincinnati	1983-86	876	4,242	4.48	‡‡68
Mike Mayweather, Army	1987-90	832	4,212	5.06	52
Jerome Persell, Western Mich.	1976-78	842	4,190	4.98	86
Napoleon McCallum, Navy	$1981-85	908	4,179	4.60	60
George Swarn, Miami (Ohio)	1983-86	881	4,172	4.74	98
Curtis Adams, Central Mich.	1981-84	761	4,162	5.47	87
Allen Pinkett, Notre Dame	1982-85	889	4,131	4.65	76
James Gray, Texas Tech	1986-89	742	4,066	5.48	72
Robert Lavette, Georgia Tech	1981-84	914	4,066	4.45	83
Stump Mitchell, Citadel	1977-80	756	4,062	5.37	77
Dalton Hilliard, Louisiana St.	1982-85	882	4,050	4.59	66
Charles Alexander, Louisiana St.	1975-78	855	4,035	4.72	64
Darrin Nelson, Stanford	1977-78, 80-81	703	4,033	5.74	80
Joe Washington, Oklahoma	1972-75	656	3,995	6.09	71
Mike Voight, North Caro.	1973-76	826	3,971	4.81	84
Jamie Morris, Michigan	1984-87	742	3,944	5.32	74
Eric Bieniemy, Colorado	1987-90	699	3,940	5.64	69
Emmitt Smith, Florida	1987-89	700	3,928	5.61	96
Ron "Po" James, New Mexico St.	1968-71	818	3,884	4.75	69
Steve Owens, Oklahoma	1967-69	905	3,867	4.27	‡‡49
Mike Williams, New Mexico	1975-78	857	3,862	4.51	36
Sonny Collins, Kentucky	1972-75	777	3,835	4.94	66
Eric Wilkerson, Kent	1985-88	735	3,830	5.21	74
Billy Sims, Oklahoma	$1975-79	538	3,813	7.09	‡‡71
James McDougald, Wake Forest	1976-79	880	3,811	4.33	62
Tony Sands, Kansas	1988-91	778	3,788	4.87	66
Reggie Dupard, Southern Methodist	1982-85	641	3,769	5.88	71
Greg Allen, Florida St.	1981-84	624	3,769	6.04	81

* Record. \$ See page 6 for explanation. ‡‡ Did not score. †† Record for minimum of 781 carries. # Record for minimum of 414 carries.

Career Yards Record Progression
(Record Yards—Player, Team, Seasons Played)

1,961—Marshall Goldberg, Pittsburgh, 1936-38; **2,105**—Tom Harmon, Michigan, 1938-40; **2,271**—Frank Sinkwich, Georgia, 1940-42; **2,301**—Bill Daley, Minnesota, 1940-42, Michigan, 1943; **2,957**—Glenn Davis, Army, 1943-46; **3,095**—Eddie Price, Tulane, 1946-49; **3,238**—John Papit, Virginia, 1947-50; **3,381**—Art Luppino, Arizona, 1953-56; **3,388**—Eugene "Mercury" Morris, West Tex. St., 1966-68; **3,867**—Steve Owens, Oklahoma, 1967-69; **4,715**—Ed Marinaro, Cornell, 1969-71; **5,177**—Archie Griffin, Ohio St., 1972-75; **6,082**—Tony Dorsett, Pittsburgh, 1973-76.

Season Yards

Player, Team	Year	Games	Plays	Yards	Avg.
Barry Sanders, Oklahoma St.	†1988	11	344	*2,628	‡7.64
Marcus Allen, Southern Cal	†1981	11	*403	2,342	5.81
Mike Rozier, Nebraska	†1983	12	275	2,148	#7.81
Tony Dorsett, Pittsburgh	†1976	11	338	1,948	5.76
Lorenzo White, Michigan St.	†1985	11	386	1,908	4.94

Player, Team	Year	Games	Plays	Yards	Avg.
Herschel Walker, Georgia	1981	11	385	1,891	4.91
Ed Marinaro, Cornell	†1971	9	356	1,881	5.28
Ernest Anderson, Oklahoma St.	†1982	11	353	1,877	5.32
Ricky Bell, Southern Cal	†1975	11	357	1,875	5.25
Paul Palmer, Temple	†1986	11	346	1,866	5.39
Charles White, Southern Cal	†1979	10	293	1,803	6.15
Anthony Thompson, Indiana	†1989	11	358	1,793	5.01
Obie Graves, Cal St. Fullerton	1978	12	275	1,789	6.51
Bo Jackson, Auburn	1985	11	278	1,786	6.42
George Rogers, South Caro.	†1980	11	297	1,781	6.00
Billy Sims, Oklahoma	†1978	11	231	1,762	7.63
Charles White, Southern Cal	1978	12	342	1,760	5.15
Robert Newhouse, Houston	1971	11	277	1,757	6.34
Herschel Walker, Georgia	1982	11	335	1,752	5.23
Earl Campbell, Texas	†1977	11	267	1,744	6.53
Mike Pringle, Cal St. Fullerton	1989	11	296	1,727	5.83
Don McCauley, North Caro.	1970	11	324	1,720	5.31

* Record. † National champion. ‡ Record for minimum of 282 carries. # Record for minimum of 214 carries.

Single-Game Yards

Yds.	Player, Team (Opponent)	Date
396	Tony Sands, Kansas (Missouri)	Nov. 23, 1991
386	Marshall Faulk, San Diego St. (Pacific, Cal.)	Sept. 14, 1991
377	Anthony Thompson, Indiana (Wisconsin)	Nov. 11, 1989
357	Mike Pringle, Cal St. Fullerton (New Mexico St.)	Nov. 4, 1989
357	Rueben Mayes, Washington St. (Oregon)	Oct. 27, 1984
356	Eddie Lee Ivery, Georgia Tech (Air Force)	Nov. 11, 1978
350	Eric Allen, Michigan St. (Purdue)	Oct. 30, 1971
349	Paul Palmer, Temple (East Caro.)	Oct. 11, 1986
347	Ricky Bell, Southern Cal (Washington St.)	Oct. 9, 1976
347	Ron Johnson, Michigan (Wisconsin)	Nov. 16, 1968
343	Tony Jeffery, Texas Christian (Tulane)	Sept. 13, 1986
342	Roosevelt Leaks, Texas (Southern Methodist)	Nov. 3, 1973
342	Charlie Davis, Colorado (Oklahoma St.)	Nov. 3, 1971
340	Eugene "Mercury" Morris, West Tex. St. (Montana St.)	Oct. 5, 1968
332	Barry Sanders, Oklahoma St. (Texas Tech)	Dec. 3, 1988
328	Derrick Fenner, North Caro. (Virginia)	Nov. 15, 1986
326	George Swarn, Miami, Ohio (Eastern Mich.)	Nov. 16, 1985
326	Fred Wendt, UTEP (New Mexico St.)	Nov. 25, 1948
322	Greg Allen, Florida St. (Western Caro.)	Oct. 31, 1981
321	Frank Mordica, Vanderbilt (Air Force)	Nov. 18, 1978
320	Barry Sanders, Oklahoma St. (Kansas St.)	Oct. 29, 1988
319	Andre Herrera, Southern Ill. (Northern Ill.)	Oct. 23, 1976
319	Jim Pilot, New Mexico St. (Hardin-Simmons)	Nov. 25, 1961
316	Emmitt Smith, Florida (New Mexico)	Oct. 21, 1989
316	Mike Adamle, Northwestern (Wisconsin)	Oct. 18, 1969
312	Mark Brus, Tulsa (New Mexico St.)	Oct. 27, 1990
312	Barry Sanders, Oklahoma St. (Kansas)	Nov. 12, 1988
310	Tony Alford, Colorado St. (Utah)	Oct. 28, 1989
310	Mitchell True, Pacific, Cal. (UC Davis)	Nov. 18, 1972
308	Stacey Robinson (QB), Northern Ill. (Fresno St.)	Oct. 6, 1990
307	Curtis Kuykendall, Auburn (Miami, Fla.)	Nov. 24, 1944
304	Barry Sanders, Oklahoma St. (Tulsa)	Oct. 1, 1988
304	Sam Dejarnette, Southern Miss. (Florida St.)	Sept. 25, 1982
304	Bill Marek, Wisconsin (Minnesota)	Nov. 23, 1974
303	Tony Dorsett, Pittsburgh (Notre Dame)	Nov. 15, 1975
302	Jason Davis, Louisiana Tech (Southwestern La.)	Sept. 29, 1990
302	Kevin Lowe, Wyoming (South Dak. St.)	Nov. 10, 1984

Annual Champions

Year	Player, Team	Class	Plays	Yards
1937	Byron "Whizzer" White, Colorado	Sr.	181	1,121
1938	Len Eshmont, Fordham	So.	132	831
1939	John Polanski, Wake Forest	So.	137	882
1940	Al Ghesquiere, Detroit Mercy	Sr.	146	957
1941	Frank Sinkwich, Georgia	Jr.	209	1,103
1942	Rudy Mobley, Hardin-Simmons	So.	187	1,281
1943	Creighton Miller, Notre Dame	Sr.	151	911
1944	Wayne "Red" Williams, Minnesota	Jr.	136	911

Year	Player, Team	Class	Plays	Yards
1945	Bob Fenimore, Oklahoma St.	Jr.	142	1,048
1946	Rudy Mobley, Hardin-Simmons	Sr.	227	1,262
1947	Wilton Davis, Hardin-Simmons	So.	193	1,173
1948	Fred Wendt, UTEP	Sr.	184	1,570
1949	John Dottley, Mississippi	Jr.	208	1,312
1950	Wilford White, Arizona St.	Sr.	199	1,502
1951	Ollie Matson, San Francisco	Sr.	245	1,566
1952	Howie Waugh, Tulsa	Sr.	164	1,372
1953	J. C. Caroline, Illinois	So.	194	1,256
1954	Art Luppino, Arizona	So.	179	1,359
1955	Art Luppino, Arizona	Jr.	209	1,313
1956	Jim Crawford, Wyoming	Sr.	200	1,104
1957	Leon Burton, Arizona St.	Sr.	117	1,126
1958	Dick Bass, Pacific (Cal.)	Jr.	205	1,361
1959	Pervis Atkins, New Mexico St.	Jr.	130	971
1960	Bob Gaiters, New Mexico St.	Sr.	197	1,338
1961	Jim Pilot, New Mexico St.	So.	191	1,278
1962	Jim Pilot, New Mexico St.	Jr.	208	1,247
1963	Dave Casinelli, Memphis St.	Sr.	219	1,016
1964	Brian Piccolo, Wake Forest	Sr.	252	1,044
1965	Mike Garrett, Southern Cal	Sr.	267	1,440
1966	Ray McDonald, Idaho	Sr.	259	1,329
1967	O. J. Simpson, Southern Cal	Jr.	266	1,415
1968	O. J. Simpson, Southern Cal	Sr.	355	1,709
1969	Steve Owens, Oklahoma	Sr.	358	1,523

Beginning in 1970, ranked on per-game (instead of total) yards

Year	Player, Team	Class	Games	Plays	Yards	Avg.
1970	Ed Marinaro, Cornell	Jr.	9	285	1,425	158.3
1971	Ed Marinaro, Cornell	Sr.	9	356	1,881	209.0
1972	Pete VanValkenburg, Brigham Young	Sr.	10	232	1,386	138.6
1973	Mark Kellar, Northern Ill.	Sr.	11	291	1,719	156.3
1974	Louie Giammona, Utah St.	Jr.	10	329	1,534	153.4
1975	Ricky Bell, Southern Cal	Jr.	11	357	1,875	170.5
1976	Tony Dorsett, Pittsburgh	Sr.	11	338	1,948	177.1
1977	Earl Campbell, Texas	Sr.	11	267	1,744	158.5
1978	Billy Sims, Oklahoma	Jr.	11	231	1,762	160.2
1979	Charles White, Southern Cal	Sr.	10	293	1,803	180.3
1980	George Rogers, South Caro.	Sr.	11	297	1,781	161.9
1981	Marcus Allen, Southern Cal	Sr.	11	*403	2,342	212.9
1982	Ernest Anderson, Oklahoma St.	Jr.	11	353	1,877	170.6
1983	Mike Rozier, Nebraska	Sr.	12	275	2,148	179.0
1984	Keith Byars, Ohio St.	Jr.	11	313	1,655	150.5
1985	Lorenzo White, Michigan St.	So.	11	386	1,908	173.5
1986	Paul Palmer, Temple	Sr.	11	346	1,866	169.6
1987	Elbert "Ickey" Woods, Nevada-Las Vegas	Sr.	11	259	1,658	150.7
1988	Barry Sanders, Oklahoma St.	Jr.	11	344	*2,628	*232.1
1989	Anthony Thompson, Indiana	Sr.	11	358	1,793	163.0
1990	Gerald Hudson, Oklahoma St.	Sr.	11	279	1,642	149.3
1991	Marshall Faulk, San Diego St.	Fr.	9	201	1,429	158.8

* Record.

QUARTERBACK RUSHING
Season Yards

Player, Team	Year	Games	Plays	Yards	TD	Avg.
Stacey Robinson, Northern Ill.	1989	11	223	*1,443	*19	6.47
Dee Dowis, Air Force	1987	12	194	1,315	10	6.78
Brian Mitchell, Southwestern La.	1989	11	237	1,311	*19	5.53
Fred Solomon, Tampa	1974	11	193	1,300	*19	6.74
Dee Dowis, Air Force	1989	12	172	1,286	18	*7.48
Stacey Robinson, Northern Ill.	1990	11	193	1,238	*19	6.41
Rob Perez, Air Force	1991	12	233	1,157	10	4.97
Jack Mildren, Oklahoma	1971	11	193	1,140	17	5.91
Nolan Cromwell, Kansas	1975	11	218	1,124	9	5.16
Michael Carter, Hawaii	1991	12	221	1,092	16	4.94
Tory Crawford, Army	1986	11	*244	1,075	15	4.41
Bart Weiss, Air Force	1985	12	180	1,032	12	5.73
Jimmy Sidle, Auburn	1963	10	185	1,006	10	5.44
Reggie Collier, Southern Miss.	1981	11	153	1,005	12	6.57
Darian Hagan, Colorado	1989	11	186	1,004	17	5.40

* Record.

Career Yards

Player, Team	Years	Games	Plays	Yards	TD	Yd. PG
Dee Dowis, Air Force	1986-89	47	543	*3,612	41	76.9
Brian Mitchell, Southwestern La.......	1986-89	43	678	3,335	*47	77.6
Fred Solomon, Tampa	1971-74	43	557	3,299	39	76.7
Stacey Robinson, Northern Ill.	1988-90	25	429	2,727	38	*109.1
Jamelle Holieway, Oklahoma	1985-88	38	505	2,699	30	71.0
Bill Hurley, Syracuse	1975-79	46	*685	2,551	19	55.5
Bill Deery, William & Mary............	1972-74	33	443	2,401	19	72.8
Reggie Collier, Southern Miss.	1979-82	39	446	2,304	26	59.1
John Bond, Mississippi St.	1980-83	44	572	2,280	24	51.8
Tory Crawford, Army..................	1984-87	31	495	2,255	34	72.7
Alton Grizzard, Navy	1987-90	38	599	2,174	15	57.2
Roy DeWalt, Texas-Arlington	1975, 77-79	38	468	2,136	27	56.2
Bucky Richardson, Texas A&M	1987-88, 90-91	41	370	2,095	30	51.1
Rocky Long, New Mexico.............	1969-71	31	469	2,071	21	66.8
Steve Davis, Oklahoma	1973-75	33	515	2,069	33	62.7
Steve Taylor, Nebraska	1985-88	37	429	2,065	30	55.8
Rick Leach, Michigan	1975-78	43	440	2,053	34	47.7
Prince McJunkins, Wichita St.........	1979-82	44	613	2,047	27	46.5
Rickey Foggie, Minnesota.............	1984-87	41	510	2,038	24	49.7
Major Harris, West Va.................	1987-89	33	386	2,030	18	51.5
Steve Gage, Tulsa	1983-84, 86	33	522	2,029	30	61.5
Darian Hagan, Colorado	1988-91	41	489	2,007	27	49.0

* Record.

PASSING

Sample Compilation of NCAA Passing Efficiency Formula

Player	G	Att.	Cmp.	Yds.	TD	Int.
Ty Detmer, Brigham Young	46	1,530	958	15,031	121	65

Completion Percentage:	62.61
Yards Per Attempted Pass:	9.82
Pct. of Passes for TDs:	7.91
Pct. of Passes Int.:	4.25

ADD the first three factors:

		Rating Points
Completion Percentage:	62.61	62.61
Yds. Per Attempted Pass:	9.82 times 8.4	82.49
Pct. of Passes for TDs:	7.91 times 3.3	26.10
		171.20

SUBTRACT the last factor:

Pct. of Passes Int.:	4.25 times 2	-8.50
	Round off to:	**162.7**

Career Passing Efficiency
(Min. 500 Completions)

Player, Team	Years	Att.	Cmp.	Int.	Pct.	Yds.	TD	Pts.
Ty Detmer, Brigham Young	1988-91	*1,530	*958	65	.626	*15,031	*121	*162.7
Jim McMahon, Brigham Young ...	1977-78, 80-81	1,060	653	34	.616	9,536	84	156.9
Steve Young, Brigham Young	1981-83	908	592	33	**.652	7,733	56	149.8
Robbie Bosco, Brigham Young ...	1983-85	997	638	36	.640	8,400	66	149.4
Chuck Long, Iowa	$1981-85	1,072	692	46	‡.646	9,210	64	147.8
Andre Ware, Houston	1987-89	1,074	660	28	.615	8,202	75	143.3
Doug Gaynor, Long Beach St.	1984-85	837	569	35	.680	6,793	35	141.6
Dan McGwire, Iowa/San Diego St.	1986-87, 89-90	973	575	30	.591	8,164	49	140.0
John Elway, Stanford	1979-82	1,246	774	39	.621	9,349	77	139.3
David Klingler, Houston	1988-91	1,261	726	38	.576	9,430	91	138.2
Scott Mitchell, Utah	1987-89	1,165	669	38	.574	8,981	68	137.7
Marc Wilson, Brigham Young	1977-79	937	535	46	.571	7,637	61	137.2
R. Cunningham, Nev.-Las Vegas ..	1982-84	1,029	597	29	.580	8,020	59	136.8
Kerwin Bell, Florida	1984-87	953	549	35	.576	7,585	56	136.5
Tom Hodson, Louisiana St.	1986-89	1,163	674	41	.580	9,115	69	136.3
Rodney Peete, Southern Cal	1985-88	972	571	32	.587	7,640	52	135.8
Joe Adams, Tennessee St.	1977-80	1,100	604	60	.549	8,649	81	134.4
Mike Gundy, Oklahoma St.	1986-89	1,037	606	37	.584	8,072	54	133.9
Todd Santos, San Diego St.	1984-87	1,484	910	57	.613	11,425	70	133.9
Tony Eason, Illinois	1981-82	856	526	29	.615	6,608	37	133.8

Player, Team	Years	Att.	Cmp.	Int.	Pct.	Yds.	TD	Pts.
Danny McCoin, Cincinnati	1984-87	899	544	26	.605	6,801	39	132.6
Rich Campbell, California	1977-80	891	574	42	.644	6,933	33	132.6
Jim Everett, Purdue	$1981-85	923	550	30	.596	7,158	40	132.5
Matt Rodgers, Iowa	1988-91	844	516	30	.611	6,308	40	132.5
Doug Flutie, Boston College	1981-84	1,270	677	54	.533	10,579	67	132.2
Jack Trudeau, Illinois	1981, 83-85	1,151	736	38	†.639	8,146	51	131.4
Kevin Sweeney, Fresno St.	$1982-86	1,336	731	48	.547	10,623	66	130.6
Bill Musgrave, Oregon	1987-90	1,018	582	38	.572	7,631	55	130.6
Gene Swick, Toledo	1972-75	938	556	45	.593	7,267	44	130.3
Brian McClure, Bowling Green ...	1982-85	1,427	900	58	.631	10,280	63	130.0

(Min. 400 Completions)

Player, Team	Years	Att.	Cmp.	Int.	Pct.	Yds.	TD	Pts.
Vinny Testaverde, Miami (Fla.)	1982, 84-86	674	413	25	.613	6,058	48	152.9
Troy Aikman, Oklahoma/UCLA	84-85, 87-88	637	401	18	.630	5,436	40	149.7
Chuck Hartlieb, Iowa..................	1985-88	716	461	17	.643	6,269	34	148.9
Gifford Nielsen, Brigham Young	1975-77	708	415	29	.586	5,833	55	145.3
Tom Ramsey, UCLA	1979-82	691	411	33	.595	5,844	48	143.9
Shawn Moore, Virginia	1987-90	762	421	32	.552	6,629	55	143.8
Jerry Rhome, Southern Meth./Tulsa ..	1961, 63-64	713	448	23	.628	5,472	47	142.6
Bernie Kosar, Miami (Fla.)	1983-84	743	463	29	.623	5,971	40	139.8
Craig Erickson, Miami (Fla.)	1987-90	752	420	22	.559	6,056	46	137.8
Dave Yarema, Michigan St.	$1982-86	727	447	29	.615	5,569	41	136.5
Gary Huff, Florida St.	1970-72	796	436	42	.548	6,378	52	133.1
Jeff Francis, Tennessee	1985-88	768	476	26	.620	5,867	31	132.7
Mike Perez, San Jose St.	1986-87	792	471	30	.595	6,194	36	132.6
Jeff Van Raaphorst, Arizona St.	1984-86	811	473	36	.583	6,250	42	131.3
Pat Sullivan, Auburn	1969-71	819	452	40	.552	6,284	53	131.2

(Min. 325 Completions)

Player, Team	Years	Att.	Cmp.	Int.	Pct.	Yds.	TD	Pts.
Jim Harbaugh, Michigan	1983-86	582	368	19	.632	5,215	31	149.6
Danny White, Arizona St.	1971-73	649	345	36	.532	5,932	59	148.9
Jim Karsatos, Ohio St.	1983-86	573	330	19	.576	4,698	36	140.6
Jerry Tagge, Nebraska	1969-71	581	348	19	.599	4,704	33	140.1
Garrett Gabriel, Hawaii................	1987-90	661	356	31	.539	5,631	47	139.5
Gary Sheide, Brigham Young	1973-74	594	358	31	.603	4,524	45	138.8
Dan Speltz, Cal St. Fullerton	1988-89	583	350	19	.600	4,595	33	138.4
Don McPherson, Syracuse	$1983-87	687	367	29	.534	5,812	46	138.1
Sam King, Nevada-Las Vegas	1979-81	625	360	29	.576	5,393	30	136.6
Jesse Freitas, Stanford/San Diego St..	1970, 72-73	547	338	33	.618	4,408	28	134.3
Jeff Blake, East Caro.	1988-91	667	360	20	.540	5,133	43	133.9
Alan Risher, Louisiana St.	1980-82	615	381	24	.620	4,585	31	133.4

* Record. ** Record for minimum of 875 attempts. ‡ Record for minimum of 1,000 attempts. † Record for minimum of 1,100 attempts. $ See page 6 for explanation.

Season Passing Efficiency
(Min. 15 Attempts Per Game)

Player, Team	Year	G.	Att.	Cmp.	Int.	Pct.	Yds.	TD	Pts.
Jim McMahon, Brigham Young	#†1980	12	445	284	18	.638	4,571	47	*176.9
Ty Detmer, Brigham Young	†1989	12	412	265	15	.643	4,560	32	175.6
Jerry Rhome, Tulsa	#†1964	10	326	224	4	.687	2,870	32	172.6
Elvis Grbac, Michigan	†1991	11	228	152	5	.667	1,955	24	169.0
Ty Detmer, Brigham Young	#†1991	12	403	249	12	.618	4,031	35	168.5
Steve Young, Brigham Young	#†1983	11	429	306	10	*.713	3,902	33	168.5
Vinny Testaverde, Miami (Fla.)	†1986	10	276	175	9	.634	2,557	26	165.8
Brian Dowling, Yale	1968	9	160	92	10	.575	1,554	19	165.8
Don McPherson, Syracuse..........	†1987	11	229	129	11	.563	2,341	22	164.3
Dave Wilson, Ball St.	1977	11	177	115	7	.650	1,589	17	164.2
Bob Berry, Oregon	1963	10	171	101	7	.591	1,675	16	164.0
Jim Harbaugh, Michigan	†1985	11	212	139	6	.656	1,913	18	163.7
Troy Aikman, UCLA.................	1987	11	243	159	6	.654	2,354	16	163.6
Turk Schonert, Stanford.............	†1979	11	221	148	6	.670	1,922	19	163.0
Brian Broomell, Temple	1979	11	214	120	11	.561	2,103	22	162.3
Dennis Shaw, San Diego St.	†1969	10	335	199	26	.594	3,185	39	162.2
Timm Rosenbach, Washington St. ...	†1988	11	302	199	10	.659	2,791	23	162.0
Davey O'Brien, Texas Christian	¢#†1938	10	167	93	4	.557	1,457	19	161.7
Chuck Hartlieb, Iowa	1987	12	299	196	8	.656	2,855	19	161.4
David Brown, Duke	1989	9	163	104	6	.638	1,479	14	161.0
Shawn Moore, Virginia	†1990	10	241	144	8	.598	2,262	21	160.7
Chuck Long, Iowa	1983	10	236	144	8	.610	2,434	14	160.4

1992 NCAA FOOTBALL

Player, Team	Year	G.	Att.	Cmp.	Int.	Pct.	Yds.	TD	Pts.
Jeff Garcia, San Jose St.	1991	9	160	99	5	.619	1,519	12	160.1
Matt Blundin, Virginia	1991	9	224	135	0	.603	1,902	19	159.6
Kerwin Bell, Florida	1985	11	288	180	8	.625	2,687	21	159.4
Mike Gundy, Oklahoma St.	1988	11	236	153	12	.648	2,163	19	158.2
Danny White, Arizona St.	1973	11	265	146	12	.551	2,609	23	157.4
Stan Heath, Nevada	#†1948	9	222	126	9	.568	2,005	22	157.2
Jim Harbaugh, Michigan	1986	11	254	167	8	.658	2,557	10	157.0
Shawn Moore, Virginia	1989	11	221	125	7	.566	2,078	18	156.1
Dan Speltz, Cal St. Fullerton	1989	11	309	214	11	.693	2,671	20	156.1
Ty Detmer, Brigham Young	1990	12	562	361	28	.642	*5,188	41	155.9
Doug Williams, Grambling	#1977	11	352	181	18	.514	3,286	38	155.2
John Huarte, Notre Dame	1964	10	205	114	11	.556	2,062	16	155.1
Jim McMahon, Brigham Young	#†1981	10	423	272	7	.643	3,555	30	155.0
Steve Sloan, Alabama	1965	10	160	97	3	.606	1,453	10	153.8
Tom Ramsey, UCLA	†1982	11	311	191	10	.614	2,824	21	153.5
Martin Vaughn, Pennsylvania	1973	9	206	114	8	.553	1,926	17	153.3
Dick Doheny, Fordham	1949	8	140	87	5	.621	1,127	13	153.3

*Record. † National champion. # National total-offense champion. ¢ Available records before 1946 do not include TD passes except for O'Brien and relatively few other passers; thus, passing efficiency points cannot be compiled for those players without TD passes.

Annual Passing Efficiency Leaders
(%Minimum 11 Attempts Per Game)

1946—Bill Mackrides, Nevada, 176.9; **1947**—Bobby Layne, Texas, 138.9; **1948**—Stan Heath, Nevada, 157.2 (#†); **1949**—Bob Williams, Notre Dame, 159.1; **1950**—Claude Arnold, Oklahoma, 157.3; **1951**—Dick Kazmaier, Princeton, 155.3 (#); **1952**—Ron Morris, Tulsa, 177.4; **1953**—Bob Garrett, Stanford, 142.2 (†); **1954**—Pete Vann, Army, 166.5; **1955**—George Welsh, Navy, 146.1 (#†); **1956**—Tom Flores, Pacific (Cal.), 147.5; **1957**—Lee Grosscup, Utah, 175.5; **1958**—John Hangartner, Arizona St., 150.1; **1959**—Charley Johnson, New Mexico St., 135.7; **1960**—Eddie Wilson, Arizona, 140.8; **1961**—Ron DiGravio, Purdue, 140.1; **1962**—John Jacobs, Arizona St., 153.9; **1963**—Bob Berry, Oregon, 164.0; **1964**—Jerry Rhome, Tulsa, 172.6 (#†).

(Minimum 15 Attempts Per Game)

1946—Ben Raimondi, Indiana, 117.0; **1947**—Charley Conerly, Mississippi, 125.8 (†); **1948**—Stan Heath, Nevada, 157.2 (#†); **1949**—Dick Doheny, Fordham, 153.3; **1950**—Dick Doheny, Fordham, 149.5; **1951**—Babe Parilli, Kentucky, 130.8; **1952**—Gene Rossi, Cincinnati, 149.7; **1953**—Bob Garrett, Stanford, 142.2 (†); **1954**—Len Dawson, Purdue, 145.8; **1955**—George Welsh, Navy, 146.1 (#†); **1956**—Bob Reinhart, San Jose St., 121.3; **1957**—Bob Newman, Washington St., 126.5 (#); **1958**—Randy Duncan, Iowa, 135.1; **1959**—Charley Johnson, New Mexico St., 135.7; **1960**—Charley Johnson, New Mexico St., 134.1; **1961**—Eddie Wilson, Arizona, 134.2; **1962**—Terry Baker, Oregon St., 146.5 (#); **1963**—Bob Berry, Oregon, 164.0; **1964**—Jerry Rhome, Tulsa, 172.6 (#†).

(Min. 15 Attempts Per Game)

Year	Player, Team	G.	Att.	Cmp.	Int.	Pct.	Yds.	TD	Pts.
1965	Steve Sloan, Alabama	10	160	97	3	.606	1,453	10	153.8
1966	Dewey Warren, Tennessee	10	229	136	7	.594	1,716	18	142.2
1967	Bill Andrejko, Villanova	10	187	114	6	.610	1,405	13	140.6
1968	Brian Dowling, Yale	9	160	92	10	.575	1,554	19	165.8
1969	#Dennis Shaw, San Diego St.	10	335	199	26	.594	3,185	39	162.2
1970	Jerry Tagge, Nebraska	11	165	104	7	.630	1,383	12	149.0
1971	Jerry Tagge, Nebraska	12	239	143	4	.598	2,019	17	150.9
1972	John Hufnagel, Penn St.	11	216	115	8	.532	2,039	15	148.0
1973	Danny White, Arizona St.	11	265	146	12	.551	2,609	23	157.4
1974	#Steve Joachim, Temple	10	221	128	13	.579	1,950	20	150.1
1975	James Kubacki, Harvard	8	137	77	9	.562	1,273	11	147.6
1976	Steve Haynes, Louisiana Tech	10	216	120	11	.556	1,981	16	146.9
1977	Dave Wilson, Ball St.	11	177	115	7	.650	1,589	17	164.2
1978	Paul McDonald, Southern Cal	11	194	111	7	.572	1,667	18	152.8

(See page 50 for annual leaders beginning in 1979)

† National champion. # National total-offense champion. % In many seasons during 1946-64, only a few passers threw as many as 15 passes per game; thus, a lower minimum was used.

		Career Yards							
Player, Team	Years	Att.	Cmp.	Int.	Pct.	Yards	TD	Long	
Ty Detmer, Brigham Young	1988-91	*1,530	*958	65	.626	*15,031	*121	76	
Todd Santos, San Diego St.	1984-87	1,484	910	57	.613	11,425	70	84	
Kevin Sweeney, Fresno St.	$1982-86	1,336	731	48	.547	10,623	66	95	
Doug Flutie, Boston College	1981-84	1,270	677	54	.533	10,579	67	80	
Brian McClure, Bowling Green . . .	1982-85	1,427	900	58	.631	10,280	63	90	
Ben Bennett, Duke	1980-83	1,375	820	57	.596	9,614	55	88	
Jim McMahon, Brigham Young . . .	1977-78, 80-81	1,060	653	34	.616	9,536	84	80	

Player, Team	Years	Att.	Cmp.	Int.	Pct.	Yards	TD	Long
Todd Ellis, South Caro.	1986-89	1,266	704	66	.556	9,519	49	97
David Klingler, Houston	1988-91	1,261	726	38	.576	9,430	91	95
Erik Wilhelm, Oregon St.	1985-88	1,480	870	61	.588	9,393	52	‡74
Jeremy Leach, New Mexico	1988-91	1,432	735	62	.513	9,382	50	82
John Elway, Stanford	1979-82	1,246	774	39	.621	9,349	77	70
T. J. Rubley, Tulsa	1987-89, 91	1,336	682	54	.510	9,324	73	75
Chuck Long, Iowa	$1981-85	1,072	692	46	‡‡.646	9,210	64	89
Mark Herrmann, Purdue	1977-80	1,218	717	*73	.589	9,188	62	75
Tom Hodson, Louisiana St.	1986-89	1,163	674	41	.580	9,115	69	80
Scott Mitchell, Utah	1987-89	1,165	669	38	.574	8,981	68	72
Joe Adams, Tennessee St.	1977-80	1,100	604	60	.549	8,649	81	71
Robbie Bosco, Brigham Young ...	1983-85	997	638	36	.640	8,400	66	‡89
Andre Ware, Houston	1987-89	1,074	660	28	.615	8,202	75	87
Dan McGwire, Iowa/San Diego St.	1986-87, 89-90	973	575	30	.591	8,164	49	71
Jack Trudeau, Illinois	1981, 83-85	1,151	736	38	†.639	8,146	51	83
Troy Taylor, California	1986-89	1,162	683	46	.588	8,126	51	79
Mike Gundy, Oklahoma St.	1986-89	1,037	606	37	.584	8,072	54	‡84
Jeff Graham, Long Beach St.	1985-88	1,175	664	42	.565	8,063	42	85
R. Cunningham, Nev.-Las Vegas ..	1982-84	1,029	597	29	.580	8,020	59	69
Steve Slayden, Duke	1984-87	1,204	699	53	.581	8,004	48	73
Dan Marino, Pittsburgh	1979-82	1,084	626	64	.577	7,905	74	65
John Holman, Northeast La.	1979-82	1,201	593	54	.494	7,827	51	85
Jack Thompson, Washington St...	1975-78	1,086	601	49	.553	7,818	53	80
Bobby Fuller, Appalachian St./ South Caro......................	1987-88, 90-91	1,061	596	32	.562	7,746	52	79
Steve Young, Brigham Young	1981-83	908	592	33	**.652	7,733	56	63
Brett Favre, Southern Miss.	1987-90	1,169	613	34	.524	7,695	52	80
Terrence Jones, Tulane	1985-88	1,042	570	41	.547	7,684	46	76
John Paye, Stanford	1983-86	1,198	715	44	.597	7,669	38	80
Rodney Peete, Southern Cal	1985-88	972	571	32	.587	7,640	52	‡68
Marc Wilson, Brigham Young	1977-79	937	535	46	.571	7,637	61	72
Scott Campbell, Purdue...........	1980-83	1,060	609	41	.575	7,636	45	77
Bill Musgrave, Oregon	1987-90	1,018	582	38	.572	7,631	55	83
Tom Tunnicliffe, Arizona	1980-83	1,069	574	56	.537	7,618	46	92
Tom Corontzos, Wyoming	1988-91	1,003	547	37	.545	7,601	47	80
Kerwin Bell, Florida	1984-87	953	549	35	.576	7,585	56	96
John Reaves, Florida..............	1969-71	1,128	603	59	.535	7,549	54	81
Jim Plunkett, Stanford	1968-70	962	530	47	.551	7,544	52	96

*Record. $ See page 6 for explanation.   ‡ Did not score.   † Record for minimum of 1,100 attempts.   ‡‡ Record for minimum of 1,000 attempts.   ** Record for minimum of 875 attempts.*

Career Yards Record Progression
(Record Yards—Player, Team, Seasons Played)

3,075—Billy Patterson, Baylor, 1936-38; **3,777**—Bud Schwenk, Washington (Mo.), 1939-41; **4,004**—Johnny Rauch, Georgia, 1945-48; **4,736**—John Ford, Hardin-Simmons, 1947-50; **4,863**—Zeke Bratkowski, Georgia, 1951-53; **5,472**—Jerry Rhome, Southern Methodist, 1961, Tulsa, 1963-64; **6,495**—Billy Stevens, UTEP, 1965-67; **7,076**—Steve Ramsey, North Texas, 1967-69; **7,544**—Jim Plunkett, Stanford, 1968-70; **7,549**—John Reaves, Florida, 1969-71; **7,818**—Jack Thompson, Washington St., 1975-78; **9,188**—Mark Herrmann, Purdue, 1977-80; **9,536**—Jim McMahon, BrighamYoung, 1977-78, 80-81; **9,614**—Ben Bennett, Duke, 1980-83; **10,579**—Doug Flutie, Boston College, 1981-84; **10,623**—Kevin Sweeney, Fresno St., $1982-86; **11,425**—Todd Santos, San Diego St., 1984-87; **15,031**—Ty Detmer, Brigham Young, 1988-91.

$ See page 6 for explanation.

Career Yards Per Game

Player, Team	Years	G.	Att.	Cmp.	Int.	Pct.	Yds.	TD	Yd. PG
Ty Detmer, Brigham Young	1988-91	46	*1,530	*958	65	.626	*15,031	*121	*326.8
Mike Perez, San Jose St.	1986-87	20	792	471	30	.595	6,194	36	309.7
Doug Gaynor, Long Beach St. ...	1984-85	22	837	569	35	.680	6,793	35	308.8
Tony Eason, Illinois	1981-82	22	856	526	29	.614	6,608	37	300.4
David Klingler, Houston	1988-91	32	1,261	726	38	.576	9,430	91	294.7
Brent Snyder, Utah St.	1987-88	22	875	472	36	.539	6,105	39	277.5
Larry Egger, Utah	1985-86	22	799	470	31	.588	5,749	39	261.3
Bernie Kosar, Miami (Fla.)........	1983-84	23	743	463	29	.623	5,971	40	259.6

*Record.

Career Touchdown Passes

Player, Team	Years	Games	TD Passes
Ty Detmer, Brigham Young	1988-91	46	*121
David Klingler, Houston	1988-91	32	91
Jim McMahon, Brigham Young	1977-78, 80-81	44	84

Player, Team	Years	Games	TD Passes
Joe Adams, Tennessee St.	1977-80	41	81
¢Troy Kopp, Pacific (Cal.)	1989-91	32	79
John Elway, Stanford	1979-82	43	77
Andre Ware, Houston	1987-89	29	75
Dan Marino, Pittsburgh	1979-82	40	74
T. J. Rubley, Tulsa	1987-89, 91	47	73
Todd Santos, San Diego St.	1984-87	46	70
Tom Hodson, Louisiana St.	1986-89	44	69
Steve Ramsey, North Texas	1967-69	29	69
Scott Mitchell, Utah	1987-89	33	68
Doug Flutie, Boston College	1981-84	42	67
Kevin Sweeney, Fresno St.	1983-86	47	66
Robbie Bosco, Brigham Young	1983-85	35	66
Chuck Long, Iowa	$1981-85	45	64

* Record.   ¢ Active player. $ See page 6 for explanation.

Season Yards

Player, Team	Year	Games	Att.	Cmp.	Int.	Pct.	Yards	TD	Long
Ty Detmer, Brigham Young	1990	12	562	361	28	.642	*5,188	41	69
David Klingler, Houston	1990	11	*643	*374	20	.582	5,140	*54	95
Andre Ware, Houston	1989	11	578	365	15	.631	4,699	46	87
Jim McMahon, Brigham Young	†1980	12	445	284	18	.638	4,571	47	80
Ty Detmer, Brigham Young	†1989	12	412	265	15	.643	4,560	32	67
Scott Mitchell, Utah	1988	11	533	323	15	.606	4,322	29	72
Robbie Bosco, Brigham Young	1985	13	511	338	24	.661	4,273	30	‡89
Ty Detmer, Brigham Young	1991	12	403	249	12	.618	4,031	35	97
Todd Santos, San Diego St.	1987	12	492	306	15	.622	3,932	26	74
Steve Young, Brigham Young	†1983	11	429	306	10	*.713	3,902	33	63
Robbie Bosco, Brigham Young	1984	12	458	283	11	.618	3,875	33	54
Dan McGwire, San Diego St.	1990	11	449	270	7	.601	3,833	27	71
Anthony Dilweg, Duke	1988	11	484	287	18	.593	3,824	24	65
Sam King, Nevada-Las Vegas	1981	12	433	255	19	.589	3,778	18	71
Troy Kopp, Pacific (Cal.)	1991	12	449	275	16	.612	3,767	37	68
Marc Wilson, Brigham Young	1979	12	427	250	15	.585	3,720	29	‡76
Dan McGwire, San Diego St.	1989	12	440	258	19	.586	3,651	16	57
Jim Everett, Purdue	1985	11	450	285	11	.633	3,651	23	70
Bernie Kosar, Miami (Fla.)	1984	12	416	262	16	.630	3,642	25	85
Jeremy Leach, New Mexico	1989	12	511	282	20	.552	3,573	22	82
Doug Gaynor, Long Beach St.	1985	12	452	321	18	.710	3,563	19	57
Jim McMahon, Brigham Young	†1981	10	423	272	7	.643	3,555	30	‡67
Todd Dillon, Long Beach St.	1982	11	504	289	21	.573	3,517	19	‡73

* Record.   † National champion.   ‡ Did not score.

Season Yards Per Game

Player, Team	Year	Games	Att.	Cmp.	Int.	Pct.	Yards	TD	Yd. PG
David Klingler, Houston	1990	11	*643	*374	20	.582	5,140	*54	*467.3
Ty Detmer, Brigham Young	1990	12	562	361	28	.642	*5,188	41	432.3
Andre Ware, Houston	1989	11	578	365	15	.631	4,699	46	427.2
Scott Mitchell, Utah	1988	11	533	323	15	.606	4,322	29	392.9
Jim McMahon, Brigham Young	†1980	12	445	284	18	.638	4,571	47	380.9
Ty Detmer, Brigham Young	†1989	12	412	265	15	.643	4,560	32	380.0
Troy Kopp, Pacific (Cal.)	1990	9	428	243	14	.568	3,311	31	367.9
Jim McMahon, Brigham Young	†1981	10	423	272	7	.643	3,555	30	355.5
Steve Young, Brigham Young	†1983	11	429	306	10	*.713	3,902	33	354.7
Dan McGwire, San Diego St.	1990	11	449	270	7	.601	3,833	27	348.5
Anthony Dilweg, Duke	1988	11	484	287	18	.593	3,824	24	347.6
Bill Anderson, Tulsa	†1965	10	509	296	14	.582	3,464	30	346.4
David Klingler, Houston	1991	10	497	278	17	.559	3,388	29	338.8
Marc Wilson, Brigham Young	1979	12	427	250	15	.585	3,720	29	338.2

* Record.   † National champion.

Season Touchdown Passes

Player, Team	Year	Games	TD Passes
David Klingler, Houston	1990	11	*54
Jim McMahon, Brigham Young	1980	12	47
Andre Ware, Houston	1989	11	46
Ty Detmer, Brigham Young	1990	12	41
Dennis Shaw, San Diego St.	1969	10	39
Doug Williams, Grambling	1977	11	38
Troy Kopp, Pacific (Cal.)	1991	12	37

Player, Team	Year	Games	TD Passes
Ty Detmer, Brigham Young	1991	12	35
Dan Marino, Pittsburgh	1981	11	34
Steve Young, Brigham Young	1983	11	33
Robbie Bosco, Brigham Young	1984	12	33
Jerry Rhome, Tulsa	1964	10	32
Ty Detmer, Brigham Young	1989	12	32
Troy Kopp, Pacific (Cal.)	1990	9	31

* *Record.*

Single-Game Yards

Yds.	Player, Team (Opponent)	Date
716	David Klingler, Houston (Arizona St.)	Dec. 2, 1990
690	Matt Vogler, Texas Christian (Houston)	Nov. 3, 1990
631	Scott Mitchell, Utah (Air Force)	Oct. 15, 1988
622	Jeremy Leach, New Mexico (Utah)	Nov. 11, 1989
621	Dave Wilson, Illinois (Ohio St.)	Nov. 8, 1980
599	Ty Detmer, Brigham Young (San Diego St.)	Nov. 16, 1991
585	Robbie Bosco, Brigham Young (New Mexico)	Oct. 19, 1985
572	David Klingler, Houston (Eastern Wash.)	Nov. 17, 1990
571	Marc Wilson, Brigham Young (Utah)	Nov. 5, 1977
568	David Lowery, San Diego St. (Brigham Young)	Nov. 16, 1991
565	Jim McMahon, Brigham Young (Utah)	Nov. 21, 1981
564	Troy Kopp, Pacific, Cal. (New Mexico St.)	Oct. 20, 1990
563	David Klingler, Houston (Texas Christian)	Nov. 3, 1990
561	Tony Adams, Utah St. (Utah)	Nov. 11, 1972
560	Ty Detmer, Brigham Young (Utah St.)	Nov. 24, 1990
558	Chuck Hartlieb, Iowa (Indiana)	Oct. 29, 1988
554	Greg Cook, Cincinnati (Ohio)	Nov. 16, 1968
538	Jim McMahon, Brigham Young (Colorado St.)	Nov. 7, 1981
537	Ty Detmer, Brigham Young (Washington St.)	Sept. 7, 1989
536	Dave Telford, Fresno St. (Pacific, Cal.)	Oct. 24, 1987
536	Todd Santos, San Diego St. (Stanford)	Oct. 17, 1987
536	David Spriggs, New Mexico St. (Southern Ill.)	Sept. 30, 1978
535	Shane Montgomery, North Caro. St. (Duke)	Nov. 11, 1989
534	Paul Justin, Arizona St. (Washington St.)	Oct. 28, 1989
533	David Klingler, Houston (Texas Tech)	Nov. 30, 1991
532	Jeff Van Raaphorst, Arizona St. (Florida St.)	Nov. 3, 1984
530	Dan McGwire, San Diego St. (New Mexico)	Nov. 17, 1990
527	Don Strock, Virginia Tech (Houston)	Oct. 7, 1972
526	Joe Theismann, Notre Dame (Southern Cal)	Nov. 28, 1970
520	Doug Flutie, Boston College (Penn St.)	Oct. 30, 1982

Career Yards Per Attempt
(Minimum 900 Attempts)

Player, Team	Years	Att.	Cmp.	Pct.	Yards	Yards Per Cmp.	Yards Per Att.
Ty Detmer, Brigham Young	1988-91	*1,530	*958	.626	*15,031	*15.69	*9.82
Jim McMahon, Brigham Young	1977-78, 80-81	1,060	653	.616	9,536	14.60	9.00
Chuck Long, Iowa	$1981-85	1,072	692	#.646	9,210	13.31	8.59
Steve Young, Brigham Young	1981-83	908	592	††.652	7,733	13.06	8.52
Robbie Bosco, Brigham Young	1983-85	997	638	.640	8,400	13.17	8.43
Dan McGwire, Iowa/San Diego St.	1986-87, 89-90	973	575	.591	8,164	14.20	8.39
Doug Flutie, Boston College	1981-84	1,270	677	.533	10,579	15.63	8.33
Marc Wilson, Brigham Young	1977-79	937	535	.571	7,637	14.27	8.15
Kerwin Bell, Florida	1984-87	953	549	.576	7,585	13.82	7.96
Kevin Sweeney, Fresno St.	$1982-86	1,336	731	.547	10,623	14.53	7.95
Joe Adams, Tennessee St.	1977-80	1,100	604	.549	8,649	14.32	7.86
Rodney Peete, Southern Cal	1985-88	972	571	.587	7,640	13.38	7.86
Tom Hodson, Louisiana St.	1986-89	1,163	674	.580	9,115	13.52	7.84
Jim Plunkett, Stanford	1968-70	962	530	.551	7,544	14.23	7.84
Randall Cunningham, Nev.-Las Vegas	1982-84	1,029	597	.580	8,020	13.43	7.79

* *Record.* \$ *See page 6 for explanation.* # *Record for minimum of 1,000 attempts.* †† *Record for minimum of 875 attempts.*

Single-Game Attempts

No.	Player, Team (Opponent)	Date
79	Matt Vogler, Texas Christian (Houston)	Nov. 3, 1990
76	David Klingler, Houston (Southern Methodist)	Oct. 20, 1990
73	Troy Kopp, Pacific, Cal. (Hawaii)	Oct. 27, 1990
73	Shane Montgomery, North Caro. St. (Duke)	Nov. 11, 1989

No.	Player, Team (Opponent)	Date
72	Matt Vogler, Texas Christian (Texas Tech)	Nov. 10, 1990
71	Sandy Schwab, Northwestern (Michigan)	Oct. 23, 1982
70	David Klingler, Houston (Texas Tech)	Nov. 30, 1991
70	David Klingler, Houston (Arizona St.)	Dec. 2, 1990
70	Dave Telford, Fresno St. (Utah St.)	Nov. 14, 1987
69	Dave Wilson, Illinois (Ohio St.)	Nov. 8, 1980
69	Chuck Hixson, Southern Methodist (Ohio St.)	Sept. 28, 1968
68	David Klingler, Houston (Baylor)	Oct. 6, 1990
68	Jeremy Leach, New Mexico (Utah)	Nov. 11, 1989
68	Steve Smith, Stanford (Notre Dame)	Oct. 7, 1989
68	Andre Ware, Houston (Arizona St.)	Sept. 23, 1989
67	Mike Hohensee, Minnesota (Ohio St.)	Nov. 7, 1981
66	Jack Trudeau, Illinois (Purdue)	Oct. 12, 1985
66	John Reaves, Florida (Auburn)	Nov. 1, 1969
65	Scott Mitchell, Utah (UTEP)	Oct. 1, 1988
65	Mike Bates, Miami, Ohio (Toledo)	Oct. 24, 1987
65	Craig Burnett, Wyoming (San Diego St.)	Nov. 15, 1986
65	Gary Schofield, Wake Forest (Maryland)	Oct. 16, 1982
65	Jim McMahon, Brigham Young (Colorado St.)	Nov. 7, 1981
65	Brooks Dawson, UTEP (UC Santa Barb.)	Sept. 14, 1968
65	Bill Anderson, Tulsa (Southern Ill.)	Oct. 30, 1965
65	Bill Anderson, Tulsa (Memphis St.)	Oct. 9, 1965

Single-Game Completions

No.	Player, Team (Opponent)	Date
48	David Klingler, Houston (Southern Methodist)	Oct. 20, 1990
45	Sandy Schwab, Northwestern (Michigan)	Oct. 23, 1982
44	Matt Vogler, Texas Christian (Houston)	Nov. 3, 1990
44	Chuck Hartlieb, Iowa (Indiana)	Oct. 29, 1988
44	Jim McMahon, Brigham Young (Colorado St.)	Nov. 7, 1981
43	Gary Schofield, Wake Forest (Maryland)	Oct. 17, 1981
43	Dave Wilson, Illinois (Ohio St.)	Nov. 8, 1980
43	Rich Campbell, California (Florida)	Sept. 13, 1980
42	Troy Kopp, Pacific, Cal. (Hawaii)	Oct. 27, 1990
42	Andre Ware, Houston (Texas Christian)	Nov. 4, 1989
42	Dan Speltz, Cal St. Fullerton (Utah St.)	Oct. 7, 1989
42	Robbie Bosco, Brigham Young (New Mexico)	Oct. 19, 1985
42	Bill Anderson, Tulsa (Southern Ill.)	Oct. 30, 1965
41	David Klingler, Houston (Texas Tech)	Nov. 30, 1991
41	David Klingler, Houston (Arizona St.)	Dec. 2, 1990
41	David Klingler, Houston (Eastern Wash.)	Nov. 17, 1990
41	Jeremy Leach, New Mexico (Utah)	Nov. 11, 1989
41	Scott Mitchell, Utah (UTEP)	Oct. 1, 1988
41	Doug Gaynor, Long Beach St. (Utah St.)	Sept. 7, 1985
40	Mike Romo, Southern Methodist (Rice)	Nov. 10, 1990
40	Andre Ware, Houston (Arizona St.)	Sept. 23, 1989
40	Dave Telford, Fresno St. (Utah St.)	Nov. 14, 1987
40	Todd Santos, San Diego St. (Stanford)	Oct. 17, 1987
40	Larry Egger, Utah (UTEP)	Nov. 29, 1986
40	John Paye, Stanford (San Diego St.)	Oct. 5, 1985
40	Gary Schofield, Wake Forest (Maryland)	Oct. 16, 1982
40	Jim McMahon, Brigham Young (North Texas)	Nov. 8, 1980

Annual Champions

Year	Player, Team	Class	Att.	Cmp.	Int.	Pct.	Yds.	TD
1937	Davey O'Brien, Texas Christian	Jr.	234	94	18	.402	969	—
1938	Davey O'Brien, Texas Christian	Sr.	167	93	4	.557	1,457	—
1939	Kay Eakin, Arkansas	Sr.	193	78	18	.404	962	—
1940	Billy Sewell, Washington St.	Sr.	174	86	17	.494	1,023	—
1941	Bud Schwenk, Washington (Mo.)	Sr.	234	114	19	.487	1,457	—
1942	Ray Evans, Kansas	Jr.	200	101	9	.505	1,117	—
1943	Johnny Cook, Georgia	Fr.	157	73	20	.465	1,007	—
1944	Paul Rickards, Pittsburgh	So.	178	84	20	.472	997	—
1945	Al Dekdebrun, Cornell	Sr.	194	90	15	.464	1,227	—
1946	Travis Tidwell, Auburn	Fr.	158	79	10	.500	943	5
1947	Charlie Conerly, Mississippi	Sr.	233	133	7	.571	1,367	18
1948	Stan Heath, Nevada	Sr.	222	126	9	.568	2,005	22
1949	Adrian Burk, Baylor	Sr.	191	110	6	.576	1,428	14
1950	Don Heinrich, Washington	Jr.	221	134	9	.606	1,846	14
1951	Don Klosterman, Loyola (Cal.)	Sr.	315	159	21	.505	1,843	9

Year	Player, Team	Class	Att.	Cmp.	Int.	Pct.	Yds.	TD
1952	Don Heinrich, Washington	Sr.	270	137	17	.507	1,647	13
1953	Bob Garrett, Stanford	Sr.	205	118	10	.576	1,637	17
1954	Paul Larson, California	Sr.	195	125	8	.641	1,537	10
1955	George Welsh, Navy	Sr.	150	94	6	.627	1,319	8
1956	John Brodie, Stanford	Sr.	240	139	14	.579	1,633	12
1957	Ken Ford, Hardin-Simmons	Sr.	205	115	11	.561	1,254	14
1958	Buddy Humphrey, Baylor	Sr.	195	112	8	.574	1,316	7
1959	Dick Norman, Stanford	Jr.	263	152	12	.578	1,963	11
1960	Harold Stephens, Hardin-Simmons	Sr.	256	145	14	.566	1,254	3
1961	Chon Gallegos, San Jose St.	Sr.	197	117	13	.594	1,480	14
1962	Don Trull, Baylor	Jr.	229	125	12	.546	1,627	11
1963	Don Trull, Baylor	Sr.	308	174	12	.565	2,157	12
1964	Jerry Rhome, Tulsa	Sr.	326	224	4	.687	2,870	32
1965	Bill Anderson, Tulsa	Sr.	509	296	14	.582	3,464	30
1966	John Eckman, Wichita St.	Jr.	458	195	*34	.426	2,339	7
1967	Terry Stone, New Mexico	Jr.	336	160	19	.476	1,946	9
1968	Chuck Hixson, Southern Methodist	So.	468	265	23	.566	3,103	21
1969	John Reaves, Florida	So.	396	222	19	.561	2,896	24

Beginning in 1970, ranked on per-game (instead of total) completions

Year	Player, Team	Cl.	G.	Att.	Cmp.	Avg.	Int.	Pct.	Yds.	TD
1970	Sonny Sixkiller, Washington	So.	10	362	186	18.6	22	.514	2,303	15
1971	Brian Sipe, San Diego St.	Sr.	11	369	196	17.8	21	.531	2,532	17
1972	Don Strock, Virginia Tech	Sr.	11	427	228	20.7	27	.534	3,243	16
1973	Jesse Freitas, San Diego St.	Sr.	11	347	227	20.6	17	.654	2,993	21
1974	Steve Bartkowski, California	Sr.	11	325	182	16.5	7	.560	2,580	12
1975	Craig Penrose, San Diego St.	Sr.	11	349	198	18.0	24	.567	2,660	15
1976	Tommy Kramer, Rice	Sr.	11	501	269	24.5	19	.537	3,317	21
1977	Guy Benjamin, Stanford	Sr.	10	330	208	20.8	15	.630	2,521	19
1978	Steve Dils, Stanford	Sr.	11	391	247	22.5	15	.632	2,943	22

Beginning in 1979, ranked on Passing Efficiency rating points (instead of per-game completions)

Year	Player, Team	Cl.	G.	Att.	Cmp.	Int.	Pct.	Yds.	TD	Pts.
1979	Turk Schonert, Stanford	Sr.	11	221	148	6	.670	1,922	19	163.0
1980	Jim McMahon, Brigham Young	Jr.	12	445	284	18	.638	4,571	47	*176.9
1981	Jim McMahon, Brigham Young	Sr.	10	423	272	7	.643	3,555	30	155.0
1982	Tom Ramsey, UCLA	Sr.	11	311	191	10	.614	2,824	21	153.5
1983	Steve Young, Brigham Young	Sr.	11	429	306	10	*.713	3,902	33	168.5
1984	Doug Flutie, Boston College	Sr.	11	386	233	11	.604	3,454	27	152.9
1985	Jim Harbaugh, Michigan	Jr.	11	212	139	6	.656	1,913	18	163.7
1986	Vinny Testaverde, Miami (Fla.)	Sr.	10	276	175	9	.634	2,557	26	165.8
1987	Don McPherson, Syracuse	Sr.	11	229	129	11	.563	2,341	22	164.3
1988	Timm Rosenbach, Washington St.	Jr.	11	302	199	10	.659	2,791	23	162.0
1989	Ty Detmer, Brigham Young	So.	12	412	265	15	.643	4,560	32	175.6
1990	Shawn Moore, Virginia	Sr.	10	241	144	8	.598	2,262	21	160.7
1991	Elvis Grbac, Michigan	Sr.	11	228	152	5	.667	1,955	24	169.0

Record.

RECEIVING

Career Catches Per Game

Player, Team	Years	Games	Catches	Yards	TD	Ct. PG
Manny Hazard, Houston	1989-90	21	220	2,635	31	*10.5
Howard Twilley, Tulsa	1963-65	26	261	3,343	32	10.0
Jason Phillips, Houston	1987-88	22	207	2,319	18	9.4
Neal Sweeney, Tulsa	1965-66	18	134	1,623	11	7.4
David Williams, Illinois	1983-85	33	245	3,195	22	7.4
James Dixon, Houston	1987-88	22	161	1,762	14	7.3
John Love, North Texas	1965-66	20	144	2,124	17	7.2
Ron Sellers, Florida St.	1966-68	30	212	3,598	23	7.1
Barry Moore, North Texas	1968-69	20	140	2,183	12	7.0
Mike Kelly, Davidson	1967-69	23	156	2,114	17	6.8
Guy Liggins, San Jose St.	1986-87	22	149	2,191	16	6.8
Dave Petzke, Northern Ill.	1977-78	22	148	1,960	16	6.7
Loren Richey, Utah	1985-86	21	140	1,746	13	6.7
Tom Reynolds, San Diego St.	1969,71	18	117	1,955	25	6.5
Tim Delaney, San Diego St.	1968-70	29	180	2,535	22	6.2
Larry Willis, Fresno St.	1983-84	23	142	2,260	14	6.2
Phil Odle, Brigham Young	1965-67	30	183	2,548	25	6.1
Mike Mikolayunas, Davidson	1968-70	29	175	1,768	14	6.0

Player, Team	Years	Games	Catches	Yards	TD	Ct. PG
Rick Eber, Tulsa	1966-67	20	119	1,902	15	6.0
Terance Mathis, New Mexico	1985-87,89	44	*263	*4,254	36	5.9
Hugh Campbell, Washington St.	1960-62	30	176	2,453	22	5.9
Vern Burke, Oregon St.	1962-63	20	117	1,801	19	5.9

* Record.

Season Catches Per Game

Player, Team	Year	Games	Catches	Yards	TD	Ct. PG
Howard Twilley, Tulsa	†1965	10	134	*1,779	16	*13.4
Manny Hazard, Houston	†1989	11	*142	1,689	*22	12.9
Jason Phillips, Houston	†1988	11	108	1,444	15	9.8
Fred Gilbert, Houston	†1991	11	106	957	7	9.6
Jerry Hendren, Idaho	†1969	10	95	1,452	12	9.5
Howard Twilley, Tulsa	†1964	10	95	1,178	13	9.5
James Dixon, Houston	1988	11	102	1,103	11	9.3
David Williams, Illinois	†1984	11	101	1,278	8	9.2
Glenn Meltzer, Wichita St.	†1966	10	91	1,115	4	9.1
Jay Miller, Brigham Young	†1973	11	100	1,181	8	9.1

* Record.   † National champion.

Career Catches

Player, Team	Years	Catches	Yards	Avg.	TD
Terance Mathis, New Mexico	1985-87, 89	*263	*4,254	16.2	36
Mark Templeton, Long Beach St. (RB)	1983-86	262	1,969	7.5	11
Howard Twilley, Tulsa	1963-65	261	3,343	12.8	32
David Williams, Illinois	1983-85	245	3,195	13.0	22
Marc Zeno, Tulane	1984-87	236	3,725	15.8	25
Manny Hazard, Houston	1989-90	220	2,635	12.0	31
Darrin Nelson, Stanford (RB)	1977-78, 80-81	214	2,368	11.1	16
Ron Sellers, Florida St.	1966-68	212	3,598	17.0	23
Jason Phillips, Houston	1987-88	207	2,319	11.2	18
Hart Lee Dykes, Oklahoma St.	1985-88	203	3,171	15.6	29

Illinois wide receiver David Williams ranks fifth in Division I-A in career pass receptions per game (7.4), fourth in career receptions (245) and ninth in career receiving yards (3,195).

Player, Team	Years	Catches	Yards	Avg.	TD
Keith Edwards, Vanderbilt.............	1980, 82-84	200	1,757	8.8	3
Bobby Slaughter, Louisiana Tech	1987-90	198	2,544	12.9	14
Richard Buchanan, Northwestern	1987-90	197	2,474	12.6	22
Gerald Harp, Western Caro...........	1977-80	197	3,305	16.8	26
Matt Bellini, Brigham Young (RB)	1987-90	196	2,544	13.0	13
Brad Muster, Stanford (FB)	1984-87	196	1,669	8.5	6
Charles Lockett, Long Beach St.........	1983-86	191	2,902	15.1	19
Clarkston Hines, Duke	1986-89	189	3,318	17.6	*38
Ricky Proehl, Wake Forest	1986-89	188	2,949	15.7	25
Boo Mitchell, Vanderbilt...............	1985-88	188	2,964	15.8	9
¢Aaron Turner, Pacific (Cal.)	1989-91	187	3,174	17.0	32
Monty Gilbreath, San Diego St.	1986-89	187	2,241	12.0	8
Eric Henley, Rice......................	1988-91	186	2,200	11.8	16
Jeff Champine, Colorado St.	1980-83	184	2,811	15.3	21
Wendell Davis, Louisiana St.	1984-85	183	2,708	14.8	19
Phil Odle, Brigham Young	1965-67	183	2,548	13.9	25
Kelly Blackwell, Texas Christian (TE) ...	1988-91	181	2,155	11.9	13
Tim Delaney, San Diego St.	1968-70	180	2,535	14.1	22
Michael Smith, Kansas St.	1988-91	179	2,457	13.7	11
Walter Murray, Hawaii	1982-85	178	2,865	16.1	20
Gordon Hudson, Brigham Young (TE) ..	1980-83	178	2,484	14.0	22
Rick Beasley, Appalachian St...........	1978-80	178	3,124	17.6	23
Stan Hunter, Bowling Green	1982-85	176	2,679	15.2	21
Rodney Carter, Purdue.................	1982-85	176	1,786	10.1	5
Hugh Campbell, Washington St.	1960-62	176	2,453	13.9	22
John Jefferson, Arizona St.	1974-77	175	2,824	16.1	19
Mike Mikolayunas, Davidson	1968-70	175	1,768	10.1	14

* Record.   ¢ Active player.

Season Catches

Player, Team	Year	Games	Catches	Yards	TD
Manny Hazard, Houston	†1989	11	*142	1,689	*22
Howard Twilley, Tulsa	†1965	10	134	*1,779	16
Jason Phillips, Houston	†1988	11	108	1,444	15
Fred Gilbert, Houston	†1991	11	106	957	7
James Dixon, Houston	1988	11	102	1,103	11
David Williams, Illinois	†1984	11	101	1,278	8
Jay Miller, Brigham Young	†1973	11	100	1,181	8
Jason Phillips, Houston	†1987	11	99	875	3
Mark Templeton, Long Beach St. (RB)	†1986	11	99	688	2
Rodney Carter, Purdue.......................	†1985	11	98	1,099	4
Keith Edwards, Vanderbilt....................	†1983	11	97	909	0
Jerry Hendren, Idaho	†1969	10	95	1,452	12
Howard Twilley, Tulsa	†1964	10	95	1,178	13
Richard Buchanan, Northwestern.............	1989	11	94	1,115	9
Aaron Turner, Pacific (Cal.)	1991	11	92	1,604	18
Dave Petzke, Northern Ill.	†1978	11	91	1,217	11
Glenn Meltzer, Wichita St....................	†1966	10	91	1,115	4

* Record.   † National champion.

Season Touchdown Receptions

Player, Team	Year	Games	TD
Manny Hazard, Houston	1989	11	*22
Desmond Howard, Michigan...	1991	11	19
Aaron Turner, Pacific (Cal.)	1991	11	18
Tom Reynolds, San Diego St.	1971	10	18
Mario Bailey, Washington	1991	11	17
Clarkston Hines, Duke	1989	11	17
Dan Bitson, Tulsa	1989	11	16
Howard Twilley, Tulsa	1965	10	16
Jason Phillips, Houston	1988	11	15
Henry Ellard, Fresno St..	1982	11	15

* Record.

Single-Game Catches

No.	Player, Team (Opponent)	Date
22	Jay Miller, Brigham Young (New Mexico)	Nov. 3, 1973
20	Rick Eber, Tulsa (Idaho St.)	Oct. 7, 1967
19	Manny Hazard, Houston (Texas)	Nov. 11, 1989
19	Manny Hazard, Houston (Texas Christian)	Nov. 4, 1989
19	Ron Fair, Arizona St. (Washington St.)	Oct. 28, 1989

No.	Player, Team (Opponent)	Date
19	Howard Twilley, Tulsa (Colorado St.)	Nov. 27, 1965
18	Richard Woodley, Texas Christian (Texas Tech)	Nov. 10, 1990
18	Mark Templeton, Long Beach St. (RB) (Utah St.)	Nov. 1, 1986
18	Howard Twilley, Tulsa (Southern Ill.)	Oct. 30, 1965
17	Loren Richey, Utah (UTEP)	Nov. 29, 1986
17	Keith Edwards, Vanderbilt (Georgia)	Oct. 15, 1983
17	Jon Harvey, Northwestern (Michigan)	Oct. 23, 1982
17	Don Roberts, San Diego St. (California)	Sept. 18, 1982
17	Tom Reynolds, San Diego St. (Utah St.)	Oct. 22, 1971
17	Mike Mikolayunas, Davidson (Richmond)	Oct. 11, 1969
17	Jerry Hendren, Idaho (Southern Miss.)	Oct. 4, 1969
17	Emilio Vallez, New Mexico (New Mexico St.)	Oct. 27, 1967
17	Chuck Hughes, UTEP (Arizona St.)	Oct. 30, 1965

Career Yards

Player, Team	Years	Catches	Yards	Avg.	TD
Terance Mathis, New Mexico	1985-87, 89	*263	*4,254	16.2	36
Marc Zeno, Tulane	1984-87	236	3,725	15.8	25
Ron Sellers, Florida St.	1966-68	212	3,598	17.0	23
Elmo Wright, Houston	1968-70	153	3,347	‡21.9	34
Howard Twilley, Tulsa	1963-65	261	3,343	12.8	32
Clarkston Hines, Duke	1986-89	189	3,318	17.6	*38
Gerald Harp, Western Caro.	1977-80	197	3,305	16.8	26
Dan Bitson, Tulsa	1987-89, 91	163	3,300	20.2	29
David Williams, Illinois	1983-85	245	3,195	13.0	22
¢Aaron Turner, Pacific (Cal.)	1989-91	187	3,174	17.0	32
Hart Lee Dykes, Oklahoma St.	1985-88	203	3,171	15.6	29
Rick Beasley, Appalachian St.	1978-80	178	3,124	17.6	23
Ricky Proehl, Wake Forest	1986-89	188	2,949	15.7	25
Henry Ellard, Fresno St.	1979-82	138	2,947	21.4	25
Kendal Smith, Utah St.	1985-88	169	2,943	17.4	25
Charles Lockett, Long Beach St.	1983-86	191	2,902	15.1	19
Chuck Hughes, UTEP	1964-66	162	2,882	17.8	19
Walter Murray, Hawaii	1982-85	178	2,865	16.1	20
Boo Mitchell, Vanderbilt	1985-88	188	2,864	15.8	9
John Jefferson, Arizona St.	1974-77	175	2,824	16.1	19

* Record. ¢ Active player. ‡ Record for minimum of 105 catches.

Career Touchdown Receptions

Player, Team	Years	Games	TD
Clarkston Hines, Duke	1986-89	44	*38
Terance Mathis, New Mexico	1985-87, 89	44	36
Elmo Wright, Houston	1968-70	30	34
¢Aaron Turner, Pacific (Cal.)	1989-91	33	32
Steve Largent, Tulsa	1973-75	30	32
Howard Twilley, Tulsa	1963-65	30	32
Manny Hazard, Houston	1989-90	21	31
Desmond Howard, Michigan	1989-91	33	30
Dan Bitson, Tulsa	1987-89, 91	44	29

* Record. ¢ Active player.

Season Yards

Player, Team	Year	Catches	Yards	Avg.	TD
Howard Twilley, Tulsa	†1965	134	*1,779	13.3	16
Manny Hazard, Houston	†1989	*142	1,689	11.9	*22
Aaron Turner, Pacific (Cal.)	†1991	92	1,604	17.4	18
Chuck Hughes, UTEP	1965	80	1,519	19.0	12
Henry Ellard, Fresno St.	1982	62	1,510	††24.4	15
Ron Sellers, Florida St.	†1968	86	1,496	17.4	12
Jerry Hendren, Idaho	†1969	95	1,452	15.3	12
Jason Phillips, Houston	†1988	108	1,444	13.4	15

* Record. † National champion. †† Record for minimum of 50 catches.

Single-Game Yards

Yds.	Player, Team (Opponent)	Date
349	Chuck Hughes, UTEP (North Texas)	Sept. 18, 1965
322	Rick Eber, Tulsa (Idaho St.)	Oct. 7, 1967
318	Harry Wood, Tulsa (Idaho St.)	Oct. 7, 1967
316	Jeff Evans, New Mexico St. (Southern Ill.)	Sept. 30, 1978
290	Tom Reynolds, San Diego St. (Utah St.)	Oct. 22, 1971

Yds.	Player, Team (Opponent)	Date
289	Wesley Walker, California (San Jose St.)	Oct. 2, 1976
288	Mike Siani, Villanova (Xavier)	Oct. 30, 1971
284	Don Clune, Pennsylvania (Harvard)	Oct. 30, 1971
283	Chris Castor, Duke (Wake Forest)	Nov. 6, 1982
282	Larry Willis, Fresno St. (Montana St.)	Nov. 17, 1984
278	Derek Graham, Princeton (Yale)	Nov. 14, 1981

Annual Champions

Year	Player, Team	Class	Ct.	Yards	TD
1937	Jim Benton, Arkansas	Sr.	47	754	—
1938	Sam Boyd, Baylor	Sr.	32	537	—
1939	Ken Kavanaugh, Louisiana St.	Sr.	30	467	—
1940	Eddie Bryant, Virginia	So.	30	222	2
1941	Hank Stanton, Arizona	Sr.	50	820	—
1942	Bill Rogers, Texas A&M	Sr.	39	432	—
1943	Neil Armstrong, Oklahoma St.	Fr.	39	317	—
1944	Reid Moseley, Georgia	So.	32	506	—
1945	Reid Moseley, Georgia	Jr.	31	662	—
1946	Neil Armstrong, Oklahoma St.	Sr.	32	479	1
1947	Barney Poole, Mississippi	Jr.	52	513	8
1948	Johnny "Red" O'Quinn, Wake Forest	Jr.	39	605	7
1949	Art Weiner, North Caro.	Sr.	52	762	7
1950	Gordon Cooper, Denver	Jr.	46	569	8
1951	Dewey McConnell, Wyoming	Sr.	47	725	9
1952	Ed Brown, Fordham	Sr.	57	774	6
1953	John Carson, Georgia	Sr.	45	663	4
1954	Jim Hanifan, California	Sr.	44	569	7
1955	Hank Burnine, Missouri	Sr.	44	594	2
1956	Art Powell, San Jose St.	So.	40	583	5
1957	Stuart Vaughan, Utah	Sr.	53	756	5
1958	Dave Hibbert, Arizona	Jr.	61	606	4
1959	Chris Burford, Stanford	Sr.	61	756	6
1960	Hugh Campbell, Washington St.	So.	66	881	10
1961	Hugh Campbell, Washington St.	Jr.	53	723	5
1962	Vern Burke, Oregon St.	Jr.	69	1,007	10
1963	Lawrence Elkins, Baylor	Jr.	70	873	8
1964	Howard Twilley, Tulsa	Jr.	95	1,178	13
1965	Howard Twilley, Tulsa	Sr.	134	*1,779	16
1966	Glenn Meltzer, Wichita St.	So.	91	1,115	4
1967	Bob Goodridge, Vanderbilt	Sr.	79	1,114	6
1968	Ron Sellers, Florida St.	Sr.	86	1,496	12
1969	Jerry Hendren, Idaho	Sr.	95	1,452	12

Beginning in 1970, ranked on per-game (instead of total) catches

Year	Player, Team	Class	G.	Ct.	Avg.	Yards	TD
1970	Mike Mikolayunas, Davidson	Sr.	10	87	8.7	1,128	8
1971	Tom Reynolds, San Diego St.	Sr.	10	67	6.7	1,070	7
1972	Tom Forzani, Utah St.	Sr.	11	85	7.7	1,169	8
1973	Jay Miller, Brigham Young	So.	11	100	9.1	1,181	8
1974	Dwight McDonald, San Diego St.	Sr.	11	86	7.8	1,157	7
1975	Bob Farnham, Brown	Jr.	9	56	6.2	701	2
1976	Billy Ryckman, Louisiana Tech	Sr.	11	77	7.0	1,382	10
1977	Wayne Tolleson, Western Caro.	Sr.	11	73	6.6	1,101	7
1978	Dave Petzke, Northern Ill.	Sr.	11	91	8.3	1,217	11
1979	Rick Beasley, Appalachian St.	Jr.	11	74	6.7	1,205	12
1980	Dave Young, Purdue	Sr.	11	67	6.1	917	8
1981	Pete Harvey, North Texas	Sr.	9	57	6.3	743	3
1982	Vincent White, Stanford	Sr.	10	68	6.8	677	8
1983	Keith Edwards, Vanderbilt	Jr.	11	97	8.8	909	8
1984	David Williams, Illinois	Jr.	11	101	9.2	1,278	8
1985	Rodney Carter, Purdue	Sr.	11	98	8.9	1,099	4
1986	Mark Templeton, Long Beach St. (RB)	Sr.	11	99	9.0	688	2
1987	Jason Phillips, Houston	Jr.	11	99	9.0	875	3
1988	Jason Phillips, Houston	Sr.	11	108	9.8	1,444	15
1989	Manny Hazard, Houston	Jr.	11	*142	12.9	1,689	*22

Beginning in 1990, ranked on both per-game catches and yards per game

Per-Game Catches

Year	Player, Team	Class	G.	Ct.	Avg.	Yards	TD
1990	Manny Hazard, Houston	Sr.	10	78	7.8	946	9
1991	Fred Gilbert, Houston	Jr.	11	106	9.6	957	7

1992 NCAA FOOTBALL

Year	Player, Team	Yards Per Game Class	G.	Ct.	Yards	Avg.	TD
1990	Patrick Rowe, San Diego St.	Jr.	11	71	1,392	126.6	8
1991	Aaron Turner, Pacific (Cal.)	Jr.	11	92	1,604	145.8	18

* Record.

SCORING

Career Points Per Game

Player, Team	Years	Games	TD	XPt.	FG	Pts.	Pt. PG
Bob Gaiters, New Mexico St.	1959-60	17	32	11	0	203	*11.9
Ed Marinaro, Cornell	1969-71	27	52	6	0	318	11.8
Bill Burnett, Arkansas	1968-70	26	49	0	0	294	11.3
Steve Owens, Oklahoma	1967-69	30	‡56	0	0	‡336	11.2
Eddie Talboom, Wyoming	1948-50	28	34	99	0	303	10.8
O. J. Simpson, Southern Cal	1967-68	19	33	0	0	198	10.4
Rudy Mobley, Hardin-Simmons	1942, 46	19	32	0	0	192	10.1
Howard Twilley, Tulsa	1963-65	26	32	67	0	259	10.0
Blaise Bryant, Iowa St.	1989-90	20	32	6	0	198	9.9
Tom Harmon, Michigan	1938-40	24	33	33	2	237	9.9
Jackie Parker, Mississippi St.	1952-53	19	24	41	0	185	9.7
Roman Anderson, Houston	1988-91	44	0	*213	70	*423	9.6
Anthony Thompson, Indiana	1986-89	41	*65	4	0	394	9.6
Johnny Bright, Drake	1949-51	25	40	0	0	240	9.6
Glenn Davis, Army	1943-46	37	59	0	0	354	9.6
Stan Koslowski, Holy Cross	1943, 45	17	23	24	0	162	9.5
Mack Herron, Kansas St.	1968-69	20	31	2	0	188	9.4
Stacey Robinson, Northern Ill. (QB)	1988-90	25	38	6	0	234	9.4
Pervis Atkins, New Mexico St.	1959-60	20	29	13	0	187	9.4
Bernard White, Bowling Green	1984-85	22	34	0	0	204	9.3
Floyd Little, Syracuse	1964-66	30	46	2	0	278	9.3
Felix "Doc" Blanchard, Army	1944-46	25	38	3	0	231	9.2
Bobby Reynolds, Nebraska	1950-52	23	28	40	1	211	9.2
Anthony Davis, Southern Cal	1972-74	33	50	2	0	302	9.2

* Record.   ‡ Three-year totals record.

Season Points Per Game

Player, Team	Year	Games	TD	XPt.	FG	Pts.	Pt. PG
Barry Sanders, Oklahoma St.	†1988	11	*39	0	0	*234	*21.3
Bobby Reynolds, Nebraska	†1950	9	22	25	0	157	17.4
Art Luppino, Arizona	†1954	10	24	22	0	166	16.6
Ed Marinaro, Cornell	†1971	9	24	4	0	148	16.4
Lydell Mitchell, Penn St.	1971	11	29	0	0	174	15.8
Marshall Faulk, San Diego St.	†1991	9	23	2	0	140	15.6
Byron "Whizzer" White, Colorado	†1937	8	16	23	1	122	15.3

* Record.   † National champion.

Career Points
(Non-Kickers)

Player, Team	Years	TD	XPt.	FG	Pts.
Anthony Thompson, Indiana	1986-89	*65	4	0	*394
Tony Dorsett, Pittsburgh	1973-76	59	2	0	356
Glenn Davis, Army	1943-46	59	0	0	354
Art Luppino, Arizona	1953-56	48	49	0	337
Steve Owens, Oklahoma	1967-69	‡56	0	0	‡336
Wilford White, Arizona St.	1947-50	48	27	4	327
Barry Sanders, Oklahoma St.	1986-88	54	0	0	324
Allen Pinkett, Notre Dame	1982-85	53	2	0	320
Ed Marinaro, Cornell	1969-71	52	6	0	318
Pete Johnson, Ohio St.	1973-76	53	0	0	318
Herschel Walker, Georgia	1980-82	52	2	0	314
James Gray, Texas Tech	1986-89	52	0	0	312
Mike Rozier, Nebraska	1981-83	52	0	0	312
Ted Brown, North Caro. St.	1975-78	51	6	0	312
John Harvey, UTEP	1985-88	51	0	0	306
Eddie Talboom, Wyoming	1948-50	34	99	0	303
Anthony Davis, Southern Cal	1972-74	50	2	0	302
Dalton Hilliard, Louisiana St.	1982-85	50	0	0	300
Billy Sims, Oklahoma	$1975-79	50	0	0	300
Charles White, Southern Cal	1976-79	49	2	0	296
Nolan Jones, Arizona St.	1958-61	30	77	13	296
Steve Bartalo, Colorado St.	1983-86	49	0	0	294

Player, Team	Years	TD	XPt.	FG	Pts.
Bill Burnett, Arkansas	1968-70	49	0	0	294
Brian Mitchell, Southwestern La.	1986-89	47	4	0	286
Keith Byars, Ohio St.	1982-85	48	0	0	286
Rick Badanjek, Maryland	1982-85	46	10	0	286

* *Record.*   ‡ *Three-year totals record.* $ *See page 6 for explanation.*

Career Points
(Kickers)

Player, Team	Years	PAT	PAT Att.	FG	FG Att.	Pts.
Roman Anderson, Houston	1988-91	*213	*217	70	101	*423
Carlos Huerta, Miami (Fla.)	1988-91	178	181	73	91	397
Derek Schmidt, Florida St.	1984-87	174	178	73	102	393
Luis Zendejas, Arizona St.	1981-84	134	135	78	*105	368
Jeff Jaeger, Washington	1983-86	118	123	*80	99	358
John Lee, UCLA	1982-85	116	117	79	92	353
Max Zendejas, Arizona	1982-85	122	124	77	104	353
Kevin Butler, Georgia	1981-84	122	125	77	98	353
Philip Doyle, Alabama	1987-90	105	108	78	*105	%345
Barry Belli, Fresno St.	1984-87	116	123	70	99	326
Jason Hanson, Washington St.	1988-91	136	141	62	95	322
R. D. Lashar, Oklahoma	1987-90	194	200	42	60	320
Collin Mackie, South Caro.	1987-90	112	113	69	95	319
Cary Blanchard, Oklahoma St.	1987-90	150	151	54	73	$314
Fuad Reveiz, Tennessee	1981-84	101	103	71	95	314
Sean Fleming, Wyoming	1988-91	150	155	54	92	312
Van Tiffin, Alabama	1983-86	135	135	59	87	312
Jess Atkinson, Maryland	1981-84	128	131	60	82	308
Gary Gussman, Miami (Ohio)	1984-87	102	104	68	94	306
Jason Elam, Hawaii	1988-91	114	117	63	75	303
Greg Cox, Miami (Fla.)	1984-87	162	169	47	64	303
Tim Lashar, Oklahoma	1983-86	168	170	43	65	297
Quin Rodriquez, Southern Cal	1987-90	139	146	52	68	295
Mike Gillette, Michigan	1985-88	125	128	56	78	293
David Browndyke, Louisiana St.	1986-89	109	109	61	75	292

* *Record.*   % *Includes one TD reception.* $ *Includes one two-point conversion.*

Season Points

Player, Team	Year	TD	XPt.	FG	Pts.
Barry Sanders, Oklahoma St.	†1988	*39	0	0	*234
Mike Rozier, Nebraska	†1983	29	0	0	174
Lydell Mitchell, Penn St.	1971	29	0	0	174
Art Luppino, Arizona	†1954	24	22	0	166
Bobby Reynolds, Nebraska	†1950	22	25	0	157
Anthony Thompson, Indiana	†1989	25	4	0	154
Fred Wendt, UTEP	†1948	20	32	0	152
Pete Johnson, Ohio St.	†1975	25	0	0	150

* *Record.*   † *National champion.*

Single-Game Points

No.	Player, Team (Opponent)	Date
48	Howard Griffith, Illinois (Southern Ill.)	Sept. 22, 1990
44	Marshall Faulk, San Diego St. (Pacific, Cal.)	Sept. 14, 1991
43	Jim Brown, Syracuse (Colgate)	Nov. 17, 1956
42	Arnold "Showboat" Boykin, Mississippi (Mississippi St.)	Dec. 1, 1951
42	Fred Wendt, UTEP (New Mexico St.)	Nov. 25, 1948
38	Dick Bass, Pacific, Cal. (San Diego St.)	Nov. 22, 1958
37	Jimmy Nutter, Wichita St. (Northern St., S.D.)	Oct. 22, 1949
36	Calvin Jones, Nebraska (Kansas)	Nov. 9, 1991
36	Blake Ezor, Michigan St. (Northwestern)	Nov. 18, 1989
36	Dee Dowis, Air Force (San Diego St.)	Sept. 2, 1989
36	Kelvin Bryant, North Caro. (East Caro.)	Sept. 12, 1981
36	Andre Herrera, Southern Ill. (Northern Ill.)	Oct. 23, 1976
36	Anthony Davis, Southern Cal (Notre Dame)	Dec. 2, 1972
36	Tim Delaney, San Diego St. (New Mexico St.)	Nov. 15, 1969
36	Tom Francisco, Virginia Tech (Va. Military)	Nov. 24, 1966
36	Howard Twilley, Tulsa (Louisville)	Nov. 6, 1965
36	Pete Pedro, West Tex. St. (UTEP)	Sept. 30, 1961
36	Tom Powers, Duke (Richmond)	Oct. 21, 1950

Annual Champions

Year	Player, Team	Class	TD	XPt.	FG	Pts.
1937	Byron "Whizzer" White, Colorado	Sr.	16	23	1	122
1938	Parker Hall, Mississippi	Sr.	11	7	0	73
1939	Tom Harmon, Michigan	Jr.	14	15	1	102
1940	Tom Harmon, Michigan	Sr.	16	18	1	117
1941	Bill Dudley, Virginia	Sr.	18	23	1	134
1942	Bob Steuber, Missouri	Sr.	18	13	0	121
1943	Steve Van Buren, Louisiana St.	Sr.	14	14	0	98
1944	Glenn Davis, Army	So.	20	0	0	120
1945	Felix "Doc" Blanchard, Army	Jr.	19	1	0	115
1946	Gene Roberts, Tenn.-Chatt.	Sr.	18	9	0	117
1947	Lou Gambino, Maryland	Jr.	16	0	0	96
1948	Fred Wendt, UTEP	Sr.	20	32	0	152
1949	George Thomas, Oklahoma	Sr.	19	3	0	117
1950	Bobby Reynolds, Nebraska	So.	22	25	0	157
1951	Ollie Matson, San Francisco	Sr.	21	0	0	126
1952	Jackie Parker, Mississippi St.	Jr.	16	24	0	120
1953	Earl Lindley, Utah St.	Sr.	13	3	0	81
1954	Art Luppino, Arizona	So.	24	22	0	166
1955	Jim Swink, Texas Christian	Jr.	20	5	0	125
1956	Clendon Thomas, Oklahoma	Jr.	18	0	0	108
1957	Leon Burton, Arizona St.	Jr.	16	0	0	96
1958	Dick Bass, Pacific (Cal.)	Jr.	18	8	0	116
1959	Pervis Atkins, New Mexico St.	Jr.	17	5	0	107
1960	Bob Gaiters, New Mexico St.	Sr.	23	7	0	145
1961	Jim Pilot, New Mexico St.	So.	21	12	0	138
1962	Jerry Logan, West Tex. St.	Sr.	13	32	0	110
1963	Cosmo Iacavazzi, Princeton	Jr.	14	0	0	84
	Dave Casinelli, Memphis St.	Sr.	14	0	0	84
1964	Brian Piccolo, Wake Forest	Sr.	17	9	0	111
1965	Howard Twilley, Tulsa	Sr.	16	31	0	127
1966	Ken Hebert, Houston	Jr.	11	41	2	113
1967	Leroy Keyes, Purdue	Jr.	19	0	0	114
1968	Jim O'Brien, Cincinnati	Jr.	12	31	13	142
1969	Steve Owens, Oklahoma	Sr.	23	0	0	138

Beginning in 1970, ranked on per-game (instead of total) points

Year	Player, Team	Class	Games	TD	XPt.	FG	Pts.	Avg.
1970	Brian Bream, Air Force	Jr.	10	20	0	0	120	12.0
	Gary Kosins, Dayton	Jr.	9	18	0	0	108	12.0
1971	Ed Marinaro, Cornell	Sr.	9	24	4	0	148	16.4
1972	Harold Henson, Ohio St.	So.	10	20	0	0	120	12.0
1973	Jim Jennings, Rutgers	Sr.	11	21	2	0	128	11.6
1974	Bill Marek, Wisconsin	Jr.	9	19	0	0	114	12.7
1975	Pete Johnson, Ohio St.	Jr.	11	25	0	0	150	13.6
1976	Tony Dorsett, Pittsburgh	Sr.	11	22	2	0	134	12.2
1977	Earl Campbell, Texas	Sr.	11	19	0	0	114	10.4
1978	Billy Sims, Oklahoma	Jr.	11	20	0	0	120	10.9
1979	Billy Sims, Oklahoma	Sr.	11	22	0	0	132	12.0
1980	Sammy Winder, Southern Miss.	Jr.	11	20	0	0	120	10.9
1981	Marcus Allen, Southern Cal	Sr.	11	23	0	0	138	12.5
1982	Greg Allen, Florida St.	So.	11	21	0	0	126	11.5
1983	Mike Rozier, Nebraska	Sr.	12	29	0	0	174	14.5
1984	Keith Byars, Ohio St.	Jr.	11	24	0	0	144	13.1
1985	Bernard White, Bowling Green	Sr.	11	19	0	0	114	10.4
1986	Steve Bartalo, Colorado St.	Sr.	11	19	0	0	114	10.4
1987	Paul Hewitt, San Diego St.	Jr.	12	24	0	0	144	12.0
1988	Barry Sanders, Oklahoma St.	Jr.	11	*39	0	0	*234	*21.3
1989	Anthony Thompson, Indiana	Sr.	11	25	4	0	154	14.0
1990	Stacey Robinson, Northern Ill. (QB)	Sr.	11	19	6	0	120	10.9
1991	Marshall Faulk, San Diego St.	Fr.	9	23	2	0	140	15.6

*Record.

INTERCEPTIONS
Career Interceptions

Player, Team	Years	No.	Yards	Avg.
Al Brosky, Illinois	1950-52	*29	356	12.3
Martin Bayless, Bowling Green	1980-83	27	266	9.9
John Provost, Holy Cross	1972-74	27	470	17.4
Tony Thurman, Boston College	1981-84	25	221	8.8

Player, Team	Years	No.	Yards	Avg.
Tom Curtis, Michigan	1967-69	25	440	17.6
Jeff Nixon, Richmond	1975-78	23	377	16.4
Bennie Blades, Miami (Fla.)	1984-87	22	355	16.1
Jim Bolding, East Caro.	1973-76	22	143	6.5
Terrell Buckley, Florida St.	1989-91	21	*501	23.9
Chuck Cecil, Arizona	1984-87	21	241	11.5
Barry Hill, Iowa St.	1972-74	21	202	9.6
Mike Sensibaugh, Ohio St.	1968-70	21	226	10.8
¢Tracy Saul, Texas Tech	1989-91	20	383	19.2
Kevin Smith, Texas A&M	1988-91	20	289	14.5
Mark Collins, Cal St. Fullerton	1982-85	20	193	9.7
Anthony Young, Temple	1981-84	20	230	11.5
Chris Williams, Louisiana St.	1977-80	20	91	4.6
Charles Jefferson, McNeese St.	1975-78	20	95	4.8
Artimus Parker, Southern Cal	1971-73	20	268	13.4
Dave Atkinson, Brigham Young	1971-73	20	222	11.1
Jackie Wallace, Arizona	1970-72	20	250	12.5
Tom Wilson, Colgate	1964-66	20	215	10.8
Lynn Chandnois, Michigan St.	1946-49	20	410	20.5
Bobby Wilson, Mississippi	1946-49	20	369	18.5

* Record. ¢ Active player.

Season Interceptions

Player, Team	Year	No.	Yards
Al Worley, Washington	†1968	*14	130
George Shaw, Oregon	†1951	13	136
Terrell Buckley, Florida St.	†1991	12	238
Cornelius Price, Houston	†1989	12	187
Bob Navarro, Eastern Mich.	†1989	12	73
Tony Thurman, Boston College	†1984	12	99
Terry Hoage, Georgia	†1982	12	51
Frank Polito, Villanova	†1971	12	261
Bill Albrecht, Washington	1951	12	140
Hank Rich, Arizona St.	†1950	12	135

* Record. † National champion.

Annual Champions

Year	Player, Team	Class	No.	Yards
1938	Elmer Tarbox, Texas Tech	Sr.	11	89
1939	Harold Van Every, Minnesota	Sr.	8	59
1940	Dick Morgan, Tulsa	Jr.	7	210
1941	Bobby Robertson, Southern Cal	Sr.	9	126
1942	Ray Evans, Kansas	Jr.	10	76
1943	Jay Stoves, Washington	Sr.	7	139
1944	Joe Stuart, California	Jr.	7	76
1945	Jake Leicht, Oregon	So.	9	195
1946	Larry Hatch, Washington	So.	8	114
1947	John Bruce, William & Mary	Jr.	9	78
1948	Jay Van Noy, Utah St.	Jr.	8	228
1949	Bobby Wilson, Mississippi	Sr.	10	70
1950	Hank Rich, Arizona St.	Sr.	12	135
1951	George Shaw, Oregon	Fr.	13	136
1952	Cecil Ingram, Alabama	Jr.	10	163
1953	Bob Garrett, Stanford	Sr.	9	80
1954	Gary Glick, Colorado St.	Jr.	8	168
1955	Sam Wesley, Oregon St.	Jr.	7	61
1956	Jack Hill, Utah St.	Sr.	7	132
1957	Ray Toole, North Texas	Sr.	7	133
1958	Jim Norton, Idaho	Jr.	9	222
1959	Bud Whitehead, Florida St.	Jr.	6	111
1960	Bob O'Billovich, Montana	Jr.	7	71
1961	Joe Zuger, Arizona St.	Sr.	10	121
1962	Byron Beaver, Houston	Sr.	10	56
1963	Dick Kern, William & Mary	Sr.	8	116
1964	Tony Carey, Notre Dame	Jr.	8	121
1965	Bob Sullivan, Maryland	Sr.	10	61
1966	Henry King, Utah St.	Sr.	11	180
1967	Steve Haterius, West Tex. St.	Sr.	11	90

Year	Player, Team	Class	No.	Yards
1968	Al Worley, Washington	Sr.	*14	130
1969	Seth Miller, Arizona St.	Sr.	11	63

Beginning in 1970, ranked on per-game (instead of total) number

Year	Player, Team	Class	Games	No.	Avg.	Yards
1970	Mike Sensibaugh, Ohio St.	Sr.	8	8	1.0	40
1971	Frank Polito, Villanova	So.	10	12	1.2	261
1972	Mike Townsend, Notre Dame	Jr.	10	10	1.0	39
1973	Mike Gow, Illinois	Jr.	11	10	0.91	142
1974	Mike Haynes, Arizona St.	Jr.	11	10	0.91	115
1975	Jim Bolding, East Caro.	Jr.	10	10	1.0	51
1976	Anthony Francis, Houston	Jr.	11	10	0.91	118
1977	Paul Lawler, Colgate	Sr.	9	7	0.78	53
1978	Pete Harris, Penn St.	Jr.	11	10	0.91	155
1979	Joe Callan, Ohio	Sr.	9	9	1.0	110
1980	Ronnie Lott, Southern Cal	Sr.	11	8	0.73	166
	Steve McNamee, William & Mary	Sr.	11	8	0.73	125
	Greg Benton, Drake.....................	Sr.	11	8	0.73	119
	Jeff Hipp, Georgia	Sr.	11	8	0.73	104
	Mike Richardson, Arizona St.	So.	11	8	0.73	89
	Vann McElroy, Baylor	Jr.	11	8	0.73	73
1981	Sam Shaffer, Temple	Sr.	10	9	0.90	76
1982	Terry Hoage, Georgia	Jr.	10	12	1.20	51
1983	Martin Bayless, Bowling Green	Sr.	11	10	0.91	64
1984	Tony Thurman, Boston College	Sr.	11	12	1.09	99
1985	Chris White, Tennessee	Sr.	11	9	0.82	168
	Kevin Walker, East Caro.	Sr.	11	9	0.82	155
1986	Bennie Blades, Miami (Fla.)	Jr.	11	10	0.91	128
1987	Keith McMeans, Virginia	Fr.	10	9	0.90	35
1988	Kurt Larson, Michigan St. (LB)	Sr.	11	8	0.73	78
	Andy Logan, Kent.......................	Sr.	11	8	0.73	54
1989	Cornelius Price, Houston	Jr.	11	12	1.09	187
	Bob Navarro, Eastern Mich.	Jr.	11	12	1.09	73
1990	Jerry Parks, Houston....................	Jr.	11	8	0.73	124
1991	Terrell Buckley, Florida St.	Jr.	12	12	1.00	238

Record.

PUNTING

Career Average (Minimum 150 Punts)

Player, Team	Years	No.	Yards	Avg.	Long
Reggie Roby, Iowa	1979-82	172	7,849	*45.6	69
Greg Montgomery, Michigan St.	1985-87	170	7,721	45.4	86
Tom Tupa, Ohio St.	1984-87	196	8,854	45.2	75
Barry Helton, Colorado	1984-87	153	6,873	44.9	68
Ray Guy, Southern Miss.	1970-72	200	8,934	44.7	93
Bucky Scribner, Kansas	1980-82	217	9,670	44.6	70
Greg Horne, Arkansas	1983-86	180	8,002	44.5	72
Ray Criswell, Florida	1982-85	161	7,153	44.4	73
Russell Erxleben, Texas	1975-78	214	9,467	44.2	80
Mark Simon, Air Force	1984-86	156	6,898	44.2	64
Johnny Evans, North Caro. St.	1974-77	185	8,143	44.0	81
Chuck Ramsey, Wake Forest	1971-73	205	9,010	44.0	70
Jimmy Colquitt, Tennessee	1981-84	201	8,816	43.9	70
John Teltschik, Texas	1982-85	217	9,496	43.8	81

Record.

Career Average (Minimum 250 Punts)

Player, Team	Years	No.	Yards	Avg.	Long
Bill Smith, Mississippi	1983-86	254	11,260	*44.3	92
Jim Arnold, Vanderbilt	1979-82	277	12,171	43.9	79
Ralf Mojsiejenko, Michigan St.	1981-84	275	11,997	43.6	72
Jim Miller, Mississippi	1976-79	266	11,549	43.4	82
Russ Henderson, Virginia	1975-78	276	11,957	43.3	74
Maury Buford, Texas Tech	1978-81	293	12,670	43.2	75
Chris Becker, Texas Christian	1985-88	265	11,407	43.0	77
Mark Bounds, West Tex. St./Texas Tech	✓1988-91	252	10,842	43.0	89
Ron Keller, New Mexico........................	1983-86	252	10,737	42.6	77
James Gargus, Texas Christian	1981-84	255	10,862	42.6	74

Record. ✓ *Transferred to Texas Tech after West Tex. St. dropped football program in 1990.*

Season Average
(Qualifiers for Championship)

Player, Team	Year	No.	Yards	Avg.
Reggie Roby, Iowa	†1981	44	2,193	*49.8
Kirk Wilson, UCLA	†1956	30	1,479	49.3
Zack Jordan, Colorado	†1950	38	1,830	48.2
Ricky Anderson, Vanderbilt	†1984	58	2,793	‡48.2
Reggie Roby, Iowa	†1982	52	2,501	48.1
Marv Bateman, Utah	†1971	68	3,269	48.1
Owen Price, UTEP	†1940	30	1,440	48.0
Jack Jacobs, Oklahoma	1940	31	1,483	47.8
Bill Smith, Mississippi	1984	44	2,099	47.7

Record. † National champion. ‡ Record for minimum of 50 punts.

Annual Champions

Year	Player, Team	Class	No.	Yards	Avg.
1937	Johnny Pingel, Michigan St.	Jr.	49	2,101	42.9
1938	Jerry Dowd, St. Mary's (Cal.)	Sr.	62	2,711	43.7
1939	Harry Dunkle, North Caro.	So.	37	1,725	46.6
1940	Owen Price, UTEP	Jr.	30	1,440	48.0
1941	Owen Price, UTEP	Sr.	40	1,813	45.3
1942	Bobby Cifers, Tennessee	Jr.	37	1,586	42.9
1943	Harold Cox, Arkansas	Fr.	37	1,518	41.0
1944	Bob Waterfield, UCLA	Sr.	60	2,575	42.9
1945	Howard Maley, Southern Methodist	Sr.	59	2,458	41.7
1946	Johnny Galvin, Purdue	Sr.	30	1,286	42.9
1947	Leslie Palmer, North Caro. St.	Sr.	65	2,816	43.3
1948	Charlie Justice, North Caro.	Jr.	62	2,728	44.0
1949	Paul Stombaugh, Furman	Sr.	57	2,550	44.7
1950	Zack Jordan, Colorado	So.	38	1,830	48.2
1951	Chuck Spaulding, Wyoming	Jr.	37	1,610	43.5
1952	Des Koch, Southern Cal	Jr.	47	2,043	43.5
1953	Zeke Bratkowski, Georgia (QB)	Sr.	50	2,132	42.6
1954	A. L. Terpening, New Mexico	Sr.	41	1,869	45.6
1955	Don Chandler, Florida	Sr.	22	975	44.3
1956	Kirk Wilson, UCLA	So.	30	1,479	49.3
1957	Dave Sherer, Southern Methodist	Jr.	36	1,620	45.0
1958	Bobby Walden, Georgia	So.	44	1,991	45.3
1959	John Hadl, Kansas	So.	43	1,960	45.6
1960	Dick Fitzsimmons, Denver	So.	25	1,106	44.2
1961	Joe Zuger, Arizona St.	Sr.	31	1,305	42.1
1962	Joe Don Looney, Oklahoma	Jr.	34	1,474	43.4
1963	Danny Thomas, Southern Methodist	Jr.	48	2,110	44.0
1964	Frank Lambert, Mississippi	Sr.	50	2,205	44.1
1965	Dave Lewis, Stanford	Jr.	29	1,302	44.9
1966	Ron Widby, Tennessee	Sr.	48	2,104	43.8
1967	Zenon Andrusyshyn, UCLA	So.	34	1,502	44.2
1968	Dany Pitcock, Wichita St.	Sr.	71	3,068	43.2
1969	Ed Marsh, Baylor	Jr.	68	2,965	43.6
1970	Marv Bateman, Utah	Jr.	65	2,968	45.7
1971	Marv Bateman, Utah	Sr.	68	3,269	48.1
1972	Ray Guy, Southern Miss.	Sr.	58	2,680	46.2
1973	Chuck Ramsey, Wake Forest	Sr.	87	3,896	44.8
1974	Joe Parker, Appalachian St.	So.	63	2,788	44.3
1975	Tom Skladany, Ohio St.	Jr.	36	1,682	46.7
1976	Russell Erxleben, Texas	So.	61	2,842	46.6
1977	Jim Miller, Mississippi	So.	66	3,029	45.9
1978	Maury Buford, Texas Tech	Fr.	71	3,131	44.1
1979	Clay Brown, Brigham Young	Jr.	43	1,950	45.3

Beginning in 1980, ranked on minimum 3.6 punts per game

Year	Player, Team	Class	No.	Yards	Long	Avg.
1980	Steve Cox, Arkansas	Sr.	47	2,186	86	46.5
1981	Reggie Roby, Iowa	Jr.	44	2,193	68	*49.8
1982	Reggie Roby, Iowa	Sr.	52	2,501	66	48.1
1983	Jack Weil, Wyoming	Sr.	52	2,369	86	45.6
1984	Ricky Anderson, Vanderbilt	Sr.	58	2,793	82	@48.2
1985	Mark Simon, Air Force	Jr.	53	2,506	71	47.3
1986	Greg Horne, Arkansas	Sr.	49	2,313	65	47.2
1987	Tom Tupa, Ohio St. (QB)	Sr.	63	2,963	72	47.0
1988	Keith English, Colorado	Sr.	51	2,297	77	45.0
1989	Tom Rouen, Colorado	So.	36	1,651	63	45.8

Year	Player, Team	Class	No.	Yards	Long	Avg.
1990	Cris Shale, Bowling Green	Sr.	66	3,087	81	46.8
1991	Mark Bounds, Texas Tech	Sr.	53	2,481	78	46.8

* Record. @ Record for minimum of 50 punts.

PUNT RETURNS
Career Average
(Minimum 1.2 Returns Per Game)

Player, Team	Years	No.	Yards	TD	Long	Avg.
Jack Mitchell, Oklahoma	1946-48	39	922	**7	70	*23.6
Gene Gibson, Cincinnati	1949-50	37	760	4	75	20.5
Eddie Macon, Pacific (Cal.)	1949-51	48	907	4	**100	18.9
Jackie Robinson, UCLA	1939-40	37	694	2	89	18.8
Mike Fuller, Auburn	1972-74	50	883	3	63	17.7
Bobby Dillon, Texas......................	1949-51	47	830	1	84	17.7
Erroll Tucker, Utah	1984-85	38	650	3	89	17.1
George Hoey, Michigan	1966-68	31	529	1	60	17.1
Jack Christiansen, Colorado St...........	1948-50	37	626	2	89	16.9
Henry Pryor, Rutgers	1948-49	37	625	1	85	16.9
Adolph Bellizeare, Pennsylvania	1972-74	33	557	3	73	16.9
Ken Hatfield, Arkansas...................	1962-64	70	1,135	5	95	16.2
Gene Rossides, Columbia	1945-48	53	851	3	70	16.1
Bill Hillenbrand, Indiana	1941-42	65	1,042	2	88	16.0

* Record. ** Record tied.

Season Average
(Minimum 1.2 Returns Per Game)

Player, Team	Year	No.	Yards	Avg.
Bill Blackstock, Tennessee	1951	12	311	*25.9
George Sims, Baylor	1948	15	375	25.0
Gene Derricotte, Michigan	1947	14	347	24.8
Erroll Tucker, Utah	†1985	16	389	24.3
George Hoey, Michigan	1967	12	291	24.3
Floyd Little, Syracuse	1965	18	423	23.5

* Record. † National champion.

Annual Champions
(Ranked on Total Yards Until 1970)

Year	Player, Team	Class	No.	Yards	Avg.
1939	Bosh Pritchard, Va. Military	So.	42	583	13.9
1940	Junie Hovious, Mississippi	Sr.	33	498	15.1
1941	Bill Geyer, Colgate	Sr.	33	616	18.7
1942	Bill Hillenbrand, Indiana	Jr.	23	481	20.9
1943	Marion Flanagan, Texas A&M	Jr.	49	475	9.7
1944	Joe Stuart, California	Jr.	39	372	9.5
1945	Jake Leicht, Oregon	So.	28	395	14.1
1946	Harry Gilmer, Alabama..............................	Jr.	37	436	11.8
1947	Lindy Berry, Texas Christian	So.	42	493	11.7
1948	Lee Nalley, Vanderbilt	Jr.	43	*791	18.4
1949	Lee Nalley, Vanderbilt	Sr.	35	498	14.2
1950	Dave Waters, Wash. & Lee	Jr.	30	445	14.8
1951	Tom Murphy, Holy Cross............................	So.	25	533	21.3
1952	Horton Nesrsta, Rice	Jr.	44	536	12.2
1953	Paul Giel, Minnesota	Sr.	17	288	16.9
1954	Dicky Maegle, Rice	Sr.	15	293	19.5
1955	Mike Sommer, Geo. Washington	So.	24	330	13.8
1956	Bill Stacy, Mississippi St.	Jr.	24	290	12.1
1957	Bobby Mulgado, Arizona St.	Sr.	14	267	19.1
1958	Howard Cook, Colorado	Sr.	24	242	10.1
1959	Pervis Atkins, New Mexico St......................	Jr.	16	241	15.1
1960	Lance Alworth, Arkansas	Jr.	18	307	17.1
1961	Lance Alworth, Arkansas	Sr.	28	336	12.0
1962	Darrell Roberts, Utah St.	Sr.	16	333	20.8
1963	Ken Hatfield, Arkansas.............................	Jr.	21	350	16.7
1964	Ken Hatfield, Arkansas.............................	Sr.	31	518	16.7
1965	Nick Rassas, Notre Dame	Sr.	24	459	19.1
1966	Vic Washington, Wyoming	Jr.	34	443	13.0
1967	Mike Battle, Southern Cal	Jr.	47	570	12.1
1968	Roger Wehrli, Missouri	Sr.	41	478	11.7
1969	Chris Farasopoulous, Brigham Young	Jr.	35	527	15.1

Year	Player, Team	Class	No.	Yards	TD	Long	Avg.
1970	Steve Holden, Arizona St.	So.	17	327	2	94	19.2
1971	Golden Richards, Brigham Young	Jr.	33	624	**4	87	18.9
1972	Randy Rhino, Georgia Tech...........	So.	25	441	1	96	17.6
1973	Gary Hayman, Penn St.	Sr.	23	442	1	83	19.2
1974	John Provost, Holy Cross	Sr.	13	238	2	85	18.3
1975	Donnie Ross, New Mexico St.........	Sr.	21	338	1	#81	16.1
1976	Henry Jenkins, Rutgers	Sr.	30	449	0	#40	15.0
1977	Robert Woods, Grambling	Sr.	††11	279	3	72	25.4
1978	Ira Matthews, Wisconsin	Sr.	16	270	3	78	16.9
1979	Jeffrey Shockley, Tennessee St.......	Sr.	27	456	1	79	16.9
1980	Scott Woerner, Georgia	Sr.	31	488	1	67	15.7
1981	Glen Young, Mississippi St.	Jr.	19	307	2	87	16.2
1982	Lionel James, Auburn................	Jr.	25	394	0	#63	15.8
1983	Jim Sandusky, San Diego St.	Sr.	20	381	1	90	19.0
1984	Ricky Nattiel, Florida	So.	22	346	1	67	15.7
1985	Erroll Tucker, Utah	Sr.	16	389	2	89	24.3
1986	Rod Smith, Nebraska	Jr.	‡‡12	227	1	63	18.9
1987	Alan Grant, Stanford	Jr.	27	446	2	77	16.5
1988	Deion Sanders, Florida St.	Sr.	33	503	1	76	15.2
1989	Larry Hargrove, Ohio	Sr.	17	309	2	83	18.2
1990	Dave McCloughan, Colorado	Sr.	32	524	2	90	16.4
1991	Bo Campbell, Virginia Tech	Jr.	15	273	0	45	18.2

* Record.   **Record tied.   # Did not score.   †† Declared champion; with three more returns (making 1.3 per game) for zero yards still would have highest average.   ‡ Ranked on minimum 1.5 returns per game, 1970-73; 1.2 from 1974.   ‡‡ Declared champion; with two more returns (making 1.2 per game) for zero yards still would have highest average.

Annual Punt Return Leaders (1939-69) Based on Average Per Return
(Minimum 1.2 Returns Per Game)

1939—Jackie Robinson, UCLA, 20.0; **1940**—Jackie Robinson, UCLA, 21.0; **1941**—Walt Slater, Tennessee, 20.4; **1942**—Billy Hillenbrand, Indiana, 20.9; **1943**—Otto Graham, Northwestern, 19.7; **1944**—Glenn Davis, Army, 18.4; **1945**—Jake Leicht, Oregon, 14.8; **1946**—Harold Griffin, Florida, 20.1; **1947**—Gene Derricotte, Michigan, 24.8; **1948**—George Sims, Baylor, 25.0; **1949**—Gene Evans, Wisconsin, 21.8; **1950**—Lindy Hanson, Boston U., 22.5; **1951**—Bill Blackstock, Tennessee, 25.9; **1952**—Gil Reich, Kansas, 17.2; **1953**—Bobby Lee, New Mexico, 19.4; **1954**—Dicky Maegle, Rice, 19.5; **1955**—Ron Lind, Drake, 21.1; **1956**—Ron Lind, Drake, 19.1; **1957**—Bobby Mulgado, Arizona St., 19.1; **1958**—Herb Hallas, Yale, 23.4; **1959**—Jacque MacKinnon, Colgate, 17.5; **1960**—Pat Fischer, Nebraska, 21.2; **1961**—Tom Larscheid, Utah St., 23.4; **1962**—Darrell Roberts, Utah St., 20.8; **1963**—Rickie Harris, Arizona, 17.4; **1964**—Ken Hatfield, Arkansas, 16.7; **1965**—Floyd Little, Syracuse, 23.5; **1966**—Don Bean, Houston, 20.2; **1967**—George Hoey, Michigan, 24.3; **1968**—Rob Bordley, Princeton, 20.5; **1969**—George Hannen, Davidson, 22.4.

KICKOFF RETURNS
Career Average
(Minimum 1.2 Returns Per Game)

Player, Team	Years	No.	Yards	Avg.
Forrest Hall, San Francisco	1946-47	22	796	*36.2
Anthony Davis, Southern Cal	1972-74	37	1,299	35.1
Overton Curtis, Utah St..................................	1957-58	32	991	31.0
Altie Taylor, Utah St...................................	1966-68	40	1,170	29.3
Stan Brown, Purdue	1968-70	49	1,412	28.8
Henry White, Colgate	1974-77	41	1,180	28.8
Donald Dennis, West Tex. St.	1964-65	27	777	28.8
Bobby Ward, Memphis St.	1973-74	27	770	28.5
Paul Loughran, Temple	1970-72	40	1,123	28.1
Jim Krieg, Washington	1970-71	31	860	27.7

* Record.

Season Average
(Minimum 1.2 Returns Per Game)

Player, Team	Year	No.	Yards	Avg.
Paul Allen, Brigham Young	1961	12	481	*40.1
Forrest Hall, San Francisco	†1946	15	573	**38.2
Tony Ball, Tenn.-Chatt.	†1947	13	473	36.4
George Marinkov, North Caro. St.	1954	13	465	35.8
Bob Baker, Cornell	1964	11	386	35.1

* Record.   † National champion.   ** Record for minimum of 1.5 returns per game.

Annual Champions
(Ranked on Total Yards Until 1970)

Year	Player, Team	Class	No.	Yards	Avg.
1939	Nile Kinnick, Iowa	Sr.	15	377	25.1
1940	Jack Emigh, Montana	Sr.	18	395	21.9
1941	Earl Ray, Wyoming	So.	23	496	21.6
1942	Frank Porto, California	Sr.	17	483	28.4
1943	Paul Copoulos, Marquette	So.	11	384	34.9
1944	Paul Copoulos, Marquette	Jr.	14	337	24.1
1945	Al Dekdebrun, Cornell	Sr.	14	321	22.9
1946	Forrest Hall, San Francisco	Jr.	15	573	*38.2
1947	Doak Walker, Southern Methodist	So.	10	387	38.7
1948	Bill Gregus, Wake Forest	Jr.	19	503	26.5
1949	Johnny Subda, Nevada	Sr.	18	444	24.7
1950	Chuck Hill, New Mexico	Jr.	27	729	27.0
1951	Chuck Hill, New Mexico	Sr.	17	504	29.6
1952	Curly Powell, Va. Military	Sr.	27	517	19.1
1953	Max McGee, Tulane	Sr.	17	371	21.8
1954	Art Luppino, Arizona	So.	20	632	31.6
1955	Sam Woolwine, Va. Military	Jr.	22	471	21.4
1956	Sam Woolwine, Va. Military	Sr.	18	503	27.9
1957	Overton Curtis, Utah St.	Jr.	23	695	30.2
1958	Sonny Randle, Virginia	Sr.	21	506	24.1
1959	Don Perkins, New Mexico	Sr.	15	520	34.7
1960	Bruce Samples, Brigham Young	Sr.	23	577	25.1
1961	Dick Mooney, Idaho	Sr.	23	494	21.5
1962	Donnie Frederick, Wake Forest	Sr.	29	660	22.8
1963	Gary Wood, Cornell	Sr.	19	618	32.5
1964	Dan Bland, Mississippi St.	Jr.	20	558	27.9
1965	Eric Crabtree, Pittsburgh	Sr.	25	636	25.4
1966	Marcus Rhoden, Mississippi St.	Sr.	26	572	22.0
1967	Joe Casas, New Mexico	Sr.	23	602	26.2
1968	Mike Adamle, Northwestern	So.	34	732	21.5
1969	Stan Brown, Purdue	Jr.	26	698	26.8

Beginning in 1970, ranked on average per return (instead of total yards)‡

Year	Player, Team	Class	No.	Yards	Avg.
1970	Stan Brown, Purdue	Sr.	19	638	33.6
1971	Paul Loughran, Temple	Jr.	15	502	33.5
1972	Larry Williams, Texas Tech	So.	16	493	30.8
1973	Steve Odom, Utah	Sr.	21	618	29.4
1974	Anthony Davis, Southern Cal	Sr.	††11	467	42.5
1975	John Schultz, Maryland	Sr.	13	403	31.0
1976	Ira Matthews, Wisconsin	So.	14	415	29.6
1977	Tony Ball, Tenn.-Chatt.	Fr.	13	473	36.4
1978	Drew Hill, Georgia Tech	Sr.	19	570	30.0
1979	Stevie Nelson, Ball St.	Fr.	18	565	31.4
1980	Mike Fox, San Diego St.	So.	†11	361	32.8
1981	Frank Minnifield, Louisville	Jr.	11	334	30.4
1982	Carl Monroe, Utah	Sr.	14	421	30.1
1983	Henry Williams, East Caro.	Jr.	19	591	31.1
1984	Keith Henderson, Texas Tech	Fr.	13	376	28.9
1985	Erroll Tucker, Utah	Sr.	24	698	29.1
1986	Terrance Roulhac, Clemson	Sr.	17	561	33.0
1987	Barry Sanders, Oklahoma St.	So.	14	442	31.6
1988	Raghib Ismail, Notre Dame	Fr.	#12	433	36.1
1989	Tony Smith, Southern Miss.	So.	14	455	32.5
1990	Dale Carter, Tennessee	Jr.	17	507	29.8
1991	Fred Montgomery, New Mexico St.	Jr.	25	734	29.4

* Record.   # Declared champion; with two more returns (making 1.3 per game) for zero yards still would have highest average.   † Declared champion; with one more return (making 1.2 per game) for zero yards still would have highest average.   †† Declared champion; with three more returns (making 1.3 per game) for zero yards still would have highest average.   ‡ Ranked on minimum 1.5 returns per game, 1970-73; 1.2 from 1974.

Annual Kickoff Return Leaders (1939-69) Based on Average Per Return
(Minimum 1.2 Returns Per Game)

1939—Nile Kinnick, Iowa, 25.1; **1940**—Bill Geyer, Colgate, 27.0; **1941**—Vern Lockard, Colorado, 24.4; **1942-45**—Not compiled; **1946**—Forrest Hall, San Francisco, 38.2; **1947**—Skippy Minisi, Pennsylvania, 28.8; **1948**—Jerry Williams, Washington St., 29.9; **1949**—Billy Conn, Georgetown, 31.1; **1950**—Johnny Turco, Holy Cross, 27.4; **1951**—Bob Mischak, Army, 31.3; **1952**—Carroll Hardy, Colorado, 32.2; **1953**—Carl Bolt, Wash. & Lee, 27.1; **1954**—George Marinkov, North Caro. St., 35.8; **1955**—Jim Brown,

Syracuse, 32.0; **1956**—Paul Hornung, Notre Dame, 31.0; **1957**—Overton Curtis, Utah St., 30.2; **1958**—Marshall Starks, Illinois, 26.3; **1959**—Don Perkins, New Mexico, 34.7; **1960**—Tom Hennessey, Holy Cross, 33.4; **1961**—Paul Allen, Brigham Young, 40.1; **1962**—Larry Coyer, Marshall, 30.2; **1963**—Gary Wood, Cornell, 32.5; **1964**—Bob Baker, Cornell, 35.1; **1965**—Tom Barrington, Ohio St., 34.3; **1966**—Frank Moore, Louisville, 27.9; **1967**—Altie Taylor, Utah St., 31.9; **1968**—Kerry Reardon, Iowa, 32.1; **1969**—Chris Farasopoulous, Brigham Young, 32.2.

ALL-PURPOSE RUNNING

Career Yards Per Game

Player, Team	Years	Rush	Rcv	Int	PR	KOR	Yds.	Yd. PG
Sheldon Canley, San Jose St.	1988-90	2,513	828	0	5	1,800	5,146	*205.8
Howard Stevens, Louisville............	§1971-72	2,723	389	0	401	360	3,873	193.7
O. J. Simpson, Southern Cal	1967-68	3,124	235	0	0	307	3,666	192.9
Ed Marinaro, Cornell	1969-71	4,715	225	0	0	0	4,940	183.0
Herschel Walker, Georgia	1980-82	5,259	243	0	0	247	5,749	174.2
Louie Giammona, Utah St.	1973-75	3,499	171	0	188	1,345	5,203	173.4
Pervis Atkins, New Mexico St.........	1959-60	1,582	769	66	459	557	3,433	171.7

Record. § *Competed two years in Division I-A and two years in Division II (Randolph-Macon, 1968-69). Four-year average: 199.1.*

Season Yards Per Game

Player, Team	Year	Rush	Rcv	Int	PR	KOR	Yds.	Yd. PG
Barry Sanders, Oklahoma St.	†1988	*2,628	106	0	95	421	*3,250	*295.5
Ryan Benjamin, Pacific (Cal.)	†1991	1,581	612	0	4	798	2,995	249.6
Byron "Whizzer" White, Colorado	†1937	1,121	0	103	587	159	1,970	246.3
Mike Pringle, Cal St. Fullerton	†1989	1,727	249	0	0	714	2,690	244.6
Paul Palmer, Temple	†1986	1,866	110	0	0	657	2,633	239.4
Marcus Allen, Southern Cal	†1981	2,342	217	0	0	0	2,559	232.6
Sheldon Canley, San Jose St.	1989	1,201	353	0	0	959	2,513	228.5
Ollie Matson, San Francisco	†1951	1,566	58	18	115	280	2,037	226.3
Art Luppino, Arizona	†1954	1,359	50	84	68	632	2,193	219.3
Chuck Weatherspoon, Houston	1989	1,146	735	0	715	95	2,391	217.4
Anthony Thompson, Indiana..........	1989	1,793	201	0	0	394	2,388	217.1
Napoleon McCallum, Navy............	†1983	1,587	166	0	272	360	2,385	216.8
Ed Marinaro, Cornell..................	†1971	1,881	51	0	0	0	1,932	214.7
Howard Stevens, Louisville............	†1972	1,294	221	0	337	240	2,132	213.2
Napoleon McCallum, Navy............	†1985	1,327	358	0	157	488	2,330	211.8
Keith Byars, Ohio St...................	†1984	1,655	453	0	0	176	2,284	207.6
Mike Rozier, Nebraska	1983	2,148	106	0	0	232	2,486	207.2

Record. † *National champion.*

Career Yards

Player, Team	Years	Rush	Rcv	Int	PR	KOR	Yds.	Yd. PP
Napoleon McCallum, Navy.......	$1981-85	4,179	796	0	858	1,339	*7,172	6.3
Darrin Nelson, Stanford	1977-78, 80-81	4,033	2,368	0	471	13	6,885	7.1
Terance Mathis, New Mexico	1985-87, 89	329	*4,254	0	115	1,993	6,691	14.6
Tony Dorsett, Pittsburgh	1973-76	*6,082	406	0	0	127	6,615	5.9
Paul Palmer, Temple	1983-86	4,895	705	0	12	997	6,609	6.1
Charles White, Southern Cal	1976-79	5,598	507	0	0	440	6,545	6.0
Anthony Thompson, Indiana.....	1986-89	4,965	713	0	0	412	6,090	5.1
Archie Griffin, Ohio St............	1972-75	5,177	286	0	0	540	6,003	6.7
Ron "Po" James, New Mexico St.	1968-71	3,884	217	0	8	1,870	5,979	6.5
Eric Wilkerson, Kent	1985-88	3,830	506	0	0	1,638	5,974	7.0
Steve Bartalo, Colorado St.	1983-86	4,813	1,079	0	0	0	5,892	4.4
Wilford White, Arizona St.	1947-50	3,173	892	212	798	791	5,866	9.2
Joe Washington, Oklahoma......	1972-75	3,995	253	0	807	726	5,781	7.3
Herschel Walker, Georgia	1980-82	5,259	243	0	0	247	‡5,749	5.6
George Swarn, Miami (Ohio)	1983-86	4,172	1,057	0	0	498	5,727	5.6
Chuck Weatherspoon, Houston ..	1987-90	3,247	1,375	0	611	482	5,715	9.7
Eric Metcalf, Texas	1985-88	2,661	1,394	0	1,076	574	5,705	6.7
George Rogers, South Caro......	1977-80	4,958	371	0	0	339	5,668	5.9
Jamie Morris, Michigan	1984-87	3,944	703	0	0	984	5,631	6.4
Joe Morris, Syracuse.............	1978-81	4,299	278	0	0	1,023	5,600	6.3
James Brooks, Auburn...........	1977-80	3,523	219	0	128	1,726	5,596	7.6
Johnny Rodgers, Nebraska	1970-72	745	2,479	0	1,515	847	‡5,586	13.8
Thurman Thomas, Oklahoma St.	1984-87	4,595	551	0	143	237	5,526	5.5
Mike Rozier, Nebraska	1981-83	4,780	216	0	0	449	‡5,445	7.7

Record. ‡ *Three-year totals.* $ *See page 6 for explanation.*

64

Season Yards

Player, Team	Year	Rush	Rcv	Int	PR	KOR	Yds.	Yd. PP
Barry Sanders, Oklahoma St.	†1988	*2,628	106	0	95	421	*3,250	8.3
Ryan Benjamin, Pacific (Cal.)	†1991	1,581	612	0	4	798	2,995	9.6
Mike Pringle, Cal St. Fullerton ...	†1989	1,727	249	0	0	714	2,690	7.6
Paul Palmer, Temple	†1986	1,866	110	0	0	657	2,633	6.8
Marcus Allen, Southern Cal	†1981	2,342	217	0	0	0	2,559	5.9
Sheldon Canley, San Jose St.	1989	1,201	353	0	0	959	2,513	7.4
Mike Rozier, Nebraska	1983	2,148	106	0	0	232	2,486	8.4
Chuck Weatherspoon, Houston ..	1989	1,146	735	0	415	95	2,391	10.7
Anthony Thompson, Indiana.....	1989	1,793	201	0	0	394	2,388	5.8
Napoleon McCallum, Navy.......	†1983	1,587	166	0	272	360	2,385	6.1
Napoleon McCallum, Navy.......	†1985	1,327	358	0	157	488	2,330	6.3
Keith Byars, Ohio St.............	†1984	1,655	453	0	0	176	2,284	6.4
Glyn Milburn, Stanford..........	†1990	729	632	0	267	594	2,222	8.4
Vaughn Dunbar, Indiana	1991	1,699	252	0	0	262	2,213	5.9
Sheldon Canley, San Jose St.	1990	1,248	386	0	5	574	2,213	6.3
Johnny Johnson, San Jose St....	1988	1,219	668	0	0	315	2,202	7.1
Art Luppino, Arizona	†1954	1,359	50	84	68	632	2,193	10.4
Rick Calhoun, Cal St. Fullerton ..	1986	1,398	125	0	138	522	2,183	7.0
Terance Mathis, New Mexico	1989	38	1,315	0	0	785	2,138	15.7
Howard Stevens, Louisville.......	†1972	1,294	221	0	377	240	2,132	6.4

* Record. † National champion.

All-Purpose Single-Game Highs

Yards	Player, Team (Opponent)	Date
422	Marshall Faulk, San Diego St. (Pacific, Cal.)	Sept. 14, 1991
417	Paul Palmer, Temple (East Caro.)	Nov. 10, 1986
417	Greg Allen, Florida St. (Western Caro.)	Oct. 31, 1981
416	Anthony Thompson, Indiana (Wisconsin)	Nov. 11, 1989
401	Chuck Hughes, UTEP (North Texas) (349 on receptions)	Sept. 18, 1965
397	Eric Allen, Michigan St. (Purdue)	Oct. 30, 1971
388	Ryan Benjamin, Pacific, Cal. (Cal St. Fullerton)	Oct. 5, 1991
387	Kendal Smith, Utah St. (San Jose St.)	Oct. 22, 1988
387	Ron Johnson, Michigan (Wisconsin)	Nov. 16, 1968
386	Barry Sanders, Oklahoma St. (Kansas)	Nov. 12, 1988
379	Glyn Milburn, Stanford (California)	Nov. 17, 1990
375	Rueben Mayes, Washington St. (Oregon St.)	Nov. 3, 1984
374	Tony Dorsett, Pittsburgh (Penn St.)	Nov. 22, 1975
373	Barry Sanders, Oklahoma St. (Oklahoma)	Nov. 5, 1988
372	Chuck Weatherspoon, Houston (Eastern Wash.)	Nov. 17, 1990

Annual Champions

Year	Player, Team	Cl.	Rush	Rcv	Int	PR	KOR	Yds.	Yd. PG
1937	Byron "Whizzer" White, Colorado	Sr.	1,121	0	103	587	159	1,970	246.3
1938	Parker Hall, Mississippi	Sr.	698	0	128	0	594	1,420	129.1
1939	Tom Harmon, Michigan	Jr.	868	110	98	0	132	1,208	151.0
1940	Tom Harmon, Michigan	Sr.	844	0	20	244	204	1,312	164.0
1941	Bill Dudley, Virginia	Sr.	968	60	76	481	89	1,674	186.0
1942	records not available	—	—	—	—	—	—	—	—
1943	Stan Koslowski, Holy Cross.............	Fr.	784	63	50	438	76	1,411	176.4
1944	Red Williams, Minnesota	Jr.	911	0	0	242	314	1,467	163.0
1945	Bob Fenimore, Oklahoma St.	Jr.	1,048	12	129	157	231	1,577	197.1
1946	Rudy Mobley, Hardin-Simmons	Sr.	1,262	13	79	273	138	1,765	176.5
1947	Wilton Davis, Hardin-Simmons..........	So.	1,173	79	0	295	251	1,798	179.8
1948	Lou Kusserow, Columbia	Sr.	766	463	19	130	359	1,737	193.0
1949	Johnny Papit, Virginia	Jr.	1,214	0	0	0	397	1,611	179.0
1950	Wilford White, Arizona St..............	Sr.	1,502	225	0	64	274	2,065	206.5
1951	Ollie Matson, San Francisco	Sr.	1,566	58	18	115	280	2,037	226.3
1952	Billy Vessels, Oklahoma	Sr.	1,072	165	10	120	145	1,512	151.2
1953	J. C. Caroline, Illinois	So.	1,256	52	0	129	33	1,470	163.3
1954	Art Luppino, Arizona	So.	1,359	50	84	68	632	2,193	219.3
1955	Jim Swink, Texas Christian	Jr.	1,283	111	46	64	198	1,702	170.2
	Art Luppino, Arizona	Jr.	1,313	74	0	62	253	1,702	170.2
1956	Jack Hill, Utah St.	Sr.	920	215	132	21	403	1,691	169.1
1957	Overton Curtis, Utah St.................	Jr.	616	193	60	44	695	1,608	160.8
1958	Dick Bass, Pacific (Cal.)	Jr.	1,361	121	5	164	227	1,878	187.8
1959	Pervis Atkins, New Mexico St...........	Jr.	971	301	23	241	264	1,800	180.0
1960	Pervis Atkins, New Mexico St...........	Sr.	611	468	23	218	293	1,613	161.3
1961	Jim Pilot, New Mexico St.	So.	1,278	20	0	161	147	1,606	160.6

Cornell's Ed Marinaro led Division I-A in all-purpose running in 1971 with 214.7 yards per game. His career average of 183.0 yards per game places him fourth on the all-time list.

Year	Player, Team	Cl.	Rush	Rcv	Int	PR	KOR	Yds.	Yd. PG
1962	Gary Wood, Cornell	Jr.	889	7	0	69	430	1,395	155.0
1963	Gary Wood, Cornell	Sr.	818	15	0	57	618	1,508	167.6
1964	Donny Anderson, Texas Tech	Jr.	966	396	0	28	320	1,710	171.0
1965	Floyd Little, Syracuse	Jr.	1,065	248	0	423	254	1,990	199.0
1966	Frank Quayle, Virginia	So.	727	420	0	30	439	1,616	161.6
1967	O. J. Simpson, Southern Cal	Jr.	1,415	109	0	0	176	1,700	188.9
1968	O. J. Simpson, Southern Cal	Sr.	1,709	126	0	0	131	1,966	196.6
1969	Lynn Moore, Army	Sr.	983	44	0	223	545	1,795	179.5
1970	Don McCauley, North Caro.	Sr.	1,720	235	0	0	66	2,021	183.7
1971	Ed Marinaro, Cornell	Sr.	1,881	51	0	0	0	1,932	214.7
1972	Howard Stevens, Louisville	Sr.	1,294	221	0	377	240	2,132	213.2
1973	Willard Harrell, Pacific (Cal.)	Jr.	1,319	18	0	88	352	1,777	177.7
1974	Louie Giammona, Utah St.	Jr.	1,534	79	0	16	355	1,984	198.4
1975	Louie Giammona, Utah St.	Sr.	1,454	33	0	124	434	2,045	185.9
1976	Tony Dorsett, Pittsburgh	Sr.	1,948	73	0	0	0	2,021	183.7
1977	Earl Campbell, Texas	Sr.	1,744	111	0	0	0	1,855	168.6
1978	Charles White, Southern Cal	Jr.	1,760	191	0	0	145	2,096	174.7
1979	Charles White, Southern Cal	Sr.	1,803	138	0	0	0	1,941	194.1
1980	Marcus Allen, Southern Cal	Jr.	1,563	231	0	0	0	1,794	179.4
1981	Marcus Allen, Southern Cal	Sr.	2,342	217	0	0	0	2,559	232.6
1982	Carl Monroe, Utah	Sr.	1,507	108	0	0	421	2,036	185.1
1983	Napoleon McCallum, Navy	Jr.	1,587	166	0	272	360	2,385	216.8
1984	Keith Byars, Ohio St.	Jr.	1,655	453	0	0	176	2,284	207.6
1985	Napoleon McCallum, Navy	Sr.	1,327	358	0	157	488	2,330	211.8
1986	Paul Palmer, Temple	Sr.	1,866	110	0	0	657	2,633	239.4
1987	Eric Wilkerson, Kent	Jr.	1,221	269	0	0	584	2,074	188.6
1988	Barry Sanders, Oklahoma St.	Jr.	*2,628	106	0	95	421	*3,250	*295.5
1989	Mike Pringle, Cal St. Fullerton	Sr.	1,727	249	0	0	714	2,690	244.6
1990	Glyn Milburn, Stanford	So.	729	632	0	267	594	2,222	202.0
1991	Ryan Benjamin, Pacific (Cal.)	Jr.	1,581	612	0	4	798	2,995	249.5

* Record.

FIELD GOALS

Career Field Goals

(One-inch tees were permitted in 1949, two-inch tees were permitted in 1965, and use of tees was eliminated in 1989. The goal posts were widened from 18 feet, 6 inches to 23 feet, 4 inches in 1959 and were narrowed back to 18 feet, 6 inches in 1991.)

Player, Team	Years	Total	Pct.	Under 40 Yds.	40 Plus	Long	‡Won
Jeff Jaeger, Washington (S)	1983-86	*80-99	.808	59-68	21-31	52	5
John Lee, UCLA (S)	1982-85	79-92	*.859	54-56	25-36	52	**10
Philip Doyle, Alabama (S)	1987-90	78-*105	.743	57-61	21-44	53	6
Luis Zendejas, Arizona St. (S)	1981-84	78-*105	.743	53-59	25-46	55	1
Kevin Butler, Georgia (S)	1981-84	77-98	.786	50-56	27-42	60	7
Max Zendejas, Arizona (S)	1982-85	77-104	.740	47-53	30-51	57	7
Carlos Huerta, Miami (Fla.) (S)	1988-91	73-91	.802	56-60	17-31	52	3
Derek Schmidt, Florida St. (S)	1984-87	73-104	.702	44-55	29-49	54	1
Fuad Reveiz, Tennessee (S)	1981-84	71-95	.747	45-53	26-42	60	7
Roman Anderson, Houston (S)	1988-91	70-101	.802	*61-*72	9-29	53	3
Barry Belli, Fresno St. (S)	1984-87	70-99	.707	47-53	23-46	55	5
Collin Mackie, South Caro. (S)	1987-90	69-95	.726	48-57	21-38	52	5
Gary Gussman, Miami (Ohio) (S)	1984-87	68-94	.723	50-57	18-37	53	2
Larry Roach, Oklahoma St. (S)	1981-84	68-101	.673	46-54	22-47	56	5
Paul Woodside, West Va. (S)	1981-84	65-81	.802	45-49	20-32	55	5
¢Jason Elam, Hawaii (S)	$1988-91	63-75	.840	40-43	23-32	55	3
John Diettrich, Ball St. (S)	1983-86	63-90	.700	42-50	21-40	62	5
Jason Hanson, Washington St. (S)	1988-91	63-96	.656	24-30	*39-*66	62	4
Kenny Stucker, Ball St. (S)	1988-91	62-87	.713	45-51	17-36	52	4
David Browndyke, Louisiana St. (S)...	1986-89	61-75	.813	49-53	12-22	52	3
Todd Gregoire, Wisconsin (S)	1984-87	61-81	.753	48-56	13-25	54	6
Jess Atkinson, Maryland (S)	1981-84	60-82	.732	40-48	20-34	50	5
Obed Ariri, Clemson (S)	1977-80	60-92	.652	47-55	13-37	57	5
Chuck Nelson, Washington (S)	1980-82	59-72	.819	47-53	12-19	51	5
Van Tiffin, Alabama (S)	1983-86	59-87	.678	32-38	27-49	57	5
John Hopkins, Stanford (S)	1987-90	59-88	.670	43-50	16-38	54	4
Jeff Ward, Texas (S)	1983-86	58-78	.744	36-41	22-37	57	**10
Jeff Shudak, Iowa St. (S)...............	1987-90	58-79	.734	38-45	20-34	55	5
Joe Worley, Kentucky (S)	1984-87	57-85	.671	40-52	17-33	53	0
Kevin Nicholl, Central Mich. (S)	1986-89	56-72	.778	28-34	28-38	54	1
Mike Gillette, Michigan (S)	1985-88	56-78	.718	44-53	12-25	56	4
Chris Gardocki, Clemson (S)	1988-90	56-80	.700	35-44	21-36	57	1
Dan Miller, Miami (Fla.) (C)	1978-81	56-83	.675	38-50	18-33	57	9
Rex Robinson, Georgia (S)	1977-80	56-84	.667	34-43	22-41	57	8
Tony Franklin, Texas A&M (S)	1975-78	56-101	.554	30-41	26-60	65	1

*Record.   **Record tied.   ‡ Number of games in which his field goal(s) provided the winning margin.   ¢ Active player. $ See page 6 for explanation.   (C) Conventional kicker.   (S) Soccer-style kicker.*

Season Field Goals

Player, Team	Year	Total	Pct.	Under 40 Yds.	40 Plus	Long	‡Won
John Lee, UCLA (S)	†1984	*29-33	.879	16-16	13-17	51	5
Paul Woodside, West Va. (S)	†1982	28-31	.903	23-23	5-8	45	2
Luis Zendejas, Arizona St. (S)	†1983	28-37	.757	19-22	9-15	52	1
Fuad Reveiz, Tennessee (S)	1982	27-31	.871	14-14	13-17	60	2
Chuck Nelson, Washington (S)	1982	25-26	*.962	22-23	3-3	49	1
Chris Jacke, UTEP (S)	1988	25-27	.926	11-11	*14-16	52	2
John Diettrich, Ball St. (S)	†1985	25-29	.862	16-17	9-12	54	2
Kendall Trainor, Arkansas (S)	†1988	24-27	.889	14-15	10-12	58	4
Carlos Reveiz, Tennessee (S)	1985	24-28	.857	12-14	12-14	52	2
Chris White, Illinois (S)...............	1984	24-28	.857	16-17	8-11	52	1
Philip Doyle, Alabama (S)	†1990	24-29	.828	16-17	8-12	47	2
Bruce Kallmeyer, Kansas (S)	1983	24-29	.828	13-14	11-15	57	1
Mike Prindle, Western Mich. (S)	1984	24-30	.800	17-20	7-10	56	1
Bobby Raymond, Florida (S)	1984	23-26	.885	18-18	5-8	51	1
Mike Bass, Illinois (S)	1982	23-26	.885	12-13	11-13	53	1
Kevin Butler, Georgia (S)..............	1984	23-28	.821	12-14	11-14	60	2
Collin Mackie, South Caro. (S)	†1987	23-30	.767	17-21	6-9	49	0
Obed Ariri, Clemson (S)	†1980	23-30	.767	18-19	5-11	52	3
Derek Schmidt, Florida St. (S)	†1987	23-31	.742	16-21	7-10	53	0

Record.   † National champion.   ‡ Number of games in which his field goal(s) provided the winning margin.   (C) Conventional kicker.   (S) Soccer-style kicker.

Single-Game Field Goals

No.	Player, Team (Opponent)	Date
7	Dale Klein, Nebraska (Missouri)	Oct. 19, 1985
7	Mike Prindle, Western Mich. (Marshall)	Sept. 29, 1984
6	Philip Doyle, Alabama (Southwestern La.)	Oct. 6, 1990
6	Sean Fleming, Wyoming (Arkansas St.)	Sept. 15, 1990
6	Bobby Raymond, Florida (Kentucky)	Nov. 17, 1984
6	John Lee, UCLA (San Diego St.)	Sept. 8, 1984
6	Bobby Raymond, Florida (Florida St.)	Dec. 3, 1983
6	Alan Smith, Texas A&M (Arkansas St.)	Sept. 17, 1983
6	Al Del Greco, Auburn (Kentucky)	Oct. 9, 1982
6	Vince Fusco, Duke (Clemson)	Oct. 16, 1976
6	Frank Nester, West Va. (Villanova)	Sept. 9, 1972
6	Charley Gogolak, Princeton (Rutgers)	Sept. 25, 1965

Annual Champions
(From 1959-90, goal posts were 23 feet, 4 inches; and from 1991, narrowed to 18 feet, 6 inches.)

Year	Player, Team	Total	PG	Pct.	Under 40 Yds.	40 Plus	Long	‡Won
1959	Karl Holzwarth, Wisconsin (C)	7-8	0.8	.875	7-8	0-0	29	4
1960	Ed Dyas, Auburn (C)	13-18	1.3	.722	13-17	0-1	37	2
1961	Greg Mather, Navy (C)	11-15	1.1	.733	9-12	2-3	45	1
1962	Bob Jencks, Miami (Ohio) (C)	8-11	0.8	.727	7-9	1-2	52	3
	Al Woodall, Auburn (C)	8-20	0.8	.400	8-13	0-7	35	0
1963	Billy Lothridge, Georgia Tech (C)	12-16	1.2	.750	10-14	2-2	41	3
1964	Doug Moreau, Louisiana St. (C)	13-20	1.3	.650	13-20	0-0	36	0
1965	Charley Gogolak, Princeton (S)	16-23	1.8	.696	7-10	9-13	54	0
1966	Jerry DePoyster, Wyoming (C)	13-*38	1.3	.342	7-13	6-*25	54	1
1967	Gerald Warren, North Caro. St. (C)	17-22	1.7	.773	13-14	4-8	47	1
1968	Bob Jacobs, Wyoming (C)	14-29	1.4	.483	10-15	4-14	51	2
1969	Bob Jacobs, Wyoming (C)	18-27	1.8	.667	13-16	5-11	43	2

Beginning in 1970, ranked on per-game (instead of total) made

Year	Player, Team	Total	PG	Pct.	Under 40 Yds.	40 Plus	Long	‡Won
1970	Kim Braswell, Georgia (C)	13-17	1.3	.765	11-14	2-3	43	0
1971	Nick Mike-Mayer, Temple (S)	12-17	1.3	.706	8-10	4-7	48	1
1972	Nick Mike-Mayer, Temple (S)	13-20	1.4	.650	10-11	3-9	44	3
1973	Rod Garcia, Stanford (S)	18-29	1.6	.621	10-14	8-15	59	2
1974	Dave Lawson, Air Force (C)	19-31	1.7	.613	13-14	6-17	60	1
1975	Don Bitterlich, Temple (S)	21-31	1.9	.677	13-14	8-17	56	0
1976	Tony Franklin, Texas A&M (S)	17-26	1.6	.654	9-12	8-14	65	0
1977	Paul Marchese, Kent (S)	18-27	1.8	.667	13-15	5-12	51	2
1978	Matt Bahr, Penn St. (S)	22-27	2.0	.815	19-20	3-7	50	3
1979	Ish Ordonez, Arkansas (S)	18-22	1.6	.818	12-14	6-8	50	2
1980	Obed Ariri, Clemson (S)	23-30	2.1	.767	18-19	5-11	52	3
1981	Bruce Lahay, Arkansas (S)	19-24	1.7	.792	12-15	7-9	49	4
	Kevin Butler, Georgia (S)	19-26	1.7	.731	11-14	8-12	52	0
	Larry Roach, Oklahoma St. (S)	19-28	1.7	.679	12-14	7-14	56	3
1982	Paul Woodside, West Va. (S)	28-31	2.6	.903	23-23	5-8	45	2
1983	Luis Zendejas, Arizona St. (S)	28-37	2.6	.757	19-22	9-15	52	1
1984	John Lee, UCLA (S)	*29-33	*2.6	.879	16-16	13-17	51	5
1985	John Diettrich, Ball St. (S)	25-29	2.3	.862	16-17	9-12	54	2
1986	Chris Kinzer, Virginia Tech (C)	22-27	2.0	.815	14-17	8-10	50	5
1987	Collin Mackie, South Caro. (S)	23-30	2.1	.767	17-21	6-9	49	0
	Derek Schmidt, Florida St. (S)	23-31	2.1	.742	16-21	7-10	53	0
1988	Kendall Trainor, Arkansas (S)	24-27	2.2	.889	14-15	10-12	58	4
1989	Philip Doyle, Alabama (S)	22-25	2.0	.880	19-19	3-6	44	2
	Gregg McCallum, Oregon (S)	22-29	2.0	.759	15-15	7-14	47	2
	Roman Anderson, Houston (S)	22-34	2.0	.647	17-20	5-14	51	0
1990	Philip Doyle, Alabama (S)	24-29	2.2	.828	16-17	8-12	47	2
1991	Doug Brien, California (S)	19-28	1.7	.679	15-20	4-8	50	2

* Record. ‡ Number of games in which his field goal(s) provided the winning margin. (C) Conventional kicker. (S) Soccer-style kicker.

LONGEST PLAYS

Since 1941, official maximum length of all plays fixed at 100 yards.

Rushing

Yds.	Player, Team (Opponent)	Year
99	Kelsey Finch, Tennessee (Florida)	1977
99	Ralph Thompson, West Tex. St. (Wichita St.)	1970

Yds.	Player, Team (Opponent)	Year
99	Max Anderson, Arizona St. (Wyoming)	1967
99	Gale Sayers, Kansas (Nebraska)	1963
98	Darrell Thompson, Minnesota (Michigan)	1987
98	George Swarn, Miami, Ohio (Western Mich.)	1984
98	Mark Malone, Arizona St. (Utah St.)	1979
98	Stanley Howell, Mississippi St. (Southern Miss.)	1979
98	Steve Atkins, Maryland (Clemson)	1978
98	Granville Amos, Va. Military (William & Mary)	1964
98	Jim Thacker, Davidson (Geo. Washington)	1952
98	Bill Powell, California (Oregon St.)	1951
98	Al Yannelli, Bucknell (Delaware)	1946
98	Meredith Warner, Iowa St. (Iowa Pre-Flight)	1943

Passing

Yds.	Passer-Receiver, Team (Opponent)	Year
99	Gino Torretta-Horace Copeland, Miami, Fla. (Arkansas)	1991
99	Scott Ankrom-James Maness, Texas Christian (Rice)	1984
99	Cris Collinsworth-Derrick Gaffney, Florida (Rice)	1977
99	Terry Peel-Robert Ford, Houston (San Diego St.)	1972
99	Terry Peel-Robert Ford, Houston (Syracuse)	1970
99	Colin Clapton-Eddie Jenkins, Holy Cross (Boston U.)	1970
99	Bo Burris-Warren McVea, Houston (Washington St.)	1966
99	Fred Owens-Jack Ford, Portland (St. Mary's, Cal.)	1947
98	Paul Oates-Sean Foster, Long Beach St. (San Diego St.)	1989
98	Barry Garrison-Al Owens, New Mexico (Brigham Young)	1987
98	Kelly Donohoe-Willie Vaughn, Kansas (Colorado)	1987
98	Jeff Martin-Mark Flaker, Drake (New Mexico St.)	1976
98	Pete Woods-Joe Stewart, Missouri (Nebraska)	1976
98	Dan Hagemann-Jack Steptoe, Utah (New Mexico)	1976
98	Bruce Shaw-Pat Kenney, North Caro. St. (Penn St.)	1972
98	Jerry Rhome-Jeff Jordan, Tulsa (Wichita St.)	1963
98	Bob Dean-Norman Dawson, Cornell (Navy)	1947

Interception Returns

Since 1941, 59 players have returned interceptions 100 yards. The most recent:

Yds.	Player, Team (Opponent)	Year
100	John Hardy, California (Wisconsin)	1990
100	Ed Givens, Army (Lafayette)	1990
100	Greg Jackson, Louisiana St. (Mississippi St.)	1988
100	Dennis Price, UCLA (California)	1987

Punt Returns

Yds.	Player, Team (Opponent)	Year
100‡	Richie Luzzi, Clemson (Georgia)	1968
100‡	Don Guest, California (Washington St.)	1966
100	Jimmy Campagna, Georgia (Vanderbilt)	1952
100	Hugh McElhenny, Washington (Southern Cal)	1951
100	Frank Brady, Navy (Maryland)	1951
100	Bert Rechichar, Tennessee (Wash. & Lee)	1950
100	Eddie Macon, Pacific, Cal. (Boston U.)	1950

‡ *Return of field-goal attempt.*

Kickoff Returns

Since 1941, 166 players have returned kickoffs 100 yards. The most recent:

Yds.	Player, Team (Opponent)	Year
100	Fred Montgomery, New Mexico St. (Long Beach St.)	1991
100	Anthony Prior, Washington St. (Southern Cal)	1991
100	Ricky Turner, Pittsburgh (West Va.)	1990
100	Kurt Johnson, Kentucky (Georgia)	1989
100	Carlos Snow, Ohio St. (Pittsburgh)	1988
100	Pierre Goode, Alabama (Mississippi)	1988
100	Eric Mortensen, Brigham Young (Utah St.)	1988

Division I-A Longest Plays

Yds.	Player, Team (Opponent)	Year
100†	Barry Sanders, Oklahoma St. (Miami, Ohio)	1988
100	Barry Sanders, Oklahoma St. (Kansas)	1987
100†	Barry Sanders, Oklahoma St. (Tulsa)	1987

† Team's first kickoff return of the season.

Punts

Yds.	Player, Team (Opponent)	Year
99	Pat Brady, Nevada (Loyola, Cal.)	1950
96	George O'Brien, Wisconsin (Iowa)	1952
94	John Hadl, Kansas (Oklahoma)	1959
94	Carl Knox, Texas Christian (Oklahoma St.)	1947
94	Preston Johnson, Southern Methodist (Pittsburgh)	1940

Field Goals

Yds.	Player, Team (Opponent)	Year
67	Joe Williams, Wichita St. (Southern Ill.)	1978
67	Steve Little, Arkansas (Texas)	1977
67	Russell Erxleben, Texas (Rice)	1977
65	Tony Franklin, Texas A&M (Baylor)	1976
64	Russell Erxleben, Texas (Oklahoma)	1977
64	Tony Franklin, Texas A&M (Baylor)	1976
63	Morten Andersen, Michigan St. (Ohio St.)	1981
63	Clark Kemble, Colorado St. (Arizona)	1975
62†	Jason Hanson, Washington St. (Nevada-Las Vegas)	1991
62	John Diettrich, Ball St. (Ohio)	1986
62	Chip Lohmiller, Minnesota (Iowa)	1986
62	Tom Whelihan, Missouri (Colorado)	1986
62	Dan Christopulos, Wyoming (Colorado St.)	1977
62	Iseed Khoury, North Texas (Richmond)	1977
62	Dave Lawson, Air Force (Iowa St.)	1975
61	Mark Porter, Kansas St. (Nebraska)	1988
61	Ralf Mojsiejenko, Michigan St. (Illinois)	1982
61	Steve Little, Arkansas (Tulsa)	1976
61	Wayne Latimer, Virginia Tech (Florida St.)	1975
61	Ray Guy, Southern Miss. (Utah St.)	1972
60	Don Shafer, Southern Cal (Notre Dame)	1986
60	Steve DeLine, Colorado St. (Air Force)	1985
60	Kevin Butler, Georgia (Clemson)	1984
60	Chris Perkins, Florida (Tulane)	1984
60	Fuad Reveiz, Tennessee (Georgia Tech)	1982
60	Russell Erxleben, Texas (Texas Tech)	1977
60	Bubba Hicks, Baylor (Rice)	1975
60	Dave Lawson, Air Force (Colorado)	1974
60	Tony Di Rienzo, Oklahoma (Kansas)	1973
60	Bill McClard, Arkansas (Southern Methodist)	1970

† Longest collegiate field goal without use of a kicking tee.

LIST OF UNDERCLASSMEN WHO WERE CERTIFIED FOR THE 1992 NATIONAL FOOTBALL LEAGUE DRAFT

Michael Bates, RB, Arizona; Michael Bonecke, QB, Arizona St.; Terrell Buckley, DB, Florida St.; Denny Chronopoulos, OG, Purdue; Marco Coleman, LB, Georgia Tech; Todd Collins, LB, Carson-Newman; Curt Douglas, LB/DT, Georgia; Shane Dronett, DE, Texas; Reggie Dwight, TE, Troy St.; Steve Emtman, DT, Washington; Sean Gilbert, DE, Pittsburgh; Marcus Grant, WR, Houston; Keith Hamilton, DE, Pittsburgh; Desmond Howard, WR/KR, Michigan; Chris Hughley, TB, Tulsa; Jay Jones, LB, Abilene Christian; Amp Lee, RB, Florida St.; Tommy Maddox, QB, UCLA; Chester McGlockton, DT, Clemson; Ostell Miles, RB, Houston; Johnny Mitchell, TE, Nebraska; Michael Moore, WR, UCLA; Lance Olberding, T, Iowa; Doug O'Neill, P, Cal Poly SLO; Corey Pargo, NT, Ohio St.; Carl Pickens, WR, Tennessee; Elliot Pilton, DL, Tennessee St.; Vince Powell, RB, Cincinnati; Joseph Randolph, WR, Elon; Mazio Royster, RB, Southern Cal; Eric Shaw, LB, Louisiana Tech; Alonzo Spellman, DE, Ohio St.; Jeff Sydner, WR/KR, Hawaii; Roosevelt Wagner, OG, Michigan St.; Sam Washington, DE, Eastern N. Mex.; Alberto White, LB, Texas; Bob Whitfield, OT, Stanford; Darryl Williams, DB, Miami (Fla.).

1992 NCAA FOOTBALL

TEAM CHAMPIONS

ANNUAL OFFENSE CHAMPIONS

Year	Total Offense	Avg.	Rushing	Avg.	Passing	Avg.
1937	Colorado	375.4	Colorado	310.0	Arkansas	185.0
1938	Fordham	341.6	Fordham	297.1	Texas Christian	164.1
1939	Ohio St.	309.3	Wake Forest	290.3	Texas Christian	148.5
1940	Lafayette	368.2	Lafayette	306.4	Cornell	186.3
1941	Duke	372.2	Missouri	307.7	Arizona	177.7
1942	Georgia	429.5	Hardin-Simmons	307.4	Tulsa	233.9
1943	Notre Dame	418.0	Notre Dame	313.7	Brown	133.1
1944	Tulsa	434.7	Army	298.6	Tulsa	206.3
1945	Army	462.7	Army	359.8	St. Mary's (Cal.)	161.3
1946	Notre Dame	441.3	Notre Dame	340.1	Nevada	198.1
1947	Michigan	412.7	Detroit Mercy	319.7	Michigan	173.9
1948	Nevada	487.0	UTEP	378.3	Nevada	255.0
1949	Notre Dame	434.8	UTEP	333.2	Fordham	183.4
1950	Arizona St.	470.4	Arizona St.	347.0	Southern Methodist	214.6
1951	Tulsa	480.1	Arizona St.	334.8	Loyola (Cal.)	210.6
1952	Tulsa	466.6	Tulsa	321.5	Fordham	225.8
1953	Cincinnati	409.5	Oklahoma	306.9	Stanford	179.5
1954	Army	448.7	Army	322.0	Purdue	177.3
1955	Oklahoma	410.7	Oklahoma	328.9	Navy	185.1
1956	Oklahoma	481.7	Oklahoma	391.0	Washington St.	206.8
1957	Arizona St.	444.9	Colorado	322.4	Utah	195.2
1958	Iowa	405.9	Pacific (Cal.)	259.6	Army	172.2
1959	Syracuse	451.5	Syracuse	313.6	Stanford	227.8
1960	New Mexico St.	419.6	Utah St.	312.0	Washington St.	185.5
1961	Mississippi	418.7	New Mexico St.	299.1	Wisconsin	188.4
1962	Arizona St.	384.4	Ohio St.	278.9	Tulsa	199.3
1963	Utah St.	395.3	Nebraska	262.6	Tulsa	244.8
1964	Tulsa	461.8	Syracuse	251.0	Tulsa	317.9
1965	Tulsa	427.8	Nebraska	290.0	Tulsa	346.4
1966	Houston	437.2	Harvard	269.0	Tulsa	272.0
1967	Houston	427.9	Houston	270.9	UTEP	301.1
1968	Houston	562.0	Houston	361.7	Cincinnati	335.8
1969	San Diego St.	532.2	Texas	363.0	San Diego St.	374.2
1970	Arizona St.	514.5	Texas	374.5	Auburn	288.5
1971	Oklahoma	566.5	Oklahoma	*472.4	San Diego St.	251.4
1972	Arizona St.	516.5	Oklahoma	368.8	Virginia Tech	304.4
1973	Arizona St.	565.5	UCLA	400.3	San Diego St.	305.0
1974	Oklahoma	507.7	Oklahoma	438.8	Colorado St.	261.8
1975	California	458.5	Arkansas St.	340.5	San Diego St.	291.3
1976	Michigan	448.1	Michigan	362.6	Brigham Young	307.8
1977	Colgate	486.1	Oklahoma	328.9	Brigham Young	341.6
1978	Nebraska	501.4	Oklahoma	427.5	Southern Meth.	276.2
1979	Brigham Young	521.4	East Caro.	368.5	Brigham Young	368.3
1980	Brigham Young	535.0	Nebraska	378.3	Brigham Young	409.8
1981	Arizona St.	498.7	Oklahoma	334.3	Brigham Young	356.9
1982	Nebraska	518.6	Nebraska	394.3	Long Beach St.	326.8
1983	Brigham Young	584.2	Nebraska	401.7	Brigham Young	381.2
1984	Brigham Young	486.5	Army	345.3	Brigham Young	346.2
1985	Brigham Young	500.2	Nebraska	374.3	Brigham Young	354.5
1986	San Jose St.	481.4	Oklahoma	404.7	San Jose St.	312.5
1987	Oklahoma	499.7	Oklahoma	428.8	San Jose St.	338.1
1988	Utah	526.8	Nebraska	382.3	Utah	395.9
1989	Houston	*624.9	Nebraska	375.3	Houston	*511.3
1990	Houston	586.8	Northern Ill.	344.6	Houston	473.9
1991	Fresno St.	541.9	Nebraska	353.2	Houston	372.8

* Record.

SCORING OFFENSE

Year	Team	Avg.	Year	Team	Avg.	Year	Team	Avg.
1937	Colorado	31.0	1942	Tulsa	42.7	1947	Michigan	38.3
1938	Dartmouth	28.2	1943	Duke	37.2	1948	Nevada	44.4
1939	Utah	28.4	1944	Army	*56.0	1949	Army	39.3
1940	Boston College	32.0	1945	Army	45.8	1950	Princeton	38.8
1941	Texas	33.8	1946	Georgia	37.2	1951	Maryland	39.2

Year	Team	Avg.	Year	Team	Avg.	Year	Team	Avg.
1952	Oklahoma	40.7	1967	UTEP	35.9	1982	Nebraska	41.1
1953	Texas Tech.	38.9	1968	Houston	42.5	1983	Nebraska	52.0
1954	UCLA	40.8	1969	San Diego St.	46.4	1984	Boston College	36.7
1955	Oklahoma	36.5	1970	Texas	41.2	1985	Fresno St.	39.1
1956	Oklahoma	46.6	1971	Oklahoma	44.9	1986	Oklahoma	42.4
1957	Arizona St.	39.7	1972	Arizona St.	46.6	1987	Oklahoma	43.5
1958	Rutgers	33.4	1973	Arizona St.	44.6	1988	Oklahoma St.	47.5
1959	Syracuse	39.0	1974	Oklahoma	43.0	1989	Houston	53.5
1960	New Mexico St.	37.4	1975	Ohio St.	34.0	1990	Houston	46.5
1961	Utah St.	38.7	1976	Michigan	38.7	1991	Fresno St.	44.2
1962	Wisconsin	31.7	1977	Grambling	42.0			
1963	Utah St.	31.7	1978	Oklahoma	40.0			
1964	Tulsa	38.4	1979	Brigham Young	40.6			
1965	Arkansas	32.4	1980	Brigham Young	46.7			
1966	Notre Dame	36.2	1981	Brigham Young	38.7			

Record.

ANNUAL TEAM DEFENSE CHAMPIONS

Year	Total Defense	Avg.	Rushing	Avg.	Passing	$Avg.
1937	Santa Clara	*69.9	Santa Clara	25.3	Harvard	31.0
1938	Alabama	77.9	Oklahoma	43.3	Penn St.	*13.1
1939	Texas A&M	76.3	Texas A&M	41.5	Kansas	34.1
1940	Navy	96.0	Texas A&M	44.3	Harvard	33.3
1941	Duquesne	110.6	Duquesne	56.0	Purdue	27.1
1942	Texas	117.3	Boston College	48.9	Harvard	45.4
1943	Duke	121.7	Duke	39.4	North Caro.	36.5
1944	Virginia	96.8	Navy	53.8	Michigan St.	26.7
1945	Alabama	109.9	Alabama	33.9	Holy Cross	37.7
1946	Notre Dame	141.7	Oklahoma	58.0	Holy Cross	53.7
1947	Penn St.	76.8	Penn St.	*17.0	North Caro. St.	39.3
1948	Georgia Tech	151.3	Georgia Tech	74.9	Northwestern	54.1
1949	Kentucky	153.8	Oklahoma	55.6	Miami (Fla.)	54.7
1950	Wake Forest	163.2	Ohio St.	64.0	Tennessee	67.5
1951	Wisconsin	154.8	San Francisco	51.6	Wash. & Lee	67.9
1952	Tennessee	166.7	Michigan St.	83.9	Virginia	50.3
1953	Cincinnati	184.3	Maryland	83.9	Richmond	40.3
1954	Mississippi	172.3	UCLA	73.2	Alabama	45.8
1955	Army	160.7	Maryland	75.9	Florida	42.0
1956	Miami (Fla.)	189.4	Miami (Fla.)	106.9	Villanova	43.8
1957	Auburn	133.0	Auburn	67.4	Georgia Tech	33.4
1958	Auburn	157.5	Auburn	79.6	Iowa St.	39.0
1959	Syracuse	96.2	Syracuse	19.3	Alabama	45.7
1960	Wyoming	149.6	Wyoming	82.4	Iowa St.	30.2
1961	Alabama	132.6	Utah St.	50.8	Pennsylvania	56.9
1962	Mississippi	142.2	Minnesota	52.2	New Mexico	56.8
1963	Southern Miss.	131.2	Mississippi	77.3	UTEP	43.8
1964	Auburn	164.7	Washington	61.3	Kent	53.6
1965	Southern Miss.	161.1	Michigan St.	45.6	Toledo	69.8
1966	Southern Miss.	163.7	Wyoming	38.5	Toledo	70.4
1967	Nebraska	157.6	Arizona St.	42.3	Nebraska	90.1
1968	Wyoming	206.8	Arizona St.	57.0	Kent	107.6
1969	Toledo	209.1	Louisiana St.	38.9	Dayton	90.0
1970	Toledo	185.8	Louisiana St.	52.2	Toledo	77.8
1971	Toledo	179.5	Michigan	63.3	Texas Tech	60.1
1972	Louisville	202.5	Louisville	82.1	Vanderbilt	80.3
1973	Miami (Ohio)	177.4	Miami (Ohio)	77.0	Nebraska	39.9
1974	Notre Dame	195.2	Notre Dame	102.8	Iowa	65.7
1975	Texas A&M	183.8	Texas A&M	80.3	Va. Military	51.1
1976	Rutgers	179.2	Rutgers	83.9	Western Mich.	78.5
1977	Jackson St.	207.0	Jackson St.	67.8	Tennessee St.	67.9
1978	Penn St.	203.9	Penn St.	54.5	Boston College	65.1
1979	Yale	175.4	Yale	75.0	Western Caro.	77.5
1980	Pittsburgh	205.5	Pittsburgh	65.3	Kansas St.	91.4
1981	Pittsburgh	224.8	Pittsburgh	62.4	Nebraska	100.1
1982	Arizona St.	228.9	Virginia Tech	49.5	Missouri	123.5
1983	Texas	212.0	Virginia Tech	69.4	Ohio	115.3
1984	Nebraska	203.3	Oklahoma	68.8	Texas Tech	114.8
1985	Oklahoma	193.5	UCLA	70.3	Oklahoma	103.6
1986	Oklahoma	169.6	Oklahoma	60.7	Oklahoma	108.9

1992 NCAA FOOTBALL

Year	Total Defense	Avg.	Rushing	Avg.	Passing	$Avg.
1987	Oklahoma	208.1	Michigan St.	61.5	Oklahoma	102.4
1988	Auburn	218.1	Auburn	63.2	Baylor	117.8
1989	Miami (Fla.)	216.5	Southern Cal	61.5	Kansas St.	129.3
1990	Clemson	216.9	Washington	66.8	Alabama	82.47
1991	Texas A&M	222.4	Clemson	53.4	Texas	77.37

* *Record.* $ *Beginning in 1990, ranked on passing-efficiency defense rating points instead of per-game yardage allowed.*

SCORING DEFENSE

Year	Team	Avg.	Year	Team	Avg.	Year	Team	Avg.
1937	Santa Clara	1.1	1957	Auburn	2.8	1977	North Caro.	7.4
1938	Duke	**0.0	1958	Oklahoma	4.9	1978	Ball St.	7.5
1939	Tennessee	**0.0	1959	Mississippi	2.1	1979	Alabama	5.3
1940	Tennessee	2.6	1960	Louisiana St.	5.0	1980	Florida St.	7.7
1941	Duquesne	2.9	1961	Alabama	2.2	1981	Southern Miss.	8.1
1942	Tulsa	3.2	1962	Louisiana St.	3.4	1982	Arkansas	10.5
1943	Duke	3.8	1963	Mississippi	3.7	1983	Virginia Tech	8.3
1944	Army	3.9	1964	Arkansas	5.7	1984	Nebraska	9.5
1945	St. Mary's (Cal.)	4.0	1965	Michigan St.	6.2	1985	Michigan	6.8
1946	Notre Dame	2.7	1966	Alabama	3.7	1986	Oklahoma	6.6
1947	Penn St.	3.0	1967	Oklahoma	6.8	1987	Oklahoma	7.5
1948	Michigan	4.9	1968	Georgia	9.8	1988	Auburn	7.2
1949	Kentucky	4.8	1969	Arkansas	7.6	1989	Miami (Fla.)	9.3
1950	Army	4.4	1970	Dartmouth	4.7	1990	Central Mich.	8.9
1951	Wisconsin	5.9	1971	Michigan	6.4	1991	Miami (Fla.)	9.1
1952	Southern Cal	4.7	1972	Michigan	5.2			
1953	Maryland	3.1	1973	Ohio St.	4.3			
1954	UCLA	4.4	1974	Michigan	6.8			
1955	Georgia Tech	4.6	1975	Alabama	6.0			
1956	Georgia Tech	3.3	1976	Michigan	7.4			
				Rutgers	7.4			

** *Record tied.*

OTHER ANNUAL TEAM CHAMPIONS

Year	Punting	#Avg.	Punt Returns	Avg.	Kickoff Returns	Avg.
1937	Iowa	43.0	—		—	
1938	Arkansas	41.6	—		—	
1939	Auburn	43.3	UCLA	16.3	Wake Forest	32.9
1940	Auburn	42.3	UCLA	16.2	Minnesota	36.4
1941	Clemson	42.3	Colgate	18.7	Tulane	32.1
1942	Tulsa	41.3	—		—	
1943	Michigan	39.2	Columbia	20.9	Navy	28.8
1944	UCLA	43.0	New York U.	22.0	—	
1945	Miami (Fla.)	39.9	—		—	
1946	UTEP	41.2	Columbia	16.8	William & Mary	31.7
1947	Duke	41.9	Florida	19.7	Southern Methodist	31.4
1948	North Caro.	44.0	Oklahoma	†22.4	Wyoming	27.4
1949	Furman	44.7	Wichita St.	18.3	Army	34.1
1950	Colorado	45.1	Texas A&M	17.6	Wyoming	29.3
1951	Alabama	41.8	Holy Cross	18.1	Marquette	25.0
1952	Colorado	43.3	Arizona St.	‡25.2	Wake Forest	25.1
1953	Georgia	41.2	Kansas St.	23.8	Texas Tech	23.8
1954	New Mexico	42.6	Miami (Fla.)	19.7	Arizona	26.1
1955	Michigan St.	41.2	North Caro.	22.5	Southern Cal	25.8
1956	Colorado St.	42.2	Cincinnati	17.7	Georgia Tech	24.6
1957	Utah St.	40.1	North Texas	17.5	Notre Dame	27.6
1958	Georgia	41.9	Notre Dame	17.6	Tulsa	25.8
1959	Brigham Young	43.2	Wyoming	16.6	Auburn	25.8
1960	Georgia	43.7	Arizona	17.7	Yale	26.7
1961	Arizona St.	42.1	Memphis St.	17.4	Harvard	25.9
1962	Wyoming	42.6	West Tex. St.	18.4	Alabama	28.9
1963	Southern Methodist	41.4	Army	18.1	Memphis St.	27.7
1964	Mississippi	44.1	UTEP	16.9	Cornell	27.1
1965	Arizona St.	44.0	Georgia Tech	23.0	Dartmouth	28.7
1966	Tennessee	43.4	Brown	21.0	Notre Dame	29.6
1967	Houston	44.4	Memphis St.	16.3	Air Force	25.3
1968	Wichita St.	43.2	Army	17.4	Louisville	25.7
1969	Georgia	43.5	Davidson	21.3	Brigham Young	28.7
1970	Utah	45.0	Wichita St.	28.5	South Caro.	26.5
1971	Utah	46.7	Mississippi St.	20.8	Miami (Fla.)	24.1

Year	Punting	#Avg.	Punt Returns	Avg.	Kickoff Returns	Avg.
1972	Southern Miss.	45.1	Georgia Tech	17.3	Michigan	26.9
1973	Wake Forest	44.1	Utah	23.4	Rice	+27.5
1974	Ohio St.	44.9	Auburn	16.6	Southern Cal	25.7
1975	Ohio St.	44.1	New Mexico St.	15.3	Maryland	$29.5
1976	Colorado St.	**44.4	Wichita St.	15.0	South Caro.	27.0
1977	Mississippi	43.4	Grambling	16.9	Miami (Ohio)	24.6
1978	Texas	41.7	McNeese St.	15.7	Utah St.	26.7
1979	Mississippi	42.4	Tennessee St.	16.9	Brigham Young	26.3
1980	Florida St.	42.6	Georgia	16.5	Oklahoma	33.2
1981	Michigan	43.1	North Caro. St.	13.4	Iowa	29.1
1982	Vanderbilt	42.1	Auburn	15.8	Utah	25.5
1983	Brigham Young	*45.0	San Diego St.	17.0	Tennessee	28.8
1984	Ohio St.	44.0	Florida	13.8	Texas Tech	25.2
1985	Colorado	43.6	Utah	20.7	Air Force	27.0
1986	Michigan	43.1	Arizona St.	17.9	Clemson	26.1
1987	Ohio St.	40.7	Stanford	15.4	Oklahoma St.	23.7
1988	Brigham Young	42.9	Florida St.	15.5	Notre Dame	24.2
1989	Colorado	43.8	Ohio	18.2	Colorado	26.1
1990	Pittsburgh	41.2	Michigan	15.6	Nebraska	27.8
1991	Texas Tech	40.6	Alabama	16.9	New Mexico St.	25.2

Beginning in 1975, ranked on net punting average.   * Record for net punting average.   ** Record for net punting average, minimum of 40 punts.   + Record for minimum of 35 kickoff returns. $ Record for minimum of 25 kickoff returns.   † Record for minimum of 30 punt returns.   ‡ Record for minimum of 15 punt returns.

ANNUAL TOUGHEST-SCHEDULE LEADERS

The NCAA's toughest-schedule program (which began in 1977) is based on what all Division I-A opponents did against other Division I-A teams when not playing the team in question. Games against non-I-A teams are deleted, and nine interdivision games are required to qualify. (Bowl games are not included.) The leaders:

Year	Team (+Record)	¢Opponents' Record			Pct.
		W	L	T	
1977	Miami (Fla.) (3-8-0)	66	42	2	.609
	Penn St. (10-1-0)	61	39	2	.608
1978	Notre Dame (8-3-0)	77	31	2	.709
	Southern Cal (11-1-0)	79	40	1	.663
1979	UCLA (5-6-0)	71	37	2	.655
	South Caro. (8-3-0)	69	38	2	.642
1980	Florida St. (10-1-0)	70	34	0	.673
	Miami (Fla.) (8-3-0)	64	33	1	.658
1981	Penn St. (9-2-0)	71	33	2	.679
	Temple (5-5-0)	71	33	2	.669
1982	Penn St. (10-1-0)	63	34	2	.646
	Kentucky (0-10-1)	63	34	5	.642
1983	Auburn (10-1-0)	70	31	3	.688
	UCLA (6-4-1)	68	37	5	.641
1984	Penn St. (6-5-0)	58	36	3	.613
	Georgia (7-4-0)	60	39	4	.602
1985	Notre Dame (5-6-0)	72	29	3	.707
	Alabama (8-2-1)	65	32	5	.662
1986	Florida (6-5-0)	64	29	3	.682
	Louisiana St. (9-2-0)	67	36	2	.648

TOP 10 TOUGHEST-SCHEDULE LEADERS FOR 1987-91

1987

	Team	¢Opp. Record	Pct.
1.	Notre Dame	71-34-2	.673
2.	Florida St.	60-29-4	.667
3.	South Caro.	55-29-0	.655
4.	Alabama	66-36-3	.643
4.	Boston College	67-37-1	.643
6.	Florida	67-38-2	.636
7.	Maryland	64-39-0	.621
8.	Iowa St.	58-38-2	.602
9.	Pittsburgh	63-42-0	.600
10.	Michigan St.	64-43-3	.595

1988

	Team	¢Opp. Record	Pct.
1.	Virginia Tech	74-36-0	.673
2.	Arizona	70-37-3	.650
3.	North Caro.	69-38-3	.641
4.	Florida St.	68-38-1	.640
5.	Southern Cal	68-39-4	.631
6.	Oregon St.	69-41-2	.625
7.	Maryland	67-40-3	.623
8.	Miami (Fla.)	68-41-2	.622
9.	Navy	66-41-1	.616
10.	East Caro.	66-43-0	.606

1989

Team	¢Opp. Record	Pct.
1. Notre Dame	74-38-4	.655
2. Louisiana St.	67-41-1	.619
3. Colorado St.	67-42-3	.612
4. Florida St.	65-41-2	.611
4. Texas	65-41-2	.611
6. South Caro.	57-36-2	.611
7. Auburn	64-42-1	.603
8. Oregon St.	64-42-3	.601
9. Tennessee	62-41-2	.600
9. Maryland	62-41-2	.600

1990

Team	¢Opp. Record	Pct.
1. Colorado	72-42-3	.628
2. Stanford	67-39-4	.627
3. Purdue	60-36-3	.621
4. Notre Dame	63-38-5	.618
5. Texas	65-40-3	.616
6. Miami (Fla.)	65-41-5	.608
7. Virginia Tech	59-38-3	.605
8. Georgia	62-41-2	.600
9. Maryland	60-40-2	.598
10. Penn St.	63-43-4	.591

1991

Team	¢Opp. Record	Pct.
1. South Caro.	57-31-2	.644
2. Florida	66-37-1	.639
3. Louisiana St.	60-38-0	.612
4. Florida St.	64-40-3	.612
5. Maryland	62-39-3	.611
6. Southern Cal	67-43-0	.609
7. Oklahoma St.	62-40-3	.605
8. Northern Ill.	44-30-4	.590
9. Tennessee	63-44-0	.589
10. Houston	61-43-2	.585

+ *Not including bowl games.*   ¢ *When not playing the team listed.*

ANNUAL MOST-IMPROVED TEAMS

		$Games Improved	From		To		Coach
1937	California	4½	1936	6-5-0	1937	*10-0-1	Stub Allison
	Syracuse	4½	1936	1-7-0	1937	5-2-1	#Ossie Solem
1938	Texas Christian	5½	1937	4-4-2	1938	*11-0-0	Dutch Meyer
1939	Texas A&M	5½	1938	4-4-1	1939	*11-0-0	Homer Norton
1940	Stanford	8	1939	1-7-1	1940	*10-0-0	#Clark Shaughnessy
1941	Vanderbilt	4½	1940	3-6-1	1941	8-2-0	Red Sanders
1942	Utah St.	5½	1941	0-8-0	1942	6-3-1	Dick Romney
1943	Purdue	8	1942	1-8-0	1943	9-0-0	Elmer Burnham
1944	Ohio St.	6	1943	3-6-0	1944	9-0-0	#Carroll Widdoes
1945	Miami (Fla.)	7	1944	1-7-1	1945	*9-1-1	Jack Harding
1946	Illinois	5	1945	2-6-1	1946	*8-2-0	Ray Eliot
	Kentucky	5	1945	2-8-0	1946	7-3-0	#Paul "Bear" Bryant
1947	California	6½	1946	2-7-0	1947	9-1-0	#Lynn "Pappy" Waldorf
1948	Clemson	6	1947	4-5-0	1948	*11-0-0	Frank Howard
1949	Tulsa	5	1948	0-9-1	1949	5-4-1	J. O. Brothers
1950	Brigham Young	5	1949	0-11-0	1950	4-5-1	Chick Atkinson
	Texas A&M	5	1949	1-8-1	1950	*7-4-0	Harry Stiteler
1951	Georgia Tech	6	1950	5-6-0	1951	*11-0-1	Bobby Dodd
1952	Alabama	4½	1951	5-6-0	1952	*10-2-0	Harold "Red" Drew
1953	Texas Tech	7	1952	3-7-1	1953	*11-1-0	DeWitt Weaver
1954	Denver	5	1953	3-5-2	1954	9-1-0	Bob Blackman
1955	Texas A&M	6½	1954	1-9-0	1955	7-2-1	Paul "Bear" Bryant
1956	Iowa	5	1955	3-5-1	1956	*9-1-0	Forest Evashevski
1957	Notre Dame	5	1956	2-8-0	1957	7-3-0	Terry Brennan
	Texas	5	1956	1-9-0	1957	+6-4-1	#Darrell Royal
1958	Air Force	6	1957	3-6-1	1958	‡9-0-1	#Ben Martin
1959	Washington	6½	1958	3-7-0	1959	*10-1-0	Jim Owens
1960	Minnesota	5½	1959	2-7-0	1960	+8-2-0	Murray Warmath
	North Caro. St.	5½	1959	1-9-0	1960	6-3-1	Earle Edwards
1961	Villanova	6	1960	2-8-0	1961	*8-2-0	Alex Bell
1962	Southern Cal	6	1961	4-5-1	1962	*11-0-0	John McKay
1963	Illinois	6	1962	2-7-0	1963	*8-1-1	Pete Elliott
1964	Notre Dame	6½	1963	2-7-0	1964	*9-1-0	#Ara Parseghian
1965	UTEP	6½	1964	0-8-2	1965	*8-3-0	#Bobby Dobbs
1966	Dayton	6½	1965	1-8-1	1966	8-2-0	John McVay
1967	Indiana	7	1966	1-8-1	1967	+9-2-0	John Pont
1968	Arkansas	5	1967	4-5-1	1968	*10-1-0	Frank Broyles
1969	UCLA	5½	1968	3-7-0	1969	8-1-1	Tommy Prothro
1970	Tulsa	5	1969	1-9-0	1970	6-4-0	#Claude Gibson

	$Games Improved		From		To		Coach
1971	Army	5	1970	1-9-1	1971	6-4-0	Tom Cahill
	Georgia	5	1970	5-5-0	1971	*11-1-0	Vince Dooley
1972	Pacific (Cal.)	5	1971	3-8-0	1972	8-3-0	Chester Caddas
	Southern Cal	5	1971	6-4-1	1972	*12-0-0	John McKay
	UCLA	5	1971	2-7-1	1972	8-3-0	Pepper Rodgers
1973	Pittsburgh	5	1972	1-10-0	1973	+6-5-1	#Johnny Majors
1974	Baylor	5½	1973	2-9-0	1974	+8-4-0	Grant Teaff
1975	Arizona St.	5	1974	7-5-0	1975	*12-0-0	Frank Kush
1976	Houston	7	1975	2-8-0	1976	*10-2-0	Bill Yeoman
1977	Miami (Ohio)	7	1976	3-8-0	1977	10-1-0	Dick Crum
1978	Tulsa	6	1977	3-8-0	1978	9-2-0	John Cooper
1979	Wake Forest	6½	1978	1-10-0	1979	+8-4-0	John Mackovic
1980	Florida	7	1979	0-10-1	1980	*8-4-0	Charley Pell
1981	Clemson	5½	1980	6-5-0	1981	*12-0-0	Danny Ford
1982	New Mexico	6	1981	4-7-1	1982	10-1-0	Joe Morrison
	Southwestern La.	6	1981	1-9-1	1982	7-3-1	Sam Robertson
1983	Kentucky	5½	1982	0-10-1	1983	+6-5-1	Jerry Claiborne
	Memphis St.	5½	1982	1-10-0	1983	6-4-1	Rex Dockery
1984	Army	6	1983	2-9-0	1984	*8-3-1	Jim Young
1985	Colorado	5½	1984	1-10-0	1985	+7-5-0	Bill McCartney
	Fresno St.	5½	1984	6-6-0	1985	*11-0-1	Jim Sweeney
1986	San Jose St.	7	1985	2-8-1	1986	*10-2-0	Claude Gilbert
1987	Syracuse	6	1986	5-6-0	1987	‡11-0-1	Dick MacPherson
1988	West Va.	5	1987	6-6-0	1988	+11-1-0	Don Nehlen
	Washington St.	5	1987	3-7-1	1988	*9-3-0	Dennis Erickson
1989	Tennessee	5½	1988	5-6-0	1989	*11-1-0	Johnny Majors
1990	Temple	6	1989	1-10-0	1990	7-4-0	Jerry Berndt
1991	Tulsa	6½	1990	3-8-0	1991	*10-2-0	Dave Rader

$ *To determine games improved, add additional victories in second year, subtract losses from previous year, then divide by two; ties not counted. Bowl victory (*), loss (+), tie (‡) included in record.* # *First year as head coach at that college.*

MOST-IMPROVED TEAMS

Games	Team (Year)	Games	Team (Year)
8	Purdue (1943)	6½	Wake Forest (1979)
8	Stanford (1940)	6½	Toledo (1967)
7	San Jose St. (1986)	6½	Dayton (1966)
7	Florida (1980)	6½	UTEP (1965)
7	Miami (Ohio) (1977)	6½	Notre Dame (1964)
7	Houston (1976)	6½	Washington (1959)
7	Indiana (1967)	6½	Texas A&M (1955)
7	Texas Tech (1953)	6½	California (1947)
7	Miami (Fla.) (1945)		
6½	Tulsa (1991)		

ALL-TIME TEAM WON-LOST RECORDS

Classified as Division I-A for the last 10 years. Won-lost-tied record includes bowl games.

PERCENTAGE (TOP 25)

Team	Yrs.	Won	Lost	Tied	Pct.†	*Bowls W	L	T	Total Games
Notre Dame#	103	702	209	40	.759	11	6	0	951
Michigan	112	722	238	33	.744	10	13	0	993
Alabama	97	669	234	43	.730	24	17	3	946
Oklahoma	97	645	233	50	.722	19	10	1	928
Texas	99	676	263	31	.713	16	16	2	970
Southern Cal	99	616	244	51	.704	22	12	0	911
Ohio St.	102	641	261	51	.699	12	12	0	953
Penn St.	105	657	284	41	.690	17	9	2	982
Nebraska$	102	653	286	40	.687	14	16	0	979
Tennessee	95	618	271	52	.684	17	15	0	941
Central Mich.	91	470	243	36	.652	3	1	0	749
Louisiana St.✓	98	566	310	46	.639	11	16	1	922
Army	102	577	316	50	.638	2	1	0	943
Miami (Ohio)	103	536	297	41	.637	5	2	0	874
Washington✓	102	546	303	49	.635	12	7	1	898

Team	Yrs.	Won	Lost	Tied	Pct.†	*Bowls W	L	T	Total Games
Arizona St.	79	432	245	24	.633	9	5	1	701
Georgia	98	574	325	53	.631	14	13	3	952
Florida St.✓	45	293	174	16	.623	12	7	2	483
Auburn✓	99	542	330	45	.616	12	9	2	917
Michigan St.	95	510	316	43	.612	5	5	0	869
Minnesota........................	108	549	343	43	.610	2	3	0	935
Colorado.........................	102	540	343	34	.607	5	11	0	917
UCLA	73	423	271	37	.604	10	7	1	731
Arkansas	98	542	349	38	.604	9	15	3	929
Pittsburgh........................	102	560	366	42	.600	8	10	0	968

ALPHABETICAL LISTING

Team	Yrs.	Won	Lost	Tied	Pct.†	*Bowls W	L	T	Total Games
Air Force	36	199	184	13	.519	6	4	1	396
Alabama	97	669	234	43	.730	24	17	3	946
Arizona	87	443	306	32	.588	2	5	1	781
Arizona St.	79	432	245	24	.633	9	5	1	701
Arkansas	98	542	349	38	.604	9	15	3	929
Army.............................	102	577	316	50	.638	2	1	0	943
Auburn✓	99	542	330	45	.616	12	9	2	917
Ball St.	67	311	249	30	.553	0	1	0	590
Baylor...........................	89	456	391	43	.537	7	7	0	890
Boston College	93	480	345	34	.579	3	4	0	859
Bowling Green...................	73	373	238	50	.602	1	3	0	661
Brigham Young	67	356	297	26	.543	5	10	1	679
Cal St. Fullerton.................	22	105	141	3	.428	0	1	0	249
California	96	517	368	51	.580	4	6	1	936
Central Mich.	91	470	243	36	.652	3	1	0	749
Cincinnati	104	434	445	51	.494	1	1	0	930
Clemson	96	512	347	45	.591	11	7	0	904
Colorado.........................	102	540	343	34	.607	5	11	0	917
Colorado St.	93	347	421	33	.454	1	1	0	801
Duke	79	409	304	31	.571	3	4	0	744
East Caro........................	56	275	254	12	.519	2	0	0	541
Eastern Mich.	99	363	362	46	.501	1	0	0	771
Florida	85	471	326	39	.587	8	11	0	836
Florida St.✓	45	293	174	16	.623	12	7	2	483
Fresno St.	70	414	272	28	.599	6	1	0	714
Georgia	98	574	325	53	.631	14	13	3	952
Georgia Tech	99	544	357	43	.599	17	8	0	944
Hawaii	76	397	279	25	.584	0	1	0	701
Houston..........................	46	277	202	14	.576	7	5	1	493
Illinois...........................	102	485	396	48	.548	4	5	0	929
Indiana..........................	104	369	478	44	.439	3	4	0	891
Iowa	103	454	419	38	.519	6	5	1	911
Iowa St.	100	414	445	45	.483	0	4	0	904
Kansas...........................	102	464	442	58	.511	1	5	0	964
Kansas St.✓	96	312	529	41	.377	0	1	0	882
Kent.............................	69	255	339	27	.432	0	1	0	621
Kentucky✓	101	480	434	44	.524	5	2	0	958
Long Beach St.	37	199	183	4	.521	0	0	1	386
Louisiana St.✓	98	566	310	46	.639	11	16	1	922
Louisville✓	73	311	340	17	.478	2	1	1	668
Maryland.........................	99	500	421	42	.541	6	9	2	963
Memphis St.✓	76	343	337	32	.504	1	0	0	712
Miami (Fla.)	65	391	256	19	.601	10	8	0	666
Miami (Ohio).....................	103	536	297	41	.637	5	2	0	874
Michigan.........................	112	722	238	33	.744	10	13	0	993
Michigan St.	95	510	316	43	.612	5	5	0	869
Minnesota........................	108	549	343	43	.610	2	3	0	935
Mississippi✓	97	499	371	35	.571	13	11	0	905
Mississippi St.✓	92	396	418	37	.487	4	3	0	851
Missouri..........................	101	501	410	50	.547	8	11	0	961
Navy	111	541	408	57	.566	3	4	1	1,006
Nebraska$	102	653	286	40	.687	14	16	0	979
Nevada-Las Vegas	24	153	109	4	.583	1	0	0	266
New Mexico......................	93	352	406	31	.466	2	2	1	789
New Mexico St.	96	352	417	32	.459	2	0	1	801

Team	Yrs.	Won	Lost	Tied	Pct.†	*Bowls W	L	T	Total Games
North Caro.	101	529	389	54	.572	6	10	0	972
North Caro. St.	100	418	425	54	.496	7	6	1	897
Northern Ill.	90	409	340	51	.543	1	0	0	800
Northwestern	104	366	506	42	.423	1	0	0	914
Notre Dame#	103	702	209	40	.759	11	6	0	951
Ohio	96	416	390	47	.515	0	2	0	853
Ohio St.	102	641	261	51	.699	12	12	0	953
Oklahoma	97	645	233	50	.722	19	10	1	928
Oklahoma St.	90	403	413	46	.494	9	3	0	862
Oregon	96	422	393	46	.517	3	5	0	861
Oregon St.	95	387	425	49	.478	2	2	0	861
Pacific (Cal.)	73	331	368	23	.474	3	1	1	722
Penn St.	105	657	284	41	.690	17	9	2	982
Pittsburgh	102	560	366	42	.600	8	10	0	968
Purdue	104	466	390	45	.542	4	1	0	901
Rice✓	80	339	432	31	.442	4	3	0	802
Rutgers	122	519	471	41	.523	0	1	0	1,031
San Diego St.	69	389	262	31	.593	2	3	0	682
San Jose St.	73	370	302	38	.548	4	3	0	709
South Caro.	98	435	423	43	.507	0	8	0	901
Southern Cal	99	616	244	51	.704	22	12	0	911
Southern Methodist	75	384	341	51	.528	4	6	1	776
Southern Miss.✓	75	407	276	25	.593	2	6	0	708
Southwestern La.	84	396	375	31	.513	0	1	0	802
Stanford	85	466	319	47	.588	7	7	1	832
Syracuse	102	567	377	48	.596	7	6	1	992
Temple	93	365	371	52	.496	1	1	0	788
Tennessee	95	618	271	52	.684	17	15	0	941
Texas	99	676	263	31	.713	16	16	2	970
Texas A&M	97	527	358	47	.591	10	8	0	932
Texas Christian	95	434	431	55	.502	4	9	1	920
Texas Tech	67	374	309	32	.545	4	13	1	715
Toledo	71	333	312	22	.516	4	1	0	667
Tulane✓	98	413	440	38	.485	2	6	0	891
Tulsa	87	466	306	26	.600	4	7	0	798
UCLA	73	423	271	37	.604	10	7	1	731
Utah	98	460	352	31	.564	2	0	0	843
Utah St.	93	400	348	31	.533	0	4	0	779
UTEP	74	289	378	29	.436	5	3	0	696
Vanderbilt	102	494	414	50	.542	1	1	1	958
Virginia	102	487	450	48	.519	2	3	0	985
Virginia Tech	98	502	369	45	.573	1	5	0	916
Wake Forest	90	316	475	33	.404	1	2	0	824
Washington✓	102	546	303	49	.635	12	7	1	898
Washington St.	95	387	389	45	.499	2	2	0	821
West Va.	99	541	374	43	.587	8	7	0	958
Western Mich.	86	399	303	22	.566	0	1	0	724
Wisconsin	102	463	394	49	.538	1	5	0	906
Wyoming	95	385	397	28	.493	4	5	0	810

The following are not listed above because of reclassification to Division I-A:

Team	Yrs.	Won	Lost	Tied	Pct.†	*Bowls W	L	T	Total Games
Akron	91	402	351	35	.532	0	0	0	788
Arkansas St.	77	343	306	36	.527	9	7	1	685
Louisiana Tech	88	446	300	37	.593	0	0	1	783
Nevada	81	374	324	32	.534	10	8	0	730

† *Ties computed as half won and half lost.* * *Record in a major bowl game only (i.e., a team's opponent was classified as a major-college team that season or it was classified as a major-college team at the time.)* # *Leader since 1948. Notre Dame displaced all-time leader Yale .8082 to .8081 after the 1947 season.* $ *Record adjusted in 1989 (8 less victories, 1 less defeat).* ✓ *Includes games forfeited or changed by action of the NCAA Council.*

VICTORIES

Team	Wins	Team	Wins	Team	Wins
Michigan	722	Nebraska$	653	Army	577
Notre Dame	702	Oklahoma	645	Georgia	574
Texas	676	Ohio St.	641	Syracuse	567
Alabama	669	Tennessee	618	Louisiana St.✓	566
Penn St.	657	Southern Cal	616	Pittsburgh	560

Team	Wins	Team	Wins	Team	Wins
Minnesota	549	Wisconsin	463	Southern Methodist	384
Washington✓	546	Utah	460	Texas Tech	374
Georgia Tech	544	Baylor	456	Bowling Green	373
Arkansas	542	Iowa	454	San Jose St.	370
Auburn✓	542	Arizona	443	Indiana	369
Navy	541	South Caro.	435	Northwestern	366
West Va.	541	Cincinnati	434	Temple	365
Colorado	540	Texas Christian	434	Eastern Mich.	363
Miami (Ohio)	536	Arizona St.	432	Brigham Young	356
North Caro.	529	UCLA	423	New Mexico	352
Texas A&M	527	Oregon	422	New Mexico St.	352
Rutgers	519	North Caro. St.	418	Colorado St.	347
California	517	Ohio	416	Memphis St.✓	343
Clemson	512	Fresno St.	414	Rice✓	339
Michigan St.	510	Iowa St.	414	Toledo	333
Virginia Tech	502	Tulane✓	413	Pacific (Cal.)	331
Missouri	501	Duke	409	Wake Forest	316
Maryland	500	Northern Ill.	409	Kansas St.✓	312
Mississippi✓	499	Southern Miss.✓	407	Ball St.	311
Vanderbilt	494	Oklahoma St.	403	Louisville✓	311
Virginia	487	Utah St.	400	Florida St.✓	293
Illinois	485	Western Mich.	399	UTEP	289
Boston College	480	Hawaii	397	Houston	277
Kentucky✓	480	Mississippi St.✓	396	East Caro.	275
Florida	471	Southwestern La.	396	Kent	255
Central Mich.	470	Miami (Fla.)	391	Air Force	199
Purdue	466	San Diego St.	389	Long Beach St.	199
Stanford	466	Oregon St.	387	Nevada-Las Vegas	153
Tulsa	466	Washington St.	387	Cal St. Fullerton	105
Kansas	464	Wyoming	385		

The following are not listed above because of reclassification to Division I-A:

Louisiana Tech 446
Akron 402
Nevada 374
Arkansas St. 343

$ *Record adjusted by Nebraska in 1989 (8 less victories).* ✓ *Includes games forfeited or changed by action of the NCAA Council.*

NATIONAL CHAMPIONS FROM 1936 TO 1949

Based on Associated Press poll of sportswriters and broadcasters, United Press International poll of coaches, Football Writers Association of America's Grantland Rice Award, and National Football Foundation and Hall of Fame's MacArthur Bowl award. The national champion was selected before bowl games as follows: AP (1936-64 and 1966-67); UP-UPI (1950-73); FWAA (1954); NFF-HF (1959-70).

Year	Team	*Record	Coach	†Years
1936	Minnesota	7-1-0	Bernie Bierman	5-15
1937	Pittsburgh	9-0-1	Jock Sutherland	13-18
1938	Texas Christian	10-0-0 W	Leo "Dutch" Meyer	5-5
1939	Texas A&M	10-0-0 W	Homer Norton	6-16
1940	Minnesota	8-0-0	Bernie Bierman	9-19
1941	Minnesota	8-0-0	Bernie Bierman	10-20
1942	Ohio St.	9-1-0	Paul Brown	2-2
1943	Notre Dame	9-1-0	Frank Leahy	3-5
1944	Army	9-0-0	Earl "Red" Blaik	4-11
1945	Army	9-0-0	Earl "Red" Blaik	5-12
1946	Notre Dame	8-0-1	Frank Leahy	4-6
1947	Notre Dame	9-0-0	Frank Leahy	5-7
1948	Michigan	9-0-0	Bennie Oosterbaan	1-1
1949	Notre Dame	10-0-0	Frank Leahy	7-9

* *Regular-season record (bowl game win or loss is indicated by W or L).* † *Years head coach at that college and total years at four-year colleges.*

NATIONAL CHAMPIONS FROM 1950

Associated Press (AP) from 1950; United Press International (UPI‡) from 1950-1990; Football Writers Association of America (FWAA) from 1954; National Football Foundation and Hall of Fame (NFF) from 1959-1990; USA Today/Cable News Network (USA/CNN) from 1991, and United Press International/National Football Foundation and Hall of Fame (UPI/NFF) from 1991.

Note: The following T-formation quarterbacks led their teams to two consecutive national championships: John Lujack, Notre Dame (1946-47); Jimmy Harris, Oklahoma (1955-56); Jerry Tagge, Nebraska (1970-

71), and Steve Davis, Oklahoma (1974-75). Bruce Smith, a single-wing tailback, led Minnesota to titles in 1940 and 1941. Lujack started the last four games for Notre Dame's 1943 national champions after Angelo Bertelli started the first six games then joined the Marines.

Year	Team	‡Selected By	*Record	Coach	†Year(s)
1950	Oklahoma	AP-UPI	10-0-0 L	Bud Wilkinson	4-4
1951	Tennessee	AP-UPI	10-0-0 L	Bob Neyland	20-20
1952	Michigan St.	AP-UPI	9-0-0	Biggie Munn	6-9
1953	Maryland	AP-UPI	10-0-0 L	Jim Tatum	7-9
1954	UCLA	UPI-FW	9-0-0	Red Sanders	6-12
	Ohio St.	AP	9-0-0 W	Woody Hayes	4-9
1955	Oklahoma	(All 3)	10-0-0 W	Bud Wilkinson	9-9
1956	Oklahoma	(All 3)	10-0-0	Bud Wilkinson	10-10
1957	Ohio St.	UPI-FW	8-1-0 W	Woody Hayes	7-12
	Auburn	AP	10-0-0	Ralph Jordan	7-7
1958	Louisiana St.	AP-UPI	10-0-0 W	Paul Dietzel	4-4
	Iowa	FW	7-1-1 W	Forest Evashevski	5-8
1959	Syracuse	(All 4)	10-0-0 W	Ben Schwartzwalder	11-14
1960	Minnesota	AP-UPI-NFF	8-1-0 L	Murray Warmath	7-9
	Mississippi	FW	9-0-1 W	John Vaught	14-14
1961	Alabama	AP-UPI-NFF	10-0-0 W	Paul "Bear" Bryant	4-17
	Ohio St.	FW	8-0-1	Woody Hayes	11-16
1962	Southern Cal	(All 4)	10-0-0 W	John McKay	3-3
1963	Texas	(All 4)	10-0-0 W	Darrell Royal	7-10
1964	Alabama	AP-UPI	10-0-0 L	Paul "Bear" Bryant	7-20
	Arkansas	FW	10-0-0 L	Frank Broyles	3-4
	Notre Dame	NFF	9-1-0	Ara Parseghian	1-14
1965	Alabama	AP-FW (tie)	8-1-1 W	Paul "Bear" Bryant	8-21
	Michigan St.	UPI-FW (tie)-NFF	10-0-0 L	Duffy Daugherty	12-12
1966	Notre Dame	AP-UPI-NFF (tie)	9-0-1	Ara Parseghian	3-17
	Michigan St.	NFF (tie)	9-0-1	Duffy Daugherty	13-13
1967	Southern Cal	(All 4)	9-1-0 W	John McKay	8-8
1968	Ohio St.	(All 4)	9-0-0 W	Woody Hayes	18-23
1969	Texas	(All 4)	10-0-0 W	Darrell Royal	13-16
1970	Nebraska	AP-FW	10-0-1 W	Bob Devaney	9-14
	Texas	UPI-NFF (tie)	10-0-0 L	Darrell Royal	14-17
	Ohio St.	NFF (tie)	9-0-0 L	Woody Hayes	20-25
1971	Nebraska	(All 4)	12-0-0 W	Bob Devaney	10-15
1972	Southern Cal	(All 4)	11-0-0 W	John McKay	13-13
1973	Notre Dame	AP-FW-NFF	10-0-0	Ara Parseghian	10-23
	Alabama	UPI	11-0-0 L	Paul "Bear" Bryant	16-29
1974	Southern Cal	UPI-FW-NFF	9-1-1 W	John McKay	15-15
	Oklahoma	AP	11-0-0	Barry Switzer	2-2
1975	Oklahoma	(All 4)	10-1-0 W	Barry Switzer	3-3
1976	Pittsburgh	(All 4)	11-1-0 W	Johnny Majors	4-9
1977	Notre Dame	(All 4)	10-1-0 W	Dan Devine	3-19
1978	Alabama	AP-FW-NFF	10-1-0 W	Paul "Bear" Bryant	21-34
	Southern Cal	UPI	11-1-0 W	John Robinson	3-3
1979	Alabama	(All 4)	11-0-0 W	Paul "Bear" Bryant	22-35
1980	Georgia	(All 4)	11-0-0 W	Vince Dooley	17-17
1981	Clemson	(All 4)	11-0-0 W	Danny Ford	#4-4
1982	Penn St.	(All 4)	10-1-0 W	Joe Paterno	17-17
1983	Miami (Fla.)	(All 4)	10-1-0 W	Howard Schnellenberger	5-5
1984	Brigham Young	(All 4)	12-0-0 W	LaVell Edwards	13-13
1985	Oklahoma	(All 4)	10-1-0 W	Barry Switzer	13-13
1986	Penn St.	(All 4)	11-0-0 W	Joe Paterno	21-21
1987	Miami (Fla.)	(All 4)	11-0-0 W	Jimmy Johnson	3-9
1988	Notre Dame	(All 4)	11-0-0 W	Lou Holtz	3-19
1989	Miami (Fla.)	(All 4)	10-1-0 W	Dennis Erickson	1-8
1990	Colorado	AP-FW-NFF	11-1-1 W	Bill McCartney	9-9
	Georgia Tech	UPI	11-0-1 W	Bobby Ross	4-14
1991	Washington	USA/CNN-UPI/NFF-FW	12-0-0 W	Don James	17-21
	Miami (Fla.)	AP	12-0-0 W	Dennis Erickson	3-10

Regular-season record (bowl game win or loss is indicated by W or L). † Years head coach at that college and total years as a head coach at four-year colleges. ‡ United Press (UP), 1950-57; UPI from 1958-90 after merger with International News Service. USA/CNN took over coaches poll in 1991. # Includes last game of 1978 season.

Pittsburgh running back Tony Dorsett capped a record-setting career in 1976 by rushing for 1,948 yards during the regular season, winning the Heisman Trophy and leading the Panthers to the national champion-ship.

NATIONAL POLL RANKINGS

DICKINSON SYSTEM

(1924-40)

The Dickinson System was a mathematical point system devised by Frank G. Dickinson, a professor of economics at Illinois. The annual Dickinson ratings were emblematic of the national championship and the basis for awarding the Rissman National Trophy and the Knute K. Rockne Intercollegiate Memorial Trophy. Notre Dame gained permanent possession of the Rissman Trophy (named for Jack F. Rissman, a Chicago clothing manufacturer) after its third victory in 1930. Minnesota retired the Rockne Trophy (named in honor of the famous Notre Dame coach) after winning it for a third time in 1940.

Subsequently, the Associated Press annual national champions were awarded the Williams Trophy and the Reverend J. Hugh O'Donnell Trophy. In 1947, Notre Dame retired the Williams Trophy (named after Dr. Henry L. Williams, Minnesota coach, and sponsored by the M Club of Minnesota). In 1956, Oklahoma retired the O'Donnell Trophy (named for Notre Dame's president and sponsored by Notre Dame alumni). Beginning with the 1957 season, the award was known as the AP Trophy, and since 1983 the award has been known as the Paul "Bear" Bryant Trophy.

Yr.		Yr.		Yr.		Yr.	
1924	Notre Dame	1929	Notre Dame	1934	Minnesota	1939	Southern Cal
1925	Dartmouth	1930	Notre Dame	1935	Southern Meth.	1940	Minnesota
1926	Stanford	1931	Southern Cal	1936	Minnesota		
1927	Illinois	1932	Michigan	1937	Pittsburgh		
1928	Southern Cal	1933	Michigan	1938	Notre Dame		

DUNKEL SYSTEM
(From 1929 to present)

A power index system devised by Dick Dunkel Sr. (1929-71); from 1972 by Dick Dunkel Jr.

Yr.		Yr.		Yr.		Yr.	
1929	Notre Dame	1949	Notre Dame	1964	Michigan	1979	Alabama
1930	Notre Dame	1950	Tennessee	1965	Michigan St.	1980	Oklahoma
1931	Southern Cal	1951	Maryland	1966	Notre Dame	1981	Penn St.
1932	Southern Cal	1952	Michigan St.	1967	Notre Dame	1982	Penn St.
1933	Ohio St.	1953	Notre Dame	1968	Ohio St.	1983	Miami (Fla.)
1934	Alabama	1954	UCLA	1969	Texas	1984	Florida
1935	Princeton	1955	Oklahoma	1970	Nebraska	1985	Oklahoma
1936	Minnesota	1956	Oklahoma	1971	Nebraska	1986	Oklahoma
1937	California	1957	Michigan St.	1972	Southern Cal	1987	Miami (Fla.)
1938	Tennessee	1958	Louisiana St.	1973	Oklahoma	1988	Notre Dame
1939	Texas A&M	1959	Mississippi	1974	Oklahoma	1989	Miami (Fla.)
1940	Tennessee	1960	Mississippi	1975	Oklahoma	1990	Florida St.
1941	Minnesota	1961	Alabama	1976	Southern Cal	1991	Washington
1942	Ohio St.	1962	Southern Cal	1977	Notre Dame		
1943	Notre Dame	1963	Texas	1978	Oklahoma		
1944	Army						
1945	Army						
1946	Notre Dame						
1947	Michigan						
1948	Michigan						

WILLIAMSON SYSTEM
(1932-63)

A power rating system chosen by Paul Williamson, a geologist and member of the Sugar Bowl committee.

Yr.		Yr.		Yr.		Yr.	
1932	Southern Cal	1942	Georgia	1952	Michigan St.	1962	Southern Cal
1933	Southern Cal	1943	Notre Dame	1953	Notre Dame	1963	Texas
1934	Alabama	1944	Army	1954	Ohio St.		
1935	Louisiana St.	1945	Army	1955	Oklahoma		
1936	Louisiana St.	1946	Georgia	1956	Oklahoma		
1937	Pittsburgh	1947	Notre Dame	1957	Auburn		
1938	Texas Christian	1948	Michigan	1958	Louisiana St.		
1939	Texas A&M	1949	Notre Dame	1959	Syracuse		
1940	Tennessee	1950	Oklahoma	1960	Mississippi		
1941	Texas	1951	Tennessee	1961	Alabama		

LITKENHOUS SYSTEM
(1934-76)

A difference-by-score formula developed by Edward E. Litkenhous, a professor of chemical engineering at Vanderbilt, and his brother, Frank.

Yr.		Yr.		Yr.		Yr.	
1934	Minnesota	1949	Notre Dame	1959	Syracuse	1969	Texas
1935	Minnesota	1950	Oklahoma	1960	Iowa	1970	Texas
1936	Minnesota	1951	Tennessee	1961	Alabama	1971	Nebraska
1937	Pittsburgh	1952	Michigan St.	1962	Mississippi	1972	Southern Cal
1938	Tennessee	1953	Notre Dame	1963	Texas	1973	Alabama
1939	Cornell	1954	UCLA	1964	Alabama	1974	Oklahoma
1940	Minnesota	1955	Oklahoma	1965	Michigan St.	1975	Ohio St.
1941	Minnesota	1956	Oklahoma	1966	Notre Dame	1976	Michigan
1942	Georgia	1957	Ohio St.	1967	Tennessee		
1943	Notre Dame	1958	Louisiana St.	1968	Georgia		
1944	Army						
1945	Army						
1946	Notre Dame						
1947	Michigan						
1948	Michigan						

ATHLETIC FOUNDATION
(1883-1982)

Originally in the name of the Helms Athletic Foundation (1936-69), the foundation was established by the founding sponsor, Paul H. Helms, Los Angeles sportsman and philanthropist. After Helms' death in 1957, United Savings & Loan Association became its benefactor during 1970-72. A merger of United Savings and Citizens Savings was completed in 1973, and the Athletic Foundation became known as

Citizens Savings Athletic Foundation. In 1982, The First Interstate Bank assumed sponsorship for its final rankings.

In 1941, Bill Schroeder, managing director of the Helms Athletic Foundation, retroactively selected the national football champions for the period beginning in 1883 (the first year of a scoring system) through 1941. Thereafter, Schroeder, who passed away in 1988, then chose, with the assistance of a Hall Board, the annual national champion after the bowl games.

Yr.		Yr.		Yr.		Yr.	
1883	Yale	1913	Harvard	1938	Texas Christian	1963	Texas
1884	Yale	1914	Army			1964	Arkansas
1885	Princeton	1915	Cornell	1939	Texas A&M	1965	Michigan St.
1886	Yale	1916	Pittsburgh	1940	Stanford	1966	Notre Dame & Michigan St.
1887	Yale	1917	Georgia Tech	1941	Minnesota		
1888	Yale	1918	Pittsburgh	1942	Wisconsin	1967	Southern Cal
1889	Princeton	1919	Harvard	1943	Notre Dame	1968	Ohio St.
1890	Harvard	1920	California	1944	Army	1969	Texas
1891	Yale	1921	Cornell	1945	Army	1970	Nebraska
1892	Yale	1922	Cornell	1946	Army & Notre Dame	1971	Nebraska
1893	Princeton	1923	Illinois			1972	Southern Cal
1894	Yale	1924	Notre Dame	1947	Michigan & Notre Dame	1973	Notre Dame
1895	Pennsylvania	1925	Alabama			1974	Oklahoma & Southern Cal
1896	Princeton	1926	Alabama & Stanford	1948	Michigan		
1897	Pennsylvania			1949	Notre Dame	1975	Ohio St. & Oklahoma
1898	Harvard	1927	Illinois	1950	Oklahoma		
1899	Harvard	1928	Georgia Tech	1951	Michigan St.	1976	Pittsburgh
1900	Yale	1929	Notre Dame	1952	Michigan St.	1977	Notre Dame
1901	Michigan	1930	Notre Dame	1953	Notre Dame	1978	Alabama, Oklahoma & Southern Cal
1902	Michigan	1931	Southern Cal	1954	UCLA & Ohio St.		
1903	Princeton	1932	Southern Cal				
1904	Pennsylvania	1933	Michigan	1955	Oklahoma	1979	Alabama
1905	Chicago	1934	Minnesota	1956	Oklahoma	1980	Georgia
1906	Princeton	1935	Minnesota	1957	Auburn	1981	Clemson
1907	Yale	1936	Minnesota	1958	Louisiana St.	1982	Penn St. & Southern Methodist
1908	Pennsylvania	1937	California	1959	Syracuse		
1909	Yale			1960	Washington		
1910	Harvard			1961	Alabama		
1911	Princeton			1962	Southern Cal		
1912	Harvard						

No. 1 vs. No. 2

The No. 1 and No. 2 teams in the Associated Press poll (begun in 1936) have faced each other 26 times (18 in regular-season games and eight in bowl games). The No. 1 team has won 16, with two games ending in ties.

Date	Score	Stadium (Site)
10-9-43	No. 1 Notre Dame 35, No. 2 Michigan 12	Michigan Stadium (Ann Arbor)
11-20-43	No. 1 Notre Dame 14, No. 2 Iowa Pre-Flight 13	Notre Dame (South Bend)
12-2-44	No. 1 Army 23, No. 2 Navy 7	Municipal (Baltimore)
11-10-45	No. 1 Army 48, No. 2 Notre Dame 0	Yankee (New York)
12-1-45	No. 1 Army 32, No. 2 Navy 13	Municipal (Philadelphia)
11-9-46	No. 1 Army 0, No. 2 Notre Dame 0 (tie)	Yankee (New York)
1-1-63	No. 1 Southern Cal 42, No. 2 Wisconsin 37 (Rose Bowl)	Rose Bowl (Pasadena)
10-12-63	No. 2 Texas 28, No. 1 Oklahoma 7	Cotton Bowl (Dallas)
1-1-64	No. 1 Texas 28, No. 2 Navy 6 (Cotton Bowl)	Cotton Bowl (Dallas)
11-19-66	No. 1 Notre Dame 10, No. 2 Michigan St. 10 (tie)	Spartan (East Lansing)
9-28-68	No. 1 Purdue 37, No. 2 Notre Dame 22	Notre Dame (South Bend)
1-1-69	No. 1 Ohio St. 27, No. 2 Southern Cal 16 (Rose Bowl)	Rose Bowl (Pasadena)
12-6-69	No. 1 Texas 15, No. 2 Arkansas 14	Razorback (Fayetteville)
11-25-71	No. 1 Nebraska 35, No. 2 Oklahoma 31	Owen Field (Norman)
1-1-72	No. 1 Nebraska 38, No. 2 Alabama 6 (Orange Bowl)	Orange Bowl (Miami)
1-1-79	No. 2 Alabama 14, No. 1 Penn St. 7 (Sugar Bowl)	Sugar Bowl (New Orleans)
9-26-81	No. 1 Southern Cal 28, No. 2 Oklahoma 24	Coliseum (Los Angeles)
1-1-83	No. 2 Penn St. 27, No. 1 Georgia 23 (Sugar Bowl)	Sugar Bowl (New Orleans)
10-19-85	No. 1 Iowa 12, No. 2 Michigan 10	Kinnick (Iowa City)
9-27-86	No. 2 Miami (Fla.) 28, No. 1 Oklahoma 16	Orange Bowl (Miami)
1-2-87	No. 2 Penn St. 14, No. 1 Miami (Fla.) 10 (Fiesta Bowl)	Fiesta Bowl (Tempe)
11-21-87	No. 2 Oklahoma 17, No. 1 Nebraska 7	Memorial (Lincoln)
1-1-88	No. 2 Miami (Fla.) 20, No. 1 Oklahoma 14 (Orange Bowl)	Orange Bowl (Miami)
11-26-88	No. 1 Notre Dame 27, No. 2 Southern Cal 10	Coliseum (Los Angeles)
9-16-89	No. 1 Notre Dame 24, No. 2 Michigan 19	Michigan (Ann Arbor)
11-16-91	No. 2 Miami (Fla.) 17, No. 1 Florida St. 16	Doak Campbell (Tallahassee)

ASSOCIATED PRESS (WRITERS AND BROADCASTERS)
FINAL POLLS

1936
Team
1. Minnesota
2. Louisiana St.
3. Pittsburgh
4. Alabama
5. Washington
6. Santa Clara
7. Northwestern
8. Notre Dame
9. Nebraska
10. Pennsylvania
11. Duke
12. Yale
13. Dartmouth
14. Duquesne
15. Fordham
16. Texas Christian
17. Tennessee
18. Arkansas
    Navy
20. Marquette

1937
Team
1. Pittsburgh
2. California
3. Fordham
4. Alabama
5. Minnesota
6. Villanova
7. Dartmouth
8. Louisiana St.
9. Notre Dame
    Santa Clara
11. Nebraska
12. Yale
13. Ohio St.
14. Holy Cross
    Arkansas
16. Texas Christian
17. Colorado
18. Rice
19. North Caro.
20. Duke

1938
Team
1. Texas Christian
2. Tennessee
3. Duke
4. Oklahoma
5. Notre Dame
6. Carnegie Tech
7. Southern Cal
8. Pittsburgh
9. Holy Cross
10. Minnesota
11. Texas Tech
12. Cornell
13. Alabama
14. California
15. Fordham
16. Michigan
17. Northwestern
18. Villanova
19. Tulane
20. Dartmouth

1939
Team
1. Texas A&M
2. Tennessee
3. Southern Cal
4. Cornell
5. Tulane
6. Missouri
7. UCLA
8. Duke
9. Iowa
10. Duquesne
11. Boston College
12. Clemson
13. Notre Dame
14. Santa Clara
15. Ohio St.
16. Georgia Tech
17. Fordham
18. Nebraska
19. Oklahoma
20. Michigan

1940
Team
1. Minnesota
2. Stanford
3. Michigan
4. Tennessee
5. Boston College
6. Texas A&M
7. Nebraska
8. Northwestern
9. Mississippi St.
10. Washington
11. Santa Clara
12. Fordham
13. Georgetown
14. Pennsylvania
15. Cornell
16. Southern Methodist
17. Hardin-Simmons
18. Duke
19. Lafayette

1941
Team
1. Minnesota
2. Duke
3. Notre Dame
4. Texas
5. Michigan
6. Fordham
7. Missouri
8. Duquesne
9. Texas A&M
10. Navy
11. Northwestern
12. Oregon St.
13. Ohio St.
14. Georgia
15. Pennsylvania
16. Mississippi St.
17. Mississippi
18. Tennessee
19. Washington St.
20. Alabama

1942
Team
1. Ohio St.
2. Georgia
3. Wisconsin
4. Tulsa
5. Georgia Tech
6. Notre Dame
7. Tennessee
8. Boston College
9. Michigan
10. Alabama
11. Texas
12. Stanford
13. UCLA
14. William & Mary
15. Santa Clara
16. Auburn
17. Washington St.
18. Mississippi St.
19. Minnesota
    Holy Cross
    Penn St.

1943
Team
1. Notre Dame
2. Iowa Pre-Flight
3. Michigan
4. Navy
5. Purdue
6. Great Lakes
7. Duke
8. Del Monte P-F
9. Northwestern
10. March Field
11. Army
12. Washington
13. Georgia Tech
14. Texas
15. Tulsa
16. Dartmouth
17. Bainbridge NTS
18. Colorado Col.
19. Pacific (Cal.)
20. Pennsylvania

1944
Team
1. Army
2. Ohio St.
3. Randolph Field
4. Navy
5. Bainbridge NTS
6. Iowa Pre-Flight
7. Southern Cal
8. Michigan
9. Notre Dame
10. March Field
11. Duke
12. Tennessee
13. Georgia Tech
    Norman P-F
15. Illinois
16. El Toro Marines
17. Great Lakes
18. Fort Pierce
19. St. Mary's P-F
20. Second Air Force

1945
Team
1. Army
2. Alabama
3. Navy
4. Indiana
5. Oklahoma St.
6. Michigan
7. St. Mary's (Cal.)
8. Pennsylvania
9. Notre Dame
10. Texas
11. Southern Cal
12. Ohio St.
13. Duke
14. Tennessee
15. Louisiana St.
16. Holy Cross
17. Tulsa
18. Georgia
19. Wake Forest
20. Columbia

1946
Team
1. Notre Dame
2. Army
3. Georgia
4. UCLA
5. Illinois
6. Michigan
7. Tennessee
8. Louisiana St.
9. North Caro.
10. Rice
11. Georgia Tech
12. Yale
13. Pennsylvania
14. Oklahoma
15. Texas
16. Arkansas
17. Tulsa
18. North Caro. St.
19. Delaware
20. Indiana

*1947
Team
1. Notre Dame
2. Michigan
3. Southern Methodist
4. Penn St.
5. Texas
6. Alabama
7. Pennsylvania
8. Southern Cal
9. North Caro.
10. Georgia Tech
11. Army
12. Kansas
13. Mississippi
14. William & Mary
15. California
16. Oklahoma
17. North Caro. St.
18. Rice
19. Duke
20. Columbia

1948
Team
1. Michigan
2. Notre Dame
3. North Caro.
4. California
5. Oklahoma
6. Army
7. Northwestern
8. Georgia
9. Oregon
10. Southern Methodist
11. Clemson
12. Vanderbilt
13. Tulane
14. Michigan St.
15. Mississippi
16. Minnesota
17. William & Mary
18. Penn St.
19. Cornell
20. Wake Forest

1949
Team
1. Notre Dame
2. Oklahoma
3. California
4. Army
5. Rice
6. Ohio St.
7. Michigan
8. Minnesota
9. Louisiana St.
10. Pacific (Cal.)
11. Kentucky
12. Cornell
13. Villanova
14. Maryland
15. Santa Clara
16. North Caro.
17. Tennessee
18. Princeton
19. Michigan St.
20. Missouri
    Baylor

1950
Team
1. Oklahoma
2. Army
3. Texas
4. Tennessee
5. California
6. Princeton
7. Kentucky
8. Michigan St.
9. Michigan
10. Clemson
11. Washington
12. Wyoming
13. Illinois
14. Ohio St.
15. Miami (Fla.)
16. Alabama
17. Nebraska
18. Wash. & Lee
19. Tulsa
20. Tulane

1951
Team
1. Tennessee
2. Michigan St.
3. Maryland
4. Illinois
5. Georgia Tech
6. Princeton
7. Stanford
8. Wisconsin
9. Baylor
10. Oklahoma
11. Texas Christian
12. California
13. Virginia
14. San Francisco
15. Kentucky
16. Boston U.
17. UCLA
18. Washington St.
19. Holy Cross
20. Clemson

1952
Team
1. Michigan St.
2. Georgia Tech
3. Notre Dame
4. Oklahoma
5. Southern Cal
6. UCLA
7. Mississippi
8. Tennessee
9. Alabama
10. Texas
11. Wisconsin
12. Tulsa
13. Maryland
14. Syracuse
15. Florida
16. Duke
17. Ohio St.
18. Purdue
19. Princeton
20. Kentucky

1953
Team
1. Maryland
2. Notre Dame
3. Michigan St.
4. Oklahoma
5. UCLA
6. Rice
7. Illinois
8. Georgia Tech
9. Iowa
10. West Va.
11. Texas
12. Texas Tech
13. Alabama
14. Army
15. Wisconsin
16. Kentucky
17. Auburn
18. Duke
19. Stanford
20. Michigan

1954
Team
1. Ohio St.
2. UCLA
3. Oklahoma
4. Notre Dame
5. Navy
6. Mississippi
7. Army
8. Maryland
9. Wisconsin
10. Arkansas
11. Miami (Fla.)
12. West Va.
13. Auburn
14. Duke
15. Michigan
16. Virginia Tech
17. Southern Cal
18. Baylor
19. Rice
20. Penn St.

1955
Team
1. Oklahoma
2. Michigan St.
3. Maryland
4. UCLA
5. Ohio St.
6. Texas Christian
7. Georgia Tech
8. Auburn
9. Notre Dame
10. Mississippi
11. Pittsburgh
12. Michigan
13. Southern Cal
14. Miami (Fla.)
15. Miami (Ohio)
16. Stanford
17. Texas A&M
18. Navy
19. West Va.
20. Army

1956
Team
1. Oklahoma
2. Tennessee
3. Iowa
4. Georgia Tech
5. Texas A&M
6. Miami (Fla.)
7. Michigan
8. Syracuse
9. Michigan St.
10. Oregon St.
11. Baylor
12. Minnesota
13. Pittsburgh
14. Texas Christian
15. Ohio St.
16. Navy
17. Geo. Washington
18. Southern Cal
19. Clemson
20. Colorado

1957
Team
1. Auburn
2. Ohio St.
3. Michigan St.
4. Oklahoma
5. Navy
6. Iowa
7. Mississippi
8. Rice
9. Texas A&M
10. Notre Dame
11. Texas
12. Arizona St.
13. Tennessee
14. Mississippi St.
15. North Caro. St.
16. Duke
17. Florida
18. Army
19. Wisconsin
20. Va. Military

1958
Team
1. Louisiana St.
2. Iowa
3. Army
4. Auburn
5. Oklahoma
6. Air Force
7. Wisconsin
8. Ohio St.
9. Syracuse
10. Texas Christian
11. Mississippi
12. Clemson
13. Purdue
14. Florida
15. South Caro.
16. California
17. Notre Dame
18. Southern Methodist
19. Oklahoma St.
20. Rutgers

1959
Team
1. Syracuse
2. Mississippi
3. Louisiana St.
4. Texas
5. Georgia
6. Wisconsin
7. Texas Christian
8. Washington
9. Arkansas
10. Alabama
11. Clemson
12. Penn St.
13. Illinois
14. Southern Cal
15. Oklahoma
16. Wyoming
17. Notre Dame
18. Missouri
19. Florida
20. Pittsburgh

1960
Team
1. Minnesota
2. Mississippi
3. Iowa
4. Navy
5. Missouri
6. Washington
7. Arkansas
8. Ohio St.
9. Alabama
10. Duke
11. Kansas
12. Baylor
13. Auburn
14. Yale
15. Michigan St.
16. Penn St.
17. New Mexico St.
18. Florida
19. Syracuse
    Purdue

1961
Team
1. Alabama
2. Ohio St.
3. Texas
4. Louisiana St.
5. Mississippi
6. Minnesota
7. Colorado
8. Michigan St.
9. Arkansas
10. Utah St.
11. Missouri
12. Purdue
13. Georgia Tech
14. Syracuse
15. Rutgers
16. UCLA
17. Rice
    Penn St.
    Arizona
20. Duke

1962
Team
1. Southern Cal
2. Wisconsin
3. Mississippi
4. Texas
5. Alabama
6. Arkansas
7. Louisiana St.
8. Oklahoma
9. Penn St.
10. Minnesota
    Only 10
    ranked

1963
Team
1. Texas
2. Navy
3. Illinois
4. Pittsburgh
5. Auburn
6. Nebraska
7. Mississippi
8. Alabama
9. Oklahoma
10. Michigan St.
    Only 10
    ranked

1964
Team
1. Alabama
2. Arkansas
3. Notre Dame
4. Michigan
5. Texas
6. Nebraska
7. Louisiana St.
8. Oregon St.
9. Ohio St.
10. Southern Cal
    Only 10
    ranked

1965
Team
1. Alabama
2. Michigan St.
3. Arkansas
4. UCLA
5. Nebraska
6. Missouri
7. Tennessee
8. Louisiana St.
9. Notre Dame
10. Southern Cal
    Only 10
    ranked

1966
Team
1. Notre Dame
2. Michigan St.
3. Alabama
4. Georgia
5. UCLA
6. Nebraska
7. Purdue
8. Georgia Tech
9. Miami (Fla.)
10. Southern Methodist
    Only 10
    ranked

1967
Team
1. Southern Cal 10-1
2. Tennessee
3. Oklahoma
4. Indiana
5. Notre Dame 8-2
6. Wyoming
7. Oregon St.
8. Alabama
9. Purdue
10. Penn St.
    Only 10
    ranked

1968
Team
1. Ohio St. 10-0
2. Penn St.
3. Texas
4. Southern Cal 9-1-1
5. Notre Dame 7-2-1
6. Arkansas
7. Kansas
8. Georgia
9. Missouri
10. Purdue
11. Oklahoma
12. Michigan
13. Tennessee
14. Southern Methodist
15. Oregon St.
16. Auburn
17. Alabama
18. Houston
19. Louisiana St.
20. Ohio

1969
Team
1. Texas
2. Penn St.
3. Southern Cal 10-0-1
4. Ohio St. 8-1
5. Notre Dame 8-2-1
6. Missouri
7. Arkansas
8. Mississippi
9. Michigan
10. Louisiana St.
11. Nebraska
12. Houston
13. UCLA
14. Florida
15. Tennessee
16. Colorado
17. West Va.
18. Purdue
19. Stanford
20. Auburn

1970
Team
1. Nebraska 11-0-1
2. Notre Dame 10-1
3. Texas
4. Tennessee
5. Ohio St. 9-1
6. Arizona St.
7. Louisiana St.
8. Stanford
9. Michigan
10. Auburn
11. Arkansas
12. Toledo
13. Georgia Tech
14. Dartmouth
15. Southern Cal
16. Air Force
17. Tulane
18. Penn St.
19. Houston
20. Oklahoma
    Mississippi

1971
Team
1. Nebraska 13-0
2. Oklahoma
3. Colorado
4. Alabama
5. Penn St.
6. Michigan
7. Georgia
8. Arizona St.
9. Tennessee
10. Stanford
11. Louisiana St.
12. Auburn
13. Notre Dame
14. Toledo
15. Mississippi
16. Arkansas
17. Houston
18. Texas
19. Washington
20. Southern Cal

1972
Team
1. Southern Cal 12-0
2. Oklahoma
3. Texas
4. Nebraska 9-2-1
5. Auburn
6. Michigan
7. Alabama
8. Tennessee
9. Ohio St. 9-2
10. Penn St.
11. Louisiana St.
12. North Caro.
13. Arizona St.
14. Notre Dame
15. UCLA
16. Colorado
17. North Caro. St.
18. Louisville
19. Washington St.
20. Georgia Tech

1973
Team
1. Notre Dame 11-0
2. Ohio St. 10-0-1
3. Oklahoma
4. Alabama
5. Penn St.
6. Michigan
7. Nebraska 9-2-1
8. Southern Cal 9-2-1
9. Arizona St.
   Houston
11. Texas Tech
12. UCLA
13. Louisiana St.
14. Texas
15. Miami (Ohio)
16. North Caro. St.
17. Missouri
18. Kansas
19. Tennessee
20. Maryland
    Tulane

1974
Team
1. Oklahoma
2. Southern Cal 10-1-1
3. Michigan
4. Ohio St. 10-2
5. Alabama
6. Notre Dame 10-2
7. Penn St.
8. Auburn
9. Nebraska 9-3
10. Miami (Ohio)
11. North Caro. St.
12. Michigan St.
13. Maryland
14. Baylor
15. Florida
16. Texas A&M
17. Mississippi St.
    Texas
19. Houston
20. Tennessee

1975
Team
1. Oklahoma
2. Arizona St.
3. Alabama
4. Ohio St. 11-1
5. UCLA
6. Texas
7. Arkansas
8. Michigan
9. Nebraska 10-2
10. Penn St.
11. Texas A&M
12. Miami (Ohio)
13. Maryland
14. California
15. Pittsburgh
16. Colorado
17. Southern Cal
18. Arizona
19. Georgia
20. West Va.

1976
Team
1. Pittsburgh
2. Southern Cal 11-1
3. Michigan
4. Houston
5. Oklahoma
6. Ohio St. 9-2-1
7. Texas A&M
8. Maryland
9. Nebraska 9-3
10. Georgia
11. Alabama
12. Notre Dame
13. Texas Tech
14. Oklahoma St.
15. UCLA
16. Colorado
17. Rutgers
18. Kentucky
19. Iowa St.
20. Mississippi St.

1977
Team
1. Notre Dame 11-1
2. Alabama
3. Arkansas
4. Texas
5. Penn St.
6. Kentucky
7. Oklahoma
8. Pittsburgh
9. Michigan
10. Washington
11. Ohio St.
12. Nebraska
13. Southern Cal
14. Florida St.
15. Stanford
16. San Diego St.
17. North Caro.
18. Arizona St.
19. Clemson
20. Brigham Young

1978
Team
1. Alabama
2. Southern Cal 12-1
3. Oklahoma
4. Penn St.
5. Michigan
6. Clemson
7. Notre Dame 9-3
8. Nebraska 9-3
9. Texas
10. Houston
11. Arkansas
12. Michigan St.
13. Purdue
14. UCLA
15. Missouri
16. Georgia
17. Stanford
18. North Caro. St.
19. Texas A&M
20. Maryland

1979
Team
1. Alabama
2. Southern Cal 11-0-1
3. Oklahoma
4. Ohio St. 11-1
5. Houston
6. Florida St.
7. Pittsburgh
8. Arkansas
9. Nebraska 10-2
10. Purdue
11. Washington
12. Texas
13. Brigham Young
14. Baylor
15. North Caro.
16. Auburn
17. Temple
18. Michigan
19. Indiana
20. Penn St.

1980
Team
1. Georgia
2. Pittsburgh
3. Oklahoma
4. Michigan
5. Florida St.
6. Alabama
7. Nebraska
8. Penn St.
9. Notre Dame
10. North Caro.
11. Southern Cal
12. Brigham Young
13. UCLA
14. Baylor
15. Ohio St.
16. Washington
17. Purdue
18. Miami (Fla.)
19. Mississippi St.
20. Southern Methodist

1981
Team
1. Clemson
2. Texas
3. Penn St.
4. Pittsburgh
5. Southern Methodist
6. Georgia
7. Alabama
8. Miami (Fla.)
9. North Caro.
10. Washington
11. Nebraska
12. Michigan
13. Brigham Young
14. Southern Cal
15. Ohio St.
16. Arizona St.
17. West Va.
18. Iowa
19. Missouri
20. Oklahoma

1982
Team
1. Penn St.
2. Southern Methodist
3. Nebraska
4. Georgia
5. UCLA
6. Arizona St.
7. Washington
8. Clemson
9. Arkansas
10. Pittsburgh
11. Louisiana St.
12. Ohio St.
13. Florida St.
14. Auburn
15. Southern Cal
16. Oklahoma
17. Texas
18. North Caro.
19. West Va.
20. Maryland

1983
Team
1. Miami (Fla.)
2. Nebraska
3. Auburn
4. Georgia
5. Texas
6. Florida
7. Brigham Young
8. Michigan
9. Ohio St.
10. Illinois
11. Clemson
12. Southern Methodist
13. Air Force
14. Iowa
15. Alabama
16. West Va.
17. UCLA
18. Pittsburgh
19. Boston College
20. East Caro.

1984 Team	1985 Team	1986 Team	1987 Team
1. Brigham Young	1. Oklahoma	1. Penn St.	1. Miami (Fla.)
2. Washington	2. Michigan	2. Miami (Fla.)	2. Florida St.
3. Florida	3. Penn St.	3. Oklahoma	3. Oklahoma
4. Nebraska	4. Tennessee	4. Arizona St.	4. Syracuse
5. Boston College	5. Florida	5. Nebraska	5. Louisiana St.
6. Oklahoma	6. Texas A&M	6. Auburn	6. Nebraska
7. Oklahoma St.	7. UCLA	7. Ohio St.	7. Auburn
8. Southern Methodist	8. Air Force	8. Michigan	8. Michigan St.
9. UCLA	9. Miami (Fla.)	9. Alabama	9. UCLA
10. Southern Cal	10. Iowa	10. Louisiana St.	10. Texas A&M
11. South Caro.	11. Nebraska	11. Arizona	11. Oklahoma St.
12. Maryland	12. Arkansas	12. Baylor	12. Clemson
13. Ohio St.	13. Alabama	13. Texas A&M	13. Georgia
14. Auburn	14. Ohio St.	14. UCLA	14. Tennessee
15. Louisiana St.	15. Florida St.	15. Arkansas	15. South Caro.
16. Iowa	16. Brigham Young	16. Iowa	16. Iowa
17. Florida St.	17. Baylor	17. Clemson	17. Notre Dame
18. Miami (Fla.)	18. Maryland	18. Washington	18. Southern Cal
19. Kentucky	19. Georgia Tech	19. Boston College	19. Michigan
20. Virginia	20. Louisiana St.	20. Virginia Tech	20. Arizona St.

1988 Team	†1989 Team	1990 Team	1991 Team
1. Notre Dame	1. Miami (Fla.)	1. Colorado	1. Miami (Fla.)
2. Miami (Fla.)	2. Notre Dame	2. Georgia Tech	2. Washington
3. Florida St.	3. Florida St.	3. Miami (Fla.)	3. Penn St.
4. Michigan	4. Colorado	4. Florida St.	4. Florida St.
5. West Va.	5. Tennessee	5. Washington	5. Alabama
6. UCLA	6. Auburn	6. Notre Dame	6. Michigan
7. Southern Cal	7. Michigan	7. Michigan	7. Florida
8. Auburn	8. Southern Cal	8. Tennessee	8. California
9. Clemson	9. Alabama	9. Clemson	9. East Caro.
10. Nebraska	10. Illinois	10. Houston	10. Iowa
11. Oklahoma St.	11. Nebraska	11. Penn St.	11. Syracuse
12. Arkansas	12. Clemson	12. Texas	12. Texas A&M
13. Syracuse	13. Arkansas	13. Florida	13. Notre Dame
14. Oklahoma	14. Houston	14. Louisville	14. Tennessee
15. Georgia	15. Penn St.	15. Texas A&M	15. Nebraska
16. Washington St.	16. Michigan St.	16. Michigan St.	16. Oklahoma
17. Alabama	17. Pittsburgh	17. Oklahoma	17. Georgia
18. Houston	18. Virginia	18. Iowa	18. Clemson
19. Louisiana St.	19. Texas Tech	19. Auburn	19. UCLA
20. Indiana	20. Texas A&M	20. Southern Cal	20. Colorado
	21. West Va.	21. Mississippi	21. Tulsa
	22. Brigham Young	22. Brigham Young	22. Stanford
	23. Washington	23. Virginia	23. Brigham Young
	24. Ohio St.	24. Nebraska	24. North Caro. St.
	25. Arizona	25. Illinois	25. Air Force

On January 6, 1948, in a special postseason poll after the Rose Bowl, the Associated Press voted Michigan No. 1 and Notre Dame No. 2. However, the postseason poll did not supersede the final regular-season poll of December 6, 1947. †*Beginning in 1989 season, AP selected top 25 teams instead of 20.*

ASSOCIATED PRESS
WEEKLY LEADERS

The weekly dates are for Tuesday, the most frequent release date of the poll, except when the final poll was taken after January 1-2 bowl games. A team's record includes its last game before the weekly poll. A new weekly leader's rank the previous week is indicated in parentheses after its record. Final poll leaders (annual champions) are in bold face. (Note: Only 10 teams were ranked in the weekly polls during 1962, 1963, 1964, 1965, 1966 and 1967; 20 were ranked in all other seasons until 1989, when 25 were ranked.)

Date	1936		
10-20	Minnesota	(3-0)	
10-27	Minnesota	(4-0)	
11-3	Northwestern	(5-0) (3)	
11-10	Northwestern	(6-0)	
11-17	Northwestern	(7-0)	
11-24	Minnesota	(7-1) (2)	
12-1	**Minnesota**	**(7-1)**	
	1937		
10-20	California	(5-0)	
10-27	California	(6-0)	
11-2	California	(7-0)	
11-9	Pittsburgh	(6-0-1) (3)	
11-16	Pittsburgh	(7-0-1)	
11-23	Pittsburgh	(8-0-1)	
11-30	**Pittsburgh**	**(9-0-1)**	
	1938		
10-18	Pittsburgh	(4-0)	
10-25	Pittsburgh	(5-0)	
11-1	Pittsburgh	(6-0)	
11-8	Texas Christian	(7-0) (2)	
11-15	Notre Dame	(7-0) (2)	
11-22	Notre Dame	(8-0)	
11-29	Notre Dame	(8-0)	
12-6	**Texas Christian**	**(10-0) (2)**	
	1939		
10-17	Pittsburgh	(3-0)	
10-24	Tennessee	(4-0) (5)	
10-31	Tennessee	(5-0)	
11-7	Tennessee	(6-0)	
11-14	Tennessee	(7-0)	
11-21	Texas A&M	(9-0) (2)	
11-28 (tie)	Texas A&M	(9-0)	
(tie)	Southern Cal	(6-0-1) (4)	
12-5	Texas A&M	(10-0)	
12-12	**Texas A&M**	**(10-0)**	
	1940		
10-15	Cornell	(2-0)	
10-22	Cornell	(3-0)	
10-29	Cornell	(4-0)	
11-5	Cornell	(5-0)	
11-12	Minnesota	(6-0) (2)	
11-19	Minnesota	(7-0)	
11-26	Minnesota	(8-0)	
12-3	**Minnesota**	**(8-0)**	
	1941		
10-14	Minnesota	(2-0)	
10-21	Minnesota	(3-0)	
10-28 (tie)	Minnesota	(4-0)	
(tie)	Texas	(5-0) (2)	
11-4	Texas	(6-0)	
11-11	Minnesota	(6-0) (2)	
11-18	Minnesota	(7-0)	
11-25	Minnesota	(8-0)	
12-2	**Minnesota**	**(8-0)**	
	1942		
10-13	Ohio St.	(3-0)	
10-20	Ohio St.	(4-0)	
10-27	Ohio St.	(5-0)	
11-3	Georgia	(7-0) (2)	
11-10	Georgia	(8-0)	
11-17	Georgia	(9-0)	
11-24	Boston College	(8-0) (3)	
12-1	**Ohio St.**	**(9-1-0) (3)**	
	1943		
10-5	Notre Dame	(2-0)	
10-12	Notre Dame	(3-0)	
10-19	Notre Dame	(4-0)	
10-26	Notre Dame	(5-0)	
11-2	Notre Dame	(6-0)	
11-9	Notre Dame	(7-0)	
11-16	Notre Dame	(8-0)	
11-23	Notre Dame	(9-0)	
11-30	**Notre Dame**	**(9-1-0)**	

	1944		
10-10	Notre Dame	(2-0)	
10-17	Notre Dame	(3-0)	
10-24	Notre Dame	(4-0)	
10-31	Army	(5-0) (2)	
11-7	Army	(6-0)	
11-14	Army	(7-0)	
11-21	Army	(8-0)	
11-28	Army	(8-0)	
12-5	**Army**	**(9-0)**	
	1945		
10-9	Army	(2-0-0)	
10-16	Army	(3-0-0)	
10-23	Army	(4-0-0)	
10-30	Army	(5-0-0)	
11-6	Army	(6-0-0)	
11-13	Army	(7-0-0)	
11-20	Army	(8-0-0)	
11-27	Army	(8-0-0)	
12-4	**Army**	**(9-0-0)**	
	1946		
10-8	Texas	(3-0-0)	
10-15	Army	(4-0-0) (2)	
10-22	Army	(5-0-0)	
10-29	Army	(6-0-0)	
11-5	Army	(7-0-0)	
11-12	Army	(7-0-1)	
11-19	Army	(8-0-1)	
11-26	Army	(8-0-1)	
12-3	**Notre Dame**	**(8-0-1) (2)**	
	1947*		
10-7	Notre Dame	(1-0-0)	
10-14	Michigan	(3-0-0) (2)	
10-21	Michigan	(4-0-0)	
10-28	Notre Dame	(4-0-0) (2)	
11-4	Notre Dame	(5-0-0)	
11-11	Notre Dame	(6-0-0)	
11-18	Michigan	(8-0-0) (2)	
11-25	Notre Dame	(8-0-0) (2)	
12-2	Notre Dame	(8-0-0)	
12-9	**Notre Dame**	**(9-0-0)**	
	1948		
10-5	Notre Dame	(2-0-0)	
10-12	North Caro.	(3-0-0) (2)	
10-19	Michigan	(4-0-0) (4)	
10-26	Michigan	(5-0-0)	
11-2	Notre Dame	(6-0-0) (2)	
11-9	Michigan	(7-0-0) (2)	
11-16	Michigan	(8-0-0)	
11-23	Michigan	(9-0-0)	
11-30	**Michigan**	**(9-0-0)**	
	1949		
10-4	Michigan	(2-0-0)	
10-11	Notre Dame	(3-0-0) (2)	
10-18	Notre Dame	(4-0-0)	
10-25	Notre Dame	(4-0-0)	
11-1	Notre Dame	(5-0-0)	
11-8	Notre Dame	(6-0-0)	
11-15	Notre Dame	(7-0-0)	
11-22	Notre Dame	(8-0-0)	
11-29	**Notre Dame**	**(9-0-0)**	
	1950		
10-3	Notre Dame	(1-0-0)	
10-10	Army	(2-0-0) (4)	
10-17	Army	(3-0-0)	
10-24	Southern Methodist	(5-0-0) (3)	
10-31	Southern Methodist	(5-0-0)	
11-7	Army	(6-0-0) (2)	
11-14	Ohio St.	(6-1-0) (2)	
11-21	Oklahoma	(8-0-0) (2)	
11-28	**Oklahoma**	**(9-0-0)**	

	1951	
10-2	Michigan St.	(2-0-0)
10-9	Michigan St.	(3-0-0)
10-16	California	(4-0-0) (2)
10-23	Tennessee	(4-0-0) (2)
10-30	Tennessee	(5-0-0)
11-6	Tennessee	(6-0-0)
11-13	Michigan St.	(7-0-0)(5)
11-20	Tennessee	(8-0-0) (2)
11-27	Tennessee	(9-0-0)
12-4	**Tennessee**	**(10-0-0)**

	1952	
9-30	Michigan St.	(1-0-0)
10-7	Wisconsin	(2-0-0) (8)
10-14	Michigan St.	(3-0-0)(2)
10-21	Michigan St.	(4-0-0)
10-28	Michigan St.	(5-0-0)
11-4	Michigan St.	(6-0-0)
11-11	Michigan St.	(7-0-0)
11-18	Michigan St.	(8-0-0)
11-25	Michigan St.	(9-0-0)
12-1	**Michigan St.**	**(9-0-0)**

	1953	
9-29	Notre Dame	(1-0-0)
10-6	Notre Dame	(2-0-0)
10-13	Notre Dame	(2-0-0)
10-20	Notre Dame	(3-0-0)
10-27	Notre Dame	(4-0-0)
11-3	Notre Dame	(5-0-0)
11-10	Notre Dame	(6-0-0)
11-17	Notre Dame	(7-0-0)
11-24	Maryland	(10-0-0) (2)
12-1	**Maryland**	**(10-0-0)**

	1954	
9-21	Oklahoma	(1-0-0)
9-28	Notre Dame	(1-0-0) (2)
10-5	Oklahoma	(2-0-0) (2)
10-12	Oklahoma	(3-0-0)
10-19	Oklahoma	(4-0-0)
10-26	Ohio St.	(5-0-0) (4)
11-2	UCLA	(7-0-0) (3)
11-9	UCLA	(8-0-0)
11-16	Ohio St.	(8-0-0) (2)
11-23	Ohio St.	(9-0-0)
11-30	**Ohio St.**	**(9-0-0)**

	1955	
9-20	UCLA	(1-0-0)
9-27	Maryland	(2-0-0) (5)
10-4	Maryland	(3-0-0)
10-11	Michigan	(3-0-0) (2)
10-18	Michigan	(4-0-0)
10-25	Maryland	(6-0-0) (2)
11-1	Maryland	(7-0-0)
11-8	Oklahoma	(7-0-0) (2)
11-15	Oklahoma	(8-0-0)
11-22	Oklahoma	(9-0-0)
11-29	**Oklahoma**	**(10-0-0)**

	1956	
9-25	Oklahoma	(0-0-0)
10-2	Oklahoma	(1-0-0)
10-9	Oklahoma	(2-0-0)
10-16	Oklahoma	(3-0-0)
10-23	Michigan St.	(4-0-0) (2)
10-30	Oklahoma	(5-0-0)
11-6	Oklahoma	(6-0-0)
11-13	Tennessee	(7-0-0) (3)
11-20	Oklahoma	(8-0-0) (2)
11-27	Oklahoma	(9-0-0)
12-4	**Oklahoma**	**(10-0-0)**

	1957	
9-24	Oklahoma	(1-0-0)
10-1	Oklahoma	(1-0-0)
10-8	Oklahoma	(2-0-0)
10-15	Michigan St.	(3-0-0) (2)
10-22	Oklahoma	(4-0-0) (2)
10-29	Texas A&M	(6-0-0) (2)
11-5	Texas A&M	(7-0-0)
11-12	Texas A&M	(8-0-0)
11-19	Michigan St.	(7-1-0)(4)
11-26	Auburn	(9-0-0) (2)
12-3	**Auburn**	**(10-0-0)**

	1958	
9-23	Ohio St.	(0-0-0)
9-30	Oklahoma	(1-0-0) (2)
10-7	Auburn	(2-0-0) (2)
10-14	Army	(3-0-0) (3)
10-21	Army	(4-0-0)
10-28	Louisiana St.	(6-0-0) (3)
11-4	Louisiana St.	(7-0-0)
11-11	Louisiana St.	(8-0-0)
11-18	Louisiana St.	(9-0-0)
11-25	Louisiana St.	(10-0-0)
12-2	**Louisiana St.**	**(10-0-0)**

	1959	
9-22	Louisiana St.	(1-0-0)
9-29	Louisiana St.	(2-0-0)
10-6	Louisiana St.	(3-0-0)
10-13	Louisiana St.	(4-0-0)
10-20	Louisiana St.	(5-0-0)
10-27	Louisiana St.	(6-0-0)
11-3	Louisiana St.	(7-0-0)
11-10	Syracuse	(7-0-0) (4)
11-17	Syracuse	(8-0-0)
11-24	Syracuse	(9-0-0)
12-1	Syracuse	(9-0-0)
12-8	**Syracuse**	**(10-0-0)**

	1960	
9-20	Mississippi	(1-0-0)
9-27	Mississippi	(2-0-0)
10-4	Syracuse	(2-0-0) (2)
10-11	Mississippi	(4-0-0) (2)
10-18	Iowa	(4-0-0) (2)
10-25	Iowa	(5-0-0)
11-1	Iowa	(6-0-0)
11-8	Minnesota	(7-0-0) (3)
11-15	Missouri	(9-0-0) (2)
11-22	Minnesota	(8-1-0) (4)
11-29	**Minnesota**	**(8-1-0)**

	1961	
9-26	Iowa	(0-0-0)
10-3	Iowa	(1-0-0)
10-10	Mississippi	(3-0-0) (2)
10-17	Michigan St.	(3-0-0) (5)
10-24	Michigan St.	(4-0-0)
10-31	Michigan St.	(5-0-0)
11-7	Texas	(7-0-0) (3)
11-14	Texas	(8-0-0)
11-21	Alabama	(9-0-0) (2)
11-28	Alabama	(9-0-0)
12-5	**Alabama**	**(10-0-0)**

	1962	
9-25	Alabama	(1-0-0)
10-2	Ohio St.	(1-0-0) (2)
10-9	Alabama	(3-0-0) (2)
10-16	Texas	(4-0-0) (2)
10-23	Texas	(5-0-0)
10-30	Northwestern	(5-0-0) (3)
11-6	Northwestern	(6-0-0)
11-13	Alabama	(8-0-0) (3)
11-20	Southern Cal	(8-0-0) (2)
11-27	Southern Cal	(9-0-0)
12-4	**Southern Cal**	**(10-0-0)**

1963

9-24	Southern Cal	(1-0-0)
10-1	Oklahoma	(1-0-0) (3)
10-8	Oklahoma	(2-0-0)
10-15	Texas	(4-0-0) (3)
10-22	Texas	(5-0-0)
10-29	Texas	(6-0-0)
11-5	Texas	(7-0-0)
11-12	Texas	(8-0-0)
11-19	Texas	(9-0-0)
11-26	Texas	(9-0-0)
12-3	Texas	(10-0-0)
12-10	**Texas**	**(10-0-0)**

1964

9-29	Texas	(2-0-0)
10-6	Texas	(3-0-0)
10-13	Texas	(4-0-0)
10-20	Ohio St.	(4-0-0)(2)
10-27	Ohio St.	(5-0-0)
11-3	Notre Dame	(6-0-0)(2)
11-10	Notre Dame	(7-0-0)
11-17	Notre Dame	(8-0-0)
11-24	Notre Dame	(9-0-0)
12-1	**Alabama**	**(10-0-0) (2)**

1965

9-21	Notre Dame	(1-0-0)
9-28	Texas	(2-0-0) (3)
10-5	Texas	(3-0-0)
10-12	Texas	(4-0-0)
10-19	Arkansas	(5-0-0) (3)
10-26	Michigan St.	(6-0-0) (2)
11-2	Michigan St.	(7-0-0)
11-9	Michigan St.	(8-0-0)
11-16	Michigan St.	(9-0-0)
11-23	Michigan St.	(10-0-0)
11-30	Michigan St.	(10-0-0)
1-4	**Alabama**	**(9-1-1) (4)**

1966

9-20	Michigan St.	(1-0-0)
9-27	Michigan St.	(2-0-0)
10-4	Michigan St.	(3-0-0)
10-11	Michigan St.	(4-0-0)
10-18	Notre Dame	(4-0-0) (2)
10-25	Notre Dame	(5-0-0)
11-1	Notre Dame	(6-0-0)
11-8	Notre Dame	(7-0-0)
11-15	Notre Dame	(8-0-0)
11-22	Notre Dame	(8-0-1)
11-29	Notre Dame	(9-0-1)
12-5	**Notre Dame**	**(9-0-1)**

1967

9-19	Notre Dame	(0-0-0)
9-26	Notre Dame	(1-0-0)
10-3	Southern Cal	(3-0-0) (2)
10-10	Southern Cal	(4-0-0)
10-17	Southern Cal	(5-0-0)
10-24	Southern Cal	(6-0-0)
10-31	Southern Cal	(7-0-0)
11-7	Southern Cal	(8-0-0)
11-14	UCLA	(7-0-1) (2)
11-21	Southern Cal	(9-1-0) (4)
11-28	**Southern Cal**	**(9-1-0)**

1968

9-17	Purdue	(0-0-0)
9-24	Purdue	(1-0-0)
10-1	Purdue	(2-0-0)
10-8	Purdue	(3-0-0)
10-15	Southern Cal	(4-0-0) (2)
10-22	Southern Cal	(5-0-0)
10-29	Southern Cal	(5-0-0)
11-5	Southern Cal	(6-0-0)
11-12	Southern Cal	(7-0-0)
11-19	Southern Cal	(8-0-0)
11-26	Ohio St.	(9-0-0) (2)
12-2	Ohio St.	(9-0-0)
12-9	**Ohio St.**	**(10-0-0)**

1969

9-23	Ohio St.	(0-0-0)
9-30	Ohio St.	(1-0-0)
10-7	Ohio St.	(2-0-0)
10-14	Ohio St.	(3-0-0)
10-21	Ohio St.	(4-0-0)
10-28	Ohio St.	(5-0-0)
11-4	Ohio St.	(6-0-0)
11-11	Ohio St.	(7-0-0)
11-18	Ohio St.	(8-0-0)
11-25	Texas	(8-0-0) (2)
12-2	Texas	(9-0-0)
12-9	Texas	(10-0-0)
1-4	**Texas**	**(11-0-0)**

1970

9-15	Ohio St.	(0-0-0)
9-22	Ohio St.	(0-0-0)
9-29	Ohio St.	(1-0-0)
10-6	Ohio St.	(2-0-0)
10-13	Ohio St.	(3-0-0)
10-20	Ohio St.	(4-0-0)
10-27	Texas	(5-0-0) (2)
11-3	Texas	(6-0-0)
11-10	Texas	(7-0-0)
11-17	Texas	(8-0-0)
11-24	Texas	(8-0-0)
12-1	Texas	(9-0-0)
12-8	Texas	(10-0-0)
1-6	**Nebraska**	**(11-0-1) (3)**

1971

9-14	Nebraska	(1-0-0)
9-21	Nebraska	(2-0-0)
9-28	Nebraska	(3-0-0)
10-5	Nebraska	(4-0-0)
10-12	Nebraska	(5-0-0)
10-19	Nebraska	(6-0-0)
10-26	Nebraska	(7-0-0)
11-2	Nebraska	(8-0-0)
11-9	Nebraska	(9-0-0)
11-16	Nebraska	(10-0-0)
11-23	Nebraska	(10-0-0)
11-30	Nebraska	(11-0-0)
12-7	Nebraska	(12-0-0)
1-4	**Nebraska**	**(13-0-0)**

1972

9-12	Southern Cal	(1-0-0)
9-19	Southern Cal	(2-0-0)
9-26	Southern Cal	(3-0-0)
10-3	Southern Cal	(4-0-0)
10-10	Southern Cal	(5-0-0)
10-17	Southern Cal	(6-0-0)
10-24	Southern Cal	(7-0-0)
10-31	Southern Cal	(8-0-0)
11-7	Southern Cal	(9-0-0)
11-14	Southern Cal	(9-0-0)
11-21	Southern Cal	(10-0-0)
11-28	Southern Cal	(10-0-0)
12-5	Southern Cal	(11-0-0)
1-3	**Southern Cal**	**(12-0-0)**

1973

9-11	Southern Cal	(0-0-0)
9-18	Southern Cal	(1-0-0)
9-25	Southern Cal	(2-0-0)
10-2	Ohio St.	(2-0-0) (3)
10-9	Ohio St.	(3-0-0)
10-16	Ohio St.	(4-0-0)
10-23	Ohio St.	(5-0-0)
10-30	Ohio St.	(6-0-0)
11-6	Ohio St.	(7-0-0)
11-13	Ohio St.	(8-0-0)
11-20	Ohio St.	(9-0-0)
11-27	Alabama	(10-0-0) (2)
12-4	Alabama	(11-0-0)
1-3	**Notre Dame**	**(11-0-0)(3)**

1974

9-10	Oklahoma	(0-0-0)
9-17	Notre Dame	(1-0-0) (2)
9-24	Ohio St.	(2-0-0) (2)
10-1	Ohio St.	(3-0-0)
10-8	Ohio St.	(4-0-0)
10-15	Ohio St.	(5-0-0)
10-22	Ohio St.	(6-0-0)
10-29	Ohio St.	(7-0-0)
11-5	Ohio St.	(8-0-0)
11-12	Oklahoma	(8-0-0) (2)
11-19	Oklahoma	(9-0-0)
11-26	Oklahoma	(10-0-0)
12-3	Oklahoma	(11-0-0)
1-3	**Oklahoma**	**(11-0-0)**

1975

9-9	Oklahoma	(0-0-0)
9-16	Oklahoma	(1-0-0)
9-23	Oklahoma	(2-0-0)
9-30	Oklahoma	(3-0-0)
10-7	Ohio St.	(4-0-0) (2)
10-14	Ohio St.	(5-0-0)
10-21	Ohio St.	(6-0-0)
10-28	Ohio St.	(7-0-0)
11-4	Ohio St.	(8-0-0)
11-11	Ohio St.	(9-0-0)
11-18	Ohio St.	(10-0-0)
11-25	Ohio St.	(11-0-0)
12-2	Ohio St.	(11-0-0)
1-3	**Oklahoma**	**(11-1-0) (3)**

1976

9-14	Michigan	(1-0-0)
9-21	Michigan	(2-0-0)
9-28	Michigan	(3-0-0)
10-5	Michigan	(4-0-0)
10-12	Michigan	(5-0-0)
10-19	Michigan	(6-0-0)
10-26	Michigan	(7-0-0)
11-2	Michigan	(8-0-0)
11-9	Pittsburgh	(9-0-0) (2)
11-16	Pittsburgh	(10-0-0)
11-23	Pittsburgh	(10-0-0)
11-30	Pittsburgh	(11-0-0)
1-5	**Pittsburgh**	**(12-0-0)**

1977

9-13	Michigan	(1-0-0)
9-20	Michigan	(2-0-0)
9-27	Oklahoma	(3-0-0) (3)
10-4	Southern Cal	(4-0-0) (2)
10-11	Michigan	(5-0-0) (3)
10-18	Michigan	(6-0-0)
10-25	Texas	(6-0-0) (2)
11-1	Texas	(7-0-0)
11-8	Texas	(8-0-0)
11-15	Texas	(9-0-0)
11-22	Texas	(10-0-0)
11-29	Texas	(11-0-0)
1-4	**Notre Dame**	**(11-1-0) (5)**

1978

9-12	Alabama	(1-0-0)
9-19	Alabama	(2-0-0)
9-26	Oklahoma	(3-0-0) (tie 3)
10-3	Oklahoma	(4-0-0)
10-10	Oklahoma	(5-0-0)
10-17	Oklahoma	(6-0-0)
10-24	Oklahoma	(7-0-0)
10-31	Oklahoma	(8-0-0)
11-7	Oklahoma	(9-0-0)
11-14	Penn St.	(10-0-0) (2)
11-21	Penn St.	(10-0-0)
11-28	Penn St.	(11-0-0)
12-5	Penn St.	(11-0-0)
1-4	**Alabama**	**(11-1-0) (2)**

1979

9-11	Southern Cal	(1-0-0)
9-18	Southern Cal	(2-0-0)
9-25	Southern Cal	(3-0-0)
10-2	Southern Cal	(4-0-0)
10-9	Southern Cal	(5-0-0)
10-16	Alabama	(5-0-0) (2)
10-23	Alabama	(6-0-0)
10-30	Alabama	(7-0-0)
11-6	Alabama	(8-0-0)
11-13	Alabama	(9-0-0)
11-20	Alabama	(10-0-0)
11-27	Alabama	(10-0-0)
12-4	Ohio St.	(11-0-0) (3)
1-3	**Alabama**	**(12-0-0) (2)**

1980

9-9	Ohio St.	(0-0-0)
9-16	Alabama	(1-0-0) (2)
9-23	Alabama	(2-0-0)
9-30	Alabama	(3-0-0)
10-7	Alabama	(4-0-0)
10-14	Alabama	(5-0-0)
10-21	Alabama	(6-0-0)
10-28	Alabama	(7-0-0)
11-4	Notre Dame	(7-0-0) (3)
11-11	Georgia	(9-0-0) (2)
11-18	Georgia	(10-0-0)
11-25	Georgia	(10-0-0)
12-2	Georgia	(11-0-0)
12-9	Georgia	(11-0-0)
1-4	**Georgia**	**(12-0-0)**

1981

9-8	Michigan	(0-0-0)
9-15	Notre Dame	(1-0-0) (4)
9-22	Southern Cal	(2-0-0) (2)
9-29	Southern Cal	(3-0-0)
10-6	Southern Cal	(4-0-0)
10-13	Texas	(4-0-0) (3)
10-20	Penn St.	(5-0-0) (2)
10-27	Penn St.	(6-0-0)
11-3	Pittsburgh	(7-0-0) (2)
11-10	Pittsburgh	(8-0-0)
11-17	Pittsburgh	(9-0-0)
11-24	Pittsburgh	(10-0-0)
12-1	Clemson	(11-0-0) (2)
1-3	**Clemson**	**(12-0-0)**

1982

9-7	Pittsburgh	(0-0-0)
9-14	Washington	(1-0-0) (2)
9-21	Washington	(2-0-0)
9-28	Washington	(3-0-0)
10-5	Washington	(4-0-0)
10-12	Washington	(5-0-0)
10-19	Washington	(6-0-0)
10-26	Pittsburgh	(6-0-0) (2)
11-2	Pittsburgh	(7-0-0)
11-9	Georgia	(9-0-0) (3)
11-16	Georgia	(10-0-0)
11-23	Georgia	(10-0-0)
11-30	Georgia	(11-0-0)
12-7	Georgia	(11-0-0)
1-3	**Penn St.**	**(11-1-0) (2)**

1986

9-9	Oklahoma	(1-0-0)
9-16	Oklahoma	(1-0-0)
9-23	Oklahoma	(2-0-0)
9-30	Miami (Fla.)	(4-0-0) (2)
10-7	Miami (Fla.)	(5-0-0)
10-14	Miami (Fla.)	(6-0-0)
10-21	Miami (Fla.)	(7-0-0)
10-28	Miami (Fla.)	(7-0-0)
11-4	Miami (Fla.)	(8-0-0)
11-11	Miami (Fla.)	(9-0-0)
11-18	Miami (Fla.)	(10-0-0)
11-25	Miami (Fla.)	(10-0-0)
12-2	Miami (Fla.)	(11-0-0)
1-4	**Penn St.**	**(12-0-0) (2)**

1983

9-6	Nebraska	(1-0-0)
9-13	Nebraska	(2-0-0)
9-20	Nebraska	(3-0-0)
9-27	Nebraska	(4-0-0)
10-4	Nebraska	(5-0-0)
10-11	Nebraska	(6-0-0)
10-18	Nebraska	(7-0-0)
10-25	Nebraska	(8-0-0)
11-1	Nebraska	(9-0-0)
11-8	Nebraska	(10-0-0)
11-15	Nebraska	(11-0-0)
11-22	Nebraska	(11-0-0)
11-29	Nebraska	(12-0-0)
12-6	Nebraska	(12-0-0)
1-3	**Miami (Fla.)**	**(11-1-0) (5)**

1987

9-8	Oklahoma	(1-0-0)
9-15	Oklahoma	(2-0-0)
9-22	Oklahoma	(2-0-0)
9-29	Oklahoma	(3-0-0)
10-6	Oklahoma	(4-0-0)
10-13	Oklahoma	(5-0-0)
10-20	Oklahoma	(6-0-0)
10-27	Oklahoma	(7-0-0)
11-3	Oklahoma	(8-0-0)
11-10	Oklahoma	(9-0-0)
11-17	Nebraska	(9-0-0) (2)
11-24	Oklahoma	(11-0-0) (2)
12-1	Oklahoma	(11-0-0)
12-8	Oklahoma	(11-0-0)
1-3	**Miami (Fla.)**	**(12-0-0) (2)**

1984

9-4	Miami (Fla.)	(2-0-0)
9-11	Nebraska	(1-0-0) (2)
9-18	Nebraska	(2-0-0)
9-25	Nebraska	(3-0-0)
10-2	Texas	(2-0-0) (2)
10-9	Texas	(3-0-0)
10-16	Washington	(6-0-0) (2)
10-23	Washington	(7-0-0)
10-30	Washington	(8-0-0)
11-6	Washington	(9-0-0)
11-13	Nebraska	(9-1-0) (2)
11-20	Brigham Young	(11-0-0) (3)
11-27	Brigham Young	(12-0-0)
12-4	Brigham Young	(12-0-0)
1-3	**Brigham Young**	**(13-0-0)**

1988

9-6	Miami (Fla.)	(1-0-0)
9-13	Miami (Fla.)	(1-0-0)
9-20	Miami (Fla.)	(2-0-0)
9-27	Miami (Fla.)	(3-0-0)
10-4	Miami (Fla.)	(4-0-0)
10-11	Miami (Fla.)	(4-0-0)
10-18	UCLA	(6-0-0) (2)
10-25	UCLA	(7-0-0)
11-1	Notre Dame	(8-0-0) (2)
11-8	Notre Dame	(9-0-0)
11-15	Notre Dame	(9-0-0)
11-22	Notre Dame	(10-0-0)
11-29	Notre Dame	(11-0-0)
12-6	Notre Dame	(11-0-0)
1-3	**Notre Dame**	**(12-0-0)**

1985

9-3	Oklahoma	(0-0-0)
9-10	Auburn	(1-0-0) (2)
9-17	Auburn	(2-0-0)
9-24	Auburn	(2-0-0)
10-1	Iowa	(3-0-0) (3)
10-8	Iowa	(4-0-0)
10-15	Iowa	(5-0-0)
10-22	Iowa	(6-0-0)
10-29	Iowa	(7-0-0)
11-5	Florida	(7-0-1)(2)
11-12	Penn St.	(9-0-0) (2)
11-19	Penn St.	(10-0-0)
11-26	Penn St.	(11-0-0)
12-3	Penn St.	(11-0-0)
1-3	**Oklahoma**	**(11-1-0) (4)**

1989

9-5	Notre Dame	(1-0-0)
9-12	Notre Dame	(1-0-0)
9-19	Notre Dame	(2-0-0)
9-26	Notre Dame	(3-0-0)
10-3	Notre Dame	(4-0-0)
10-10	Notre Dame	(5-0-0)
10-17	Notre Dame	(6-0-0)
10-24	Notre Dame	(7-0-0)
10-31	Notre Dame	(8-0-0)
11-7	Notre Dame	(9-0-0)
11-14	Notre Dame	(10-0-0)
11-21	Notre Dame	(11-0-0)
11-28	Colorado	(11-0-0) (2)
12-5	Colorado	(11-0-0)
1-2	**Miami (Fla.)**	**(11-1-0) (2)**

	1990			1991	
9-4	Miami (Fla.)	(0-0-0)	9-3	Florida St.	(1-0-0)
9-11	Notre Dame	(0-0-0) (2)	9-10	Florida St.	(2-0-0)
9-18	Notre Dame	(1-0-0)	9-17	Florida St.	(3-0-0)
9-25	Notre Dame	(2-0-0)	9-23	Florida St.	(3-0-0)
10-2	Notre Dame	(3-0-0)	9-30	Florida St.	(4-0-0)
10-9	Michigan	(3-1-0) (3)	10-7	Florida St.	(5-0-0)
10-16	Virginia	(6-0-0) (2)	10-14	Florida St.	(6-0-0)
10-23	Virginia	(7-0-0)	10-21	Florida St.	(7-0-0)
10-30	Virginia	(7-0-0)	10-28	Florida St.	(8-0-0)
11-6	Notre Dame	(7-1-0) (2)	11-4	Florida St.	(9-0-0)
11-13	Notre Dame	(8-1-0)	11-11	Florida St.	(10-0-0)
11-20	Colorado	(10-1-1) (2)	11-18	Miami (Fla.)	(9-0-0) (2)
11-27	Colorado	(10-1-1)	11-25	Miami (Fla.)	(10-0-0)
12-4	Colorado	(10-1-1)	12-2	Miami (Fla.)	(11-0-0)
1-2	**Colorado**	**(11-1-1)**	**1-2**	**Miami (Fla.)**	**(12-0-0)**

On January 6, 1948, in a special postseason poll after the Rose Bowl, the Associated Press voted Michigan No. 1 and Notre Dame No. 2. However, the postseason poll did not supersede the final regular-season poll of December 6, 1947.

UNITED PRESS INTERNATIONAL/ NATIONAL FOOTBALL FOUNDATION

United Press (UP), 1950-57; United Press International (UPI) from 1958 after merger with International News Service (INS). Coaches' poll until 1991 when it was taken over by USA Today/Cable News Network (CNN) poll.

1950
Team
1. Oklahoma
2. Texas
3. Tennessee
4. California
5. Army
6. Michigan
7. Kentucky
8. Princeton
9. Michigan St.
10. Ohio St.
11. Illinois
12. Clemson
13. Miami (Fla.)
14. Wyoming
15. Washington
　　Baylor
17. Alabama
18. Wash. & Lee
19. Navy
20. Nebraska
　　Wisconsin
　　Cornell

1951
Team
1. Tennessee
2. Michigan St.
3. Illinois
4. Maryland
5. Georgia Tech
6. Princeton
7. Stanford
8. Wisconsin
9. Baylor
10. Texas Christian
11. Oklahoma
12. California
13. Notre Dame
14. San Francisco
　　Purdue
　　Washington St.
17. Holy Cross
　　UCLA
　　Kentucky
20. Kansas

1952
Team
1. Michigan St.
2. Georgia Tech
3. Notre Dame
4. Oklahoma
　　Southern Cal
6. UCLA
7. Mississippi
8. Tennessee
9. Alabama
10. Wisconsin
11. Texas
12. Purdue
13. Maryland
14. Princeton
15. Ohio St.
　　Pittsburgh
17. Navy
18. Duke
19. Houston
　　Kentucky

1953
Team
1. Maryland
2. Notre Dame
3. Michigan St.
4. UCLA
5. Oklahoma
6. Rice
7. Illinois
8. Texas
9. Georgia Tech
10. Iowa
11. Alabama
12. Texas Tech
13. West Va.
14. Wisconsin
15. Kentucky
16. Army
17. Stanford
18. Duke
19. Michigan
20. Ohio St.

1954
Team
1. UCLA
2. Ohio St.
3. Oklahoma
4. Notre Dame
5. Navy
6. Mississippi
7. Army
8. Arkansas
9. Miami (Fla.)
10. Wisconsin
11. Southern Cal
　　Maryland
　　Georgia Tech
14. Duke
15. Michigan
16. Penn St.
17. Southern Methodist
18. Denver
19. Rice
20. Minnesota

1955
Team
1. Oklahoma
2. Michigan St.
3. Maryland
4. UCLA
5. Ohio St.
6. Texas Christian
7. Georgia Tech
8. Auburn
9. Mississippi
10. Notre Dame
11. Pittsburgh
12. Southern Cal
13. Michigan
14. Texas A&M
15. Army
16. Duke
17. West Va.
18. Miami (Fla.)
19. Iowa
20. Navy
　　Stanford
　　Miami (Ohio)

1956
Team
1. Oklahoma
2. Tennessee
3. Iowa
4. Georgia Tech
5. Texas A&M
6. Miami (Fla.)
7. Michigan
8. Syracuse
9. Minnesota
10. Michigan St.
11. Baylor
12. Pittsburgh
13. Oregon St.
14. Texas Christian
15. Southern Cal
16. Wyoming
17. Yale
18. Colorado
19. Navy
20. Duke

1957
Team
1. Ohio St.
2. Auburn
3. Michigan St.
4. Oklahoma
5. Iowa
6. Navy
7. Rice
8. Mississippi
9. Notre Dame
10. Texas A&M
11. Texas
12. Arizona St.
13. Army
14. Duke
　　Wisconsin
16. Tennessee
17. Oregon
18. Clemson
　　UCLA
20. North Caro. St.

1958

Team
1. Louisiana St.
2. Iowa
3. Army
4. Auburn
5. Oklahoma
6. Wisconsin
7. Ohio St.
8. Air Force
9. Texas Christian
10. Syracuse
11. Purdue
12. Mississippi
13. Clemson
14. Notre Dame
15. Florida
16. California
17. Northwestern
18. Southern Methodist

1959

Team
1. Syracuse
2. Mississippi
3. Louisiana St.
4. Texas
5. Georgia
6. Wisconsin
7. Washington
8. Texas Christian
9. Arkansas
10. Penn St.
11. Illinois
12. Southern Cal
13. Alabama
14. Penn St.
15. Oklahoma
16. Northwestern
    Michigan St.
18. Wyoming
19. Auburn
    Missouri

1960

Team
1. Minnesota
2. Iowa
3. Mississippi
4. Missouri
5. Wisconsin
6. Navy
7. Arkansas
8. Ohio St.
9. Kansas
10. Alabama
11. Duke
    Baylor
    Michigan St.
14. Auburn
15. Purdue
16. Florida
17. Texas
18. Yale
19. New Mexico St.
    Tennessee

1961

Team
1. Alabama
2. Ohio St.
3. Louisiana St.
4. Texas
5. Mississippi
6. Minnesota
7. Colorado
8. Arkansas
9. Michigan St.
10. Utah St.
11. Purdue
    Missouri
13. Georgia Tech
14. Duke
15. Kansas
16. Syracuse
17. Wyoming
18. Wisconsin
19. Miami (Fla.)
    Penn St.

1962

Team
1. Southern Cal
2. Wisconsin
3. Mississippi
4. Texas
5. Alabama
6. Arkansas
7. Oklahoma
8. Louisiana St.
9. Penn St.
10. Minnesota
11. Georgia Tech
12. Missouri
13. Ohio St.
14. Duke
    Washington
16. Northwestern
    Oregon St.
18. Arizona St.
    Illinois
    Miami (Fla.)

1963

Team
1. Texas
2. Navy
3. Pittsburgh
4. Illinois
5. Nebraska
6. Auburn
7. Mississippi
8. Oklahoma
9. Alabama
10. Michigan St.
11. Mississippi St.
12. Syracuse
13. Arizona St.
14. Memphis St.
15. Washington
16. Penn St.
    Southern Cal
    Missouri
19. North Caro.
20. Baylor

1964

Team
1. Alabama
2. Arkansas
3. Notre Dame
4. Michigan
5. Texas
6. Nebraska
7. Louisiana St.
8. Oregon St.
9. Ohio St.
10. Southern Cal
11. Florida St.
12. Syracuse
13. Princeton
14. Penn St.
    Utah
16. Illinois
    New Mexico
18. Tulsa
    Missouri
20. Mississippi
    Michigan St.

1965

Team
1. Michigan St.
2. Arkansas
3. Nebraska
4. Alabama
5. UCLA
6. Missouri
7. Tennessee
8. Notre Dame
9. Southern Cal
10. Texas Tech
11. Ohio St.
12. Florida
13. Purdue
14. Louisiana St.
15. Georgia
16. Tulsa
17. Mississippi
18. Kentucky
19. Syracuse
20. Colorado

1966

Team
1. Notre Dame
2. Michigan St.
3. Alabama
4. Georgia
5. UCLA
6. Purdue
7. Nebraska
8. Georgia Tech
9. Southern Methodist
10. Miami (Fla.)
11. Florida
12. Mississippi
13. Arkansas
14. Tennessee
15. Wyoming
16. Syracuse
17. Houston
18. Southern Cal
19. Oregon St.
20. Virginia Tech

1967

Team
1. Southern Cal *10-1*
2. Tennessee
3. Oklahoma
4. Notre Dame *8-2*
5. Wyoming
6. Indiana
7. Alabama
8. Oregon St.
9. Purdue
10. UCLA
11. Penn St.
12. Syracuse
13. Colorado
14. Minnesota
15. Florida St.
16. Miami (Fla.)
17. North Caro. St.
18. Georgia
19. Houston
20. Arizona St.

1968

Team
1. Ohio St.
2. Southern Cal *9-1-1*
3. Penn St.
4. Georgia
5. Texas
6. Kansas
7. Tennessee
8. Notre Dame *7-2-1*
9. Arkansas
10. Oklahoma
11. Purdue
12. Alabama
13. Oregon St.
14. Florida St.
15. Michigan
16. Southern Methodist
17. Missouri
18. Ohio
    Minnesota
20. Houston
    Stanford

1969

Team
1. Texas
2. Penn St.
3. Arkansas
4. Southern Cal *10-0-1*
5. Ohio St.
6. Missouri
7. Louisiana St.
8. Michigan
9. Notre Dame *8-2-1*
10. UCLA
11. Tennessee
12. Nebraska
13. Mississippi
14. Stanford
15. Auburn
16. Houston
17. Florida
18. Purdue
    San Diego St.
    West Va.

Division I-A National Poll Rankings

95

1970
Team
1. Texas
2. Ohio St.
3. Nebraska
4. Tennessee
5. Notre Dame 10-1
6. Louisiana St.
7. Michigan
8. Arizona St.
9. Auburn
10. Stanford
11. Air Force
12. Arkansas
13. Houston
    Dartmouth
15. Oklahoma
16. Colorado
17. Georgia Tech
    Toledo
19. Penn St.
    Southern Cal

1971
Team
1. Nebraska
2. Alabama
3. Oklahoma
4. Michigan
5. Auburn
6. Arizona St.
7. Colorado
8. Georgia
9. Tennessee
10. Louisiana St.
11. Penn St.
12. Texas
13. Toledo
14. Houston
15. Notre Dame
16. Stanford
17. Iowa St.
18. North Caro.
19. Florida St.
20. Arkansas
    Mississippi

1972
Team
1. Southern Cal 12-0
2. Oklahoma
3. Ohio St.
4. Alabama
5. Texas
6. Michigan
7. Auburn
8. Penn St.
9. Nebraska
10. Louisiana St.
11. Tennessee
12. Notre Dame
13. Arizona St.
14. Colorado
    North Caro.
16. Louisville
17. UCLA
    Washington St.
19. Utah St.
20. San Diego St.

1973
Team
1. Alabama
2. Oklahoma
3. Ohio St.
4. Notre Dame
5. Penn St.
6. Michigan
7. Southern Cal 9-2-1
8. Texas
9. UCLA
10. Arizona St.
11. Nebraska
    Texas Tech
13. Houston
14. Louisiana St.
15. Kansas
    Tulane
17. Miami (Ohio)
18. Maryland
19. San Diego St.
    Florida

*1974
Team
1. Southern Cal 10-1-1
2. Alabama
3. Ohio St.
4. Notre Dame
5. Michigan
6. Auburn
7. Penn St.
8. Nebraska
9. North Caro. St.
10. Miami (Ohio)
11. Houston
12. Florida
13. Maryland
14. Baylor
15. Texas A&M
    Tennessee
17. Mississippi St.
18. Michigan St.
19. Tulsa

1975
Team
1. Oklahoma
2. Arizona St.
3. Alabama
4. Ohio St.
5. UCLA
6. Arkansas
7. Texas
8. Michigan
9. Nebraska
10. Penn St.
11. Maryland
12. Texas A&M
13. Arizona
    Pittsburgh
15. California
16. Miami (Ohio)
17. Notre Dame
    West Va.
19. Georgia
    Southern Cal

1976
Team
1. Pittsburgh
2. Southern Cal 11-1
3. Michigan
4. Houston
5. Ohio St.
6. Oklahoma
7. Nebraska
8. Texas A&M
9. Alabama
10. Georgia
11. Maryland
12. Notre Dame
13. Texas Tech
14. Oklahoma St.
15. UCLA
16. Colorado
17. Rutgers
18. Iowa St.
19. Baylor
    Kentucky

1977
Team
1. Notre Dame
2. Alabama
3. Arkansas
4. Penn St.
5. Texas
6. Oklahoma
7. Pittsburgh
8. Michigan
9. Washington
10. Nebraska
11. Florida St.
12. Ohio St.
    Southern Cal
14. North Caro.
15. Stanford
16. North Texas
    Brigham Young
18. Arizona St.
19. San Diego St.
    North Caro. St.

1978
Team
1. Southern Cal 12-1
2. Alabama
3. Oklahoma
4. Penn St.
5. Michigan
6. Notre Dame
7. Clemson
8. Nebraska
9. Texas
10. Arkansas
11. Houston
12. UCLA
13. Purdue
14. Missouri
15. Georgia
16. Stanford
17. Navy
18. Texas A&M
19. Arizona St.
    North Caro. St.

1979
Team
1. Alabama
2. Southern Cal 11-0-1
3. Oklahoma
4. Ohio St.
5. Houston
6. Pittsburgh
7. Nebraska
8. Florida St.
9. Arkansas
10. Purdue
11. Washington
12. Brigham Young
13. Texas
14. North Caro.
15. Baylor
16. Indiana
17. Temple
18. Penn St.
19. Michigan
20. Missouri

1980
Team
1. Georgia 12-0
2. Pittsburgh 11-1
3. Oklahoma 10-2
4. Michigan 10-2
5. Florida St. 10-2
6. Alabama 10-2
7. Nebraska 10-2
8. Penn St. 10-2
9. North Caro. 11-1
10. Notre Dame 9-2-1
11. Brigham Young
12. Southern Cal
13. Baylor
14. UCLA
15. Ohio St.
16. Purdue
17. Washington
18. Miami (Fla.)
19. Florida
20. Southern Methodist

1981
Team
1. Clemson
2. Pittsburgh
3. Penn St.
4. Texas
5. Georgia
6. Alabama
7. Washington
8. North Caro.
9. Nebraska
10. Michigan
11. Brigham Young
12. Ohio St.
13. Southern Cal
14. Oklahoma
15. Iowa
16. Arkansas
17. Mississippi St.
18. West Va.
19. Southern Miss.
20. Missouri

Consensus all-American tailback Charles White (left) rushed for 1,760 yards and quarterback Paul McDonald threw 18 touchdown passes to lead Southern Cal to the No. 1 ranking in the 1978 UPI poll.

1982

Team
1. Penn St.
2. Southern Methodist
3. Nebraska
4. Georgia
5. UCLA
6. Arizona St.
7. Washington
8. Arkansas
9. Pittsburgh
10. Florida St.
11. Louisiana St.
12. Ohio St.
13. North Caro.
14. Auburn
15. Michigan
16. Oklahoma
17. Alabama
18. Texas
19. West Va.
20. Maryland

1983

Team
1. Miami (Fla.) 11-1
2. Nebraska 12-1
3. Auburn 11-1
4. Georgia 10-1-1
5. Texas 11-1
6. Florida 9-2-1
7. Brigham Young 11-1
8. Ohio St. 9-3
9. Michigan 9-3
10. Illinois 10-2
11. Southern Methodist
12. Alabama
13. UCLA
14. Iowa
15. Air Force
16. West Va.
17. Penn St.
18. Oklahoma St.
19. Pittsburgh
20. Boston College

1984

Team
1. Brigham Young
2. Washington
3. Nebraska
4. Boston College
5. Oklahoma St.
6. Oklahoma
7. Florida
8. Southern Methodist
9. Southern Cal
10. UCLA
11. Maryland
12. Ohio St.
13. South Caro.
14. Auburn
15. Iowa
16. Louisiana St.
17. Virginia
18. West Va.
19. Kentucky
    Florida St.

1985

Team
1. Oklahoma
2. Michigan
3. Penn St.
4. Tennessee
5. Air Force
6. UCLA
7. Texas A&M
8. Miami (Fla.)
9. Iowa
10. Nebraska
11. Ohio St.
12. Arkansas
13. Florida St.
14. Alabama
15. Baylor
16. Fresno St.
17. Brigham Young
18. Georgia Tech
19. Maryland
20. Louisiana St.

Division I-A National Poll Rankings

1986 Team	**1987** Team	**1988** Team	**1989** Team
1. Penn St.	1. Miami (Fla.)	1. Notre Dame	1. Miami (Fla.)
2. Miami (Fla.)	2. Florida St.	2. Miami (Fla.)	2. Florida St.
3. Oklahoma	3. Oklahoma	3. Florida St.	3. Notre Dame
4. Nebraska	4. Syracuse	4. Michigan	4. Colorado
5. Arizona St.	5. Louisiana St.	5. West Va.	5. Tennessee
6. Ohio St.	6. Nebraska	6. UCLA	6. Auburn
7. Michigan	7. Auburn	7. Auburn	7. Alabama
8. Auburn	8. Michigan St.	8. Clemson	8. Michigan
9. Alabama	9. Texas A&M	9. Southern Cal	9. Southern Cal
10. Arizona	10. Clemson	10. Nebraska	10. Illinois
11. Louisiana St.	11. UCLA	11. Oklahoma St.	11. Clemson
12. Texas A&M	12. Oklahoma St.	12. Syracuse	12. Nebraska
13. Baylor	13. Tennessee	13. Arkansas	13. Arkansas
14. UCLA	14. Georgia	14. Oklahoma	14. Penn St.
15. Iowa	15. South Caro.	15. Georgia	15. Virginia
16. Arkansas	16. Iowa	16. Washington St.	16. Texas Tech
17. Washington	17. Southern Cal	17. North Caro. St.	Michigan St.
18. Boston College	18. Michigan	Alabama	18. Brigham Young
19. Clemson	19. Texas	19. Indiana	19. Pittsburgh
20. Florida St.	20. Indiana	20. Wyoming	20. Washington

#1990 Team	**1991** Team
1. Georgia Tech	1. Washington
2. Colorado	2. Miami (Fla.)
3. Miami (Fla.)	3. Penn St.
4. Florida St.	4. Florida St.
5. Washington	5. Alabama
6. Notre Dame	6. Michigan
7. Tennessee	7. Florida
8. Michigan	8. California
9. Clemson	9. East Caro.
10. Penn St.	10. Iowa
11. Texas	11. Syracuse
12. Louisville	12. Notre Dame
13. Texas A&M	13. Texas A&M
14. Michigan St.	14. Tennessee
15. Virginia	15. Nebraska
16. Iowa	16. Oklahoma
17. Brigham Young	17. Clemson
Nebraska	18. Colorado
19. Auburn	19. UCLA
20. San Jose St.	20. Georgia
21. Syracuse	21. Tulsa
22. Southern Cal	22. Stanford
23. Mississippi	23. North Caro. St.
24. Illinois	24. Brigham Young
25. Virginia Tech	25. Ohio St.

Beginning in 1974, by agreement with the American Football Coaches Association, teams on probation by the NCAA were ineligible for ranking and national championship consideration by the UPI Board of Coaches. # Beginning in 1990 season, UPI selected top 25 teams instead of 20.

1992 NCAA FOOTBALL

USA TODAY/CABLE NEWS NETWORK (COACHES)
(Since 1982)
Took over as coaches' poll in 1991.

1982
Team
1. Penn St.
2. Southern Methodist
3. Nebraska
4. Georgia
5. UCLA
6. Arizona St.
7. Pittsburgh
8. Arkansas
9. Clemson
10. Washington
11. Louisiana St.
12. Florida St.
13. Ohio St.
14. Southern Cal
15. Oklahoma
16. Auburn
17. West Va.
18. Maryland
19. North Caro.
20. Texas
21. Michigan
22. Alabama
23. Tulsa
24. Iowa
25. Florida

1983
Team
1. Miami (Fla.)
2. Auburn
3. Nebraska
4. Georgia
5. Texas
6. Brigham Young
7. Michigan
8. Ohio St.
9. Florida
10. Clemson
11. Illinois
12. Southern Methodist
13. Alabama
14. Air Force
15. West Va.
16. Iowa
17. Tennessee
18. UCLA
19. Pittsburgh
20. Penn St.
21. Oklahoma
22. Boston College
23. Oklahoma St.
24. Maryland
25. East Caro.

1984
Team
1. Brigham Young
2. Washington
3. Florida
4. Nebraska
5. Oklahoma
6. Boston College
7. Oklahoma St.
8. Southern Methodist
9. Maryland
10. South Caro.
11. Southern Cal
12. UCLA
13. Louisiana St.
14. Ohio St.
15. Auburn
16. Miami (Fla.)
17. Florida St.
18. Virginia
19. Kentucky
20. Iowa
21. West Va.
22. Army
23. Georgia
24. Air Force
25. Notre Dame

1985
Team
1. Oklahoma
2. Penn St.
3. Michigan
4. Tennessee
5. Florida
6. Miami (Fla.)
7. Air Force
8. Texas A&M
9. UCLA
10. Iowa
11. Nebraska
12. Alabama
13. Ohio St.
14. Florida St.
15. Arkansas
16. Brigham Young
17. Maryland
18. Georgia Tech
19. Baylor
20. Auburn
21. Louisiana St.
22. Army
23. Fresno St.
24. Georgia
25. Oklahoma St.

1986
Team
1. Penn St.
2. Miami (Fla.)
3. Oklahoma
4. Nebraska
5. Arizona St.
6. Ohio St.
7. Auburn
8. Michigan
9. Alabama
10. Louisiana St.
11. Arizona
12. Texas A&M
13. UCLA
14. Baylor
15. Boston College
16. Iowa
17. Arkansas
18. Clemson
19. Washington
20. Virginia Tech
21. Florida St.
22. Stanford
23. Georgia
24. North Caro. St.
25. San Diego St.

1987
Team
1. Miami (Fla.)
2. Florida St.
3. Oklahoma
4. Syracuse
5. Nebraska
6. Louisiana St.
7. Auburn
8. Michigan St.
9. Texas A&M
10. UCLA
11. Clemson
12. Oklahoma St.
13. Georgia
14. Tennessee
15. Iowa
16. Notre Dame
17. Southern Cal
18. South Caro.
19. Michigan
20. Texas
21. Pittsburgh
22. Indiana
23. Penn St.
24. Ohio St.
25. Alabama

1988
Team
1. Notre Dame
2. Miami (Fla.)
3. Florida St.
4. UCLA
5. Michigan
6. West Va.
7. Southern Cal
8. Nebraska
9. Auburn
10. Clemson
11. Oklahoma St.
12. Syracuse
13. Oklahoma
14. Arkansas
15. Washington St.
16. Georgia
17. Alabama
18. North Caro. St.
19. Houston
20. Indiana
21. Wyoming
22. Louisiana St.
23. Colorado
24. Southern Miss.
25. Brigham Young

1989
Team
1. Miami (Fla.)
2. Notre Dame
3. Florida St.
4. Colorado
5. Tennessee
6. Auburn
7. Southern Cal
8. Michigan
9. Alabama
10. Illinois
11. Nebraska
12. Clemson
13. Arkansas
14. Houston
15. Penn St.
16. Virginia
17. Michigan St.
18. Texas Tech
19. Pittsburgh
20. Texas A&M
21. West Va.
22. Brigham Young
23. Syracuse
24. Ohio St.
25. Washington

1990
Team
1. Colorado
2. Georgia Tech
3. Miami (Fla.)
4. Florida St.
5. Washington
6. Notre Dame
7. Tennessee
8. Michigan
9. Clemson
10. Texas
11. Penn St.
12. Houston
13. Florida
14. Louisville
15. Michigan St.
16. Texas A&M
17. Oklahoma
18. Iowa
19. Auburn
20. Brigham Young
21. Mississippi
22. Southern Cal
23. Nebraska
24. Illinois
25. Virginia

1991
Team
1. Washington
2. Miami (Fla.)
3. Penn St.
4. Florida St.
5. Alabama
6. Michigan
7. California
8. Florida
9. East Caro.
10. Iowa
11. Syracuse
12. Notre Dame
13. Texas A&M
14. Oklahoma
15. Tennessee
16. Nebraska
17. Clemson
18. UCLA
19. Georgia
20. Colorado
21. Tulsa
22. Stanford
23. Brigham Young
24. Air Force
25. North Caro. St.

GAMES IN WHICH A NO. 1-RANKED
TEAM WAS DEFEATED OR TIED

Listed here are 98 games in which the No. 1-ranked team in the Associated Press poll was defeated or tied. An asterisk (*) indicates the home team, an (N) a neutral site. In parentheses following the winning or tying team is its rank in the previous week's poll (NR indicates it was not ranked), its won-lost record entering the game and score. The defeated or tied No. 1-ranked team follows with its score, and in parentheses is its rank in the poll the following week.

Note: Only 10 teams were ranked in the weekly polls during 1962, 1963, 1964, 1965, 1966 and 1967; 20 teams all other seasons until 1989, when 25 teams were ranked.

10-31-36	*Northwestern (3, 4-0) 6, Minnesota 0 (2)
11-21-36	*Notre Dame (11, 5-2) 26, Northwestern 6 (7)
10-30-37	(Tie) Washington (NR, 3-2-1) 0, *California 0 (2)
10-29-38	Carnegie Tech (t19, 4-1) 20, *Pittsburgh 10 (3)
12-2-38	*Southern Cal (8, 7-2) 13, Notre Dame 0 (5)
10-14-39	Duquesne (NR, 3-0) 21, *Pittsburgh 13 (18)
11-8-41	(Tie) Baylor (NR, 3-4) 7, *Texas 7 (2)
10-31-42	*Wisconsin (6, 5-0-1) 17, Ohio St. 7 (6)
11-21-42	(N) Auburn (NR, 4-4-1) 27, Georgia 13 (5)
11-28-42	Holy Cross (NR, 4-4-1) 55, *Boston College 12 (8)
11-27-43	*Great Lakes NTS (NR, 9-2-0) 19, Notre Dame 14 (1)
11-9-46	(Tie) (N) Notre Dame (2, 5-0-0) 0, Army 0 (1)
10-8-49	Army (7, 2-0) 21, *Michigan 7 (7)
10-7-50	Purdue (NR, 0-1) 28, *Notre Dame 14 (10)
11-4-50	*Texas (7, 4-1) 23, Southern Methodist 20 (7)
11-18-50	*Illinois (10, 6-1) 14, Ohio St. 7 (8)
1-1-51	(Sugar Bowl) Kentucky (7, 10-1-0) 13, Oklahoma 7 (1)
10-20-51	Southern Cal (11, 4-1) 21, California 14 (9)
10-11-52	*Ohio St. (NR, 1-1-0) 23, Wisconsin 14 (12)
11-21-53	(Tie) Iowa (20, 5-3-0) 14, *Notre Dame 14 (2)
10-2-54	Purdue (19, 1-0-0) 27, *Notre Dame 14 (8)
9-24-55	*Maryland (5, 1-0-0) 7, UCLA 0 (7)
10-27-56	*Illinois (NR, 1-3-0) 20, Michigan St. 13 (4)
10-19-57	Purdue (NR, 0-3-0) 20, Michigan St. 13 (8)
11-16-57	*Rice (20, 4-3-0) 7, Texas A&M 6 (4)
10-25-58	(Tie) *Pittsburgh (NR, 4-1-0) 14, Army 14 (3)
11-7-59	*Tennessee (13, 4-1-1) 14, Louisiana St. 13 (3)
11-5-60	*Minnesota (3, 6-0-0) 27, Iowa 10 (5)
11-12-60	Purdue (NR, 2-4-1) 23, *Minnesota 14 (4)
11-19-60	Kansas (NR, 6-2-1) 23, *Missouri 7 (5)

11-4-61	*Minnesota (NR, 4-1-0) 13, Michigan St. 0 (6)
11-18-61	Texas Christian (NR, 2-4-1) 6, *Texas 0 (5)
10-6-62	*UCLA (NR, 0-0-0) 9, Ohio St. 7 (10)
10-27-62	(Tie) *Rice (NR, 0-3-1) 14, Texas 14 (5)
11-10-62	*Wisconsin (8, 5-1-0) 37, Northwestern 6 (9)
11-17-62	*Georgia Tech (NR, 5-2-1) 7, Alabama 6 (6)
9-28-63	Oklahoma (3, 1-0-0) 17, *Southern Cal 12 (8)
10-12-63	(N)Texas (2, 3-0-0) 28, Oklahoma 7 (6)
10-17-64	Arkansas (8, 4-0-0) 14, Texas 13 (6)
11-28-64	*Southern Cal (NR, 6-3-0) 20, Notre Dame 17 (3)
9-25-65	*Purdue (6, 1-0-0) 25, Notre Dame 21 (8)
10-16-65	*Arkansas (3, 4-0-0) 27, Texas 24 (5)
1-1-66	(Rose Bowl) UCLA (5, 7-2-1) 14, Michigan St. 12 (2)
11-19-66	(Tie) *Michigan St. (2, 9-0-0) 10, Notre Dame 10 (1)
9-30-67	*Purdue (10, 1-0-0) 28, Notre Dame 21 (6)
11-11-67	*Oregon St. (NR, 5-2-1) 3, Southern Cal 0 (4)
11-18-67	*Southern Cal (4, 8-1-0) 21, UCLA 20 (4)
10-12-68	*Ohio St. (4, 2-0-0) 13, Purdue 0 (5)
11-22-69	*Michigan (12, 7-2-0) 24, Ohio St. 12 (4)
1-1-71	(Cotton Bowl) Notre Dame (6, 8-1-1) 24, Texas 11 (3)
9-29-73	(Tie) Oklahoma (8, 1-0-0) 7, *Southern Cal 7 (4)
11-24-73	(Tie) *Michigan (4, 10-0-0) 10, Ohio St. 10 (3)
12-31-73	(Sugar Bowl) Notre Dame (3, 10-0-0) 24, Alabama 23 (4)
11-9-74	*Michigan St. (NR, 4-3-1) 16, Ohio St. 13 (4)
1-1-76	(Rose Bowl) UCLA (11, 8-2-1) 23, Ohio St. 10 (4)
11-6-76	*Purdue (NR, 3-5-0) 16, Michigan 14 (4)
10-8-77	Alabama (t7, 3-1-0) 21, Southern Cal 20 (6)
10-22-77	*Minnesota (NR, 4-2-0) 16, Michigan 0 (6)
1-2-78	(Cotton Bowl) Notre Dame (5, 10-1-0) 38, Texas 10 (4)
9-23-78	(N) Southern Cal (7, 2-0-0) 24, Alabama 14 (3)
11-11-78	*Nebraska (4, 8-1-0) 17, Oklahoma 14 (4)
1-1-79	(Sugar Bowl) Alabama 14 (2, 10-1-0) 14, Penn St. 7 (4)
10-13-79	(Tie) Stanford (NR, 3-2-0) 21, Southern Cal 21 (4)
1-1-80	(Rose Bowl) Southern Cal (3, 10-0-1) 17, Ohio St. 16 (4)
11-1-80	(N) Mississippi St. (NR, 6-2-0) 6, Alabama 3 (6)
11-8-80	(Tie) *Georgia Tech (NR, 1-7-0) 3, Notre Dame 3 (6)
9-12-81	*Wisconsin (NR, 0-0-0) 21, Michigan 14 (11)
9-19-81	*Michigan (11, 0-1-0) 25, Notre Dame 7 (13)
10-10-81	Arizona (NR, 2-2-0) 13, *Southern Cal 10 (7)
10-17-81	*Arkansas (NR, 4-1-0) 42, Texas 11 (10)
10-31-81	*Miami (Fla.) (NR, 4-2-0) 17, Penn St. 14 (5)
11-28-81	Penn St. (11, 8-2-0) 48, *Pittsburgh 14 (10)
11-6-82	Notre Dame (NR, 5-1-1) 31, *Pittsburgh 16 (8)
1-1-83	(Sugar Bowl) Penn St. (2, 10-1-0) 27, Georgia 23 (4)
1-2-84	(Orange Bowl) Miami (Fla.) (5, 10-1-0) 31, Nebraska 30 (4)
9-8-84	*Michigan (14, 0-0-0) 22, Miami (Fla.) 14 (5)
9-29-84	*Syracuse (NR, 2-1-0) 17, Nebraska 9 (8)
10-13-84	(N) (Tie) Oklahoma (3, 4-0-0) 15, Texas 15 (3)
11-10-84	*Southern Cal (12, 7-1-0) 16, Washington 7 (5)
11-17-84	Oklahoma (6, 7-1-1) 17, *Nebraska 7 (7)
9-28-85	*Tennessee (NR, 0-0-1) 38, Auburn 20 (14)
11-2-85	*Ohio St. (7, 6-1-0) 22, Iowa 13 (6)
11-9-85	(N) Georgia (17, 6-1-1) 24, Florida 3 (11)
1-1-86	(Orange Bowl) Oklahoma (4, 9-1-0) 25, Penn St. 10 (3)
9-27-86	*Miami (Fla.) (2, 3-0-0) 28, Oklahoma 16 (6)
1-2-87	(Fiesta Bowl) Penn St. (2, 11-0-0) 14, Miami (Fla.) 10 (2)
11-21-87	Oklahoma (2, 11-0-0) 17, *Nebraska 7 (5)
1-1-88	(Orange Bowl) Miami (Fla.) (2, 11-1-0) 20, Oklahoma 14 (3)
10-15-88	*Notre Dame (4, 5-0-0) 31, Miami (Fla.) 30 (4)
10-29-88	Washington St. (NR, 4-3-0) 34, *UCLA 30 (6)
11-25-89	*Miami (Fla.) (7, 9-1-0) 27, Notre Dame 10 (5)
1-1-90	(Orange Bowl) Notre Dame (4, 11-1-0) 21, Colorado 6 (4)
9-8-90	*Brigham Young (16, 1-0-0) 28, Miami (Fla.) 21 (10)
10-6-90	Stanford (NR, 1-3-0) 36, *Notre Dame 31 (8)
10-13-90	Michigan St. (NR, 1-2-1) 28, *Michigan 27 (10)
11-3-90	Georgia Tech (16, 6-0-1) 41, Virginia 38 (11)
11-17-90	Penn St. (18, 7-2-0) 24, *Notre Dame 21 (7)
11-16-91	Miami (Fla.) (2, 8-0-0) 17, *Florida St. 16 (3)

UNDEFEATED, UNTIED TEAMS

Regular-season games only, minimum of five games played against opponents above the high-school level. Subsequent bowl win is indicated by (†), loss (‡) and tie ($). Unscored-on teams are indicated by (●).

Year	College	Wins	Year	College	Wins	Year	College	Wins
78	Princeton	6	12	Harvard	9	26	Alabama	$9
82	Yale	8		Notre Dame	7		Stanford	$10
83	Yale	8		Penn St.	8		Utah	7
85	Princeton	9		Washington	6	27	(None)	
87	Yale	9		Wisconsin	7	28	Boston College	9
88	Yale	●13	13	Auburn	8		Detroit	9
89	Princeton	10		Chicago	7		Georgia Tech	†9
90	Harvard	11		Harvard	9	29	Notre Dame	9
91	Yale	●13		Michigan St.	7		Pittsburgh	‡9
92	Minnesota	5		Nebraska	8		Purdue	8
	Purdue	8		Notre Dame	7		Tulane	9
	Yale	●13		Washington	7		Utah	7
93	Minnesota	6	14	Army	9	30	Alabama	†9
	Princeton	11		Illinois	7		Notre Dame	10
94	Pennsylvania	12		Tennessee	9		Utah	8
	Va. Military	5		Texas	8		Washington St.	‡9
	Yale	16		Wash. & Lee	9	31	Tulane	‡11
95	Pennsylvania	14	15	Colorado St.	7	32	Colgate	●9
96	Louisiana St.	6		Columbia	5		Michigan	9
97	Pennsylvania	15		Cornell	9		Southern Cal	†9
98	Harvard	11		Nebraska	8	33	Princeton	9
	Kentucky	●7		Oklahoma	10	34	Alabama	†9
	Michigan	10		Pittsburgh	8		Minnesota	8
	North Caro.	9		Washington	7	35	Minnesota	8
99	Kansas	10		Washington St.	†6		Princeton	9
	Sewanee	12	16	Army	9		Southern Meth.	‡12
00	Clemson	6		Ohio St.	7	36	(None)	
	Texas	6		Pittsburgh	8	37	Alabama	‡9
	Tulane	●5		Tulsa	10		Colorado	‡8
	Yale	12	17	Denver	9		Santa Clara	‡8
01	Harvard	12		Georgia Tech	9	38	Duke	‡●9
	Michigan	†●10		Pittsburgh	9		Georgetown	8
	Wisconsin	9		Texas A&M	●8		Oklahoma	‡10
02	Arizona	●5		Washington St.	6		Tennessee	†10
	California	8	18	Michigan	5		Texas Christian	†10
	Michigan	11		Oklahoma	6		Texas Tech	‡10
	Nebraska	●10		Texas	9	39	Cornell	8
03	Nebraska	11		Virginia Tech	7		Tennessee	‡●10
	Princeton	11		Washington (Mo.)	6		Texas A&M	†10
04	Auburn	5	19	Notre Dame	9	40	Boston College	†10
	Michigan	10		Texas A&M	●10		Lafayette	9
	Minnesota	13	20	Boston College	8		Minnesota	8
	Pennsylvania	12		California	†8		Stanford	†9
	Pittsburgh	10		Notre Dame	9		Tennessee	‡10
	Vanderbilt	9		Ohio St.	‡7	41	Duke	‡9
05	Chicago	10		Southern Cal	6		Duquesne	8
	Stanford	8		Texas	9		Minnesota	8
	Yale	10		Va. Military	9	42	Tulsa	‡10
06	New Mexico St.	5	21	California	$9	43	Purdue	9
	Washington St.	●6		Cornell	8	44	Army	9
	Wisconsin	5		Iowa	7		Ohio St.	9
07	Oregon St.	●6	22	California	9	45	Alabama	†9
08	Kansas	9		Cornell	8		Army	9
	Louisiana St.	10		Drake	7		Oklahoma St.	†8
09	Arkansas	7		Iowa	7	46	Georgia	†10
	Colorado	●6		Princeton	8		Hardin-Simmons	10
	Washington	7		Tulsa	7		UCLA	‡10
	Yale	●10	23	Colorado	9	47	Michigan	†9
10	Colorado	6		Cornell	8		Notre Dame	9
	Illinois	●7		Illinois	8		Penn St.	$9
	Pittsburgh	●9		Michigan	8	48	California	‡10
	Washington	6		Southern Methodist	9		Clemson	†10
11	Colorado	6		Yale	8		Michigan	9
	Oklahoma	8	24	Notre Dame	†9	49	Army	9
	Utah St.	●5	25	Alabama	†9		California	‡10
	Washington	7		Dartmouth	8		Notre Dame	10

Year	College	Wins	Year	College	Wins	Year	College	Wins
	Oklahoma †10		64	Alabama ‡10		75	Arizona St. †11	
50	Oklahoma ‡10			Arkansas †10			Arkansas St. 11	
	Princeton 9			Princeton 9			Ohio St. ‡11	
	Wyoming †9		65	Arkansas ‡10		76	Maryland ‡11	
51	Maryland †9			Dartmouth 9			Pittsburgh †11	
	Michigan St. 9			Michigan St. ‡10			Rutgers 11	
	Princeton 9			Nebraska ‡10		77	Texas ‡11	
	San Francisco 9		66	Alabama †10		78	Penn St. ‡11	
	Tennessee ‡10		67	Wyoming ‡10		79	Alabama †11	
52	Georgia Tech †11		68	Ohio ‡10			Brigham Young ‡11	
	Michigan St. 9			Ohio St. †9			Florida St. ‡11	
53	Maryland ‡10			Penn St. †10			McNeese St. ‡11	
54	Ohio St. †9		69	Penn St. †10			Ohio St. ‡11	
	Oklahoma 10			San Diego St. †10		80	Georgia †11	
	UCLA 9			Texas †10		81	Clemson †11	
55	Maryland ‡10			Toledo †10		82	Georgia ‡11	
	Oklahoma †10		70	Arizona St. †10		83	Nebraska ‡12	
56	Oklahoma 10			Dartmouth 9			Texas ‡11	
	Tennessee ‡10			Ohio St. ‡9		84	Brigham Young ‡12	
	Wyoming 10			Texas ‡10		85	Penn St. ‡11	
57	Arizona St. 10			Toledo †11			Bowling Green ‡11	
	Auburn 10		71	Alabama ‡11		86	Penn St. ‡11	
58	Louisiana St. †10			Michigan ‡11			Miami (Fla.) ‡11	
59	Syracuse †10			Nebraska ‡12		87	Miami (Fla.) †11	
60	New Mexico St. †10			Toledo †11			Syracuse $11	
	Yale 9		72	Southern Cal †11			Oklahoma ‡11	
61	Alabama †10		73	Alabama ‡11		88	Notre Dame †11	
	Rutgers 9			Miami (Ohio) †10			West Va. ‡11	
62	Dartmouth 9			Notre Dame †10		89	Colorado ‡11	
	Mississippi †9			Penn St. †11		90	(None)	
	Southern Cal †10		74	Alabama ‡11		91	Miami (Fla.) †11	
63	Texas †10			Oklahoma 11			Washington †11	

THE SPOILERS

(From 1937 Season)

Following is a list of the spoilers of major-college teams that lost their perfect (undefeated, untied) record in their **final** game of the season, including a bowl game (in parentheses). Confrontations of two undefeated, untied teams at the time are in bold face. An asterisk (*) indicates the home team in a regular-season game, a dagger (†) indicates a neutral site.

Date	Spoiler	Victim	Score
1-1-38	California	Alabama (Rose)	13-0
1-1-38	Rice	Colorado (Cotton)	28-14
12-3-38	*Southern Cal	Notre Dame	13-0
1-2-39	Southern Cal	Duke (Rose)	7-3
1-2-39	**Tennessee**	**Oklahoma (Orange)**	17-0
1-2-39	St. Mary's (Cal.)	Texas Tech (Cotton)	20-13
12-2-39	*Duquesne	Detroit Mercy	tie 10-10
1-1-41	**Boston College**	**Tennessee (Sugar)**	19-13
1-1-42	Oregon St.	Duke (Rose)	20-16
11-27-43	*Great Lakes	Notre Dame	19-14
11-25-44	*Virginia	Yale	tie 6-6
1-1-47	Illinois	UCLA (Rose)	45-14
1-1-48	Southern Methodist	Penn St. (Cotton)	tie 13-13
11-27-48	†Navy	Army	tie 21-21
12-2-48	*Southern Cal	Notre Dame	tie 14-14
1-1-49	Northwestern	California (Rose)	20-14
1-2-50	Ohio St.	California (Rose)	17-14
12-2-50	†Navy	Army	14-2
1-1-51	Kentucky	Oklahoma (Sugar)	13-7
1-1-52	**Maryland**	**Tennessee (Sugar)**	28-13
11-22-52	Southern Cal	*UCLA	14-12
1-1-54	Oklahoma	Maryland (Orange)	7-0
1-2-56	**Oklahoma**	**Maryland (Orange)**	20-6
1-1-57	Baylor	Tennessee (Sugar)	13-7
11-28-64	*Southern Cal	Notre Dame	20-17

Date	Spoiler	Victim	Score
1-1-65	Texas	Alabama (Orange)	21-17
11-20-65	**Dartmouth**	**Princeton**	28-14
1-1-66	UCLA	Michigan St. (Rose)	14-12
1-1-66	Alabama	Nebraska (Orange)	39-28
1-1-66	Louisiana St.	Arkansas (Cotton)	14-7
11-19-66	**Notre Dame**	***Michigan St.**	tie 10-10
1-1-68	Louisiana St.	Wyoming (Sugar)	20-13
11-23-68	*Harvard	Yale	tie 29-29
12-27-68	Richmond	Ohio (Tangerine)	49-42
11-22-69	*Michigan	Ohio St.	24-12
11-22-69	*Princeton	Dartmouth	35-7
11-21-70	*Ohio St.	Michigan	20-9
1-1-71	Stanford	Ohio St. (Rose)	27-17
1-1-71	Notre Dame	Texas (Cotton)	24-11
1-1-72	Stanford	Michigan (Rose)	13-12
1-1-72	**Nebraska**	**Alabama (Orange)**	38-6
11-25-72	*Ohio St.	Michigan	14-11
11-24-73	**Ohio St.**	***Michigan**	tie 10-10
12-31-73	**Notre Dame**	**Alabama (Sugar)**	24-23
11-23-74	*Ohio St.	Michigan	12-10
11-23-74	*Harvard	Yale	21-16
1-1-75	Notre Dame	Alabama (Orange)	13-11
1-1-76	UCLA	Ohio St. (Rose)	23-10
1-1-77	Houston	Maryland (Cotton)	30-21
11-19-77	*Delaware	Colgate	21-3
1-2-78	Notre Dame	Texas (Cotton)	38-10
1-1-79	Alabama	Penn St. (Sugar)	14-7
11-17-79	Harvard	*Yale	22-7
12-15-79	Syracuse	McNeese St. (Independence)	31-7
12-21-79	Indiana	Brigham Young (Holiday)	38-37
1-1-80	Southern Cal	Ohio St. (Rose)	17-16
1-1-80	Oklahoma	Florida St. (Orange)	24-7
1-1-83	Penn St.	Georgia (Sugar)	27-23
1-2-84	Georgia	Texas (Cotton)	10-9
1-2-84	Miami (Fla.)	Nebraska (Orange)	31-30
12-14-85	Fresno St.	Bowling Green (California)	51-7
1-1-86	Oklahoma	Penn St. (Orange)	25-10
1-2-87	**Penn St.**	**Miami (Fla.) (Fiesta)**	14-10
1-1-88	Auburn	Syracuse (Sugar)	tie 16-16
1-1-88	**Miami (Fla.)**	**Oklahoma (Orange)**	20-14
1-2-89	**Notre Dame**	**West Va. (Fiesta)**	34-21
1-1-90	Notre Dame	Colorado (Orange)	21-6

LONGEST WINNING STREAKS
(Includes Bowl Games)

Wins	Team	Years	Ended by	Score
47	Oklahoma	1953-57	Notre Dame	7-0
39	Washington	1908-14	Oregon St.	0-0
37	Yale	1890-93	Princeton	6-0
37	Yale	1887-89	Princeton	10-0
35	Toledo	1969-71	Tampa	21-0
34	Pennsylvania	1894-96	Lafayette	6-4
31	Oklahoma	1948-50	Kentucky	*13-7
31	Pittsburgh	1914-18	Cleveland Naval Reserve	10-9
31	Pennsylvania	1896-98	Harvard	10-0
30	Texas	1968-70	Notre Dame	*24-11
29	Michigan	1901-03	Minnesota	6-6
28	Alabama	1978-80	Mississippi St.	6-3
28	Oklahoma	1973-75	Kansas	23-3
28	Michigan St.	1950-53	Purdue	6-0
27	Nebraska	1901-04	Colorado	6-0
26	Cornell	1921-24	Williams	14-7
26	Michigan	1903-05	Chicago	2-0
25	Brigham Young	1983-85	UCLA	27-24
25	Michigan	1946-49	Army	21-7
25	Army	1944-46	Notre Dame	0-0

Wins	Team	Years	Ended by	Score
25	Southern Cal	1931-33	Oregon St.	0-0
24	Princeton	1949-52	Pennsylvania	13-7
24	Minnesota	1903-05	Wisconsin	16-12
24	Yale	1894-95	Boston AC	0-0
24	Harvard	1890-91	Yale	10-0
24	Yale	1882-84	Princeton	0-0
23	Notre Dame	1988-89	Miami (Fla.)	27-10
23	Nebraska	1970-71	UCLA	20-17
23	Penn St.	1968-70	Colorado	41-13
23	Tennessee	1937-39	Southern Cal	*14-0
23	Harvard	1901-02	Yale	23-0
22	Nebraska	1982-83	Miami (Fla.)	*31-30
22	Ohio St.	1967-69	Michigan	24-12
22	Arkansas	1963-65	Louisiana St.	*14-7
22	Harvard	1912-14	Penn St.	13-13
22	Yale	1904-06	Princeton	0-0
21	Arizona St.	1969-71	Oregon St.	24-18
21	San Diego St.	1968-70	Long Beach St.	27-11
21	Notre Dame	1946-48	Southern Cal	14-14
21	Minnesota	1933-36	Northwestern	6-0
21	Colorado	1908-12	Colorado St.	21-0
21	Pennsylvania	1903-05	Lafayette	6-6
21	Yale	1900-01	Army	5-5
21	Harvard	1898-99	Yale	0-0
20	Oklahoma	1986-87	Miami (Fla.)	*20-14
20	Tennessee	1950-51	Maryland	*28-13
20	Notre Dame	1929-31	Northwestern	0-0
20	Alabama	1924-26	Stanford	*7-7
20	Iowa	1920-23	Illinois	9-6
20	Notre Dame	1919-21	Iowa	10-7

* Streak ended in bowl game.

LONGEST UNBEATEN STREAKS
(Includes Bowl Games; Must Have At Least One Tie)

No.	Wins	Ties	Team	Years	Ended by	Score
63	59	4	Washington	1907-17	California	27-0
56	55	1	Michigan	1901-05	Chicago	2-0
50	46	4	California	1920-25	Olympic Club	15-0
48	47	1	Oklahoma	1953-57	Notre Dame	7-0
48	47	1	Yale	1885-89	Princeton	10-0
47	42	5	Yale	1879-85	Princeton	6-5
44	42	2	Yale	1894-96	Princeton	24-6
42	39	3	Yale	1904-08	Harvard	4-0
39	37	2	Notre Dame	1946-50	Purdue	28-14
37	36	1	Oklahoma	1972-75	Kansas	23-3
35	34	1	Minnesota	1903-05	Wisconsin	16-12
34	33	1	Nebraska	1912-16	Kansas	7-3
34	32	2	Princeton	1884-87	Harvard	12-0
34	29	5	Princeton	1877-82	Harvard	1-0
33	30	3	Tennessee	1926-30	Alabama	18-6
33	31	2	Georgia Tech	1914-18	Pittsburgh	32-0
33	30	3	Harvard	1911-15	Cornell	10-0
32	31	1	Nebraska	1969-71	UCLA	20-17
32	30	2	Army	1944-47	Columbia	21-20
32	31	1	Harvard	1898-00	Yale	28-0
31	30	1	Penn St.	1967-70	Colorado	41-13
31	30	1	San Diego St.	1967-70	Long Beach St.	27-11
31	29	2	Georgia Tech	1950-53	Notre Dame	27-14
30	25	5	Penn St.	1919-22	Navy	14-0
30	28	2	Pennsylvania	1903-06	Swarthmore	4-0
28	26	2	Southern Cal	1978-80	Washington	20-10
28	26	2	Army	1947-50	Navy	14-2
28	24	4	Minnesota	1933-36	Northwestern	6-0
28	26	2	Tennessee	1930-33	Duke	10-2
27	26	1	Southern Cal	1931-33	Stanford	13-7
27	24	3	Notre Dame	1910-14	Yale	28-0

LONGEST HOME WINNING STREAKS
(Includes Bowl Games)

Wins	Team	Years	Ended by	Score
57	Alabama	1963-82	Southern Miss.	38-29
45	Miami (Fla.)	1985-92	Still current	—
40	Notre Dame	1907-18	Great Lakes	7-7
33	Nebraska	1901-06	Iowa St.	14-2
30	Auburn	1952-61	Kentucky	14-12
27	Vanderbilt	1903-07	Michigan	8-0
25	Ohio St.	1972-76	Missouri	22-21
24	Georgia	1980-83	Auburn	13-7
24	Georgia Tech	1916-19	Wash. & Lee	3-0
24	Virginia	1899-04	Navy	5-0
23	Tulane	1929-32	Vanderbilt	6-6
23	Michigan St.	1904-08	Michigan	0-0
22	Wyoming	1965-70	Air Force	41-17
22	Minnesota	1933-37	Notre Dame	7-6
21	Mississippi	1952-59	Louisiana St.	10-10
21	North Caro.	1893-00	Virginia Tech	0-0
20	Fresno St.	1987-90	Utah St.	24-24
20	Rutgers	1974-78	Colgate	14-9
20	Mississippi St.	1939-45	Mississippi	7-6
20	Southern Cal	1927-29	California	15-7
20	Southern Cal	1919-23	California	13-7

LONGEST LOSING STREAKS

Losses	Team	Years	Ended by	Score
34	Northwestern	1979-82	Northern Ill.	31-6
28	Virginia	1958-61	William & Mary	21-6
28	Kansas St.	1944-48	Arkansas St.	37-6
27	New Mexico St.	1988-90	Cal St. Fullerton	43-9
27	Eastern Mich.	1980-82	Kent	9-7
20	Florida St.	1972-74	Miami (Fla.)	21-14
18	Wake Forest	1962-63	South Caro.	20-19
17	Memphis St.	1981-82	Arkansas St.	12-0
17	Tulane	1961-63	South Caro.	20-7
17	Kansas	1953-55	Washington St.	13-0
16	Indiana	1983-85	Louisville	41-28
16	Vanderbilt	1961-62	Tulane	20-0

MOST-PLAYED RIVALRIES

Games	Opponents (Series leader listed first)	Rivalry Record	First Game
101	Minnesota-Wisconsin	55-38-8	1890
100	Missouri-Kansas	47-44-9	1891
98	Nebraska-Kansas	74-21-3	1892
98	Texas Christian-Baylor	46-45-1	1899
98	Texas-Texas A&M	64-29-5	1894
96	North Caro.-Virginia	52-40-4	1892
96	Miami (Ohio)-Cincinnati	52-38-6	1888
95	Auburn-Georgia	45-43-7	1892
95	Oregon-Oregon St.	46-39-10	1894
94	Purdue-Indiana	57-31-6	1891
94	Stanford-California	46-37-11	1892
92	Navy-Army	43-42-7	1890
91	Penn St.-Pittsburgh	46-41-4	1893
91	#Auburn-Georgia Tech	47-39-4	1892
89	Louisiana St.-Tulane	*60-22-7	1893
89	Clemson-South Caro.	53-32-4	1896
89	Kansas-Kansas St.	60-24-5	1902
89	Oklahoma-Kansas	60-23-6	1903

Games	Opponents (Series leader listed first)	Rivalry Record	First Game
89	Utah-Utah St.	58-27-4	1892
88	Michigan-Ohio St.	50-33-5	1897
88	Mississippi-Mississippi St.	51-31-6	1901
87	Tennessee-Kentucky	55-23-9	1893
86	Texas-Oklahoma	50-32-4	1900
86	Oklahoma-Oklahoma St.	69-11-6	1904
86	Georgia-Georgia Tech	46-35-5	1893
85	Tennessee-Vanderbilt	54-26-5	1892
84	Michigan-Michigan St.	55-24-5	1898
84	Pittsburgh-West Va.	55-26-3	1895
84	Washington-Washington St.	54-24-6	1900

Did not play in 1990 or 1991.   *Disputed series record: Tulane claims 23-59-7 record.

ADDITIONAL RECORDS

Longest Uninterrupted Series
- 89 games—Kansas-Oklahoma (from 1903)
- 86 games—Kansas-Nebraska (from 1906)
- 85 games—Minnesota-Wisconsin (from 1907)
- 82 games—Wake Forest-North Caro. (from 1910)

Most Consecutive Wins Over a Major Opponent in an Uninterrupted Series
- 32—Oklahoma over Kansas St., 1937-68
- 26—Texas over Rice, 1966-91

Most Consecutive Current Wins Over a Major Opponent
- 28—Notre Dame over Navy, 1964-91 (55-9-1 in the rivalry)
- 23—Nebraska over Kansas, 1969-91 (74-21-3 in the rivalry)
- 23—Nebraska over Kansas St., 1969-91 (64-10-2 in the rivalry)
- 21—Oklahoma over Kansas St., 1971-91 (62-11-4 in the rivalry)

Most Consecutive Games Without a Loss Against a Major Opponent
- 34—Oklahoma over Kansas St., 1935-68 (1 tie)

CLIFFHANGERS

Regular-season Division I-A games won on the final play (since 1971, when first recorded). The extra point is listed when it provided the margin of victory after the winning touchdown on the game's final play.

Date	Opponents, Score	Game-winning play
9-25-71	Marshall 15, Xavier (Ohio) 13	Terry Gardner 13 pass from Reggie Oliver
10-9-71	California 30, Oregon St. 27	Steve Sweeney 7 pass from Jay Cruze
10-23-71	Washington St. 24, Stanford 23	Don Sweet 27 FG
11-6-71	Kentucky 14, Vanderbilt 7	Darryl Bishop 43 interception return
11-4-72	Louisiana St. 17, Mississippi 16	Brad Davis 10 pass from Bert Jones (Rusty Jackson kick)
11-18-72	California 24, Stanford 21	Steve Sweeney 7 pass from Vince Ferragamo
9-15-73	Lamar 21, Howard Payne 17	Larry Spears 14 pass from Jabo Leonard
9-22-73	Hawaii 13, Fresno St. 10	Reinhold Stuprich 29 FG
11-17-73	New Mexico 23, Wyoming 21	Bob Berg 43 FG
11-23-74	Stanford 22, California 20	Mike Langford 50 FG
9-20-75	Indiana St. 23, Southern Ill. 21	Dave Vandercook 50 FG
10-18-75	Cal St. Fullerton 32, UC Riverside 31	John Choukair 52 FG
11-8-75	West Va. 17, Pittsburgh 14	Bill McKenzie 38 FG
11-8-75	Stanford 13, Southern Cal 10	Mike Langford 37 FG
11-15-75	North Caro. 17, Tulane 15	Tom Biddle 40 FG
11-6-76	Eastern Mich. 30, Central Mich. 27	Ken Dudal 38 FG
9-30-78	Virginia Tech 22, William & Mary 19	Ron Zollicoffer 50 pass from David Lamie
10-21-78	Arkansas St. 6, McNeese St. 3	Doug Dobbs 42 FG
11-9-78	San Jose St. 33, Pacific (Cal.) 31	Rick Parma 5 pass from Ed Luther
10-6-79	Stanford 27, UCLA 24	Ken Naber 56 FG
10-20-79	Nevada-Las Vegas 43, Utah 41	Todd Peterson 49 FG
10-27-79	Michigan 27, Indiana 21	Anthony Carter 45 pass from John Wangler
11-10-79	Penn St. 9, North Caro. St. 7	Herb Menhardt 54 FG
11-17-79	Air Force 30, Vanderbilt 29	Andy Bark 14 pass from Dave Ziebart
11-24-79	Arizona 27, Arizona St. 24	Brett Weber 27 FG

Date	Opponents, Score	Game-winning play
9-13-80	Southern Cal 20, Tennessee 17	Eric Hipp 47 FG
9-13-80	Illinois 20, Michigan St. 17	Mike Bass 38 FG
9-20-80	Notre Dame 29, Michigan 27	Harry Oliver 51 FG
9-27-80	Tulane 26, Mississippi 24	Vince Manalla 29 FG
10-18-80	Connecticut 18, Holy Cross 17	Ken Miller 4 pass from Ken Sweitzer (Keith Hugger pass from Sweitzer)
10-18-80	Washington 27, Stanford 24	Chuck Nelson 25 FG
11-1-80	Tulane 24, Kentucky 22	Vince Manalla 22 FG
11-15-80	Florida 17, Kentucky 15	Brian Clark 34 FG
10-16-82	Arizona 16, Notre Dame 13	Max Zendejas 48 FG
10-23-82	Illinois 29, Wisconsin 28	Mike Bass 46 FG
11-20-82	California 25, Stanford 20	57 (5 laterals) kickoff return involving, in order: Kevin Moen, Richard Rodgers, Dwight Garner, Rodgers, Mariet Ford and Moen
10-8-83	Iowa St. 38, Kansas 35	Marc Bachrodt 47 FG
10-29-83	Bowling Green 15, Central Mich. 14	Stan Hunter 8 pass from Brian McClure
11-5-83	Baylor 24, Arkansas 21	Marty Jimmerson 24 FG
11-12-83	Pacific (Cal.) 30, San Jose St. 26	Ron Woods 85 pass from Mike Pitz
11-12-83	Miami (Fla.) 17, Florida St. 16	Jeff Davis 19 FG
11-26-83	Arizona 17, Arizona St. 15	Max Zendejas 45 FG
9-8-84	Southwestern La. 17, Louisiana Tech 16	Patrick Broussard 21 FG
9-15-84	Syracuse 13, Northwestern 12	Jim Tait 2 pass from Todd Norley (Don McAulay kick)
10-13-84	UCLA 27, Washington St. 24	John Lee 47 FG
11-17-84	Southwestern La. 18, Tulsa 17	Patrick Broussard 45 FG
11-17-84	Temple 19, West Va. 17	Jim Cooper 36 FG
11-23-84	Boston College 47, Miami (Fla.) 45	Gerard Phelan 48 pass from Doug Flutie
9-14-85	Clemson 20, Virginia Tech 17	David Treadwell 36 FG
9-14-85	Oregon St. 23, California 20	Jim Nielsen 20 FG
9-14-85	Utah 29, Hawaii 27	Andre Guardi 19 FG
9-21-85	New Mexico St. 22, UTEP 20	Andy Weiler 32 FG
10-5-85	Mississippi St. 31, Memphis St. 28	Artie Cosby 54 FG
10-5-85	Illinois 31, Ohio St. 28	Chris White 38 FG
10-12-85	Tulsa 37, Long Beach St. 35	Jason Staurovsky 46 FG
10-19-85	Northwestern 17, Wisconsin 14	John Duvic 42 FG
10-19-85	Iowa 12, Michigan 10	Rob Houghtlin 29 FG
10-19-85	Utah 39, San Diego St. 37	Andre Guardi 42 FG
11-30-85	Alabama 25, Auburn 23	Van Tiffin 52 FG
9-13-86	Oregon 32, Colorado 30	Matt MacLeod 35 FG
9-13-86	Wyoming 23, Pacific (Cal.) 20	Greg Worker 38 FG
9-20-86	Clemson 31, Georgia 28	David Treadwell 46 FG
9-20-86	Southern Cal 17, Baylor 14	Don Shafer 32 FG
10-18-86	Michigan 20, Iowa 17	Mike Gillette 34 FG
10-25-86	Syracuse 27, Temple 24	Tim Vesling 32 FG
11-1-86	North Caro. St. 23, South Caro. 22	Danny Peebles 33 pass from Erik Kramer
11-1-86	North Caro. 32, Maryland 30	Lee Gliarmis 28 FG
11-8-86	Southern Miss. 23, East Caro. 21	Rex Banks 31 FG
11-15-86	Minnesota 20, Michigan 17	Chip Lohmiller 30 FG
11-29-86	Notre Dame 38, Southern Cal 37	John Carney 19 FG
9-12-87	Youngstown St. 20, Bowling Green 17	John Dowling 36 FG
9-19-87	Utah 31, Wisconsin 28	Scott Lieber 39 FG
10-10-87	Marshall 34, Louisville 31	Keith Baxter 31 pass from Tony Petersen
10-17-87	Texas 16, Arkansas 14	Tony Jones 18 pass from Bret Stafford
11-12-88	New Mexico 24, Colorado St. 23	Tony Jones 28 pass from Jeremy Leach
9-16-89	Southern Methodist 31, Connecticut 30	Mike Bowen 4 pass from Mike Romo
9-30-89	Kansas St. 20, North Texas 17	Frank Hernandez 12 pass from Carl Straw
10-7-89	Florida 16, Louisiana St. 13	Arden Czyzewski 41 FG
10-14-89	Southern Miss. 16, Louisville 10	Darryl Tillman 79 pass from Brett Favre
10-28-89	Virginia 16, Louisville 15	Jake McInerney 37 FG
11-4-89	Toledo 19, Western Mich. 18	Romauldo Brown 9 pass from Kevin Meger
11-4-89	Northern Ill. 23, Southwestern La. 20	Stacey Robinson 7 run
9-8-90	Utah 35, Minnesota 29	Lavon Edwards 91 run of blocked FG
9-29-90	North Caro. St. 12, North Caro. 9	Damon Hartman 56 FG
10-20-90	Alabama 9, Tennessee 6	Philip Doyle 47 FG
10-6-90	Colorado 33, Missouri 31	Charles S. Johnson 1 run
11-3-90	Southern Miss. 14, Southwestern La. 13	Michael Welch 11 pass from Brett Favre (Jim Taylor kick)
11-17-90	Stanford 27, California 25	John Hopkins 39 FG
11-24-90	Michigan 16, Ohio St. 13	J. D. Carlson 37 FG
9-7-91	Central Mich. 27, Southwestern La. 24	L. J. Muddy 2 pass from Jeff Bender

Date	Opponents, Score	Game-winning play
9-21-91	Georgia Tech 24, Virginia 21	Scott Sisson 33 FG
9-21-91	Louisiana Tech 17, Eastern Mich. 14	Chris Bonoil 54 FG
10-12-91	Ball St. 10, Eastern Mich. 8	Kenny Stucker 41 FG
11-2-91	Kentucky 20, Cincinnati 17	Doug Pelphrey 53 FG
11-2-91	Tulsa 13, Southern Miss. 10	Eric Lange 24 FG

"Cardiac Seasons"
(From 1937; won-lost record in parentheses)
Games Decided by Two Points or Less

6—Kansas, 1973 (3-2-1): Tennessee 27-28, Nebraska 9-10, Iowa St. 22-20, Oklahoma St. 10-10, Colorado 17-15, Missouri 14-13 (season record: 7-3-1)

5—Columbia, 1971 (4-1-0): Princeton 22-20, Harvard 19-21, Yale 15-14, Rutgers 17-16, Dartmouth 31-29 (season record: 6-3-0)

5—Missouri, 1957 (2-2-1): Vanderbilt 7-7, Southern Methodist 7-6, Nebraska 14-13, Kansas St. 21-23, Kansas 7-9 (season record: 5-4-1)

Games Decided by Three Points or Less

7—Bowling Green, 1980 (2-5-0): Ohio 20-21, Ball St. 24-21, Western Mich. 17-14, Kentucky 20-21, Long Beach St. 21-23, Eastern Mich. 16-18, Richmond 17-20 (season record: 4-7-0)

7—Columbia, 1971 (4-3-0): Lafayette 0-3, Princeton 22-20, Harvard 19-21, Yale 15-14, Rutgers 17-16, Cornell 21-24, Dartmouth 31-29 (season record: 6-3-0)

6—Central Mich., 1991 (2-0-4): Ohio 17-17, Southwestern La. 27-24, Akron 31-29, Toledo 16-16, Miami (Ohio) 10-10, Eastern Mich. 14-14 (season record: 6-1-4)

6—Air Force, 1967 (2-2-2): Oklahoma St. 0-0, California 12-14, North Caro. 10-8, Tulane 13-10, Colorado St. 17-17, Army 7-10 (season record: 2-6-2)

6—Missouri, 1957 (3-2-1): Vanderbilt 7-7, Southern Methodist 7-6, Nebraska 14-13, Colorado 9-6, Kansas St. 21-23, Kansas 7-9 (season record: 5-4-1)

DIVISION I-A FOOTBALL STADIUMS

Stadiums used by NCAA Division I-A football teams, ranked by capacity.
(107 Teams, 111 Stadiums)

Rank	Stadium	Home Team	Conference	Year Built	Capacity	Surface
1.	Michigan	Michigan	Big Ten	1927	102,000†	PAT
2.	✓Rose Bowl	UCLA	Pacific-10	1922	99,563	Grass
3.	Beaver	Penn St.	Big Ten	1960	93,000	Grass
4.	✓Los Angeles Coliseum	Southern Cal	Pacific-10	1923	92,516	Grass
5.	Neyland	Tennessee	Southeastern	1921	91,902	Turf
6.	Ohio	Ohio St.	Big Ten	1922	91,470	PAT
7.	Stanford	Stanford	Pacific-10	1921	85,500	Grass
8.	Sanford	Georgia	Southeastern	1929	85,434	Grass
9.	Jordan-Hare	Auburn	Southeastern	1939	85,214	Grass
10.	Florida Field	Florida	Southeastern	1929	83,000	Grass
11.	Tiger	Louisiana St.	Southeastern	1924	80,140	Grass
12.	Memorial	Clemson	Atlantic Coast	1942	79,853	Grass
13.	Memorial	Texas	Southwest	1924	77,809	Turf
14.	Camp Randall	Wisconsin	Big Ten	1917	77,745	Turf
15.	Spartan	Michigan St.	Big Ten	1957	76,000	Turf
	✓Giants	*Rutgers	Big East	1976	76,000	Turf
17.	✓Legion Field	#Alabama	Southeastern	1927	75,952	Turf
18.	Memorial	California	Pacific-10	1923	75,662	Turf
19.	Owen Field	Oklahoma	Big Eight	1923	75,004	Turf
20.	Sun Devil	Arizona St.	Pacific-10	1958	74,783	Grass
21.	✓Orange Bowl	Miami (Fla.)	Big East	1935	74,244	PAT
22.	Memorial	Nebraska	Big Eight	1923	73,650	Turf
23.	✓Superdome@	Tulane	Independent	1975	72,704	Turf
24.	Husky	Washington	Pacific-10	1920	72,500	Turf
25.	Williams-Brice	South Caro.	Southeastern	1934	72,400	Grass
26.	Kinnick	Iowa	Big Ten	1929	70,311	PAT
27.	Kyle Field	Texas A&M	Southwest	1925	70,210	Turf
28.	Bryant-Denny	#Alabama	Southeastern	1929	70,123	PAT
29.	Rice	Rice	Southwest	1950	70,000	Turf
30.	Memorial	Illinois	Big Ten	1923	69,200	Turf

The Louisiana Superdome in New Orleans is the largest of the four indoor stadiums used by Division I-A teams. The Superdome, which is Tulane's home field, seats 72,704 for football.

Rank	Stadium	Home Team	Conference	Year Built	Capacity	Surface
31.	Ross-Ade	Purdue	Big Ten	1924	67,861	PAT
32.	✓Veterans	Temple	Big East	1971	66,592	Turf
33.	Cougar	Brigham Young	Western Athletic	1964	65,000	Grass
34.	Mountaineer Field	West Va.	Big East	1980	63,500	Turf
35.	✓Jack Murphy	San Diego St.	Western Athletic	1967	62,809	Grass
36.	✓Miss. Memorial	$Mississippi	Southeastern	1953	62,500	Grass
		$Mississippi St.	Southeastern	1953	62,500	Grass
37.	✓Liberty Bowl	Memphis St.	Independent	1965	62,425	PAT
38.	✓Metrodome@	Minnesota	Big Ten	1982	62,345	Turf
39.	Faurot Field	Missouri	Big Eight	1926	62,000	Turf
40.	Doak Campbell	Florida St.	Atlantic Coast	1950	60,519	PAT
41.	✓Astrodome@	Houston	Southwest	1965	60,000	Turf
42.	Notre Dame	Notre Dame	Independent	1930	59,075	Grass
43.	Carter-Finley	North Caro. St.	Atlantic Coast	1966	59,000%	Grass
44.	Commonwealth	Kentucky	Southeastern	1973	57,800	Grass
45.	Pitt	Pittsburgh	Big East	1925	56,500	Turf
46.	Arizona	Arizona	Pacific-10	1928	56,167	Grass
47.	Falcon	Air Force	Western Athletic	1962	53,533	Grass
48.	✓War Memorial	Arkansas	Southeastern	1948	53,250	Turf
49.	Razorback	Arkansas	Southeastern	1938	52,860	Turf
50.	Memorial	Indiana	Big Ten	1960	52,354	Turf
51.	Kenan	North Caro.	Atlantic Coast	1927	52,000	Grass
	✓Sun Bowl	UTEP	Western Athletic	1963	52,000	Turf
53.	Folsom Field	Colorado	Big Eight	1924	51,748	Turf
54.	Lane	Virginia Tech	Big East	1965	51,000	Grass
55.	Lewis	Oklahoma St.	Big Eight	1920	50,440	Turf
56.	Memorial	Kansas	Big Eight	1921	50,250	Turf
57.	✓Aloha	Hawaii	Western Athletic	1975	50,000	Turf
	Jack Trice Field	Iowa St.	Big Eight	1975	50,000	Turf
	Carrier Dome@	Syracuse	Big East	1980	50,000	Turf
60.	Dyche	Northwestern	Big Ten	1926	49,256	Turf
61.	Floyd Casey	Baylor	Southwest	1950	48,500	Turf
62.	Jones	Texas Tech	Southwest	1947	47,000	Turf

110

Rank	Stadium	Home Team	Conference	Year Built	Capacity	Surface
63.	Dodd/Grant Field	Georgia Tech	Atlantic Coast	1914	46,000	Turf
	Amon Carter	Texas Christian	Southwest	1929	46,000	Turf
65.	Byrd	Maryland	Atlantic Coast	1950	45,000	Grass
66.	Vaught-Hemingway	$Mississippi	Southeastern	1941	42,573	Grass
67.	KSU	Kansas St.	Big Eight	1968	42,000	Turf
	Scott	Virginia	Atlantic Coast	1931	42,000	Turf
69.	Autzen	Oregon	Pacific-10	1967	41,678	Turf
70.	Scott Field	$Mississippi St.	Southeastern	1935	41,200	Grass
71.	Vanderbilt	Vanderbilt	Southeastern	1922**	41,000	Turf
72.	Parker	Oregon St.	Pacific-10	1953	40,593	Turf
73.	Bulldog	Fresno St.	Western Athletic	1980	40,513	Grass
74.	Skelly	Tulsa	Independent	1930	40,385	Turf
75.	Martin	Washington St.	Pacific-10	1972	40,000	Turf
76.	Michie	Army	Independent	1924	39,929	Turf
77.	✓Cardinal	Louisville	Independent	1956	35,500	Turf
78.	✓Rubber Bowl	Akron	Mid-American	1940	35,482	Turf
79.	Nippert	Cincinnati	Independent	1916	35,000	Turf
	Ficklen Memorial	East Caro.	Independent	1963	35,000	Grass
	Rice	Utah	Western Athletic	1927	35,000	Turf
82.	Wallace Wade	Duke	Atlantic Coast	1929	33,941	Grass
83.	War Memorial	Wyoming	Western Athletic	1950	33,500	Grass
84.	Indian	Arkansas St.	Independent	1974	33,410	Grass
85.	Roberts	Southern Miss.	Independent	1976	33,000	Grass
86.	Alumni	Boston College	Big East	1957	32,000	Turf
	✓Silver Bowl	Nevada-Las Vegas	Big West	1971	32,000	Turf
88.	Groves	Wake Forest	Atlantic Coast	1968	31,500	Grass
89.	Spartan	San Jose St.	Big West	1932	31,218	Grass
90.	Cajun Field	Southwestern La.	Independent	1971	31,000	Grass
91.	Huskie	Northern Ill.	Independent	1965	30,998	Turf
92.	University	New Mexico	Western Athletic	1960	30,646	Grass
93.	Doyt Perry	Bowling Green	Mid-American	1966	30,599	Grass
94.	Dix	Kent	Mid-American	1969	30,520	Grass
95.	Joe Aillet	Louisiana Tech	Independent	1968	30,500	Grass
96.	Mackay	Nevada	Big West	1965	30,485	Grass
97.	Aggie Memorial	New Mexico St.	Big West	1978	30,343	Grass
98.	Romney	Utah St.	Big West	1968	30,257	Grass
99.	Hughes	Colorado St.	Western Athletic	1968	30,000	Grass
	Rynearson	Eastern Mich.	Mid-American	1969	30,000	Turf
	Navy-MC Memorial	Navy	Independent	1959	30,000	Grass
	Stagg Memorial	Pacific (Cal.)	Big West	1950	30,000	Grass
	Waldo	Western Mich.	Mid-American	1939	30,000	Grass
104.	Glass Bowl	Toledo	Mid-American	1937	26,248	Turf
105.	Fred Yager	Miami (Ohio)	Mid-American	1983	25,183	Grass
106.	Rutgers	Rutgers	Big East	1938	25,000	Grass
107.	Ownby	"Southern Methodist	Southwest	1926	23,783	Turf
108.	Kelly/Shorts	Central Mich.	Mid-American	1972	20,086	Turf
109.	Peden	Ohio	Mid-American	1929	20,000	Grass
110.	Ball St.	Ball St.	Mid-American	1967	16,319	Grass
111.	Titan	Cal St. Fullerton	Big West	1992	10,000	Grass

✓ Not located on campus.   @ Indoor facility.

Stadiums listed alphabetically by school.

School	Stadium	Conference	Year Built	Capacity	Surface
Air Force	Falcon	Western Athletic	1962	53,533	Grass
Akron	✓Rubber Bowl	Mid-American	1940	35,482	Turf
Alabama	✓Legion Field	Southeastern	1927	75,952	Turf
	Bryant-Denny	Southeastern	1929	70,123	PAT
Arizona	Arizona	Pacific-10	1928	56,167	Grass
Arizona St.	Sun Devil	Pacific-10	1958	74,783	Grass
Arkansas	✓War Memorial	Southeastern	1948	53,250	Turf
	Razorback	Southeastern	1938	52,860	Turf
Arkansas St.	Indian	Independent	1974	33,410	Grass
Army	Michie	Independent	1924	39,929	Turf
Auburn	Jordan-Hare	Southeastern	1939	85,214	Grass
Ball St.	Ball St.	Mid-American	1967	16,319	Grass

School	Stadium	Conference	Year Built	Capacity	Surface
Baylor	Floyd Casey	Southwest	1950	48,500	Turf
Boston College	Alumni	Big East	1957	32,000	Turf
Bowling Green	Doyt Perry	Mid-American	1966	30,599	Grass
Brigham Young	Cougar	Western Athletic	1964	65,000	Grass
Cal St. Fullerton	Titan	Big West	1992	10,000	Grass
California	Memorial	Pacific-10	1923	75,662	Turf
Central Mich.	Kelly/Shorts	Mid-American	1972	20,086	Turf
Cincinnati	Nippert	Independent	1916	35,000	Turf
Clemson	Memorial	Atlantic Coast	1942	79,853	Grass
Colorado	Folsom Field	Big Eight	1924	51,748	Turf
Colorado St.	Hughes	Western Athletic	1968	30,000	Grass
Duke	Wallace Wade	Atlantic Coast	1929	33,941	Grass
East Caro.	Ficklen Memorial	Independent	1963	35,000	Grass
Eastern Mich.	Rynearson	Mid-American	1969	30,000	Turf
Florida	Florida Field	Southeastern	1929	83,000	Grass
Florida St.	Doak Campbell	Atlantic Coast	1950	60,519	PAT
Fresno St.	Bulldog	Western Athletic	1980	40,513	Grass
Georgia	Sanford	Southeastern	1929	82,122	Grass
Georgia Tech	Dodd/Grant Field	Atlantic Coast	1914	46,000	Turf
Hawaii	✓Aloha	Western Athletic	1975	50,000	Turf
Houston	✓Astrodome@	Southwest	1965	60,000	Turf
Illinois	Memorial	Big Ten	1923	69,200	Turf
Indiana	Memorial	Big Ten	1960	52,354	Turf
Iowa	Kinnick	Big Ten	1929	70,311	PAT
Iowa St.	Jack Trice Field	Big Eight	1975	50,000	Turf
Kansas	Memorial	Big Eight	1921	50,250	Turf
Kansas St.	KSU	Big Eight	1968	42,000	Turf
Kent	Dix	Mid-American	1969	30,520	Grass
Kentucky	Commonwealth	Southeastern	1973	57,800	Grass
Louisiana St.	Tiger	Southeastern	1924	80,140	Grass
Louisiana Tech	Joe Aillet	Independent	1968	30,500	Grass
Louisville	✓Cardinal	Independent	1956	35,500	Turf
Maryland	Byrd	Atlantic Coast	1950	45,000	Grass
Memphis St.	✓Liberty Bowl	Independent	1965	62,425	PAT
Miami (Fla.)	✓Orange Bowl	Big East	1935	74,244	PAT
Miami (Ohio)	Fred Yager	Mid-American	1983	25,183	Grass
Michigan	Michigan	Big Ten	1927	102,000†	PAT
Michigan St.	Spartan	Big Ten	1957	76,000	Turf
Minnesota	✓Metrodome@	Big Ten	1982	62,345	Turf
Mississippi	✓Miss. Memorial	Southeastern	1953	62,500	Grass
	Vaught-Hemingway	Southeastern	1941	42,573	Grass
Mississippi St.	✓Miss. Memorial	Southeastern	1953	62,500	Grass
	Scott Field	Southeastern	1935	41,200	Grass
Missouri	Faurot Field	Big Eight	1926	62,000	Turf
Navy	Navy-MC	Independent	1959	30,000	Grass
Nebraska	Memorial	Big Eight	1923	73,650	Turf
Nevada	Mackay	Big West	1965	30,485	Grass
Nevada-Las Vegas	✓Silver Bowl	Big West	1971	32,000	Turf
New Mexico	University	Western Athletic	1960	30,646	Grass
New Mexico St.	Aggie Memorial	Big West	1978	30,343	Grass
North Caro.	Kenan	Atlantic Coast	1927	52,000	Grass
North Caro. St.	Carter-Finley	Atlantic Coast	1966	59,000	Grass
Northern Ill.	Huskie	Independent	1965	30,998	Turf
Northwestern	Dyche	Big Ten	1926	49,256	Turf
Notre Dame	Notre Dame	Independent	1930	59,075	Grass
Ohio	Peden	Mid-American	1929	20,000	Grass
Ohio St.	Ohio	Big Ten	1922	91,470	PAT
Oklahoma	Owen Field	Big Eight	1923	75,004	Turf
Oklahoma St.	Lewis	Big Eight	1920	50,440	Turf
Oregon	Autzen	Pacific-10	1967	41,678	Turf
Oregon St.	Parker	Pacific-10	1953	40,593	Turf
Pacific (Cal.)	Stagg Memorial	Big West	1950	30,000	Grass

School	Stadium	Conference	Year Built	Capacity	Surface
Penn St.	Beaver	Big Ten	1960	93,000	Grass
Pittsburgh	Pitt	Big East	1925	56,500	Turf
Purdue	Ross-Ade	Big Ten	1924	67,861	PAT
Rice	Rice	Southwest	1950	70,000	Turf
Rutgers	✓Giants	Big East	1976	76,000	Turf
	Rutgers	Big East	1938	25,000	Grass
San Diego St.	✓Jack Murphy	Western Athletic	1967	62,809	Grass
San Jose St.	Spartan	Big West	1932	31,218	Grass
South Caro.	Williams-Brice	Southeastern	1934	72,400	Grass
Southern Cal	✓Los Angeles Coliseum	Pacific-10	1923	92,516	Grass
Southern Methodist	"Ownby	Southwest	1926	23,783	Turf
Southern Miss.	Roberts	Independent	1976	33,000	Grass
Southwestern La.	Cajun Field	Independent	1971	31,000	Grass
Stanford	Stanford	Pacific-10	1921	85,500	Grass
Syracuse	Carrier Dome@	Big East	1980	50,000	Turf
Temple	✓Veterans	Big East	1971	66,592	Turf
Tennessee	Neyland	Southeastern	1921	91,902	Turf
Texas	Memorial	Southwest	1924	77,809	Turf
Texas A&M	Kyle Field	Southwest	1925	70,210	Turf
Texas Christian	Amon Carter	Southwest	1929	46,000	Turf
Texas Tech	Jones	Southwest	1947	47,000	Turf
Toledo	Glass Bowl	Mid-American	1937	26,248	Turf
Tulane...........................	✓Superdome@	Independent	1975	72,704	Turf
Tulsa	Skelly	Independent	1930	40,385	Turf
UCLA	✓Rose Bowl	Pacific-10	1922	99,563	Grass
UTEP	✓Sun Bowl	Western Athletic	1963	52,000	Turf
Utah	Rice	Western Athletic	1927	35,000	Turf
Utah St.	Romney	Big West	1968	30,257	Grass
Vanderbilt	Vanderbilt	Southeastern	1922**	41,000	Turf
Virginia	Scott	Atlantic Coast	1931	42,000	Turf
Virginia Tech	Lane	Big East	1965	51,000	Grass
Wake Forest.....................	Groves	Atlantic Coast	1968	31,500	Grass
Washington	Husky	Pacific-10	1920	72,500	Turf
Washington St...................	Martin	Pacific-10	1972	40,000	Turf
West Va..........................	Mountaineer Field	Big East	1980	63,500	Turf
Western Mich....................	Waldo	Mid-American	1939	30,000	Grass
Wisconsin	Camp Randall	Big Ten	1917	77,745	Turf
Wyoming.........................	War Memorial	Western Athletic	1950	33,500	Grass

✓ *Not located on campus.* @ *Indoor facility.*

NOTES:

† *Michigan Stadium currently is being renovated, with new capacity not yet determined; however, it will be more than 102,000.*

* *Giants Stadium, located in East Rutherford, New Jersey, is the home of NFL teams the New York Giants and New York Jets. Rutgers also plays home games in its on-campus facility (Rutgers Stadium, capacity 25,000) in Piscataway, New Jersey.*

Legion Field in Birmingham has been home to Alabama for approximately half of its home games. Alabama plays the remainder of its home contests at Bryant-Denny Stadium in Tuscaloosa (capacity 70,123).

** *Vanderbilt Stadium was renovated almost completely in 1981.*

$ *Mississippi plays several home games a year at Mississippi Memorial Stadium in Jackson (capacity 62,500). Mississippi plays its on-campus games in Vaught-Hemingway Stadium (capacity 42,577) in Oxford. Mississippi St. also plays home games at Mississippi Memorial Stadium in Jackson.*

% *59,000 capacity includes 12,000 allowed to sit in grassy area at south end of field.*

" *Southern Methodist plays one game a year at the Cotton Bowl (capacity 72,032).*

NOTES ON OFF-CAMPUS FACILITIES:

Legion Field is located in Birmingham and is home to approximately half of Alabama's home games.
War Memorial Stadium is located in Little Rock.
Aloha Stadium is located in Honolulu.
The Astrodome is located approximately 10 miles from the Houston campus.
The Metrodome is the home of the Minnesota Vikings (capacity 62,345).
Mississippi plays several home games a year at Mississippi Memorial Stadium in Jackson (capacity 62,500). Mississippi St. also plays home games at Mississippi Memorial Stadium.
Giants Stadium is the home of the New York Giants and the New York Jets and is located in East Rutherford, New Jersey.
Jack Murphy Stadium is the home of the San Diego Chargers.
The Los Angeles Coliseum is the home of the Los Angeles Raiders.

Veterans Stadium is the home of the Philadelphia Eagles (capacity 66,592).
The Louisiana Superdome is the home of the New Orleans Saints.

Surface Legend: *Turf—Any of several types of artificial turfs (name brands include AstroTurf, All-Pro, Omniturf, SuperTurf, etc.); Grass—Natural grass surface; PAT—Prescription Athletic Turf (a "natural-artificial" surface featuring a network of pipes connected to pumps capable of sucking water from the natural turf or watering it. The pipes are located 18 inches from the surface and covered with a mixture of sand and filler. The turf also is lined with heating coils to keep it from freezing in temperatures below 32 degrees).*

MAJOR-COLLEGE STATISTICS TRENDS†

(Average Per Game, Both Teams)

Year	Rushing			Passing					Total Offense			Scoring		
	Plays	Yds.	Avg.	Att.	Cmp.	Pct.	Yds.	Av. Att.	Plays	Yds.	Avg.	TD	FG	Pts.
1937	—	267.6	—	26.0	9.9	.381	129.0	4.96	—	396.8	—	—	—	20.2
1938	81.6	280.2	3.43	28.0	10.4	.371	140.2	5.01	109.6	420.4	3.85	3.50	0.12	23.5
1939	81.6	271.8	3.33	27.6	10.3	.374	132.8	4.81	109.2	404.6	3.70	3.32	0.18	22.7
1940	83.8	281.0	3.35	29.6	11.5	.386	156.0	5.26	113.4	437.0	3.85	3.94	0.16	26.6
1941	84.4	282.4	3.35	30.0	11.7	.392	161.2	5.38	114.4	443.6	3.88	4.06	0.12	27.5
1946	84.6	304.8	3.60	31.0	12.1	.389	176.6	5.69	115.6	481.4	4.16	4.78	0.08	32.1
1947	84.6	317.4	3.75	30.5	12.6	.414	180.2	5.91	115.1	497.6	4.32	4.73	0.07	31.8
1948	87.4	324.4	3.71	31.7	13.4	.423	188.4	5.95	119.0	513.0	4.31	5.04	0.09	34.2
1949	94.4	361.2	3.83	35.3	15.1	.431	220.1	6.24	129.7	581.3	4.48	5.71	0.08	38.8
1950	94.0	360.3	3.83	35.0	15.3	.438	216.9	6.19	129.0	577.2	4.47	5.58	0.07	37.8
1951	97.1	365.0	3.76	37.7	16.8	.446	227.1	6.02	134.9	592.1	4.39	5.72	0.09	38.8
1952	96.6	352.7	3.65	36.7	16.2	.441	223.6	6.09	133.4	576.3	4.32	5.36	0.14	36.7
1953	90.1	353.1	3.92	30.4	13.0	.428	183.4	6.03	120.5	536.4	4.45	5.07	0.09	34.2
1954	90.9	368.1	*4.05	29.7	13.0	.437	182.2	6.14	120.6	550.2	4.56	5.17	0.09	34.7
1955	92.1	353.3	3.83	27.1	11.8	.435	169.3	6.24	119.2	522.6	4.38	4.74	0.10	32.1
1956	98.3	386.2	3.93	28.2	12.3	.437	171.8	6.09	126.5	558.0	4.41	4.90	0.09	33.0
1957	98.5	355.0	3.60	28.8	12.8	.444	171.0	5.94	127.2	526.0	4.14	4.61	0.11	31.1
1958	94.2	341.4	3.62	32.2	14.7	.458	195.3	6.06	126.4	536.7	4.24	4.61	0.18	32.0
1959	92.4	332.0	3.59	33.0	14.9	.451	197.0	5.96	125.4	529.0	4.21	4.50	0.34	31.7
1960	90.6	339.7	3.75	31.5	14.3	.454	187.1	5.94	122.1	526.8	4.31	4.37	0.38	31.1
1961	91.1	333.3	3.66	31.8	14.3	.448	189.4	5.95	122.9	522.7	4.25	4.46	0.47	32.0
1962	90.5	328.0	3.63	34.4	15.9	.463	209.9	6.10	124.9	537.9	4.31	4.59	0.42	32.7
1963	88.2	320.0	3.63	35.2	16.2	.461	210.5	5.98	123.4	530.6	4.30	4.38	0.53	31.6
1964	87.4	299.3	3.43	35.8	16.9	.472	219.9	6.14	123.2	519.2	4.21	4.13	0.59	30.1
1965	90.2	298.7	3.31	41.5	19.3	.464	246.4	5.93	131.7	545.0	4.14	4.51	0.83	33.3
1966	88.5	297.3	3.36	43.9	20.6	.470	266.3	6.07	132.3	563.6	4.26	4.70	0.84	34.9
1967	94.6	309.3	3.27	45.8	21.4	.467	279.6	6.10	140.4	588.9	4.19	4.95	0.91	36.8
1968	99.4	341.5	3.44	50.7	24.1	.474	315.4	6.22	*150.1	657.0	4.38	5.77	0.92	42.4
1969	98.9	343.6	3.47	50.9	24.0	.471	314.1	6.17	149.8	657.7	4.39	5.80	1.08	43.2
1970	98.5	351.3	3.57	49.9	23.3	.467	305.3	6.12	148.4	656.6	4.42	5.66	1.13	42.6
1971	99.3	364.3	3.67	43.4	20.1	.463	264.6	6.10	142.6	628.9	4.41	5.38	1.08	40.4
1972	99.6	369.0	3.70	43.9	20.3	.462	273.7	6.24	143.5	642.7	4.48	5.42	1.22	41.1
1973	100.2	385.5	3.85	40.8	19.2	.472	261.7	6.41	141.0	647.2	4.59	5.50	1.29	41.9
1974	103.7	403.6	3.89	37.6	17.8	.474	244.6	6.50	141.3	648.2	4.59	5.27	1.26	40.3
1975	*103.8	*408.9	3.94	36.7	17.3	.473	239.2	6.52	140.5	648.1	4.61	5.14	1.48	40.1
1976	102.7	397.5	3.87	38.1	18.1	.474	246.9	6.49	140.8	644.4	4.58	5.13	1.49	40.0
1977	102.5	389.2	3.80	40.3	19.5	.483	269.0	6.67	142.9	658.2	4.61	5.34	1.46	41.5
1978	101.7	385.2	3.79	42.4	20.6	.486	277.7	6.55	144.1	662.9	4.60	5.28	1.51	41.1
1979	98.1	375.8	3.83	43.1	21.2	.491	278.6	6.47	141.2	654.4	4.63	5.09	1.53	39.9
1980	95.3	356.6	3.74	46.6	23.3	.500	303.7	6.52	141.9	660.3	4.65	5.22	1.61	41.0
1981	92.6	338.8	3.66	50.6	25.4	.502	329.4	6.51	143.2	668.2	4.67	5.14	1.73	41.0
1982	90.2	338.5	3.75	55.2	28.9	.522	364.8	6.61	145.4	703.3	4.84	5.42	2.04	43.8
1983	89.2	338.9	3.80	53.9	28.8	.536	365.5	6.79	143.1	704.5	4.92	5.45	2.11	44.2
1984	89.4	336.2	3.76	53.5	28.2	.527	362.2	6.77	142.9	698.4	4.89	5.32	2.30	44.1
1985	89.1	338.3	3.80	54.5	29.3	.537	372.2	6.82	143.6	710.5	4.95	5.48	2.18	44.7
1986	88.4	335.8	3.80	54.4	29.2	.537	370.2	6.81	142.8	706.0	4.95	5.59	2.14	45.4
1987	88.8	348.4	3.92	54.1	28.5	.526	367.1	6.78	142.9	715.5	5.01	5.65	2.25	46.1
1988	88.0	349.1	3.97	54.1	28.6	.529	371.5	6.87	142.1	720.6	5.07	5.82	*2.31	47.5
1989	85.4	332.8	3.90	*57.0	*30.8	*.540	*401.8	*7.05	142.4	*734.6	*5.16	5.94	2.26	48.2
1990	86.1	335.3	3.90	56.6	30.2	.534	394.3	6.96	142.7	729.6	5.11	*6.07	2.16	*48.8
1991	86.6	339.4	3.91	54.4	29.1	.535	379.2	6.98	141.0	718.7	5.10	5.90	1.77	46.2

* Record. † Records not compiled in 1942-45 except for Scoring Points Per Game: 1942 (31.3); 1943 (31.3); 1944 (32.6); 1945 (32.2).

1992 NCAA FOOTBALL

ADDITIONAL MAJOR-COLLEGE STATISTICS TRENDS†

Rules changes and statistics changes affecting trends: PUNTING—Beginning in 1965, 20 yards not deducted from a punt into the end zone for a touchback. INTERCEPTIONS—Interception yards not compiled, 1958-65. KICKOFF RETURNS—During 1937-45, if a kickoff went out of bounds, the receiving team put the ball in play on its 35-yard line instead of a second kickoff; in 1984 (rescinded in 1985), a 30-yard-line touchback for kickoffs crossing the goal line in flight and first touching the ground out of the end zone; in 1986, kickoffs from the 35-yard line. PUNT RETURNS—In 1967, interior linemen restricted from leaving until the ball is kicked.

	Punting		Net	Interceptions			Punt Returns			Kickoff Returns			
					Avg.			Avg.			Avg.		Pct.
Year	No.	Avg.	Avg.	No.	Ret.	Yds.	No.	Ret.	Yds.	No.	Ret.	Yds.	Ret'd
1937	18.4	36.3	—	3.36	—	—	—	—	—	—	—	—	—
1938	18.6	37.2	—	3.40	9.19	31.6	—	—	—	—	—	—	—
1939	*18.7	36.7	—	3.34	9.84	33.0	*8.84	9.40	83.2	4.28	19.3	82.6	.764
1940	18.1	36.6	—	3.58	10.05	36.0	8.41	10.58	89.0	4.64	*20.4	95.0	.753
1941	17.7	36.1	—	*3.62	11.28	40.8	8.54	11.10	*94.8	4.82	20.2	97.2	.768
1946	14.6	35.7	—	3.50	11.79	41.2	7.40	11.32	83.8	6.02	18.9	113.8	.870
1947	13.4	36.4	30.3	3.21	11.93	38.3	6.94	11.73	81.4	6.07	18.9	114.5	.884
1948	12.6	36.3	30.2	3.20	12.59	40.3	6.18	*12.16	75.1	6.34	18.5	117.2	.873
1949	12.5	36.6	30.3	3.37	*13.23	*44.6	6.41	12.13	77.7	7.02	17.9	125.5	.885
1950	12.0	36.3	30.8	3.21	11.99	38.5	6.07	10.72	65.1	6.92	16.6	114.8	.889
1951	12.8	35.9	30.7	3.34	12.00	40.1	6.20	10.58	65.6	7.06	17.0	119.7	.884
1952	12.5	36.4	31.6	3.19	11.60	37.0	6.13	9.95	61.0	6.89	17.6	121.4	.908
1953	10.4	34.9	29.7	2.74	12.12	33.2	5.13	10.66	54.7	6.54	17.8	116.4	.903
1954	9.7	34.9	29.4	2.71	12.48	33.8	4.84	11.16	54.0	6.64	18.4	122.0	*.910
1955	9.8	34.9	29.8	2.52	12.96	33.5	4.78	10.54	50.4	6.17	18.5	114.4	.892
1956	10.1	35.1	30.1	2.57	12.86	33.1	4.97	10.07	50.1	6.37	18.0	114.8	.906
1957	10.6	34.8	30.2	2.52	11.95	30.1	5.06	9.57	48.4	6.09	18.7	114.1	.897
1958	11.1	35.4	30.9	2.65	—	—	5.13	9.70	49.8	6.03	18.9	113.9	.880
1959	11.0	35.9	31.5	2.66	—	—	5.34	9.06	48.4	6.18	18.7	115.6	.892
1960	10.2	36.0	31.4	2.48	—	—	4.78	9.73	46.5	6.09	18.8	114.6	.890
1961	10.3	35.5	31.1	2.44	—	—	4.85	9.44	45.8	6.12	18.3	112.2	.873
1962	10.4	35.7	31.3	2.50	—	—	4.72	9.66	45.6	6.20	19.6	121.4	.876
1963	10.3	36.3	32.5	2.38	—	—	4.68	9.71	45.4	6.15	20.1	123.7	.880
1964	10.6	36.4	32.5	2.39	—	—	4.65	8.99	41.8	5.86	19.6	114.6	.862
1965	11.7	38.5	33.9	2.84	—	—	5.46	9.99	54.5	6.30	18.8	118.6	.849
1966	11.8	37.5	33.5	3.00	12.07	36.2	5.26	8.82	46.4	6.48	18.7	121.6	.849
1967	12.9	36.8	31.6	3.04	11.39	34.6	6.83	9.92	67.7	6.61	18.7	123.3	.831
1968	13.3	37.4	33.3	3.22	11.51	37.1	6.01	8.95	53.8	7.27	19.1	139.1	.829
1969	13.1	37.5	33.4	3.39	11.07	37.5	6.00	9.00	54.0	7.34	18.9	138.7	.818
1970	12.6	37.4	33.2	3.32	11.65	38.7	5.78	9.28	53.7	7.37	19.0	140.2	.828
1971	12.3	37.6	33.4	2.97	11.75	34.9	5.78	9.04	52.3	7.14	19.2	137.2	.834
1972	12.1	37.2	33.4	3.07	11.54	35.4	5.44	8.61	46.8	6.99	19.0	132.8	.803
1973	11.6	37.8	34.1	2.72	11.30	30.8	5.03	8.65	43.5	7.08	19.6	138.4	.797
1974	11.2	37.6	34.2	2.46	11.30	27.8	4.80	7.92	38.0	6.75	19.1	128.5	.784
1975	10.8	38.1	35.0	2.42	11.26	27.2	4.77	7.19	34.3	6.39	19.3	123.3	.733
1976	11.3	38.0	35.1	2.45	11.44	28.0	4.83	6.83	33.0	6.28	18.3	114.7	.722
1977	11.5	38.0	35.0	2.51	11.05	27.8	4.89	7.10	34.6	6.32	18.4	116.1	.711
1978	12.0	38.0	34.9	2.68	10.83	29.0	5.02	7.39	37.1	6.36	18.7	119.1	.665
1979	11.6	37.7	34.8	2.62	10.66	27.9	4.76	7.09	33.8	6.03	18.8	113.7	.637
1980	11.6	38.3	35.4	2.74	10.85	29.7	4.88	7.01	34.2	5.81	19.0	110.2	.651
1981	11.9	38.9	35.9	2.76	10.22	28.2	4.90	7.22	35.4	5.72	18.8	107.8	.636
1982	11.7	*39.8	*36.5	2.78	10.70	29.7	4.79	8.00	38.3	5.37	19.3	103.7	.561
1983	11.0	39.5	35.9	2.74	10.43	28.6	4.94	7.95	39.3	5.29	19.2	101.6	.549
1984	11.1	39.7	36.3	2.61	10.07	26.3	4.94	7.61	37.6	6.05	18.6	112.3	.621
1985	11.0	39.6	36.1	2.59	10.47	27.1	4.89	7.92	38.8	5.88	19.4	114.0	.603
1986	10.7	39.2	35.4	2.59	10.99	28.5	5.01	8.23	41.3	7.55	19.8	149.2	.770
1987	10.7	38.6	34.7	2.64	10.82	28.6	4.95	8.31	41.1	7.78	19.1	149.0	.780
1988	10.4	38.4	34.7	2.47	11.17	28.0	4.78	7.96	38.1	*7.94	19.4	154.2	.778
1989	10.4	38.5	34.3	2.56	10.75	27.6	4.72	8.46	39.9	7.83	19.7	*154.3	.776
1990	10.6	38.6	34.3	2.46	11.40	28.0	4.89	9.33	45.7	7.58	19.6	148.9	.738
1991	10.5	38.4	34.3	2.35	11.30	26.6	5.00	8.74	43.7	6.86	19.4	133.1	.741

† Records not compiled in 1942-45.   * Record.

MAJOR-COLLEGE TIE GAMES

The record for most tie games in a single week is six—on October 27, 1962; September 28, 1963, and October 9, 1982.

Year	No.	Games	Pct.	Scoreless	Year	No.	Games	Pct.	Scoreless
1954	15	551	2.72	2	1974	18	749	2.40	0
1955	22	536	4.10	1	1975	16	785	2.04	0
1956	28	558	5.02	2	1976	13	796	1.63	1
1957	24	570	4.21	4	1977	16	849	1.88	1
*1958	19	578	3.29	2	1978	16	816	1.96	1
1959	13	578	2.25	4	1979	17	811	2.10	1
1960	23	596	3.86	4	1980	12	810	1.48	0
1961	11	574	1.92	1	1981	17	788	2.16	0
1962	20	602	3.32	2	1982	14	599	2.34	0
1963	25	605	4.13	4	1983	13	631	2.06	†1
1964	19	613	3.10	2	1984	15	626	2.40	0
1965	19	619	3.07	4	1985	13	623	2.09	0
1966	13	626	2.08	0	1986	10	619	1.62	0
1967	14	611	2.29	1	1987	13	615	2.11	0
1968	17	615	2.76	1	1988	12	616	1.94	0
1969	9	621	1.45	0	1989	15	614	2.44	0
1970	7	667	1.05	0	1990	15	623	2.41	0
1971	12	726	1.65	1	1991	14	617	2.27	0
1972	14	720	1.94	1					
1973	18	741	2.43	2					

*First year of two-point conversion rule.   † Last scoreless tie game: Nov. 19, 1983, Oregon vs. Oregon St.

HIGHEST-SCORING TIE GAMES

(Home team is listed first)

Score	Date	Opponents	Score	Date	Opponents
52-52	11-16-91	San Diego St.-Brigham Young	35-35	10-7-78	Ohio St.-Southern Methodist
48-48	9-8-79	San Jose St.-Utah St.	35-35	10-19-74	Idaho-Montana
43-43	11-12-88	Duke-North Caro. St.	35-35	10-9-71	New Mexico-New Mexico St.
41-41	9-23-89	San Diego St.-Cal St.	35-35	9-27-69	Minnesota-Ohio
		Fullerton	35-35	9-21-68	Washington-Rice
40-40	11-8-75	Idaho-Weber St.	35-35	11-18-67	Navy-Vanderbilt
39-39	11-7-82	Texas Tech-Texas Christian	35-35	12-11-48	†Pacific (Cal.)—Hardin-
37-37	9-23-67	*Alabama-Florida St.			Simmons
36-36	9-30-72	Georgia Tech-Rice	34-34	10-6-90	Iowa St.-Kansas
35-35	11-16-91	San Jose St.-Hawaii	33-33	10-1-83	California-Arizona
35-35	12-9-89	Hawaii-Air Force	33-33	9-24-49	Texas Christian-Oklahoma St.
35-35	9-23-89	Colorado St.-Eastern Mich.	33-33	10-31-31	Yale-Dartmouth

* At Birmingham.   † Grape Bowl, Lodi, Calif.

HOME-FIELD RECORDS

(Includes host teams at neutral-site games)

Year	Games	Home Team Won	Lost	Tied	Pct.	Year	Games	Home Team Won	Lost	Tied	Pct.
1966	626	365	248	13	.594	1981	788	457	314	17	.591
1967	611	333	264	14	.557	1982	599	368	217	14	.626
1968	615	348	250	17	.580	1983	631	364	254	13	.587
1969	621	366	246	9	.596	1984	626	371	240	15	.605
1970	667	399	261	7	.603	1985	623	371	239	13	.606
1971	726	416	298	12	.581	1986	619	363	246	10	.595
1972	720	441	265	14	.622	1987	615	387	215	13	*.640
1973	741	439	284	18	.605	1988	616	370	234	12	.610
1974	749	457	274	18	.622	1989	614	365	234	15	.607
1975	785	434	335	16	.563	1990	623	373	235	15	.611
1976	796	463	320	13	.590	1991	617	362	241	14	.598
1977	849	501	332	16	.600						
1978	816	482	318	16	.601						
1979	811	460	334	17	.578						
1980	809	471	327	12	.589						

* Record.

FIELD-GOAL TRENDS
(1938-1968)

(Goal posts widened from 18 feet, 6 inches to 23 feet, 4 inches in 1959)

Year	Made	Year	Made	Year	Made	Atts.	Pct.
1938	47	1951	53	1960	224		
1939	80	1952	83	1961	277		
1940	84	1953	50	1962	261		
1941	59	1954	48	1963	314		
1942-45	*	1955	57	1964	368		
1946	44	1956	53	1965	484	1,035	.468
1947	38	1957	64	1966	522	1,125	.464
1948	53	1958	103	1967	555	1,266	.438
1949	46	1959	199	1968	566	1,287	.440
1950	46						

* Records not compiled.

FIELD-GOAL TRENDS (FROM 1969)

(Includes Field Goal Attempts by Divisions I-AA, II and III Opponents)

	Totals							Breakdown by Distances					
Year	Made	Atts.	Pct.	16-39	Pct.	16-49	Pct.	40-49	Pct.	50 Plus	Pct.	60 Plus	
1969	669	1,402	.477	538-872	.617	654-1,267	.516	116-395	.294	15-135	.111	0-8	
1970	754	1,548	.487	614-990	.620	740-1,380	.536	126-390	.323	14-168	.083	1-9	
1971	780	1,625	.480	607-1,022	.594	760-1,466	.518	153-444	.345	20-159	.126	0-11	
1972	876	1,828	.479	705-1,150	.613	855-1,641	.521	150-491	.305	21-187	.112	1-12	
1973	958	1,920	.499	728-1,139	.639	914-1,670	.547	186-531	.350	44-250	.176	1-21	
1974	947	1,905	.497	706-1,096	.644	906-1,655	.547	200-559	.358	41-250	.164	1-17	
1975	1,164	2,237	.520	849-1,255	.676	1,088-1,896	.574	239-641	.373	76-341	.223	4-32	
1976	1,187	2,330	.509	854-1,301	.656	1,131-1,997	.566	277-696	.398	56-333	.168	3-24	
1977	1,238	2,514	.492	882-1,315	.671	1,160-2,088	.556	278-773	.360	78-426	.183	6-40	
1978	1,229	2,113	.582	938-1,361	.689	1,193-1,982	.602	255-621	.411	36-131	.275	1-4	

Year	Made	Atts.	Pct.	Under 20	20-29	30-39	40-49	50-59	60 Plus
1979	1,241	2,129	.583	34-43	455-601	425-706	286-600	41-173	0-6
1980	1,302	2,241	.581	31-39	408-529	452-696	317-682	37-175	0-7
1981	1,360	2,254	.603	42-48	471-598	461-731	335-698	58-169	1-10
1982	1,224	1,915	.639	31-34	384-475	415-597	319-604	73-190	2-15
1983	1,329	2,025	.656	34-37	417-508	477-636	329-628	72-201	0-15
1984	1,442	2,112	.683	44-49	450-532	503-681	363-630	80-206	2-14
1985	1,360	2,106	.646	40-47	416-511	478-657	341-647	84-227	1-17
1986	1,326	2,034	.652	45-48	445-525	448-641	340-629	44-182	4-9
1987	1,381	2,058	.671	45-48	484-559	469-638	311-604	72-200	0-9
1988	1,421	2,110	.673	33-35	487-573	495-664	337-610	68-217	1-11
1989#	1,389	2,006	*.692	50-53	497-565	471-655	319-573	52-154	0-6
1990	1,348	2,011	.670	39-42	477-546	454-626	319-625	59-167	0-5
1991$	1,092	1,831	.595	31-32	395-519	366-612	254-531	45-132	1-5

* Record.   # First year after kicking tee became illegal. $ First year after goal-post width narrowed back to 18'6" from 23'4".

FIELD-GOAL TRENDS BY SOCCER-STYLE AND CONVENTIONAL KICKERS

(Pete Gogolak of Cornell was documented as the first soccer-style kicker in college football history. The Hungarian-born kicker played at Cornell from 1961 through 1963. He set a national major-college record of 44 consecutive extra-point conversions and finished 54 of 55 for his career. His younger brother, Charley, also a soccer-styler, kicked at Princeton from 1963 through 1965.)

(Division I-A Kickers Only)
Soccer-Style

	Totals							Breakdown by Distances					
Year	†No.	Made	Atts.	Pct.	16-39	Pct.	16-49	Pct.	40-49	Pct.	50 Plus	Pct.	60 Plus
1975	70	528	1,012	.522	370-540	.685	479-816	.587	109-276	.395	49-196	.250	1-17
1976	84	517	1,019	.507	350-517	.677	477-831	.574	127-314	.404	40-188	.213	3-16
1977	96	665	1,317	.505	450-649	.693	615-1,047	.587	165-398	.415	50-270	.185	2-27
1978	98	731	1,244	.588	540-768	.703	703-1,148	.612	163-380	.429	28-96	.292	1-3

Year	†No.	Made	Atts.	Pct.	Under 20	20-29	30-39	40-49	50-59	60 Plus
1979	116	839	1,413	.594	23-28	288-380	282-455	214-419	32-126	0-5
1980	121	988	1,657	.596	26-32	327-416	342-522	261-540	32-147	0-5
1981	138	1,108	1,787	.620	32-36	377-476	376-576	279-551	43-142	1-6

Year	†No.	Made	Atts.	Pct.	Under 20	20-29	30-39	40-49	50-59	60 Plus
1982	105	1,026	1,548	.663	26-27	317-375	346-482	273-495	62-156	2-13
1983	110	1,139	1,724	.661	29-31	345-416	403-541	294-543	68-179	0-14
1984	127	1,316	1,898	*.694	43-47	414-480	438-589	341-572	78-197	2-13
1985	133	1,198	1,838	.652	35-41	369-452	415-578	306-560	72-191	1-16
1986	128	1,201	1,829	.657	37-40	398-467	410-575	313-576	39-162	4-9
1987	122	1,275	1,892	.674	40-43	458-523	424-574	290-566	63-177	0-9
1988	140	1,317	1,947	.676	31-33	445-521	468-630	311-562	61-201	1-11
1989	138	1,313	1,897	.692	49-52	462-526	441-612	310-551	51-150	0-6
1990	135	1,282	1,890	.678	36-38	450-515	432-589	308-590	56-154	0-4
1991	132	1,048	1,763	.594	30-31	381-500	349-589	243-512	44-130	1-1

Conventional

	Totals				Breakdown by Distances								
Year	†No.	Made	Atts.	Pct.	16-39	Pct.	16-49	Pct.	40-49	Pct.	50 Plus	Pct.	60 Plus
1975	116	564	1,085	.520	427-640	.667	541-959	.564	114-319	.357	23-126	.183	3-13
1976	101	608	1,192	.510	460-720	.639	594-1,065	.558	134-345	.388	14-127	.110	0-7
1977	98	513	1,054	.487	384-586	.655	487-916	.532	103-330	.312	26-138	.188	4-14
1978	86	440	761	.578	352-516	.682	434-729	.595	82-213	.385	6-32	.188	0-0

Year	†No.	Made	Atts.	Pct.	Under 20	20-29	30-39	40-49	50-59	60 Plus
1979	70	333	585	.569	10-14	140-185	111-198	63-150	9-37	0-1
1980	62	258	471	.548	5-7	81-113	110-174	56-142	6-33	0-2
1981	50	195	367	.531	8-9	70-97	69-126	41-112	7-22	0-1
1982	25	103	195	.528	3-4	36-50	34-62	25-59	5-18	0-2
1983	23	112	181	.619	4-5	40-55	46-58	22-50	0-12	0-1
1984	10	44	76	.579	0-1	17-26	20-33	7-15	0-1	0-0
1985	12	81	138	.587	3-4	22-29	29-40	19-44	8-20	0-1
1986	8	58	89	.652	4-4	21-28	17-27	14-24	2-6	0-0
1987	4	35	50	.700	4-4	10-14	14-16	6-9	1-7	0-0
1988	5	26	40	.650	0-0	17-21	5-7	4-10	0-2	0-0
1989	2	37	47	*.787	1-1	19-20	12-16	5-9	0-1	0-0
1990	2	23	38	.605	1-1	8-10	8-9	4-13	2-5	0-0
1991	2	16	24	.667	0-0	5-9	6-7	5-7	0-1	0-0

* Record.   † Number of kickers attempting at least one field goal.

AVERAGE YARDAGE OF FIELD GOALS

(Division I-A Kickers Only)

	Soccer-Style			Conventional			Nation		
Year	Made	Missed	Total	Made	Missed	Total	Made	Missed	Total
1975	35.1	43.2	39.0	33.1	41.3	37.0	34.1	42.2	37.9
1976	35.0	43.1	39.0	33.2	40.7	36.9	34.0	41.8	37.9
1977	34.7	44.3	39.5	33.3	41.9	37.7	34.1	43.2	38.7
1978	34.0	39.9	36.4	31.9	38.3	34.6	33.2	39.3	35.7
1979	33.7	39.9	36.2	31.9	38.0	34.5	33.2	39.3	35.7
1980	34.0	40.7	36.7	33.4	39.6	36.2	33.8	40.4	36.6
1981	33.9	40.1	36.2	33.2	38.6	35.7	33.8	39.8	36.1
1982	34.8	41.8	37.2	34.0	39.8	36.7	34.7	41.5	37.1
1983	34.7	42.1	37.2	32.3	40.5	35.5	34.5	41.9	37.0
1984	34.4	41.8	36.7	32.3	34.9	33.4	34.3	41.5	36.5
1985	34.5	41.3	36.8	35.4	41.7	38.0	34.5	41.3	36.9
1986	33.9	41.6	36.6	32.5	38.6	34.7	33.9	41.4	36.5
1987	33.5	41.8	36.2	32.3	41.4	35.1	33.5	41.8	36.2
1988	33.9	41.7	36.4	30.0	37.6	32.7	32.0	39.3	34.4
1989	33.5	41.2	35.9	30.5	39.6	32.4	33.4	41.2	35.8
1990	33.4	41.3	36.0	33.4	42.0	36.7	33.4	41.3	36.0
1991	33.2	40.7	35.8	28.6	31.9	40.7	35.9	40.4	36.1

DIVISION I-A EXTRA-POINT TRENDS

(From start of two-point attempts)

		Percent of Total Tries		Kick Attempts			Two-Point Attempts		
Year	Games	Kick	2-Pt.	Atts.	Made	Pct.	Atts.	Made	Pct.
1958	578	.486	*.514	1,295	889	.686	*1,371	*613	.447
1959	578	.598	.402	1,552	1,170	.754	1,045	421	.403
1960	596	.701	.299	1,849	1,448	.783	790	345	.437
1961	574	.723	.277	1,842	1,473	.800	706	312	.442
1962	602	.724	.276	1,987	1,549	.780	757	341	.450

		Percent of Total Tries		Kick Attempts			Two-Point Attempts		
Year	Games	Kick	2-Pt.	Atts.	Made	Pct.	Atts.	Made	Pct.
1963	605	.776	.224	2,057	1,659	.807	595	256	.430
1964	613	.814	.186	2,053	1,704	.830	469	189	.403
1965	619	.881	.119	2,460	2,083	.847	331	134	.405
1966	626	.861	.139	2,530	2,167	.857	410	165	.402
1967	611	.869	.131	2,629	2,252	.857	397	160	.403
1968	615	.871	.129	3,090	2,629	.851	456	181	.397
1969	621	.880	.120	3,168	2,781	.878	432	170	.394
1970	667	.862	.138	3,255	2,875	.883	522	246	*.471
1971	726	.889	.111	3,466	3,081	.889	433	173	.400
1972	720	.872	.128	3,390	3,018	.890	497	219	.441
1973	741	.893	.107	3,637	3,258	.896	435	180	.414
1974	749	.885	.115	3,490	3,146	.901	455	211	.464
1975	785	.891	.109	3,598	3,266	.908	440	171	.389
1976	796	.877	.123	3,579	3,241	.906	502	203	.404
1977	849	.891	.109	*4,041	*3,668	.908	495	209	.422
1978	816	.884	.116	3,808	3,490	.916	498	208	.418
1979	811	.897	.103	3,702	3,418	.923	424	176	.415
1980	810	.895	.105	3,785	3,480	.919	442	170	.384
1981	788	.901	.099	3,655	3,387	.927	403	172	.427
1982	599	.901	.099	2,920	2,761	.946	320	120	.375
1983	631	.896	.104	3,080	2,886	.937	356	151	.424
1984	626	.889	.111	2,962	2,789	.942	370	173	.468
1985	623	.899	.101	3,068	2,911	.949	345	121	.351
1986	619	.905	.095	3,132	2,999	.958	330	131	.397
1987	615	.892	.108	3,094	2,935	.949	375	163	.435
1988	616	.899	.101	3,215	3,074	.956	363	156	.430
1989	614	.888	.112	3,233	3,090	.956	409	179	.438
1990	623	*.911	.089	3,429	3,291	*.960	335	138	.412
1991	617	.906	.094	3,279	3,016	.920	342	128	.374

* Record.

DIVISION I-A EXTRA-POINT KICK ATTEMPTS
(1938-1957)

Year	Pct. Made	Year	Pct. Made	Year	Pct. Made	Year	Pct. Made
1938	.608	1946	.657	1951	.711	1956	.666
1939	.625	1947	.657	1952	.744	1957	.653
1940	.607	1948	.708	1953	.650		
1941	.638	1949	.738	1954	.656		
1942-45	*	1950	.713	1955	.669		

* Not compiled.

ALL-DIVISIONS DEFENSIVE EXTRA-POINT TRENDS

In 1988, the NCAA Football Rules Committee adopted a rule that gave defensive teams an opportunity to score two points on point-after-touchdown tries. The two points were awarded for returning an interception or advancing a blocked kick for a touchdown on point-after tries.

DIVISION I-A

Year	Games	Kick Ret./TDs	Int. Ret./TDs	Total Ret./TDs
1988	616	8/2	6/0	14/2
1989	614	12/3	9/2	21/5
1990	623	9/3	5/2	14/5
1991	617	9/3	10/3	19/6

DIVISION I-AA

Year	Games	Kick Ret./TDs	Int. Ret./TDs	Total Ret./TDs
1988	553	4/1	7/1	11/2
1989	554	11/4	4/2	15/6
1990	548	7/3	4/2	11/5
1991	560	12/3	9/2	21/5

DIVISION II

Year	Games	Kick Ret./TDs	Int. Ret./TDs	Total Ret./TDs
1988	580	19/4	9/0	28/4
1989	590	18/8	11/3	29/11
1990	596	9/3	2/2	11/5
1991	575	10/3	8/2	18/5

DIVISION III		Kick	Int.	Total
Year	Games	Ret./TDs	Ret./TDs	Ret./TDs
1988	994	29/8	25/3	54/11
1989	1,012	16/5	13/4	29/9
1990	1,020	25/10	16/6	41/16
1991	1,006	18/7	14/5	32/12
ALL DIVISIONS—NATIONWIDE		Kick	Int.	Total
Year	Games	Ret./TDs	Ret./TDs	Ret./TDs
1988	2,743	60/15	47/4	107/19
1989	2,770	57/20	37/11	94/31
1990	2,787	50/19	27/12	77/31
1991	2,758	49/16	41/12	90/28

ALL-DIVISIONS FUMBLE-RECOVERY RETURNS

In 1990, the NCAA Football Rules Committee adopted a rule that gave the defense an opportunity to advance fumbles that occur beyond the neutral zone (or line of scrimmage). Here are the number of fumble recoveries by division that were advanced, and whether a score resulted.

DIVISION I-A

Year	Games	Fumble Rec./TDs
1990	623	51/17
1991	617	60/16

DIVISION I-AA

Year	Games	Fumble Rec./TDs
1990	548	34/16
1991	560	42/13

DIVISION II

Year	Games	Fumble Rec./TDs
1990	596	46/25
1991	575	43/19

DIVISION III

Year	Games	Fumble Rec./TDs
1990	1,020	55/19
1991	1,006	62/22

ALL DIVISIONS—NATIONWIDE

Year	Games	Fumble Rec./TDs
1990	2,787	186/77
1991	2,758	207/70

COLLEGE FOOTBALL RULES CHANGES

THE BALL

1869	Round, rubber Association ball.
1875	Egg-shaped, leather-covered Rugby ball.
1896	Prolate spheroid, without specific measurements.
1912	28-28½ inches around ends, 22½-23 inches around middle, weight 14-15 ounces.
1952	Ball may be inclined no more than 45 degrees by snapper.
1956	Rubber-covered ball permitted.
1973	Teams allowed to use ball of their choice while in possession.
1978	Ball may not be altered, and new or nearly new balls added.
1982	10⅞ to 11⁷⁄₁₆ inches long, 20¾ to 21¼ inches around middle, and 27¾ to 28½ inches long circumference.

THE FIELD

1869	120 yards by 75 yards; uprights 24 feet apart.
1871	166⅔ yards by 100 yards.
1872	133⅓ yards by 83⅓ yards.
1873	Uprights 25 feet apart.
1876	110 yards by 53⅓ yards. Uprights 18½ feet apart; crossbar 10 feet high.
1882	Field marked with transverse lines every five yards. This distance to be gained in three downs to retain possession.
1912	Field 120 yards by 53⅓ yards, including two 10-yard end zones.
1927	Goal posts moved back 10 yards, to end line.
1957	Team area at 35-yard lines.
1959	Uprights widened to 23 feet, 4 inches.
1966	Pylons placed in corners of end zone and at goal lines.
1991	Uprights moved back to 18 feet, 6 inches.

POINTS

1869	All goals count 1 each.
1883	Safety 1, touchdown 2, goal after TD 4, goal from field 5.
1884	Safety 2, touchdown 4, goal after TD 2.
1898	Touchdown 5, goal after TD 1.
1904	Goal from field 4.
1909	Goal from field 3.
1912	Touchdown 6.
1922	Try-for-point by scrimmage play from 5-yard line.
1929	Try-for-point by scrimmage play from 2-yard line.
1958	One-point & two-point conversion (from 3-yard line).
1958	One-point safety added.
1974	Ball must go between the uprights for a successful field goal, over the uprights previously scored.
1976	Forfeit score changed from 1-0 to score at time of forfeit if the offended team is ahead at time of forfeit.
1984	Try may be eliminated at end of game if both captains agree.

PLAYERS

1869	Each team consisted of 25 players.
1873	Each team consisted of 20 players.
1876	Each team consisted of 15 players.
1880	Each team consisted of 11 players.
1895	Only one man in motion forward before the snap. No more than three players behind the line. One player permitted in motion toward own goal line.
1910	Seven players required on line.
1911	Illegal to conceal ball beneath a player's clothing.
1915	Numbering of players recommended.
1937	Number front and back mandatory with 6-inch Arabic in front and 10-inch in the rear.
1939	All players must wear head protectors.
1951	Face masks legal.
1966	Mandatory numbering of five players on the line 50-79.
1982	Tearaway jersey eliminated by charging a timeout.
1983	Mandatory white jersey for visiting teams.

SUBSTITUTIONS

1876	Fifteen players to a team and few if any substitutions.
1882	Replacements for disqualified or injured players.
1897	Substitutions may enter the game any time at discretion of captains.
1922	Players withdrawn during the first half may be returned during the second half. A player withdrawn in the second half may not return.
1941	A player may substitute any time but may not be withdrawn or the outgoing player returned to the game until one play had intervened. Platoon football made possible.
1948	Unlimited substitution on change of team possession.
1953	Two-platoon abolished and players allowed to enter the game only once in each quarter.
1954-64	Changes each year toward more liberalized substitution rule and platoon football.
1965	Platoon football returns. Unlimited substitutions between periods, after a score or try.
1974	Substitutes must be in for one play and replaced players out for one play.

PASSING GAME

1906	One forward pass legalized behind the line if made five yards right or left of center. Ball went to opponents if it failed to touch a player of either side before touching the ground. Either team could recover a pass touched by an opponent. One pass each scrimmage down.
1910	Pass interference does not apply 20 yards beyond the line of scrimmage. Passer must be five yards behind the line of scrimmage. One forward pass permitted during each down.
1914	Roughing the passer added.
1923	Handing the ball forward is an illegal forward pass and receivers going out of bounds and returning prohibited.
1934	Three changes encourage use of pass. (1) First forward pass in series of downs can be incomplete in the end zone without loss of ball except on fourth down. (2) Circumference of ball reduced, making it easier to throw. (3) Five-yard penalty for more than one incomplete pass in same series of downs eliminated.
1941	Fourth-down forward pass incomplete in end zone no longer a touchback. Ball goes to opponent at spot where put in play.
1945	Forward pass may be thrown from anywhere behind the line, encouraging use of modern T formation.
1968	Compulsory numbering system makes only players numbered other than 50-79 eligible forward-pass receivers.
1976	Offensive blocking changed to provide half extension of arms to assist pass blocking.

College Football Rules Changes

1980	Retreat blocking added with full arm extension to assist pass blocking, and illegal use of hands reduced to five yards.
1982	Pass interference only on a catchable forward pass. Forward pass intentionally grounded to conserve time permitted.
1983	First down added to roughing the passer.
1985	Retreat block deleted and open hands and extended arms permitted anywhere on the field.

GENERAL CHANGES

1876	Holding and carrying the ball permitted.
1880	Eleven players on a side and a scrimmage line established.
1882	Downs and yards to gain enter the rules.
1883	Scoring system established.
1906	Forward passes permitted. Ten yards for first down.
1920	Clipping defined.
1922	Try-for-point introduced. Ball brought out five yards from goal line for scrimmage, allowing try for extra point by place kick, drop kick, run or forward pass.
1925	Kickoff returned to 40-yard line. Clipping made a violation, with penalty of 25 yards.
1927	One-second pause imposed on shift. Thirty seconds allowed for putting ball in play. Huddle limited to 15 seconds. To encourage use of lateral pass, missed backward pass other than from center declared dead ball when it hits the ground and cannot be recovered by opponents.
1929	All fumbles ruled dead at point of recovery.
1932	Most far-reaching changes in nearly a quarter of a century set up safeguards against hazards of game. (1) Ball declared dead when any portion of player in possession, except his hands or feet, touches ground. (2) Use of flying block and flying tackle barred under penalty of five yards. (3) Players on defense forbidden to strike opponents on head, neck or face. (4) Hard and dangerous equipment must be covered with padding.
1937	Numerals on front and back of jerseys required.
1941	Legal to hand ball forward behind the neutral zone.
1948	One-inch kicking tees permitted.
1949	Blockers required to keep hands against their chest.
1951	Fair catch restored.
1952	Penalty for striking with forearm, elbow or locked hands, or for flagrantly rough play or unsportsmanlike conduct, changed from 15 yards to mandatory suspension.
1957	Penalty for grabbing face mask.
1959	Distance penalties limited to one-half distance to offending team's goal line.
1965	Two-inch kicking tees permitted.
1967	Coaching from sideline permitted.
1971	Crack-back block (blocking below waist) illegal.
1972	Freshman eligibility restored.
1977	Clock started on snap after a penalty.
1978	Unsuccessful field goal returned to the previous spot.
1983	Offensive encroachment changed . . . no offensive player permitted in or beyond the neutral zone after snapper touches ball.
1985	One or both feet on ground required for blocking below waist foul.
1986	Kickoff from the 35-yard line.
1988	Defensive team allowed to score two points on return of blocked extra-point kick attempt or interception of extra-point pass attempt.
1989	Kicking tees eliminated for field goals and extra-point attempts.
1990	Defense allowed to advance fumbles that occur beyond the neutral zone.
1991	Width between goal-post uprights reduced from 23 feet, 4 inches to 18 feet, 6 inches. Kickoffs out of bounds allow receiving team to elect to take ball 30 yards beyond yard line where kickoff occurred.
1992	Defense allowed to advance fumbles regardless of where they occur. Changes ruling of 1990 fumble advancement.

DIVISION I-AA RECORDS

Marshall quarterback Michael Payton set a Division I-AA record for season passing efficiency (181.3 rating) last year to lead the Thundering Herd to an 8-3 record and an appearance in the Division I-AA title game,

INDIVIDUAL RECORDS

TOTAL OFFENSE
(Rushing Plus Passing)

Most Plays
Quarter
31—Mike Hanlin, Morehead St. vs. Austin Peay, Oct. 10, 1981 (4th)
Half
48—John Witkowski, Columbia vs. Dartmouth, Nov. 6, 1982 (2nd)
Game
89—Thomas Leonard, Mississippi Val. vs. Texas Southern, Oct. 25, 1986 (440 yards)
Season
611—Neil Lomax, Portland St., 1979 (3,966 yards)
Career
1,901—Neil Lomax, Portland St., 1977-80 (13,345 yards)

Most Plays Per Game
Season
56.4—Willie Totten, Mississippi Val., 1984 (564 in 10)
Career
45.3—Willie Totten, Mississippi Val., 1982-85 (1,812 in 40)

Most Plays by a Freshman
Game
79—Adrian Breen, Morehead St. vs. Austin Peay, Oct. 8, 1983 (206 yards)
Season
462—Greg Wyatt, Northern Ariz., 1986 (2,695 yards)
Per-game record—44.7, Jason Whitmer, Idaho St., 1987 (402 in 9)

Most Yards Gained
Quarter
278—Willie Totten, Mississippi Val. vs. Kentucky St., Sept. 1, 1984 (2nd)
Half
404—Todd Hammel, Stephen F. Austin vs. Northeast La., Nov. 11, 1989 (1st)
Game
643—Jamie Martin, Weber St. vs. Idaho St., Nov. 23, 1991 (624 passing, 19 rushing)
Season
4,572—Willie Totten, Mississippi Val., 1984 (4,557 passing, 15 rushing)
2 Yrs
8,314—Willie Totten, Mississippi Val., 1984-85 (8,255 passing, 59 rushing)
3 Yrs
11,647—Neil Lomax, Portland St., 1978-80 (11,550 passing, 97 rushing)
Career
(4 yrs.) 13,345—Neil Lomax, Portland St., 1977-80 (13,220 passing, 125 rushing)

Most Yards Gained Per Game
Season
457.2—Willie Totten, Mississippi Val., 1984 (4,572 in 10)
Career
325.2—Willie Totten, Mississippi Val., 1982-85 (13,007 in 40)

Most Seasons Gaining 3,000 Yards or More
3—Sean Payton, Eastern, Ill., 1984-86; Neil Lomax, Portland St., 1978-80

Most Yards Gained by a Freshman
Game
478—Steve McNair, Alcorn St. vs. Howard, Oct. 5, 1991 (42 plays)
Season
3,137—Steve McNair, Alcorn St., 1991
Also holds per-game record at 313.7

Most Yards Gained, Two, Three and Four Consecutive Games
2 Games
1,088—Willie Totten, Mississippi Val., 1984 (561 vs. Southern-B.R., Sept. 29; 527 vs. Grambling, Oct. 13)
3 Games
1,576—Willie Totten, Mississippi Val., 1984 (488 vs. Jackson St., Sept. 22; 561 vs. Southern-B.R., Sept. 29; 527 vs. Grambling, Oct. 13)
4 Games
2,068—Willie Totten, Mississippi Val., 1984 (561 vs. Southern-B.R., Sept. 29; 527 vs. Grambling, Oct. 13; 359 vs. Texas Southern, Oct. 20; 621 vs. Prairie View, Oct. 27)

Most Games Gaining 300 Yards or More
Season
10—Willie Totten, Mississippi Val., 1984; Neil Lomax, Portland St., 1980
Career
28—Neil Lomax, Portland St., 1977-80

Most Consecutive Games Gaining 300 Yards or More
Season
10—Willie Totten, Mississippi Val., 1984
Career
13—Neil Lomax, Portland St., 1979-80

Most Games Gaining 400 Yards or More
Season
7—Willie Totten, Mississippi Val., 1984
Career
13—Willie Totten, Mississippi Val., 1982-85

Most Consecutive Games Gaining 400 Yards or More
Season
5—Willie Totten, Mississippi Val., 1984

Most Games Gaining 500 Yards or More
Season
4—Willie Totten, Mississippi Val., 1984
Also holds career record at 4 (1982-85)

Most Yards Gained Against One Opponent
Career
1,713—Willie Totten, Mississippi Val. vs. Prairie View, 1982-85
Also holds per-game record at 428.3 (1,713 in 4)

Gaining 1,000 Yards Rushing and 1,000 Yards Passing
Season
Tracy Ham (QB), Ga. Southern, 1986 (1,048 rushing, 1,772 passing)

Gaining 2,000 Yards Rushing and 4,000 Yards Passing

Career
Tracy Ham (QB), Ga. Southern, 1984-86 (2,506 rushing, 4,871 passing)

Highest Average Gain Per Play

Game
(Min. 39 plays) 12.2—Todd Hammel, Stephen F. Austin vs. Northeast La., Nov. 11, 1989 (46 for 562)
(Min. 50 plays) 9.76—Michael Proctor, Murray St. vs. Akron, Oct. 21, 1989 (51 for 498)
(Min. 60 plays) 9.70—Willie Totten, Mississippi Val. vs. Prairie View, Oct. 27, 1984 (64 for 621)

Season
(Min. 2,500 yards) 9.57—Frank Baur, Lafayette, 1988 (285 for 2,727)
(Min. 3,300 yards) 8.36—Jeff Wiley, Holy Cross, 1987 (445 for 3,722)

Career
(Min. 4,000 yards) 7.55—Reggie Lewis, Sam Houston St., 1986-87 (653 for 4,929)
(Min. 5,000 yards) 7.18—Willie Totten, Mississippi Val., 1982-85 (1,812 for 13,007)

Most Touchdowns Responsible For (TDs Scored and Passed For)

Game
9—Willie Totten, Mississippi Val. vs. Prairie View, Oct. 27, 1984 (passed for 8, scored 1) &

vs. Kentucky St., Sept. 1, 1984 (passed for 9); Neil Lomax, Portland St. vs. Delaware St., Nov. 8, 1980 (passed for 8, scored 1)

Season
61—Willie Totten, Mississippi Val., 1984 (passed for 56, scored 5)
Also holds per-game record at 6.1 (61 in 10)

Career
157—Willie Totten, Mississippi Val., 1982-85 (passed for 139, scored 18)
Also holds per-game record at 3.93 (157 in 40)

Most Points Responsible For (Points Scored and Passed For)

Game
56—Willie Totten, Mississippi Val. vs. Kentucky St., Sept. 1, 1984 (passed for 9 TDs and 1 two-point conversion)

Season
368—Willie Totten, Mississippi Val., 1984 (passed for 56 TDs, scored 5 TDs and passed for 1 two-point conversion)
Also holds per-game record at 36.8 (368 in 10)

Career
946—Willie Totten, Mississippi Val., 1982-85 (passed for 139 TDs, scored 18 TDs and passed for 1 two-point conversion)
Also holds per-game record at 23.7 (946 in 40)

RUSHING

Most Rushes

Quarter
19—Mal Najarian, Boston U. vs. Northeastern, Sept. 30, 1978 (4th)

Half
32—David Clark, Dartmouth vs. Pennsylvania, Nov. 18, 1989 (2nd)

Game
52—James Black, Akron vs. Austin Peay, Nov. 19, 1983 (295 yards)

Season
351—James Black, Akron, 1983 (1,568 yards)

Career
963—Kenny Gamble, Colgate, 1984-87 (5,220 yards)

Most Rushes Per Game

Season
34.0—James Black, Akron, 1982 (306 in 9)

Career
23.7—Paul Lewis, Boston U., 1981-84 (878 in 37)

Most Consecutive Carries by Same Player

Game
14—Dave Mixon, Tennessee Tech vs. Morehead St., Oct. 22, 1983 (during 4 series)

Most Yards Gained

Quarter
194—Otto Kelly, Nevada vs. Idaho, Nov. 12, 1983 (3rd, 8 rushes)

Half
263—Joe Delaney, Northwestern (La.) vs. Nicholls St., Oct. 28, 1978 (2nd, 19 rushes)

Game
345—Russell Davis, Idaho vs. Portland St., Oct. 3, 1981 (20 rushes)

Season
1,883—Rich Erenberg, Colgate, 1983 (302 rushes)

Career
5,333—Frank Hawkins, Nevada, 1977-80 (945 rushes)

Most Yards Gained Per Game

Season
172.2—Gene Lake, Delaware St., 1984 (1,722 in 10)

Career
(2 yrs.) 124.7—Rich Erenberg, Colgate, 1982-83 (2,618 in 21 games)
(3 yrs.) 133.0—Mike Clark, Akron, 1984-86 (4,257 in 32)
(4 yrs.) 124.3—Kenny Gamble, Colgate, 1984-87 (5,220 in 42)

Most Yards Gained by a Freshman

Game
304—Tony Citizen, McNeese St. vs. Prairie View, Sept. 6, 1986 (30 rushes)

Season
1,620—Markus Thomas, Eastern Ky., 1989 (232 rushes)

Most Yards Gained Per Game by a Freshman

Season
147.3—Markus Thomas, Eastern Ky., 1989 (1,620 in 11)

Most Yards Gained by a Quarterback

Game
286—Gene Brown, Citadel vs. Va. Military, Nov. 12, 1988 (15 rushes)

Season
1,152—Jack Douglas, Citadel, 1991 (266 rushes)
Also holds per-game record at 104.7

Career
2,748—Jack Douglas, Citadel, 1989-91 (654 rushes)

Most Games Gaining 100 Yards or More

Season
11—Frank Hawkins, Nevada, 1980

Career
29—Kenny Gamble, Colgate, 1984-87 (42 games); Frank Hawkins, Nevada, 1977-80 (43 games)

Most Consecutive Games Gaining 100 Yards or More
Season
11—Frank Hawkins, Nevada, 1980
Career
20—Frank Hawkins, Nevada, 1979-80

Most Games Gaining 200 Yards or More
Season
4—Kenny Gamble, Colgate, 1986; Rich Erenberg, Colgate, 1983
Career
6—Kenny Gamble, Colgate, 1984-87

Most Consecutive Games Gaining 200 Yards or More
Season
4—Rich Erenberg, Colgate, 1983

Most Yards Gained, Two, Three and Four Consecutive Games
2 Games
568—Gene Lake, Delaware St., 1984 (232 vs. Howard, Nov. 3; 336 vs. Liberty, Nov. 10)
3 Games
711—Gene Lake, Delaware St., 1984 (143 vs. Central St., Ohio, Oct. 27; 232 vs. Howard, Nov. 3; 336 vs. Liberty, Nov. 10)
4 Games
874—Gene Lake, Delaware St., 1984 (163 vs. Towson St., Oct. 20; 143 vs. Central St., Ohio, Oct. 27; 232 vs. Howard, Nov. 3; 336 vs. Liberty, Nov. 10)

Most Seasons Gaining 1,000 Yards or More
Career
3—By 14 players. Most recent: Joe Segreti, Holy Cross, 1988-90; Elroy Harris, Eastern Ky., 1985, 87-88; Kenny Gamble, Colgate, 1985-87; James Crawford, Eastern Ky., 1985-87

Two Players, Same Team, Each Gaining 1,000 Yards or More
Yale, 1991—Chris Kouri (1,101) & Nick Crawford (1,024); William & Mary, 1990—Robert Green (1,185) & Tyrone Shelton (1,020); Citadel, 1988—Adrian Johnson (1,091) & Gene Brown (1,006); Eastern Ky., 1986—Elroy Harris (1,152) & James Crawford (1,070); Eastern Ky., 1985—James Crawford (1,282) & Elroy Harris (1,134); Nevada, 1983—Otto Kelly (1,090) & Tony Corley (1,006); Jackson St., 1978—Perry Harrington (1,105) & Jeffrey Moore (1,094)

Most Yards Gained by Two Players, Same Team
Game
445—Joe Delaney (299) & Brett Knecht (146), Northwestern (La.) vs. Nicholls St., Oct. 28, 1978

Season
2,429—Frank Hawkins (1,683) & John Vicari (746), Nevada, 1979

Most Yards Gained in an Opening Game of a Season
304—Tony Citizen, McNeese St. vs. Prairie View, Sept. 6, 1986 (30 rushes)

Most Yards Gained in First Game of a Career
304—Tony Citizen, McNeese St. vs. Prairie View, Sept. 6, 1986 (30 rushes)

Highest Average Gain Per Rush
Game
(Min. 15 rushes) 19.1—Gene Brown, Citadel vs. Va. Military, Nov. 12, 1988 (15 for 286)
(Min. 20 rushes) 17.3—Russell Davis, Idaho vs. Portland St., Oct. 3, 1981 (20 for 345)
Season
(Min. 150 rushes) 7.74—Harvey Reed, Howard, 1986 (179 for 1,386)
(Min. 200 rushes) 7.29—Mike Clark, Akron, 1986 (245 for 1,786)
Career
(Min. 350 rushes) 7.30—Keith Williams, Southwest Mo. St., 1982-85 (369 for 2,694)
(Min. 600 rushes) 6.52—Harvey Reed, Howard, 1984-87 (635 for 4,142)

Most Touchdowns Scored by Rushing
Game
6—Gene Lake, Delaware St. vs. Howard, Nov. 3, 1984; Gill Fenerty, Holy Cross vs. Columbia, Oct. 29, 1983; Henry Odom, South Caro. St. vs. Morgan St., Oct. 18, 1980
Season
24—Geoff Mitchell, Weber St., 1991
Career
55—Kenny Gamble, Colgate, 1984-87

Most Touchdowns Scored Per Game by Rushing
Season
2.2—Geoff Mitchell, Weber St., 1991 (24 in 11)
Career
1.52—Elroy Harris, Eastern Ky., 1985, 87-88 (47 in 31)

Most Touchdowns Scored by Rushing by a Quarterback
Season
18—Tracy Ham, Ga. Southern, 1986
Career
36—DeAndre Smith, Southwest Mo. St., 1987-90

Per-game record—1.06, Jack Douglas, Citadel, 1989-91 (35 in 33)

Longest Play
99—Phillip Collins, Southwest Mo. St. vs. Western Ill., Sept. 16, 1989; Pedro Bacon, Western Ky. vs. Livingston, Sept. 13, 1986 (only rush of the game); Hubert Owens, Mississippi Val. vs. Ark.-Pine Bluff, Sept. 20, 1980

PASSING

Highest Passing Efficiency Rating Points
Game
(Min. 15 atts.) 322.9—Mike Smith, Northern Iowa vs. Indiana St., Nov. 13, 1986 (16 attempts, 14 completions, 0 interceptions, 252 yards, 5 TD passes)
(Min. 25 atts.) 283.3—Mike Smith, Northern Iowa vs. McNeese St., Nov. 8, 1986 (27 attempts, 22 completions, 0 interceptions, 413 yards, 6 TD passes)
(Min. 45 atts.) 220.8—Todd Hammel, Stephen F. Austin vs. Northeast La., Nov. 11, 1989 (45 attempts, 31 completions, 3 interceptions, 571 yards, 8 TD passes)

Season

(Min. 15 atts. per game) 181.3—Michael Payton, Marshall, 1991 (216 attempts, 143 completions, 5 interceptions, 2,333 yards, 19 TD passes)

Career

(Min. 400 comps.) 146.8—Willie Totten, Mississippi Val., 1982-85 (1,555 attempts, 907 completions, 75 interceptions, 12,711 yards, 139 TD passes)

Most Passes Attempted

Quarter

28—Paul Peterson, Idaho St. vs. Cal Poly SLO, Oct. 22, 1983 (4th)

Half

42—Doug Pederson, Northeast La. vs. Stephen F. Austin, Nov. 11, 1989 (1st, completed 27); Mike Machurek, Idaho St. vs. Weber St., Sept. 20, 1980 (2nd, completed 18)

Game

77—Neil Lomax, Portland St. vs. Northern Colo., Oct. 20, 1979 (completed 44)

Season

518—Willie Totten, Mississippi Val., 1984 (completed 324)

Also holds per-game record at 51.8

Career

1,606—Neil Lomax, Portland St., 1977-80 (completed 938)

Per-game record—42.9, Stan Greene, Boston U., 1989-90 (944 in 22)

Most Passes Attempted by a Freshman

Game

66—Chris Swartz, Morehead St. vs. Tennessee Tech, Oct. 17, 1987 (completed 35)

Season

392—Greg Wyatt, Northern Ariz., 1987 (completed 250)

Per-game record—37.8, Jason Whitmer, Idaho St., 1987 (340 in 9)

Most Passes Completed

Quarter

18—Kirk Schulz, Villanova vs. Central Conn. St., Oct. 10, 1987 (3rd); Willie Totten, Mississippi Val. vs. Grambling, Oct. 31, 1984 (2nd) & vs. Kentucky St., Sept. 1, 1984 (2nd)

Half

27—Doug Pederson, Northeast La. vs. Stephen F. Austin, Nov. 11, 1989 (1st, attempted 42)

Game

47—Jamie Martin, Weber St. vs. Idaho St., Nov. 23, 1991 (attempted 62)

Season

324—Willie Totten, Mississippi Val., 1984 (attempted 518)

Also holds per-game record at 32.4

Career

938—Neil Lomax, Portland St., 1977-80 (attempted 1,606)

Per-game record—23.8, Stan Greene, Boston U., 1989-90 (524 in 22)

Most Passes Completed by a Freshman

Game

35—Chris Swartz, Morehead St. vs. Tennessee Tech, Oct. 17, 1987 (attempted 66)

Season

250—Greg Wyatt, Northern Ariz., 1986 (attempted 392)

Also holds per-game record at 22.7 (250 in 11)

Most Passes Completed, Freshman and Sophomore Seasons

518—Greg Wyatt, Northern Ariz., 1986-87 (attempted 804)

Most Consecutive Passes Completed

Game

19—Kirk Schulz, Villanova vs. Central Conn. St., Oct. 10, 1987

Most Consecutive Pass Completions to Start Game

18—Scott Auchenbach, Bucknell vs. Colgate, Nov. 11, 1989

Highest Percentage of Passes Completed

Game

(Min. 20 comps.) 84.8%—John Friesz, Idaho vs. Montana St., Oct. 14, 1989 (28 of 33)

(Min. 30 comps.) 81.6%—Eric Beavers, Nevada vs. Idaho St., Nov. 17, 1984 (31 of 38)

Season

(Min. 200 atts.) 68.2%—Jason Garrett, Princeton, 1988 (204 of 299)

Career

(Min. 500 atts.) 66.9%—Jason Garrett, Princeton, 1987-88 (366 of 550)

(Min. 750 atts.) 61.3%—Greg Wyatt, Northern Ariz., 1986-89 (926 of 1,510)

Most Passes Had Intercepted

Game

7—Dan Crowley, Towson St. vs. Maine, Nov. 16, 1991 (53 attempts); Carlton Jenkins, Mississippi Val. vs. Prairie View, Oct. 31, 1987 (34 attempts); Charles Hebert, Southeastern La. vs. Northwestern (La.), Nov. 12, 1983 (23 attempts); Mick Spoon, Idaho St. vs. Montana, Oct. 21, 1978 (attempted 35)

Season

29—Willie Totten, Mississippi Val., 1985 (492 attempts)

Also holds per-game record at 2.64 (29 in 11)

Career

75—Willie Totten, Mississippi Val., 1982-85

Per-game record—2.0, John Witkowski, Columbia, 1981-83 (60 in 30)

Lowest Percentage of Passes Had Intercepted

Season

(Min. 175 atts.) 0.84%—Jeff Mladenich, Boise St., 1991 (2 of 239)

(Min. 325 atts.) 1.57%—Jeff Cesarone, Western Ky., 1985 (7 of 447)

Career

(Min. 500 atts.) 1.82%—Jason Garrett, Princeton, 1987-88 (10 of 550)

(Min. 750 atts.) 2.89%—Stan Yagiello, William & Mary, 1981-85 (36 of 1,247)

Most Passes Attempted Without Interception

Game

68—Tony Petersen, Marshall vs. Western Caro., Nov. 14, 1987 (completed 34)

Most Consecutive Passes Attempted Without Interception

Season

176—Jason Garrett, Princeton, 1988 (in 7 games, from Sept. 17 through Oct. 29)

Career

199—Thomas Debow, Tennessee Tech, began Sept. 17, 1988, ended Oct. 14, 1989

Most Yards Gained

Quarter

278—Willie Totten, Mississippi Val. vs. Kentucky St., Sept. 1, 1984 (2nd)

Half
  383—Michael Payton, Marshall vs. Va. Military, Nov. 16, 1991 (1st)
Game
  624—Jamie Martin, Weber St. vs. Idaho St., Nov. 23, 1991
Season
  4,557—Willie Totten, Mississippi Val., 1984
Career
  13,220—Neil Lomax, Portland St., 1977-80

Most Yards Gained Per Game
Season
  455.7—Willie Totten, Mississippi Val., 1984 (4,557 in 10)
Career
  320.1—Tom Ehrhardt, Rhode Island, 1984-85 (6,722 in 21)

Most Yards Gained by a Freshman
Game
  469—Jason Whitmer, Idaho St. vs. Weber St., Nov. 21, 1987
Season
  2,895—Steve McNair, Alcorn St., 1991
  Also holds per-game record at 289.5 (2,895 in 10)

Most Yards Gained, Freshman and Sophomore Seasons
  5,864—Greg Wyatt, Northern Ariz., 1986-87

Most Yards Gained, Two, Three and Four Consecutive Games
2 Games
  1,105—Todd Hammel, Stephen F. Austin, 1989 (534 vs. Sam Houston St., Nov. 4; 571 vs. Northeast La., Nov. 11)
3 Games
  1,624—Willie Totten, Mississippi Val., 1984 (526 vs. Jackson St., Sept. 22; 553 vs. Southern-B.R., Sept. 29; 545 vs. Grambling, Oct. 13)
4 Games
  2,065—Willie Totten, Mississippi Val., 1984 (553 vs. Southern-B.R., Sept. 29; 545 vs. Grambling, Oct. 13; 368 vs. Texas Southern, Oct. 20; 599 vs. Prairie View, Oct. 27)

Most Games Gaining 200 Yards or More
Season
  11—By 11 players. Most recent: Jamie Martin, Weber St., 1991; John Friesz, Idaho, 1989; Todd Hammel, Stephen F. Austin, 1989
Career
  36—Neil Lomax, Portland St., 1977-80 (42 games)

Most Consecutive Games Gaining 200 Yards or More
Season
  11—By nine players. Most recent: Jamie Martin, Weber St., 1991; Jeff Wiley, Holy Cross, 1987; Tony Petersen, Marshall, 1987
Career
  28—Neil Lomax, Portland St., 1978-80

Most Games Gaining 300 Yards or More
Season
  10—John Friesz, Idaho, 1989; Willie Totten, Mississippi Val., 1984
Career
  28—Neil Lomax, Portland St., 1977-80

Most Consecutive Games Gaining 300 Yards or More
Season
  10—John Friesz, Idaho, 1989; Willie Totten, Mississippi Val., 1984

Career
  13—Neil Lomax, Portland St., 1979-80

Most Yards Gained Against One Opponent
Career
  1,675—Willie Totten, Mississippi Val. vs. Prairie View, 1982-85
  Also holds per-game record at 418.8 (1,675 in 4)

Most Yards Per Attempt
Game
  (Min. 30 atts.) 16.1—Gilbert Renfroe, Tennessee St. vs. Dist. Columbia, Nov. 5, 1983 (30 for 484)
  (Min. 45 atts.) 12.69—Todd Hammel, Stephen F. Austin vs. Northeast La., Nov. 11, 1989 (45 for 571)
Season
  (Min. 250 atts.) 10.31—Mike Smith, Northern Iowa, 1986 (303 for 3,125)
  (Min. 325 atts.) 9.51—John Friesz, Idaho, 1989 (425 for 4,041)
Career
  (Min. 500 atts.) 8.72—Mike Smith, Northern Iowa, 1984-87 (943 for 8,219)
  (Min. 1,000 atts.) 8.23—Neil Lomax, Portland St., 1977-80 (1,606 for 13,220)

Most Yards Gained Per Completion
Game
  (Min. 15 comps.) 22.79—Matt Griffin, New Hampshire vs. Hofstra, Sept. 21, 1991 (19 for 433)
  (Min. 20 comps.) 22.55—Michael Payton, Marshall vs. Va. Military, Nov. 16, 1991 (22 for 496)
Season
  (Min. 200 comps.) 16.4—Todd Hammel, Stephen F. Austin, 1989 (238 for 3,914)
Career
  (Min. 400 comps.) 15.31—Todd Hammel, Stephen F. Austin, 1986-89 (443 for 6,784)

Most Touchdown Passes
Quarter
  7—Neil Lomax, Portland St. vs. Delaware St., Nov. 8, 1980 (1st)
Half
  7—Neil Lomax, Portland St. vs. Delaware St., Nov. 8, 1980 (1st)
Game
  9—Willie Totten, Mississippi Val. vs. Kentucky St., Sept. 1, 1984
Season
  56—Willie Totten, Mississippi Val., 1984
  Also holds per-game record at 5.60 (56 in 10)
Career
  139—Willie Totten, Mississippi Val., 1982-85
  Also holds per-game record at 3.48 (139 in 40)

Most Consecutive Games Throwing a Touchdown Pass
Career
  27—Willie Totten, Mississippi Val., 1983-85

Most Touchdown Passes, Same Passer and Receiver
Season
  27—Willie Totten to Jerry Rice, Mississippi Val., 1984
Career
  47—Willie Totten to Jerry Rice, Mississippi Val., 1982-84

Highest Percentage of Passes for Touchdowns
Season
   (Min. 200 atts.) 11.7%—Mike Williams, Grambling, 1980 (28 of 239)
   (Min. 300 atts.) 10.8%—Willie Totten, Mississippi Val., 1984 (56 of 518)

Career
   (Min. 500 atts.) 8.46%—Mike Williams, Grambling, 1977-80 (44 of 520)
   (Min. 750 atts.) 7.06%—Eric Beavers, Nevada, 1983-86 (77 of 1,094)

RECEIVING

Most Passes Caught
Game
   24—Jerry Rice, Mississippi Val. vs. Southern-B.R., Oct. 1, 1983 (219 yards)
Season
   115—Brian Forster, Rhode Island, 1985 (1,617 yards)
Career
   301—Jerry Rice, Mississippi Val., 1981-84 (4,693 yards)

Most Passes Caught Per Game
Season
   11.5—Brian Forster, Rhode Island, 1985 (115 in 10)
Career
   7.3—Jerry Rice, Mississippi Val., 1981-84 (301 in 41)

Most Passes Caught by a Tight End
Game
   18—Brian Forster, Rhode Island, 1985 (327 yards)
Season
   115—Brian Forster, Rhode Island, 1985 (1,617 yards)
   Also holds per-game record at 11.5 (115 in 10)
Career
   245—Brian Forster, Rhode Island, 1983-85, 87 (3,410 yards)

Most Passes Caught by a Running Back
Game
   21—David Pandt, Montana St. vs. Eastern Wash., Sept. 21, 1985 (169 yards)
Season
   78—Gordie Lockbaum, Holy Cross, 1987 (1,152 yards)
2 Yrs
   135—Gordie Lockbaum, Holy Cross, 1986-87 (2,012 yards)
   Also holds per-game record at 6.1 (135 in 22)
Career
   182—Merril Hoge, Idaho St., 1983-86 (1,734 yards)

Most Passes Caught by Two Players, Same Team
Season
   183—Jerry Rice (103 for 1,682 yards and 27 TDs) & Joe Thomas (80 for 1,119 yards and 11 TDs), Mississippi Val., 1984
Career
   420—Darrell Colbert (217 for 3,177 yards and 33 TDs) & Donald Narcisse (203 for 2,429 yards and 26 TDs), Texas Southern, 1983-86

Most Yards Gained
Game
   370—Michael Lerch, Princeton vs. Brown, Oct. 12, 1991 (caught 9)
Season
   1,682—Jerry Rice, Mississippi Val., 1984 (caught 103)
Career
   4,693—Jerry Rice, Mississippi Val., 1981-84 (caught 301)

Most Yards Gained Per Game
Season
   168.2—Jerry Rice, Mississippi Val., 1984 (1,682 in 10)
Career
   114.5—Jerry Rice, Mississippi Val., 1981-84 (4,693 in 41)

Most Yards Gained by a Tight End
Game
   327—Brian Forster, Rhode Island vs. Brown, Sept. 28, 1985 (caught 18)
Season
   1,617—Brian Forster, Rhode Island, 1985 (caught 115)
   Also holds per-game record at 161.7 (1,617 in 10)
Career
   3,410—Brian Forster, Rhode Island, 1983-85, 87 (caught 245)

Most Yards Gained by a Running Back
Game
   220—Alvin Atkinson, Davidson vs. Furman, Nov. 3, 1979 (caught 9)
Season
   1,152—Gordie Lockbaum, Holy Cross, 1987 (caught 78)
   Also holds per-game record at 104.7 (1,152 in 11)

Most Yards Gained by Two Players, Same Team
Season
   2,801—Jerry Rice (1,682, 103 caught and 27 TDs) & Joe Thomas (1,119, 80 caught and 11 TDs), Mississippi Val., 1984
Career
   5,806—Roy Banks (3,177, 184 caught and 38 TDs) & Cal Pierce (2,629, 163 caught and 13 TDs), Eastern Ill., 1983-86

Highest Average Gain Per Reception
Game
   (Min. 5) 44.6—John Taylor, Delaware St. vs. St. Paul's, Sept. 21, 1985 (5 for 223)
   (Min. 10) 23.9—Jimmy Smith, Jackson St. vs. Delaware St., Oct. 5, 1991 (10 for 239)
Season
   (Min. 30) 26.3—Brian Allen, Idaho, 1983 (31 for 814)
   (Min. 40) 25.0—Mark Stock, Va. Military, 1986 (45 for 1,123)
   (Min. 60) 20.7—Golden Tate, Tennessee St., 1983 (63 for 1,307)
Career
   (Min. 90) 24.3—John Taylor, Delaware St., 1982-85 (100 for 2,426)
   (Min. 125) 20.0—Tracy Singleton, Howard, 1979-82 (159 for 3,187)

Most Games Gaining 100 Yards or More
Career
   23—Jerry Rice, Mississippi Val., 1981-84 (in 41 games played)

Most Touchdown Passes Caught

Game
5—Rennie Benn, Lehigh vs. Indiana (Pa.), Sept. 14, 1985 (266 yards); Jerry Rice, Mississippi Val. vs. Prairie View, Oct. 27, 1984 & vs. Kentucky St., Sept. 1, 1984

Season
27—Jerry Rice, Mississippi Val., 1984

Career
50—Jerry Rice, Mississippi Val., 1981-84

Most Touchdown Passes Caught Per Game

Season
2.7—Jerry Rice, Mississippi Val., 1984 (27 in 10)

Career
1.22—Jerry Rice, Mississippi Val., 1981-84 (50 in 41)

Most Games Catching a Touchdown Pass

Season
10—Jerry Rice, Mississippi Val., 1984
Also holds consecutive record at 10 (1984)

Career
26—Jerry Rice, Mississippi Val., 1981-84
Also holds consecutive record at 17 (1983-84)

PUNTING

Most Punts

Game
16—Matt Stover, Louisiana Tech vs. Northeast La., Nov. 18, 1988 (567 yards)

Season
98—Barry Hickingbotham, Louisiana Tech, 1987 (3,821 yards)

Career
301—Barry Bowman, Louisiana Tech, 1983-86 (11,441 yards)

Highest Average Per Punt

Game
(Min. 5) 55.7—Jody Farmer, Montana vs. Ne-

vada, Oct. 1, 1988 (9 for 501)
(Min. 10) 52.2—Stuart Dodds, Montana St. vs. Northern Ariz., Oct. 20, 1979 (10 for 522)

Season
(Min. 60) 47.0—Harold Alexander, Appalachian St., 1991 (64 for 3,009)

Career
(Min. 150) 44.4—Pumpy Tudors, Tenn.-Chatt., 1989-91 (181 for 8,041)

Longest Punt
91—Bart Helsley, North Texas vs. Northeast La., Nov. 17, 1990

INTERCEPTIONS

Most Passes Intercepted

Game
5—Mark Cordes, Eastern Wash. vs. Boise St., Sept. 6, 1986 (48 yards); Michael Richardson, Northwestern (La.) vs. Southeastern La., Nov. 12, 1983 (128 yards); Karl Johnson, Jackson St. vs. Grambling, Oct. 23, 1982 (29 yards)

Season
12—Dean Cain, Princeton, 1987 (98 yards)
Also holds per-game record at 1.2 (12 in 10)

Career
28—Dave Murphy, Holy Cross, 1986-89 (309 yards)
Per-game record—0.73, Dean Cain, Princeton, 1985-87 (22 in 30)

Most Yards on Interception Returns

Game
216—Keiron Bigby, Brown vs. Yale, Sept. 29, 1984 (3 interceptions) (first career game)

Season
216—Keiron Bigby, Brown, 1984 (3 interceptions)

Career
452—Rick Harris, East Tenn. St., 1986-88 (20 interceptions)

Most Touchdowns Scored on Interception Returns

Game
2—By three players. Most recent: Keiron Bigby, Brown vs. Yale, Sept. 29, 1984

Season
4—Robert Turner, Jackson St., 1990 (9 interceptions, 212 yards)

Career
4—Robert Turner (DB), Jackson St., 1990 (9 interceptions); Ken Braden (LB), Southwest Mo. St., 1984-87 (8 interceptions); Roger Robinson (DB), Tennessee St., 1981-84 (12 interceptions)

Highest Average Gain Per Interception

Game
(Min. 3) 72.0—Keiron Bigby, Brown vs. Yale, Sept. 29, 1984 (3 for 216)

Season
(Min. 3) 72.0—Keiron Bigby, Brown, 1984 (3 for 216)

Career
(Min. 12) 24.9—Roger Robinson, Tennessee St., 1981-84 (12 for 299)

PUNT RETURNS

Most Punt Returns

Game
9—By 11 players. Most recent: Ricardo Clark, Marshall vs. Tenn.-Chatt., Oct. 22, 1988 (43 yards)

Season
55—Tommy Houk, Murray St., 1980 (442 yards)
Also holds per-game record at 5.0 (55 in 11)

Career
117—David McCrary, Tenn.-Chatt., 1982-85 (1,230 yards)

Per-game record—3.8, Tommy Houk, Murray St., 1979-80 (84 in 22)

Most Yards on Punt Returns

Game
216—Gary Harrell, Howard vs. Morgan St., Nov. 3, 1990 (7 returns); Willie Ware, Mississippi Val. vs. Washburn, Sept. 15, 1984 (7 returns)

130

Season

561—Willie Ware, Mississippi Val., 1985 (31 returns)
Also holds per-game record at 51.0 (561 in 11)

Career

1,230—David McCrary, Tenn.-Chatt., 1982-85 (117 returns)

Highest Average Gain Per Return

Game

(Min. 5) 30.9—Gary Harrell, Howard vs. Morgan St., Nov. 3, 1990 (7 for 216); Willie Ware, Mississippi Val. vs. Washburn, Sept. 15, 1984 (7 for 216)

Season

(Min. 1.2 per game) 23.0—Tim Egerton, Delaware St., 1988 (16 for 368)

Career

(Min. 1.2 per game) 16.4—Willie Ware, Mississippi Val., 1982-85 (61 for 1,003)

Most Touchdowns Scored on Punt Returns

Game

2—By four players. Most recent: Sebron Spivey, Southern Ill. vs. Southeast Mo. St., Oct. 19, 1985

Season

4—Howard Huckaby, Florida A&M, 1988 (26 returns)

Career

5—Tim Egerton, Delaware St., 1986-88; Willie Ware, Mississippi Val., 1982-85

Longest Punt Return

98—Barney Bussey, South Caro. St. vs. Johnson Smith, Oct. 10, 1981

Consecutive Games Returning Punt for Touchdown

3—Troy Jones, McNeese St., 1989 (vs. Mississippi Col., Sept. 2; vs. Samford, Sept. 9; vs. Northeast La., Sept. 16)

KICKOFF RETURNS

Most Kickoff Returns

Game

10—Merril Hoge, Idaho St. vs. Weber St., Oct. 25, 1986 (179 yards)

Season

50—David Primus, Samford, 1989 (1,411 yards)

Career

118—Clarence Alexander, Mississippi Val., 1986-89 (2,439 yards)

Most Kickoff Returns Per Game

Season

4.55—David Primus, Samford, 1989 (50 in 11)

Career

2.95—Clarence Alexander, Mississippi Val., 1986-89 (118 in 40); Lorenza Rivers, Tennessee Tech, 1985, 87 (62 in 21)

Most Yards on Kickoff Returns

Game

262—Herman Hunter, Tennessee St. vs. Mississippi Val., Nov. 13, 1982 (6 returns)

Season

1,411—David Primus, Samford, 1989 (50 returns)

Career

2,439—Clarence Alexander, Mississippi Val., 1986-89 (118 returns)

Most Yards Per Game on Kickoff Returns

Season

128.3—David Primus, Samford, 1989 (1,411 in 11)

Career

60.98—Clarence Alexander, Mississippi Val., 1986-89 (2,439 in 40)

Highest Average Gain Per Return

Game

(Min. 5) 45.6—Jerome Stelly, Western Ill. vs. Youngstown St., Nov. 7, 1981 (5 for 228)

Season

(Min. 1.2 per game) 34.7—Craig Richardson, Eastern Wash., 1984 (21 for 729)

Career

(Min. 1.2 per game) 29.3—Charles Swann, Indiana St., 1989-91 (45 for 1,319)

Most Touchdowns Scored on Kickoff Returns

Game

2—Paul Ashby, Alabama St. vs. Grambling, Nov. 9, 1991 (97 & 94 yards); David Lucas, Florida A&M vs. North Caro. A&T, Oct. 12, 1991 (99 & 93 yards); Jerome Stelly, Western Ill. vs. Youngstown St., Nov. 7, 1981 (99 & 97 yards)

Season

3—Troy Brown, Marshall, 1991; David Lucas, Florida A&M, 1991

Career

3—By seven players. Most recent: David Lucas, Florida A&M, 1991

TOTAL KICK RETURNS
(Combined Punt and Kickoff Returns)

Most Kick Returns

Game

12—Craig Hodge, Tennessee St. vs. Morgan St., Oct. 24, 1987 (8 punts, 4 kickoffs, 318 yards)

Season

64—Joe Markus, Connecticut, 1981 (34 punts, 30 kickoffs, 939 yards)

Career

199—Herman Hunter, Tennessee St., 1981-84 (103 punts, 96 kickoffs, 3,232 yards)

Most Yards on Kick Returns

Game

319—Craig Hodge, Tennessee St. vs. Morgan St., Oct. 24, 1987 (12 returns, 206 on punts, 113 on kickoffs)

Season

1,469—David Primus, Samford, 1989 (1,411 on kickoffs, 58 on punts)
Also holds per-game record at 133.5 (1,469 in 11)

Career
3,232—Herman Hunter, Tennessee St., 1981-84 (974 on punts, 2,258 on kickoffs)
Also holds per-game record at 75.2 (3,232 in 43)

Gaining 1,000 Yards on Punt Returns and 1,000 Yards on Kickoff Returns
Career
Joe Markus, Connecticut, 1979-82 (1,012 and 1,185)

Highest Average Per Kick Return
Game
(Min. 6) 42.3—Herman Hunter, Tennessee St. vs. Mississippi Val., Nov. 13, 1982 (7 for 296)

Season
(Min. 40) 26.7—David Primus, Samford, 1989 (55 for 1,469)
Career
(Min. 60) 20.9—Bill LaFreniere, Northeastern, 1978-81 (112 for 2,336)

Most Touchdowns Scored on Kick Returns
Season
4—Troy Brown, Marshall, 1991 (3 kickoffs and 1 punt); Howard Huckaby, Florida A&M, 1988 (4 punts); Willie Ware, Mississippi Val., 1985 (2 punts and 2 kickoffs)
Career
7—Willie Ware, Mississippi Val., 1982-85 (5 punts and 2 kickoffs)

ALL-PURPOSE RUNNING
(Yardage Gained From Rushing, Receiving and All Runbacks)
Most Plays

Game
54—Ron Darby, Marshall vs. Western Caro., Nov. 12, 1988 (47 rushes, 4 receptions, 3 kickoff returns; 329 yards)
Season
357—Lorenzo Bouier, Maine, 1980 (349 rushes, 8 receptions; 1,639 yards)
Career
1,096—Kenny Gamble, Colgate, 1984-87 (963 rushes, 43 receptions, 10 punt returns, 80 kickoff returns; 7,623 yards)

Most Yards Gained
Game
463—Michael Lerch, Princeton vs. Brown, Oct. 12, 1991 (15 rushing, 370 receiving, 78 kickoff returns; 16 plays)
Season
2,425—Kenny Gamble, Colgate, 1986 (1,816 rushing, 178 receiving, 40 punt returns, 391 kickoff returns; 343 plays)
Career
7,623—Kenny Gamble, Colgate, 1984-87 (5,220 rushing, 536 receiving, 104 punt returns, 1,763 kickoff returns; 1,096 plays)

Most Yards Gained Per Game
Season
220.5—Kenny Gamble, Colgate, 1986 (2,425 in 11)
Career
189.1—David Meggett, Towson St., 1987-88 (3,403 in 18)

Most Yards Gained by a Freshman
Season
1,656—Markus Thomas, Eastern Ky., 1989

Highest Average Gain Per Play
Game
(Min. 20 plays) 20.6—Herman Hunter, Tennessee St. vs. Mississippi Val., Nov. 13, 1982 (453 on 22)
Season
(Min. 1,000 yards, 100 plays) 19.68—Otis Washington, Western Caro., 1988 (2,086 on 106)

Maine running back Lorenzo Bouier set a Division I-AA single-season record for most plays with 357 in 1980 (349 rushes, eight receptions).

Career
(Min. 4,000 yards, 350 plays) 14.8—Pete Mandley, Northern Ariz., 1979-80, 82-83 (5,925 on 401)

SCORING
Most Points Scored
Game
36—By five players. Most recent: Erwin Matthews, Richmond vs. Massachusetts, Sept. 19, 1987 (6 TDs, including 1 TD and 6 points in OT)

Season
170—Geoff Mitchell, Weber St., 1991 (28 TDs, 2 PATs)
Career
385—Marty Zendejas, Nevada, 1984-87 (72 FGs, 169 PATs)

Most Points Scored Per Game
Season
16.2—Jerry Rice, Mississippi Val., 1984 (162 in 10)
Career
10.0—David Meggett, Towson St., 1987-88 (180 in 18)

Most Touchdowns Scored
Game
6—By five players. Most recent: Erwin Matthews, Richmond vs. Massachusetts, Sept. 19, 1987 (1 TD in OT)
Season
28—Geoff Mitchell, Weber St., 1991
Career
60—Charvez Foger, Nevada, 1985-88

Most Touchdowns Scored Per Game
Season
2.7—Jerry Rice, Mississippi Val., 1984 (27 in 10)
Career
1.67—David Meggett, Towson St., 1987-88 (30 in 18)

Most Touchdowns Scored by a Freshman
Season
18—Charvez Foger, Nevada, 1985
Also holds per-game record at 1.8 (18 in 10)

Most Extra Points Attempted by Kicking
Game
15—John Kincheloe, Portland St. vs. Delaware St., Nov. 8, 1980 (15 made)
Season
74—John Kincheloe, Portland St., 1980 (70 made)
Per-game record—7.2, Jonathan Stokes, Mississippi Val., 1984 (72 in 10)
Career
175—Thayne Doyle, Idaho, 1988-91 (160 made); Marty Zendejas, Nevada, 1984-87 (169 made)

Most Extra Points Made by Kicking
Game
15—John Kincheloe, Portland St. vs. Delaware St., Nov. 8, 1980 (15 attempts)
Season
70—John Kincheloe, Portland St., 1980 (74 attempts)

Per-game record—6.8, Jonathan Stokes, Mississippi Val., 1984 (68 in 10)
Career
169—Marty Zendejas, Nevada, 1984-87 (175 attempts)
Also holds per-game record at 3.84 (169 in 44)

Best Perfect Record of Extra Points Made
Season
51 of 51—Jim Hodson, Lafayette, 1988

Highest Percentage of Extra Points Made
Career
(Min. 100 atts.) 100%—Anders Larsson, Montana St., 1985-88 (101 of 101)
(Min. 120 atts.) 99.2%—Brian Mitchell, Marshall/Northern Iowa, 1987, 89-91 (130 of 131)

Most Consecutive Extra Points Made
Game
15—John Kincheloe, Portland St. vs. Delaware St., Nov. 8, 1980
Season
51—Jim Hodson, Lafayette, 1988
Career
105—Tim McMonigle, Idaho, 1982-84

Most Points Scored by Kicking
Game
24—Goran Lingmerth, Northern Ariz. vs. Idaho, Oct. 25, 1986 (8 FGs)
Season
109—Brian Mitchell, Northern Iowa, 1990 (26 FGs, 31 PATs)
Career
385—Marty Zendejas, Nevada, 1984-87 (72 FGs, 169 PATs)

Most Points Scored by Kicking Per Game
Season
9.9—Brian Mitchell, Northern Iowa, 1990 (109 in 11)
Career
9.09—Tony Zendejas, Nevada, 1981-83 (300 in 33)

Most Two-Point Attempts
Season
11—Jamie Martin, Weber St., 1990; Brent Woods, Princeton, 1982

Most Successful Two-Point Passes
Game
3—Brent Woods, Princeton vs. Lafayette, Nov. 6, 1982 (attempted 3)
Season
5—Jamie Martin, Weber St., 1990 (attempted 11); Brent Woods, Princeton, 1982 (attempted 11)

DEFENSIVE EXTRA POINTS

Most Defensive Extra-Point Returns, One Game, Single Player
2—Joe Lee Johnson, Western Ky. vs. Indiana St., Nov. 10, 1990 (both kick returns, scored on neither)

Most Defensive Extra Points Scored
Game
1—By many players
Season
2—Jackie Kellogg, Eastern Wash. vs. Weber St., Oct. 6, 1990 (90-yard interception return) & vs. Portland St., Oct. 27, 1990 (94-yard interception return)

Longest Return of a Defensive Extra Point
Game
100—Morgan Ryan (DB), Montana St. vs. Sam Houston St., Sept. 7, 1991 (interception return)

First Defensive Extra-Point Attempts
Mike Rogers (DB), Davidson vs. Lehigh, Sept. 10, 1988 (30-yard interception return); Dave Benna (LB), Towson St. vs. Northeastern, Sept. 10, 1988 (35-yard interception return)

FIELD GOALS

Most Field Goals Attempted

Game

8—Goran Lingmerth, Northern Ariz. vs. Idaho, Oct. 25, 1986 (made 8)

Season

33—Tony Zendejas, Nevada, 1982 (made 26)

Career

102—Kirk Roach, Western Caro., 1984-87 (made 71)

Most Field Goals Made

Quarter

4—Ryan Weeks, Tennessee Tech vs. Tenn.-Chatt., Sept. 9, 1989 (3rd); Tony Zendejas, Nevada vs. Northern Ariz., Oct. 16, 1982 (4th)

Half

5—Ryan Weeks, Tennessee Tech vs. Tenn.-Chatt., Sept. 9, 1989 (2nd); Tony Zendejas, Nevada vs. Northern Ariz., Oct. 16, 1982 (2nd); Dean Biasucci, Western Caro. vs. Mars Hill, Sept. 18, 1982 (1st)

Game

8—Goran Lingmerth, Northern Ariz. vs. Idaho, Oct. 25, 1986 (39, 18, 20, 33, 46, 27, 22, 35 yards; by quarters—1, 3, 2, 2), 8 attempts

Season

26—Brian Mitchell, Northern Iowa, 1990 (27 attempts); Tony Zendejas, Nevada, 1982 (33 attempts)

Career

72—Marty Zendejas, Nevada, 1984-87 (90 attempts)

Most Field Goals Made Per Game

Season

2.36—Brian Mitchell, Northern Iowa, 1990 (26 in 11); Tony Zendejas, Nevada, 1982 (26 in 11)

Career

2.12—Tony Zendejas, Nevada, 1981-83 (70 in 33)

Highest Percentage of Field Goals Made

Season

(Min. 20 atts.) 96.3%—Brian Mitchell, Northern Iowa, 1990 (26 of 27)

Career

(Min. 50 atts.) 81.4%—Tony Zendejas, Nevada, 1981-83 (70 of 86)

Most Consecutive Field Goals Made

Game

8—Goran Lingmerth, Northern Ariz. vs. Idaho, Oct. 25, 1986

Season

21—Brian Mitchell, Northern Iowa, 1990

Career

26—Brian Mitchell, Northern Iowa, 1990-91

Most Consecutive Games Kicking a Field Goal

Career

33—Tony Zendejas, Nevada, 1981-83 (at least one in every game played)

Most Field Goals Made, 50 Yards or More

Game

3—Jesse Garcia, Northeast La. vs. McNeese St., Oct. 29, 1983 (52, 56, 53 yards)

Season

7—Kirk Roach, Western Caro., 1987 (12 attempts); Jesse Garcia, Northeast La., 1983 (12 attempts)

Career

11—Kirk Roach, Western Caro., 1984-87 (26 attempts)

Highest Percentage of Field Goals Made, 50 Yards or More

Season

(Min. 6 atts.) 83.3%—Tim Foley, Ga. Southern, 1987 (5 of 6)

Career

(Min. 10 atts.) 90.9%—Tim Foley, Ga. Southern, 1984-87 (10 of 11)

Most Field Goals Made, 40 Yards or More

Season

12—Marty Zendejas, Nevada, 1985 (15 attempts)

Career

30—Marty Zendejas, Nevada, 1984-87 (45 attempts)

Highest Percentage of Field Goals Made, 40 Yards or More

Season

(Min. 8) 100.0%—Tim Foley, Ga. Southern, 1985 (8 of 8)

Career

(Min. 15) 72.0%—Tim Foley, Ga. Southern, 1984-87 (18 of 25)

Highest Percentage of Field Goals Made, 40-49 Yards

Season

(Min. 8) 90.0%—Marty Zendejas, Nevada, 1985 (9 of 10)

Career

(Min. 12) 72.0%—Tony Zendejas, Nevada, 1981-83 (18 of 25)

Highest Percentage of Field Goals Made, Under 40 Yards

Season

(Min. 15) 100.0%—Brian Mitchell, Northern Iowa, 1990 (23 of 23); Kirk Roach, Western Caro., 1986 (17 of 17); Matt Stover, Louisiana Tech, 1986 (15 of 15)

Career

(Min. 25) 93.3%—Marty Zendejas, Nevada, 1984-87 (42 of 45)

Most Times Kicking Two or More Field Goals in a Game

Season

10—Brian Mitchell, Northern Iowa, 1991

Career

25—Kirk Roach, Western Caro., 1984-87

Most Times Kicking Three or More Field Goals in a Game

Season

7—Brian Mitchell, Northern Iowa, 1991

Career

11—Brian Mitchell, Marshall/Northern Iowa, 1987, 89-91

Most Consecutive Quarters Kicking a Field Goal

Season

7—Scott Roper, Arkansas St., 1986 (last 3 vs. McNeese St., Oct. 25; all 4 vs. North Texas, Nov. 1)

Longest Average Distance Field Goals Made

Game

(Min. 3) 53.7—Jesse Garcia, Northeast La. vs. McNeese St., Oct. 29, 1983 (52, 56, 53 yards)

Season

(Min. 14) 45.0—Jesse Garcia, Northeast La., 1983 (15 made)

Career
(Min. 35) 37.5—Roger Ruzek, Weber St., 1979-82 (46 made)

Longest Average Distance Field Goals Attempted
Season
(Min. 20 atts.) 45.9—Jesse Garcia, Northeast La., 1983 (26 attempts)
Career
(Min. 60 atts.) 40.5—Kirk Roach, Western Caro., 1984-87 (102 attempts)

Longest Field Goal Made
63—Scott Roper, Arkansas St. vs. North Texas, Nov. 7, 1987; Tim Foley, Ga. Southern vs. James Madison, Nov. 7, 1987

Longest Field Goal Made by a Freshman
60—David Cool, Ga. Southern vs. James Madison, Nov. 5, 1988

Most Field Goals Made by a Freshman Game
5—Chuck Rawlinson, Stephen F. Austin vs. Prairie View, Sept. 10, 1988 (5 attempts); Marty Zendejas, Nevada vs. Idaho St., Nov. 17, 1984 (5 attempts); Mike Powers, Colgate vs. Army, Sept. 10, 1983 (6 attempts)
Season
22—Marty Zendejas, Nevada, 1984 (27 attempts)

Most Field Goals Made in First Game of a Career
5—Mike Powers, Colgate vs. Army, Sept. 10, 1983 (6 attempts)

Most Games in Which Field Goal(s) Provided the Winning Margin
Career
11—John Dowling, Youngstown St., 1984-87

Longest Return of a Missed Field Goal
89—Pat Bayers, Western Ill. vs. Youngstown St., Nov. 6, 1982 (TD)

TEAM RECORDS

SINGLE GAME—OFFENSE
TOTAL OFFENSE

Most Plays
113—Villanova vs. Connecticut, Oct. 7, 1989 (553 yards)

Most Plays, Both Teams
196—Villanova (113) & Connecticut (83), Oct. 7, 1989 (904 yards)

Most Yards Gained
876—Weber St. vs. Idaho St., Nov. 23, 1991 (252 rushing, 624 passing)

Most Yards Gained, Both Teams
1,418—Howard (740) & Bethune-Cookman (678), Sept. 19, 1987 (161 plays)

Most Yards Gained by a Losing Team
678—Bethune-Cookman vs. Howard, Sept. 19, 1987 (lost 51-58)

Fewest Yards Gained by a Winning Team
31—Middle Tenn. St. vs. Murray St., Oct. 17, 1981 (won 14-9)

Highest Average Gain Per Play (Min. 55 Plays)
12.7—Marshall vs. Va. Military, Nov. 16, 1991 (62 for 789)

Most Touchdowns Scored by Rushing and Passing
14—Portland St. vs. Delaware St., Nov. 8, 1980 (10 passing, 4 rushing)

RUSHING

Most Rushes
90—Va. Military vs. East Tenn. St., Nov. 17, 1990 (311 yards)

Most Rushes, Both Teams
125—Austin Peay (81) & Murray St. (44), Nov. 17, 1990 (443 yards); Southwest Mo. St. (71) & Northern Ill. (54), Oct. 17, 1987 (375 yards)

Fewest Rushes
11—Western Ill. vs. Northern Iowa, Oct. 24, 1987 (-11 yards); Mississippi Val. vs. Kentucky St., Sept. 1, 1984 (17 yards)

Most Yards Gained
681—Southwest Mo. St. vs. Mo. Southern St., Sept. 10, 1988 (83 rushes)

Most Yards Gained, Both Teams
762—Arkansas St. (604) & East Tex. St. (158), Sept. 26, 1987 (102 rushes)

Most Yards Gained by a Losing Team
429—Nevada vs. Weber St., Nov. 6, 1982 (lost 43-46, 3 OT)

Highest Average Gain Per Rush (Min. 45 Rushes)
11.2—Southwest Mo. St. vs. Northeast Mo. St., Oct. 5, 1985 (45 for 505)

Most Touchdowns Scored by Rushing
10—Arkansas St. vs. East Tex. St., Sept. 26, 1987

PASSING

Most Passes Attempted
77—Portland St. vs. Northern Colo., Oct. 20, 1979 (completed 44 for 499 yards)

Most Passes Attempted, Both Teams
122—Idaho (62) & Idaho St. (60), Sept. 24, 1983 (completed 48 for 639 yards)

Fewest Passes Attempted
1—By many teams. Most recent: Northeastern vs. Towson St., Sept. 9, 1989 (completed 1)

Fewest Passes Attempted, Both Teams
11—Western Ky. (6) & North Caro. A&T (5), Nov. 19, 1988 (completed 2); Arkansas St. (8) & Memphis St. (3), Nov. 27, 1982 (completed 6)

Most Passes Attempted Without Interception
72—Marshall vs. Western Caro., Nov. 14, 1987 (completed 35)

Most Passes Completed
50—Mississippi Val. vs. Prairie View, Oct. 27, 1984 (attempted 66 for 642 yards); Mississippi Val. vs. Southern-B.R., Sept. 29, 1984 (attempted 70 for 633 yards)

Most Passes Completed, Both Teams I-AA
77—Northeast La. (46) & Stephen F. Austin (31), Nov. 11, 1989 (attempted 116 for 1,190 yards)

Most Passes Completed, Both Teams
80—Hofstra (50) & Fordham (30), Oct. 19, 1991 (attempted 120 for 987 yards)

Fewest Passes Completed
0—By many teams. Most recent: Delaware St. vs. North Caro. A&T, Nov. 9, 1991; Morgan St. vs. Cheyney, Nov. 10, 1990; Arkansas St. vs. Illinois St., Nov. 11, 1989; Va. Military vs. Marshall, Oct. 28, 1989; Ga. Southern vs. Central Fla., Oct. 21, 1989

Fewest Passes Completed, Both Teams
2—North Caro. A&T (0) & Western Ky. (2), Nov. 19, 1988 (attempted 11)

Highest Percentage Completed
(Min. 30 atts.) 81.6%—Nevada vs. Idaho St., Nov. 17, 1984 (31 of 38)
(Min. 45 atts.) 75.7%—Mississippi Val. vs. Prairie View, Oct. 27, 1984 (50 of 66)

Lowest Percentage Completed
(Min. 20 atts.) 9.5%—Florida A&M vs. Central St. (Ohio), Oct. 11, 1986 (2 of 21)

Most Passes Had Intercepted
10—Boise St. vs. Montana, Oct. 28, 1989 (55 attempts); Mississippi Val. vs. Grambling, Oct. 17, 1987 (47 attempts)

Most Yards Gained
699—Mississippi Val. vs. Kentucky St., Sept. 1, 1984

Most Yards Gained, Both Teams
1,190—Northeast La. (619) & Stephen F. Austin (571), Nov. 11, 1989

Most Yards Gained Per Attempt (Min. 25 Atts.)
17.4—Marshall vs. Va. Military, Nov. 16, 1991 (37 for 642)

Most Yards Gained Per Completion
(Min. 10 comps.) 33.0—Jackson St. vs. Southern-B. R., Oct. 13, 1990 (14 for 462)
(Min. 25 comps.) 22.9—Marshall vs. Va. Military, Nov. 16, 1991 (28 for 642)

Most Touchdown Passes
11—Mississippi Val. vs. Kentucky St., Sept. 1, 1984

Most Touchdown Passes, Both Teams
14—Mississippi Val. (8) & Texas Southern (6), Oct. 26, 1985

PUNTING

Most Punts
16—Louisiana Tech vs. Northeast La., Nov. 19, 1988 (567 yards)

Highest Average Per Punt (Min. 5 Punts)
55.7—Montana vs. Nevada, Oct. 1, 1988 (9 for 501)

Highest Average Per Punt (Min. 10 Punts)
52.2—Montana St. vs. Northern Ariz., Oct. 20, 1979 (10 for 522)

Fewest Punts
0—By many teams. Most recent: Dartmouth vs. Brown, Nov. 16, 1991; Yale vs. Harvard, Nov. 17, 1990; Citadel vs. Wofford, Nov. 10, 1990; Sam Houston St. vs. Northwestern (La.), Nov. 3, 1990; Mississippi Val. vs. Texas Southern, Oct. 20, 1990; Va. Military vs. West Va. Tech, Oct. 20, 1990; Bucknell vs. Towson St., Oct. 6, 1990; Indiana St. vs. Murray St., Oct. 6, 1990; Stephen F. Austin vs. Southwest Tex. St., Oct. 6, 1990; Howard vs. Morris Brown, Sept. 8, 1990

Fewest Punts, Both Teams
0—Ga. Southern & James Madison, Nov. 15, 1986

Most Opponents' Punts Blocked By
4—Middle Tenn. St. vs. Mississippi Val., Oct. 8, 1988 (7 punts); Montana vs. Montana St., Oct. 31, 1987 (13 punts)

PUNT RETURNS

Most Punt Returns
12—Northern Iowa vs. Youngstown St., Oct. 20, 1984 (83 yards)

Most Yards on Punt Returns
221—Howard vs. Morgan St., Nov. 3, 1990 (8 returns)

Highest Average Gain Per Return (Min. 6 Returns)
30.9—Mississippi Val. vs. Washburn, Sept. 15, 1984 (7 for 216, 2 TDs)

Most Touchdowns Scored on Punt Returns
2—By nine teams. Most recent: Lehigh vs. Davidson, Sept. 10, 1988 (includes a blocked punt return)

KICKOFF RETURNS

Most Kickoff Returns
15—Delaware St. vs. Portland St., Nov. 8, 1980 (209 yards)

Most Yards on Kickoff Returns
277—Idaho St. vs. Texas A&I, Sept. 12, 1987 (10 returns)

Highest Average Gain Per Return
(Min. 3 rets.) 50.5 — Eastern Ky. vs. Murray St., Oct. 28, 1978 (4 for 202)
(Min. 6 rets.) 39.1 — Tennessee St. vs. Mississippi Val., Nov. 13, 1982 (7 for 274)

Most Touchdowns Scored on Kickoff Returns
2 — Western Ill. vs. Youngstown St., Nov. 7, 1981

TOTAL KICK RETURNS
(Combined Punt and Kickoff Returns)

Most Yards on Kick Returns
318 — Tennessee St. vs. Morgan St., Oct. 24, 1987 (12 returns)

Highest Average Gain Per Return
(Min. 6 rets.) 46.8 — Connecticut vs. Yale, Sept. 24, 1983 (6 for 281)

SCORING

Most Points Scored
105 — Portland St. vs. Delaware St., Nov. 8, 1980 (15 TDs, 15 PATs)

Most Points Scored, Both Teams
122 — Weber St. (63) & Eastern Wash. (59), Sept. 28, 1991 (17 TDs, 14 PATs, 2 FGs)

Most Points Scored by a Losing Team
59 — Eastern Wash. vs. Weber St., Sept. 28, 1991

Most Points Scored Each Quarter
1st: 49 — Portland St. vs. Delaware St., Nov. 8, 1980
2nd: 50 — Alabama St. vs. Prairie View, Oct. 26, 1991
3rd: 35 — Portland St. vs. Delaware St., Nov. 8, 1980
4th: 35 — Southeastern La. vs. Delta St., Nov. 8, 1980

Most Points Scored Each Half
1st: 73 — Montana St. vs. Eastern Ore., Sept. 14, 1985
2nd: 49 — Northern Iowa vs. Wis.-Whitewater, Oct. 13, 1984; Southeastern La. vs. Delta St., Nov. 8, 1980

Most Touchdowns Scored
15 — Portland St. vs. Delaware St., Nov. 8, 1980

Most Touchdowns Scored, Both Teams
17 — Weber St. (9) & Eastern Wash. (8), Sept. 28, 1991; Furman (9) & Davidson (8), Nov. 3, 1979

Most Extra Points Made by Kicking
15 — Portland St. vs. Delaware St., Nov. 8, 1980 (15 attempts)

Most Two-Point Attempts Made
5 — Weber St. vs. Eastern Wash., Oct. 6, 1990 (5 passes attempted)

Most Field Goals Made
8 — Northern Ariz. vs. Idaho, Oct. 25, 1986 (8 attempts)

Most Field Goals Attempted
8 — Northern Ariz. vs. Idaho, Oct. 25, 1986 (made 8)

Most Field Goals Made, Both Teams
9 — Nevada (5) & Weber St. (4), Nov. 6, 1982 (11 attempts, 3 OT); Nevada (5) & Northern Ariz. (4), Oct. 9, 1982 (12 attempts)

Most Safeties Scored
3 — Alabama St. vs. Albany St. (Ga.), Oct. 15, 1988

Most Defensive Extra Points Scored
2 — Va. Military vs. Davidson, Nov. 4, 1989 (2 interception returns)

Most Defensive Extra-Point Attempts
2 — Western Ky. vs. Indiana St., Nov. 10, 1990 (2 interception returns); Va. Military vs. Davidson, Nov. 4, 1989 (2 interception returns)

FIRST DOWNS

Most First Downs
46 — Weber St. vs. Idaho St., Nov. 23, 1991 (12 rushing, 31 passing, 3 penalty)

Most First Downs, Both Teams
72 — Bethune-Cookman (40) & Howard (32), Sept. 19, 1987

Most First Downs by Rushing
29 — By six teams. Most recent: Arkansas St. vs.

Southern Ill., Nov. 5, 1988; Southwest Mo. St. vs. Mo. Southern St., Sept. 10, 1988

Most First Downs by Passing
31 — Weber St. vs. Idaho St., Nov. 23, 1991

Most First Downs by Penalty
11 — Towson St. vs. Liberty, Oct. 21, 1990

FUMBLES

Most Fumbles
16 — Delaware St. vs. Portland St., Nov. 8, 1980 (lost 6)

Most Fumbles, Both Teams
20 — Prairie View (11) & Southern-B.R. (9), Sept. 24, 1983 (lost 7); Morgan St. (11) & South Caro. St. (9), Oct. 14, 1978 (lost 9)

Most Fumbles Lost
8 — By four teams. Most recent: Morgan St. vs. North Caro. A&T, Sept. 22, 1990 (12 fumbles)

Most Fumbles Lost, Both Teams
12 — Austin Peay (8) & Mars Hill (4), Nov. 17, 1979 (18 fumbles); Virginia St. (7) & Howard (5), Oct. 13, 1979 (16 fumbles)

PENALTIES

Most Penalties Against
22—By three teams. Most recent: Grambling vs. Texas Southern, Nov. 1, 1986 (198 yards)

Most Penalties, Both Teams
39—In four games. Most recent: Jackson St. (22) & Grambling (17), Oct. 24, 1987 (370 yards)

Most Yards Penalized
260—Southern-B.R. vs. Howard, Nov. 4, 1978 (22 penalties)

Most Yards Penalized, Both Teams
423—Southern-B.R. (260) & Howard (163), Nov. 4, 1978 (37 penalties)

TURNOVERS
(Passes Had Intercepted and Fumbles Lost)

Most Turnovers
12—Texas Southern vs. Lamar, Sept. 6, 1980 (4 interceptions, 8 fumbles lost)

Most Turnovers, Both Teams
15—Stephen F. Austin (8) & Nicholls St. (7), Sept. 22, 1990 (8 interceptions, 7 fumbles lost); Bucknell (8) & Hofstra (7), Sept. 8, 1990 (10 interceptions, 5 fumbles lost)

SINGLE GAME—DEFENSE
TOTAL DEFENSE

Fewest Plays Allowed
31—Howard vs. Dist. Columbia, Sept. 2, 1989 (32 yards)

Fewest Yards Allowed
Minus 12—Eastern Ill. vs. Kentucky St., Nov. 13, 1982 (-67 rushing, 55 passing)

RUSHING DEFENSE

Fewest Rushes Allowed
11—Northern Iowa vs. Western Ill., Oct. 24, 1987 (-11 yards)

Fewest Rushing Yards Allowed
Minus 88—Austin Peay vs. Morehead St., Oct. 8, 1983 (31 rushes)

PASS DEFENSE

Fewest Attempts Allowed
1—By five teams. Most recent: Towson St. vs. Northeastern, Sept. 9, 1989 (1 completed)

Fewest Completions Allowed
0—By many teams. Most recent: Colgate vs. Army, Nov. 18, 1989 (2 attempts); Illinois St. vs. Arkansas St., Nov. 11, 1989 (3 attempts); Marshall vs. Va. Military, Oct. 28, 1989 (4 attempts)

Lowest Completion Percentage Allowed (Min. 30 Atts.)
11.8%—Southern-B.R. vs. Nicholls St., Oct. 11, 1980 (4 of 34)

Fewest Yards Allowed
Minus 2—Florida A&M vs. Albany St. (Ga.), Oct. 16, 1982

Most Passes Intercepted By
10—Montana vs. Boise St., Oct. 28, 1989 (55 attempts); Grambling vs. Mississippi Val., Oct. 17, 1987 (47 attempts)

Most Times Opponent Tackled for Loss Attempting to Pass
13—Austin Peay vs. Morehead St., Oct. 8, 1983 (110 yards)

Most Interceptions Returned for Touchdowns
3—Delaware St. vs. Akron, Oct. 17, 1987 (5 for 124 yards); Montana vs. Eastern Wash., Nov. 12, 1983 (4 for 134 yards); Tenn.-Chatt. vs. Southwestern La., Sept. 17, 1983 (4 for 122 yards)

DEFENSIVE EXTRA POINTS

Most Defensive Extra Points Scored
2—Va. Military vs. Davidson, Nov. 4, 1989 (Jeff Barnes, 95-yard interception return, and Wayne Purcell, 90-yard interception return)

SEASON—OFFENSE
TOTAL OFFENSE

Most Yards Gained Per Game
640.1—Mississippi Val., 1984 (6,401 in 10)

Highest Average Gain Per Play
7.39—Mississippi Val., 1984 (866 for 6,401)

Most Plays Per Game
89.6—Weber St., 1991 (986 in 11)

Most Touchdowns by Rushing and Passing Per Game
8.4—Mississippi Val., 1984 (84 in 10)

RUSHING

Most Yards Gained Per Game
381.6—Howard, 1987 (3,816 in 10)

Highest Average Gain Per Rush
6.60—Howard, 1987 (578 for 3,816)

Most Rushes Per Game
69.8—Northeastern, 1986 (698 in 10)

Most Touchdowns by Rushing Per Game
4.50—Howard, 1987 (45 in 10)

PASSING

Most Yards Gained Per Game
496.8—Mississippi Val., 1984 (4,968 in 10)

Highest Average Gain Per Attempt
(Min. 250 atts.) 10.17—Marshall, 1991 (298 for 3,032)
(Min. 400 atts.) 9.25—Idaho, 1989 (445 for 4,117)

Highest Average Gain Per Completion
(Min. 125 comps.) 19.27—Jackson St., 1990 (156 for 3,006)
(Min. 200 comps.) 16.6—Stephen F. Austin, 1989 (240 for 3,985)

Most Passes Attempted Per Game
55.8—Mississippi Val., 1984 (558 in 10)

Most Passes Completed Per Game
35.1—Mississippi Val., 1984 (351 in 10)

Highest Percentage Completed
(Min. 200 atts.) 68.4%—Princeton, 1988 (206 of 301)
(Min. 450 atts.) 62.9%—Mississippi Val., 1984 (351 of 558)

Lowest Percentage Had Intercepted
(Min. 200 atts.) 1.00%—Princeton, 1988 (3 of 301)
(Min. 400 atts.) 1.22%—Lamar, 1988 (5 of 411)

Most Consecutive Passes Attempted Without an Interception
275—Lamar, 1988 (during 8 games, Sept. 3 to Oct. 29)

Most Touchdown Passes Per Game
6.4—Mississippi Val., 1984 (64 in 10)

Highest Passing Efficiency Rating Points
173.5—Marshall, 1991 (298 attempts, 186 completions, 8 interceptions, 3,032 yards, 28 TDs)

PUNTING

Most Punts Per Game
9.64—Louisiana Tech, 1987 (106 in 11)

Fewest Punts Per Game
2.40—Howard, 1987 (24 in 10)

Highest Punting Average
47.0—Appalachian St., 1991 (64 for 3,009)

Highest Net Punting Average
42.8—Western Caro., 1984 (49 for 2,127 yards; 32 yards returned)

Most Punts Had Blocked
8—Western Ky., 1982

PUNT RETURNS

Most Punt Returns Per Game
5.4—Murray St., 1980 (59 in 11)

Fewest Punt Returns Per Game
0.64—Southern Ill., 1991 (7 in 11); Prairie View, 1991 (7 in 11); Youngstown St., 1990 (7 in 11)

Most Punt-Return Yards Per Game
56.1—South Caro. St., 1981 (617 in 11)

Highest Average Gain Per Punt Return
(Min. 20 rets.) 18.6—Richmond, 1985 (23 for 427)
(Min. 30 rets.) 18.1—Mississippi Val., 1985 (31 for 561)

Most Touchdowns Scored on Punt Returns
5—Southern Ill., 1985

KICKOFF RETURNS

Most Kickoff Returns Per Game
7.0—Prairie View, 1991 (77 in 11; 1,128 yards); Idaho St., 1987 (77 in 11; 1,577 yards); Davidson, 1986 (63 in 9; 1,104 yards)

Fewest Kickoff Returns Per Game
1.4—North Texas, 1983 (15 in 11)

Most Kickoff-Return Yards Per Game
143.4—Idaho St., 1987 (1,577 in 11; 77 returns)

Highest Average Gain Per Kickoff Return
(Min. 20 rets.) 29.5—Eastern Ky., 1986 (34 for 1,022)

COMBINED RETURNS
(Interceptions, Punt Returns and Kickoff Returns)

Most Touchdowns Scored
9—Delaware St., 1987 (5 interceptions, 3 punt returns, 1 kickoff return)

SCORING

Most Points Per Game
60.9—Mississippi Val., 1984 (609 in 10)

Most Touchdowns Per Game
8.7—Mississippi Val., 1984 (87 in 10)

Most Extra Points Made by Kicking Per Game
7.7—Mississippi Val., 1984 (77 in 10)

Most Consecutive Extra Points Made by Kicking
51—Lafayette, 1988

Most Two-Point Attempts Made
8—Bethune-Cookman, 1991 (11 attempts)

Most Defensive Extra-Point Attempts
2—Va. Military, 1989

Most Defensive Extra Points Scored
2—Va. Military, 1989 (2 interception returns)

Most Field Goals Made Per Game
2.4—Northern Iowa, 1990 (26 in 11); Nevada, 1982 (26 in 11)

Most Safeties Scored
5—Jackson St., 1986

FIRST DOWNS

Most First Downs Per Game
31.7—Mississippi Val., 1984 (317 in 10)

Most Rushing First Downs Per Game
17.9—Howard, 1987 (179 in 10)

Most Passing First Downs Per Game
21.4—Mississippi Val., 1984 (214 in 10)

Most First Downs by Penalty Per Game
3.7—Texas Southern, 1987 (41 in 11; 134 penalties by opponents); Alabama St., 1984 (41 in 11; 109 penalties by opponents)

FUMBLES

Most Fumbles Per Game
5.3—Prairie View, 1984 (58 in 11)

Most Fumbles Lost Per Game
3.1—Delaware St., 1980 (31 in 10); Idaho, 1978 (31 in 10)

Fewest Own Fumbles Lost
3—By four teams. Most recent: Tennessee St., 1987 (10 fumbles)

PENALTIES

Most Penalties Per Game
13.7—Grambling, 1984 (151 in 11; 1,206 yards)

Most Yards Penalized Per Game
125.5—Tennessee St., 1982 (1,255 in 10; 132 penalties)

TURNOVERS

Fewest Turnovers
10—Appalachian St., 1985 (3 fumbles, 7 interceptions)

Most Turnovers
59—Texas Southern, 1980 (27 fumbles, 32 interceptions)

Highest Turnover Margin Per Game Over Opponents
2.5—Appalachian St., 1985; Florida A&M, 1981

SEASON—DEFENSE
TOTAL DEFENSE

Fewest Yards Allowed Per Game
149.9—Florida A&M, 1978 (1,649 in 11)

Fewest Rushing and Passing Touchdowns Allowed Per Game
0.7—Western Mich., 1982 (8 in 11)

Lowest Average Yards Allowed Per Play
2.4—South Caro. St., 1978 (719 for 1,736)

RUSHING DEFENSE

Fewest Yards Allowed Per Game
44.5—Grambling, 1984 (489 in 11)

Lowest Average Yards Allowed Per Rush
1.3—Florida A&M, 1978 (419 for 535)

Fewest Rushing Touchdowns Allowed Per Game
0.3—Florida A&M, 1978 (3 in 11)

PASS DEFENSE

Fewest Yards Allowed Per Game
59.9—Bethune-Cookman, 1981 (659 in 11)

Fewest Yards Allowed Per Attempt (Min. 200 Atts.)
3.98—Middle Tenn. St., 1988 (251 for 999)

Fewest Yards Allowed Per Completion (Min. 100 Comps.)
9.08—Middle Tenn. St., 1988 (110 for 999)

Lowest Completion Percentage Allowed
(Min. 200 atts.) 32.3%—Alcorn St., 1979 (76 of 235)
(Min. 300 atts.) 34.2%—Tennessee St., 1986 (107 of 313)

Fewest Touchdowns Allowed by Passing
1—Middle Tenn. St., 1990; Nevada, 1978

Lowest Passing Efficiency Defense Rating (Since 1990)
70.01—South Caro. St., 1991 (278 attempts, 97 completions, 21 interceptions, 1,360 yards, 8 TDs)

Most Passes Intercepted By, Per Game
3.2—Florida A&M, 1981 (35 in 11)

Highest Percentage Intercepted By
13.4—Florida A&M, 1981 (35 of 262)

Most Yards Gained on Interceptions
498—Jackson St., 1985 (28 interceptions)

Most Yards Gained Per Game on Interceptions
49.8—Jackson St., 1985 (498 for 10)

Highest Average Per Interception Return (Min. 15 Rets.)
21.6—Jackson St., 1986 (23 for 497)

Most Touchdowns on Interception Returns
7—Jackson St., 1985

PUNTING

Most Opponents' Punts Blocked By
9—Middle Tenn. St., 1988 (73 punts)

PUNT RETURNS

Lowest Average Yards Allowed Per Punt Return
0.96—Yale, 1988 (24 for 23)

Fewest Returns Allowed
7—Furman, 1984 (11 games, 8 yards)

KICKOFF RETURNS

Lowest Average Yards Allowed Per Kickoff Return
11.0—Lafayette, 1980 (20 for 220)

SCORING

Fewest Points Allowed
6.5—South Caro. St., 1978 (72 in 11)

FUMBLES

Most Opponents' Fumbles Recovered
29—Western Ky., 1982 (43 fumbles)

TURNOVERS

Most Opponents' Turnovers Per Game
4.8—Grambling, 1985 (53 in 11)

ADDITIONAL RECORDS

Most Consecutive Victories
20—Holy Cross, 1990-91

Most Consecutive Games Without Defeat (Must Have at Least One Tie)
19—Eastern Ky., 1982-83 (includes 1 tie)

Most Consecutive Home Victories
38—Ga. Southern, from Oct. 5, 1985, through Sept. 22, 1990 (includes 10 I-AA playoff games)

Most Consecutive Losses
44—Columbia, from Nov. 12, 1983, through Oct. 1, 1988 (ended Oct. 8, 1988, with 16-13 win over Princeton)

Most Consecutive Games Without a Win
47—Columbia, from Oct. 22, 1983, through Oct. 1, 1988, including two ties (ended Oct. 8, 1988, with 16-13 win over Princeton)

Most Consecutive Games Without Being Shut Out
193—Boise St., from Sept. 21, 1968, through Nov. 10, 1984

Most Shutouts in a Season
5—South Caro. St., 1978

Most Consecutive Quarters Holding Opponents Scoreless
14—McNeese St., 1985; Bucknell, 1979

Most Consecutive Games Without a Tie
304—Richmond (current)

Last Scoreless-Tie Game
Oct. 26, 1985—McNeese St. & North Texas

Most Consecutive Passes Attempted Without an Interception
297—Lamar (in 9 games from Nov. 21, 1987, to Oct. 29, 1988)

Most Points Overcome to Win a Game
35—Nevada (55) vs. Weber St. (49), Nov. 2, 1991 (trailed 14-49 with 12:16 remaining in the 3rd quarter)
32—Morehead St. (36) vs. Wichita St. (35), Sept. 20, 1986 (trailed 3-35 with 9:03 remaining in the 3rd quarter)

Most Points Overcome in Fourth Quarter to Win a Game
28—Delaware St. (38) vs. Liberty (37), Oct. 6, 1990 (trailed 9-37 with 13:00 remaining in 4th quarter)

Most Overtime Periods in a Game
6—Rhode Island vs. Maine, Sept. 18, 1982 (score after regulation time was 21-21; Rhode Island won, 58-55)

Score By Periods

				Regulation
Rhode Island	7	7	0	7—21
Maine	0	7	0	14—21

					Overtime
Rhode Island	7	7	3	7	7	6—58
Maine	7	7	3	7	7	3—55

There were 15 TDs, 14 PATs, 3 FGs. Game time was 3:46, including 51 minutes of overtime. Rhode Island's T. J. Del Santo scored the winning TD on a 2-yard run (his fourth TD of the game) after Maine kicked a field goal in the sixth overtime.

6—Villanova vs. Connecticut, Oct. 7, 1989 (score after regulation time was 21-21; Villanova won, 41-35)

Score By Periods

				Regulation		
Connecticut	0	14	0	7—21		
Villanova	0	0	14	7—21		
				Overtime		
Connecticut	0	0	7	0	7	0—35
Villanova	0	0	7	0	7	6—41

There were 11 TDs, 10 PATs. Game time was 3:40. Villanova's Jeff Johnson scored the winning TD on a 3-yard run (his third TD of the game).

Most Consecutive Overtime Games Played
2—Connecticut, 1989 (Connecticut 35, Villanova 41, 6 OT, Oct. 7; and Connecticut 39, Massachusetts 33, 1 OT, Oct. 14); Maine, 1982 (Maine 55, Rhode Island 58, 6 OT, Sept. 18; and Maine 45, Boston U. 48, 4 OT, Sept. 25)

Most Consecutive Extra-Point Kicks Made
134—Boise St. (began Oct. 27, 1984; ended Nov. 12, 1988)

Most Consecutive Winning Seasons
27—Grambling (1960-86)

Most Improved Won-Lost Record
9½ games—Montana St., 1984 (12-2-0, including 3 Division I-AA playoff games) from 1983 (1-10-0)

ANNUAL CHAMPIONS, ALL-TIME LEADERS

TOTAL OFFENSE
Career Yards Per Game

Player, Team	Years	Games	Plays	Yards	TDR‡	Yd. PG
Willie Totten, Mississippi Val.	1982-85	40	1,812	13,007	*157	*325.2
Neil Lomax, Portland St.	1977-80	42	*1,901	*13,345	120	317.7
Tom Ehrhardt, Rhode Island	#1984-85	21	1,010	6,492	66	309.1
Tod Mayfield, West Tex. St.	¢1984-86	24	1,165	7,316	58	304.8
Stan Greene, Boston U.	1989-90	22	1,167	6,408	49	291.3
John Friesz, Idaho	1986-89	35	1,459	10,187	79	291.1
Vern Harris, Idaho St.	1984-85	19	813	5,302	36	279.1
Grady Bennett, Montana	1988-90	31	1,389	8,304	69	267.9
Sean Payton, Eastern Ill.	1983-86	39	1,690	10,298	91	264.1
John Witkowski, Columbia	1981-83	30	1,330	7,748	58	258.3
Dave Stireman, Weber St.	1984-85	21	762	5,396	43	257.0
Ken Hobart, Idaho	1980-83	44	1,847	11,127	105	252.9
Mike Machurek, Idaho St.	1980-81	20	805	4,974	43	248.7
Tony Petersen, Marshall	1986-87	20	756	4,940	31	247.0
Jeff Wiley, Holy Cross	1985-88	40	1,428	9,877	76	246.9
Doug Butler, Princeton	1983-85	29	1,137	7,157	52	246.8
Tom Ciaccio, Holy Cross	1988-91	37	1,283	9,066	87	245.0
Greg Wyatt, Northern Ariz.	1986-89	42	1,753	10,277	75	244.7
Chris Hakel, William & Mary	1988-91	28	915	6,458	56	239.2
Bob Jean, New Hampshire	1985-88	32	1,287	7,621	59	238.2
Michael Proctor, Murray St.	1986-89	43	1,577	9,886	66	230.0
Jason Garrett, Princeton	1987-88	20	731	4,555	24	227.8
Paul Peterson, Idaho St.	1982-83	22	1,057	4,967	36	225.8
Frank Baur, Lafayette	1985, 87-89	38	1,312	8,579	72	225.8
Eric Beavers, Nevada	1983-86	40	1,307	9,025	85	225.6

* Record. ‡ Touchdowns-responsible-for are player's TDs scored and passed for. # Two years in Division I-AA and two years in Division II (LIU-C. W. Post). Four-year totals: 9,793 yards and 232.2 average. ¢ Two years in Division I-AA (1984-85) and one year in Division II (1986).

Season Yards Per Game

Player, Team	Year	Games	Plays	Yards	TDR‡	Yd. PG
Willie Totten, Mississippi Val.	†1984	10	564	*4,572	*61	*457.2
Jamie Martin, Weber St.	†1991	11	591	4,337	37	394.3
Neil Lomax, Portland St.	†1980	11	550	4,157	42	377.9
Neil Lomax, Portland St.	†1979	11	*611	3,966	31	360.5
John Friesz, Idaho	†1989	11	464	3,853	31	350.3
Todd Hammel, Stephen F. Austin	1989	11	487	3,822	38	347.5
Tom Ehrhardt, Rhode Island	†1985	10	529	3,460	35	346.0
Ken Hobart, Idaho	†1983	11	578	3,800	37	345.5
Dave Stireman, Weber St.	1985	11	502	3,759	33	341.7
Willie Totten, Mississippi Val.	1985	11	561	3,742	43	340.2
Jeff Wiley, Holy Cross	†1987	11	445	3,722	34	338.4
Jamie Martin, Weber St.	†1990	11	508	3,713	25	337.6

Player, Team	Year	Games	Plays	Yards	TDR‡	Yd. PG
Sean Payton, Eastern Ill.	1984	11	584	3,661	31	332.8
Tod Mayfield, West Tex. St.	1985	10	526	3,328	21	332.8
Neil Lomax, Portland St.	†1978	11	519	3,524	27	320.4

Record. † National champion. ‡ Touchdowns-responsible-for are player's TDs scored and passed for.

Career Yards

Player, Team	Years	Plays	Yards	Avg.
Neil Lomax, Portland St.	1977-80	*1,901	*13,345	7.02
Willie Totten, Mississippi Val.	1982-85	1,812	13,007	*7.18
Ken Hobart, Idaho	1980-83	1,847	11,127	6.02
Sean Payton, Eastern Ill.	1983-86	1,690	10,298	6.09
Greg Wyatt, Northern Ariz.	1986-89	1,753	10,277	5.86
John Friesz, Idaho	1986-89	1,459	10,187	6.98
Michael Proctor, Murray St.	1986-89	1,577	9,886	6.27
Jeff Wiley, Holy Cross	1985-88	1,428	9,877	6.92
Matt DeGennaro, Connecticut	1987-90	1,619	9,269	5.73
¢Jamie Martin, Weber St.	1989-91	1,289	9,158	7.10
Tom Ciaccio, Holy Cross............................	1988-91	1,283	9,066	7.07
Eric Beavers, Nevada	1983-86	1,307	9,025	6.91
Marty Horn, Lehigh	1982-85	1,612	8,956	5.56
Kirk Schulz, Villanova	1986-89	1,534	8,900	5.80
Chris Swartz, Morehead St.	1987-90	1,559	8,648	5.55
Frank Baur, Lafayette 1985, 87-89		1,312	8,579	6.54
Steve Calabria, Colgate	1981-84	1,342	8,532	6.36
Mike Buck, Maine.....................................	1986-89	1,288	8,457	6.57
Jason Whitmer, Idaho St.	1987-90	1,618	8,449	5.22
Scott Davis, North Texas	1987-90	1,548	8,436	5.45
Grady Bennett, Montana............................	1988-90	1,389	8,304	5.98
Stan Yagiello, William & Mary	$1981-85	1,492	8,168	5.47
Mike Smith, Northern Iowa	1984-87	1,163	8,145	7.00
Bob Bleier, Richmond	1983-86	1,313	7,991	6.09
Alan Hooker, North Caro. A&T	1984-87	1,476	7,787	5.28
John Witkowski, Columbia...........................	1981-83	1,330	7,748	5.83
Kelly Bradley, Montana St.	1983-86	1,547	7,740	5.00
Jeff Cesarone, Western Ky.	1984-87	1,502	7,694	5.12
Chris Goetz, Towson St.	1987-90	1,361	7,643	5.62
Bob Jean, New Hampshire...........................	1985-88	1,287	7,621	5.92
Scott Linehan, Idaho 1982, 84-86		1,223	7,550	6.17

Record. $ See page 6 for explanation. ¢ Active player.

Season Yards

Player, Team	Year	Games	Plays	Yards	Avg.
Willie Totten, Mississippi Val.	†1984	10	564	*4,572	8.11
Jamie Martin, Weber St.	†1991	11	591	4,337	7.34
Neil Lomax, Portland St.	†1980	11	550	4,157	7.56
Neil Lomax, Portland St.	†1979	11	*611	3,966	6.49
John Friesz, Idaho	†1989	11	464	3,853	8.30
Todd Hammel, Stephen F. Austin	1989	11	487	3,822	7.85
Ken Hobart, Idaho	†1983	11	578	3,800	6.57
Dave Stireman, Weber St.	1985	11	502	3,759	7.49
Willie Totten, Mississippi Val.	1985	11	561	3,742	6.67
Jeff Wiley, Holy Cross..........................	†1987	11	445	3,722	*8.36
Jamie Martin, Weber St.	†1990	11	508	3,713	7.31
Sean Payton, Eastern Ill.	1984	11	584	3,661	6.27
Todd Brunner, Lehigh	1989	11	504	3,639	7.22
Neil Lomax, Portland St.	†1978	11	519	3,524	6.79
Glenn Kempa, Lehigh...........................	1991	11	513	3,511	6.84
John Friesz, Idaho	1987	11	543	3,489	6.43
Doug Nussmeier, Idaho	1991	11	472	3,460	7.33
Tom Ehrhardt, Rhode Island	†1985	10	529	3,460	6.54
Kelly Bradley, Montana St.	1984	11	598	3,455	5.78

Record. † National champion.

Single-Game Yards

Yds.	Player, Team (Opponent)	Date
643	Jamie Martin, Weber St. (Idaho St.)	Nov. 23, 1991
621	Willie Totten, Mississippi Val. (Prairie View)	Oct. 27, 1984
595	Doug Pederson, Northeast La. (Stephen F. Austin)	Nov. 11, 1989

Yds.	Player, Team (Opponent)	Date
587	Vern Harris, Idaho St. (Montana)	Oct. 12, 1985
566	Tom Ehrhardt, Rhode Island (Connecticut)	Nov. 16, 1985
562	Todd Hammel, Stephen F. Austin (Northeast La.)	Nov. 11, 1989
561	Willie Totten, Mississippi Val. (Southern-B.R.)	Sept. 29, 1984
547	Tod Mayfield, West Tex. St. (New Mexico St.)	Nov. 16, 1985
546	Dave Stireman, Weber St. (Montana)	Nov. 2, 1985
543	Ken Hobart, Idaho (Southern Colo.)	Sept. 10, 1983
536	Willie Totten, Mississippi Val. (Kentucky St.)	Sept. 1, 1984
527	Willie Totten, Mississippi Val. (Grambling)	Oct. 13, 1984
519	Bernard Hawk, Bethune-Cookman (Ga. Southern)	Oct. 6, 1984

Annual Champions

Year	Player, Team	Class	Games	Plays	Yards	Avg.
1978	Neil Lomax, Portland St.	So.	11	519	3,524	320.4
1979	Neil Lomax, Portland St.	Jr.	11	*611	3,966	360.5
1980	Neil Lomax, Portland St.	Sr.	11	550	4,157	377.9
1981	Mike Machurek, Idaho St.	Sr.	9	363	2,645	293.9
1982	Brent Woods, Princeton	Sr.	10	577	3,079	307.9
1983	Ken Hobart, Idaho	Sr.	11	578	3,800	345.5
1984	Willie Totten, Mississippi Val.	Jr.	10	564	*4,572	*457.2
1985	Tom Ehrhardt, Rhode Island	Sr.	10	529	3,460	346.0
1986	Brent Pease, Montana	Sr.	10	499	3,094	309.4
1987	Jeff Wiley, Holy Cross	Jr.	11	445	3,722	338.4
1988	John Friesz, Idaho	Jr.	10	424	2,751	275.1
1989	John Friesz, Idaho	Sr.	11	464	3,853	350.3
1990	Jamie Martin, Weber St.	So.	11	508	3,713	337.6
1991	Jamie Martin, Weber St.	Jr.	11	591	4,337	394.3

* Record.

RUSHING
Career Yards Per Game§

Player, Team	Years	Games	Plays	Yards	TD	Yd. PG
Mike Clark, Akron	1984-86	32	804	4,257	24	*133.0
Rich Erenberg, Colgate	1982-83	21	464	2,618	22	124.7
Kenny Gamble, Colgate	1984-87	42	*963	5,220	*55	124.3
Frank Hawkins, Nevada	1977-80	43	945	*5,333	39	124.0
Elroy Harris, Eastern Ky.	1985, 87-88	31	648	3,829	47	123.5
Gill Fenerty, Holy Cross	1983-85	30	622	3,618	26	120.6
Buford Jordan, McNeese St.	1982-83	19	436	2,123	17	111.7
Derrick Harmon, Cornell	1981-83	28	545	3,074	26	109.8
Paul Lewis, Boston U.	1982-84	37	878	3,995	50	108.0
Derrick Franklin, Indiana St.	1989-91	30	710	3,231	23	107.7
Charvez Foger, Nevada	1985-88	42	864	4,484	52	106.8
James Crawford, Eastern Ky.	1985-87	32	661	3,404	22	106.4
Bryan Keys, Pennsylvania	1987-89	30	609	3,137	34	104.6
Fine Unga, Weber St.	1987-88	22	406	2,298	19	104.5
Judd Garrett, Princeton	1987-89	30	687	3,109	32	103.6
Stanford Jennings, Furman	1982-83	22	390	2,267	25	103.0

* Record. § The following players competed two years in Division I-AA and two years in Division I-A:
Rich Erenberg, Colgate (four years: 3,689 yards and 94.6 average); Buford Jordan, McNeese St. (four years: 4,106 yards and 100.1 average), and Stanford Jennings, Furman (four years: 3,868 yards and 90.0 average).

Season Yards Per Game

Player, Team	Year	Games	Plays	Yards	TD	Yd. PG
Gene Lake, Delaware St.	†1984	10	238	1,722	20	*172.2
Rich Erenberg, Colgate	†1983	11	302	*1,883	20	171.2
Kenny Gamble, Colgate	†1986	11	307	1,816	**21	165.1
Mike Clark, Akron	1986	11	245	1,786	8	162.4
Frank Hawkins, Nevada	†1980	11	307	1,719	14	156.3
Brad Baxter, Alabama St.	1986	11	302	1,705	13	155.0
Elroy Harris, Eastern Ky.	1988	10	277	1,543	**21	154.3
Frank Hawkins, Nevada	†1979	11	293	1,683	13	153.0
Carl Smith, Maine	†1989	11	305	1,680	20	152.7
Harvey Reed, Howard	†1987	10	211	1,512	20	151.2
John Settle, Appalachian St.	1986	11	317	1,661	20	151.0
Garry Pearson, Massachusetts	†1982	11	312	1,631	13	148.3
Lorenzo Bouier, Maine	1980	11	349	1,622	9	147.5

* Record. ** Record tied. † National champion.

Career Yards@

Player, Team	Years	Plays	Yards	Avg.	Long
Frank Hawkins, Nevada	1977-80	945	*5,333	5.64	50
Kenny Gamble, Colgate	1984-87	*963	5,220	5.42	91
Cedric Minter, Boise St.	1977-80	752	4,475	5.95	77
John Settle, Appalachian St.	1983-86	891	4,409	4.95	88
Mike Clark, Akron	1984-86	804	4,257	5.29	†65
Warren Marshall, James Madison	$1982-86	737	4,168	5.66	59
Harvey Reed, Howard	1984-87	635	4,142	*6.52	85
Paul Lewis, Boston U.	1981-84	878	3,995	4.55	80
Joe Ross, Ga. Southern	1987-90	687	3,876	5.64	75
Garry Pearson, Massachusetts	1979-82	808	3,859	4.78	71
Elroy Harris, Eastern Ky. 1985, 87-88		648	3,829	5.91	64
Lorenzo Bouier, Maine	1979-82	879	3,827	4.35	77
Lewis Tillman, Jackson St.	$1984-88	779	3,824	4.91	39
Joe Campbell, Middle Tenn. St.	1988-91	638	3,823	5.99	81
Carl Smith, Maine	1988-91	759	3,815	5.03	89
Brad Baxter, Alabama St.	1985-88	773	3,732	4.83	71
¢Markus Thomas, Eastern Ky.	1989-91	546	3,651	6.69	90
Gill Fenerty, Holy Cross	1983-85	622	3,618	5.82	76
Burton Murchison, Lamar	1984-87	665	3,598	5.41	76

* Record.   † Did not score.   ¢ Active player. $ See page 6 for explanation.   @ The following players competed two years in Division I-AA and two years in Division I-A: Rich Erenberg, Colgate (four years: 3,689 yards); Buford Jordan, McNeese St. (four years: 4,106 yards), and Stanford Jennings, Furman (four years: 3,868 yards).

Season Yards

Player, Team	Year	Games	Plays	Yards	Avg.
Rich Erenberg, Colgate	†1983	11	302	*1,883	6.24
Kenny Gamble, Colgate	†1986	11	307	1,816	5.92
Mike Clark, Akron	1986	11	245	1,786	‡7.29
Gene Lake, Delaware St.	†1984	10	238	1,722	7.24
Frank Hawkins, Nevada	†1980	11	307	1,719	5.60
Brad Baxter, Alabama St.	1986	11	302	1,705	5.65
Frank Hawkins, Nevada	†1979	11	293	1,683	5.74
Carl Smith, Maine	†1989	11	305	1,680	5.51
John Settle, Appalachian St.	1986	11	317	1,661	5.24
Garry Pearson, Massachusetts	†1982	11	312	1,631	5.23
Lorenzo Bouier, Maine	1980	11	349	1,622	4.65
Markus Thomas, Eastern Ky.	1989	11	232	1,620	6.98
James Black, Akron	1983	11	*351	1,568	4.47
Burton Murchison, Lamar	†1985	11	265	1,547	5.84
Jerome Bledsoe, Massachusetts	†1991	11	264	1,545	5.85
Elroy Harris, Eastern Ky.	1988	10	277	1,543	5.57
Cedric Minter, Boise St.	1978	11	258	1,526	5.91

* Record.   † National champion.   ‡ Record for minimum of 200 carries.

Single-Game Yards

Yds.	Player, Team (Opponent)	Date
345	Russell Davis, Idaho (Portland St.)	Oct. 3, 1981
337	Gill Fenerty, Holy Cross (Columbia)	Oct. 29, 1983
336	Gene Lake, Delaware St. (Liberty)	Nov. 10, 1984
323	Matt Johnson, Harvard (Brown)	Nov. 9, 1991
305	Lucius Floyd, Nevada (Montana St.)	Sept. 27, 1986
304	Tony Citizen, McNeese St. (Prairie View)	Sept. 6, 1986
302	Lorenzo Bouier, Maine (Northeastern)	Nov. 1, 1980
300	Markus Thomas, Eastern Ky. (Marshall)	Oct. 21, 1989
299	Joe Delaney, Northwestern, La. (Nicholls St.)	Oct. 28, 1978
293	Terence Thompson, Eastern Ky. (Akron)	Sept. 26, 1981
293	Frank Hawkins, Nevada (San Fran. St.)	Sept. 30, 1978

Annual Champions

Year	Player, Team	Class	Games	Plays	Yards	Avg.
1978	Frank Hawkins, Nevada	So.	10	259	1,445	144.5
1979	Frank Hawkins, Nevada	Jr.	11	293	1,683	153.0
1980	Frank Hawkins, Nevada	Sr.	11	307	1,719	156.3
1981	Gregg Drew, Boston U.	Jr.	10	309	1,257	125.7
1982	Garry Pearson, Massachusetts	Sr.	11	312	1,631	148.3
1983	Rich Erenberg, Colgate	Sr.	11	302	*1,883	171.2
1984	Gene Lake, Delaware St.	Jr.	10	238	1,722	*172.2
1985	Burton Murchison, Lamar	So.	11	265	1,547	140.6

Year	Player, Team	Class	Games	Plays	Yards	Avg.
1986	Kenny Gamble, Colgate	Jr.	11	307	1,816	165.1
1987	Harvey Reed, Howard................	Sr.	10	211	1,512	151.2
1988	Elroy Harris, Eastern Ky.	Jr.	10	277	1,543	154.3
1989	Carl Smith, Maine....................	So.	11	305	1,680	152.7
1990	Walter Dean, Grambling	Sr.	11	221	1,401	127.4
1991	Al Rosier, Dartmouth.................	Sr.	10	258	1,432	143.2

* *Record.*

QUARTERBACK RUSHING
Career Yards (Since 1978)

Player, Team	Years	Games	Plays	Yards	TD	Yd. PG
Jack Douglas, Citadel...............	1989-91	33	654	2,748	35	83.3
Tracy Ham, Ga. Southern	1984-86	33	511	2,506	32	75.9
Raymond Gross, Ga. Southern	1987-90	42	695	2,290	20	54.5
Dwane Brown, Arkansas St.	1984-87	42	595	2,192	33	52.2
Roy Johnson, Arkansas St.	1988-91	43	558	2,182	22	50.7
DeAndre Smith, Southwest Mo. St. ...	1987-90	42	558	2,140	36	50.9
¢Tony Scales, Va. Military	1989-91	33	414	1,898	16	57.5
Ken Hobart, Idaho	1980-83	44	628	1,827	26	41.5
¢Bill Vergantino, Delaware	1989-91	33	518	1,783	21	54.0
Darin Kehler, Yale	1987-90	28	402	1,643	13	58.7

¢ *Active player.*

Season Yards (Since 1978)

Player, Team	Year	Games	Plays	Yards	TD	Avg.
Tony Scales, Va. Military	1991	11	185	1,105	8	5.97
Tracy Ham, Ga. Southern	1986	11	207	1,048	18	5.06
Nick Crawford, Yale	1991	10	210	1,024	8	4.98
Gene Brown, Citadel................	1988	9	152	1,006	13	6.62
Roy Johnson, Arkansas St.	1989	11	193	925	6	4.79
Darin Kehler, Yale	1989	10	210	903	6	4.30
Jim O'Leary, Northeastern	1986	10	195	884	10	4.53
Earl Easley, Arkansas St.	1988	11	196	861	11	4.39
Brad Brown, Northwestern (La.)	1990	11	192	843	8	4.39
DeAndre Smith, Southwest Mo. St. ..	1989	11	176	841	12	4.78
Jack Douglas, Citadel...............	1990	11	211	836	13	3.96
Ken Hobart, Idaho	1980	11	209	829	7	3.97

PASSING
Career Passing Efficiency
(Minimum 300 Completions)

Player, Team	Years	Att.	Cmp.	Int.	Pct.	Yards	TD	Pts.
Willie Totten, Mississippi Val.	1982-85	1,555	907	*75	.583	12,711	*139	*146.8
Kenneth Biggles, Tennessee St......	1981-84	701	397	28	.566	5,933	57	146.6
Mike Smith, Northern Iowa	1984-87	943	557	43	.591	8,219	58	143.5
Neil Lomax, Portland St.	1977-80	*1,606	*938	55	.584	*13,220	106	142.5
Tom Ciaccio, Holy Cross............	1988-91	1,073	658	46	.613	8,603	72	142.2
Jim Zaccheo, Nevada	1987-88	554	326	27	.588	4,750	35	142.0
Eric Beavers, Nevada	1983-86	1,094	646	37	.591	8,626	77	141.8
Jason Garrett, Princeton	1987-88	550	368	10	*.669	4,274	20	140.6
Connell Maynor, Winston-Salem/ North Caro. A&T	1987, 89-91	661	365	31	.552	5,390	50	139.3
Ricky Jones, Alabama St.	1988-91	644	324	30	.503	5,472	49	137.5
Jeff Carlson, Weber St..............	1984, 86-88	723	384	33	.531	6,147	47	136.9
Chris Hakel, William & Mary	1988-91	812	489	26	.602	6,447	40	136.7
Jeff Wiley, Holy Cross	1985-88	1,208	723	63	.599	9,698	71	136.3
Tom Ehrhardt, Rhode Island	††1984-85	919	526	35	.572	6,722	66	134.8
Mike Buck, Maine	1986-89	1,134	637	41	.562	8,721	68	133.4
Frankie DeBusk, Furman............	1987-90	634	333	29	.525	5,414	35	133.3
Frank Novak, Lafayette	1981-83	834	478	36	.573	6,378	51	133.1
Rick Worman, Eastern Wash.	**1982-84, 85	673	382	23	.568	5,013	41	132.6
Glenn Kempa, Lehigh	1989-91	901	520	27	.577	6,722	49	132.3
Gilbert Renfroe, Tennessee St.	1982-85	721	370	23	.513	5,556	48	131.6
Tod Mayfield, West Tex. St..........	##1984-86	1,035	630	38	.609	7,424	55	131.3
Tracy Ham, Ga. Southern	1984-86	568	301	31	.530	4,881	29	131.1
Matt DeGennaro, Connecticut	1987-90	1,319	803	49	.609	9,288	73	130.9
Ken Hobart, Idaho	1980-83	1,219	629	42	.516	9,300	79	130.2

* *Record.* $ *See page 6 for explanation.* ** *At Fresno St. in 1982.* ## *Two years in Division I-AA (1984-85) and one year in Division II (1986).* †† *Two years in Division I-AA and two years in Division II (LIU-C. W. Post).*

Season Passing Efficiency
(Minimum 15 Attempts Per Game)

Player, Team	Year	G	Att.	Cmp.	Int.	Pct.	Yards	TD	Pts.
Michael Payton, Marshall	†1991	9	216	143	5	.622	2,333	19	*181.3
Frank Baur, Lafayette	†1988	10	256	164	11	.641	2,621	23	171.1
Bobby Lamb, Furman	†1985	11	181	106	6	.586	1,856	18	170.9
Mike Smith, Northern Iowa	†1986	11	303	190	16	.627	3,125	27	168.2
Willie Totten, Mississippi Val.	†1983	9	279	174	9	.624	2,566	29	167.5
Eriq Williams, James Madison	1991	11	192	107	7	.557	1,914	19	164.8
Willie Totten, Mississippi Val.	†1984	10	*518	*324	22	.626	*4,557	*56	163.6
Jeff Wiley, Holy Cross	†1987	11	400	265	17	.663	3,677	34	163.0
Todd Hammel, Stephen F. Austin	†1989	11	401	238	13	.594	3,914	34	162.8
Mike Williams, Grambling	†1980	11	239	127	5	.531	2,116	28	162.0
John Friesz, Idaho	1989	11	425	260	8	.612	4,041	31	161.4
David Charpia, Furman	1983	9	155	99	4	.635	1,419	12	160.1
Joe Aliotti, Boise St.	†1979	11	219	144	7	.658	1,870	19	159.7
Gilbert Renfroe, Tennessee St.	1984	11	165	95	5	.576	1,458	17	159.7
Mike Buck, Maine	1989	11	264	170	3	.644	2,315	19	159.5
Bobby Lamb, Furman	1984	11	191	106	7	.555	1,781	19	159.3
Kenneth Biggles, Tennessee St.	1984	11	258	157	8	.609	2,242	24	159.1
Hugh Swilling, Furman	1991	9	153	85	5	.556	1,422	14	157.3
Connell Maynor, North Caro. A&T	†1990	11	191	123	10	.644	1,699	16	156.3
Neil Lomax, Portland St.	1980	11	473	296	12	.626	4,094	37	156.0

*Record. † National champion.

Career Yards

Player, Team	Years	Att.	Cmp.	Int.	Pct.	Yards	TD
Neil Lomax, Portland St.	1977-80	*1,606	*938	55	.584	*13,220	106
Willie Totten, Mississippi Val.	1982-85	1,555	907	*75	.583	12,711	*139
John Friesz, Idaho	1986-89	1,350	801	40	.593	10,697	77
Greg Wyatt, Northern Ariz.	1986-89	1,510	926	49	.613	10,697	70
Sean Payton, Eastern Ill.	1983-86	1,408	756	55	.537	10,655	75
Jeff Wiley, Holy Cross	1985-88	1,208	723	63	.599	9,698	71
Kirk Schulz, Villanova	1986-89	1,297	774	70	.597	9,305	70
Ken Hobart, Idaho	1980-83	1,219	629	42	.516	9,300	79
Matt DeGennaro, Connecticut	1987-90	1,319	803	49	.609	9,288	73
Marty Horn, Lehigh	1982-85	1,390	744	64	.535	9,120	62
Jason Whitmer, Idaho St.	1987-90	1,349	721	53	.534	9,081	55
Chris Swartz, Morehead St.	1987-90	1,408	774	47	.550	9,027	56
¢Jamie Martin, Weber St.	1989-91	1,081	652	42	.603	9,000	67
Mike Buck, Maine	1986-89	1,134	637	41	.562	8,721	68
Michael Proctor, Murray St.	1986-89	1,148	578	45	.503	8,682	52
Eric Beavers, Nevada	1983-86	1,094	646	37	.590	8,626	77
Tom Ciaccio, Holy Cross	1988-91	1,073	658	46	.613	8,603	72
Steve Calabria, Colgate	1981-84	1,143	626	68	.548	8,555	54
Jeff Cesarone, Western Ky.	1984-87	1,339	714	39	.533	8,404	45
Mike Buck, Maine	1986-89	1,102	636	46	.577	8,399	62
Frank Baur, Lafayette	1985, 87-89	1,103	636	46	.577	8,399	62
Stan Yagiello, William & Mary	$1981-85	1,247	737	36	.591	8,249	51
Mike Smith, Northern Iowa	1984-87	943	557	43	.591	8,219	58
Kelly Bradley, Montana St.	1983-86	1,238	714	45	.577	8,152	60
Bob Bleier, Richmond	1983-86	1,169	672	56	.575	8,057	54
John Gregory, Marshall	#85, 86, 88-89	1,074	552	45	.513	7,896	59
Chris Goetz, Towson St.	1987-90	1,172	648	51	.553	7,882	42
Paul Singer, Western Ill.	1985-88	1,171	646	43	.552	7,850	61
John Witkowski, Columbia	1981-83	1,176	613	60	.521	7,849	56
Grady Bennett, Montana	1987-90	1,097	641	42	.584	7,778	55
Bernard Hawk, Bethune-Cookman	1982-85	1,120	554	51	.495	7,737	56
Bob Jean, New Hampshire	1985-88	1,126	567	49	.504	7,704	51

*Record. $ See page 6 for explanation.   # At Southeastern La. in 1985.   ¢ Active player.

Career Yards Per Game

Player, Team	Years	G	Att.	Cmp.	Yards	TD	Yd. PG
Willie Totten, Mississippi Val.	1982-85	40	1,555	907	12,711	*139	*317.8
Neil Lomax, Portland St.	1977-80	42	*1,606	*938	*13,220	106	314.8
John Friesz, Idaho	1986-89	35	1,350	801	10,697	77	305.6
Sean Payton, Eastern Ill.	1983-86	37	1,408	756	10,655	75	288.0
Greg Wyatt, Northern Ariz.	1986-89	42	1,510	926	10,697	70	254.7

*Record.

Career Touchdown Passes

Player, Team	Years	Games	TD Passes
Willie Totten, Mississippi Val.	1982-85	40	*139
Neil Lomax, Portland St.	1977-80	42	106
Ken Hobart, Idaho	1980-83	44	79
John Friesz, Idaho	1986-89	35	77
Eric Beavers, Nevada	1983-86	40	77
Sean Payton, Eastern Ill.	1983-86	39	75
Matt DeGennaro, Connecticut	1987-90	43	73
Tom Ciaccio, Holy Cross	1988-91	37	72
Jeff Wiley, Holy Cross	1985-88	41	71
Greg Wyatt, Northern Ariz.	1986-89	42	70
Kirk Schulz, Villanova	1986-89	42	70

* Record.

Special Note: Tom Ehrhardt played two years at LIU-C. W. Post (Division II) and two years at Rhode Island (Division I-AA) and totaled 92 career touchdown passes. For I-AA, he totaled 66.

Season Touchdown Passes

Player, Team	Year	Games	TD Passes
Willie Totten, Mississippi Val.	1984	10	*56
Willie Totten, Mississippi Val.	1985	11	39
Neil Lomax, Portland St.	1980	11	37
Jamie Martin, Weber St.	1991	11	35
Tom Ehrhardt, Rhode Island	1985	10	35
Todd Hammel, Stephen F. Austin	1989	11	34
Jeff Wiley, Holy Cross	1987	11	34
Doug Hudson, Nicholls St.	1986	11	32
Ken Hobart, Idaho	1983	11	32
Glenn Kempa, Lehigh	1991	11	31
John Friesz, Idaho	1989	11	31
Brent Pease, Montana	1986	11	30
Kelly Bradley, Montana St.	1984	11	30

* Record.

Season Yards

Player, Team	Year	G	Att.	Cmp.	Int.	Pct.	Yards	TD
Willie Totten, Mississippi Val.	†1984	10	*518	*324	22	.626	*4,557	*56
Jamie Martin, Weber St.	1991	11	500	310	17	.620	4,125	35
Neil Lomax, Portland St.	1980	11	473	296	12	.626	4,094	37
John Friesz, Idaho	1989	11	425	260	8	.612	4,041	31
Neil Lomax, Portland St.	1979	11	516	299	16	.579	3,950	26
Todd Hammel, Stephen F. Austin	†1989	11	401	238	13	.594	3,914	34
Sean Payton, Eastern Ill.	1984	11	473	270	15	.571	3,843	28
Jamie Martin, Weber St.	1990	11	428	256	15	.598	3,700	23
Willie Totten, Mississippi Val.	1985	11	492	295	29	.600	3,698	39
Jeff Wiley, Holy Cross	†1987	11	400	265	17	.663	3,677	34
John Friesz, Idaho	1987	11	502	311	14	.620	3,677	28
Ken Hobart, Idaho	1983	11	477	268	19	.562	3,618	32
Glenn Kempa, Lehigh	1991	11	474	286	15	.603	3,565	31
Tom Ehrhardt, Rhode Island	1985	10	497	283	19	.569	3,542	35
Tony Petersen, Marshall	1987	11	466	251	25	.539	3,529	22
Todd Brunner, Lehigh	1989	11	450	273	19	.607	3,516	26
Kelly Bradley, Montana St.	1984	11	499	289	20	.579	3,508	30
Neil Lomax, Portland St.	†1978	11	436	241	22	.553	3,506	25

* Record.   † National champion.

Single-Game Yards

Yds.	Player, Team (Opponent)	Date
624	Jamie Martin, Weber St. (Idaho St.)	Nov. 23, 1991
619	Doug Pederson, Northeast La. (Stephen F. Austin)	Nov. 11, 1989
599	Willie Totten, Mississippi Val. (Prairie View)	Oct. 27, 1984
589	Vern Harris, Idaho St. (Montana)	Oct. 12, 1985
571	Todd Hammel, Stephen F. Austin (Northeast La.)	Nov. 11, 1989
566	Tom Ehrhardt, Rhode Island (Connecticut)	Nov. 16, 1985
553	Willie Totten, Mississippi Val. (Southern-B.R.)	Sept. 29, 1984
545	Willie Totten, Mississippi Val. (Grambling)	Oct. 13, 1984
537	Tod Mayfield, West Tex. St. (New Mexico St.)	Nov. 16, 1985
536	Willie Totten, Mississippi Val. (Kentucky St.)	Sept. 1, 1984
534	Todd Hammel, Stephen F. Austin (Sam Houston St.)	Nov. 4, 1989
527	Bernard Hawk, Bethune-Cookman (Ga. Southern)	Oct. 6, 1984

Yds.	Player, Team (Opponent)	Date
527	Ken Hobart, Idaho (Southern Colo.)	Sept. 10, 1983
526	Willie Totten, Mississippi Val. (Jackson St.)	Sept. 22, 1984

Single-Game Attempts

No.	Player, Team (Opponent)	Date
77	Neil Lomax, Portland St. (Northern Colo.)	Oct. 20, 1979
74	Paul Peterson, Idaho St. (Nevada)	Oct. 1, 1983
71	Doug Pederson, Northeast La. (Stephen F. Austin)	Nov. 11, 1989
70	Greg Farland, Rhode Island (Boston U.)	Oct. 18, 1986
68	Tony Petersen, Marshall (Western Caro.)	Nov. 14, 1987
67	Vern Harris, Idaho St. (Montana)	Oct. 12, 1985
67	Rick Worman, Eastern Wash. (Nevada)	Oct. 12, 1985
67	Tod Mayfield, West Tex. St. (Indiana St.)	Oct. 5, 1985
67	Tom Ehrhardt, Rhode Island (Brown)	Sept. 28, 1985
66	Chris Swartz, Morehead St. (Tennessee Tech)	Oct. 17, 1987
66	Sean Cook, Texas Southern (Texas A&I)	Sept. 6, 1986
66	Kelly Bradley, Montana St. (Eastern Wash.)	Sept. 21, 1985
66	Bernard Hawk, Bethune-Cookman (Ga. Southern)	Oct. 6, 1984
66	Willie Totten, Mississippi Val. (Southern-B.R.)	Sept. 29, 1984
66	Paul Peterson, Idaho St. (Cal Poly SLO)	Oct. 22, 1983

Single-Game Completions

No.	Player, Team (Opponent)	Date
47	Jamie Martin, Weber St. (Idaho St.)	Nov. 23, 1991
46	Doug Pederson, Northeast La. (Stephen F. Austin)	Nov. 11, 1989
46	Willie Totten, Mississippi Val. (Southern-B.R.)	Sept. 29, 1984
45	Willie Totten, Mississippi Val. (Prairie View)	Oct. 27, 1984
44	Neil Lomax, Portland St. (Northern Colo.)	Oct. 20, 1979
42	Tod Mayfield, West Tex. St. (Indiana St.)	Oct. 5, 1985
42	Kelly Bradley, Montana St. (Eastern Wash.)	Sept. 21, 1985
42	Rusty Hill, North Texas (Tulsa)	Nov. 20, 1982

Annual Champions

Year	Player, Team	Cl.	G.	Att.	Cmp.	Avg.	Int.	Pct.	Yds.	TD
1978	Neil Lomax, Portland St.	So.	11	436	241	21.9	22	.553	3,506	25

Beginning in 1979, ranked on Passing Efficiency Rating Points (instead of per-game completions)

Year	Player, Team	Cl.	G.	Att.	Cmp.	Int.	Pct.	Yds.	TD	Pts.
1979	Joe Aliotti, Boise St.	Jr.	11	219	144	7	.658	1,870	19	159.7
1980	Mike Williams, Grambling	Sr.	11	239	127	5	.531	2,116	28	162.0
1981	Mike Machurek, Idaho St.	Sr.	9	313	188	11	.601	2,752	22	150.1
1982	Frank Novak, Lafayette	Jr.	10	257	154	12	.599	2,257	20	150.0
1983	Willie Totten, Mississippi Val.	So.	9	279	174	9	.624	2,566	29	167.5
1984	Willie Totten, Mississippi Val.	Jr.	10	*518	*324	22	.626	*4,557	*56	163.6
1985	Bobby Lamb, Furman	Sr.	11	181	106	6	.586	1,856	18	170.9
1986	Mike Smith, Northern Iowa	Jr.	11	303	190	16	.627	3,125	27	168.2
1987	Jeff Wiley, Holy Cross	Jr.	11	400	265	17	.663	3,677	34	163.0
1988	Frank Baur, Lafayette	Jr.	10	256	164	11	.641	2,621	23	171.1
1989	Todd Hammel, Stephen F. Austin	Sr.	11	401	238	13	.594	3,914	34	162.8
1990	Connell Maynor, North Caro. A&T	Jr.	11	191	123	10	.644	1,699	16	156.3
1991	Michael Payton, Marshall	Jr.	9	216	143	5	.662	2,333	19	*181.3

* Record.

RECEIVING
Career Catches Per Game

Player, Team	Years	Games	Catches	Yards	TD	Ct. PG
Jerry Rice, Mississippi Val.	1981-84	41	*301	*4,693	*50	*7.3
Kevin Guthrie, Princeton	1981-83	28	193	2,645	16	6.9
Eric Yarber, Idaho	1984-85	19	129	1,920	17	6.8
Brian Forster, Rhode Island (TE)	1983-85, 87	38	245	3,410	31	6.5
Kasey Dunn, Idaho	1988-91	42	268	3,847	25	6.4
Gordie Lockbaum, Holy Cross (RB)	‡1986-87	22	135	2,012	17	6.1
Derek Graham, Princeton	1981, 83-84	29	176	2,819	19	6.1
Stuart Gaussoin, Portland St.	1978-80	23	135	1,909	14	5.9
Don Lewis, Columbia	1981-83	30	176	2,207	11	5.9
Mike Barber, Marshall	1985-88	36	209	3,250	20	5.8
Sebastian Brown, Bethune-Cookman	1984-85	20	116	1,830	17	5.8
Rennie Benn, Lehigh	1982-85	41	237	3,662	44	5.8
Daren Altieri, Boston U.	1987-90	39	225	2,518	15	5.8
Bill Reggio, Columbia	1981-83	30	170	2,384	26	5.7

* Record. ‡ Defensive back in 1984-85.

Boise State quarterback Joe Aliotti led Division I-AA in passing efficiency in 1979 with a rating of 159.7. He completed 65.8 percent of his passes and threw just seven interceptions in 11 games.

Season Catches Per Game

Player, Team	Year	Games	Catches	Yards	TD	Ct. PG
Brian Forster, Rhode Island (TE)	†1985	10	*115	1,617	12	*11.5
Jerry Rice, Mississippi Val.	1984	10	103	*1,682	*27	10.3
Jerry Rice, Mississippi Val.	†1983	10	102	1,450	14	10.2
Stuart Gaussoin, Portland St.	†1979	9	90	1,132	8	10.0
Kevin Guthrie, Princeton	1983	10	88	1,259	9	8.8
Alfred Pupunu, Weber St. (TE)	†1991	11	93	1,204	12	8.5
Derek Graham, Princeton	1983	10	84	1,363	11	8.4
Don Lewis, Columbia	†1982	10	84	1,000	6	8.4
Peter Macon, Weber St.	†1989	11	92	1,047	6	8.4
Marvin Walker, North Texas	1982	11	91	934	11	8.3

* Record.   † National champion.

Career Catches

Player, Team	Years	Catches	Yards	Avg.	TD
Jerry Rice, Mississippi Val.	1981-84	*301	*4,693	15.6	*50
Kasey Dunn, Idaho	1988-91	268	3,847	14.4	25
Brian Forster, Rhode Island	1983-85, 87	245	3,410	13.9	31
Mark Didio, Connecticut	1988-91	239	3,535	14.8	21
Rennie Benn, Lehigh	1982-85	237	3,662	15.5	44
Daren Altieri, Boston U.	1987-90	225	2,518	11.2	15
Darrell Colbert, Texas Southern	1983-86	217	3,177	14.6	33
Mike Barber, Marshall	1985-88	209	3,520	16.8	20
William Brooks, Boston U.	1982-85	204	3,154	15.5	26
Donald Narcisse, Texas Southern	1983-86	203	2,429	12.0	26
Shawn Collins, Northern Ariz.	1985-88	201	2,764	13.8	24
Leland Melvin, Richmond	1982-85	198	2,669	13.5	16
Curtis Olds, New Hampshire	1985-88	193	3,028	15.7	23
Kevin Guthrie, Princeton	1981-83	193	2,645	13.7	16
Sergio Hebra, Maine	1984-87	189	2,612	13.8	17
Joe Thomas, Mississippi Val.	1982-85	186	2,816	15.1	36
Glenn Antrum, Connecticut	1985-88	186	2,552	13.7	14

Player, Team	Years	Catches	Yards	Avg.	TD
Roy Banks, Eastern Ill.	1983-86	184	3,177	17.3	38
Merril Hoge, Idaho St. (RB)	1983-86	182	1,734	9.5	13
George Delaney, Colgate	1988-91	181	2,938	16.2	25
Robert Brady, Villanova	1986-89	180	2,725	15.1	28
Cisco Richard, Northeast La................	1987-90	179	1,874	10.5	12
Peter Macon, Weber St.	1986-89	177	2,151	12.1	16
Derek Graham, Princeton	1981, 83-84	176	2,819	16.0	19
Don Lewis, Columbia	1981-83	176	2,207	12.5	11

* Record.

Season Catches

Player, Team	Year	Games	Catches	Yards	TD
Brian Forster, Rhode Island (TE)	†1985	10	*115	1,617	12
Jerry Rice, Mississippi Val.	†1984	10	103	*1,682	*27
Jerry Rice, Mississippi Val.	†1983	10	102	1,450	14
Alfred Pupunu, Weber St. (TE)	†1991	11	93	1,204	12
Peter Macon, Weber St.	†1989	11	92	1,047	6
Marvin Walker, North Texas	1982	11	91	934	11
Stuart Gaussoin, Portland St.	†1979	9	90	1,132	8
Mark Didio, Connecticut	1991	11	88	1,354	8
Kasey Dunn, Idaho	†1990	11	88	1,164	7
Donald Narcisse, Texas Southern	†1986	11	88	1,074	15
Kevin Guthrie, Princeton	1983	10	88	1,259	9
Kasey Dunn, Idaho	1991	11	85	1,263	6
Derek Graham, Princeton	1983	10	84	1,363	11
Don Lewis, Columbia	†1982	10	84	1,000	6

* Record. † National champion.

Single-Game Catches

No.	Player, Team (Opponent)	Date
24	Jerry Rice, Mississippi Val. (Southern-B.R.)...Oct. 1, 1983	
22	Marvin Walker, North Texas.(Tulsa) ....Nov. 20, 1982	
21	David Pandt, Montana St. (Eastern Wash.) ....Sept. 21, 1985	
18	Jerome Williams, Morehead St. (Eastern Ky.) ....Nov. 18, 1989	
18	Brian Forster, Rhode Island (Brown)...Sept. 28, 1985	
17	Lifford Jackson, Louisiana Tech (Kansas St.) ....Oct. 1, 1988	
17	Brian Forster, Rhode Island (Lehigh)...Oct. 12, 1985	
17	Jerry Rice, Mississippi Val. (Southern-B.R.) ....Sept. 29, 1984	
17	Jerry Rice, Mississippi Val. (Kentucky St.) ....Sept. 1, 1984	

Career Yards

Player, Team	Years	Catches	Yards	Avg.	TD
Jerry Rice, Mississippi Val.	1981-84	*301	*4,693	15.6	*50
Kasey Dunn, Idaho	1988-91	268	3,847	14.4	25
Rennie Benn, Lehigh........................	1982-85	237	3,662	15.5	44
Mark Didio, Connecticut	1988-91	239	3,535	14.8	21
Mike Barber, Marshall	1985-88	209	3,520	16.8	20
Brian Forster, Rhode Island (TE)	1983-85, 87	245	3,410	13.9	31
Tracy Singleton, Howard	1979-82	159	3,187	‡20.0	16
Roy Banks, Eastern Ill.	1983-86	184	3,177	17.3	38
Darrell Colbert, Texas Southern	1983-86	217	3,177	14.6	33
William Brooks, Boston U.	1982-85	204	3,154	15.5	26

* Record. ‡ Record for minimum of 125 catches.

Season Yards

Player, Team	Year	Catches	Yards	Avg.	TD
Jerry Rice, Mississippi Val.	†1984	103	*1,682	16.3	*27
Brian Forster, Rhode Island	†1985	*115	1,617	14.1	12
Jerry Rice, Mississippi Val.	†1983	102	1,450	14.2	14
Derek Graham, Princeton	1983	84	1,363	16.2	11
Mark Didio, Connecticut	†1991	88	1,354	15.4	8
Golden Tate, Tennessee St.	1983	63	1,307	20.7	13

* Record. † National champion.

Single-Game Yards

Yds.	Player, Team (Opponent)	Date
370	Michael Lerch, Princeton (Brown)..Oct. 12, 1991	
330	Nate Singleton, Grambling (Virginia Union) ....Sept. 14, 1991	
327	Brian Forster, Rhode Island (Brown)..Sept. 28, 1985	
299	Treamelle Taylor, Nevada (Montana)...Oct. 14, 1989	

Division I-AA Annual Champions, All-Time Leaders   151

Yds.	Player, Team (Opponent)	Date
299	Brian Forster, Rhode Island (Lehigh)	Oct. 12, 1985
294	Jerry Rice, Mississippi Val. (Kentucky St.)	Sept. 1, 1984
285	Jerry Rice, Mississippi Val. (Jackson St.)	Sept. 22, 1984
279	Jerry Rice, Mississippi Val. (Southern-B.R.)	Oct. 1, 1983
266	Rennie Benn, Lehigh (Indiana, Pa.)	Sept. 14, 1985
263	Mark Stock, Va. Military (East Tenn. St.)	Nov. 22, 1986
262	Andre Motley, Marshall (Tenn.-Chatt.)	Oct. 20, 1990
262	Kenneth Gilstrap, Tennessee Tech (Morehead St.)	Oct. 17, 1987
253	Chris Johnson, Indiana St. (Illinois St.)	Oct. 18, 1986
252	Jeff Sanders, William & Mary (Miami, Ohio)	Sept. 11, 1982
251	Lifford Jackson, Louisiana Tech (Kansas St.)	Oct. 1, 1988

Annual Champions

Year	Player, Team	Class	G.	Ct.	Avg.	Yards	TD
1978	Dan Ross, Northeastern	Sr.	11	68	6.2	988	7
1979	Stuart Gaussoin, Portland St.	Jr.	9	90	10.0	1,132	8
1980	Kenny Johnson, Portland St.	So.	11	72	6.5	1,011	11
1981	Ken Harvey, Northern Iowa	Sr.	11	78	7.1	1,161	15
1982	Don Lewis, Columbia	Jr.	10	84	8.4	1,000	6
1983	Jerry Rice, Mississippi Val.	Jr.	10	102	10.2	1,450	14
1984	Jerry Rice, Mississippi Val.	Sr.	10	103	10.3	*1,682	*27
1985	Brian Forster, Rhode Island (TE)	Jr.	10	*115	*11.5	1,617	12
1986	Donald Narcisse, Texas Southern	Sr.	11	88	8.0	1,074	15
1987	Mike Barber, Marshall	Jr.	11	78	7.1	1,237	7
	Gordie Lockbaum, Holy Cross (RB)	Sr.	11	78	7.1	1,152	9
1988	Glenn Antrum, Connecticut	Sr.	11	77	7.0	1,130	7
1989	Peter Macon, Weber St.	Sr.	11	92	8.4	1,047	6

Beginning in 1990, ranked on both per-game catches and yards per game

Per-Game Catches

Year	Player, Team	Class	G.	Ct.	Avg.	Yards	TD
1990	Kasey Dunn, Idaho	Jr.	11	88	8.0	1,164	7
1991	Alfred Pupunu, Weber St. (TE)	Sr.	11	93	8.5	1,204	12

Yards Per Game

Year	Player, Team	Class	G.	Ct.	Yards	Avg.	TD
1990	Kasey Dunn, Idaho	Jr.	11	88	1,164	105.8	7
1991	Mark Didio, Connecticut	Sr.	11	88	1,354	123.1	8

* *Record.*

SCORING

Career Points Per Game §

Player, Team	Years	Games	TD	XPt.	FG	Pts.	Pt. PG
David Meggett, Towson St.	1987-88	18	30	0	0	180	*10.0
Elroy Harris, Eastern Ky.	1985, 87-88	31	47	6	0	288	9.3
Tony Zendejas, Nevada	1981-83	33	0	90	70	300	9.1
Gerald Harris, Ga. Southern	1984-86	31	45	2	0	272	8.8
Marty Zendejas, Nevada	1984-87	44	0	*169	*72	*385	8.8
Charvez Foger, Nevada	1985-88	42	*60	2	0	362	8.6
Paul Lewis, Boston U.	1981-84	37	51	2	0	308	8.3
Judd Garrett, Princeton	1987-89	30	41	1	0	248	8.3
Andre Garron, New Hampshire	1982-85	30	41	0	0	246	8.2
Micky Penaflor, Northern Ariz.	1986-88	22	0	66	38	180	8.2
Kenny Gamble, Colgate	1984-87	42	57	0	0	342	8.1
Jerry Rice, Mississippi Val.	1981-84	41	50	2	0	302	7.4
Joel Sigel, Portland St.	1977-80	41	50	2	0	302	7.4
Brian Mitchell, Marshall/Northern Iowa	1987, 89-91	44	0	130	64	322	7.3
George Benyola, Louisiana Tech	1984-85	22	0	40	40	160	7.3
Roberto Moran, Boise St.	1985-86	22	0	57	34	159	7.2
Harvey Reed, Howard	1984-87	41	48	6	0	294	7.2
Thayne Doyle, Idaho	1988-91	43	0	160	49	307	7.1
Dwight Stone, Middle Tenn. St.	1985-86	22	26	0	0	156	7.1
Stanford Jennings, Furman	1982-83	22	26	0	0	156	7.1
Rich Erenberg, Colgate	1982-83	21	23	10	0	148	7.0

* *Record.*   § *The following players competed two years in Division I-AA and two years in Division I-A: Stanford Jennings, Furman (four years: 262 points and 6.1 average); Rich Erenberg, Colgate (four years: 202 points and 5.2 average), and Buford Jordan, McNeese St. (four years: 266 points and 6.5 average).*

Season Points Per Game

Player, Team	Year	Games	TD	XPt.	FG	Pts.	Pt. PG
Jerry Rice, Mississippi Val.	†1984	10	27	0	0	162	*16.2
Geoff Mitchell, Weber St.	†1991	11	*28	1	0	*170	15.5
Elroy Harris, Eastern Ky.	†1988	10	21	2	0	128	12.8
Sean Sanders, Weber St.	†1987	10	21	0	0	126	12.6
Rich Erenberg, Colgate	†1983	11	21	10	0	136	12.4
Harvey Reed, Howard	1987	10	20	2	0	122	12.2
Paul Lewis, Boston U.	1983	10	20	2	0	122	12.2
Gordie Lockbaum, Holy Cross	1987	11	22	0	0	132	12.0
Gordie Lockbaum, Holy Cross	†1986	11	22	0	0	132	12.0
Gene Lake, Delaware St.	1984	10	20	0	0	120	12.0
Ernest Thompson, Ga. Southern	1988	10	19	2	0	116	11.6
Barry Bourassa, New Hampshire	1991	11	21	0	0	126	11.5
Kenny Gamble, Colgate	1986	11	21	0	0	126	11.5
Gerald Harris, Ga. Southern	1984	9	17	0	0	102	11.3
Harvey Reed, Howard	1986	10	18	2	0	110	11.0
Carl Smith, Maine	†1989	11	20	0	0	120	10.9
Joe Segreti, Holy Cross	1988	11	20	0	0	120	10.9
Luther Turner, Sam Houston St.	1987	11	20	0	0	120	10.9
John Settle, Appalachian St.	1986	11	20	0	0	120	10.9

* Record.   † National champion.

Career Points (Non-Kickers)

Player, Team	Years	TD	XPt.	Pts.
Charvez Foger, Nevada	1985-88	*60	2	362
Kenny Gamble, Colgate	1984-87	57	0	342
Paul Lewis, Boston U.	1981-84	51	2	308
Erick Torain, Lehigh	1987-90	50	6	306
Jerry Rice, Mississippi Val.	1981-84	50	2	302
Joel Sigel, Portland St.	1977-80	50	2	302
Harvey Reed, Howard	1984-87	48	6	294
Elroy Harris, Eastern Ky.	1985, 87-88	47	6	288
Joe Campbell, Middle Tenn. St.	1988-91	45	2	272
Gerald Harris, Ga. Southern	1984-86	45	2	272
Norm Ford, New Hampshire	1986-89	45	0	270
John Settle, Appalachian St.	1983-86	44	4	268
Ernest Thompson, Ga. Southern	1985, 87-89	44	2	266
Rennie Benn, Lehigh	1982-85	44	2	266
Joe Segreti, Holy Cross	1987-90	44	0	264
Gordie Lockbaum, Holy Cross	1984-87	44	0	264
Frank Hawkins, Nevada	1977-80	44	0	264

* Record.

Career Points (Kickers)

Player, Team	Years	PAT	PAT Att.	FG	FG Att.	Pts.
Marty Zendejas, Nevada	1984-87	*169	*175	*72	90	*385
Brian Mitchell, Marshall/Northern Iowa	1987, 89-91	130	131	64	81	322
Thayne Doyle, Idaho	1988-91	160	174	49	75	307
Kirk Roach, Western Caro.	1984-87	89	91	71	*102	302
Tim Foley, Ga. Southern	1984-87	151	156	50	62	301
Dewey Klein, Marshall	1988-91	156	165	48	66	300
Tony Zendejas, Nevada	1981-83	90	96	70	86	300
Steve Christie, William & Mary	1986-89	108	116	57	83	279
Mike Black, Boise St.	1988-91	122	127	51	75	275
Kirk Duce, Montana	1988-91	131	141	47	78	272
Paul Hickert, Murray St.	1984-87	116	121	49	79	263
Dean Biasucci, Western Caro.	1980-83	101	106	54	80	263
$Matt Stover, Louisiana Tech	1986-89	70	72	64	88	262
Kelly Potter, Middle Tenn. St.	1981-84	105	109	52	78	261
Billy Hayes, Sam Houston St.	1985-88	117	120	47	71	258
Jim Hodson, Lafayette	1987-90	134	140	40	66	254
Dave Parkinson, Delaware St.	1985-88	134	143	40	77	254
Chuck Rawlinson, Stephen F. Austin	1988-91	106	110	49	69	253
Paul Politi, Illinois St.	1983-86	101	103	50	78	251
Teddy Garcia, Northeast La.	1984-87	78	81	56	88	246
Paul McFadden, Youngstown St.	1980-83	87	90	52	90	243

* Record. $ Member of Division I-A 1989 only.

Player, Team	Year	TD	XPt.	FG	Pts.
Geoff Mitchell, Weber St.	†1991	*28	2	0	*170
Jerry Rice, Mississippi Val.	†1984	27	0	0	162
Rich Erenberg, Colgate	†1983	21	10	0	136
Gordie Lockbaum, Holy Cross	1987	22	0	0	132
Gordie Lockbaum, Holy Cross	†1986	22	0	0	132
Elroy Harris, Eastern Ky.	†1988	21	1	0	128
Barry Bourassa, New Hampshire	1991	21	0	0	126
Sean Sanders, Weber St.	†1987	21	0	0	126
Kenny Gamble, Colgate	1986	21	0	0	126
Harvey Reed, Howard	1987	20	2	0	122
Paul Lewis, Boston U.	1983	20	2	0	122
Carl Smith, Maine	†1989	20	0	0	120
Joe Segreti, Holy Cross	1988	20	0	0	120
Luther Turner, Sam Houston St.	1987	20	0	0	120
John Settle, Appalachian St.	1986	20	0	0	120
Gene Lake, Delaware St.	1984	20	0	0	120

Record.   † National champion.

Annual Champions

Year	Player, Team	Class	Games	TD	XPt.	FG	Pts.	Avg.
1978	Frank Hawkins, Nevada	So.	10	17	0	0	102	10.2
1979	Joel Sigel, Portland St.	Jr.	10	16	0	0	96	9.6
1980	Ken Jenkins, Bucknell	Jr.	10	16	0	0	96	9.6
1981	Paris Wicks, Youngstown St.	Jr.	11	17	2	0	104	9.5
1982	Paul Lewis, Boston U.	So.	10	18	0	0	108	10.8
1983	Rich Erenberg, Colgate	Sr.	11	21	10	0	136	12.4
1984	Jerry Rice, Mississippi Val.	Sr.	10	27	0	0	162	*16.2
1985	Charvez Foger, Nevada	Fr.	10	18	0	0	108	10.8
1986	Gordie Lockbaum, Holy Cross	Jr.	11	22	0	0	132	12.0
1987	Sean Sanders, Weber St.	Sr.	10	21	0	0	126	12.6
1988	Elroy Harris, Eastern Ky.	Jr.	10	21	1	0	128	12.8
1989	Carl Smith, Maine	So.	11	20	0	0	120	10.9
1990	Barry Bourassa, New Hampshire	So.	9	16	0	0	96	10.7
1991	Geoff Mitchell, Weber St.	Sr.	11	*28	1	0	*170	15.5

Record.

PUNTING

Career Average (Minimum 150 Punts)

Player, Team	Years	No.	Yards	Long	Avg.
Pumpy Tudors, Tenn.-Chatt.	1989-91	181	8,041	79	*44.4
Case de Bruijn, Idaho St.	1978-81	256	11,184	76	43.7
George Cimadevilla, East Tenn. St.	1983-86	225	9,676	72	43.0
John Christopher, Morehead St.	1979-82	298	12,633	62	42.4
Russell Griffith, Utah St./Weber St.	1983, 85-86	187	7,908	67	42.3
Bret Wright, Southeastern La.	1981-83	165	6,963	66	42.2
Jeff Kaiser, Idaho St.	1982-84	156	6,571	88	42.1
Greg Davis, Citadel	1983-86	263	11,076	81	42.1
Mark Royals, Appalachian St.	1983-85	223	9,372	67	42.0

Record.

Season Average
(Qualifiers for Championship)

Player, Team	Year	No.	Yards	Avg.
Harold Alexander, Appalachian St.	†1991	64	3,009	*47.0
Case de Bruijn, Idaho St.	†1981	42	1,928	45.9
Colin Godfrey, Tennessee St.	†1990	57	2,614	45.9
Stuart Dodds, Montana St.	†1979	59	2,689	45.6
Pumpy Tudors, Tenn.-Chatt.	1991	53	2,414	45.6
Paul Asbury, Southwest Tex. St.	1990	39	1,749	44.9
Tom Sugg, Idaho	1991	53	2,371	44.7
Mike Rice, Montana	†1985	62	2,771	44.7
Case de Bruijn, Idaho St.	1979	73	3,261	44.7
George Cimadevilla, East Tenn. St.	1985	66	2,948	44.7
Greg Davis, Citadel	†1986	61	2,723	44.6
Pumpy Tudors, Tenn.-Chatt.	1990	63	2,810	44.6
Pat Velarde, Marshall	†1983	64	2,852	44.6
Bart Bradley, Sam Houston St.	1986	44	1,957	44.5
Curtis Moody, Texas Southern	1985	64	2,844	44.4

Player, Team	Year	No.	Yards	Avg.
Terry Belden, Northern Ariz.	1991	43	1,908	44.4
Bret Wright, Southeastern La.	1983	66	2,923	44.3
George Cimadevilla, East Tenn. St.	1986	65	2,876	44.3
Case de Bruijn, Idaho St.	†1980	67	2,945	44.0

* Record.   † National champion.

Annual Champions

Year	Player, Team	Class	No.	Yards	Avg.
1978	Nick Pavich, Nevada	So.	47	1,939	41.3
1979	Stuart Dodds, Montana St.	Sr.	59	2,689	45.6
1980	Case de Bruijn, Idaho St.	Jr.	67	2,945	44.0
1981	Case de Bruijn, Idaho St.	Sr.	42	1,928	45.9
1982	John Christopher, Morehead St.	Sr.	93	4,084	43.9
1983	Pat Velarde, Marshall	Sr.	64	2,852	44.6
1984	Steve Kornegay, Western Caro.	Jr.	49	2,127	43.4
1985	Mike Rice, Montana	Jr.	62	2,771	44.7
1986	Greg Davis, Citadel	Sr.	61	2,723	44.6
1987	Eric Stein, Eastern Wash.	Sr.	74	3,193	43.2
1988	Mike McCabe, Illinois St.	Sr.	69	3,042	44.1
1989	Pumpy Tudors, Tenn.-Chatt.	So.	65	2,817	43.3
1990	Colin Godfrey, Tennessee St.	So.	57	2,614	45.9
1991	Harold Alexander, Appalachian St.	Jr.	64	3,009	*47.0

* Record.

INTERCEPTIONS
Career Interceptions

Player, Team	Years	No.	Yards	Avg.
Dave Murphy, Holy Cross	1986-89	*28	309	11.0
Issiac Holt, Alcorn St.	1981-84	24	319	13.3
Bill McGovern, Holy Cross	1981-84	24	168	7.0
Kevin Smith, Rhode Island	1987-90	23	287	12.5
Mike Prior, Illinois St.	1981-84	23	211	9.2
Frank Robinson, Boise St.	1988-91	22	203	9.2
Dean Cain, Princeton	1985-87	22	203	9.2
¢William Carroll, Florida A&M	1989-91	21	328	15.6
George Floyd, Eastern Ky.	1978-81	21	318	15.1
Kevin Dent, Jackson St.	1985-88	21	280	13.3
Chris Demarest, Northeastern	1984-87	21	255	12.1
Greg Greely, Nicholls St.	1981-84	21	218	10.4
Mark Seals, Boston U.	1985-88	21	169	8.0
Jeff Smith, Illinois St.	1985-88	21	152	7.2
Rick Harris, East Tenn. St.	1986-88	20	*452	22.6
Leslie Frazier, Alcorn St.	1977-80	20	269	13.5
Mark Kelso, William & Mary	1981-84	20	171	8.6
Ricky Thomas, South Caro. St.	1988-91	19	374	19.7
Michael Richardson, Northwestern (La.)	1981-84	19	344	18.1
Mike Genetti, Northeastern	1980-83	19	296	15.6
George Schmitt, Delaware	1980-82	19	280	14.7
Joe Burton, Delaware St.	1983-86	19	248	13.1
Dwayne Harper, South Caro. St.	1984-87	19	163	8.6

* Record.   ¢ Active player.

Season Interceptions

Player, Team	Year	No.	Yards
Dean Cain, Princeton	†1987	*12	98
Aeneas Williams, Southern-B. R.	‡1990	11	173
Claude Pettaway, Maine	‡1990	11	161
Everson Walls, Grambling.................	†1980	11	145
Anthony Young, Jackson St.	†1978	11	108
Bill McGovern, Holy Cross	†1984	11	102
Kevin Dent, Jackson St.	‡1986	10	192
George Schmitt, Delaware	†1982	10	186
Neale Henderson, Southern-B.R.	†1979	10	151
Mike Genetti, Northeastern	†1981	10	144
Chris Demarest, Northeastern	1987	10	129
Eric Thompson, New Hampshire...........	‡1986	10	94
Bob Mahr, Lafayette......................	1981	10	48

Player, Team	Year	No.	Yards
Mike Armentrout, Southwest Mo. St.	†1983	10	42
Anthony Anderson, Grambling	†1986	10	37
Cedric Walker, Stephen F. Austin......................	1990	10	11

* Record.   † National champion.   ‡ National championship shared.

Annual Champions
(Ranked on Per-Game Average)

Year	Player, Team	Class	Games	No.	Avg.	Yards
1978	Anthony Young, Jackson St.	Sr.	11	11	1.00	108
1979	Neale Henderson, Southern-B.R.	Sr.	11	10	0.91	151
1980	Everson Walls, Grambling.................	Sr.	11	11	1.00	145
1981	Mike Genetti, Northeastern	So.	10	10	1.00	144
1982	George Schmitt, Delaware	Sr.	11	10	0.91	186
1983	Mike Armentrout, Southwest Mo. St.	Jr.	11	10	0.91	42
1984	Bill McGovern, Holy Cross	Sr.	11	11	1.00	102
1985	Mike Cassidy, Rhode Island	Sr.	10	9	0.90	169
	George Duarte, Northern Ariz.	Jr.	10	9	0.90	150
1986	Kevin Dent, Jackson St.	So.	11	10	0.91	192
	Eric Thompson, New Hampshire..........	Sr.	11	10	0.91	94
	Anthony Anderson, Grambling	Sr.	11	10	0.91	37
1987	Dean Cain, Princeton	Sr.	10	*12	*1.20	98
1988	Kevin Smith, Rhode Island	So.	10	9	0.90	94
1989	Mike Babb, Weber St.	Sr.	11	9	0.82	90
1990	Aeneas Williams, Southern-B. R.	Sr.	11	11	1.00	173
	Claude Pettaway, Maine..................	Sr.	11	11	1.00	161
1991	Warren McIntire, Delaware	Jr.	11	9	0.82	208

* Record.

PUNT RETURNS
Career Average
(Minimum 1.2 Returns Per Game)

Player, Team	Years	No.	Yards	Avg.
Willie Ware, Mississippi Val.	1982-85	61	1,003	*16.4
Tim Egerton, Delaware St.	1986-89	59	951	16.1
Chris Darrington, Weber St.	1984-86	26	415	16.0
John Armstrong, Richmond	1984-85	31	449	14.5
Joe Fuller, Northern Iowa	1982-85	69	888	12.9
Eric Yarber, Idaho	1984-85	32	406	12.7
Trumaine Johnson, Grambling	1979-82	53	662	12.5
Tony Merriwether, North Texas......................	1982-83	41	507	12.4
Thaylen Armstead, Grambling	1989-91	44	540	12.3
Barney Bussey, South Caro. St.	1980-83	47	573	12.2
John Taylor, Delaware St.	1982-85	48	576	12.0

* Record.

Season Average
(Minimum 1.2 Returns Per Game and Qualifiers for Championship)

Player, Team	Year	No.	Yards	Avg.
Tim Egerton, Delaware St.	†1988	16	368	*23.0
Ryan Priest, Lafayette................................	†1982	12	271	22.6
Craig Hodge, Tennessee St.	†1987	19	398	21.0
John Armstrong, Richmond	†1985	19	391	20.6
Willie Ware, Mississippi Val.	†1984	19	374	19.7
Mark Hurt, Alabama St.	1988	10	185	18.5
Howard Huckaby, Florida A&M	1988	26	478	18.4
Ashley Ambrose, Mississippi Val.	†1991	28	514	18.4
Barney Bussey, South Caro. St.	†1981	14	255	18.2
Chris Darrington, Weber St.	†1986	16	290	18.1
Willie Ware, Mississippi Val.	1985	31	*561	18.1
Clarence Alexander, Mississippi Val.	1986	22	380	17.3
Henry Richard, Northeast La.	†1989	15	258	17.2
Carl Williams, Texas Southern	1981	16	269	16.8
Jerome Bledsoe, Massachusetts	1988	17	285	16.8

* Record.   † National champion.

Annual Champions

Year	Player, Team	Class	No.	Yards	Avg.
1978	Ray Smith, Northern Ariz.............................	Sr.	13	181	13.9
1979	Joseph Markus, Connecticut.........................	Fr.	17	219	12.9

1992 NCAA FOOTBALL

Year	Player, Team	Class	No.	Yards	Avg.
1980	Trumaine Johnson, Grambling	So.	††13	226	17.4
1981	Barney Bussey, South Caro. St.	So.	14	255	18.2
1982	Ryan Priest, Lafayette	Fr.	12	271	22.6
1983	Joe Fuller, Northern Iowa	So.	22	344	15.6
1984	Willie Ware, Mississippi Val.	Jr.	19	374	19.7
1985	John Armstrong, Richmond	Sr.	19	391	20.6
1986	Chris Darrington, Weber St.	Sr.	16	290	18.1
1987	Craig Hodge, Tennessee St.	Sr.	19	398	21.0
1988	Tim Egerton, Delaware St.	Jr.	16	368	*23.0
1989	Henry Richard, Northeast La.	Jr.	15	258	17.2
1990	Gary Harrell, Howard	Fr.	26	417	16.0
1991	Ashley Ambrose, Mississippi Val.	Sr.	28	514	18.4

Record. †† Declared champion; with one more return (making 1.3 per game) for zero yards still would have highest average.*

KICKOFF RETURNS
Career Average
(Minimum 1.2 Returns Per Game)

Player, Team	Years	No.	Yards	Avg.
Charles Swann, Indiana St.	1989-91	45	1,319	*29.3
Craig Richardson, Eastern Wash.	1983-86	71	2,021	28.5
Daryl Holcombe, Eastern Ill.	1986-89	49	1,379	28.1
Curtis Chappell, Howard	1984-87	42	1,177	28.0
Jerry Parrish, Eastern Ky.	1978-81	61	1,668	27.3
Tony James, Eastern Ky.	1982-84	57	1,552	27.2
Frank Selto, Idaho St.	1986-87	30	803	26.8
Chris Pollard, Dartmouth	1986-88	52	1,376	26.5
John Jarvis, Howard	1986-88	39	1,031	26.4
Ronald Scott, Southern-B.R.	1982-85	38	1,003	26.4
Vernon Williams, Eastern Wash.	1986-88	40	1,052	26.3
Steve Ortman, Pennsylvania	1982-84	31	808	26.1
John Armstrong, Richmond	1984-85	32	826	25.8
Renard Coleman, Montana	1985-88	57	1,465	25.7
Michael Haynes, Northern Ariz.	1986-87	36	925	25.7
Kevin Gainer, Bethune-Cookman	1988-90	42	1,070	25.5
Archie Herring, Youngstown St.	1987-90	79	2,005	25.4
Jerome Stelly, Western Ill.	1981-82	42	1,024	24.4
Albert Brown, Western Ill.	1985-86	30	723	24.1
Sylvester Stamps, Jackson St.	1980, 82-83	42	1,012	24.1
Ray Brown, Southeastern La.	1983-84	30	719	24.0
Mike Wilt, Fordham	1990-91	26	620	23.9
Robert Alford, Middle Tenn. St.	1984-87	52	1,234	23.7
Michael Clemons, William & Mary	1983-86	43	1,013	23.6
Herman Hunter, Tennessee St.	1981-84	96	2,258	23.5
Dennis Smith, Northwestern (La.)	1986-89	69	1,622	23.5

Record.

Season Average
(Minimum 1.2 Returns Per Game)

Player, Team	Year	No.	Yards	Avg.
Craig Richardson, Eastern Wash.	†1984	21	729	*34.7
Dave Meggett, Towson St.	†1988	13	418	32.2
Charles Swann, Indiana St.	†1990	20	642	32.1
Archie Herring, Youngstown St.	1990	18	575	31.9
Davlin Mullen, Western Ky.	†1982	18	574	31.9
Danny Copeland, Eastern Ky.	†1986	26	812	31.2
Chris Chappell, Howard	1986	17	528	31.1
Dave Loehle, New Hampshire	†1978	15	460	30.7
Paul Ashby, Alabama St.	†1991	17	520	30.6
Juan Jackson, North Caro. A&T	1986	16	487	30.4
Kevin Gainer, Bethune-Cookman	1990	21	635	30.2
Howard Huckaby, Florida A&M	†1987	20	602	30.1
Tony James, Eastern Ky.	†1983	17	511	30.1
Jerry Parrish, Eastern Ky.	†1981	18	534	29.7
John Armstrong, Richmond	1984	18	531	29.5
Renard Coleman, Montana	1987	20	588	29.4

Record. † National champion.

Year	Player, Team	Class	No.	Yards	Avg.
1978	Dave Loehle, New Hampshire.........................	Jr.	15	460	30.7
1979	Garry Pearson, Massachusetts.......................	Fr.	12	348	29.0
1980	Danny Thomas, North Caro. A&T....................	Fr.	15	381	25.4
1981	Jerry Parrish, Eastern Ky.	Sr.	18	534	29.7
1982	Davlin Mullen, Western Ky.	Sr.	18	574	31.9
1983	Tony James, Eastern Ky.	Jr.	17	511	30.1
1984	Craig Richardson, Eastern Wash.	So.	21	729	*34.7
1985	Rodney Payne, Murray St.	Fr.	16	464	29.0
1986	Danny Copeland, Eastern Ky.	Jr.	26	812	31.2
1987	Howard Huckaby, Florida A&M	So.	20	602	30.1
1988	Dave Meggett, Towson St.	Sr.	13	418	32.2
1989	Scott Thomas, Liberty	Fr.	13	373	28.7
1990	Charles Swann, Indiana St.	Jr.	20	642	32.1
1991	Paul Ashby, Alabama St.	Jr.	17	520	30.6

* Record.

ALL-PURPOSE RUNNING

Career Yards Per Game

Player, Team	Years	Rush	Rcv	Int.	PR	KOR	Yds.	Yd. PG
Dave Meggett, Towson St.	1987-88	1,658	788	0	212	745	3,403	*189.1
Kenny Gamble, Colgate	1984-87	5,220	536	0	104	1,763	*7,623	181.5
Rich Erenberg, Colgate	#1982-83	2,618	423	0	268	315	3,624	172.6
Fine Unga, Weber St.	1987-88	2,298	391	0	7	967	3,663	166.5
Gill Fenerty, Holy Cross	1983-85	3,618	477	0	1	731	4,827	160.9
Judd Garrett, Princeton	1987-89	3,109	1,385	0	0	10	4,510	150.3
Treamelle Taylor, Nevada........	1987-90	0	1,926	0	662	687	3,275	148.9
Andre Garron, New Hampshire ..	1982-85	2,901	809	0	8	651	4,369	145.6
Carl Boyd, Northern Iowa	1983, 85-87	2,735	1,987	0	0	183	4,905	144.3
Merril Hoge, Idaho St............	1983-86	2,713	1,734	0	1	1,005	5,453	139.8
Pete Mandley, Northern Ariz.....	79-80, 82-83	436	2,598	11	901	1,979	5,925	137.8
Frank Hawkins, Nevada	1977-80	*5,333	519	0	0	0	5,852	136.1
Derrick Harmon, Cornell	1981-83	3,074	679	0	5	42	3,800	135.7
Dorron Hunter, Morehead St.	1977-80	1,336	1,320	0	510	1,970	5,136	135.2

* Record.   # Two years in Division I-AA and two years in Division I-A. Four-year totals: 5,695 yards and 146.0 average.

Season Yards Per Game

Player, Team	Year	Rush	Rcv	Int.	PR	KOR	Yds.	Yd. PG
Kenny Gamble, Colgate	†1986	1,816	178	0	40	391	*2,425	*220.5
Michael Clemons, William & Mary .	1986	1,065	516	0	330	423	2,334	212.2
Rich Erenberg, Colgate	†1983	*1,883	214	0	126	18	2,241	203.7
Dave Meggett, Towson St.	†1987	814	572	0	78	327	1,791	199.0
Gordie Lockbaum, Holy Cross	1986	827	860	34	0	452	2,173	197.6
Gill Fenerty, Holy Cross	†1985	1,368	187	0	1	414	1,970	197.0
Barry Bourassa, New Hampshire ..	†1991	1,130	426	0	0	596	2,152	195.6
Barry Bourassa, New Hampshire ..	†1990	957	276	0	133	368	1,734	192.7
Merril Hoge, Idaho St..............	1985	1,041	708	0	0	364	2,113	192.1
Andre Garron, New Hampshire	1983	1,009	539	0	0	359	1,907	190.7
Kenny Gamble, Colgate	1987	1,411	151	0	64	471	2,097	190.6
Otis Washington, Western Caro. ...	†1988	64	907	0	0	1,113	2,086	189.6
Ken Jenkins, Bucknell	†1980	1,270	293	0	65	256	1,884	188.4
Kenny Gamble, Colgate	1985	1,361	162	0	0	520	2,043	185.7
Gordie Lockbaum, Holy Cross	1987	403	1,152	0	209	277	2,041	185.6
Dominic Corr, Eastern Wash........	†1989	796	52	0	0	807	1,655	183.9
Al Rosier, Dartmouth	1991	1,432	113	0	0	290	1,835	183.5
Jerome Bledsoe, Massachusetts ...	1991	1,545	178	0	0	293	2,016	183.3
Mark Stock, Va. Military	1988	90	1,161	0	260	500	2,011	182.8
Jamie Jones, Eastern Ill.	1991	1,403	299	0	0	305	2,007	182.5
Pete Mandley, Northern Ariz........	†1982	36	1,067	0	344	532	1,979	179.9
Dave Meggett, Towson St.	1988	844	216	0	134	418	1,612	179.1
Carl Smith, Maine	1989	1,680	169	0	0	120	1,969	179.0

* Record.   † National champion.

Career Yards §

Player, Team	Years	Rush	Rcv	Int.	PR	KOR	Yds.	Yd. PP
Kenny Gamble, Colgate	1984-87	5,220	536	0	104	1,763	*7,623	7.0
Pete Mandley, Northern Ariz.....	1979-80, 82-83	436	2,598	11	901	1,979	5,925	*14.8
Frank Hawkins, Nevada	1977-80	*5,333	519	0	0	0	5,852	5.8

Player, Team	Years	Rush	Rcv	Int.	PR	KOR	Yds.	Yd. PP
Jamie Jones, Eastern Ill.	1988-91	3,466	816	0	66	1,235	5,583	6.2
Merril Hoge, Idaho St...........	1983-86	2,713	1,734	0	1	1,005	5,453	6.6
Herman Hunter, Tennessee St. ...	1981-84	1,049	1,129	0	974	*2,258	5,410	10.5
Cedric Minter, Boise St.	1977-80	4,475	525	0	49	267	5,316	6.5
Charvez Foger, Nevada	1985-88	4,484	821	0	0	0	5,305	5.7
Garry Pearson, Massachusetts ..	1979-82	3,859	466	0	0	952	5,277	5.9
John Settle, Appalachian St.	1983-86	4,409	526	0	0	319	5,254	5.3
Dorron Hunter, Morehead St. ...	1977-80	1,336	1,320	0	510	1,970	5,136	9.6

* Record.   § Rich Erenberg, Colgate, competed two years in Division I-AA and two years in Division I-A (four-year total: 5,695 yards), and Dwight Walker, Nicholls St., competed two years in Division I-AA and two years in Division II (four-year total: 5,200 yards).

Season Yards

Player, Team	Year	Rush	Rcv	Int.	PR	KOR	Yds.	Yd. PP
Kenny Gamble, Colgate	†1986	1,816	178	0	40	391	*2,425	7.1
Michael Clemons, William & Mary	1986	1,065	516	0	330	423	2,334	6.7
Rich Erenberg, Colgate	†1983	*1,883	214	0	126	18	2,241	6.7
Gordie Lockbaum, Holy Cross	1986	827	860	34	0	452	2,173	9.7
Barry Bourassa, New Hampshire	†1991	1,130	426	0	0	596	2,152	7.5
Merril Hoge, Idaho St................	1985	1,041	708	0	0	364	2,113	7.4
Kenny Gamble, Colgate	1987	1,411	151	0	64	471	2,097	6.5
Otis Washington, Western Caro.	†1988	66	907	0	0	1,113	2,086	*19.7
Kenny Gamble, Colgate	1985	1,361	162	0	0	520	2,043	7.3
Gordie Lockbaum, Holy Cross	1987	403	1,152	0	209	277	2,041	10.4
Jerome Bledsoe, Massachusetts	1991	1,545	178	0	0	293	2,016	6.7
Mark Stock, Va. Military	1988	90	1,161	0	260	500	2,011	14.0
Jamie Jones, Eastern Ill.	1991	1,403	299	0	0	305	2,007	7.2
Pete Mandley, Northern Ariz............	†1982	36	1,067	0	344	532	1,979	18.7
Gill Fenerty, Holy Cross	†1985	1,368	187	0	1	414	1,970	6.8

* Record.   † National champion.

All-Purpose Single-Game Highs

Yds.	Player, Team (Opponent)	Date
463	Michael Lerch, Princeton (Brown)	Oct. 12, 1991
453	Herman Hunter, Tennessee St. (Mississippi Val.)	Nov. 13, 1982
395	Scott Oliaro, Cornell (Yale)	Nov. 3, 1990
386	Gill Fenerty, Holy Cross (Columbia)	Oct. 29, 1983
378	Joe Delaney, Northwestern, La. (Nicholls St.)	Oct. 28, 1978
372	Gary Harrell, Howard (Morgan St.)	Nov. 3, 1990
372	Treamelle Taylor, Nevada (Montana)	Oct. 14, 1989
369	Flip Johnson, McNeese St. (Southwestern La.)	Nov. 15, 1986
367	Chris Darrington, Weber St. (Idaho St.)..	Oct. 25, 1986
365	Erwin Matthews, Richmond (Delaware)	Sept. 26, 1987
352	Andre Garron, New Hampshire (Lehigh)	Oct. 15, 1983
345	Russell Davis, Idaho (Weber St.)	Oct. 2, 1982
341	Barry Bourassa, New Hampshire (Delaware)	Oct. 5, 1991
340	Gene Lake, Delaware St. (Liberty)	Nov. 10, 1984
335	Judd Garrett, Princeton (Harvard)	Oct. 22, 1988
329	Barry Bourassa, New Hampshire (Maine)	Sept. 22, 1990
329	Ron Darby, Marshall (Youngstown St.)	Nov. 19, 1988
329	Keith Williams, Southwest Mo. St. (Illinois St.)	Sept. 14, 1985

Annual Champions

Year	Player, Team	Cl.	Rush	Rcv	Int.	PR	KOR	Yds.	Yd. PG
1978	Frank Hawkins, Nevada	So.	1,445	211	0	0	0	1,656	165.6
1979	Frank Hawkins, Nevada	Jr.	1,683	123	0	0	0	1,806	164.2
1980	Ken Jenkins, Bucknell	Jr.	1,270	293	0	65	256	1,884	188.4
1981	Garry Pearson, Massachusetts	Jr.	1,026	105	0	0	450	1,581	175.7
1982	Pete Mandley, Northern Ariz.........	Jr.	36	1,067	0	344	532	1,979	179.9
1983	Rich Erenberg, Colgate	Sr.	*1,883	214	0	126	18	2,241	203.7
1984	Gene Lake, Delaware St.	Jr.	1,722	37	0	0	0	1,759	175.9
1985	Gill Fenerty, Holy Cross	Sr.	1,368	187	0	1	414	1,970	197.0
1986	Kenny Gamble, Colgate	Jr.	1,816	178	0	40	391	*2,425	*220.5
1987	Dave Meggett, Towson St.	Jr.	814	572	0	78	327	1,791	199.0
1988	Otis Washington, Western Caro.	Sr.	66	907	0	0	1,113	2,086	189.6
1989	Dominic Corr, Eastern Wash.........	Sr.	796	52	0	0	807	1,655	183.9
1990	Barry Bourassa, New Hampshire	So.	957	276	0	133	368	1,734	192.7
1991	Barry Bourassa, New Hampshire	Jr.	1,130	426	0	0	596	2,152	195.6

* Record.

FIELD GOALS

Career Field Goals

Player, Team	Years	Total	Pct.	Under 40 Yds.	40 Plus	Long
Marty Zendejas, Nevada (S)	1984-87	*72-90	.800	42-45	30-45	54
Kirk Roach, Western Caro. (S)	1984-87	71-*102	.696	45-49	26-53	57
Tony Zendejas, Nevada (S)	1981-83	70-86	*.814	45-49	25-37	58
Brian Mitchell, Marshall/Northern Iowa (S)	1987, 89-91	64-81	.790	48-55	16-26	57
Matt Stover, Louisiana Tech (S)	1986-89	64-88	.727	36-42	28-46	57
Steve Christie, William & Mary (S)	1986-89	57-83	.686	39-49	18-34	53
Teddy Garcia, Northeast La. (S)	1984-87	56-88	.636	35-43	21-45	55
Bjorn Nittmo, Appalachian St. (S)	1985-88	55-74	.743	35-40	20-34	54
Kelly Potter, Middle Tenn. St. (S)	1981-84	52-78	.667	37-49	15-29	57
Paul McFadden, Youngstown St. (S)	1980-83	52-90	.578	28-42	24-48	54
Mike Black, Boise St. (S)	1988-91	51-75	.680	35-43	16-32	48
Tim Foley, Ga. Southern (S)	1984-87	50-62	.806	32-37	18-25	**63
Paul Politi, Illinois St. (S)	1983-86	50-78	.641	34-48	16-30	50
Thayne Doyle, Idaho (S)	1988-91	49-75	.653	35-51	14-24	52
Chuck Rawlinson, Stephen F. Austin (S)	1988-91	49-69	.710	34-43	15-26	58
Scott Roper, Texas-Arlington/Ark. St. (S)	1985, 86-87	49-75	.653	35-43	14-32	**63
Paul Hickert, Murray St. (S)	1984-87	49-79	.620	34-48	15-31	62
Dewey Klein, Marshall (S)	1988-91	48-66	.727	37-47	11-19	54
John Dowling, Youngstown St. (S)	1984-87	48-76	.632	36-44	12-32	49
Kirk Duce, Montana (S)	1988-91	47-78	.603	37-51	10-27	51
Billy Hayes, Sam Houston St. (S)	1985-88	47-71	.662	37-55	10-16	54
Roger Ruzek, Weber St. (S)	1979-82	46-78	.590	28-37	18-41	51

*Record. ** Record tied. (S) Soccer-style kicker.

Season Field Goals

Player, Team	Year	Total	Pct.	Under 40 Yds.	40 Plus	Long
Brian Mitchell, Northern Iowa (S)	†1990	**26-27	*.963	23-23	3-4	45
Tony Zendejas, Nevada (S)	†1982	**26-*33	.788	18-20	8-13	52
Kirk Roach, Western Caro. (S)	†1986	24-28	.857	17-17	7-11	52
George Benyola, Louisiana Tech (S)	†1985	24-31	.774	15-18	9-13	53
Goran Lingmerth, Northern Ariz. (S)	1986	23-29	.793	16-19	7-10	55
Tony Zendejas, Nevada (S)	†1983	23-29	.793	14-15	9-14	58
Marty Zendejas, Nevada (S)	†1984	22-27	.815	12-13	10-14	52
Kevin McKelvie, Nevada (S)	1990	21-24	.875	16-17	5-7	52
Tony Zendejas, Nevada (S)	†1981	21-24	.875	13-14	8-10	55
Matt Stover, Louisiana Tech (S)	1986	21-25	.840	15-15	6-10	53
Scott Roper, Arkansas St. (S)	1986	21-28	.750	15-17	6-11	50
Steve Christie, William & Mary (S)	†1989	20-29	.690	16-17	4-12	53
Darren Goodman, Idaho St. (S)	1990	20-28	.714	12-14	8-14	53
Teddy Garcia, Northeast La. (S)	1987	20-28	.714	10-11	10-17	55

*Record. † National champion. ** Record tied. (S) Soccer-style kicker.

Annual Champions

Year	Player, Team	Total	PG	Pct.	Under 40 Yds.	40 Plus	Long
1978	Tom Sarette, Boise St. (S)	12-20	1.2	.600	8-10	4-10	47
1979	Wilfredo Rosales, Alcorn St. (S)	13-20	1.3	.650	10-11	3-9	45
	Sandro Vitiello, Massachusetts (S)	13-22	1.3	.591	10-12	3-10	47
1980	Scott Norwood, James Madison (S)	15-21	1.5	.714	10-11	5-10	48
1981	Tony Zendejas, Nevada (S)	21-24	1.9	.875	13-14	8-10	55
1982	Tony Zendejas, Nevada (S)	**26-*33	**2.4	.788	18-20	8-13	52
1983	Tony Zendejas, Nevada (S)	23-29	2.1	.793	14-15	9-14	58
1984	Marty Zendejas, Nevada (S)	22-27	2.0	.815	12-13	10-14	52
1985	George Benyola, Louisiana Tech (S)	24-31	2.2	.774	15-18	9-13	53
1986	Kirk Roach, Western Caro. (S)	24-28	2.2	.857	17-17	7-11	52
1987	Micky Penaflor, Northern Ariz. (S)	19-27	1.9	.704	12-16	7-11	51
1988	Chris Lutz, Princeton (S)	19-24	1.9	.792	19-21	0-3	39
1989	Steve Christie, William & Mary (S)	20-29	1.8	.690	16-17	4-12	53
1990	Brian Mitchell, Northern Iowa (S)	**26-27	**2.4	*.963	23-23	3-4	45
1991	Brian Mitchell, Northern Iowa (S)	19-24	1.7	.792	15-16	4-8	57

*Record. ** Record tied. (S) Soccer-style kicker.

LONGEST PLAYS

Since 1941, official maximum length of all plays fixed at 100 yards.

Rushing

Yds.	Player, Team (Opponent)	Year
99	Phillip Collins, Southwest Mo. St. (Western Ill.)	1989
99	Pedro Bacon, Western Ky. (Livingston)	1986
99	Hubert Owens, Mississippi Val. (Ark.-Pine Bluff)	1980
98	Johnny Gordon, Nevada (Montana St.)	1984
97	David Clark, Dartmouth (Harvard)	1989
97	David Clark, Dartmouth (Princeton)	1988
96	Andre Lockhart, Tenn.-Chatt. (East Tenn. St.)	1986
95	Joe Sparksman, James Madison (William & Mary)	1990
94	Mark Vigil, Idaho (Simon Fraser)	1980
93	Jimmy Henderson, Columbia (Yale)	1984
93	Terence Thompson, Eastern Ky. (Akron)	1981

Passing

Yds.	Passer-Receiver, Team (Opponent)	Year
99	Todd Donnan-Troy Brown, Marshall (East Tenn. St.)	1991
99	Antoine Ezell-Tyrone Davis, Florida A&M (Bethune-Cookman)	1991
99	Jay Johnson-Kenny Shedd, Northern Iowa (Oklahoma St.)	1990
99	John Bonds-Hendricks Johnson, Northern Ariz. (Boise St.)	1990
99	Scott Stoker-Victor Robinson, Northwestern, La. (Northeast La.)	1989
98	Antoine Ezell-Tim Daniel, Florida A&M (Delaware St.)	1991
98	John Friesz-Lee Allen, Idaho (Northern Ariz.)	1989
98	Fred Gatlin-Treamelle Taylor, Nevada (Montana)	1989
98	Steve Monaco-Emerson Foster, Rhode Island (Holy Cross)	1988
98	Frank Baur-Maurice Caldwell, Lafayette (Columbia)	1988
98	David Gabianelli-Craig Morton, Dartmouth (Columbia)	1986
98	Joe Pizzo-Bryan Calder, Nevada (Eastern Wash.)	1984
98	Bobby Hebert-Randy Liles, Northwestern, La. (Southeastern La.)	1980
97	Nate Harrison-Brian Thomas, Southern-B.R. (Dist. Columbia)	1989
97	Jerome Baker-John Taylor, Delaware St. (St. Paul's)	1985
97	John McKenzie-Chris Burkett, Jackson St. (Mississippi Val.)	1983
96	Greg Wyatt-Shawn Collins, Northern Ariz. (Montana St.)	1988
96	Rick Fahnestock-Albert Brown, Western Ill. (Northern Iowa)	1986
96	Jeff Cesarone-Keith Paskett, Western Ky. (Akron)	1985
96	Mike Williams-Trumaine Johnson, Grambling (Jackson St.)	1980

Interception Returns

Yds.	Player, Team (Opponent)	Year
100	Derek Grier, Marshall (East Tenn. St.)	1991
100	Ricky Fields, Samford (Concord, West Va.)	1990
100	Warren Smith, Stephen F. Austin (Nicholls St.)	1990
100	Rob Pouliot, Montana St. (Boise St.)	1988
100	Rick Harris, East Tenn. St. (Davidson)	1986
100	Bruce Alexander, Stephen F. Austin (Lamar)	1986
100	Guy Carbone, Rhode Island (Lafayette)	1985
100	Moses Aimable, Northern Iowa (Western Ill.)	1985
100	Kervin Fontennette, Southeastern La. (Nicholls St.)	1985
100	Jim Anderson, Princeton (Cornell)	1984
100	Keiron Bigby, Brown (Yale)	1984
100	Vencie Glenn, Indiana St. (Wayne St., Mich.)	1984
100	George Floyd, Eastern Ky. (Youngstown St.)	1980

Punt Returns

Yds.	Player, Team (Opponent)	Year
98	Willie Ware, Mississippi Val. (Bishop)	1985
98	Barney Bussey, South Caro. St. (Johnson Smith)	1981
96	Carl Williams, Texas Southern (Grambling)	1981
95	Clarence Weathers, Delaware St. (Salisbury St.)	1980
93	Joe Fuller, Northern Iowa (Wis.-Whitewater)	1984

Kickoff Returns

Twenty-eight players have returned kickoffs 100 yards. The most recent:

Yds.	Player, Team (Opponent)	Year
100	Eddie Godfrey, Western Ky. (Louisville)	1990
100	Roman Carter, Idaho (Cal St. Chico)	1990

Yds.	Player, Team (Opponent)	Year
100	Dominic Corr, Eastern Wash. (Weber St.)	1989
100	Leon Brown, Eastern Ky. (Austin Peay)	1989
100	Dave Meggett, Towson St. (Northeastern)	1988
100	Dominic Corr, Eastern Wash. (Illinois St.)	1987
100	Barry Chubb, Colgate (Lafayette)	1986
100	Marco Kornegay, Morgan St. (Norfolk St.)	1986

Punts

Yds.	Player, Team (Opponent)	Year
91	Bart Helsley, North Texas (Northeast La.)	1990
89	Jim Carriere, Connecticut (Maine)	1987
88	Jeff Kaiser, Idaho St. (UTEP)	1983
87	John Starnes, North Texas (Texas-Arlington)	1983
85	Don Alonzo, Nicholls St. (Northwestern, La.)	1980
84	Billy Smith, Tenn.-Chatt. (Appalachian St.)	1988
83	Jason Harkins, Appalachian St. (Citadel)	1986
82	Tim Healy, Delaware (Boston U.)	1987
82	John Howell, Tenn.-Chatt. (Vanderbilt)	1982

Field Goals

Yds.	Player, Team (Opponent)	Year
63	Scott Roper, Arkansas St. (North Texas)	1987
63	Tim Foley, Ga. Southern (James Madison)	1987
62	Paul Hickert, Murray St. (Eastern Ky.)	1986
58	Rich Emke, Eastern Ill. (Northern Iowa)	1986
58	Tony Zendejas, Nevada (Boise St.)	1983

TEAM CHAMPIONS

OFFENSE

Year	Total Offense	Avg.	Rushing	Avg.
1978	Portland St.	477.4	Jackson St.	314.5
1979	Portland St.	460.7	Jackson St.	288.4
1980	Portland St.	504.3	North Caro. A&T	322.1
1981	Idaho	438.8	Idaho	266.3
1982	Drake	444.8	Delaware	258.4
1983	Idaho	479.5	Furman	287.1
1984	Mississippi Val.	*640.1	Delaware St.	377.3
1985	Weber St.	516.1	Southwest Mo. St.	298.7
1986	Nevada	492.0	Northeastern	336.0
1987	Holy Cross	552.2	Howard	*381.6
1988	Lehigh	485.6	Eastern Ky.	303.0
1989	Idaho	495.9	Ga. Southern	329.2
1990	William & Mary	498.7	Delaware St.	298.7
1991	Weber St.	581.4	Va. Military	316.9

Year	Scoring	Avg.	Passing	Avg.
1978	Nevada	35.6	Portland St.	367.1
1979	Portland St.	34.3	Portland St.	368.9
1980	Portland St.	49.2	Portland St.	434.9
1981	Delaware	34.1	Idaho St.	325.7
1982	Delaware	34.1	West Tex. St.	313.7
1983	Mississippi Val.	39.2	Idaho	336.1
1984	Mississippi Val.	*60.9	Mississippi Val.	*496.8
1985	Mississippi Val.	41.5	Rhode Island	384.3
1986	Nevada	39.4	Eastern Ill.	326.1
1987	Holy Cross	46.5	Holy Cross	358.4
1988	Lafayette	38.2	Lehigh	330.1
1989	Grambling	37.1	Idaho	374.3
1990	Jackson St.	38.0	Weber St.	342.2
1991	Nevada	45.1	Weber St.	389.1

DEFENSE

Year	Total Defense	Avg.	Rushing	Avg.
1978	Florida A&M	*149.9	Florida A&M	48.6
1979	Alcorn St.	166.3	Alcorn St.	56.7

On the strength of quarterback Jamie Martin's arm, Weber State led Division I-AA in total offense (581.4 yards per game) and passing offense (389.1) in 1991. Martin passed for 4,125 yards, the second-highest total in Division I-AA history.

Year	Total Defense	Avg.	Rushing	Avg.
1980	Massachusetts	193.5	South Caro. St.	61.8
1981	South Caro. St.	204.0	South Caro. St.	60.8
1982	South Caro. St.	191.4	South Caro. St.	59.4
1983	Grambling	206.0	Jackson St.	79.2
1984	Tennessee St.	187.0	Grambling	*44.5
1985	Arkansas St.	258.8	Jackson St.	63.0
1986	Tennessee St.	178.5	Eastern Ky.	62.8
1987	Southern-B.R.	202.8	Southern-B.R.	64.5
1988	Alcorn St.	215.4	Stephen F. Austin	83.5
1989	Howard	220.0	Montana	70.2
1990	Middle Tenn. St.	244.8	Delaware St.	77.2
1991	South Caro. St.	208.9	Boise St.	84.4

Year	Scoring	Avg.	Passing	$Avg.
1978	South Caro. St.	*6.5	Southern-B.R.	85.6
1979	Lehigh	7.2	Mississippi Val.	64.2
1980	Murray St.	9.1	Howard	93.8
1981	Jackson St.	9.4	Bethune-Cookman	*59.9
1982	Western Mich.	7.1	Northeastern	98.8
1983	Grambling	8.6	Louisiana Tech	111.4
1984	Northwestern (La.)	9.0	Louisiana Tech	105.5
1985	Appalachian St.	9.9	Dartmouth	110.3
1986	Tennessee St.	8.3	Bethune-Cookman	99.8
1987	Holy Cross	10.0	Alcorn St.	101.3
1988	Furman	9.7	Middle Tenn. St.	90.8
1989	Howard	10.5	Tenn.-Chatt.	104.4
1990	Middle Tenn. St.	9.2	Middle Tenn. St.	78.83
1991	Villanova	12.0	South Caro. St.	*70.01

* *Record.* $ *Beginning in 1990, ranked on passing-efficiency defense rating points instead of per-game yardage allowed.*

ANNUAL TOUGHEST-SCHEDULE LEADERS

The Division I-AA toughest-schedule program, which began in 1982, is based on what all Division I-AA opponents did against other Division I-AA and Division I-A teams when *not* playing the team in question. Games against non-I-AA and I-A teams are deleted. (Playoff games are not included.) The top two leaders by year:

Year	Team (+Record)	W	L	T	Pct.
				¢Opponents' Record	
1982	Massachusetts (5-6-0)	50	30	1	.623
	Lehigh (4-6-0)	44	31	0	.587
1983	Florida A&M (7-4-0)	42	23	3	.640
	Grambling (8-1-2)	49	31	0	.613
1984	North Texas (2-9-0)	55	35	2	.609
	Va. Military (1-9-0)	53	37	2	.587
1985	South Caro. St. (5-6-0)	43	20	1	.680
	Lehigh (5-6-0)	47	33	1	.586
1986	James Madison (5-5-1)	46	28	1	.620
	Bucknell (3-7-0)	43	27	0	.614
1987	Ga. Southern (8-3-0)	47	31	0	.603
	Northeastern (6-5-0)	50	37	0	.575
1988	Northwestern (La.) (9-2-0)	54	36	2	.598
	Ga. Southern (9-2-0)	43	31	1	.580
1989	Liberty (7-3-0)	39	22	2	.635
	Western Caro. (3-7-1)	46	34	2	.573
1990	Ga. Southern (8-3-0)	53	25	1	.677
	Western Ky. (2-8-0)	55	36	1	.603
1991	Bucknell (1-9-0)	53	29	1	.645
	William & Mary (5-6-0)	62	43	0	.590

+ *Not including playoff games.* ¢ *When not playing the team listed.*

ALL-TIME WON-LOST RECORDS

Includes records as a senior college only, minimum of 20 seasons of competition. Bowl and playoff games are included, and each tie game is computed as half won and half lost.

BY PERCENTAGE

Team	Yrs.	Won	Lost	Tied	Pct.	Total Games
Yale	119	766	251	55	.740	1,072
Tennessee St.†	64	414	138	30	.737	582
Grambling	49	371	134	15	.728	520
Florida A&M	59	408	157	18	.715	583
Boise St.	24	191	82	2	.698	275
Princeton	122	690	285	49	.698	1,024
Harvard	117	695	308	50	.684	1,053
Jackson St.	46	292	159	12	.644	463
Dartmouth	110	576	319	45	.637	940
Eastern Ky.	68	401	234	27	.626	662
Pennsylvania	115	677	406	42	.620	1,125
South Caro. St.	65	345	206	27	.620	578
Southern-B.R.	70	398	241	25	.618	664
Bethune-Cookman	53	289	179	22	.612	490
Ga. Southern	23	146	93	7	.608	246
Appalachian St.	62	373	236	29	.607	638
Middle Tenn. St.	75	413	269	27	.602	709
Alcorn St.	68	329	213	37	.600	579
Western Ky.	73	391	258	31	.598	680
Fordham	89	407	270	50	.594	727
Morgan St.	71	348	233	30	.594	611
Holy Cross	96	513	347	55	.591	915
McNeese St.	41	245	168	14	.590	427
Cornell	104	537	368	34	.590	939
Delaware	100	487	340	42	.585	869
Northern Iowa	93	443	312	47	.582	802
Southwest Tex. St.	77	386	276	26	.580	688
Youngstown St.	51	272	206	15	.567	493
Colgate	101	473	359	49	.565	881
Furman	78	423	327	36	.561	786

Team	Yrs.	Won	Lost	Tied	Pct.	Total Games
Alabama St.	86	344	326	41	.513	711
Alcorn St.	68	329	213	37	.600	579
Appalachian St.	62	373	236	29	.607	638
Austin Peay	55	212	318	16	.403	546
Bethune–Cookman	53	289	179	22	.612	490
Boise St.	24	191	82	2	.698	275
Boston U.	72	286	331	28	.465	645
Brown	106	471	459	40	.506	970
Bucknell	106	468	429	51	.521	948
Citadel	91	373	391	32	.489	796
Colgate	101	473	359	49	.565	881
Columbia	101	308	490	41	.392	839
Connecticut	93	362	398	38	.477	798
Cornell	104	537	368	34	.590	939
Dartmouth	110	576	319	45	.637	940
Delaware	100	487	340	42	.585	869
Delaware St.	46	200	223	8	.473	431
East Tenn. St.	68	274	330	27	.631	631
Eastern Ill.	91	348	386	43	.476	777
Eastern Ky.	68	401	234	27	.626	662
Eastern Wash.	81	341	289	23	.540	653
Florida A&M	69	408	157	18	.715	583
Fordham	89	407	270	50	.594	727
Furman	78	423	327	36	.561	786
Ga. Southern	23	146	93	7	.608	246
Grambling	49	371	134	15	.728	520
Harvard	117	695	308	50	.684	1,053
Holy Cross	96	513	347	55	.591	915
Howard	95	371	303	42	.547	716
Idaho	94	340	421	25	.448	786
Idaho St.	87	372	319	20	.537	711
Illinois St.	92	340	399	63	.463	802
Indiana St.	75	286	317	20	.475	623
Jackson St.	46	292	159	12	.644	463
Lafayette	110	551	443	36	.552	1,030
Lehigh	108	499	488	44	.505	1,031
Maine	100	385	353	38	.521	776
Marshall	88	352	427	44	.454	823
Massachusetts	109	413	435	51	.488	899
McNeese St.	41	245	168	14	.590	427
Middle Tenn. St.	75	413	269	27	.602	709
Mississippi Val.	39	162	194	9	.456	365
Montana	92	332	415	26	.446	773
Montana St.	88	335	345	34	.493	714
Morehead St.	62	215	319	22	.406	556
Morgan St.	71	348	233	30	.594	611
Murray St.	67	345	271	34	.557	650
New Hampshire	95	386	340	53	.530	779
Nicholls St.	20	105	113	3	.482	221
North Caro. A&T	68	324	272	39	.541	635
North Texas	76	394	307	32	.559	733
Northeast La.	41	186	227	8	.451	421
Northeastern	56	208	245	16	.461	469
Northern Ariz.	67	281	299	22	.485	602
Northern Iowa	93	443	312	47	.582	802
Northwestern (La.)	83	383	309	33	.551	725
Pennsylvania	115	677	406	42	.620	1,125
Prairie View	65	327	285	31	.533	643
Princeton	122	690	285	49	.698	1,024
Rhode Island	91	313	392	41	.447	746
Richmond	108	374	505	52	.430	931
Sam Houston St.	76	338	337	32	.501	707
Samford	75	296	301	46	.496	643
South Caro. St.	65	345	206	27	.620	578
Southeast Mo. St.	79	338	320	37	.513	695
Southern-B.R.	70	398	241	25	.618	664
Southern Ill.	76	302	361	33	.458	696
Southwest Mo. St.	80	348	332	40	.511	720

Team	Yrs.	Won	Lost	Tied	Pct.	Total Games
Southwest Tex. St.	77	386	276	26	.580	688
Stephen F. Austin#	65	249	364	28	.410	641
Tenn.-Chatt.	84	410	354	33	.535	797
Tenn.-Martin	35	159	193	5	.452	357
Tennessee St.†	64	414	138	30	.737	582
Tennessee Tech	70	291	346	31	.459	668
Texas Southern	46	222	226	27	.496	475
Towson St.	23	128	105	4	.549	237
Troy St.	61	295	261	14	.530	570
Va. Military	101	414	462	43	.474	919
Villanova	94	430	358	41	.543	829
Weber St.	30	150	162	3	.481	315
Western Caro.	58	235	312	23	.432	570
Western Ill.	88	359	322	37	.526	717
Western Ky.	73	391	258	31	.598	680
William & Mary	96	406	434	37	.484	877
Yale	119	766	251	55	.740	1,072
Youngstown St.	51	272	206	15	.567	493

I-AA teams lacking 20 seasons:

Team	Yrs.	Won	Lost	Tied	Pct.	Total Games
Central Fla.	13	67	70	1	.489	138
James Madison	19	110	90	3	.549	203
Liberty	19	88	97	4	.476	189

† *Tennessee State's participation in 1981 and 1982 Division I-AA championships (1-2 record) voided.*   # *Stephen F. Austin's participation in 1989 Division I-AA championship (3-1 record) voided.*

VICTORIES

Team	Wins	Team	Wins	Team	Wins
Yale	766	Maine	385	Samford	296
Harvard	695	Northwestern (La.)	383	Troy St.	295
Princeton	690	Richmond	374	Jackson St.	292
Pennsylvania	677	Appalachian St.	373	Tennessee Tech	291
Dartmouth	576	Citadel	373	Bethune-Cookman	289
Lafayette	551	Idaho St.	372	Boston U.	286
Cornell	537	Grambling	371	Indiana St.	286
Holy Cross	513	Howard	371	Northern Ariz.	281
Lehigh	499	Connecticut	362	East Tenn. St.	274
Delaware	487	Western Ill.	359	Youngstown St.	272
Colgate	473	Marshall	352	Stephen F. Austin#	249
Brown	471	Eastern Ill.	348	McNeese St.	245
Bucknell	468	Morgan St.	348	Western Caro.	235
Northern Iowa	443	Southwest Mo. St.	348	Texas Southern	222
Villanova	430	Murray St.	345	Morehead St.	215
Furman	423	South Caro. St.	345	Austin Peay	212
Tennessee St.†	414	Alabama St.	344	Northeastern	208
Va. Military	414	Eastern Wash.	341	Delaware St.	200
Massachusetts	413	Idaho	340	Boise St.	191
Middle Tenn. St.	413	Illinois St.	340	Northeast La.	186
Tenn.-Chatt.	410	Sam Houston St.	338	Mississippi Val.	162
Florida A&M	408	Southeast Mo. St.	338	Tenn.-Martin	159
Fordham	407	Montana St.	335	Weber St.	150
William & Mary	406	Montana	332	Ga. Southern	146
Eastern Ky.	401	Alcorn St.	329	Towson St.	128
Southern-B.R.	398	Prairie View	327	James Madison	110
North Texas	394	North Caro. A&T	324	Nicholls St.	105
Western Ky.	391	Rhode Island	313	Liberty	88
New Hampshire	386	Columbia	308	Central Fla.	67
Southwest Tex. St.	386	Southern Ill.	302		

† *Tennessee State's participation in 1981 and 1982 Division I-AA championships (1-2 record) voided.*   # *Stephen F. Austin's participation in 1989 Division I-AA championship (3-1 record) voided.*

UNDEFEATED, UNTIED TEAMS

Regular-season games only, from 1978.
Subsequent loss in Division I-AA championship is indicated by (††).

Yr.	College	Wins	Yr.	College	Wins
1978	Nevada	††11	1987	Holy Cross	11
1982	*Eastern Ky.	10	1989	*Ga. Southern	11
1984	Tennessee St.	11	1990	Youngstown St.	††11
	Alcorn St.	††9	1991	Holy Cross	11
1985	Middle Tenn. St.	††11		Nevada	††11
1986	Nevada	††11			
	Pennsylvania	10			

* Won Division I-AA championship.

DIVISION I-AA FINAL POLL LEADERS

(Released before division championship playoffs)

Year	Team, Record*	Coach	†Record in Championship
1978	Nevada (10-0-0)	Chris Ault	0-1 Lost in semifinals
1979	Grambling (8-2-0)	Eddie Robinson	Did not compete
1980	South Caro. St. (10-0-0)	Bill Davis	Did not compete
1981	Eastern Ky. (9-1-0)	Roy Kidd	2-1 Runner-up
1982	Eastern Ky. (10-0-0)	Roy Kidd	3-0 Champion
1983	Southern Ill. (10-1-0)	Rey Dempsey	3-0 Champion
1984	Alcorn St. (9-0-0)	Marino Casem	0-1 Lost in quarterfinals
1985	Middle Tenn. St. (11-0-0)	James Donnelly	0-1 Lost in quarterfinals
1986	Nevada (11-0-0)	Chris Ault	2-1 Lost in semifinals
1987	Holy Cross (11-0-0)	Mark Duffner	Did not compete
1988	Idaho (9-1-0)	Keith Gilbertson	2-1 Lost in semifinals
1989	Ga. Southern (11-0-0)	Erk Russell	4-0 Champion
1990	Middle Tenn. St. (10-1-0)	James Donnelly	1-1 Lost in quarterfinals
1991	Nevada (11-0-0)	Chris Ault	1-1 Lost in quarterfinals

* Final poll record; in some cases, a team had one or two games remaining before the championship playoffs.   † Number of teams in the championship: 4 (1978-80); 8 (1981); 12 (1982-85); 16 (1986-).

THE SPOILERS

(From 1978 Season)

Following is a list of the spoilers of Division I-AA teams that lost their perfect (undefeated, untied) record in their **season-ending** game, including the Division I-AA championship playoffs. An asterisk (*) indicates a championship playoff game and a dagger (†) indicates the home team in a regular-season game.

Date	Spoiler	Victim	Score
12-9-78	*Massachusetts	Nevada	44-21
11-15-80	†Grambling	South Caro. St.	26-3
11-22-80	†Murray St.	Western Ky.	49-0
12-1-84	*Louisiana Tech	Alcorn St.	44-21
12-7-85	*Ga. Southern	Middle Tenn. St.	28-21
11-22-86	Boston College	†Holy Cross	56-26
12-19-86	*Ga. Southern	Nevada	48-38
11-19-88	*Cornell	Pennsylvania	19-6
11-24-90	*Central Fla.	Youngstown St.	20-17
12-7-91	*Youngstown St.	Nevada	30-28

MOST-PLAYED RIVALRIES

(Current Rivalry)

Games	Opponents (Rivalry leader listed first)	Rivalry Record	First Game
127	Lafayette-Lehigh	69-53-5	1884
114	Yale-Princeton	63-41-10	1873
108	Yale-Harvard	59-41-8	1875
101	William & Mary-Richmond	49-47-5	1898
98	Pennsylvania-Cornell	54-39-5	1893
96	Yale-Brown	68-23-5	1880
95	Harvard-Dartmouth	50-40-5	1882
91	Montana-Montana St.	54-32-5	1897
91	Harvard-Brown	67-22-2	1893
84	Princeton-Harvard	45-32-7	1877
83	Princeton-Pennsylvania	58-24-1	1876
82	Connecticut-Rhode Island	42-32-8	1897
80	Illinois St.-Eastern Ill.	39-33-8	1901
79	Maine-New Hampshire	36-35-8	1903
79	Cornell-Columbia	52-24-3	1889
77	Cornell-Colgate	45-29-3	1896

CLIFFHANGERS

Regular-season Division I-AA games won on the final play in regulation time. The extra point is listed when it provided the margin of victory after the winning touchdown on the game's final play.

Date	Opponents, Score	Game-winning play
10-21-78	Western Ky. 17, Eastern Ky. 16	Kevin McGrath 25 FG
9-8-79	Northern Ariz. 22, Portland St. 21	Ken Fraser 15 pass from Brian Potter (Mike Jenkins pass from Potter)
10-18-80	Connecticut 18, Holy Cross 17	Ken Miller 4 pass from Ken Sweitzer (Keith Hugger pass from Sweitzer)
11-15-80	Morris Brown 19, Bethune-Cookman 18	Ray Mills 1 run (Carlton Johnson kick)
9-26-81	Abilene Christian 41, Northwestern (La.) 38	David Russell 17 pass from Loyal Proffitt
10-10-81	LIU-C. W. Post 37, James Madison 36	Tom DeBona 10 pass from Tom Ehrhardt
11-13-82	Pennsylvania 23, Harvard 21	Dave Shulman 27 FG
10-1-83	Connecticut 9, New Hampshire 7	Larry Corn 7 run
9-8-84	Southwestern La. 17, Louisiana Tech 16	Patrick Broussard 21 FG
9-15-84	Lehigh 10, Connecticut 7	Dave Melick 45 FG
9-15-84	William & Mary 23, Delaware 21	Jeff Sanders 18 pass from Stan Yagiello
10-13-84	Lafayette 20, Connecticut 13	Ryan Priest 2 run
10-20-84	Central Fla. 28, Illinois St. 24	Jeff Farmer 30 punt return
10-27-84	Western Ky. 33, Morehead St. 31	Arnold Grier 50 pass from Jeff Cesarone
9-7-85	Central Fla. 39, Bethune-Cookman 37	Ed O'Brien 55 FG
10-26-85	Va. Military 39, William & Mary 38	Al Comer 3 run (James Wright run)
8-30-86	Texas Southern 38, Prairie View 35	Don Espinoza 23 FG
9-20-86	Delaware 33, West Chester 31	Fred Singleton 3 run
10-4-86	Northwestern (La.) 17, Northeast La. 14	Keith Hodnett 27 FG
10-11-86	Eastern Ill. 31, Northern Iowa 30	Rich Ehmke 58 FG
9-12-87	Youngstown St. 20, Bowling Green 17	John Dowling 36 FG
10-3-87	Northeast La. 33, Northwestern (La.) 31	Jackie Harris 48 pass from Stan Humphries
10-10-87	Marshall 34, Louisville 31	Keith Baxter 31 pass from Tony Petersen
10-17-87	Princeton 16, Lehigh 15	Rob Goodwin 38 FG
11-12-87	South Caro. St. 15, Grambling 13	William Wrighten 23 FG
9-24-88	Holy Cross 30, Princeton 26	70 kickoff return; Tim Donovan 55 on lateral from Darin Cromwell (15)
10-15-88	Weber St. 37, Nevada 31	Todd Beightol 57 pass from Jeff Carlson
10-29-88	Nicholls St. 13, Southwest Tex. St. 10	Jim Windham 33 FG
9-2-89	Alabama St. 16, Troy St. 13	Reggie Brown 28 pass from Antonius Smith
9-16-89	Western Caro. 26, Tenn.-Chatt. 20	Terrell Wagner 68 interception return
9-23-89	Northwestern (La.) 18, McNeese St. 17	Chris Hamler 25 FG
10-14-89	East Tenn. St. 24, Tenn.-Chatt. 23	George Searcy 1 run
9-29-90	Southwest Tex. St. 33, Nicholls St. 30	Robbie Roberson 32 FG
10-6-90	Grambling 27, Alabama A&M 20	Dexter Butcher 28 pass from Shawn Burras

1992 NCAA FOOTBALL

LONGEST WINNING STREAKS

(From 1978. Includes playoff games and must have been I-AA members during that period)

Wins	Team	Years	Ended by	Score
20	Holy Cross	1990-92	Still Active	
18	Eastern Ky.	1982-83	Western Ky.	10-10
16	Ga. Southern	1989-90	Middle Tenn. St.	13-16
14	Delaware	1979-80	Lehigh	20-27
13	Holy Cross	1988-89	Army	9-45
13	Nevada	1986	Ga. Southern	38-48
13	Tennessee St.	1983-85	Western Ky.	17-22
12	Nevada	1989-90	Boise St.	14-30
12	Furman	1989	Stephen F. Austin	19-21
12	Holy Cross	1987-88	Army	3-23
12	Southern Ill.	1982-83	Wichita St.	6-28
12	Florida A&M	1978-79	Tennessee St.	3-20

LONGEST UNBEATEN STREAKS

(From 1978. Includes playoff games and must include at least one tie)

No.	Wins	Ties	Team	Years	Ended by
19	18	1	Eastern Ky.	1982-83	Murray St.
17	16	1	Grambling	1977-78	Florida A&M
16	15	1	Alabama St.	1990-91	Still Active
13	12	1	Mississippi Val.	1983-84	Alcorn St.
13	12	1	Eastern Ill.	1981-82	Tennessee St.
12	11	1	Tennessee St.	1985-86	Alabama St.
12	11	1	Tennessee St.	1981-83	Jackson St.
10	9	1	Stephen F. Austin	1989	Ga. Southern
10	9	1	Holy Cross	1983	Boston College
10	9	1	Jackson St.	1980	Grambling

HOME WINNING STREAKS

(From 1978. Must have been I-AA members during that period)

Wins	Team	Years	Ended by
38	Ga. Southern	1985-90	Eastern Ky.
30	Eastern Ky.	1978-83	Western Ky.
23	Northern Iowa	1983-87	Montana
22	Nevada	1989-91	Youngstown St.
20	Arkansas St.	1984-87	Northwestern (La.)
16	Southwest Tex. St.	1981-83	Central St. (Ohio)
16	Citadel	1980-82	East Tenn. St.
15	Holy Cross	1987-89	Massachusetts
13	William & Mary	1988-91	Delaware
12	Idaho	1988-89	Eastern Ill.
12	Delaware St.	1983-86	Northeastern
12	Eastern Ill.	1981-83	Indiana St.

REGULAR-SEASON OVERTIME GAMES

In 1981, the NCAA Football Rules Committee approved an overtime tie-breaker system to decide a tie game for the purpose of determining a conference champion. The following conferences have used the tie-breaker system to decide conference-only tie games.

BIG SKY CONFERENCE

Date	Opponents, Score	No. OTs	Score, Reg.
10-31-81	Northern Ariz. 24, ‡Weber St. 23	1	17-17
11-21-81	‡Idaho St. 33, Weber St. 30	3	23-23
10-2-82	‡Montana St. 30, Idaho St. 27	3	17-17

Date	Opponents, Score	No. OTs	Score, Reg.
11-6-82	Nevada 46, ‡Weber St. 43	3	30-30
10-13-84	‡Montana St. 44, Nevada 41	4	21-21
9-17-88	Boise St. 24, ‡Northern Ariz. 21	2	14-14
10-15-88	‡Montana 33, Northern Ariz. 26	2	26-26
9-15-90	‡Weber St. 45, Idaho St. 38	2	31-31
9-29-90	‡Nevada 31, Idaho 28	1	28-28
11-3-90	Eastern Wash. 33, ‡Idaho St. 26	1	26-26
11-10-90	Montana St. 28, ‡Eastern Wash. 25	1	25-25
10-26-91	Eastern Wash. 34, ‡Idaho 31	2	24-24
11-16-91	Montana 35, ‡Idaho 34	1	28-28

MID-EASTERN ATHLETIC CONFERENCE

Date	Opponents, Score	No. OTs	Score, Reg.
11-1-86	‡North Caro. A&T 30, Bethune-Cookman 24	1	24-24

OHIO VALLEY CONFERENCE

Date	Opponents, Score	No. OTs	Score, Reg.
10-13-84	Youngstown St. 17, Austin Peay 13	1	10-10
11-3-84	‡Murray St. 20, Austin Peay 13.............................	2	10-10
10-19-85	‡Middle Tenn. St. 31, Murray St. 24	2	17-17
11-2-85	‡Middle Tenn. St. 28, Youngstown St. 21	2	14-14
10-4-86	‡Austin Peay 7, Middle Tenn. St. 0	1	0-0
10-10-87	‡Austin Peay 20, Morehead St. 13..........................	1	13-13
11-7-87	‡Youngstown St. 20, Murray St. 13..........................	1	13-13
10-1-88	Tennessee Tech 16, ‡Murray St. 13	1	10-10
10-29-88	Eastern Ky. 31, ‡Murray St. 24	1	24-24
11-18-89	Eastern Ky. 38, ‡Morehead St. 31	3	24-24
11-10-90	‡Tennessee Tech 20, Austin Peay 14	1	14-14
11-17-90	Murray St. 31, ‡Austin Peay 24.............................	3	24-24

YANKEE CONFERENCE

Date	Opponents, Score	No. OTs	Score, Reg.
9-18-82	Rhode Island 58, ‡Maine 55................................	6	21-21
9-25-82	‡Boston U. 48, Maine 45	4	24-24
10-27-84	Maine 13, ‡Connecticut 10	1	10-10
9-13-86	New Hampshire 28, ‡Delaware 21	1	21-21
11-15-86	‡Connecticut 21, Rhode Island 14	1	14-14
9-19-87	‡Richmond 52, Massachusetts 51...........................	4	28-28
9-19-87	New Hampshire 27, ‡Boston U. 20...........................	3	17-17
10-31-87	Maine 59, ‡Delaware 56...................................	2	49-49
11-21-87	‡Delaware 17, Boston U. 10................................	1	10-10
9-24-88	Villanova 31, ‡Boston U. 24	1	24-24
10-8-88	‡Richmond 23, New Hampshire 17	1	17-17
10-7-89	‡Villanova 41, Connecticut 35	6	21-21
11-16-91	Boston U. 29, ‡Connecticut 26.............................	2	23-23

‡ *Home team.*

DIVISION I-AA FOOTBALL STADIUMS

Stadiums used by NCAA Division I-AA football teams, ranked by capacity.
(89 Teams, 89 Stadiums)

Rank	Stadium	Home Team	Conference	Year Built	Capacity	Surface
1.	Yale Bowl	Yale	Ivy	1914	70,896	Grass
2.	✓Florida Citrus Bowl...	Central Fla.	Independent	*1989	70,000	Grass
3.	✓Mississippi Memorial .	Jackson St.	Southwestern	1949	62,512	Grass
4.	✓Franklin Field	Pennsylvania	Ivy	1895	60,546	Turf
5.	Palmer	Princeton	Ivy	1914	45,725	Grass
6.	Harvard	Harvard	Ivy	1903	37,289	Grass
7.	Marshall	Marshall	Southern	1991	28,000	Turf
8.	Schoelkopf...........	Cornell	Ivy	1915	27,000	Turf
9.	Bragg Memorial	Florida A&M	Mid-Eastern	1957	25,500	Grass
10.	(Not named)	Alcorn St.	Southwestern	1992	25,000	Grass

Rank	Stadium	Home Team	Conference	Year Built	Capacity	Surface
	✓Robertson	Texas Southern	Southwestern	1965	25,000	Grass
12.	✓Cramton Bowl	Alabama St.	Southwestern	N/A	24,600	Grass
13.	Mumford	Southern-B.R.	Southwestern	1928	24,000	Grass
14.	Fitton Field	Holy Cross	Patriot	1924	23,500	Grass
15.	Malone	Northeast La.	Southland	1978	23,277	Grass
16.	Delaware	Delaware	Yankee	1952	23,000	Grass
17.	Bronco	Boise St.	Big Sky	1970	22,600	Turf
18.	Johnson Hagood.....	Citadel	Southern	1948	22,500	Grass
	Richmond	Richmond	Yankee	1929	22,500	Turf
20.	Robinson.............	Grambling	Southwestern	1983	22,000	Grass
21.	Memorial	Indiana St.	Gateway	1970	20,500	Turf
22.	Memorial Field	Dartmouth	Ivy	1923	20,416	Grass
23.	Brown...............	Brown	Ivy	1925	20,000	Grass
	Hanger Field	Eastern Ky.	Ohio Valley	1969	20,000	Grass
	Cowboy	McNeese St.	Southland	1965	20,000	Grass
	Fouts Field	North Texas	Southland	1952	20,000	Turf
27.	Kidd Brewer.........	Appalachian St.	Southern	1962	18,000	Turf
	Paulson	Ga. Southern	Southern	1984	18,000	Grass
29.	Aggie	North Caro. A&T	Mid-Eastern	1981	17,500	Grass
	Wildcat	Weber St.	Big Sky	1966	17,500	Grass
	L. T. Smith	Western Ky.	Gateway	1968	17,500	Grass
32.	Nickerson Field	Boston U.	Yankee	1930	17,369	Turf
33.	McAndrew	Southern Ill.	Gateway	1975	17,324	Turf
34.	Lawrence Wien.......	Columbia	Ivy	1984	17,000	Grass
35.	Stewart..............	Murray St.	Ohio Valley	1973	16,800	Turf
36.	Turpin	Northwestern (La.)	Southland	1976	16,522	Turf
37.	Tucker	Tennessee Tech	Ohio Valley	1966	16,500	Turf
38.	UNI-Dome@	Northern Iowa	Gateway	1976	16,400	Turf
39.	Memorial	Connecticut	Yankee	1953	16,200	Grass
40.	Paladin	Furman	Southern	1981	16,000	Grass
	Kibbie Dome@	Idaho	Big Sky	1975	16,000	Turf
	Goodman	Lehigh	Patriot	1988	16,000	Grass
	McGuirk	Massachusetts	Yankee	1965	16,000	Grass
	W. J. Hale	Tennessee St.	Ohio Valley	1953	16,000	Grass
	Stambaugh	Youngstown St.	Independent	1982	16,000	Turf
46.	Washington-Grizzly ..	Montana	Big Sky	1986	15,400	Grass
47.	Walkup Skydome@ ..	Northern Ariz.	Big Sky	1977	15,300	Turf
48.	Reno Sales	Montana St.	Big Sky	1973	15,197	Grass
49.	Hancock	Illinois St.	Gateway	1963	15,000	Turf
	Bridgeforth	James Madison	Independent	1975	15,000	Turf
	Johnny Floyd	Middle Tenn. St.	Ohio Valley	1969	15,000	Turf
	Hanson Field	Western Ill.	Gateway	1948	15,000	Grass
	Cary Field	William & Mary	Independent	1935	15,000	Grass
54.	Homer Bryce.........	Stephen F. Austin	Southland	1973	14,575	Turf
55.	Bobcat	Southwest Tex. St.	Southland	1981	14,104	Grass
56.	Bowers	Sam Houston St.	Southland	1986	14,000	Turf
	Dawson Bulldog	South Caro. St.	Mid-Eastern	1955	14,000	Grass
58.	Fisher Field	Lafayette	Patriot	1926	13,500	Grass
	Cowell	New Hampshire	Yankee	1936	13,500	Grass
60.	Villanova.............	Villanova	Yankee	1929	13,400	Turf
61.	Mathewson...........	Bucknell	Patriot	1924	13,100	Grass
62.	John Guidry	Nicholls St.	Independent	1972	12,800	Grass
63.	Memorial Center@ ...	East Tenn. St.	Southern	1977	12,000	Turf
	Holt Arena@	Idaho St.	Big Sky	1970	12,000	Turf
	Liberty	Liberty	Independent	1989	12,000	Turf
	Memorial	Troy St.	Independent	1950	12,000	Grass
	Whitmire	Western Caro.	Southern	1974	12,000	Turf
68.	Chamberlain	Tenn.-Chatt.	Southern	1947	10,501	Grass
69.	Magnolia	Mississippi Val.	Southwestern	1958	10,500	Grass
70.	Andy Kerr	Colgate	Patriot	1937	10,221	Grass
71.	Municipal	Austin Peay	Ohio Valley	1946	10,000	Turf
	Memorial	Bethune-Cookman	Mid-Eastern	N/A	10,000	Grass
	O'Brien.............	Eastern Ill.	Gateway	1970	10,000	Grass
	Alumni	Maine	Yankee	1942	10,000	Grass
	Jayne	Morehead St.	Ohio Valley	1964	10,000	Turf
	Hughes	Morgan St.	Mid-Eastern	N/A	10,000	Grass
	Meade...............	Rhode Island	Yankee	1928	10,000	Grass
	Houck...............	Southeast Mo. St.	Independent	1930	10,000	Grass
	Alumni Field	Va. Military	Southern	1962	10,000	Grass

Division I-AA Football Stadiums

Rank	Stadium	Home Team	Conference	Year Built	Capacity	Surface
80.	Briggs	Southwest Mo. St.	Gateway	1940	9,000	Turf
81.	Greene	Howard	Mid-Eastern	1986	7,500	Turf
	Pacer................	Tenn.-Martin	Ohio Valley	1964	7,500	Grass
83.	Jack Coffey Field	Fordham	Patriot	1930	7,000	Grass
	E. S. Parsons	Northeastern	Independent	1933	7,000	Turf
85.	Siebert	Samford	Independent	N/A	6,700	Grass
86.	Blackshear	Prairie View	Southwestern	N/A	6,600	Grass
87.	Woodard	Eastern Wash.#	Big Sky	1967	6,000	Grass
88.	Alumni Field	Delaware St.	Mid-Eastern	1957	5,000	Grass
	Minnegan	Towson St.	Independent	1978	5,000	Grass

✓ *Not located on campus.* @ *Indoor facility.*

Stadiums listed alphabetically by school.

School	Stadium	Conference	Year Built	Capacity	Surface
Alabama St.	✓Cramton Bowl	Southwestern	N/A	24,600	Grass
Alcorn St.	(Not named)	Southwestern	1992	25,000	Grass
Appalachian St.	Kidd Brewer	Southern	1962	18,000	Turf
Austin Peay	Municipal	Ohio Valley	1946	10,000	Turf
Bethune-Cookman	Memorial	Mid-Eastern	N/A	10,000	Grass
Boise St.	Bronco	Big Sky	1970	22,600	Turf
Boston U.	Nickerson Field	Yankee	1930	17,369	Turf
Brown...................	Brown	Ivy	1925	20,000	Grass
Bucknell	Mathewson	Patriot	1924	13,100	Grass
Central Fla.	✓Florida Citrus Bowl	Independent	*1989	70,000	Grass
Citadel	Johnson Hagood	Southern	1948	22,500	Grass
Colgate	Andy Kerr	Patriot	1937	10,221	Grass
Columbia	Lawrence Wien	Ivy	1984	17,000	Grass
Connecticut.............	Memorial	Yankee	1953	16,200	Grass
Cornell	Schoelkopf	Ivy	1915	27,000	Turf
Dartmouth	Memorial Field	Ivy	1923	20,416	Grass
Delaware................	Delaware	Yankee	1952	23,000	Grass
Delaware St.	Alumni Field	Mid-Eastern	1957	5,000	Turf
East Tenn. St.	Memorial Center@	Southern	1977	12,000	Turf
Eastern Ill................	O'Brien	Gateway	1970	10,000	Grass
Eastern Ky.	Hanger Field	Ohio Valley	1969	20,000	Grass
Eastern Wash.#	Woodard	Big Sky	1967	6,000	Grass
Florida A&M	Bragg Memorial	Mid-Eastern	1957	25,500	Grass
Fordham	Jack Coffey Field	Patriot	1930	7,000	Grass
Furman	Paladin	Southern	1981	16,000	Grass
Ga. Southern............	Paulson	Southern	1984	18,000	Grass
Grambling	Robinson	Southwestern	1983	22,000	Grass
Harvard	Harvard	Ivy	1903	37,289	Grass
Holy Cross	Fitton Field	Patriot	1924	23,500	Grass
Howard	Greene	Mid-Eastern	1986	7,500	Turf
Idaho	Kibbie Dome@	Big Sky	1975	16,000	Turf
Idaho St.	Holt Arena@	Big Sky	1970	12,000	Turf
Illinois St.	Hancock	Gateway	1963	15,000	Turf
Indiana St.	Memorial	Gateway	1970	20,500	Turf
Jackson St.	✓Mississippi Memorial	Southwestern	1949	62,512	Grass
James Madison	Bridgeforth	Independent	1975	15,000	Turf
Lafayette	Fisher Field	Patriot	1926	13,500	Grass
Lehigh	Goodman	Patriot	1988	16,000	Grass
Liberty	Liberty	Independent	1989	12,000	Turf
Maine	Alumni	Yankee	1942	10,000	Grass
Marshall.................	Marshall	Southern	1991	28,000	Turf
Massachusetts	McGuirk	Yankee	1965	16,000	Grass
McNeese St.	Cowboy	Southland	1965	20,000	Grass
Middle Tenn. St.........	Johnny Floyd	Ohio Valley	1969	15,000	Turf
Mississippi Val..........	Magnolia	Southwestern	1958	10,500	Grass
Montana	Washington-Grizzly	Big Sky	1986	15,400	Grass
Montana St.	Reno Sales	Big Sky	1973	15,197	Grass
Morehead St.............	Jayne	Ohio Valley	1964	10,000	Turf
Morgan St.	Hughes	Mid-Eastern	N/A	10,000	Grass
Murray St................	Stewart	Ohio Valley	1973	16,800	Turf
New Hampshire	Cowell	Yankee	1936	13,500	Grass
Nicholls St...............	John Guidry	Independent	1972	12,800	Grass
North Caro. A&T	Aggie	Mid-Eastern	1981	17,500	Grass

School	Stadium	Conference	Year Built	Capacity	Surface
North Texas	Fouts Field	Southland	1952	20,000	Turf
Northeast La.	Malone	Southland	1978	23,277	Grass
Northeastern	E. S. Parsons	Independent	1933	7,000	Turf
Northern Ariz.	Walkup Skydome@	Big Sky	1977	15,300	Turf
Northern Iowa	UNI-Dome@	Gateway	1976	16,400	Turf
Northwestern (La.)	Turpin	Southland	1976	16,522	Turf
Pennsylvania	✓Franklin Field	Ivy	1895	60,546	Turf
Prairie View	Blackshear	Southwestern	N/A	6,600	Grass
Princeton	Palmer	Ivy	1914	45,725	Grass
Rhode Island	Meade	Yankee	1928	10,000	Grass
Richmond	Richmond	Yankee	1929	22,611	Turf
Sam Houston St.	Bowers	Southland	1986	14,000	Turf
Samford	Siebert	Independent	N/A	6,700	Grass
South Caro. St.	Dawson Bulldog	Mid-Eastern	1955	14,000	Grass
Southeast Mo. St.	Houck	Independent	1930	10,000	Grass
Southern-B.R.	Mumford	Southwestern	1928	24,000	Grass
Southern Ill.	McAndrew	Gateway	1975	17,324	Turf
Southwest Mo. St.	Briggs	Gateway	1941	17,107	Turf
Southwest Tex. St.	Bobcat	Southland	1981	14,104	Grass
Stephen F. Austin	Homer Bryce	Southland	1973	14,575	Turf
Tenn.-Chatt.	Chamberlain	Southern	1947	10,501	Grass
Tenn.-Martin	Pacer	Ohio Valley	1964	7,500	Grass
Tennessee St.	W. J. Hale	Ohio Valley	1953	16,000	Grass
Tennessee Tech	Tucker	Ohio Valley	1966	16,500	Turf
Texas Southern	✓Robertson	Southwestern	1965	25,000	Grass
Towson St.	Minnegan	Independent	1978	5,000	Grass
Troy St.	Memorial	Independent	1950	12,000	Grass
Va. Military	Alumni Field	Southern	1962	10,000	Grass
Villanova	Villanova	Yankee	1929	13,400	Turf
Weber St.	Wildcat	Big Sky	1966	17,500	Grass
Western Caro.	Whitmire	Southern	1974	12,000	Turf
Western Ill.	Hanson Field	Gateway	1948	15,000	Grass
Western Ky.	L. T. Smith	Gateway	1968	17,500	Grass
William & Mary	Cary Field	Independent	1935	15,000	Grass
Yale	Yale Bowl	Ivy	1914	70,896	Grass
Youngstown St.	Stambaugh	Independent	1982	16,000	Turf

✓ Not located on campus.   @ Indoor facility.

* Renovated by adding 19,000 seats in 1989. An earlier renovation in 1975 brought attendance from 9,000 to 51,000.   # Also plays some "home" games at Albi Stadium (33,891) in Spokane, Washington.

Surface Legend: Turf—Any of several types of artificial turfs (name brands include AstroTurf, All-Pro, Omniturf, SuperTurf, etc.); Grass—Natural grass surface.

STATISTICS TRENDS

(Average Per Game, Both Teams)

	Rushing				Passing				Total Offense			Scoring		
Year	Plays	Yds.	Avg.	Att.	Cmp.	Pct.	Yds.	Avg. Att.	Plays	Yds.	Avg.	TD	FG	Pts.
1978	*96.7	*343.5	3.55	41.4	19.1	46.2	258.6	6.24	138.1	602.1	4.36	5.20	1.03	39.0
1979	94.1	329.3	3.50	40.9	18.4	45.0	250.4	6.13	135.0	579.7	4.30	4.79	1.23	36.9
1980	90.3	329.6	3.65	44.8	20.8	46.5	288.8	6.45	135.1	618.4	4.58	5.15	1.18	39.2
1981	88.5	309.9	3.50	49.7	23.7	47.7	322.9	6.49	138.2	632.8	4.58	5.42	1.38	41.7
1982	88.8	313.1	3.53	52.2	25.6	48.9	332.0	6.35	141.0	645.1	4.57	5.24	1.59	41.0
1983	87.8	310.3	3.54	52.4	25.9	49.4	334.5	6.38	140.2	644.8	4.60	5.38	1.58	42.1
1984	85.7	305.1	3.56	55.7	27.9	50.0	361.9	6.49	141.4	666.9	4.72	5.59	1.60	43.6
1985	84.7	315.2	3.72	*57.7	*29.1	50.4	*374.6	6.49	*142.4	689.8	4.84	5.67	1.61	44.2
1986	84.8	315.8	3.72	56.5	28.1	49.7	372.8	6.60	141.3	688.6	4.87	5.80	1.72	45.4
1987	86.2	317.2	3.68	54.2	27.1	50.1	351.1	6.48	140.4	668.3	4.76	5.55	1.81	44.0
1988	86.3	322.5	3.74	52.9	26.5	50.2	345.4	6.53	139.2	667.9	4.80	5.59	*1.81	44.2
1989	84.9	320.4	3.77	55.4	28.4	51.3	372.0	6.71	140.3	692.4	4.93	5.43	1.49	45.5
1990	85.3	323.0	3.79	55.6	28.1	50.6	374.0	6.73	140.9	697.0	4.95	5.96	1.67	46.4
1991	86.4	341.2	*3.95	53.7	27.9	*51.9	369.3	*6.87	140.1	*710.5	*5.07	*6.38	1.33	*48.1

* Record.

ADDITIONAL STATISTICS TRENDS

(Average Per Game, Both Teams)

Year	Punting			Interceptions			Punt Returns			Kickoff Returns			
	No.	Avg.	Net Avg.	No.	Avg. Ret.	Yds.	No.	Avg. Ret.	Yds.	No.	Avg. Ret.	Yds.	Pct. Rtrnd
1978	*12.2	36.5	33.6	2.84	11.92	33.9	4.78	7.49	35.8	6.45	18.4	118.4	77.3
1979	11.9	36.5	33.4	2.88	11.39	32.8	4.82	7.46	35.9	6.11	18.4	112.3	74.9
1980	11.6	37.0	33.7	2.74	10.06	27.6	4.87	7.94	38.7	6.17	17.4	107.4	72.9
1981	11.8	37.2	33.9	*3.19	10.63	*33.9	4.99	7.77	38.8	6.54	18.4	120.1	73.2
1982	12.0	37.1	34.0	2.99	10.15	30.3	4.88	7.63	37.2	6.15	19.0	116.8	68.9
1983	11.9	37.3	34.1	3.03	9.99	30.2	*5.17	7.58	39.2	6.11	18.6	113.8	67.3
1984	11.6	37.3	33.9	3.05	10.40	31.7	5.10	7.84	40.0	6.46	18.6	120.0	69.5
1985	11.4	37.6	*34.2	3.02	10.56	31.9	5.09	7.52	38.3	6.39	18.1	115.7	67.9
1986	11.2	*37.6	34.0	3.01	10.90	32.8	5.09	7.92	40.3	*8.04	*19.4	*155.7	83.6
1987	11.2	36.8	33.4	2.80	10.57	29.7	4.96	7.51	37.3	7.91	19.0	149.1	*83.6
1988	10.9	36.3	32.8	2.68	10.61	28.4	4.80	7.96	38.3	7.90	18.8	148.6	83.2
1989	11.0	36.1	32.8	2.62	10.40	27.3	4.63	7.93	36.7	7.92	18.9	149.4	83.2
1990	10.8	36.7	32.7	2.76	*11.94	32.9	4.97	8.46	42.0	8.03	18.9	151.7	81.5
1991	10.6	36.6	32.6	2.70	10.81	29.1	4.92	*8.57	*42.2	7.68	19.1	146.7	80.8

Record.

I-AA FINAL REGULAR-SEASON TOP 20 POLLS

1982
Team
1. Eastern Ky.
2. Louisiana Tech
3. Delaware
4. Tennessee St.
5. Eastern Ill.
6. Furman
7. South Caro. St.
8. Jackson St.
9. Colgate
10. Grambling
11. Idaho
12. Northern Ill.
13. Holy Cross
14. Bowling Green
15. Boise St.
16. Western Mich.
17. Tenn.-Chatt.
18. Northwestern (La.)
19. Montana
20. Lafayette

1983
Team
1. Southern Ill.
2. Furman
3. Holy Cross
4. North Texas
5. Indiana St.
6. Eastern Ill.
7. Colgate
8. Eastern Ky.
9. Western Caro.
10. Grambling
11. Nevada
12. Idaho St.
13. Boston U.
    Northeast La.
15. Jackson St.
16. Middle Tenn. St.
17. Tennessee St.
18. South Caro. St.
19. Mississippi Val.
20. New Hampshire

1984
Team
1. Alcorn St.
2. Montana St.
   Rhode Island
4. Boston U.
5. Indiana St.
6. Middle Tenn. St.
   Mississippi Val.
8. Eastern Ky.
9. Louisiana Tech
10. Arkansas St.
11. New Hampshire
12. Richmond
13. Murray St.
14. Western Caro.
15. Holy Cross
16. Furman
17. Tenn.-Chatt.
18. Northern Iowa
19. Delaware
20. McNeese St.

1985
Team
1. Middle Tenn. St.
2. Furman
   Nevada
4. Northern Iowa
5. Idaho
6. Arkansas St.
7. Rhode Island
8. Grambling
9. Ga. Southern
10. Akron
11. Eastern Wash.
12. Appalachian St.
    Delaware St.
14. Louisiana Tech
15. Jackson St.
16. William & Mary
17. Murray St.
18. Richmond
19. Eastern Ky.
20. Alcorn St.

1986
Team
1. Nevada
2. Arkansas St.
3. Eastern Ill.
4. Ga. Southern
5. Holy Cross
6. Appalachian St.
7. Pennsylvania
8. William & Mary
9. Jackson St.
10. Eastern Ky.
11. Sam Houston St.
12. Nicholls St.
13. Delaware
14. Tennessee St.
15. Furman
16. Idaho
17. Southern Ill.
18. Murray St.
19. Connecticut
20. North Caro. A&T

1987
Team
1. Holy Cross
2. Appalachian St.
3. Northeast La.
4. Northern Iowa
5. Idaho
6. Ga. Southern
7. Eastern Ky.
8. James Madison
9. Jackson St.
10. Weber St.
11. Western Ky.
12. Arkansas St.
13. Maine
14. Marshall
15. Youngstown St.
16. North Texas
17. Richmond
18. Howard
19. Sam Houston St.
20. Delaware St.

1988
Team
1. Stephen F. Austin
2. Idaho
3. Ga. Southern
4. Western Ill.
5. Furman
6. Jackson St.
7. Marshall
8. Eastern Ky.
9. Citadel
10. Northwestern (La.)
11. Massachusetts
12. North Texas
13. Boise St.
14. Florida A&M
    Pennsylvania
16. Western Ky.
17. Connecticut
18. Grambling
19. Montana
20. New Hampshire

1989
Team
1. Ga. Southern
2. Furman
3. Stephen F. Austin
4. Holy Cross
   Idaho
6. Montana
7. Appalachian St.
8. Maine
9. Southwest Mo. St.
10. Middle Tenn. St.
    William & Mary
12. Eastern Ky.
13. Grambling
14. Youngstown St.
15. Eastern Ill.
16. Villanova
17. Jackson St.
18. Connecticut
19. Nevada
20. Northern Iowa

1990

Team
1. Middle Tenn. St.
2. Youngstown St.
3. Ga. Southern
4. Nevada
5. Eastern Ky.
6. Southwest Mo. St.
7. William & Mary
8. Holy Cross
9. Massachusetts
10. Boise St.
11. Northern Iowa
12. Furman
13. Idaho
14. Northeast La.
15. Citadel
16. Jackson St.
17. Dartmouth
18. Central Fla.
19. New Hampshire
    North Caro. A&T

1991

Team (Record)	How Season Ended
1. Nevada (12-1)	Eliminated by Youngstown St., 28-30, in championship quarterfinals.
2. Eastern Ky. (12-2)	Eliminated by Marshall, 7-14, in championship semifinals.
3. Holy Cross (11-0)	Ended regular season with 28-3 victory over Colgate.
4. Northern Iowa (11-2)	Eliminated by Marshall, 13-41, in championship quarterfinals.
5. Alabama St. (10-0-1)	Defeated North Caro. A&T, 36-13, in the Heritage Bowl.
6. Delaware (10-2)	Eliminated by James Madison, 35-42, in championship first round.
7. Villanova (10-2)	Eliminated by Youngstown St., 16-17, in championship first round.
8. Marshall (11-3)	Lost to Youngstown St., 17-25, in Division I-AA championship.
9. Middle Tenn. St. (9-4) ..	Eliminated by Eastern Ky., 13-23, in championship quarterfinals.
10. Samford (12-2)	Eliminated by Youngstown St., 0-10, in championship semifinals.
11. New Hampshire (9-3) ...	Eliminated by Samford, 13-29, in championship first round.
12. Sam Houston St. (8-3-1)	Eliminated by Middle Tenn. St., 19-20, in championship first round.
13. Youngstown St. (11-3)...	Defeated Marshall, 25-17, in Division I-AA championship.
14. Western Ill. (7-4-1)	Eliminated by Marshall, 17-20, in championship first round.
15. Weber St. (8-4)	Eliminated by Northern Iowa, 21-38, in championship first round.
16. James Madison (9-4)	Eliminated by Samford, 21-24, in championship quarterfinals.
17. Appalachian St. (8-4)	Eliminated by Eastern Ky., 3-14, in championship first round.
18. Northeast La. (7-3-1)	Ended regular season with 44-21 victory over North Texas.
19. McNeese St. (6-4-2)	Eliminated by Nevada, 16-22, in championship first round.
20. Citadel (7-4)	Ended regular season with 10-6 victory over Furman.
Furman (7-4)	Ended regular season with 6-10 loss to Citadel.

1991 WEEK-BY-WEEK I-AA FOOTBALL POLLS

Final Poll—Nov. 25	11/18	11/11	11/4	10/28	10/21	10/14	10/7	9/30	9/23	9/16	9/9	8/19
1. Nevada	1	1	1	1	1	1	1	1	1	1	2	5
2. Eastern Ky.	2	2	2	2	2	2	3	3	3t	3t	5	2
3. Holy Cross	3	3	3	3	3	3	5	7	9	10	14	13
4. Northern Iowa	4	4	4	4	4	5	7	9	17	5	7	7
5. Alabama St.	5	5	5	6	7	11	11t	11	15	15	18	19
6. Delaware	6	6	8	9	11	14	16	5	6	8	12	—
7. Villanova	7	7	9	10t	12t	4	6	8	13	16	16	—
8. Marshall	8	10	15	19	6	8	13	18	19t	**	—	14t
9. Middle Tenn. St.	9	11	6	7	8	7	9	12t	16	7	10	12
10. Samford	11	14	14	18	**	19	**	**	**	**	—	—
11. New Hampshire ...	12	15	7	8	9	12	14	20t	19t	20	**	8
12. Sam Houston St. ..	13	8	10	5	5	6	8	10	11	12t	17	**
13. Youngstown St. ...	14t	16	**	**	—	**	18	**	**	**	8	9
14. Western Ill.	14t	13	16	12	14	17t	**	—	—	—	—	—
15. Weber St.	16	20t	**	**	**	17t	**	**	—	—	—	—
16. James Madison ...	17	17	12	14	17	10	11t	17	**	—	**	—
17. Appalachian St. ...	18	18	20	10t	12t	16	17	—	—	19	—	—
18. Northeast La.......	19t	19	**	16	20	15	10	16	18t	18	—	16
19. McNeese St.	19t	**	19	**	—	**	—	—	—	—	—	—
20. Citadel	**	**	18	**	**	**	—	—	—	—	19t	—
Furman	10	12	11	13	15	9	2	2	3t	3t	6	6

t *Tie.*   ** *Received votes.*   — *Not ranked.*

DIVISION II RECORDS

Southern Utah running back Zed Robinson led all of college football in rushing yardage last year with 1,828 yards on 254 carries, an average of

Official national statistics for all nonmajor four-year colleges began in 1946 with a limited postseason survey. In 1948, the service was expanded to include weekly individual and team statistics rankings in all categories except interceptions, punt returns and kickoff returns; these categories were added to official individual rankings and records in 1970.

From 1946, individual rankings were by totals. Beginning in 1970, most season individual rankings were by per-game averages. In total offense, rushing and scoring, yards or points per game determine rankings; in receiving and interceptions, catches per game; in punt and kickoff returns, yards per return; and in field goals, number made per game. Punting always has been by average, and all team rankings have been per game.

Beginning in 1979, passers were ranked in all divisions on Efficiency Rating Points (see page 6 for explanation).

Before 1967, rankings and records included all four-year colleges that reported their statistics to the NCAA. Beginning with the 1967 season, rankings and records included only members of the NCAA.

In 1973, College Division teams were divided into Division II and Division III under a three-division reorganization plan adopted by the special NCAA Convention on August 1, 1973. Career records of players who played in both Divisions II and III will be found where they played the majority of their careers (i.e., two of the last three or three of the last four years). In the event an individual's four-year or two-year career is divided evenly between classifications (or between member or nonmember status), the player's career statistics are entered in the collegiate record category.

Collegiate records for all NCAA divisions can be determined by comparing records for all four divisions. Collegiate records are listed only if they involve players with divided careers.

All individual and team statistics rankings include regular-season games only.

INDIVIDUAL RECORDS

TOTAL OFFENSE
(Rushing Plus Passing)

Most Plays

Game
85—Dave Walter, Michigan Tech vs. Ferris St., Oct. 18, 1986 (457 yards)
Season
594—Chris Hegg, Northeast Mo. St., 1985 (3,782 yards)
Per-game record—58.3, Dave Walter, Michigan Tech, 1986 (525 in 9)
2 Yrs
1,107—Pat Brennan, Franklin, 1983-84 (6,487 yards)
Also holds per-game record at 55.4 (1,107 in 20)
3 Yrs
1,542—Earl Harvey, N.C. Central, 1985-87 (8,266 yards)
Career
(4 yrs.) 2,045—Earl Harvey, N.C. Central, 1985-88 (10,667 yards)
Also holds per-game record at 52.4 (2,045 in 39)

Most Plays by a Freshman

Season
538—Earl Harvey, N.C. Central, 1985 (3,008 yards)
Also holds per-game record at 53.8 (538 in 10)

Most Yards Gained

Game
584—Tracy Kendall, Alabama A&M vs. Clark Atlanta, Nov. 4, 1989 (70 rushing, 514 passing)
Season
3,782—Chris Hegg, Northeast Mo. St., 1985 (41 rushing, 3,741 passing)
2 Yrs
6,487—Pat Brennan, Franklin, 1983-84 (-344 rushing, 6,831 passing)
3 Yrs
8,266—Earl Harvey, N.C. Central, 1985-87 (14 rushing, 8,252 passing)
Career
(4 yrs.) 10,667—Earl Harvey, N.C. Central, 1985-88 (46 rushing, 10,621 passing)

Most Yards Gained Per Game
Season
350.4—Rob Tomlinson, Cal St. Chico, 1989 (3,504 in 10)
Career
281.0—Jayson Merrill, Western St., 1990-91 (5,619 in 20)

Most Seasons Gaining 3,000 Yards or More
2—Pat Brennan, Franklin, 1983 (3,239) & 1984 (3,248)

Most Seasons Gaining 2,500 Yards or More
3—Jim Lindsey, Abilene Christian, 1968 (2,740), 1969 (2,646) & 1970 (2,654)

Gaining 2,500 Yards Rushing and 3,000 Yards Passing
Career
Jeff Bentrim, North Dak. St., 1983-86 (2,946 rushing, 3,453 passing)

Most Yards Gained by a Freshman
Game
482—Matthew Montgomery, Hampton vs. Tuskegee, Oct. 26, 1991
Season
3,008—Earl Harvey, N.C. Central, 1985 (538 plays)
Also holds per-game record at 300.8 (3,008 in 10)

Most Games Gaining 300 Yards or More
Season
8—Chris Hegg, Northeast Mo. St., 1985

Career
15—June Jones, Portland St., 1975-76; Jim Lindsey, Abilene Christian, 1967-70

Highest Average Gain Per Play
Season
(Min. 350 plays) 8.33—Bob Toledo, San Fran. St., 1967 (409 for 3,407)
Career
(Min. 950 plays) 7.64—Doug Williams, Grambling, 1974-77 (1,072 for 8,195)

Most Touchdowns Responsible For (TDs Scored and Passed For)
Game
10—Bruce Swanson, North Park vs. North Central, Oct. 12, 1968 (passed for 10)
Also holds record for Most Points Responsible For at 60
Season
46—Bob Toledo, San Fran. St., 1967 (scored 1, passed for 45)
Also holds per-game record at 4.6 (46 in 10) and record for Most Points Responsible For at 276
Career
106—Earl Harvey, N.C. Central, 1985-88 (scored 20, passed for 86)

Most Points Responsible For (Points Scored and Passed For)
Career
636—Earl Harvey, N.C. Central, 1985-88 (scored 120, passed for 516)

RUSHING

Most Rushes
Game
62—Nelson Edmonds, Northern Mich. vs. Wayne St. (Mich.), Oct. 26, 1991 (291 yards)
Season
350—Leon Burns, Long Beach St., 1969 (1,659 yards)
Per-game record—38.6, Mark Perkins, Hobart, 1968
2 Yrs
648—Steve Roberts, Butler, 1987-88 (2,917 yards)
Career
1,072—Bernie Peeters, Luther, 1968-71 (4,435 yards)
Also holds per-game record at 29.8 (1,072 in 36)

Most Consecutive Rushes by the Same Player
Game
13—Randy Walker, Wheaton (Ill.) vs. North Park, Nov. 4, 1972 (during one ball possession)

Most Yards Gained
Game
382—Kelly Ellis, Northern Iowa vs. Western Ill., Oct. 13, 1979 (40 rushes)
Season
2,011—Johnny Bailey, Texas A&I, 1986 (271 rushes)
2 Yrs
3,609—Johnny Bailey, Texas A&I, 1986-87 (488 rushes)
3 Yrs
5,051—Johnny Bailey, Texas A&I, 1986-88 (717 rushes)
Career
6,320—Johnny Bailey, Texas A&I, 1986-89 (885 rushes)

Most Yards Gained Per Game
Season
182.8—Johnny Bailey, Texas A&I, 1986 (2,011 in 11)
2 Yrs
171.9—Johnny Bailey, Texas A&I, 1986-87 (3,609 in 21)
Career
(Min. 3,000 yds.) 162.1—Johnny Bailey, Texas A&I, 1986-89 (6,320 in 39)

Most Yards Gained by a Freshman
Game
370—Jim Hissam, Marietta vs. Bethany (W. Va.), Nov. 15, 1958 (22 rushes)
Season
2,011—Johnny Bailey, Texas A&I, 1986 (271 rushes)
Also holds per-game record at 182.8 (2,011 in 11)

Most Yards Gained in First Game of a Career
238—Johnny Bailey, Texas A&I vs. Texas Southern, Sept. 6, 1986

Most Yards Gained by Two Players, Same Team
Game
476—Ed Tillison (272) & Jeremy Wilson (204), Northwest Mo. St. vs. Neb.-Kearney, Nov. 11, 1990
Season
3,526—Johnny Bailey (2,011) & Heath Sherman (1,515), Texas A&I, 1986
Also hold per-game record at 320.5 (3,526 in 11)
Career
(3 yrs.) 8,594—Johnny Bailey (5,051) & Heath Sherman (3,543), Texas A&I, 1986-88 (1,317 rushes)

Two Players, Same Team, Each Gaining 200 Yards or More
Game
Ed Tillison, 272 (29 rushes, 2 TDs) & Jeremy Wilson, 204 (18 rushes, 1 TD), Northwest Mo. St. vs. Neb.-Kearney, Nov. 11, 1990; Jeremy Monroe, 220 (23 rushes, 5 TDs) & Mark Kieliszewski, 212 (18 rushes, 1 TD), Michigan Tech vs. Trinity (Ill.), Nov. 3, 1990; Johnny Bailey, 207 (23 rushes, 0 TDs) & Heath Sherman, 206 (17 rushes, 3 TDs), Texas A&I vs. East Central Okla., Sept. 20, 1986; Johnny Bailey, 244 (21 rushes, 3 TDs) & Heath Sherman, 216 (22 rushes, 4 TDs), Texas A&I vs. North Dak., Sept. 13, 1986 (consecutive games)

Two Players, Same Team, Each Gaining 1,000 Yards or More
Season
11 times. Most recent: Pittsburg St., 1991—Darren Dawson (1,176) & Ronald Moore (1,040); Pittsburg St., 1990—Darren Dawson (1,170) & Ronald Moore (1,013)

Most Games Gaining 100 Yards or More
Season
11—Johnny Bailey, Texas A&I, 1986
Also holds freshman record at 11
Career
33—Johnny Bailey, Texas A&I, 1986-89 (39 games)

Most Consecutive Games Gaining 100 Yards or More
Season
11—Johnny Bailey, Texas A&I, 1986
Also holds freshman record at 11
Career
24—Peter Gorniewicz, Colby, 1971-73

Most Games Gaining 200 Yards or More
Season
5—Johnny Bailey, Texas A&I, 1986
Also holds freshman record at 5
Career
11—Johnny Bailey, Texas A&I, 1986-89 (39 games)

Most Consecutive Games Gaining 200 Yards or More
Season
4—Johnny Bailey, Texas A&I, 1986 (first games of his career)

Most Yards Gained, Four and Five Consecutive Games
4 Games
975—Zed Robinson, Southern Utah, Oct. 5-Oct. 26, 1991
5 Games
1,075—Zed Robinson, Southern Utah, Oct. 5-Nov. 2, 1991

Most Yards Gained by a Quarterback
Game
323—Shawn Graves, Wofford vs. Lenoir-Rhyne, Sept. 15, 1990 (23 rushes)
Season
1,483—Shawn Graves, Wofford, 1989 (241 rushes)

Career
4,138—Shawn Graves, Wofford, 1989-91 (570 rushes)

Most Rushes by a Quarterback
Career
603—Jeff Bentrim, North Dak. St., 1983-86

Most Yards Gained by a Freshman in First Game of Career
238—Johnny Bailey, Texas A&I vs. Texas Southern, Sept. 6, 1986

Most Seasons Gaining 1,000 Yards or More
Career
4—Johnny Bailey, Texas A&I, 1986-89; Vincent Allen, Indiana St., 1973-75, 77

Highest Average Gain Per Rush
Game
(Min. 20 rushes) 17.5—Don Polkinghorne, Washington (Mo.) vs. Wash. & Lee, Nov. 23, 1957 (21 for 367)
Season
(Min. 140 rushes) 10.5—Billy Johnson, Widener, 1972 (148 for 1,556)
(Min. 200 rushes) 8.13—Bob White, Western N. Mex., 1951 (202 for 1,643)
(Min. 250 rushes) 7.42—Johnny Bailey, Texas A&I, 1986 (271 for 2,011)
Career
(Min. 300 rushes) 9.09—Billy Johnson, Widener, 1971-73 (411 for 3,735)
(Min. 500 rushes) 8.49—Bill Rhodes, Western St., 1953-56 (506 for 4,294)

Most Touchdowns Scored by Rushing
Game
8—Junior Wolf, Panhandle St. vs. St. Mary (Kan.), Nov. 8, 1958
Season
28—Terry Metcalf, Long Beach St., 1971
Career
66—Johnny Bailey, Texas A&I, 1986-89
Per-game record—1.83, Jeff Bentrim, North Dak. St., 1983-86 (64 in 35)

Most Touchdowns Scored by Rushing by a Freshman
Season
24—Shawn Graves, Wofford, 1989
Also holds per-game record at 2.18 (24 in 11)

Most Touchdowns Scored by Rushing by a Quarterback
Season
24—Shawn Graves, Wofford, 1989
Per-game record—2.3, Jeff Bentrim, North Dak. St. (23 in 10)
Career
64—Jeff Bentrim, North Dak. St., 1983-86
Also holds per-game record at 1.83 (64 in 35)

Most Touchdowns Scored by Rushing by Two Players, Same Team
Season
41—Heath Sherman (23) & Johnny Bailey (18), Texas A&I, 1986
Also hold per-game record at 3.73 (41 in 11)
Career
106—Heath Sherman (55) & Johnny Bailey (51), Texas A&I, 1985-88

PASSING

Highest Passing Efficiency Rating Points

Season
(Min. 15 atts. per game) 210.1—Boyd Crawford, Col. of Idaho, 1953 (120 attempts, 72 completions, 6 interceptions, 1,462 yards, 21 TD passes)
(Min. 100 comps.) 189.0—Chuck Green, Wittenberg, 1963 (182 attempts, 114 completions, 8 interceptions, 2,181 yards, 19 TD passes)
(Min. 200 comps.) 159.7—Chris Petersen, UC Davis, 1986 (311 attempts, 218 completions, 7 interceptions, 2,622 yards, 22 TD passes)
Career
(Min. 375 comps.) 164.0—Chris Petersen, UC Davis, 1985-86 (553 attempts, 385 completions, 13 interceptions, 4,988 yards, 39 TD passes)

Most Passes Attempted

Game
72—Kurt Otto, North Dak. vs. Texas A&I, Sept. 13, 1986 (completed 41); Kaipo Spencer, Santa Clara vs. Portland St., Oct. 11, 1975 (completed 37); Joe Stetser, Cal St. Chico vs. Oregon Tech, Sept. 23, 1967 (completed 38)
Season
515—Tod Mayfield, West Tex. St., 1986 (completed 317)
Career
1,442—Earl Harvey, N.C. Central, 1985-88 (completed 690)

Most Passes Attempted Per Game

Season
50.2—Pat Brennan, Franklin, 1984 (502 in 10)
Career
46.2—Tim Von Dulm, Portland St., 1969-70 (924 in 20)

Most Passes Completed

Game
44—Tom Bonds, Cal Lutheran vs. St. Mary's (Cal.), Nov. 22, 1986 (attempted 59)
Season
317—Tod Mayfield, West Tex. St., 1986 (attempted 515)
Career
690—Earl Harvey, N.C. Central, 1985-88 (attempted 1,442)

Most Passes Completed Per Game

Season
28.8—Tod Mayfield, West Tex. St., 1986 (317 in 11)
Career
25.0—Tim Von Dulm, Portland St., 1969-70 (500 in 20)

Most Passes Completed by a Freshman

Game
41—Neil Lomax, Portland St. vs. Montana St., Nov. 19, 1977 (59 attempts, 469 yards, 6 TDs)

Most Consecutive Passes Completed

Game
20—Rod Bockwoldt, Weber St. vs. South Dak. St., Nov. 6, 1976
Season
23—Mike Ganey, Allegheny, 1967 (completed last 16 attempts vs. Carnegie Mellon, Oct. 9 and first 7 vs. Oberlin, Oct. 16)

Highest Percentage of Passes Completed

Game
(Min. 20 comps.) 90.9%—Rod Bockwoldt, Weber St. vs. South Dak. St., Nov. 6, 1976 (20 of 22)
(Min. 35 comps.) 70.1%—Kurt Beathard, Towson St. vs. Lafayette, Nov. 2, 1985 (40 of 51)
Season
(Min. 225 atts.) 70.1%—Chris Petersen, UC Davis, 1986 (218 of 311)
(Min. 350 atts.) 65.2%—George Bork, Northern Ill., 1963 (244 of 374)
Career
(Min. 500 atts.) 69.6%—Chris Petersen, UC Davis, 1985-86 (385 of 553)

Most Passes Had Intercepted

Game
9—Pat Brennan, Franklin vs. Saginaw Valley, Sept. 24, 1983; Henry Schafer, Johns Hopkins vs. Haverford, Oct. 16, 1965
Season
32—Joe Stetser, Cal St. Chico, 1967 (attempted 464)
Career
83—Mike Houston, St. Joseph's (Ind.), 1978-81 (attempted 1,031)

Lowest Percentage of Passes Had Intercepted

Season
(Min. 200 atts.) 0.75%—Larry Caswell, Rhode Island, 1967 (2 of 266)
(Min. 300 atts.) 1.93%—Scott Jones, South Dak., 1985 (6 of 311)
Career
(Min. 500 atts.) 2.35%—Chris Petersen, UC Davis, 1985-86 (13 of 553)
(Min. 700 atts.) 2.63%—Jack Hull, Grand Valley St., 1988-91 (22 of 835)

Most Passes Attempted Without Interception

Game
70—Tim Von Dulm, Portland St. vs. Eastern Wash., Nov. 21, 1970
Season
113—Jeff Allen, New Hampshire, 1975

Most Consecutive Passes Attempted Without Interception

176—Larry Caswell, Rhode Island, during 6 games from Oct. 14 to Nov. 18, 1967

Most Yards Gained

Game
592—John Charles, Portland St. vs. Cal Poly SLO, Nov. 16, 1991
Season
3,741—Chris Hegg, Northeast Mo. St., 1985
2 Yrs
6,831—Pat Brennan, Franklin, 1983-84
3 Yrs
8,252—Earl Harvey, N.C. Central, 1985-87
Career
10,621—Earl Harvey, N.C. Central, 1985-88

Most Yards Gained Per Game

Season
351.3—Bob Toledo, San Fran. St., 1967 (3,513 in 10)
Career
298.4—Tim Von Dulm, Portland St., 1969-70 (5,967 in 20)

Most Yards Gained by a Freshman
Game
469—Neil Lomax, Portland St. vs. Montana St., Nov. 19, 1977
Season
3,190—Earl Harvey, N.C. Central, 1985

Most Games Gaining 200 Yards or More
Season
11—Tod Mayfield, West Tex. St., 1986; Chris Hegg, Northeast Mo. St., 1985
Career
29—Dave DenBraber, Ferris St., 1984-87

Most Consecutive Games Gaining 200 Yards or More
Career
15—Tim Von Dulm, Portland St., 1969-70

Most Games Gaining 300 Yards or More
Season
8—Earl Harvey, N.C. Central, 1985; Chris Hegg, Northeast Mo. St., 1985
Career
15—Earl Harvey, N.C. Central, 1987-88

Most Consecutive Games Gaining 300 Yards or More
Season
5—Earl Harvey, N.C. Central, 1985; Tim Von Dulm, Portland St., 1970; Jim Lindsey, Abilene Christian, 1968
Career
8—Earl Harvey, N.C. Central, 1985-86

Western State quarterback Jayson Merrill holds Division II season and career passing records for yards per attempt and yards per completion. He also holds the division's career mark of 281 yards per game in total offense.

Most Yards Gained Per Attempt
Season
(Min. 300 atts.) 11.28—Jayson Merrill, Western St., 1991 (309 for 3,484)
Career
(Min. 500 atts.) 10.05—Jayson Merrill, Western St., 1990-91 (580 for 5,830)
(Min. 700 atts.) 9.02—Bruce Upstill, Col. of Emporia, 1960-63 (769 for 6,935)

Most Yards Gained Per Completion
Season
(Min. 125 comps.) 18.70—Matt Cook, Mo. Southern St., 1991 (141 for 2,637)
(Min. 175 comps.) 17.87—Jayson Merrill, Western St., 1991 (195 for 3,484)
Career
(Min. 300 comps.) 17.77—Jayson Merrill, Western St., 1990-91 (328 for 5,830)
(Min. 450 comps.) 17.38—Doug Williams, Grambling, 1974-77 (484 for 8,411)

Most Touchdown Passes
Quarter
5—Kevin Russell, Calif. (Pa.) vs. Frostburg St., Nov. 5, 1983 (2nd quarter)
Game
10—Bruce Swanson, North Park vs. North Central, Oct. 12, 1968
Season
45—Bob Toledo, San Fran. St., 1967
Also holds per-game record at 4.5 (45 in 10)
Career
93—Doug Williams, Grambling, 1974-77
Per-game record—2.7, Bob Toledo, San Fran. St., 1966-67 (53 in 20)

Most Touchdown Passes by a Freshman
Game
6—Earl Harvey, N.C. Central vs. Johnson Smith, Nov. 9, 1985
Season
22—Earl Harvey, N.C. Central, 1985

Highest Percentage of Passes for Touchdowns
Season
(Min. 150 atts.) 16.0%—John Ford, Hardin-Simmons, 1949 (26 of 163)
(Min. 300 atts.) 11.4%—Bob Toledo, San Fran. St., 1967 (45 of 396)
Career
(Min. 500 atts.) 12.2%—Al Niemela, West Chester, 1985-88 (73 of 600)

Most Consecutive Games Throwing a Touchdown Pass
Career
21—Earl Harvey, N.C. Central, 1985-87 (last 5 in 1985, all 10 in 1986, first 6 in 1987)

Most Games Throwing a Touchdown Pass
Career
38—Doug Williams, Grambling, 1974-77 (played in 40 games)

RECEIVING

Most Passes Caught
Game
23—Barry Wagner, Alabama A&M vs. Clark Atlanta, Nov. 4, 1989 (370 yards)
Season
106—Barry Wagner, Alabama A&M, 1989 (1,812 yards)
Career
253—Chris Myers, Kenyon, 1967-70 (3,897 yards)

Most Passes Caught Per Game
Season
10.1—Bruce Cerone, Emporia St., 1968 (91 in 9)
Career
8.6—Ed Bell, Idaho St., 1968-69 (163 in 19)

Most Consecutive Games Catching a Pass
Career
41—Cedric Tillman, Northern Colo., 1986-89 (41 of 42 games played)

Most Passes Caught by a Tight End
Game
15—By six players. Most recent: Mark Martin, Cal St. Chico vs. San Fran. St., Oct. 21, 1989 (223 yards)
Season
77—Bob Tucker, Bloomsburg, 1967 (1,325 yards)
Career
199—Barry Naone, Portland St., 1985-88 (2,237 yards)

Most Passes Caught by a Running Back
Season
94—Billy Joe Masters, Evansville, 1987 (960 yards)
Also holds per-game record at 9.4 (94 in 10)
Career
200—Mark Steinmeyer, Kutztown, 1988-91 (2,118 yards)
Per-game record—5.4, Mark Marana, Northern Mich., 1979-80 (107 in 20)

Most Passes Caught by a Freshman
Season
66—Don Hutt, Boise St., 1971 (928 yards)

Most Passes Caught by Two Players, Same Team
Career
363—Robert Clark (210) & Robert Green (153), N.C. Central, 1983-86 (6,528 yards, 49 TDs)

Most Yards Gained
Game
370—Barry Wagner, Alabama A&M vs. Clark Atlanta, Nov. 4, 1989 (caught 23)
Season
1,812—Barry Wagner, Alabama A&M, 1989 (caught 106)
Career
4,354—Bruce Cerone, Yankton/Emporia St., 1966-69 (caught 241)

Most Yards Gained Per Game
Season
164.7—Barry Wagner, Alabama A&M, 1989 (1,812 in 11)
Career
137.3—Ed Bell, Idaho St., 1968-69 (2,608 in 19)

Most Yards Gained by a Tight End
Game
290—Bob Tucker, Bloomsburg vs. Susquehanna, Oct. 7, 1967 (caught 15)
Season
1,325—Bob Tucker, Bloomsburg, 1967 (caught 77)
Career
2,494—Dan Anderson, Northwest Mo. St., 1982-85 (caught 186)

Most Yards Gained by a Running Back
Game
209—Don Lenhard, Bucknell vs. Delaware, Nov. 19, 1966 (caught 11)
Season
960—Billy Joe Masters, Evansville, 1987 (caught 94)
Also holds per-game record at 96.0 (960 in 10)
Career
2,118—Mark Steinmeyer, Kutztown, 1988-91 (caught 200)

Most Yards Gained by Two Players, Same Team
Career
6,528—Robert Clark (4,231) & Robert Green (2,297), N.C. Central, 1983-86 (caught 363, 49 TDs)

Highest Average Gain Per Reception
Season
(Min. 30) 32.5—Tyrone Johnson, Western St., 1991 (32 for 1,039)
(Min. 40) 27.6—Chris Harkness, Ashland, 1987 (41 for 1,131)
(Min. 55) 24.0—Rod Smith, Mo. Southern St., 1991 (60 for 1,439)
Career
(Min. 135) 21.8—Willie Richardson, Jackson St., 1959-62 (166 for 3,616)
(Min. 180) 20.1—Robert Clark, N.C. Central, 1983-86 (210 for 4,231)

Highest Average Gain Per Reception by a Running Back
Season
(Min. 40) 19.4—John Smith, Boise St., 1975 (45 for 854)
Career
(Min. 80) 18.1—John Smith, Boise St., 1972-75 (89 for 1,608)

Most Touchdown Passes Caught
Game
8—Paul Zaeske, North Park vs. North Central, Oct. 12, 1968 (11 receptions)
Season
20—Ed Bell, Idaho St., 1969 (96 receptions)
Per-game record—2.0, Shannon Sharpe, Savannah St., 1989 (18 in 9); Ed Bell, Idaho St., 1969 (20 in 10)
Career
49—Bruce Cerone, Yankton/Emporia St., 1966-69 (241 receptions)
Per-game record—1.6, Ed Bell, Idaho St., 1968-69 (30 in 19)

Most Touchdown Passes Caught by a Tight End
Game
5—Mike Palomino, Portland St. vs. Cal Poly SLO, Nov. 16, 1991; Alex Preuss, Grand Valley St. vs. Winona St., Sept. 17, 1988
Season
13—Bob Tucker, Bloomsburg, 1967

Most Touchdown Passes Caught by a Running Back

Season
11—John Smith, Boise St., 1975

Career
24—John Smith, Boise St., 1972-75

Most Touchdown Passes Caught by a Freshman

Season
11—Douglas Grant, Savannah St., 1990; Harold Roberts, Austin Peay, 1967

Highest Percentage of Passes Caught for Touchdowns

Season
(Min. 10 TDs) 68.8%—Jim Callahan, Temple, 1966 (11 of 16)

Career
(Min. 20 TDs) 30.0%—Bob Cherry, Wittenberg, 1960-63 (27 of 90)

Most Consecutive Passes Caught for Touchdowns

Season
10—Jim Callahan, Temple, 1966 (first 5 games, first games of career)

Most Consecutive Games Catching a Touchdown Pass

Career
14—Jeff Tiefenthaler, South Dak. St., from Oct. 27, 1984, through Nov. 9, 1985

Most Games Catching a Touchdown Pass

Career
25—Jeff Tiefenthaler, South Dak. St., 1983-86 (in 36 games)

PUNTING

Most Punts

Game
32—Jan Jones, Sam Houston St. vs. East Tex. St., Nov. 2, 1946 (1,203 yards)

Season
98—John Tassi, Lincoln (Mo.), 1981 (3,163 yards)

Career
328—Dan Brown, Nicholls St., 1976-79 (12,883 yards)

Highest Average Per Punt

Game
(Min. 5) 57.5—Tim Baer, Colorado Mines vs. Fort Lewis, Oct. 25, 1986 (8 for 460)

Season
(Min. 20) 49.1—Steve Ecker, Shippensburg, 1965 (32 for 1,570)
(Min. 40) 46.3—Mark Bounds, West Tex. St., 1990 (69 for 3,198)

Career
(Min. 200) 44.3—Tim Baer, Colorado Mines, 1986-89 (235 for 10,406)

INTERCEPTIONS (From 1970)

Most Passes Intercepted

Quarter
3—Anthony Devine, Millersville vs. Cheyney, Oct. 13, 1990 (3rd; 90 yards); Mike McDonald, Southwestern La. vs. Lamar, Oct. 24, 1970 (4th; 25 yards)

Game
5—By five players. Most recent: Gary Evans, Northeast Mo. St. vs. Missouri-Rolla, Oct. 18, 1975

Season
14—By five players. Most recent: Luther Howard, Delaware St., 1972 (99 yards); Eugene Hunter, Fort Valley St., 1972 (211 yards)

Career
37—Tom Collins, Indianapolis, 1982-85 (390 yards)

Most Passes Intercepted by Per Game

Season
1.56—Luther Howard, Delaware St., 1972 (14 in 9); Eugene Hunter, Fort Valley St., 1972 (14 in 9); Tom Rezzuti, Northeastern, 1971 (14 in 9)

Most Yards on Interception Returns

Game
152—Desmond Brown, Tuskegee vs. Morris Brown, Sept. 15, 1990 (2 interceptions)

Season
300—Mike Brim, Virginia Union, 1986 (8 interceptions)

Career
504—Anthony Leonard, Virginia Union, 1973-76 (17 interceptions)

Highest Average Gain Per Interception

Season
(Min. 6) 37.5—Mike Brim, Virginia Union, 1986 (8 for 300)

Career
(Min. 10) 37.4—Greg Anderson, Montana, 1974-76 (11 for 411)
(Min. 15) 29.6—Anthony Leonard, Virginia Union, 1973-76 (17 for 504)

Most Touchdowns Scored on Interceptions

Season
4—Clay Blalack, Tenn.-Martin, 1976 (8 interceptions)

PUNT RETURNS (From 1970)

Most Punt Returns

Game
10—Armin Anderson, UC Davis vs. Cal St. Chico, Oct. 22, 1983 (42 yards)

Season
61—Armin Anderson, UC Davis, 1984 (516 yards)

Career
153—Armin Anderson, UC Davis, 1983-85 (1,207 yards)

Most Yards on Punt Returns

Game
265—Billy Johnson, Widener vs. St. John's (N.Y.), Sept. 23, 1972 (4 returns)

Season
603—Rob Richmond, Hampden-Sydney, 1971 (46 returns)

Career
1,207—Armin Anderson, UC Davis, 1983-85 (153 returns)

Highest Average Gain Per Return
Game
   (Min. 4) 66.3—Billy Johnson, Widener vs. St. John's (N.Y.), Sept. 23, 1972 (4 for 265)
Season
   (Min. 1.2 per game) 34.1—Billy Johnson, Widener, 1972 (15 for 511)
Career
   (Min. 1.2 per game) 24.7—Billy Johnson, Widener, 1971-73 (40 for 989)

Most Touchdowns Scored on Punt Returns
Game
   3—By four players. Most recent: Virgil Seay, Troy St. vs. Livingston, Sept. 29, 1979
Season
   4—Michael Fields, Mississippi Col., 1984; Billy Johnson, Widener, 1972
Career
   7—Billy Johnson, Widener, 1971-73

KICKOFF RETURNS (From 1970)

Most Kickoff Returns
Game
   9—Darron Turner, Tenn.-Martin vs. Jacksonville St., Oct. 21, 1989; Thad Kuehnl, Michigan Tech vs. Northern Mich., Sept. 5, 1987; Matthew Williams, Northeast La. vs. Jacksonville St., Nov. 3, 1973
Season
   47—Sean Tarrant, Lincoln (Mo.), 1986 (729 yards)
   Also holds per-game record at 4.3 (47 in 11)
Career
   115—Sean Tarrant, Lincoln (Mo.), 1985-88 (1,901 yards)

Most Yards on Kickoff Returns
Game
   276—Matt Pericolosi, Central Conn. St. vs. Hofstra, Sept. 14, 1991 (6 returns); Tom Dufresne, Hamline vs. Minn.-Duluth, Sept. 30, 1972 (7 returns)
Season
   983—Doug Parrish, San Fran. St., 1990 (34 returns)

Career
   2,291—Joe Wingate, Northwest Mo. St., 1970-73 (99 returns)

Highest Average Gain Per Return
Game
   (Min. 3) 71.7—Clarence Martin, Cal Poly SLO vs. Cal Poly Pomona, Nov. 20, 1982 (3 for 215)
Season
   (Min. 1.2 per game) 36.1—Roscoe Word, Jackson St., 1973 (18 for 650)
Career
   (Min. 1.2 per game) 34.0—Glen Printers, Southern Colo., 1973-74 (25 for 851)

Most Touchdowns Scored on Kickoff Returns
Game
   2—Clarence Martin, Cal Poly SLO vs. Cal Poly Pomona, Nov. 20, 1982 (successive); Tom Dufresne, Hamline vs. Minn.-Duluth, Sept. 30, 1972
Season
   3—Otha Hill, Central St. (Ohio), 1979
Career
   4—Kurt Johnson, Grand Valley St., 1978-81

TOTAL KICK RETURNS
(Combined Punt and Kickoff Returns)

Most Kick Returns
Season
   63—Bobby Yates, Central Mo. St., 1990 (31 kickoffs, 32 punts, 840 yards)

Most Consecutive Touchdowns on Kick Returns
Game
   2—Victor Barnes, Nebraska-Omaha vs. Neb.-Kearney, Sept. 8, 1990 (1 kickoff return, 94 yards & 1 punt return, 79 yards)

ALL RUNBACKS
(Combined Interceptions, Punt Returns and Kickoff Returns)

Most Touchdowns Scored on Interceptions, Punt Returns and Kickoff Returns
Season
   6—Anthony Leonard, Virginia Union, 1974 (2 interceptions, 2 punt returns, 2 kickoff returns)
Career
   13—Anthony Leonard, Virginia Union, 1973-76 (3 interceptions, 6 punt returns, 4 kickoff returns)

Most Touchdowns Scored on Punt Returns and Kickoff Returns
Career
   10—Anthony Leonard, Virginia Union, 1973-76 (6 punt returns, 4 kickoff returns)

Longest Defensive Extra Point Blocked-Kick Return
Game
   97—Dominic Kurtyan (DB), West Chester vs. Kutztown, Oct. 7, 1988 (TD)

Longest Defensive Extra Point Interception-Fumble Return
Game
   87—Rod Beauchamp (DB), Colorado Mines vs. Hastings, Sept. 3, 1988 (fumble return, TD)

OPPONENTS' PUNTS BLOCKED
Career
   13—Bernard Ford, Central Fla., 1985-87

ALL-PURPOSE RUNNING

(Yardage Gained From Rushing, Receiving and All Runbacks)

Most Plays

Season
415—Steve Roberts, Butler, 1989 (325 rushes, 49 receptions, 21 punt returns, 20 kickoff returns)

Career
1,195—Steve Roberts, Butler, 1986-89 (1,026 rushes, 120 receptions, 21 punt returns, 28 kickoff returns)

Most Yards Gained

Game
525—Andre Johnson, Ferris St. vs. Clarion, Sept. 16, 1989 (19 rushing, 235 receiving, 10 punt returns, 261 kickoff returns; 17 plays)

Season
2,669—Steve Roberts, Butler, 1989 (1,450 rushing, 532 receiving, 272 punt returns, 415 kickoff returns; 415 plays)
Freshman record (2,425) and freshman per-game record (220.5) held by Johnny Bailey, Texas A&I (11 games)

Career
7,803—Johnny Bailey, Texas A&I, 1986-89 (6,302 rushing, 452 receiving, 20 punt returns, 1,011 kickoff returns)

Most Yards Gained by Two Players, Same Team

Season
4,076—Johnny Bailey (2,425) and Heath Sherman (1,651), Texas A&I, 1986
Also hold per-game record at 370.5 (4,076 in 11)

Most Yards Gained Per Game

Season
266.9—Steve Roberts, Butler, 1989 (2,669 in 10)

Career
205.1—Howard Stevens, Randolph-Macon, 1968-69 (3,691 in 18)
Also holds collegiate per-game record at 199.1 (7,564 in 38) at Randolph-Macon, 1968-69, and Louisville, 1971-72

Highest Average Gain Per Play

Game
(Min. 15 plays) 30.9—Andre Johnson, Ferris St. vs. Clarion, Sept. 16, 1989 (525 on 17)

Season
(Min. 1,500 yards, 150 plays) 12.94—Billy Johnson, Widener, 1972 (2,265 on 175)

Career
(Min. 4,000 yards, 300 plays) 11.28—Billy Johnson, Widener, 1971-73 (5,404 on 479)

SCORING

Most Points Scored

Game
48—Paul Zaeske, North Park vs. North Central, Oct. 12, 1968 (8 TDs); Junior Wolf, Panhandle St. vs. St. Mary (Kan.), Nov. 8, 1958 (8 TDs)

Season
178—Terry Metcalf, Long Beach St., 1971 (29 TDs, 4 PATs)

3 Yrs
400—Walter Payton, Jackson St., 1972-74 (59 TDs, 40 PATs, 2 FGs)

Career
464—Walter Payton, Jackson St., 1971-74 (66 TDs, 53 PATs, 5 FGs)

Most Points Scored Per Game

Season
21.0—Carl Herakovich, Rose-Hulman, 1958 (168 in 8)

Career
13.4—Ole Gunderson, St. Olaf, 1969-71 (362 in 27)

Most Touchdowns Scored

Game
8—Paul Zaeske, North Park vs. North Central, Oct. 12, 1968 (all on pass receptions); Junior Wolf, Panhandle St. vs. St. Mary (Kan.), Nov. 8, 1958 (all by rushing)

Season
29—Terry Metcalf, Long Beach St., 1971

Career
(3 yrs.) 62—Billy Johnson, Widener, 1971-73
(4 yrs.) 70—Johnny Bailey, Texas A&I, 1986-89

Most Touchdowns Scored Per Game

Season
3.1—Carl Herakovich, Rose-Hulman, 1958 (25 in 8)

Career
2.2—Billy Johnson, Widener, 1971-73 (62 in 28)

Most Touchdowns and Points Scored by a Freshman

Season
24 & 144—Shawn Graves, Wofford, 1989
Also holds per-game records at 2.2 & 13.1 (24 & 144 in 11)

Ole Gunderson scored 362 points in 27 games for St. Olaf from 1969 to 1971, a Division II career record 13.4 per game.

Most Touchdowns and Points Scored by a Quarterback

Season
24 & 144—Shawn Graves, Wofford, 1989
Per-game records—2.3 &13.8, Jeff Bentrim, North Dak. St., 1986 (23 & 138 in 10)

Career
64 & 386—Jeff Bentrim, North Dak. St., 1983-86
Also holds per-game records at 1.8 & 11.0 (64 & 386 in 35)

Most Touchdowns and Points Scored by Two Players, Same Team

Season
42 & 254—Heath Sherman (23 & 138) & Johnny Bailey (19 & 116), Texas A&I, 1986
Also hold per-game records at 3.8 & 23.1 (42 & 254 in 11)

3 Yrs
110 & 666—Heath Sherman (56 & 336) & Johnny Bailey (54 & 330), Texas A&I, 1986-88

Most Consecutive Games Scoring a Touchdown

Career
25—Billy Johnson, Widener, 1971-73

Most Field Goals Made

Game
6—Steve Huff, Central Mo. St. vs. Southeast Mo. St., Nov. 2, 1985 (37, 45, 37, 24, 32, 27 yards), 6 attempts

Season
20—Pat Beaty, North Dak., 1988 (26 attempts); Tom Jurich, Northern Ariz., 1977 (29 attempts)

Career
64—Mike Wood, Southeast Mo. St., 1974-77 (109 attempts)

Most Field Goals Made Per Game

Season
1.9—Dennis Hochman, Sonoma St., 1986 (19 in 10); Jaime Nunez, Weber St., 1971 (19 in 10)

Career
1.5—Mike Wood, Southeast Mo. St., 1974-77 (64 in 44)

Most Consecutive Field Goals Made

Career
14—Keith Kasnic, Tenn.-Martin, 1982-83; Kurt Seibel, South Dak., 1982-83

Longest Field Goal

67—Tom Odle, Fort Hays St. vs. Washburn, Nov. 5, 1988
Special reference: Ove Johannson, Abilene Christian (not an NCAA-member college at the time), kicked a 69-yard field goal against East Tex. St., Oct. 16, 1976

Most Field Goals Attempted

Game
7—Jim Turcotte, Mississippi Col. vs. Troy St., Oct. 3, 1981 (made 2)

Season
35—Mike Wood, Southeast Mo. St., 1977 (made 16)
Per-game record—3.3, Skipper Butler, Texas-Arlington, 1968 (33 in 10)

Career
109—Mike Wood, Southeast Mo. St., 1974-77 (made 64)
Per-game record—2.7, Jaime Nunez, Weber St., 1969-71 (83 in 31)

Highest Percentage of Field Goals Made

Season
(Min. 15 atts.) 88.2%—Howie Guarini, Shippensburg, 1990 (15 of 17); Kurt Seibel, South Dak., 1983 (15 of 17)
(Min. 20 atts.) 86.4%—Dennis Hochman, Sonoma St., 1986 (19 of 22)

Career
(Min. 35 made) 80.0%—Billy May, Clarion, 1977-80 (48 of 60)

Longest Return of a Missed Field Goal

100—Kalvin Simmons, Clark Atlanta vs. Morris Brown, Sept. 5, 1987 (actually from 6 yards in the end zone)

Most Extra Points Made by Kicking

Game
14—Art Anderson, North Park vs. North Central, Oct. 12, 1968 (attempted 15); Matt Johnson, Connecticut vs. Newport Naval Training, Oct. 22, 1949 (attempted 17)

Season
65—Miguel Sagaro, Grand Valley St., 1989 (attempted 66)

Career
156—James Jenkins, Pittsburg St., 1988-91 (attempted 179)

Most Extra Points Attempted by Kicking

Game
17—Matt Johnson, Connecticut vs. Newport Naval Training, Oct. 22, 1949 (made 14)

Season
74—Bill McFarland, Pacific (Cal.), 1949 (made 54)

Career
179—James Jenkins, Pittsburg St., 1988-91 (made 156)

Highest Percentage of Extra Points Made by Kicking

Season
(Min. 50 atts.) 100.0%—Bryan Thompson, Angelo St., 1989 (51 of 51); Dave Austinson, Northeast Mo. St., 1982 (50 of 50); Ken Blazei, North Dak. St., 1968 (50 of 50)

Career
(Min. 90 atts.) 98.9%—Mark DeMoss, Liberty, 1980-83 (92 of 93)
(Min. 100 atts.) 97.1%—Dan Worrell, Montana, 1968-71 (101 of 104)

Most Consecutive Extra Points Made by Kicking

Season
51—Bryan Thompson, Angelo St., 1989 (51 attempts)

Career
82—Mark DeMoss, Liberty, 1980-83

Most Points Scored by Kicking

Game
20—Clarence Joseph, Central St. (Ohio) vs. Kentucky St., Oct. 16, 1982 (5 FGs, 5 PATs)

Season
92—Tom Jurich, Northern Ariz., 1977 (20 FGs, 32 PATs)
Per-game record—8.8, Jay Masek, Chadron St., 1990 (88 in 10)

Career
266—Eddie Loretto, UC Davis, 1985-88 (46 FGs, 128 PATs)
Per-game record *(Min. 145 pts.)*—8.3, Dave Austinson, Northeast Mo. St., 1981-82 (149 in 18)
Per-game record *(Min. 175 pts.)*—6.65, Eddie Loretto, UC Davis, 1985-88 (266 in 40)

DEFENSIVE EXTRA POINTS

Most Defensive Extra Points Scored
Game and Season
1—Seven times. Most recent: Rob Greenwood (LB), North Dak. St. vs. Augustana (S.D.), Oct. 27, 1990 (70-yard blocked kick return)

TEAM RECORDS

SINGLE GAME—OFFENSE
TOTAL OFFENSE

Most Yards Gained
910—Hanover vs. Franklin, Oct. 30, 1948 (426 rushing, 484 passing; 75 plays)

Most Plays
117—Texas A&I vs. Angelo St., Oct. 30, 1982 (96 rushes, 21 passes; 546 yards)

Highest Average Gain Per Play
12.1—Hanover vs. Franklin, Oct. 30, 1948 (75 for 910)

Most Touchdowns Scored by Rushing and Passing
15—North Park vs. North Central, Oct. 12, 1968 (4 by rushing, 11 by passing)

Most Touchdowns Scored by Rushing and Passing, Both Teams
20—North Park (15) & North Central (5), Oct. 12, 1968

Most Yards Gained by a Losing Team
645—Texas A&I vs. West Tex. St., Nov. 1, 1986 (lost 49-54)

RUSHING

Most Yards Gained
719—Coe vs. Beloit, Oct. 16, 1971 (73 rushes)

Most Rushes
97—Hobart vs. Union (N.Y.), Oct. 23, 1971 (444 yards)

Highest Average Gain Per Rush
(Min. 50 rushes)
10.5—St. Olaf vs. Beloit, Nov. 8, 1969 (51 for 537)

Most Touchdowns Scored by Rushing
12—Coe vs. Beloit, Oct. 16, 1971

Most Players, One Team, Each Gaining
100 Yards or More
5—South Dak. vs. St. Cloud St., Nov. 1, 1986 (James Hambrick 125, Darryl Colvin 123, Tony Higgins 118, Dave Elle 109, Joe Longueville [QB] 106; team gained 581)

PASSING

Most Passes Attempted
76—Portland St. vs. Eastern Wash., Nov. 21, 1970 (completed 44)

Most Passes Attempted, Both Teams
121—Franklin (68) & Saginaw Valley (53), Sept. 22, 1984 (completed 63)

Most Passes Completed
44—Cal Lutheran vs. St. Mary's (Cal.), Nov. 22, 1986 (attempted 59); Portland St. vs. Eastern Wash., Nov. 21, 1970 (attempted 76)

Most Passes Completed, Both Teams
67—Indiana (Pa.) (34) & Lehigh (33), Sept. 14, 1985 (attempted 92)

Most Passes Had Intercepted
11—Hamline vs. Concordia-M'head, Nov. 5, 1955; Rhode Island vs. Brown, Oct. 8, 1949

Most Passes Attempted Without Interception
63—Hamline vs. St. John's (Minn.), Oct. 8, 1955 (completed 34)

Highest Percentage of Passes Completed
(Min. 20 atts.) 90.0%—Northwestern (La.) vs. Southwestern La., Nov. 12, 1966 (20 of 22)

Most Yards Gained
678—Portland St. vs. Eastern Mont., Nov. 20, 1976

Most Yards Gained, Both Teams
904—New Haven (455) & West Chester (449), Oct. 5, 1990

Most Touchdown Passes
11—North Park vs. North Central, Oct. 12, 1968

Most Touchdown Passes, Both Teams
14—North Park (11) & North Central (3), Oct. 12, 1968

PUNTING

Most Punts
32—Sam Houston St. vs. East Tex. St., Nov. 2, 1946 (1,203 yards)

Most Punts, Both Teams
63—Sam Houston St. (32) & East Tex. St. (31), Nov. 2, 1946

Highest Average Per Punt (Min. 5 punts)
57.5—Colorado Mines vs. Fort Lewis, Oct. 21, 1989 (8 for 460)

PUNT RETURNS

Most Yards on Punt Returns
265—Widener vs. St. John's (N.Y.), Sept. 23, 1972 (4 returns)

Most Touchdowns Scored on Punt Returns
3—Troy St. vs. Livingston, Sept. 29, 1979; Widener vs. St. John's (N.Y.), Sept. 23, 1972

SCORING

Most Points Scored
125—Connecticut vs. Newport Naval Training, Oct. 22, 1949

Most Points Scored Against a College Opponent
106—Fort Valley St. vs. Knoxville, Oct. 11, 1969 (14 TDs, 2 PATs, 9 two-point conversions, 1 safety)

Most Points Scored by a Losing Team
60—New Haven vs. Southern Conn. St. (64), Oct. 25, 1991

Most Points Scored, Both Teams
136—North Park (104) & North Central (32), Oct. 12, 1968

Most Points Scored in Two Consecutive Games
172—Tuskegee, 1966 (93-0 vs. Morehouse, Oct. 14; 79-0 vs. Lane, Oct. 22)

Most Touchdowns Scored
17—Connecticut vs. Newport Naval Training, Oct. 22, 1949

Most Touchdowns Scored Against a College Opponent
15—North Park vs. North Central, Oct. 12, 1968; Alcorn St. vs. Paul Quinn, Sept. 9, 1967;

Iowa Wesleyan vs. William Penn, Oct. 31, 1953

Most Points After Touchdowns Made by Kicking
14—North Park vs. North Central, Oct. 12, 1968 (attempted 15); Connecticut vs. Newport Naval Training, Oct. 22, 1949 (attempted 17)

Most Two-Point Attempts
11—Fort Valley St. vs. Knoxville, Oct. 11, 1969 (made 9)

Most Two-Point Attempts Made
9—Fort Valley St. vs. Knoxville, Oct. 11, 1969 (attempted 11)

Most Field Goals Made
6—Central Mo. St. vs. Southeast Mo. St., Nov. 2, 1985 (6 attempts)

Most Defensive Extra Points Scored
1—By seven teams. Most recent: North Dak. St. vs. Augustana (S.D.), Oct. 27, 1990 (70-yard blocked kick return)

Most Defensive Extra-Point Opportunities
2—North Dak. St. vs. Augustana (S.D.), Sept. 24, 1988 (2 interceptions; none scored)

FIRST DOWNS

Most Total First Downs
42—Delaware vs. Baldwin-Wallace, Oct. 6, 1973

Most First Downs by Penalty
14—La Verne vs. Northern Ariz., Oct. 11, 1958

Most Total First Downs, Both Teams
66—North Dak. (36) & Texas A&I (30), Sept. 13, 1986; Ferris St. (33) & Northwood (33), Oct. 26, 1985

PENALTIES

Most Penalties
28—Northern Ariz. vs. La Verne, Oct. 11, 1958 (155 yards)

Most Penalties, Both Teams
42—N.C. Central (23) & St. Paul's (19), Sept. 13, 1986 (453 yards)

Most Yards Penalized
293—Cal Poly SLO vs. Portland St., Oct. 31, 1981 (26 penalties)

Most Yards Penalized, Both Teams
453—N.C. Central (256) & St. Paul's (197), Sept. 13, 1986 (42 penalties)

FUMBLES

Most Fumbles
16—Carthage vs. North Park, Nov. 14, 1970 (lost 7)

SINGLE GAME—DEFENSE
TOTAL DEFENSE

Fewest Total Offense Plays Allowed
29—North Park vs. Concordia (Ill.), Sept. 26, 1964

Fewest Total Offense Yards Allowed
Minus 55—San Diego St. vs. U.S. Int'l, Nov. 27, 1965 (59 plays)

Fewest Rushes Allowed
7—Indianapolis vs. Valparaiso, Oct. 30, 1982 (-57 yards)

Fewest Rushing Yards Allowed
Minus 95—San Diego St. vs. U.S. Int'l, Nov. 27, 1965 (35 plays)

Fewest Pass Completions Allowed
0—By many teams. Most recent: Livingston vs. Jacksonville St., Nov. 12, 1988 (3 attempts)

Fewest Passing Yards Allowed
Minus 19—Ashland vs. Heidelberg, Sept. 25, 1948 (4 completions)

Most Times an Opponent Tackled for
Loss Attempting to Pass
  19—Southern Conn. St. vs. Albany (N.Y.), Oct.
  6, 1984

PUNTING

Most Opponents' Punts Blocked By
  5—Winston-Salem vs. N.C. Central, Oct. 4,
  1986; Southeastern La. vs. Troy St., Oct. 7,
  1978 (holds record for most consecutive
  punts blocked with 4)

INTERCEPTIONS

Most Passes Intercepted By
  11—St. Cloud St. vs. Bemidji St., Oct. 31, 1970
  (45 attempts); Concordia-M'head vs. Hamline, Nov. 5, 1955 (37 attempts)

Most Touchdowns on Interception Returns
  3—By many teams. Most recent: Fort Valley St.
  vs. North Ala., Oct. 12, 1991

SEASON—OFFENSE
TOTAL OFFENSE

Most Yards Gained Per Game
  624.1—Hanover, 1948 (4,993 in 8)

Most Yards Gained
  5,969—Texas A&I, 1986 (899 plays, 11 games)

Highest Average Gain Per Play
  9.20—Hanover, 1948 (543 for 4,993)

Highest Average Gain Per Play
(Min. 800 plays)
  6.64—Texas A&I, 1986 (899 for 5,969)

Most Plays Per Game
  88.7—Cal St. Chico, 1967 (887 in 10)

RUSHING

Most Yards Gained Per Game
  404.7—Col. of Emporia, 1954 (3,643 in 9)

Most Yards Gained
  4,347—Texas A&I, 1986 (689 rushes, 11 games)

Highest Average Gain Per Rush
  8.38—Hanover, 1948 (382 for 3,203)

Highest Average Gain Per Rush
(Min. 500 rushes)
  7.07—William Jewell, 1952 (537 for 3,795)

Highest Average Gain Per Rush
(Min. 600 rushes)
  6.31—Texas A&I, 1986 (689 for 4,347)

Most Rushes Per Game
  78.9—Panhandle St., 1963 (789 in 10)

PASSING

Most Yards Gained Per Game
  404.1—Portland St., 1976 (4,445 in 11)

Highest Average Gain Per Attempt
  (Min. 175 atts.) 10.8—Western St., 1991 (330 for
  3,574)

Highest Average Gain Per Completion
  (Min. 100 comps.) 19.4—Calif. (Pa.), 1966 (116
  for 2,255)
  (Min. 200 comps.) 17.6—Western St., 1991 (203
  for 3,574)

Most Passes Attempted Per Game
  51.8—Portland St., 1970 (518 in 10)

Most Passes Completed Per Game
  29.9—West Tex. St., 1986 (329 in 11)

Fewest Passes Completed Per Game
  0.4—Hobart, 1971 (4 in 9)

Highest Percentage Completed
  (Min. 200 atts.) 70.2%—UC Davis, 1986 (226 of
  322)
  (Min. 350 atts.) 65.3%—Northern Ill., 1962 (237
  of 363)

Lowest Percentage of Passes
Had Intercepted
  (Min. 275 atts.) 1.34%—UC Davis, 1988 (4 of
  298)

Most Touchdown Passes Per Game
  4.9—San Fran. St., 1967 (49 in 10)

Highest Passing Efficiency Rating Points
  (Min. 200 atts.) 183.8—Wittenberg, 1963 (216
  attempts, 138 completions, 10 interceptions,
  2,457 yards, 22 TDs)
  (Min. 300 atts.) 180.2—Western St., 1991 (330
  attempts, 203 completions, 12 interceptions,
  3,574 yards, 35 TDs)

PUNTING

Most Punts Per Game
  10.0—Wash. & Lee, 1968 (90 in 9)

Fewest Punts Per Game
  1.9—Kent, 1954 (17 in 9)

Highest Punting Average
  48.0—Adams St., 1966 (36 for 1,728)

190

PUNT RETURNS

Most Punt Returns
64—UC Davis, 1984 (557 yards)

Most Touchdowns Scored on Punt Returns
4—Eastern N. Mex., 1991; Mississippi Col., 1984; Widener, 1972

KICKOFF RETURNS

Most Kickoff Returns
70—Wayne St. (Neb.), 1988 (926 yards)

SCORING

Most Points Per Game
54.7—Florida A&M, 1961 (492 in 9)

Most Touchdowns Per Game
7.7—Pacific (Cal.), 1949 (85 in 11)

**Most Consecutive Extra Points
Made by Kicking**
51—Angelo St., 1989

Most Consecutive Field Goals Made
13—UC Davis, 1976

Most Two-Point Attempts Per Game
6.8—Florida A&M, 1961 (61 in 9, scored 69 TDs)

Most Two-Point Attempts Made Per Game
3.6—Florida A&M, 1961 (32 in 9, attempted 61)

Most Field Goals Made
20—North Dak., 1988 (attempted 26); Northern Ariz., 1977 (attempted 29)

Most Defensive Extra Points Scored
1—North Dak. St., 1990; Central Okla., 1989; Jacksonville St., 1989; New Haven, 1989; Colorado Mines, 1988; Springfield, 1988; Norfolk St., 1988; West Chester, 1988

Most Defensive Extra-Point Opportunities
3—Central Okla., 1989 (2 blocked kick returns, 1 interception; one scored); Northern Colo., 1988 (2 blocked kick returns, 1 interception; none scored)

PENALTIES

Most Penalties Against
143—N.C. Central, 1986 (1,288 yards)
Also holds per-game record at 14.3 (143 in 10)

Most Yards Penalized
1,356—Hampton, 1977 (124 penalties, 11 games)

TURNOVERS (GIVEAWAYS) (From 1985)
(Passes Had Intercepted and Fumbles Lost)

Fewest Turnovers
9—North Dak. St., 1991 (1 interception, 8 fumbles lost)

Fewest Turnovers Per Game
1.0—North Dak. St., 1991 (9 in 9)

Most Turnovers
61—Cheyney, 1990 (36 interceptions, 25 fumbles lost)

Most Turnovers Per Game
5.8—Livingstone, 1986 (58 in 10)

SEASON—DEFENSE
TOTAL DEFENSE

Fewest Yards Allowed Per Game
44.4—John Carroll, 1962 (311 in 7)

Lowest Average Yards Allowed Per Play
1.0—John Carroll, 1962 (310 for 311 yards)

**Lowest Average Yards Allowed Per Play
(Min. 500 plays)**
1.51—Tennessee St., 1966 (511 for 771)

**Lowest Average Yards Allowed Per Play
(Min. 600 plays)**
1.81—Alcorn St., 1976 (603 for 1,089)

**Fewest Rushing and Passing Touchdowns
Allowed Per Game**
0.0—Albany St. (Ga.), 1960 (0 in 9)

RUSHING DEFENSE

Fewest Yards Allowed Per Game
Minus 16.7—Tennessee St., 1967 (-150 in 9)

Lowest Average Yards Allowed Per Rush
Minus 0.5—Tennessee St., 1967 (296 for -150 yards)

**Lowest Average Yards Allowed Per Rush
(Min. 325 rushes)**
0.41—Merchant Marine, 1969 (359 for 146)

**Lowest Average Yards Allowed Per Rush
(Min. 400 rushes)**
1.25—Luther, 1971 (414 for 518)

PASS DEFENSE

Fewest Yards Allowed Per Game
10.1—Ashland, 1948 (91 in 9)

Fewest Yards Allowed Per Attempt
(Min. 200 atts.) 3.07—Virginia St., 1971 (205 for

630)
(Min. 300 atts.) 3.16—Southwest Mo. St., 1966 (315 for 996)

Fewest Yards Allowed Per Completion
  (Min. 100 comps.) 8.78—Long Beach St., 1965
  (144 for 1,264)

Lowest Completion Percentage Allowed
  (Min. 250 atts.) 24.1%—Southwest Mo. St.,
  1966 (76 of 315)

Most Passes Intercepted By Per Game
  3.9—Whitworth, 1959 (35 in 9); Delaware, 1946
  (35 in 9)

Fewest Passes Intercepted By
  (Min. 150 atts.) 1—Gettysburg, 1972 (175 attempts; 0 yards returned)

Highest Percentage Intercepted By
  (Min. 150 atts.) 21.7%—Stephen F. Austin, 1949
  (35 of 161)
  (Min. 275 atts.) 11.8%—Missouri-Rolla, 1978
  (35 of 297)

Most Touchdowns on Interception Returns
  7—Fort Valley St., 1991 (15 interceptions);
  Virginia Union, 1986 (31 interceptions)

**Lowest Passing Efficiency Rating Points
by Opponents**
  (Min. 250 atts.) 41.7—Fort Valley St., 1985
  (allowed 283 attempts, 90 completions, 1,039
  yards, 2 TDs and intercepted 33)

BLOCKED KICKS

Most Blocked Kicks
  27—Winston-Salem, 1986 (16 punts, 7 field
  goal attempts, 4 point-after-touchdown kicks)

SCORING

Fewest Points Allowed Per Game
  0.0—Albany St. (Ga.), 1960 (0 in 9 games)

Most Points Allowed Per Game
  64.5—Rose-Hulman, 1961 (516 in 8)

Most Defensive Extra-Point Opportunities
  3—Central Okla., 1989 (2 blocked kick returns,
  1 interception; one scored); Northern Colo.,
  1988 (2 blocked kick returns, 1 interception;
  none scored)

TURNOVERS (TAKEAWAYS) (From 1985)
(Opponents' Passes Intercepted and Fumbles Recovered)

**Highest Margin of Turnovers Per Game
Over Opponents**
  2.5—North Ala., 1990 (plus 25 in 10; 14 giveaways vs. 39 takeaways); St. Joseph's (Ind.),
  1986 (plus 25 in 10; 18 giveaways vs. 43
  takeaways)

Most Opponents' Turnovers Per Game
  4.73—East Tex. St., 1990 (52 in 11)

Most Opponents' Turnovers
  52—East Tex. St., 1990 (31 interceptions, 21
  fumble recoveries)

ADDITIONAL RECORDS

Most Consecutive Victories
  41—Missouri Valley, 1941-48 (did not field
  teams during 1943-45)
  Special reference: Texas A&I, from Nov. 17,
  1973, through Oct. 1, 1977 (a period during
  which it was not an NCAA-member college),
  won 42 consecutive games. The streak ended
  Oct. 8, 1977, with a 25-25 tie vs. Abilene
  Christian

Most Consecutive Games Unbeaten (From 1946)
  38—Doane, 1965-70 (2 ties)
  Special reference: Texas A&I, from Nov. 17,
  1973, through Oct. 29, 1977 (a period during
  which it was not an NCAA-member college),
  was unbeaten during 46 games (including
  one tie). The streak ended Nov. 5, 1977, with
  a 7-6 loss to East Tex. St.

**Most Consecutive Games Without
Being Shut Out**
  178—North Dak. (from Oct. 7, 1967, through
  Nov. 10, 1984; ended with 41-0 loss to Northern Ariz., Aug. 31, 1985)

Most Points Overcome to Win a Game
  27—New Haven (58) vs. West Chester (57),
  Oct. 5, 1990 (trailed 24-51 with 5:51 remaining
  in 3rd quarter)

Most Consecutive Losses
  39—St. Paul's, 1948-53

Most Consecutive Games Without a Victory
  49—Paine, 1954-61 (1 tie)

Most Consecutive Games Without a Tie
  329—West Chester (from Oct. 26, 1945, to Oct.
  31, 1980; ended with 24-24 tie vs. Cheyney,
  Nov. 8, 1980)

Most Tie Games in a Season
  5—Wofford, 1948 (consecutive)

Highest-Scoring Tie Game
  43-43—Trinity (Conn.) & Rensselaer, Oct. 11,
  1969

**Most Consecutive Quarters Without
Yielding a Rushing Touchdown**
  51—Butler (from Sept. 25, 1982, to Oct. 15,
  1983)

**Most Consecutive Point-After-Touchdown
Kicks Made**
  123—Liberty (1978-83)

Most Improved Won-Lost Record
  11 games—Northern Mich., 1975 (13-1-0),
  including 3 Division II playoff victories, from
  1974 (0-10-0)

TOTAL OFFENSE

Career Yards

Player, Team	Years	Plays	Yards
Earl Harvey, N.C. Central	1985-88	*2,045	*10,667
Sam Mannery, Calif. (Pa.)	1987-90	1,669	9,125
Steward Perez, Chadron St.	1988-91	1,072	8,443
Jim Lindsey, Abilene Christian	1967-70	1,510	8,385
Dave Walter, Michigan Tech	1983-86	1,660	8,345
Maurice Heard, Tuskegee	1988-91	1,289	8,321
Jack Hull, Grand Valley St.	1988-91	1,196	8,221
Doug Williams, Grambling	1974-77	1,072	8,195
Dave DenBraber, Ferris St.	1984-87	1,522	8,115
Tracy Kendall, Alabama A&M	1988-91	1,480	8,112
Ned Cox, Angelo St.	1983-86	1,831	8,097
Steve Wray, Franklin	1978-82	1,370	7,606
Carl Wright, Virginia Union	1989-91	1,104	7,517
John Schultz, Augustana (S.D.)	1982-85	1,328	7,474
Tom Nelson, St. Cloud St.	1980-83	1,421	7,430
Donald Smith, Langston	1958-61	998	7,376
Tom Bonds, Cal Lutheran	1984-87	1,439	7,374
Al Niemela, West Chester	1985-88	1,259	7,359
Loyal Proffitt, Abilene Christian	1981-84	1,418	7,337
Pat Brennan, Franklin	1981-84	1,286	7,316
Chris Crawford, Portland St.	1985-88	1,178	7,310
Ted Wahl, South Dak. St.	1985-88	1,172	7,253
Scott Butler, Delta St.	1981-84	1,358	7,229
Bruce Upstill, Col. of Emporia	1960-63	922	7,122
Mike Houston, St. Joseph's (Ind.)	1978-81	1,298	7,104

* Record.

Season Yards

Player, Team	Year	Games	Plays	Yards
Chris Hegg, Northeast Mo. St.	†1985	11	*594	*3,782
Tod Mayfield, West Tex. St.	†1986	11	555	3,533
Rob Tomlinson, Cal St. Chico	†1989	10	533	3,504
June Jones, Portland St.	†1976	11	465	3,463
Bob Toledo, San Fran. St.	†1967	10	409	3,407
Jayson Merrill, Western St.	†1991	10	337	3,400
Richard Strasser, San Fran. St.	1985	10	536	3,259
Pat Brennan, Franklin	†1984	10	583	3,248
Pat Brennan, Franklin	†1983	10	524	3,239
Phil Basso, Liberty	1984	11	456	3,227
Andy Breault, Kutztown	†1990	11	562	3,173
Jim McMillan, Boise St.	†1974	10	403	3,101
Tracy Kendall, Alabama A&M	1989	11	451	3,079
Darin Slack, Central Fla.	1987	11	491	3,037
Dan Koster, Southwest St. (Minn.)	1983	11	567	3,032
Earl Harvey, N.C. Central	1985	10	538	3,008
Jim Zorn, Cal Poly Pomona	†1973	11	499	3,000

* Record. † National champion.

Single-Game Yards

Yds.	Player, Team (Opponent)	Date
584	Tracy Kendall, Alabama A&M (Clark Atlanta)	Nov. 4, 1989
571	John Charles, Portland St. (Cal Poly SLO)	Nov. 16, 1991
562	Bob Toledo, San Fran. St. (Cal St. Hayward)	Oct. 21, 1967
555	A. J. Vaughn, Wayne St., Mich. (Wis.-Milwaukee)	Sept. 30, 1967
536	Earl Harvey, N.C. Central (Jackson St.)	Aug. 30, 1986
528	Rob Tomlinson, Cal St. Chico (Southern Conn. St.)	Oct. 7, 1989
526	Dwayne Butler, Dist. Columbia (Central St., Ohio)	Nov. 20, 1982
526	Dennis Shaw, San Diego St. (Southern Miss.)	Nov. 9, 1968
519	Maurice Heard, Tuskegee (Alabama A&M)	Nov. 10, 1990
517	Jeff Petrucci, Calif., Pa. (Edinboro)	Nov. 9, 1968
506	Kurt Otto, North Dak. (Texas A&I)	Sept. 13, 1986
505	Jim Zorn, Cal Poly Pomona (Southern Utah)	Sept. 14, 1974

Career Yards Per Game

Player, Team	Years	Games	Plays	Yards	Yd. PG
Jayson Merrill, Western St.	1990-91	20	641	5,619	*281.0
Chris Petersen, UC Davis	1985-86	20	735	5,532	276.6
Tim Von Dulm, Portland St.	1969-70	20	989	5,501	275.1
Earl Harvey, N.C. Central	1985-88	41	*2,045	*10,667	260.2
Chris Hegg, Northeast Mo. St.	‡1982, 84-85	21	932	5,412	257.7
Jim Zorn, Cal Poly Pomona	1973-74	21	946	5,364	255.4
Pat Brennan, Franklin	1981-84	30	1,286	7,316	243.9
June Jones, Hawaii/Portland St.	1974, 75-76	23	760	5,601	243.5
Carl Wright, Virginia Union	1989-91	31	1,104	7,517	242.5
Steve Wray, Franklin	1978-82	32	1,370	7,606	237.7
Jim Lindsey, Abilene Christian	1967-70	36	1,510	8,385	232.9

* Record. ‡ Played in one game at Northern Iowa in 1982.

Season Yards Per Game

Player, Team	Year	Games	Plays	Yards	Yd. PG
Rob Tomlinson, Cal St. Chico	†1989	10	533	3,504	*350.4
Chris Hegg, Northeast Mo. St.	†1985	11	*594	*3,782	343.8
Bob Toledo, San Fran. St.	†1967	10	409	3,407	340.7
Jayson Merrill, Western St.	†1991	10	337	3,400	340.0
George Bork, Northern Ill.	†1963	9	413	2,945	327.2
Richard Strasser, San Fran. St.	1985	10	536	3,259	325.9
Pat Brennan, Franklin	†1984	10	583	3,248	324.8
Pat Brennan, Franklin	†1983	10	524	3,239	323.9
Tod Mayfield, West Tex. St.	†1986	11	555	3,533	321.2
June Jones, Portland St.	†1976	11	465	3,463	314.8
Jim McMillan, Boise St.	†1974	10	403	3,101	310.1

* Record. † National champion.

Annual Champions

Year	Player, Team	Class	Plays	Yards
1946	Buster Dixon, Abilene Christian	Sr.	170	960
1947	Jim Peterson, Hanover	So.	108	1,449
1948	Jim Peterson, Hanover	Jr.	130	1,589
1949	Connie Callahan, Morningside	Sr.	311	2,006
1950	Bob Heimerdinger, Northern Ill.	Jr.	286	1,782
1951	Bob Heimerdinger, Northern Ill.	Sr.	292	1,775
1952	Don Gottlob, Sam Houston St.	Sr.	303	2,470
1953	Ralph Capitani, Northern Iowa	Jr.	317	1,755
1954	Bill Engelhardt, Nebraska-Omaha	So.	243	1,645
1955	Jim Stehlin, Brandeis	Sr.	222	1,455
1956	Dick Jamieson, Bradley	So.	240	1,925
1957	Stan Jackson, Cal Poly Pomona	Jr.	301	2,145
1958	Stan Jackson, Cal Poly Pomona	Sr.	334	2,478
1959	Gary Campbell, Whittier	Sr.	309	2,383
1960	Charles Miller, Austin	Sr.	287	1,966
1961	Denny Spurlock, Whitworth	Sr.	224	1,684
1962	George Bork, Northern Ill.	Jr.	397	2,398
1963	George Bork, Northern Ill.	Sr.	413	2,945
1964	Jerry Bishop, Austin	Jr.	332	2,152
1965	Ron Christian, Northern Ill.	Sr.	377	2,307
1966	Joe Stetser, Cal St. Chico	Jr.	406	2,382
1967	Bob Toledo, San Fran. St.	Sr.	409	3,407
1968	Terry Bradshaw, Louisiana Tech	Jr.	426	2,987
1969	Tim Von Dulm, Portland St.	Jr.	462	2,736

Beginning in 1970, ranked on per-game (instead of total) yards

Year	Player, Team	Cl.	G	Plays	Yards	Avg.
1970	Jim Lindsey, Abilene Christian	Sr.	9	440	2,654	294.9
1971	Randy Mattingly, Evansville	Jr.	9	402	2,234	248.2
1972	Bob Biggs, UC Davis	Sr.	9	381	2,356	261.8
1973	Jim Zorn, Cal Poly Pomona	Jr.	11	499	3,000	272.7
1974	Jim McMillan, Boise St.	Sr.	10	403	3,101	310.1
1975	Lynn Hieber, Indiana (Pa.)	Sr.	10	402	2,503	250.3
1976	June Jones, Portland St.	Sr.	11	465	3,463	314.8
1977	Steve Mariucci, Northern Mich.	Sr.	8	270	1,780	222.5
1978	Charlie Thompson, Western St.	Jr.	9	304	2,138	237.6
1979	Phil Kessel, Northern Mich.	Jr.	9	368	2,164	240.4
1980	Curt Strasheim, Southwest St. (Minn.)	Jr.	10	501	2,565	256.5
1981	Steve Wray, Franklin	Jr.	10	488	2,726	272.6

Year	Player, Team	Cl.	G	Plays	Yards	Avg.
1982	Steve Wray, Franklin	Sr.	8	382	2,114	264.3
1983	Pat Brennan, Franklin	Jr.	10	524	3,239	323.9
1984	Pat Brennan, Franklin	Sr.	10	583	3,248	324.8
1985	Chris Hegg, Northeast Mo. St.	Sr.	11	*594	*3,782	343.8
1986	Tod Mayfield, West Tex. St.	Sr.	11	555	3,533	312.2
1987	Randy Hobson, Evansville	Sr.	10	457	2,964	296.4
1988	Mark Sedinger, Northern Colo.	Sr.	10	413	2,828	282.8
1989	Rob Tomlinson, Cal St. Chico	So.	10	533	3,504	*350.4
1990	Andy Breault, Kutztown	Jr.	11	562	3,173	288.5
1991	Jayson Merrill, Western St.	Sr.	10	337	3,400	340.0

* Record.

RUSHING

Career Yards

Player, Team	Years	Plays	Yards	Avg.
Johnny Bailey, Texas A&I	1986-89	885	*6,320	7.14
Chris Cobb, Eastern Ill.	1976-79	930	5,042	5.42
Harry Jackson, St. Cloud St.	1986-89	915	4,890	5.34
Jerry Linton, Panhandle St.	1959-62	648	4,839	7.47
Jim VanWagner, Michigan Tech	1973-76	958	4,788	5.00
Heath Sherman, Texas A&I	1985-88	804	4,654	5.79
Steve Roberts, Butler	1986-89	1,026	4,623	4.51
Don Aleksiewicz, Hobart	1969-72	819	4,525	5.53
Dale Mills, Northeast Mo. St.	1957-60	751	4,502	5.99
Leo Lewis, Lincoln (Mo.)	1951-54	623	4,458	7.16
Bernie Peeters, Luther	1968-71	*1,072	4,435	4.14
Larry Schreiber, Tennessee Tech	1966-69	878	4,421	5.04
Brad Rowland, McMurry	1947-50	683	4,347	6.36
Vincent Allen, Indiana St.	1973-75, 77	832	4,335	5.21
Bill Rhodes, Western St.	1953-56	506	4,294	*8.49
Lem Harkey, Col. of Emporia	1951-54	502	4,232	8.43
Curtis Delgardo, Portland St.	1987-90	703	4,178	5.94
Ricke Stonewall, Millersville	1981-84	648	4,169	6.43

* Record.

Season Yards

Player, Team	Year	Games	Plays	Yards	Avg.
Johnny Bailey, Texas A&I	†1986	11	271	*2,011	7.42
Zed Robinson, Southern Utah	1991	11	254	1,828	7.20
Jim Holder, Panhandle St.	†1963	10	275	1,775	6.45
Mike Thomas, Nevada-Las Vegas	†1973	11	274	1,741	6.35
Terry Metcalf, Long Beach St.	1971	12	273	1,673	6.13
Troy Mills, Cal St. Sacramento	1991	10	223	1,668	7.48
Leon Burns, Long Beach St.	†1969	11	*350	1,659	4.74
Chad Guthrie, Northeast Mo. St.	1991	11	302	1,649	5.46
Bob White, Western N. Mex.	†1951	9	202	1,643	8.13
Don Aleksiewicz, Hobart	†1971	9	276	1,616	5.86

* Record.   † National champion.

Single-Game Yards

Yds.	Player, Team (Opponent)	Date
382	Kelly Ellis, Northern Iowa (Western Ill.)	Oct. 13, 1979
373	Dallas Garber, Marietta (Wash. & Jeff.)	Nov. 7, 1959
370	Jim Baier, Wis.-River Falls (Wis.-Stevens Point)	Nov. 5, 1966
370	Jim Hissam, Marietta (Bethany, W. Va.)	Nov. 15, 1958
367	Don Polkinghorne, Washington, Mo. (Wash. & Lee)	Nov. 23, 1957
363	Richie Weaver, Widener (Moravian)	Oct. 17, 1970
356	Ole Gunderson, St. Olaf (Monmouth, Ill.)	Oct. 11, 1969
350	Ricke Stonewall, Millersville (New Haven)	Nov. 13, 1982
343	Zed Robinson, Southern Utah (Santa Clara)	Oct. 12, 1991
343	Jesse Lakes, Central Mich. (Wis.-Milwaukee)	Sept. 27, 1969
337	Harry Jackson, St. Cloud St. (South Dak.)	Nov. 4, 1989
327	Bill Rhodes, Western St. (Adams St.)	Oct. 20, 1956
323	Shawn Graves, Wofford (Lenoir-Rhyne)	Sept. 15, 1990
323	Gary Nelson, Wartburg (Buena Vista)	Oct. 26, 1968
322	Jimmy Smith, Northern Ariz. (Cal St. Northridge)	Oct. 27, 1973

Career Yards Per Game

Player, Team	Years	Games	Plays	Yards	Yd. PG
Johnny Bailey, Texas A&I	1986-89	39	885	*6,320	*162.1
Ole Gunderson, St. Olaf	1969-71	27	639	4,060	150.4
Brad Hustad, Luther	1957-59	27	655	3,943	146.0
Joe Iacone, West Chester	1960-62	27	565	3,767	139.5
Billy Johnson, Widener	1971-73	28	411	3,737	133.5
Don Aleksiewicz, Hobart	1969-72	34	819	4,525	133.1
Jim VanWagner, Michigan Tech	1973-76	36	958	4,788	133.0
Steve Roberts, Butler	1986-89	35	1,026	4,623	132.1

* Record.

Season Yards Per Game

Player, Team	Year	Games	Plays	Yards	TD	Yd. PG
Johnny Bailey, Texas A&I	†1986	11	271	*2,011	18	*182.8
Bob White, Western N. Mex.	†1951	9	202	1,643	20	182.6
Kevin Mitchell, Saginaw Valley	†1989	8	236	1,460	6	182.5
Don Aleksiewicz, Hobart	†1971	9	276	1,616	19	179.6
Jim Holder, Panhandle St.	†1963	10	275	1,775	9	177.5
Jim Baier, Wis.-River Falls	†1966	9	240	1,587	17	176.3
Billy Johnson, Widener	†1972	9	148	1,556	23	172.9
Hank Treesh, Hanover	†1948	8	100	1,383	17	172.9
Dave Kiarsis, Trinity (Conn.)	†1970	8	201	1,374	10	171.8

* Record.   † National champion.

Annual Champions

Year	Player, Team	Class	Plays	Yards
1946	V. T. Smith, Abilene Christian	So.	99	733
1947	John Williams, Jacksonville St.	Jr.	150	931
1948	Hank Treesh, Hanover	Jr.	100	1,383
1949	Odie Posey, Southern-B.R.	Jr.	121	1,399
1950	Meriel Michelson, Eastern Wash.	Sr.	180	1,234
1951	Bob White, Western N. Mex.	Jr.	202	1,643
1952	Al Conway, William Jewell	Sr.	134	1,325
1953	Elroy Payne, McMurry	So.	183	1,274
1954	Lem Harkey, Col. of Emporia	Sr.	121	1,146
1955	Gene Scott, Centre	Sr.	107	1,138
1956	Bill Rhodes, Western St.	Sr.	130	1,200
1957	Brad Hustad, Luther	So.	219	1,401
1958	Dale Mills, Northeast Mo. St.	So.	186	1,358
1959	Dale Mills, Northeast Mo. St.	Jr.	248	1,385
1960	Joe Iacone, West Chester	So.	199	1,438
1961	Bobby Lisa, St. Mary (Kan.)	Jr.	156	1,082
1962	Jerry Linton, Panhandle St.	Sr.	272	1,483
1963	Jim Holder, Panhandle St.	Sr.	275	1,775
1964	Jim Allison, San Diego St.	Sr.	174	1,186
1965	Allen Smith, Findlay	Jr.	207	1,240
1966	Jim Baier, Wis.-River Falls	Sr.	240	1,587
1967	Dickie Moore, Western Ky.	Jr.	208	1,444
1968	Howard Stevens, Randolph-Macon	Fr.	191	1,468
1969	Leon Burns, Long Beach St.	Jr.	*350	1,659

Beginning in 1970, ranked on per-game (instead of total) yards

Year	Player, Team	Cl.	G	Plays	Yards	Avg.
1970	Dave Kiarsis, Trinity (Conn.)	Sr.	8	201	1,374	171.8
1971	Don Aleksiewicz, Hobart	Jr.	9	276	1,616	179.6
1972	Billy Johnson, Widener	So.	9	148	1,556	172.9
1973	Mike Thomas, Nevada-Las Vegas	Jr.	11	274	1,741	158.3
1974	Jim VanWagner, Michigan Tech	So.	9	246	1,453	161.4
1975	Jim VanWagner, Michigan Tech	Jr.	9	289	1,331	147.9
1976	Ted McKnight, Minn.-Duluth	Sr.	10	220	1,482	148.2
1977	Bill Burnham, New Hampshire	Sr.	10	281	1,422	142.2
1978	Mike Harris, Northeast Mo. St.	Sr.	11	329	1,598	145.3
1979	Chris Cobb, Eastern Ill.	Sr.	11	293	1,609	146.3
1980	Louis Jackson, Cal Poly SLO	Sr.	10	287	1,424	142.4
1981	Rick Porter, Slippery Rock	Sr.	9	208	1,179	131.0
1982	Ricke Stonewall, Millersville	So.	10	191	1,387	138.7
1983	Mark Corbin, Central St. (Ohio)	So.	10	208	1,502	150.2
1984	Charles Sanders, Slippery Rock	Jr.	10	269	1,280	128.0
1985	Dan Sonnek, South Dak. St.	So.	11	303	1,518	138.0
1986	Johnny Bailey, Texas A&I	Fr.	11	271	*2,011	*182.8

Year	Player, Team	Cl.	G	Plays	Yards	Avg.
1987	Johnny Bailey, Texas A&I	So.	10	217	1,598	159.8
1988	Johnny Bailey, Texas A&I	Jr.	10	229	1,442	144.2
1989	Kevin Mitchell, Saginaw Valley	Jr.	8	236	1,460	182.5
1990	David Jones, Chadron St.	Sr.	10	225	1,570	157.0
1991	Quincy Tillmon, Emporia St.	So.	9	259	1,544	171.6

* Record.

PASSING

Career Passing Efficiency
(Min. 375 Completions)

Player, Team	Years	Att.	Cmp.	Int.	Pct.	Yds.	TD	Pts.
Chris Petersen, UC Davis	1985-86	553	385	13	*.696	4,988	39	*164.0
Jim McMillan, Boise St.	1971-74	640	382	29	.597	5,508	58	152.8
Jack Hull, Grand Valley St.	1988-91	835	485	22	.581	7,120	64	149.7
Bruce Upstill, Col. of Emporia	1960-63	769	438	36	.570	6,935	48	144.0
George Bork, Northern Ill.	1960-63	902	577	33	.640	6,782	60	141.8
Steve Mariucci, Northern Mich.	1974-77	678	380	33	.561	6,022	41	140.9
Scott Barry, UC Davis	1982-84	588	377	16	.641	4,421	33	140.4
June Jones, Hawaii/Portland St.	1974, 75-76	666	376	35	.565	5,809	41	139.5
Doug Williams, Grambling	1974-77	1,009	484	52	.480	8,411	*93	138.1
Chris Crawford, Portland St.	1985-88	954	588	35	.616	7,543	48	137.3
Dan Miles, Southern Ore.	1964-67	871	577	56	.662	6,531	52	136.1
Al Niemela, West Chester	1985-88	1,063	600	36	.564	7,853	73	134.4
Steward Perez, Chadron St.	1988-91	1,015	565	60	.557	8,186	69	134.0
Denny Spurlock, Whitworth	1958-61	723	388	48	.537	5,526	63	133.4
Jeff Tisdel, Nevada	1974-77	776	394	34	.508	6,098	59	133.1

* Record.

Season Passing Efficiency
(Minimum 15 Attempts Per Game)

Player, Team	Year	G	Att.	Cmp.	Int.	Pct.	Yds.	TD	Pts.
Boyd Crawford, Col. of Idaho	†1953	8	120	72	6	.600	1,462	21	*210.1
Chuck Green, Wittenberg	†1963	9	182	114	8	.626	2,181	19	189.0
Jayson Merrill, Western St.	†1991	10	309	195	11	.631	3,484	35	187.9
Jim Feely, Johns Hopkins	†1967	7	110	69	5	.627	1,264	12	186.2
John Charles, Portland St.	1991	11	247	147	7	.595	2,619	32	185.5
Jim Peterson, Hanover	†1948	8	125	81	12	.648	1,571	12	182.9
John Wristen, Southern Colo.	†1982	8	121	68	2	.562	1,358	13	182.5
Richard Basil, Savannah St.	†1989	9	211	120	7	.569	2,148	29	180.9
Jim Cahoon, Ripon	†1964	8	127	74	7	.583	1,206	19	176.4
Tony Aliucci, Indiana (Pa.)	†1990	10	181	111	10	.613	1,801	21	172.0
John Costello, Widener	†1956	9	149	74	10	.497	1,702	17	169.8
Chris Petersen, UC Davis	†1985	10	242	167	6	.690	2,366	17	169.4
Mike Rieker, Lehigh	†1977	11	230	137	14	.596	2,431	23	169.2
Steve Michuta, Grand Valley St.	†1981	8	173	114	11	.659	1,702	17	168.3
James Armendariz, Southern Utah ..	1991	11	184	109	5	.592	1,839	17	168.0
Mitch Nicholson, Winston-Salem ...	1990	11	171	85	5	.497	1,651	22	167.2
Dave Alfaro, Santa Clara	†1979	9	168	110	9	.655	1,721	13	166.3

* Record. † National champion.

Annual Passing Efficiency Leaders
(Minimum 11 Attempts Per Game)

1948—Jim Peterson, Hanover, 182.9; **1949**—John Ford, Hardin-Simmons, 179.6; **1950**—Edward Ludorf, Trinity (Conn.), 167.8; **1951**—Vic Lesch, Western Ill., 182.4; **1952**—Jim Gray, East Tex. St., 205.5; **1953**—Boyd Crawford, Col. of Idaho, *210.1; **1954**—Bill Englehardt, Nebraska-Omaha, 170.7; **1955**—Robert Alexander, Trinity (Conn.), 208.7; **1956**—John Costello, Widener, 169.8; **1957**—Doug Maison, Hillsdale, 200.0; **1958**—Kurt Duecker, Ripon, 161.7; **1959**—Fred Whitmire, Humboldt St., 188.7; **1960**—Larry Cline, Otterbein, 195.2.

* Record.

(Minimum 15 Attempts Per Game)

Year	Player, Team	G	Att.	Cmp.	Int.	Pct.	Yds.	TD	Pts.
1961	Denny Spurlock, Whitworth	10	189	115	16	.609	1,708	26	165.2
1962	Roy Curry, Jackson St.................	10	194	104	8	.536	1,862	15	151.5
1963	Chuck Green, Wittenberg	9	182	114	8	.626	2,181	19	189.0
1964	Jim Cahoon, Ripon	8	127	74	7	.583	1,206	19	176.4
1965	Ed Buzzell, Ottawa	9	238	118	5	.496	2,170	31	165.0
1966	Jim Alcorn, Clarion	9	199	107	4	.538	1,714	24	161.9

Year	Player, Team	G	Att.	Cmp.	Int.	Pct.	Yds.	TD	Pts.
1967	Jim Feely, Johns Hopkins	7	110	69	5	.627	1,264	12	186.2
1968	Larry Green, Doane	9	182	97	7	.533	1,592	22	159.0
1969	George Kaplan, Northern Colo.	9	155	92	5	.594	1,396	16	162.6
1970	Gary Wichard, LIU-C. W. Post	9	186	100	5	.538	1,527	12	138.6
1971	Peter Mackey, Middlebury	8	180	101	4	.561	1,597	19	161.0
1972	David Hamilton, Fort Valley St.	9	180	99	9	.550	1,571	24	162.3
1973	Jim McMillan, Boise St.	11	179	110	5	.615	1,525	17	158.8
1974	Jim McMillan, Boise St.	10	313	192	15	.613	2,900	33	164.4
1975	Joe Sterrett, Lehigh	11	228	135	13	.592	2,114	22	157.5
1976	Mike Makings, Western St.	10	179	90	6	.503	1,617	14	145.3
1977	Mike Rieker, Lehigh	11	230	137	14	.596	2,431	23	169.2
1978	Mike Moroski, UC Davis	10	205	119	9	.581	1,689	17	145.9

(See page 201 for annual leaders beginning in 1979.)

Career Yards

Player, Team	Years	Att.	Cmp.	Int.	Pct.	Yards	TD
Earl Harvey, N.C. Central	1985-88	*1,442	*690	81	.479	*10,621	86
Sam Mannery, Calif. (Pa.)	1987-90	1,283	649	68	.506	8,680	64
Dave DenBraber, Ferris St.	1984-87	1,254	661	45	.527	8,536	52
Jim Lindsey, Abilene Christian	1967-70	1,237	642	69	.519	8,521	61
Maurice Heard, Tuskegee	1988-91	1,134	556	54	.490	8,434	87
Doug Williams, Grambling	1974-77	1,009	484	52	.480	8,411	*93
Steward Perez, Chadron St.	1988-91	1,015	565	60	.557	8,186	69
Steve Wray, Franklin	1978-82	1,230	592	48	.481	8,123	62
Al Niemela, West Chester	1985-88	1,063	600	36	.564	7,853	73
Ned Cox, Angelo St.	1983-86	1,205	589	58	.489	7,843	56
Loyal Proffitt, Abilene Christian	1981-84	1,157	550	80	.475	7,824	54
Tom Bonds, Cal Lutheran	1984-87	1,137	625	52	.550	7,773	57
Pat Brennan, Franklin	1981-84	1,123	535	62	.476	7,717	53
Chris Crawford, Portland St.	1985-88	954	588	35	.616	7,543	48
Tom Bertoldi, Northern Mich.	1980-83	987	524	50	.531	7,330	45
Tracy Kendall, Alabama A&M	1988-91	1,117	564	54	.505	7,205	49
Jack Hull, Grand Valley St.	1988-91	835	485	22	.581	7,120	64
Bob Caress, Bradley	1962-65	1,156	610	62	.528	7,115	64
Greg Calcagno, Santa Clara	1984-87	1,004	566	39	.564	7,011	43
Kim McQuilken, Lehigh	1971-73	925	516	42	.558	6,996	37
Bruce Upstill, Emporia St.	1960-63	769	438	36	.570	6,935	48
Scott Butler, Delta St.	1981-84	995	491	41	.493	6,917	38
John Schultz, Augustana (S.D.)	1982-85	998	503	57	.504	6,881	40
David Walter, Michigan Tech	1983-86	1,079	545	59	.505	6,876	48
Loren Snyder, Northern Colo.	1984-86	1,043	570	50	.547	6,874	48

* *Record.*

Season Yards

Player, Team	Year	Games	Att.	Cmp.	Int.	Pct.	Yards	TD
Chris Hegg, Northeast Mo. St.	1985	11	503	284	20	.565	*3,741	32
Tod Mayfield, West Tex. St.	1986	11	*515	*317	20	.615	3,664	31
June Jones, Portland St.	†1976	11	423	238	24	.563	3,518	25
Bob Toledo, San Fran. St.	1967	10	396	211	24	.533	3,513	*45
Pat Brennan, Franklin	1983	10	458	226	30	.493	3,491	25
Jayson Merrill, Western St.	†1991	10	309	195	11	.631	3,484	35
Pat Brennan, Franklin	1984	10	502	238	20	.474	3,340	18
Phil Basso, Liberty	1984	11	426	250	15	.587	3,326	24
Richard Strasser, San Fran. St.	1985	10	452	250	19	.553	3,317	20
Rob Tomlinson, Cal St. Chico	1989	10	437	254	16	.581	3,237	19
Earl Harvey, N.C. Central	1985	10	392	188	19	.480	3,190	22
Andy Breault, Kutztown	1990	11	474	269	19	.568	3,143	23
Jay McLucas, New Haven	1990	10	402	209	18	.520	3,114	23
George Bork, Northern Ill.	†1963	9	374	244	12	.652	3,077	32
Darin Slack, Central Fla.	1987	11	420	219	18	.521	3,054	26
Randy Hobson, Evansville	1987	10	386	242	16	.626	3,042	23
Tim Von Dulm, Portland St.	†1970	10	490	259	23	.529	3,041	25

* *Record.* † *National champion.*

Single-Game Yards

Yds.	Player, Team (Opponent)	Date
592	John Charles, Portland St. (Cal Poly SLO)	Nov. 16, 1991
568	Bob Toledo, San Fran. St. (Cal St. Hayward)	Oct. 21, 1967
550	Earl Harvey, N.C. Central (Jackson St.)	Aug. 30, 1986
539	Maurice Heard, Tuskegee (Alabama A&M)	Nov. 10, 1990

1992 NCAA FOOTBALL

Yds.	Player, Team (Opponent)	Date
525	Rob Tomlinson, Cal St. Chico (Southern Conn. St.)	Oct. 7, 1989
524	Dennis Shaw, San Diego St. (Southern Miss.)	Nov. 9, 1968
514	Tracy Kendall, Alabama A&M (Clark Atlanta)	Nov. 4, 1989
506	Tod Mayfield, West Tex. St. (Texas A&I)	Nov. 1, 1986
502	Mike Packer, Lock Haven (Delaware Valley)	Oct. 24, 1970
501	Bob Toledo, San Fran. St. (Humboldt St.)	Nov. 4, 1967
500	Jerry Bishop, Austin (East Cent. Okla.)	Nov. 2, 1963

Single-Game Attempts

No.	Player, Team (Opponent)	Date
72	Kurt Otto, North Dak. (Texas A&I)	Sept. 13, 1986
72	Kaipo Spencer, Santa Clara (Portland St.)	Oct. 11, 1975
72	Joe Stetser, Cal St. Chico (Oregon Tech)	Sept. 23, 1967
71	Pat Brennan, Franklin (Ashland)	Nov. 3, 1984

Single-Game Completions

No.	Player, Team (Opponent)	Date
44	Tom Bonds, Cal Lutheran (St. Mary's, Cal.)	Nov. 22, 1986
43	George Bork, Northern Ill. (Central Mich.)	Nov. 9, 1963
42	Chris Teal, West Ga. (Valdosta St.)	Oct. 19, 1991
42	Tim Von Dulm, Portland St. (Eastern Wash.)	Nov. 21, 1970
41	Kurt Otto, North Dak. (Texas A&I)	Sept. 13, 1986
41	Neil Lomax, Portland St. (Montana St.)	Nov. 19, 1977
40	Kurt Beathard, Towson St. (Lafayette)	Nov. 2, 1985
39	Pat Brennan, Franklin (Saginaw Valley)	Sept. 22, 1984
39	Mark Beans, Shippensburg (Edinboro)	Sept. 24, 1983
39	Curt Strasheim, Southwest St., Minn. (Moorhead St.)	Nov. 14, 1981
39	Craig Blackford, Evansville (Ball St.)	Oct. 17, 1970

Career Yards Per Game

Player, Team	Years	G.	Att.	Cmp.	Int.	Pct.	Yards	TD	Avg.
Tim Von Dulm, Portland St.	1969-70	20	924	500	41	.541	5,967	51	*298.4
Jayson Merrill, Western St.	1990-91	20	580	328	25	.566	5,830	56	291.5
Earl Harvey, N.C. Central	1985-88	40	*1,442	*690	81	.479	*10,621	86	265.5
Pat Brennan, Franklin	1981-84	30	1,123	535	62	.476	7,717	53	257.2
Jay McLucas, New Haven	1989-90	20	699	370	30	.529	5,139	37	257.0
Steve Wray, Franklin	1978-82	32	1,230	592	48	.481	8,123	62	253.8
Chris Hegg, Northeast Mo. St.	‡1982, 84-85	21	772	410	33	.531	5,306	44	252.7
Chris Petersen, UC Davis	1985-86	20	553	385	13	*.696	4,988	39	249.4
Jeff Phillips, Central Mo. St.	1986-88	26	892	496	54	.556	6,294	46	242.1
June Jones, Hawaii/Portland St.	1974, 75-76	24	666	376	35	.565	5,809	41	242.0
Rex Lamberti, Abilene Christian	1984-86	24	829	439	29	.530	5,807	56	242.0
Rich Ingold, Indiana (Pa.)	#1981, 83-85	27	862	503	36	.584	6,494	50	240.5
Joe Stetser, Cal St. Chico	1966-67	20	813	394	48	.485	4,803	40	240.2
Leonard Williams, Tenn.-Martin	1990-91	19	594	305	21	.513	4,518	40	237.8
Jim Lindsey, Abilene Christian	1967-70	36	1,237	642	69	.519	8,521	61	236.7

*Record. ‡ Played in one game at Northern Iowa in 1982. # Played in one game at South Carolina in 1981.

Season Yards Per Game

Player, Team	Year	Games	Att.	Cmp.	Int.	Pct.	Yards	TD	Avg.
Bob Toledo, San Fran. St.	1967	10	396	211	24	.533	3,513	*45	*351.3
Pat Brennan, Franklin	1983	10	458	226	30	.493	3,491	25	349.1
Jayson Merrill, Western St.	†1991	10	309	195	11	.631	3,484	35	348.4
George Bork, Northern Ill.	†1963	9	374	244	12	.652	3,077	32	341.9
Chris Hegg, Northeast Mo. St.	†1985	11	503	284	20	.565	*3,741	32	340.1
Pat Brennan, Franklin	1984	10	502	238	20	.474	3,340	18	334.0
Tod Mayfield, West Tex. St.	1986	11	*515	*317	20	.615	3,664	31	333.1
Richard Strasser, San Fran. St.	1985	10	452	250	19	.553	3,317	20	331.7
Rob Tomlinson, Cal St. Chico	1989	10	437	254	16	.581	3,237	19	323.7
June Jones, Portland St.	†1976	11	423	238	24	.563	3,518	25	319.8
Earl Harvey, N.C. Central	1985	10	392	188	19	.480	3,190	22	319.0
Jay McLucas, New Haven	1990	10	402	209	18	.520	3,114	23	311.4
Randy Hobson, Evansville	1987	10	386	242	16	.626	3,042	23	304.2
Tim Von Dulm, Portland St.	†1970	10	490	259	23	.529	3,041	25	304.1
Phil Basso, Liberty/No. Ill.	1984	11	426	250	15	.587	3,326	24	302.4

*Record. † National champion.

Northern Illinois quarterback George Bork ranks fifth in Division II in career passing efficiency (141.8), and his average of 341.9 passing yards per game in 1963 is the division's fourth best.

Annual Champions

Year	Player, Team	Cl.	Att.	Cmp.	Int.	Pct.	Yds.	TD
1946	Hank Caver, Presbyterian	Sr.	128	59	13	.461	790	7
1947	James Batchelor, East Tex. St.	Sr.	184	94	10	.511	1,114	9
1948	Sam Gary, Swarthmore	Jr.	153	93	11	.608	1,218	16
1949	Sam McGowan, New Mexico St.	Sr.	219	112	22	.511	1,712	12
1950	Andy MacDonald, Central Mich.	Jr.	200	109	12	.545	1,577	15
1951	Andy MacDonald, Central Mich.	Sr.	183	114	7	.623	1,560	12
1952	Wes Bair, Illinois St.	So.	242	135	18	.558	1,375	14
1953	Pence Dacus, Southwest Tex. St.	Sr.	207	113	10	.546	1,654	11
1954	Tommy Egan, Brandeis	Sr.	144	87	8	.604	1,050	11
1955	Jerry Foley, Hamline	Fr.	167	87	8	.521	1,034	6
1956	James Stehlin, Brandeis	Sr.	206	116	11	.563	1,155	6
1957	Jay Roelen, Pepperdine	Sr.	214	106	16	.495	1,428	13
1958	Stan Jackson, Cal Poly Pomona	Sr.	256	123	14	.480	1,994	16
1959	Gary Campbell, Whittier	Sr.	183	111	4	.607	1,717	12
1960	Denny Spurlock, Whitworth	Jr.	257	135	16	.525	1,892	14
1961	Tom Gryzwinski, Defiance	Jr.	258	127	17	.492	1,684	14
1962	George Bork, Northern Ill.	Jr.	356	232	11	.652	2,506	22
1963	George Bork, Northern Ill.	Sr.	374	244	12	.652	3,077	32
1964	Jerry Bishop, Austin	Jr.	300	182	16	.607	2,246	17
1965	Bob Caress, Bradley	Sr.	393	210	21	.534	2,167	24
1966	Paul Krause, Dubuque	Sr.	318	179	22	.563	2,210	16
1967	Joe Stetser, Cal St. Chico	Sr.	464	220	*32	.474	2,446	14
1968	Jim Lindsey, Abilene Christian	So.	396	204	19	.515	2,717	18
1969	Tim Von Dulm, Portland St.	Jr.	434	241	18	.555	2,926	26

Beginning in 1970, ranked on per-game (instead of total) completions

Year	Player, Team	Cl.	G.	Att.	Cmp.	Avg.	Int.	Pct.	Yds.	TD
1970	Tim Von Dulm, Portland St.	Sr.	10	490	259	*25.9	23	.529	3,041	25
1971	Bob Baron, Rensselaer.............	Sr.	9	302	168	18.7	13	.556	2,105	15
1972	Bob Biggs, UC Davis	Sr.	9	327	186	20.7	16	.569	2,291	15
1973	Kim McQuilken, Lehigh	Sr.	11	326	196	17.8	13	.601	2,603	19
1974	Jim McMillan, Boise St.	Sr.	10	313	192	19.2	15	.613	2,900	13
1975	Dan Hayes, UC Riverside	Sr.	10	316	171	17.1	20	.541	2,215	21
1976	June Jones, Portland St.	Sr.	11	423	238	21.6	24	.563	3,518	25
1977	Ed Schultz, Moorhead St.	Sr.	10	304	187	18.7	16	.615	1,943	21
1978	Jeff Knapple, Northern Colo.......	Sr.	10	349	178	17.8	21	.510	2,191	16

Beginning in 1979, ranked on Passing Efficiency Rating Points (instead of per-game completions)

Year	Player, Team	Cl.	G.	Att.	Cmp.	Int.	Pct.	Yds.	TD	Pts.
1979	Dave Alfaro, Santa Clara	Jr.	9	168	110	9	.655	1,721	13	166.3
1980	Willie Tullis, Troy St.	Sr.	10	203	108	8	.532	1,880	15	147.5
1981	Steve Michuta, Grand Valley St.	Sr.	8	173	114	11	.659	1,702	17	168.3
1982	John Wristen, Southern Colo.	Jr.	8	121	68	2	.562	1,358	13	182.5
1983	Kevin Parker, Fort Valley St.	Jr.	9	168	87	8	.518	1,539	18	154.6
1984	Brian Quinn, Northwest Mo. St.	Sr.	10	178	96	2	.539	1,561	14	151.3
1985	Chris Petersen, UC Davis	Jr.	10	242	167	6	.690	2,366	17	169.4
1986	Chris Petersen, UC Davis	Sr.	10	311	218	7	‡.701	2,622	22	159.7
1987	Dave Biondo, Ashland	Jr.	10	177	95	11	.536	1,828	14	154.0
1988	Al Niemela, West Chester	Sr.	10	217	138	9	.635	1,932	21	161.9
1989	Richard Basil, Savannah St.	Sr.	9	211	120	7	.568	2,148	29	180.9
1990	Tony Aliucci, Indiana (Pa.)	Jr.	10	181	111	10	.613	1,801	21	172.0
1991	Jayson Merrill, Western St.	Sr.	10	309	195	11	.631	3,484	35	187.9

* *Record.* ‡ *Record for minimum of 225 attempts.*

RECEIVING

Career Catches

Player, Team	Years	No.	Yards	TD
Chris Myers, Kenyon	1967-70	*253	3,897	33
Bruce Cerone, Yankton/Emporia St.	1966-67, 68-69	241	*4,354	*49
Harold "Red" Roberts, Austin Peay	1967-70	232	3,005	31
Jerry Hendren, Idaho	1967-69	230	3,435	27
Mike Healey, Valparaiso	1982-85	228	3,212	26
William Mackall, Tenn.-Martin	1985-88	224	2,488	16
Robert Clark, N.C. Central	1983-86	210	4,231	38
Terry Fredenberg, Wis.-Milwaukee	1965-68	206	2,789	24
Dan Bogar, Valparaiso	1981-84	204	2,816	26
Rich Otte, Northeast Mo. St.	1980-83	202	2,821	16
Mark Steinmeyer, Kutztown (RB)	1988-91	200	2,118	23
Barry Naone, Portland St. (TE)	1985-88	199	2,237	8
Jon Braff, St. Mary's (Cal.) (TE)	1985-88	193	2,461	20
Shannon Sharpe, Savannah St.	1986-89	192	3,744	40
Bill Wick, Carroll (Wis.)	1966-69	190	2,967	20
Don Hutt, Boise St.	1971-73	187	2,716	30
Steve Hansley, Northwest Mo. St.	1983-85	186	2,898	24
Dan Anderson, Northwest Mo. St. (TE)	1982-85	186	2,494	16

* *Record.*

Season Catches

Player, Team	Year	Games	No.	Yards	TD
Barry Wagner, Alabama A&M	†1989	11	*106	1,812	17
Mike Healey, Valparaiso	†1985	10	101	1,279	11
Ed Bell, Idaho St.	†1969	10	96	1,522	*20
Dick Hewins, Drake	†1968	10	95	1,316	13
Billy Joe Masters, Evansville	†1987	10	¢94	¢960	4
Stan Carraway, West Tex. St.	†1986	11	94	1,175	9
Manley Sarnowsky, Drake	†1966	10	92	1,114	7
Bruce Cerone, Emporia St.	1968	9	91	1,479	15
Harvey Tanner, Murray St.	†1967	10	88	1,019	3

* *Record.* † *National champion.* ¢ *Record for a running back.*

Single-Game Catches

No.	Player, Team (Opponent)	Date
23	Barry Wagner, Alabama A&M (Clark Atlanta)	Nov. 4, 1989
20	Harold Roberts, Austin Peay (Murray St.)	Nov. 8, 1969
19	Aaron Marsh, Eastern Ky. (Northwood)	Oct. 14, 1967
19	George LaPorte, Union, N.Y. (Rensselaer)	Oct. 16, 1965
18	Carl Bruere, N.M. Highlands (Western St.)	Oct. 12, 1991
18	Billy Joe Masters, Evansville (Ashland)	Oct. 31, 1987
18	Bruce Cerone, Emporia St. (Washburn)	Nov. 9, 1968
18	Dick Donlin, Hamline (St. John's, Minn.)	Oct. 8, 1955

Career Catches Per Game

Player, Team	Years	Games	No.	Yards	TD	Ct. PG
Ed Bell, Idaho St.	1968-69	19	163	2,608	30	*8.6
Jerry Hendren, Idaho	1967-69	30	230	3,435	27	7.7
Gary Garrison, San Diego St.	1964-65	20	148	2,188	26	7.4
Chris Myers, Kenyon	1967-70	35	*253	3,897	33	7.2

* *Record.*

Season Catches Per Game

Player, Team	Year	Games	No.	Yards	TD	Ct. PG
Bruce Cerone, Emporia St.	1968	9	91	1,479	15	*10.1
Mike Healey, Valparaiso	†1985	10	101	1,279	11	10.1
Barry Wagner, Alabama A&M	†1989	11	*106	*1,812	17	9.6
Ed Bell, Idaho St.	†1969	10	96	1,522	*20	9.6
Jerry Hendren, Idaho	1968	9	86	1,457	14	9.6
Dick Hewins, Drake	†1968	10	95	1,316	13	9.5
Billy Joe Masters, Evansville	†1987	10	¢94	¢960	4	¢9.4
Joe Dittrich, Southwest St. (Minn.)	†1980	9	83	974	7	9.2
Manley Sarnowsky, Drake................	†1966	10	92	1,114	7	9.2

* Record.   † National champion.   ¢ Record for a running back.

Career Yards

Player, Team	Years	Catches	Yards	Avg.	TD
Bruce Cerone, Yankton/Emporia St. ...	1966-67, 68-69	241	*4,345	18.1	*49
Robert Clark, N.C. Central	1983-86	210	4,231	‡‡20.1	38
Chris Myers, Kenyon	1967-70	*253	3,897	15.4	33
Shannon Sharpe, Savannah St.	1986-89	192	3,744	19.5	40
Jeff Tiefenthaler, South Dak. St.	1983-86	173	3,621	20.9	31
Willie Richardson, Jackson St.	1959-62	166	3,616	††21.8	36

* Record.   ‡‡ Record for a minimum of 180 catches.   †† Record for a minimum of 135 catches.

Season Yards

Player, Team	Year	Catches	Yards	Avg.	TD
Barry Wagner, Alabama A&M	†1989	*106	*1,812	17.1	17
Dan Fulton, Nebraska-Omaha	1976	67	1,581	23.6	16
Jeff Tiefenthaler, South Dak. St...........	1986	73	1,534	21.0	11
Ed Bell, Idaho St.	†1969	96	1,522	15.9	*20
Bruce Cerone, Emporia St.	1968	91	1,479	16.3	15
Jerry Hendren, Idaho	1968	86	1,457	16.9	14

* Record.   † National champion.

Annual Champions

Year	Player, Team	Class	No.	Yards	TD
1946	Hugh Taylor, Oklahoma City	Jr.	23	457	8
1947	Bill Klein, Hanover	So.	52	648	12
1948	Bill Klein, Hanover	Jr.	43	812	6
1949	Cliff Coggin, Southern Miss.	Sr.	53	1,087	9
1950	Jack Bighead, Pepperdine	Jr.	38	551	6
1951	Jim Stefoff, Kalamazoo	Jr.	45	680	5
1952	Jim McKinzie, Northern Ill.........................	Sr.	44	703	6
1953	Dick Beetsch, Northern Iowa	So.	54	837	9
1954	R. C. Owens, Col. of Idaho	Sr.	48	905	7
1955	Dick Donlin, Hamline	Sr.	41	480	2
1956	Tom Rychlec, American Int'l	Sr.	40	353	3
1957	Tom Whitaker, Nevada	Jr.	40	527	4
1958	Bruce Shenk, West Chester	Sr.	39	580	9
1959	Fred Tunnicliffe, UC Santa Barb.	So.	48	1,087	11
1960	Ken Gregory, Whittier	Sr.	74	1,018	4
1961	Marty Baumhower, Defiance	Jr.	57	708	4
1962	Hugh Rohrschneider, Northern Ill.	Jr.	76	795	5
1963	Hugh Rohrschneider, Northern Ill.	Sr.	75	1,036	14
1964	Steve Gilliatt, Parsons	So.	81	984	12
1965	George LaPorte, Union (N.Y.)	Sr.	74	724	5
1966	Manley Sarnowsky, Drake...........................	Sr.	92	1,114	7
1967	Harvey Tanner, Murray St..........................	Jr.	88	1,019	3
1968	Dick Hewins, Drake	Sr.	95	1,316	13
1969	Ed Bell, Idaho St...................................	Sr.	96	1,522	*20

Beginning in 1970, ranked on per-game (instead of total) catches

Year	Player, Team	Cl.	G	Ct.	Avg.	Yards	TD
1970	Steve Mahaffey, Wash. & Lee	Sr.	9	74	8.2	897	2
1971	Kalle Kontson, Rensselaer	Sr.	9	69	7.7	1,031	7
1972	Freddie Scott, Amherst	Jr.	8	66	8.3	936	12
1973	Ron Gustafson, North Dak.	Jr.	10	67	6.7	1,210	10
1974	Andy Sanchez, Cal Poly Pomona	Sr.	10	62	6.2	903	0
1975	Butch Johnson, UC Riverside	Sr.	8	67	8.4	1,027	8
1976	Bo Darden, Shaw	So.	9	57	6.3	863	4
1977	Jeff Tesch, Moorhead St..................	Sr.	10	67	6.7	760	9

Year	Player, Team	Cl.	G	Ct.	Avg.	Yards	TD
1978	Mike Chrobot, Butler	Sr.	10	55	5.5	628	5
	Tom Ferguson, Cal St. Hayward	Jr.	10	55	5.5	698	6
	Mark McDaniel, Northern Colo.	Sr.	10	55	5.5	761	6
1979	Robbie Ray, Franklin	Sr.	10	63	6.3	987	3
1980	Joe Dittrich, Southwest St. (Minn.)	Sr.	9	83	9.2	974	7
1981	Paul Choudek, Southwest St. (Minn.)	Sr.	10	70	7.0	747	5
1982	Jay Barnett, Evansville	Sr.	10	81	8.1	1,181	12
1983	Perry Kemp, Calif. (Pa.)	Sr.	10	74	7.4	1,101	9
1984	Dan Bogar, Valparaiso	Sr.	10	73	7.3	861	11
1985	Mike Healey, Valparaiso	Sr.	10	101	10.1	1,279	11
1986	Stan Carraway, West Tex. St.	Sr.	11	94	8.5	1,175	9
1987	Billy Joe Masters, Evansville	Sr.	10	¢94	¢9.4	¢960	4
1988	Todd Smith, Morningside	Sr.	11	86	7.8	1,006	8
1989	Barry Wagner, Alabama A&M	Sr.	11	*106	9.6	*1,812	17
1990	Mark Steinmeyer, Kutztown	Jr.	11	86	7.8	940	5
1991	Jesse Lopez, Cal St. Hayward	Sr.	10	86	8.6	861	4

* Record.   ¢ Record for a running back.

Receiving Yards Per Game

Year	Player, Team	Cl.	G	Ct.	Yards	Avg.	TD
1990	Ernest Priester, Edinboro	Sr.	8	45	1,060	132.5	14
1991	Rod Smith, Mo. Western St.	Jr.	11	60	1,439	130.8	15

SCORING

Career Points

Player, Team	Years	TD	XPt.	FG	Pts.
Walter Payton, Jackson St.	1971-74	66	53	5	*464
Johnny Bailey, Texas A&I	1986-89	*70	3	0	426
Dale Mills, Northeast Mo. St.	1957-60	64	23	0	407
Garney Henley, Huron	1956-59	63	16	0	394
Steve Roberts, Butler	1986-89	63	4	0	386
Jeff Bentrim, North Dak. St.	1983-86	64	2	0	386
Leo Lewis, Lincoln (Mo.)	1951-54	64	0	0	384
Heath Sherman, Texas A&I	1985-88	63	0	0	378
Billy Johnson, Widener	1971-73	62	0	0	372
¢Shawn Graves, Wofford	1989-91	61	4	0	370
Tank Younger, Grambling	1945-48	60	9	0	369
Bill Cooper, Muskingum	1957-60	54	37	1	364

* Record.   ¢ Active player.

Season Points

Player, Team	Year	TD	XPt.	FG	Pts.
Terry Metcalf, Long Beach St.	1971	*29	4	0	*178
Jim Switzer, Col. of Emporia	†1963	28	0	0	168
Carl Herakovich, Rose-Hulman	†1958	25	18	0	168
Ted Scown, Sul Ross St.	†1948	28	0	0	168
Leon Burns, Long Beach St.	†1969	27	2	0	164
Billy Johnson, Widener	†1972	27	0	0	162
Mike Deutsch, North Dak.	1972	27	0	0	162

* Record.   † National champion.

Career Points Per Game

Player, Team	Years	Games	TD	XPt.	FG	Pts.	Pt. PG
Ole Gunderson, St. Olaf	1969-71	27	60	2	0	362	*13.4
Billy Johnson, Widener	1971-73	28	62	0	0	372	13.3
Leon Burns, Long Beach St.	1969-70	22	47	2	0	284	12.9
Dale Mills, Northeast Mo. St.	1957-60	36	64	23	0	407	11.3
Walter Payton, Jackson St.	1971-74	42	66	53	5	*464	11.0
Steve Roberts, Butler	1986-89	35	63	4	0	386	11.0
Jeff Bentrim, North Dak. St.	1983-86	35	64	2	0	386	11.0
Johnny Bailey, Texas A&I	1986-89	39	*70	3	0	426	10.9
Garney Henley, Huron	1956-59	37	63	16	0	394	10.6

* Record.

Season Points Per Game

Player, Team	Year	Games	TD	XPt.	FG	Pts.	Pt. PG
Carl Herakovich, Rose-Hulman	†1958	8	25	18	0	168	*21.0
Jim Switzer, Col. of Emporia	†1963	9	28	0	0	168	18.7
Billy Johnson, Widener	†1972	9	27	0	0	162	18.0
Carl Garrett, N. M. Highlands	†1966	9	26	2	0	158	17.6
Ted Scown, Sul Ross St.	†1948	10	28	0	0	168	16.8

* Record.   † National champion.

Annual Champions

Year	Player, Team	Class	TD	XPt.	FG	Pts.
1946	Joe Carter, Florida N&I............................	So.	21	26	0	152
1947	Darwin Horn, Pepperdine	Jr.	19	1	0	115
	Chuck Schoenherr, Wheaton (Ill.)	So.	19	1	0	115
1948	Ted Scown, Sul Ross St.	So.	28	0	0	168
1949	Sylvester Polk, Md.-East. Shore	Jr.	19	15	0	129
1950	Carl Taseff, John Carroll	Sr.	23	0	0	138
1951	Paul Yackey, Heidelberg	Jr.	22	0	0	132
1952	Al Conway, William Jewell	Sr.	22	1	0	133
1953	Leo Lewis, Lincoln (Mo.)	Jr.	22	0	0	132
1954	Jim Podoley, Central Mich.........................	Jr.	18	1	0	109
	Dick Nyers, Indianapolis	Sr.	16	13	0	109
1955	Nate Clark, Hillsdale	Jr.	24	0	0	144
1956	Larry Houdek, Kan. Wesleyan......................	Sr.	19	0	0	114
1957	Lenny Lyles, Louisville	Sr.	21	6	0	132
1958	Carl Herakovich, Rose-Hulman	Sr.	25	18	0	168
1959	Garney Henley, Huron	Sr.	22	9	0	141
1960	Bill Cooper, Muskingum	Sr.	23	14	0	152
1961	John Murio, Whitworth.............................	Jr.	15	33	2	129
1962	Mike Goings, Bluffton.............................	So.	22	0	0	132
1963	Jim Switzer, Col. of Emporia	Sr.	28	0	0	168
1964	Henry Dyer, Grambling	Jr.	17	2	0	104
	Dunn Marteen, Cal St. Los Angeles	Sr.	11	38	0	104
1965	Allen Smith, Findlay	Jr.	24	2	0	146
1966	Carl Garrett, N. M. Highlands	So.	26	2	0	158
1967	Bert Nye, West Chester	Jr.	19	13	0	127
1968	Howard Stevens, Randolph-Macon	Fr.	23	4	0	142
1969	Leon Burns, Long Beach St.	Jr.	27	2	0	164

Beginning in 1970, ranked on per-game (instead of total) points

Year	Player, Team	Class	G	TD	XPt.	FG	Pts.	Avg.
1970	Mike DiBlasi, Mount Union	Sr.	9	22	0	0	132	14.7
1971	Larry Ras, Michigan Tech	Sr.	9	24	0	0	144	16.0
1972	Billy Johnson, Widener	Jr.	9	27	0	0	162	18.0
1973	Walter Payton, Jackson St.	Jr.	11	24	13	1	160	14.5
1974	Walter Payton, Jackson St.	Sr.	10	19	6	1	123	12.3
1975	Dale Kasowski, North Dak..............	Sr.	7	16	4	0	100	14.3
1976	Ted McKnight, Minn.-Duluth	Sr.	10	24	0	0	144	14.4
1977	Bill Burnham, New Hampshire	Sr.	10	22	0	0	132	13.2
1978	Marschell Brunfield, Youngstown St.	Sr.	9	14	0	0	84	9.3
	Charlie Thompson, Western St.	Sr.	9	14	0	0	84	9.3
1979	Robby Robson, Youngstown St.	Jr.	10	20	0	0	120	12.0
1980	Amory Bodin, Minn.-Duluth	Sr.	10	19	2	0	116	11.6
1981	George Works, Northern Mich...........	Jr.	10	21	0	0	126	12.6
1982	George Works, Northern Mich...........	Sr.	10	23	0	0	138	13.8
1983	Clarence Johnson, North Ala............	Jr.	10	16	0	0	96	9.6
1984	Jeff Bentrim, North Dak. St.............	So.	9	14	0	0	84	9.3
1985	Jeff Bentrim, North Dak. St.............	Jr.	8	18	2	0	110	††13.8
1986	Jeff Bentrim, North Dak. St.............	Sr.	10	23	0	0	138	13.8
1987	Johnny Bailey, Texas A&I	So.	10	20	0	0	120	12.0
1988	Steve Roberts, Butler	Jr.	10	23	4	0	142	14.2
1989	Jimmy Allen, St. Joseph's (Ind.)	Jr.	10	23	0	0	138	13.8
1990	Ernest Priester, Edinboro	Sr.	8	16	0	0	96	12.0
1991	Quincy Tillmon, Emporia St.	So.	9	19	0	0	114	12.7

†† Declared champion; with one more game (to meet 75 percent of games played minimum) for zero points, still would have highest per-game average.

204   *1992 NCAA FOOTBALL*

PUNTING

Career Average
(Minimum 100 Punts)

Player, Team	Years	No.	Yards	Avg.
Tim Baer, Colorado Mines	1986-89	235	10,406	*44.3
Jeff Guy, Western St.	1983-85	113	4,967	44.0
Russ Pilcher, Carroll (Mont.)	1964-66	124	5,424	43.7
Russell Gonzales, Morris Brown	1976-77	111	4,833	43.5
Gerald Circo, Cal St. Chico	1964-65	103	4,470	43.4
Trent Morgan, Cal St. Northridge	1987-88	128	5,531	43.2
Bryan Wagner, Cal St. Northridge	1981-84	203	8,762	43.2
Tom Kolesar, Nevada	1973-74	140	6,032	43.1
Don Geist, Northern Colo.	1981-84	263	11,247	42.8
Jan Chapman, San Diego	1958-60	106	4,533	42.8
Warner Robertson, Md.-East. Shore	1968-70	131	5,578	42.6

* Record.

Season Average
(Qualifiers for Championship)

Player, Team	Year	No.	Yards	Avg.
Steve Ecker, Shippensburg	†1965	32	1,570	*49.1
Don Cockroft, Adams St.	†1966	36	1,728	48.0
Jack Patterson, William Jewell	1965	29	1,377	47.5
Art Calandrelli, Canisius	†1949	25	1,177	47.1
Grover Perkins, Southern-B.R.	†1961	22	1,034	47.0
Erskine Valrie, Alabama A&M	1966	36	1,673	46.5
Mark Bounds, West Tex. St.	†1990	69	3,198	46.3
Bruce Swanson, North Park	†1967	53	2,455	46.3
Lyle Johnston, Weber St.	1965	29	1,340	46.2

* Record.   † National champion.

Annual Champions

Year	Player, Team	Class	No.	Yards	Avg.
1948	Arthur Teixeira, Central Mich.	Sr.	42	1,867	44.5
1949	Art Calandrelli, Canisius	Jr.	25	1,177	47.1
1950	Flavian Weidekamp, Butler	Sr.	41	1,762	43.0
1951	Curtiss Harris, Savannah St.	Sr.	42	1,854	44.1
1952	Virgil Stan, Western St.	Sr.	37	1,622	43.8
1953	Bill Bradshaw, Bowling Green	Jr.	50	2,199	44.0
1954	Bill Bradshaw, Bowling Green	Sr.	28	1,228	43.9
1955	Don Baker, North Texas	Sr.	30	1,349	45.0
1956	Marion Zody, Ashland	Jr.	34	1,475	43.4
1957	Lawson Persley, Mississippi Val.	Sr.	36	1,659	46.1
1958	Tom Lewis, Lake Forest	Jr.	24	1,089	45.4
1959	Buck Grover, Salem	Fr.	27	1,203	44.6
1960	Joe Roy, N. M. Highlands	So.	40	1,744	43.6
1961	Grover Perkins, Southern-B.R.	Fr.	22	1,034	47.0
1962	Ron Crouse, Catawba	Jr.	37	1,653	44.7
1963	Steve Bailey, Kentucky St.	Sr.	39	1,747	44.8
1964	Russ Pilcher, Carroll (Mont.)	So.	34	1,545	45.4
1965	Steve Ecker, Shippensburg	Sr.	32	1,570	*49.1
1966	Don Cockroft, Adams St.	Sr.	36	1,728	48.0
1967	Bruce Swanson, North Park	Jr.	53	2,455	46.3
1968	Warner Robertson, Md.-East. Shore	Fr.	61	2,699	44.2
1969	Warner Robertson, Md.-East. Shore	So.	37	1,629	44.0
1970	John Bonner, Tenn.-Chatt.	Sr.	73	3,243	44.4
1971	Ken Gamble, Fayetteville St.	Sr.	47	2,092	44.5
1972	Raymond Key, Jackson St.	Jr.	44	1,883	42.8
1973	Jerry Pope, Louisiana Tech	Fr.	48	2,064	43.0
1974	Mike Shawen, Middle Tenn. St.	Sr.	62	2,720	43.9
1975	Mike Wood, Southeast Mo. St.	Jr.	40	1,729	43.2
1976	Russell Gonzales, Morris Brown	So.	54	2,474	45.8
1977	Jeff Gossett, Eastern Ill.	Jr.	62	2,668	43.0
1978	Bill Moats, South Dak.	Sr.	77	3,377	43.9
1979	Bob Fletcher, Northeast Mo. St.	Sr.	79	3,409	43.2
1980	Sean Landeta, Towson St.	So.	47	2,038	43.4
1981	Gregg Lowery, Jacksonville St.	Jr.	64	2,787	43.5
1982	Don Geist, Northern Colo.	So.	66	2,966	44.4

Year	Player, Team	Class	No.	Yards	Avg.
1983	Jeff Guy, Western St.	So.	39	1,734	44.5
1984	Jeff Guy, Western St.	Jr.	46	2,012	43.7
1985	Jeff Williams, Slippery Rock	Sr.	46	1,977	43.0
1986	Tim Baer, Colorado Mines	Fr.	62	2,797	45.1
1987	Jeff McComb, Southern Utah	Sr.	42	1,863	44.4
1988	Tim Baer, Colorado Mines	Jr.	65	2,880	43.9
1989	Tim Baer, Colorado Mines	Sr.	55	2,382	43.3
1990	Mark Bounds, West Tex. St.	Jr.	69	3,198	46.3
1991	Doug O'Neill, Cal Poly SLO	Sr.	42	1,895	45.1

* Record.

INTERCEPTIONS
Career Interceptions

Player, Team	Years	No.	Yards	Avg.
Tom Collins, Indianapolis	1982-85	*37	390	10.5
Dean Diaz, Humboldt St.	1980-83	31	328	10.6
Scott Wiedeman, Adams St.	1988-91	31	289	9.3
Bill Grantham, Missouri-Rolla	1977-80	29	263	9.1
Tony Woods, Bloomsburg	1982-85	26	105	4.0
Gary Rubeling, Towson St.	1980-83	25	122	4.9

* Record.

Season Interceptions

Player, Team	Year	No.	Yards
Eugene Hunter, Fort Valley St.	†1972	**14	211
Luther Howard, Delaware St.	†1972	**14	99
Tom Rezzuti, Northeastern	†1971	**14	153
Jim Blackwell, Southern-B.R.	†1970	**14	196
Carl Ray Harris, Fresno St.	1970	**14	98

** Record tied.   † National champion.

Annual Champions

Year	Player, Team	Class	Games	No.	Avg.	Yards
1970	Jim Blackwell, Southern-B.R.	Sr.	11	**14	1.27	196
1971	Tom Rezzuti, Northeastern	Jr.	9	**14	**1.56	153
1972	Eugene Hunter, Fort Valley St.	So.	9	**14	**1.56	211
	Luther Howard, Delaware St.	Sr.	9	**14	**1.56	99
1973	Mike Pierce, Northern Colo.	Sr.	7	7	1.00	158
	James Smith, Shaw	So.	8	8	1.00	94
1974	Terry Rusin, Wayne St. (Mich.)	Fr.	10	10	1.00	62
1975	Jim Poettgen, Cal Poly Pomona	Jr.	11	12	1.09	156
1976	Johnny Tucker, Tennessee Tech	Sr.	11	10	0.91	74
1977	Mike Ellis, Norfolk St.	So.	11	12	1.09	257
	Cornelius Washington, Winston-Salem	Sr.	11	12	1.09	128
1978	Bill Grantham, Missouri-Rolla	So.	11	11	1.00	109
1979	Jeff Huffman, Michigan Tech	Sr.	10	11	1.10	97
1980	Mike Lush, East Stroudsburg	Sr.	10	12	1.20	208
1981	Bobby Futrell, Elizabeth City St.	So.	9	11	1.22	159
1982	Greg Maack, Central Mo. St.	Sr.	10	11	1.10	192
1983	Matt Didio, Wayne St. (Mich.)	Sr.	10	13	1.30	131
1984	Bob Jahelka, LIU-C. W. Post	Sr.	8	9	1.13	83
1985	Duvaal Callaway, Fort Valley St.	Sr.	11	10	0.91	175
	Tony Woods, Bloomsburg	Sr.	11	10	0.91	10
1986	Doug Smart, Winona St.	Jr.	8	10	1.25	56
1987	Mike Petrich, Minn.-Duluth	Jr.	11	9	0.82	151
1988	Pete Jaros, Augustana (S.D.)	Jr.	11	13	1.18	120
1989	Jacque DeMatteo, Clarion	Jr.	8	6	0.75	21
1990	Eric Turner, East Tex. St.	Jr.	11	10	0.91	105
1991	Jeff Fickes, Shippensburg	Sr.	11	12	1.09	154

** Record tied.

PUNT RETURNS

Career Average
(Minimum 1.2 Returns Per Game)

Player, Team	Years	No.	Yards	Avg.
Billy Johnson, Widener	1971-73	40	989	*24.7
Robbie Martin, Cal Poly SLO	1978-80	69	1,168	16.9
Roscoe Word, Jackson St.	1970-73	35	554	15.8
Darryl Skinner, Hampton	1983-86	53	835	15.8
Michael Fields, Mississippi Col.	1984-85	50	695	13.9

* Record.

Season Average
(Minimum 1.2 Returns Per Game)

Player, Team	Year	No.	Yards	Avg.
Billy Johnson, Widener	†1972	15	511	*34.1
William Williams, Livingstone	†1976	16	453	28.3
Terry Egerdahl, Minn.-Duluth	†1975	13	360	27.7
Ennis Thomas, Bishop	†1971	18	450	25.0
Chuck Goehl, Monmouth (Ill.)	1972	17	416	24.5

* Record. † National champion.

Annual Champions

Year	Player, Team	Class	No.	Yards	Avg.
1970	Kevin Downs, Ill. Benedictine	Jr.	11	255	23.2
1971	Ennis Thomas, Bishop	So.	18	450	25.0
1972	Billy Johnson, Widener	Jr.	15	511	*34.1
1973	Roscoe Word, Jackson St.	Sr.	19	316	16.6
1974	Greg Anderson, Montana	So.	13	263	20.2
1975	Terry Egerdahl, Minn.-Duluth	Sr.	13	360	27.7
1976	William Williams, Livingstone	So.	16	453	28.3
1977	Armando Olivieri, New York Tech	So.	14	270	19.3
1978	Dwight Walker, Nicholls St.	Fr.	16	284	17.8
1979	Ricky Eberhart, Morris Brown	Fr.	18	401	22.3
1980	Ron Bagby, Puget Sound	So.	16	242	15.1
1981	Ron Trammell, East Tex. St.	Jr.	29	467	16.1
1982	Darrel Green, Texas A&I	Sr.	19	392	20.6
1983	Steve Carter, Albany St. (Ga.)	Sr.	27	511	18.9
1984	Michael Fields, Mississippi Col.	Jr.	23	487	21.2
1985	Darryl Skinner, Hampton	Jr.	19	426	22.4
1986	Ben Frazier, Cheyney	So.	14	246	17.6
1987	Ronald Day, Savannah St.	Sr.	12	229	19.1
1988	Donnie Morris, Norfolk St.	Jr.	12	283	23.6
1989	Dennis Mailhot, East Stroudsburg	Jr.	16	284	17.8
1990	Ron West, Pittsburg St.	Jr.	23	388	16.9
1991	Douglas Grant, Savannah St.	So.	19	331	17.4

* Record.

KICKOFF RETURNS

Career Average
(Minimum 1.2 Returns Per Game)

Player, Team	Years	No.	Yards	Avg.
Glen Printers, Southern Colo.	1973-74	25	851	*34.0
Clarence Chapman, Eastern Mich.	1973-75	45	1,278	28.4
Greg Wilson, East Tenn. St.	1975-78	37	1,032	27.9
Bernie Rose, Samford/North Ala.	1973, 74-76	64	1,715	26.8
Roscoe Word, Jackson St.	1970-73	74	1,980	26.8

* Record.

Season Average
(Minimum 1.2 Returns Per Game)

Player, Team	Year	No.	Yards	Avg.
Roscoe Word, Jackson St.	†1973	18	650	*36.1
Steve Levenseller, Puget Sound	†1978	17	610	35.9
Winston Horshaw, Shippensburg	†1991	15	536	35.7
Anthony Rivera, Western St.	1991	18	635	35.3
Mike Scullin, Baldwin-Wallace	†1970	14	492	35.1
Rufus Smith, Eastern N. Mex.	†1985	11	386	35.1
Greg Anderson, Montana	†1974	10	335	33.5
Kevin McDevitt, Butler	†1975	12	395	32.9

* Record. † National champion.

Year	Player, Team	Class	No.	Yards	Avg.
1970	Mike Scullin, Baldwin-Wallace	So.	14	492	35.1
1971	Joe Brockmeyer, Western Md.	Jr.	16	500	31.3
1972	Rick Murphy, Indiana St.	Jr.	22	707	32.1
1973	Roscoe Word, Jackson St.	Sr.	18	650	*36.1
1974	Greg Anderson, Montana	So.	10	335	33.5
1975	Kevin McDevitt, Butler	Jr.	12	395	32.9
1976	Henry Vereen, Nevada-Las Vegas	So.	20	628	31.4
1977	Dickie Johnson, Southern Colo.	Jr.	13	385	29.6
1978	Steve Levenseller, Puget Sound	Sr.	17	610	35.9
1979	Otha Hill, Central St. (Ohio)	Sr.	18	526	29.2
1980	Charlie Taylor, Southeast Mo. St.	Sr.	13	396	30.5
1981	Willie Canady, Fort Valley St.	Jr.	13	415	31.9
1982	Clarence Martin, Cal Poly SLO	So.	11	360	32.7
1983	David Anthony, Southern Ore.	Jr.	14	436	31.1
1984	Larry Winters, St. Paul's	Sr.	20	644	32.2
1985	Rufus Smith, Eastern N. Mex.	Fr.	11	386	35.1
1986	John Barron, Butler	So.	21	653	31.1
1987	Albert Fann, Cal St. Northridge	Fr.	16	468	29.3
1988	Pierre Fils, New Haven	So.	12	378	31.5
1989	Dennis Mailhot, East Stroudsburg	Jr.	11	359	32.6
1990	Alfred Banks, Livingston	Sr.	17	529	31.1
1991	Winston Horshaw, Shippensburg	Jr.	15	536	35.7

* Record.

FIELD GOALS

Career Field Goals

Player, Team	Years	Made	Atts.	Pct.
Mike Wood, Southeast Mo. St. (S)	1974-77	*64	*109	.587
Pat Beaty, North Dak. (S)	1985-88	52	82	.634
Bob Gilbreath, Eastern N. Mex. (S)	1986-89	50	77	.649
Ed O'Brien, Central Fla. (S)	1984-87	50	77	.649
Bill May, Clarion (C)	1977-80	48	60	*.800
Mike Thomas, Angelo St. (S)	1980-83	47	68	.691
Steve Huff, Central Mo. St. (C)	1982-85	47	80	.588
Phil Brandt, Central Mo. St. (S)	1987-90	46	66	.697
Howie Guarini, Shippensburg (S)	1988-91	45	62	.726
James Knowles, North Ala. (C)	1982-85	45	77	.584
Ed Hotz, Southeast Mo. St. (S)	1978-81	45	77	.584
Kurt Seibel, South Dak. (C)	1980-83	44	62	.710
Pat Bolton, Montana St. (C)	1972-75	44	76	.579
Skipper Butler, Texas-Arlington (C)	1966-69	44	101	.436

* Record.   (C) Conventional kicker.   (S) Soccer-style kicker.

Season Field Goals

Player, Team	Year	Made	Atts.	Pct.
Pat Beaty, North Dak. (S)	†1988	**20	26	.769
Tom Jurich, Northern Ariz. (C)	†1977	**20	29	.690
Dennis Hochman, Sonoma St. (S)	†1986	19	22	.864
Cory Solberg, North Dak. (S)	†1989	19	27	.704
Jaime Nunez, Weber St. (S)	†1971	19	32	.594
Bernard Henderson, Albany St. (Ga.) (S)	†1985	18	26	.692
Ki Tok Chu, Tenn.-Martin (S)	1988	17	22	.773
Jack McTyre, Valdosta St. (S)	1990	17	23	.739
Dino Beligrinis, Winston-Salem (S)	1988	17	23	.739
Ed O'Brien, Central Fla. (S)	†1987	17	26	.654
Mike Wood, Southeast Mo. St. (S)	1976	17	33	.515

** Record tied.   (C) Conventional kicker.   (S) Soccer-style kicker.

Annual Champions

Year	Player, Team	Class	Made	Atts.	Pct.	PG
1970	Chris Guerrieri, Alfred (S)	Sr.	11	21	.524	1.38
1971	Jaime Nunez, Weber St. (S)	Sr.	19	32	.594	**1.90
1972	Randy Walker, Northwestern (La.) (C)	Jr.	13	19	.684	1.30
1973	Reinhold Struprich, Hawaii (S)	Jr.	15	23	.652	1.36
1974	Mike Wood, Southeast Mo. St. (S)	Fr.	16	23	.696	1.45
1975	Wolfgang Taylor, Western St. (S)	Sr.	14	21	.667	1.56
1976	Rolf Benirschke, UC Davis (S)	Sr.	14	19	.737	1.56

Year	Player, Team	Class	Made	Atts.	Pct.	PG
1977	Tom Jurich, Northern Ariz. (C)	Sr.	**20	29	.690	1.81
1978	Frank Friedman, Cal St. Northridge (S)	Jr.	15	22	.682	1.50
1979	Bill May, Clarion (C)	Jr.	16	21	.762	1.60
1980	Nelson McMurain, North Ala. (S)	Jr.	14	22	.636	1.40
	Sean Landeta, Towson St. (S).................	So.	14	28	.500	1.40
1981	Russ Meier, South Dak. St. (S)	Fr.	16	21	.762	1.60
1982	Joey Malone, Alabama A&M (C)	Fr.	15	21	.714	1.36
	Rick Ruszkiewicz, Edinboro (S)	Sr.	15	24	.625	1.36
1983	Mike Thomas, Angelo St. (S)	Sr.	16	22	.727	1.45
1984	Terry Godfrey, South Dak. (S)................	Jr.	16	26	.615	1.60
1985	Bernard Henderson, Albany St. (Ga.) (S)	Sr.	18	26	.692	1.64
1986	Dennis Hochman, Sonoma St. (S)	Sr.	19	22	.864	**1.90
1987	Ed O'Brien, Central Fla. (S)	Sr.	17	26	.654	1.70
1988	Pat Beaty, North Dak. (S)	Sr.	**20	26	.769	1.82
1989	Cory Solberg, North Dak. (S)	Jr.	19	27	.704	1.73
1990	Jack McTyre, Valdosta St. (S)	Sr.	17	23	.739	1.70
1991	Billy Watkins, East Tex. St. (S)	So.	15	24	.625	1.36

** *Record tied.* (C) *Conventional kicker.* (S) *Soccer-style kicker.*

LONGEST PLAYS

Since 1941, official maximum length of all plays fixed at 100 yards.

Rushing

Yds.	Player, Team (Opponent)	Year
99	Lester Frye, Edinboro (Calif., Pa.)	1991
99	Kelvin Minefee, Southern Utah (Mesa St.).....................................	1988
99	Fred Deutsch, Springfield (Wagner)	1977
99	Sammy Croom, San Diego (Asuza Pacific)	1972
99	John Stenger, Swarthmore (Widener)	1970
99	Jed Knuttila, Hamline (St. Thomas, Minn.)	1968
99	Dave Lanoha, Colorado Col. (Texas Lutheran)	1967
99	Tom Pabst, UC Riverside (Cal Tech)	1965
99	George Phillips, Concord (Davis & Elkins)	1961
99	Gerry White, Connecticut (Rhode Island)	1960
99	Leo Williams, St. Augustine's (Morris)	1960
99	George Phelps, Cornell College (Monmouth, Ill.)	1959
99	Mark Lydon, Tufts (Bowdoin)	1958
99	David Wells, Tufts (Williams)	1956
99	Jack Moskal, Case Reserve (Case Tech)	1956
99	Lou Mariano, Kent (Case Reserve)	1954
99	Ron Temple, Cal St. Chico (Southern Ore.)	1953
99	Ellis Horton, Eureka (Rose-Hulman)	1952
99	Pat Abbruzzi, Rhode Island (New Hampshire)	1951

Passing

Pass plays have resulted in 99-yard completions 12 times. The most recent:

Yds.	Passer-Receiver, Team (Opponent)	Year
99	Bret Comp-Ken Kopetchny, East Stroudsburg (Mansfield).......................	1990
99	Mike Turk-Titus Dixon, Troy St. (Nicholls St.)	1986
99	Keith Young-John Ragin, Dist. Columbia (Fayetteville St.)	1985
99	Nick Pannunzo-Herman Heard, Southern Colo. (Adams St.)	1982
99	Tim Ebersole-Ed Noon, Shippensburg (Indiana, Pa.)...........................	1982
99	John Guercio-Tom Bennett, LIU-C. W. Post (Juniata)	1980
99	Mike Moroski-Calvin Ellison, UC Davis (Puget Sound)	1978
99	Gary Duesenberg-Harvey King, North Park (Ill. Wesleyan)......................	1970

Field Goals

Yds.	Player, Team (Opponent)	Year
67	Tom Odle, Fort Hays St. (Washburn)	1988
63	Joe Duren, Arkansas St. (McNeese St.)	1974
62	Mike Flater, Colorado Mines (Western St.)	1973
61	Duane Christian, Cameron (Southwestern Okla.)	1976
61	Mike Wood, Southeast Mo. St. (Lincoln, Mo.)	1975
61	Bill Shear, Cortland St. (Hobart)	1966
60	Mike Panasuk, Ferris St. (St. Joseph's, Ind.)	1990
60	Ed Beaulac, Sonoma St. (St. Mary's, Cal.)	1989

Yds.	Player, Team (Opponent)	Year
60	Roger McCoy, Grand Valley St. (Grand Rapids)	1976
60	Skipper Butler, Texas-Arlington (East Tex. St.)	1968

Punts

Yds.	Player, Team (Opponent)	Year
97	Earl Hurst, Emporia St. (Central Mo. St.)	1964
96	Gary Frens, Hope (Olivet)	1966
96	Jim Jarrett, North Dak. (South Dak.)	1957
93	Elliot Mills, Carleton (Monmouth, Ill.)	1970
93	Kaspar Fitins, Taylor (Georgetown, Ky.)	1966
93	Leeroy Sweeney, Pomona (UC Riverside)	1960

Since 1941, many players have returned interceptions, punts and kickoffs 100 yards. For the 1991 season leaders, see page 527.

TEAM CHAMPIONS AND WINNING STREAKS

ANNUAL TEAM OFFENSE CHAMPIONS

Year	Total Offense Team	Avg.	Rushing Team	Avg.	Passing Team	Avg.
1948	Hanover	*624.1	Hanover	400.4	Hanover	223.8
1949	Pacific (Cal.)	505.3	Southern-B.R.	382.9	Baldwin-Wallace	196.9
1950	West Tex. St.	465.3	St. Lawrence	356.1	Northern Ill.	187.0
1951	Western Ill.	473.6	Western N. Mex.	379.2	Central Mich.	213.8
1952	Sam Houston St.	448.2	William Jewell	345.0	Sam Houston St.	263.0
1953	Col. of Idaho	476.3	McPherson	375.9	Southern Conn. St.	193.5
1954	Col. of Emporia	469.7	Col. of Emporia	*404.8	Northern Iowa	206.1
1955	Centre	431.0	Centre	373.4	Hamline	210.7
1956	Florida A&M	475.0	Tufts	359.9	Widener	207.7
1957	Denison	430.8	Denison	372.1	Cal Poly Pomona	236.0
1958	Mo. Valley	449.6	Huron	353.3	Cal Poly Pomona	217.6
1959	Whittier	461.3	Bemidji St.	326.6	Whittier	199.3
1960	Muskingum	456.4	Muskingum	355.2	Whitworth	213.6
1961	Florida A&M	413.6	Huron	313.1	Cal Poly Pomona	244.1
1962	Baker	438.4	Northern St.	355.3	Northern Ill.	285.6
1963	Col. of Emporia	517.1	Luther	356.0	Northern Ill.	349.3
1964	San Diego St.	422.6	Cal St. Los Angeles	325.9	Parsons	301.3
1965	Long Beach St.	439.5	Huron	303.3	Southern Ore.	268.9
1966	Weber St.	460.1	Neb.-Kearney	370.1	San Diego St.	268.1
1967	San Fran. St.	490.0	North Dak. St.	299.6	San Fran. St.	387.0
1968	Louisiana Tech	459.1	Delaware	315.8	Louisiana Tech	316.4
1969	Delaware	488.9	St. Olaf	369.1	Portland St.	308.6
1970	Grambling	457.7	Delaware	385.9	Portland St.	313.8
1971	Delaware	515.6	Delaware	371.2	LIU-C. W. Post	262.5
1972	Hobart	457.3	Hobart	380.7	Maryville (Tenn.)	277.8
1973	Boise St.	466.5	Bethune-Cookman	308.8	Lehigh	275.0
1974	Boise St.	516.9	Central Mich.	324.6	Boise St.	334.5
1975	Portland St.	472.4	North Dak.	344.4	Portland St.	361.7
1976	Portland St.	497.5	Montana St.	287.5	Portland St.	*404.1
1977	Portland St.	506.7	South Caro. St.	321.5	Portland St.	378.5
1978	Western St.	487.0	Western St.	320.2	Northern Mich.	242.3
1979	Delaware	450.5	Mississippi Col.	314.5	Northern Mich.	284.2
1980	Southwest Tex. St.	423.0	Minn.-Duluth	307.3	Northern Mich.	269.6
1981	Southwest Tex. St.	482.3	Millersville	322.9	Franklin	306.5
1982	Northern Mich.	450.4	Mississippi Col.	297.0	Evansville	313.0
1983	Central St. (Ohio)	491.1	Jamestown	297.7	Franklin	358.0
1984	North Dak. St.	455.3	North Dak. St.	334.7	Franklin	334.0
1985	Northeast Mo. St.	471.4	Saginaw Valley	300.4	Northeast Mo. St.	345.1
1986	Texas A&I	542.6	Texas A&I	395.2	West Tex. St.	345.5
1987	Texas A&I	486.4	Texas A&I	330.5	Evansville	306.6
1988	Cal St. Sacramento	486.0	North Dak. St.	373.1	Central Fla.	292.2
1989	Grand Valley St.	480.8	Wofford	373.7	Cal St. Chico	328.8
1990	Chadron St.	479.6	North Dak. St.	364.2	New Haven	335.4
1991	Western St.	549.8	Wofford	347.9	Western St.	357.4

1992 NCAA FOOTBALL

Quarterback Phil Kessel led Northern Michigan to its second and third straight passing-offense crowns in 1979 and 1980. Kessel passed for 4,793 yards and 36 touchdowns over those two seasons.

Scoring Offense

Year	Team	Avg.	Year	Team	Avg.
1948	Sul Ross St.	43.1	1971	Michigan Tech	42.4
1949	Pacific (Cal.)	50.0	1972	Fort Valley St.	45.0
1950	West Tex. St.	37.2	1973	Western Ky.	37.7
1951	Western Ill.	42.1	1974	Boise St.	44.6
1952	East Tex. St.	49.6	1975	Bethune-Cookman	37.9
1953	Col. of Idaho	42.4	1976	Northern Mich.	43.0
1954	Col. of Emporia	43.2	1977	South Caro. St.	38.4
1955	Central Mich.	36.3	1978	Western St.	45.2
1956	Florida A&M	45.9	1979	Delaware	35.5
1957	Denison	38.6	1980	Minn.-Duluth	35.4
1958	Wheaton (Ill.)	44.6	1981	Southwest Tex. St.	37.5
1959	Florida A&M	42.6	1982	Northeast Mo. St.	40.0
1960	Florida A&M	52.8	1983	Central St. (Ohio)	43.6
1961	Florida A&M	*54.7	1984	North Dak. St.	39.0
1962	Florida A&M	42.0	1985	UC Davis	37.6
1963	Col. of Emporia	42.4	1986	Texas A&I	43.1
1964	San Diego St.	42.3	1987	West Chester	34.5
1965	Ottawa	43.2		Central Fla.	34.5
1966	N. M. Highlands	48.1	1988	North Dak. St.	39.6
1967	Waynesburg	53.7		Texas A&I	39.6
1968	Doane	52.9	1989	Grand Valley St.	44.5
1969	St. Olaf	45.2	1990	Indiana (Pa.)	44.2
1970	Wittenberg	40.0	1991	Western St.	46.1

* Record.

ANNUAL TEAM DEFENSE CHAMPIONS

Year	Total Defense — Team	Avg.	Rushing Defense — Team	Avg.	Pass Defense — Team	$Avg.
1948	Morgan St.	104.4	Morgan St.	44.8	Ashland	*10.1
1949	Southern Conn. St.	95.6	Hanover	43.5	Wilmington (Ohio)	39.8
1950	Southern Conn. St.	93.6	Lewis & Clark	50.3	Vermont	34.4
1951	Southern Conn. St.	84.3	Southern Conn. St.	17.1	Alfred	52.0
1952	West Chester	128.4	East Tex. St.	48.5	Cortland St.	45.9
1953	Shippensburg	81.9	Shippensburg	53.6	Shippensburg	28.3
1954	Geneva	106.3	Tennessee St.	29.2	St. Augustine's	26.5
1955	Col. of Emporia	102.0	Muskingum	52.5	Ithaca	15.5
1956	Tennessee St.	118.9	Hillsdale	51.1	West Va. Tech	29.1
1957	West Chester	90.2	West Chester	27.9	Lake Forest	25.0
1958	Rose-Hulman	95.8	Ithaca	48.4	Coast Guard	25.4
1959	Maryland St.	75.3	Maryland St.	36.3	Huron	21.9
1960	Maryland St.	104.8	West Chester	41.4	Susquehanna	27.3
1961	Florida A&M	85.3	Florida A&M	20.1	Westminster (Utah)	24.8
1962	John Carroll	*44.4	John Carroll	-1.0	Principia	27.8
1963	West Chester	100.8	St. John's (Minn.)	12.9	Western Caro.	39.3
1964	Morgan St.	126.4	Fort Valley St.	39.7	Eastern Mont.	44.1
1965	Morgan St.	91.5	Morgan St.	15.0	Minot St.	44.5
1966	Tennessee St.	85.7	Tennessee St.	13.9	Manchester	54.7
1967	Tennessee St.	61.6	Tennessee St.	*-16.7	Mount Union	61.4
1968	Alcorn St.	103.4	Alcorn St.	8.8	Bridgeport	47.6
1969	Livingstone	148.5	Kings Point	16.2	Wabash	72.0
1970	Delaware St.	103.5	Delaware St.	-4.9	Hampden-Sydney	62.9
1971	Hampden-Sydney	115.6	Northern Colo.	27.5	Western Ky.	57.7
1972	Wis.-Whitewater	143.8	Alcorn St.	49.8	Howard	48.8
1973	Livingstone	114.9	Alcorn St.	45.9	East Stroudsburg	37.6
1974	Livingstone	120.5	Livingstone	53.0	Tennessee St.	52.6
1975	South Caro. St.	100.6	Alcorn St.	15.9	N.C. Central	60.2
1976	Alcorn St.	108.9	Alcorn St.	32.5	Morris Brown	60.8
1977	Virginia Union	160.3	Virginia Union	63.6	Delaware St.	64.3
1978	East Stroudsburg	153.8	East Stroudsburg	52.2	Concordia-M'head	55.8
1979	Virginia Union	138.2	Virginia Union	41.0	Kentucky St.	62.3
1980	Concordia-M'head	191.7	Missouri-Rolla	34.6	Norfolk St.	71.5
1981	Fort Valley St.	148.3	Fort Valley St.	46.9	Bowie St.	75.7
1982	Jamestown	187.9	Butler	71.1	Elizabeth City St.	49.0
1983	Virginia Union	143.7	Butler	38.2	Elizabeth City St.	65.0
1984	Virginia St.	180.6	Norfolk St.	53.8	Virginia St.	80.4
1985	Fort Valley St.	162.2	Norfolk St.	50.9	Fort Valley St.	94.5
1986	Virginia Union	163.5	Central St. (Ohio)	44.5	Virginia Union	84.7
1987	Alabama A&M	167.1	West Chester	67.2	Alabama A&M	72.5
1988	Alabama A&M	175.8	Cal Poly SLO	56.4	Alabama A&M	84.3
1989	Winston-Salem	185.7	Texas A&I	60.7	Mo. Southern St.	93.0
1990	Sonoma St.	218.5	Sonoma St.	58.3	Angelo St.	65.4
1991	Ashland	195.5	Sonoma St.	63.6	Carson-Newman	64.9

Scoring Defense

Year	Team	Avg.	Year	Team	Avg.
1959	Huron	2.1	1976	South Caro. St.	3.4
1960	Albany St. (Ga.)	*0.0	1977	Minn.-Duluth	7.8
1961	Florida A&M	2.8	1978	Southwestern La.	7.1
1962	John Carroll	2.9	1979	Virginia Union	6.1
1963	Massachusetts	1.3	1980	Minn.-Duluth	7.6
1964	Central (Iowa)	4.8	1981	Moorhead St.	5.0
1965	St. John's (Minn.)	2.2	1982	Jamestown	5.9
1966	Morgan St.	3.6	1983	Towson St.	5.8
1967	Waynesburg	4.3	1984	Cal Poly SLO	9.0
1968	Central Conn. St.	4.4	1985	Fort Valley St.	6.3
1969	Carthage	6.0	1986	North Dak. St.	6.8
1970	Hampden-Sydney	2.8	1987	Tuskegee	9.1
1971	Hampden-Sydney	3.4	1988	Alabama A&M	7.5
1972	Ashland	5.6	1989	Jacksonville St.	7.0
1973	Virginia Union	3.8	1990	Cal Poly SLO	11.3
1974	Minn.-Duluth	5.5	1991	Butler	7.1
1975	South Caro. St.	2.9			

Record. $ Beginning in 1990, based on passing efficiency ranking instead of yards per game.

1992 NCAA FOOTBALL

** LONGEST STREAKS
(From 1937; includes postseason games)

Winning Streaks

Wins	Team	Years
41	Mo. Valley	†1941-48
34	Hillsdale	1954-57
32	Wilkes....................	1965-69
32	Morgan St.	1965-68
29	East Tex. St..............	1951-53
26	Delaware	†1941-47
25	San Diego St.	1965-67
25	Peru St.	1951-54
25	Maryland St..............	1948-51
24	North Dak. St.............	1964-66
24	Wesleyan	1945-48

Unbeaten Streaks

No.	Wins	Ties	Team	Years
54	47	7	Morgan St.	1931-38
38	36	2	Doane	1965-70
37	35	2	Southern-B.R.............	1947-51
35	34	1	North Dak. St.............	1968-71
32	31	1	Delaware	†1940-47
31	29	2	St. Ambrose	†1935-38
30	29	1	Wittenberg	1961-65
30	29	1	East Tex. St..............	1951-53
28	27	1	Wesleyan	‡1942-48
28	27	1	Case Reserve	1934-37
27	26	1	Juniata..................	1956-59

** During 1973-77 (a period when it was not an NCAA-member college), Texas A&I won 42 consecutive games and was unbeaten during 46 consecutive games (including one tie).   † Did not field teams 1943-45.   ‡ Did not field teams 1943-44.

MOST-PLAYED RIVALRIES

Games	Opponents (Series leader listed first)	Series Record	First Game
96	North Dak.-North Dak. St.....................................	52-41-3	1894
91	South Dak.-South Dak. St.	47-37-7	1889
88	Colorado Mines-Colorado Col.	46-37-5	1889
82	South Dak.-Morningside	50-27-5	1898
81	Tuskegee-Morehouse	51-24-6	1902
80	Virginia Union-Hampton	41-37-2	1906
78	North Dak. St.-South Dak. St.	40-33-5	1903

ALL-TIME WON-LOST RECORDS

Includes records as a senior college only, minimum of 20 seasons of competition since 1937. Postseason games are included, and each tie game is computed as half won and half lost.

TOP 25—BY PERCENTAGE

Team	Yrs.	Won	Lost	Tied	Pct.
West Chester..................	63	404	164	16	.705
Texas A&I	63	423	190	16	.685
Neb.-Kearney	68	380	210	26	.638
Central Okla.	86	470	262	46	.634
Indiana (Pa.)	62	340	193	22	.632
Minn.-Duluth	59	302	178	22	.624
Grand Valley St.	21	131	79	1	.623
Virginia Union................	91	423	248	43	.623
Tuskegee.....................	94	474	280	49	.621
Pittsburg St..................	84	456	276	46	.616
Northeast Mo. St.	84	426	262	35	.613
Angelo St.....................	28	181	114	6	.611
Hillsdale.....................	99	475	296	45	.610
Carson-Newman	68	379	238	29	.609
East Stroudsburg	64	325	208	18	.606
North Dak. St.	95	464	296	34	.606
Fort Valley St.	46	252	161	20	.605
Virginia St.	80	395	252	48	.603
Butler.......................	102	461	307	35	.596
Jacksonville St.	59	313	210	26	.594
North Dak.	95	441	304	28	.589
Santa Clara	70	346	238	26	.589
St. Mary's (Cal.)	63	307	220	19	.580
Southern Conn. St.	44	229	166	10	.578
Central Ark.	80	387	280	40	.576

TOP 25—BY VICTORIES

Team	Wins
Hillsdale	475
Tuskegee	474
Central Okla.	470
North Dak. St.	464
Butler.......................	461
Pittsburg St.	456
North Dak.	441
Northeast Mo. St...........	426
Texas A&I	423
Virginia Union	423
Washburn	414
South Dak. St.	410
South Dak.	405
Springfield	405
West Chester	404
Virginia St.	395
Central Ark.	387
East Tex. St.	385
Neb.-Kearney	380
Carson-Newman	379
Mississippi Col.............	377
Hampton	376
Presbyterian	372
Elon	371
Lenoir-Rhyne..............	369

Team	Yrs.	Won	Lost	Tied	Pct.
Abilene Christian	70	352	285	32	.550
Adams St.	57	252	214	16	.539
Alabama A&M	52	246	215	25	.532
Albany St. (Ga.)	46	204	200	20	.505
American Int'l	55	222	226	20	.496
Angelo St.	28	181	114	6	.611
Ashland	69	312	261	29	.542
Augustana (S.D.)	71	272	323	13	.458
Bemidji St.	66	216	300	23	.422
Bloomsburg	64	246	263	20	.484
Bowie St.	20	68	117	5	.371
Butler	102	461	307	35	.596
Cal Poly SLO	51	272	206	8	.568
Cal St. Chico	68	280	309	21	.476
Cal St. Hayward	28	120	153	7	.441
Cal St. Northridge	30	136	170	4	.445
Cal St. Sacramento	38	170	204	7	.455
Calif. (Pa.)	62	232	258	19	.474
Cameron	24	135	106	8	.558
Carson-Newman	68	379	238	29	.609
Catawba	72	342	327	26	.511
Central Ark.	80	387	280	40	.576
Central Conn. St.	53	199	220	22	.476
Central Mo. St.	95	361	413	50	.468
Central Okla.	86	470	262	46	.634
Chadron St.	77	326	281	15	.536
Cheyney	38	79	247	4	.245
Clarion	63	288	220	17	.565
Clark Atlanta	53	167	247	23	.408
Colorado Mines	102	304	420	30	.423
Delta St.	62	286	280	20	.505
East Stroudsburg	64	325	208	18	.606
East Tex. St.	74	385	284	31	.572
Eastern N. Mex.	48	241	224	12	.518
Edinboro	63	219	271	23	.449
Elizabeth City St.	50	219	210	17	.510
Elon	70	371	288	18	.561
Emporia St.	94	364	399	44	.478
Fayetteville St.	46	151	248	22	.385
Ferris St.	63	207	282	32	.428
Fort Hays St.	70	307	327	46	.485
Fort Lewis	28	100	154	3	.395
Fort Valley St.	46	252	161	20	.605
Gardner-Webb	22	103	125	2	.452
Grand Valley St.	21	131	79	1	.623
Hampton	90	376	314	33	.543
Henderson St.	84	363	303	42	.542
Hillsdale	99	475	296	45	.610
Humboldt St.	64	283	248	18	.532
Indiana (Pa.)	62	340	193	22	.632
Indianapolis	54	231	236	21	.495
Jacksonville St.	59	313	210	26	.594
Johnson Smith	64	258	277	34	.483
Kentucky St.	63	268	308	25	.467
Kutztown	61	200	281	20	.419
Lenoir-Rhyne	72	369	293	34	.555
Livingston	50	189	253	14	.430
Livingstone	43	167	213	14	.442
Lock Haven	63	240	298	24	.448
Mankato St.	66	278	259	27	.517
Mansfield	62	195	289	30	.409
Mars Hill	28	125	145	9	.464
Mesa St.	16	106	58	5	.642
Michigan Tech	69	235	233	17	.502
Miles	22	43	145	6	.237
Millersville	60	255	229	20	.526
Minn.-Duluth	59	302	178	22	.624
Mississippi Col.	79	377	285	33	.566

Team	Yrs.	Won	Lost	Tied	Pct.
Missouri-Rolla	86	328	372	35	.470
Mo. Southern St.	24	129	108	6	.543
Mo. Western St.	22	93	128	7	.423
Morehouse	92	314	325	49	.492
Morningside	90	321	296	34	.519
Morris Brown	66	298	264	37	.528
N.C. Central	61	308	228	24	.571
Neb.-Kearney	68	380	210	26	.638
Nebraska-Omaha	75	313	301	30	.509
New Haven	19	87	91	4	.489
Newberry	78	286	416	33	.412
N. M. Highlands	65	218	286	25	.436
Norfolk St.	31	155	135	6	.534
North Ala.	43	238	182	15	.564
North Dak.	95	441	304	28	.589
North Dak. St.	95	464	296	34	.606
Northeast Mo. St.	84	426	262	35	.613
Northern Colo.	79	294	315	24	.483
Northern Mich.	78	321	234	25	.575
Northwest Mo. St.	74	298	331	32	.475
Northwood	30	123	139	6	.470
Pittsburg St.	84	456	276	46	.616
Portland St.	37	185	189	7	.495
Presbyterian	79	372	349	35	.515
Saginaw Valley	17	85	88	3	.491
San Fran. St.	59	234	283	21	.454
Santa Clara	70	346	238	26	.589
Savannah St.	39	142	200	13	.418
Shepherd	68	280	253	26	.524
Shippensburg	62	295	239	20	.551
Slippery Rock	64	302	231	28	.563
Sonoma St.	13	50	81	1	.383
South Dak.	96	405	373	34	.520
South Dak. St.	94	410	344	38	.542
Southern Conn. St.	44	229	166	10	.578
Southern Utah	29	144	128	5	.529
Southwest Baptist	9	37	50	2	.427
Springfield	98	405	356	55	.530
St. Cloud St.	64	292	238	21	.549
St. Joseph's (Ind.)	72	227	273	22	.456
St. Mary's (Cal.)	63	307	220	19	.580
Texas A&I	63	423	190	16	.685
Troy St.	61	295	261	14	.530
Tuskegee	94	474	280	49	.621
UC Davis	73	339	286	31	.540
Valdosta St.	10	57	44	2	.563
Valparaiso	71	280	316	24	.471
Virginia St.	80	395	252	48	.603
Virginia Union	91	423	248	43	.623
Washburn	100	414	430	40	.491
Wayne St. (Mich.)	74	257	320	29	.448
Wayne St. (Neb.)	66	275	322	37	.463
West Chester	63	404	164	16	.705
West Ga.	13	54	78	0	.409
West Liberty St.	65	315	248	35	.556
West Tex. St.	80	353	370	22	.489
Western St.	69	272	296	13	.479
Wingate	6	27	31	0	.466
Winona St.	91	245	392	31	.390
Winston-Salem	48	246	195	19	.555
Wofford	83	348	380	35	.479

WIRE SERVICE NATIONAL CHAMPIONS

(1958-74)

(For what was then known as College Division teams. Selections by United Press International from 1958 and Associated Press from 1960.)

Year	Team	Coach	*Record
1958	Southern Miss.	Thad "Pie" Vann	9-0-0
1959	Bowling Green	Doyt Perry	9-0-0
1960	Ohio	Bill Hess	10-0-0
1961	Pittsburg St.	Carnie Smith	9-0-0
1962	Southern Miss. (UPI)	Thad "Pie" Vann	9-1-0
	Florida A&M (AP)	Jake Gaither	9-0-0
1963	Delaware (UPI)	Dave Nelson	8-0-0
	Northern Ill. (AP)	Howard Fletcher	9-0-0
1964	Cal St. Los Angeles (UPI)	Homer Beatty	9-0-0
	Wittenberg (AP)	Bill Edwards	8-0-0
1965	North Dak. St.	Darrell Mudra	10-0-0
1966	San Diego St.	Don Coryell	10-0-0
1967	San Diego St.	Don Coryell	9-1-0
1968	San Diego St. (UPI)	Don Coryell	9-0-1
	North Dak. St. (AP)	Ron Erhardt	9-0-0
1969	North Dak. St.	Ron Erhardt	9-0-0
1970	Arkansas St.	Bennie Ellender	10-0-0
1971	Delaware	Harold "Tubby" Raymond	9-1-0
1972	Delaware	Harold "Tubby" Raymond	10-0-0
1973	Tennessee St.	John Merritt	10-0-0
1974	Louisiana Tech (UPI)	Maxie Lambright	10-0-0
	Central Mich. (AP)	Roy Kramer	9-1-0

* Regular season.

NCAA DIVISION II FINAL POLL LEADERS

(Released before the division championship playoffs)

Year	Team, Record*	Coach	†Record in Championship Playoffs
1975	North Dak. (9-0-0)	Jerry Olson	0-1 Lost in first round
1976	Northern Mich. (10-0-0)	Gil Krueger	1-1 Lost in semifinals
1977	North Dak. St. (8-1-1)	Jim Wacker	1-1 Lost in semifinals
1978	Winston-Salem (10-0-0)	Bill Hayes	Did not compete
1979	Delaware (9-1-0)	Harold "Tubby" Raymond	3-0 Champion
1980	Eastern Ill. (8-2-0)	Darrell Mudra	2-1 Runner-up
1981	Southwest Tex. St. (9-0-0)	Jim Wacker	3-0 Champion
1982	Southwest Tex. St. (11-0-0)	Jim Wacker	3-0 Champion
1983	UC Davis (9-0-0)	Jim Sochor	1-1 Lost in semifinals
1984	North Dak. St. (9-1-0)	Don Morton	2-1 Runner-up
1985	UC Davis (9-1-0)	Jim Sochor	0-1 Lost in first round
1986	North Dak. St. (10-0-0)	Earle Solomonson	3-0 Champion
1987	Texas A&I (9-1-0)	Ron Harms	Did not compete
1988	North Dak. St. (9-0-0)	Rocky Hager	4-0 Champion
1989	Texas A&I (10-0-0)	Ron Harms	0-1 Lost in first round
1990	North Dak. St. (10-0-0)	Rocky Hager	4-0 Champion
1991	Indiana (Pa.) (10-0-0)	Frank Cignetti	2-1 Lost in semifinals

* Final poll record; in some cases, a team had one game remaining before the championship play-offs.   † Number of teams in the championship: 8 (1975-87); 16 (1988-).

UNDEFEATED, UNTIED TEAMS

(Regular-season games only)

In 1948, official national statistics rankings began to include all nonmajor four-year colleges. Until the 1967 season, rankings and records included all four-year colleges that reported their statistics to the NCAA. Beginning with the 1967 season, statistics (and won-lost records) included only members of the NCAA.

Since 1981, conference playoff games have been included in a team's regular-season statistics and won-lost record (previously, such games were considered postseason contests).

The regular-season list includes games in which a home team served as a predetermined, preseason host of a "bowl game" regardless of its record and/or games scheduled before the season, thus eliminating as postseason designation the Orange Blossom Classic, annually hosted by Florida A&M, and the Prairie View Bowl, annually hosted by Prairie View, for example.

Figures are regular-season wins only. A subsequent postseason win(s) is indicated by (*), loss (†) and tie (‡).

Year	College	Wins	Year	College	Wins	Year	College	Wins
1948	Alma	8		N'western Col. (Wis.)	6		West Chester	9
	Bloomsburg	9		Peru St.	8	1958	Calif. (Pa.)	8
	Denison	8		Prairie View	10		Chadron St.	8
	Heidelberg	9		Shippensburg	8		Gust. Adolphus	†8
	Michigan Tech	7		St. Olaf	8		Missouri Valley	†8
	Missouri Valley	†‡9		Westminster (Pa.)	8		Neb.-Kearney	9
	Occidental	*8		Wis.-La Crosse	‡9		Northeastern Okla.	**9
	Southern-B.R.	*11		Wis.-Platteville	6		Northern Ariz.	*†10
	Sul Ross St.	‡10	1954	Ashland	7		Rochester	8
	Wesleyan	8		Carleton	8		Rose-Hulman	8
1949	Ball St.	8		Central Conn. St.	6		Sewanee	8
	Emory & Henry	*†10		Col. of Emporia	†9		Southern Miss.	9
	Gannon	8		Delta St.	8		St. Benedict's	†10
	Hanover	†8		Hastings	*8		Wheaton (Ill.)	8
	Lewis	8		Hobart	8	1959	Bowling Green	9
	Md.-East. Shore	8		Juniata	8		Butler	9
	Morgan St.	8		Luther	9		Coe	8
	Pacific (Cal.)	11		Miles	*9		Fairmont St.	9
	St. Ambrose	8		Nebraska-Omaha	*9		Florida A&M	10
	St. Vincent	*9		N'western Col. (Wis.)	6		Hofstra	9
	Trinity (Conn.)	8		Pomona-Pitzer	7		John Carroll	7
	Wayne St. (Neb.)	9		Principia	7		Lenoir-Rhyne	*†9
	Wofford	11		Southeastern La.	*9		San Fran. St.	10
1950	Abilene Christian	*10		Tennessee St.	†10		Western Ill.	9
	Canterbury	8		Trinity (Conn.)	7	1960	Albright	9
	Florida St.	8		Trinity (Tex.)	9		Arkansas Tech	†10
	Frank. & Marsh.	9		Whitworth	8		Humboldt St.	*†10
	Lehigh	9		Widener	7		Langston	9
	Lewis & Clark	*8		Worcester Tech	6		Lenoir-Rhyne	*‡10
	Md.-East. Shore	8	1955	Alfred	8		Montclair St.	8
	Mission House	6		Centre	8		Muskingum	9
	New Hampshire	8		Coe	8		Northern Iowa	†9
	St. Lawrence	8		Col. of Emporia	9		Ohio	10
	St. Norbert	7		Drexel	8		Ottawa	9
	Thiel	7		Grambling	10		Wagner	9
	Valparaiso	†9		Heidelberg	9		West Chester	9
	West Liberty St.	*8		Hillsdale	9		Whitworth	9
	Wis.-La Crosse	*9		Juniata	‡8		Willamette	8
	Wis.-Whitewater	6		Md.-East. Shore	9	1961	Albion	8
1951	Bloomsburg	8		Miami (Ohio)	9		Baldwin-Wallace	9
	Bucknell	9		Muskingum	8		Butler	9
	Col. of Emporia	8		Northern St.	†9		Central Okla.	9
	Ill. Wesleyan	8		Parsons	8		Florida A&M	10
	Lawrence	7		Shepherd	8		Fresno St.	*9
	Northern Ill.	9		Southeast Mo. St.	9		Linfield	*†10
	Principia	6		Trinity (Conn.)	7		Mayville St.	8
	South Dak. Tech	8		Whitworth	9		Millikin	8
	St. Michael's	6		Wis.-Stevens Point	8		Northern St.	9
	Susquehanna	6	1956	Alfred	7		Ottawa	9
	Trenton St.	6		Central Mich.	9		Pittsburg St.	**9
	Valparaiso	9		Hillsdale	9		Wash. & Lee	9
	Western Md.	8		Lenoir-Rhyne	10		Wheaton (Ill.)	8
1952	Beloit	8		Milton	6		Whittier	†9
	Clarion	*8		Montana St.	‡9	1962	Carthage	8
	East Tex. St.	*10		Neb.-Kearney	9		Central Okla.	**9
	Fairmont St.	6		Redlands	9		Col. of Emporia	†10
	Idaho St.	8		Sam Houston St.	*9		Earlham	8
	Lenoir-Rhyne	†8		Southern Conn. St.	9		East Stroudsburg	†8
	Northeastern Okla.	†9		St. Thomas (Minn.)	8		John Carroll	7
	Peru St.	10		Tennessee St.	10		Kalamazoo	8
	Rochester	8		Westminster (Pa.)	8		Lenoir-Rhyne	*†10
	Shippensburg	7	1957	Elon	6		Northern St.	†9
	St. Norbert	6		Fairmont St.	7		Parsons	9
	West Chester	7		Florida A&M	9		St. John's (Minn.)	9
1953	Cal Poly SLO	9		Hillsdale	†9		Susquehanna	9
	Col. of Emporia	8		Hobart	6		Wittenberg	9
	Col. of Idaho	†8		Idaho St.	9	1963	Alabama A&M	8
	Defiance	8		Jamestown	7		Central Wash.	9
	East Tex. St.	‡10		Juniata	7		Coast Guard	†8
	Florida A&M	10		Lock Haven	8		Col. of Emporia	10
	Indianapolis	8		Middle Tenn. St.	10		Delaware	8
	Iowa Wesleyan	†9		Pittsburg St.	*10		John Carroll	7
	Juniata	7		Ripon	8		Lewis & Clark	8
	Northern St.	8		St. Norbert	8		Luther	9

Year	College	Wins
	McNeese St. 8	
	Neb.-Kearney.......†9	
	Northeastern ....†8	
	Northeastern Okla. ..*10	
	Northern Ill. *9	
	Prairie View ....*†9	
	Ripon 8	
	Sewanee 8	
	Southwest Mo. St. ...†9	
	Southwest Tex. St. ...10	
	St. John's (Minn.) ...**8	
	Wis.-Eau Claire 7	
1964	Albion 8	
	Amherst 8	
	Cal St. Los Angeles ...9	
	Concordia-M'head ..*‡9	
	Frank. & Marsh........8	
	Montclair St. 7	
	Prairie View 9	
	Wagner 10	
	Western St. ....†9	
	Westminster (Pa.) 8	
	Wittenberg 8	
1965	Ball St...............‡9	
	East Stroudsburg *9	
	Fairmont St. ....†8	
	Georgetown (Ky.) 9	
	Ill. Wesleyan 8	
	Ithaca 8	
	Middle Tenn. St. 10	
	Morgan St.............9	
	North Dak. St. *10	
	Northern Ill...........†9	
	Ottawa 9	
	Springfield 9	
	St. John's (Minn.) ...**9	
	Sul Ross St. ....†10	
	Tennessee St........‡9	
1966	Central (Iowa) ....†9	
	Clarion...............9	
	Defiance 9	
	Morgan St............*8	
	Muskingum ....†9	
	Northwestern (La.)....9	
	San Diego St.........*10	
	Tennessee St. *9	

Year	College	Wins
	Waynesburg **9	
	Wilkes 8	
	Wis.-Whitewater ....*†9	

*Beginning in 1967,
NCAA members only.*

Year	College	Wins
1967	Alma 8	
	Central (Iowa) 9	
	Doane ....‡8	
	Lawrence 8	
	Morgan St.............8	
	North Dak. St. ....†9	
	Northern Mich. ......†9	
	Wagner 9	
	West Chester ....*†9	
	Wilkes 8	
1968	Alma 8	
	Doane *9	
	East Stroudsburg ....‡8	
	Indiana (Pa.).........†9	
	North Dak. St.........*9	
	Randolph-Macon 9	
1969	Albion 8	
	Carthage.............9	
	Defiance 9	
	Doane 8	
	Montana...........†10	
	North Dak. St........*9	
	Northern Colo. 10	
	Wesleyan 8	
	Wittenberg *9	
1970	Arkansas St. *10	
	Jacksonville St. 10	
	Montana ....†10	
	St. Olaf 9	
	Tennessee St. *10	
	Westminster (Pa.) ..**8	
	#Wittenberg 9	
1971	Alfred 8	
	Hampden-Sydney ..†10	
	Westminster (Pa.) ..‡8	
1972	Ashland 11	
	Bridgeport *10	
	Delaware 10	
	Doane ....†10	
	Frank. & Marsh.......9	

Year	College	Wins
	Heidelberg **9	
	Louisiana Tech *11	
	Middlebury 8	
	Monmouth (Ill.) 9	
1973	Tennessee St.........10	
	Western Ky........**†10	
1974	Louisiana Tech ....*†10	
	Michigan Tech 9	
	Nevada-Las Vegas .*†11	
1975	East Stroudsburg *9	
	North Dak. ....†9	
1976	East Stroudsburg ...‡9	
1977	Florida A&M 11	
	UC Davis ....*†10	
	Winston-Salem .....†11	
1978	Western St. ....*†9	
	Winston-Salem ....*†10	
1979	(None)	
1980	Minn.-Duluth 10	
	Missouri-Rolla 10	
1981	Northern Mich. ....*†10	
	Shippensburg ....**†11	
	Virginia Union ......†11	
1982	North Dak. St. .....*†11	
	Southwest Tex. St. **†11	
	UC Davis ....***†10	
1983	Central St. (Ohio) **†10	
	UC Davis ....*†10	
1984	(None)	
1985	Bloomsburg ....*†11	
1986	North Dak. St. ....***†10	
	UC Davis ....†10	
	Virginia Union ......†11	
1987	(None)	
1988	North Dak. St. ...****10	
	St. Mary's (Cal.)......10	
1989	Grand Valley St. ....†11	
	Jacksonville St. ..***†10	
	Pittsburg St. ....*†11	
	Texas A&I ....†10	
1990	North Dak. St. ...****10	
	Pittsburg St. ......**†10	
1991	Carson-Newman ...†10	
	Indiana (Pa.)......**†10	
	Jacksonville St. ...***†9	

Later forfeited all games.

THE SPOILERS

(Compiled since 1973, when the three-division reorganization plan was adopted by the special NCAA Convention.)

Following is a list of the spoilers of Division II teams that lost their perfect (undefeated, untied) record in their **season-ending** game, including the Division II championship playoffs. An asterisk (*) indicates an NCAA championship playoff game, a pound sign (#) indicates an NAIA championship playoff game, and a dagger (†) indicates the home team in a regular-season game. A game involving two undefeated, untied teams is in bold face.

Date	Spoiler	Victim	Score
12-15-73	*Louisiana Tech	Western Ky.	34-0
11-30-74	*Louisiana Tech	Western Caro.	10-7
11-15-75	†LIU-C. W. Post	American Int'l	21-0
11-15-75	Eastern N. Mex.	†Northern Colo.	16-14
11-29-75	*Livingston	North Dak.	34-14
11-20-76	†Shippensburg	East Stroudsburg	tie14-14
12-3-77	‡South Caro. St.	Winston-Salem	10-7
12-3-77	*Lehigh	UC Davis	39-30
12-2-78	*Delaware	Winston-Salem	41-0
11-28-81	*Shippensburg	Virginia Union	40-27

Date	Spoiler	Victim	Score
12-5-81	*North Dak. St.	Shippensburg	18-6
12-5-81	*Southwest Tex. St.	Northern Mich.	62-0
12-4-82	*UC Davis	North Dak. St.	19-14
12-11-82	**Southwest Tex. St.**	**UC Davis**	**34-9**
12-3-83	*North Dak. St.	UC Davis	26-17
12-10-83	*North Dak. St.	Central St. (Ohio)	41-21
12-7-85	*North Ala.	Bloomsburg	34-0
11-15-86	West Chester	†Millersville	7-3
11-29-86	*Troy St.	Virginia Union	31-7
11-29-86	*South Dak.	UC Davis	26-23
12-10-88	*Adams St.	Pittsburg St.	13-10
11-18-89	*Mississippi Col.	Texas A&I	34-19
11-18-89	*Indiana (Pa.)	Grand Valley St.	34-24
11-25-89	*Angelo St.	Pittsburg St.	24-21
12-9-89	*Mississippi Col.	Jacksonville St.	3-0
12-1-90	**North Dak. St.**	**Pittsburg St.**	**39-29**
11-23-91	#Western St.	Carson-Newman	38-21
12-7-91	**Jacksonville St.**	**Indiana (Pa.)**	**27-20**
12-14-91	*Pittsburg St.	Jacksonville St.	23-6

‡ *Gold Bowl.*

CLIFFHANGERS

Regular-season Division II games *won on the final play of the game* (from 1973). The extra point is listed when it provided the margin of victory after the winning touchdown.

Date	Opponents, Score	Game-winning play
10-12-74	Westminster (Pa.) 23, Indiana (Pa.) 20	Rick Voltz 20 FG
11-23-74	Arkansas St. 22, McNeese St. 20	Joe Duren 56 FG
10-11-75	Indiana (Pa.) 16, Westminster (Pa.) 14	Tom Alper 37 FG
10-18-75	Cal St. Fullerton 32, UC Riverside 31	John Choukair 52 FG
9-25-76	Portland St. 50, Montana 49	Dave Stief 2 pass from June Jones
10-30-76	South Dak. St. 16, Northern Iowa 13	Monte Mosiman 53 pass from Dick Weikert
10-27-77	Albany (N.Y.) 42, Maine 39	Larry Leibowitz 19 FG
10-6-79	Indiana (Pa.) 31, Shippensburg 24	Jeff Heath 4 run
9-6-80	Ferris St. 20, St. Joseph's (Ind.) 15	Greg Washington 17 pass from (holder) John Gibson (after bad snap on 34 FG attempt)
11-15-80	Morris Brown 19, Bethune-Cookman 18	Ray Mills 1 run (Carlton Jackson kick)
11-15-80	Tuskegee 23, Alabama A&M 21	Korda Joseph 45 FG
9-26-81	Abilene Christian 41, Northwestern (La.) 38	David Russell 17 pass from Loyal Proffitt
9-26-81	Cal St. Chico 10, Santa Clara 7	Mike Sullivan 46 FG
10-10-81	LIU-C. W. Post 37, James Madison 36	Tom Ehrhardt 10 pass from Tom Ehrhardt (Ehrhardt run)
10-9-82	Westminster (Pa.) 3, Indiana (Pa.) 0	Ron Bauer 35 FG
9-17-83	Central Mo. St. 13, Sam Houston St. 10	Steve Huff 27 FG
9-29-84	Angelo St. 18, Eastern N. Mex. 17	Ned Cox 3 run
10-13-84	Northwest Mo. St. 35, Central Mo. St. 34	Pat Johnson 20 FG
10-13-84	UC Davis 16, Cal St. Chico 13	Ray Sullivan 48 FG
11-3-84	Bloomsburg 34, West Chester 31	Curtis Still 50 pass from Jay Dedea
11-20-84	Central Fla. 28, Illinois St. 24	Jeff Farmer 30 punt return
9-7-85	Central Fla. 39, Bethune-Cookman 37	Ed O'Brien 55 FG
9-13-86	Michigan Tech 34, St. Norbert 30	Jim Wallace 41 pass from Dave Walter
9-20-86	Delaware 33, West Chester 31	Fred Singleton 3 run
10-18-86	Indianapolis 25, Evansville 24	Ken Bruce 18 FG
10-24-87	Indianapolis 27, Evansville 24	Doug Sabotin 2 pass from Tom Crowell
11-7-87	Central Mo. St. 35, Northeast Mo. St. 33	Phil Brandt 25 FG
9-3-88	Alabama A&M 17, North Ala. 16	Edmond Allen 30 FG
9-17-89	Morehouse 22, Fort Valley St. 21	David Boone 18 pass from Jimmie Davis
11-11-89	East Stroudsburg 22, Central Conn. St. 19	Frank Magolon 4 pass from Tom Taylor
10-13-90	East Stroudsburg 23, Bloomsburg 21	Ken Kopetchny 3 pass from Bret Comp
11-10-90	Southern Conn. St. 12, Central Conn. St. 10	Paul Boulanger 48 FG
9-21-91	Livingston 22, Albany St. (Ga.) 21	Matt Carman 24 pass from Deon Timmons (Anthony Armstrong kick)
10-26-91	Central Mo. St. 38, Northeast Mo. St. 37	Chris Pyatt 45 FG

DIVISION II STATISTICS TRENDS

(For valid comparisons from 1973, when College Division teams
were divided into Division II and Division III)

(Average Per Game, Both Teams)

Year	Rushing				Passing				Total Offense			Scoring		
	Plays	Yds.	Avg.	Att.	Cmp.	Pct.	Yds.	Av. Att.	Plays	Yds.	Avg.	TD	FG	Pts.
1973	95.1	339.1	3.57	40.0	17.6	.442	243.0	6.08	135.1	582.1	4.31	5.06	0.83	36.4
1974	95.1	312.6	3.29	38.9	17.3	.445	244.8	6.28	134.0	557.3	4.16	5.10	0.86	37.9
1975	94.6	337.1	3.56	38.9	17.4	.448	241.2	6.21	133.5	578.3	4.33	4.98	0.89	37.1
1976	94.7	331.4	3.50	39.8	18.2	.457	251.8	6.32	134.5	583.2	4.34	5.03	0.93	37.4
1977	*96.7	*347.6	3.59	40.6	18.4	.453	252.4	6.21	137.3	599.9	4.37	5.16	0.91	38.2
1978	95.9	338.5	3.52	41.1	18.4	.448	248.5	6.05	137.0	587.0	4.29	5.11	0.98	38.6
1979	91.6	309.4	3.38	41.9	18.9	.450	251.6	6.00	133.4	560.9	4.20	4.73	1.03	35.8
1980	90.5	307.5	3.40	44.7	20.7	.463	275.2	6.16	135.2	582.6	4.31	5.02	1.04	37.8
1981	89.1	293.2	3.29	47.9	21.9	.457	291.7	6.09	137.0	584.9	4.27	4.95	1.08	37.4
1982	86.5	288.2	3.32	52.2	24.5	.469	322.0	6.17	138.6	610.2	4.40	5.25	1.24	39.6
1983	86.3	290.7	3.37	52.1	25.0	.479	329.0	6.31	138.4	619.7	4.48	5.27	1.23	39.2
1984	83.8	284.3	3.39	52.0	26.4	.481	329.5	6.33	135.8	613.8	4.52	5.25	1.23	38.7
1985	83.3	288.0	3.46	*54.8	*26.4	.483	341.2	6.23	138.1	629.2	4.56	5.46	1.30	41.8
1986	83.6	297.7	3.56	53.7	26.0	.484	336.8	6.27	137.3	634.5	4.62	5.78	1.27	43.9
1987	85.6	303.7	3.55	49.2	23.8	.483	311.0	6.31	134.9	614.7	4.56	5.29	1.28	40.4
1988	87.7	318.8	3.64	49.2	23.8	.484	319.5	6.49	136.9	638.3	4.66	5.83	1.29	44.2
1989	87.3	332.0	3.80	50.1	24.3	*.485	323.0	6.45	137.4	655.0	4.77	5.94	1.24	45.1
1990	87.3	336.6	*3.86	52.8	25.6	.485	*346.6	*6.57	*140.0	*683.2	*4.88	*6.19	1.29	*46.7
1991	87.4	335.5	3.84	52.7	25.5	.484	344.8	6.54	140.0	680.3	4.86	6.09	*1.31	46.4

* Record.

ADDITIONAL DIVISION II STATISTICS TRENDS

(Average Per Game, Both Teams)

Year	†Teams	Games	Punting		Kick Attempts		Two-Point Attempts		Field Goals
			No.	Avg.	Pct. Made	Pct. of Total Tries	Pct. Made	Pct. of Total Tries	Pct. Made
1973	131	1,326	11.5	36.0	.833	.876	.419	.124	.439
1974	136	1,388	11.4	*36.8	.830	.859	.432	.141	.472
1975	126	1,282	11.0	36.3	.837	.874	.464	.126	.476
1976	122	1,244	11.6	36.2	.841	.878	.419	.122	.461
1977	124	1,267	11.7	36.1	.832	.874	.436	.126	.442
1978	91	921	11.9	35.9	.830	.880	.452	.120	.519
1979	99	1,016	12.1	35.2	.854	.861	.459	.139	.543
1980	103	1,040	11.7	35.6	.852	.864	.438	.136	.512
1981	113	1,138	*12.2	35.6	.856	.861	.440	.139	.531
1982	118	1,196	12.2	36.4	.862	.877	.431	.123	.560
1983	115	1,175	11.9	36.1	.866	.847	.428	.153	.564
1984	112	1,150	11.8	36.4	.876	.875	.448	.125	.567
1985	107	1,098	11.5	35.9	*.905	.864	.414	.136	.549
1986	109	1,124	11.1	36.5	.870	.865	.466	.135	*.576
1987	105	1,100	11.4	35.7	.857	.865	.435	.135	.547
1988	111	1,114	11.2	35.6	.886	.868	.399	.132	.555
1989	106	1,084	10.9	36.7	.873	.845	.376	*.155	.567
1990	105	1,065	11.3	35.7	.876	*.885	*.474	.115	.568
1991	114	1,150	10.9	36.1	.882	.880	.426	.120	.572

* Record.   † Teams reporting statistics, not the total number of teams in the division.

DIVISION III RECORDS

Running back Stanley Drayton set Division III season records for touchdowns scored (28), points scored (168) and points per game (16.8) in 1991 to pace a high-powered Allegheny attack that finished third in the division in scoring offense (37.5 points per game).

Division III football records are based on the performances of Division III teams since the three-division reorganization plan was adopted by the special NCAA Convention in August 1973.

INDIVIDUAL RECORDS

TOTAL OFFENSE

(Rushing Plus Passing)

Most Plays

Quarter
32—Mike Wallace, Ohio Wesleyan vs. Denison, Oct. 3, 1981 (4th)

Half
59—Mike Wallace, Ohio Wesleyan vs. Denison, Oct. 3, 1981 (2nd)

Game
89—Rhett Bonner, Bethel (Minn.) vs. Gust. Adolphus, Nov. 2, 1985 (78 passes, 11 rushes; 407 yards)

Season
614—Tim Peterson, Wis.-Stout, 1989 (3,244 yards)

2 Yrs
1,165—Kirk Baumgartner, Wis.-Stevens Point, 1987-88 (7,502 yards)

3 Yrs
1,695—Kirk Baumgartner, Wis.-Stevens Point, 1987-89 (11,042 yards)

Career
(4 Yrs.) 2,007—Kirk Baumgartner, Wis.-Stevens Point, 1986-89 (12,767 yards)

Most Plays Per Game

Season
61.4—Tim Peterson, Wis.-Stout, 1989 (614 in 10)

2 Yrs
55.6—Keith Bishop, Wheaton (Ill.), 1984-85 (1,000 in 18)

3 Yrs
53.0—Kirk Baumgartner, Wis.-Stevens Point, 1987-89 (1,695 in 32)

Career
(4 Yrs.) 49.0—Kirk Baumgartner, Wis.-Stevens Point, 1986-89 (2,007 in 41)

Most Plays by a Freshman

Season
479—Jason Cooperider, Denison, 1989 (2,301 yards)
Also holds per-game record at 47.9 (479 in 10)

Most Yards Gained

Game
596—John Love, North Park vs. Elmhurst, Oct. 13, 1990 (533 passing, 63 rushing)

Season
3,790—Kirk Baumgartner, Wis.-Stevens Point, 1988 (-38 rushing, 3,828 passing)

2 Yrs
7,502—Kirk Baumgartner, Wis.-Stevens Point, 1987-88 (-81 rushing, 7,583 passing)

3 Yrs
11,042—Kirk Baumgartner, Wis.-Stevens Point, 1987-89 (-233 rushing, 11,275 passing)

Career
(4 Yrs.) 12,767—Kirk Baumgartner, Wis.-Stevens Point, 1986-89 (-261 rushing, 13,028 passing)

Most Yards Gained Per Game

Season
354.8—Keith Bishop, Wheaton (Ill.), 1983 (3,193 in 9)

2 Yrs
349.0—Kirk Baumgartner, Wis.-Stevens Point, 1988-89 (7,330 in 21)

3 Yrs
345.1—Kirk Baumgartner, Wis.-Stevens Point, 1987-89 (11,042 in 32)

Career
311.4—Kirk Baumgartner, Wis.-Stevens Point, 1986-89 (12,767 in 41)

Most Yards Gained by a Freshman

Season
2,554—Brad Hensley, Kenyon, 1991 (441 plays)
Per-game record—260.0, Dennis Bogacz, Wis.-Oshkosh, 1988 (2,080 in 8)

Most Games Gaining 300 Yards or More

Season
8—Kirk Baumgartner, Wis.-Stevens Point, 1989

Career
26—Kirk Baumgartner, Wis.-Stevens Point, 1986-89

Most Consecutive Games Gaining 300 Yards or More

Season
6—Kirk Baumgartner, Wis.-Stevens Point, 1987

Gaining 4,000 Yards Rushing and 2,000 Yards Passing

Career
Chris Spriggs, Denison, 1983-86 (4,248 rushing & 2,799 passing)
Also holds record for yards gained by a running back at 7,047

Gaining 3,000 Yards Rushing and 3,000 Yards Passing

Career
Clay Sampson (TB), Denison, 1977-80 (3,726 rushing & 3,194 passing)

Highest Average Gain Per Play

Season
(Min. 2,500 yards) 11.97—Willie Reyna, La Verne, 1991 (220 for 2,633)

Career
(Min. 6,000 yards) 6.96—Walter Briggs, Montclair St., 1983-86 (972 for 6,769)
(Min. 7,000 yards) 6.46—Gary Collier, Emory & Henry, 1984-87 (1,089 for 7,036)

Most Touchdowns Responsible For (TDs Scored and Passed For)

Career
123—Kirk Baumgartner, Wis.-Stevens Point, 1986-89 (110 passing, 13 rushing)
Also holds per-game record at 3.00 (123 in 41)

222   *1992 NCAA FOOTBALL*

RUSHING

Most Rushes
Game
58—Bill Kaiser, Wabash vs. DePauw, Nov. 9, 1985 (211 yards)
Season
380—Mike Birosak, Dickinson, 1989 (1,798 yards)
Career
1,112—Mike Birosak, Dickinson, 1986-89 (4,662 yards)

Most Rushes Per Game
Season
38.0—Mike Birosak, Dickinson, 1989 (380 in 10)
Career
32.7—Chris Sizemore, Bridgewater (Va.), 1972-74 (851 in 26)

Most Rushes by a Quarterback
Season
231—Jeff Saveressig, Wis.-River Falls, 1988 (1,095 yards)
Also holds per-game record at 25.7 (231 in 9)

Most Consecutive Rushes by the Same Player
Game
46—Dan Walsh, Montclair St. vs. Ramapo, Sept. 30, 1989 (during 13 ball possessions)
Season
51—Dan Walsh, Montclair St., 1989 (Sept. 23 to Sept. 30)

Most Yards Gained
Half
310—Leroy Horn, Montclair St. vs. Jersey City St., Nov. 9, 1985 (21 rushes)
Game
382—Pete Baranek, Carthage vs. North Central, Oct. 5, 1985 (24 rushes)
Season
2,035—Ricky Gales, Simpson, 1989 (297 rushes)
2 Yrs
3,326—Ricky Gales, Simpson, 1988-89 (530 rushes)
3 Yrs
4,476—Joe Dudek, Plymouth St., 1983-85 (662 rushes)
Career
(4 Yrs.) 5,570—Joe Dudek, Plymouth St., 1982-85 (785 rushes)

Most Yards Gained Per Game
Season
203.5—Ricky Gales, Simpson, 1989 (2,035 in 10)
2 Yrs
175.1—Ricky Gales, Simpson, 1988-89 (3,326 in 19)
3 Yrs
165.3—Terry Underwood, Wagner, 1986-88 (3,803 in 23)
Career
151.8—Terry Underwood, Wagner, 1985-88 (5,010 in 33)

Most Yards Gained by a Freshman
Season
1,283—Jason Wooley, Worcester Tech, 1990 (209 rushes)
Per-game record—148.4, Chris Harper, Carthage, 1990 (1,187 in 8)

Most Rushing Yards Gained by a Quarterback
Game
235—Mark Cota, Wis.-River Falls vs. Minn.-Morris, Sept. 13, 1986 (27 rushes)

Season
1,279—Mark Cota, Wis.-River Falls, 1986 (227 rushes)
Also holds per-game record at 127.9 (1,279 in 10)
Career
2,171—Sam Juarascio, DePauw, 1972-75 (407 rushes)

Longest Gain by a Quarterback
Game
98—Jon Hinds, Principia vs. Illinois Col., Sept. 20, 1986 (TD)

Most Games Gaining 100 Yards or More
Career
30—Joe Dudek, Plymouth St., 1982-85 (41 games)

Most Consecutive Games Gaining 100 Yards or More
Career
18—Hank Wineman, Albion, 1990-91

Most Games Gaining 200 Yards or More
Season
8—Ricky Gales, Simpson, 1989 (consecutive)
Career
11—Ricky Gales, Simpson, 1988-89

Most Seasons Gaining 1,000 Yards or More
Career
4—Joe Dudek, Plymouth St., 1982-85; Rich Kowalski, Hobart, 1972-75

Two Players, Same Team, Each Gaining 1,000 Yards or More
Season
By six teams. Most recent: Beloit, 1990 (Shane Stadler, WB, 1,227 & Steve Dixon, FB, 1,008)

Most Yards Gained Rushing by Two Players, Same Team
Game
472—Jon Warga (TB) 264 & Jeff Stockdale (FB) 208, Wittenberg vs. Emory & Henry, Oct. 27, 1990
Season
2,590—Jon Warga (TB) 1,836 & Jeff Stockdale (FB) 727, Wittenberg, 1990 (10 games)

Highest Average Gain Per Rush
Game
(Min. 15 rushes) 19.1—Billy Johnson, Widener vs. Swarthmore, Nov. 10, 1973 (15 for 286)
(Min. 24 rushes) 15.9—Pete Baranek, Carthage vs. North Central, Oct. 5, 1985 (24 for 382)
Season
(Min. 140 rushes) 8.89—Billy Johnson, Widener, 1973 (168 for 1,494)
(Min. 195 rushes) 7.49—Sandy Rogers, Emory & Henry, 1986 (231 for 1,730)
Career
(Min. 500 rushes) 7.10—Joe Dudek, Plymouth St., 1982-85 (785 for 5,570)

Most Touchdowns Scored by Rushing
Game
6—Rob Sinclair, Simpson vs. Upper Iowa, Nov. 10, 1990
Season
27—Stanley Drayton, Allegheny, 1991
Also holds per-game record at 3.0 (27 in 9)
Career
76—Joe Dudek, Plymouth St., 1982-85
Also holds per-game record at 1.85 (76 in 41)

Most Touchdowns Scored by Rushing by a Quarterback

Season

16—Mark Cota, Wis.-River Falls, 1986
Also holds per-game record at 1.60 (16 in 10)

PASSING

Highest Passing Efficiency Rating Points

Season

(Min. 15 atts. per game) *203.3—Joe Blake, Simpson, 1989 (144 attempts, 93 completions, 3 interceptions, 1,705 yards, 19 TDs)

(Min. 20 atts. per game) 175.4—Jimbo Fisher, Samford, 1987 (252 attempts, 139 completions, 5 interceptions, 2,394 yards, 34 TDs)

Career

(Min. 325 comps.) 153.3—Joe Blake, Simpson, 1987-90 (672 attempts, 399 completions, 15 interceptions, 6,183 yards, 43 TDs)

* *Declared champion; with six more pass attempts (making 15 per game), all interceptions, still would have highest efficiency (187.3).*

Most Passes Attempted

Quarter

31—Mike Wallace, Ohio Wesleyan vs. Denison, Oct. 3, 1981 (4th)

Half

57—Mike Wallace, Ohio Wesleyan vs. Denison, Oct. 3, 1981 (2nd)

Game

79—Mike Wallace, Ohio Wesleyan vs. Denison, Oct. 3, 1981 (completed 47)

Season

527—Kirk Baumgartner, Wis.-Stevens Point, 1988 (completed 276)

2 Yrs

993—Kirk Baumgartner, Wis.-Stevens Point, 1987-88 (completed 519)

3 Yrs

1,448—Kirk Baumgartner, Wis.-Stevens Point, 1987-89 (completed 766)

Career

(4 Yrs.) 1,696—Kirk Baumgartner, Wis.-Stevens Point, 1986-89 (completed 883)

Most Passes Attempted by a Freshman

Season

384—Brad Hensley, Kenyon, 1991 (completed 198)

Most Passes Attempted Per Game

Season

50.8—Keith Bishop, Wheaton (Ill.), 1985 (457 in 9)

Career

42.3—Keith Bishop, Ill. Wesleyan, 1981; Wheaton (Ill.), 1983-85 (1,311 in 31)

Most Passes Attempted Per Game by a Freshman

Season

46.3—Jordan Poznick, Principia, 1990 (278 in 6)

Most Passes Completed

Quarter

21—Rob Bristow, Pomona-Pitzer vs. Whittier, Oct. 19, 1985 (4th)

Half

36—Mike Wallace, Ohio Wesleyan vs. Denison, Oct. 3, 1981 (2nd)

Game

50—Tim Lynch, Hofstra vs. Fordham, Oct. 19, 1991 (attempted 69)

Season

276—Kirk Baumgartner, Wis.-Stevens Point, 1988 (attempted 527)

2 Yrs

523—Kirk Baumgartner, Wis.-Stevens Point, 1988-89 (attempted 982)

3 Yrs

766—Kirk Baumgartner, Wis.-Stevens Point, 1987-89 (attempted 1,448)

Career

(4 Yrs.) 883—Kirk Baumgartner, Wis.-Stevens Point, 1986-89 (attempted 1,696)

Most Passes Completed by a Freshman

Season

199—Luke Hanks, Otterbein, 1990 (attempted 370)

Most Passes Completed Per Game

Season

29.1—Keith Bishop, Wheaton (Ill.), 1985 (262 in 9)

Career

24.9—Keith Bishop, Ill. Wesleyan, 1981; Wheaton (Ill.), 1983-85 (772 in 31)

Most Passes Completed Per Game by a Freshman

Season

21.8—Jordan Poznick, Principia, 1990 (131 in 6)

Highest Percentage of Passes Completed

Game

(Min. 20 comps.) 84.6%—Bob Krepfle, Wis.-La Crosse vs. Anderson, Oct. 6, 1984 (22 of 26)

(Min. 25 comps.) 83.3%—Scott Driggers, Colorado Col. vs. Neb. Wesleyan, Sept. 10, 1983 (35 of 42)

Season

(Min. 250 atts.) 63.7%—Willie Reyna, La Verne, 1991 (170 of 267)

Career

(Min. 550 atts.) 62.2%—Brian Moore, Baldwin-Wallace, 1981-84 (437 of 703)

(Min. 750 atts.) 60.0%—Scott Driggers, Colorado Col., 1981-84 (613 of 1,022)

Most Consecutive Passes Completed

Game

17—William Snyder, Carnegie Mellon vs. Wooster, Oct. 20, 1990

Season

20—Dick Puccio, Cortland St. vs. Brockport St., Oct. 12, and Albany (N.Y.), Oct. 19, 1991

Most Passes Had Intercepted

Game

8—Jason Clark, Ohio Northern vs. John Carroll, Nov. 9, 1991; Jim Higgins, Brockport St. vs. Buffalo St., Sept. 29, 1990; Dennis Bogacz, Wis.-Oshkosh vs. Wis.-Stevens Point, Oct. 29, 1988; Kevin Karwath, Canisius vs. Liberty, Nov. 19, 1979

Season

43—Steve Hendry, Wis.-Superior, 1982 (attempted 480)
Also holds per-game record at 3.9 (43 in 11)

Career

117—Steve Hendry, Wis.-Superior, 1980-83 (attempted 1,343)
Per-game record—3.2, Willie Martinez, Oberlin, 1973-74 (58 in 18)

Lowest Percentage of Passes Had Intercepted
Season
(Min. 150 atts.) 0.89% — Brett Russ, Union (N.Y.), 1991 (2 of 224)
Career
(Min. 600 atts.) 1.93% — Mark Casale, Montclair St., 1980-83 (16 of 828)

Most Passes Attempted Without Interception
Game
61 — Mark Krajnik, Occidental vs. La Verne, Oct. 18, 1986 (32 completions); Brion Demski, Wis.-Stevens Point vs. Wis.-Superior, Oct. 16, 1981 (31 completions)
Season
124 — Tim Tenhet, Sewanee, 1982

Most Consecutive Passes Attempted Without an Interception
Season
205 — Kirk Baumgartner, Wis.-Stevens Point, 1989 (during 6 games; began Sept. 16 vs. Wis.-Platteville, ended Oct. 21 vs. Wis.-Whitewater)

Most Yards Gained
Game
585 — Tim Lynch, Hofstra vs. Fordham, Oct. 19, 1991
Season
3,828 — Kirk Baumgartner, Wis.-Stevens Point, 1988
2 Yrs
7,583 — Kirk Baumgartner, Wis.-Stevens Point, 1987-88
3 Yrs
11,275 — Kirk Baumgartner, Wis.-Stevens Point, 1987-89
Career
(4 Yrs.) 13,028 — Kirk Baumgartner, Wis.-Stevens Point, 1986-89

Most Yards Gained by a Freshman
Season
2,520 — Brad Hensley, Kenyon, 1991

Most Yards Gained Per Game
Season
369.2 — Kirk Baumgartner, Wis.-Stevens Point, 1989 (3,692 in 10)
Career
317.8 — Kirk Baumgartner, Wis.-Stevens Point, 1986-89 (13,028 in 41)

Most Yards Gained Per Game by a Freshman
Season
268.8 — Dennis Bogacz, Wis.-Oshkosh, 1988 (2,150 in 8)

Most Games Passing for 200 Yards or More
Season
10 — Kirk Baumgartner, Wis.-Stevens Point, 1989, 1988, 1987
Career
32 — Kirk Baumgartner, Wis.-Stevens Point, 1986-89

Most Consecutive Games Passing for 200 Yards or More
Season
10 — Kirk Baumgartner, Wis.-Stevens Point, 1989 (entire season)
Career
27 — Keith Bishop, Ill. Wesleyan, 1981; Wheaton (Ill.), 1983-85

Most Games Passing for 300 Yards or More
Season
9 — Kirk Baumgartner, Wis.-Stevens Point, 1989

Career
24 — Kirk Baumgartner, Wis.-Stevens Point, 1986-89

Most Consecutive Games Passing for 300 Yards or More
Season
9 — Kirk Baumgartner, Wis.-Stevens Point, 1989 (began Sept. 9 vs. St. Norbert, through Nov. 4 vs. Wis.-Superior)
Career
13 — Kirk Baumgartner, Wis.-Stevens Point, 1988-89 (began Oct. 22, 1988, vs. Wis.-Stout, through Nov. 4, 1989, vs. Wis.-Superior)

Most Yards Gained by Two Opposing Players
Game
928 — Brion Demski, Wis.-Stevens Point (477) & Steve Hendry, Wis.-Superior (451), Oct. 17, 1981 (completed 70 of 123)

Most Yards Gained Per Attempt
Season
(Min. 175 atts.) 10.49 — George Muller, Hofstra, 1980 (189 for 1,983)
(Min. 275 atts.) 8.73 — Keith Bishop, Wheaton (Ill.), 1983 (375 for 3,274)
Career
(Min. 600 atts.) 9.20 — Joe Blake, Simpson, 1987-90 (672 for 6,183)
(Min. 950 atts.) 8.22 — John Clark, Wis.-Eau Claire, 1987-90 (1,119 for 9,196)

Most Yards Gained Per Completion
Season
(Min. 100 comps.) 19.7 — David Parker, Bishop, 1981 (114 for 2,242)
(Min. 200 comps.) 15.5 — Kirk Baumgartner, Wis.-Stevens Point, 1987 (243 for 3,755)
Career
(Min. 300 comps.) 18.3 — David Parker, Bishop, 1981-84 (378 for 6,934)
(Min. 425 comps.) 15.1 — Rob Light, Moravian, 1986-89 (438 for 6,624)

Most Touchdown Passes
Quarter
4 — By five players. Most recent: Kirk Baumgartner, Wis.-Stevens Point vs. Wis.-Whitewater, Oct. 21, 1989 (3rd)
Game
8 — Kirk Baumgartner, Wis.-Stevens Point vs. Wis.-Superior, Nov. 4, 1989
Season
39 — Kirk Baumgartner, Wis.-Stevens Point, 1989
Also holds per-game record at 3.90 (39 in 10)
Career
110 — Kirk Baumgartner, Wis.-Stevens Point, 1986-1989
Also holds per-game record at 2.68 (110 in 41)

Highest Percentage of Passes for Touchdowns
Season
(Min. 200 atts.) 13.49% — Jimbo Fisher, Samford, 1987 (34 of 252)
(Min. 300 atts.) 8.87% — Craig Solomon, Rhodes, 1978 (29 of 327)
Career
(Min. 625 atts.) 10.84% — Gary Collier, Emory & Henry, 1984-87 (80 of 738)
(Min. 800 atts.) 7.59% — Scott Scesney, St. John's (N.Y.), 1986-89 (71 of 935)

Most Touchdown Passes by a Freshman
Season
25 — David Parker, Bishop, 1981
Per-game record — 2.44, Jim Ballard, Wilmington (Ohio), 1990 (22 in 9)

Career
27—Dan Stewart, Union (N.Y.) (from Nov. 14, 1981, through Nov. 10, 1984)

RECEIVING

Most Passes Caught
Game
20—Rich Johnson, Pace vs. Fordham, Nov. 7, 1987 (206 yards); Pete Thompson, Carroll (Wis.) vs. Augustana (Ill.), Nov. 4, 1978 (224 yards)
Season
106—Theo Blanco (RB), Wis.-Stevens Point, 1987 (1,616 yards)
Career
258—Bill Stromberg, Johns Hopkins, 1978-81 (3,776 yards)

Most Passes Caught Per Game
Season
10.2—Scott Faessler, Framingham St., 1990 (92 in 9)
Career
7.2—Bill Stromberg, Johns Hopkins, 1978-81 (258 in 36)

Most Passes Caught by a Tight End
Game
16—Shawn Graham, St. Thomas (Minn.) vs. Hamline, Nov. 13, 1982
Season
72—Don Moehling, Wis.-Stevens Point, 1988 (1,290 yards)
Career
171—Jim Maransky, Albright, 1986-89 (2,128 yards)

Most Passes Caught by a Running Back
Game
17—Theo Blanco, Wis.-Stevens Point vs. Wis.-Oshkosh, Oct. 31, 1987 (271 yards); Tim Mowery, Wis.-Superior vs. Wis.-Stevens Point, Oct. 17, 1981 (154 yards)
Season
106—Theo Blanco, Wis.-Stevens Point, 1987 (1,616 yards)
Career
169—Mike Christman, Wis.-Stevens Point, 1983-86 (2,190 yards)

Most Passes Caught by a Freshman
Season
67—Bill Stromberg, Johns Hopkins, 1978 (1,027 yards)

Most Passes Caught by Two Players, Same Team
Season
158—Theo Blanco (RB) 106 & Aatron Kenney (WR) 52, Wis.-Stevens Point, 1987 (2,713 yards, 24 TDs)

Most Passes Caught by Three Players, Same Team
Season
217—Theo Blanco (WR) 80, Don Moehling (TE) 72 & Jim Mares (RB) 65, Wis.-Stevens Point, 1988. Totaled 2,959 yards and 19 TDs (team totals: 285-3,924-26)

Most Consecutive Games Catching a Pass
Career
36—David Lauber, Wheaton (Ill.), 1985, 87-89; Bill Stromberg, Johns Hopkins, 1978-81 (entire career)

Most Yards Gained
Game
309—Dale Amos, Frank. & Marsh. vs. Western Md., Oct. 24, 1987 (caught 12)
Season
1,616—Theo Blanco (RB), Wis.-Stevens Point, 1987 (caught 106)
Career
3,846—Dale Amos, Frank. & Marsh., 1986-89 (caught 233)

Most Yards Gained Per Game
Season
164.8—Jim Myers, Kenyon, 1974 (1,483 in 9)
Career
110.1—Tim McNamara, Trinity (Conn.), 1981-84 (2,313 in 21)

Most Yards Gained by a Tight End
Game
267—Tom Mullady, Rhodes vs. Rose-Hulman, Nov. 11, 1978 (caught 13)
Season
1,290—Don Moehling, Wis.-Stevens Point, 1988 (caught 72)
Career
2,663—Don Moehling, Wis.-Stevens Point, 1986-89 (caught 152)

Most Yards Gained by a Running Back
Game
271—Theo Blanco, Wis.-Stevens Point vs. Wis.-Oshkosh, Oct. 31, 1987 (caught 17)
Season
1,616—Theo Blanco, Wis.-Stevens Point, 1987 (caught 106)
Career
2,190—Mike Christman, Wis.-Stevens Point, 1983-86 (caught 169)

Most Yards Gained by Two Players, Same Team
Season
2,713—Theo Blanco (RB) 1,616 & Aatron Kenney (WR) 1,097, Wis.-Stevens Point, 1987 (158 receptions, 24 TDs)

Highest Average Gain Per Reception
Game
(Min. 3) 68.3—Paul Jaeckel, Elmhurst vs. Ill. Wesleyan, Oct. 8, 1983 (3 for 205)
(Min. 5) 56.8—Tom Casperson, Trenton St. vs. Ramapo, Nov. 15, 1980 (5 for 284)
Season
(Min. 35) 26.9—Marty Redlawsk, Concordia (Ill.), 1985 (38 for 1,022)
(Min. 50) 23.5—Evan Elkington, Worcester Tech, 1989 (52 for 1,220)
Career
(Min. 125) 20.0—Marty Redlawsk, Concordia (Ill.), 1984-87 (131 for 2,620)
(Min. 150) 19.4—John Aromando, Trenton St., 1981-84 (165 for 3,197)

Highest Average Gain Per Reception by a Running Back
Season
(Min. 50) 17.5—Barry Rose, Wis.-Stevens Point, 1989 (67 for 1,171)

Most Touchdown Passes Caught

Game

5—By nine players. Most recent: Chris Della Camera, Iona vs. FDU-Madison, Nov. 10, 1990

Season

20—John Aromando, Trenton St., 1983
Also holds per-game record at 2.0 (20 in 10)

Career

43—¢Chris Bisaillon, Ill. Wesleyan, 1989-91 (169 receptions)
Per-game record—1.08, Bill Stromberg, Johns Hopkins, 1978-81 (39 in 36)

¢ Active player.

Most Touchdown Passes Caught by a Freshman

Season

12—Chris Bisaillon, Ill. Wesleyan, 1989

Highest Percentage of Passes Caught for Touchdowns

Season

(Min. 12 TDs) 54.3%—Keith Gilliam, Randolph-Macon, 1984 (19 of 35)

Career

(Min. 20 TDs) 28.0%—Pat Schwanke, Lawrence, 1979-82 (28 of 100)

Most Consecutive Passes Caught for Touchdowns

9—Keith Gilliam, Randolph-Macon, 1984 (during four games)

PUNTING

Most Punts

Game

17—Jerry Williams, Frostburg St. vs. Salisbury St., Sept. 30, 1978

Season

106—Bob Blake, Wis.-Superior, 1977 (3,404 yards)
Per-game record—11.0, Mark Roedelbronn, FDU-Madison, 1990 (99 in 9)

Career

263—Chris Gardner, Loras, 1987-90 (9,394 yards)

Highest Average Per Punt

Season

(Min. 40) 44.9—Bob Burwell, Rose-Hulman, 1978 (61 for 2,740)

Career

(Min. 110) 42.1—Mike Manson, Ill. Benedictine, 1975-78 (120 for 5,056)

INTERCEPTIONS

Most Passes Intercepted

Game

5—By seven players. Most recent: Teel Bruner, Centre vs. Rose-Hulman, Oct. 20, 1984

Season

15—Mark Dorner, Juniata, 1987 (202 yards)
Also holds per-game record at 1.50 (15 in 10)

Career

34—Ralph Gebhardt, Rochester, 1972-75 (406 yards)

Most Consecutive Games Intercepting a Pass

Season

8—Vic Harris, Mount Union, 1985
Also holds career record at 8

Most Yards on Interception Returns

Game

164—Rick Conner, Western Md. vs. Dickinson, Oct. 15, 1983 (89-yard interception and 75-yard lateral after an interception)

Season

358—Rod Pesek, Whittier, 1987 (10 interceptions)

Career

479—Eugene Hunter, Fort Valley St., 1972-74 (29 interceptions)

Highest Average Gain Per Interception

Season

(Min. 7) 35.8—Rod Pesek, Whittier, 1987 (10 for 358)

Career

(Min. 20) 20.4—Todd Schoelzel, Wis.-Oshkosh, 1985-88 (22 for 448)

Most Touchdowns Scored on Interceptions

Game

2—By many players. Most recent: Aaron Brown, Capital vs. Bethany (W. Va.), Sept. 14, 1991

Season

3—By six players. Most recent: Richard Matthews, Coe, 1990

PUNT RETURNS

Most Punt Returns

Game

10—Ellis Wangelin, Wis.-River Falls vs. Wis.-Platteville, Oct. 12, 1985 (87 yards)

Season

48—Rick Bealer, Lycoming, 1989 (492 yards)

Career

126—Mike Caterbone, Frank. & Marsh., 1980-83 (1,141 yards)

Most Yards on Punt Returns

Game

212—Melvin Dillard, Ferrum vs. Newport News App., Oct. 13, 1990 (6 returns)

Season

688—Melvin Dillard, Ferrum, 1990 (25 returns)

Career

1,198—Chuck Downey, Stony Brook, 1984-87 (59 returns)

Highest Average Gain Per Return

Season

(Min. 1.2 per game) 31.2—Chuck Downey, Stony Brook, 1986 (17 for 530)

Career

(Min. 1.2 per game) 22.9—Keith Winston, Knoxville, 1986-87 (30 for 686)
(Min. 50) 20.3—Chuck Downey, Stony Brook, 1984-87 (59 for 1,198)

Most Touchdowns Scored on Punt Returns

Game

2—By five players. Most recent: Michael Clarke, Glassboro St. vs. Norwich, Sept. 15, 1990 (64 & 58 yards)

Season

4—Chris Warren, Ferrum, 1989 (18 returns); Keith Winston, Knoxville, 1986 (14 returns); Chuck Downey, Stony Brook, 1986 (17 returns); Matt Pekarske, Wis.-La Crosse, 1986 (37 returns)

Career
7—Chuck Downey, Stony Brook, 1984-87 (59 returns)

KICKOFF RETURNS

Most Kickoff Returns
Game
9—Larry Schurder, North Park vs. Elmhurst, Sept. 17, 1983 (229 yards)
Season
42—Phil Puryear, Wooster, 1990 (834 yards); Dirk Blood, Ohio Northern, 1987 (973 yards)
Career
85—Tom Southall, Colorado Col., 1981-84 (1,876 yards)

Most Yards on Kickoff Returns
Game
279—Chuck Downey, Stony Brook vs. Trenton St., Oct. 5, 1984 (7 returns)
Season
973—Dirk Blood, Ohio Northern, 1987 (42 returns)
Career
1,876—Tom Southall, Colorado Col., 1981-84 (85 returns)

Highest Average Gain Per Return
Game
(Min. 3) 68.0—Victor Johnson, Elmhurst vs. Wheaton (Ill.), Sept. 15, 1979 (3 for 204)
Season
(Min. 1.2 per game) *41.5—Mike Askew, Kean, 1980 (10 for 415)
Career
(Min. 1.2 per game) 29.2—Daryl Brown, Tufts, 1974-76 (38 for 1,111)

* *Declared record; with one more return (making 1.2 per game) for zero yards, still would have highest average (37.7).*

Most Touchdowns Scored on Kickoff Returns
Game
2—By many players. Most recent: Bill Nashwinter, Buffalo St. vs. Alfred, Oct. 27, 1990
Season
4—Byron Womack, Iona, 1989
Career
6—Byron Womack, Iona, 1988-91

Stony Brook's Chuck Downey set or tied 13 Division III punt- and kickoff-return records from 1984 to 1987. His career punt-return average of 20.3 is a collegiate record for a minimum of 50 returns.

TOTAL KICK RETURNS
(Combined Punt and Kickoff Returns)

Most Yards on Kick Returns
Game
354—Chuck Downey, Stony Brook vs. Trenton St., Oct. 5, 1984 (7 kickoff returns for 279 yards, 1 punt return for 75 yards)

Gaining 1,000 Yards on Punt Returns and 1,000 Yards on Kickoff Returns
Career
Chuck Downey, Stony Brook, 1984-87 (1,281 on kickoff returns, 1,198 on punt returns)

Most Touchdowns on Kick Returns
Game
3—Chuck Downey, Stony Brook vs. Trenton St., Oct. 5, 1984 (2 kickoff returns 98 & 95 yards, 1 punt return 75 yards)
Season
5—Chris Warren, Ferrum, 1989 (4 punt returns, 1 kickoff return); Chuck Downey, Stony Brook, 1986 (4 punt returns, 1 kickoff return)

Career
10—Chuck Downey, Stony Brook, 1984-87 (7 punt returns, 3 kickoff returns)

Highest Average Per Kick Return
(Min. 1.2 Returns Per Game Each)
Career
23.6—Chuck Downey, Stony Brook, 1984-87 (59 for 1,198 on punt returns; 46 for 1,281 on kickoff returns)

Averaging 20 Yards Each on Punt Returns and Kickoff Returns
(Min. 1.2 Returns Per Game Each)
Career
Chuck Downey, Stony Brook, 1984-87 (20.3 on punt returns, 59 for 1,198; 27.8 on kickoff returns, 46 for 1,281)

ALL RUNBACKS

(Combined Interceptions, Punt Returns and Kickoff Returns)

Most Touchdowns on Interceptions, Punt Returns and Kickoff Returns

Season
6—Chuck Downey, Stony Brook, 1986 (4 punt returns, 1 kickoff return, 1 interception return)

Career
11—Chuck Downey, Stony Brook, 1984-87 (7 punt returns, 3 kickoff returns, 1 interception return)

ALL-PURPOSE RUNNING

(Yardage Gained From Rushing, Receiving and All Runbacks)

Most Plays

Season
383—Mike Birosak, Dickinson, 1989 (380 rushes, 3 receptions)

Career
1,158—Eric Frees, Western Md., 1988-91 (1,059 rushes, 34 receptions, 58 kickoff returns, 7 punt returns)

Most Yards Gained

Game
402—Dan Nienhuis, Carleton vs. Hamline, Sept. 28, 1985 (88 rushing, 94 receiving, 66 punt returns, 154 kickoff returns; 33 plays)

Season
2,418—Theo Blanco, Wis.-Stevens Point, 1987 (454 rushing, 1,616 receiving, 245 punt returns, 103 kickoff returns; 271 plays)

Career
6,878—Eric Frees, Western Md., 1988-91 (5,281 rushing, 392 receiving, 47 punt returns, 1,158 kickoff returns; 1,158 plays)

Most Yards Gained Per Game

Season
238.5—Ricky Gales, Simpson, 1989 (2,385 in 10)

Career
197.4—Gary Trettel, St. Thomas (Minn.), 1988-90 (5,724 in 29)

Highest Average Gain Per Play

Season
(Min. 1,500 yards, 125 plays) 10.21—Billy Johnson, Widener, 1973 (1,868 on 183)

Career
(Min. 4,000 yards, 300 plays) 10.82—Theo Blanco, Wis.-Stevens Point, 1985-88 (4,698 yards on 434). Successively played RB, TE, RB and WR during his career

PUNTS BLOCKED BY

Most Punts Blocked By

Game
3—Jim Perryman, Millikin vs. Carroll (Wis.), Nov. 1, 1980

Season
9—Jim Perryman, Millikin, 1980

Career
13—Frank Lyle, Millsaps, 1979-82 (Daryl Hobson, Ill. Benedictine DB, blocked 9 punts during 17 games in 1987-88)

SCORING

Most Points Scored

Season
168—Stanley Drayton, Allegheny, 1991 (28 TDs)

Career
474—Joe Dudek, Plymouth St., 1982-85 (79 TDs)

Most Points Scored Per Game

Season
16.8—Stanley Drayton, Allegheny, 1991 (168 in 10)

Career
11.6—Joe Dudek, Plymouth St., 1982-85 (474 in 41)

Two Players, Same Team, Each Scoring 100 Points or More

Season
Denis McDermott (126) & Manny Tsantes (102), St. John's (N.Y.), 1989; Theo Blanco (102) & Aatron Kenney (102), Wis.-Stevens Point, 1987

Most Touchdowns Scored

Season
28—Stanley Drayton, Allegheny, 1991

Career
79—Joe Dudek, Plymouth St., 1982-85

Most Touchdowns Scored Per Game

Season
2.8—Stanley Drayton, Allegheny, 1991 (28 in 10)

Career
1.93—Joe Dudek, Plymouth St., 1982-85 (79 in 41)

Most Games Scoring a Touchdown

Career
33—Joe Dudek, Plymouth St., 1982-85 (41 games)

Most Games Scoring Two or More Touchdowns

Career
24—Joe Dudek, Plymouth St., 1982-85 (41 games)

Most Field Goals Made

Game
6—Jim Hever, Rhodes vs. Millsaps, Sept. 22, 1984 (30, 24, 42, 44, 46, 30 yards; attempted 8)

Season
20—Ken Edelman, Mount Union, 1990 (attempted 27)

Career
52—Ken Edelman, Mount Union, 1987-90, (attempted 71)

Most Field Goals Made Per Game

Season
2.00—Ken Edelman, Mount Union, 1990 (20 in 10)

Career
(Min. 30) 1.30—Ken Edelman, Mount Union, 1987-90 (52 in 40)

Most Field Goals Attempted
Game
8—Jim Hever, Rhodes vs. Millsaps, Sept. 22, 1984 (made 6)
Season
29—Scott Ryerson, Central Fla., 1981 (made 18)
Career
71—Ken Edelman, Mount Union, 1987-90 (made 52); Doug Hart, Grove City, 1985-88 (made 40)

Highest Percentage of Field Goals Made
Season
(Min. 15 atts.) 93.8%—Steve Graeca, John Carroll, 1988 (15 of 16)
Career
(Min. 50 atts.) *77.6%—Mike Duvic, Dayton, 1986-89 (38 of 49)
* Declared champion; with one more attempt (making 50), failed, still would have highest percentage (76.0).

Longest Field Goal Made
62—Dom Antonini, Glassboro St. vs. Salisbury St., Sept. 18, 1976

Most Field Goals Attempted Without Success
Season
11—Scott Perry, Moravian, 1986

Most Extra Points Attempted by Kicking
Game
14—Kurt Christenson, Concordia-M'head vs. Macalester, Sept. 24, 1977 (made 13)
Season
63—Tim Mercer, Ferrum, 1989 (made 62)
Career
194—Tim Mercer, Ferrum, 1987-90 (made 183)

Most Extra Points Made by Kicking
Game
13—Kurt Christenson, Concordia-M'head vs. Macalester, Sept. 24, 1977 (attempted 14)
Season
62—Tim Mercer, Ferrum, 1989 (attempted 63)
Career
183—Tim Mercer, Ferrum, 1987-90 (attempted 194)

Highest Percentage of Extra Points Made (Best Perfect Season)
(Min. 40 atts.) Mike Duvic, Dayton, 1989 (46 of 46)

Highest Percentage of Extra Points Made
Career
(Min. 80 atts.) 100.0%—Mike Farrell, Adrian, 1983-85 (84 of 84)
(Min. 100 atts.) 98.5%—Rims Roof, Coe, 1982-85 (135 of 137)

Most Consecutive Extra Points Made by Kicking
Game
13—Kurt Christenson, Concordia-M'head vs. Macalester, Sept. 24, 1977

Career
102—Rims Roof, Coe (from Sept. 24, 1983, through Nov. 9, 1985)

Most Points Scored by Kicking
Game
20—Jim Hever, Rhodes vs. Millsaps, Sept. 22, 1984 (6 FGs, 2 PATs)
Season
102—Ken Edelman, Mount Union, 1990 (20 FGs, 42 PATs)
Career
274—Ken Edelman, Mount Union, 1987-90 (52 FGs, 118 PATs)

Most Points Per Game Scored by Kicking
Season
10.2—Ken Edelman, Mount Union, 1990 (102 in 10)
Career
6.9—Ken Edelman, Mount Union, 1987-90 (274 in 40)

Most Successful Two-Point Pass Attempts
Game
4—Rob Bristow, Pomona-Pitzer vs. Whittier, Oct. 19, 1985 (all in 4th quarter); Dave Geissler, Wis.-Stevens Point vs. Wis.-La Crosse, Sept. 21, 1985 (all in 4th quarter)
Season
7—Kirk Baumgartner, Wis.-Stevens Point, 1988 (8 attempts); Gary Collier, Emory & Henry, 1987 (11 attempts); Dave Geissler, Wis.-Stevens Point, 1985 (8 attempts)
Career
11—Dave Geissler, Wis.-Stevens Point, 1982-85 (14 attempts)
Rob Bristow, Pomona-Pitzer, 1983-86, holds record for highest percentage of successful two-point pass attempts (best perfect record) at 9 of 9

Most Two-Point Passes Caught
Season
4—Don Moehling, Wis.-Stevens Point, 1988; Mike Christman, Wis.-Stevens Point, 1985

Most Defensive Extra Points Scored
Game
1—By many players
Season
2—Dan Fichter, Brockport St., 1990 (2 blocked kick returns)

Longest Defensive Extra Point Blocked Kick Return
95—Brian Adcock (CB), Wheaton (Ill.) vs. North Park, Oct. 28, 1989 (scored)

Longest Defensive Extra Point Interception
100—By four players. Most recent: Chris Schleeper (FS), Quincy vs. Ill. Wesleyan, Sept. 29, 1990 (scored)

First Defensive Extra Point Scored
Steve Nieves (DB), St. John's (N.Y.) vs. Iona, Sept. 10, 1988 (83-yard blocked kick return)

TEAM RECORDS

SINGLE GAME—OFFENSE
TOTAL OFFENSE

Most Plays
112—Gust. Adolphus vs. Bethel (Minn.), Nov. 2, 1985 (65 passes, 47 rushes; 493 yards)

Most Plays, Both Teams
214—Gust. Adolphus (112) & Bethel (Minn.) (102), Nov. 2, 1985 (143 passes, 71 rushes; 930 yards)

Most Yards Gained
727—Concordia-M'head vs. Macalester, Sept. 24, 1977 (604 rushing, 123 passing)
Most Yards Gained, Both Teams
1,360—Millikin (694) & Wheaton (Ill.) (666), Nov. 12, 1983 (166 plays)

Most Touchdowns Scored by Rushing and Passing
14—Concordia-M'head vs. Macalester, Sept. 24, 1977 (12 rushing, 2 passing)

RUSHING

Most Rushes
92—Wis.-River Falls vs. Wis.-Platteville, Oct. 21, 1989 (464 yards)
Most Yards Gained Rushing
642—Wis.-River Falls vs. Wis.-Superior, Oct. 14, 1989 (88 rushes)

Most Touchdowns Scored by Rushing
12—Concordia-M'head vs. Macalester, Sept. 24, 1977

PASSING

Most Passes Attempted
79—Ohio Wesleyan vs. Denison, Oct. 3, 1981 (completed 47)
Most Passes Attempted, Both Teams
143—Bethel (Minn.) (78) & Gust. Adolphus (65), Nov. 2, 1985 (completed 65)
Most Passes Attempted Without an Interception
61—Occidental vs. La Verne, Oct. 18, 1986 (completed 32); Wis.-Stevens Point vs. Wis.-Superior, Oct. 16, 1981 (completed 31)
Most Passes Completed
50—Hofstra vs. Fordham, Oct. 19, 1991 (attempted 69)
Most Passes Completed, Both Teams
80—Hofstra (50) & Fordham (30), Oct. 19, 1991 (attempted 120)

Highest Percentage of Passes Completed
(Min. 35 atts.) 78.9%—Wheaton (Ill.) vs. North Park, Oct. 8, 1983 (30 of 38)
Most Yards Gained
585—Hofstra vs. Fordham, Oct. 19, 1991
Most Yards Gained, Both Teams
1,036—Knox (576) & Cornell College (460), Oct. 11, 1986 (attempted 92, completed 59)
Most Touchdown Passes
8—Wis.-Stevens Point vs. Wis.-Superior, Nov. 4, 1989
Most Touchdown Passes, Both Teams
11—Emory & Henry (6) & Samford (5), Oct. 24, 1987; Cornell College (6) & Knox (5), Oct. 11, 1986

PUNT RETURNS

Most Touchdowns Scored on Punt Returns
2—By many teams. Most recent: Widener vs. Susquehanna, Oct. 20, 1990; Widener vs. Albright, Oct. 13, 1990 (consecutive games, 3 returns on blocked punts)

KICKOFF RETURNS

Most Yards on Kickoff Returns
279—Stony Brook vs. Trenton St., Oct. 5, 1984

SCORING

Most Points Scored
97—Concordia-M'head vs. Macalester, Sept. 24, 1977
Most Points Scored, Both Teams
111—Carroll (Wis.) (58) & Ill. Wesleyan (53), Nov. 11, 1989
Most Points Scored by a Losing Team
53—Ill. Wesleyan vs. Carroll (Wis.) (58), Nov. 11, 1989
Most Points Scored in First Varsity Game
63—Bentley vs. Brooklyn (26), Sept. 24, 1988
Most Touchdowns Scored
14—Concordia-M'head vs. Macalester, Sept. 24, 1977
Most Extra Points Made by Kicking
13—Concordia-M'head vs. Macalester, Sept. 24, 1977 (attempted 14)

Most Field Goals Made
6—Rhodes vs. Millsaps, Sept. 22, 1984 (attempted 8)
Most Field Goals Attempted
8—Rhodes vs. Millsaps, Sept. 22, 1984 (made 6)
Most Defensive Extra-Point Returns Scored
1—By many teams
Most Defensive Extra-Point Opportunities
2—Wis.-River Falls vs. Wis.-La Crosse, Nov. 11, 1989 (2 kick returns; 1 scored); Wis.-Platteville vs. Wis.-Oshkosh, Oct. 15, 1988 (2 interceptions; none scored); Buffalo St. vs. Brockport St., Oct. 1, 1988 (1 interception & 1 kick return; none scored)

TURNOVERS

(Most Times Losing the Ball on Interceptions and Fumbles)

Most Turnovers
13—St. Olaf vs. St. Thomas (Minn.), Oct. 12, 1985 (10 interceptions, 3 fumbles); Mercy- hurst vs. Buffalo St., Oct. 23, 1982 (12 fumbles, 1 interception); Albany (N.Y.) vs. Rochester Inst., Oct. 1, 1977

FIRST DOWNS

Most Total First Downs
38—Beloit vs. Grinnell, Sept. 22, 1990 (28 rushing, 8 passing, 2 by penalty)

PENALTIES

Most Penalties Against
25—Norwich vs. Coast Guard, Sept. 29, 1985 (192 yards)

SINGLE GAME—DEFENSE
TOTAL DEFENSE

Fewest Yards Allowed
Minus 50—Ithaca vs. Springfield, Oct. 11, 1975 (-94 rushing, 44 passing)

RUSHING DEFENSE

Fewest Rushes Allowed
10—Augustana (Ill.) vs. Ill. Wesleyan, Oct. 11, 1983 (28 yards); Wis.-Superior vs. Wis.-Stevens Point, Oct. 17, 1981 (-3 yards)

Fewest Yards Allowed
Minus 112—Coast Guard vs. Wesleyan, Oct. 7, 1989 (23 plays)

PASS DEFENSE

Fewest Attempts Allowed
0—By many teams. Most recent: Wis.-Eau Claire vs. Wis.-River Falls, Sept. 22, 1990

Fewest Completions Allowed
0—By many teams. Most recent: Lawrence vs. Chicago, Oct. 6, 1990 (4 attempts)

Fewest Yards Allowed
Minus 6—Central (Iowa) vs. Simpson, Oct. 19, 1985 (1 completion)

Most Passes Intercepted By
10—St. Thomas (Minn.) vs. St. Olaf, Oct. 12, 1985 (91 yards; 50 attempts)

Most Players Intercepting a Pass
8—Samford vs. Anderson, Oct. 11, 1986 (8 interceptions in the game)

PUNTING

Most Opponents' Punts Blocked By
4—Ill. Benedictine vs. Olivet Nazarene, Oct. 22, & vs. Aurora, Oct. 29, 1988 (consecutive games, resulting in 4 TDs and 1 safety).

Blocked 9 punts in three consecutive games, vs. MacMurray, Oct. 15, Olivet Nazarene and Aurora, resulting in 4 TDs and 2 safeties

FIRST DOWNS

Fewest First Downs Allowed
0—Case Reserve vs. Wooster, Sept. 21, 1985

SEASON—OFFENSE
TOTAL OFFENSE

Most Yards Gained Per Game
523.1—Samford, 1987 (5,231 in 10)

Highest Average Gain Per Play
8.14—Ferrum, 1990 (534 for 4,350)

Most Plays Per Game
85.6—Hampden-Sydney, 1978 (856 in 10)

Most Touchdowns Scored Per Game by Rushing and Passing
7.0—Samford, 1987 (70 in 10; 40 passing, 30 rushing)

RUSHING

Most Yards Gained Per Game
434.7—Ferrum, 1990 (3,912 in 9)

Highest Average Gain Per Rush
8.32—Ferrum, 1990 (470 for 3,912)

Most Rushes Per Game
71.4—Wis.-River Falls, 1988 (714 in 10)

Most Touchdowns Scored Per Game by Rushing
5.4—Ferrum, 1990 (49 in 9)

PASSING

Most Yards Gained Per Game
403.5—Hofstra, 1991 (4,035 in 10)

Fewest Yards Gained Per Game
18.4—Wis.-River Falls, 1983 (184 in 10)

Highest Average Gain Per Attempt
(Min. 250 atts.) 9.86—Ill. Benedictine, 1974 (259

for 2,554)
(Min. 325 atts.) 8.71—Wheaton (Ill.), 1983 (393 for 3,424)

Highest Average Gain Per Completion
(Min. 200 comps.) 15.4—Wis.-Stevens Point, 1987 (249 for 3,836)

Most Passes Attempted Per Game
58.5—Hofstra, 1991 (585 in 10)
Fewest Passes Attempted Per Game
4.0—Wis.-River Falls, 1988 (40 in 10)
Most Passes Completed Per Game
34.4—Hofstra, 1991 (344 in 10)
Fewest Passes Completed Per Game
1.3—Wis.-River Falls, 1983 (13 in 10)
Highest Percentage Completed
(Min. 200 atts.) 65.2%—Kenyon, 1978 (148 of
227)
(Min. 300 atts.) 62.6%—Wheaton (Ill.), 1983
(246 of 393)

Lowest Percentage of Passes Had Intercepted
(Min. 150 atts.) 0.7%—San Diego, 1990 (1 of
153)

Most Touchdown Passes Per Game
4.0—Samford, 1987 (40 in 10)

Highest Passing Efficiency Rating Points
(Min. 15 atts. per game) 191.7—Simpson, 1989
(163 attempts, 101 completions, 3 interceptions, 1,804 yards, 20 TDs)
(Min. 300 atts.) 171.7—Samford, 1987 (303
attempts, 165 completions, 7 interceptions,
2,825 yards, 40 TDs)

PUNTING

Most Punts Per Game
11.0—FDU-Madison, 1990 (99 in 9)
Fewest Punts Per Game
2.4—Frostburg St., 1990 (24 in 10)

Highest Punting Average
44.6—Occidental, 1982 (55 for 2,454)

SCORING

Most Points Per Game
51.7—Samford, 1987 (517 in 10)

Most Touchdowns Per Game
7.4—Samford, 1987 (74 in 10)

**Best Perfect Record on
Extra Points Made by Kicking**
49 of 49—Dayton, 1989

Most Two-Point Attempts Per Game
2.8—N'western Col. (Wis.), 1990 (17 in 6)

Most Field Goals Made Per Game
2.0—Mount Union, 1990 (20 in 10)

Highest Scoring Margin
38.2—Hofstra, 1990 (averaged 47.2 and allowed
9.0 in 10 games)
Most Touchdowns on Blocked Punt Returns
5—Widener, 1990
Most Safeties
4—Wis.-Stevens Point, 1990
Most Defensive Extra-Point Returns Scored
2—Eureka, 1991; Brockport St., 1990
Most Defensive Extra Point Blocked Kick Returns
3—Brockport St., 1990 (2 scored)
Most Defensive Extra Point Interceptions
2—Swarthmore, 1989 (1 scored); Wis.-Platte-
ville, 1988 (none scored)

TURNOVERS (GIVEAWAYS) (FROM 1985)

(Passes Had Intercepted and Fumbles Lost)

Fewest Turnovers
8—North Central, 1989 (7 interceptions, 1
fumble lost); Occidental, 1988 (2 interceptions, 6 fumbles lost)
Fewest Turnovers Per Game
0.89—North Central, 1989 (8 in 9); Occidental,
1988 (8 in 9)

Most Turnovers
52—William Penn, 1985 (19 interceptions, 33
fumbles lost)

Most Turnovers Per Game
5.2—William Penn, 1985 (52 in 10)

SEASON—DEFENSE
TOTAL DEFENSE

Fewest Yards Allowed Per Game
94.0—Knoxville, 1977 (940 in 10)
Lowest Average Yards Allowed Per Play
(Min. 500 plays) 1.76—Bowie St., 1978 (576 for
1,011)

(Min. 650 plays) 2.03—Plymouth St., 1987 (733
for 1,488)
**Fewest Rushing and Passing Touchdowns
Allowed Per Game**
0.3—Montclair St., 1984 (3 in 10)

RUSHING DEFENSE

Fewest Yards Allowed Per Game
Minus 2.3—Knoxville, 1977 (-23 in 10 games)
Lowest Average Yards Allowed Per Rush
(Min. 275 rushes) Minus 0.07—Knoxville, 1977
(333 for -23)

(Min. 400 rushes) 1.00—Lycoming, 1976 (400
for 399)
Fewest Touchdowns by Rushing Allowed
0—Union (N.Y.), 1983 (9 games); New Haven,
1978 (9 games)

PASS DEFENSE

Fewest Yards Allowed Per Game
48.5—Mass. Maritime, 1976 (388 in 8)
Fewest Yards Allowed Per Attempt
(Min. 150 atts.) 2.87—Plymouth St., 1982 (170

for 488)
(Min. 225 atts.) 3.27—Plymouth St., 1987 (281
for 919)

Fewest Yards Allowed Per Completion
(Min. 100 comps.) 8.64—Baldwin-Wallace, 1990 (151 for 1,305)

Lowest Completion Percentage Allowed
(Min. 150 atts.) 24.3%—Doane, 1973 (41 of 169)
(Min. 250 atts.) 33.5%—Plymouth St., 1987 (94 of 281)

Highest Percentage Intercepted By
(Min. 200 atts.) 15.2%—Rose-Hulman, 1977 (32 of 210)

Most Passes Intercepted By Per Game
3.4—Montclair St., 1981 (34 in 10)

Most Passes Intercepted By
35—Plymouth St., 1987 (12 games, 281 attempts against, 348 yards returned)

Fewest Passes Intercepted By
(Min. 125 atts.) 1—Bates, 1987 (134 attempts against in 8 games, 0 yards returned)

Most Yards on Interception Returns
576—Emory & Henry, 1987 (31 interceptions)

Most Touchdowns Scored on Interceptions
6—Augustana (Ill.), 1987 (23 interceptions, 229 passes against)

Fewest Touchdown Passes Allowed
0—By many teams. Most recent: Dayton, 1980 (11 games)

Lowest Passing Efficiency Rating Points Allowed Opponents
(Min. 150 atts.) 27.82—Plymouth St., 1982 (allowed 170 attempts, 53 completions, 488 yards, 1 TD & intercepted 25 passes)
(Min. 275 atts.) 43.06—Plymouth St., 1987 (allowed 281 attempts, 94 completions, 919 yards, 6 TDs & intercepted 35 passes)

PUNTING

Most Opponents' Punts Blocked By
11—Ill. Benedictine, 1987 (78 punts against in 10 games). Blocked 17 punts in 18 games during 1987-88, resulting in 5 TDs and 3 safeties

SCORING

Fewest Points Allowed Per Game
3.4—Millsaps, 1980 (31 in 9)

Fewest Touchdowns Allowed
4—Baldwin-Wallace, 1981 (10 games); Millsaps, 1980 (9 games); Bentley, 1990 (8 games)

Most Points Allowed Per Game
59.1—Macalester, 1977 (532 in 9; 76 TDs, 64 PATs, 4 FGs)

Most Defensive Extra-Point Attempts by Opponents
3—Muskingum, 1989 (3 blocked kick returns; none scored); Brockport St., 1988 (1 interception; scored 2 blocked kick returns; LIU-C.W. Post, 1988 (1 blocked kick return, 2 interceptions; none scored)

TURNOVERS (TAKEAWAYS) (FROM 1985)

(Opponents' Passes Intercepted and Fumbles Recovered)

Highest Margin of Turnovers Per Game Over Opponents
2.90—Macalester, 1986 (29 in 10; 29 giveaways vs. 58 takeaways)

Most Opponents' Turnovers Per Game
5.80—Macalester, 1986 (58 in 10)

Most Opponents' Turnovers
58—Macalester, 1986 (28 interceptions, 30 fumbles lost)

ADDITIONAL RECORDS

Most Consecutive Victories
37—Augustana (Ill.) (from Sept. 17, 1983, through 1985 Division III playoffs; ended with 0-0 tie vs. Elmhurst, Sept. 13, 1986)

Most Consecutive Regular-Season Victories
49—Augustana (Ill.) (from Oct. 25, 1980, through 1985; ended with 0-0 tie vs. Elmhurst, Sept. 13, 1986)

Most Consecutive Games Without Defeat
60—Augustana (Ill.), 1983-87 (including 1 tie). Began Sept. 17, 1983, and ended with a 36-38 loss to Dayton, Nov. 29, 1987, in Division III playoffs

Most Consecutive Regular-Season Games Without Defeat
70—Augustana (Ill.) (from Oct. 25, 1980, through Oct. 1, 1988; ended with 21-24 loss to Carroll, Wis., Oct. 8, 1988)

Most Consecutive Games Without Being Shut Out
186—Carnegie Mellon (current from Sept. 30, 1972)

Most Consecutive Losses
50—Macalester (from Oct. 5, 1974, to Nov. 10, 1979; ended with 17-14 win over Mount Senario, Sept. 6, 1980)

Most Consecutive Games Without a Tie
371—Widener (from Oct. 29, 1949, to Nov. 11, 1989; ended with 14-14 tie against Gettysburg, Sept. 8, 1990)

Highest-Scoring Tie Game
40-40—Wagner & Montclair St., Sept. 11, 1982

Last Scoreless Tie Game
Sept. 10, 1988—Wis.-Oshkosh & Valparaiso

Most Shutouts in a Season
6—Cortland St., 1989; Plymouth St., 1982 (consecutive)

Most Consecutive Shutouts in a Season
6—Plymouth St., 1982

Most Consecutive Quarters Without Yielding a Touchdown by Rushing
61—Augustana (Ill.) (in 16 games from Sept. 27, 1986, to Nov. 7, 1987; 77 including four 1986 Division III playoff games); Union (N.Y.) (in 16 games from Oct. 23, 1982, to Sept. 29, 1984)

Most Consecutive Quarters Without Yielding a Touchdown by Passing
44—Swarthmore (from Oct. 31, 1981, to Nov. 13, 1982)

Most Turnovers by Both Teams in a Game
24—Albany (N.Y.) (13) & Rochester Inst. (11), Oct. 1, 1977

Most Points Overcome to Win a Game
33—Salisbury St. vs. Randolph-Macon, Sept. 15, 1984 (trailed 33-0 with 14:18 left in 2nd quarter; won 34-33); Wis.-Platteville vs. Wis.-Eau Claire, Nov. 8, 1980 (trailed 33-0 with 7:00 left in 2nd quarter; won 52-43)

Most Points Scored in a Brief Period of Time
21 in 2:11—Merchant Marine vs. Bentley, Sept. 30, 1989 (turned 0-0 game into 21-0 in 1st quarter; won 30-14)
32 in 4:04—Wis.-Stevens Point vs. Wis.-La Crosse, Sept. 21, 1985 (trailed 3-27 and 11-35 in the 4th quarter; ended in 35-35 tie)

Most Improved Won-Lost Record (Including Postseason Games)
7 games—Susquehanna, 1986 (11-1-0) from 1985 (3-7-0); Maryville (Tenn.), 1976 (7-2-0) from 1975 (0-9-0)

Most Consecutive Winning Seasons
34—Wittenberg (from 1955 through 1988; ended with 4-5 record in 1989)

ANNUAL CHAMPIONS, ALL-TIME LEADERS

TOTAL OFFENSE
Career Yards

Player, Team	Years	Plays	Yards
Kirk Baumgartner, Wis.-Stevens Point	1986-89	*2,007	*12,767
Tim Peterson, Wis.-Stout	1986-89	1,558	9,701
Keith Bishop, Ill. Wesleyan/Wheaton (Ill.)	1981, 83-85	1,467	9,052
Dave Geissler, Wis.-Stevens Point	1982-85	1,695	8,990
Dennis Bogacz, Wis.-Oshkosh/Wis.-Whitewater	1988-89, 90-91	1,394	8,850
John Clark, Wis.-Eau Claire	1987-90	1,354	8,838
Matt Jozokos, Plymouth St.	1987-90	1,234	8,188
Darryl Kosut, William Penn	1983-86	1,583	7,817
Steve Osterberger, Drake	1987-90	1,263	7,520
David Parker, Bishop	1981-84	1,257	7,516
John Rooney, Ill. Wesleyan	1982-84	1,260	7,393
Larry Barretta, Lycoming	1983-86	1,205	7,320
Shane Fulton, Heidelberg	1983-86	1,344	7,203
Scott Scesney, St. John's (N.Y.)	1986-89	1,048	7,196
Ron Devorsky, Hiram	1984-87	1,178	7,059
Ed Dougherty, Lycoming	1988-91	1,320	7,055
Craig Solomon, Rhodes	1975-78	1,261	7,055
Chris Spriggs, Denison	1983-86	1,219	7,047
Gary Collier, Emory & Henry	1984-87	1,089	7,036
Clay Sampson, Denison	1977-80	1,225	6,920
Rob Light, Moravian	1986-89	1,226	6,886
Mike Culver, Juniata	1983-86	1,098	6,834
Paul Brandenburg, Ripon	1984-87	1,301	6,769
Walter Briggs, Montclair St.	1983-86	972	6,769
Steve Kinne, Alma	1987-90	1,125	6,714

* Record.

Season Yards

Player, Team	Year	Games	Plays	Yards
Kirk Baumgartner, Wis.-Stevens Point	†1988	11	604	*3,790
Kirk Baumgartner, Wis.-Stevens Point	1987	11	561	3,712
Kirk Baumgartner, Wis.-Stevens Point	†1989	10	530	3,540
Tim Peterson, Wis.-Stout	1989	10	*614	3,244
Keith Bishop, Wheaton (Ill.)	†1983	9	421	3,193
Tim Peterson, Wis.-Stout	1987	11	393	3,052
Keith Bishop, Wheaton (Ill.)	†1985	9	521	2,951
Dennis Bogacz, Wis.-Oshkosh	1989	10	417	2,939
Brion Demski, Wis.-Stevens Point	†1981	10	503	2,895
Larry Barretta, Lycoming	†1986	10	453	2,875
Shane Fulton, Heidelberg	1985	10	485	2,858
Mark Peterson, Neb. Wesleyan	1983	10	425	2,846
Keith Bishop, Wheaton (Ill.)	†1984	9	479	2,777
Rhory Moss, Hofstra	†1990	9	372	2,775
Dave Geissler, Wis.-Stevens Point	1985	11	456	2,756
Bill Lech, Coe	1989	9	404	2,743
Chris Creighton, Kenyon	1990	10	452	2,731

* Record. † National champion.

Single-Game Yards

Yds.	Player, Team (Opponent)	Date
596	John Love, North Park (Elmhurst)	Oct. 13, 1990
564	Tim Lynch, Hofstra (Fordham)	Oct. 19, 1991
527	Rob Shippy, Concordia, Ill. (Concordia, Wis.)	Oct. 5, 1985
515	Seamus Crotty, Hamilton (Middlebury)	Oct. 27, 1984
512	Bob Monroe, Knox (Cornell College)	Oct. 11, 1986
511	Kirk Baumgartner, Wis.-Stevens Point (Wis.-Superior)	Nov. 4, 1989
511	Kirk Baumgartner, Wis.-Stevens Point (Wis.-Stout)	Oct. 24, 1987
509	Craig Solomon, Rhodes (Rose-Hulman)	Nov. 11, 1978
507	George Beisel, Hofstra (LIU-C. W. Post)	Sept. 28, 1991
506	Todd Coolidge, Susquehanna (Muhlenberg)	Sept. 12, 1987
504	Jeff Hagan, Coast Guard (Trinity, Conn.)	Oct. 26, 1985
502	Tim Nielson, Carleton (Gust. Adolphus)	Oct. 8, 1988
498	Kirk Baumgartner, Wis.-Stevens Point (Wis.-River Falls)	Nov. 5, 1988
497	Keith Bishop, Wheaton, Ill. (North Park)	Oct. 12, 1985
496	John Guglielmo, Johns Hopkins (Georgetown)	Oct. 26, 1991
495	Willie Reyna, La Verne (Occidental)	Nov. 9, 1991
492	Mike Fanger, Lewis & Clark (Simon Fraser)	Sept. 17, 1988
491	Trent Merzon, Dubuque (Simpson)	Sept. 30, 1989
490	John Nielson, Carleton (Gust. Adolphus)	Oct. 20, 1990
489	Bob Krepfle, Wis.-La Crosse (Wis.-River Falls)	Nov. 12, 1983

Career Yards Per Game

Player, Team	Years	Games	Plays	Yards	Yd. PG
Kirk Baumgartner, Wis.-Stevens Point	1986-89	41	*2,007	*12,767	*311.4
Keith Bishop, Ill. Wesleyan/Wheaton (Ill.)	1981, 83-85	31	1,467	9,052	292.0
John Rooney, Ill. Wesleyan	1982-84	27	1,260	7,393	273.8
Tim Peterson, Wis.-Stout	1986-89	36	1,558	9,701	269.5
Robert Farra, Claremont-M-S	1978-79	16	690	4,179	261.2
Dennis Bogacz, Wis.-Oshkosh/ Wis.-Whitewater	1988-89, 90-91	38	1,394	8,850	232.9
John Clark, Wis.-Eau Claire	1987-90	38	1,354	8,838	232.6
Mark Peterson, Neb. Wesleyan	1982-84	28	1,151	6,367	227.4
Scott Scesney, St. John's (N.Y.)	1986-89	32	1,048	7,196	224.9
Rob Bristow, Pomona-Pitzer	1983-86	29	1,290	6,465	222.9
Dave Geissler, Wis.-Stevens Point	1982-85	42	1,695	8,990	214.0
Jeff Beer, Bethany (W. Va.)	1978-80	25	878	5,228	209.1
John Love, North Park	1988-90	27	1,182	5,613	207.9
Jeff Voris, DePauw	1986-89	28	993	5,788	206.7
Seamus Crotty, Hamilton	1982-85	31	1,225	6,402	206.5
Matt Jozokos, Plymouth St.	1987-90	40	1,234	8,188	204.7
Steve Osterberger, Drake	1987-90	37	1,263	7,520	203.2
Marty Barrett, Buffalo	1980-82	32	1,280	6,466	202.1

* Record.

Season Yards Per Game

Player, Team	Year	Games	Plays	Yards	Yd. PG
Keith Bishop, Wheaton (Ill.)	†1983	9	421	3,193	*354.8
Kirk Baumgartner, Wis.-Stevens Point	†1989	10	530	3,540	354.0
Kirk Baumgartner, Wis.-Stevens Point	†1988	11	604	*3,790	344.5
Kirk Baumgartner, Wis.-Stevens Point	1987	11	561	3,712	337.5
Willie Reyna, La Verne	†1991	8	220	2,633	329.1
Keith Bishop, Wheaton (Ill.)	†1985	9	521	2,951	327.9
Tim Peterson, Wis.-Stout	1989	10	*614	3,244	324.4
Keith Bishop, Wheaton (Ill.)	†1984	9	479	2,777	308.6
Rhory Moss, Hofstra	†1990	9	372	2,775	308.3
Bill Lech, Coe	1989	9	404	2,743	304.8
Robert Farra, Claremont-M-S	†1978	9	427	2,685	298.3
Rob Shippy, Concordia (Ill.)	1985	9	370	2,682	298.0
Brett Butler, Wabash	1989	9	449	2,666	296.2
Dennis Bogacz, Wis.-Oshkosh	1989	10	417	2,939	293.9
Brion Demski, Wis.-Stevens Point	†1981	10	503	2,895	289.5

* Record. † National champion.

Annual Champions

Year	Player, Team	Cl.	G	Plays	Yards	Avg.
1973	Bob Dulich, San Diego	Jr.	11	340	2,543	231.2
1974	Larry Cenotto, Pomona-Pitzer	Sr.	9	436	2,127	236.3
1975	Ricky Haygood, Millsaps	Jr.	9	332	2,176	241.8
1976	Rollie Wiebers, Buena Vista	So.	9	353	2,198	244.2

1992 NCAA FOOTBALL

Year	Player, Team	Cl.	G	Plays	Yards	Avg.
1977	Tom Hamilton, Occidental	Sr.	9	358	2,050	227.8
1978	Robert Farra, Claremont-M-S	Jr.	9	427	2,685	298.3
1979	Clay Sampson, Denison	Jr.	9	412	2,255	250.6
1980	Jeff Beer, Bethany (W. Va.)	Sr.	9	372	2,331	259.0
1981	Brion Demski, Wis.-Stevens Point	Sr.	10	503	2,895	289.5
1982	Dave McCarrell, Wheaton (Ill.)	Sr.	9	387	2,503	278.1
1983	Keith Bishop, Wheaton (Ill.)	So.	9	421	3,193	*354.8
1984	Keith Bishop, Wheaton (Ill.)	Jr.	9	479	2,777	308.6
1985	Keith Bishop, Wheaton (Ill.)	Sr.	9	521	2,951	327.9
1986	Larry Barretta, Lycoming	Sr.	10	453	2,875	287.5
1987	Todde Greenough, Willamette	Jr.	9	436	2,567	285.2
1988	Kirk Baumgartner, Wis.-Stevens Point	Jr.	11	604	*3,790	344.5
1989	Kirk Baumgartner, Wis.-Stevens Point	Sr.	10	530	3,540	354.0
1990	Rhory Moss, Hofstra	Jr.	9	372	2,775	308.3
1991	Willie Reyna, La Verne	Jr.	8	220	2,633	329.1

* Record.

RUSHING

Career Yards

Player, Team	Years	Plays	Yards	Avg.
Joe Dudek, Plymouth St.........................	1982-85	785	*5,570	‡7.10
Eric Frees, Western Md.	1988-91	1,059	5,281	4.99
Terry Underwood, Wagner	1985-88	742	5,010	6.75
Mike Birosak, Dickinson	1986-89	*1,112	4,662	4.19
Rich Kowalski, Hobart	1972-75	907	4,631	5.11
Remon Smith, Randolph-Macon	1984-87	737	4,249	5.77
Chris Spriggs, Denison	1983-86	787	4,248	5.40
Scott Reppert, Lawrence	1979-82	757	4,211	5.56
Alonzo Patterson, Wagner	1979-82	816	4,177	5.12
Peter Gorniewicz, Colby	1971-74	1,024	4,113	4.02
Bryce Tuohy, Heidelberg	1986-89	905	4,067	4.49
Ricky Gales, Nebraska-Omaha; Simpson	1986-87; 88-89	701	4,061	5.79
Brian Grandison, Wooster......................	1988-91	899	4,042	4.50
Jay Wessler, Illinois Col.	1977-80	807	4,016	4.98
Sandy Rogers, Emory & Henry	1983-86	641	4,005	6.25
Tim McDaniel, Centre..........................	1988-91	920	3,897	4.24
Ted Pretasky, Wis.-La Crosse	1985-88	698	3,877	5.55
Roscoe Mitchell, Fort Valley St.	1976-79	848	3,869	4.56
Evan Lipp, Marietta	1984-87	900	3,844	4.27
Pedro Bowman, Duquesne......................	1981-84	801	3,830	4.78
Joe Thompson, Augustana (Ill.)................	1973-76	729	3,779	5.18
Scott Dudak, Gettysburg.......................	1978-81	736	3,774	5.13

* Record.   ‡ Record for minimum of 500 carries.

Season Yards

Player, Team	Year	Games	Plays	Yards	Avg.
Ricky Gales, Simpson........................	†1989	10	297	*2,035	6.85
Jon Warga, Wittenberg............................	†1990	10	254	1,836	7.23
Terry Underwood, Wagner	†1988	9	245	1,809	6.75
Mike Birosak, Dickinson	1989	10	*380	1,798	4.73
Sandy Rogers, Emory & Henry	†1986	11	231	1,730	$7.49
Anthony Russo, St. John's (N.Y.)	†1991	10	287	1,685	5.87
John Bernatavitz, Dickinson	1990	10	266	1,666	6.26
Hank Wineman, Albion..............................	1991	9	307	1,629	5.31
Gary Trettel, St. Thomas (Minn.)	1990	10	293	1,620	5.53
Joe Dudek, Plymouth St............................	†1985	11	216	1,615	7.48
Eric Frees, Western Md............................	1990	10	295	1,594	5.40
George Rainey, Wis.-Whitewater	1987	11	279	1,567	5.62
Eric Frees, Western Md............................	1991	10	304	1,545	5.08
Clay Sampson, Denison	†1979	9	323	1,517	4.70
Chuck Evans, Ferris St.	1976	10	224	1,509	6.74
Chris Babirad, Wash. & Jeff.	1991	9	224	1,508	6.73
Gary Trettel, St. Thomas (Minn.)	1989	10	256	1,502	5.87
Billy Johnson, Widener	†1973	9	168	1,494	+8.89
Alonzo Patterson, Wagner	1981	10	256	1,487	5.81
Chris Dabrow, Claremont-M-S......................	†1987	9	265	1,486	5.61

* Record.   † National champion.   + Record for minimum of 140 carries. $ Record for minimum of 195 carries.

Simpson running back Ricky Gales set Division III season marks for rushing yards (2,035) and rushing yards per game (203.5) in 1989.

Single-Game Yards

Yds.	Player, Team (Opponent)	Date
382	Pete Baranek, Carthage (North Central)	Oct. 5, 1985
363	Terry Underwood, Wagner (Hofstra)	Oct. 15, 1988
354	Terry Underwood, Wagner (Western Conn. St.)	Oct. 3, 1986
342	Dave Bednarek, Wis.-River Falls (Wis.-Stevens Point)	Oct. 29, 1983
337	Kirk Matthieu, Maine Maritime (Curry)	Oct. 27, 1990
337	Ted Helsel, St. Francis, Pa. (Gallaudet)	Nov. 3, 1979
334	Oliver Bridges, Stony Brook (Pace)	Nov. 16, 1991
329	Don Williams, Lowell (Colby)	Oct. 4, 1985
326	Mike Krueger, Tufts (Amherst)	Oct. 25, 1980
321	Jack Davis, Hobart (Brockport St.)	Nov. 5, 1977
312	Don Taylor, Central, Iowa (Dubuque)	Oct. 9, 1976
311	Jason Wooley, Worcester Tech (MIT)	Nov. 10, 1990
311	Mike Birosak, Dickinson (Gettysburg)	Nov. 4, 1989
311	Roy Heffernan, Middlebury (Worcester Tech)	Oct. 4, 1975

Career Yards Per Game

Player, Team	Years	Games	Plays	Yards	Yd. PG
Terry Underwood, Wagner	1985-88	33	742	5,010	*151.8
Joe Dudek, Plymouth St.	1982-85	41	785	*5,570	135.9
Eric Frees, Western Md.	1988-91	40	1,059	5,281	132.0
Rich Kowalski, Hobart	1972-75	36	907	4,631	128.6
Peter Gorniewicz, Colby	1971-74	32	1,024	4,113	128.5
Scott Reppert, Lawrence	1979-82	33	757	4,211	127.6
Tim Barrett, John Carroll	1972-74	29	662	3,621	124.9

* Record.

Season Yards Per Game

Player, Team	Year	Games	Plays	Yards	TD	Yd. PG
Ricky Gales, Simpson	†1989	10	297	*2,035	26	*203.5
Terry Underwood, Wagner	†1988	9	245	1,809	21	201.0
Jon Warga, Wittenberg	†1990	10	254	1,836	15	183.6
Hank Wineman, Albion	†1991	9	307	1,629	14	181.0
Eric Grey, Hamilton	1991	8	217	1,439	13	179.9
Mike Birosak, Dickinson	1989	10	*380	1,798	18	179.8
Clay Sampson, Denison	†1979	9	323	1,517	13	168.6
Anthony Russo, St. John's (N.Y.)	1991	10	287	1,685	18	168.5
Chris Babirad, Wash. & Jeff.	1991	9	224	1,508	18	167.6
John Bernatavitz, Dickinson	1990	10	266	1,666	15	166.6
Billy Johnson, Widener	†1973	9	168	1,494	21	166.0
Scott Reppert, Lawrence	†1982	8	254	1,323	14	165.4
Chris Dabrow, Claremont-M-S	†1987	9	265	1,486	13	165.1
Gary Trettel, St. Thomas (Minn.)	1990	10	293	1,620	19	162.0
Tom Shaffner, Defiance	1973	9	251	1,450	19	161.1

* Record.   † National champion.

Annual Champions

Year	Player, Team	Cl.	G	Plays	Yards	Avg.
1973	Billy Johnson, Widener	Sr.	9	168	1,494	166.0
1974	Tim Barrett, John Carroll	Sr.	9	256	1,409	156.6
1975	Ron Baker, Monmouth (Ill.)	Sr.	8	200	1,116	139.5
1976	Chuck Evans, Ferris St.	Jr.	10	224	1,509	150.9
1977	Don Taylor, Central (Iowa)	Sr.	9	267	1,329	147.7
1978	Dino Hall, Glassboro St.	Sr.	10	239	1,330	133.0
1979	Clay Sampson, Denison	Jr.	9	323	1,517	168.6
1980	Scott Reppert, Lawrence	So.	8	223	1,223	152.9
1981	Scott Reppert, Lawrence	Jr.	9	250	1,410	156.7
1982	Scott Reppert, Lawrence	Sr.	8	254	1,323	165.4
1983	John Franco, Wagner	Sr.	8	175	1,166	145.8
1984	Gary Errico, Lowell	Sr.	9	165	1,404	156.0
1985	Bruce Montella, Chicago	Sr.	9	265	1,372	152.4
1986	Sandy Rogers, Emory & Henry	Sr.	11	231	1,730	157.3
1987	Chris Dabrow, Claremont-M-S	Sr.	9	265	1,486	165.1
1988	Terry Underwood, Wagner	Sr.	9	245	1,809	201.0
1989	Ricky Gales, Simpson	Sr.	10	297	*2,035	*203.5
1990	Jon Warga, Wittenberg	Sr.	10	254	1,836	183.6
1991	Hank Wineman, Albion	Sr.	9	307	1,629	181.0

* Record.

PASSING

Career Passing Efficiency
(Min. 325 Completions)

Player, Team	Years	Att.	Cmp.	Int.	Pct.	Yds.	TD	Pts.
Joe Blake, Simpson	1987-90	672	399	15	.594	6,183	43	*153.3
Gary Collier, Emory & Henry	1984-87	738	386	33	.523	6,103	80	148.6
Greg Heeres, Hope	1981-84	630	347	21	.537	5,120	53	144.4
Bruce Crosthwaite, Adrian	1984-87	618	368	31	.596	4,959	45	141.0
Matt Jozokos, Plymouth St.	1987-90	1,003	527	39	.525	7,658	95	140.2
Joe Coviello, Frank. & Marsh.	1973-76	591	334	36	.565	4,651	52	139.5
John Clark, Wis.-Eau Claire	1987-90	1,119	645	42	.576	9,196	63	137.7
Joe Shield, Trinity (Conn.)	1981-84	845	476	39	.563	6,646	52	133.5
David Broecker, Wabash	1979-82	633	369	45	.583	4,895	45	132.5
Dick Puccio, Cortland St.	1988-91	727	451	34	.620	5,301	40	131.9
Mike Culver, Juniata	1983-86	756	406	41	.537	5,799	56	131.7
Robb Disbennett, Salisbury St.	1982-85	633	359	40	.567	5,023	40	131.6
Kirk Baumgartner, Wis.-Stevens Point	1986-89	*1,696	*883	57	.521	*13,028	*110	131.3
Walter Briggs, Montclair St.	1983-86	832	417	36	.501	6,489	59	130.4
Brian Cox, Beloit	1988-91	620	337	43	.544	4,641	50	130.0
Randy Muetzel, St. Thomas (Minn.)	1979-82	613	339	20	.553	4,462	36	129.3
Larry Barretta, Lycoming	1983-86	732	361	26	.493	5,345	57	129.3
Ed Dougherty, Lycoming	1988-91	1,025	589	47	.575	7,108	69	128.7
Keith Bishop, Ill. Wesleyan/Wheaton (Ill.)	1981, 83-5	1,311	772	65	.589	9,579	71	128.2
Kevin King, Ripon	1978-81	635	348	43	.548	5,029	39	128.1

* Record.

Season Passing Efficiency
(Minimum 15 Attempts Per Game)

Player, Team	Year	G	Att.	Cmp.	Int.	Pct.	Yds.	TD	Pts.
Joe Blake, Simpson	††1989	10	144	93	3	.645	1,705	19	*203.3
Mitch Sanders, Bridgeport	1973	10	151	84	7	.556	1,551	23	182.9
Pat Mayew, St. John's (Minn.)	†1991	9	247	154	4	.623	2,408	30	181.0
Jimbo Fisher, Samford	†1987	10	252	139	5	.551	2,394	34	‡175.4
Gary Collier, Emory & Henry	1987	11	249	152	10	.610	2,317	33	174.8
James Grant, Ramapo	1989	9	147	91	7	.619	1,441	17	172.7
Gary Urwiler, Eureka	1991	10	171	103	5	.602	1,656	18	170.3
Robb Disbennett, Salisbury St......	†1985	10	153	94	6	.614	1,462	16	168.4
Scott Scesney, St. John's (N.Y.)	1989	10	244	131	9	.536	2,314	31	167.8
Chuck Hooker, Cornell College	1985	9	186	108	10	.581	1,818	21	166.7
Steve Varley, St. John's (Minn.)	1989	9	162	106	8	.654	1,476	16	164.6
Brad Forsyth, Ill. Wesleyan	1989	9	159	100	4	.628	1,380	16	163.9
Cody Dearing, Randolph-Macon....	†1984	10	226	125	12	.553	2,139	27	163.4
Paul Foye, Amherst	1985	8	133	87	7	.654	1,161	14	163.0
Matt Dillon, Cornell College........	1978	9	166	98	7	.590	1,567	16	161.7
Aaron Van Dyke, Cornell College ...	1976	9	154	91	12	.591	1,611	14	161.4
John Koz, Baldwin-Wallace	1991	10	239	153	4	.640	1,014	21	160.5
George Muller, Hofstra	†1980	10	189	115	14	.608	1,983	15	160.4
Larry Cummings, Plymouth St.	1984	10	168	94	4	.560	1,516	17	160.3

*Record. † National champion. †† Declared champion; with six more pass attempts (making 15 per game), all interceptions, still would have highest efficiency (187.3). ‡ Record for minimum of 20 attempts per game.

Career Yards

Player, Team	Years	Att.	Cmp.	Int.	Pct.	Yards	TD
Kirk Baumgartner, Wis.-Stevens Point	1986-89	*1,696	*883	57	.521	*13,028	*110
Keith Bishop, Ill. Wesleyan/Wheaton (Ill.) ..	1981, 83-85	1,311	772	65	.589	9,579	71
Dennis Bogacz, Wis.-Oshkosh/Wis.-Whitewater	1988-89, 90-91	1,275	654	59	.513	9,536	66
Dave Geissler, Wis.-Stevens Point	1982-85	1,346	789	57	.586	9,518	65
John Clark, Wis.-Eau Claire	1987-90	1,119	645	42	.576	9,196	63
Tim Peterson, Wis.-Stout	1986-89	1,185	653	62	.551	8,881	59
Matt Jozokos, Plymouth St.	1987-90	1,003	527	39	.525	7,658	95
Shane Fulton, Heidelberg	1983-86	1,024	587	55	.573	7,372	50
Paul Brandenburg, Ripon	1984-87	1,181	607	66	.514	7,320	39
Craig Solomon, Rhodes	1975-78	1,022	542	70	.530	7,314	71
Rob Bristow, Pomona-Pitzer	1983-86	1,155	628	60	.544	7,120	27
Ed Dougherty, Lycoming	1988-91	1,025	589	47	.575	7,108	69
Steve Osterberger, Drake	1987-90	981	536	33	.546	7,021	53
Ron Devorsky, Hiram	1984-87	1,028	542	59	.527	7,012	50
Gary Walljasper, Wartburg	1981-84	974	521	50	.535	6,992	49
Marty Barrett, Buffalo	1980-83	956	513	53	.537	6,945	44
David Parker, Bishop	1981-84	938	378	63	.403	6,934	69
Scott Scesney, St. John's (N.Y.)	1986-89	945	463	44	.490	6,914	72
Scott Driggers, Colorado Col..............	1981-84	1,022	612	54	.599	6,709	40

*Record.

Season Yards

Player, Team	Year	Games	Att.	Cmp.	Int.	Pct.	Yards	TD
Kirk Baumgartner, Wis.-Stevens Point	1988	11	*527	*276	16	.524	*3,828	25
Kirk Baumgartner, Wis.-Stevens Point	1987	11	466	243	22	.521	3,755	31
Kirk Baumgartner, Wis.-Stevens Point	1989	10	455	247	9	.542	3,692	*39
Keith Bishop, Wheaton (Ill.)	1983	9	375	236	19	*.629	3,274	24
Keith Bishop, Wheaton (Ill.)	1985	9	457	262	22	.573	3,171	25
Dennis Bogacz, Wis.-Oshkosh	1989	10	378	219	18	.579	3,051	18
Keith Bishop, Wheaton (Ill.)	1984	9	440	259	21	.589	2,968	21
Tim Peterson, Wis.-Stout	1989	10	445	256	15	.575	2,956	20
Brion Demski, Wis.-Stevens Point	1981	10	452	222	20	.491	2,889	16
Shane Fulton, Heidelberg	1985	10	393	222	24	.565	2,876	19
Tim Peterson, Wis.-Stout	1987	11	302	180	19	.596	2,871	18
Chris Creighton, Kenyon	1990	10	398	231	18	.580	2,843	29
Kevin Enterlein, Pace	1986	10	427	205	28	.480	2,829	20
John Clark, Wis.-Eau Claire	1989	10	344	199	14	.578	2,785	22
Robert Farra, Claremont-M-S	†1978	9	359	196	15	.546	2,770	20

*Record. † National champion.

Single-Game Yards

Yds.	Player, Team (Opponent)	Date
585	Tim Lynch, Hofstra (Fordham)	Oct. 19, 1991
533	John Love, North Park (Elmhurst)	Oct. 13, 1990
532	Bob Monroe, Knox (Cornell College)	Oct. 11, 1986
523	Kirk Baumgartner, Wis.-Stevens Point (Wis.-Stout)	Oct. 24, 1987
513	Craig Solomon, Rhodes (Rose-Hulman)	Nov.11, 1978
509	Bob Krepfle, Wis.-La Crosse (Wis.-River Falls)	Nov. 12, 1983
507	George Beisel, Hofstra (LIU-C. W. Post)	Sept. 28, 1991
506	Keith Bishop, Wheaton, Ill. (Ill. Wesleyan)	Oct. 29, 1983
505	Kirk Baumgartner, Wis.-Stevens Point (Wis.-Superior)	Nov. 4, 1989
504	Rob Shippy, Concordia, Ill. (Concordia, Wis.)	Oct. 5, 1985
503	Dave Detrick, Wis.-Superior (Wis.-Oshkosh)	Sept. 16, 1989
501	Keith Bishop, Wheaton, Ill. (North Park)	Oct. 12, 1985

Single-Game Completions

Cmp.	Player, Team (Opponent)	Date
50	Tim Lynch, Hofstra (Fordham)	Oct. 19, 1991
47	Mike Wallace, Ohio Wesleyan (Denison)	Oct. 3, 1981
42	Tim Lynch, Hofstra (Towson St.)	Nov. 2, 1991
42	Keith Bishop, Wheaton, Ill. (Millikin)	Sept. 14, 1985
41	Michael Doto, Hofstra (Central Conn. St.)	Sept. 14, 1991
41	Todd Monken, Knox (Cornell College)	Oct. 8, 1988
40	Dave Geissler, Wis.-Stevens Point (Wis.-Eau Claire)	Nov. 12, 1983
39	Rob Bristow, Pomona-Pitzer (La Verne)	Oct. 12, 1985
39	Steve Hendry, Wis.-Superior (Wis.-Stevens Point)	Oct. 17, 1981
38	Jeff Voris, DePauw (Findlay)	Oct. 31, 1987
38	Todde Greenough, Willamette (Southern Ore.)	Sept. 26, 1987
38	Pat Moyer, Maryville, Tenn. (Cumberland)	Oct. 5, 1985

Career Yards Per Game

Player, Team	Years	G	Att.	Cmp.	Int.	Pct.	Yards	TD	Avg.
Kirk Baumgartner, Wis.-Stevens Pt.	1986-89	41	*1,696	*883	57	.521	*13,028	*110	*317.8
Keith Bishop, Ill. Wes./Wheaton ...	1981, 83-85	31	1,311	772	65	.589	9,579	71	309.0
Robert Farra, Claremont-M-S	1978-79	16	579	313	24	.541	4,360	31	272.5
Dennis Bogacz, Wis.-Oshkosh/ Wis.-Whitewater	1988-89, 90-1	38	1,275	654	59	.513	9,536	66	250.9
Tim Peterson, Wis.-Stout	1986-89	36	1,185	653	62	.551	8,881	59	246.7
Rob Bristow, Pomona-Pitzer	1983-86	29	1,155	628	60	.544	7,120	27	245.5
John Rooney, Ill. Wesleyan	1982-84	27	986	489	47	.496	6,576	55	243.6
John Clark, Wis.-Eau Claire	1987-90	38	1,119	645	42	.576	9,196	63	242.0
Dave Geissler, Wis.-Stevens Pt. ...	1982-85	42	1,346	789	57	.586	9,518	65	226.6
Scott Scesney, St. John's (N.Y.) ...	1986-89	32	945	463	44	.490	6,914	72	216.1
Jeff Voris, DePauw	1986-89	28	910	504	25	.554	6,035	56	215.5
Paul Brandenburg, Ripon	1984-87	34	1,181	607	66	.514	7,320	39	215.3

* Record.

Season Yards Per Game

Player, Team	Year	G	Att.	Cmp.	Int.	Pct.	Yards	TD	Avg.
Kirk Baumgartner, Wis.-Stevens Point ..	1989	10	455	247	9	.543	3,692	*39	*369.2
Keith Bishop, Wheaton (Ill.)	1983	9	375	236	19	*.629	3,274	24	363.8
Keith Bishop, Wheaton (Ill.)	1985	9	457	262	22	.573	3,171	25	352.3
Kirk Baumgartner, Wis.-Stevens Point ..	1988	11	*527	*276	16	.524	*3,828	25	348.0
Kirk Baumgartner, Wis.-Stevens Point ..	1987	11	466	243	22	.521	3,755	31	341.4
Keith Bishop, Wheaton (Ill.)	1984	9	440	259	21	.589	2,968	21	329.8
Willie Reyna, La Verne	1991	8	267	170	6	.636	2,543	16	317.9
Robert Farra, Claremont-M-S	†1978	9	359	196	15	.546	2,770	20	307.8
Dennis Bogacz, Wis.-Oshkosh	1989	10	378	219	18	.580	3,051	18	305.1

* Record.   † National champion.

Annual Champions

Year	Player, Team	Cl.	G	Att.	Cmp.	Avg.	Int.	Pct.	Yds.	TD
1973	Pat Clements, Kenyon	Jr.	9	239	133	14.8	17	.556	1,738	12
1974	Larry Cenotto, Pomona-Pitzer	Sr.	9	294	147	16.3	23	.500	2,024	15
1975	Ron Miller, Elmhurst	Sr.	8	205	118	14.8	15	.576	1,398	7
1976	Tom Hamilton, Occidental	Jr.	8	235	131	16.4	10	.557	1,988	10
1977	Tom Hamilton, Occidental	Sr.	9	323	171	19.0	17	.529	2,132	13
1978	Robert Farra, Claremont-M-S	Jr.	9	359	196	21.8	15	.546	2,770	20

Beginning in 1979, ranked on Passing Efficiency Rating Points, minimum of 15 attempts per game (instead of per-game completions).

Year	Player, Team	Cl.	G	Att.	Cmp.	Int.	Pct.	Yds.	TD	Pts.
1979	David Broecker, Wabash	Fr.	9	145	81	9	.559	1,311	13	149.0
1980	George Muller, Hofstra	Sr.	10	189	115	14	.608	1,983	15	160.4
1981	Larry Atwater, Coe	Sr.	9	172	92	10	.535	1,615	15	147.2
1982	Mike Bennett, Cornell College	Sr.	9	154	83	8	.539	1,436	17	158.3
1983	Joe Shield, Trinity (Conn.)	Jr.	8	238	135	13	.567	2,185	19	149.1
1984	Cody Dearing, Randolph-Macon...	Sr.	10	226	125	12	.553	2,139	27	163.4
1985	Robb Disbennett, Salisbury St......	Sr.	10	153	94	6	.614	1,462	16	168.4
1986	Gary Collier, Emory & Henry	Jr.	11	171	88	6	.514	1,509	21	158.9
1987	Jimbo Fisher, Samford	Sr.	10	252	139	5	.551	2,394	34	175.4
1988	Steve Flynn, Central (Iowa)	Jr.	8	133	82	6	.616	1,190	10	152.5
1989	Joe Blake, Simpson	††Jr.	10	144	93	3	.645	1,705	19	*203.3
1990	Dan Sharley, Dayton	†††Sr.	10	149	95	2	.637	1,377	12	165.1
1991	Pat Mayew, St. John's (Minn.)	Sr.	9	247	154	4	.623	2,408	30	181.0

* Record. †† Declared champion; with six more pass attempts (making 15 per game), all interceptions, still would have highest efficiency (187.3). ††† Declared champion; with one more attempt (making 15 per game), an interception, still would have highest efficiency (162.8).

Annual Passing Efficiency Leaders (Before 1979)
(Minimum 15 Attempts Per Game)

Year	Player, Team	G	Att.	Cmp.	Int.	Pct.	Yds.	TD	Pts.
1973	Mitch Sanders, Bridgeport	10	151	84	7	.556	1,551	23	182.9
1974	Tom McGuire, Ill. Benedictine.........	10	221	142	16	.643	2,206	16	157.5
1975	Jim Morrow, Wash. & Jeff.	9	137	82	7	.599	1,283	11	154.8
1976	Aaron Van Dyke, Cornell College	9	154	91	12	.591	1,611	14	161.4
1977	Matt Winslow, Middlebury	8	130	79	5	.608	919	17	155.6
1978	Matt Dillon, Cornell College...........	9	166	98	7	.590	1,567	16	161.7

RECEIVING

Career Catches

Player, Team	Years	No.	Yards	TD
Bill Stromberg, Johns Hopkins........................	1978-81	*258	3,776	39
Dale Amos, Frank. & Marsh.	1986-89	233	*3,846	35
Scott Fredrickson, Wis.-Stout	1986-89	233	3,390	23
Mike Whitehouse, St. Norbert	1986-89	230	3,480	37
Mike Funk, Wabash	1985, 87-89	228	2,858	33
Dan Daley, Pomona-Pitzer	1985-88	227	2,598	10
Jim Jorden, Wheaton (Ill.)	1982-85	225	3,022	22
Theo Blanco, Wis.-Stevens Point.....................	1985-88	223	3,139	18
Ed Brady, Ill. Wesleyan	1981-84	220	2,907	22
Walter Kalinowski, Catholic	1983-86	219	2,430	16
Jim Bradford, Carleton.............................	1988-91	212	3,719	32
Mike Cottle, Juniata...............................	1985-88	212	2,607	36
John Ward, Cornell College........................	1979-82	211	3,085	30
Ron Severance, Otterbein.........................	1989-91	207	2,378	17
Vince Dortch, Jersey City St........................	1983-86	206	3,037	28
Rick Fry, Occidental	1974-77	200	3,073	18
Todd Stoner, Kenyon..............................	1981-84	197	3,191	31
Steve Feyrer, Ripon	1983-86	196	2,611	19

* Record.

Season Catches

Player, Team	Year	Games	No.	Yards	TD
Theo Blanco, Wis.-Stevens Point..................	1987	11	*106	*1,616	8
Ron Severance, Otterbein........................	1990	10	92	1,049	8
Scott Faessler, Framingham St.	†1990	9	92	916	5
Mike Funk, Wabash	†1989	9	87	1,169	12
Ted Taggart, Kenyon	1989	10	87	1,004	7
Jim Jorden, Wheaton (Ill.)	†1985	9	87	1,011	8
Ron Severance, Otterbein........................	†1991	10	85	929	4
Scott Fredrickson, Wis.-Stout	1989	10	83	1,102	7
Rick Fry, Occidental	†1977	9	82	1,222	5
Jim Myers, Kenyon	†1974	9	82	1,483	12
Wayne Morris, Hofstra	1991	10	80	890	7
Theo Blanco, Wis.-Stevens Point.................	†1988	10	80	1,009	7
Bob Glanville, Lewis & Clark	1985	9	80	1,054	9
Ed Brady, Ill. Wesleyan	†1983	9	80	873	7
Roger Little, Dubuque	1988	10	79	1,025	7
Walt Kalinowski, Catholic	1985	11	79	875	4

* Record. † National champion.

Single-Game Catches

No.	Player, Team (Opponent)	Date
20	Rich Johnson, Pace (Fordham)	Nov. 7, 1987
20	Pete Thompson, Carroll, Wis. (Augustana, Ill.)	Nov. 4, 1978
17	Dan Daley, Pomona-Pitzer (Occidental)	Oct. 15, 1988
17	Theo Blanco, Wis.-Stevens Point (Wis.-Oshkosh)	Oct. 31, 1987
17	Tim Mowery, Wis.-Superior (Wis.-Stevens Point)	Oct. 17, 1971

Career Catches Per Game

Player, Team	Years	Games	No.	Yards	TD	Ct. PG
Bill Stromberg, Johns Hopkins	1978-81	36	*258	3,776	39	*7.2
Tim McNamara, Trinity (Conn.)	1981-84	21	146	2,313	19	7.0
Ron Severance, Otterbein	1989-91	30	207	2,378	17	6.9
Chuck Braun, Wis.-Stevens Point	1980-81	18	124	1,914	19	6.9
Jim Jorden, Wheaton (Ill.)	1982-85	33	225	3,022	22	6.8
Mike Whitehouse, St. Norbert	1986-89	35	230	3,480	37	6.6
Dan Daley, Pomona-Pitzer	1985-88	35	227	2,598	10	6.5
Rich Johnson, Pace	1985-87	29	188	2,614	8	6.5
Rick Fry, Occidental	1974-77	33	200	3,073	18	6.1
Mike Funk, Wabash	1985, 87-89	38	228	2,858	33	6.0
Ted Taggart, Kenyon	1988-90	28	165	2,034	20	5.9
Pat McNamara, Trinity (Conn.)	1977-79	24	141	2,280	20	5.9
Theo Blanco, Wis.-Stevens Point	1985-88	38	223	3,139	18	5.9
Dale Amos, Frank. & Marsh.	1986-89	40	233	*3,846	35	5.8
Scott Fredrickson, Wis.-Stout	1986-89	40	233	3,390	23	5.8
Steve Feyrer, Ripon	1983-86	34	196	2,611	19	5.8

* Record.

Season Catches Per Game

Player, Team	Year	Games	No.	Yards	TD	Ct. PG
Scott Faessler, Framingham St.	†1990	9	92	916	5	*10.2
Mike Funk, Wabash	†1989	9	87	1,169	12	9.7
Jim Jorden, Wheaton (Ill.)	†1985	9	87	1,011	8	9.7
Theo Blanco, Wis.-Stevens Point	1987	11	*106	*1,616	8	9.6
Rick Fry, Occidental	†1976	8	74	1,214	8	9.3
Ron Severance, Otterbein	1990	10	92	1,049	8	9.2
Rick Fry, Occidental	†1977	9	82	1,222	5	9.1
Jim Myers, Kenyon	†1974	9	82	1,483	12	9.1
Bob Glanville, Lewis & Clark	1985	9	80	1,054	9	8.9
Ed Brady, Ill. Wesleyan	†1983	9	80	873	7	8.9
John Tucci, Amherst	†1986	8	70	1,025	8	8.8
Ted Taggart, Kenyon	1989	10	87	1,004	7	8.7

* Record.   † National champion.

Annual Champions (Catches Per Game)

Year	Player, Team	Cl.	G	No.	Avg.	Yards	TD
1973	Ron Duckett, Trinity (Conn.)	Sr.	8	57	7.1	834	7
1974	Jim Myers, Kenyon	Sr.	9	82	9.1	1,483	12
1975	C. J. DeWitt, Bridgewater (Va.)	Sr.	9	64	7.1	836	2
1976	Rick Fry, Occidental	Jr.	8	74	9.3	1,214	8
1977	Rick Fry, Occidental	Sr.	9	82	9.1	1,222	5
1978	Pat McNamara, Trinity (Conn.)	Jr.	8	67	8.4	1,024	11
1979	Theodore Anderson, Fisk	Jr.	7	49	7.0	699	2
1980	Bill Stromberg, Johns Hopkins	Jr.	9	66	7.3	907	11
1981	Bill Stromberg, Johns Hopkins	Sr.	9	78	8.7	924	10
1982	Jim Gustafson, St. Thomas (Minn.)	Sr.	10	72	7.2	990	5
1983	Ed Brady, Ill. Wesleyan	Jr.	9	80	8.9	873	7
1984	Tim McNamara, Trinity (Conn.)	Sr.	8	67	8.4	1,004	10
1985	Jim Jorden, Wheaton (Ill.)	Sr.	9	87	9.7	1,011	8
1986	John Tucci, Amherst	Sr.	8	70	8.8	1,025	8
1987	Chris Vogel, Knox	So.	9	78	8.7	1,326	15
1988	Theo Blanco, Wis.-Stevens Point	Sr.	10	80	8.0	1,009	7
1989	Mike Funk, Wabash	Sr.	9	87	9.7	1,169	12
1990	Scott Faessler, Framingham St.	So.	9	92	*10.2	916	5
1991	Ron Severance, Otterbein	Sr.	10	85	8.5	929	4

* Record.

Annual Champions (Yards Per Game)

Year	Player, Team	Cl.	G	No.	Yards	TD	Avg.
1990	Ray Shelley, Juniata	Sr.	10	54	1,147	12	114.7
1991	Rodd Patten, Framingham St.	So.	8	49	956	13	119.5

Career Yards

Player, Team	Years	Catches	Yards	Avg.	TD
Dale Amos, Frank. & Marsh.	1986-89	233	*3,846	16.5	35
Bill Stromberg, Johns Hopkins............	1978-81	*258	3,776	14.6	39
Jim Bradford, Carleton...................	1988-91	212	3,719	17.5	32
Mike Whitehouse, St. Norbert	1986-89	230	3,480	15.1	37
Scott Fredrickson, Wis.-Stout	1986-89	233	3,390	14.5	23
John Aromando, Trenton St.	1981-84	165	3,197	19.4	39
Todd Stoner, Kenyon.....................	1981-84	197	3,191	16.2	31
Theo Blanco, Wis.-Stevens Point..........	1985-88	223	3,139	14.1	18
John Ward, Cornell College...............	1979-82	211	3,085	14.6	30
Rick Fry, Occidental	1974-77	200	3,073	15.4	18

* Record.

Season Yards

Player, Team	Year	Catches	Yards	Avg.	TD
Theo Blanco, Wis.-Stevens Point.........	1987	*106	*1,616	15.2	8
Jim Myers, Kenyon	†1974	82	1,483	18.1	12
Beau Almodobar, Norwich	1984	71	1,375	19.4	10
Chris Vogel, Knox.......................	†1987	78	1,326	17.0	15
Dale Amos, Frank. & Marsh.	1989	72	1,302	18.1	15
Don Moehling, Wis.-Stevens Point	1988	72	1,290	17.9	7
Jim Bradford, Carleton...................	1989	69	1,238	17.9	6
Rick Fry, Occidental	†1977	82	1,222	14.9	5
Evan Elkington, Worcester Tech	1989	52	1,220	+23.5	16
Rick Fry, Occidental	†1976	74	1,214	16.4	8
Mike Howey, Moravian	1989	61	1,203	19.7	7
Scott Fredrickson, Wis.-Stout	1987	70	1,185	16.9	7
Bill Bagley, Frostburg St..................	1984	70	1,182	16.9	10

* Record.   † National champion.   + Record for minimum of 50 receptions.

SCORING
Career Points

Player, Team	Years	TD	XPt.	FG	Pts.
Joe Dudek, Plymouth St..........................	1982-85	*79	0	0	*474
Terry Underwood, Wagner	1985-88	58	0	0	348
Cary Osborn, Wis.-Eau Claire	1987-90	55	0	0	330
Tim McDaniel, Centre............................	1988-91	54	0	0	324
A. J. Pagano, Wash. & Jeff.	1984-87	53	5	0	323
Ricky Gales, Nebraska-Omaha; Simpson	1986-87; 88-89	51	10	0	316
Greg Corning, Wis.-River Falls	1984-87	52	2	0	314
Vance Mueller, Occidental	1982-85	51	8	0	314
Scott Barnyak, Carnegie Mellon	1987-90	49	14	0	308
Prentes Wilson, Ill. Benedictine	1987-90	50	0	0	300
Eric Frees, Western Md...........................	1988-91	49	4	0	298
Michael Waithe, Curry	1984-87	49	0	0	294
Jeff Norman, St. John's (Minn.)	1974-77	25	119	8	293
Joe Thompson, Augustana (Ill.)..................	1973-76	48	4	0	292
Ryan Kolpin, Coe	1987-90	48	0	0	288

* Record.

Season Points

Player, Team	Year	TD	XPt.	FG	Pts.
Stanley Drayton, Allegheny	†1991	*28	0	0	*168
Ricky Gales, Simpson......................................	†1989	26	10	0	166
Joe Dudek, Plymouth St....................................	1985	25	0	0	150
Bruce Naszimento, Jersey City St.	1973	25	0	0	150
Scott Barnyak, Carnegie Mellon	†1990	22	6	0	138
Ryan Kolpin, Coe	†1990	23	0	0	138
Ron Corbett, Cornell College	1982	23	0	0	138
Billy Johnson, Widener	†1973	23	0	0	138
Chris Babirad, Wash. & Jeff.	1991	22	2	0	134
Tim McDaniel, Centre......................................	1990	22	0	0	132
Chris Hipsley, Cornell College	†1976	14	42	2	132
Karl Kohl, Catholic...	1989	21	2	0	128
Denis McDermott, St. John's (N.Y.)	1989	21	0	0	126
Terry Underwood, Wagner	†1988	21	0	0	126
Prentes Wilson, Ill. Benedictine	1988	21	0	0	126
Joe Dudek, Plymouth St....................................	†1984	21	0	0	126

* Record.   † National champion.

Player, Team	Years	Games	TD	XPt.	FG	Pts.	Pt. PG
Joe Dudek, Plymouth St...............	1982-85	41	*79	0	0	*474	*11.6
Terry Underwood, Wagner	1985-88	33	58	0	0	348	10.5
Ryan Kolpin, Coe	1987-90	28	48	0	0	288	10.3
A. J. Pagano, Wash. & Jeff.	1984-87	36	53	5	0	323	9.0
Gary Trettel, St. Thomas (Minn.)	1988-90	29	43	0	0	258	8.9
Vance Mueller, Occidental	1982-85	36	51	8	0	314	8.7
Jeff Norman, St. John's (Minn.)	1974-77	34	25	119	8	293	8.6
Denis McDermott, St. John's (N.Y.) ...	1987-89	30	43	0	0	258	8.6
Joe Thompson, Augustana (Ill.).......	1973-76	34	48	4	0	292	8.6
Tim McDaniel, Centre................	1988-91	38	54	0	0	324	8.5
Jay Wessler, Illinois Col.	1977-80	34	46	6	0	282	8.3
Scott Reppert, Lawrence	1979-82	33	45	0	0	270	8.2
Pedro Bowman, Duquesne............	1981-84	34	46	2	0	278	8.2

* Record.

Season Points Per Game

Player, Team	Year	Games	TD	XPt.	FG	Pts.	Pt. PG
Stanley Drayton, Allegheny	†1991	10	*28	0	0	*168	*16.8
Ricky Gales, Simpson..................	†1989	10	26	10	0	166	16.6
Billy Johnson, Widener	†1973	9	23	0	0	138	15.3
Bruce Naszimento, Jersey City St.	1973	10	25	0	0	150	15.0
Chris Babirad, Wash. & Jeff.	1991	9	22	2	0	134	14.9
Chris Hipsley, Cornell College	†1976	9	14	42	2	132	14.7
Michael Waithe, Curry	†1987	8	19	0	0	114	14.3
Rick Bell, St. John's (Minn.)	†1982	9	21	2	0	128	14.2
Terry Underwood, Wagner	†1988	9	21	0	0	126	14.0
Scott Barnyak, Carnegie Mellon	†1990	10	22	6	0	138	13.8
Ryan Kolpin, Coe	†1990	10	23	0	0	138	13.8
Kevin Weaver, Wash. & Lee	†1985	8	17	8	0	110	13.8
Joe Dudek, Plymouth St................	1985	11	25	0	0	150	13.6

* Record.   † National champion.

Annual Champions

Year	Player, Team	Class	G	TD	XPt.	FG	Pts.	Avg.
1973	Billy Johnson, Widener	Sr.	9	23	0	0	138	15.3
1974	Joe Thompson, Augustana (Ill.).........	So.	9	17	0	0	102	11.3
1975	Ron Baker, Monmouth (Ill.)	Sr.	8	15	2	0	92	11.5
1976	Chris Hipsley, Cornell College	So.	9	14	42	2	132	14.7
1977	Chip Zawoiski, Widener	Sr.	9	18	0	0	108	12.0
1978	Roger Andrachik, Baldwin-Wallace	Sr.	8	16	0	0	96	12.0
1979	Jay Wessler, Illinois Col.	Jr.	8	16	4	0	100	12.5
1980	Daryl Johnson, Wabash................	Jr.	9	20	0	0	120	13.3
1981	Scott Reppert, Lawrence	Jr.	9	15	0	0	90	10.0
	Daryl Johnson, Wabash................	Sr.	9	15	0	0	90	10.0
1982	Rick Bell, St. John's (Minn.)	Sr.	9	21	2	0	128	14.2
1983	John Aromando, Trenton St.	Jr.	10	20	0	0	120	12.0
1984	Joe Dudek, Plymouth St................	Jr.	10	21	0	0	126	12.6
1985	Kevin Weaver, Wash. & Lee	Jr.	8	17	8	0	110	13.8
1986	Jim Korfonta, Hamilton	Sr.	8	16	0	0	96	12.0
	Russ Kring, Mount Union	Jr.	10	20	0	0	120	12.0
1987	Michael Waithe, Curry	Sr.	8	19	0	0	114	14.3
1988	Terry Underwood, Wagner	Sr.	9	21	0	0	126	14.0
1989	Ricky Gales, Simpson..................	Sr.	10	26	10	0	166	16.6
1990	Scott Barnyak, Carnegie Mellon	Sr.	10	22	6	0	138	13.8
	Ryan Kolpin, Coe	Sr.	10	23	0	0	138	13.8
1991	Stanley Drayton, Allegheny	Jr.	10	*28	0	0	*168	*16.8

* Record.

PUNTING
Career Average
(Minimum 100 Punts)

Player, Team	Years	No.	Yards	Avg.
Mike Manson, Ill. Benedictine	1975-78	120	5,056	*42.13
Kirk Seufert, Memphis St./Rhodes	1981, 83-84	109	4,587	42.08
Dan Osborn, Occidental	1981-83	157	6,528	41.6
Thomas Murray, Catholic	1983-84	122	5,028	41.2
Scott Lanz, Bethany (W. Va.)	1975-78	235	9,592	40.8
Jim Allshouse, Adrian	1972-75	210	8,525	40.6

* Record.

Season Average
(Qualifiers for Championship)

Player, Team	Year	No.	Yards	Avg.
Bob Burwell, Rose-Hulman	†1978	61	2,740	*44.9
Charles McPherson, Clark Atlanta	1978	50	2,237	44.7
Dan Osborn, Occidental	†1982	55	2,454	44.6
Mike Manson, Ill. Benedictine	†1976	36	1,587	44.1
Linc Welles, Bloomsburg	†1973	39	1,708	43.8
Kirk Seufert, Rhodes	†1983	44	1,921	43.7
Kelvin Albert, Knoxville	†1987	30	1,308	43.6

* Record.   † National champion.

Annual Champions

Year	Player, Team	Class	No.	Yards	Avg.
1973	Linc Welles, Bloomsburg	Sr.	39	1,708	43.8
1974	Sylvester Cunningham, Fort Valley St.	So.	40	1,703	42.6
1975	Larry Hersh, Shepherd	Jr.	58	2,519	43.4
1976	Mike Manson, Ill. Benedictine	So.	36	1,587	44.1
1977	Scott Lanz, Bethany (W. Va.)	Jr.	78	3,349	42.9
1978	Bob Burwell, Rose-Hulman	Sr.	61	2,740	*44.9
1979	Jay Lenstrom, Neb. Wesleyan	Sr.	64	2,641	41.3
1980	Duane Harrison, Bridgewater (Va.)	Sr.	43	1,792	41.7
1981	Dan Paro, Denison	Jr.	54	2,223	41.2
1982	Dan Osborn, Occidental	Jr.	55	2,454	44.6
1983	Kirk Seufert, Rhodes	Jr.	44	1,921	43.7
1984	Thomas Murray, Catholic	Sr.	59	2,550	43.2
1985	Dave Lewis, Muhlenberg	So.	55	2,290	41.6
	Mike Matzen, Coe	Sr.	55	2,290	41.6
1986	Darren Estes, Millsaps	Jr.	45	1,940	43.1
1987	Kelvin Albert, Knoxville	So.	30	1,308	43.6
1988	Bobby Graves, Sewanee	So.	57	2,445	42.9
1989	Paul Becker, Kenyon	Sr.	57	2,307	40.5
1990	Bill Nolan, Carroll (Wis.)	Sr.	33	1,322	40.1
1991	Jeff Stolte, Chicago	So.	54	2,295	42.5

* Record.

INTERCEPTIONS

Career Interceptions

Player, Team	Years	No.	Yards	Avg.
Ralph Gebhardt, Rochester	1972-75	*34	406	11.9
Eugene Hunter, Fort Valley St.	1972-74	29	*479	16.5
Brian Fetterolf, Aurora	1986-89	28	390	13.9
Rick Bealer, Lycoming	1987-90	28	279	10.0
Tim Lennon, Curry	1986-89	27	190	7.0
Mike Hintz, Wis.-Platteville	1983-86	27	183	6.8
Mark Dorner, Juniata	1984-87	26	443	17.0
Neal Guggemos, St. Thomas (Minn.)	1982-85	25	377	15.1
Dave Adams, Carleton	1984-87	25	327	13.1
Will Hill, Bishop	1983-86	25	261	10.4
Tom Devine, Juniata	1979-82	25	248	9.9
Gary Ellis, Rose-Hulman	1974-77	25	226	9.1

* Record.

Season Interceptions

Player, Team	Year	No.	Yards
Mark Dorner, Juniata	†1987	*15	202
Steve Nappo, Buffalo	†1986	13	155
Chris McMahon, Catholic	†1984	13	105
Ralph Gebhardt, Rochester	†1973	13	105
Brian Barr, Gettysburg	1985	12	144
John Bernard, Buffalo	†1983	12	143
Mick McConkey, Neb. Wesleyan	†1982	12	111
Tom Devine, Juniata	†1981	12	91

* Record.   † National champion.

Annual Champions
(Ranked on Average Per Game)

Year	Player, Team	Class	Games	No.	Avg.	Yards
1973	Ralph Gebhardt, Rochester	So.	9	13	1.44	105
1974	Kevin Birkholz, Carleton	Jr.	9	11	1.22	137

Year	Player, Team	Class	Games	No.	Avg.	Yards
1975	Mark Persichetti, Wash. & Jeff.	So.	9	10	1.11	97
1976	Gary Jantzer, Southern Ore.	Sr.	9	10	1.11	63
1977	Greg Jones, FDU-Madison	So.	9	10	1.11	106
	Mike Jones, Norwich	So.	9	10	1.11	98
1978	Don Sutton, San Fran. St.	Fr.	8	10	1.25	43
1979	Greg Holland, Simpson	Fr.	9	11	1.22	150
1980	Tim White, Lawrence	Sr.	8	10	1.25	131
1981	Tom Devine, Juniata	Sr.	9	12	1.33	91
1982	Mick McConkey, Neb. Wesleyan	Sr.	9	12	1.33	111
1983	John Bernard, Buffalo	Sr.	10	12	1.20	143
1984	Chris McMahon, Catholic	Sr.	9	13	1.44	140
1985	Kim McManis, Lane	Sr.	9	11	1.22	165
1986	Steve Nappo, Buffalo	Sr.	11	13	1.18	155
1987	Mark Dorner, Juniata	Sr.	10	*15	*1.50	202
1988	Tim Lennon, Curry	Jr.	9	11	1.22	86
1989	Ron Davies, Coast Guard	So.	9	11	1.22	90
1990	Craig Garritano, FDU-Madison	Jr.	9	10	1.11	158
	Brad Bohn, Neb. Wesleyan	So.	9	10	1.11	90
	Frank Greer, Sewanee	So.	9	10	1.11	67
	Harold Krebs, Merchant Marine	Sr.	9	10	1.11	19
1991	Murray Meadows, Millsaps	Sr.	9	11	1.22	46

* Record.

PUNT RETURNS
Career Average
(Minimum 1.2 Returns Per Game)

Player, Team	Years	No.	Yards	Avg.
Keith Winston, Knoxville	1986-87	30	686	*22.9
Robert Middlebrook, Knoxville	1984-85	21	473	22.5
Kevin Doherty, Mass. Maritime	1976-78, 80	45	939	20.9
Chuck Downey, Stony Brook	1984-87	59	*1,198	+20.3
Mike Askew, Kean	1980-81	28	555	19.8
Willie Canady, Fort Valley St.	1979-82	41	772	18.8

* Record.   + Record for minimum of 50 returns.

Season Average
(Minimum 1.2 Returns Per Game)

Player, Team	Year	No.	Yards	Avg.
Chuck Downey, Stony Brook	†1986	17	530	*31.2
Kevin Doherty, Mass. Maritime	†1976	11	332	30.2
Robert Middlebrook, Knoxville	†1984	9	260	28.9
Joe Troise, Kean	†1974	12	342	28.5
Melvin Dillard, Ferrum	†1990	25	*688	27.5
Chris Warren, Ferrum	†1989	18	421	23.4
Kevin Doherty, Mass. Maritime	1978	11	246	22.4

* Record.   † National champion.

Annual Champions

Year	Player, Team	Class	No.	Yards	‡Avg.
1973	Al Shepherd, Monmouth (Ill.)	Sr.	18	347	19.3
1974	Joe Troise, Kean	Fr.	12	342	28.5
1975	Mitch Brown, St. Lawrence	So.	25	430	17.2
1976	Kevin Doherty, Mass. Maritime	Fr.	11	332	30.2
1977	Charles Watkins, Knoxville	Sr.	15	278	18.5
1978	Dennis Robinson, Wesleyan	Sr.	††9	263	29.2
1979	Steve Moffett, Maryville (Tenn.)	Jr.	19	357	18.8
1980	Mike Askew, Kean	Jr.	16	304	19.0
1981	Mike Askew, Kean	Sr.	12	251	20.9
1982	Tom Southall, Colorado Col.	So.	13	281	21.6
1983	Edmond Donald, Millsaps	Jr.	15	320	21.3
1984	Robert Middlebrook, Knoxville	So.	9	260	28.9
1985	Dan Schone, Illinois Col.	Fr.	11	231	21.0
1986	Chuck Downey, Stony Brook	Jr.	17	530	*31.2
1987	Keith Winston, Knoxville	Sr.	16	343	21.4
1988	Dennis Tarr, Framingham St.	Jr.	9	178	19.8
1989	Chris Warren, Ferrum	Sr.	18	421	23.4
1990	Melvin Dillard, Ferrum	Sr.	25	*688	27.5
1991	Jordan Nixon, Augustana (Ill.)	Sr.	27	473	17.5

* Record.   ‡ Ranked on minimum of 1.5 returns per game in 1973; 1.2 from 1974.   †† Declared champion; with one more return (making 1.25 per game) for zero yards still would have highest average.

KICKOFF RETURNS

Career Average
(Minimum 1.2 Returns Per Game)

Player, Team	Years	No.	Yards	Avg.
Daryl Brown, Tufts	1974-76	38	1,111	*29.2
Mike Askew, Kean	1980-81	33	938	28.4
Chuck Downey, Stony Brook	1984-87	46	1,281	27.8
Scott Reppert, Lawrence	1979-82	44	1,134	25.8
Rick Rosenfeld, Western Md.	1973-76	69	1,732	25.1

* Record.

Season Average
(Minimum 1.2 Returns Per Game)

Player, Team	Year	No.	Yards	Avg.
Mike Askew, Kean	††1980	10	415	*41.5
Nate Kirtman, Pomona-Pitzer	†1990	14	515	36.8
Tom Myers, Coe	†1983	11	401	36.5
Ron Scott, Occidental	1983	10	363	36.3
Al White, Wm. Paterson	1990	12	427	35.6
Byron Womack, Iona	†1989	15	531	35.4
Darnell Marshall, Carroll (Wis.)	1989	17	586	34.5
Daryl Brown, Tufts	†1976	11	377	34.3
Anthony Drakeford, Ferrum	†1987	15	507	33.8
Sean Healy, Coe	1989	11	372	33.8
Glenn Koch, Tufts	†1986	14	472	33.7

* Record.   † National champion.   †† Declared champion; with one more return (making 1.2 per game) for zero yards still would have highest average (37.7).

Annual Champions

Year	Player, Team	Class	No.	Yards	‡Avg.
1973	Greg Montgomery, Wis.-Whitewater	So.	17	518	30.5
1974	Tom Oleksa, Muhlenberg	Sr.	15	467	31.1
1975	Jeff Levant, Beloit	Jr.	15	434	28.9
1976	Daryl Brown, Tufts	Sr.	11	377	34.3
1977	Charlie Black, Marietta	Jr.	14	465	33.2
1978	Russ Atchison, Centre	So.	11	284	25.8
1979	Jim Iannone, Rochester	Jr.	13	411	31.6
1980	Mike Askew, Kean	So.	††10	415	*41.5
1981	Gene Cote, Wesleyan	Sr.	16	521	32.6
1982	Jim Hachey, Bri'water (Mass.)	Jr.	16	477	29.8
1983	Tom Myers, Coe	So.	11	401	36.5
1984	Mike Doetsch, Trinity (Conn.)	Jr.	13	434	33.4
1985	Gary Newsom, Lane	So.	10	319	31.9
1986	Glenn Koch, Tufts	Sr.	14	472	33.7
1987	Anthony Drakeford, Ferrum	Sr.	15	507	33.8
1988	Harold Owens, Wis.-La Crosse	Jr.	10	508	29.9
1989	Byron Womack, Iona	Sr.	15	531	35.4
1990	Nate Kirtman, Pomona-Pitzer	Jr.	14	515	36.8
1991	Tom Reason, Albion	So.	13	423	32.5

* Record.   ‡ Ranked on minimum of 1.5 returns per game in 1973; 1.2 from 1974.   †† Declared champion; with one more return (making 1.2 per game) for zero yards still would have highest average (37.7).

FIELD GOALS

Career Field Goals

Player, Team	Years	Made	Atts.	Pct.
Ken Edelman, Mount Union (S)	1987-90	*52	**71	.732
Ted Swan, Colorado Col. (S)	1973-76	43	57	.754
Jim Hever, Rhodes (S)	1982-85	42	66	.636
Manny Matsakis, Capital (C)	1980-83	40	66	.606
Doug Hart, Grove City (S)	1985-88	40	**71	.563
Mike Duvic, Dayton (S)	1986-89	38	49	$.776
Jeff Reitz, Lawrence (C)	1974-77	37	60	.617
Dan Deneher, Montclair St. (S)	1978-79, 81-82	37	65	.569
Jim Flynn, Gettysburg (S)	1982-85	37	68	.544

* Record.   ** Record tied. $ Declared record; with one more attempt (making 50), failed, still would have highest percentage (.760).   (C) Conventional kicker.   (S) Soccer-style kicker.

1992 NCAA FOOTBALL

Season Field Goals

Player, Team	Year	Made	Atts.	Pct.
Ken Edelman, Mount Union (S)	†1990	*20	27	.741
Scott Ryerson, Central Fla. (S)	†1981	18	*29	.621
Steve Graeca, John Carroll (S)	†1988	15	16	*.938
Ken Edelman, Mount Union (S)	1988	15	17	.882
Gary Potter, Hamline (C)	†1984	15	21	.714
Jeff Reitz, Lawrence (C)	†1975	15	26	.577

Record.   † National champion.   (C) Conventional kicker.   (S) Soccer-style kicker.

Annual Champions

Year	Player, Team	Class	Made	Atts.	Pct.	PG
1973	Chuck Smeltz, Susquehanna (C)	Jr.	10	14	.714	1.11
1974	Ted Swan, Colorado Col. (S)	So.	13	15	.867	1.44
1975	Jeff Reitz, Lawrence (C)	So.	15	26	.577	1.67
1976	Mark Sniegocki, Bethany (W. Va.) (C)	So.	11	14	.786	1.22
1977	Bob Unruh, Wheaton (Ill.) (S)	Jr.	11	14	.786	1.22
1978	Craig Walker, Western Md. (C)	So.	13	24	.542	1.44
1979	Jeff Holter, Concordia-M'head (S)	Jr.	12	15	.800	1.33
1980	Jeff Holter, Concordia-M'head (S)	Sr.	13	19	.684	1.30
1981	Scott Ryerson, Central Fla. (S)	So.	18	*29	.621	1.80
1982	Manny Matsakis, Capital (C)	Jr.	13	20	.650	1.44
1983	Mike Farrell, Adrian (S)	So.	12	21	.571	1.33
1984	Gary Potter, Hamline (C)	Jr.	15	21	.714	1.50
1985	Joe Bevelhimer, Wabash (C)	Sr.	14	22	.636	1.40
	Jim Hever, Rhodes (S)	Sr.	14	23	.609	1.40
1986	Tim Dewberry, Occidental (C)	Sr.	13	21	.619	1.44
1987	Doug Dickason, John Carroll (S)	Sr.	13	21	.619	1.44
1988	Steve Graeca, John Carroll (S)	Fr.	15	16	*.938	1.67
1989	Dave Bergmann, San Diego (S)	So.	14	18	.778	1.56
	Rich Egal, Merchant Marine (S)	Fr.	14	22	.636	1.56
1990	Ken Edelman, Mount Union (S)	Sr.	*20	27	.741	*2.00
1991	Greg Harrison, Union (N.Y.) (S)	So.	12	16	.750	1.33

Record.   (C) Conventional kicker.   (S) Soccer-style kicker.

LONGEST PLAYS

Since 1941, official maximum length of all plays fixed at 100 yards.

Rushing

Yds.	Player, Team (Opponent)	Year
99	Reese Wilson, MacMurray (Eureka)	1986
99	Don Patria, Rensselaer (Mass.-Lowell)	1981
99	Kevin Doherty, Mass. Maritime (New Haven)	1980
99	Sam Halliston, Albany, N.Y. (Norwich)	1977
98	Ted Pretasky, Wis.-La Crosse (Wis.-River Falls)	1987
98	Jon Hinds, Principia (Illinois Col.)	1986
98	Alex Schmidt, Muhlenberg (Lebanon Valley)	1984
98	Eric Batt, Ohio Northern (Ohio Wesleyan)	1982
98	Mike Shannon, Centre (Sewanee)	1978

Passing

Yds.	Passer-Receiver, Team (Opponent)	Year
99	Carlos Nazario-Ray Marshall, St. Peter's (Georgetown)	1991
99	Mike Jones-Warren Tweedy, Frostburg St. (Waynesburg)	1990
99	Chris Etzler-Andy Nowlin, Bluffton (Urbana)	1990
99	John Clark-Pete Balistrieri, Wis.-Eau Claire (Minn.-Duluth)	1989
99	Kelly Sandidge-Mark Green, Centre (Sewanee)	1988
99	Mike Francis-John Winter, Carleton (Trinity, Tex.)	1983
99	Rich Boling-Lewis Borsellino, DePauw (Valparaiso)	1976
99	John Wicinski-Donnell Lipford, John Carroll (Allegheny)	1975
99	Jack Berry-Mercer West, Wash. & Lee (Hampden-Sydney)	1974
99	Gary Shope-Rick Rudolph, Juniata (Moravian)	1973

Interceptions Returns
Sixteen players have returned interceptions 100 yards. The most recent:

Yds.	Player, Team (Opponent)	Year
100	Randy Ashe, Loras (Quincy)	1991
100	Bill Zagger, Stony Brook (Merchant Marine)	1990
100	Dana Cruickshank, Dubuque (Upper Iowa)	1987
100	Todd Schoelzel, Wis.-Oshkosh (Wis.-Platteville)	1987
100	John Gutsmiedle, UC San Diego (Pomona-Pitzer)	1986

Punt Returns

Yds.	Player, Team (Opponent)	Year
99	Robert Middlebrook, Knoxville (Miles)	1985
98	Mark Griggs, Wooster (Oberlin)	1980
98	Ron Mabry, Emory & Henry (Maryville, Tenn.)	1973
97	Rob Allard, Nichols (Curry)	1991
96	Marvin Robbins, Salisbury St. (Wesley)	1987
96	Gary Martin, Muskingum (Wooster)	1976
95	Stan Thompson, Knoxville (Livingstone)	1982

Kickoff Returns
Thirty-nine players have returned kickoffs 100 yards. The most recent:

Yds.	Player, Team (Opponent)	Year
100	Nate Kirtman, Pomona-Pitzer (Redlands)	1990
100	Phil Bryant, Wilmington, Ohio (Tiffin)	1990
100	Steve Burns, Mass.-Boston (Curry)	1989
100	Wayne Morris, Hofstra (Pace)	1989
100	Brian Haberstock, Mercyhurst (Brockport St.)	1988
100	Gary Trettel, St. Thomas, Minn. (Concordia-M'head)	1988

Punts

Yds.	Player, Team (Opponent)	Year
90	Dan Heeren, Coe (Lawrence)	1974
86	David Anastasi, Buffalo (John Carroll)	1989
86	Dana Loucks, Buffalo (Frostburg St.)	1987
86	John Pavlik, Wabash (Centre)	1978
82	John Massab, Albion (Adrian)	1982
82	Mike Manson, Ill. Benedictine (Monmouth, Ill.)	1976
81	Jason Berg, Mass. Maritime (Lowell)	1990
81	Tom Ilig, Ohio Wesleyan (Wittenberg)	1975

Field Goals

Yds.	Player, Team (Opponent)	Year
62	Dom Antonini, Glassboro St. (Salisbury St.)	1976
59	Chris Gustafson, Carroll, Wis. (North Park)	1985
59	Hartmut Strecker, Dayton (Iowa St.)	1977
57	Scott Fritz, Wartburg (Simpson)	1982
57	Kevin Shea, St. Mary's, Cal. (Oregon Tech)	1976

TEAM CHAMPIONS AND WINNING STREAKS

ANNUAL TEAM OFFENSE CHAMPIONS

Year	Total Offense Team	Avg.	Rushing Team	Avg.	Passing Team	Avg.
1973	San Diego	441.0	Widener	361.7	San Diego	231.7
1974	Ithaca	487.9	Albany (N.Y.)	361.6	Ill. Benedictine	255.4
1975	Frank. & Marsh.	439.4	Widener	345.8	St. Norbert	227.7
1976	St. John's (Minn.)	451.8	St. John's (Minn.)	348.9	Occidental	255.4
1977	St. John's (Minn.)	437.5	St. John's (Minn.)	315.3	Southwestern	257.8
1978	Lawrence	432.6	Ithaca	320.1	Claremont-M-S	331.7
1979	Norwich	465.2	Norwich	383.1	Claremont-M-S	250.1
1980	Widener	459.0	Widener	317.5	Occidental	255.9
1981	Middlebury	446.5	Augustana (Ill.)	313.6	Wis.-Stevens Point	288.9
1982	West Ga.	470.6	West Ga.	319.6	Wheaton (Ill.)	308.7
1983	Elmhurst	483.3	Augustana (Ill.)	345.7	Wheaton (Ill.)	*380.4
1984	Alma	465.1	Augustana (Ill.)	338.4	Wheaton (Ill.)	351.6
1985	St. Thomas (Minn.)	446.9	Denison	351.0	Wheaton (Ill.)	371.6
1986	Mount Union	452.8	Wis.-River Falls	361.4	Pace	286.9
1987	Samford	*523.1	Augustana (Ill.)	369.1	Wis.-Stout	314.6

Year	Team	Avg.	Team	Avg.	Team	Avg.
1988	Wagner	465.9	Tufts	369.0	Wis.-Stevens Point	356.7
1989	Simpson	514.0	Wis.-River Falls	388.5	Wis.-Stevens Point	380.4
1990	Hofstra	505.7	Ferrum	*434.7	Hofstra	342.2
1991	St. John's (Minn.)	503.8	Ferrum	361.4	St. John's (Minn.)	302.8

Record.

Norwich quarterback Randy Grenier splits the defense with a pass to Walt Hannon during a 34-20 win over Middlebury in 1979, when Norwich led Division III in total offense (465.2 yards per game) and rushing offense (383.1).

Scoring Offense

Year	Team	Avg.	Year	Team	Avg.
1973	San Diego	40.1	1983	Elmhurst	38.1
1974	Frank. & Marsh.	45.1	1984	Hope	40.3
1975	Frank. & Marsh.	38.2	1985	Salisbury St.	39.5
1976	St. John's (Minn.)	42.5	1986	Dayton	40.8
1977	Lawrence	38.2	1987	Samford	*51.7
1978	Georgetown	36.5	1988	Central (Iowa)	37.6
1979	Wittenberg	39.7	1989	Ferrum	46.7
1980	Widener	43.3	1990	Ferrum	47.3
1981	Lawrence	35.3	1991	Union (N.Y.)	46.1
1982	West Ga.	42.1			

Record.

ANNUAL TEAM DEFENSE CHAMPIONS

	Total Defense		Rushing Defense		Pass Defense	
Year	Team	Avg.	Team	Avg.	Team	$Avg.
1973	Doane	144.3	Oregon Col.	61.2	Nichols	53.0
1974	Alfred	153.6	Millersville	57.2	Findlay	49.2
1975	Lycoming	133.1	Cal Lutheran	62.4	Wash. & Jeff.	56.0

Total Defense

Year	Team	Avg.
1976	Albion	129.9
1977	Knoxville	*94.0
1978	Bowie St.	112.3
1979	Catholic	116.9
1980	Maine Maritime	127.2
1981	Millsaps	147.6
1982	Plymouth St.	122.2
1983	Lycoming	154.5
1984	Swarthmore	159.2
1985	Augustana (Ill.)	149.1
1986	Augustana (Ill.)	136.2
1987	Plymouth St.	135.3
1988	Plymouth St.	143.6
1989	Frostburg St.	119.7
1990	Bentley	139.8
1991	Wash. & Jeff.	143.0

Rushing Defense

Team	Avg.
Lycoming	44.3
Knoxville	*-2.3
Western Md.	43.4
Catholic	46.4
Maine Maritime	3.2
Augustana (Ill.)	30.7
Lycoming	34.2
DePauw	41.6
Swarthmore	40.0
Augustana (Ill.)	35.1
Dayton	13.5
Lycoming	35.4
Worcester St.	43.9
Frostburg St.	49.7
Ohio Wesleyan	18.9
Wash. & Jeff.	64.6

Pass Defense

Team	$Avg.
Mass. Maritime	*48.5
Hofstra	49.4
Bowie St.	64.7
Wagner	59.5
Williams	63.8
Plymouth St.	66.9
Plymouth St.	48.8
Muhlenberg	76.4
Bri'water (Mass.)	68.7
Bri'water (Mass.)	77.3
Knoxville	83.2
Jersey City St.	67.0
Colorado Col.	78.9
Frostburg St.	70.0
Bentley	47.4
Wash. & Jeff.	50.3

*Record. $ Beginning in 1990, ranked on passing efficiency defense rating points instead of per-game yardage allowed.

Scoring Defense

Year	Team	Avg.	Year	Team	Avg.
1973	Fisk	6.4	1983	Carnegie Mellon	5.3
	Slippery Rock	6.4	1984	Union (N.Y.)	4.6
1974	Central (Iowa)	6.9	1985	Augustana (Ill.)	4.7
	Rhodes	6.9	1986	Augustana (Ill.)	5.1
1975	Millsaps	5.0	1987	Plymouth St.	6.2
1976	Albion	5.4			
1977	Central (Iowa)	5.0	1988	Plymouth St.	6.5
1978	Minn.-Morris	5.9	1989	Millikin	4.8
1979	Carnegie Mellon	4.9	1990	Bentley	4.5
1980	Millsaps	*3.4	1991	Mass.-Lowell	5.4
1981	Baldwin-Wallace	3.9			
1982	West Ga.	4.6			

*Record.

LONGEST STREAKS
(Minimum two seasons in Division III; includes postseason games.)

Winning Streaks

Wins	Team	Years
37	Augustana (Ill.)	1983-85
24	Allegheny	1990-91
22	Augustana (Ill.)	1986-87
21	Williams	1988-90
21	Dayton	1979-81
20	Plymouth St.	1987-88
19	Plymouth St.	1981-82
18	Lawrence	1980-81
18	Ithaca	1979-80
18	Cal Lutheran	1974-75
18	Heidelberg	1971-73

Unbeaten Streaks

No.	Wins	Ties	Team	Years
60	59	1	Augustana (Ill.)	1983-87
24	23	1	Wabash	1979-81
22	21	1	Dayton	1979-81
21	20	1	Baldwin-Wallace	1977-79
20	18	2	St. John's (Minn.)	1975-76

LONGEST DIVISION III SERIES

Games	Opponents (Series leader listed first)	Series Record	First Game
106	Williams-Amherst	57-45-4	1884
105	Albion-Kalamazoo	67-34-4	1896
103	Bowdoin-Colby	59-36-8	1892
102	Monmouth (Ill.)-Knox	47-45-10	1891
101	Coe-Cornell College	54-43-4	1891
98	DePauw-Wabash	45-45-8	1890
97	Amherst-Wesleyan	50-38-9	1882
97	Williams-Wesleyan	57-35-5	1881
96	Hampden-Sydney—Randolph-Macon	49-36-11	1893
96	Union (N.Y.)-Hamilton	46-38-12	1890
94	Colby-Bates	49-37-8	1893

ALL-TIME WON-LOST RECORDS

Includes records as a senior college only, minimum 20 seasons of competition since 1937. Postseason games are included, and each tie game is computed as half won and half lost.

TOP 25—BY PERCENTAGE

Team	Yrs.	Won	Lost	Tied	Pct.
Plymouth St.	22	145	57	6	.712
Wis.-La Crosse	67	389	176	39	.676
St. John's (Minn.)	81	382	193	22	.658
Cal Lutheran	30	192	100	6	.654
Ithaca	59	299	165	11	.641
Montclair St.	61	304	175	20	.629
Gust. Adolphus	76	374	218	21	.627
Wittenberg	98	529	310	31	.626
Wis.-Whitewater	67	337	197	21	.626
Augustana (Ill.)	79	393	229	28	.626
Concordia-M'head	72	358	208	36	.625
Baldwin-Wallace	87	417	255	30	.615
Millikin	86	421	263	28	.611
Hofstra	51	286	182	9	.609
Lawrence	98	439	279	29	.607
St. Thomas (Minn.)	86	406	262	32	.603
Widener	111	509	330	37	.602
Williams	106	496	322	45	.601
Dayton	84	457	304	26	.597
Salisbury St.	20	115	77	4	.597
Central (Iowa)	83	398	266	26	.596
Georgetown	80	381	256	31	.594
Wis.-River Falls	66	310	209	31	.592
Wash. & Jeff.	100	495	336	39	.591
Wabash	105	468	324	58	.585

TOP 25—BY VICTORIES

Team	Wins
Wittenberg	529
Widener	509
Frank. & Marsh.	496
Williams	496
Wash. & Jeff.	495
Amherst	490
Wabash	468
Dayton	457
Denison	452
Gettysburg	452
Ohio Wesleyan	451
Albion	443
Centre	443
Lawrence	439
Muskingum	433
Drake	429
Tufts	426
Mount Union	425
Coe	424
DePauw	424
Millikin	421
Swarthmore	421
Wesleyan	420
Baldwin-Wallace	417
Trinity (Conn.)	417

ALPHABETICAL
(No minimum seasons of competition.)

Team	Yrs.	Won	Lost	Tied	Pct.
Adrian	89	283	356	17	.444
Ala.-Birmingham	1	4	3	2	.556
Albany (N.Y.)	19	111	74	0	.600
Albion	105	443	316	43	.579
Albright	79	319	362	21	.469
Alfred	93	361	273	44	.565
Allegheny	97	358	331	44	.518
Alma	95	377	318	27	.541
Amherst	112	490	356	53	.575
Assumption	4	8	24	1	.258
Augsburg	60	129	335	18	.286
Augustana (Ill.)	79	393	229	28	.626
Aurora	6	30	19	1	.610
Baldwin-Wallace	87	417	255	30	.615
Bates	96	277	387	46	.423
Beloit	101	335	404	47	.456
Bentley	4	21	11	1	.652
Bethany (W. Va.)	91	275	425	33	.398
Bethel (Minn.)	39	111	224	8	.335
Bluffton	69	221	301	23	.427
Bowdoin	98	335	376	43	.473
Bri'water (Mass.)	32	125	139	6	.474
Bridgewater (Va.)	47	114	252	10	.316
Brockport St.	45	111	237	2	.320
Buena Vista	87	338	303	28	.526
Buffalo	78	279	314	29	.472
Buffalo St.	11	38	60	0	.388
Cal Lutheran	30	192	100	6	.654
Canisius	46	199	153	23	.561
Capital	68	269	254	26	.514
Carleton	97	398	293	25	.573
Carnegie Mellon	82	370	293	29	.556
Carroll (Wis.)	88	337	264	38	.557
Carthage	95	349	317	41	.523
Case Reserve	22	85	112	2	.432

Team	Yrs.	Won	Lost	Tied	Pct.
Catholic	46	179	187	12	.489
Central (Iowa)	83	398	266	26	.596
Centre	99	443	330	38	.570
Charleston So.	1	3	6	0	.333
Chicago	72	309	291	33	.514
Claremont-M-S	34	118	178	4	.400
Coe	99	424	314	38	.571
Colby	98	276	393	32	.417
Coast Guard	68	232	299	49	.442
Colorado Col.	106	412	367	34	.528
Concordia (Ill.)	53	160	233	18	.411
Concordia-M'head	72	358	208	36	.625
Cornell College	101	405	343	33	.540
Cortland St.	65	264	222	27	.541
Curry	27	92	130	5	.416
Davidson	94	317	457	44	.414
Dayton	84	457	304	26	.597
Delaware Valley	44	168	193	10	.466
Denison	102	452	345	54	.563
DePauw	104	424	390	39	.520
Dickinson	103	359	452	53	.446
Drake	98	429	417	27	.507
Dubuque	69	257	284	25	.476
Duquesne	44	180	188	18	.490
Earlham	101	294	434	23	.407
Elmhurst	72	227	340	22	.404
Emory & Henry	76	382	317	19	.545
Eureka	58	120	304	26	.296
Evansville	66	236	339	22	.414
FDU-Madison	18	41	112	1	.269
Ferrum	7	54	22	1	.708
Fitchburg St.	8	7	63	0	.100
Framingham St.	18	67	91	1	.425
Frank. & Marsh.	104	496	353	47	.580
Franklin	91	326	380	30	.463
Frostburg St.	31	129	153	6	.458
Gallaudet	92	201	398	19	.341
Gannon	4	23	12	0	.657
Georgetown	80	381	256	31	.594
Gettysburg	99	452	381	41	.541
Glassboro St.	32	139	140	7	.498
Grinnell	101	328	436	33	.432
Grove City	97	376	372	60	.502
Guilford	86	223	450	25	.337
Gust. Adolphus	76	374	218	21	.627
Hamilton	98	313	372	47	.460
Hamline	100	337	337	30	.500
Hampden-Sydney	97	400	348	28	.534
Heidelberg	96	379	374	40	.503
Hiram	93	230	442	32	.349
Hobart	98	339	394	40	.464
Hofstra	51	286	182	9	.609
Hope	82	314	249	37	.554
Ill. Benedictine	70	226	263	23	.464
Illinois Col.	95	329	365	36	.475
Ill. Wesleyan	100	406	322	41	.555
Iona	14	60	75	3	.446
Ithaca	59	299	165	11	.641
Jersey City St.	24	85	136	2	.386
John Carroll	69	306	249	35	.548
Johns Hopkins	107	339	403	56	.460
Juniata	69	297	247	21	.544
Kalamazoo	97	318	373	41	.462
Kean	20	79	111	5	.418
Ky. Wesleyan	31	86	124	16	.416
Kenyon	102	290	459	44	.393
Knox	98	334	418	43	.447
La Verne	66	241	289	17	.456
Lake Forest	99	335	354	55	.487
Lawrence	98	439	279	29	.607

Team	Yrs.	Won	Lost	Tied	Pct.
Lebanon Valley	91	324	405	36	.447
LIU-C.W. Post	35	191	139	4	.578
Loras	63	262	216	30	.545
Luther	78	338	264	21	.559
Lycoming	42	198	157	10	.556
Macalester	89	224	391	29	.370
MacMurray	7	27	37	1	.423
Maine Maritime	46	184	168	9	.522
Marietta	97	329	421	34	.441
Marist	14	44	78	2	.363
Maryville (Tenn.)	94	358	381	35	.485
MIT	4	10	18	1	.362
Mass.-Boston	4	12	23	1	.347
Mass.-Dartmouth	4	14	22	0	.389
Mass.-Lowell	12	61	50	1	.549
Mass. Maritime	19	95	72	1	.568
Menlo	6	28	25	1	.528
Merchant Marine	47	196	221	12	.471
Mercyhurst	11	55	40	2	.577
Middlebury	95	315	332	42	.488
Millikin	86	421	263	28	.611
Millsaps	69	289	264	35	.521
Monmouth (Ill.)	99	405	370	39	.521
Montclair St.	61	304	175	20	.629
Moravian	58	239	232	20	.507
Mount Union	95	425	377	34	.529
Muhlenberg	92	379	392	40	.492
Muskingum	97	433	312	37	.577
Neb. Wesleyan	83	362	317	42	.531
Nichols	33	137	120	5	.532
North Central	87	304	337	34	.476
North Park	34	70	224	4	.242
N'western Col. (Wis.)	93	282	297	30	.488
Norwich	93	276	385	31	.421
Oberlin	101	350	423	39	.455
Occidental	90	369	311	26	.541
Ohio Northern	93	341	378	34	.475
Ohio Wesleyan	101	451	387	44	.536
Olivet	91	257	403	32	.395
Otterbein	102	327	463	41	.418
Pace	14	55	74	2	.427
Plymouth St.	22	145	57	6	.712
Pomona-Pitzer	94	318	348	31	.478
Principia	58	171	265	16	.396
Quincy	6	27	28	1	.491
Ramapo	12	57	52	2	.523
Randolph-Macon	104	375	369	55	.504
Redlands	82	352	337	27	.510
Rensselaer	102	263	469	46	.368
Rhodes	80	287	293	36	.495
Ripon	102	389	283	46	.574
Rochester	103	416	368	38	.529
Rose-Hulman	96	319	401	29	.445
Sacred Heart	1	5	4	0	.556
Salisbury St.	20	115	77	4	.597
San Diego	24	105	112	7	.484
Sewanee	97	401	357	39	.528
Siena	4	9	27	0	.250
Simpson	86	337	401	36	.459
St. Francis (Pa.)	43	133	190	11	.415
St. John Fisher	4	13	24	0	.351
St. John's (Minn.)	81	382	193	22	.658
St. John's (N.Y.)	23	114	89	7	.560
St. Lawrence	97	333	329	29	.503
St. Norbert	58	258	215	20	.544
St. Olaf	74	336	242	20	.579
St. Peter's	20	37	115	1	.245
St. Thomas (Minn.)	86	406	262	32	.603
Stonehill	4	17	15	2	.529
Stony Brook	9	35	43	1	.449

Division III All-Time Won-Lost Records

Team	Yrs.	Won	Lost	Tied	Pct.
Susquehanna	93	319	376	38	.461
Swarthmore	111	421	399	35	.513
Thiel	87	290	334	36	.467
Thomas More	2	13	6	0	.684
Trenton St.	67	237	244	30	.493
Trinity (Conn.)	107	417	309	42	.570
Trinity (Tex.)	87	302	390	49	.441
Tufts	110	426	413	45	.507
Union (N.Y.)	104	370	378	62	.495
Upper Iowa	89	266	346	25	.437
Upsala	66	229	299	18	.436
Ursinus	99	289	466	54	.391
Wabash	105	468	324	58	.585
Wagner	61	260	231	17	.529
Wartburg	56	214	247	12	.465
Washington (Mo.)	94	363	382	38	.488
Wash. & Jeff.	100	495	336	39	.591
Wash. & Lee	98	376	411	38	.479
Waynesburg	88	332	300	37	.524
Wesley	6	18	37	0	.327
Wesleyan	110	420	409	42	.506
Western Conn. St.	20	63	122	2	.342
Western Md.	97	401	368	46	.520
Western New Eng.	11	40	57	0	.412
Westfield St.	10	39	55	0	.415
Wheaton (Ill.)	78	314	287	29	.521
Whittier	82	398	278	36	.584
Widener	111	509	330	37	.602
Wilkes	46	166	214	7	.438
Wm. Paterson	20	81	110	4	.426
William Penn	91	255	419	35	.384
Williams	106	496	322	45	.601
Wilmington (Ohio)	59	231	248	13	.483
Wis.-Eau Claire	73	272	277	34	.496
Wis.-La Crosse	67	389	176	39	.676
Wis.-Oshkosh	65	209	281	30	.431
Wis.-Platteville	83	280	271	31	.508
Wis.-River Falls	66	310	209	31	.592
Wis.-Stevens Point	65	281	239	31	.538
Wis.-Stout	72	194	358	33	.360
Wis.-Superior	65	193	343	34	.368
Wis.-Whitewater	67	337	197	21	.626
Wittenberg	98	529	310	31	.626
Wooster	93	390	341	40	.532
Worcester St.	7	30	29	0	.508
Worcester Tech	102	231	388	30	.379

NCAA DIVISION III FINAL POLL LEADERS

(Released before the division championship playoffs.)

Year	Team, Record*	Coach	†Record in Championship Playoffs
1975	Ithaca (8-0-0)	Jim Butterfield	2-1 Runner-up
1976	St. John's (Minn.) (7-0-1)	John Gagliardi	3-0 Champion
1977	Wittenberg (8-0-0)	Dave Maurer	Did not compete
1978	Minn.-Morris (9-0-0)	Al Molde	1-1 Lost in semifinals
1979	Wittenberg (8-0-0)	Dave Maurer	2-1 Runner-up
1980	Ithaca (10-0-0)	Jim Butterfield	2-1 Runner-up
1981	Widener (9-0-0)	Bill Manlove	3-0 Champion
1982	Baldwin-Wallace (10-0-0)	Bob Packard	0-1 Lost in first round
1983	Augustana (Ill.) (9-0-0)	Bob Reade	3-0 Champion
1984	Augustana (Ill.) (9-0-0)	Bob Reade	3-0 Champion
1985	Augustana (Ill.) (9-0-0)	Bob Reade	4-0 Champion
1986	Dayton (10-0-0)	Mike Kelly	0-1 Lost in first round
1987	Augustana (Ill.) (9-0-0)	Bob Reade	1-1 Lost in quarterfinals

1992 NCAA FOOTBALL

Year	Team, Record*	Coach	†Record in Championship Playoffs
1988	**East Region**		
	Cortland St. (9-0-0)	Dennis Kayser	1-1 Lost in quarterfinals
	North Region		
	Dayton (9-1-0)	Mike Kelly	0-1 Lost in first round
	South Region		
	Ferrum (9-0-0)	Hank Norton	2-1 Lost in semifinals
	West Region		
	Central (Iowa) (8-0-0)	Ron Schipper	3-1 Runner-up
1989	**East Region**		
	Union (N.Y.) (9-0-0)	Al Bagnoli	3-1 Runner-up
	North Region		
	Dayton (8-0-1)	Mike Kelly	4-0 Champion
	South Region		
	Rhodes (7-0-0)	Mike Clary	Did not compete
	West Region		
	Central (Iowa) (8-0-0)	Ron Schipper	1-1 Lost in quarterfinals
1990	**East Region**		
	Hofstra (9-0-0)	Joe Gardi	2-1 Lost in semifinals
	North Region		
	Dayton (9-0-0)	Mike Kelly	1-1 Lost in quarterfinals
	South Region		
	Ferrum (8-0-0)	Hank Norton	0-1 Lost in first round
	West Region		
	Wis.-Whitewater (9-0-0)	Bob Berezowitz	0-1 Lost in first round
1991	**East Region**		
	Ithaca (7-1-0)	Jim Butterfield	4-0 Champion
	North Region		
	Allegheny (10-0-0)	Ken O'Keefe	1-1 Lost in quarterfinals
	South Region		
	Lycoming (8-0-0)	Frank Girardi	1-1 Lost in quarterfinals
	West Region		
	St. John's (Minn.) (9-0-0)	John Gagliardi	1-1 Lost in quarterfinals

* *Final poll record.*
† *Number of teams in the championship: 8 (1975-84); 16 (1985-).*

UNDEFEATED, UNTIED TEAMS

(Regular-season games only.)

Following is a list of undefeated and untied teams since 1973, when College Division teams were divided into Division II and Division III under a three-division reorganization plan adopted by the special NCAA Convention on August 1, 1973.

Since 1981, conference playoff games have been included in a team's won-lost record (previously, such games were considered postseason contests).

Figures indicate the regular-season wins (minimum seven games against four-year varsity opponents). A subsequent postseason win(s) in the Division III championship or a conference playoff game (before 1981) is indicated by (*), loss (†) and tie (‡).

Year	College	Wins	Year	College	Wins	Year	College	Wins
1973	Fisk	9		Tufts	8	1983	Augustana (Ill.)	***9
	Wittenberg	***9		Widener	*†9		Carnegie Mellon	†9
1974	Albany (N.Y.)	9		Wittenberg	***†8		Hofstra	†10
	Central (Iowa)	**9	1980	Adrian	9		Worcester Tech	8
	Frank. & Marsh.	9		Baldwin-Wallace	†9	1984	Amherst	8
	Ithaca	*†9		Bethany (W. Va.)	†9		Augustana (Ill.)	***9
	Towson St.	10		Dayton	***11		Case Reserve	9
1975	Cal Lutheran	*†9		Ithaca	**†10		Central (Iowa)	**†9
	Ithaca	**†8		Millsaps	9		Dayton	†10
	Widener	*†9		Widener	*†10		Hope	9
	Wittenberg	***†9	1981	Alfred	†10		Occidental	†10
1976	Albion	9		Augustana (Ill.)	†9		Plymouth St.	†10
1977	Central (Iowa)	†9		Lawrence	*†9	1985	Augustana (Ill.)	***†9
	Cornell College	†8		West Ga.	†9		Carnegie Mellon	†8
	Wittenberg	†9		Widener	***†10		Central (Iowa)	**†9
1978	Baldwin-Wallace	‡***8	1982	Augustana (Ill.)	**†9		Denison	†10
	Illinois Col.	9		Baldwin-Wallace	**†10		Lycoming	†10
	Minn.-Morris	*†10		Plymouth St.	10		Mount Union	*†10
	Wittenberg	‡**†8		St. John's (Minn.)	†9		Union (N.Y.)	†9
1979	Carnegie Mellon	*†9		St. Lawrence	*†9	1986	Central (Iowa)	*†10
	Dubuque	†9		Wabash	10		Dayton	†10
	Jamestown	7		West Ga.	***9		Ithaca	**†9

Year	College	Wins	Year	College	Wins	Year	College	Wins
	Mount Union ......*†10			Union (N.Y.) .....***†10			Baldwin-Wallace ...†10	
	Salisbury St. .....***†10			Williams..............8			Dayton ....***†10	
	Susquehanna......*†10		1990	Carnegie Mellon....†10			Dickinson ....†10	
	Union (N.Y.) ....†9			Dayton ....*†10			Eureka...............10	
1987	Augustana (Ill.) .....*†9			Hofstra ....**†10			Lycoming...........*†9	
	Gust. Adolphus.....†10			Lycoming.........***†9			Mass.-Lowell ....†10	
	Wash. & Jeff. ....*†9			Mount Union ......†10			Simpson............†10	
1988	Cortland St. ....*†10			Wash. & Jeff. ....*†9			St. John's (Minn.) ..**†9	
	Ferrum.............**†9			Williams..............8			Thomas More 10	
1989	Central (Iowa) ......*†9			Wis.-Whitewater ....†10			Union (N.Y.) ....*†9	
	Millikin.............*†9		1991	Allegheny ....*†10				

THE SPOILERS

(Since 1973, when the three-division reorganization plan was adopted by the special NCAA Convention, creating Divisions II and III.)

Following is a list of the spoilers of Division III teams that lost their perfect (undefeated, untied) record in their **season-ending** game, including the Division III championship playoffs. An asterisk (*) indicates a Division III championship playoff game and a dagger (†) indicates the home team in a regular-season game. A game involving two undefeated, untied teams is in bold face.

Date	Spoiler	Victim	Score
11-17-73	†Williams	Amherst	30-14
12-7-74	*Central (Iowa)	Ithaca	10-8
11-8-75	Cornell College	†Lawrence	17-16
11-22-75	*Ithaca	Widener	23-14
12-6-75	*Wittenberg	Ithaca	28-0
11-12-77	Norwich	†Middlebury	34-20
11-12-77	Ripon	†Cornell College	10-7
11-19-77	†Baldwin-Wallace	Wittenberg	14-7
11-19-77	*Widener	Central (Iowa)	19-0
11-25-78	*Wittenberg	Minn.-Morris	35-14
11-17-79	*Ithaca	Dubuque	27-7
11-17-79	‡Findlay	Jamestown	41-15
11-24-79	*Wittenberg	Widener	17-14
11-24-79	*Ithaca	Carnegie Mellon	15-6
12-1-79	*Ithaca	Wittenberg	14-10
11-8-80	DePauw	†Wabash	tie 22-22
11-22-80	*Widener	Bethany (W. Va.)	43-12
11-22-80	*Dayton	Baldwin-Wallace	34-0
11-29-80	*Dayton	Widener	28-24
12-6-80	#*Dayton	Ithaca	63-0
11-14-81	†DePauw	Wabash	21-14
11-14-81	†St. Mary's (Cal.)	San Diego	31-14
11-21-81	*Widener	West Ga.	10-3
11-21-81	*Dayton	Augustana (Ill.)	19-7
11-21-81	*Montclair St.	Alfred	13-12
11-28-81	*Dayton	Lawrence	38-0
11-13-82	†Widener	Swarthmore	24-7
11-20-82	‡Northwestern (Iowa)	St. John's (Minn.)	33-28
11-20-82	*Augustana (Ill.)	Baldwin-Wallace	28-22
11-27-82	*Augustana (Ill.)	St. Lawrence	14-0
12-4-82	**West Ga.**	**Augustana (Ill.)**	14-0
11-19-83	*Salisbury St.	Carnegie Mellon	16-14
11-19-83	*Union (N.Y.)	Hofstra	51-19
11-10-84	St. John's (N.Y.)	†Hofstra	19-16
11-10-84	†St. Olaf	Hamline	tie 7-7
11-17-84	*Union (N.Y.)	Plymouth St.	26-14
11-17-84	*Central (Iowa)	Occidental	23-22
11-17-84	*Augustana (Ill.)	Dayton	14-13
12-8-84	**Augustana (Ill.)**	**Central (Iowa)**	21-12
11-23-85	*Gettysburg	Lycoming	14-10
11-23-85	**Mount Union**	**Denison**	35-3
11-23-85	*Salisbury St.	Carnegie Mellon	35-22
11-23-85	*Ithaca	Union (N.Y.)	13-12
12-7-85	**Augustana (Ill.)**	**Central (Iowa)**	14-7
11-15-86	†Lawrence	Coe	14-10

1992 NCAA FOOTBALL

Date	Spoiler	Victim	Score
11-22-86	*Mount Union	Dayton	42-36
11-22-86	*Ithaca	Union (N.Y.)	OT 24-17
11-29-86	*Concordia-M'head	Central (Iowa)	17-14
11-29-86	*Salisbury St.	Susquehanna	31-17
11-29-86	*Augustana (Ill.)	Mount Union	16-7
12-6-86	*Salisbury St.	Ithaca	44-40
12-13-86	*Augustana (Ill.)	Salisbury St.	31-3
11-11-87	St. Norbert	†Monmouth (Ill.)	20-15
11-21-87	*St. John's (Minn.)	Gust. Adolphus	7-3
11-28-87	*Emory & Henry	Wash. & Jeff.	23-16
11-28-87	$*Dayton	Augustana (Ill.)	38-36
11-12-88	†St. Norbert	Monmouth (Ill.)	12-0
11-19-88	Coast Guard	†Plymouth St.	28-19
11-26-88	*Ithaca	Cortland St.	24-17
12-3-88	*Ithaca	Ferrum	62-28
11-11-89	†Baldwin-Wallace	John Carroll	25-19
11-11-89	†Bri'water (Mass.)	Mass.-Lowell	14-10
11-11-89	†Centre	Rhodes	13-10
11-18-89	†Alfred	Bri'water (Mass.)	30-27
11-25-89	*St. John's (Minn.)	Central (Iowa)	27-24
11-25-89	*Dayton	Millikin	28-16
12-9-89	*Dayton	Union (N.Y.)	17-7
11-10-90	Trenton St.	†Ramapo	9-0
11-10-90	†Waynesburg	Frostburg St.	28-18
11-17-90	*Allegheny	Mount Union	26-15
11-17-90	*Lycoming	Carnegie Mellon	17-7
11-17-90	*St. Thomas (Minn.)	Wis.-Whitewater	24-23
11-24-90	*Allegheny	Dayton	31-23
11-24-90	*Lycoming	Wash. & Jeff.	24-0
12-1-90	*Lycoming	Hofstra	20-10
12-8-90	*Allegheny	Lycoming	OT 21-14
11-9-91	†Coe	Beloit	26-10
11-23-91	*Union (N.Y.)	Mass.-Lowell	55-16
11-23-91	*Dayton	Baldwin-Wallace	27-10
11-30-91	*Dayton	Allegheny	OT 28-25
11-30-91	*Ithaca	Union (N.Y.)	35-23
11-30-91	*Susquehanna	Lycoming	31-24
12-7-91	*Dayton	St. John's (Minn.)	34-20

‡ NAIA championship playoff game. # Defeated three consecutive perfect-record teams in the Division III championship playoffs. $ Ended Augustana's (Ill.) 60-game undefeated streak.

CLIFFHANGERS

Regular-season Division III games won on the final play of the game in regulation time (from 1973). The extra point is listed when it provided the margin of victory after the winning touchdown.

Date	Opponents, Score	Game-winning play
9-22-73	Hofstra 21, Seton Hall 20	Tom Calder 15 pass from Steve Zimmer (Jim Hogan kick)
9-18-76	Ohio Wesleyan 23, DePauw 20	Tom Scurfield 48 pass from Bob Mauck
10-27-77	Albany (N.Y.) 42, Maine 39	Larry Leibowitz 19 FG
9-22-79	Augustana (Ill.) 19, Carthage 18	John Stockton 14 pass from Mark Schick
10-6-79	Carleton 17, Lake Forest 14	Tim Schoonmaker 46 FG
11-10-79	Dayton 24, St. Norbert 22	Jim Fullenkamp 21 FG
9-13-80	Cornell College 14, Lawrence 13	John Bryant 8 pass from Matt Dillon (Keith Koehler kick)
9-27-80	Muhlenberg 41, Johns Hopkins 38	Mickey Mottola 1 run
10-25-80	Lowell 15, Marist 13	Ed Kulis 3 run
10-17-81	Carleton 22, Ripon 21	John Winter 23 pass from Billy Ford (Dave Grein kick)
10-2-82	Frostburg St. 10, Mercyhurst 7	Mike Lippold 34 FG
11-6-82	Williams 27, Wesleyan 24	Marc Hummon 33 pass from Robert Connolly
10-7-83	Johns Hopkins 19, Ursinus 17	John Tucker 10 pass from Mark Campbell
10-8-83	Susquehanna 17, Widener 14	Todd McCarthy 20 FG
10-29-83	Frank. & Marsh. 16, Swarthmore 15	Billy McLean 51 pass from Niall Rosenzweig
9-24-84	Muhlenberg 3, Frank. & Marsh. 0	Tom Mulroy 26 FG
10-26-85	Buffalo 13, Brockport St. 11	Dan Friedman 37 FG

Date	Opponents, Score	Game-winning play
11-9-85	Frank. & Marsh. 29, Johns Hopkins 28	Brad Ramsey 1 run (Ken Scalet pass from John Travagline)
9-18-86	Beloit 16, Lakeland 13	Sean Saturnio 38 pass from Ed Limon
10-18-86	Ill. Wesleyan 25, Elmhurst 23	Dave Anderson 11 pass from Doug Moews
9-5-87	Wash. & Jeff. 17, Ohio Wesleyan 16	John Ivory 28 FG
10-3-87	Wis.-Whitewater 10, Wis.-Platteville 7	Dave Emond 25 FG
10-24-87	Geneva 9, St. Francis (Pa.) 7	John Moores 19 FG
10-1-88	Canisius 17, Rochester 14	Jim Ehrig 34 FG
10-1-88	Cortland St. 24, Western Conn. St. 21	Ted Nagengast 35 FG
10-8-88	UC Santa Barbara 20, Sonoma St. 18	Harry Konstantinopoulos 52 FG
10-8-88	Hamilton 13, Bowdoin 10	Nate O'Steen 19 FG
11-5-88	Colby 20, Middlebury 18	Eric Aulenback 1 run
11-12-88	Wis.-River Falls 24, Wis.-Stout 23	Andy Feil 45 FG
10-7-89	Moravian 13, Juniata 10	Mike Howey 75 pass from Rob Light
10-21-89	Western New Eng. 17, Bentley 14	Leo Coughlin 17 FG
10-21-89	Thiel 19, Carnegie Mellon 14	Bill Barber 4 pass from Jeff Sorenson
9-8-90	Emory & Henry 22, Wash. & Lee 21	Todd Woodall 26 pass from Pat Walker
9-15-90	Otterbein 20, Capital 17	Korey Brown 39 FG
11-10-90	Colby 23, Bowdoin 20	Paul Baisley 10 pass from Bob Ward

REGULAR-SEASON OVERTIME GAMES

In 1981, the NCAA Football Rules Committee approved an overtime tie-breaker system to decide a tie game for the purpose of determining a conference champion. The following conferences are currently using the tie-breaker system to decide conference-only tie games. The number of overtimes is indicated in parentheses.

IOWA INTERCOLLEGIATE ATHLETIC CONFERENCE

Date	Opponents, Score	Date	Opponents, Score
9-26-81	William Penn 24, Wartburg 21 (1 OT)	10-4-86	Luther 28, Wartburg 21 (1 OT)
9-25-82	Dubuque 16, Buena Vista 13 (1 OT)	9-26-87	William Penn 19, Upper Iowa 13 (2 OT)
10-2-82	Luther 25, Dubuque 22 (1 OT)	11-7-87	William Penn 17, Loras 10 (1 OT)
10-30-82	Wartburg 27, Dubuque 24 (3 OT)		

MIDWEST COLLEGIATE ATHLETIC CONFERENCE

Date	Opponents, Score	Date	Opponents, Score
10-25-86	Lake Forest 30, Chicago 23 (1 OT)	9-30-89	Illinois Col. 26, Ripon 20 (3 OT)
10-26-86	Lawrence 7, Beloit 0 (1 OT)	10-27-90	Beloit 16, St. Norbert 10 (1 OT)

NEW ENGLAND FOOTBALL CONFERENCE
(From 1987)

Date	Opponents, Score	Date	Opponents, Score
10-31-87	Nichols 21, Mass.-Lowell 20 (1 OT)	9-30-89	Worcester St. 23, Southeastern Mass. 20 (1 OT)
9-17-88	Lowell 22, Worcester St. 19 (2 OT)	10-28-89	Worcester St. 27, Nichols 20 (1 OT)

SOUTHERN CALIFORNIA INTERCOLLEGIATE ATHLETIC CONFERENCE

Date	Opponents, Score	Date	Opponents, Score
10-18-86	La Verne 53, Occidental 52 (1 OT)	10-27-90	Occidental 47, Claremont-M-S 41 (1 OT)
9-26-87	Claremont-M-S 33, Occidental 30 (1 OT)		

ALL-TIME WINNINGEST NON-NCAA MEMBER TEAMS

Minimum of 20 seasons of varsity competition. Postseason games are included, and each tie game is computed as half won and half lost.

BY PERCENTAGE

Team	Yrs.	Won	Lost	Tied	Pct.	Post-season
Missouri Valley	68	437	164	33	.715	7-6-2
Northwestern (Iowa)	32	207	103	6	.665	13-7-0
Linfield	77	376	208	30	.637	14-11-0
Central St. (Ohio)	70	379	213	31	.633	12-9-0
William Jewell	103	488	280	52	.627	1-1-0
Northern St.	86	422	246	33	.626	0-4-0
Arkansas Tech	71	390	228	35	.624	0-1-0
Minot St.	67	280	164	29	.623	0-2-0
Pacific Lutheran	57	305	187	27	.614	15-8-1
St. Ambrose	58	289	182	27	.607	0-1-0

Team	Yrs.	Won	Lost	Tied	Pct.	Post-season
Westminster (Pa.)	96	456	305	50	.593	21-7-1
Baker	84	415	286	39	.587	4-3-0
Dickinson St.	66	269	188	25	.584	4-6-0
Central Wash.	73	323	232	22	.579	5-7-0
Carroll (Mont.)	70	276	200	16	.577	1-4-0
Central Ark.	80	387	280	40	.576	11-11-2
Puget Sound	83	359	264	35	.572	0-1-0
Peru St.	91	414	306	48	.570	6-2-0
Minn.-Morris	30	160	120	10	.569	3-5-0
Hastings	93	383	288	51	.566	2-2-0
Doane	96	413	314	49	.564	1-1-1
Valley City St.	78	300	232	28	.561	1-2-0
Northeastern Okla. St.	69	329	260	28	.556	6-8-0
Ouachita Baptist	85	387	305	42	.556	1-3-0
Western Ore.	76	302	242	17	.553	0-3-0
Bethany (Kan.)	80	370	296	29	.553	2-6-0
Fairmont St.	78	335	267	44	.553	5-3-0
Southern Ark.	60	305	245	21	.553	1-0-1
Jamestown	71	298	239	26	.552	0-1-0
Willamette	91	370	305	39	.546	0-2-0
Henderson St.	84	363	303	42	.542	3-2-0
Ottawa	84	376	315	38	.542	0-0-0
Benedictine	59	280	236	17	.541	1-1-0
Southwestern (Kan.)	86	396	333	47	.541	2-3-0
Moorhead St.	74	317	268	28	.540	0-4-0
Concord	67	298	270	26	.524	4-7-0
Lewis & Clark	46	209	190	12	.523	1-2-0
Southwestern Okla. St.	82	355	327	37	.519	2-1-0
East Central (Okla.)	79	362	335	38	.518	1-5-0
South Dak. Tech	89	312	295	43	.513	0-0-0
Hanover	99	357	342	30	.510	1-7-0
Geneva	97	396	383	50	.508	2-1-0
Howard Payne	86	363	354	41	.506	1-1-0
Austin	91	360	365	39	.497	2-4-0
Concordia (Neb.)	52	215	221	20	.493	0-0-0
Southern Ore.	58	231	239	16	.492	0-0-0
Black Hills St.	89	305	316	35	.492	0-0-0
Langston	68	283	295	29	.490	1-4-0
Anderson	45	192	200	11	.490	1-2-0
Teikyo Westmar	77	277	296	34	.484	0-1-0
Kansas Wesleyan	82	311	333	38	.484	0-0-0
Huron	89	300	322	39	.483	0-1-0
Southeastern Okla. St.	81	325	351	43	.482	1-1-0
West Va. Tech	72	262	288	35	.478	0-1-0
Western Wash.	75	266	293	34	.477	0-0-0
Midland Lutheran	97	329	365	40	.475	0-0-0
Northwood	30	123	139	6	.470	0-0-0
McMurry	66	273	326	33	.458	1-2-0

Records of Non-NCAA Teams

INDIVIDUAL COLLEGIATE RECORDS

Houston kicker Roman Anderson scored 69 points in 1991 to move into fourth place on the career scoring list with 423. He finished his career as

Individual collegiate records are determined by comparing the best records in all four divisions (I-A, I-AA, II and III) in comparable categories. Included are career records of players who played half their careers in two divisions (e.g., Dennis Shaw of San Diego St., Howard Stevens of Randolph-Macon and Louisville, and Tom Ehrhardt of LIU-C. W. Post and Rhode Island).

TOTAL OFFENSE
Career Yards Per Game

Player, Team (Division[s])	Years	Games	Plays	Yards	TDR‡	Yd. PG
Willie Totten, Mississippi Val. (I-AA)	1982-85	40	1,812	13,007	*157	*325.2
Ty Detmer, Brigham Young (I-A)	1988-91	46	1,795	*14,665	135	318.8
Neil Lomax, Portland St. (II; I-AA)	1977; 78-80	42	1,901	13,345	120	317.7
Kirk Baumgartner, Wis.-Stevens Point (III)	1986-89	41	*2,007	12,767	110	311.4
Mike Perez, San Jose St. (I-A)	1986-87	20	875	6,182	37	309.1
Doug Gaynor, Long Beach St. (I-A)	1984-85	22	1,067	6,710	45	305.0
Tod Mayfield, West Tex. St. (I-AA; II)	1984-85; 86	24	1,165	7,316	58	304.8
Tony Eason, Illinois (I-A)	1981-82	22	1,016	6,589	43	299.5
Keith Bishop, Ill. Wes./Wheaton (III.) (III) . .	1981, 83-85	31	1,467	9,052	77	292.0
David Klingler, Houston (I-A)	1988-91	32	1,431	9,327	93	291.5
Stan Greene, Boston U. (I-AA)	1989-90	22	1,167	6,408	49	291.3
John Friesz, Idaho (I-AA)	1986-89	35	1,459	10,187	79	291.1
Steve Young, Brigham Young (I-A)	1981-83	31	1,177	8,817	74	284.4
Jayson Merrill, Western St. (II)	1990-91	20	641	5,619	57	281.0
Vern Harris, Idaho St. (I-AA)	1984-85	19	813	5,302	36	279.1
Andre Ware, Houston (I-A)	1987-89	29	1,194	8,058	81	277.9
Chris Petersen, UC Davis (II)	1985-86	20	735	5,532	52	276.6
Tim Von Dulm, Portland St. (II)	1969-70	20	989	5,501	51	275.1
John Rooney, Ill. Wesleyan (III)	1982-84	27	1,260	7,363	71	273.8
Tim Peterson, Wis.-Stout (III)	1986-89	36	1,558	9,701	59	269.5
Doug Flutie, Boston College (I-A)	1981-84	42	1,558	11,317	74	269.5
Bret Snyder, Utah St. (I-A)	1987-88	22	1,040	5,916	43	268.9
Dennis Shaw, San Diego St. (II; I-A)	1968; 69	20	682	5,371	72	268.6

* Record.   ‡ Touchdowns-responsible-for are player's TDs scored and passed for.

Season Yards Per Game

Player, Team (Division)	Year	Games	Plays	Yards	TDR‡	Yd. PG
David Klingler, Houston (I-A)	†1990	11	*704	*5,221	55	*474.6
Willie Totten, Mississippi Val. (I-AA)	†1984	10	564	4,572	*61	457.2
Andre Ware, Houston (I-A)	†1989	11	628	4,661	49	423.7
Ty Detmer, Brigham Young (I-A)	1990	12	635	5,022	45	418.5
Steve Young, Brigham Young (I-A)	†1983	11	531	4,346	41	395.1
Jamie Martin, Weber St. (I-AA)	†1991	11	591	4,337	37	394.3
Scott Mitchell, Utah (I-A)	†1988	11	589	4,299	29	390.8
Jim McMahon, Brigham Young (I-A)	†1980	12	540	4,627	53	385.6
Neil Lomax, Portland St. (I-AA)	†1980	11	550	4,157	42	377.9
Ty Detmer, Brigham Young (I-A)	1989	12	497	4,433	38	369.4
Troy Kopp, Pacific (Cal.) (I-A)	1990	9	485	3,276	32	364.0
Neil Lomax, Portland St. (I-AA)	†1979	11	611	3,966	31	360.5
Keith Bishop, Wheaton (Ill.) (III)	†1983	9	421	3,193	24	354.8
Kirk Baumgartner, Wis.-Stevens Point (III) . . .	†1989	10	530	3,540	39	354.0
Rob Tomlinson, Cal St. Chico (II)	†1989	10	533	3,504	26	350.4
John Friesz, Idaho (I-AA)	†1989	11	464	3,853	31	350.3
Todd Hammel, Stephen F. Austin (I-AA)	1989	11	487	3,822	38	347.5
Tom Ehrhardt, Rhode Island (I-AA)	†1985	10	529	3,460	35	346.0
Jim McMahon, Brigham Young (I-A)	†1981	10	487	3,458	30	345.8
Ken Hobart, Idaho (I-AA)	†1983	11	578	3,800	37	345.5
Kirk Baumgartner, Wis.-Stevens Point (III) . . .	†1988	11	604	3,790	27	344.5
Chris Hegg, Northeast Mo. St. (II)	†1985	11	594	3,782	35	343.8
Dave Stireman, Weber St. (I-AA)	1985	11	502	3,759	33	341.7
Bob Toledo, San Fran. St. (II)	†1967	10	409	3,407	46	340.7
Willie Totten, Mississippi Val. (I-AA)	1985	11	561	3,742	43	340.2

* Record.   † National champion.   ‡ Touchdowns-responsible-for are player's TDs scored and passed for.

Career Yards

Player, Team (Division[s])	Years	Plays	Yards	Avg.
Ty Detmer, Brigham Young (I-A)	1988-91	1,795	*14,665	*8.17
Neil Lomax, Portland St. (II; I-AA)	1977; 78-80	1,901	13,345	7.02
Willie Totten, Mississippi Val. (I-AA)	1982-85	1,812	13,007	7.18
Kirk Baumgartner, Wis.-Stevens Point (III)	1986-89	2,007	12,767	6.36
Doug Flutie, Boston College (I-A)...................	1981-84	1,558	11,317	7.26
Ken Hobart, Idaho (I-AA)	1980-83	1,847	11,127	6.02
Earl Harvey, N.C. Central (II)	1985-88	*2,045	10,667	5.22
Todd Santos, San Diego St. (I-A)	1984-87	1,722	10,513	6.11
Sean Payton, Eastern Ill. (I-AA)	1983-86	1,690	10,298	6.09
Greg Wyatt, Northern Ariz. (I-AA)	1986-89	1,753	10,277	5.86
Kevin Sweeney, Fresno St. (I-A)..................	$1982-86	1,700	10,252	6.03
John Friesz, Idaho (I-AA)	1986-89	1,459	10,187	6.98
Michael Proctor, Murray St. (I-AA)	1986-89	1,577	9,886	6.27
Jeff Wiley, Holy Cross (I-AA).....................	1985-88	1,428	9,877	6.92
Tom Ehrhardt, LIU-C. W. Post (II); R. I. (I-AA)	1981-82; 84-85	1,674	9,793	5.85
Brian McClure, Bowling Green (I-A)	1982-85	1,630	9,774	6.00
Jim McMahon, Brigham Young (I-A)	1977-78, 80-81	1,325	9,723	7.34
Tim Peterson, Wis.-Stout (III)	1986-89	1,558	9,701	6.23
Terrence Jones, Tulane (I-A)	1985-88	1,620	9,445	5.83
David Klingler, Houston (I-A)	1988-91	1,431	9,327	6.52
Matt DeGennaro, Connecticut (I-AA)	1987-90	1,619	9,269	5.73
¢Jamie Martin, Weber St. (I-AA)	1989-91	1,289	9,158	7.10
Sam Mannery, Calif. (Pa.) (II)	1987-90	1,669	9,125	5.47
T. J. Rubley, Tulsa (I-A)	1987-89, 91	1,541	9,080	5.89
John Elway, Stanford (I-A)	1979-82	1,505	9,070	6.03
Tom Ciaccio, Holy Cross (I-AA)	1988-91	1,283	9,066	7.07
Erik Wilhelm, Oregon St. (I-A)	1985-88	1,689	9,062	5.37
Ben Bennett, Duke (I-A)	1980-83	1,582	9,061	5.73
Keith Bishop, Ill. Wesleyan/Wheaton (Ill.) (III)	1981, 83-85	1,467	9,052	6.17
Chuck Long, Iowa (I-A)	$1981-85	1,411	9,034	6.40

* Record. \$ See page 6 for explanation. ¢ Active player.

Season Yards

Player, Team (Division)	Year	Games	Plays	Yards	Avg.
David Klingler, Houston (I-A)	†1990	11	*704	*5,221	7.42
Ty Detmer, Brigham Young (I-A)	1990	12	635	5,022	7.91
Andre Ware, Houston (I-A)........................	†1989	11	628	4,661	7.42
Jim McMahon, Brigham Young (I-A)...............	†1980	12	540	4,627	8.57
Willie Totten, Mississippi Val. (I-AA)	†1984	10	564	4,572	8.11
Ty Detmer, Brigham Young (I-A)	1989	12	497	4,433	@8.92
Steve Young, Brigham Young (I-A)................	†1983	11	531	4,346	8.18
Jamie Martin, Weber St. (I-AA)...................	†1991	11	591	4,337	7.34
Scott Mitchell, Utah (I-A)........................	†1988	11	589	4,299	7.30
Neil Lomax, Portland St. (I-AA)	†1980	11	550	4,157	7.56
Robbie Bosco, Brigham Young (I-A)	1985	13	578	4,141	7.16
Ty Detmer, Brigham Young (I-A)	†1991	12	478	4,001	8.37
Neil Lomax, Portland St. (I-AA)	†1979	11	611	3,966	6.49
Robbie Bosco, Brigham Young (I-A)	†1984	12	543	3,932	7.24
John Friesz, Idaho (I-AA)	†1989	11	464	3,853	8.30
Todd Hammel, Stephen F. Austin (I-AA)	1989	11	487	3,822	7.85
Ken Hobart, Idaho (I-AA)	1983	11	578	3,800	6.57
Kirk Baumgartner, Wis.-Stevens Point (III)	†1988	11	604	3,790	6.27
Chris Hegg, Northeast Mo. St. (II)	†1985	11	594	3,782	6.37
Dave Stireman, Weber St. (I-AA)	1985	11	502	3,759	7.49
Willie Totten, Mississippi Val. (I-AA)	1985	11	561	3,742	6.67
Jeff Wiley, Holy Cross (I-AA).....................	†1987	11	445	3,722	8.36
Jamie Martin, Weber St. (I-AA)	1990	11	508	3,713	7.31
Anthony Dilweg, Duke (I-A)......................	1988	11	539	3,713	6.89
Kirk Baumgartner, Wis.-Stevens Point (III)	1987	11	561	3,712	6.62

* Record. † National champion. @ Record for minimum of 3,000 yards.

Single-Game Yards

Yds.	Div.	Player, Team (Opponent)	Date
732	I-A	David Klingler, Houston (Arizona St.)...................................	Dec. 2, 1990
696	I-A	Matt Vogler, Texas Christian (Houston)	Nov. 3, 1990
643	I-AA	Jamie Martin, Weber St. (Idaho St.)	Nov. 23, 1991
625	I-A	David Klingler, Houston (Texas Christian)	Nov. 3, 1990
625	I-A	Scott Mitchell, Utah (Air Force).......................................	Oct. 15, 1988

Yd	iv.	Player, Team (Opponent)	Date
6'	AA	Willie Totten, Mississippi Val. (Prairie View)	Oct. 27, 1984
6౦౦	I-A	Ty Detmer, Brigham Young (San Diego St.)	Nov. 16, 1991
601	I-A	Troy Kopp, Pacific, Cal. (New Mexico St.)	Oct. 20, 1990
599	I-A	Virgil Carter, Brigham Young (UTEP)	Nov. 5, 1966
596	III	John Love, North Park (Elmhurst)	Oct. 13, 1990
595	I-AA	Doug Pederson, Northeast La. (Stephen F. Austin)	Nov. 11, 1989
594	I-A	Jeremy Leach, New Mexico (Utah)	Nov. 11, 1989
587	I-AA	Vern Harris, Idaho St. (Montana)	Oct. 12, 1985
585	I-A	Dave Wilson, Illinois (Ohio St.)	Nov. 8, 1980
584	II	Tracy Kendall, Alabama A&M (Clark Atlanta)	Nov. 4, 1989
582	I-A	Marc Wilson, Brigham Young (Utah)	Nov. 5, 1977
578	I-A	David Klingler, Houston (Eastern Wash.)	Nov. 17, 1990
571	II	John Charles, Portland St. (Cal Poly SLO)	Nov. 16, 1991
566	I-AA	Tom Ehrhardt, Rhode Island (Connecticut)	Nov. 16, 1985
564	III	Tim Lynch, Hofstra (Fordham)	Oct. 19, 1991
562	I-AA	Todd Hammel, Stephen F. Austin (Northeast La.)	Nov. 11, 1989
562	I-A	Ty Detmer, Brigham Young (Washington St.)	Sept. 7, 1989
562	II	Bob Toledo, San Fran. St. (Cal St. Hayward)	Oct. 21, 1967
561	I-AA	Willie Totten, Mississippi Val. (Southern-B.R.)	Sept. 29, 1984
555	II	A. J. Vaughn, Wayne St., Mich. (Wis.-Milwaukee)	Sept. 30, 1967

RUSHING

Career Yards Per Game

Player, Team (Division[s])	Years	G	Plays	Yards	TD	Yd. PG
Ed Marinaro, Cornell (I-A)	1969-71	27	918	4,715	50	*174.6
O.J. Simpson, Southern Cal (I-A)	1967-68	19	621	3,214	33	164.4
Johnny Bailey, Texas A&I (II)	1986-89	39	885	*6,320	66	162.1
Herschel Walker, Georgia (I-A)	1980-82	33	994	5,259	49	159.4
Terry Underwood, Wagner (III)	1985-88	33	742	5,010	52	151.8
Ole Gunderson, St. Olaf (II)	1969-71	27	639	4,060	56	150.4
Brad Hustad, Luther (II)	1957-59	27	655	3,943	25	146.0
Tony Dorsett, Pittsburgh (I-A)	1973-76	43	1,074	6,082	55	141.4
Joe Iacone, West Chester (II)	1960-62	27	565	3,767	40	139.5
Howard Stevens, Rand.-Macon (II); Louisville (I-A)	1968-69; 71-72	38	891	5,297	58	139.4
Mike Rozier, Nebraska (I-A)	1981-83	35	668	4,780	50	136.6
Joe Dudek, Plymouth St. (III)	1982-85	41	785	5,570	*76	135.9
Jerome Persell, Western Mich. (I-A)	1976-78	31	842	4,190	39	135.2

* Record.

Season Yards Per Game

Player, Team (Division)	Year	Games	Plays	Yards	TD	Yd. PG
Barry Sanders, Oklahoma St. (I-A)	†1988	11	344	*2,628	*37	*232.1
Marcus Allen, Southern Cal (I-A)	†1981	11	*403	2,342	22	212.9
Ed Marinaro, Cornell (I-A)	†1971	9	356	1,881	24	209.0
Ricky Gales, Simpson (III)	†1989	10	297	2,035	26	203.5
Terry Underwood, Wagner (III)	†1988	9	245	1,809	21	201.0
Jon Warga, Wittenberg (III)	†1990	10	254	1,836	15	183.6
Johnny Bailey, Texas A&I (II)	†1986	11	271	2,011	18	182.8
Bob White, Western New Mex. (II)	†1951	9	202	1,643	20	182.6
Kevin Mitchell, Saginaw Valley (II)	1989	8	236	1,460	6	182.5
Hank Wineman, Albion (III)	†1991	9	307	1,629	14	181.0
Charles White, Southern Cal (I-A)	†1979	10	293	1,803	18	180.3
Eric Grey, Hamilton (III)	1991	8	217	1,439	13	179.9
Mike Birosak, Dickinson (III)	1989	10	380	1,798	18	179.8
Don Aleksiewicz, Hobart (II)	†1971	9	276	1,616	19	179.6
Mike Rozier, Nebraska (I-A)	†1983	12	275	2,148	29	179.0
Jim Holder, Panhandle St. (II)	†1963	10	275	1,775	9	177.5
Tony Dorsett, Pittsburgh (I-A)	†1976	11	338	1,948	21	177.1
Jim Baier, Wis.-River Falls (II)	†1966	9	240	1,587	17	176.3
Ollie Matson, San Francisco (I-A)	†1951	9	245	1,566	20	174.0

* Record. † National champion.

Career Yards

Player, Team (Division[s])	Years	Plays	Yards	Avg.
Johnny Bailey, Texas A&I (II)	1986-89	885	*6,320	7.14
Tony Dorsett, Pittsburgh (I-A)	1973-76	1,074	6,082	5.66
Charles White, Southern Cal (I-A)	1976-79	1,023	5,598	5.47
Joe Dudek, Plymouth St. (III)	1982-85	785	5,570	7.10
Frank Hawkins, Nevada (I-AA)	1977-80	945	5,333	5.64

Player, Team (Division[s])	Years	Plays	Yards	Avg.
Howard Stevens, Rand.-Macon (II); Louisville (I-A)	1968-69; 71-72	891	5,297	5.95
Eric Frees, Western Md. (III)	1988-91	1,059	5,281	4.99
Herschel Walker, Georgia (I-A)	1980-82	994	5,259	5.29
Kenny Gamble, Colgate (I-AA)	1984-87	963	5,220	5.42
Archie Griffin, Ohio St. (I-A)	1972-75	845	5,177	6.13
Chris Cobb, Eastern III. (II)	1976-79	930	5,042	5.42
Darren Lewis, Texas A&M (I-A)	1987-90	909	5,012	5.51
Terry Underwood, Wagner (III)	1985-88	742	5,010	6.75
Anthony Thompson, Indiana (I-A)	1986-89	1,089	4,965	4.56
George Rogers, South Caro. (I-A)	1977-80	902	4,958	5.50
Paul Palmer, Temple (I-A)	1983-86	948	4,895	5.16
Harry Jackson, St. Cloud St. (II)	1986-89	915	4,890	5.34
Jerry Linton, Panhandle St. (II)	1959-62	648	4,839	‡7.47
Steve Bartalo, Colorado St. (I-A)	1983-86	*1,215	4,813	3.96

* Record.   ‡ Record for minimum of 600 carries.

Season Yards

Player, Team (Division)	Year	Games	Plays	Yards	Avg.
Barry Sanders, Oklahoma St. (I-A)	†1988	11	344	*2,628	@7.64
Marcus Allen, Southern Cal (I-A)	†1981	11	*403	2,342	5.81
Mike Rozier, Nebraska (I-A)	†1983	12	275	2,148	††7.81
Ricky Gales, Simpson (III)	†1989	10	297	2,035	6.85
Johnny Bailey, Texas A&I (II)	†1986	11	271	2,011	7.42
Tony Dorsett, Pittsburgh (I-A)	†1976	11	338	1,948	5.76
Lorenzo White, Michigan St. (I-A)	†1985	11	386	1,908	4.94
Herschel Walker, Georgia (I-A)	†1981	11	385	1,891	4.91
Rich Erenberg, Colgate (I-AA)	†1983	11	302	1,883	6.24
Ed Marinaro, Cornell (I-A)	†1971	9	356	1,881	5.28
Ernest Anderson, Oklahoma St. (I-A)	†1982	11	353	1,877	5.32
Ricky Bell, Southern Cal (I-A)	†1975	11	357	1,875	5.25
Paul Palmer, Temple (I-A)	†1986	11	346	1,866	5.39
Jon Warga, Wittenberg (III)	†1990	10	254	1,836	7.23
Zed Robinson, Southern Utah (II)	1991	11	254	1,828	7.20
Kenny Gamble, Colgate (I-AA)	†1986	11	307	1,816	5.92
Terry Underwood, Wagner (III)	†1988	9	245	1,809	6.75
Charles White, Southern Cal (I-A)	†1979	10	293	1,803	6.15

* Record.   † National champion.   †† Record for minimum of 214 carries.   @ Record for minimum of 282 carries.

Single-Game Yards

Yds.	Div.	Player, Team (Opponent)	Date
396	I-A	Tony Sands, Kansas (Missouri)	Nov. 23, 1991
386	I-A	Marshall Faulk, San Diego St. (Pacific, Cal.)	Sept. 14, 1991
382	III	Pete Baranek, Carthage (North Central)	Oct. 5, 1985
382	II	Kelly Ellis, Northern Iowa (Western III.)	Oct. 13, 1979
377	I-A	Anthony Thompson, Indiana (Wisconsin)	Nov. 11, 1989
373	II	Dallas Garber, Marietta (Wash. & Jeff.)	Nov. 7, 1959
370	II	Jim Baier, Wis.-River Falls (Wis.-Stevens Point)	Nov. 5, 1966
370	II	Jim Hissam, Marietta (Bethany, W. Va.)	Nov. 15, 1958
367	II	Don Polkinghorne, Washington, Mo. (Wash. & Lee)	Nov. 23, 1957
363	III	Terry Underwood, Wagner (Hofstra)	Oct. 15, 1988
363	II	Richie Weaver, Widener (Moravian)	Oct. 17, 1970
357	I-A	Mike Pringle, Cal St. Fullerton (New Mexico St.)	Nov. 4, 1989
357	I-A	Rueben Mayes, Washington St. (Oregon)	Oct. 27, 1984
356	I-A	Eddie Lee Ivery, Georgia Tech (Air Force)	Nov. 11, 1978
356	II	Ole Gunderson, St. Olaf (Monmouth, III.)	Oct. 11, 1969
354	III	Terry Underwood, Wagner (Western Conn. St.)	Oct. 3, 1986
350	II	Ricke Stonewall, Millersville (New Haven)	Nov. 13, 1982
350	I-A	Eric Allen, Michigan St. (Purdue)	Oct. 30, 1971

PASSING

Career Passing Efficiency
(Min. 475 Completions)

Player, Team (Division[s])	Years	Att.	Cmp.	Int.	Pct.	Yds.	TD	Pts.
Ty Detmer, Brigham Young (I-A)	1988-91	1,530	*958	65	.626	*15,031	121	*162.7
Jim McMahon, Brigham Young (I-A) ...	1977-78, 80-81	1,060	653	34	.616	9,536	84	156.9
Steve Young, Brigham Young (I-A)	1981-83	908	592	33	.652	7,733	56	149.8
Jack Hull, Grand Valley St. (II)	1988-91	835	485	22	.581	7,120	64	149.7
Robbie Bosco, Brigham Young (I-A) ...	1983-85	997	638	36	.640	8,400	66	149.4

Player, Team (Division[s])	Years	Att.	Cmp.	Int.	Pct.	Yds.	TD	Pts.
Chuck Long, Iowa (I-A)	$1981-85	1,072	692	46	.646	9,210	64	147.8
Willie Totten, Mississippi Val. (I-AA)	1982-85	1,555	907	*75	.583	12,711	*139	146.8
Mike Smith, Northern Iowa (I-AA)	1984-87	943	557	43	.591	8,219	58	143.5
Neil Lomax, Portland St. (II; I-AA)	1977; 78-80	*1,606	938	55	.584	13,220	106	142.5
Tom Ciaccio, Holy Cross (I-AA)	1988-91	1,073	658	46	.613	8,603	72	142.2
George Bork, Northern Ill. (II)	1960-63	902	577	33	.640	6,782	60	141.8
Eric Beavers, Nevada (I-AA)	1983-86	1,094	646	37	.591	8,626	77	141.8
Doug Gaynor, Long Beach St. (I-A)	1984-85	837	569	35	.680	6,793	35	141.6
Matt Jozokos, Plymouth St. (III)........	1987-90	1,003	527	39	.525	7,658	95	140.2
Dan McGwire, Iowa/San Diego St. (I-A) .	1986-87, 89-90	973	575	30	.591	8,164	49	140.0
John Elway, Stanford (I-A)	1979-82	1,246	774	39	.621	9,349	77	139.3
David Klingler, Houston (I-A)	1988-91	1,261	726	38	.576	9,430	91	138.2
Doug Williams, Grambling (II; I-A)	1974-76; 77	1,009	484	52	.480	8,411	93	138.1

* Record. $ See page 6 for explanation.

Career Passing Efficiency
(Min. 325 Completions)

Player, Team (Division[s])	Years	Att.	Cmp.	Int.	Pct.	Yds.	TD	Pts.
Tony Aliucci, Indiana (Pa.) (II)	1988-91	579	350	24	.604	5,655	53	*164.4
Jayson Merrill, Western St. (II)	1990-91	580	328	25	.566	5,830	56	164.2
Chris Petersen, UC Davis (II)	1985-86	553	385	13	*.696	4,988	39	164.0
Dennis Shaw, San Diego St. (II; I-A) ...	1968; 69	575	333	41	.579	5,324	58	154.7
Joe Blake, Simpson (III)	1987-90	672	399	15	.594	6,183	43	153.3
Jim McMillan, Boise St. (II)	1971-74	640	382	29	.597	5,508	58	152.8
Troy Aikman, Oklahoma/UCLA (I-A)...	84-85, 87-88	637	401	18	.630	5,436	40	149.7
Jim Harbaugh, Michigan (I-A)	1983-86	582	368	19	.632	5,215	31	149.6
Chuck Hartlieb, Iowa (I-A)	1985-88	716	461	17	.643	6,269	34	148.9
Danny White, Arizona St. (I-A)	1971-73	649	345	36	.532	5,932	59	148.9
Gary Collier, Emory & Henry (III)	1984-87	738	386	33	.523	6,103	80	148.6
Kenneth Biggles, Tennessee St. (I-AA) ..	1981-84	701	397	28	.566	5,933	57	146.6
Gifford Nielsen, Brigham Young (I-A) ..	1975-77	708	415	29	.586	5,833	55	145.3
Greg Heeres, Hope (III)	1981-84	630	347	21	.537	5,120	53	144.4
Bruce Upstill, Col. of Emporia (II)	1960-63	769	438	36	.570	6,935	48	144.0
Tom Ramsey, UCLA (I-A)	1979-82	691	411	33	.595	5,844	48	143.9
Shawn Moore, Virginia (I-A)	1987-90	762	421	32	.552	6,629	55	143.8
Jerry Rhome, SMU/Tulsa (I-A)	1961, 63-64	713	448	23	.628	5,472	47	142.6
Jim Zaccheo, Nevada (I-AA)	1987-88	554	326	27	.588	4,750	35	142.0
Bruce Crosthwaite, Adrian (III).........	1984-87	618	368	31	.596	4,959	45	141.0
Steve Mariucci, Northern Mich. (II).....	1974-77	678	380	33	.561	6,022	41	140.9
Jim Karsatos, Ohio St. (I-A)	1983-86	573	330	19	.576	4,698	36	140.6
Jason Garrett, Princeton (I-AA)	1987-88	550	368	10	.669	4,274	20	140.6
Scott Barry, UC Davis (II)	1982-84	588	377	16	.641	4,421	33	140.4
Jerry Tagge, Nebraska (I-A)............	1969-71	581	348	19	.599	4,704	33	140.1

* Record.

Season Passing Efficiency
(Min. 30 Attempts Per Game)

Player, Team (Division)	Year	G	Att.	Cmp.	Int.	Pct.	Yds.	TD	Pts.
Jayson Merrill, Western St. (II)	†1991	10	309	195	11	.631	3,484	35	*187.9
Jim McMahon, Brigham Young (I-A) ..	†1980	12	445	284	18	.638	4,571	47	176.9
Ty Detmer, Brigham Young (I-A)	†1989	12	412	265	15	.643	4,560	32	175.6
Jerry Rhome, Tulsa (I-A)	†1964	10	326	224	4	.687	2,870	32	172.6
Ty Detmer, Brigham Young (I-A)	1991	12	403	249	12	.618	4,031	35	168.5
Steve Young, Brigham Young (I-A) ...	†1983	11	429	306	10	*.713	3,902	33	168.5
Willie Totten, Mississippi Val. (I-AA) ...	†1983	9	279	174	9	.624	2,566	29	167.5
Jim McMillan, Boise St. (II)	†1974	10	313	192	15	.613	2,900	33	164.4
Willie Totten, Mississippi Val. (I-AA) ...	†1984	10	518	324	22	.626	4,557	*56	163.6
Jeff Wiley, Holy Cross (I-AA)..........	†1987	11	400	265	17	.663	3,677	34	163.0
Todd Hammel, Stephen F. Austin (I-AA)	†1989	11	401	238	13	.594	3,914	34	162.8
Dennis Shaw, San Diego St. (I-A)	†1969	10	335	199	26	.594	3,185	39	162.2
John Friesz, Idaho (I-AA)	1989	11	425	260	8	.612	4,041	31	161.4
Willie Reyna, La Verne (III)	1991	8	267	170	6	.636	2,543	16	158.8
George Bork, Northern Ill. (II)	1963	9	374	244	12	.652	2,824	32	156.2
Neil Lomax, Portland St. (I-AA)	1980	11	473	296	12	.626	4,094	37	156.0
Ty Detmer, Brigham Young (I-A)	1990	12	562	361	28	.642	*5,188	41	155.9
Doug Williams, Grambling (I-AA)	1977	11	352	181	18	.514	3,286	38	155.2
Jim McMahon, Brigham Young (I-A) ..	†1981	10	423	272	7	.643	3,555	30	155.0
Andy Breault, Kutztown (II)	1991	10	360	225	20	.625	2,927	37	153.4
Chuck Long, Iowa (I-A)	1985	11	351	231	15	.658	2,978	26	153.0
Doug Flutie, Boston College (I-A).....	1984	11	386	233	11	.604	3,454	27	152.9

* Record. † National champion.

Season Passing Efficiency
(Min. 15 Attempts Per Game)

Player, Team (Division)	Year	G	Att.	Cmp.	Int.	Pct.	Yds.	TD	Pts.
Boyd Crawford, Col. of Idaho (II)	†1953	8	120	72	6	.600	1,462	21	*210.1
Chuck Green, Wittenberg (II)	†1963	9	182	114	8	.626	2,181	19	189.0
Jim Feeley, Johns Hopkins (III)	†1967	7	110	69	5	.627	1,264	12	186.2
John Charles, Portland St. (II)	1991	11	247	147	7	.595	2,619	32	185.5
Mitch Sanders, Bridgeport (III)	†1973	10	151	84	7	.556	1,551	23	182.9
Jim Peterson, Hanover (II)	†1948	8	125	81	12	.648	1,571	12	182.9
John Wristen, Southern Colo. (II)	†1982	8	121	68	2	.562	1,358	13	182.5
Michael Payton, Marshall (I-AA)	†1991	9	216	143	5	.622	2,333	19	181.3
Pat Mayew, St. John's (Minn.) (III)	†1991	9	247	154	4	.623	2,408	30	181.0
Richard Basil, Savannah St. (II)	†1989	9	211	120	7	.568	2,148	29	180.9
Jim Cahoon, Ripon (II)...............	†1964	8	127	74	7	.583	1,206	19	176.4
Jimbo Fisher, Samford (III)............	†1987	10	252	139	5	.551	2,394	34	175.4
Gary Collier, Emory & Henry (III)	1987	11	249	152	10	.610	2,317	33	174.8
James Grant, Ramapo (III)	1989	9	147	91	7	.619	1,441	17	172.7
Tony Aliucci, Indiana (Pa.) (II)	†1990	10	181	111	10	.613	1,801	21	172.0
Frank Baur, Lafayette (I-AA)	†1988	10	256	164	11	.641	2,621	23	171.1
Bobby Lamb, Furman (I-AA)	†1985	11	181	106	6	.586	1,856	18	170.9
Gary Urwiler, Eureka (III).............	1991	10	171	103	5	.602	1,656	18	170.3
John Costello, Widener (II)	†1956	9	149	74	10	.497	1,702	17	169.8
Chris Petersen, UC Davis (II)	†1985	10	242	167	6	.690	2,366	17	169.4

* Record. † National champion.

Career Yards

Player, Team (Division[s])	Years	Att.	Cmp.	Int.	Pct.	Yds.	TD
Ty Detmer, Brigham Young (I-A)	1988-91	1,530	*958	65	.626	*15,031	121
Neil Lomax, Portland St. (II; I-AA).............	1977; 78-80	1,606	938	55	.584	13,220	106
Kirk Baumgartner, Wis.-Stevens Point (III)	1986-89	*1,696	883	57	.521	13,028	110
Willie Totten, Mississippi Val. (I-AA)	1982-85	1,555	907	*75	.583	12,711	*139
Todd Santos, San Diego St. (I-A)	1984-87	1,484	910	57	.613	11,425	70
John Friesz, Idaho (I-AA)	1986-89	1,350	801	40	.593	10,697	77
Greg Wyatt, Northern Ariz. (I-AA)	1986-89	1,510	926	49	.613	10,697	70
Sean Payton, Eastern Ill. (I-AA)	1983-86	1,408	756	55	.537	10,655	75
Kevin Sweeney, Fresno St. (I-A)...............	$1982-86	1,336	731	48	.547	10,623	66
Earl Harvey, N.C. Central (II)	1985-88	1,442	690	81	.479	10,621	86
Doug Flutie, Boston College (I-A).............	1981-84	1,270	677	54	.533	10,579	67
Tom Ehrhardt, LIU-C.W. Post (II); R. I. (I-AA) .	1981-82; 84-85	1,489	833	63	.559	10,325	92
Brian McClure, Bowling Green (I-A)	1982-85	1,427	900	58	.631	10,280	63
Jeff Wiley, Holy Cross (I-AA)	1985-88	1,208	723	63	.599	9,698	71
Ben Bennett, Duke (I-A)	1980-83	1,375	820	57	.596	9,614	53
Keith Bishop, Ill. Wes./Wheaton (Ill.) (III)......	1981, 83-85	1,311	772	65	.589	9,579	71
Dennis Bogacz, Wis.-Oshkosh/ Wis.-Whitewater (III)	1988-89, 90-91	1,275	654	59	.513	9,536	66
Jim McMahon, Brigham Young (I-A)..........	1977-78, 80-81	1,060	653	34	.616	9,536	84
Todd Ellis, South Caro. (I-A)	1986-89	1,266	704	66	.556	9,519	97
Dave Geissler, Wis.-Stevens Point (III)	1982-85	1,346	789	57	.586	9,518	65
David Klingler, Houston (I-A)	1988-91	1,261	726	38	.576	9,430	91
Erik Wilhelm, Oregon St. (I-A)................	1985-88	1,480	870	61	.588	9,393	52
Jeremy Leach, New Mexico (I-A)	1988-91	1,432	735	62	.513	9,382	50
John Elway, Stanford (I-A)	1979-82	1,246	774	39	.621	9,349	77
Kirk Schulz, Villanova (I-AA)	1986-89	1,297	774	70	.597	9,305	70
Ken Hobart, Idaho (I-AA)	1980-83	1,219	629	42	.516	9,300	79

* Record. $ See page 6 for explanation.

Career Yards Per Game

Player, Team (Division[s])	Years	G	Att.	Cmp.	Int.	Pct.	Yds.	TD	Yd. PG
Ty Detmer, Brigham Young (I-A)	1988-91	46	1,530	*958	65	.626	*15,031	121	*326.8
Willie Totten, Mississippi Val. (I-AA) ...	1982-85	40	1,555	907	*75	.583	12,711	*139	317.8
Kirk Baumgartner, Wis.-Stevens Pt. (III)	1986-89	41	*1,696	883	57	.521	13,028	110	317.8
Neil Lomax, Portland St. (II; I-AA).....	77;78-80	42	1,606	938	55	.584	13,220	106	314.8
Mike Perez, San Jose St. (I-A)	1986-87	20	792	471	30	.595	6,194	36	309.7
Keith Bishop, Ill. Wes./Wheaton (Ill.) (III)	81,83-85	31	1,311	772	65	.589	9,579	71	309.0
Doug Gaynor, Long Beach St. (I-A) ...	1984-85	22	837	569	35	.680	6,793	35	308.8
John Friesz, Idaho (I-AA)	1986-89	35	1,350	801	40	.593	10,697	77	305.6
Tony Eason, Illinois (I-A)..............	1981-82	22	856	526	29	.615	6,608	37	300.4

* Record.

Career Touchdown Passes

Player, Team (Division[s])	Years	Att.	Cmp.	Int.	Pct.	Yds.	TD
Willie Totten, Mississippi Val. (I-AA)	1982-85	1,555	907	*75	.583	12,711	*139
Ty Detmer, Brigham Young (I-A)	1988-91	1,530	*958	65	.626	*15,031	121
Kirk Baumgartner, Wis.-Stevens Point (III)	1986-89	*1,696	883	57	.521	13,028	110
Neil Lomax, Portland St. (II; I-AA)	1977; 78-80	1,606	938	55	.584	13,220	106
Matt Jozokos, Plymouth St. (III)..............	1987-90	1,003	527	39	.525	7,658	95
Doug Williams, Grambling (II; I-A)	1974-76; 77	1,009	484	52	.480	8,411	93
Tom Ehrhardt, LIU-C. W. Post (II); Rhode Island (I-AA)	1981-82; 84-85	1,489	833	63	.559	10,325	92
David Klingler, Houston (I-A)	1988-91	1,261	726	38	.576	9,430	91
Earl Harvey, N. C. Central (II)	1985-88	1,442	690	81	.479	10,621	86
Jim McMahon, Brigham Young (I-A)	1977-78, 80-81	1,060	653	34	.616	9,536	84
Joe Adams, Tennessee St. (I-A)	1977-80	1,100	604	60	.549	8,649	81
Gary Collier, Emory & Henry (III)	1984-87	738	386	33	.523	6,103	80
¢Troy Kopp, Pacific (Cal.) (I-A)	1989-91	1,118	657	38	.588	8,588	79
Ken Hobart, Idaho (I-AA)	1980-83	1,219	629	42	.516	9,300	79

Record. ¢ *Active player.*

Season Yards

Player, Team (Division)	Year	G	Att.	Cmp.	Int.	Pct.	Yds.	TD
Ty Detmer, Brigham Young (I-A)	†1990	12	562	361	28	.642	*5,188	41
David Klingler, Houston (I-A)	1990	11	*643	*374	20	.582	5,140	54
Andre Ware, Houston (I-A)...................	†1989	11	578	365	15	.631	4,699	46
Jim McMahon, Brigham Young (I-A)	†1980	12	445	284	18	.638	4,571	47
Ty Detmer, Brigham Young (I-A)	1989	12	412	265	15	.643	4,560	32
Willie Totten, Mississippi Val. (I-AA)	†1984	10	518	324	22	.626	4,557	*56
Scott Mitchell, Utah (I-A)...................	1988	11	533	323	15	.606	4,322	29
Robbie Bosco, Brigham Young (I-A)	1985	13	511	338	24	.661	4,257	30
Jamie Martin, Weber St. (I-AA)	1991	11	500	310	17	.620	4,125	35
Neil Lomax, Portland St. (I-AA)	1980	11	473	296	12	.626	4,094	37
John Friesz, Idaho (I-AA)	†1989	11	425	260	8	.612	4,041	31
Ty Detmer, Brigham Young (I-A)	1991	12	403	249	12	.618	4,031	35
Neil Lomax, Portland St. (I-AA)	1979	11	516	299	16	.579	3,950	26
Todd Santos, San Diego St. (I-A)	1987	12	492	306	15	.622	3,932	26
Todd Hammel, Stephen F. Austin (I-AA)	1989	11	401	238	13	.594	3,914	34
Steve Young, Brigham Young (I-A)...........	†1983	11	429	306	10	*.713	3,902	33
Robbie Bosco, Brigham Young (I-A)	1984	12	458	283	11	.618	3,875	33
Sean Payton, Eastern Ill. (I-AA)	1984	11	473	270	15	.571	3,843	28
Dan McGwire, San Diego St. (I-A)	1990	11	449	270	7	.601	3,833	27
Kirk Baumgartner, Wis.-Stevens Point (III) ...	1988	11	527	276	16	.524	3,828	25
Anthony Dilweg, Duke (I-A).................	1988	11	484	287	18	.593	3,824	24
Sam King, Nevada-Las Vegas (I-A)	1981	12	433	255	19	.589	3,778	18
Troy Kopp, Pacific (Cal.) (I-A)...............	1991	12	449	275	16	.612	3,767	37
Kirk Baumgartner, Wis.-Stevens Point (III) ...	1987	11	466	243	22	.521	3,755	31
Chris Hegg, Northeast Mo. St. (II)	1985	11	503	284	20	.565	3,741	32
Marc Wilson, Brigham Young (I-A)...........	1979	12	427	250	15	.585	3,720	29

Record. † *National champion.*

Season Yards Per Game

Player, Team (Division)	Year	G	Att.	Cmp.	Int.	Pct.	Yds.	TD	Yd. PG
David Klingler, Houston (I-A)	1990	11	*643	*374	20	.582	5,140	54	*467.3
Willie Totten, Mississippi Val. (I-AA) ...	1984	10	518	324	22	.626	4,557	*56	455.7
Ty Detmer, Brigham Young (I-A)	1990	12	562	361	28	.642	*5,188	41	432.3
Andre Ware, Houston (I-A)............	1989	11	578	365	15	.631	4,699	46	427.2
Scott Mitchell, Utah (I-A)..............	1988	11	533	323	15	.606	4,322	29	392.9
Jim McMahon, Brigham Young (I-A)..	1980	12	445	284	18	.638	4,571	47	380.9
Ty Detmer, Brigham Young (I-A)	1989	12	412	265	15	.643	4,560	32	380.0

Record.

Season Touchdown Passes

Player, Team (Division)	Year	Att.	Cmp.	Int.	Pct.	Yds.	TD
Willie Totten, Mississippi Val. (I-AA)	1984	518	324	22	.626	4,557	*56
David Klingler, Houston (I-A)	1990	*643	*374	20	.582	5,140	54
Jim McMahon, Brigham Young (I-A)	1980	445	284	18	.638	4,571	47
Andre Ware, Houston (I-A)....................	1989	578	365	15	.631	4,699	46
Bob Toledo, San Fran. St. (II)	1967	396	211	24	.533	3,513	45
Ty Detmer, Brigham Young (I-A)	1990	562	361	28	.642	*5,188	41
Kirk Baumgartner, Wis.-Stevens Point (III)	1989	455	247	9	.542	3,692	39
Willie Totten, Mississippi Val. (I-AA)	1985	492	295	29	.600	3,698	39
Dennis Shaw, San Diego St. (I-A)	1969	335	199	26	.594	3,185	39

Player, Team (Division)	Year	Att.	Cmp.	Int.	Pct.	Yds.	TD
Doug Williams, Grambling (I-A)	1977	352	181	18	.514	3,286	38
Troy Kopp, Pacific (Cal.) (I-A)	1991	449	275	16	.613	3,767	37
Andy Breault, Kutztown (II)	1991	360	225	20	.625	2,927	37
Neil Lomax, Portland St. (I-AA)	1980	473	296	12	.626	4,094	37
Ty Detmer, Brigham Young (I-A)	1991	403	249	12	.618	4,031	35
Jamie Martin, Weber St. (I-AA)	1991	500	310	17	.620	4,125	35
Jayson Merrill, Western St. (II)	1991	309	195	11	.631	3,484	35
Tom Ehrhardt, Rhode Island (I-AA)	1985	497	283	19	.569	3,542	35

* Record.

Single-Game Yards

Yds.	Div.	Player, Team (Opponent)	Date
716	I-A	David Klingler, Houston (Arizona St.)..................................Dec. 2, 1990
690	I-A	Matt Vogler, Texas Christian (Houston) ....Nov. 3, 1990
631	I-A	Scott Mitchell, Utah (Air Force)......................................Oct. 15, 1988
624	I-AA	Jamie Martin, Weber St. (Idaho St.) ....Nov. 23, 1991
622	I-A	Jeremy Leach, New Mexico (Utah) ....Nov. 11, 1989
621	I-A	Dave Wilson, Illinois (Ohio St.) ....Nov. 8, 1980
619	I-AA	Doug Pederson, Northeast La. (Stephen F. Austin)......................Nov. 11, 1989
599	I-A	Ty Detmer, Brigham Young (San Diego St.) ....Nov. 16, 1991
599	I-AA	Willie Totten, Mississippi Val. (Prairie View) ....Oct. 27, 1984
592	II	John Charles, Portland St. (Cal Poly SLO) ....Nov. 16, 1991
589	I-AA	Vern Harris, Idaho St. (Montana) ....Oct. 12, 1985
585	III	Tim Lynch, Hofstra (Fordham) ....Oct. 19, 1991
585	I-A	Robbie Bosco, Brigham Young (New Mexico)..........................Oct. 19, 1985
572	I-A	David Klingler, Houston (Eastern Wash.) ....Nov. 17, 1990
571	I-AA	Todd Hammel, Stephen F. Austin (Northeast La.) ....Nov. 11, 1989
571	I-A	Marc Wilson, Brigham Young (Utah) ....Nov. 5, 1977
568	I-A	David Lowery, San Diego St. (Brigham Young) ....Nov. 16, 1991
568	II	Bob Toledo, San Fran. St. (Cal St. Hayward) ....Oct. 21, 1967
566	I-AA	Tom Ehrhardt, Rhode Island (Connecticut) ....Nov. 16, 1985
565	I-A	Jim McMahon, Brigham Young (Utah) ....Nov. 21, 1981
564	I-A	Troy Kopp, Pacific, Cal. (New Mexico St.) ....Oct. 20, 1990
563	I-A	David Klingler, Houston (Texas Christian) ....Nov. 3, 1990
561	I-A	Tony Adams, Utah St. (Utah)..Nov. 11, 1972

Texas Christian quarterback Matt Vogler tied a collegiate record on November 3, 1990, when he attempted 79 passes in a game against Houston. His total of 690 yards passing in that game is the second-highest in history.

Single-Game Attempts

Atts.	Div.	Player, Team (Opponent)	Date
79	I-A	Matt Vogler, Texas Christian (Houston)	Nov. 3, 1990
79	III	Mike Wallace, Ohio Wesleyan (Denison)	Oct. 3, 1981
77	I-AA	Neil Lomax, Portland St. (Northern Colo.)	Oct. 20, 1979
76	I-A	David Klingler, Houston (Southern Methodist)	Oct. 20, 1990
74	I-AA	Paul Peterson, Idaho St. (Nevada)	Oct. 1, 1983
73	I-A	Troy Kopp, Pacific, Cal. (Hawaii)	Oct. 27, 1990
73	I-A	Shane Montgomery, North Caro. St. (Duke)	Nov. 11, 1989
72	I-A	Matt Vogler, Texas Christian (Texas Tech)	Nov. 10, 1990
72	II	Kurt Otto, North Dak. (Texas A&I)	Sept. 13, 1986
72	III	Bob Lockhart, Millikin (Franklin)	Nov. 12, 1977
72	II	Kaipo Spencer, Santa Clara (Portland St.)	Oct. 11, 1975
72	II	Joe Stetser, Cal St. Chico (Oregon Tech)	Sept. 23, 1967

Single-Game Completions

Cmp.	Div.	Player, Team (Opponent)	Date
50	III	Tim Lynch, Hofstra (Fordham)	Oct. 19, 1991
48	I-A	David Klingler, Houston (Southern Methodist)	Oct. 20, 1990
47	I-AA	Jamie Martin, Weber St. (Idaho St.)	Nov. 23, 1991
47	III	Mike Wallace, Ohio Wesleyan (Denison)	Oct. 3, 1981
46	I-AA	Doug Pederson, Northeast La. (Stephen F. Austin)	Nov. 11, 1989
46	I-AA	Willie Totten, Mississippi Val. (Southern-B.R.)	Sept. 29, 1984
45	I-AA	Willie Totten, Mississippi Val. (Prairie View)	Oct. 27, 1984
45	I-A	Sandy Schwab, Northwestern (Michigan)	Oct. 23, 1982
44	I-A	Matt Vogler, Texas Christian (Houston)	Nov. 3, 1990
44	I-A	Chuck Hartlieb, Iowa (Indiana)	Oct. 29, 1988
44	II	Tom Bonds, Cal Lutheran (St. Mary's, Cal.)	Nov. 22, 1986
44	I-A	Jim McMahon, Brigham Young (Colorado St.)	Nov. 7, 1981
44	I-AA	Neil Lomax, Portland St. (Northern Colo.)	Oct. 20, 1979
43	I-A	Gary Schofield, Wake Forest (Maryland)	Oct. 17, 1981
43	I-A	Dave Wilson, Illinois (Ohio St.)	Nov. 8, 1980
43	I-A	Rich Campbell, California (Florida)	Sept. 13, 1980
43	II	George Bork, Northern Ill. (Central Mich.)	Nov. 9, 1963

RECEIVING
Career Catches

Player, Team (Division[s])	Years	Catches	Yards	Avg.	TD
Jerry Rice, Mississippi Val. (I-AA)	1981-84	*301	*4,693	15.6	*50
Kasey Dunn, Idaho (I-AA)	1988-91	268	3,847	14.4	25
Terance Mathis, New Mexico (I-A)	1985-87, 89	263	4,254	16.2	36
Mark Templeton, Long Beach St. (I-A) (RB)	1983-86	¢262	1,969	7.5	11
Howard Twilley, Tulsa (I-A)	1963-65	261	3,343	12.8	32
Bill Stromberg, Johns Hopkins (III)	1978-81	258	3,776	14.6	39
Chris Myers, Kenyon (II)	1967-70	253	3,897	15.4	33
Brian Forster, Rhode Island (I-AA) (TE)	1983-85, 87	#245	#3,410	13.9	31
David Williams, Illinois (I-A)	1983-85	245	3,195	13.0	22
Bruce Cerone, Yankton/Emporia St. (II)	1966-67, 68-69	241	4,354	18.1	49
Mark Didio, Connecticut (I-AA)	1988-91	239	3,535	14.8	21
Rennie Benn, Lehigh (I-AA)	1982-85	237	3,662	15.5	44
Marc Zeno, Tulane (I-A)	1984-87	236	3,725	15.8	25
Dale Amos, Frank. & Marsh. (III)	1986-89	233	3,846	16.5	35
Scott Fredrickson, Wis.-Stout (III)	1986-89	233	3,390	14.5	23
Harold "Red" Roberts, Austin Peay (II)	1967-70	232	3,005	13.0	31
Mike Whitehouse, St. Norbert (III)	1986-89	230	3,480	15.1	37
Jerry Hendren, Idaho (II; I-A)	1967-68; 69	230	3,435	14.9	27

Record. ¢ Record for a running back. # Record for a tight end.

Career Catches Per Game

Player, Team (Division[s])	Years	G	Catches	Yds.	TD	Ct. PG
Manny Hazard, Houston (I-A)	1989-90	21	220	2,635	31	*10.5
Howard Twilley, Tulsa (I-A)	1963-65	26	261	3,343	32	10.0
Jason Phillips, Houston (I-A)	1987-88	22	207	2,319	18	9.4
Ed Bell, Idaho St. (II)	1968-69	19	163	2,608	30	8.6
Jerry Hendren, Idaho (II)	1967-69	30	230	3,435	27	7.7
Neal Sweeney, Tulsa (I-A)	1965-66	18	134	1,623	11	7.4
David Williams, Illinois (I-A)	1983-85	33	245	3,195	22	7.4
Gary Garrison, San Diego St. (II)	1964-65	20	148	2,188	26	7.4
Jerry Rice, Mississippi Val. (I-AA)	1981-84	41	*301	*4,693	*50	7.3
James Dixon, Houston (I-A)	1987-88	22	161	1,762	14	7.3

Record.

1992 NCAA FOOTBALL

Career Touchdown Receptions

Player, Team (Division[s])	Years	Games	TD
Jerry Rice, Mississippi Val. (I-AA)	1981-84	41	*50
Bruce Cerone, Yankton/Emporia St. (II)	1966-67, 68-69	42	49
Rennie Benn, Lehigh (I-AA)................................	1982-85	41	44
¢Chris Bisaillon, Ill. Wesleyan (III)	1989-91	27	43
Shannon Sharpe, Savannah St. (II)	1986-89	42	40
John Aromando, Trenton St. (III)	1981-84	40	39
Bill Stromberg, Johns Hopkins (III)	1978-81	40	39
Clarkston Hines, Duke (I-A)...............................	1986-89	44	38
Robert Clark, N. C. Central (II)	1983-86	40	38
Roy Banks, Eastern Ill. (I-AA)	1983-86	38	38
Mike Jones, Tennessee St. (I-AA)	1979-82	42	38
Chris Holder, Tuskegee (II)	1988-91	40	37
Mike Whitehouse, St. Norbert (III)	1986-89	38	37
Terance Mathis, New Mexico (I-A)	1985-87, 89	44	36
Mike Cottle, Juniata (III)	1985-88	37	36
Joe Thomas, Mississippi Val. (I-AA).......................	1982-85	41	36
Willie Richardson, Jackson St. (II)	1959-62	38	36

Record. ¢ Active player.

Season Catches

Player, Team (Division)	Year	G	Catches	Yards	TD
Manny Hazard, Houston (I-A)........................	†1989	11	*142	1,689	22
Howard Twilley, Tulsa (I-A)........................	†1965	10	134	1,779	16
Brian Forster, Rhode Island (I-AA) (TE)	†1985	10	115	1,617	12
Fred Gilbert, Houston (I-A)	†1991	11	106	957	7
Barry Wagner, Alabama A&M (II)	†1989	11	106	*1,812	17
Theo Blanco, Wis.-Stevens Point (III) (RB)	1987	11	#106	#1,616	8
Jerry Rice, Mississippi Val. (I-AA)	†1984	10	103	1,682	*27
Jerry Rice, Mississippi Val. (I-AA)	†1983	10	102	1,450	14
Mike Healey, Valparaiso (II)	†1985	10	101	1,279	11
David Williams, Illinois (I-A)	†1984	11	101	1,278	8
Jay Miller, Brigham Young (I-A)	†1973	11	100	1,181	8
Jason Phillips, Houston (I-A)	†1987	11	99	875	3
Mark Templeton, Long Beach St. (I-A) (RB)	†1986	11	99	688	2
Rodney Carter, Purdue (I-A)	†1985	11	98	1,099	4
Keith Edwards, Vanderbilt (I-A)	†1983	11	97	909	0

Record. † National champion. # Record for a running back.

Season Catches Per Game

Player, Team (Division)	Year	G	Catches	Yds.	TD	Ct. PG
Howard Twilley, Tulsa (I-A).................	†1965	10	134	1,779	16	*13.4
Manny Hazard, Houston (I-A)	†1989	11	*142	1,689	22	12.9
Brian Forster, Rhode Island (I-AA) (TE)	†1985	10	115	1,617	12	11.5
Jerry Rice, Mississippi Val. (I-AA)	†1984	10	103	1,682	*27	10.3
Scott Faessler, Framingham St. (III)	†1990	9	92	916	5	10.2
Jerry Rice, Mississippi Val. (I-AA)	†1983	10	102	1,450	14	10.2
Mike Healy, Valparaiso (II)	†1985	10	101	1,279	11	10.1
Bruce Cerone, Emporia St. (II)	†1968	9	91	1,479	15	10.1
Stuart Gaussoin, Portland St. (I-AA)	†1979	9	90	1,132	8	10.0

Record. † National champion.

Single-Game Catches

No.	Div.	Player, Team (Opponent)	Date
24	I-AA	Jerry Rice, Mississippi Val. (Southern-B.R.)............................	Oct. 1, 1983
23	II	Barry Wagner, Alabama A&M (Clark Atlanta)............................	Nov. 4, 1989
22	I-AA	Marvin Walker, North Texas (Tulsa)	Nov. 20, 1982
22	I-A	Jay Miller, Brigham Young (New Mexico)	Nov. 3, 1973
21#	I-AA	David Pandt, Montana St. (Eastern Wash.)	Sept. 21, 1985
20	III	Rich Johnson, Pace (Fordham)	Nov. 7, 1987
20	III	Pete Thompson, Carroll, Wis. (Augustana, Ill.)	Nov. 4, 1978
20	II	Harold "Red" Roberts, Austin Peay (Murray St.)......................	Nov. 8, 1969
20	I-A	Rick Eber, Tulsa (Idaho St.)	Oct. 7, 1967

 # Record for a running back.

Career Yards

Player, Team (Division[s])	Years	Catches	Yards	Avg.	TD
Jerry Rice, Mississippi Val. (I-AA)	1981-84	*301	*4,693	15.6	*50
Bruce Cerone, Yankton/Emporia St. (II)	1966-67, 68-69	241	4,354	18.1	49
Terance Mathis, New Mexico (I-A)	1985-87, 89	263	4,254	16.2	36

Player, Team (Division[s])	Years	Catches	Yards	Avg.	TD
Robert Clark, N.C. Central (II)	1983-86	210	4,231	‡20.1	38
Chris Myers, Kenyon (II)	1967-70	253	3,897	15.4	33
Kasey Dunn, Idaho (I-AA)	1988-91	268	3,847	14.4	25
Dale Amos, Frank. & Marsh. (III)	1986-89	233	3,846	16.5	35
Bill Stromberg, Johns Hopkins (III)	1978-81	258	3,776	14.6	39
Shannon Sharpe, Savannah St. (II)	1986-89	192	3,744	19.5	40
Marc Zeno, Tulane (I-A)................	1984-87	236	3,725	15.8	25
Jim Bradford, Carleton (III)	1988-91	212	3,719	17.5	32
Rennie Benn, Lehigh (I-AA)	1982-85	237	3,662	15.5	44
Jeff Tiefenthaler, South Dak. St. (II)	1983-86	173	3,621	20.9	31
Willie Richardson, Jackson St. (II)	1959-62	166	3,616	21.8	36
Ron Sellers, Florida St. (I-A)	1966-68	212	3,598	17.0	23

* Record. ‡ Record for minimum of 180 catches.

Season Yards

Player, Team (Division)	Year	Catches	Yards	Avg.	TD
Barry Wagner, Alabama A&M (II)	†1989	106	*1,812	17.1	17
Howard Twilley, Tulsa (I-A)	†1965	134	1,779	13.3	16
Manny Hazard, Houston (I-A)	†1989	*142	1,689	11.9	22
Jerry Rice, Mississippi Val. (I-AA)	†1984	103	1,682	16.3	*27
Brian Forster, Rhode Island (I-AA) (TE) ...	†1985	115	1,617	14.1	12
Theo Blanco, Wis.-Stevens Point (III) (RB)	1987	#106	#1,616	15.2	8
Aaron Turner, Pacific (Cal.) (I-A)	†1991	92	1,604	17.4	18
Dan Fulton, Nebraska-Omaha (II)	1976	67	1,581	23.6	16
Jeff Tiefenthaler, South Dak. St. (II)	1986	73	1,534	21.0	11
Ed Bell, Idaho St. (II)	†1969	96	1,522	15.9	20
Chuck Hughes, UTEP (I-A)	1965	80	1,519	19.0	12
Henry Ellard, Fresno St. (I-A)	1982	62	1,510	††24.4	15
Ron Sellers, Florida St. (I-A)	†1968	86	1,496	17.4	12

* Record. † National champion. †† Record for minimum of 55 catches. # Record for a running back.

Season Touchdown Receptions

Player, Team (Division)	Year	Games	TD
Jerry Rice, Mississippi Val. (I-AA)	1984	10	*27
Manny Hazard, Houston (I-A)	1989	11	22
John Aromando, Trenton St. (III)	1983	10	20
Ed Bell, Idaho St. (II)	1969	10	20
Desmond Howard, Michigan (I-A)	1991	11	19
Aaron Turner, Pacific (Cal.) (I-A)	1991	11	18
Tom Reynolds, San Diego St. (I-A).................................	1971	10	18
Mario Bailey, Washington (I-A)....................................	1991	11	17
Chris Bisaillon, Ill. Wesleyan (III)	1991	9	17
Clarkston Hines, Duke (I-A)	1989	11	17
Barry Wagner, Alabama A&M (II)	1989	11	17
Dameon Reilly, Rhode Island (I-AA)	1985	11	17
Dan Bitson, Tulsa (I-A)..	1989	11	16
Evan Elkington, Worcester Tech (III)	1989	10	16
Dan Fulton, Nebraska-Omaha (II).................................	1976	10	16
Howard Twilley, Tulsa (I-A)..	1965	10	16

Single-Game Yards

Yds.	Div.	Player, Team (Opponent)	Date
370	I-AA	Michael Lerch, Princeton (Brown)..	Oct. 12, 1991
370	II	Barry Wagner, Alabama A&M (Clark Atlanta).............................	Nov. 4, 1989
363	II	Tom Nettles, San Diego St. (Southern Miss.)	Nov. 9, 1968
354	II	Robert Clark, N.C. Central (Jackson St.)	Aug. 30, 1986
349	I-A	Chuck Hughes, UTEP (North Texas)	Sept. 18, 1965
330	I-AA	Nate Singleton, Grambling (Virginia Union)	Sept. 14, 1991
327@	I-AA	Brian Forster, Rhode Island (Brown)....................................	Sept. 28, 1985
325	II	Paul Zaeske, North Park (North Central)	Oct. 12, 1968
322	I-A	Rick Eber, Tulsa (Idaho St.)	Oct. 7, 1967
318	I-A	Harry Wood, Tulsa (Idaho St.)	Oct. 7, 1967
317	II	Dan Fulton, Nebraska-Omaha (South Dak.)	Sept. 4, 1976
316	I-A	Jeff Evans, New Mexico St. (Southern Ill.)	Sept. 30, 1978
310	II	Mike Collodi, Colorado Mines (Westminster, Utah)	Oct. 3, 1970
309	III	Dale Amos, Frank. & Marsh. (Western Md.).............................	Oct. 24, 1987

@ Record for a tight end.

1992 NCAA FOOTBALL

INTERCEPTIONS

Career Interceptions

Player, Team (Division[s])	Years	No.	Yards	Avg.
Tom Collins, Indianapolis (II)	1982-85	*37	390	10.5
Ralph Gebhardt, Rochester (III)	1972-75	34	406	11.9
Dean Diaz, Humboldt St. (II)	1980-83	31	328	10.6
Scott Wiedeman, Adams St. (II)	1988-91	31	289	9.3
Eugene Hunter, Fort Valley St. (III)	1972-74	29	479	16.5
Al Brosky, Illinois (I-A)	1950-52	29	356	12.3
Bill Grantham, Missouri-Rolla (II)	1977-80	29	263	9.1
Brian Fetterolf, Aurora (III)	1986-89	28	390	13.9
Dave Murphy, Holy Cross (I-AA)	1986-89	28	309	11.0
Rick Bealer, Lycoming (III)	1987-90	28	279	10.0
John Provost, Holy Cross (I-A)	1972-74	27	470	17.4
Martin Bayless, Bowling Green (I-A)	1980-83	27	266	9.9
Tim Lennon, Curry (III)	1986-89	27	190	7.0
Mike Hintz, Wis.-Platteville (III)	1983-86	27	183	6.8
Tony Woods, Bloomsburg (II)	1982-85	26	105	4.0

Record.

Season Interceptions

Player, Team (Division)	Year	No.	Yards
Mark Dorner, Juniata (III)	†1987	*15	202
Eugene Hunter, Fort Valley St. (II)	†1972	14	211
Jim Blackwell, Southern-B.R. (II)	†1970	14	196
Tom Rezzuti, Northeastern (II)	†1971	14	153
Al Worley, Washington (I-A)	†1968	14	130
Luther Howard, Delaware St. (II)	†1972	14	99
Carl Ray Harris, Fresno St. (II)	†1970	14	98

Record.   *† National champion.*

PUNT RETURNS

Career Average
(Min. 1.2 Returns Per Game)

Player, Team (Division[s])	Years	No.	Yards	Avg.
Billy Johnson, Widener (II; III)	1971-72; 73	40	989	*24.7
Jack Mitchell, Oklahoma (I-A)	1946-48	39	922	23.6
Keith Winston, Knoxville (III)	1986-87	30	686	22.9
Robert Middlebrook, Knoxville (III)	1984-85	21	473	22.5
Kevin Doherty, Mass. Maritime (III)	1976-78, 80	45	939	20.9
Chuck Downey, Stony Brook (III)	1984-87	59	1,198	**20.3
Mike Askew, Kean (III)	1980-81	28	555	19.8
Eddie Macon, Pacific (Cal.) (I-A)	1949-51	48	907	18.9
Willie Canady, Fort Valley St. (III)	1979-82	41	772	18.8
Jackie Robinson, UCLA (I-A)	1939-40	37	694	18.8

*Record.   ** Record for minimum of 50 returns.*

Season Average
(Min. 1.2 Returns Per Game)

Player, Team (Division)	Year	No.	Yards	Avg.
Billy Johnson, Widener (II)	†1972	15	511	*34.1
Chuck Downey, Stony Brook (III)	†1986	17	530	31.2
Kevin Doherty, Mass. Maritime (III)	†1976	11	332	30.2
Dennis Robinson, Wesleyan (III)	†1978	9	263	29.2
Robert Middlebrook, Knoxville (III)	†1984	9	260	28.9
Joe Troise, Kean (III)	†1974	12	342	28.5
William Williams, Livingstone (II)	†1976	16	453	28.3
Terry Egerdahl, Minn.-Duluth (II)	†1975	13	360	27.7
Melvin Dillard, Ferrum (III)	†1990	25	688	27.5
Bill Blackstock, Tennessee (I-A)	1951	12	311	25.9
Ennis Thomas, Bishop (II)	†1971	18	450	25.0
George Sims, Baylor (I-A)	1948	15	375	25.0

Record.   † National champion.

KICKOFF RETURNS

Career Average
(Min. 1.2 Returns Per Game)

Player, Team (Division[s])	Years	No.	Yards	Avg.
Forrest Hall, San Francisco (I-A)	1946-47	22	796	*36.2
Anthony Davis, Southern Cal (I-A)	1972-74	37	1,299	35.1
Glen Printers, Southern Colo. (II)	1973-74	25	851	34.0
Overton Curtis, Utah St. (I-A)	1957-58	32	991	31.0
Charles Swann, Indiana St. (I-AA)	1989-91	45	1,319	29.3
Altie Taylor, Utah St. (I-A)	1966-68	40	1,170	29.3
Daryl Brown, Tufts (III)	1974-76	38	1,111	29.2
Stan Brown, Purdue (I-A)	1968-70	49	1,412	28.8
Henry White, Colgate (I-A)	1974-77	41	1,180	28.8
Donald Dennis, West Tex. St. (I-A)	1964-65	27	777	28.8
Bobby Ward, Memphis St. (I-A)	1973-74	27	770	28.5
Craig Richardson, Eastern Wash. (I-AA)	1983-86	71	2,021	28.5

* Record.

Season Average
(Min. 1.2 Returns Per Game)

Player, Team (Division)	Year	No.	Yards	Avg.
Paul Allen, Brigham Young (I-A)	1961	12	481	*40.1
Forrest Hall, San Francisco (I-A)	1946	15	573	@38.2
Nate Kirtman, Pomona-Pitzer (III)	†1990	14	515	36.8
Tom Myers, Coe (III)	†1983	11	401	36.5
Tony Ball, Tenn.-Chatt. (I-A)	†1977	13	473	36.4
Ron Scott, Occidental (III)	1983	10	363	36.3
Roscoe Word, Jackson St. (II)	†1973	18	650	36.1
Steve Levenseller, Puget Sound (II)	†1978	17	610	35.9
George Marinkov, North Caro. St. (I-A)	1954	13	465	35.8

* Record.   † National champion.   @ Record for minimum of 1.5 returns per game.

FIELD GOALS

Career Field Goals
(One-inch tees were permitted in 1949, two-inch tees were permitted in 1965, and use of tees was eliminated before 1989 season. The goal posts were widened from 18 feet, 6 inches to 23 feet, 4 inches in 1959 and were narrowed back to 18 feet, 6 inches before 1991 season.)

Player, Team (Division[s])	Years	FGM	FGA	Pct.
Jeff Jaeger, Washington (S) (I-A)	1983-86	*80	99	.808
John Lee, UCLA (S) (I-A)	1982-85	79	92	*.859
Philip Doyle, Alabama (S) (I-A)	1987-90	78	*105	.743
Luis Zendejas, Arizona St. (S) (I-A)	1981-84	78	*105	.743
Kevin Butler, Georgia (S) (I-A)	1981-84	77	98	.786
Max Zendejas, Arizona (S) (I-A)	1982-85	77	104	.740
Carlos Huerta, Miami (Fla.) (S) (I-A)	1988-91	73	91	.802
Derek Schmidt, Florida St. (S) (I-A)	1984-87	73	104	.702
Marty Zendejas, Nevada (S) (I-AA)	1984-87	72	90	.800
Fuad Reveiz, Tennessee (S) (I-A)	1981-84	71	95	.747
Kirk Roach, Western Caro. (S) (I-AA)	1984-87	71	102	.696
Tony Zendejas, Nevada (S) (I-AA)	1981-83	70	86	.814
Barry Belli, Fresno St. (S) (I-A)	1984-87	70	99	.707
Roman Anderson, Houston (S) (I-A)	1988-91	70	101	.693
Collin Mackie, South Caro. (S) (I-A)	1987-90	69	95	.726
Gary Gussman, Miami (Ohio) (S) (I-A)	1984-87	68	94	.723
Larry Roach, Oklahoma St. (S) (I-A)	1981-84	68	101	.673
Paul Woodside, West Va. (S) (I-A)	1981-84	65	81	.802

* Record.   (C) Conventional kicker.   (S) Soccer-style kicker.

Season Field Goals

Player, Team (Division)	Year	FGM	FGA	Pct.
John Lee, UCLA (S) (I-A)	1984	*29	33	.879
Paul Woodside, West Va. (S) (I-A)	1982	28	31	.903
Luis Zendejas, Arizona St. (S) (I-A)	1983	28	37	.757
Fuad Reveiz, Tennessee (S) (I-A)	1982	27	31	.871
Brian Mitchell, Northern Iowa (S) (I-AA)	1990	26	27	*.963
Tony Zendejas, Nevada (S) (I-AA)	1982	26	33	.788
Chuck Nelson, Washington (S) (I-A)	1982	25	26	.962
Chris Jacke, UTEP (S) (I-A)	1988	25	27	.926

Player, Team (Division)	Year	FGM	FGA	Pct.
John Diettrich, Ball St. (S) (I-A)	1985	25	29	.862
Kendall Trainor, Arkansas (S) (I-A)	1988	24	27	.889
Kirk Roach, Western Caro. (S) (I-AA)	1986	24	28	.857
Carlos Reveiz, Tennessee (S) (I-A)	1985	24	28	.857
Chris White, Illinois (S) (I-A)	1984	24	28	.857
Philip Doyle, Alabama (S) (I-A)	1990	24	29	.828
Bruce Kallmeyer, Kansas (S) (I-A)	1983	24	29	.828
Mike Prindle, Western Mich. (S) (I-A)	1984	24	30	.800
George Benyola, Louisiana Tech (S) (I-AA)	1985	24	31	.774

* *Record.* (C) *Conventional kicker.* (S) *Soccer-style kicker.*

(Record for attempts is 38)

Longest Field Goals

Yards	Div.	Player, Team (Opponent)	Year
67	II	Tom Odle, Fort Hays St. (Washburn)	1988
67	I-A	Joe Williams, Wichita St. (Southern Ill.)	1978
67	I-A	Steve Little, Arkansas (Texas)	1977
67	I-A	Russell Erxleben, Texas (Rice)	1977
65	I-A	Tony Franklin, Texas A&M (Baylor)	1976
64	I-A	Russell Erxleben, Texas (Oklahoma)	1977
64	I-A	Tony Franklin, Texas A&M (Baylor)	1976
63	I-AA	Scott Roper, Arkansas St. (North Texas)	1987
63	I-AA	Tim Foley, Ga. Southern (James Madison)	1987
63	I-A	Morten Andersen, Michigan St. (Ohio St.)	1981
63	I-A	Clark Kemble, Colorado St. (Arizona)	1975
63	II	Joe Duren, Arkansas St. (McNeese St.)	1974
62*	I-A	Jason Hanson, Washington St. (Nevada-Las Vegas)	1991
62	I-A	John Diettrich, Ball St. (Ohio)	1986
62	I-AA	Paul Hickert, Murray St. (Eastern Ky.)	1986
62	I-A	Chip Lohmiller, Minnesota (Iowa)	1986
62	I-A	Tom Whelihan, Missouri (Colorado)	1986
62	I-A	Dan Christopulos, Wyoming (Colorado St.)	1977
62	I-A	Iseed Khoury, North Texas (Richmond)	1977
62	III	Dom Antonini, Glassboro St. (Salisbury St.)	1976
62	I-A	Dave Lawson, Air Force (Iowa St.)	1975
62	II	Mike Flater, Colorado Mines (Western St.)	1973

* *Longest collegiate field goal without use of a tee.*

Special Reference: Ove Johannson, Abilene Christian (not an NCAA-member college at the time), kicked a 69-yard field goal against East Tex. St., Oct. 16, 1976.

PUNTING

Career Punting Average
(Minimum 150 Punts)

Player, Team (Division[s])	Years	No.	Yards	Avg.
Reggie Roby, Iowa (I-A)............................	1979-82	172	7,849	*45.6
Greg Montgomery, Michigan St. (I-A)	1985-87	170	7,721	45.4
Tom Tupa, Ohio St. (I-A)	1984-87	196	8,854	45.2
Barry Helton, Colorado (I-A)	1984-87	153	6,873	44.9
Ray Guy, Southern Miss. (I-A)	1970-72	200	8,934	44.7
Bucky Scribner, Kansas (I-A)	1980-82	217	9,670	44.6
Greg Horne, Arkansas (I-A)	1983-86	180	8,002	44.5
Ray Criswell, Florida (I-A).........................	1982-85	161	7,153	44.4
Pumpy Tudors, Tenn.-Chatt. (I-AA)	1988-91	181	8,041	44.4
Bill Smith, Mississippi (I-A)	1983-86	254	11,260	44.3
Tim Baer, Colorado Mines (II)	1986-89	235	10,406	44.3
Russell Erxleben, Texas (I-A)	1975-78	214	9,467	44.2
Mark Simon, Air Force (I-A)	1984-86	156	6,898	44.2
Johnny Evans, North Caro. St. (I-A)	1974-77	185	8,143	44.0
Chuck Ramsey, Wake Forest (I-A)	1971-73	205	9,010	44.0

* *Record.*

Season Punting Average
(Qualifiers for the Championship)

Player, Team (Division)	Year	No.	Yards	Avg.
Reggie Roby, Iowa (I-A)............................	†1981	44	2,193	*49.8
Kirk Wilson, UCLA (I-A)............................	†1956	30	1,479	49.3
Steve Ecker, Shippensburg (II)	†1965	32	1,570	49.1
Zack Jordan, Colorado (I-A)	†1950	38	1,830	48.2

Player, Team (Division)	Year	No.	Yards	Avg.
Ricky Anderson, Vanderbilt (I-A)	†1984	58	2,793	48.2
Reggie Roby, Iowa (I-A)	†1982	52	2,501	48.1
Marv Bateman, Utah (I-A)	†1971	68	3,269	48.1
Don Cockroft, Adams St. (II)	†1966	36	1,728	48.0
Owen Price, UTEP (I-A)	†1940	30	1,440	48.0
Jack Jacobs, Oklahoma (I-A)	1940	31	1,483	47.8
Bill Smith, Mississippi (I-A)	1984	44	2,099	47.7

Record.   † National champion.

Longest Punts

Yards	Div.	Player, Team (Opponent)	Year
99	I-A	Pat Brady, Nevada (Loyola, Cal.)	1950
97	II	Earl Hurst, Emporia St. (Central Mo. St.)	1964
96	II	Gary Frens, Hope (Olivet)	1966
96	II	Jim Jarrett, North Dak. (South Dak.)	1957
96	I-A	George O'Brien, Wisconsin (Iowa)	1952
94	I-A	John Hadl, Kansas (Oklahoma)	1959
94	I-A	Carl Knox, Texas Christian (Oklahoma St.)	1947
94	I-A	Preston Johnson, Southern Methodist (Pittsburgh)	1940
93	II	Elliot Mills, Carleton (Monmouth, Ill.)	1970
93	II	Kasper Fitins, Taylor (Georgetown, Ky.)	1966
93	II	Leroy Sweeney, Cal Poly Pomona (UC Riverside)	1960
93	I-A	Bob Handke, Drake (Wichita St.)	1949

ALL-PURPOSE RUNNING

Career Yards

Player, Team (Division[s])	Years	Rush	Rcv	PR	KO	Yds.
Johnny Bailey, Texas A&I (II)	1986-89	*6,320	452	20	1,011	*7,803
Kenny Gamble, Colgate (I-AA)	1984-87	5,220	536	104	1,763	7,623
Howard Stevens, Rand.-Macon (II); Louisville (I-A)	1968-69; 71-72	5,297	738	781	748	7,564
Napoleon McCallum, Navy (I-A)	$1981-85	4,179	796	858	1,339	7,172
Albert Fann, Cal St. Northridge (II)	1987-90	4,090	803	0	2,141	7,032
Curtis Delgardo, Portland St. (II)	$1986-90	4,178	1,258	318	1,188	6,942
Darrin Nelson, Stanford (I-A)	1977-78, 80-81	4,033	2,368	471	13	6,885
Eric Frees, Western Md. (III)	1988-91	5,281	392	47	1,158	6,878
Steve Roberts, Butler (II)	1986-89	4,623	1,201	272	578	6,674
Tony Dorsett, Pittsburgh (I-A)	1973-76	6,082	406	0	127	6,615
Paul Palmer, Temple (I-A)	1983-86	4,895	705	0	997	6,609
Charles White, Southern Cal (I-A)	1976-79	5,598	507	0	440	6,545
Joe Dudek, Plymouth St. (III)	1982-85	5,570	348	0	243	6,509
Chris Cobb, Eastern Ill. (II)	1976-79	5,042	520	37	478	6,077
Don Aleksiewicz, Hobart (II)	1969-72	4,525	470	320	748	6,063
Gary Trettel, St. Thomas (Minn.) (III)	1988-90	3,724	853	0	1,467	6,044
Archie Griffin, Ohio St. (I-A)	1972-75	5,177	286	0	540	6,003
Ron "Po" James, New Mexico St. (I-A)	1968-71	3,884	217	8	1,870	5,979
Eric Wilkerson, Kent (I-A)	1985-88	3,830	506	0	1,638	5,974

Record. $ See page 6 for explanation.

Career Yards Per Game

Player, Team (Division[s])	Years	G	Rush	Rcv	PR	KO	Yds.	Yd. PG
Sheldon Canley, San Jose St. (I-A)	1988-90	25	2,513	828	5	1,800	5,146	*205.8
Johnny Bailey, Texas A&I (II)	1986-89	39	*6,320	452	20	1,011	*7,803	200.1
Howard Stevens, Randolph Macon (II); Louisville (I-A)	1968-69; 71-72	38	5,297	738	781	748	7,564	199.1
Gary Trettel, St. Thomas (Minn.) (III)	1988-90	29	3,483	834	0	1,407	5,724	197.4
Billy Johnson, Widener (II; III)	1971-72; 73	28	3,737	27	43	989	5,404	193.0
O. J. Simpson, Southern Cal (I-A)	1967-68	19	3,124	235	0	307	3,666	192.9
Dave Meggett, Towson St. (I-AA)	1987-88	18	1,658	788	212	745	3,403	189.1

Record.

Season Yards

Player, Team (Division)	Year	Rush	Rcv	PR	KO	Yds.
Barry Sanders, Oklahoma St. (I-A)	†1988	*2,628	106	95	421	*3,250
Ryan Benjamin, Pacific (Cal.) (I-A)	†1991	1,581	612	4	798	2,995
Mike Pringle, Cal St. Fullerton (I-A)	†1989	1,727	249	0	714	2,690
Steve Roberts, Butler (II)	†1989	1,450	532	272	415	2,669
Paul Palmer, Temple (I-A)	†1986	1,866	110	0	657	2,633
Marcus Allen, Southern Cal (I-A)	†1981	2,342	217	0	0	2,559

Player, Team (Division)	Year	Rush	Rcv	PR	KO	Yds.
Sheldon Canley, San Jose St. (I-A)	1989	1,201	353	0	959	2,513
Mike Rozier, Nebraska (I-A)	1983	2,148	106	0	232	2,486
Johnny Bailey, Texas A&I (II)	†1986	2,011	54	20	340	2,425
Kenny Gamble, Colgate (I-AA)	†1986	1,816	198	40	391	2,425
Theo Blanco, Wis.-Stevens Point (III)	1987	454	1,616	245	103	2,418
Rick Wegher, South Dak. St. (II)	1984	1,317	264	0	824	2,405
Chuck Weatherspoon, Houston (I-A)	1989	1,146	735	415	95	2,391
Anthony Thompson, Indiana (I-A)	1989	1,793	201	0	394	2,388
Ricky Gales, Simpson (III)	†1989	2,035	102	0	248	2,385
Napoleon McCallum, Navy (I-A)	†1983	1,587	166	272	360	2,385
Gary Trettel, St. Thomas (Minn.) (III).............	1989	1,502	337	0	496	2,335
Michael Clemons, William & Mary (I-AA)	1986	1,065	516	330	423	2,334
Napoleon McCallum, Navy (I-A)	†1985	1,327	358	157	488	2,330
Gary Trettel, St. Thomas (Minn.) (III)	1990	1,620	388	0	319	2,327
Keith Byars, Ohio St. (I-A)	†1984	1,655	453	0	176	2,284

* *Record.*   † *National champion.*

Season Yards Per Game

Player, Team (Division)	Year	G	Rush	Rcv	PR	KO	Yds.	Yd. PG
Barry Sanders, Oklahoma St. (I-A)	†1988	11	*2,628	106	0	95	*3,250	*295.5
Steve Roberts, Butler (II)	†1989	10	1,450	532	272	415	2,669	266.9
Billy Johnson, Widener (II)	†1972	9	1,556	40	511	115	%2,265	251.7
Ryan Benjamin, Pacific (Cal.) (I-A)..........	†1991	12	1,581	612	4	798	2,995	249.6
Byron "Whizzer" White, Colorado (I-A)	†1937	8	1,121	0	587	159	$1,970	246.3
Mike Pringle, Cal St. Fullerton (I-A)	1989	11	1,727	249	0	714	2,690	244.6
Paul Palmer, Temple (I-A)	†1986	11	1,866	110	0	657	2,633	239.4
Ricky Gales, Simpson (III)	†1989	10	2,035	102	0	248	2,385	238.5
Gary Trettel, St. Thomas (Minn.) (III)........	1989	10	1,502	337	0	496	2,335	233.5
Gary Trettel, St. Thomas (Minn.) (III)........	1990	10	1,620	388	0	319	2,327	232.7

* *Record.*   † *National champion.*   % *Also includes 43 yards in interception returns.* $ *Also includes 103 yards in interception returns.*

SCORING

Career Points

Player, Team (Division[s])	Years	TD	XPt.	FG	Pts.
Joe Dudek, Plymouth St. (III)	1982-85	*79	0	0	*474
Walter Payton, Jackson St. (II)	1971-74	66	53	5	464
Johnny Bailey, Texas A&I (II)	1986-89	70	3	0	426
Roman Anderson, Houston (I-A)........................	1988-91	0	*213	70	423
Howard Stevens, Randolph-Macon (II); Louisville (I-A) ..	1968-69; 71-72	69	4	0	418
Dale Mills, Northeast Mo. St. (II)	1957-60	64	23	0	407
Carlos Huerta, Miami (Fla.) (I-A)	1988-91	0	178	73	397
Anthony Thompson, Indiana (I-A)	1986-89	65	4	0	394
Garney Henley, Huron (II)	1956-59	63	16	0	394
Derek Schmidt, Florida St. (I-A)........................	1984-87	0	174	73	393
Steve Roberts, Butler (II)	1986-89	63	4	0	386
Jeff Bentrim, North Dak. St. (II)	1983-86	64	2	0	††386
Marty Zendejas, Nevada (I-AA)	1984-87	0	169	72	385
Leo Lewis, Lincoln (Mo.) (II)	1951-54	64	0	0	384
Heath Sherman, Texas A&I (II)	1985-88	63	0	0	378
Billy Johnson, Widener (II; III)	1971-72; 73	62	0	0	372
¢Shawn Graves, Wofford (II)	1989-91	61	4	0	370
Tank Younger, Grambling (II)	1945-48	60	9	0	369
Luis Zendejas, Arizona St. (I-A)	1981-84	0	134	78	368
Bill Cooper, Muskingum (II)	1957-60	54	37	1	364
Charvez Foger, Nevada (I-AA)	1985-88	60	2	0	362
Ole Gunderson, St. Olaf (II)	1969-71	60	2	0	362
Jeff Jaeger, Washington (I-A)	1983-86	0	118	*80	358
Tony Dorsett, Pittsburgh (I-A)	1973-76	59	2	0	356
Glenn Davis, Army (I-A)	1943-46	59	0	0	354

* *Record.*   †† *Record for a quarterback.*   ¢ *Active player.*

Season Points

Player, Team (Division)	Year	TD	XPt.	FG	Pts.
Barry Sanders, Oklahoma St. (I-A)	†1988	*39	0	0	*234
Terry Metcalf, Long Beach St. (II)	1971	29	4	0	178
Mike Rozier, Nebraska (I-A)	†1983	29	0	0	174
Lydell Mitchell, Penn St. (I-A)	1971	29	0	0	174

Individual Collegiate Records

Player, Team (Division)	Year	TD	XPt.	FG	Pts.
Geoff Mitchell, Weber St. (I-AA)	†1991	28	1	0	170
Stanley Drayton, Allegheny (III)	†1991	28	0	0	168
Jim Switzer, Col. of Emporia (II)	†1963	28	0	0	168
Carl Herakovich, Rose-Hulman (II)	†1958	25	18	0	168
Ted Scown, Sul Ross St. (II)	†1948	28	0	0	168
Ricky Gales, Simpson (III)	†1989	26	10	0	166
Art Luppino, Arizona (I-A)	†1954	24	22	0	166
Leon Burns, Long Beach St. (II)	†1969	27	2	0	164
Jerry Rice, Mississippi Val. (I-AA)	†1984	27	0	0	162
Billy Johnson, Widener (II)	†1972	27	0	0	162
Mike Deutsch, North Dak. (II)	1972	27	0	0	162
Bobby Reynolds, Nebraska (I-A)	†1950	22	25	0	157

* Record.   † National champion.

Single-Game Points

Pts.	Div.	Player, Team (Opponent)	Date
48	I-A	Howard Griffith, Illinois (Southern Ill.)	Sept. 22, 1990
48	II	Paul Zaeske, North Park (North Central)	Oct. 12, 1968
48	II	Junior Wolf, Panhandle St. (St. Mary's, Kan.)	Nov. 8, 1958
44	I-A	Marshall Faulk, San Diego St. (Pacific, Cal.)	Sept. 14, 1991
43	I-A	Jim Brown, Syracuse (Colgate)	Nov. 17, 1956
42	I-A	Arnold "Showboat" Boykin, Mississippi (Mississippi St.)	Dec. 1, 1951
42	I-A	Fred Wendt, UTEP (New Mexico St.)	Nov. 25, 1948

1992 NCAA FOOTBALL

AWARD WINNERS

Florida State linebacker Marvin Jones was the only sophomore named to the 1991 consensus all-America team, and he will be the only returning defensive all-American in 1992. Three other underclassmen

CONSENSUS ALL-AMERICA SELECTIONS

103 Years of All-Americas, 1889-1991

In 1950, the National Collegiate Athletic Bureau (the NCAA's service bureau) compiled the first official comprehensive roster of all-time all-Americans.

The compilation of the all-America roster was supervised by a panel of analysts working in large part with the historical records contained in the files of the Dr. Baker Football Information Service.

The roster consists of only those players who were **first-team** selections on one or more of the all-America teams that were selected for the national audience and received nationwide circulation.

Not included are the thousands of players who received mention on all-America second or third teams, nor the numerous others who were selected by newspapers or agencies with circulations that were not primarily national and with viewpoints, therefore, that were not normally nationwide in scope.

Listed on the following pages are the consensus all-Americans (i.e., the players who were accorded a majority of votes at their positions by the selectors). (Included are the selections of 1889-97, 1909-12 and 1922 when there was only one selector.)

Symbols for Selectors

AA—All-America Board
AP—Associated Press
C—Walter Camp (published in Harper's Weekly 1897; in Collier's Magazine 1898-1924)
COL—Collier's Magazine (selections by Grantland Rice 1925-47; published American Football Coaches Association teams 1948-56, listed under FC)
CP—Central Press
FBW—Football World Magazine
FC—American Football Coaches Association (published in Saturday Evening Post Magazine 1945-47; in Collier's Magazine 1948-56; sponsored by General Mills 1957-59 and by Eastman Kodak from 1960)
FN—Football News
FW—Football Writers Association of America (published in Look Magazine 1946-70)
INS—International News Service (merged with United Press in 1958 to form UPI)
L—Look Magazine (published Football Writers Association of America teams, 1946-70, listed under FW)
LIB—Liberty Magazine
M—Frank Menke Syndicate
NM—Newsweek Magazine
NANA—North American Newspaper Alliance
NEA—Newspaper Enterprise Association
SN—Sporting News
UP—United Press (merged with International News Service in 1958 to form UPI)
UPI—United Press International
W—Caspar Whitney (published in The Week's Sport in association with Walter Camp 1889-90; published in Harper's Weekly 1891-96 and in Outing Magazine, which he owned, 1898-1908; Walter Camp substituted for Whitney, who was on a world sports tour, and selected Harper's Weekly's team for 1897)
WCF—Walter Camp Foundation

All-America Selections

Yr.	1889-1899 W	C		Yr.	1924-1934 C	INS	NEA	FBW	AA	LIB	AP	COL	UP	NANA	SN
89	X			24	X	X	X	X	X	X					
90	X			25		X	X	X	X	X	X	X	X		
91	X			26		X	X		X		X	X	X		
92	X			27		X	X		X		X	X	X	X	
93	X			28		X	X		X		X	X	X	X	
94	X			29		X	X		X		X	X	X	X	
95	X			30		X	X		X		X	X	X	X	
96	X			31		X	X		X	X	X	X	X		
97	X			32		X	X		X	X	X	X	X	X	
98	X	X		33		X	X		X	X	X	X	X	X	
99	X	X		34		X	X		X	X	X	X	X	X	X

1900-1912

Yr.	W	C
00	X	X
01	X	X
02	X	
03	X	X
04	X	X
05	X	X
06	X	X
07	X	X
08	X	
09		X
10		X
11		X
12		X

1913-1923

Yr.	C	INS	M	NEA	FBW
13	X	X			
14	X	X			
15	X	X			
16	X	X	X		
17	(*)	X	X	X	
18	X		X		
19	X		X		
20	X	X	X		
21	X				X
22	X				
23	X				X

1935-1936

Yr.	C	INS	NEA	FBW	AA	LIB	AP	COL	UP	NANA	SN
35		X	X		X	X	X	X	X	X	X
36		X	X		X	X	X	X	X	X	X

1937-1941

Yr.	INS	NEA	AA	LIB	AP	COL	UP	NANA	SN	N
37	X	X	X	X	X	X	X	X	X	X
38	X	X	X	X	X	X	X		X	X
39	X	X	X	X	X	X	X		X	X
40	X	X	X	X	X	X	X		X	X
41	X	X	X		X	X	X		X	X

1942-1957

Yr.	INS	NEA	AA	AP	COL	UP	SN	N	L	FBN	FW	FC
42	X	X	X	X	X	X	X	X	X			
43	X		X	X	X	X	X		X			
44	X	X	X	X	X	X	X	X	X	X		
45	X	X	X	X	X	X	X				X	X
46	X	X	X	X	X	X	X		(†)		X	X
47	X			X	X	X	X				X	X
48	(#)X			X	(‡)	X	X				X	X
49	X	X		X		X	X				X	X
50	X	X	X	X		X	X				X	X
51	X	X	X	X		X	X				X	X
52	X	X	X	X		X	X				X	X
53	X	X	X	X		X	X				X	X
54	X	X	X	X		X	X				X	X
55	X	X	X	X		X	X				X	X
56	X	X		X		X	X				X	X
57	X	X		X		X	X				X	X

1958-1962

Yr.	NEA	AP	UPI	SN	FW	FC
58	X	X	X	X	X	X
59	X	X	X	X	X	X
60	X	X	X	X	X	X
61	X	X	X	X	X	X
62	X	X	X	X	X	X

1963-1971

Yr.	NEA	AP	UPI	SN	FW	FC	CP
63	X	X	X	X	X	X	X
64	X	X	X		X	X	X
65	X	X	X		X	X	X
66	X	X	X		X	X	X
67	X	X	X		X	X	X
68	X	X	X		X	X	X
69	X	X	X		X	X	X
70	X	X	X		X	X	X
71	X	X	X		X	X	

1972-1974

Yr.	NEA	AP	UPI	FW	FC	WCF
72	X	X	X	X	X	X
73	X	X	X	X	X	X
74		X	X	X	X	X

1975-1982

Yr.	AP	UPI	FW	FC
75	X	X	X	X
76	X	X	X	X
77	X	X	X	X
78	X	X	X	X
79	X	X	X	X
80	X	X	X	X
81	X	X	X	X
82	X	X	X	X

1983-1986

Yr.	AP	UPI	FW	FC	WCF
83	X	X	X	X	X
84	X	X	X	X	X
85	X	X	X	X	X
86	X	X	X	X	X

1987-1991

Yr.	AP	UPI	FW	FC	WCF
87	X	X	X	X	X
88	X	X	X	X	X
89	X	X	X	X	X
90	X	X	X	X	X
91	X	X	X	X	X

* In 1917, Walter Camp selected an all-Service, all-America team composed of military personnel. † During 1946-70, Look Magazine published the Football Writers Association of America's selections, listed under FW. ‡ During 1948-56, Collier's Magazine published American Football Coaches Association's selections, listed under FC. # International News Service was the first to select offensive and defensive teams.

1889

E—Amos Alonzo Stagg, Yale; Arthur Cumnock, Harvard; T—Hector Cowan, Princeton; Charles Gill, Yale; G—Pudge Heffelfinger, Yale; John Cranston, Harvard; C—William George, Princeton; B— Edgar Allan Poe, Princeton; Roscoe Channing, Princeton; Knowlton Ames, Princeton; James Lee, Harvard.

1890

E—Frank Hallowell, Harvard; Ralph Warren, Princeton; T—Marshall Newell, Harvard; William Rhodes, Yale; G—Pudge Heffelfinger, Yale; Jesse Riggs, Princeton; C—John Cranston, Harvard; B— Thomas McClung, Yale; Sheppard Homans, Princeton; Dudley Dean, Harvard; John Corbett, Harvard.

1891

E—Frank Hinkey, Yale; John Hartwell, Yale; T—Wallace Winter, Yale; Marshall Newell, Harvard; G—Pudge Heffelfinger, Yale; Jesse Riggs, Princeton; C—John Adams, Pennsylvania; B—Philip King, Princeton; Everett Lake, Harvard; Thomas McClung, Yale; Sheppard Homans, Princeton.

1892

E—Frank Hinkey, Yale; Frank Hallowell, Harvard; T—Marshall Newell, Harvard; A. Hamilton Wallis, Yale; G—Arthur Wheeler, Princeton; Bertram Waters, Harvard; C—William Lewis, Harvard; B—Charles Brewer, Harvard; Vance McCormick, Yale; Philip King, Princeton; Harry Thayer, Pennsylvania.

1893

E—Frank Hinkey, Yale; Thomas Trenchard, Princeton; T—Langdon Lea, Princeton; Marshall Newell, Harvard; G—Arthur Wheeler, Princeton; William Hickok, Yale; C—William Lewis, Harvard; B—Philip King, Princeton; Charles Brewer, Harvard; Franklin Morse, Princeton; Frank Butterworth, Yale.

1894

E—Frank Hinkey, Yale; Charles Gelbert, Pennsylvania; T—Bertram Waters, Harvard; Langdon Lea, Princeton; G—Arthur Wheeler, Princeton; William Hickok, Yale; C—Philip Stillman, Yale; B—George Adee, Yale; Arthur Knipe, Pennsylvania; George Brooke, Pennsylvania; Frank Butterworth, Yale.

1895

E—Norman Cabot, Harvard; Charles Gelbert, Pennsylvania; T—Langdon Lea, Princeton; Fred Murphy, Yale; G—Charles Wharton, Pennsylvania; Dudley Riggs, Princeton; C—Alfred Bull, Pennsylvania; B—Clinton Wyckoff, Cornell; Samuel Thorne, Yale; Charles Brewer, Harvard; George Brooke, Pennsylvania.

1896

E—Norman Cabot, Harvard; Charles Gelbert, Pennsylvania; T—William Church, Princeton; Fred Murphy, Yale; G—Charles Wharton, Pennsylvania; Wylie Woodruff, Pennsylvania; C—Robert Gailey, Princeton; B—Clarence Fincke, Yale; Edgar Wrightington, Harvard; Addison Kelly, Princeton; John Baird, Princeton.

1897

E—Garrett Cochran, Princeton; John Hall, Yale; T—Burr Chamberlain, Yale; John Outland, Pennsylvania; G—T. Truxton Hare, Pennsylvania; Gordon Brown, Yale; C—Alan Doucette, Harvard; B— Charles DeSaulles, Yale; Benjamin Dibblee, Harvard; Addison Kelly, Princeton; John Minds, Pennsylvania.

1898

E—Lew Palmer, Princeton; John Hallowell, Harvard; T—Arthur Hillebrand, Princeton; Burr Chamberlain, Yale; G—T. Truxton Hare, Pennsylvania; Gordon Brown, Yale; Walter Boal, Harvard; C—Pete Overfield, Pennsylvania; William Cunningham, Michigan; B—Charles Daly, Harvard; Benjamin Dibblee, Harvard; John Outland, Pennsylvania; Clarence Herschberger, Chicago; Malcolm McBride, Yale; Charles Romeyn, Army.

1899

E—David Campbell, Harvard; Arthur Poe, Princeton; T—Arthur Hillebrand, Princeton; George Stillman, Yale; G—T. Truxton Hare, Pennsylvania; Gordon Brown, Yale; C—Pete Overfield, Pennsylvania; B—Charles Daly, Harvard; Josiah McCracken, Pennsylvania; Malcolm McBride, Yale; Isaac Seneca, Carlisle; Albert Sharpe, Yale; Howard Reiter, Princeton.

1900

E—John Hallowell, Harvard; David Campbell, Harvard; William Smith, Army; T—George Stillman, Yale; James Bloomer, Yale; G—Gordon Brown, Yale; T. Truxton Hare, Pennsylvania; C—Herman Olcott, Yale; Walter Bachman, Lafayette; B—Bill Morley, Columbia; George Chadwick, Yale; Perry Hale, Yale; William Fincke, Yale; Charles Daly, Harvard; Raymond Starbuck, Cornell.

1901

E— David Campbell, Harvard; Ralph Davis, Princeton; Edward Bowditch, Harvard; Neil Snow, Michigan; T—Oliver Cutts, Harvard; Paul Bunker, Army; Crawford Blagden, Harvard; G—William Warner, Cornell; William Lee, Harvard; Charles Barnard, Harvard; Sanford Hunt, Cornell; C—Henry Holt, Yale; Walter Bachman, Lafayette; B—Robert Kernan, Harvard; Charles Daly, Army; Thomas Graydon, Harvard; Harold Weekes, Columbia; Bill Morley, Columbia.

1902

E—Thomas Shevlin, Yale; Edward Bowditch, Harvard; T—Ralph Kinney, Yale; James Hogan, Yale; Paul Bunker, Army; G—Edgar Glass, Yale; John DeWitt, Princeton; William Warner, Cornell; C—Henry Holt, Yale; Robert Boyers, Army; B—Foster Rockwell, Yale; George Chadwick, Yale; Thomas Graydon, Harvard; Thomas Barry, Brown.

1903

E—Howard Henry, Princeton; Charles Rafferty, Yale; T—Daniel Knowlton, Harvard; James Hogan, Yale; Fred Schacht, Minnesota; G—John DeWitt, Princeton; Andrew Marshall, Harvard; James Bloomer, Yale; C—Henry Hooper, Dartmouth; B— Willie Heston, Michigan; J. Dana Kafer, Princeton; James Johnson, Carlisle; Richard Smith, Columbia; Myron Witham, Dartmouth; W. Ledyard Mitchell, Yale.

1904

E—Thomas Shevlin, Yale; Fred Speik, Chicago; T—James Hogan, Yale; James Cooney, Princeton; G—Frank Piekarski, Pennsylvania; Joseph Gilman, Dartmouth; Ralph Kinney, Yale; C—Arthur Tipton, Army; B—Daniel Hurley, Harvard; Walter Eckersall, Chicago; Vincent Stevenson, Pennsylvania; Willie Heston, Michigan; Andrew Smith, Pennsylvania; Foster Rockwell, Yale; Henry Torney, Army.

1905

E—Thomas Shevlin, Yale; Ralph Glaze, Dartmouth; Mark Catlin, Chicago; T—Otis Lamson, Pennsylvania; Beaton Squires, Harvard; Karl Brill, Harvard; G—Roswell Tripp, Yale; Francis Burr, Harvard; C—Robert Torrey, Pennsylvania; B—Walter Eckersall, Chicago; Howard Roome, Yale; John Hubbard, Amherst; James McCormick, Princeton; Guy Hutchinson, Yale; Daniel Hurley, Harvard; Henry Torney, Army.

1906

E—Robert Forbes, Yale; L. Casper Wister, Princeton; T—L. Horatio Biglow, Yale; James Cooney, Princeton; Charles Osborne, Harvard; G—Francis Burr, Harvard; Elmer Thompson, Cornell; August Ziegler, Pennsylvania; C—William Dunn, Penn St.; William Newman, Cornell; B—Walter Eckersall, Chicago; Hugh Knox, Yale; Edward Dillon, Princeton; John Mayhew, Brown; William Hollenback, Pennsylvania; Paul Veeder, Yale.

1907

E—Bill Dague, Navy; Clarence Alcott, Yale; Albert Exendine, Carlisle; L. Casper Wister, Princeton; T—Dexter Draper, Pennsylvania; L. Horatio Biglow, Yale; G—August Ziegler, Pennsylvania; William Erwin, Army; C—Adolph Schulz, Michigan; Patrick Grant, Harvard; B—John Wendell, Harvard; Thomas A. D. Jones, Yale; Edwin Harlan, Princeton; James McCormick, Princeton; Edward Coy, Yale; Peter Hauser, Carlisle.

1908

E—Hunter Scarlett, Pennsylvania; George Schildmiller, Dartmouth; T—Hamilton Fish, Harvard; Frank Horr, Syracuse; Percy Northcroft, Navy; G—Clark Tobin, Dartmouth; William Goebel, Yale; Hamlin Andrus, Yale; Bernard O'Rourke, Cornell; C—Charles Nourse, Harvard; B—Edward Coy, Yale; Frederick Tibbott, Princeton; William Hollenback, Pennsylvania; Walter Steffen, Chicago; Ed Lange, Navy; Hamilton Corbett, Harvard.

1909

E—Adrian Regnier, Brown; John Kilpatrick, Yale; T—Hamilton Fish, Harvard; Henry Hobbs, Yale; G—Albert Benbrook, Michigan; Hamlin Andrus, Yale; C—Carroll Cooney, Yale; B—Edward Coy, Yale; John McGovern, Minnesota; Stephen Philbin, Yale; Wayland Minot, Harvard.

1910

E—John Kilpatrick, Yale; Stanfield Wells, Michigan; T—Robert McKay, Harvard; James Walker, Minnesota; G—Robert Fisher, Harvard; Albert Benbrook, Michigan; C—Ernest Cozens, Pennsylvania; B—E. LeRoy Mercer, Pennsylvania; Percy Wendell, Harvard; Earl Sprackling, Brown; Talbot Pendleton, Princeton.

1911

E—Douglass Bomeisler, Yale; Sanford White, Princeton; T—Edward Hart, Princeton; Leland Devore, Army; G—Robert Fisher, Harvard; Joseph Duff, Princeton; C—Henry Ketcham, Yale; B—Jim Thorpe, Carlisle; Percy Wendell, Harvard; Arthur Howe, Yale; Jack Dalton, Navy.

1912

E—Samuel Felton, Harvard; Douglass Bomeisler, Yale; T—Wesley Englehorn, Dartmouth; Robert Butler, Wisconsin; G—Stanley Pennock, Harvard; John Logan, Princeton; C—Henry Ketcham, Yale; B—Charles Brickley, Harvard; Jim Thorpe, Carlisle; George Crowther, Brown; E. LeRoy Mercer, Pennsylvania.

1913

E—Robert Hogsett, Dartmouth; Louis Merrillat, Army; T—Harold Ballin, Princeton; Nelson Talbott, Yale; Miller Pontius, Michigan; Harvey Hitchcock, Harvard; G—John Brown, Navy; Stanley Pennock, Harvard; Ray Keeler, Wisconsin; C—Paul Des Jardien, Chicago; B—Charles Brickley, Harvard; Edward Mahan, Harvard; Jim Craig, Michigan; Ellery Huntington, Colgate; Gus Dorais, Notre Dame.

1914

E—Huntington Hardwick, Harvard; John O'Hearn, Cornell; Perry Graves, Illinois; T—Harold Ballin, Princeton; Walter Trumbull, Harvard; G—Stanley Pennock, Harvard; Ralph Chapman, Illinois; Clarence Spears, Dartmouth; C—John McEwan, Army; B—John Maulbetsch, Michigan; Edward Mahan, Harvard; Charles Barrett, Cornell; John Spiegel, Wash. & Jeff.; Harry LeGore, Yale.

1915

E—Murray Shelton, Cornell; Guy Chamberlin, Nebraska; T—Joseph Gilman, Harvard; Howard Buck, Wisconsin; G—Clarence Spears, Dartmouth; Harold White, Syracuse; C—Robert Peck, Pittsburgh; B—Charles Barrett, Cornell; Edward Mahan, Harvard; Richard King, Harvard; Bart Macomber, Illinois; Eugene Mayer, Virginia; Neno Jerry DaPrato, Michigan St.

1916

E—Bert Baston, Minnesota; James Herron, Pittsburgh; T—Clarence Horning, Colgate; D. Belford West, Colgate; G—Clinton Black, Yale; Harrie Dadmun, Harvard; Frank Hogg, Princeton; C—Robert Peck, Pittsburgh; B—Elmer Oliphant, Army; Oscar Anderson, Colgate; Fritz Pollard, Brown; Charles Harley, Ohio St.

1917

E—Charles Bolen, Ohio St.; Paul Robeson,

Rutgers; Henry Miller, Pennsylvania; T—Alfred Cobb; Syracuse; George Hauser, Minnesota; G—Dale Seis, Pittsburgh; John Sutherland, Pittsburgh; Eugene Neely, Dartmouth; C—Frank Rydzewski, Notre Dame; B—Elmer Oliphant, Army; Ben Boynton, Williams; Everett Strupper, Georgia Tech; Charles Harley, Ohio St.

1918

E—Paul Robeson, Rutgers; Bill Fincher, Georgia Tech; T—Wilbur Henry, Wash. & Jeff.; Leonard Hilty, Pittsburgh; Lou Usher, Syracuse; Joe Guyon, Georgia Tech; G—Joe Alexander, Syracuse; Lyman Perry, Navy; C—Ashel Day, Georgia Tech; John Depler, Illinois; B—Frank Murrey, Princeton; Tom Davies, Pittsburgh; Wolcott Roberts, Navy; George McLaren, Pittsburgh.

1919

E—Bob Higgins, Penn St.; Henry Miller, Pennsylvania; Lester Belding, Iowa; T—Wilbur Henry, Wash. & Jeff.; D. Belford West, Colgate; G—Joe Alexander, Syracuse; Adolph Youngstrom, Dartmouth; C—James Weaver, Centre; Charles Carpenter, Wisconsin; B—Charles Harley, Ohio St.; Ira Rodgers, West Va.; Edward Casey, Harvard; Bo McMillin, Centre; Ben Boynton, Williams.

1920

E—Luke Urban, Boston College; Charles Carney, Illinois; Bill Fincher, Georgia Tech; T—Stan Keck, Princeton; Ralph Scott, Wisconsin; G—Tim Callahan, Yale; Tom Woods, Harvard; Iolas Huffman, Ohio St.; C—Herb Stein, Pittsburgh; B—George Gipp, Notre Dame; Donold Lourie, Princeton; Gaylord Stinchcomb, Ohio St.; Charles Way, Penn St.

1921

E—Brick Muller, California; Eddie Anderson, Notre Dame; T—Dan McMillan, California; Iolas Huffman, Ohio St.; G—Frank Schwab, Lafayette; John Brown, Harvard; Stan Keck, Princeton; C—Herb Stein, Pittsburgh; B—Aubrey Devine, Iowa; Glenn Killinger, Penn St.; Bo McMillin, Centre; Malcolm Aldrich, Yale; Edgar Kaw, Cornell.

1922

E—Brick Muller, California; Wendell Taylor, Navy; T—C. Herbert Treat, Princeton; John Thurman, Pennsylvania; G—Frank Schwab, Lafayette; Charles Hubbard, Harvard; C—Ed Garbisch, Army; B—Harry Kipke, Michigan; Gordon Locke, Iowa; John Thomas, Chicago; Edgar Kaw, Cornell.

1923

E—Pete McRae, Syracuse; Ray Ecklund, Minnesota; Lynn Bomar, Vanderbilt; T—Century Milstead, Yale; Marty Below, Wisconsin; G—Charles Hubbard, Harvard; James McMillen, Illinois; C—Jack Blott, Michigan; B—George Pfann, Cornell; Red Grange, Illinois; William Mallory, Yale; Harry Wilson, Penn St.

Beginning in 1924, unanimous selections are indicated by (*).

1924

E—Jim Lawson, Stanford, 5-11, 190, Long Beach, Calif.; (tie) E—Dick Luman, Yale, 6-1, 176, Pinedale, Wyo.; E—Henry Wakefield, Vanderbilt, 5-10, 160, Petersburg, Tenn.; T—Ed McGinley, Pennsylvania, 5-11, 185, Swarthmore, Pa.; T—Ed Weir, Nebraska, 6-1, 194, Superior, Neb.; G—Joe Pondelik, Chicago, 5-11, 215, Cicero, Ill.; G—Carl Diehl, Dartmouth, 6-1, 205, Chicago, Ill.; C—Edwin Horrell, California, 5-11, 185, Pasadena, Calif.; B—*Red Grange, Illinois, 5-10, 170, Wheaton, Ill.; B—Harry Stuhldreher, Notre Dame, 5-7, 151, Massillon, Ohio; B—Jimmy Crowley, Notre Dame, 5-11, 162, Green Bay, Wis.; B—Elmer Layden, Notre Dame, 6-0, 162, Davenport, Ia.

1925

E—Bennie Oosterbaan, Michigan, 6-0, 180, Muskegon, Mich.; E—George Tully, Dartmouth, 5-10, 175, Orange, N.J.; T—*Ed Weir, Nebraska, 6-1, 194, Superior, Neb.; T—Ralph Chase, Pittsburgh, 6-3, 202, Easton, Pa.; G—Carl Diehl, Dartmouth, 6-1, 205, Chicago, Ill.; G—Ed Hess, Ohio St., 6-1, 190, Cincinnati, Ohio; C—Ed McMillan, Princeton, 6-0, 208, Pittsburgh, Pa.; B—*Andy Oberlander, Dartmouth, 6-0, 197, Everett, Mass.; B—Red Grange, Illinois, 5-10, 170, Wheaton, Ill.; B—Ernie Nevers, Stanford, 6-0, 200, Superior, Wis.; (tie) B—Benny Friedman, Michigan, 5-8, 170, Cleveland, Ohio; B—George Wilson, Washington, 5-11, 190, Everett, Wash.

1926

E—Bennie Oosterbaan, Michigan, 6-0, 186, Muskegon, Mich.; E—Vic Hanson, Syracuse, 5-10, 174, Syracuse, N.Y.; T—*Frank Wickhorst, Navy, 6-0, 218, Oak Park, Ill.; T—Bud Sprague, Army, 6-2, 210, Dallas, Tex.; G—Harry Connaughton, Georgetown, 6-2, 275, Philadelphia, Pa.; G—Bernie Shively, Illinois, 6-4, 208, Oliver, Ill.; C—Bud Boeringer, Notre Dame, 6-1, 186, St. Paul, Minn.; B—Benny Friedman, Michigan, 5-8, 172, Cleveland, Ohio; B—Mort Kaer, Southern Cal, 5-11, 167, Red Bluff, Calif.; B—Ralph Baker, Northwestern, 5-10, 172, Rockford, Ill.; B—Herb Joesting, Minnesota, 6-1, 192, Owatonna, Minn.

1927

E—*Bennie Oosterbaan, Michigan, 6-0, 186, Muskegon, Mich.; E—Tom Nash, Georgia, 6-3, 200, Washington, Ga.; T—Jesse Hibbs, Southern Cal, 5-11, 185, Glendale, Calif.; T—Ed Hake, Pennsylvania, 6-0, 190, Philadelphia, Pa.; G—Bill Webster, Yale, 6-0, 200, Shelton, Conn.; G—John Smith, Notre Dame, 5-9, 164, Hartford, Conn.; (tie) C—Larry Bettencourt, St. Mary's (Cal.), 5-10, 187, Centerville, Calif.; C—John Charlesworth, Yale, 5-11, 198, North Adams, Mass.; B—*Gibby Welch, Pittsburgh, 5-11, 170, Parkersburg, W. Va.; B—Morley Drury, Southern Cal, 6-0, 185, Long Beach, Calif.; B—Red Cagle, Army, 5-9, 167, Merryville, La.; B—Herb Joesting, Minnesota, 6-1, 192, Owatonna, Minn.

1928

E—Irv Phillips, California, 6-1, 188, Salinas, Calif.; E—Wes Fesler, Ohio St., 6-0, 173, Youngstown, Ohio; T—Otto Pommerening, Michigan, 6-0, 178, Ann Arbor, Mich.; T—Mike Getto, Pittsburgh, 6-2, 198, Jeannette, Pa.; G—Seraphim Post, Stanford, 6-0, 190, Berkeley, Calif.; (tie) Don Robesky, Stanford, 5-11, 198, Bakersfield, Calif.; G—Edward Burke, Navy, 6-0, 180, Larksville, Pa.; C—Pete Pund, Georgia

1992 NCAA FOOTBALL

Tech, 6-0, 195, Augusta, Ga.; B—*Red Cagle, Army, 5-9, 167, Merryville, La.; B—Paul Scull, Pennsylvania, 5-8, 187, Bala, Pa.; B—Ken Strong, New York U., 6-0, 201, West Haven, Conn.; (tie) Howard Harpster, Carnegie Tech, 6-1, 160, Akron, Ohio; B—Charles Carroll, Washington, 6-0, 190, Seattle, Wash.

1929

E—*Joe Donchess, Pittsburgh, 6-0, 175, Youngstown, Ohio; E—Wes Fesler, Ohio St., 6-0, 183, Youngstown, Ohio; T—Bronko Nagurski, Minnesota, 6-2, 217, International Falls, Minn.; T—Elmer Sleight, Purdue, 6-2, 193, Morris, Ill.; G—Jack Cannon, Notre Dame, 5-11, 193, Columbus, Ohio; G—Ray Montgomery, Pittsburgh, 6-1, 188, Wheeling, W. Va.; C—Ben Ticknor, Harvard, 6-2, 193, New York, N.Y.; B—*Frank Carideo, Notre Dame, 5-7, 175, Mount Vernon, N.Y.; B—Ralph Welch, Purdue, 6-1, 189, Whitesboro, Tex.; B—Red Cagle, Army, 5-9, 167, Merryville, La.; B—Gene McEver, Tennessee, 5-10, 185, Bristol, Va.

1930

E—*Wes Fesler, Ohio St., 6-0, 185, Youngstown, Ohio; E—Frank Baker, Northwestern, 6-2, 175, Cedar Rapids, Ia.; T—*Fred Sington, Alabama, 6-2, 215, Birmingham, Ala.; T—Milo Lubratovich, Wisconsin, 6-2, 216, Duluth, Minn.; G—Ted Beckett, California, 6-1, 190, Oroville, Calif.; G—Barton Koch, Baylor, 5-10, 195, Temple, Tex.; C—*Ben Ticknor, Harvard, 6-2, 193, New York, N.Y.; B—*Frank Carideo, Notre Dame, 5-7, 175, Mount Vernon, N.Y.; B—Marchy Schwartz, Notre Dame, 5-11, 172, Bay St. Louis, Miss.; B—Erny Pinckert, Southern Cal, 6-0, 189, San Bernardino, Calif.; B—Leonard Macaluso, Colgate, 6-2, 210, East Aurora, N.Y.

1931

E—*Jerry Dalrymple, Tulane, 5-10, 175, Arkadelphia, Ark.; E—Vernon Smith, Georgia, 6-2, 190, Macon, Ga.; T—Jesse Quatse, Pittsburgh, 5-8, 198, Greensburg, Pa.; (tie) T—Jack Riley, Northwestern, 6-2, 218, Wilmette, Ill.; T—Dallas Marvil, Northwestern, 6-3, 227, Laurel, Del.; G—Biggie Munn, Minnesota, 5-10, 217, Minneapolis, Minn.; G—John Baker, Southern Cal, 5-10, 185, Kingsburg, Calif.; C—Tommy Yarr, Notre Dame, 5-11, 197, Chimacum, Wash.; G—Gus Shaver, Southern Cal, 5-11, 185, Covina, Calif.; B—Marchy Schwartz, Notre Dame, 5-11, 178, Bay St. Louis, Miss.; B—Pug Rentner, Northwestern, 6-1, 185, Joliet, Ill.; B—Barry Wood, Harvard, 6-1, 173, Milton, Mass.

1932

E—*Paul Moss, Purdue, 6-2, 185, Terre Haute, Ind.; E—Joe Skladany, Pittsburgh, 5-10, 185, Larksville, Pa.; T—*Joe Kurth, Notre Dame, 6-2, 204, Madison, Wis.; T—*Ernie Smith, Southern Cal, 6-2, 215, Los Angeles, Calif.; G—Milt Summerfelt, Army, 6-0, 181, Benton Harbor, Mich.; G—Bill Corbus, Stanford, 5-11, 188, Vallejo, Calif.; C—Pete Gracey, Vanderbilt, 6-0, 188, Franklin, Tenn.; B—*Harry Newman, Michigan, 5-7, 175, Detroit, Mich.; B—*Warren Heller, Pittsburgh, 6-0, 170, Steelton, Pa.; B—Don Zimmerman, Tulane, 5-10, 190, Lake Charles, La.; B—Jimmy Hitchcock, Auburn, 5-11, 172, Union Springs, Ala.

1933

E—Joe Skladany, Pittsburgh, 5-10, 190, Larksville, Pa.; E—Paul Geisler, Centenary, 6-2, 189, Berwick, La.; T—Fred Crawford, Duke, 6-2, 195, Waynesville, N.C.; T—Francis Wistert, Michigan, 6-3, 212, Chicago, Ill.; G—Bill Corbus, Stanford, 5-11, 195, Vallejo, Calif.; G—Aaron Rosenberg, Southern Cal, 6-0, 210, Los Angeles, Calif.; C—*Chuck Bernard, Michigan, 6-2, 215, Benton Harbor, Mich.; B—*Cotton Warburton, Southern Cal, 5-7, 147, San Diego, Calif.; B—George Sauer, Nebraska, 6-2, 195, Lincoln, Neb.; B—Beattie Feathers, Tennessee, 5-10, 180, Bristol, Va.; B—Duane Purvis, Purdue, 6-1, 190, Mattoon, Ill.

1934

E—Don Hutson, Alabama, 6-1, 185, Pine Bluff, Ark.; E—Frank Larson, Minnesota, 6-3, 190, Duluth, Minn.; T—Bill Lee, Alabama, 6-2, 225, Eutaw, Ala.; T—Bob Reynolds, Stanford, 6-4, 220, Okmulgee, Okla.; G—Chuck Hartwig, Pittsburgh, 6-0, 190, Benwood, W. Va.; G—Bill Bevan, Minnesota, 5-11, 194, St. Paul, Minn.; C—Jack Robinson, Notre Dame, 6-3, 195, Huntington, N.Y.; B—Bobby Grayson, Stanford, 5-11, 186, Portland, Ore.; B—Pug Lund, Minnesota, 5-11, 185, Rice Lake, Wis.; B—Dixie Howell, Alabama, 5-10, 164, Hartford, Ala.; B—Fred Borries, Navy, 6-0, 175, Louisville, Ky.

1935

E—Wayne Millner, Notre Dame, 6-0, 184, Salem, Mass.; (tie) E—James Moscrip, Stanford, 6-0, 186, Adena, Ohio; E—Gaynell Tinsley, Louisiana St., 6-0, 188, Homer, La.; T—Ed Widseth, Minnesota, 6-2, 220, McIntosh, Minn.; T—Larry Lutz, California, 6-0, 201, Santa Ana, Calif.; G—John Weller, Princeton, 6-0, 195, Wynnewood, Pa.; (tie) G—Sidney Wagner, Michigan St., 5-11, 186, Lansing, Mich.; G—J. C. Wetsel, Southern Methodist, 6-0, 185, Dallas, Tex.; (tie) C—Gomer Jones, Ohio St., 5-8, 210, Cleveland, Ohio; C—Darrell Lester, Texas Christian, 6-4, 218, Jacksboro, Tex.; B—*Jay Berwanger, Chicago, 6-0, 195, Dubuque, Ia.; B—*Bobby Grayson, Stanford, 5-11, 190, Portland, Ore.; B—Bobby Wilson, Southern Methodist, 5-10, 147, Corsicana, Tex.; B—Riley Smith, Alabama, 6-1, 195, Columbus, Miss.

1936

E—*Larry Kelley, Yale, 6-1, 190, Williamsport, Pa.; E—*Gaynell Tinsley, Louisiana St., 6-0, 196, Homer, La.; T—*Ed Widseth, Minnesota, 6-2, 220, McIntosh, Minn.; T—Averell Daniell, Pittsburgh, 6-3, 200, Mt. Lebanon, Pa.; G—Steve Reid, Northwestern, 5-9, 192, Chicago, Ill.; G—Max Starcevich, Washington, 5-10, 198, Duluth, Minn.; (tie) C—Alex Wojciechowicz, Fordham, 6-0, 192, South River, N.J.; C—Mike Basrak, Duquesne, 6-1, 210, Bellaire, Ohio; B—Sammy Baugh, Texas Christian, 6-2, 180, Sweetwater, Tex.; B—Ace Parker, Duke, 5-11, 175, Portsmouth, Va.; B—Ray Buivid, Marquette, 6-1, 193, Port

Washington, Wis.; B—Sam Francis, Nebraska, 6-1, 207, Oberlin, Kans.

1937

E—Chuck Sweeney, Notre Dame, 6-0, 190, Bloomington, Ill.; E—Andy Bershak, North Caro., 6-0, 190, Clairton, Pa.; T—Ed Franco, Fordham, 5-8, 196, Jersey City, N.J.; T—Tony Matisi, Pittsburgh, 6-0, 224, Endicott, N.Y.; G—Joe Routt, Texas A&M, 6-0, 193, Chappel Hill, Tex.; G—Leroy Monsky, Alabama, 6-0, 198, Montgomery, Ala.; C—Alex Wojciechowicz, Fordham, 6-0, 196, South River, N.J.; B—*Clint Frank, Yale, 5-10, 190, Evanston, Ill.; B—Marshall Goldberg, Pittsburgh, 5-11, 185, Elkins, W. Va.; B—Byron "Whizzer" White, Colorado, 6-1, 185, Wellington, Colo.; B—Sam Chapman, California, 6-0, 190, Tiburon, Calif.

1938

E—Waddy Young, Oklahoma, 6-2, 203, Ponca City, Okla.; (tie) E—Brud Holland, Cornell, 6-1, 205, Auburn, N.Y.; E—Bowden Wyatt, Tennessee, 6-1, 190, Kingston, Tenn.; T— *Ed Beinor, Notre Dame, 6-2, 207, Harvey, Ill.; T—Alvord Wolff, Santa Clara, 6-2, 220, San Francisco, Calif.; G—*Ralph Heikkinen, Michigan, 5-10, 185, Ramsey, Mich.; G—Ed Bock, Iowa St., 6-0, 202, Fort Dodge, Ia.; C—Ki Aldrich, Texas Christian, 5-11, 195, Temple, Tex.; B—*Davey O'Brien, Texas Christian, 5-7, 150, Dallas, Tex.; B—*Marshall Goldberg, Pittsburgh, 6-0, 190, Elkins, W. Va.; B—Bob MacLeod, Dartmouth, 6-0, 190, Glen Ellyn, Ill.; B—Vic Bottari, California, 5-9, 182, Vallejo, Calif.

1939

E—Esco Sarkkinen, Ohio St., 6-0, 192, Fairport Harbor, Ohio; E—Ken Kavanaugh, Louisiana St., 6-3, 203, Little Rock, Ark.; T—Nick Drahos, Cornell, 6-3, 200, Cedarhurst, N.Y.; T—Harley McCollum, Tulane, 6-4, 235, Wagoner, Okla.; G—*Harry Smith, Southern Cal, 5-11, 218, Ontario, Calif.; G—Ed Molinski, Tennessee, 5-10, 190, Massillon, Ohio; C—John Schiechl, Santa Clara, 6-2, 220, San Francisco, Calif.; B—Nile Kinnick, Iowa, 5-8, 167, Omaha, Neb.; B—Tom Harmon, Michigan, 6-0, 195, Gary, Ind.; B—John Kimbrough, Texas A&M, 6-2, 210, Haskell, Tex.; B—George Cafego, Tennessee, 6-0, 174, Scarbro, W. Va.

1940

E—Gene Goodreault, Boston College, 5-10, 184, Haverhill, Mass.; E—Dave Rankin, Purdue, 6-1, 190, Warsaw, Ind.; T—Nick Drahos, Cornell, 6-3, 212, Cedarhurst, N.Y.; (tie) T—Alf Bauman, Northwestern, 6-1, 210, Chicago, Ill.; T—Urban Odson, Minnesota, 6-3, 247, Clark, S.D.; G—*Bob Suffridge, Tennessee, 6-0, 190, Knoxville, Tenn.; G—Marshall Robnett, Texas A&M, 6-1, 205, Klondike, Tex.; C—Rudy Mucha, Washington, 6-2, 210, Chicago, Ill.; B—*Tom Harmon, Michigan, 6-0, 195, Gary, Ind.; B—*John Kimbrough, Texas A&M, 6-2, 221, Haskell, Tex.; B—Frank Albert, Stanford, 5-9, 170, Glendale, Calif.; B—George Franck, Minnesota, 6-0, 175, Davenport, Ia.

1941

E—Holt Rast, Alabama, 6-1, 185, Birmingham, Ala.; E—Bob Dove, Notre Dame, 6-2, 195, Youngstown, Ohio; T—Dick Wildung, Minnesota, 6-0, 210, Luverne, Minn.; T—Ernie Blandin, Tulane, 6-3, 245, Keighley, Kans.; G—*Endicott Peabody, Harvard, 6-0, 181, Syracuse, N.Y.; G—Ray Frankowski, Washington, 5-10, 210, Hammond, Ind.; C—Darold Jenkins, Missouri, 6-0, 195, Higginsville, Mo.; B—Bob Westfall, Michigan, 5-8, 190, Ann Arbor, Mich.; B—Bruce Smith, Minnesota, 6-0, 193, Faribault, Minn.; B—Frank Albert, Stanford, 5-9, 173, Glendale, Calif.; (tie) B—Bill Dudley, Virginia, 5-10, 175, Bluefield, Va.; B—Frank Sinkwich, Georgia, 5-8, 180, Youngstown, Ohio.

1942

E—*Dave Schreiner, Wisconsin, 6-2, 198, Lancaster, Wis.; E—Bob Dove, Notre Dame, 6-2, 195, Youngstown, Ohio; T—Dick Wildung, Minnesota, 6-0, 215, Luverne, Minn.; T—Albert Wistert, Michigan, 6-2, 205, Chicago, Ill.; G—Chuck Taylor, Stanford, 5-11, 200, San Jose, Calif.; (tie) G—Harvey Hardy, Georgia Tech, 5-10, 185, Thomaston, Ga.; G—Julie Franks, Michigan, 6-0, 187, Hamtramck, Mich.; C—Joe Domnanovich, Alabama, 6-1, 200, South Bend, Ind.; B—*Frank Sinkwich, Georgia, 5-8, 185, Youngstown, Ohio; B—Paul Governali, Columbia, 5-11, 186, New York, N.Y.; B—Mike Holovak, Boston College, 6-2, 214, Lansford, Pa.; B—Billy Hillenbrand, Indiana, 6-0, 195, Evansville, Ind.

1943

E—Ralph Heywood, Southern Cal, 6-2, 195, Huntington Park, Calif.; E—John Yonakor, Notre Dame, 6-4, 220, Dorchester, Mass.; T—Jim White, Notre Dame, 6-2, 210, Edgewater, N.J.; T—Don Whitmire, Navy, 5-11, 215, Decatur, Ala.; G—Alex Agase, Purdue, 5-10, 190, Evanston, Ill.; G—Pat Filley, Notre Dame, 5-8, 175, South Bend, Ind.; C—*Casimir Myslinski, Army, 5-11, 186, Steubenville, Ohio; B—*Bill Daley, Michigan, 6-2, 206, St. Cloud, Minn.; B—Angelo Bertelli, Notre Dame, 6-1, 173, West Springfield, Mass.; B—Creighton Miller, Notre Dame, 6-0, 185, Wilmington, Del.; B—Bob Odell, Pennsylvania, 5-11, 182, Sioux City, Ia.

1944

E—Phil Tinsley, Georgia Tech, 6-1, 188, Bessemer, Ala.; (tie) E—Paul Walker, Yale, 6-3, 203, Oak Park, Ill.; E—Jack Dugger, Ohio St., 6-3, 210, Canton, Ohio; T—*Don Whitmire, Navy, 5-11, 215, Decatur, Ala.; T—John Ferraro, Southern Cal, 6-3, 235, Maywood, Calif.; G—Bill Hackett, Ohio St., 5-9, 191, London, Ohio; G—Ben Chase, Navy, 6-1, 195, San Diego, Calif.; C—John Tavener, Indiana, 6-0, 220, Granville, Ohio; B—*Les Horvath, Ohio St., 5-10, 167, Parma, Ohio; B—Glenn Davis, Army, 5-9, 170, Claremont, Calif.; B—Doc Blanchard, Army, 6-0, 205, Bishopville, S. C.; B—Bob Jenkins, Navy, 6-1, 195, Talladega, Ala.

1945

E—Dick Duden, Navy, 6-2, 203, New York, N.Y.; E—(tie) Hubert Bechtol, Texas, 6-2, 190, Lubbock, Tex.; E—Bob Ravensberg, Indiana, 6-1, 180, Bellevue, Ky.; E—Max Morris, Northwestern, 6-2, 195, West Frankfort, Ill.; T—Tex Coulter, Army, 6-3, 220, Fort Worth, Tex.; T—George Savitsky, Pennsylvania, 6-3, 250, Camden, N.J.; G—*Warren Amling, Ohio St., 6-0, 197, Pana, Ill.; G—John Green, Army, 5-11, 190, Shelbyville, Ky.; C—Vaughn Mancha, Alabama, 6-0, 235, Birmingham, Ala.; B—*Glenn Davis, Army, 5-9, 170, Claremont, Calif.; B—*Doc Blanchard, Army, 6-0, 205, Bishopville, S.C.; B—*Herman Wedemeyer, St. Mary's (Cal.), 5-10, 173, Honolulu, Hawaii; B—Bob Fenimore, Oklahoma St., 6-2, 188, Woodward, Okla.

1946

E—*Burr Baldwin, UCLA, 6-1, 196, Bakersfield, Calif.; E—(tie) Hubert Bechtol, Texas, 6-2, 201, Lubbock, Tex.; E—Hank Foldberg, Army, 6-1, 200, Dallas, Tex.; T—George Connor, Notre Dame, 6-3, 225, Chicago, Ill.; (tie) T—Warren Amling, Ohio St., 6-0, 197, Pana, Ill.; T—Dick Huffman, Tennessee, 6-2, 230, Charleston, W. Va.; G—Alex Agase, Illinois, 5-10, 191, Evanston, Ill.; G—Weldon Humble, Rice, 6-1, 214, San Antonio, Tex.; C—Paul Duke, Georgia Tech, 6-1, 210, Atlanta, Ga.; B—*John Lujack, Notre Dame, 6-0, 180, Connellsville, Pa.; B—*Charley Trippi, Georgia, 5-11, 185, Pittston, Pa.; B—*Glenn Davis, Army, 5-9, 170, Claremont, Calif.; B—*Doc Blanchard, Army, 6-0, 205, Bishopville, S.C.

1947

E—Paul Cleary, Southern Cal, 6-1, 195, Santa Ana, Calif.; E—Bill Swiacki, Columbia, 6-2, 198, Southbridge, Mass.; T—Bob Davis, Georgia Tech, 6-4, 220, Columbus, Ga.; T—George Connor, Notre Dame, 6-3, 225, Chicago, Ill.; G—Joe Steffy, Army, 5-11, 190, Chattanooga, Tenn.; G—Bill Fischer, Notre Dame, 6-2, 230, Chicago, Ill.; C—Chuck Bednarik, Pennsylvania, 6-3, 220, Bethlehem, Pa.; B—*John Lujack, Notre Dame, 6-0, 180, Connellsville, Pa.; B—*Bob Chappuis, Michigan, 6-0, 180, Toledo, Ohio; B—Doak Walker, Southern Methodist, 5-11, 170, Dallas, Tex.; (tie) B—Charley Conerly, Mississippi, 6-0, 184, Clarksdale, Miss.; B—Bobby Layne, Texas, 6-0, 191, Dallas, Tex.

1948

E—Dick Rifenburg, Michigan, 6-3, 197, Saginaw, Mich.; E—Leon Hart, Notre Dame, 6-4, 225, Turtle Creek, Pa.; T—Leo Nomellini, Minnesota, 6-2, 248, Chicago, Ill.; T—Alvin Wistert, Michigan, 6-3, 218, Chicago, Ill.; G—Buddy Burris, Oklahoma, 5-11, 214, Muskogee, Okla.; G—Bill Fischer, Notre Dame, 6-2, 233, Chicago, Ill.; C—Chuck Bednarik, Pennsylvania, 6-3, 220, Bethlehem, Pa.; B—*Doak Walker, Southern Methodist, 5-11, 168, Dallas, Tex.; B—Charlie Justice, North Caro., 5-10, 165, Asheville, N.C.; B—Jackie Jensen, California, 5-11, 195, Oakland, Calif.; (tie) B—Emil Sitko, Notre Dame, 5-8, 180, Fort Wayne, Ind.; B—Clyde Scott, Arkansas, 6-0, 175, Smackover, Ark.

1949

E—*Leon Hart, Notre Dame, 6-5, 260, Turtle Creek, Pa.; E—James Williams, Rice, 6-0, 197, Waco, Tex.; T—Leo Nomellini, Minnesota, 6-2, 255, Chicago, Ill.; T—Alvin Wistert, Michigan, 6-3, 223, Chicago, Ill.; G—*Rod Franz, California, 6-1, 198, San Francisco, Calif.; G—Ed Bagdon, Michigan St., 5-10, 200, Dearborn, Mich.; C—*Clayton Tonnemaker, Minnesota, 6-3, 240, Minneapolis, Minn.; B—*Emil Sitko, Notre Dame, 5-8, 180, Fort Wayne, Ind.; B—Doak Walker, Southern Methodist, 5-11, 170, Dallas, Tex.; B—Arnold Galiffa, Army, 6-2, 190, Donora, Pa.; B—Bob Williams, Notre Dame, 6-1, 180, Baltimore, Md.

1950

E—*Dan Foldberg, Army, 6-1, 185, Dallas, Tex.; E—Bill McColl, Stanford, 6-4, 225, San Diego, Calif.; T—Bob Gain, Kentucky, 6-3, 230, Weirton, W. Va.; T—Jim Weatherall, Oklahoma, 6-4, 220, White Deer, Tex.; G—Bud McFadin, Texas, 6-3, 225, Iraan, Tex.; G—Les Richter, California, 6-2, 220, Fresno, Calif.; C—Jerry Groom, Notre Dame, 6-3, 215, Des Moines, Ia.; B—*Vic Janowicz, Ohio St., 5-9, 189, Elyria, Ohio; B—Kyle Rote, Southern Methodist, 6-0, 190, San Antonio, Tex.; B—Babe Parilli, Kentucky, 6-1, 183, Rochester, Pa.; B—Leon Heath, Oklahoma, 6-1, 195, Hollis, Okla.

1951

E—*Bill McColl, Stanford, 6-4, 225, San Diego, Calif.; E—Bob Carey, Michigan St., 6-5, 215, Charlevoix, Mich.; T—*Don Coleman, Michigan St., 5-10, 185, Flint, Mich.; T—*Jim Weatherall, Oklahoma, 6-4, 230, White Deer, Tex.; G—*Bob Ward, Maryland, 5-10, 185, Elizabeth, N.J.; G—Les Richter, California, 6-2, 230, Fresno, Calif.; C—Dick Hightower, Southern Methodist, 6-1, 215, Tyler, Tex.; B—*Dick Kazmaier, Princeton, 5-11, 171, Maumee, Ohio; B—*Hank Lauricella, Tennessee, 5-10, 169, New Orleans, La.; B—Babe Parilli, Kentucky, 6-1, 188, Rochester, Pa.; B—Johnny Karras, Illinois, 5-11, 171, Argo, Ill.

1952

E—Frank McPhee, Princeton, 6-3, 203, Youngstown, Ohio; E—Bernie Flowers, Purdue, 6-1, 189, Erie, Pa.; T—Dick Modzelewski, Maryland, 6-0, 235, West Natrona, Pa.; T—Hal Miller, Georgia Tech, 6-4, 235, Kingsport, Tenn.; G—John Michels, Tennessee, 5-10, 195, Philadelphia, Pa.; G—Elmer Wilhoite, Southern Cal, 6-2, 216, Winton, Calif.; C—Donn Moomaw, UCLA, 6-4, 220, Santa Ana, Calif.; B—*Jack Scarbath, Maryland, 6-1, 190, Baltimore, Md.; B—*Johnny Lattner, Notre Dame, 6-1, 190, Chicago, Ill.; B—Billy Vessels, Oklahoma, 6-0, 185, Cleveland, Okla.; B—Jim Sears, Southern Cal, 5-9, 167, Inglewood, Calif.

1953

E—Don Dohoney, Michigan St., 6-1, 193, Ann Arbor, Mich.; E—Carlton Massey, Texas, 6-4, 210, Rockwall, Tex.; T—*Stan Jones, Maryland, 6-0, 235, Lemoyne, Pa.; T—Art Hunter, Notre Dame, 6-2, 226, Akron, Ohio; G—J. D. Roberts, Oklahoma, 5-10, 210, Dallas, Tex.; G—Crawford Mims, Mississippi, 5-10, 200, Greenwood, Miss.; C—Larry Morris, Georgia Tech, 6-0, 205, Decatur, Ga.; B—*Johnny Lattner, Notre Dame, 6-1, 190, Chicago, Ill.; B—*Paul Giel, Minnesota, 5-11, 185, Winona, Minn.; B—

Paul Cameron, UCLA, 6-0, 185, Burbank, Calif.; B—J. C. Caroline, Illinois, 6-0, 184, Columbia, S.C.

1954

E—Max Boydston, Oklahoma, 6-2, 207, Muskogee, Okla.; E—Ron Beagle, Navy, 6-0, 185, Covington, Ky.; T—Jack Ellena, UCLA, 6-3, 214, Susanville, Calif.; T—Sid Fournet, Louisiana St., 5-11, 225, Baton Rouge, La.; G—*Bud Brooks, Arkansas, 5-11, 200, Wynne, Ark.; G—Calvin Jones, Iowa, 6-0, 200, Steubenville, Ohio; C—Kurt Burris, Oklahoma, 6-1, 209, Muskogee, Okla.; B—*Ralph Guglielmi, Notre Dame, 6-0, 185, Columbus, Ohio; B—*Howard Cassady, Ohio St., 5-10, 177, Columbus, Ohio; B—*Alan Ameche, Wisconsin, 6-0, 215, Kenosha, Wis.; B—Dicky Maegle, Rice, 6-0, 175, Taylor, Tex.

1955

E—*Ron Beagle, Navy, 6-0, 186, Covington, Ky.; E—Ron Kramer, Michigan, 6-3, 218, East Detroit, Mich.; T—Norman Masters, Michigan St., 6-2, 225, Detroit, Mich.; T—Bruce Bosley, West Va., 6-2, 225, Green Bank, W. Va.; G—Bo Bolinger, Oklahoma, 5-10, 206, Muskogee, Okla.; (tie) G—Calvin Jones, Iowa, 6-0, 220, Steubenville, Ohio; G—Hardiman Cureton, UCLA, 6-0, 213, Duarte, Calif.; C—*Bob Pellegrini, Maryland, 6-2, 225, Yatesboro, Pa.; B—*Howard Cassady, Ohio St., 5-10, 172, Columbus, Ohio; B—*Jim Swink, Texas Christian, 6-1, 180, Rusk, Tex.; B—Earl Morrall, Michigan St., 6-1, 180, Muskegon, Mich.; B—Paul Hornung, Notre Dame, 6-2, 205, Louisville, Ky.

1956

E—*Joe Walton, Pittsburgh, 5-11, 205, Beaver Falls, Pa.; E—*Ron Kramer, Michigan, 6-3, 220, East Detroit, Mich.; T—John Witte, Oregon St., 6-2, 232, Klamath Falls, Ore.; T—Lou Michaels, Kentucky, 6-2, 229, Swoyersville, Pa.; G—*Jim Parker, Ohio St., 6-2, 251, Toledo, Ohio; G—*Bill Glass, Baylor, 6-4, 220, Corpus Christi, Tex.; C—*Jerry Tubbs, Oklahoma, 6-2, 205, Breckenridge, Tex.; B—*Jim Brown, Syracuse, 6-2, 212, Manhasset, N.Y.; B—*John Majors, Tennessee, 5-10, 162, Huntland, Tenn.; B—Tommy McDonald, Oklahoma, 5-9, 169, Albuquerque, N.M.; B—John Brodie, Stanford, 6-1, 190, Oakland, Calif.

1957

E—*Jimmy Phillips, Auburn, 6-2, 205, Alexander City, Ala.; E—Dick Wallen, UCLA, 6-0, 185, Alhambra, Calif.; T—Lou Michaels, Kentucky, 6-2, 235, Swoyersville, Pa.; T—Alex Karras, Iowa, 6-2, 233, Gary, Ind.; G—Bill Krisher, Oklahoma, 6-1, 213, Midwest City, Okla.; G—Al Ecuyer, Notre Dame, 5-10, 190, New Orleans, La.; C—Dan Currie, Michigan St., 6-3, 225, Detroit, Mich.; B—*John David Crow, Texas A&M, 6-2, 214, Springhill, La.; B—Walt Kowalczyk, Michigan St., 6-0, 205, Westfield, Mass.; B—Bob Anderson, Army, 6-2, 200, Cocoa, Fla.; B—Clendon Thomas, Oklahoma, 6-2, 188, Oklahoma City, Okla.

1958

E—Buddy Dial, Rice, 6-1, 185, Magnolia, Tex.; E—Sam Williams, Michigan St., 6-5, 225, Dansville, Mich.; T—Ted Bates, Oregon St., 6-2, 215, Los Angeles, Calif.; T—Brock Strom, Air Force, 6-0, 217, Ironwood, Mich.; G—John Guzik, Pittsburgh, 6-3, 223, Lawrence, Pa.; (tie) G—Zeke Smith, Auburn, 6-2, 210, Uniontown, Ala.; G—George Deiderich, Vanderbilt, 6-1, 198, Toronto, Ohio; C—Bob Harrison, Oklahoma, 6-2, 206, Stamford, Tex.; B—*Randy Duncan, Iowa, 6-0, 180, Des Moines, Ia.; B—*Pete Dawkins, Army, 6-1, 197, Royal Oak, Mich.; B—*Billy Cannon, Louisiana St., 6-1, 200, Baton Rouge, La.; B—Bob White, Ohio St., 6-2, 212, Covington, Ky.

1959

E—Bill Carpenter, Army, 6-2, 210, Springfield, Pa.; E—Monty Stickles, Notre Dame, 6-4, 225, Poughkeepsie, N.Y.; T—*Dan Lanphear, Wisconsin, 6-2, 214, Madison, Wis.; T—Don Floyd, Texas Christian, 6-3, 215, Midlothian, Tex.; G—*Roger Davis, Syracuse, 6-2, 228, Solon, Ohio; G—Bill Burrell, Illinois, 6-0, 210, Chebanse, Ill.; C—Maxie Baughan, Georgia Tech, 6-1, 212, Bessemer, Ala.; B—Richie Lucas, Penn St., 6-1, 185, Glassport, Pa.; B—Billy Cannon, Louisiana St., 6-1, 208, Baton Rouge, La.; B—Charlie Flowers, Mississippi, 6-0, 198, Marianna, Ark.; B—Ron Burton, Northwestern, 5-9, 185, Springfield, Ohio.

1960

E—*Mike Ditka, Pittsburgh, 6-3, 215, Aliquippa, Pa.; E—*Danny LaRose, Missouri, 6-4, 220, Crystal City, Mo.; T—*Bob Lilly, Texas Christian, 6-5, 250, Throckmorton, Tex.; T—Ken Rice, Auburn, 6-3, 250, Bainbridge, Ga.; G—*Tom Brown, Minnesota, 6-0, 225, Minneapolis, Minn.; G—Joe Romig, Colorado, 5-10, 197, Lakewood, Colo.; C—E. J. Holub, Texas Tech, 6-4, 215, Lubbock, Tex.; B—*Jake Gibbs, Mississippi, 6-0, 185, Grenada, Miss.; B—*Joe Bellino, Navy, 5-9, 181, Winchester, Mass.; B—*Bob Ferguson, Ohio St., 6-0, 217, Troy, Ohio; B—Ernie Davis, Syracuse, 6-2, 205, Elmira, N.Y.

1961

E—Gary Collins, Maryland, 6-3, 205, Williamstown, Pa.; E—Bill Miller, Miami (Fla.) 6-0, 188, McKeesport, Pa.; T—*Billy Neighbors, Alabama, 5-11, 229, Tuscaloosa, Ala.; T—Merlin Olsen, Utah St., 6-5, 265, Logan, Utah; G—*Roy Winston, Louisiana St., 6-1, 225, Baton Rouge, La.; G—Joe Romig, Colorado, 5-10, 199, Lakewood, Colo.; C—Alex Kroll, Rutgers, 6-2, 228, Leechburg, Pa.; B—*Ernie Davis, Syracuse, 6-2, 210, Elmira, N.Y.; B—*Bob Ferguson, Ohio St., 6-0, 217, Troy, Ohio; B—*Jimmy Saxton, Texas, 5-11, 160, Palestine, Tex.; B—Sandy Stephens, Minnesota, 6-0, 215, Uniontown, Pa.

1962

E—Hal Bedsole, Southern Cal, 6-5, 225, Northridge, Calif.; E—Pat Richter, Wisconsin, 6-5, 229, Madison, Wis.; T—*Bobby Bell, Minnesota, 6-4, 214, Shelby, N.C.; T—Jim Dunaway, Mississippi, 6-4, 260, Columbia, Miss.; G—*Johnny Treadwell, Texas, 6-1, 194, Austin, Tex.; G—Jack Cvercko, Northwestern, 6-0, 230, Campbell, Ohio; C—*Lee Roy Jordan, Alabama, 6-2, 207, Monroeville, Ala.; B—*Terry Baker, Oregon St., 6-3, 191, Portland, Ore.; B—*Jerry Stovall, Louisiana St., 6-2, 195, West

Monroe, La.; B—Mel Renfro, Oregon, 5-11, 190, Portland, Ore.; B—George Saimes, Michigan St., 5-10, 186, Canton, Ohio.

1963

E—Vern Burke, Oregon St., 6-4, 195, Bakersfield, Calif.; E—Lawrence Elkins, Baylor, 6-1, 187, Brownwood, Tex.; T—*Scott Appleton, Texas, 6-3, 235, Brady, Tex.; T—Carl Eller, Minnesota, 6-6, 241, Winston-Salem, N.C.; G—*Bob Brown, Nebraska, 6-5, 259, Cleveland, Ohio; G—Rick Redman, Washington, 5-11, 210, Seattle, Wash.; C—*Dick Butkus, Illinois, 6-3, 234, Chicago, Ill.; B—*Roger Staubach, Navy, 6-2, 190, Cincinnati, Ohio; B—Sherman Lewis, Michigan St., 5-8, 154, Louisville, Ky.; B—Jim Grisham, Oklahoma, 6-2, 205, Olney, Tex.; (tie) B—Gale Sayers, Kansas, 6-0, 196, Omaha, Neb.; B—Paul Martha, Pittsburgh, 6-1, 180, Wilkinsburg, Pa.

1964

E—Jack Snow, Notre Dame, 6-2, 210, Long Beach, Calif.; E—Fred Biletnikoff, Florida St., 6-1, 186, Erie, Pa.; T—*Larry Kramer, Nebraska, 6-2, 240, Austin, Minn.; T—*Ralph Neely, Oklahoma, 6-5, 243, Farmington, N.M.; G—Rick Redman, Washington, 5-11, 215, Seattle, Wash.; G—Glenn Ressler, Penn St., 6-2, 230, Dornsife, Pa.; C—Dick Butkus, Illinois, 6-3, 237, Chicago, Ill.; B—John Huarte, Notre Dame, 6-0, 180, Anaheim, Calif.; B—Gale Sayers, Kansas, 6-0, 194, Omaha, Neb.; B—Lawrence Elkins, Baylor, 6-1, 187, Brownwood, Tex.; B—Tucker Frederickson, Auburn, 6-2, 210, Hollywood, Fla.

Beginning in 1965, offense and defense selected.

1965
Offense

E—*Howard Twilley, Tulsa, 5-10, 180, Galena Park, Tex.; E—Freeman White, Nebraska, 6-5, 220, Detroit, Mich.; T—Sam Ball, Kentucky, 6-4, 241, Henderson, Ky.; T—Glen Ray Hines, Arkansas, 6-5, 235, El Dorado, Ark.; G—*Dick Arrington, Notre Dame, 5-11, 232, Erie, Pa.; G—Stas Maliszewski, Princeton, 6-1, 215, Davenport, Ia.; C—Paul Crane, Alabama, 6-2, 188, Prichard, Ala.; B—*Mike Garrett, Southern Cal, 5-9, 185, Los Angeles, Calif.; B—*Jim Grabowski, Illinois, 6-2, 211, Chicago, Ill.; B—Bob Griese, Purdue, 6-1, 185, Evansville, Ind.; B—Donny Anderson, Texas Tech, 6-3, 210, Stinnett, Tex.

Defense

E—Aaron Brown, Minnesota, 6-4, 230, Port Arthur, Tex.; E—Bubba Smith, Michigan St., 6-7, 268, Beaumont, Tex.; T—Walt Barnes, Nebraska, 6-3, 235, Chicago, Ill.; T—Loyd Phillips, Arkansas, 6-3, 221, Longview, Tex.; T—Bill Yearby, Michigan, 6-3, 222, Detroit, Mich.; LB—Carl McAdams, Oklahoma, 6-3, 215, White Deer, Tex.; LB—Tommy Nobis, Texas, 6-2, 230, San Antonio, Tex.; LB—Frank Emanuel, Tennessee, 6-3, 228, Newport News, Va.; B—George Webster, Michigan St., 6-4, 204, Anderson, S.C.; B—Johnny Roland, Missouri, 6-2, 198, Corpus Christi, Tex.; B—Nick Rassas, Notre Dame, 6-0, 185, Winnetka, Ill.

1966
Offense

E—*Jack Clancy, Michigan, 6-1, 192, Detroit, Mich.; E—Ray Perkins, Alabama, 6-0, 184, Petal, Miss.; T—*Cecil Dowdy, Alabama, 6-0, 206, Cherokee, Ala.; T—Ron Yary, Southern Cal, 6-6, 265, Bellflower, Calif.; G—Tom Regner, Notre Dame, 6-1, 245, Kenosha, Wis.; G—LaVerne Allers, Nebraska, 6-0, 209, Davenport, Ia.; C—Jim Breland, Georgia Tech, 6-2, 223, Blacksburg, Va.; B—*Steve Spurrier, Florida, 6-2, 203, Johnson City, Tenn.; B—*Nick Eddy, Notre Dame, 6-0, 195, Lafayette, Calif.; B—Mel Farr, UCLA, 6-2, 208, Beaumont, Tex.; B—Clint Jones, Michigan St., 6-0, 206, Cleveland, Ohio.

Defense

E—*Bubba Smith, Michigan St., 6-7, 283, Beaumont, Tex.; E—Alan Page, Notre Dame, 6-5, 238, Canton, Ohio; T—*Loyd Phillips, Arkansas, 6-3, 230, Longview, Tex.; T—Tom Greenlee, Washington, 6-0, 195, Seattle, Wash.; MG—Wayne Meylan, Nebraska, 6-0, 239, Bay City, Mich.; MG—John LaGrone, Southern Methodist, 5-10, 232, Borger, Tex.; LB—*Jim Lynch, Notre Dame, 6-1, 225, Lima, Ohio; LB—Paul Naumoff, Tennessee, 6-1, 209, Columbus, Ohio; B—*George Webster, Michigan St., 6-4, 218, Anderson, S.C.; B—Tom Beier, Miami (Fla.), 5-11, 197, Fremont, Ohio; B—Nate Shaw, Southern Cal, 6-2, 205, San Diego, Calif.

1967
Offense

E—Dennis Homan, Alabama, 6-0, 182, Muscle Shoals, Ala.; E—Ron Sellers, Florida St., 6-4, 187, Jacksonville, Fla.; T—*Ron Yary, Southern Cal, 6-6, 245, Bellflower, Calif.; T—Ed Chandler, Georgia, 6-2, 222, Cedartown, Ga.; G—Harry Olszewski, Clemson, 5-11, 237, Baltimore, Md.; G—Rich Stotter, Houston, 5-11, 225, Shaker Heights, Ohio; C—*Bob Johnson, Tennessee, 6-4, 232, Cleveland, Tenn.; B—Gary Beban, UCLA, 6-0, 191, Redwood City, Calif.; B—*Leroy Keyes, Purdue, 6-3, 199, Newport News, Va.; B—*O. J. Simpson, Southern Cal, 6-2, 205, San Francisco, Calif.; B—*Larry Csonka, Syracuse, 6-3, 230, Stow, Ohio.

Defense

E—*Ted Hendricks, Miami (Fla.), 6-8, 222, Miami Springs, Fla.; E—Tim Rossovich, Southern Cal, 6-5, 235, Mountain View, Calif.; T—Dennis Byrd, North Caro. St., 6-4, 250, Lincolnton, N.C.; MG—*Granville Liggins, Oklahoma, 5-11, 216, Tulsa, Okla.; MG—Wayne Meylan, Nebraska, 6-0, 231, Bay City, Mich.; LB—Adrian Young, Southern Cal, 6-1, 210, La Puente, Calif.; LB—Don Manning, UCLA, 6-2, 204, Culver City, Calif.; B—Tom Schoen, Notre Dame, 5-11, 178, Euclid, Ohio; B—Frank Loria, Virginia Tech, 5-9, 174, Clarksburg, W. Va.; B—Bobby Johns, Alabama, 6-1, 180, Birmingham, Ala.; B—Dick Anderson, Colorado, 6-2, 204, Boulder, Colo.

Consensus All-America Selections   291

1968
Offense

E—*Ted Kwalick, Penn St., 6-4, 230, McKees Rocks, Pa.; E—Jerry LeVias, Southern Methodist, 5-10, 170, Beaumont, Tex.; T—*Dave Foley, Ohio St., 6-5, 246, Cincinnati, Ohio; T—George Kunz, Notre Dame, 6-5, 240, Arcadia, Calif.; G—*Charles Rosenfelder, Tennessee, 6-1, 220, Humboldt, Tenn.; (tie) G—Jim Barnes, Arkansas, 6-4, 227, Pine Bluff, Ark.; G—Mike Montler, Colorado, 6-4, 235, Columbus, Ohio; C—*John Didion, Oregon St., 6-4, 242, Woodland, Calif.; B—*O. J. Simpson, Southern Cal, 6-2, 205, San Francisco, Calif.; B—*Leroy Keyes, Purdue, 6-3, 205, Newport News, Va.; B—Terry Hanratty, Notre Dame, 6-1, 200, Butler, Pa.; B—Chris Gilbert, Texas, 5-11, 176, Spring, Tex.

Defense

E—*Ted Hendricks, Miami (Fla.), 6-8, 222, Miami Springs, Fla.; E—John Zook, Kansas, 6-4, 230, Larned, Kans.; T—Bill Stanfill, Georgia, 6-5, 245, Cairo, Ga.; T—Joe Greene, North Tex. St., 6-4, 274, Temple, Tex.; MG—Ed White, California, 6-3, 245, Palm Desert, Calif.; MG—Chuck Kyle, Purdue, 6-1, 225, Fort Thomas, Ky.; LB—Steve Kiner, Tennessee, 6-1, 205, Tampa, Fla.; LB—Dennis Onkotz, Penn St., 6-2, 205, Northampton, Pa.; B—Jake Scott, Georgia, 6-1, 188, Arlington, Va.; B—Roger Wehrli, Missouri, 6-0, 184, King City, Mo.; B—Al Worley, Washington, 6-0, 175, Wenatchee, Wash.

1969
Offense

E—Jim Mandich, Michigan, 6-3, 222, Solon, Ohio; (tie) E—Walker Gillette, Richmond, 6-5, 200, Capron, Va.; E—Carlos Alvarez, Florida, 5-11, 180, Miami, Fla.; T—Bob McKay, Texas, 6-6, 245, Crane, Tex.; T—John Ward, Oklahoma St., 6-5, 248, Tulsa, Okla.; G—Chip Kell, Tennessee, 6-0, 255, Decatur, Ga.; G—Bill Bridges, Houston, 6-2, 230, Carrollton, Tex.; C—Rodney Brand, Arkansas, 6-2, 218, Newport, Ark.; B—*Mike Phipps, Purdue, 6-3, 206, Columbus, Ind.; B—*Steve Owens, Oklahoma, 6-2, 215, Miami, Okla.; B—Jim Otis, Ohio St., 6-0, 214, Celina, Ohio; B—Bob Anderson, Colorado, 6-0, 208, Boulder, Colo.

Defense

E—Jim Gunn, Southern Cal, 6-1, 210, San Diego, Calif.; E—Phil Olsen, Utah St., 6-5, 255, Logan, Utah; T—*Mike Reid, Penn St., 6-3, 240, Altoona, Pa.; T—*Mike McCoy, Notre Dame, 6-5, 274, Erie, Pa.; MG—Jim Stillwagon, Ohio St., 6-0, 216, Mount Vernon, Ohio; LB—*Steve Kiner, Tennessee, 6-1, 215, Tampa, Fla.; LB—Dennis Onkotz, Penn St., 6-2, 212, Northampton, Pa.; LB—Mike Ballou, UCLA, 6-3, 230, Los Angeles, Calif.; B—Jack Tatum, Ohio St., 6-0, 204, Passaic, N.J.; B—Buddy McClinton, Auburn, 5-11, 190, Montgomery, Ala.; B—Tom Curtis, Michigan, 6-1, 190, Aurora, Ohio.

1970
Offense

E—Tom Gatewood, Notre Dame, 6-2, 208, Baltimore, Md.; E—Ernie Jennings, Air Force, 6-0, 172, Kansas City, Mo.; E—Elmo Wright, Houston, 6-0, 195, Brazoria, Tex.; T—Dan Dierdorf, Michigan, 6-4, 250, Canton, Ohio; (tie) T—Bobby Wuensch, Texas, 6-3, 230, Houston, Tex.; T—Bob Newton, Nebraska, 6-4, 248, LaMirada, Calif.; G—*Chip Kell, Tennessee, 6-0, 240, Decatur, Ga.; G—Larry DiNardo, Notre Dame, 6-1, 235, New York, N.Y.; C—Don Popplewell, Colorado, 6-2, 240, Raytown, Mo.; QB—Jim Plunkett, Stanford, 6-3, 204, San Jose, Calif.; RB—Steve Worster, Texas, 6-0, 210, Bridge City, Tex.; RB—Don McCauley, North Caro., 6-0, 211, Garden City, N.Y.

Defense

E—Bill Atessis, Texas, 6-3, 255, Houston, Tex.; E—Charlie Weaver, Southern Cal, 6-2, 214, Richmond, Calif.; T—Rock Perdoni, Georgia Tech, 5-11, 236, Wellesley, Mass.; T—Dick Bumpas, Arkansas, 6-1, 225, Fort Smith, Ark.; MG—*Jim Stillwagon, Ohio St., 6-0, 220, Mount Vernon, Ohio; LB—Jack Ham, Penn St., 6-3, 212, Johnstown, Pa.; LB—Mike Anderson, Louisiana St., 6-3, 225, Baton Rouge, La.; B—*Jack Tatum, Ohio St., 6-0, 208, Passaic, N.J.; B—Larry Willingham, Auburn, 6-1, 185, Birmingham, Ala.; B—Dave Elmendorf, Texas A&M, 6-1, 190, Houston, Tex.; B—Tommy Casanova, Louisiana St., 6-1, 191, Crowley, La.

1971
Offense

E—*Terry Beasley, Auburn, 5-11, 184, Montgomery, Ala.; E—Johnny Rodgers, Nebraska, 5-10, 171, Omaha, Neb.; T—*Jerry Sisemore, Texas, 6-4, 255, Plainview, Tex.; T—Dave Joyner, Penn St., 6-0, 235, State College, Pa.; G—*Royce Smith, Georgia, 6-3, 240, Savannah, Ga.; G—Reggie McKenzie, Michigan, 6-4, 232, Highland Park, Mich.; C—Tom Brahaney, Oklahoma, 6-2, 231, Midland, Tex.; QB—*Pat Sullivan, Auburn, 6-0, 191, Birmingham, Ala.; RB—*Ed Marinaro, Cornell, 6-3, 210, New Milford, N.J.; RB—*Greg Pruitt, Oklahoma, 5-9, 176, Houston, Tex.; RB—Johnny Musso, Alabama, 5-11, 194, Birmingham, Ala.

Defense

E—*Walt Patulski, Notre Dame, 6-5, 235, Liverpool, N.Y.; E—Willie Harper, Nebraska, 6-3, 207, Toledo, Ohio; T—Larry Jacobson, Nebraska, 6-6, 250, Sioux Falls, S.D.; T—Mel Long, Toledo, 6-1, 230, Toledo, Ohio; T—Sherman White, California, 6-5, 250, Portsmouth, N.H.; LB—*Mike Taylor, Michigan, 6-2, 224, Detroit, Mich.; LB—Jeff Siemon, Stanford, 6-2, 225, Bakersfield, Calif.; B—*Bobby Majors, Tennessee, 6-1, 197, Sewanee, Tenn.; B—Clarence Ellis, Notre Dame, 6-0, 178, Grand Rapids, Mich.; B—Ernie Jackson, Duke, 5-10, 170, Hopkins, S.C.; B—Tommy Casanova, Louisiana St., 6-2, 195, Crowley, La.

1972
Offense
WR—*Johnny Rodgers, Nebraska, 5-9, 173, Omaha, Neb.; TE—*Charles Young, Southern Cal, 6-4, 228, Fresno, Calif.; T—*Jerry Sisemore, Texas, 6-4, 260, Plainview, Tex.; T—Paul Seymour, Michigan, 6-5, 250, Berkley, Mich.; G—*John Hannah, Alabama, 6-3, 282, Albertville, Ala.; G—Ron Rusnak, North Caro., 6-1, 223, Prince George, Va.; C—Tom Brahaney, Oklahoma, 6-2, 227, Midland, Tex.; QB—Bert Jones, Louisiana St., 6-3, 205, Ruston, La.; RB—*Greg Pruitt, Oklahoma, 5-9, 177, Houston, Tex.; RB—Otis Armstrong, Purdue, 5-11, 197, Chicago, Ill.; RB—Woody Green, Arizona St., 6-1, 190, Portland, Ore.

Defense
E—Willie Harper, Nebraska, 6-2, 207, Toledo, Ohio; E—Bruce Bannon, Penn St., 6-3, 224, Rockaway, N.J.; T—*Greg Marx, Notre Dame, 6-5, 265, Redford, Mich.; T—Dave Butz, Purdue, 6-7, 279, Park Ridge, Ill.; MG—*Rich Glover, Nebraska, 6-1, 234, Jersey City, N.J.; LB—Randy Gradishar, Ohio St., 6-3, 232, Champion, Ohio; LB—John Skorupan, Penn St., 6-2, 208, Beaver, Pa.; B—*Brad VanPelt, Michigan St., 6-5, 221, Owosso, Mich.; B—Cullen Bryant, Colorado, 6-2, 215, Colo. Springs, Colo.; B—Robert Popelka, Southern Methodist, 6-1, 190, Temple, Tex.; B—Randy Logan, Michigan, 6-2, 192, Detroit, Mich.

1973
Offense
WR—Lynn Swann, Southern Cal, 6-0, 180, Foster City, Calif.; TE—Dave Casper, Notre Dame, 6-3, 252, Chilton, Wis.; T—*John Hicks, Ohio St., 6-3, 258, Cleveland, Ohio; T—Booker Brown, Southern Cal, 6-3, 270, Santa Barbara, Calif.; G—Buddy Brown, Alabama, 6-2, 242, Tallahassee, Fla.; G—Bill Yoest, North Caro. St., 6-0, 235, Pittsburgh, Pa.; C—Bill Wyman, Texas, 6-2, 235, Spring, Tex.; QB—Dave Jaynes, Kansas, 6-2, 212, Bonner Springs, Kans.; RB—*John Cappelletti, Penn St., 6-1, 206, Upper Darby, Pa.; RB—Roosevelt Leaks, Texas, 5-11, 209, Brenham, Tex.; RB—Woody Green, Arizona St., 6-1, 202, Portland, Ore.; RB—Kermit Johnson, UCLA, 6-0, 185, Los Angeles, Calif.

Defense
L—*John Dutton, Nebraska, 6-7, 248, Rapid City, S.D.; L—Dave Gallagher, Michigan, 6-4, 245, Piqua, Ohio; L—*Lucious Selmon, Oklahoma, 5-11, 236, Eufaula, Okla.; L—Tony Cristiani, Miami (Fla.), 5-10, 215, Brandon, Fla.; LB—*Randy Gradishar, Ohio St., 6-3, 236, Champion, Ohio; LB—Rod Shoate, Oklahoma, 6-1, 214, Spiro, Okla.; LB—Richard Wood, Southern Cal, 6-2, 217, Elizabeth, N.J.; B—Mike Townsend, Notre Dame, 6-3, 183, Hamilton, Ohio; B—Artimus Parker, Southern Cal, 6-3, 215, Sacramento, Calif.; B—Dave Brown, Michigan, 6-1, 188, Akron, Ohio; B—Randy Rhino, Georgia Tech, 5-10, 179, Charlotte, N.C.

1974
Offense
WR—Pete Demmerle, Notre Dame, 6-1, 190, New Canaan, Conn.; TE—Bennie Cunningham, Clemson, 6-5, 252, Seneca, S.C.; T—Kurt Schumacher, Ohio St., 6-4, 250, Lorain, Ohio; T—Marvin Crenshaw, Nebraska, 6-6, 240, Toledo, Ohio; G—Ken Huff, North Caro., 6-4, 261, Coronado, Calif.; G—John Roush, Oklahoma, 6-0, 252, Arvada, Colo.; G—Gerry DiNardo, Notre Dame, 6-1, 237, New York, N.Y.; C—Steve Myers, Ohio St., 6-2, 244, Kent, Ohio; QB—Steve Bartkowski, California, 6-4, 215, Santa Clara, Calif.; RB—*Archie Griffin, Ohio St., 5-9, 184, Columbus, Ohio; RB—*Joe Washington, Oklahoma, 5-10, 178, Port Arthur, Tex.; RB—*Anthony Davis, Southern Cal, 5-9, 183, San Fernando, Calif.

Defense
L—*Randy White, Maryland, 6-4, 238, Wilmington, Del.; L—Mike Hartenstine, Penn St., 6-4, 233, Bethlehem, Pa.; L—Pat Donovan, Stanford, 6-5, 240, Helena, Mont.; L—Jimmy Webb, Mississippi St., 6-5, 245, Florence, Miss.; L—Leroy Cook, Alabama, 6-4, 205, Abbeville, Ala.; MG—Louie Kelcher, Southern Methodist, 6-5, 275, Beaumont, Tex.; MG—Rubin Carter, Miami (Fla.), 6-3, 260, Ft. Lauderdale, Fla.; LB—*Rod Shoate, Oklahoma, 6-1, 213, Spiro, Okla.; LB—Richard Wood, Southern Cal, 6-2, 213, Elizabeth, N.J.; LB—Ken Bernich, Auburn, 6-2, 240, Gretna, La.; LB—Woodrow Lowe, Alabama, 6-0, 211, Phenix City, Ala.; B—*Dave Brown, Michigan, 6-1, 188, Akron, Ohio; B—Pat Thomas, Texas A&M, 5-9, 180, Plano, Tex.; B—John Provost, Holy Cross, 5-10, 180, Quincy, Mass.

1975
Offense
E—Steve Rivera, California, 6-0, 185, Wilmington, Cal.; E—Larry Seivers, Tennessee, 6-4, 198, Clinton, Tenn.; T—Bob Simmons, Texas, 6-5, 245, Temple, Tex.; T—Dennis Lick, Wisconsin, 6-3, 262, Chicago, Ill.; G—Randy Johnson, Georgia, 6-2, 250, Rome, Ga.; G—Ted Smith, Ohio St., 6-1, 242, Gibsonburg, Ohio; C—*Rik Bonness, Nebraska, 6-4, 223, Bellevue, Neb.; QB—John Sciarra, UCLA, 5-10, 178, Alhambra, Calif.; RB—*Archie Griffin, Ohio St., 5-9, 182, Columbus, Ohio; RB—*Ricky Bell, Southern Cal, 6-2, 215, Los Angeles, Calif.; RB—Chuck Muncie, California, 6-3, 220, Uniontown, Pa.

Defense
E—*Leroy Cook, Alabama, 6-4, 205, Abbeville, Ala.; E—Jimbo Elrod, Oklahoma, 6-0, 210, Tulsa, Okla.; T—*Lee Roy Selmon, Oklahoma, 6-2, 256, Eufaula, Okla.; T—*Steve Niehaus, Notre Dame, 6-5, 260, Cincinnati, Ohio; MG—Dewey Selmon, Oklahoma, 6-1, 257, Eufaula, Okla.; LB—*Ed Simonini, Texas A&M, 6-0, 215, Las Vegas, Nev.; LB—Greg Buttle, Penn St., 6-3, 220, Linwood, N.J.; LB—Sammy Green, Florida, 6-2, 228, Ft. Meade, Fla.; B—*Chet Moeller, Navy, 6-0, 189, Kettering, Ohio; B—Tim Fox, Ohio St., 6-0, 186, Canton, Ohio; B—Pat Thomas, Texas A&M, 5-10, 180, Plano, Tex.

1976
Offense

TE—Ken MacAfee, Notre Dame, 6-4, 251, Brockton, Mass.; SE—Larry Seivers, Tennessee, 6-4, 200, Clinton, Tenn.; T—Mike Vaughan, Oklahoma, 6-5, 275, Ada, Okla.; T—Chris Ward, Ohio St., 6-4, 274, Dayton, Ohio; G—Joel Parrish, Georgia, 6-3, 232, Douglas, Ga.; G—Mark Donahue, Michigan, 6-3, 245, Oak Lawn, Ill.; C—Derrel Gofourth, Oklahoma St., 6-2, 250, Parsons, Kans.; QB—Tommy Kramer, Rice, 6-2, 190, San Antonio, Tex.; RB—*Tony Dorsett, Pittsburgh, 5-11, 192, Aliquippa, Pa.; RB—*Ricky Bell, Southern Cal, 6-2, 218, Los Angeles, Calif.; RB—Rob Lytle, Michigan, 6-1, 195, Fremont, Ohio; PK—Tony Franklin, Texas A&M, 5-10, 170, Fort Worth, Tex.

Defense

E—*Ross Browner, Notre Dame, 6-3, 248, Warren, Ohio; E—Bob Brudzinski, Ohio St., 6-4, 228, Fremont, Ohio; T—Wilson Whitley, Houston, 6-3, 268, Brenham, Tex.; T—Gary Jeter, Southern Cal, 6-5, 255, Cleveland, Ohio; T—Joe Campbell, Maryland, 6-6, 255, Wilmington, Del.; MG—Al Romano, Pittsburgh, 6-3, 230, Solvay, N.Y.; LB—*Robert Jackson, Texas A&M, 6-2, 228, Houston, Tex.; LB—Jerry Robinson, UCLA, 6-3, 208, Santa Rosa, Calif.; B—*Bill Armstrong, Wake Forest, 6-4, 205, Randolph, N.J.; B—Gary Green, Baylor, 5-11, 182, San Antonio, Tex.; B—Dennis Thurman, Southern Cal, 5-11, 170, Santa Monica, Calif.; B—Dave Butterfield, Nebraska, 5-10, 182, Kersey, Colo.

UCLA linebacker Jerry Robinson makes one of the more than 470 tackles that helped him earn consensus all-America honors in 1976, 1977 and 1978.

1977
Offense

TE—*Ken MacAfee, Notre Dame, 6-4, 250, Brockton, Mass.; WR—John Jefferson, Arizona St., 6-1, 184, Dallas, Tex.; WR—Ozzie Newsome, Alabama, 6-4, 210, Leighton, Ala.; T—*Chris Ward, Ohio St., 6-4, 272, Dayton, Ohio; T—Dan Irons, Texas Tech, 6-7, 260, Lubbock, Tex.; G—*Mark Donahue, Michigan, 6-3, 245, Oak Lawn, Ill.; G—Leotis Harris, Arkansas, 6-1, 254, Little Rock, Ark.; C—Tom Brzoza, Pittsburgh, 6-3, 240, New Castle, Pa.; QB—Guy Benjamin, Stanford, 6-4, 202, Sepulveda, Calif.; RB—*Earl Campbell, Texas, 6-1, 220, Tyler, Tex.; RB—*Terry Miller, Oklahoma St., 6-0, 196, Colorado Springs, Colo.; RB—Charles Alexander, Louisiana St., 6-1, 215, Galveston, Tex.; K—Steve Little, Arkansas, 6-0, 179, Overland Park, Kans.

Defense

L—*Ross Browner, Notre Dame, 6-3, 247, Warren, Ohio; L—*Art Still, Kentucky, 6-8, 247, Camden, N.J.; L—*Brad Shearer, Texas, 6-4, 255, Austin, Tex.; L—Randy Holloway, Pittsburgh, 6-6, 228, Sharon, Pa.; L—Dee Hardison, North Caro., 6-4, 252, Newton Grove, N.C.; LB—*Jerry Robinson, UCLA, 6-3, 208, Santa Rosa, Calif.; LB—Tom Cousineau, Ohio St., 6-3, 228, Fairview Park, Ohio; LB—Gary Spani, Kansas St., 6-2, 222, Manhattan, Kans.; B—*Dennis Thurman, Southern Cal, 5-11, 173, Santa Monica, Calif.; B—*Zac Henderson, Oklahoma, 6-1, 184, Burkburnett, Tex.; B—Luther Bradley, Notre Dame, 6-2, 204, Muncie, Ind.; B—Bob Jury, Pittsburgh, 6-0, 190, Library, Pa.

1992 NCAA FOOTBALL

1978
Offense
TE—Kellen Winslow, Missouri, 6-6, 235, East St. Louis, Ill.; WR—Emanuel Tolbert, Southern Methodist, 5-10, 180, Little Rock, Ark.; T—*Keith Dorney, Penn St., 6-5, 257, Allentown, Pa.; T—Kelvin Clark, Nebraska, 6-4, 275, Odessa, Tex.; G—*Pat Howell, Southern Cal, 6-6, 255, Fresno, Calif.; G—*Greg Roberts, Oklahoma, 6-3, 238, Nacogdoches, Tex.; C—Dave Huffman, Notre Dame, 6-5, 245, Dallas, Tex.; C—Jim Ritcher, North Caro. St., 6-3, 242, Hinckley, Ohio; QB—*Chuck Fusina, Penn St., 6-1, 195, McKees Rocks, Pa.; RB—*Billy Sims, Oklahoma, 6-0, 205, Hooks, Tex.; RB—*Charles White, Southern Cal, 5-11, 183, San Fernando, Calif.; RB—Ted Brown, North Caro. St., 5-10, 195, High Point, N.C.; RB—Charles Alexander, Louisiana St., 6-1, 214, Galveston, Tex.

Defense
L—*Al Harris, Arizona St., 6-5, 240, Wheeler AFB, Hawaii; L—*Bruce Clark, Penn St., 6-3, 246, New Castle, Pa.; L—Hugh Green, Pittsburgh, 6-2, 215, Natchez, Miss.; L—Mike Bell, Colorado St., 6-5, 265, Wichita, Kans.; L—Marty Lyons, Alabama, 6-6, 250, St. Petersburg, Fla.; LB—*Bob Golic, Notre Dame, 6-3, 244, Willowick, Ohio; LB—*Jerry Robinson, UCLA, 6-3, 209, Santa Rosa, Calif.; LB—Tom Cousineau, Ohio St., 6-3, 227, Fairview Park, Ohio; B—*Johnnie Johnson, Texas, 6-2, 183, LaGrange, Tex.; B—Kenny Easley, UCLA, 6-2, 202, Chesapeake, Va.; B—Jeff Nixon, Richmond, 6-4, 195, Glendale, Ariz.

1979
Offense
TE—*Junior Miller, Nebraska, 6-4, 222, Midland, Tex.; WR—Ken Margerum, Stanford, 6-1, 175, Fountain Valley, Calif.; T—*Greg Kolenda, Arkansas, 6-1, 258, Kansas City, Kans.; T—Jim Bunch, Alabama, 6-2, 240, Mechanicsville, Va.; G—*Brad Budde, Southern Cal, 6-5, 253, Kansas City, Mo.; G—Ken Fritz, Ohio St., 6-3, 238, Ironton, Ohio; C—*Jim Ritcher, North Caro. St., 6-3, 245, Hinckley, Ohio; QB—*Marc Wilson, Brigham Young, 6-5, 204, Seattle, Wash.; RB—*Charles White, Southern Cal, 6-0, 185, San Fernando, Calif.; RB—*Billy Sims, Oklahoma, 6-0, 205, Hooks, Tex.; RB—Vagas Ferguson, Notre Dame, 6-1, 194, Richmond, Ind.; PK—Dale Castro, Maryland, 6-1, 170, Shady Side, Md.

Defense
L—*Hugh Green, Pittsburgh, 6-2, 220, Natchez, Miss.; L—*Steve McMichael, Texas, 6-2, 250, Freer, Tex.; L—Bruce Clark, Penn St., 6-3, 255, New Castle, Pa.; L—Jim Stuckey, Clemson, 6-5, 241, Cayce, S.C.; MG—Ron Simmons, Florida St., 6-1, 235, Warner Robins, Ga.; LB—*George Cumby, Oklahoma, 6-0, 205, Tyler, Tex.; LB—Ron Simpkins, Michigan, 6-2, 220, Detroit, Mich.; LB—Mike Singletary, Baylor, 6-1, 224, Houston, Tex.; B—*Kenny Easley, UCLA, 6-3, 204, Chesapeake, Va.; B—*Johnnie Johnson, Texas, 6-2, 190, LaGrange, Tex.; B—Roland James, Tennessee, 6-2, 182, Jamestown, Ohio; P—Jim Miller, Mississippi, 5-11, 183, Ripley, Miss.

1980
Offense
WR—*Ken Margerum, Stanford, 6-1, 175, Fountain Valley, Calif.; TE—*Dave Young, Purdue, 6-6, 242, Akron, Ohio; L—*Mark May, Pittsburgh, 6-6, 282, Oneonta, N.Y.; L—Keith Van Horne, Southern Cal, 6-7, 265, Fullerton, Calif.; L—Nick Eyre, Brigham Young, 6-5, 276, Las Vegas, Nev.; L—Louis Oubre, Oklahoma, 6-4, 262, New Orleans, La.; L—Randy Schleusener, Nebraska, 6-7, 242, Rapid City, S.D.; C—*John Scully, Notre Dame, 6-5, 255, Huntington, N.Y.; QB—*Mark Herrmann, Purdue, 6-4, 187, Carmel, Ind.; RB—*George Rogers, South Caro., 6-2, 220, Duluth, Ga.; RB—*Herschel Walker, Georgia, 6-2, 220, Wrightsville, Ga.; RB—Jarvis Redwine, Nebraska, 5-11, 204, Inglewood, Calif.

Defense
L—*Hugh Green, Pittsburgh, 6-2, 222, Natchez, Miss.; L—*E. J. Junior, Alabama, 6-3, 227, Nashville, Tenn.; L—Kenneth Sims, Texas, 6-6, 265, Groesbeck, Tex.; L—Leonard Mitchell, Houston, 6-7, 270, Houston, Tex.; MG—Ron Simmons, Florida St., 6-1, 230, Warner Robins, Ga.; LB—*Mike Singletary, Baylor, 6-1, 232, Houston, Tex.; LB—*Lawrence Taylor, North Caro., 6-3, 237, Williamsburg, Va.; LB—David Little, Florida, 6-1, 228, Miami, Fla.; LB—Bob Crable, Notre Dame, 6-3, 222, Cincinnati, Ohio; B—*Kenny Easley, UCLA, 6-3, 206, Chesapeake, Va.; B—*Ronnie Lott, Southern Cal, 6-2, 200, Rialto, Calif.; B—John Simmons, Southern Methodist, 5-11, 188, Little Rock, Ark.

1981
Offense
WR—*Anthony Carter, Michigan, 5-11, 161, Riviera Beach, Fla.; TE—*Tim Wrightman, UCLA, 6-3, 237, San Pedro, Calif.; L—*Sean Farrell, Penn St., 6-3, 266, Westhampton Beach, N.Y.; L—Roy Foster, Southern Cal, 6-4, 265, Overland Park, Kans.; L—Terry Crouch, Oklahoma, 6-1, 275, Dallas, Tex.; L—Ed Muransky, Michigan, 6-7, 275, Youngstown, Ohio; L—Terry Tausch, Texas, 6-4, 265, New Braunfels, Tex.; L—Kurt Becker, Michigan, 6-6, 260, Aurora, Ill.; C—*Dave Rimington, Nebraska, 6-3, 275, Omaha, Neb.; QB—*Jim McMahon, Brigham Young, 6-0, 185, Roy, Utah; RB—*Marcus Allen, Southern Cal, 6-2, 202, San Diego, Calif.; RB—*Herschel Walker, Georgia, 6-2, 222, Wrightsville, Ga.

Defense
L—*Billy Ray Smith, Arkansas, 6-4, 228, Plano, Tex.; L—*Kenneth Sims, Texas, 6-6, 265, Groesbeck, Tex.; L—Andre Tippett, Iowa, 6-4, 235, Newark, N.J.; L—Tim Krumrie, Wisconsin, 6-3, 237, Mondovi, Wis.; LB—Bob Crable, Notre Dame, 6-3, 225, Cincinnati, Ohio; LB—Jeff Davis, Clemson, 6-0, 223, Greensboro, N.C.; LB—Sal Sunseri, Pittsburgh, 6-0, 220, Pittsburgh, Pa.; DB—Tommy Wilcox,

Alabama, 5-11, 187, Harahan, La.; DB—Mike Richardson, Arizona St., 6-1, 192, Compton, Calif.; DB—Terry Kinard, Clemson, 6-1, 183, Sumter, S.C.; DB—Fred Marion, Miami (Fla.), 6-3, 194, Gainesville, Fla.; P—Reggie Roby, Iowa, 6-3, 215, Waterloo, Iowa.

1982
Offense
WR—*Anthony Carter, Michigan, 5-11, 161, Riviera Beach, Fla.; TE—*Gordon Hudson, Brigham Young, 6-4, 224, Salt Lake City, Utah; L—*Don Mosebar, Southern Cal, 6-7, 270, Visalia, Calif.; L—*Steve Korte, Arkansas, 6-2, 270, Littleton, Colo.; L—Jimbo Covert, Pittsburgh, 6-5, 279, Conway, Pa.; L—Bruce Matthews, Southern Cal, 6-5, 265, Arcadia, Calif.; C—*Dave Rimington, Nebraska, 6-3, 290, Omaha, Neb.; QB—*John Elway, Stanford, 6-4, 202, Northridge, Calif.; RB—*Herschel Walker, Georgia, 6-1, 222, Wrightsville, Ga.; RB—*Eric Dickerson, Southern Methodist, 6-2, 215, Sealy, Tex.; RB—Mike Rozier, Nebraska, 5-11, 210, Camden, N.J.; PK—*Chuck Nelson, Washington, 5-11, 178, Everett, Wash.

Defense
L—*Billy Ray Smith, Arkansas, 6-3, 228, Plano, Tex.; L—Vernon Maxwell, Arizona St., 6-2, 225, Carson, Calif.; L—Mike Pitts, Alabama, 6-5, 255, Baltimore, Md.; L—Wilber Marshall, Florida, 6-1, 230, Titusville, Fla.; L—Gabriel Rivera, Texas Tech, 6-3, 270, San Antonio, Tex.; L—Rick Bryan, Oklahoma, 6-4, 260, Coweta, Okla.; MG—George Achica, Southern Cal, 6-5, 260, San Jose, Calif.; LB—*Darryl Talley, West Va., 6-4, 210, East Cleveland, Ohio; LB—Ricky Hunley, Arizona, 6-1, 230, Petersburg, Va.; LB—Marcus Marek, Ohio St., 6-2, 224, Masury, Ohio; DB—*Terry Kinard, Clemson, 6-1, 189, Sumter, S.C.; DB—Mike Richardson, Arizona St., 6-0, 190, Compton, Calif.; DB—Terry Hoage, Georgia, 6-3, 196, Huntsville, Tex.; P—*Jim Arnold, Vanderbilt, 6-3, 205, Dalton, Ga.

1983
Offense
WR—*Irving Fryar, Nebraska, 6-0, 200, Mount Holly, N.J.; TE—*Gordon Hudson, Brigham Young, 6-4, 231, Salt Lake City, Utah; L—*Bill Fralic, Pittsburgh, 6-5, 270, Penn Hills, Pa.; L—Terry Long, East Caro., 6-0, 280, Columbia, S.C.; L—Dean Steinkuhler, Nebraska, 6-3, 270, Burr, Neb.; L—Doug Dawson, Texas, 6-3, 263, Houston, Tex.; C—Tony Slaton, Southern Cal, 6-4, 260, Merced, Calif.; QB—*Steve Young, Brigham Young, 6-1, 198, Greenwich, Conn.; RB—*Mike Rozier, Nebraska, 5-11, 210, Camden, N.J.; RB—Bo Jackson, Auburn, 6-1, 222, Bessemer, Ala.; RB—Greg Allen, Florida St., 6-0, 200, Milton, Fla.; RB—Napoleon McCallum, Navy, 6-2, 208, Milford, Ohio; PK—Luis Zendejas, Arizona St., 5-9, 186, Chino, Calif.

Defense
L—*Rick Bryan, Oklahoma, 6-4, 260, Coweta, Okla.; L—*Reggie White, Tennessee, 6-5, 264, Chattanooga, Tenn.; L—William Perry, Clemson, 6-3, 320, Aiken, S.C.; L—William Fuller, North Caro., 6-4, 250, Chesapeake, Va.; LB—*Ricky Hunley, Arizona, 6-2, 230, Petersburg, Va.; LB—Wilber Marshall, Florida, 6-1, 230, Titusville, Fla.; LB—Ron Rivera, California, 6-3, 225, Monterey, Calif.; LB—Jeff Leiding, Texas, 6-4, 240, Tulsa, Okla.; DB—*Russell Carter, Southern Methodist, 6-3, 193, Ardmore, Pa.; DB—Jerry Gray, Texas, 6-1, 183, Lubbock, Tex.; DB—Terry Hoage, Georgia, 6-3, 196, Huntsville, Tex.; DB—Don Rogers, UCLA, 6-2, 208, Sacramento, Calif.; P—Jack Weil, Wyoming, 5-11, 171, Northglenn, Colo.

1984
Offense
WR—*David Williams, Illinois, 6-3, 195, Los Angeles, Calif.; WR—Eddie Brown, Miami (Fla.), 6-0, 185, Miami, Fla.; TE—Jay Novacek, Wyoming, 6-4, 211, Gothenburg, Neb.; T—*Bill Fralic, Pittsburgh, 6-5, 285, Penn Hills, Pa.; T—Lomas Brown, Florida, 6-5, 277, Miami, Fla.; G—Del Wilkes, South Caro., 6-3, 255, Columbia, S.C.; G—Jim Lachey, Ohio St., 6-6, 274, St. Henry, Ohio; G—Bill Mayo, Tennessee, 6-3, 280, Dalton, Ga.; C—*Mark Traynowicz, Nebraska, 6-6, 265, Bellevue, Neb.; QB—*Doug Flutie, Boston College, 5-9, 177, Natick, Mass.; RB—*Keith Byars, Ohio St., 6-2, 233, Dayton, Ohio; RB—*Kenneth Davis, Texas Christian, 5-11, 205, Temple, Tex.; RB—Rueben Mayes, Washington St., 6-0, 200, North Battleford, Saskatchewan, Can.; PK—Kevin Butler, Georgia, 6-1, 190, Stone Mountain, Ga.

Defense
DL—Bruce Smith, Virginia Tech, 6-4, 275, Norfolk, Va.; DL—Tony Degrate, Texas, 6-4, 280, Snyder, Tex.; DL—Ron Holmes, Washington, 6-4, 255, Lacey, Wash.; DL—Tony Casillas, Oklahoma, 6-3, 272, Tulsa, Okla.; LB—Gregg Carr, Auburn, 6-2, 215, Birmingham, Ala.; LB—Jack Del Rio, Southern Cal, 6-4, 235, Hayward, Calif.; LB—Larry Station, Iowa, 5-11, 233, Omaha, Neb.; DB—*Jerry Gray, Texas, 6-1, 183, Lubbock, Tex.; DB—Tony Thurman, Boston College, 6-0, 179, Lynn, Mass.; DB—Jeff Sanchez, Georgia, 6-0, 183, Yorba Linda, Calif.; DB—David Fulcher, Arizona St., 6-3, 220, Los Angeles, Calif.; DB—Rod Brown, Oklahoma St., 6-3, 188, Gainesville, Tex.; P—*Ricky Anderson, Vanderbilt, 6-2, 190, St. Petersburg, Fla.

1985
Offense
WR—*David Williams, Illinois, 6-3, 195, Los Angeles, Calif.; WR—Tim McGee, Tennessee, 5-10, 181, Cleveland, Ohio; TE—Willie Smith, Miami (Fla.), 6-2, 230, Jacksonville, Fla.; L—*Jim Dombrowski, Virginia, 6-5, 290, Williamsville, N.Y.; L—Jeff Bregel, Southern Cal, 6-4, 280, Granada Hills, Calif.; L—Brian Jozwiak, West Va., 6-6, 290, Catonsville, Md.; L—John Rienstra, Temple, 6-4, 280, Colorado Springs, Colo.; L—J. D. Maarleveld, Maryland, 6-5, 300, Rutherford, N.J.; L—Jamie Dukes, Florida St., 6-0, 272, Orlando, Fla.; C—Pete Anderson, Georgia, 6-3, 264, Glen Ridge, N.J.; QB—*Chuck Long,

Iowa, 6-4, 213, Wheaton, Ill.; RB—*Bo Jackson, Auburn, 6-1, 222, Bessemer, Ala.; RB—*Lorenzo White, Michigan St., 5-11, 205, Fort Lauderdale, Fla.; RB—Thurman Thomas, Oklahoma St., 5-11, 186, Missouri City, Tex.; RB—Reggie Dupard, Southern Methodist, 6-0, 201, New Orleans, La.; RB—Napoleon McCallum, Navy, 6-2, 214, Milford, Ohio; PK—*John Lee, UCLA, 5-11, 187, Downey, Calif.

Defense

L—*Tim Green, Syracuse, 6-2, 246, Liverpool, N.Y.; L—*Leslie O'Neal, Oklahoma St., 6-3, 245, Little Rock, Ark.; L—Tony Casillas, Oklahoma, 6-3, 280, Tulsa, Okla.; L—Mike Ruth, Boston College, 6-2, 250, Norristown, Pa.; L—Mike Hammerstein, Michigan, 6-4, 240, Wapakoneta, Ohio; LB—*Brian Bosworth, Oklahoma, 6-2, 234, Irving, Tex.; LB—*Larry Station, Iowa, 5-11, 227, Omaha, Neb.; LB—Johnny Holland, Texas A&M, 6-2, 219, Hempstead, Tex.; DB—David Fulcher, Arizona St., 6-3, 228, Los Angeles, Calif.; DB—Brad Cochran, Michigan, 6-3, 219, Royal Oak, Mich.; DB—Scott Thomas, Air Force, 6-0, 185, San Antonio, Tex.; P—Barry Helton, Colorado, 6-3, 195, Simla, Colo.

1986
Offense

WR—Cris Carter, Ohio St., 6-3, 194, Middletown, Ohio; TE—*Keith Jackson, Oklahoma, 6-3, 241, Little Rock, Ark.; L—Jeff Bregel, Southern Cal, 6-4, 280, Granada Hills, Calif.; L—Randy Dixon, Pittsburgh, 6-4, 286, Clewiston, Fla.; L—Danny Villa, Arizona St., 6-5, 284, Nogales, Ariz.; L—John Clay, Missouri, 6-5, 285, St. Louis, Mo.; C—*Ben Tamburello, Auburn, 6-3, 268, Birmingham, Ala.; QB—*Vinny Testaverde, Miami (Fla.), 6-5, 218, Elmont, N.Y.; RB—*Brent Fullwood, Auburn, 5-11, 209, St. Cloud, Fla.; RB—*Paul Palmer, Temple, 5-10, 180, Potomac, Md.; RB—Terrence Flagler, Clemson, 6-1, 200, Fernandina Beach, Fla.; RB—Brad Muster, Stanford, 6-3, 226, Novato, Calif.; RB—D. J. Dozier, Penn St., 6-1, 204, Virginia Beach, Va.; PK—Jeff Jaeger, Washington, 5-11, 191, Kent, Wash.

Defense

L—*Jerome Brown, Miami (Fla.), 6-2, 285, Brooksville, Fla.; L—*Danny Noonan, Nebraska, 6-4, 280, Lincoln, Neb.; L—Tony Woods, Pittsburgh, 6-4, 240, Newark, N.J.; L—Jason Buck, Brigham Young, 6-6, 270, St. Anthony, Idaho; L—Reggie Rogers, Washington, 6-6, 260, Sacramento, Calif.; LB—*Cornelius Bennett, Alabama, 6-4, 235, Birmingham, Ala.; LB—Shane Conlan, Penn St., 6-3, 225, Frewsburg, N.Y.; LB—Brian Bosworth, Oklahoma, 6-2, 240, Irving, Tex.; LB—Chris Spielman, Ohio St., 6-2, 227, Massillon, Ohio; DB—*Thomas Everett, Baylor, 5-9, 180, Daingerfield, Tex.; DB—Tim McDonald, Southern Cal, 6-3, 205, Fresno, Calif.; DB—Bennie Blades, Miami (Fla.), 6-0, 207, Ft. Lauderdale, Fla.; DB—Rod Woodson, Purdue, 6-0, 195, Fort Wayne, Ind.; DB—Garland Rivers, Michigan, 6-1, 187, Canton, Ohio; P—Barry Helton, Colorado, 6-4, 200, Simla, Colo.

1987
Offense

WR—*Tim Brown, Notre Dame, 6-0, 195, Dallas, Tex.; WR—Wendell Davis, Louisiana St., 6-0, 186, Shreveport, La.; TE—*Keith Jackson, Oklahoma, 6-3, 248, Little Rock, Ark.; L—*Mark Hutson, Oklahoma, 6-4, 282, Fort Smith, Ark.; L—Dave Cadigan, Southern Cal, 6-5, 280, Newport Beach, Calif.; L—John Elliott, Michigan, 6-7, 306, Lake Ronkonkoma, N.Y.; L—Randall McDaniel, Arizona St., 6-5, 261, Avondale, Ariz.; C—*Nacho Albergamo, Louisiana St., 6-2, 257, Marrera, La.; QB—*Don McPherson, Syracuse, 6-0, 182, West Hempstead, N.Y.; RB—Lorenzo White, Michigan St., 5-11, 211, Fort Lauderdale, Fla.; RB—Craig Heyward, Pittsburgh, 6-0, 260, Passaic, N.J.; PK—David Treadwell, Clemson, 6-1, 165, Jacksonville, Fla.

Defense

L—*Daniel Stubbs, Miami (Fla.), 6-4, 250, Red Bank, N.J.; L—*Chad Hennings, Air Force, 6-5, 260, Elboron, Iowa; L—Tracy Rocker, Auburn, 6-3, 258, Atlanta, Ga.; L—Ted Gregory, Syracuse, 6-1, 260, East Islip, N.Y.; L—John Roper, Texas A&M, 6-2, 215, Houston, Tex.; LB—*Chris Spielman, Ohio St., 6-2, 236, Massillon, Ohio; LB—Aundray Bruce, Auburn, 6-6, 236, Montgomery, Ala.; LB—Dante Jones, Oklahoma, 6-2, 235, Dallas, Tex.; DB—*Bennie Blades, Miami (Fla.), 6-0, 215, Fort Lauderdale, Fla.; DB—*Deion Sanders, Florida St., 6-0, 192, Fort Myers, Fla.; DB—Rickey Dixon, Oklahoma, 5-10, 184, Dallas, Tex.; DB—Chuck Cecil, Arizona, 6-0, 185, Red Bluff, Calif.; P—*Tom Tupa, Ohio St., 6-5, 215, Brecksville, Ohio.

1988
Offense

WR—Jason Phillips, Houston, 5-9, 175, Houston, Tex.; WR—Hart Lee Dykes, Oklahoma St., 6-4, 220, Bay City, Tex.; TE—Marv Cook, Iowa, 6-4, 243, West Branch, Iowa; L—*Tony Mandarich, Michigan St., 6-6, 315, Oakville, Ontario, Can.; L—*Anthony Phillips, Oklahoma, 6-3, 286, Tulsa, Okla.; L—Mike Utley, Washington St., 6-6, 302, Seattle, Wash.; L—Mark Stepnoski, Pittsburgh, 6-3, 265, Erie, Pa.; C—Jake Young, Nebraska, 6-5, 260, Midland, Tex.; C—John Vitale, Michigan, 6-1, 273, Detroit, Mich.; QB—Steve Walsh, Miami (Fla.), 6-3, 195, St. Paul, Minn.; QB—Troy Aikman, UCLA, 6-4, 217, Henryetta, Okla.; RB—*Barry Sanders, Oklahoma St., 5-8, 197, Wichita, Kans.; RB—Anthony Thompson, Indiana, 6-0, 205, Terre Haute, Ind.; RB—Tim Worley, Georgia, 6-2, 216, Lumberton, N.C.; PK—Kendall Trainor, Arkansas, 6-2, 205, Fredonia, Kans.

Defense

L—*Mark Messner, Michigan, 6-3, 244, Hartland, Mich.; L—*Tracy Rocker, Auburn, 6-3, 278, Atlanta, Ga.; L—Wayne Martin, Arkansas, 6-5, 263, Cherry Valley, Ark.; L—Frank Stams, Notre Dame, 6-4, 237, Akron, Ohio; L—Bill Hawkins, Miami (Fla.), 6-6, 260, Hollywood, Fla.; LB—*Derrick Thomas, Alabama, 6-4, 230, Miami, Fla.; LB—*Broderick Thomas, Nebraska, 6-3, 235, Houston, Tex.; LB—Michael Stonebreaker, Notre Dame, 6-1, 228, River Ridge, La.; DB—*Deion Sanders, Florida St., 6-0, 195, Fort

Myers, Fla.; DB—Donnell Woolford, Clemson, 5-10, 195, Fayetteville, N.C.; DB—Louis Oliver, Florida, 6-2, 222, Bell Glade, Fla.; DB—Darryl Henley, UCLA, 5-10, 165, Ontario, Calif.; P—Keith English, Colorado, 6-3, 215, Greeley, Colo.

1989
Offense
WR—*Clarkston Hines, Duke, 6-1, 170, Chapel Hill, N.C.; WR—Terance Mathis, New Mexico, 5-9, 167, Stone Mountain, Ga.; TE—Mike Busch, Iowa St., 6-5, 252, Donahue, Iowa; L—Jim Mabry, Arkansas, 6-4, 262, Memphis, Tenn.; L—Bob Kula, Michigan St., 6-4, 282, West Bloomfield, Mich.; L—Mohammed Elewonibi, Brigham Young, 6-5, 290, Kamloops, British Columbia, Can.; L—Joe Garten, Colorado, 6-3, 280, Placentia, Calif.; L—*Eric Still, Tennessee, 6-3, 283, Germantown, Tenn.; C—Jake Young, Nebraska, 6-4, 270, Midland, Tex.; QB—Andre Ware, Houston, 6-2, 205, Dickinson, Tex.; RB—*Anthony Thompson, Indiana, 6-0, 209, Terre Haute, Ind.; RB—*Emmitt Smith, Florida, 5-10, 201, Pensacola, Fla.; PK—*Jason Hanson, Washington St., 6-0, 164, Spokane, Wash.

Defense
L—Chris Zorich, Notre Dame, 6-1, 268, Chicago, Ill.; L—Greg Mark, Miami (Fla.), 6-4, 255, Pennsauken, N.J.; L—Tim Ryan, Southern Cal, 6-5, 260, San Jose, Calif.; L—*Moe Gardner, Illinois, 6-2, 250, Indianapolis, Ind.; LB—*Percy Snow, Michigan St., 6-3, 240, Canton, Ohio; LB—*Keith McCants, Alabama, 6-5, 256, Mobile, Ala.; LB—Alfred Williams, Colorado, 6-6, 230, Houston, Tex.; DB—*Todd Lyght, Notre Dame, 6-1, 181, Flint, Mich.; DB—*Mark Carrier, Southern Cal, 6-1, 185, Long Beach, Calif.; DB—*Tripp Welborne, Michigan, 6-1, 193, Greensboro, N.C.; DB—LeRoy Butler, Florida St., 6-0, 194, Jacksonville, Fla.; P—Tom Rouen, Colorado, 6-3, 220, Littleton, Colo.

1990
Offense
WR—*Raghib Ismail, Notre Dame, 5-10, 175, Wilkes-Barre, Pa.; WR—Herman Moore, Virginia, 6-5, 197, Danville, Va.; TE—*Chris Smith, Brigham Young, 6-4, 230, La Canada, Calif.; OL—*Antone Davis, Tennessee, 6-4, 310, Fort Valley, Ga.; OL—*Joe Garten, Colorado, 6-3, 280, Placentia, Calif.; OL—*Ed King, Auburn, 6-4, 284, Phenix City, Ala.; OL—Stacy Long, Clemson, 6-2, 275, Griffin, Ga.; C—John Flannery, Syracuse, 6-4, 301, Pottsville, Pa.; QB—Ty Detmer, Brigham Young, 6-0, 175, San Antonio, Tex.; RB—*Eric Bieniemy, Colorado, 5-7, 195, West Covina, Calif.; RB—Darren Lewis, Texas A&M, 6-0, 220, Dallas, Tex.; PK—*Philip Doyle, Alabama, 6-1, 190, Birmingham, Ala.

Defense
DL—*Russell Maryland, Miami (Fla.), 6-2, 273, Chicago, Ill.; DL—*Chris Zorich, Notre Dame, 6-1, 266, Chicago, Ill.; DL—Moe Gardner, Illinois, 6-2, 258, Indianapolis, Ind.; DL—David Rocker, Auburn, 6-4, 264, Atlanta, Ga.; LB—*Alfred Williams, Colorado, 6-6, 236, Houston, Tex.; LB—*Michael Stonebreaker, Notre Dame, 6-1, 228, River Ridge, La.; LB—Maurice Crum, Miami (Fla.), 6-0, 222, Tampa, Fla.; DB—*Tripp Welborne, Michigan, 6-1, 201, Greensboro, N.C.; DB—*Darryll Lewis, Arizona, 5-9, 186, West Covina, Calif.; DB—*Ken Swilling, Georgia Tech, 6-3, 230, Toccoa, Ga.; DB—Todd Lyght, Notre Dame, 6-1, 184, Flint, Mich.; P—Brian Greenfield, Pittsburgh, 6-1, 210, Sherman Oaks, Calif.

1991
Offense
WR—*Desmond Howard, Michigan, 5-9, 176, Cleveland, Ohio; WR—Mario Bailey, Washington, 5-9, 167, Seattle, Wash.; TE—Kelly Blackwell, Texas Christian, 6-2, 242, Fort Worth, Tex.; OL—*Greg Skrepenak, Michigan, 6-8, 322, Wilkes-Barre, Pa.; OL—Bob Whitfield, Stanford, 6-7, 300, Carson, Calif.; OL—Jeb Flesch, Clemson, 6-3, 266, Morrow, Ga.; OL—(tie) Jerry Ostroski, Tulsa, 6-4, 305, Collegeville, Pa.; Mirko Jurkovic, Notre Dame, 6-4, 289, Calumet City, Ill.; C—*Jay Leeuwenburg, Colorado, 6-3, 265, Kirkwood, Mo.; QB—Ty Detmer, Brigham Young, 6-0, 175, San Antonio, Tex.; RB—*Vaughn Dunbar, Indiana, 6-0, 207, Fort Wayne, Ind.; RB—(tie) Trevor Cobb, Rice, 5-9, 180, Houston, Tex.; Russell White, California, 6-0, 210, Van Nuys, Calif.; PK—Carlos Huerta, Miami (Fla.), 5-9, 186, Miami, Fla.

Defense
DL—*Steve Emtman, Washington, 6-4, 280, Cheney, Wash.; DL—*Santana Dotson, Baylor, 6-5, 264, Houston, Tex.; DL—Brad Culpepper, Florida, 6-2, 263, Tallahassee, Fla.; DL—Leroy Smith, Iowa, 6-2, 214, Sicklerville, N. J.; LB—*Robert Jones, East Caro., 6-3, 234, Blackstone, Va.; LB—Marvin Jones, Florida St., 6-2, 220, Miami, Fla.; LB—Levon Kirkland, Clemson, 6-2, 245, Lamar, S.C.; DB—*Terrell Buckley, Florida St., 5-10, 175, Pascagoula, Miss.; DB—Dale Carter, Tennessee, 6-2, 182, Oxford, Ga.; DB—Kevin Smith, Texas A&M, 6-0, 180, Orange, Tex.; DB—Darryl Williams, Miami (Fla.), 6-2, 190, Miami, Fla.; P—*Mark Bounds, Texas Tech, 5-11, 185, Stamford, Tex.

(1991 Selectors: Associated Press, United Press International, Football Writers Association of America, American Football Coaches Association and Walter Camp Foundation.)

* Indicates unanimous selection.

CONSENSUS ALL-AMERICANS BY COLLEGE
Beginning in 1924, unanimous selections are indicated by (*).

AIR FORCE
58— Brock Strom, T
70— Ernie Jennings, E
85— Scott Thomas, DB
87—*Chad Hennings, DL

ALABAMA
30—*Fred Sington, T
34— Don Hutson, E
 Bill Lee, T
 Dixie Howell, B
35— Riley Smith, B
37— Leroy Monsky, G
41— Holt Rast, E
42— Joe Domnanovich, C
45— Vaughn Mancha, C

61—*Billy Neighbors, T
62—*Lee Roy Jordan, C
65— Paul Crane, C
66— Ray Perkins, E
   *Cecil Dowdy, T
67— Dennis Homan, E
   Bobby Johns, DB
71— Johnny Musso, B
72—*John Hannah, G
73— Buddy Brown, G
74— Leroy Cook, DL
   Woodrow Lowe, LB
75—*Leroy Cook, DE
77— Ozzie Newsome, WR
78— Marty Lyons, DL
79— Jim Bunch, T
80—*E.J. Junior, DL
81— Tommy Wilcox, DB
82— Mike Pitts, DL
86—*Cornelius Bennett, LB
88—*Derrick Thomas, LB
89—*Keith McCants, LB
90—*Philip Doyle, PK

AMHERST
05— John Hubbard, B

ARIZONA
82— Ricky Hunley, LB
83—*Ricky Hunley, LB
87— Chuck Cecil, DB
90—*Darryll Lewis, DB

ARIZONA ST.
72— Woody Green, B
73— Woody Green, B
77— John Jefferson, WR
78—*Al Harris, DL
81— Mike Richardson, DB
82— Mike Richardson, DB
   Vernon Maxwell, DL
83— Luis Zendejas, PK
84— David Fulcher, DB
85— David Fulcher, DB
86— Danny Villa, OL
87— Randall McDaniel, OL

ARKANSAS
48— Clyde Scott, B
54—*Bud Brooks, G
65— Glen Ray Hines, T
   Loyd Phillips, DT
66—*Loyd Phillips, DT
68— Jim Barnes, G
69— Rodney Brand, C
70— Dick Bumpas, DT
77— Leotis Harris, G
   Steve Little, K
79—*Greg Kolenda, T
81—*Billy Ray Smith, DL
82—*Billy Ray Smith, DL
   *Steve Korte, OL
88— Kendall Trainor, PK
   Wayne Martin, DL
89— Jim Mabry, OL

ARMY
98— Charles Romeyn, B
00— William Smith, E
01— Paul Bunker, T
   Charles Daly, B
02— Paul Bunker, T-B
   Robert Boyers, C
04— Arthur Tipton, C
   Henry Torney, B
05— Henry Torney, B
07— William Erwin, G
11— Leland Devore, T

13— Louis Merillat, E
14— John McEwan, C
16— Elmer Oliphant, B
17— Elmer Oliphant, B
22— Ed Garbisch, C
26— Bud Sprague, T
27— Red Cagle, B
28—*Red Cagle, B
29— Red Cagle, B
32— Milt Summerfelt, G
43—*C. Myslinski, C
44— Glenn Davis, B
   Doc Blanchard, B
45— Tex Coulter, T
   John Green, G
   *Glenn Davis, B
   *Doc Blanchard, B
46— Hank Foldberg, E
   *Glenn Davis, B
   *Doc Blanchard, B
47— Joe Steffy, G
49— Arnold Galiffa, B
50—*Dan Foldberg, E
57— Bob Anderson, B
58—*Pete Dawkins, B
59— Bill Carpenter, E

AUBURN
32— Jimmy Hitchcock, B
57—*Jimmy Phillips, E
58—*Zeke Smith, G
60— Ken Rice, T
64— T. Frederickson, B
69— B. McClinton, DB
70—*L. Willingham, DB
71—*Pat Sullivan, QB
   *Terry Beasley, E
74— Ken Bernich, LB
83— Bo Jackson, RB
84— Gregg Carr, LB
85—*Bo Jackson, RB
86—*Ben Tamburello, C
   *Brent Fullwood, RB
87— Tracy Rocker, DL
   Aundray Bruce, LB
88—*Tracy Rocker, DL
90—*Ed King, OL
   David Rocker, DL

BAYLOR
30— Barton Koch, G
56—*Bill Glass, G
63— Lawrence Elkins, E
64— Lawrence Elkins, B
76— Gary Green, DB
79— Mike Singletary, LB
80—*Mike Singletary, LB
86—*Thomas Everett, DB
91—*Santana Dotson, DL

BOSTON COLLEGE
20— Luke Urban, E
40— Gene Goodreault, E
42— Mike Holovak, B
84—*Doug Flutie, QB
   Tony Thurman, DB
85— Mike Ruth, DL

BRIGHAM YOUNG
79—*Marc Wilson, QB
80— Nick Eyre, OL
81—*Jim McMahon, QB
82—*Gordon Hudson, TE
83—*Gordon Hudson, TE
   *Steve Young, QB
86— Jason Buck, DL
89— M. Elewonibi, OL
90— Ty Detmer, QB

   *Chris Smith, TE
91— Ty Detmer, QB

BROWN
02— Thomas Barry, B
06— John Mayhew, B
09— Adrian Regnier, E
10— Earl Sprackling, B
12— George Crowther, B
16— Fritz Pollard, B

CALIFORNIA
21— Brick Muller, E
   Dan McMillan, T
22— Brick Muller, E
24— Edwin Horrell, C
28— Irv Phillips, E
30— Ted Beckett, G
35— Larry Lutz, T
37— Sam Chapman, B
38— Vic Bottari, B
48— Jackie Jensen, B
49—*Rod Franz, G
50— Les Richter, G
51— Les Richter, G
68— Ed White, MG
71— Sherman White, DT
74— Steve Bartkowski, QB
75— Chuck Muncie, RB
   Steve Rivera, E
83— Ron Rivera, LB
91— Russell White, RB

CARLISLE
99— Isaac Seneca, B
03— James Johnson, B
07— Albert Exendine, E
   Peter Hauser, B
11— Jim Thorpe, B
12— Jim Thorpe, B

CARNEGIE TECH
28— Howard Harpster, B
CENTENARY
33— Paul Geisler, E
CENTRE
19— James Weaver, C
   Bo McMillin, B
21— Bo McMillin, B

CHICAGO
98— C. Herschberger, B
04— Fred Speik, E
   Walter Eckersall, B
05— Mark Catlin, E
   Walter Eckersall, B
06— Walter Eckersall, B
08— Walter Steffen, B
13— Paul Des Jardien, C
22— John Thomas, B
24— Joe Pondelik, G
35—*Jay Berwanger, B

CLEMSON
67— Harry Olszewski, G
74— B. Cunningham, TE
79— Jim Stuckey, DL
81— Jeff Davis, LB
   Terry Kinard, DB
82—*Terry Kinard, DB
83— William Perry, DL
86— Terrence Flagler, RB
87— David Treadwell, PK
88— Donnell Woolford, DB
90— Stacy Long, OL
91— Jeb Flesch, OL
   Levon Kirkland, LB

COLGATE
13— Ellery Huntington, B
16— Clarence Horning, T
    D. Belford West, T
    Oscar Anderson, B
19— D. Belford West, T
30— L. Macaluso, B

COLORADO
37— Byron White, B
60— Joe Romig, G
61— Joe Romig, G
67— Dick Anderson, DB
68— Mike Montler, G
69— Bob Anderson, B
70— Don Popplewell, C
72— Cullen Bryant, DB
85— Barry Helton, P
86— Barry Helton, P
88— Keith English, P
89— Joe Garten, OL
    Alfred Williams, LB
    Tom Rouen, P
90—*Eric Bieniemy, RB
    *Joe Garten, OL
    *Alfred Williams, LB
91—*Jay Leeuwenburg, OL

COLORADO ST.
78— Mike Bell, DL

COLUMBIA
00— Bill Morley, B
01— Harold Weekes, B
    Bill Morley, B
03— Richard Smith, B
42— Paul Governali, B
47— Bill Swiacki, E

CORNELL
95— Clinton Wyckoff, B
00— R. Starbuck, B
01— William Warner, G
    Sanford Hunt, G
02— William Warner, G
06— Elmer Thompson, G
    William Newman, C
08— B. O'Rourke, G
14— John O'Hearn, E
    Charles Barrett, B
15— Murray Shelton, E
    Charles Barrett, B
21— Edgar Kaw, B
22— Edgar Kaw, B
23— George Pfann, B
38— Brud Holland, E
39— Nick Drahos, T
40— Nick Drahos, T
71—*Ed Marinaro, B

DARTMOUTH
03— Henry Hooper, C
    Myron Witham, B
04— Joseph Gilman, G
05— Ralph Glaze, E
08— Geo. Schildmiller, E
    Clark Tobin, G
12— W. Englehorn, T
13— Robert Hogsett, E
14— Clarence Spears, G
15— Clarence Spears, G
17— Eugene Neely, G
19— A. Youngstrom, G
24— Carl Diehl, G
25— Carl Diehl, G
    George Tully, E
    *A. Oberlander, B
38— Bob MacLeod, B

DUKE
33— Fred Crawford, T
36— Ace Parker, B
71— Ernie Jackson, DB
89—*Clarkston Hines, WR

DUQUESNE
36— Mike Basrak, C

EAST CARO.
83— Terry Long, OL
91—*Robert Jones, LB

FLORIDA
66—*Steve Spurrier, B
69— Carlos Alvarez, E
75— Sammy Green, LB
80— David Little, LB
82— Wilber Marshall, DL
83— Wilber Marshall, DL
84— Lomas Brown, OT
88— Louis Oliver, DB
89—*Emmitt Smith, RB
91— Brad Culpepper, DL

FLORIDA ST.
64— Fred Biletnikoff, E
67— Ron Sellers, E
79— Ron Simmons, MG
80— Ron Simmons, MG
83— Greg Allen, RB
85— Jamie Dukes, OL
87—*Deion Sanders, DB
88—*Deion Sanders, DB
89— LeRoy Butler, DB
91—*Terrell Buckley, DB
    Marvin Jones, LB

FORDHAM
36— A. Wojciechowicz,
    C
37— Ed Franco, T
    A. Wojciechowicz,
    C

GEORGETOWN
26— H. Connaughton, G

GEORGIA
27— Tom Nash, E
31— Vernon Smith, E
41— Frank Sinkwich, B
42—*Frank Sinkwich, B
46—*Charley Trippi, B
67— Ed Chandler, T
68— Bill Stanfill, DT
    Jake Scott, DB
71—*Royce Smith, G
75— Randy Johnson, G
76— Joel Parrish, G
80—*Herschel Walker, RB
81—*Herschel Walker, RB
82—*Herschel Walker, RB
    Terry Hoage, DB
83— Terry Hoage, DB
84— Kevin Butler, PK
    Jeff Sanchez, DB
85— Pete Anderson, C
88— Tim Worley, RB

GEORGIA TECH
17— Everett Strupper, B
18— Bill Fincher, E
    Joe Guyon, T
    Ashel Day, C
20— Bill Fincher, E
28— Pete Pund, C
42— Harvey Hardy, G
44— Phil Tinsley, E
46— Paul Duke, C

47— Bob Davis, T
52— Hal Miller, T
53— Larry Morris, C
59— Maxie Baughan, C
66— Jim Breland, C
70— Rock Perdoni, DT
73— Randy Rhino, DB
90—*Ken Swilling, DB

HARVARD
89— Arthur Cumnock, E
    John Cranston, G
    James Lee, B
90— Frank Hallowell, E
    Marshall Newell, T
    John Cranston, C
    Dudley Dean, B
    John Corbett, B
91— Marshall Newell, T
    Everett Lake, B
92— Frank Hallowell, E
    Marshall Newell, T
    Bertram Waters, G
    William Lewis, C
    Charles Brewer, B
93— Marshall Newell, T
    William Lewis, C
    Charles Brewer, B
94— Bertram Waters, T
95— Norman Cabot, E
    Charles Brewer, B
96— Norman Cabot, E
    E. Wrightington, B
97— Alan Doucette, C
    Benjamin Dibblee, B
98— John Hallowell, E
    Walter Boal, G
    Charles Daly, B
    Benjamin Dibblee, B
99— David Campbell, E
    Charles Daly, B
00— John Hallowell, E
    David Campbell, E
    Charles Daly, B
01— David Campbell, E
    Edward Bowditch, E
    Oliver Cutts, T
    Crawford Blagden, T
    William Lee, G
    Charles Barnard, G
    Robert Kernan, B
    Thomas Graydon, B
02— Edward Bowditch, E
    Thomas Graydon, B
03— Daniel Knowlton, T
    Andrew Marshall, G
04— Daniel Hurley, B
05— Beaton Squires, T
    Karl Brill, T
    Francis Burr, G
    Daniel Hurley, B
06— Charles Osborne, T
    Francis Burr, G
07— Patrick Grant, C
    John Wendell, B
08— Hamilton Fish, T
    Charles Nourse, C
    Hamilton Corbett, B
09— Hamilton Fish, T
    Wayland Minot, B
10— Robert McKay, T
    Robert Fisher, G
    Percy Wendell, B
11— Robert Fisher, G
    Percy Wendell, B

12— Samuel Felton, E
　　Stanley Pennock, G
　　Charles Brickley, B
13— Harvey Hitchcock, T
　　Stanley Pennock, G
　　Charles Brickley, B
　　Edward Mahan, B
14— H. Hardwick, E
　　Walter Trumbull, T
　　Stanley Pennock, G
　　Edward Mahan, B
15— Joseph Gilman, T
　　Edward Mahan, B
　　Richard King, B
16— Harrie Dadmun, G
19— Edward Casey, B
20— Tom Woods, G
21— John Brown, G
22— Charles Hubbard, G
23— Charles Hubbard, G
29— Ben Ticknor, C
30—*Ben Ticknor, C
31— Barry Wood, B
41—*E. Peabody, G

HOLY CROSS
74— John Provost, DB

HOUSTON
67— Rich Stotter, G
69— Bill Bridges, G
70— Elmo Wright, E
76— Wilson Whitley, DT
80— Leonard Mitchell, DL
88— Jason Phillips, WR
89— Andre Ware, QB

ILLINOIS
14— Perry Graves, E
　　Ralph Chapman, G
15— Bart Macomber, B
18— John Depler, C
20— Charles Carney, E
23— James McMillen, G
　　Red Grange, B
24—*Red Grange, B
25— Red Grange, B
26— Bernie Shively, G
46— Alex Agase, G
51— Johnny Karras, B
53— J. C. Caroline, B
59— Bill Burrell, G
63—*Dick Butkus, C
64— Dick Butkus, C
65—*Jim Grabowski, B
84—*David Williams, WR
85—*David Williams, WR
89—*Moe Gardner, DL
90— Moe Gardner, DL

INDIANA
42— Billy Hillenbrand, B
44— John Tavener, C
45— Bob Ravensberg, E
88— Anthony Thompson, RB
89—*Anthony Thompson, RB
91—*Vaughn Dunbar, RB

IOWA
19— Lester Belding, E
21— Aubrey Devine, B
22— Gordon Locke, B
39— Nile Kinnick, B
54— Calvin Jones, G
55— Calvin Jones, G
57— Alex Karras, T
58—*Randy Duncan, B
81— Andre Tippett, DL

　　Reggie Roby, P
84— Larry Station, LB
85—*Chuck Long, QB
　　*Larry Station, LB
88— Marv Cook, TE
91— Leroy Smith, DL

IOWA ST.
38— Ed Bock, G
89— Mike Busch, TE

KANSAS
63— Gale Sayers, B
64— Gale Sayers, B
68— John Zook, DE
73— David Jaynes, QB

KANSAS ST.
77— Gary Spani, LB

KENTUCKY
50— Bob Gain, T
　　Babe Parilli, B
51— Babe Parilli, B
56— Lou Michaels, T
57— Lou Michaels, T
65— Sam Ball, T
77—*Art Still, DL

LAFAYETTE
00— Walter Bachman, C
01— Walter Bachman, C
21— Frank Schwab, G
22— Frank Schwab, G

LOUISIANA ST.
35— Gaynell Tinsley, E
36—*Gaynell Tinsley, E
39— Ken Kavanaugh, E
54— Sid Fournet, T
58—*Billy Cannon, B
59— Billy Cannon, B
61—*Roy Winston, G
62—*Jerry Stovall, B
70— Mike Anderson, LB
　　T. Casanova, DB
71— T. Casanova, DB
72— Bert Jones, QB
77— C. Alexander, RB
78— C. Alexander, RB
87— Wendell Davis, WR
　　*Nacho Albergamo, C

MARQUETTE
36— Ray Buivid, B

MARYLAND
51—*Bob Ward, G
52— Dick Modzelewski, T
　　*Jack Scarbath, B
53—*Stan Jones, T
55—*Bob Pellegrini, C
61— Gary Collins, E
74—*Randy White, DL
76— Joe Campbell, DT
79— Dale Castro, PK
85— J.D. Maarleveld, OL

MIAMI (FLA.)
61— Bill Miller, E
66— Tom Beier, DB
67—*Ted Hendricks, DE
68—*Ted Hendricks, DE
73— Tony Cristiani, DL
74— Rubin Carter, MG
81— Fred Marion, DB
84— Eddie Brown, WR
85— Willie Smith, TE
86—*Vinny Testaverde, QB
　　*Jerome Brown, DL
　　Bennie Blades, DB

87—*Daniel Stubbs, DL
　　*Bennie Blades, DB
88— Steve Walsh, QB
　　Bill Hawkins, DL
89— Greg Mark, DL
90— Maurice Crum, LB
　　*Russell Maryland, DL
91— Carlos Huerta, PK
　　Darryl Williams, DB

MICHIGAN
98— W. Cunningham, C
01— Neil Snow, E
03— Willie Heston, B
04— Willie Heston, B
07— Adolph Schulz, C
09— Albert Benbrook, G
10— Stanfield Wells, E
　　Albert Benbrook, G
13— Miller Pontius, T
　　Jim Craig, B
14— John Maulbetsch, B
22— Harry Kipke, B
23— Jack Blott, C
25— B. Oosterbaan, E
　　Benny Friedman, B
26— B. Oosterbaan, E
　　Benny Friedman, B
27—*B. Oosterbaan, E
28— O. Pommerening, T
32—*Harry Newman, B
33— Francis Wistert, T
　　*Chuck Bernard, C
38—*Ralph Heikkinen, G
39— Tom Harmon, B
40—*Tom Harmon, B
41— Bob Westfall, B
42— Albert Wistert, T
　　Julie Franks, G
43—*Bill Daley, B
47—*Bob Chappuis, B
48— Dick Rifenburg, E
　　Alvin Wistert, T
49— Alvin Wistert, T
55— Ron Kramer, E
56—*Ron Kramer, E
65— Bill Yearby, DT
66—*Jack Clancy, E
69—*Jim Mandich, E
　　Tom Curtis, DB
70— Dan Dierdorf, T
71— Reggie McKenzie, G
　　*Mike Taylor, LB
72— Paul Seymour, T
　　Randy Logan, DB
73— Dave Gallagher, DL
　　Dave Brown, DB
74—*Dave Brown, DB
76— Rob Lytle, RB
　　Mark Donahue, G
77—*Mark Donahue, G
79— Ron Simpkins, LB
81—*Anthony Carter, WR
　　Ed Muransky, OL
　　Kurt Becker, OL
82—*Anthony Carter, WR
85— Mike Hammerstein, DL
　　Brad Cochran, DB
86— Garland Rivers, DB
87— John Elliott, OL
88— John Vitale, C
　　*Mark Messner, DL
89—*Tripp Welborne, DB
90—*Tripp Welborne, DB
91—*Desmond Howard, WR
　　*Greg Skrepenak, OL

MICHIGAN ST.
15— N. Jerry DaPrato, B
35— Sidney Wagner, G
49— Ed Bagdon, G
51— Bob Carey, E
　　*Don Coleman, T
53— Don Dohoney, E
55— Norman Masters, T
　　Earl Morrall, B
57— Dan Currie, C
　　Walt Kowalczyk, B
58— Sam Williams, E
62— George Saimes, B
63— Sherman Lewis, B
65— Bubba Smith, DE
　　*George Webster, DB
66— Clint Jones, B
　　*Bubba Smith, DE
　　*George Webster, DB
72— *Brad VanPelt, DB
85— *Lorenzo White, RB
87— Lorenzo White, RB
88— Tony Mandarich, OL
89— *Percy Snow, LB
　　Bob Kula, OL

MINNESOTA
03— Fred Schacht, T
09— John McGovern, B
10— James Walker, T
16— Bert Baston, E
17— George Hauser, T
23— Ray Ecklund, E
26— Herb Joesting, B
27— Herb Joesting, B
29— Bronko Nagurski, T
31— Biggie Munn, G
34— Frank Larson, E
　　Bill Bevan, G
　　Pug Lund, B
35— Ed Widseth, T
36— *Ed Widseth, T
40— Urban Odson, T
　　George Franck, B
41— Dick Wildung, T
　　Bruce Smith, B
42— Dick Wildung, T
48— Leo Nomellini, T
49— Leo Nomellini, T
　　*C. Tonnemaker, C
53— *Paul Giel, B
60— *Tom Brown, G
61— Sandy Stephens, B
62— *Bobby Bell, T
63— Carl Eller, T
65— Aaron Brown, DE

MISSISSIPPI
47— Charley Conerly, B
53— Crawford Mims, G
59— Charlie Flowers, B
60— *Jake Gibbs, B
62— Jim Dunaway, T
79— Jim Miller, P

MISSISSIPPI ST.
74— Jimmy Webb, DL

MISSOURI
41— Darold Jenkins, C
60— *Danny LaRose, E
65— Johnny Roland, DB
68— Roger Wehrli, DB
78— Kellen Winslow, TE
86— John Clay, OL

NAVY
07— Bill Dague, E

08— Percy Northcroft, T
　　Ed Lange, B
11— Jack Dalton, B
13— John Brown, G
18— Lyman Perry, G
　　Wolcott Roberts, B
22— Wendell Taylor, T
26— *Frank Wickhorst, T
28— Edward Burke, G
34— Fred Borries, B
43— Don Whitmire, T
44— *Don Whitmire, T
　　Ben Chase, G
　　Bob Jenkins, B
45— Dick Duden, E
54— Ron Beagle, E
55— *Ron Beagle, E
60— *Joe Bellino, B
63— *Roger Staubach, B
75— *Chet Moeller, DB
83— Napoleon McCallum, RB
85— Napoleon McCallum, RB

NEBRASKA
15— Guy Chamberlin, E
24— Ed Weir, T
25— *Ed Weir, T
33— George Sauer, B
36— Sam Francis, B
63— *Bob Brown, G
64— *Larry Kramer, T
65— Freeman White, E
　　Walt Barnes, DT
66— LaVerne Allers, G
　　Wayne Meylan, MG
67— Wayne Meylan, MG
70— Bob Newton, T
71— Johnny Rodgers, FL
　　Willie Harper, DE
　　Larry Jacobson, DT
72— *Johnny Rodgers, FL
　　Willie Harper, DE
　　*Rich Glover, MG
73— *John Dutton, DL
74— M. Crenshaw, OT
75— *Rik Bonness, C
76— Dave Butterfield, DB
78— Kelvin Clark, OT
79— *Junior Miller, TE
80— R. Schleusener, OL
　　Jarvis Redwine, RB
81— *Dave Rimington, C
82— *Dave Rimington, C
　　Mike Rozier, RB
83— *Irving Fryar, WR
　　Dean Steinkuhler, OL
　　*Mike Rozier, RB
84— *Mark Traynowicz, C
86— *Danny Noonan, DL
88— Jake Young, C
　　*Broderick Thomas, LB
89— Jake Young, C

NEW MEXICO
89— Terance Mathis, WR

NEW YORK U.
28— Ken Strong, B

NORTH CARO.
37— Andy Bershak, E
48— Charlie Justice, B
70— Don McCauley, B
72— Ron Rusnak, G
74— Ken Huff, G
77— Dee Hardison, DL
80— *Lawrence Taylor, LB
83— William Fuller, DL

NORTH CARO. ST.
67— Dennis Byrd, DT
73— Bill Yoest, G
78— Jim Ritcher, C
　　Ted Brown, RB
79— *Jim Ritcher, C

NORTH TEXAS
68— Joe Greene, DT

NORTHWESTERN
26— Ralph Baker, B
30— Frank Baker, E
31— Jack Riley, T
　　Dallas Marvil, T
　　Pug Rentner, B
36— Steve Reid, G
40— Alf Bauman, T
45— Max Morris, E
59— Ron Burton, B
62— Jack Cvercko, G

NOTRE DAME
13— Gus Dorais, B
17— Frank Rydzewski, C
20— George Gipp, B
21— Eddie Anderson, E
24— Harry Stuhldreher, B
　　Jimmy Crowley, B
　　Emer Layden, B
26— Bud Boeringer, C
27— John Smith, G
29— Jack Cannon, G
　　*Frank Carideo, B
30— *Frank Carideo, B
　　Marchy Schwartz, B
31— Tommy Yarr, C
　　Marchy Schwartz, B
32— *Joe Kurth, T
34— Jack Robinson, C
35— Wayne Millner, E
37— Chuck Sweeney, E
38— *Ed Beinor, T
41— Bob Dove, E
42— Bob Dove, E
43— John Yonakor, E
　　Jim White, T
　　Pat Filley, G
　　Angelo Bertelli, B
　　Creighton Miller, B
46— George Connor, T
　　*John Lujack, B
47— George Connor, T
　　Bill Fischer, G
　　*John Lujack, B
48— Leon Hart, E
　　Bill Fischer, G
　　Emil Sitko, B
49— *Leon Hart, E
　　*Emil Sitko, B
　　Bob Williams, B
50— Jerry Groom, C
52— *Johnny Lattner, B
53— Art Hunter, T
　　*Johnny Lattner, B
54— *Ralph Guglielmi, B
55— Paul Hornung, B
57— Al Ecuyer, G
59— Monty Stickles, E
64— Jack Snow, E
　　John Huarte, B
65— *Dick Arrington, G
　　Nick Rassas, B
66— Tom Regner, G
　　*Nick Eddy, B
　　Alan Page, DE
　　*Jim Lynch, LB

67— Tom Schoen, DB
68— George Kunz, T
     Terry Hanratty, QB
69— *Mike McCoy, DT
70— Tom Gatewood, E
     Larry DiNardo, G
71— *Walt Patulski, DE
     Clarence Ellis, DB
72— *Greg Marx, DT
73— Dave Casper, TE
     Mike Townsend, DB
74— Pete Demmerle, WR
     Gerry DiNardo, G
75— *Steve Niehaus, DT
76— Ken MacAfee, TE
     *Ross Browner, DE
77— *Ken MacAfee, TE
     *Ross Browner, DE
     Luther Bradley, DB
78— Dave Huffman, C
     *Bob Golic, LB
79— Vagas Ferguson, RB
80— *John Scully, C
     Bob Crable, LB
81— Bob Crable, LB
87— *Tim Brown, WR
88— Frank Stams, DL
     Michael Stonebreaker, LB
89— *Todd Lyght, DB
     Chris Zorich, DL
90— *Raghib Ismail, WR/RB
     Todd Lyght, DB
     *Michael Stonebreaker, LB
     *Chris Zorich, DL
91— Mirko Jurkovic, OL

OHIO ST.
16— Charles Harley, B
17— Charles Bolen, E
     Charles Harley, B
19— Charles Harley, B
20— Iolas Huffman, G
     G. Stinchcomb, B
21— Iolas Huffman, T
25— Ed Hess, G
28— Wes Fesler, E
29— Wes Fesler, E
30— *Wes Fesler, E
35— Gomer Jones, C
39— Esco Sarkkinen, E
44— Jack Dugger, E
     Bill Hackett, G
     *Les Horvath, B
45— *Warren Amling, G
46— Warren Amling, T
50— *Vic Janowicz, B
54— *Howard Cassady, B
55— *Howard Cassady, B
56— *Jim Parker, G
58— Bob White, B
60— *Bob Ferguson, B
61— *Bob Ferguson, B
68— *Dave Foley, T
69— Jim Otis, B
     Jim Stillwagon, MG
     Jack Tatum, DB
70— *Jim Stillwagon, MG
     *Jack Tatum, DB
72— Randy Gradishar, LB
73— *John Hicks, OT
     *Randy Gradishar, LB
74— K. Schumacher, OT
     Steve Myers, C
     *Archie Griffin, RB
75— *Archie Griffin, RB

Ted Smith, G
Tim Fox, DB
76— Chris Ward, T
     Bob Brudzinski, DE
77— *Chris Ward, T
     Tom Cousineau, LB
78— Tom Cousineau, LB
79— Ken Fritz, G
82— Marcus Marek, LB
84— Jim Lachey, OG
     *Keith Byars, RB
86— Cris Carter, WR
     Chris Spielman, LB
87— *Chris Spielman, LB
     *Tom Tupa, P

OKLAHOMA
38— Waddy Young, E
48— Buddy Burris, G
50— Jim Weatherall, T
     Leon Heath, B
51— *Jim Weatherall, T
52— Billy Vessels, B
53— J. D. Roberts, G
54— Max Boydston, E
     Kurt Burris, C
55— Bo Bolinger, G
56— *Jerry Tubbs, C
     Tommy McDonald, B
57— Bill Krisher, G
     Clendon Thomas, B
58— Bob Harrison, C
63— Jim Grisham, B
64— Ralph Neely, T
65— Carl McAdams, LB
67— *G. Liggins, MG
69— *Steve Owens, B
71— *Greg Pruitt, B
     Tom Brahaney, C
72— *Greg Pruitt, B
     Tom Brahaney, C
73— *Lucious Selmon, DL
     Rod Shoate, LB
74— John Roush, G
     *Joe Washington, RB
     *Rod Shoate, LB
75— *Lee Roy Selmon, DT
     Dewey Selmon, MG
     Jimbo Elrod, DE
76— *Mike Vaughan, OT
77— *Zac Henderson, DB
78— *Greg Roberts, G
     *Billy Sims, RB
79— *Billy Sims, RB
     *George Cumby, LB
80— Louis Oubre, OL
81— Terry Crouch, OL
82— Rick Bryan, DL
83— *Rick Bryan, DL
84— Tony Casillas, DL
85— Tony Casillas, DL
     *Brian Bosworth, LB
86— *Keith Jackson, TE
     *Brian Bosworth, LB
87— *Keith Jackson, TE
     *Mark Hutson, OL
     Dante Jones, LB
     Rickey Dixon, DB
88— *Anthony Phillips, OL

OKLAHOMA ST.
45— Bob Fenimore, B
69— John Ward, T
76— Derrel Gofourth, C
77— *Terry Miller, RB
84— Rod Brown, DB

85— Thurman Thomas, RB
     *Leslie O'Neal, DL
88— Hart Lee Dykes, WR
     *Barry Sanders, RB
OREGON
62— Mel Renfro, B
OREGON ST.
56— John Witte, T
58— Ted Bates, T
62— *Terry Baker, B
63— Vern Burke, E
68— *John Didion, C
PENN ST.
06— William Dunn, C
19— Bob Higgins, E
20— Charles Way, B
21— Glenn Killinger, B
23— Harry Wilson, B
59— Richie Lucas, B
64— Glenn Ressler, G
68— *Ted Kwalick, E
     Dennis Onkotz, LB
69— *Mike Reid, DT
     Dennis Onkotz, LB
70— Jack Ham, LB
71— Dave Joyner, T
72— Bruce Bannon, DE
     John Skorupan, LB
73— *John Cappelletti, B
74— M. Hartenstine, DL
75— Greg Buttle, LB
78— *Keith Dorney, OT
     *Chuck Fusina, QB
     *Bruce Clark, DL
79— *Bruce Clark, DL
81— *Sean Farrell, OL
86— D. J. Dozier, RB
     Shane Conlan, LB

PENNSYLVANIA
91— John Adams, C
92— Harry Thayer, B
94— Charles Gelbert, E
     Arthur Knipe, B
     George Brooke, B
95— Charles Gelbert, E
     Charles Wharton, G
     Alfred Bull, C
     George Brooke, B
96— Charles Gelbert, E
     Charles Wharton, G
     Wylie Woodruff, G
97— John Outland, T
     T. Truxton Hare, G
     John Minds, B
98— T. Truxton Hare, G
     Pete Overfield, C
     John Outland, B
99— T. Truxton Hare, G
     Pete Overfield, C
     Josiah McCracken, B
00— T. Truxton Hare, G
04— Frank Piekarski, G
     V. Stevenson, B
     Andrew Smith, B
05— Otis Lamson, T
     Robert Torrey, C
06— August Ziegler, G
     Wm. Hollenback, B
07— Dexter Draper, T
     August Ziegler, G
08— Hunter Scarlett, E
     Wm. Hollenback, B
10— Ernest Cozens, C
     E. LeRoy Mercer, B

12— E. LeRoy Mercer, B
17— Henry Miller, E
19— Henry Miller, E
22— John Thurman, T
24— Ed McGinley, T
27— Ed Hake, T
28— Paul Scull, B
43— Bob Odell, B
45— George Savitsky, T
47— Chuck Bednarik, C
48— Chuck Bednarik, C
PITTSBURGH
15— Robert Peck, C
16— James Herron, E
    Robert Peck, C
17— Dale Seis, G
    John Sutherland, G
18— Leonard Hilty, T
    Tom Davies, B
    George McLaren, B
20— Herb Stein, C
21— Herb Stein, C
25— Ralph Chase, T
27—*Gibby Welch, B
28— Mike Getto, T
29—*Joe Donchess, E
    Ray Montgomery, G
31— Jesse Quatse, T
32— Joe Skladany, E
    *Warren Heller, B
33— Joe Skladany, E
34— Chuck Hartwig, G
36— Averell Daniell, T
37— Tony Matisi, T
    Marshall Goldberg, B
38—*Marshall Goldberg, B
56—*Joe Walton, B
58— John Guzik, G
60—*Mike Ditka, E
63— Paul Martha, B
76—*Tony Dorsett, RB
    Al Romano, MG
77— Tom Brzoza, C
    Randy Holloway, DL
    Bob Jury, DB
78— Hugh Green, DL
79—*Hugh Green, DL
80—*Hugh Green, DL
    *Mark May, OL
81— Sal Sunseri, LB
82— Jimbo Covert, OL
83—*Bill Fralic, OL
84—*Bill Fralic, OT
86— Randy Dixon, OL
    Tony Woods, DL
87— Craig Heyward, RB
88— Mark Stepnoski, OL
90— Brian Greenfield, P
PRINCETON
89— Hector Cowan, T
    William George, C
    Edgar Allan Poe, B
    Roscoe Channing, B
    Knowlton Ames, B
90— Ralph Warren, E
    Jesse Riggs, G
    Sheppard Homans, B
91— Jesse Riggs, G
    Philip King, B
    Sheppard Homans, B
92— Arthur Wheeler, G
    Philip King, B
93— Thomas Trenchard, E
    Langdon Lea, T

Arthur Wheeler, G
    Philip King, B
    Franklin Morse, B
94— Langdon Lea, T
    Arthur Wheeler, G
95— Langdon Lea, T
    Dudley Riggs, G
96— William Church, T
    Robert Gailey, C
    Addison Kelly, B
    John Baird, B
97— Garrett Cochran, E
    Addison Kelly, B
98— Lew Palmer, E
    Arthur Hillebrand, T
99— Arthur Hillebrand, T
    Arthur Poe, E
    Howard Reiter, B
01— Ralph Davis, E
02— John DeWitt, G
03— Howard Henry, E
    John DeWitt, G
    J. Dana Kafer, G
04— James Cooney, T
05— James McCormick, B
06— L. Casper Wister, E
    James Cooney, T
    Edward Dillon, B
07— L. Casper Wister, E
    Edwin Harlan, B
    James McCormick, B
08—*Frederick Tibbott, B
10— Talbot Pendleton, B
11— Sanford White, E
    Edward Hart, T
    Joseph Duff, G
12— John Logan, G
13— Harold Ballin, T
14— Harold Ballin, T
16— Frank Hogg, G
18— Frank Murrey, B
20— Stan Keck, T
    Donold Lourie, B
21— Stan Keck, G
22— C. Herbert Treat, T
25— Ed McMillan, C
35— John Weller, G
51—*Dick Kazmaier, B
52— Frank McPhee, E
65— Stas Maliszewski, G
PURDUE
29— Elmer Sleight, T
    Ralph Welch, B
32—*Paul Moss, E
33— Duane Purvis, B
40— Dave Rankin, E
43— Alex Agase, G
52— Bernie Flowers, E
65— Bob Griese, QB
67—*Leroy Keyes, B
68—*Leroy Keyes, B
    Chuck Kyle, MG
69—*Mike Phipps, QB
72— Otis Armstrong, B
    Dave Butz, DT
80—*Dave Young, TE
    *Mark Herrmann, QB
86— Rod Woodson, DB
RICE
46— Weldon Humble, G
49— James Williams, E
54— Dicky Maegle, B
58— Buddy Dial, E
76— Tommy Kramer, QB

91— Trevor Cobb, RB
RICHMOND
69— Walker Gillette, E
78— Jeff Nixon, DB
RUTGERS
17— Paul Robeson, E
18— Paul Robeson, E
61— Alex Kroll, C

SANTA CLARA
38— Alvord Wolff, T
39— John Schiechl, C
SOUTH CARO.
80—*George Rogers, RB
84— Del Wilkes, OG

SOUTHERN CAL
26— Mort Kaer, B
27— Jesse Hibbs, T
    Morley Drury, B
30— Erny Pinckert, B
31— John Baker, G
    Gus Shaver, B
32—*Ernie Smith, T
33— Aaron Rosenberg, G
    *C. Warburton, B
39—*Harry Smith, G
43—*Ralph Heywood, E
44— John Ferraro, T
47— Paul Cleary, E
52— Elmer Willhoite, G
    Jim Sears, B
62— Hal Bedsole, E
65—*Mike Garrett, B
66— Ron Yary, T
    Nate Shaw, DB
67—*Ron Yary, T
    *O. J. Simpson, B
    Tim Rossovich, DE
    Adrian Young, LB
68—*O. J. Simpson, B
69— Jim Gunn, DE
70— Charlie Weaver, DE
72—*Charles Young, TE
73— Lynn Swann, WR
    Booker Brown, OT
    Richard Wood, LB
    Artimus Parker, DB
74—*Anthony Davis, RB
    Richard Wood, LB
75—*Ricky Bell, RB
76—*Ricky Bell, RB
    Gary Jeter, DT
    Dennis Thurman, DB
77—*Dennis Thurman, DB
78—*Pat Howell, G
    *Charles White, RB
79—*Brad Budde, G
    *Charles White, RB
80— Keith Van Horne, OL
    *Ronnie Lott, DB
81— Roy Foster, OL
    *Marcus Allen, RB
82—*Don Mosebar, OL
    Bruce Matthews, OL
    George Achica, MG
83— Tony Slaton, C
84— Jack Del Rio, LB
85— Jeff Bregel, OL
86— Jeff Bregel, OL
    Tim McDonald, DB
87— Dave Cadigan, OL
89—*Mark Carrier, DB
    Tim Ryan, DL

SOUTHERN METHODIST
35— J. C. Wetsel, G
    Bobby Wilson, B
47— Doak Walker, B
48— *Doak Walker, B
49— Doak Walker, B
50— Kyle Rote, B
51— Dick Hightower, C
66— John LaGrone, MG
68— Jerry LeVias, E
72— Robert Popelka, DB
74— Louie Kelcher, G
78— Emanuel Tolbert, WR
80— John Simmons, DB
82— *Eric Dickerson, RB
83— *Russell Carter, DB
85— Reggie Dupard, RB

ST. MARY'S (CAL.)
27— Larry Bettencourt, C
45— *H.Wedemeyer, B

STANFORD
24— Jim Lawson, E
25— Ernie Nevers, B
28— Seraphim Post, G
    Don Robesky, G
32— Bill Corbus, G
33— Bill Corbus, G
34— Bob Reynolds, T
    Bobby Grayson, B
35— James Moscrip, E
    *Bobby Grayson, B
40— Frank Albert, B
41— Frank Albert, B
42— Chuck Taylor, G
50— Bill McColl, E
51— *Bill McColl, E
56— John Brodie, QB
70— Jim Plunkett, QB
71— Jeff Siemon, LB
74— Pat Donovan, DL
77— Guy Benjamin, QB
79— Ken Margerum, WR
80— *Ken Margerum, WR
82— *John Elway, QB
86— Brad Muster, RB
91— Bob Whitfield, OL

SYRACUSE
08— Frank Horr, T
15— Harold White, G
17— Alfred Cobb, T
18— Lou Usher, T
    Joe Alexander, G
19— Joe Alexander, G
23— Pete McRae, E
26— Vic Hanson, E
56— *Jim Brown, B
59— *Roger Davis, G
60— Ernie Davis, B
61— *Ernie Davis, B
67— *Larry Csonka, B
85— *Tim Green, DL
87— *Don McPherson, QB
    Ted Gregory, DL
90— John Flannery, C

TEMPLE
85— John Rienstra, OL
86— *Paul Palmer, RB

TENNESSEE
29— Gene McEver, B
33— Beattie Feathers, B
38— Bowden Wyatt, E
39— Ed Molinski, G
    George Cafego, B

40— *Bob Suffridge, G
46— Dick Huffman, T
51— *Hank Lauricella, B
52— John Michels, G
56— *John Majors, B
65— Frank Emanuel, LB
66— Paul Naumoff, LB
67— *Bob Johnson, C
68— *C. Rosenfelder, G
    Steve Kiner, LB
69— Chip Kell, G
    *Steve Kiner, LB
70— *Chip Kell, G
71— *Bobby Majors, DB
75— Larry Seivers, E
76— Larry Seivers, SE
79— Roland James, DB
83— *Reggie White, DL
84— Bill Mayo, OG
85— Tim McGee, WR
89— *Eric Still, OL
90— *Antone Davis, OL
91— Dale Carter, DB

TEXAS
45— Hubert Bechtol, E
46— Hubert Bechtol, E
47— Bobby Layne, B
50— *Bud McFadin, G
53— Carlton Massey, E
61— *Jimmy Saxton, B
62— *J. Treadwell, G
63— *Scott Appleton, T
65— Tommy Nobis, LB
68— Chris Gilbert, B
69— Bob McKay, T
70— Bobby Wuensch, T
    Steve Worster, B
    Bill Atessis, DE
71— *Jerry Sisemore, T
72— *Jerry Sisemore, T
73— *Bill Wyman, C
    Roosevelt Leaks, B
75— Bob Simmons, T
77— *Earl Campbell, RB
    *Brad Shearer, DL
78— *Johnnie Johnson, DB
79— *Steve McMichael, DL
    *Johnnie Johnson, DB
80— Kenneth Sims, DL
81— Terry Tausch, OL
    *Kenneth Sims, DL
83— Doug Dawson, OL
    Jeff Leiding, LB
    Jerry Gray, DB
84— Tony Degrate, DL
    *Jerry Gray, DB

TEXAS A&M
37— Joe Routt, G
39— John Kimbrough, B
40— Marshall Robnett, G
    *John Kimbrough, B
57— *John D. Crow, B
70— Dave Elmendorf, DB
74— Pat Thomas, DB
75— *Ed Simonini, LB
    Pat Thomas, DB
76— Tony Franklin, PK
    *Robert Jackson, LB
85— Johnny Holland, LB
87— John Roper, DL
90— Darren Lewis, RB
91— Kevin Smith, DB

TEXAS CHRISTIAN
35— Darrell Lester, C

36— Sammy Baugh, B
38— Ki Aldrich, C
    *Davey O'Brien, B
55— *Jim Swink, B
59— Don Floyd, T
60— *Bob Lilly, T
84— *Kenneth Davis, RB
91— Kelly Blackwell, TE

TEXAS TECH
60— E. J. Holub, C
65— Donny Anderson, B
77— Dan Irons, T
82— Gabriel Rivera, DL
91— *Mark Bounds, P

TOLEDO
71— Mel Long, DT

TULANE
31— *Jerry Dalrymple, E
32— Don Zimmerman, B
39— Harley McCollum, T
41— Ernie Blandin, T

TULSA
65— *Howard Twilley, E
91— Jerry Ostroski, OL

UCLA
46— *Burr Baldwin, E
52— Donn Moomaw, C
53— Paul Cameron, B
54— Jack Ellena, T
55— H. Cureton, G
57— Dick Wallen, E
66— Mel Farr, B
67— *Gary Beban, B
    Don Manning, LB
69— Mike Ballou, LB
73— Kermit Johnson, B
75— John Sciarra, QB
76— Jerry Robinson, LB
77— *Jerry Robinson, LB
78— *Jerry Robinson, LB
    Kenny Easley, DB
79— *Kenny Easley, DB
80— *Kenny Easley, DB
81— *Tim Wrightman, TE
83— Don Rogers, DB
85— *John Lee, PK
88— Troy Aikman, QB
    Darryl Henley, DB

UTAH ST.
61— Merlin Olsen, T
69— Phil Olsen, DE

VANDERBILT
23— Lynn Bomar, E
24— Henry Wakefield, E
32— Pete Gracey, C
58— George Deiderich, G
82— Jim Arnold, P
84— *Ricky Anderson, P

VIRGINIA
15— Eugene Mayer, B
41— Bill Dudley, B
85— *Jim Dombrowski, OL
90— Herman Moore, WR

VIRGINIA TECH
67— Frank Loria, DB
84— Bruce Smith, DL

WAKE FOREST
76— *Bill Armstrong, DB

WASH. & JEFF.
14— John Spiegel, B
18— Wilbur Henry, T
19— Wilbur Henry, T

WASHINGTON
25— George Wilson, B
28— Charles Carroll, B
36— Max Starcevich, G
40— Rudy Mucha, C
41— Ray Frankowski, G
63— Rick Redman, G
64— Rick Redman, G
66— Tom Greenlee, DT
68— Al Worley, DB
82—*Chuck Nelson, PK
84— Ron Holmes, DL
86— Jeff Jaeger, PK
    Reggie Rogers, DL
91—*Steve Emtman, DL
    Mario Bailey, WR

WASHINGTON ST.
84— Rueben Mayes, RB
88— Mike Utley, OL
89—*Jason Hanson, PK

WEST VA.
19— Ira Rodgers, B
55— Bruce Bosley, T
82—*Darryl Talley, LB
85— Brian Jozwiak, OL

WILLIAMS
17— Ben Boynton, B
19— Ben Boynton, B

WISCONSIN
12— Robert Butler, T
13— Ray Keeler, G
15— Howard Buck, T
19— C. Carpenter, C
20— Ralph Scott, T
23— Marty Below, T
30— Milo Lubratovich, T
42—*Dave Schreiner, E
54—*Alan Ameche, B
59—*Dan Lanphear, T
62— Pat Richter, E
75— Dennis Lick, T
81— Tim Krumrie, DL

WYOMING
83— Jack Weil, P
84— Jay Novacek, TE

YALE
89— Amos A. Stagg, E

Charles Gill, T
P. Heffelfinger, G
90— William Rhodes, T
P. Heffelfinger, G
Thomas McClung, B
91— Frank Hinkey, E
John Hartwell, E
Wallace Winter, T
P. Heffelfinger, G
Thomas McClung, B
92— Frank Hinkey, E
A. H. Wallis, T
V. McCormick, B
93— Frank Hinkey, E
William Hickok, G
Frank Butterworth, B
94— Frank Hinkey, E
William Hickok, G
Philip Stillman, C
George Adee, B
Frank Butterworth, B
95— Fred Murphy, T
Samuel Thorne, B
96— Fred Murphy, T
Clarence Fincke, B
97— John Hall, E
Burr Chamberlin, T
Gordon Brown, G
C. DeSaulles, B
98— Burr Chamberlin, T
Gordon Brown, G
Malcolm McBride, B
99— George Stillman, T
Gordon Brown, G
Malcolm McBride, B
Albert Sharpe, B
00— George Stillman, T
James Bloomer, T
Gordon Brown, G
Herman Olcott, C
George Chadwick, B
Perry Hale, B
William Fincke, B
01— Henry Holt, C
02— Thomas Shevlin, E
Ralph Kinney, T
James Hogan, T
Edgar Glass, G
Henry Holt, C
Foster Rockwell, B

George Chadwick, B
03— Charles Rafferty, E
James Hogan, T
James Bloomer, G
W. L. Mitchell, B
04— Thomas Shevlin, E
James Hogan, T
Ralph Kinney, G
Foster Rockwell, B
05— Thomas Shevlin, E
Roswell Tripp, G
Howard Roome, B
Guy Hutchinson, B
06— Robert Forbes, E
L. Horatio Biglow, T
Hugh Knox, B
Paul Veeder, B
07— Clarence Alcott, E
L. Horatio Biglow, T
T. A. D. Jones, B
Edward Coy, B
08— William Goebel, G
Hamlin Andrus, G
Edward Coy, B
09— John Kilpatrick, E
Henry Hobbs, T
Hamlin Andrus, G
Carroll Cooney, C
Edward Coy, B
Stephen Philbin, B
10— John Kilpatrick, E
11— D. Bomeisler, E
Henry Ketcham, C
Arthur Howe, B
12— D. Bomeisler, E
Henry Ketcham, C
13— Nelson Talbott, T
14— Harry LeGore, B
16— Clinton Black, G
20— Tim Callahan, G
21— Malcolm Aldrich, B
23— Century Milstead, T
William Mallory, B
24— Dick Luman, E
27— Bill Webster, G
J. Charlesworth, C
36— Larry Kelley, E
37—*Clint Frank, B
44— Paul Walker, E

TEAM LEADERS IN CONSENSUS ALL-AMERICANS
(Ranked on total number of selections)

Team	No.	Players	Team	No.	Players
Yale	100	69	Michigan St.	24	21
Notre Dame	89	74	Navy	23	20
Harvard	89	59	UCLA	23	19
Michigan	65	53	Miami (Fla.)	21	19
Princeton	65	49	Illinois	21	16
Southern Cal	57	50	Auburn	20	18
Ohio St.	53	38	California	20	18
Oklahoma	52	43	Georgia	20	16
Pittsburgh	46	39	Cornell	19	15
Pennsylvania	46	32	Colorado	18	14
Nebraska	38	31	Georgia Tech	17	16
Army	37	28	Purdue	17	16
Alabama	32	31	Arkansas	17	15
Texas	32	28	Dartmouth	17	15
Minnesota	29	25	Syracuse	17	15
Tennessee	28	25	Southern Methodist	16	14
Penn St	25	23	Louisiana St.	16	12
Stanford	25	20	Washington	15	14

Team	No.	Players	Team	No.	Players
Iowa	15	13	Houston	7	7
Texas A&M	15	13	Kentucky	7	5
Wisconsin	13	13	Boston College	6	6
Clemson	13	12	Brown	6	6
Arizona St.	12	9	Mississippi	6	6
Brigham Young	11	9	Missouri	6	6
Chicago	11	9	Rice	6	6
Florida St.	11	9	Vanderbilt	6	6
Maryland	10	10	Carlisle	6	5
Northwestern	10	10	Colgate	6	5
Florida	10	9	Columbia	6	5
Oklahoma St.	9	9	Indiana	6	5
Texas Christian	9	9	Oregon St.	5	5
Baylor	9	7	Texas Tech	5	5
North Caro.	8	8	North Caro. St.	5	4

SPECIAL AWARDS

HEISMAN MEMORIAL TROPHY

(Originally presented in 1935 as the DAC Trophy by the Downtown Athletic Club of New York City to the best college player east of the Mississippi River. In 1936, players across the country were eligible and the award was renamed the Heisman Memorial Trophy to honor former college coach and DAC athletics director John W. Heisman. The award now goes to the outstanding college football player in the United States.)

Year	Player, College, Pos.
1935	Jay Berwanger, Chicago, HB
1936	Larry Kelley, Yale, E
1937	Clint Frank, Yale, HB
1938	Davey O'Brien, Texas Christian, QB
1939	Nile Kinnick, Iowa, HB
1940	Tom Harmon, Michigan, HB
1941	Bruce Smith, Minnesota, HB
1942	Frank Sinkwich, Georgia, HB
1943	Angelo Bertelli, Notre Dame, QB
1944	Les Horvath, Ohio St., QB
1945	*Doc Blanchard, Army, FB
1946	Glenn Davis, Army, HB
1947	John Lujack, Notre Dame, QB
1948	*Doak Walker, Southern Methodist, HB
1949	Leon Hart, Notre Dame, E
1950	*Vic Janowicz, Ohio St., HB
1951	Dick Kazmaier, Princeton, HB
1952	Billy Vessels, Oklahoma, HB
1953	John Lattner, Notre Dame, HB
1954	Alan Ameche, Wisconsin, FB
1955	Howard Cassady, Ohio St., HB
1956	Paul Hornung, Notre Dame, QB
1957	John Crow, Texas A&M, HB
1958	Pete Dawkins, Army, HB
1959	Billy Cannon, Louisiana St., HB
1960	Joe Bellino, Navy, HB
1961	Ernie Davis, Syracuse, HB
1962	Terry Baker, Oregon St., QB
1963	*Roger Staubach, Navy, QB
1964	John Huarte, Notre Dame, QB
1965	Mike Garrett, Southern Cal, HB
1966	Steve Spurrier, Florida, QB
1967	Gary Beban, UCLA, QB
1968	O. J. Simpson, Southern Cal, HB
1969	Steve Owens, Oklahoma, HB
1970	Jim Plunkett, Stanford, QB
1971	Pat Sullivan, Auburn, QB
1972	Johnny Rodgers, Nebraska, FL
1973	John Cappelletti, Penn St., HB
1974	*Archie Griffin, Ohio St., HB
1975	Archie Griffin, Ohio St., HB
1976	Tony Dorsett, Pittsburgh, HB

Year	Player, College, Pos.
1977	Earl Campbell, Texas, HB
1978	*Billy Sims, Oklahoma, HB
1979	Charles White, Southern Cal, HB
1980	George Rogers, South Caro., HB
1981	Marcus Allen, Southern Cal, HB
1982	*Herschel Walker, Georgia, HB

Stanford quarterback Jim Plunkett earned the 1970 Heisman Trophy by passing for 2,715 yards and 18 touchdowns and leading his team to the Pacific-8 Conference championship.

Year	Player, College, Pos.		Year	Player, College, Pos.
1983	Mike Rozier, Nebraska, HB		1988	*Barry Sanders, Oklahoma St., RB
1984	Doug Flutie, Boston College, QB		1989	*Andre Ware, Houston, QB
1985	Bo Jackson, Auburn, HB		1990	*Ty Detmer, Brigham Young, QB
1986	Vinny Testaverde, Miami (Fla.), QB		1991	#Desmond Howard, Michigan, WR
1987	Tim Brown, Notre Dame, WR			

* Juniors (all others seniors).   # Had one year of eligibility remaining.

1991 HEISMAN VOTING

1. #Desmond Howard, WR, Michigan 2,077
2. Casey Weldon, QB, Florida St. 503
3. Ty Detmer, QB, Brigham Young 445
4. *Steve Emtman, DT, Washington 357
5. *Shane Matthews, QB, Florida 246
6. Vaughn Dunbar, RB, Indiana 173
7. Jeff Blake, QB, East Caro. 114
8. *Terrell Buckley, DB, Florida St. 102
9. ¢Marshall Faulk, RB, San Diego St. 52
10. Bucky Richardson, QB, Texas A&M 45

* Junior, ¢ Freshman (all others seniors).   # Had one year of eligibility remaining.

OUTLAND TROPHY

(Honoring the outstanding interior lineman in the nation, first presented in 1946 by the Football Writers Association of America. The award is named for its benefactor, Dr. John H. Outland.)

Year	Player, College, Pos.		Year	Player, College, Pos.
1946	George Connor, Notre Dame, T		1970	Jim Stillwagon, Ohio St., MG
1947	Joe Steffy, Army, G		1971	Larry Jacobson, Nebraska, DT
1948	Bill Fischer, Notre Dame, G		1972	Rich Glover, Nebraska, MG
1949	Ed Bagdon, Michigan St., G		1973	John Hicks, Ohio St., OT
1950	Bob Gain, Kentucky, T		1974	Randy White, Maryland, DE
1951	Jim Weatherall, Oklahoma, T		1975	Lee Roy Selmon, Oklahoma, DT
1952	Dick Modzelewski, Maryland, T			
1953	J. D. Roberts, Oklahoma, G		1976	*Ross Browner, Notre Dame, DE
1954	Bill Brooks, Arkansas, G		1977	Brad Shearer, Texas, DT
1955	Calvin Jones, Iowa, G		1978	Greg Roberts, Oklahoma, G
			1979	Jim Ritcher, North Caro. St., C
1956	Jim Parker, Ohio St., G		1980	Mark May, Pittsburgh, OT
1957	Alex Karras, Iowa, T			
1958	Zeke Smith, Auburn, G		1981	*Dave Rimington, Nebraska, C
1959	Mike McGee, Duke, T		1982	Dave Rimington, Nebraska, C
1960	Tom Brown, Minnesota, G		1983	Dean Steinkuhler, Nebraska, G
			1984	Bruce Smith, Virginia Tech, DT
1961	Merlin Olsen, Utah St., T		1985	Mike Ruth, Boston College, NG
1962	Bobby Bell, Minnesota, T		1986	Jason Buck, Brigham Young, DT
1963	Scott Appleton, Texas, T		1987	Chad Hennings, Air Force, DT
1964	Steve DeLong, Tennessee, T		1988	Tracy Rocker, Auburn, DT
1965	Tommy Nobis, Texas, G		1989	Mohammed Elewonibi, Brigham Young, G
1966	Loyd Phillips, Arkansas, T			
1967	Ron Yary, Southern Cal, T		1990	Russell Maryland, Miami (Fla.), DT
1968	Bill Stanfill, Georgia, T		1991	*Steve Emtman, Washington, DT
1969	Mike Reid, Penn St., DT			

VINCE LOMBARDI/ROTARY AWARD

(Honoring the outstanding college lineman of the year, first presented in 1970 by the Rotary Club of Houston, Tex. The award is named after professional football coach Vince Lombardi, a member of the legendary "Seven Blocks of Granite" at Fordham in the 1930s.)

Year	Player, College, Pos.		Year	Player, College, Pos.
1970	Jim Stillwagon, Ohio St., MG		1981	Kenneth Sims, Texas, DT
1971	Walt Patulski, Notre Dame, DE		1982	Dave Rimington, Nebraska, C
1972	Rich Glover, Nebraska, MG		1983	Dean Steinkuhler, Nebraska, G
1973	John Hicks, Ohio St., OT		1984	Tony Degrate, Texas, DT
1974	Randy White, Maryland, DT			
1975	Lee Roy Selmon, Oklahoma, DT		1985	Tony Casillas, Oklahoma, NG
1976	Wilson Whitley, Houston, DT		1986	Cornelius Bennett, Alabama, LB
1977	Ross Browner, Notre Dame, DE		1987	Chris Spielman, Ohio St., LB
1978	Bruce Clark, Penn St., DT		1988	Tracy Rocker, Auburn, DT
1979	Brad Budde, Southern Cal, G		1989	Percy Snow, Michigan St., LB
1980	Hugh Green, Pittsburgh, DE		1990	Chris Zorich, Notre Dame, NT
			1991	Steve Emtman, Washington, DT

MAXWELL AWARD

(Honoring the nation's outstanding college football player, first presented in 1937 by the Maxwell Memorial Football Club of Philadelphia. The award is named after Robert "Tiny" Maxwell, a Philadelphia native who played at the University of Chicago as a lineman near the turn of the century.)

Year	Player, College, Pos.	Year	Player, College, Pos.
1937	Clint Frank, Yale, HB	1965	Tommy Nobis, Texas, LB
1938	Davey O'Brien, Texas Christian, QB	1966	Jim Lynch, Notre Dame, LB
1939	Nile Kinnick, Iowa, HB	1967	Gary Beban, UCLA, QB
1940	Tom Harmon, Michigan, HB	1968	O. J. Simpson, Southern Cal, RB
1941	Bill Dudley, Virginia, HB	1969	Mike Reid, Penn St., DT
1942	Paul Governali, Columbia, QB	1970	Jim Plunkett, Stanford, QB
1943	Bob Odell, Pennsylvania, HB	1971	Ed Marinaro, Cornell, RB
1944	Glenn Davis, Army, HB	1972	Brad VanPelt, Michigan St., DB
1945	Doc Blanchard, Army, FB	1973	John Cappelletti, Penn St., RB
1946	Charley Trippi, Georgia, HB	1974	Steve Joachim, Temple, QB
1947	Doak Walker, Southern Methodist, HB	1975	Archie Griffin, Ohio St., RB
1948	Chuck Bednarik, Pennsylvania, C	1976	Tony Dorsett, Pittsburgh, RB
1949	Leon Hart, Notre Dame, E	1977	Ross Browner, Notre Dame, DE
1950	Reds Bagnell, Pennsylvania, HB	1978	Chuck Fusina, Penn St., QB
1951	Dick Kazmaier, Princeton, HB	1979	Charles White, Southern Cal, RB
1952	John Lattner, Notre Dame, HB	1980	Hugh Green, Pittsburgh, DE
1953	John Lattner, Notre Dame, HB	1981	Marcus Allen, Southern Cal, RB
1954	Ron Beagle, Navy, E	1982	Herschel Walker, Georgia, RB
1955	Howard Cassady, Ohio St., HB	1983	Mike Rozier, Nebraska, RB
1956	Tommy McDonald, Oklahoma, HB	1984	Doug Flutie, Boston College, QB
1957	Bob Reifsnyder, Navy, T	1985	Chuck Long, Iowa, QB
1958	Pete Dawkins, Army, HB	1986	Vinny Testaverde, Miami (Fla.), QB
1959	Rich Lucas, Penn St., QB	1987	Don McPherson, Syracuse, QB
1960	Joe Bellino, Navy, HB	1988	Barry Sanders, Oklahoma St., RB
1961	Bob Ferguson, Ohio St., FB	1989	Anthony Thompson, Indiana, RB
1962	Terry Baker, Oregon St., QB	1990	Ty Detmer, Brigham Young, QB
1963	Roger Staubach, Navy, QB	1991	Desmond Howard, Michigan, WR
1964	Glenn Ressler, Penn St., C		

BUTKUS AWARD

(First presented in 1985 to honor the nation's best collegiate linebacker by the Downtown Athletic Club of Orlando, Fla. The award is named after Dick Butkus, two-time consensus all-America at Illinois and six-time all-pro linebacker with the Chicago Bears.)

Year	Player, College	Year	Player, College
1985	Brian Bosworth, Oklahoma	1989	Percy Snow, Michigan St.
1986	Brian Bosworth, Oklahoma	1990	Alfred Williams, Colorado
1987	Paul McGowan, Florida St.	1991	Erick Anderson, Michigan
1988	Derrick Thomas, Alabama		

JIM THORPE AWARD

(First presented in 1986 to honor the nation's best defensive back by the Jim Thorpe Athletic Club of Oklahoma City. The award is named after Jim Thorpe, Olympic champion, two-time consensus all-America halfback at Carlisle, and professional football player.)

Year	Player, College	Year	Player, College
1986	Thomas Everett, Baylor	1989	Mark Carrier, Southern Cal
1987	(tie) Bennie Blades, Miami (Fla.)	1990	Darryll Lewis, Arizona
	Rickey Dixon, Oklahoma	1991	Terrell Buckley, Florida St.
1988	Deion Sanders, Florida St.		

DAVEY O'BRIEN NATIONAL QUARTERBACK AWARD

(First presented in 1977 as the O'Brien Memorial Trophy, the award went to the outstanding player in the Southwest. In 1981, the Davey O'Brien Educational and Charitable Trust of Fort Worth, Tex., renamed the award the Davey O'Brien National Quarterback Award, and it now honors the nation's best quarterback.)

Memorial Trophy

Year	Player, College	Year	Player, College
1977	Earl Campbell, Texas, RB	1979	Mike Singletary, Baylor, LB
1978	Billy Sims, Oklahoma, RB	1980	Mike Singletary, Baylor, LB

National QB Award

Year	Player, College	Year	Player, College
1981	Jim McMahon, Brigham Young	1984	Doug Flutie, Boston College
1982	Todd Blackledge, Penn St.	1985	Chuck Long, Iowa
1983	Steve Young, Brigham Young	1986	Vinny Testaverde, Miami (Fla.)

Year	Player, College	Year	Player, College
1987	Don McPherson, Syracuse	1990	Ty Detmer, Brigham Young
1988	Troy Aikman, UCLA	1991	Ty Detmer, Brigham Young
1989	Andre Ware, Houston		

DOAK WALKER NATIONAL RUNNING BACK AWARD

(Presented for the first time in 1990 to honor the nation's best running back among Division I-A juniors or seniors who combine outstanding achievements on the field, in the classroom and in the community. Sponsored by the GTE/Southern Methodist Athletic Forum in Dallas, Tex., a $10,000 scholarship is donated to the recipient's university in his name. It is voted on by a 16-member panel of media and former college football standouts. The award is named after Doak Walker, Southern Methodist's three-time consensus all-America halfback and 1948 Heisman Trophy winner.)

Year	Player, College
1990	Greg Lewis, Washington
1991	Trevor Cobb, Rice

AMERICAN FOOTBALL COACHES ASSOCIATION "COACHES' CHOICE" PLAYER OF THE YEAR

(Did not select any players in 1990 & 1991)

Division I-A
1988—Barry Sanders, Oklahoma St., RB   1989—Anthony Thompson, Indiana, RB

Division I-AA
1988—Mike Barber, Marshall, WR   1989—John Friesz, Idaho, QB

College Division I
1988—Johnny Bailey, Texas A&I, RB   1989—Johnny Bailey, Texas A&I, RB

College Division II
1988—Terry Underwood, Wagner, RB   1989—Ricky Gales, Simpson, RB

WALTER PAYTON PLAYER OF THE YEAR AWARD

(First presented in 1987 to honor the top Division I-AA football player by the Sports Network and voted on by Division I-AA sports information directors. The award is named after Walter Payton, former Jackson St. player and the National Football League's all-time leading rusher.)

Year	Player, College	Year	Player, College
1987	Kenny Gamble, Colgate, RB	1990	Walter Dean, Grambling, RB
1988	Dave Meggett, Towson St., RB	1991	*Jamie Martin, Weber St., QB
1989	John Friesz, Idaho, QB		

* Junior.

HARLON HILL TROPHY

(First presented in 1986 to honor the best Division II player by Division II sports information directors. The award is named after Harlon Hill, former receiver at North Alabama and the National Football League's most valuable player for the Chicago Bears in 1955.)

Year	Player, College	Year	Player, College
1986	Jeff Bentrim, North Dak. St., QB	1989	Johnny Bailey, Texas A&I, RB
1987	Johnny Bailey, Texas A&I, RB	1990	Chris Simdorn, North Dak. St., QB
1988	Johnny Bailey, Texas A&I, RB	1991	Ronnie West, Pittsburg St., WR

COLLEGE FOOTBALL HALL OF FAME

Established: In 1947, by the National Football Foundation and College Hall of Fame, Inc. The first class of enshrinees was inducted in 1951 and the present College Football Hall of Fame was opened in 1978 in Kings Island, Ohio. **Eligibility:** A nominated player must be out of college at least 10 years and a first-team all-America selection by a major selector during his career. Coaches must be retired three years. The voting is done by a 12-member panel made up of athletics directors, conference and bowl officials, and media representatives.

Class of 1992 (to be inducted at the National Football Foundation awards dinner, December 8, in New York City): Players—RB Ron Johnson, Michigan (1966-68); LB Jim Lynch, Notre Dame (1964-66); OL Lou Michaels, Kentucky (1955-57); LB Larry Morris, Georgia Tech (1951-54); QB Craig Morton, California (1962-64); RB Bob Odell, Pennsylvania (1941-43); DL Loyd Phillips, Arkansas (1964-66); WR Howard Twilley, Tulsa (1963-65); OL Jim Weatherall, Oklahoma (1948-51); WR Art Weiner, North Caro. (1946-49), and DL Jack Youngblood, Florida (1968-70). Coaches—John Ralston, Utah St. (1959-63) and Stanford (1963-71), and Earl Banks, Morgan St. (1960-73).

Member players are listed with final year they played in college, and member coaches are listed with year of induction. (†) Indicates deceased members.

Players

Player, College	Year	Player, College	Year
†Earl Abell, Colgate	1915	Alex Agase, Purdue/Illinois	1946

Player, College	Year
†Harry Agganis, Boston U.	1952
Frank Albert, Stanford	1941
†Ki Aldrich, Texas Christian	1938
†Malcolm Aldrich, Yale	1921
†Joe Alexander, Syracuse	1920
Lance Alworth, Arkansas	1961
†Alan Ameche, Wisconsin	1954
†Knowlton Ames, Princeton	1889
Warren Amling, Ohio St.	1946
Donny Anderson, Texas Tech	1966
†Hunk Anderson, Notre Dame	1921
Doug Atkins, Tennessee	1952
Everett Bacon, Wesleyan	1912
Reds Bagnell, Pennsylvania	1950
†Hobey Baker, Princeton	1913
†John Baker, Southern Cal	1931
†Moon Baker, Northwestern	1926
Terry Baker, Oregon St.	1962
†Harold Ballin, Princeton	1914
†Bill Banker, Tulane	1929
Vince Banonis, Detroit Mercy	1941
†Stan Barnes, California	1921
†Charles Barrett, Cornell	1915
†Bert Baston, Minnesota	1916
†Cliff Battles, West Va. Wesleyan	1931
Sammy Baugh, Texas Christian	1936
Maxie Baughan, Georgia Tech	1959
†James Bausch, Kansas	1930
Ron Beagle, Navy	1955
Gary Beban, UCLA	1967
Hub Bechtol, Texas	1946
†John Beckett, Oregon	1916
Chuck Bednarik, Pennsylvania	1948
Forrest Behm, Nebraska	1940
Bobby Bell, Minnesota	1962
Joe Bellino, Navy	1960
Marty Below, Wisconsin	1923
†Al Benbrook, Michigan	1910
†Charlie Berry, Lafayette	1924
Angelo Bertelli, Notre Dame	1943
Jay Berwanger, Chicago	1935
†Lawrence Bettencourt, St. Mary's (Cal.)	1927
Fred Biletnikoff, Florida St.	1964
Doc Blanchard, Army	1946
†Al Blozis, Georgetown	1942
Ed Bock, Iowa St.	1938
Lynn Bomar, Vanderbilt	1924
†Bo Bomeisler, Yale	1913
†Albie Booth, Yale	1931
†Fred Borries, Navy	1934
Bruce Bosely, West Va.	1955
Don Bosseler, Miami (Fla.)	1956
Vic Bottari, California	1938
†Ben Boynton, Williams	1920
†Charles Brewer, Harvard	1895
†Johnny Bright, Drake	1951
John Brodie, Stanford	1956
†George Brooke, Pennsylvania	1895
George Brown, Navy/San Diego St.	1947
†Gordon Brown, Yale	1900
†John Brown Jr., Navy	1913
†Johnny Mack Brown, Alabama	1925
Tay Brown, Southern Cal	1932
†Paul Bunker, Army	1902
Ron Burton, Northwestern	1959
Dick Butkus, Illinois	1964
†Robert Butler, Wisconsin	1912
George Cafego, Tennessee	1939
†Red Cagle, Southwestern La./Army	1929

Player, College	Year
†John Cain, Alabama	1932
Ed Cameron, Wash. & Lee	1924
†David Campbell, Harvard	1901
Earl Campbell, Texas	1977
†Jack Cannon, Notre Dame	1929
†Frank Carideo, Notre Dame	1930
†Charles Carney, Illinois	1921
J. C. Caroline, Illinois	1954
Bill Carpenter, Army	1959
†Hunter Carpenter, Virginia Tech	1905
Charles Carroll, Washington	1928
†Edward Casey, Harvard	1919
Howard Cassady, Ohio St.	1955
†Guy Chamberlin, Nebraska	1915
Sam Chapman, California	1938
Bob Chappuis, Michigan	1947
†Paul Christman, Missouri	1940
†Dutch Clark, Colorado Col.	1929
Paul Cleary, Southern Cal	1947
†Zora Clevenger, Indiana	1903
Jack Cloud, William & Mary	1948
†Gary Cochran, Princeton	1897
†Josh Cody, Vanderbilt	1919
Don Coleman, Michigan St.	1951
Charlie Conerly, Mississippi	1947
George Connor, Holy Cross/Notre Dame	1947
†William Corbin, Yale	1888
William Corbus, Stanford	1933
†Hector Cowan, Princeton	1889
†Edward (Tad) Coy, Yale	1909
†Fred Crawford, Duke	1933
John David Crow, Texas A&M	1957
†Jim Crowley, Notre Dame	1924
Larry Csonka, Syracuse	1967
Slade Cutter, Navy	1934
†Ziggie Czarobski, Notre Dame	1947
Carroll Dale, Virginia Tech	1959
†Gerald Dalrymple, Tulane	1931
John Dalton, Navy	1911
Charles Daly, Harvard/Army	1902
Averell Daniell, Pittsburgh	1936
†James Daniell, Ohio St.	1941
†Tom Davies, Pittsburgh	1921
†Ernie Davis, Syracuse	1961
Glenn Davis, Army	1946
Robert Davis, Georgia Tech	1947
Pete Dawkins, Army	1958
Al DeRogatis, Duke	1948
†Paul DesJardien, Chicago	1914
†Aubrey Devine, Iowa	1921
†John DeWitt, Princeton	1903
Mike Ditka, Pittsburgh	1960
Glenn Dobbs, Tulsa	1942
†Bobby Dodd, Tennessee	1930
Holland Donan, Princeton	1950
†Joseph Donchess, Pittsburgh	1929
†Nathan Dougherty, Tennessee	1909
Nick Drahos, Cornell	1940
†Paddy Driscoll, Northwestern	1917
†Morley Drury, Southern Cal	1927
Bill Dudley, Virginia	1941
Kenny Easley, UCLA	1980
†Walter Eckersall, Chicago	1906
†Turk Edwards, Washington St.	1931
†William Edwards, Princeton	1899
†Ray Eichenlaub, Notre Dame	1914
Bump Elliott, Michigan/Purdue	1947
Ray Evans, Kansas	1947
†Albert Exendine, Carlisle	1907

Special Awards

311

Player, College	Year
Nello Falaschi, Santa Clara	1936
Tom Fears, Santa Clara/UCLA	1947
†Beattie Feathers, Tennessee	1933
Bob Fenimore, Oklahoma St.	1946
†Doc Fenton, Louisiana St.	1909
John Ferraro, Southern Cal	1944
Wes Fesler, Ohio St.	1930
†Bill Fincher, Georgia Tech	1920
Bill Fischer, Notre Dame	1948
†Hamilton Fish, Harvard	1909
†Robert Fisher, Harvard	1911
†Allen Flowers, Georgia Tech	1920
Danny Fortmann, Colgate	1935
Sam Francis, Nebraska	1936
Ed Franco, Fordham	1937
Clint Frank, Yale	1937
Rodney Franz, California	1949
†Benny Friedman, Michigan	1926
Roman Gabriel, North Caro. St.	1961
Bob Gain, Kentucky	1950
†Arnold Galiffa, Army	1949
Hugh Gallarneau, Stanford	1940
†Edgar Garbisch, Wash. & Jeff./Army	1924
Mike Garrett, Southern Cal	1965
†Charles Gelbert, Pennsylvania	1896
†Forest Geyer, Oklahoma	1915
Paul Giel, Minnesota	1953
Frank Gifford, Southern Cal	1951
†Walter Gilbert, Auburn	1936
†George Gipp, Notre Dame	1920
†Chet Gladchuk, Boston College	1940
Bill Glass, Baylor	1956
Marshall Goldberg, Pittsburgh	1938
Gene Goodreault, Boston College	1940
†Walter Gordon, California	1918
†Paul Governali, Columbia	1942
Otto Graham, Northwestern	1943
†Red Grange, Illinois	1925
†Bobby Grayson, Stanford	1935
†Jack Green, Tulane/Army	1945
Joe Greene, North Texas	1968
Bob Griese, Purdue	1966
Archie Griffin, Ohio St.	1975
†Merle Gulick, Toledo/Hobart	1929
†Joe Guyon, Georgia Tech	1918
†Edwin Hale, Mississippi Col.	1921
L. Parker Hall, Mississippi	1938
Jack Ham, Penn St.	1970
Bob Hamilton, Stanford	1935
Tom Hamilton, Navy	1926
†Vic Hanson, Syracuse	1926
†Tack Hardwick, Harvard	1914
†T. Truxton Hare, Pennsylvania	1900
†Chick Harley, Ohio St.	1919
†Tom Harmon, Michigan	1940
†Howard Harpster, Carnegie Mellon	1928
†Edward Hart, Princeton	1911
Leon Hart, Notre Dame	1949
Bill Hartman, Georgia	1937
†Homer Hazel, Rutgers	1924
†Matt Hazeltine, California	1954
†Ed Healey, Dartmouth	1916
†Pudge Heffelfinger, Yale	1891
†Mel Hein, Washington St.	1930
†Don Heinrich, Washington	1952
Ted Hendricks, Miami (Fla.)	1968
†Wilbur Henry, Wash. & Jeff.	1919
†C. Herschberger, Chicago	1898
†Robert Herwig, California	1937
†Willie Heston, Michigan	1904

Player, College	Year
†Herman Hickman, Tennessee	1931
†William Hickok, Yale	1894
Dan Hill, Duke	1938
†Art Hillebrand, Princeton	1899
†Frank Hinkey, Yale	1894
Carl Hinkle, Vanderbilt	1937
Clarke Hinkle, Bucknell	1931
Elroy Hirsch, Wisconsin/Michigan	1943
†James Hitchcock, Auburn	1932
Frank Hoffmann, Notre Dame	1931
†James J. Hogan, Yale	1904
†Brud Holland, Cornell	1938
†Don Holleder, Army	1955
†Bill Hollenback, Pennsylvania	1908
Mike Holovak, Boston College	1942
E. J. Holub, Texas Tech	1960
Paul Hornung, Notre Dame	1956
Edwin Horrell, California	1924
Les Horvath, Ohio St.	1944
†Arthur Howe, Yale	1911
†Dixie Howell, Alabama	1934
†Cal Hubbard, Centenary	1926
†John Hubbard, Amherst	1906
†Pooley Hubert, Alabama	1925
Sam Huff, West Va.	1955
Weldon Humble, Rice	1946
†Joel Hunt, Texas A&M	1927
Ellery Huntington, Colgate	1914
Don Hutson, Alabama	1934
†Jonas Ingram, Navy	1906
†Cecil Isbell, Purdue	1937
†J. Jablonsky, Army/Washington	1933
Vic Janowicz, Ohio St.	1951
†Darold Jenkins, Missouri	1941
†Jackie Jensen, California	1948
†Herbert Joesting, Minnesota	1927
Bob Johnson, Tennessee	1967
†Jimmie Johnson, Carlisle/Northwestern	1903
†Calvin Jones, Iowa	1955
†Gomer Jones, Ohio St.	1935
Lee Roy Jordan, Alabama	1962
†Frank Juhan, Sewanee	1910
Charlie Justice, North Caro.	1949
Mort Kaer, Southern Cal	1926
Alex Karras, Iowa	1957
Ken Kavanaugh, Louisiana St.	1939
†Edgar Kaw, Cornell	1922
Dick Kazmaier, Princeton	1951
†James Keck, Princeton	1921
Larry Kelley, Yale	1936
†Wild Bill Kelly, Montana	1926
Doug Kenna, Army	1944
†George Kerr, Boston College	1941
†Henry Ketcham, Yale	1913
Leroy Keyes, Purdue	1968
†Glenn Killinger, Penn St.	1921
†John Kilpatrick, Yale	1910
John Kimbrough, Texas A&M	1940
†Frank Kinard, Mississippi	1937
†Phillip King, Princeton	1893
†Nile Kinnick, Iowa	1939
†Harry Kipke, Michigan	1923
†John Kirkpatrick, Yale	1910
†John Kitzmiller, Oregon	1930
†Barton Koch, Baylor	1931
†Walt Koppisch, Columbia	1924
Ron Kramer, Michigan	1956
Charlie Krueger, Texas A&M	1957
Malcolm Kutner, Texas	1941
Ted Kwalick, Penn St.	1968

Player, College	Year	Player, College	Year
†Steve Lach, Duke	1941	†John Minds, Pennsylvania	1897
†Myles Lane, Dartmouth	1927	Skip Minisi, Pennsylvania/Navy	1947
Johnny Lattner, Notre Dame	1953	†Alex Moffat, Princeton	1883
Hank Lauricella, Tennessee	1952	†Ed Molinski, Tennessee	1940
†Lester Lautenschlaeger, Tulane	1925	Cliff Montgomery, Columbia	1933
†Elmer Layden, Notre Dame	1924	Donn Moomaw, UCLA	1952
†Bobby Layne, Texas	1947	†William Morley, Columbia	1902
†Langdon Lea, Princeton	1895	George Morris, Georgia Tech	1952
Eddie LeBaron, Pacific (Cal.)	1949	†Bill Morton, Dartmouth	1931
†James Leech, Va. Military	1920	†Monk Moscrip, Stanford	1935
Darrell Lester, Texas Christian	1935	†Brick Muller, California	1922
Bob Lilly, Texas Christian	1960	†Bronko Nagurski, Minnesota	1929
†Augie Lio, Georgetown	1940	†Ernie Nevers, Stanford	1925
Floyd Little, Syracuse	1966	†Marshall Newell, Harvard	1893
†Gordon Locke, Iowa	1922	Harry Newman, Michigan	1932
Don Lourie, Princeton	1921	Tommy Nobis, Texas	1965
Richie Lucas, Penn St.	1959	Leo Nomellini, Minnesota	1949
Sid Luckman, Columbia	1938	†Andrew Oberlander, Dartmouth	1925
Johnny Lujack, Notre Dame	1947	†Davey O'Brien, Texas Christian	1938
Pug Lund, Minnesota	1934	†Pat O'Dea, Wisconsin	1899
Robert MacLeod, Dartmouth	1938	†Jack O'Hearn, Cornell	1915
†Bart Macomber, Illinois	1915	Robin Olds, Army	1942
Dick Maegle, Rice	1954	†Elmer Oliphant, Army/Purdue	1917
†Ned Mahon, Harvard	1915	Merlin Olsen, Utah St.	1961
Johnny Majors, Tennessee	1956	†Bennie Oosterbaan, Michigan	1927
†William Mallory, Yale	1923	Charles O'Rourke, Boston College	1940
Vaughn Mancha, Alabama	1947	†John Orsi, Colgate	1931
†Gerald Mann, Southern Methodist	1927	†Win Osgood, Cornell	1892
Archie Manning, Mississippi	1970	Bill Osmanski, Holy Cross	1938
Edgar Manske, Northwestern	1933	†George Owen, Harvard	1922
Ed Marinaro, Cornell	1971	Jim Owens, Oklahoma	1949
Vic Markov, Washington	1937	Steve Owens, Oklahoma	1969
†Bobby Marshall, Minnesota	1906	Jack Pardee, Texas A&M	1956
Ollie Matson, San Francisco	1952	Babe Parilli, Kentucky	1951
Ray Matthews, Texas Christian	1927	Ace Parker, Duke	1936
†John Maulbetsch, Michigan	1914	Jackie Parker, Mississippi St.	1953
†Pete Mauthe, Penn St.	1912	Jim Parker, Ohio St.	1956
†Robert Maxwell, Chicago/Swarthmore	1906	†Vince Pazzetti, Lehigh	1912
George McAfee, Duke	1939	†Chub Peabody, Harvard	1941
†Thomas McClung, Yale	1891	†Robert Peck, Pittsburgh	1916
Bill McColl, Stanford	1951	†Stan Pennock, Harvard	1914
†Jim McCormick, Princeton	1907	George Pfann, Cornell	1923
Tommy McDonald, Oklahoma	1956	†H. D. Phillips, Sewanee	1904
†Jack McDowall, North Caro. St.	1927	Pete Pihos, Indiana	1946
Hugh McElhenny, Washington	1951	†Erny Pinckert, Southern Cal	1931
†Gene McEver, Tennessee	1931	John Pingel, Michigan St.	1938
†John McEwan, Army	1916	Jim Plunkett, Stanford	1970
Banks McFadden, Clemson	1939	†Arthur Poe, Princeton	1899
Bud McFadin, Texas	1950	†Fritz Pollard, Brown	1916
Mike McGee, Duke	1959	B. Poole, Miss./North Caro./Army	1947
†Edward McGinley, Pennsylvania	1924	Merv Pregulman, Michigan	1943
†John McGovern, Minnesota	1910	†Eddie Price, Tulane	1949
Thurman McGraw, Colorado St.	1949	†Peter Pund, Georgia Tech	1928
†Mike McKeever, Southern Cal	1960	Garrard Ramsey, William & Mary	1942
†George McLaren, Pittsburgh	1918	†Claude Reeds, Oklahoma	1913
†Dan McMillan, Southern Cal/California	1922	Mike Reid, Penn St.	1969
†Bo McMillin, Centre	1921	Steve Reid, Northwestern	1936
†Bob McWhorter, Georgia	1913	†William Reid, Harvard	1899
†LeRoy Mercer, Pennsylvania	1912	Mel Renfro, Oregon	1963
Don Meredith, Southern Methodist	1959	†Pug Rentner, Northwestern	1932
†Bert Metzger, Notre Dame	1930	Bob Reynolds, Stanford	1935
Wayne Meylan, Nebraska	1967	†Bobby Reynolds, Nebraska	1952
Abe Mickal, Louisiana St.	1935	Les Richter, California	1951
Creighton Miller, Notre Dame	1943	Jack Riley, Northwestern	1931
†Don Miller, Notre Dame	1924	†Charles Rinehart, Lafayette	1897
†Eugene Miller, Penn St.	1913	†Ira Rodgers, West Va.	1919
†Fred Miller, Notre Dame	1928	†Edward Rogers, Carlisle/Minnesota	1903
†Rip Miller, Notre Dame	1924	Joe Romig, Colorado	1961
Wayne Millner, Notre Dame	1935	†Aaron Rosenberg, Southern Cal	1933
†C. A. Milstead, Wabash/Yale	1923	Kyle Rote, Southern Methodist	1950

Player, College	Year	Player, College	Year
†Harry Young, Wash. & Lee	1916	Gust Zarnas, Ohio St.	1937
†Waddy Young, Oklahoma	1938		

Coaches

Coach	Year	Coach	Year
†Joe Aillet	1989	Dave Maurer	1991
†Bill Alexander	1951	Charley McClendon	1986
†Ed Anderson	1971	Herb McCracken	1973
†Ike Armstrong	1957	†Dan McGugin	1951
†Charlie Bachman	1978	John McKay	1988
†Harry Baujan	1990	Allyn McKeen	1991
†Matty Bell	1955	†Tuss McLaughry	1962
†Hugo Bezdek	1954	†Dutch Meyer	1956
†Dana X. Bible	1951	†Jack Mollenkopf	1988
†Bernie Bierman	1955	†Bernie Moore	1954
Bob Blackman	1987	†Scrappy Moore	1980
†Earl (Red) Blaik	1965	†Ray Morrison	1954
Frank Broyles	1983	†George Munger	1976
†Paul (Bear) Bryant	1986	†Clarence (Biggie) Munn	1959
†Charlie Caldwell	1961	†Bill Murray	1974
†Walter Camp	1951	†Frank Murray	1983
Len Casanova	1977	†Ed (Hooks) Mylin	1974
†Frank Cavanaugh	1954	†Earle (Greasy) Neale	1967
†Dick Colman	1990	†Jess Neely	1971
†Fritz Crisler	1954	†David Nelson	1987
†Duffy Daugherty	1984	†Robert Neyland	1956
Bob Devaney	1981	†Homer Norton	1971
Dan Devine	1985	†Frank (Buck) O'Neill	1951
†Gil Dobie	1951	†Bennie Owen	1951
†Michael Donohue	1951	Ara Parseghian	1980
†Gus Dorais	1954	†Doyt Perry	1988
†Bill Edwards	1986	†Jimmy Phelan	1973
†Rip Engle	1973	Tommy Prothro	1991
Don Faurot	1961	†E. N. Robinson	1955
Jake Gaither	1973	†Knute Rockne	1951
Sid Gillman	1989	†Dick Romney	1954
†Ernest Godfrey	1972	†Bill Roper	1951
Ray Graves	1990	Darrell Royal	1983
†Andy Gustafson	1985	†George Sanford	1971
†Edward Hall	1951	†Francis Schmidt	1971
†Jack Harding	1980	Ben Schwartzwalder	1982
†Richard Harlow	1954	†Clark Shaughnessy	1968
†Harvey Harman	1981	†Buck Shaw	1972
†Jesse Harper	1971	†Andy Smith	1951
†Percy Haughton	1951	†Carl Snavely	1965
†Woody Hayes	1983	†Amos Alonzo Stagg	1951
†John W. Heisman	1954	†Jock Sutherland	1951
†Robert Higgins	1954	†Jim Tatum	1984
†Babe Hollingberry	1979	†Frank Thomas	1951
Frank Howard	1989	†Thad Vann	1987
†Bill Ingram	1973	Johnny Vaught	1979
†Morley Jennings	1973	†Wallace Wade	1955
†Biff Jones	1954	†Lynn (Pappy) Waldorf	1966
†Howard Jones	1951	†Glenn (Pop) Warner	1951
†Tad Jones	1958	†E. E. (Tad) Wieman	1956
†Lloyd Jordan	1978	†John Wilce	1954
†Ralph (Shug) Jordan	1982	Bud Wilkinson	1969
†Andy Kerr	1951	†Henry Williams	1951
†Frank Leahy	1970	†George Woodruff	1963
†George Little	1955	Warren Woodson	1989
†Lou Little	1960	†Fielding (Hurry Up) Yost	1951
†Slip Madigan	1974	†Bob Zuppke	1951

FIRST-TEAM ALL-AMERICA SELECTIONS BELOW DIVISION I-A

(Selected by the Associated Press and
the American Football Coaches Association)

Selection of Associated Press Little All-America Teams began in 1934. Early AP selectors were not bound by NCAA statistical classifications; therefore, 26 current Division I-A teams are included in this list.

The American Football Coaches Association began selecting all-America teams below Division I-A in 1967 for two College-Division classifications. Its College-Division I team includes NCAA Division II and National Association of Intercollegiate Athletics (NAIA) Division I players. The AFCA College-Division II team includes NCAA Division III and NAIA Division II players. The AFCA added a Division I-AA team in 1979; AP began selecting a Division I-AA team in 1982, and these players are included. In 1990, the Champion USA Division III team was added, selected by a panel of 25 sports information directors.

Nonmembers of the NCAA are included in this list, as are colleges that no longer play varsity football.

Players selected to a Division I-AA all-America team are indicated by (†). Current members of Division I-A are indicated by (*).

All-Americans are listed by college, year selected and position.

ABILENE CHRISTIAN (16)
48— V. T. Smith, B
51— Lester Wheeler, OT
52— Wallace Bullington, DB
65— Larry Cox, OT
69— Chip Bennett, LB
70— Jim Lindsey, QB
73— Wilbert Montgomery, RB
74— Chip Martin, DL
77— Chuck Sitton, DB
82— Grant Feasel, C
83— Mark Wilson, DB
84— Dan Remsberg, OT
87— Richard Van Druten, OT
89— John Layfield, OG
90— Dennis Brown, PK
91— Jay Jones, LB

ADAMS ST. (3)
79— Ronald Johnson, DB
84— Bill Stone, RB
87— Dave Humann, DB

AKRON* (9)
69— John Travis, OG
71— Michael Hatch, DB
76— Mark Van Horn, OG
       Steve Cockerham, LB
77— Steve Cockerham, LB
80—†Brad Reece, LB
81—†Brad Reece, LB
85—†Wayne Grant, DL
86—†Mike Clark, RB

ALABAMA A&M (3)
87— Howard Ballard, OL
88— Fred Garner, DB
89— Barry Wagner, WR

ALABAMA ST. (3)
90—†Eddie Robinson, LB
91—†Patrick Johnson, OL
       †Eddie Robinson, LB

ALBANY ST. (GA.) (1)
72— Harold Little, DE

ALBION (6)
40— Walter Ptak, G
58— Tom Taylor, E
76— Steve Spencer, DL
86— Joe Felton, OG
       Mike Grant, DB
91— Hank Wineman, RB

ALBRIGHT (3)
36— Richard Riffle, B
37— Richard Riffle, B
75— Chris Simcic, OL

ALCORN ST. (11)
69— David Hadley, DB
70— Fred Carter, DT
71— Harry Gooden, LB
72— Alex Price, DT
73— Leonard Fairley, DB
74— Jerry Dismuke, OG
75— Lawrence Pillers, DE
76— Augusta Lee, RB
       Larry Warren, DT
79—†Leslie Frazier, DB
84—†Issiac Holt, DB

ALFRED (6)
51— Ralph DiMicco, B
52— Ralph DiMicco, B
55— Charles Schultz, E
56— Charles Schultz, E
75— Joseph Van Cura, DE
82— Brian O'Neil, DB

ALLEGHENY (9)
75— Charles Slater, OL
87— Mike Mates, OL
88— Mike Parker, DL
90— Jeff Filkovski, QB
       David LaCarte, DB
       John Marzca, C
91— Ron Bendekovic, OT
       Stanley Drayton, RB
       Tony Bifulco, DB

AMERICAN INT'L (10)
71— Bruce Laird, RB
80— Ed Cebula, C
82— Paul Thompson, DT
85— Keith Barry, OL
86— Jon Provost, OL
87— Jon Provost, OL
88— Greg Doherty, OL
89— Lamont Cato, DB
90— George Patterson, DL
91— Gabe Mokwuah, DL

AMHERST (3)
42— Adrian Hasse, E
72— Richard Murphy, QB
73— Fred Scott, FL

ANGELO ST. (10)
75— James Cross, DB
78— Jerry Aldridge, RB
       Kelvin Smith, LB
81— Clay Weishuhn, LB
82— Mike Elarms, WR
83— Mike Thomas, K
85— Henry Jackson, LB
86— Pierce Holt, DL
87— Pierce Holt, DL

88— Henry Alsbrooks, LB

APPALACHIAN ST. (8)
48— John Caskey, E
63— Greg Van Orden, G
85—†Dino Hackett, LB
87—†Anthony Downs, DE
88—†Bjorn Nittmo, PK
89—†Derrick Graham, OL
       †Keith Collins, DB
91—†Harold Alexander, P

ARIZONA* (1)
41— Henry Stanton, E

ARKANSAS ST.* (17)
53— Richard Woit, B
64— Dan Summers, OG
65— Dan Summers, OG
68— Bill Bergey, LB
69— Dan Buckley, C
       Clovis Swinney, DT
70— Bill Phillips, OG
       Calvin Harrell, HB
71— Calvin Harrell, RB
       Dennis Meyer, DB
       Wayne Dorton, OG
73— Doug Lowrey, OG
84—†Carter Crawford, DL
85—†Carter Crawford, DL
86—†Randy Barnhill, OG
87—†Jim Wiseman, C
       †Charlie Fredrick, DT

ARKANSAS TECH (2)
58— Edward Meador, B
61— Powell McClellan, E

ASHLAND (7)
70— Len Pettigrew, LB
78— Keith Dare, DL
85— Jeff Penko, OL
86— Vince Mazza, PK
89— Douglas Powell, DB
90— Morris Furman, LB
91— Ron Greer, LB

AUGUSTANA (ILL.) (9)
72— Willie Van, DT
73— Robert Martin, OT
83— Kurt Kapischke, OL
84— Greg King, C
86— Lynn Thomsen, DL
87— Carlton Beasley, DL
88— John Bothe, OL
90— Barry Reade, PK
91— Mike Hesler, DB

AUGUSTANA (S.D.) (3)
60— John Simko, E

87— Tony Adkins, DL
88— Pete Jaros, DB
AUSTIN (9)
37— Wallace Johnson, C
79— Price Clifford, LB
80— Chris Luper, DB
81— Larry Shillings, QB
83— Ed Holt, DL
84— Jeff Timmons, PK
87— Otis Amy, WR
88— Otis Amy, WR
90— Jeff Cordell, DB
AUSTIN PEAY (7)
65— Tim Chilcutt, DB
66— John Ogles, FB
70— Harold Roberts, OE
77— Bob Bible, LB
78— Mike Betts, DB
80— Brett Williams, DE
82— Charlie Tucker, OL
AZUSA PACIFIC (1)
86— Christian Okoye, RB
BAKER (3)
83— Chris Brown, LB
85— Kevin Alewine, RB
90— John Campbell, OL
BALDWIN-WALLACE (9)
50— Norbert Hecker, E
68— Bob Quackenbush, DT
78— Jeff Jenkins, OL
80— Dan Delfino, DE
82— Pete Primeau, DL
83— Steve Varga, K
89— Doug Halbert, DL
91— John Koz, QB
　　Jim Clardy, LB
BALL ST.* (4)
67— Oscar Lubke, OT
68— Amos Van Pelt, HB
72— Douglas Bell, C
73— Terry Schmidt, DB
BATES (1)
81— Larry DiGammarino, WR
BEMIDJI ST. (1)
83— Bruce Ecklund, TE
BENEDICTINE (1)
36— Leo Deutsch, E
BETHANY (W. VA.) (1)
77— Scott Lanz, P
BETHEL (KAN.) (1)
80— David Morford, C
BETHUNE-COOKMAN (2)
75— Willie Lee, DE
81— Booker Reese, DE
**BIRMINGHAM-
SOUTHERN (1)**
37— Walter Riddle, T
BISHOP (1)
81— Carlton Nelson, DL
BLOOMSBURG (7)
79— Mike Morucci, RB
82— Mike Blake, TE
83— Frank Sheptock, LB
84— Frank Sheptock, LB
85— Frank Sheptock, LB
　　Tony Woods, DB
91— Eric Jonassen, OL
BOISE ST. (20)
72— Al Marshall, OE
73— Don Hutt, WR

74— Jim McMillan, QB
75— John Smith, FL
77— Chris Malmgren, DT
　　Terry Hutt, WR
　　Harold Cotton, OT
79—†Joe Aliotti, QB
　　†Doug Scott, DT
80—†Randy Trautman, DT
81—†Randy Trautman, DT
　　†Rick Woods, DB
82—†John Rade, DL
　　†Carl Keever, LB
84—†Carl Keever, LB
85—†Marcus Koch, DL
87—†Tom DeWitz, OG
　　†Pete Kwiatkowski, DT
90—†Erik Helgeson, DL
91—†Frank Robinson, DB
BOSTON U. (14)
67— Dick Farley, DB
68— Bruce Taylor, DB
69— Bruce Taylor, DB
79—†Mal Najarian, RB
　　†Tom Pierzga, DL
81—†Bob Speight, OT
　　†Gregg Drew, RB
82—†Mike Mastrogiacomo,
　　OG
83—†Paul Lewis, RB
84—†Paul Lewis, RB
86—†Kevin Murphy, DT
87—†Mark Seals, DB
88—†Mark Seals, DB
89—†Daren Altieri, WR
BOWDOIN (1)
77— Steve McCabe, OL
BOWIE ST. (2)
80— Victor Jackson, CB
81— Marco Tongue, DB
BOWLING GREEN* (2)
59— Bob Zimpfer, T
82—†Andre Young, DL
BRADLEY (1)
38— Ted Panish, B
BRANDEIS (2)
54— William McKenna, E
56— James Stehlin, B
BRIDGEPORT (1)
72— Dennis Paldin, DB
BRIDGEWATER (VA.) (1)
75— C. J. DeWitt, SE
BROCKPORT ST. (1)
90— Ed Smart, TE
BUCKNELL (7)
51— George Young, DT
60— Paul Terhes, B
64— Tom Mitchell, OE
65— Tom Mitchell, OE
74— Larry Schoenberger, LB
80— Mike McDonald, OT
90—†Mike Augsberger, DB
BUENA VISTA (4)
72— Joe Kotval, OG
73— Joe Kotval, OG
76— Keith Kerkhoff, DL
87— Jim Higley, LB
BUFFALO (2)
84— Gerry Quinlivan, LB
87— Steve Wojciechowski, LB
BUTLER (1)
88— Steve Roberts, RB

CAL LUTHERAN (2)
72— Brian Kelley, LB
79— Mike Hagen, SE
CAL POLY SLO (13)
53— Stan Sheriff, C
58— Charles Gonzales, G
66— David Edmondson, C
72— Mike Amos, DB
73— Fred Stewart, OG
78— Louis Jackson, RB
80— Louis Jackson, RB
　　Robbie Martin, FL
81— Charles Daum, OL
84— Nick Frost, DB
89— Robert Morris, DL
90— Pat Moore, DL
91— Doug O'Neill, P
CAL ST. CHICO (1)
87— Chris Verhulst, TE
CAL ST. HAYWARD (3)
75— Greg Blankenship, LB
84— Ed Lively, DT
86— Fred Williams, OL
CAL ST. NORTHRIDGE (5)
75— Mel Wilson, DB
82— Pat Hauser, OT
83— Pat Hauser, OT
87— Kip Dukes, DB
91— Don Goodman, OL
CAL ST. SACRAMENTO (3)
64— William Fuller, OT
91— Troy Mills, RB
　　Jim Crouch, PK
CALIF. (PA.) (1)
83— Perry Kemp, WR
CANISIUS (2)
87— Tom Doctor, LB
88— Marty Hurley, DB
CAPITAL (3)
74— Greg Arnold, OG
80— John Phillips, DL
　　Steve Wigton, C
CARLETON (1)
90— Jim Bradford, WR
CARNEGIE MELLON (3)
81— Ken Murawski, LB
85— Robert Butts, OL
91— Chuck Jackson, OT
CARROLL (MONT.) (5)
76— Richard Dale, DB
79— Don Diggins, DL
87— Jeff Beaudry, DB
88— Paul Petrino, QB
89— Suitoa Keleti, OL
CARROLL (WIS.) (2)
74— Robert Helf, TE
90— Bill Nolan, P
CARSON-NEWMAN (4)
78— Tank Black, FL
80— Brad Payne, SAF
83— Dwight Wilson, OL
90— Robert Hardy, RB
CASE RESERVE (4)
41— Mike Yurcheshen, E
52— Al Feeny, DE
84— Fred Manley, DE
85— Mark Raiff, OL
CATAWBA (5)
34— Charles Garland, T
35— Charles Garland, T

45— Carroll Bowen, B
72— David Taylor, OT
74— Mike McDonald, LB
CATHOLIC (1)
84— Chris McMahon, DB
CENTRAL ARK. (3)
80— Otis Chandler, MG
84— David Burnette, DT
91— David Henson, DL
CENTRAL CONN. ST. (4)
74— Mike Walton, C
84— Sal Cintorino, LB
88— Doug Magazu, DL
89— Doug Magazu, DL
CENTRAL FLA. (2)
87— Bernard Ford, WR
Ed O'Brien, PK
CENTRAL (IOWA) (8)
70— Vernon Den Herder, DT
74— Al Dorenkamp, LB
77— Donald Taylor, RB
84— Scott Froehle, DB
85— Rich Thomas, DL
88— Mike Stumberg, DL
89— Mike Estes, DL
Kris Reis, LB
CENTRAL MICH.* (4)
42— Warren Schmakel, G
59— Walter Beach, B
62— Ralph Soffredine, G
74— Rick Newsome, DL
CENTRAL MO. ST. (3)
68— Jim Urczyk, OT
85— Steve Huff, PK
88— Jeff Wright, DL
CENTRAL OKLA. (2)
65— Jerome Bell, OE
78— Gary Smith, TE
CENTRAL ST. (OHIO) (6)
83— Mark Corbin, RB
84— Dave Dunham, OT
85— Mark Corbin, RB
86— Terry Morrow, RB
89— Kenneth Vines, OG
90— Eric Williams, OL
CENTRAL WASH. (4)
48— Robert Osgood, G
50— Jack Hawkins, G
88— Mike Estes, DL
91— Eric Lamphere, OL
CENTRE (6)
55— Gene Scott, B
84— Teel Bruner, DB
85— Teel Bruner, DB
86— Jeff Leonard, OL
88— John Gohmann, DL
89— Jeff Bezold, LB
CHADRON ST. (3)
74— Dennis Fitzgerald, DB
78— Rick Mastey, OL
90— David Jones, RB
CHICAGO (2)
91— Neal Cawi, DE
Jeff Stolte, P
CITADEL (6)
82— Jim Ettari, DL
84— Jim Gabrish, OL
85— Jim Gabrish, OL
86— Scott Thompson, DT
88—†Carlos Avalos, OL
90—†DeRhon Robinson, OL

CLARION (7)
78— Jeff Langhans, OL
80— Steve Scillitani, MG
Gary McCauley, TE
81— Gary McCauley, TE
83— Elton Brown, RB
85— Chuck Duffy, OL
87— Lou Weiers, DL
CLARK ATLANTA (1)
79— Curtis Smith, OL
COAST GUARD (2)
90— Ron Davies, DB
91— Ron Davies, DB
COE (4)
74— Dan Schmidt, OG
76— Paul Wagner, OT
85— Mike Matzen, P
90— Richard Matthews, DB
COLGATE (7)
82—†Dave Wolf, LB
83—†Rich Erenberg, RB
84—†Tom Stenglein, WR
85—†Tom Stenglein, WR
86—†Kenny Gamble, RB
87—†Kenny Gamble, RB
†Greg Manusky, LB
COLLEGE OF EMPORIA (1)
51— William Chai, OG
COLLEGE OF IDAHO (2)
53— Norman Hayes, T
54— R. C. Owens, E
COLORADO COL. (3)
72— Ed Smith, DE
73— Darryl Crawford, DB
82— Ray Bridges, DL
COLORADO MINES (5)
39— Lloyd Madden, B
41— Dick Moe, T
59— Vince Tesone, B
72— Roger Cirimotich, DB
86— Tim Baer, P
CONCORD (1)
86— Kevin Johnson, LB
CONCORDIA-M'HEAD (3)
77— Barry Bennett, DT
90— Mike Gindorff, DT
Shayne Lindsay, NG
CONNECTICUT (6)
45— Walter Trojanowski, B
73— Richard Foye, C
80—†Reggie Eccleston, WR
83—†John Dorsey, LB
88—†Glenn Antrum, WR
89—†Troy Ashley, LB
91—†Mark Didio, WR
CORNELL (2)
82—†Dan Suren, TE
86—†Tom McHale, DE
CORNELL COLLEGE (1)
82— John Ward, WR
CORTLAND ST. (5)
67— Rodney Verkey, DE
89— Jim Cook, OL
90— Chris Lafferty, OG
Vinny Swanda, LB
91— Vinny Swanda, LB
CUMBERLAND (KY.) (2)
87— David Carmichael, DB
89— Ralph McWilliams, OL

DAKOTA WESLEYAN (1)
45— Robert Kirkman, T
DARTMOUTH (1)
91—†Al Rosier, RB
DAVIDSON (1)
34— John Mackorell, B
DAYTON (8)
36— Ralph Niehaus, T
78— Rick Chamberlin, LB
81— Chris Chaney, DB
84— David Kemp, LB
86— Gerry Meyer, OL
89— Mike Duvic, PK
90— Steve Harder, OL
91— Brian Olson, OG
DELAWARE (27)
42— Hugh Bogovich, G
46— Tony Stalloni, T
54— Don Miller, B
63— Mike Brown, B
66— Herb Slattery, OT
69— John Favero, LB
70— Conway Hayman, OG
71— Gardy Kahoe, RB
72— Joe Carbone, DE
Dennis Johnson, DT
73— Jeff Cannon, DT
74— Ed Clark, LB
Ray Sweeney, OG
75— Sam Miller, DE
76— Robert Pietuszka, DB
78— Jeff Komlo, QB
79—†Herb Beck, OG
†Scott Brunner, QB
80—†Gary Kuhlman, OT
81—†Gary Kuhlman, OL
82—†George Schmitt, DB
85—†Jeff Rosen, OL
86—†Darrell Booker, LB
87—†James Anderson, WR
88—†Mike Renna, DL
89—†Mike Renna, DL
91—†Warren McIntire, DB
DELAWARE ST. (3)
84— Gene Lake, RB
86— Joe Burton, DB
91—†Rod Milstead, OL
DELTA ST. (1)
67— Leland Hughes, OG
DENISON (5)
47— William Hart, E
48— William Wehr, C
75— Dennis Thome, DL
79— Clay Sampson, RB
86— Dan Holland, DL
DePAUW (1)
63— Richard Dean, C
DETROIT TECH (1)
39— Mike Kostiuk, T
DICKINSON ST. (2)
81— Tony Moore, DL
91— Shaughn White, DB
DOANE (1)
66— Fred Davis, OT
DRAKE (3)
72— Mike Samples, DT
82— Pat Dunsmore, TE
Craig Wederquist, OT
DREXEL (2)
55— Vincent Vidas, T
56— Vincent Vidas, T

EAST CARO.* (1)
64— Bill Cline, HB
EAST CENTRAL (OKLA.) (1)
84— Don Wilson, C
EAST STROUDSBURG (6)
65— Barry Roach, DB
75— William Stem, DB
79— Ronald Yakavonis, DL
83— Mike Reichenbach, LB
84— Andy Baranek, QB
91— Curtis Bunch, DB
EAST TENN. ST. (5)
53— Hal Morrison, E
68— Ron Overbay, DB
70— William Casey, DB
85— George Cimadevilla, P
86— George Cimadevilla, P
EAST TEX. ST. (13)
38— Darrell Tully, B
53— Bruno Ashley, G
58— Sam McCord, B
59— Sam McCord, B
68— Chad Brown, OT
70— William Lewis, C
72— Curtis Wester, OG
73— Autry Beamon, DB
84— Alan Veingrad, OG
88— Kim Morton, DL
90— Terry Bagsby, DL
91— Eric Turner, DB
      Dwayne Phorne, OL
EASTERN ILL. (16)
72— Nate Anderson, RB
76— Ted Petersen, C
78— James Warring, WR
79— Chris Cobb, RB
      Pete Catan, DE
80— Pete Catan, DE
81— †Kevin Grey, DB
82—†Robert Williams, DB
      †Bob Norris, OG
83—†Robert Williams, DB
      †Chris Nicholson, DT
84—†Jerry Wright, WR
86—†Roy Banks, WR
88—†John Jurkovic, DL
89—†John Jurkovic, DL
90—†Tim Lance, DB
EASTERN KY. (21)
69— Teddy Taylor, MG
74— Everett Talbert, RB
75— Junior Hardin, MG
76— Roosevelt Kelly, OL
79—†Bob McIntyre, LB
80—†George Floyd, DB
81—†George Floyd, DB
      †Kevin Greve, OG
82—†Steve Bird, WR
83—†Chris Sullivan, OL
84—†Chris Sullivan, C
85—†Joe Spadafino, OL
86—†Fred Harvey, LB
87—†Aaron Jones, DL
88—†Elroy Harris, RB
      †Jessie Small, DL
89—†Al Jacevicius, DL
90—†Kelly Blount, LB
      †Al Jacevicius, OL
91—†Carl Satterly, OL
      †Ernest Thompson, DL
EASTERN MICH.* (5)
68— John Schmidt, C
69— Robert Lints, MG

70— Dave Pureifory, DT
71— Dave Pureifory, DT
73— Jim Pietrzak, OT
EASTERN N. MEX. (5)
81— Brad Beck, RB
83— Kevin Kott, QB
87— Earl Jones, OL
89— Murray Garrett, DL
90— Anthony Pertile, DB
EASTERN WASH. (7)
57— Richard Huston, C
65— Mel Stanton, HB
73— Scott Garske, TE
81— John Tighe, OL
86— Ed Simmons, OT
87—†Eric Stein, P
91—†Kevin Sargent, OL
EDINBORO (3)
82— Rick Ruszkiewicz, K
89— Elbert Cole, RB
90— Ernest Priester, WR
ELMHURST (1)
82— Lindsay Barich, OL
ELON (9)
50— Sal Gero, T
68— Richard McGeorge, OE
69— Richard McGeorge, OE
73— Glenn Ellis, DT
76— Ricky Locklear, DT
      Dan Bass, OL
77— Dan Bass, OL
80— Bobby Hedrick, RB
86— Ricky Sigmon, OL
EMORY & HENRY (12)
50— Robert Miller, B
51— Robert Miller, B
56— William Earp, C
68— Sonny Wade, B
85— Keith Furr, DB
      Rob McMillen, DL
86— Sandy Rogers, RB
87— Gary Collier, QB
88— Steve Bowman, DL
89— Doug Reavis, DB
90— Billy Salyers, OL
91— Jason Grooms, DL
EMPORIA ST. (5)
35— James Fraley, B
37— Harry Klein, E
68— Bruce Cerone, OE
69— Bruce Cerone, OE
91— Quincy Tillmon, RB
EVANSVILLE (1)
46— Robert Hawkins, T
FAIRMONT ST. (3)
67— Dave Williams, DT
84— Ed Coleman, WR
88— Lou Mabin, DB
FAYETTEVILLE ST. (1)
90— Terrence Smith, LB
FDU-MADISON (3)
84— Ira Epstein, DL
86— Eric Brey, DB
87— Frank Illidge, DL
FERRIS ST. (1)
76— Charles Evans, RB
FERRUM (5)
87— Dave Harper, LB
88— Dave Harper, LB
89— Chris Warron, RB
90— Melvin Dillard, DB/KR

91— John Sheets, OG
FINDLAY (4)
65— Allen Smith, HB
80— Nelson Bolden, FB
85— Dana Wright. RB
90— Tim Russ, OL
FLORIDA A&M (12)
61— Curtis Miranda, C
62— Robert Paremore, B
67— Major Hazelton, DB
      John Eason, OE
73— Henry Lawrence, OT
75— Frank Poole, LB
77— Tyrone McGriff, OG
78— Tyrone McGriff, OG
79—†Tyrone McGriff, OG
      †Kiser Lewis, C
80—†Gifford Ramsey, DB
83—†Ray Alexander, WR
FLORIDA ST.* (1)
51— William Dawkins, OG
FORT LEWIS (1)
89— Eric Fadness, P
FORT VALLEY ST. (4)
74— Fred Harris, OT
80— Willie Canady, DB
81— Willie Canady, DB
83— Tugwan Taylor, DB
FRANK. & MARSH. (8)
35— Woodrow Sponaugle, C
38— Sam Roeder, B
40— Alex Schibanoff, T
47— William Iannicelli, E
50— Charles Cope, C
81— Vin Carioscia, OL
82— Vin Carioscia, OL
89— Dale Amos, WR
FRANKLIN (1)
82— Joe Chester, WR
FRESNO ST.* (5)
39— Jack Mulkey, E
40— Jack Mulkey, E
60— Douglas Brown, G
68— Tom McCall, LB
      Erv Hunt, DB
FROSTBURG ST. (7)
80— Terry Beamer, LB
82— Steve Forsythe, WR
83— Kevin Walsh, DL
85— Bill Bagley, WR
86— Marcus Wooley, LB
88— Ken Boyd, DB
89— Ken Boyd, DB
FURMAN (9)
82—†Ernest Gibson, DB
83—†Ernest Gibson, DB
84—†Rock Hurst, LB
85—†Gene Reeder, C
88—†Jeff Blankenship, LB
89—†Kelly Fletcher, DL
90—†Steve Duggan, C
      †Kevin Kendrick, LB
91—†Eric Walter, OL
GA. SOUTHERN (13)
85—†Vance Pike, OL
      †Tim Foley, PK
86—†Fred Stokes, OT
      †Tracy Ham, QB
87—†Flint Matthews, LB
      †Dennis Franklin, C
      †Tim Foley, PK
88—†Dennis Franklin, C

†Darren Alford, DL
89— †Joe Ross, RB
†Giff Smith, DL
90— †Giff Smith, DL
91— †Rodney Oglesby, DB

GA. SOUTHWESTERN (2)
85— Roger Glover, LB
86— Roger Glover, LB

GALLAUDET (1)
87— Shannon Simon, OL

GARDNER-WEBB (2)
73— Richard Grissom, LB
87— Jeff Parker, PK

GEORGETOWN (3)
73— Robert Morris, DE
74— Robert Morris, DE
91— Chris Murphy, DE

GEORGETOWN (KY.) (7)
74— Charles Pierson, DL
78— John Martinelli, OL
85— Rob McCrary, RB
87— Chris Reed, C
88— Chris Reed, OL
89— Steve Blankenbaker, DL
91— Chris Hogan, DL

GETTYSBURG (4)
66— Joseph Egresitz, DE
83— Ray Condren, RB
84— Ray Condren, RB
85— Brian Barr, DB

GLASSBORO ST. (1)
78— Dino Hall, RB

GLENVILLE ST. (3)
73— Scotty Hamilton, DB
83— Byron Brooks, RB
84— Mike Payne, DB

GONZAGA (2)
34— Ike Peterson, B
39— Tony Canadeo, B

GRAMBLING (27)
62— Junious Buchanan, T
64— Alphonse Dotson, OT
65— Willie Young, OG
Frank Cornish, DT
69— Billy Manning, C
70— Richard Harris, DE
Charles Roundtree, DT
71— Solomon Freelon, OG
John Mendenhall, DE
72— Steve Dennis, DB
Gary Johnson, DT
73— Gary Johnson, DT
Willie Bryant, DB
74— Gary Johnson, DT
75— Sammie White, WR
James Hunter, DB
79— †Joe Gordon, DT
†Aldrich Allen, LB
†Robert Salters, DB
80— †Trumaine Johnson, WR
†Mike Barker, DT
81— †Andre Robinson, LB
82— †Trumaine Johnson, WR
83— †Robert Smith, DL
85— †James Harris, LB
90— †Walter Dean, RB
†Jake Reed, WR

GRAND VALLEY ST. (3)
79— Ronald Essink, OL
89— Todd Tracey, DL
91— Chris Tiede, C

GROVE CITY (1)
87— Doug Hart, PK

GUILFORD (2)
75— Steve Musulin, OT
91— Rodney Alexander, DE

GUST. ADOLPHUS (7)
37— Wendell Butcher, B
50— Calvin Roberts, T
51— Haldo Norman, OE
52— Calvin Roberts, DT
54— Gene Nei, G
67— Richard Jaeger, LB
84— Kurt Ploeger, DL

HAMILTON (2)
86— Joe Gilbert, OL
91— Eric Grey, RB

HAMLINE (4)
55— Dick Donlin, E
84— Kevin Graslewicz, WR
85— Ed Hitchcock, OL
89— Jon Voss, TE

HAMPDEN-SYDNEY (8)
48— Lynn Chewning, B
54— Stokeley Fulton, C
72— Michael Leidy, LB
74— Ed Kelley, DE
75— Ed Kelley, DE
77— Robert Wilson, OL
78— Tim Smith, DL
86— Jimmy Hondroulis, PK

HAMPTON (2)
84— Ike Readon, MG
85— Ike Readon, DL

HANOVER (2)
86— Jon Pinnick, QB
88— Mike Luker, WR

HARDIN-SIMMONS (5)
37— Burns McKinney, B
39— Clyde Turner, C
40— Owen Goodnight, B
42— Rudy Mobley, B
46— Rudy Mobley, B

HARDING (2)
74— Barney Crawford, DL
91— Pat Gill, LB

HARVARD (2)
82— †Mike Corbat, OL
84— †Roger Caron, OL

HASTINGS (1)
84— Dennis Sullivan, OL

HAWAII* (2)
41— Nolle Smith, B
68— Tim Buchanan, LB

HENDERSON ST. (1)
90— Todd Jones, OL

HILLSDALE (9)
49— William Young, B
55— Nate Clark, B
56— Nate Clark, B
75— Mark Law, OG
81— Mike Broome, OG
82— Ron Gladnick, DE
86— Al Huge, DL
87— Al Huge, DL
88— Rodney Patterson, LB

HOBART (3)
72— Don Aleksiewicz, RB
75— Rich Kowalski, RB
86— Brian Verdon, DB

HOFSTRA (4)
83— Chuck Choinski, DL
86— Tom Salamone, P
88— Tom Salamone, DB
90— George Tischler, LB

HOLY CROSS (12)
83— †Bruce Kozerski, OT
Steve Raquet, DL
84— †Bill McGovern, DB
Kevin Garvey, OG
85— †Gil Fenerty, RB
86— †Gordie Lockbaum, RB-DB
87— †Jeff Wiley, QB
†Gordie Lockbaum, WR-SP
88— †Dennis Golden, OL
89— †Dave Murphy, DB
90— †Craig Callahan, LB
91— †Jerome Fuller, RB

HOPE (2)
79— Craig Groendyk, OL
82— Kurt Brinks, C

HOWARD (2)
75— Ben Harris, DL
87— †Harvey Reed, RB

HOWARD PAYNE (3)
61— Ray Jacobs, T
72— Robert Woods, LB
73— Robert Woods, LB

HUMBOLDT ST. (5)
61— Drew Roberts, E
62— Drew Roberts, E
76— Michael Gooing, OL
82— David Rush, MG
83— Dean Diaz, DB

HURON (1)
76— John Aldridge, OL

IDAHO (7)
83— †Ken Hobart, QB
85— †Eric Yarber, WR
88— †John Friesz, QB
89— †John Friesz, QB
†Lee Allen, WR
90— †Kasey Dunn, WR
91— †Kasey Dunn, WR

IDAHO ST. (6)
69— Ed Bell, OE
77— Ray Allred, MG
81— †Case de Bruijn, P
†Mike Machurek, QB
83— †Jeff Kaiser, P
84— †Steve Anderson, DL

ILL. BENEDICTINE (1)
72— Mike Rogowski, LB

ILL. WESLEYAN (3)
34— Tony Blazine, T
74— Caesar Douglas, OT
91— Chris Bisaillon, WR

ILLINOIS COLL. (1)
81— Joe Aiello, DL

ILLINOIS ST. (4)
68— Denny Nelson, OT
85— †Jim Meyer, OL
86— †Brian Gant, LB
88— †Mike McCabe, P

INDIANA (PA.) (12)
75— Lynn Hieber, QB
76— Jim Haslett, DE
77— Jim Haslett, DE
78— Jim Haslett, DE

79— Terrence Skelley, OE
80— Joe Cuigari, DT
84— Gregg Brenner, WR
86— Jim Angelo, OL
87— Troy Jackson, LB
88— Dean Cottrill, LB
90— Andrew Hill, WR
91— Tony Aliucci, QB

INDIANA ST. (7)
69— Jeff Keller, DE
75— Chris Hicks, OL
    Vince Allen, RB
83—†Ed Martin, DE
84—†Wayne Davis, DB
85—†Vencie Glenn, DB
86—†Mike Simmonds, OL

INDIANAPOLIS (6)
83— Mark Bless, DL
84— Paul Loggan, DB
85— Tom Collins, DB
86— Dan Jester, TE
87— Thurman Montgomery, DL
91— Greg Matheis, DL

IOWA WESLEYAN (1)
87— Mike Wiggins, P

ITHACA (9)
72— Robert Wojnar, OT
74— David Remick, RB
75— Larry Czarnecki, DT
79— John Laper, LB
80— Bob Ferrigno, HB
84— Bill Sheerin, DL
85— Tim Torrey, LB
90— Jeff Wittman, FB
91— Jeff Wittman, FB

JACKSON ST. (16)
62— Willie Richardson, E
69— Joe Stephens, OG
71— Jerome Barkum, OE
74— Walter Payton, RB
    Robert Brazile, LB
78— Robert Hardy, DT
80—†Larry Werts, LB
81— Mike Fields, OT
85—†Jackie Walker, LB
86—†Kevin Dent, DB
87—†Kevin Dent, DB
88—†Lewis Tillman, RB
    †Kevin Dent, DB
89—†Darion Conner, LB
90—†Robert Turner, DB
91—†Deltrich Lockridge, OL

JACKSONVILLE ST. (8)
52— Jodie Connell, OG
66— Ray Vinson, DB
70— Jimmy Champion, C
77— Jesse Baker, DT
78— Jesse Baker, DT
82— Ed Lett, QB
86— Joe Billingsley, OT
88— Joe Billingsley, OT

JAMES MADISON (6)
77— Woody Bergeria, DT
78— Rick Booth, OL
85—†Charles Haley, LB
86—†Carlo Bianchini, OG
89—†Steve Bates, DL
90—†Eupton Jackson, DB

JAMESTOWN (2)
76— Brent Tischer, OL
81— Ron Hausauer, OL

JOHN CARROLL (2)
50— Carl Taseff, B
74— Tim Barrett, RB

JOHNS HOPKINS (2)
80— Bill Stromberg, WR
81— Bill Stromberg, WR

JOHNSON SMITH (2)
82— Dan Beauford, DE
88— Ronald Capers, LB

JUNIATA (3)
54— Joe Veto, T
86— Steve Yerger, OL
87— Mark Dorner, DB

KANSAS WESLEYAN (2)
35— Virgil Baker, G
56— Larry Houdek, B

KEAN (1)
87— Kevin McGuirl, TE

KENTUCKY ST. (1)
72— Wiley Epps, LB

LAFAYETTE (4)
79—†Rich Smith, TE
81—†Joe Skladany, LB
82—†Tony Green, DL
88—†Frank Baur, QB

LAKELAND (1)
89— Jeff Ogiego, P

LAMAR (5)
57— Dudley Meredith, T
61— Bobby Jancik, B
67— Spergon Wynn, OG
83—†Eugene Seale, LB
85—†Burton Murchison, RB

LANE (1)
73— Edward Taylor, DT

LANGSTON (1)
73— Thomas Henderson, DE

LAWRENCE (9)
49— Claude Radtke, E
67— Charles McKee, QB

Ithaca halfback Bob Ferrigno breaks clear for a 58-yard touchdown run against Alfred in 1979. He led the Bombers with 906 yards rushing that year, helping them to the Division III title. He received all-America honors the following season.

KENYON (1)
74— Jim Myers, WR

KNOX (2)
86— Rich Schiele, TE
87— Chris Vogel, WR

KNOXVILLE (1)
77— Dwight Treadwell, OL

KUTZTOWN (1)
77— Steve Head, OG

LA SALLE (2)
38— George Somers, T
39— Frank Loughney, G

LA VERNE (2)
72— Dana Coleman, DT
91— Willie Reyna, QB

77— Frank Bouressa, C
78— Frank Bouressa, C
80— Scott Reppert, HB
81— Scott Reppert, HB
82— Scott Reppert, RB
83— Murray McDonough, DB
86— Dan Galante, DL

LEHIGH (16)
49— Robert Numbers, C
50— Dick Doyne, B
57— Dan Nolan, B
59— Walter Meincke, T
69— Thad Jamula, OT
71— John Hill, C
73— Kim McQuilken, QB
75— Joe Sterrett, QB

77— Steve Kreider, WR
Mike Reiker, QB
79—†Dave Melone, OT
†Jim McCormick, DL
80—†Bruce Rarig, LB
83—†John Shigo, LB
85—†Rennie Benn, WR
90—†Keith Petzold, OL
LENOIR-RHYNE (3)
52— Steve Trudnak, B
62— Richard Kemp, B
67— Eddie Joyner, OT
LEWIS & CLARK (2)
68— Bill Bailey, DT
91— Dan Ruhl, RB
LIBERTY (2)
82— John Sanders, LB
86— Mark Mathis, DB
LINCOLN (MO.) (2)
53— Leo Lewis, B
54— Leo Lewis, B
LINFIELD (8)
57— Howard Morris, G
64— Norman Musser, C
72— Bernard Peterson, OE
75— Ken Cutcher, OL
78— Paul Dombroski, DB
80— Alan Schmidlin, QB
83— Steve Lopes, OL
84— Steve Boyea, OL
LIU-C. W. POST (5)
71— Gary Wichard, QB
77— John Mohring, DE
78— John Mohring, DE
81— Tom DeBona, WR
89— John Levelis, DL
LIVINGSTON (3)
82— Charles Martin, DT
84— Andrew Fields, WR
87— Ronnie Glanton, DL
LIVINGSTONE (1)
84— Jo Jo White, RB
LOCK HAVEN (1)
45— Robert Eyer, E
LONG BEACH ST.* (4)
68— Bill Parks, OE
69— Leon Burns, FB
70— Leon Burns, RB
71— Terry Metcalf, RB
LORAS (2)
47— Robert Hanlon, B
84— James Drew, P
LOS ANGELES ST. (1)
64— Walter Johnson, OG
LOUISIANA COLLEGE (1)
50— Bernard Calendar, E
LOUISIANA TECH (15)
41— Garland Gregory, G
46— Mike Reed, G
68— Terry Bradshaw, QB
69— Terry Bradshaw, QB
72— Roger Carr, WR
73— Roger Carr, FL
74— Mike Barber, TE
Fred Dean, DT
82—†Matt Dunigan, QB
84—†Doug Landry, LB
†Walter Johnson, DE
85—†Doug Landry, LB
86—†Walter Johnson, LB-DE
87—†Glenell Sanders, LB

88—†Glenell Sanders, LB
LOUISVILLE* (1)
57— Leonard Lyles, B
LOYOLA (CAL.) (1)
42— Vince Pacewic, B
LOYOLA (ILL.) (2)
35— Billy Roy, B
37— Clay Calhoun, B
LUTHER (1)
57— Bruce Hartman, T
LYCOMING (7)
83— John Whalen, OL
85— Walt Zataveski, OL
89— Rick Bealer, DB
90— Rick Bealer, DB
91— Darrin Kenney, OT
Don Kinney, DL
Bill Small, LB
MAINE (6)
65— John Huard, LB
66— John Huard, LB
80—†Lorenzo Bouier, RB
89—†Carl Smith, RB
†Scott Hough, OL
90—†Claude Pettaway, DB
MANKATO ST. (3)
73— Marty Kranz, DB
87— Duane Goldammer, OG
91— John Kelling, DB
MARS HILL (3)
78— Alan Rice, OL
79— Steven Campbell, DB
87— Lee Marchman, LB
MARSHALL (9)
37— William Smith, E
40— Jackie Hunt, B
41— Jackie Hunt, B
87—†Sean Doctor, TE
†Mike Barber, WR
88—†Mike Barber, WR
†Sean Doctor, TE
90—†Eric Ihnat, TE
91—†Phil Ratliff, OL
MARYVILLE (TENN.) (3)
67— Steve Dockery, DB
73— Earl McMahon, OG
77— Wayne Dunn, LB
MASSACHUSETTS (18)
52— Tony Chambers, OE
63— Paul Graham, T
64— Milt Morin, DE
67— Greg Landry, QB
71— William DeFlavio, MG
72— Steve Schubert, OE
73— Tim Berra, OE
75— Ned Deane, OL
76— Ron Harris, DB
77— Kevin Cummings, TE
Bruce Kimball, OL
78— Bruce Kimball, OG
80—†Bob Manning, DB
81—†Garry Pearson, RB
82—†Garry Pearson, RB
85—†Mike Dwyer, DL
88—†John McKeown, LB
90—†Paul Mayberry, OL
McMURRY (6)
49— Brad Rowland, B
50— Brad Rowland, B
58— Charles Davis, G
68— Telly Windham, DE

74— Randy Roemisch, OT
80— Rick Nolly, OL
McNEESE ST. (5)
52— Charles Kuehn, DE
69— Glenn Kidder, OG
72— James Moore, TE
74— James Files, OT
82—†Leonard Smith, DB
MD.-EAST. SHORE (2)
64— John Smith, DT
68— Bill Thompson, DB
MEMPHIS ST.* (1)
54— Robert Patterson, G
MERCHANT MARINE (3)
52— Robert Wiechard, LB
69— Harvey Adams, DE
90— Harold Krebs, DB
MESA ST. (8)
82— Dean Haugum, DT
83— Dean Haugum, DL
84— Don Holmes, DB
85— Mike Berk, OL
86— Mike Berk, OL
88— Tracy Bennett, PK
89— Jeff Russell, OT
90— Brian Johnson, LB
MIAMI (FLA.)* (2)
45— Ed Cameron, G
William Levitt, C
MIAMI (OHIO)* (1)
82—†Brian Pillman, MG
MICHIGAN TECH (1)
76— Jim VanWagner, RB
MIDDLE TENN. ST. (9)
64— Jimbo Pearson, SAF
65— Keith Atchley, LB
83—†Robert Carroll, OL
84—†Kelly Potter, PK
85—†Don Griffin, DB
88—†Don Thomas, LB
90—†Joe Campbell, RB
91—†Steve McAdoo, OL
†Joe Campbell, RB
MIDDLEBURY (2)
36— George Anderson, G
83— Jonathan Good, DL
MIDLAND LUTHERAN (2)
76— Dave Marreel, DE
79— Scott Englehardt, OL
MILLERSVILLE (4)
76— Robert Parr, DB
80— Rob Riddick, RB
81— Mark Udovich, C
86— Jeff Hannis, DL
MILLIKIN (1)
42— Virgil Wagner, B
MILLSAPS (9)
72— Rowan Torrey, DB
73— Michael Reams, LB
76— Rickie Haygood, QB
78— David Culpepper, LB
79— David Culpepper, LB
83— Edmond Donald, RB
85— Tommy Powell, LB
90— Sean Brewer, DL
91— Sean Brewer, DL
MINN.-DULUTH (4)
74— Mark Johnson, DB
75— Terry Egerdahl, RB
76— Ted McKnight, RB
82— Gary Birkholz, OG

MISSISSIPPI COL. (9)
72— Ricky Herzog, FL
79— Calvin Howard, RB
80— Bert Lyles, DE
82— Major Everett, RB
83— Wayne Frazier, OL
85— Earl Conway, DL
88— Terry Fleming, DL
89— Terry Fleming, DL
90— Fred McAfee, RB

MISSISSIPPI VAL. (6)
79—†Carl White, OG
83—†Jerry Rice, WR
84—†Jerry Rice, WR
    †Willie Totten, QB
87—†Vincent Brown, LB
91—†Ashley Ambrose, DB

MISSOURI-ROLLA (4)
41— Ed Kromka, T
69— Frank Winfield, OG
74— Merle Dillow, TE
80— Bill Grantham, SAF

MISSOURI VALLEY (3)
47— James Nelson, G
48— James Nelson, G
49— Herbert McKinney, T

MONMOUTH (ILL.) (1)
75— Ron Baker, RB

MONTANA (10)
67— Bob Beers, LB
70— Ron Stein, DB
76— Greg Anderson, DB
79—†Jim Hard, FL
83—†Brian Salonen, TE
85—†Mike Rice, P
87—†Larry Clarkson, OL
88—†Tim Hauck, DB
89—†Kirk Scafford, OL
    †Tim Hauck, DB

MONTANA ST. (10)
66— Don Hass, HB
67— Don Hass, HB
70— Gary Gustafson, LB
73— Bill Kollar, DT
75— Steve Kracher, RB
76— Lester Leininger, DL
78— Jon Borchardt, OT
81—†Larry Rubens, OL
84—†Mark Fellows, LB
    †Dirk Nelson, P

MONTANA TECH (3)
73— James Persons, OT
80— Steve Hossler, HB
81— Craig Opatz, OL

MONTCLAIR ST. (11)
75— Barry Giblin, OL
77— Mario Benimeo, DT
79— Tom Morton, OL
80— Sam Mills, LB
81— Terrance Porter, WR
82— Mark Casale, QB
84— Jim Rennae, OL
85— Dan Zakashefski, DL
86— Dan Zakashefski, DL
89— Paul Cioffi, LB
90— Paul Cioffi, LB

MOORHEAD ST. (2)
76— Rocky Gullickson, OG
84— Randy Sullivan, DB

MOREHEAD ST. (5)
38— John Horton, C
42— Vincent Zachem, C

69— Dave Haverdick, DT
82—†John Christopher, P
86—†Randy Poe, OG

MORGAN ST. (7)
65— Willie Lanier, LB
67— Jeff Queen, DE
70— Willie Germany, DB
72— Stan Cherry, LB
73— Eugene Simms, LB
78— Joe Fowlkes, DB
80— Mike Holston, WR

MORNINGSIDE (2)
49— Connie Callahan, B
91— Jorge Diaz, PK

MOUNT UNION (4)
84— Troy Starr, LB
87— Russ Kring, RB
90— Ken Edelman, PK
    Dave Lasecki, LB

MUHLENBERG (2)
46— George Bibighaus, E
47— Harold Bell, B

MURRAY ST. (4)
37— Elmer Cochran, G
73— Don Clayton, RB
79—†Terry Love, DB
86—†Charley Wiles, OL

MUSKINGUM (4)
40— Dave Evans, T
60— Bill Cooper, B
66— Mark DeVilling, DT
75— Jeff Heacock, DB

N.C. CENTRAL (4)
68— Doug Wilkerson, MG
69— Doug Wilkerson, OT
74— Charles Smith, DE
88— Earl Harvey, QB

NEB.-KEARNEY (2)
76— Dale Mitchell Johnson, DB
78— Doug Peterson, DL

NEB. WESLEYAN (2)
90— Brad Bohn, DB
91— Darren Stohlmann, TE

NEBRASKA-OMAHA (9)
64— Gerald Allen, HB
68— Dan Klepper, OG
76— Dan Fulton, WR
77— Dan Fulton, OE
80— Tom Sutko, LB
82— John Walker, DT
83— Tim Carlson, LB
84— Ron Petersen, OT
86— Keith Coleman, LB

NEVADA* (23)
52— Neil Garrett, DB
74— Greg Grouwinkel, DB
78— James Curry, MG
    Frank Hawkins, RB
79—†Frank Hawkins, RB
    †Lee Fobbs, DB
80—†Frank Hawkins, RB
    †Bubba Puha, DL
81—†John Ramatici, LB
    †Tony Zendejas, K
82—†Tony Zendejas, K
    †Charles Mann, DT
83—†Tony Zendejas, K
    †Jim Werbeckes, OG
    †Tony Shaw, DB
85—†Greg Rea, OL
    †Marty Zendejas, PK

    †Pat Hunter, DB
86—†Henry Rolling, DE-LB
88—†Bernard Ellison, DB
90—†Bernard Ellison, DB
    †Treamelle Taylor, KR
91—†Matt Clafton, LB

NEVADA-LAS VEGAS* (3)
73— Mike Thomas, RB
74— Mike Thomas, RB
75— Joseph Ingersoll, DL

NEW HAMPSHIRE (10)
50— Ed Douglas, G
68— Al Whittman, DT
75— Kevin Martell, C
76— Bill Burnham, RB
77— Bill Burnham, RB
    Grady Vigneau, OT
85—†Paul Dufault, OL
87—†John Driscoll, OL
91—†Barry Bourassa, RB
    †Dwayne Sabb, LB

NEW HAVEN (4)
85— David Haubner, OL
87— Erik Lesinski, LB
88— Rob Thompson, OL
90— Jay McLucas, QB

NEWBERRY (2)
40— Dominic Collangelo, B
81— Stan Stanton, DL

NICHOLLS ST. (6)
76— Gerald Butler, OE
77— Rusty Rebowe, LB
81—†Dwight Walker, WR
82—†Clint Conque, LB
84—†Dewayne Harrison, TE
86—†Mark Carrier, WR

NICHOLS (1)
81— Ed Zywien, LB

N.M. HIGHLANDS (6)
66— Carl Garrett, HB
67— Carl Garrett, HB
68— Carl Garrett, HB
81— Jay Lewis, DL
85— Neil Windham, LB
86— Tim Salz, PK

NORFOLK ST. (2)
79— Mike Ellis, DB
89— Arthur Jimmerson, LB

NORTH ALA. (5)
82— Don Smith, C
84— Daryl Smith, DB
85— Bruce Jones, DB
90— James Davis, LB
    Mike Nord, OL

NORTH CARO. A&T (5)
69— Merl Code, DB
70— Melvin Holmes, OT
81—†Mike West, OL
86—†Ernest Riddick, NG
88—†Demetrius Harrison, LB

NORTH DAK. (14)
55— Steve Myhra, G
56— Steve Myhra, G
63— Neil Reuter, T
65— Dave Lince, DE
66— Roger Bonk, LB
71— Jim LeClair, LB
    Dan Martinsen, DB
72— Mike Deutsch, RB
75— Bill Deutsch, RB
79— Paul Muckenhirn, TE
80— Todd Thomas, OT

First-Team All-America Selections Below Division I-A

81— Milson Jones, RB
89— Cory Solberg, PK
91— Shannon Burnell, RB
NORTH DAK. ST. (25)
34— Melvin Hanson, B
46— Cliff Rothrock, C
66— Walt Odegaard, MG
67— Jim Ferge, LB
68— Jim Ferge, DT
Paul Hatchett, B
69— Paul Hatchett, HB
Joe Cichy, DB
70— Joe Cichy, DB
74— Jerry Dahl, DE
76— Rick Budde, LB
77— Lew Curry, OL
81— Wayne Schluchter, DB
82— Cliff Carmody, OG
Steve Garske, LB
83— Mike Whetstone, OG
84— Greg Hagfors, C
86— Jeff Bentrim, QB
Jim Dick, LB
87— Mike Favor, C
88— Matt Tracy, OL
Mike Favor, C
Yorrick Byers, LB
90— Phil Hansen, DL
Chris Simdorn, QB
NORTH PARK (2)
72— Greg Nugent, OE
90— John Love, QB
NORTH TEXAS (6)
47— Frank Whitlow, T
51— Ray Renfro, DB
83—†Ronnie Hickman, DE
†Rayford Cooks, DL
88—†Rex Johnson, DL
90—†Mike Davis, DL
NORTHEAST LA. (15)
67— Vic Bender, C
70— Joe Profit, RB
72— Jimmy Edwards, RB
73— Glenn Fleming, MG
74— Glenn Fleming, MG
77— Steve Powell, RB
82—†Arthur Christophe, C
Bruce Daigle, DB
83—†Mike Grantham, OG
84—†Mike Grantham, OG
85—†Mike Turner, DB
87—†John Clement, OT
†Claude Brumfield, DT
88—†Cyril Crutchfield, DB
89—†Jackie Harris, E
NORTHEAST MO. ST. (3)
60— Dale Mills, B
65— Richard Rhodes, OT
85— Chris Hegg, QB
NORTHEASTERN (2)
72— Tom Rezzuti, DB
78— Dan Ross, TE
NORTHEASTERN OKLA. ST. (4)
69— Manuel Britto, HB
71— Roosevelt Manning, DT
74— Kevin Goodlet, DB
82— Cedric Mack, WR
NORTHERN ARIZ. (12)
66— Rick Ries, LB
67— Bill Hanna, DE
68— Larry Small, OG
77— Larry Friedrichs, OL

Tom Jurich, K
78— Jerry Lumpkin, LB
79—†Ed Judie, LB
82—†Pete Mandley, WR
83—†Pete Mandley, WR
†James Gee, DT
86—†Goran Lingmerth, PK
89—†Darrell Jordan, LB
NORTHERN COLO. (7)
68— Jack O'Brien, DB
80— Todd Volkart, DT
81— Brad Wimmer, OL
82— Mark Mostek, OG
Kevin Jelden, PK
89— Vance Lechman, DB
90— Frank Wainwright, TE
NORTHERN ILL.* (2)
62— George Bork, B
63— George Bork, B
NORTHERN IOWA (11)
52— Lou Bohnsack, C
60— George Asleson, G
61— Wendell Williams, G
64— Randy Schultz, FB
65— Randy Schultz, FB
67— Ray Pedersen, MG
75— Mike Timmermans, OT
85— Joe Fuller, DB
87—†Carl Boyd, RB
90—†Brian Mitchell, PK
91—†Brian Mitchell, PK
NORTHERN MICH. (6)
75— Daniel Stencil, OL
76— Maurice Mitchell, FL
77— Joseph Stemo, DB
82— George Works, RB
87— Jerry Woods, DB
88— Jerry Woods, DB
NORTHERN ST. (1)
76— Larry Kolbo, DL
NORTHWEST MO. ST. (3)
39— Marion Rogers, G
84— Steve Hansley, WR
89— Jason Agee, DB
NORTHWESTERN (IOWA) (1)
71— Kevin Korvor, DE
NORTHWESTERN (LA.) (9)
66— Al Dodd, DB
80—†Warren Griffith, C
†Joe Delaney, RB
81—†Gary Reasons, LB
82—†Gary Reasons, LB
83—†Gary Reasons, LB
84—†Arthur Berry, DT
87—†John Kulakowski, DE
91—†Andre Carron, LB
NORTHWOOD (3)
73— Bill Chandler, DT
74— Bill Chandler, DT
NORWICH (3)
79— Milt Williams, RB
84— Beau Almodobar, WR
85— Mike Norman, OL
OBERLIN (1)
45— James Boswell, B
OCCIDENTAL (6)
76— Rick Fry, LB
77— Rick Fry, SE
82— Dan Osborn, P
83— Ron Scott, DB
89— David Hodges, LB

90— Peter Tucker, OL
OHIO* (2)
35— Art Lewis, T
60— Dick Grecni, C
OHIO WESLEYAN (7)
34— John Turley, B
51— Dale Bruce, OE
71— Steve Dutton, DE
83— Eric DiMartino, LB
90— Jeff Court, OG
Neil Ringers, DL
91— Kevin Rucker, DL
OTTERBEIN (3)
82— Jim Hoyle, K
90— Ron Severance, WR
91— Ron Severance, WR
OUACHITA BAPTIST (1)
79— Ezekiel Vaughn, LB
PACIFIC (CAL.)* (4)
34— Cris Kjeldsen, G
47— Eddie LeBaron, B
48— Eddie LeBaron, B
49— Eddie LeBaron, B
PACIFIC LUTHERAN (9)
40— Marv Tommervik, B
41— Marv Tommervik, B
47— Dan D'Andrea, C
52— Ron Billings, DB
65— Marvin Peterson, C
78— John Zamberlin, LB
85— Mark Foege, PK
Tim Shannon, DL
88— Jon Kral, DL
PANHANDLE ST. (2)
82— Tom Rollison, DB
83— Tom Rollison, DB
PENNSYLVANIA (3)
86—†Marty Peterson, OL
88—†John Zinser, OL
90—†Joe Valerio, OL
PEPPERDINE (2)
47— Darwin Horn, B
55— Wixie Robinson, G
PERU ST. (4)
52— Robert Lade, OT
53— Robert Lade, T
81— Alvin Holder, RB
91— Tim Herman, DL
PILLSBURY (1)
85— Calvin Addison, RB
PITTSBURG ST. (7)
61— Gary Snadon, B
70— Mike Potchard, OT
78— Brian Byers, OL
88— Jesse Wall, OL
89— John Roderique, LB
90— Ron West, WR
91— Ron West, WR
PLYMOUTH ST. (6)
74— Robert Gibson, DB
82— Mark Barrows, LB
83— Joe Dudek, RB
84— Joe Dudek, RB
85— Joe Dudek, RB
91— Scott Allen, LB
POMONA-PITZER (1)
74— Larry Cenotto, QB
PORTLAND ST. (10)
76— June Jones, QB
77— Dave Stief, OE

324

79—†Stuart Gaussoin, SE
   †Kurt Ijanoff, OT
80—†Neil Lomax, QB
84— Doug Mikolas, DL
88— Bary Naone, TE
   Chris Crawford, QB
89— Darren Del'Andrae, QB
91— James Fuller, DB

PRAIRIE VIEW (2)
64— Otis Taylor, OE
70— Bivian Lee, DB

PRESBYTERIAN (8)
45— Andy Kavounis, G
46— Hank Caver, B
52— Joe Kirven, OE
68— Dan Eckstein, DB
71— Robert Norris, LB
78— Roy Walker, OL
79— Roy Walker, OL
83— Jimmie Turner, LB

PRINCETON (2)
87—†Dean Cain, DB
89—†Judd Garrett, RB

PUGET SOUND (9)
56— Robert Mitchell, G
63— Ralph Bauman, G
66— Joseph Peyton, OE
75— Bill Linnenkohl, LB
76— Dan Kuehl, DL
81— Bob Jackson, MG
82— Mike Bos, WR
83— Larry Smith, DB
87— Mike Oliphant, RB

RANDOLPH-MACON (6)
47— Albert Oley, G
57— Dave Young, G
79— Rick Eades, DL
80— Rick Eades, DL
84— Cody Dearing, QB
88— Aaron Boston, OL

REDLANDS (1)
77— Randy Van Horn, OL

RHODE ISLAND (7)
55— Charles Gibbons, T
82—†Richard Pelzer, OL
83—†Tony DeLuca, DL
84—†Brian Forster, TE
85—†Brian Forster, TE
   †Tom Ehrhardt, QB
90—†Kevin Smith, DB

RHODES (5)
36— Henry Hammond, E
38— Gaylon Smith, B
76— Conrad Bradburn, DB
85— Jim Hever, PK
88— Larry Hayes, OL

RICHMOND (1)
84—†Eddie Martin, OL

RIPON (5)
57— Peter Kasson, E
75— Dick Rehbein, C
76— Dick Rehbein, OL
79— Art Peters, TE
82— Bob Wallner, OL

ROANOKE (1)
38— Kenneth Moore, E

ROCHESTER (5)
51— Jack Wilson, DE
52— Donald Bardell, DG
67— Dave Ragusa, LB
75— Ralph Gebhardt, DB

90— Craig Chodak, P
ROCKHURST (1)
41— Joe Kiernan, T
ROLLINS (1)
40— Charles Lingerfelt, E
ROSE-HULMAN (1)
77— Gary Ellis, DB
SAGINAW VALLEY (3)
81— Eugene Marve, LB
84— Joe Rice, DL
90— David Cook, DB
SALISBURY ST. (4)
82— Mark Lagowski, LB
84— Joe Mammano, OL
85— Robb Disbennett, QB
86— Tom Kress, DL
SAM HOUSTON ST. (3)
49— Charles Williams, E
52— Don Gottlob, B
91—†Michael Bankston, DL
SAMFORD (1)
36— Norman Cooper, C
SAN DIEGO (2)
73— Bob Dulich, QB
81— Dan Herbert, DB
SAN DIEGO ST.* (6)
35— John Butler, G
66— Don Horn, QB
67— Steve Duich, OT
   Haven Moses, OE
68— Fred Dryer, DE
   Lloyd Edwards, OE
SAN FRAN. ST. (7)
51— Robert Williamson, OT
60— Charles Fuller, B
67— Joe Koontz, OE
76— Forest Hancock, LB
78— Frank Duncan, DB
82— Poncho James, RB
84— Jim Jones, TE
SAN FRANCISCO (1)
42— John Sanchez, T

SAN JOSE ST.* (2)
38— Lloyd Thomas, E
39— LeRoy Zimmerman, B
SANTA CLARA (8)
64— Lou Pastorini, LB
71— Ronald Sani, C
79— Jim Leonard, C
80— Brian Sullivan, K
82— Gary Hoffman, OT
83— Alex Vlahos, C
   Mike Rosselli, LB
85— Brent Jones, TE
SAVANNAH ST. (2)
79— Timothy Walker, DL
89— Shannon Sharpe, TE
SEWANEE (8)
63— Martin Agnew, B
73— Mike Lumpkin, DE
77— Nino Austin, DB
79— John Hill, DB
80— Mallory Nimocs, TE
81— Greg Worsowicz, DB
86— Mark Kent, WR
90— Ray McGowan, DL
SHIPPENSBURG (2)
53— Robert Adams, G
91— Jeff Fickes, DB

SIMON FRASER (1)
90— Nick Mazzoli, WR
SIMPSON (1)
89— Ricky Gales, RB
SLIPPERY ROCK (6)
74— Ed O'Reilly, RB
75— Jerry Skocik, TE
76— Chris Thull, LB
77— Bob Schrantz, TE
78— Bob Schrantz, TE
85— Jeff Williams, P
SONOMA ST. (1)
86— Mike Henry, LB
SOUTH CARO. ST. (18)
67— Tyrone Caldwell, DE
71— James Evans, LB
72— Barney Chavous, DE
73— Donnie Shell, DB
75— Harry Carson, DE
76— Robert Sims, DL
77— Ricky Anderson, RB
79—†Phillip Murphy, DL
80—†Edwin Bailey, OG
81—†Anthony Reed, FB
   †Dwayne Jackson, DL
82—†Dwayne Jackson, DE
   †Anthony Reed, RB
   †Ralph Green, OT
   †John Courtney, DT
83—†Ralph Green, OT
89—†Eric Douglas, OL
91—†Robert Porcher, DL
SOUTH DAK. (10)
68— John Kohler, OT
69— John Kohler, OT
71— Gene Macken, OG
72— Gary Kipling, OG
78— Bill Moats, DB
79— Benjamin Long, LB
83— Kurt Seibel, K
86— Jerry Glinsky, C
   Todd Salat, DB
88— Doug VanderEsch, LB
SOUTH DAK. ST. (9)
67— Darwin Gonnerman, HB
68— Darwin Gonnerman, FB
74— Lynn Boden, OT
77— Bill Matthews, DE
79— Charles Loewen, OL
84— Rick Wegher, RB
85— Jeff Tiefenthaler, WR
86— Jeff Tiefenthaler, WR
91— Kevin Tetzlaff, DL

SOUTH DAK. TECH (1)
73— Charles Waite, DB
SOUTHEAST MO. ST. (1)
37— Wayne Goddard, T

SOUTHEASTERN LA. (3)
70— Ronnie Hornsby, LB
83—†Bret Wright, P
85—†Willie Shepherd, DL

SOUTHERN ARK. (2)
84— Greg Stuman, LB
85— Greg Stuman, LB

SOUTHERN-B.R. (5)
70— Isiah Robertson, LB
72— James Wright, OG
73— Godwin Turk, LB
79—†Ken Times, DL
87—†Gerald Perry, OT

SOUTHERN CONN. ST. (5)
82— Mike Marshall, DB
83— Kevin Gray, OL
84— William Sixsmith, LB
86— Rick Atkinson, DB
91— Ron Lecointe, OL

SOUTHERN ILL. (4)
70— Lionel Antoine, OE
71— Lionel Antoine, OE
83—†Donnell Daniel, DB
     †Terry Taylor, DB

SOUTHERN MISS.* (4)
53— Hugh Pepper, B
56— Don Owens, T
58— Robert Yencho, E
59— Hugh McInnis, E

SOUTHERN ORE. ST. (1)
75— Dennis Webber, LB

SOUTHERN UTAH (4)
79— Lane Martino, DL
87— Jeff McComb, P
89— Randy Bostic, C
90— Randy Bostic, C

SOUTHWEST MO. ST. (5)
66— William Stringer, OG
87—†Matt Soraghan, LB
89—†Mark Christenson, OL
90—†DeAndre Smith, QB
91—†Bill Walter, DL

SOUTHWEST ST. (MINN.) (2)
87— James Ashley, WR
91— Wayne Hawkins, DE

SOUTHWEST TEX. ST. (10)
53— Pence Dacus, B
63— Jerry Cole, E
64— Jerry Cole, DB
72— Bob Daigle, C
75— Bobby Kotzur, DT
82— Tim Staskus, LB
83— Tim Staskus, LB
84—†Scott Forester, C
90—†Reggie Rivers, RB
91—†Ervin Thomas, C

SOUTHWESTERN (KAN.) (2)
82— Tom Audley, DL
84— Jackie Jenson, RB

SOUTHWESTERN LA.* (1)
69— Glenn LaFleur, LB

**SOUTHWESTERN
OKLA. ST. (2)**
77— Louis Blanton, DB
82— Richard Lockman, LB

SPRINGFIELD (11)
68— Dick Dobbert, C
70— John Curtis, OE
76— Roy Samuelsen, MG
78— Jack Quinn, DB
79— Jack Quinn, DB
80— Steve Foster, OT
81— Jon Richardson, LB
83— Wally Case, DT
     Ed Meachum, TE
85— Jim Anderson, LB
91— Fran Papasedero, DL

ST. AMBROSE (4)
40— Nick Kerasiotis, G
51— Robert Flanagan, B
58— Robert Webb, B
87— Jerry Klosterman, DL

ST. BONAVENTURE (2)
46— Phil Colella, B

48— Frank LoVuola, E

ST. CLOUD ST. (1)
85— Mike Lambrecht, DL

ST. JOHN'S (MINN.) (5)
65— Pat Whalin, DB
79— Ernie England, MG
82— Rick Bell, RB
83— Chris Biggins, TE
91— Pat Mayew, QB

ST. JOHN'S (N.Y.) (1)
83— Todd Jamison, QB

ST. LAWRENCE (2)
51— Ken Spencer, LB
77— Mitch Brown, DB

ST. MARY (KAN.) (1)
86— Joe Brinson, RB

ST. MARY'S (CAL.) (3)
79— Fran McDermott, DB
80— Fran McDermott, DB
88— Jon Braff, TE

ST. MARY'S (TEX.) (1)
36— Douglas Locke, B

ST. NORBERT (2)
57— Norm Jarock, B
64— Dave Jauquet, DE

ST. OLAF (3)
53— John Gustafson, E
78— John Nahorniak, LB
80— Jon Anderson, DL

ST. THOMAS (MINN.) (6)
45— Theodore Molitor, E
48— Jack Salscheider, B
84— Neal Guggemos, DB
85— Neal Guggemos, DB
90— Gary Trettel, RB
91— Kevin DeVore, OL

STEPHEN F. AUSTIN (6)
51— James Terry, DE
79— Ronald Haynes, DL
85— James Noble, WR
86—†Darrell Harkless, DB
88—†Eric Lokey, LB
89—†David Whitmore, DB

STONY BROOK (2)
87— Chuck Downey, DB
88— David Lewis, P

SUL ROSS ST. (2)
65— Tom Nelson, DE
88— Francis Jones, DB

SUSQUEHANNA (2)
51— James Hazlett, C
90— Keith Henry, DL

SWARTHMORE (1)
89— Marshall Happer, OL

TAMPA (5)
65— John Perry, DB
68— Ron Brown, MG
70— Leon McQuay, RB
71— Ron Mikolajczyk, OT
     Sammy Gellerstedt, MG

TENN.-CHATT. (22)
35— Robert Klein, E
38— Robert Sutton, G
39— Jack Gregory, T
45— Thomas Stewart, T
46— Gene Roberts, B
48— Ralph Hutchinson, T
49— Vincent Sarratore, G
51— Chester LaGod, DT
52— Chester LaGod, DT

54— Richard Young, B
57— Howard Clark, E
58— John Green, B
60— Charles Long, T
64— Jerry Harris, SAF
66— Harry Sorrell, OG
76— Tim Collins, LB
86—†Mike Makins, DL
89—†Pumpy Tudors, P
     †Junior Jackson, LB
90—†Troy Boeck, DL
     †Tony Hill, DL
     †Pumpy Tudors, P

TENN.-MARTIN (3)
68— Julian Nunnamaker, OG
88— Emanuel McNeil, DL
91— Oscar Bunch, TE

TENNESSEE ST. (16)
67— Claude Humphrey, DT
68— Jim Marsalis, DB
69— Joe Jones, DE
70— Vernon Holland, OT
71— Cliff Brooks, DB
     Joe Gilliam, QB
72— Robert Woods, OT
     Waymond Bryant, LB
73— Waymond Bryant, LB
     Ed Jones, DE
74— Cleveland Elam, DE
81—†Mike Jones, WR
     †Malcolm Taylor, DT
82—†Walter Tate, OL
86—†Onzy Elam, LB
90—†Colin Godfrey, P

TENNESSEE TECH (10)
52— Tom Fann, OT
59— Tom Hackler, E
60— Tom Hackler, E
61— David Baxter, T
69— Larry Schreiber, HB
71— Jim Youngblood, LB
72— Jim Youngblood, LB
74— Elois Grooms, DE
76— Ed Burns, OT
89—†Ryan Weeks, PK

TEXAS A&I (40)
40— Stuart Clarkson, C
41— Stuart Clarkson, C
59— Gerald Lambert, G
60— William Crafts, T
62— Douglas Harvey, C
63— Sid Banks, B
65— Randy Johnson, QB
66— Dwayne Nix, OE
67— Dwayne Nix, OE
68— Dwayne Nix, OE
     Ray Hickl, OG
70— Dwight Harrison, DB
     Margarito Guerrero, MG
71— Eldridge Small, OE
     Levi Johnson, DB
72— Ernest Price, DE
74— Don Hardeman, RB
75— David Hill, TE
76— Richard Ritchie, QB
     Larry Grunewald, LB
77— Larry Collins, RB
     John Barefield, DE
78— Billy John, OT
79— Andy Hawkins, LB
80— Don Washington, CB
81— Durwood Roquemore, DB
82— Darrell Green, DB

83— Loyd Lewis, OG
84— Neal Lattue, PK
85— Charles Smith, C
86— Johnny Bailey, RB
Moses Horn, OG
87— Johnny Bailey, RB
Moses Horn, OG
88— Rod Mounts, OL
Johnny Bailey, RB
John Randle, DL
89— Johnny Bailey, RB
90— Keithen DeGrate, OL
91— Brian Nielsen, OL

TEXAS-ARLINGTON (5)
66— Ken Ozee, DT
67— Robert Diem, OG
Robert Willbanks, SAF
83— †Mark Cannon, C
84— †Bruce Collie, OL

TEXAS LUTHERAN (3)
73— David Wehmeyer, RB
74— D. W. Rutledge, LB
75— Jerry Ellis, OL

TEXAS SOUTHERN (2)
70— Nathaniel Allen, DB
76— Freddie Dean, OL

TEXAS TECH* (2)
35— Herschel Ramsey, E
45— Walter Schlinkman, B

TOLEDO* (1)
38— Dan Buckwick, G

TOWSON ST. (9)
75— Dan Dullea, QB
76— Skip Chase, OE
77— Randy Bielski, DB
78— Ken Snoots, SE
82— Sean Landeta, P
83— Gary Rubeling, DB
84— Terry Brooks, OG
85— Stan Eisentooth, OL
86— David Haden, LB

TRENTON ST. (3)
74— Eric Hamilton, C
83— John Aromando, WR
91— Chris Shaw, C

TRINITY (CONN.) (6)
35— Mickey Kobrosky, B
36— Mickey Kobrosky, B
55— Charles Sticka, B
59— Roger LeClerc, C
70— David Kiarsis, HB
78— Pat McNamara, FL

TRINITY (TEX.) (4)
54— Alvin Beal, B
55— Hubert Cook, C
56— Milton Robichaux, E
67— Marvin Upshaw, DT

TROY ST. (10)
39— Sherrill Busby, E
73— Mark King, C
74— Mark King, C
76— Perry Griggs, OE
78— Tim Tucker, LB
80— Willie Tullis, QB
84— Mitch Geier, OG
86— Freddie Thomas, DB
87— Mike Turk, QB
Freddie Thomas, QB

TUFTS (6)
34— William Grinnell, E
76— Tim Whelan, RB
78— Mark Buben, DL

79— Chris Connors, QB
80— Mike Brown, OL
86— Bob Patz, DL

TULSA* (1)
34— Rudy Prochaska, C

UC DAVIS (10)
72— Bob Biggs, QB
David Roberts, OT
76— Andrew Gagnon, OL
77— Chuck Fomasi, DT
78— Casey Merril, DL
79— Jeffrey Allen, DB
82— Ken O'Brien, QB
83— Bo Eason, DB
84— Scott Barry, QB
85— Mike Wise, DL

UC RIVERSIDE (1)
75— Michael Johnson, SE

UC SANTA BARB. (3)
36— Douglas Oldershaw, G
37— Douglas Oldershaw, G
67— Paul Vallerga, DB

UNION (N.Y.) (8)
39— Sam Hammerstrom, B
82— Steve Bodmer, DL
83— Tim Howell, LB
84— Brian Cox, DE
85— Anthony Valente, DL
86— Rich Romer, DL
87— Rich Romer, DL
91— Greg Harrison, PK

UNION (TENN.) (2)
41— James Jones, B
42— James Jones, B

UPSALA (1)
64— Dick Giessuebel, LB

U.S. INT'L (2)
72— Jerry Robinson, DB
75— Steve Matson, FL

VA. MILITARY (1)
88— †Mark Stock, WR

VALDOSTA ST. (4)
82— Mark Catano, OL
86— Jessie Tuggle, LB
89— Randy Fisher, WR
90— Deon Searcy, DB

VALPARAISO (5)
51— Joe Pahr, B
71— Gary Puetz, OT
72— Gary Puetz, OT
76— John Belskis, DB
85— Mike Healey, WR

VILLANOVA (3)
88— †Paul Berardelli, OL
89— †Bryan Russo, OL
91— †Curtis Eller, LB

VIRGINIA ST. (3)
71— Larry Brooks, DT
84— John Greene, LB
85— James Ward, DL

VIRGINIA UNION (12)
73— Herb Scott, OG
74— Herb Scott, OG
75— Anthony Leonard, DB
77— Frank Dark, DB
79— Plummer Bullock, DE
80— William Dillon, DB
81— William Dillon, DB
82— William Dillon, DB
83— Larry Curtis, DT
88— Leroy Gause, LB

91— Paul DeBerry, DB
Kevin Williams, LB

WABASH (5)
76— Jimmy Parker, DB
77— David Harvey, QB
81— Pete Metzelaars, TE
88— Tim Pliske, PK
89— Mike Funk, WR

WAGNER (9)
67— John Gloistein, OT
80— Phil Theis, OL
81— Alonzo Patterson, RB
82— Alonzo Patterson, RB
83— Selwyn Davis, OT
86— Charles Stinson, DL
87— Rich Negrin, OT
88— Terry Underwood, RB
91— Walter Lopez, PK

WASH. & JEFF. (4)
84— Ed Kusko, OL
87— A. J. Pagano, RB
91— Chris Babirad, RB
Gilbert Floyd, DB

WASH. & LEE (4)
76— Tony Perry, OE
81— Mike Pressler, DL
83— Glenn Kirschner, OL
86— John Packett, OL

WASHBURN (2)
64— Robert Hardy, DB
88— Troy Slusser, WR

WASHINGTON (MO.) (4)
72— Shelby Jordan, LB
73— Stu Watkins, OE
74— Marion Stallings, DB
88— Paul Matthews, TE

WAYNE ST. (NEB.) (2)
84— Herve Roussel, PK
85— Ruben Mendoza, OL

WAYNESBURG (1)
41— Nick George, G

WEBER ST. (13)
66— Ronald McCall, DE
67— Lee White, FB
Jim Schmedding, OG
69— Carter Campbell, DE
70— Henry Reed, DE
71— David Taylor, OT
77— Dennis Duncanson, DB
78— Dennis Duncanson, DB
Randy Jordan, WR
80— †Mike Humiston, LB
89— †Peter Macon, WR
91— †Jamie Martin, QB
†Alfred Pupunu, WR

WESLEY (1)
91— Fran Naselli, KR

WESLEYAN (6)
46— Bert VanderClute, G
48— Jack Geary, T
72— Robert Heller, C
73— Robert Heller, C
76— John McVicar, DL
77— John McVicar, DL

WEST CHESTER (8)
52— Charles Weber, DG
58— Richard Emerich, T
61— Joe Iacone, B
62— Joe Iacone, B
72— Tim Pierantozzi, QB
76— William Blystone, RB

First-Team All-America Selections Below Division I-A

87— Ralph Tamm, OL
88— Bill Hess, WR
WEST TEX. ST. (2)
86— Stan Carraway, WR
90— Mark Bounds, P
WEST VA.* (1)
34— Tod Goodwin, E
WEST VA. TECH (3)
82— Elliott Washington, DB
86— Calvin Wallace, DL
89— Phil Hudson, WR
WEST VA. WESLEYAN (2)
36— George Mike, T
82— Jerry Free, T
WESTERN CARO. (12)
49— Arthur Byrd, G
71— Steve Williams, DT
73— Mark Ferguson, OT
74— Jerry Gaines, SE
  Steve Yates, LB
84—†Louis Cooper, DL
  †Kirk Roach, PK
  †Steve Kornegay, P
85—†Clyde Simmons, DL
86—†Alonzo Carmichael, TE
  †Kirk Roach, PK
87—†Kirk Roach, PK
WESTERN ILL. (14)
59— Bill Larson, B
61— Leroy Jackson, B
74— John Passananti, OT
76— Scott Levenhagen, TE
  Greg Lee, DB
77— Craig Phalen, DT
78— Bill Huskisson, DL
80— Mike Maher, TE
  Don Greco, OG
83—†Chris Gunderson, MG
84—†Chris Gunderson, T
86—†Frank Winters, C
  †Todd Auer, DL
88—†Marlin Williams, DL
WESTERN KY. (15)
64— Dale Lindsey, LB
70— Lawrence Brame, DE
73— Mike McKoy, DB
74— John Bushong, DL
  Virgil Livers, DB
75— Rick Green, LB
77— Chip Carpenter, OL
80—†Pete Walters, OG
  †Tim Ford, DL
81—†Donnie Evans, DE
82—†Paul Gray, LB
83—†Paul Gray, LB
87—†James Edwards, DB
88—†Dean Tiebout, OL
  †Joe Arnold, RB
WESTERN MD. (3)
51— Victor Makovitch, DG
78— Ricci Bonaccorsy, DL
79— Ricci Bonaccorsy, DL

WESTERN MICH.* (1)
82—†Matt Meares, OL
WESTERN NEW MEX. (2)
83— Jay Ogle, WR
88— Pat Maxwell, P
WESTERN ST. (4)
56— Bill Rhodes, B
78— Bill Campbell, DB
80— Justin Cross, OT

84— Jeff Guy, P
WESTERN WASH. (2)
51— Norman Hash, DB
79— Patrick Locker, RB
WESTMINSTER (PA.) (9)
73— Robert Pontius, DB
77— Rex Macey, FL
82— Gary DeGruttola, LB
83— Scott Higgins, DB
86— Joe Keaney, LB
88— Kevin Myers, LB
89— Joe Micchia, QB
90— Brad Tokar, RB
91— Brian DeLorenzo, DL
WHEATON (ILL.) (5)
55— Dave Burnham, B
58— Robert Bakke, T
77— Larry Wagner, LB
78— Scott Hall, QB
83— Keith Bishop, QB
WHITTIER (3)
38— Myron Claxton, T
62— Richard Peter, T
77— Michael Ciacci, DB
WHITWORTH (4)
52— Pete Swanson, OG
54— Larry Paradis, T
85— Wayne Ralph, WR
86— Wayne Ralph, WR
WIDENER (11)
72— Billy Johnson, RB
73— Billy Johnson, RB
75— John Warrington, DB
76— Al Senni, OL
77— Chip Zawoiski, RB
79— Tom Deery, DB
80— Tom Deery, DB
81— Tom Deery, DB
82— Tony Stefanoni, DL
88— Ron Nesbitt, OL
  Dave Duffy, DL
WILKES (1)
73— Jeff Grandinetti, DT
WILLAMETTE (11)
34— Loren Grannis, G
35— John Oravec, B
36— Richard Weisgerber, B
46— Marvin Goodman, E
58— William Long, C
59— Marvin Cisneros, G
64— Robert Burles, DT
65— Robert Burles, DT
69— Calvin Lee, LB
75— Gary Johnson, DL
82— Richard Milroy, DB
WILLIAM & MARY (4)
83—†Mario Shaffer, OL
86—†Michael Clemons, RB
89—†Steve Christie, P
90—†Pat Crowley, DL
WILLIAM JEWELL (4)
52— Al Conway, B
73— John Strada, OE
81— Guy Weber, DL
83— Mark Mundel, OL
WILLIAM PENN (1)
72— Bruce Polen, DB
WILLIAMS (5)
51— Charles Salmon, DG
69— Jack Maitland, HB
74— John Chandler, LB

78— Greg McAleenan, DB
90— George Rogers, DL
WILMINGTON (1)
72— William Roll, OG
WINGATE (1)
89— Jimmy Sutton, OT
WINSTON-SALEM (4)
77— Cornelius Washington, DB
78— Tim Newsome, RB
84— Danny Moore, OG
87— Barry Turner, G
WIS.-EAU CLAIRE (1)
81— Roger Vann, RB
WIS.-LA CROSSE (8)
52— Ted Levanhagen, LB
72— Bryon Buelow, DB
78— Joel Williams, LB
83— Jim Byrne, DL
85— Tom Newberry, OL
88— Ted Pretasky, RB
89— Terry Strouf, OL
91— Jon Lauscher, LB
WIS.-MILWAUKEE (1)
70— Pete Papara, LB
WIS.-PLATTEVILLE (2)
73— William Vander Velden, DE
86— Mike Hintz, DB
WIS.-RIVER FALLS (3)
80— Gerald Sonsalla, OG
82— Roland Hall, LB
87— Greg Corning, RB
WIS.-STEVENS POINT (2)
77— Reed Giordana, QB
81— Chuck Braun, WR
WIS.-STOUT (1)
79— Joseph Bullis, DL
WIS.-SUPERIOR (3)
66— Mel Thake, DB
83— Larry Banks, MG
85— Phil Eiting, LB
WIS.-WHITEWATER (4)
75— William Barwick, OL
79— Jerry Young, WR
82— Daryl Schleim, DE
90— Reggie White, OL

WITTENBERG (17)
62— Donald Hunt, G
63— Bob Cherry, E
64— Chuck Green, QB
68— Jim Felts, DE
73— Steve Drongowski, OT
74— Arthur Thomas, LB
75— Robert Foster, LB
76— Dean Caven, DL
78— Dave Merritt, RB
79— Joe Govern, DL
80— Mike Dowds, DE
81— Bill Beach, DB
83— Bryant Lemon, DL
87— Eric Horstman, OL
88— Ken Bonner, OT
  Eric Horstman, OL
90— Jon Warga, RB

WOFFORD (10)
42— Aubrey Faust, E
47— Ken Dubard, T
49— Elbert Hammett, T
51— Jack Beeler, DB
57— Charles Bradshaw, B
61— Dan Lewis, G

70— Sterling Allen, OG
79— Keith Kinard, OL
90— David Wiley, OL
91— Tom Cotter, OL
WOOSTER (1)
79— Blake Moore, C
XAVIER (OHIO) (1)
51— Tito Carinci, LB

YALE (1)
84—†John Zanieski, DL
YOUNGSTOWN ST. (12)
74— Don Calloway, DB
75— Don Calloway, DB
78— Ed McGlasson, OL
79— James Ferranti, OE
Jeff Lear, OT

80— Jeff Gergel, LB
81—†Paris Wicks, RB
82—†Paris Wicks, RB
88—†Jim Zdelar, OL
89—†Paul Soltis, LB
90—†Tony Bowens, DL
91—†Pat Danko, DL

NCAA POSTGRADUATE SCHOLARSHIP WINNERS

Following are football players who are NCAA postgraduate scholarship winners, whether or not they were able to accept the grant, plus all alternates indicated by (*) who accepted grants. The program began with the 1964 season. (Those who played in 1964 are listed as 1965 winners, those who played in 1965 as 1966 winners, etc.) To qualify, student-athletes must maintain a 3.000 grade-point average (on a 4.000 scale) during their collegiate careers and perform with distinction in varsity football.

ABILENE CHRISTIAN
71— James Lindsey
83—*Grant Feasel
85— Daniel Remsberg
86—*James Embry
Craig Huff
90— William Clayton
AIR FORCE
65— Edward Fausti
67— James Hogarty
68— Kenneth Zagzebski
69—*Richard Rivers Jr.
70— Charles Longnecker
*Alfred Wurglitz
71— Ernest Jennings
Robert Parker Jr.
72— Darryl Haas
73— Mark Prill
75—*Joseph Debes
84— Jeffrey Kubiak
86— Derek Brown
88— Chad Hennings
89— David Hlatky
90— Steven Wilson
91— Christopher Howard
92— Ronald James
ALABAMA
69— Donald Sutton
72— John Musso Jr.
75— Randy Hall
80— Steadman Shealy
ALABAMA ST.
92— Edward Robinson Jr.
ALBANY (N.Y.)
88—*Thomas Higgins
ALBION
81— Joel Manby
ALBRIGHT
67—*Paul Chaiet
ALLEGHENY
65— David Wion
92— Darren Hadlock
ALMA
67— Keith Bird Jr.
79— Todd Friesner
AMHERST
66— David Greenblatt
76— Geoffrey Miller
85— Raymond Nurme

APPALACHIAN ST.
78— Gill Beck
ARIZONA
69— William Michael Moody
78— Jon Abbott
80— Jeffrey Whitton
88— Charles Cecil
ARIZONA ST.
78— John Harris
90— Mark Tingstad
ARKANSAS
70— Terry Stewart
71— William Burnett
79— William Bradford Shoup
85—*Mark Lee
ARKANSAS ST.
72— John Meyer
77— Thomas Humphreys
ARMY
66— Samuel Champi Jr.
68— Bohdan Neswiacheny
69— James McCall Jr.
Thomas Wheelock
70— Theodore Shadid Jr.
78— Curtis Downs
81—*Stanley March
86— Donald Smith
Douglas Black
88— William Conner
90— Michael Thorson
ASHLAND
78— Daniel Bogden
88— David Biondo
90— Douglas Powell
AUBURN
66— John Cochran
69—*Roger Giffin
85— Gregg Carr
90— James Lyle IV
AUGSBURG
90— Terry Mackenthun
AUGUSTANA (ILL.)
69—*Jeffrey Maurus
71— Kenneth Anderson
77— Joe Thompson
86— Steven Sanders
AUGUSTANA (S.D.)
72— Michael Olson
75— David Zelinsky

77— James Clemens
78— Dee Donlin
Roger Goebel
90—*David Gubbrud
91— Scott Boyens
BALL ST.
67—*John Hostrawser
73— Gregory Mack
77— Arthur Yaroch
84— Richard Chitwood
88— Ronald Duncan
90— Theodore Ashburn
BATES
79— Christopher Howard
BAYLOR
65— Michael Kennedy
66— Edward Whiddon
BOISE ST.
72— Brent McIver
76—*Glenn Sparks
79— Samuel Miller
82— Kip Bedard
92— Larry Stayner
BOSTON COLLEGE
66—*Lawrence Marzetti
67— Michael O'Neill
69— Gary Andrachik
70— Robert Bouley
78— Richard Scudellari
87— Michael Degnan
BOSTON U.
69— Suren Donabedian Jr.
81— David Bengtson
BOWDOIN
65— Steven Ingram
67— Thomas Allen
BOWIE ST.
92— Mark Fitzgerald
BOWLING GREEN
77— Richard Preston
78— Mark Miller
91— Patrick Jackson
BRIDGEPORT
70— Terry Sparker
BRIGHAM YOUNG
67— Virgil Carter
76— Orrin Olsen
77—*Stephen Miller

First-Team All-America Selections Below Division I-A

78— Gifford Nielsen
80— Marc Wilson
82— Daniel Plater
83— Bart Oates
84— Steve Young
85— Marvin Allen
89— Charles Cutler

BROWN
65— John Kelly Jr.
70— James Lukens
74— Douglas Jost
75— William Taylor
77— Scott Nelson
78— Louis Cole
79— Robert Forster
82— Travis Holcombe

BUCKNELL
71—*Kenneth Donahue
74— John Dailey
75— Steve Leskinen
77— Lawrence Brunt
85— David Kucera

BUENA VISTA
77— Steven Trost
87— Michael Habben

BUFFALO ST.
87— James Dunbar

BUTLER
72— George Yearsich
78— William Ginn
85— Stephen Kollias

CAL LUTHERAN
90—*Gregory Maw

CAL POLY SLO
69— William Creighton

CAL TECH
67— William Mitchell
68— John Frazzini
74— Frank Hobbs Jr.

CALIFORNIA
66— William Krum
67— John Schmidt
68— Robert Crittenden
70— James Calkins
71— Robert Richards
83— Harvey Salem

CANISIUS
84— Thomas Schott

CAPITAL
84—*Michael Linton

CARLETON
67— Robert Paarlberg
73— Mark Williams
83— Paul Vaaler

CARNEGIE MELLON
80— Gusty Sunseri
91— Robert O'Toole

CARROLL (WIS.)
77— Stephen Thompson

CARTHAGE
70— William Radakovitz

CASE RESERVE
89— Christopher Nutter
91— James Meek

CENTRAL (IOWA)
71— Vernon Den Herder
87— Scott Lindell
89— Eric Perry
92— Richard Kacmarynski

CENTRAL MICH.
77— John Wunderlich
80—*Michael Ball
85— Kevin Egnatuk
88— Robert Stebbins
92— Jeffrey Bender

CENTRAL WASH.
70— Danny Collins

CENTRE
69— Glenn Shearer
86— Casteel "Teel" Bruner II
88—*Robert Clark
90— James Ellington

CHEYNEY
76— Steven Anderson

CHICAGO
86—*Bruce Montella
89— Paul Haar

CINCINNATI
71—*Earl Willson

CITADEL
74— Thomas Leitner
79— Kenneth Caldwell
84—*William West IV

CLAREMONT-M-S
68— Craig Dodel
70—*Gregory Long
71— Stephen Endemano
73— Christopher Stecher
74— Samuel Reece

CLEMSON
65— James Bell Jr.
68— James Addison
73— Benjamin Anderson
79— Stephen Fuller

COAST GUARD
73— Rodney Leis
74— Leonard Kelly
81— Bruce Hensel
89—*Ty Rinoski
   *Jeffery Peters
90— Richard Schachner
91— John Freda

COE
67— Lynn Harris

COLBY
71— Ronald Lupton
   Frank Apantaku

COLGATE
73— Kenneth Nelson
80— Angelo Colosimo
89— Donald Charney

COLORADO COL.
69— Steven Ehrhart
72— Randy Bobier
75— Bruce Kolbezen
84— Herman Motz III

COLORADO MINES
66— Stuart Bennett
67— Michael Greensburg
   Charles Kirby
75— David Chambers

COLORADO ST.
65— Russel Mowrer
76— Mark Driscoll
87— Stephan Bartalo
88— Joseph Brookhart

COLUMBIA
72— John Sefcik
80— Mario Biaggi Jr.

CONNECTICUT
77—*Bernard Palmer

CORNELL
68— Ronald Kipicki
72— Thomas Albright
84— Derrick Harmon

CORNELL COLLEGE
65— Steven Miller
72— David Hilmers
73— Robert Ash
79— Brian Farrell
79— Thomas Zinkula
81—*Timothy Garry
83— John Ward

DARTMOUTH
66— Anthony Yezer
68— Henry Paulson Jr.
69— Randolph Wallick
71— Willie Bogan
73— Frederick Radke
74— Thomas Csatari
   *Robert Funk
77— Patrick Sullivan
89— Paul Sorensen

DAVIDSON
66— Stephen Smith
71— Rick Lyon
72— Robert Norris
86—*Louis Krempel

DAYTON
73— Timothy Quinn
76— Roy Gordon III
83—*Michael Pignatiello
91— Daniel Sharley

DELAWARE
86— Brian Farrell

DELAWARE VALLEY
85— Daniel Glowatski

DELTA ST.
76— William Hood

DENISON
70— Richard Trumball
73— Steven Smiljanich
76—*Dennis Thome
78— David Holcombe
86— Brian Gearinger
88— Grant Jones
92— Jonathan Fortkamp

DePAUW
68— Bruce Montgomerie
78— Mark Frazer
81— Jay True
85— Richard Bonaccorsi
86— Anthony deNicola
92— Thomas Beaulieu

DICKINSON
66— Robert Averback
71—*John West
75—*Gerald Urich

DOANE
68— John Lothrop
70— Richard Held

DRAKE
73— Joseph Worobec

DREXEL
72— Blake Lynn Ferguson

DUBUQUE
82— Timothy Finn

DUKE
68— Robert Lasky

71—*Curt Rawley

EAST CARO.
92— Keith Arnold

EAST TENN. ST.
82— Jay Patterson

EASTERN KY.
78— Steven Frommeyer

EASTERN N. MEX.
66— Richard James

ELIZABETH CITY ST.
73— Darnell Johnson
80— David Nickelson

ELMHURST
80— Richard Green

EMORY & HENRY
82— Thomas Browder Jr.

EVANSVILLE
75— David Mattingly
76— Charles Uhde Jr.
79—*Neil Saunders

FERRIS ST.
79— Robert Williams

FLORIDA
72— Carlos Alvarez
77— Darrell Carpenter
85— Garrison Rolle
87— Bret Wiechmann
90—*Cedric Smith
91— Huey Richardson

FLORIDA ST.
88— David Palmer
91— David Roberts

FORDHAM
91— Eric Schweiker

FRANK. & MARSH.
69— Frank deGenova
83—*Robert Shepardson

FRESNO ST.
70—*Henry Corda
74— Dwayne Westphal
83— William Griever Jr.

FURMAN
77— Thomas Holcomb III
82— Charles Anderson
84— Ernest Gibson
86—*David Jager
87— Stephen Squire
90— Christopher Roper
92— Paul Siffri
    Eric Von Walter

GEORGETOWN
75— James Chesley Jr.

GEORGIA
68— Thomas Lawhorne Jr.
69— William Payne
71— Thomas Lyons
72— Thomas Nash Jr.
    Raleigh Mixon Robinson
78— Jeffrey Lewis
80— Jeffrey Pyburn
81— Christopher Welton
84— Terrell Hoage
88— Kim Stephens
89— Richard Tardits

GEORGIA TECH
68— William Eastman
75— James Robinson
81— Sheldon Fox
83— Ellis Gardner
86— John Ivemeyer

GETTYSBURG
70—*Herbert Ruby III
80— Richard Swartz

GRAMBLING
73— Stephen Dennis

GRINNELL
72— Edward Hirsch
80—*Derek Muehrcke

GUST. ADOLPHUS
74— James Goodwin
81—*David Najarian

HAMLINE
85— Kyle Aug
91— Robert Hackney

HAMPDEN-SYDNEY
78—*Wilson Newell
80— Timothy Maxa

HARVARD
68— Alan Bersin
71—*Richard Frisbie
75— Patrick McInally
76— William Emper
81— Charles Durst
85— Brian Bergstrom
87— Scott Collins

HAWAII
68— James Roberts
73—*Don Satterlee

HIRAM
68— Sherman
    Riemenschneider
74— Donald Brunetti

HOLY CROSS
84—*Bruce Kozerski
89— Jeffrey Wiley
91— John Lavalette

HOPE
74— Ronald Posthuma
80— Craig Groendyk
83— Kurt Brinks
85—*Scott Jecmen

HOUSTON
86— Gary Schoppe
87— Robert Brezina

IDAHO
67— Michael Lavens
67— Joseph McCollum Jr.
84— Boyce Bailey

IDAHO ST.
76— Richard Rodgers
92— Steven Boyenger

ILL. BENEDICTINE
70— David Cyr
71— Thomas Danaher

ILLINOIS
72— Robert Bucklin
73— Laurence McCarren Jr.
91— Curtis Lovelace
92— Michael Hopkins

INDIANA
73— Glenn Scolnik
79— David Abrams
81— Kevin Speer

INDIANA (PA.)
78—*John Mihota
84— Kenneth Moore

INDIANA ST.
86— Jeffrey Miller

INDIANAPOLIS
76— Rodney Pawlik

IONA
81— Neal Kurtti
82—*Paul Rupp

IOWA
69— Michael Miller
76— Robert Elliott
78— Rodney Sears
86— Larry Station Jr.
88— Michael Flagg
89— Charles Hartlieb

IOWA ST.
70— William Bliss

JACKSON ST.
80—*Lester Walls

JACKSONVILLE ST.
79— Dewey Barker

JAMES MADISON
79— Warren Coleman
90— Mark Kiefer

JOHNS HOPKINS
73— Joseph Ouslander
74— Gunter Glocker

JUNIATA
72— Maurice Taylor
87— Robert Crossey

KANSAS
65— Ronald Oelschlager
69— David Morgan
72— Michael McCoy
73— John Schroll
78— Tom Fitch
87— Mark Henderson

KANSAS ST.
66—*Larry Anderson
83— James Gale
88— Matthew Garver

KENTUCKY
76— Thomas Ranieri
79— James Kovach
84—*Keith Martin

KENTUCKY ST.
68— James Jackson

KENYON
75— Patrick Clements

KNOX
88— Robert Monroe

LAFAYETTE
71— William Sprecher
76— Michael Kline
78— Victor Angeline III

LAMAR
73—*Richard Kubiak

LAWRENCE
68— Charles McKee
83— Christopher Matheus

LEBANON VALLEY
74—*Alan Shortell

LEHIGH
66— Robert Adelaar
68— Richard Miller
73—*Thomas Benfield
75— James Addonizio
76—*Robert Liptak
77—*Michael Yaszemski
80— David Melone

LIU-C. W. POST
79— John Luchsinger

LONG BEACH ST.
84— Joseph Donohue

LOUISIANA ST.
79— Robert Dugas
83— James Britt
88— Ignazio Albergamo
91— Solomon Graves

LUTHER
67— Thomas Altemeier
78—*Mark Larson
85— Larry Bonney

MANKATO ST.
70— Bernard Maczuga

MARYLAND
78— Jonathan Claiborne

MARYVILLE (TENN.)
67— Frank Eggers II

McNEESE ST.
81— Daryl Burckel
86— Ross Leger

MEMPHIS ST.
77—*James Mincey Jr.

MERCHANT MARINE
70— Robert Lavinia
76—*John Castagna

MIAMI (FLA.)
90— Robert Chudzinski
91— Michael Sullivan

MICHIGAN
67— David Fisher
74— David Gallagher
81—*John Wangler
82— Norm Betts
84— Stefan Humphries
84— Thomas Dixon
86— Clayton Miller
87— Kenneth Higgins

MICHIGAN ST.
69— Allen Brenner
70— Donald Baird

MICHIGAN TECH
72— Larry Ras
74— Bruce Trusock
75— Daniel Rhude

MIDDLE TENN. ST.
73—*Edwin Zaunbrecher

MIDDLEBURY
79— Franklin Kettle

MIDLAND LUTHERAN
76— Thomas Hale

MILLERSVILLE
92— Thomas Burns III

MILLIKIN
90—*Charles Martin

MILLSAPS
67— Edward Weller
73—*Russell Gill
92— David Harrison Jr.

MINNESOTA
69— Robert Stein
71— Barry Mayer
73— Douglas Kingsriter
78— Robert Weber

MISSISSIPPI
66— Stanley Hindman
69— Steve Hindman
81— Kenneth Toler Jr.
86— Richard Austin
87— Jeffrey Noblin
88— Daniel Hoskins
89— Charles Walls
91— Todd Sandroni

MISSISSIPPI COL.
80— Stephen Johnson

MISSISSIPPI ST.
69— William Nelson
73— Frank Dowsing Jr.
75— James Webb
77— William Coltharp

MISSOURI
66— Thomas Lynn
67— James Whitaker
69—*Charles Weber
71— John Weisenfels
79— Christopher Garlich
82— Van Darkow

MISSOURI-ROLLA
69— Robert Nicodemus
73— Kim Colter
81— Paul Janke

MIT
91— Darcy Prather
92— Rodrigo Rubiano

MONMOUTH (ILL.)
72— Dale Brooks
90— Brent Thurness

MONTANA
75— Rock Svennungsen
79— Steven Fisher
84— Brian Salonen
91— Michael McGowan

MONTANA ST.
65— Gene Carlson
68— Russell Dodge
71— Jay Groepper
77— Bert Markovich
79— Jon Borchardt
        James Mickelson
90— Derrick Isackson
92— Travis Annette

MORAVIAN
73— Daniel Joseph

MOREHEAD ST.
92— James Appel

MORNINGSIDE
65— Larry White

MORRIS BROWN
83— Arthur Knight Jr.

MOUNT UNION
89— Paul Hrics

MUHLENBERG
73— Edward Salo
76— Eric Butler
78— Mark Stull
81— Arthur Scavone
91— Michael Hoffman

MURRAY ST.
71— Matthew Haug
78— Edward McFarland
81—*Kris Robbins
90— Eric Crigler

NAVY
65— William Donnelly
69— William Newton
70— Daniel Pike
75—*Timothy Harden
76— Chester Moeller II
81— Theodore Dumbauld

N.C. CENTRAL
91— Anthony Cooley

NEBRASKA
70— Randall Reeves

71—*John Decker
72— Larry Jacobson
73— David Mason
74— Daniel Anderson
76— Thomas Heiser
77— Vince Ferragamo
78— Ted Harvey
79— James Pillen
80— Timothy Smith
81— Randy Schleusener
        Jeffrey Finn
82— Eric Lindquist
85— Scott Strasburger
88— Jeffrey Jamrog
89— Mark Blazek
90— Gerald Gdowski
        Jacob Young III
91— David Edeal
        Patrick Tyrance Jr.
92— Patrick Engelbert

NEBRASKA-OMAHA
84— Kirk Hutton
84— Clark Toner

NEW HAMPSHIRE
85— Richard Leclerc

NEW MEXICO
72— Roderick Long
76— Robert Berg
79— Robert Rumbaugh
83— George Parks

NEW MEXICO ST.
76— Ralph Jackson
77—*Joseph Fox

NORTH ALA.
82—*Warren Moore

NORTH CARO.
75— Christopher Kupec
81— William Donnalley
83— David Drechsler
91— Kevin Donnalley

NORTH CARO. ST.
75— Justus Everett
82—*Calvin Warren Jr.

NORTH DAK.
79— Dale Lian
81— Douglas Moen
82— Paul Franzmeier
85— Glen Kucera
88— Kurt Otto
89— Matthew Gulseth

NORTH DAK. ST.
66— James Schindler
69—*Stephen Stephens
71— Joseph Cichy
75— Paul Cichy
84— Doug Hushka
89— Charles Stock

NORTH TEXAS
68— Ruben Draper
77— Peter Morris

NORTHEAST MO. ST.
83— Roy Pettibone

NORTHERN ARIZ.
78— Larry Friedrichs

NORTHERN COLO.
76— Robert Bliss
91— Thomas Langer

NORTHERN IOWA
81— Owen Dockter

NORTHERN MICH.
73— Guy Falkenhagen

81— Phil Kessel
86— Keith Nelsen

NORTHWEST MO. ST.
82— Robert Gregory

NORTHWESTERN
70— *Bruce Hubbard
74— Steven Craig
77— Randolph Dean
81— Charles Kern

NORWICH
68— Richard Starbuck
74— Matthew Hincks

NOTRE DAME
67— Frederick Schnurr
68— James Smithberger
69— George Kunz
70— Michael Oriard
71— Lawrence DiNardo
72— Thomas Gatewood
73— Gregory Marx
74— David Casper
75— Peter Demmerle
75— Reggie Barnett
79— Joseph Restic
81— Thomas Gibbons
82— John Krimm Jr.
86— Gregory Dingens
89— Reginald Ho

OCCIDENTAL
66— James Wanless
67— Richard Verry
69— John St. John
78— Richard Fry
80— *Timothy Bond
89— *Curtis Page

OHIO
78— *Robert Weidaw
80— Mark Geisler

OHIO NORTHERN
79— Mark Palmer
82— Larry Egbert

OHIO ST.
65— Arnold Chonko
66— Donald Unverferth
67— Ray Pryor
69— David Foley
71— Rex Kern
74— Randolph Gradishar
76— Brian Baschnagel
77— William Lukens
80— James Laughlin
84— John Frank
85— David Crecelius
86— Michael Lanese

OKLAHOMA
72— Larry Jack Mildren Jr.
73— Joe Wylie
81— Jay Jimerson
89— Anthony Phillips
91— Michael Sawatzky

OKLAHOMA ST.
83— *Doug Freeman

OLIVET
75— William Ziem

OREGON
79— *Willie Blasher Jr.
91— William Musgrave

OREGON ST.
69— William Enyart
69— *Jerry Belcher

PACIFIC (CAL.)
72— *Byron Cosgrove
78— Brian Peets
80— Bruce Filarsky

PENN ST.
66— Joseph Bellas
67— John Runnells III
71— Robert Holuba
72— David Joyner
73— Bruce Bannon
74— Mark Markovich
75— John Baiorunos
79— *Charles Correal
80— *Michael Guman
81— John Walsh
84— Harry Hamilton
85— Douglas Strange
87— Brian Silverling
90— Roger Thomas Duffy

PENNSYLVANIA
68— Ben Mortensen

PITTSBURGH
79— Jeff Delaney
86— Robert Schilken
89— Mark Stepnoski

POMONA-PITZER
69— *Lee Piatek
77— Scott Borg
83— *Calvin Oishi
85— *Derek Watanabe
88— Edward Irick

PORTLAND ST.
79— John Urness

PRINCETON
67— Charles Peters
69— Richard Sandler
70— Keith Mauney
76— Ronald Beible
81— Mark Bailey
83— Brent Woods
86— James Petrucci
87— John Hammond

PUGET SOUND
68— Stephen Doolittle
79— *Patrick O'Loughlin
83— *Anthony Threlkeld

PURDUE
70— Michael Phipps
74— Robert Hoftiezer
75— Lawrence Burton

REDLANDS
65— Robert Jones

RENSSELAER
67— Robert Darnall
69— John Contento

RHODES
71— John Churchill
79— *Philip Mischke
81— Jeffrey Lane
83— *Russell Ashford
85— *John Foropoulos
89— James Augustine

RICE
81— *Lamont Jefferson
91— Donald Hollas

RICHMOND
86— Leland Melvin

RIPON
65— Phillip Steans
69— Steven Thompson
80— Thomas Klofta

RUTGERS
90— Steven Tardy

SANTA CLARA
72— Ronald Sani
77— Mark Tiernan
81— *David Alfaro
85— Alexis Vlahos
87— Patrick Sende

SEWANEE
65— Frank Stubblefield
66— Douglas Paschall
69— James Beene
71— John Popham IV
77— Dudley West
82— Gregory Worsowicz
82— Domenick Reina
83— Michael York
84— Michael Jordan

SHIPPENSBURG
77— Anthony Winter

SIMPSON
71— Richard Clogg
74— Hugh Lickiss
90— Roger Grover

SOUTH CARO.
67— Steven Stanley Juk Jr.

SOUTH DAK.
79— Michael Schurrer
87— Todd Salat

SOUTH DAK. ST.
80— Charles Loewen
81— Paul Kippley
88— Daniel Sonnek

SOUTHEASTERN LA.
74— William Percy Jr.

SOUTHERN-B.R.
70— Alden Roche

SOUTHERN CAL
66— Charles Arrobio
69— Steven Sogge
70— Harry Khasigian
　　　Steve Lehmer
74— Monte Doris
75— Patrick Haden
76— Kevin Bruce
78— Gary Bethel
80— Brad Budde
　　　Paul McDonald
81— Gordon Adams
　　　*Jeffrey Fisher
85— Duane Bickett
86— Anthony Colorito
　　　*Matthew Koart
87— Jeffrey Bregel
90— John Jackson

SOUTHERN COLO.
70— Gregory Smith
73— Collon Kennedy III

SOUTHERN METHODIST
83—*Brian O'Meara
85—*Monte Goen
87— David Adamson

SOUTHERN MISS.
83— Richard Thompson
84— Stephen Carmody

SOUTHERN UTAH
92— Stephen McDowell

SOUTHWEST MO. ST.
80— Richard Suchenski
　　　Mitchel Ware
85— Michael Armentrout

SOUTHWEST TEX. ST.
82— Michael Miller

SOUTHWESTERN LA.
71—*George Coussa

ST. CLOUD ST.
90— Richard Rodgers

ST. FRANCIS (PA.)
87— Christopher Tantlinger

ST. JOHN'S (MINN.)
92— Denis McDonough

ST. JOSEPH'S (IND.)
80— Michael Bettinger

ST. NORBERT
66— Michael Ryan
88— Matthew Lang

ST. PAUL'S
80— Gerald Hicks

ST. THOMAS (MINN.)
75— Mark Dienhart

STANFORD
65—*Joe Neal
66—*Terry DeSylvia
68— John Root
71— John Sande III
72— Jackie Brown
74— Randall Poltl
75—*Keith Rowen
76— Gerald Wilson
77— Duncan McColl
81— Milton McColl
84— John Bergren
85— Scott Carpenter
86— Matthew Soderlund
87— Brian Morris
88— Douglas Robison

SUSQUEHANNA
77— Gerald Hueseken
82— Daniel Distasio

SWARTHMORE
72— Christopher Leinberger
83—*John Walsh

SYRACUSE
78—*Robert Avery
86— Timothy Green

TEMPLE
74— Dwight Fulton

TENN.-CHATT.
67— Harvey Ouzts
72—*Frank Webb
74— John McBrayer
76— Russell Gardner

TENNESSEE
71— Donald Denbo
     Timothy Priest
77— Michael Mauck
81— Timothy Irwin

TEXAS
69— Corbin Robertson Jr.
71— Willie Zapalac Jr.
73—*Michael Bayer
74— Patrick Kelly
75— Wade Johnston
76— Robert Simmons
77— William Hamilton

TEXAS A&M
69— Edward Hargett
71— David Elmendorf
72— Stephen Luebbehusen
88— Kip Corrington

TEXAS-ARLINGTON
69— Michael Baylor

TEXAS CHRISTIAN
67— John Richards
68— Eldon Gresham Jr.
73— Scott Walker
75— Terry Drennan
88— J. Clinton Hailey

TEXAS SOUTHERN
65— Leon Hardy

TEXAS TECH
65— James Ellis Jr.
68— John Scovell
75— Jeffrey Jobe
78—*Richard Arledge
85—*Bradford White
90— Thomas Mathiasmeier

TOLEDO
82— Tad Wampfler
89— Kenneth Moyer

TRINITY (CONN.)
67—*Howard Wrzosek
68— Keith Miles

TRINITY (TEX.)
84—*Peter Broderick

TROY ST.
75— Mark King

TUFTS
65— Peter Smith
70— Robert Bass
79—*Don Leach
80—*James Ford
82—*Brian Gallagher
87— Robert Patz
92— Paulo Oliveira

TULSA
67—*Larry Williams
75— James Mack Lancaster II

TUSKEGEE
68— James Greene

UC DAVIS
76— Daniel Carmazzi
     David Gellerman
77— Rolf Benirschke
79— Mark Markel
86— Robert Hagenau
90—*James Tomasin
92— Robert Kincade
     Michael Shepard

UC RIVERSIDE
72— Tyrone Hooks
74— Gary Van Jandegian

UCLA
67—*Raymond Armstrong
     Dallas Grider
70— Gregory Jones
74— Steven Klosterman
76— John Sciarra
77— Jeffrey Dankworth
78— John Fowler Jr.
83— Cormac Carney
84— Richard Neuheisel
86— Michael Hartmeier
90— Richard Meyer

UNION (N.Y.)
88— Richard Romer

UTAH
81— James Baldwin

UTAH ST.
67— Ronnie Edwards

68— Garth Hall
70— Gary Anderson
76— Randall Stockham

UTEP
80— Eddie Forkerway
89— Patrick Hegarty
92— Robert Sesich

VA. MILITARY
79— Robert Bookmiller
80— Richard Craig Jones

VALPARAISO
75—*Richard Seall

VANDERBILT
73— Barrett Sutton Jr.
75— Douglas Martin

VILLANOVA
77— David Graziano
89— Richard Spugnardi

VIRGINIA
67— Frederick Jones
83— Patrick Chester

VIRGINIA TECH
73— Thomas Carpenito

WABASH
74—*Mark Nicolini
81—*Melvin Gore
83— David Broecker
87— James Herrmann
92— William Padgett

WAKE FOREST
70— Joseph Dobner
74—*Daniel Stroup
76— Thomas Fehring
78—*Michael McGlamry
83— Philip Denfeld
87— Toby Cole Jr.

WARTBURG
75— Conrad Mandsager
76— James Charles Peterson
82—*Rod Feddersen

WASH. & JEFF.
70— Edward Guna
82— Max Regula
91— David Conn

WASH. & LEE
70— Michael Thornton
74— William Wallace Jr.
78— Jeffrey Slatcoff
79— Richard Wiles
80—*Scott Smith
81— Lonnie Nunley III
89— Michael Magoline

WASHINGTON
65— William Douglas
67— Michael Ryan
72—*James Krieg
73— John Brady
77— Scott Phillips
78— Blair Bush
80— Bruce Harrell
82— Mark Jerue
83— Charles Nelson
     Mark Stewart
88— David Rill
92— Edward Cunningham

WASHINGTON ST.
67— Richard Sheron
68— A. Douglas Flansburg
83— Gregory Porter
84— Patrick Lynch Jr.
85— Daniel Lynch

334

WAYNE ST. (MICH.)
76— Edward Skowneski Jr.
81— Phillip Emery
WEBER ST.
68— Phillip Tuckett
74—*Douglas Smith
92— David Hall
WESLEYAN
67— John Dwyer
69— Stuart Blackburn
71— James Lynch
78— John McVicar
WEST TEX. ST.
75—*Ben Bentley
82— Kevin Dennis
WEST VA.
74— Ade Dillion
74—*Daniel Larcamp
82— Oliver Luck
WESTERN ILL.
89— Paul Singer
WESTERN KY.
72— Jimmy Barber
80— Charles DeLacey
WESTERN MICH.
68— Martin Barski
71— Jonathan Bull

WESTERN N. MEX.
68— Richard Mahoney
WHEATON (ILL.)
89— David Lauber
WHITTIER
76— John Getz
79— Mark Deven
87—*Timothy Younger
WILLAMETTE
87—*Gerry Preston
WILLIAM & MARY
78— G. Kenneth Smith
80— Clarence Gaines
85— Mark Kelso
WILLIAM JEWELL
66— Charles Scrogin
70— Thomas Dunn
      John Johnston
WILLIAMS
65— Jerry Jones
72— John Murray
WINSTON-SALEM
84— Eddie Sauls
WIS.-PLATTEVILLE
87— Michael Hintz

WISCONSIN
66— David Fronek
80— Thomas Stauss
82—*David Mohapp
83— Mathew Vanden Boom
WITTENBERG
82— William Beach
WOOSTER
80— Edward Blake Moore
WYOMING
74— Steven Cockreham
85— Bob Gustafson
89— Randall Welniak
XAVIER (OHIO)
65— William Eastlake
YALE
66—*James Groninger
67— Howard Hilgendorf Jr.
69— Frederick Morris
71— Thomas Neville
72— David Bliss
75— John Burkus
77—*Stone Phillips
79— William Crowley
82— Richard Diana
91— Vincent Mooney

ACADEMIC ALL-AMERICA HALL OF FAME

Since its inception in 1988, 19 former NCAA football players have been inducted into the GTE Academic All-America Hall of Fame. They were selected from among nominees by the College Sports Information Directors of America (CoSIDA) from past academic all-Americans of the 1950s, '60s and '70s. Following are the selections, the year selected, team, position and last year played:

1988
Pete Dawkins, Army, HB, 1958
Pat Haden, Southern Cal, QB, 1974
Rev. Donn Moomaw, UCLA, LB, 1953
Merlin Olsen, Utah St., T, 1961

1989
Carlos Alvarez, Florida, WR, 1971
Willie Bogan, Dartmouth, DB, 1970

Steve Bramwell, Washington, DB, 1965
Joe Romig, Colorado, G, 1961
Jim Swink, Texas Christian, B, 1956
John Wilson, Michigan St., DB, 1952

1990
Joe Theismann, Notre Dame, QB, 1970
Howard Twilley, Tulsa, TE, 1965

1991
Terry Baker, Oregon St., QB, 1962
Joe Holland, Cornell, RB, 1978
David Joyner, Penn St., OT, 1971
Brock Strom, Air Force, T, 1958
1992
Alan Ameche, Wisconsin, RB, 1954
Stephen Eisenhauer, Navy, G, 1953
Randy Gradishar, Ohio St., LB, 1973

FIRST-TEAM ACADEMIC ALL-AMERICA SELECTIONS

Since 1952, academic all-America teams have been selected by the College Sports Information Directors of America. To be eligible, student-athletes must be regular performers and have at least a 3.200 grade-point average (on a 4.000 scale) during their college careers. University division teams (I-A and I-AA) are complete in this list, but college division teams (II, III, NAIA) before 1970 are missing from CoSIDA archives, with few exceptions. Following are all known first-team selections:

ABILENE CHRISTIAN
63—Jack Griggs, LB
70—Jim Lindsey, QB
74—Greg Stirman, E
76—Bill Curbo, T
77—Bill Curbo, T

87—Bill Clayton, DL
88—Bill Clayton, DL
89—Bill Clayton, DL
90—Sean Grady, WR
ADRIAN
84—Steve Dembowski, QB

AIR FORCE
58—Brock Strom, T
59—Rich Mayo, B
60—Rich Mayo, B
70—Ernie Jennings, E
71—Darryl Haas, LB,K

Utah State tackle Merlin Olsen, who won the Outland Trophy and was a first-team academic all-American in 1961, was among the inaugural class of inductees into the GTE Academic All-America Hall of Fame.

72—Bob Homburg, DE
     Mark Prill, LB
73—Joe Debes, OT
74—Joe Debes, OT
78—Steve Hoog, WR
81—Mike France, LB
83—Jeff Kubiak, P
86—Chad Hennings, DL
87—Chad Hennings, DL
88—David Hlatky, OL
90—Chris Howard, RB

AKRON
80—Andy Graham, PK

ALABAMA
61—Tommy Brooker, E
     Pat Trammell, B
64—Gaylon McCollough, C
65—Steve Sloan, QB
     Dennis Homan, OHB
67—Steve Davis, K
     Bob Childs, LB
70—Johnny Musso, HB
71—Johnny Musso, HB
73—Randy Hall, DT
74—Randy Hall, DT
75—Danny Ridgeway, KS
79—Major Ogilvie, RB

ALABAMA A&M
89—Tracy Kendall, QB
90—Tracy Kendall, QB

ALBANY (N.Y.)
86—Thomas Higgins, OT
87—Thomas Higgins, OT

ALBION
82—Bruce Drogosch, LB
86—Michael Grant, DB
90—Scott Bissell, DB

ALFRED
89—Mark Szynkowski, OL

ALLEGHENY
81—Kevin Baird, P
91—Adam Lechman, OL
     Darren Hadlock, LB

ALMA
86—Greg Luczak, TE

AMERICAN INT'L
81—Todd Scyocurka, LB

APPALACHIAN ST.
77—Gill Beck, C

ARIZONA
68—Mike Moody, OG
75—Jon Abbott, LB
76—Jon Abbott, T/LB
77—Jon Abbott, T/LB
79—Jeffrey Whitton, DL
87—Charles Cecil, DB

ARIZONA ST.
66—Ken Dyer, OE
88—Mark Tingstad, LB

ARKANSAS
57—Gerald Nesbitt, FB
61—Lance Alworth, B
64—Ken Hatfield, B
65—Randy Stewart, C
     Jim Lindsey, OHB
     Jack Brasuell, DB
68—Bob White, K
69—Bill Burnett, OHB
     Terry Stewart, DB
78—Brad Shoup, DHB

ARKANSAS-MONTICELLO
85—Ray Howard, OG
88—Sean Rochelle, QB

ARKANSAS ST.
59—Larry Zabrowski, OT
61—Jim McMurray, QB

ARKANSAS TECH
90—Karl Kuhn, TE
91—Karl Kuhn, TE

ARMY
55—Ralph Chesnauskas, E
57—James Kernan, C
     Pete Dawkins, HB
58—Pete Dawkins, HB
59—Don Usry, E
65—Sam Champi, DE
67—Bud Neswiacheny, DE
69—Theodore Shadid, C
89—Michael Thorson, DB

ASHLAND
73—Mark Gulling, DB
74—Ron Brown, LB
76—Dan Bogden, E
77—Bruce Niehm, LB
81—Mark Braun, C
91—Thomas Shiban, RB

AUBURN
57—Jimmy Phillips, E
59—Jackie Burkett, C
60—Ed Dyas, B
65—Bill Cody, LB
69—Buddy McClinton, DB
74—Bobby Davis, LB
75—Chuck Fletcher, DT
76—Chris Vacarella, RB
84—Gregg Carr, LB

AUGSBURG
81—Paul Elliott, DL

AUGUSTANA (ILL.)
75—George Wesbey, T
80—Bill Dannehl, WR
84—Steve Sanders, OT
85—Steve Sanders, OT

AUGUSTANA (S.D.)
72—Pat McNerney, T
73—Pat McNerney, T
74—Jim Clemens, G
75—Jim Clemens, C
77—Stan Biondi, K
86—David Gubbrud, DL
87—David Gubbrud, DL
88—David Gubbrud, LB
89—David Gubbrud, LB

AUSTIN
81—Gene Branum, PK

AUSTIN PEAY
74—Gregory Johnson, G

BAKER
61—John Jacobs, B

BALDWIN-WALLACE
70—Earl Stolberg, DHB
72—John Yezerski, G
78—Roger Andrachik, RB
　　Greg Monda, LB
81—Chuck Krajacic, OG
88—Shawn Gorman, P
91—Tom Serdinak, P

BALL ST.
83—Rich Chitwood, C
85—Ron Duncan, TE
86—Ron Duncan, TE
87—Ron Duncan, TE
88—Ted Ashburn, OL
　　Greg Shackelford, DL
89—Ted Ashburn, OL
　　David Haugh, DB
91—Troy Hoffer, DB

BATES
82—Neal Davidson, DB

BAYLOR
61—Ronnie Bull, RB
62—Don Trull, QB
63—Don Trull, QB
76—Cris Quinn, DE
89—Mike Welch, DB
90—Mike Welch, DB

BELOIT
90—Shane Stadler, RB

BETHANY (KAN.)
86—Wade Gaeddert, DB

BLOOMSBURG
83—Dave Pepper, DL

BOISE ST.
71—Brent McIver, IL
73—Glenn Sparks, G
78—Sam Miller, DB

BOSTON COLLEGE
77—Richard Scudellari, LB
86—Michael Degnan, DL

BOSTON U.
83—Steve Shapiro, K
85—Brad Hokin, DB

BOWDOIN
84—Mike Siegel, P

BOWLING GREEN
75—John Boles, DE
89—Pat Jackson, LB
90—Pat Jackson, TE

BRIGHAM YOUNG
73—Steve Stratton, RB
80—Scott Phillips, RB
81—Dan Plater, WR
87—Chuck Cutler, WR
88—Chuck Cutler, WR
　　Tim Clark, DL
89—Fred Whittingham, RB
90—Andy Boyce, WR

BROWN
81—Travis Holcombe, OG
82—Dave Folsom, DB
86—Marty Edwards, C
87—John Cuozzo, C

BUCKNELL
72—Douglas Nauman, T
　　John Ondrasik, DB
73—John Dailey, LB
74—Steve Leskinen, T
75—Larry Brunt, E
76—Larry Brunt, E
84—Rob Masonis, RB
　　Jim Reilly, TE
86—Mike Morrow, WR
91—David Berardinelli, WR

BUFFALO
63—Gerry Philbin, T
84—Gerry Quinlivan, LB
85—James Dunbar, C
86—James Dunbar, C

BUFFALO ST.
87—Clint Morano, OT

BUTLER
84—Steve Kollias, L

CAL LUTHERAN
81—John Walsh, OT

CALIFORNIA
67—Bob Crittenden, DG
70—Robert Richards, OT
82—Harvey Salem, OT

CANISIUS
82—Tom Schott, WR
83—Tom Schott, TE
86—Mike Panepinto, RB

CAPITAL
70—Ed Coy, E
83—Mike Linton, G
85—Kevin Sheets, WR

CARNEGIE MELLON
76—Rick Lackner, E
　　Dave Nackoul, E
84—Roger Roble, WR

87—Bryan Roessler, DL
　　Chris Haupt, LB
89—Robert O'Toole, LB
90—Frank Bellante, RB
　　Robert O'Toole, LB

CARROLL (WIS.)
76—Stephen Thompson, QB

CARSON-NEWMAN
61—David Dale, E

CARTHAGE
61—Bob Halsey, B
77—Mark Phelps, QB

CASE RESERVE
75—John Kosko, T
82—Jim Donnelly, RB
83—Jim Donnelly, RB
84—Jim Donnelly, RB
88—Chris Hutter, TE
90—Michael Bissler, DB

CENTRAL (IOWA)
79—Chris Adkins, LB
85—Scott Lindrell, LB
86—Scott Lindrell, LB
91—Rich Kacmarynski, RB

CENTRAL MICH.
70—Ralph Burde, DL
74—Mike Franckowiak, QB
　　John Wunderlich, T
79—Mike Ball, WR
84—John DeBoer, WR
91—Jeff Bender, QB

CENTRE
84—Teel Bruner, DB
85—Teel Bruner, DB
89—Bryan Ellington, DB
91—Eric Horstmeyer, WR

CHADRON ST.
73—Jerry Sutton, LB
75—Bob Lacey, KS
79—Jerry Carder, TE

CHEYNEY
75—Steve Anderson, G

CHICAGO
87—Paul Haar, OG
88—Paul Haar, OL

CINCINNATI
81—Kari Yli-Renko, OT
90—Kyle Stroh, DL
91—Kris Bjorson, TE

CITADEL
63—Vince Petno, E
76—Kenny Caldwell, LB
77—Kenny Caldwell, LB
78—Kenny Caldwell, LB
87—Thomas Frooman, RB
89—Thomas Frooman, RB

CLEMSON
59—Lou Cordileone, T
78—Steve Fuller, QB

COAST GUARD
70—Charles Pike, LB
71—Bruce Melnick, DHB
81—Mark Butt, DB

COLGATE
78—Angelo Colosimo, RB
79—Angelo Colosimo, RB
85—Tom Stenglein, WR
89—Jeremy Garvey, TE

COLORADO
60—Joe Romig, G

61—Joe Romig, G
67—Kirk Tracy, OG
70—Jim Cooch, DB
73—Rick Stearns, LB
74—Rick Stearns, LB
75—Steve Young, DT
87—Eric McCarty, LB
90—Jim Hansen, OL
91—Jim Hansen, OL

COLORADO MINES
72—Dave Chambers, RB
83—Charles Lane, T

COLORADO ST.
55—Gary Glick, B
69—Tom French, OT
86—Steve Bartalo, RB

COLUMBIA
52—Mitch Price, B
53—John Gasella, T
56—Claude Benham, B
71—John Sefcik, OHB

CORNELL
77—Joseph Holland, RB
78—Joseph Holland, RB
82—Derrick Harmon, RB
83—Derrick Harmon, RB
85—Dave Van Metre, DL

CORNELL COLLEGE
72—Rob Ash, QB
　　Dewey Birkhofer, S
76—Joe Lauterbach, G
　　Tom Zinkula, DT
77—Tom Zinkula, DT
78—Tom Zinkula, DL
82—John Ward, WR
91—Bruce Feldmann, QB

DARTMOUTH
70—Willie Bogan, DB
83—Michael Patsis, DB
87—Paul Sorensen, LB
88—Paul Sorensen, LB
90—Brad Preble, DB
91—Mike Bobo, WR
　　Tom Morrow, LB

DAYTON
71—Tim Quinn, LB
72—Tim Quinn, DT
79—Scott Terry, QB
84—Greg French, K
　　David Kemp, LB
　　Jeff Slayback, L
85—Greg French, K
86—Gerry Meyer, OT
91—Brett Cuthbert, DB
　　Dan Rosenbaum, DB

DEFIANCE
80—Jill Bailey, OT
　　Mark Bockelman, TE

DELAWARE
70—Yancey Phillips, T
71—Robert Depew, DE
72—Robert Depew, DE

DELAWARE VALLEY
84—Dan Glowatski, WR

DELTA ST.
70—Hal Posey, RB
74—Billy Hood, E
　　Ricky Lewis, LB
　　Larry Miller, RB
75—Billy Hood, E
78—Terry Moody, DHB
79—Charles Stavley, G

DENISON
75—Dennis Thome, LB
87—Grant Jones, DB

DePAUW
70—Jim Ceaser, LB
71—Jim Ceaser, LB
73—Neil Oslos, RB
80—Jay True, WR
85—Tony deNicola, QB
87—Michael Sherman, DB
90—Tom Beaulieu, DL
91—Tom Beaulieu, DL
　　Matt Nelson, LB

DICKINSON
74—Gerald Urich, RB
79—Scott Mumma, RB

DRAKE
74—Todd Gaffney, KS
83—Tom Holt, RB

DREXEL
70—Lynn Ferguson, S

DUBUQUE
80—Tim Finn, RB

DUKE
66—Roger Hayes, DE
67—Bob Lasky, DT
70—Curt Rawley, DT
86—Mike Diminick, DB
87—Mike Diminick, DB
88—Mike Diminick, DB
89—Doug Key, DL

EAST STROUDSBURG
84—Ernie Siegrist, TE

EAST TENN. ST.
71—Ken Oster, DHB

EAST TEX. ST.
77—Mike Hall, OT

EASTERN KY.
77—Steve Frommeyer, S

EASTERN N. MEX.
80—Tom Sager, DL
81—Tom Sager, DL

ELON
73—John Rascoe, E
79—Bryan Burney, DB

EMORY & HENRY
71—Tom Wilson, LB

EMPORIA ST.
79—Tom Lingg, DL

EVANSVILLE
74—David Mattingly, S
76—Michael Pociask, C
87—Jeffery Willman, TE

FERRIS ST.
81—Vic Trecha, OT

FLORIDA
65—Charles Casey, E
69—Carlos Alvarez, OE
71—Carlos Alvarez, OE
76—David Posey, KS
77—Wes Chandler, RB
80—Cris Collinsworth, WR
91—Brad Culpepper, DL

FLORIDA A&M
90—Irvin Clark, DL

FLORIDA ST.
72—Gary Huff, QB
79—William Jones, DB
　　Phil Williams, WR

80—William Jones, DB
81—Rohn Stark, P

FORDHAM
90—Eric Schweiker, OL

FORT HAYS ST.
75—Greg Custer, RB
82—Ron Johnson, P
85—Paul Nelson, DL
86—Paul Nelson, DL
89—Dean Gengler, OL

FORT LEWIS
72—Dee Tennison, E

FRANK. & MARSH.
77—Joe Fry, DB
78—Joe Fry, DB

FURMAN
76—Jeff Holcomb, T
85—Brian Jager, RB
88—Kelly Fletcher, DL
89—Kelly Fletcher, DL
　　Chris Roper, LB
91—Eric Walter, OL

GA. SOUTHWESTERN
87—Gregory Slappery, RB

GEORGETOWN
71—Gerry O'Dowd, HB
86—Andrew Phelan, OG

GEORGETOWN (KY.)
89—Eric Chumbley, OL

GEORGIA
60—Francis Tarkenton, B
65—Bob Etter, K
66—Bob Etter, K
　　Lynn Hughes, DB, S
68—Bill Stanfill, DT
71—Tom Nash, OT
　　Mixon Robinson, DE
77—Jeff Lewis, LB
82—Terry Hoage, DB
83—Terry Hoage, DB

GEORGIA TECH
52—Ed Gossage, T
　　Cecil Trainer, DE
　　Larry Morris, LB
55—Wade Mitchell, B
56—Allen Ecker, G
66—Jim Breland, C
　　W. J. Blaine, LB
　　Bill Eastman, DB
67—Bill Eastman, DB
80—Sheldon Fox, DLB
90—Stefen Scotton, RB

GETTYSBURG
79—Richard Swartz, LB

GRAMBLING
72—Floyd Harvey, RB

GRAND VALLEY ST.
91—Mark Smith, OL
　　Todd Wood, DB

GRINNELL
71—Edward Hirsch, E
81—David Smiley, TE

GROVE CITY
74—Pat McCoy, LB
89—Travis Croll, P

GUST. ADOLPHUS
80—Dave Najarian, DL
81—Dave Najarian, LB

HAMLINE
73—Thomas Dufresne, E

89—Jon Voss, TE
HAMPDEN-SYDNEY
82—John Dickinson, OG
90—W. R. Jones, OL
91—David Brickhill, PK
HARVARD
84—Brian Bergstrom, DB
HEIDELBERG
82—Jeff Kurtzman, DL
HILLSDALE
61—James Richendollar, T
72—John Cervini, G
81—Mark Kellogg, LB
HOLY CROSS
83—Bruce Kozerski, T
85—Kevin Reilly, OT
87—Jeff Wiley, QB
91—Pete Dankert, DL
HOPE
73—Ronald Posthuma, T
79—Craig Groendyk, T
80—Greg Bekius, PK
82—Kurt Brinks, C
84—Scott Jecmen, DB
86—Timothy Chase, OG
HOUSTON
64—Horst Paul, E
76—Mark Mohr, DB
    Kevin Rollwage, OT
77—Kevin Rollwage, OT
IDAHO
70—Bruce Langmeade, T
IDAHO ST.
84—Brent Koetter, DB
91—Steve Boyenger, DB
ILL. WESLEYAN
71—Keith Ihlanfeldt, DE
80—Jim Eaton, DL
    Rick Hanna, DL
    Mike Watson, DB
81—Mike Watson, DB
91—Chris Bisaillon, WR
ILLINOIS
52—Bob Lenzini, DT
64—Jim Grabowski, B
65—Jim Grabowski, B
66—John Wright, E
70—Jim Rucks, DE
71—Bob Bucklin, DE
80—Dan Gregus, DL
81—Dan Gregus, DL
82—Dan Gregus, DL
91—Mike Hopkins, DB
ILLINOIS COL.
80—Jay Wessler, RB
ILLINOIS ST.
76—Tony Barnes, C
80—Jeff Hembrough, DL
89—Dan Hackman, OL
INDIANA
67—Harry Gonso, HB
72—Glenn Scolnik, RB
80—Kevin Speer, C
INDIANA (PA.)
82—Kenny Moore, DB
83—Kenny Moore, DB
INDIANA ST.
71—Gary Brown, E
72—Michael Eads, E

INDIANAPOLIS
76—William Willan, E
IONA
80—Neal Kurtti, DL
IOWA
52—Bill Fenton, DE
53—Bill Fenton, E
75—Bob Elliott, DB
85—Larry Station, LB
IOWA ST.
52—Max Burkett, DB
82—Mark Carlson, LB
ITHACA
72—Dana Hallenbeck, LB
85—Brian Dougherty, DB
89—Peter Burns, OL
JACKSONVILLE ST.
77—Dewey Barker, OE
78—Dewey Barker, TE
JAMES MADISON
78—Warren Coleman, OT
JOHN CARROLL
83—Nick D'Angelo, LB
    Jim Sferra, DL
85—Joe Burrello, LB
86—Joe Burrello, LB
JOHNS HOPKINS
77—Charles Hauck, DT
JUNIATA
70—Ray Grabiak, DL
71—Ray Grabiak, DE
71—Maurice Taylor, ILM
KANSAS
64—Fred Elder, T
67—Mike Sweatman, LB
68—Dave Morgan, LB
71—Mike McCoy, C
76—Tom Fitch, S
KANSAS ST.
74—Don Lareau, LB
77—Floyd Dorsey, OG
81—Darren Gale, DB
82—Darren Gale, DB
    Mark Hundley, RB
85—Troy Faunce, P
KENT
72—Mark Reiheld, DB
91—Brad Smith, RB
KENTUCKY
74—Tom Ranieri, LB
78—Mark Keene, C
    Jim Kovach, LB
85—Ken Pietrowiak, C
KENYON
77—Robert Jennings, RB
85—Dan Waldeck, TE
LA VERNE
82—Scott Shier, OT
LAFAYETTE
70—William Sprecher, T
74—Mike Kline, DB
79—Ed Rogusky, RB
80—Ed Rogusky, RB
LAWRENCE
81—Chris Matheus, DL
    Scott Reppert, RB
82—Chris Matheus, DL
LEHIGH
90—Shon Harker, DB

LEWIS & CLARK
61—Pat Clock, G
81—Dan Jones, WR
LIU-C.W. POST
70—Art Canario, T
75—Frank Prochilo, RB
84—Bob Jahelka, DB
LONG BEACH ST.
83—Joe Donohue, LB
LORAS
84—John Coyle, DL
    Pete Kovatsis, DB
85—John Coyle, DL
91—Mark Goedken, DL
LOUISIANA ST.
59—Mickey Mangham, E
60—Charles Strange, C
61—Billy Booth, T
71—Jay Michaelson, KS
73—Tyler Lafauci, OG
    Joe Winkler, DB
74—Brad Davis, RB
77—Robert Dugas, OT
84—Juan Carlos Betanzos, K
LOWELL
85—Don Williams, RB
LUTHER
83—Larry Bonney, DL
84—Larry Bonney, DL
89—Larry Anderson, RB
90—Joel Nerem, DL
91—Joel Nerem, DL
LYCOMING
74—Thomas Vanaskie, DB
85—Mike Kern, DL
MACALESTER
82—Lee Schaefer, OG
MANKATO ST.
74—Dan Miller, C
MANSFIELD
83—John Delate, DB
MARIETTA
83—Matt Wurtzbacher, DL
MARYLAND
53—Bernie Faloney, B
75—Kim Hoover, DE
78—Joe Muffler, DL
McGILL
87—Bruno Pietrobon, WR
McNEESE ST.
78—Jim Downing, OT
79—Jim Downing, OT
90—David Easterling, DB
MIAMI (FLA.)
59—Fran Curci, B
84—Bernie Kosar, QB
MIAMI (OHIO)
73—Andy Pederzolli, DB
MICHIGAN
52—Dick Balzhiser, B
55—Jim Orwig, T
57—Jim Orwig, T
64—Bob Timberlake, QB
66—Dave Fisher, FB
    Dick Vidmer, FB
69—Jim Mandich, OE
70—Phil Seymour, DE
71—Bruce Elliott, DHB
72—Bill Hart, OG
74—Kirk Lewis, OG

75—Dan Jilek, DE
81—Norm Betts, TE
82—Stefan Humphries, OG
    Robert Thompson, LB
83—Stefan Humphries, OG
85—Clay Miller, OT
86—Kenneth Higgins, WR

MICHIGAN ST.
52—John Wilson, DB
53—Don Dohoney, E
55—Buck Nystrom, G
57—Blanche Martin, HB
65—Don Bierowicz, DT
    Don Japinga, DB
66—Pat Gallinagh, DT
68—Al Brenner, OE, DB
69—Ron Saul, OG
    Rich Saul, DE
73—John Shinsky, DT
79—Alan Davis, DB
85—Dean Altobelli, DB
86—Dean Altobelli, DB
86—Shane Bullough, LB

MICHIGAN TECH
71—Larry Ras, HB
73—Bruce Trusock, C
76—Jim Van Wagner, RB

MILLERSVILLE
91—Tom Burns, OL

MILLIKIN
61—Gerald Domesick, B
75—Frank Stone, G
78—Charlie Sammis, K
79—Eric Stevens, WR
83—Marc Knowles, WR
84—Tom Kreller, RB
85—Cary Bottorff, LB
    Tom Kreller, RB
90—Tim Eimermann, PK

MINNESOTA
56—Bob Hobert, T
60—Frank Brixius, T
68—Bob Stein, DE
70—Barry Mayer, RB
89—Brent Herbel, P

MISSISSIPPI
54—Harold Easterwood, C
59—Robert Khayat, T
    Charlie Flowers, B
61—Doug Elmore, B
65—Stan Hindman, G
68—Steve Hindman, OHB
69—Julius Fagan, K
74—Greg Markow, DE
77—Robert Fabris, OE
    George Plasketes, DE
80—Ken Toler, WR
86—Danny Hoskins, OG
87—Danny Hoskins, OG
88—Wesley Walls, TE
89—Todd Sandroni, DB

MISSISSIPPI COL.
75—Anthony Saway, S
78—Steve Johnson, OT
79—Steve Johnson, OT
83—Wayne Frazier, C

MISSISSIPPI ST.
53—Jackie Parker, B
56—Ron Bennett, E
72—Frank Dowsing, DB
73—Jimmy Webb, DE
76—Will Coltharp, DE
89—Stacy Russell, DB

MISSOURI
62—Tom Hertz, G
66—Dan Schuppan, DE
    Bill Powell, DT
68—Carl Garber, MG
70—John Weisenfels, LB
72—Greg Hill, KS
81—Van Darkow, LB

MISSOURI-ROLLA
72—Kim Colter, DB
80—Paul Janke, OG
86—Tom Reed, RB
87—Jim Pfeiffer, OT
88—Jim Pfeiffer, OL
91—Don Huff, DB

MIT
89—Anthony Lapes, WR
90—Darcy Prather, LB
91—Rodrigo Rubiano, DL

MO. SOUTHERN ST.
85—Mike Testman, DB

MONMOUTH (ILL.)
83—Robb Long, QB

MONTANA
77—Steve Fisher, DE
79—Ed Cerkovnik, DB
88—Michael McGowan, LB
89—Michael McGowan, LB
90—Michael McGowan, LB

MONTANA ST.
84—Dirk Nelson, P
88—Anders Larsson, PK

MONTCLAIR ST.
70—Bill Trimmer, DL
82—Daniel Deneher, KS

MOORHEAD ST.
88—Brad Shamla, DL

MORAVIAN
87—Jeff Pollock, WR

MOREHEAD ST.
74—Don Russell, KS
90—James Appel, OL
91—James Appel, OL

MOUNT UNION
71—Dennis Montgomery, QB
84—Rick Marabito, L
86—Scott Gindlesberger, QB
87—Paul Hrics, C

MUHLENBERG
70—Edward Salo, G
71—Edward Salo, ILM
72—Edward Salo, C
75—Keith Ordemann, LB
80—Arthur Scavone, OT
89—Joe Zeszotarski, DL
90—Mike Hoffman, DB

MURRAY ST.
76—Eddie McFarland, DB

MUSKINGUM
78—Dan Radalia, DL
79—Dan Radalia, DL

NAVY
53—Steve Eisenhauer, G
57—Tom Forrestal, QB
58—Joe Tranchini, B
69—Dan Pike, RB
80—Ted Dumbauld, LB

NEB.-KEARNEY
70—John Makovicka, RB
75—Tim Brodahl, E

NEB. WESLEYAN
87—Pat Sweeney, DB
88—Pat Sweeney, DB
    Mike Surls, LB
89—Scott Shaffer, RB
    Scott Shipman, DB

NEBRASKA
62—James Huge, E
63—Dennis Calridge, B
66—Marv Mueller, DB
69—Randy Reeves, DB
71—Larry Jacobson, DT
    Jeff Kinney, HB
73—Frosty Anderson, OE
75—Rik Bonness, C
    Tom Heiser, RB
76—Vince Ferragamo, QB
    Ted Harvey, DB
77—Ted Harvey, DB
78—George Andrews, DL
    James Pillen, DHB
79—Rod Horn, DL
    Kelly Saalfeld, C
    Randy Schleusener, OG
80—Jeff Finn, TE
    Randy Schleusener, OG
81—Eric Lindquist, DB
    David Rimington, C
    Randy Theiss, OT
82—David Rimington, C
83—Scott Strasburger, DL
    Rob Stuckey, DL
84—Scott Strasburger, DL
    Rob Stuckey, DL
    Mark Traynowicz, C
86—Dale Klein, K
    Thomas Welter, OT
87—Jeffrey Jamrog, DL
    Mark Blazek, DB
88—Mark Blazek, DB
    John Kroeker, P
89—Gerry Gdowski, QB
    Jake Young, OL
90—David Edeal, OL
    Pat Tyrance, LB
    Jim Wanek, OL
91—Pat Engelbert, DL
    Mike Stigge, P

NEBRASKA-OMAHA
82—Kirk Hutton, DB
    Clark Toner, LB
83—Kirk Hutton, DB
84—Jerry Kripal, QB

NEVADA
82—David Heppe, P

NEW HAMPSHIRE
52—John Driscoll, T
84—Dave Morton, OL

NEW MEXICO
75—Bob Johnson, S
77—Robert Rumbaugh, DT
78—Robert Rumbaugh, DL

NEW MEXICO ST.
66—Jim Bohl, B
74—Ralph Jackson, OG
75—Ralph Jackson, OG
85—Andy Weiler, KS

NICHOLS
89—David Kane, DB

NORTH CARO.
64—Ken Willard, QB
71—Charles Putnik, ILM
85—Kevin Anthony, QB

NORTH CARO. ST.
60—Roman Gabriel, QB
63—Joe Scarpati, B
67—Steve Warren, OT
71—Craig John, OG
73—Justus Everett, C
      Stan Fritts, RB
74—Justus Everett, C
80—Calvin Warren, P

NORTH DAK.
87—Kurt Otto, QB
88—Chuck Clairmont, OL
      Matt Gulseth, DB

NORTH DAK. ST.
71—Tomm Smail, DT

NORTH PARK
83—Mike Lilgegren, DB
85—Scott Love, WR
86—Todd Love, WR
87—Todd Love, WR

NORTH TEXAS
75—Pete Morris, LB
76—Pete Morris, LB

NORTHEAST LA.
70—Tom Miller, KS
74—Mike Bialas, T

NORTHEAST MO. ST.
73—Tom Roberts, T
78—Keith Driscoll, LB
79—Keith Driscoll, LB

NORTHEASTERN
85—Shawn O'Malley, LB

NORTHERN ARIZ.
89—Chris Baniszewski, WR

NORTHERN COLO.
81—Duane Hirsch, DL
      Ray Sperger, DB
82—Jim Bright, RB
89—Mike Yonkovich, DL
      Tom Langer, LB
90—Tom Langer, LB

NORTHERN MICH.
83—Bob Stefanski, WR

NORTHWEST MO. ST.
81—Robert "Chip" Gregory, LB

NORTHWESTERN
56—Al Viola, G
58—Andy Cvercko, T
61—Larry Onesti, C
62—Paul Flatley, B
63—George Burman, E
70—Joe Zigulich, OG
76—Randolph Dean, OE
80—Jim Ford, OT
86—Michael Baum, OT
      Bob Dirkes, DL
      Todd Krehbiel, DB
87—Mike Baum, OT
88—Mike Baum, OL
90—Ira Adler, PK

NORTHWESTERN (IOWA)
83—Mark Muilenberg, RB

NORTHWESTERN (OKLA.)
61—Stewart Arthurs, B

NORWICH
70—Gary Fry, RB

NOTRE DAME
52—Joe Heap, B
53—Joe Heap, B
54—Joe Heap, B

55—Don Schaefer, B
58—Bob Wetoska, E
63—Bob Lehmann, G
66—Tom Regner, OG
      Jim Lynch, LB
67—Jim Smithberger, DB
68—George Kunz, OT
69—Jim Reilly, OT
70—Tom Gatewood, OE
      Larry DiNardo, OG
      Joe Theismann, QB
71—Greg Marx, DT
      Tom Gatewood, OE
72—Michael Creaney, OE
      Greg Marx, OT
73—David Casper, OE
      Gary Potempa, LB
      Robert Thomas, KS
74—Reggie Barnett, DB
      Pete Demmerle, E
77—Ken MacAfee, OE
      Joe Restic, S
      Dave Vinson, OG
78—Joe Restic, DHB
80—Bob Burger, OG
      Tom Gibbons, DB
81—John Krimm, DB
85—Greg Dingens, DL
87—Ted Gradel, PK
      Vince Phelan, P

OCCIDENTAL
88—Curtis Page, DL

OHIO
71—John Rousch, HB

OHIO NORTHERN
76—Jeff McFarlin, S
79—Robert Coll, WR
86—David Myers, DL
90—Chad Hummell, OL

OHIO ST.
52—John Borton, B
54—Dick Hilinski, T
58—Bob White, B
61—Tom Perdue, E
65—Bill Ridder, MG
66—Dave Foley, OT
68—Dave Foley, OT
      Mark Stier, LB
69—Bill Urbanik, DT
71—Rick Simon, OG
73—Randy Gradishar, LB
74—Brian Baschnagel, RB
75—Brian Baschnagel, RB
76—Pete Johnson, RB
      Bill Lukens, OG
77—Jeff Logan, RB
80—Marcus Marek, LB
82—John Frank, TE
      Joseph Smith, OT
83—John Frank, TE
84—David Crecelius, DL
      Michael Lanese, WR
85—Michael Lanese, WR
89—Joseph Staysniak, OL

OHIO WESLEYAN
70—Tony Heald, LB
      Tom Liller, E
81—Ric Kinnan, WR
85—Kevin Connell, OG

OKLAHOMA
52—Tom Catlin, C
54—Carl Allison, E
56—Jerry Tubbs, C

57—Doyle Jenning, T
58—Ross Coyle, E
62—Wayne Lee, C
63—Newt Burton, G
64—Newt Burton, G
66—Ron Shotts, OHB
67—Ron Shotts, OHB
68—Eddie Hinton, DB
70—Joe Wylie, RB
71—Jack Mildren, QB
72—Joe Wylie, RB
74—Randy Hughes, S
75—Dewey Selmon, LB
      Lee Roy Selmon, DT
80—Jay Jimerson, DB
86—Brian Bosworth, LB

OKLAHOMA ST.
54—Dale Meinert, G
72—Tom Wolf, OT
73—Doug Tarrant, LB
74—Tom Wolf, OT
77—Joe Avanzini, DE

OREGON
62—Steve Barnett, T
65—Tim Casey, LB
86—Mike Preacher, P
90—Bill Musgrave, QB

OREGON ST.
62—Terry Baker, B
67—Bill Enyart, FB
68—Bill Enyart, FB

OUACHITA BAPTIST
78—David Cowling, OG

PACIFIC (CAL.)
78—Bruce Filarsky, OG
79—Bruce Filarsky, DL

PACIFIC LUTHERAN
82—Curt Rodin, TE

PANHANDLE ST.
76—Larry Johnson, G

PENN ST.
65—Joe Bellas, T
      John Runnells, LB
66—John Runnells, LB
67—Rich Buzin, OT
69—Charlie Pittman, OHB
      Dennis Onkotz, LB
71—Dave Joyner, OT
72—Bruce Bannon, DE
73—Mark Markovich, OG
76—Chuck Benjamin, OT
78—Keith Dorney, OG
82—Todd Blackledge, QB
      Harry Hamilton, DB
      Scott Radicec, LB
83—Harry Hamilton, LB
84—Lance Hamilton, DB
      Carmen Masciantonio, LB
85—Lance Hamilton, DB
86—John Shaffer, QB

PENNSYLVANIA
86—Rich Comizio, RB

PITTSBURG ST.
72—Jay Sperry, RB
89—Brett Potts, DL
91—Mike Brockel, OL

PITTSBURGH
52—Dick Deitrick, DT
54—Lou Palatella, T
56—Joe Walton, E
58—John Guzik, G
76—Jeff Delaney, LB

80—Greg Meisner, DL
81—Rob Fada, OG
82—Rob Fada, OG
    J. C. Pelusi, DL
88—Mark Stepnoski, OL

PORTLAND ST.
72—Bill Dials, T
77—John Urness, OE
78—John Urness, WR

PRINCETON
68—Dick Sandler, DT
76—Kevin Fox, OG
82—Kevin Guthrie, WR
83—Kevin Guthrie, WR

PUGET SOUND
82—Buster Crook, DB

PURDUE
56—Len Dawson, B
60—Jerry Beabout, T
65—Sal Ciampi, G
67—Jim Beirne, OE
    Lance Olssen, DT
68—Tim Foley, DB
69—Tim Foley, DB
    Mike Phipps, QB
    Bill Yanchar, DT
73—Bob Hoftiezer, DE
79—Ken Loushin, DL
80—Tim Seneff, DB
81—Tim Seneff, DB
89—Bruce Brineman, OL

RHODE ISLAND
76—Richard Moser, RB
77—Richard Moser, RB

RHODES
90—Robert Heck, DL

RICE
52—Richard Chapman, DG
53—Richard Chapman, DG
54—Dick Maegle, B
69—Steve Bradshaw, DG
79—LaMont Jefferson, LB
83—Brian Patterson, DB

ROCHESTER
82—Bob Cordaro, LB

ROSE-HULMAN
78—Rick Matovich, DL
79—Scott Lindner, DL
80—Scott Lindner, DL
    Jim Novacek, P
83—Jack Grote, LB
84—Jack Grote, LB
88—Greg Kremer, LB
    Shawn Ferron, PK
89—Shawn Ferron, PK
90—Ed Huonden, WR

SAM HOUSTON ST.
72—Walter Anderson, KS
73—Walter Anderson, KS

SAN DIEGO
87—Bryan Day, DB
88—Bryan Day, DB

SAN JOSE ST.
75—Tim Toews, OG

SANTA CLARA
71—Ron Sani, ILM
73—Alex Damascus, RB
74—Steve Lagorio, LB
75—Mark Tiernan, LB
76—Lou Marengo, KS
    Mark Tiernan, LB

80—Dave Alfaro, QB

SHIPPENSBURG
76—Tony Winter, LB
82—Dave Butler, DL

SOUTH CARO.
87—Mark Fryer, OT
88—Mark Fryer, OL
91—Joe Reeves, LB

SOUTH DAK.
78—Scott Pollock, QB
82—Jerus Campbell, DL
83—Jeff Sime, T
87—Dan Sonnek, RB

SOUTH DAK. ST.
74—Bob Gissler, E
75—Bill Matthews, T
77—Bill Matthews, DE
79—Tony Harris, PK
    Paul Kippley, DB

SOUTHERN CAL
52—Dick Nunis, DB
59—Mike McKeever, G
60—Mike McKeever, G
    Marlin McKeever, E
65—Charles Arrobio, T
67—Steve Sogge, QB
68—Steve Sogge, QB
69—Harry Khasigian, OG
73—Pat Haden, QB
74—Pat Haden, QB
78—Rich Dimler, DL
79—Brad Budde, OG
    Paul McDonald, QB
    Keith Van Horne, T
84—Duane Bickett, LB
85—Matt Koart, DL
86—Jeffrey Bregel, OG
88—John Jackson, WR
89—John Jackson, WR

SOUTHERN COLO.
83—Dan DeRose, LB

SOUTHERN CONN. ST.
84—Gerald Carbonaro, OL

SOUTHERN ILL.
70—Sam Finocchio, G
88—Charles Harmke, RB
91—Dwayne Summers, DL
    Jon Manley, LB

SOUTHERN METHODIST
52—Dave Powell, E
53—Darrell Lafitte, G
54—Raymond Berry, E
55—David Hawk, G
57—Tom Koenig, G
58—Tom Koenig, G
62—Raymond Schoenke, T
66—John LaGrone, MG
    Lynn Thornhill, OG
68—Jerry LeVias, OE
72—Cleve Whitener, LB
83—Brian O'Meara, T

SOUTHERN UTAH
88—Jim Andrus, RB
90—Steve McDowell, P

SOUTHWEST MO. ST.
73—Kent Stringer, QB
75—Kent Stringer, QB
78—Steve Newbold, WR

SOUTHWEST ST. (MINN.)
88—Bruce Saugstad, DB

SOUTHWEST TEX. ST.
72—Jimmy Jowers, LB
73—Jimmy Jowers, LB
78—Mike Ferris, OG
79—Mike Ferris, G
    Allen Kiesling, DL
81—Mike Miller, QB

SPRINGFIELD
71—Bruce Rupert, LB
84—Sean Flanders, DL
85—Sean Flanders, DL

ST. CLOUD ST.
88—Rick Rodgers, DB
89—Rick Rodgers, DB

ST. JOHN'S (MINN.)
72—Jim Kruzich, E
79—Terry Geraghty, DB

ST. JOSEPH'S (IND.)
77—Mike Bettinger, DB
78—Mike Bettinger, DB
79—Mike Bettinger, DB
85—Ralph Laura, OT
88—Keith Woodason, OL
89—Jeff Fairchild, P

ST. NORBERT
86—Matthew Lang, LB
    Karl Zacharias, P
87—Karl Zacharias, PK
    Matthew Lang, LB
88—Mike Whitehouse, WR
89—Mike Whitehouse, WR

ST. OLAF
61—Dave Hindermann, T

ST. THOMAS (MINN.)
73—Mark Dienhart, T
74—Mark Dienhart, T
77—Tom Kelly, OG
80—Doug Groebner, C

STANFORD
70—John Sande, C
    Terry Ewing, DB
75—Don Stevenson, RB
76—Don Stevenson, RB
77—Guy Benjamin, QB
78—Vince Mulroy, WR
    Jim Stephens, OG
79—Pat Bowe, TE
    Milt McColl, LB
    Joe St. Geme, DB
81—John Bergren, DL
    Darrin Nelson, RB
82—John Bergren, DL
83—John Bergren, DL
85—Matt Soderlund, LB
87—Brad Muster, RB
90—Ed McCaffrey, WR
91—Tommy Vardell, RB

SUL ROSS ST.
73—Archie Nexon, RB

SUSQUEHANNA
75—Gerry Huesken, T
76—Gerry Huesken, T
80—Dan Distasio, LB

SYRACUSE
60—Fred Mautino, E
71—Howard Goodman, LB
83—Tony Romano, LB
84—Tim Green, DL
85—Tim Green, DL

TARLETON ST.
81—Ricky Bush, RB
90—Mike Loveless, OL

TENN.-MARTIN
74—Randy West, E
TENNESSEE
56—Charles Rader, T
57—Bill Johnson, G
65—Mack Gentry, DT
67—Bob Johnson, C
70—Tim Priest, DB
80—Timothy Irwin, OT
82—Mike Terry, DL
TENNESSEE TECH
87—Andy Rittenhouse, DL
TEXAS
59—Maurice Doke, G
61—Johnny Treadwell, G
62—Johnny Treadwell, G
Pat Culpepper, B
63—Duke Carlisle, B
66—Gene Bledsoe, OT
67—Mike Perrin, DE
Corby Robertson, LB
68—Corby Robertson, LB
Scott Henderson, LB
69—Scott Henderson, LB
Bill Zapalac, DE
70—Bill Zapalac, LB
Scott Henderson, LB
72—Mike Bayer, DB
Tommy Keel, S
Steve Oxley, T
73—Tommy Keel, S
83—Doug Dawson, G
88—Lee Brockman, DL
TEXAS A&I
72—Floyd Goodwin, T
73—Johnny Jackson, E
76—Wade Whitmer, T
77—Joe Henke, LB
Wade Whitmer, DL
78—Wade Whitmer, DL
TEXAS A&M
56—Jack Pardee, B
71—Steve Luebbehusen, LB
76—Kevin Monk, LB
77—Kevin Monk, LB
85—Kip Corrington, DB
86—Kip Corrington, DB
87—Kip Corrington, DB
TEXAS CHRISTIAN
52—Marshall Harris, T
55—Hugh Pitts, C
Jim Swink, B
56—Jim Swink, B
57—John Nikkel, E
68—Jim Ray, G
72—Scott Walker, C
74—Terry Drennan, DB
80—John McClean, DL
TEXAS TECH
72—Jeff Jobe, E
79—Maury Buford, P
83—Chuck Alexander, DB
TOLEDO
83—Michael Matz, DL
TUFTS
70—Bruce Zinsmeister, DL
81—Brian Gallagher, OG
83—Richard Guiunta, G
TULANE
71—David Hebert, DHB
TULSA
64—Howard Twilley, E

65—Howard Twilley, E
74—Mack Lancaster, T
UC DAVIS
72—Steve Algeo, LB
75—Dave Gellerman, LB
90—Mike Shepard, DL
UC RIVERSIDE
71—Tyrone Hooks, HB
UCLA
52—Ed Flynn, G
Donn Moomaw, LB
53—Ira Pauly, C
54—Sam Boghosian, G
66—Ray Armstrong, OE
75—John Sciarra, QB
77—John Fowler, LB
81—Cormac Carney, WR
Tim Wrightman, TE
82—Cormac Carney, WR
85—Mike Hartmeier, OG
UNION (N.Y.)
71—Tom Anacher, LB
73—Dave Ricks, DB
87—Richard Romer, DL
URSINUS
86—Chuck Odgers, DB
87—Chuck Odgers, LB
UTAH
64—Mel Carpenter, T
71—Scott Robbins, DHB
73—Steve Odom, RB
76—Dick Graham, E
UTAH ST.
61—Merlin Olsen, T
69—Gary Anderson, LB
74—Randy Stockham, DE
75—Randy Stockham, DE
UTEP
88—Pat Hegarty, QB
VA. MILITARY
78—Craig Jones, PK
79—Craig Jones, PK
84—David Twillie, OL
86—Dan Young, DL
88—Anthony McIntosh, DB
VANDERBILT
58—Don Donnell, C
68—Jim Burns, DB
74—Doug Martin, OE
75—Damon Regen, LB
77—Greg Martin, K
83—Phil Roach, WR
VILLANOVA
86—Ron Sency, RB
88—Peter Lombardi, RB
VIRGINIA
72—Tom Kennedy, OG
75—Bob Meade, DT
VIRGINIA TECH
67—Frank Loria, DB
72—Tommy Carpenito, LB
WABASH
70—Roscoe Fouts, DHB
71—Kendrick Shelburne, DT
82—Dave Broecker, QB
WARTBURG
75—James Charles Peterson, DB
76—Randy Groth, DB
77—Neil Mandsager, LB
90—Jerrod Staack, OL

WASH. & LEE
75—John Cocklereece, DB
78—George Ballantyne, LB
WASHINGTON
55—Jim Houston, E
63—Mike Briggs, T
64—Rick Redman, G
65—Steve Bramwell, DB
79—Bruce Harrell, LB
81—Mark Jerue, LB
Chuck Nelson, PK
82—Chuck Nelson, PK
86—David Rill, LB
87—David Rill, LB
91—Ed Cunningham, OL
WASHINGTON ST.
89—Jason Hanson, PK
90—Lee Tilleman, DL
Jason Hanson, PK
91—Jason Hanson, PK
WAYNE ST. (MICH.)
71—Gary Schultz, DHB
72—Walt Stasinski, DB
WAYNESBURG
77—John Culp, RB
78—John Culp, RB
89—Andrew Barrish, OL
90—Andrew Barrish, OL
91—Karl Petrof, OL
WEST CHESTER
83—Eric Wentling, K
86—Gerald Desmond, K
WEST VA.
52—Paul Bischoff, E
54—Fred Wyant, B
55—Sam Huff, T
70—Kim West, K
80—Oliver Luck, QB
81—Oliver Luck, QB
83—Jeff Hostetler, QB
WESTERN CARO.
75—Mike Wade, E
76—Mike Wade, LB
84—Eddie Maddox, RB
WESTERN ILL.
61—Jerry Blew, G
85—Jeff McKinney, RB
91—David Fierke, OL
WESTERN KY.
71—James Barber, LB
81—Tim Ford, DL
84—Mark Fatkin, OL
85—Mark Fatkin, OG
WESTERN MD.
73—Chip Chaney, S
WESTERN MICH.
70—Jon Bull, OT
WESTERN OREGON
61—Francis Tresler, C
WESTERN ST.
78—Bill Campbell, DHB
88—Damon Lockhart, RB
WESTMINSTER (PA.)
73—Bob Clark, G
77—Scott McLuckey, LB
WHEATON (ILL.)
73—Bill Hyer, G
75—Eugene Campbell, RB
76—Eugene Campbell, RB
88—Paul Sternenberg, DL

First-Team Academic All-America Selections   343

WHITTIER
86—Brent Kane, DL
WILKES
70—Al Kenney, C
WILLAMETTE
61—Stuart Hall
WILLIAM & MARY
74—John Gerdelman, RB
75—Ken Smith, DB
77—Ken Smith, DB
78—Robert Musculus, TE
84—Mark Kelso, DB
88—Chris Gessner, DB
90—Jeff Nielsen, LB

WIS.-EAU CLAIRE
74—Mark Anderson, RB
80—Mike Zeihen, DB
WIS.-PLATTEVILLE
85—Mark Hintz, DB
   Mark Rae, P
86—Mike Hintz, QB

87—Mark Rae, P
WIS.-RIVER FALLS
91—Mike Olson, LB
WISCONSIN
52—Bob Kennedy, DG
53—Alan Ameche, B
54—Alan Ameche, B
58—Jon Hobbs, B
59—Dale Hackbart, B
62—Pat Richter, E
63—Ken Bowman, C
72—Rufus Ferguson, RB
82—Kyle Borland, LB
87—Don Davey, DL
88—Don Davey, DL
89—Don Davey, DL
90—Don Davey, DL
WITTENBERG
80—Bill Beach, DB
81—Bill Beach, DB
82—Tom Jones, OT
88—Paul Kungl, WR

90—Victor Terebuh, DB
WOOSTER
73—Dave Foy, LB
77—Blake Moore, C
78—Blake Moore, C
79—Blake Moore, C
80—Dale Fortner, DB
   John Weisensell, OG
WYOMING
65—Bob Dinges, DE
67—George Mills, OG
73—Mike Lopiccolo, OT
84—Bob Gustafson, OT
87—Patrick Arndt, OG
YALE
68—Fred Morris, C
70—Tom Neville, DT
78—William Crowley, LB
81—Rich Diana, RB
   Frederick Leone, DL
89—Glover Lawrence, DL
91—Scott Wagner, DB

COLLEGE FOOTBALL ASSOCIATION SCHOLAR-ATHLETE TEAM

Following are football players acknowledged by the College Football Association for successfully balancing athletics and academics. The team was chosen for the first time in 1991 by a panel that included faculty members, athletics administrators, football coaches, academic advisers and sports information directors. The criteria included a cumulative grade-point average between 3.000 and 4.000 (4.000 scale), standing as at least a junior athletically, completion of 50 percent of degree requirements, completion of at least one year at the nominating institution, and playing time as a starter or significant reserve.

ARKANSAS
91—Mick Thomas, LB
ARMY
91—Michael McElrath, DB
CINCINNATI
91—Kris Bjorson, WR

CLEMSON
91—Bruce Batton, OL
COLORADO
91—James Hansen, OL
FLORIDA
91—Cal Dixon, OL
   Brad Culpepper, DL
KENTUCKY
91—Greg Lahr, OL

LOUISIANA ST.
91—Scott Wharton, DL
LOUISVILLE
91—Eric Watts, QB
MIAMI (FLA.)
91—Carlos Huerta, PK
MISSISSIPPI
91—James Singleton, DL

MISSISSIPPI ST.
91—Daniel Boyd, LB
NEBRASKA
91—Pat Engelbert, DL
   Mike Stigge, P
OKLAHOMA ST.
91—Stacey Satterwhite, DL

PITTSBURGH
91—Dave Moore, WR
RICE
91—Howard Teichelman, OL
SOUTH CARO.
91—Joe Reaves, LB
SOUTHERN METHODIST
91—Cary Brabham, DB
TEMPLE
91—Tony Schmitz, DB
VIRGINIA TECH
91—Will Furrer, QB
WEST VA.
91—Alex Shook, WR
WYOMING
91—Tom Corontzos, QB

BOWL/ALL-STAR
GAME RESULTS

Miami (Florida) fullback Larry Jones rushed for 144 yards and one touchdown and was named most valuable player in the Hurricanes' 22-0 victory over Nebraska in the 1992 Federal Express Orange Bowl. It was the Hurricanes' ninth straight bowl appearance.

RESULTS OF MAJOR BOWL GAMES

ROSE BOWL

Present Site: Pasadena, Cal.
Stadium (Capacity): Rose Bowl (99,563)
Playing Surface: Grass
Playing Sites: Tournament Park, Pasadena (1902, 1916-22); Rose Bowl, Pasadena (1923-41); Duke Stadium, Durham, N.C. (1942); Rose Bowl (since 1943)

1-1-02—Michigan 49, Stanford 0
1-1-16—Washington St. 14, Brown 0
1-1-17—Oregon 14, Pennsylvania 0
1-1-18—Mare Island 19, Camp Lewis 7
1-1-19—Great Lakes 17, Mare Island 0
1-1-20—Harvard 7, Oregon 6
1-1-21—California 28, Ohio St. 0
1-2-22—Wash. & Jeff. 0, California 0
1-1-23—Southern Cal 14, Penn St. 3
1-1-24—Navy 14, Washington 14
1-1-25—Notre Dame 27, Stanford 10
1-1-26—Alabama 20, Washington 19
1-1-27—Alabama 7, Stanford 7
1-2-28—Stanford 7, Pittsburgh 6
1-1-29—Georgia Tech 8, California 7
1-1-30—Southern Cal 47, Pittsburgh 14
1-1-31—Alabama 24, Washington St. 0
1-1-32—Southern Cal 21, Tulane 12
1-2-33—Southern Cal 35, Pittsburgh 0
1-1-34—Columbia 7, Stanford 0
1-1-35—Alabama 29, Stanford 13
1-1-36—Stanford 7, Southern Methodist 0
1-1-37—Pittsburgh 21, Washington 0
1-1-38—California 13, Alabama 0
1-2-39—Southern Cal 7, Duke 3
1-1-40—Southern Cal 14, Tennessee 0
1-1-41—Stanford 21, Nebraska 13
1-1-42—Oregon St. 20, Duke 16 (at Durham)
1-1-43—Georgia 9, UCLA 0
1-1-44—Southern Cal 29, Washington 0
1-1-45—Southern Cal 25, Tennessee 0
1-1-46—Alabama 34, Southern Cal 14
1-1-47—Illinois 45, UCLA 14
1-1-48—Michigan 49, Southern Cal 0
1-1-49—Northwestern 20, California 14
1-2-50—Ohio St. 17, California 14
1-1-51—Michigan 14, California 6
1-1-52—Illinois 40, Stanford 7
1-1-53—Southern Cal 7, Wisconsin 0
1-1-54—Michigan St. 28, UCLA 20

1-1-55—Ohio St. 20, Southern Cal 7
1-2-56—Michigan St. 17, UCLA 14
1-1-57—Iowa 35, Oregon St. 19
1-1-58—Ohio St. 10, Oregon 7
1-1-59—Iowa 38, California 12
1-1-60—Washington 44, Wisconsin 8
1-2-61—Washington 17, Minnesota 7
1-1-62—Minnesota 21, UCLA 3
1-1-63—Southern Cal 42, Wisconsin 37
1-1-64—Illinois 17, Washington 7
1-1-65—Michigan 34, Oregon St. 7
1-1-66—UCLA 14, Michigan St. 12
1-2-67—Purdue 14, Southern Cal 13
1-1-68—Southern Cal 14, Indiana 3
1-1-69—Ohio St. 27, Southern Cal 16
1-1-70—Southern Cal 10, Michigan 3
1-1-71—Stanford 27, Ohio St. 17
1-1-72—Stanford 13, Michigan 12
1-1-73—Southern Cal 42, Ohio St. 17
1-1-74—Ohio St. 42, Southern Cal 21
1-1-75—Southern Cal 18, Ohio St. 17
1-1-76—UCLA 23, Ohio St. 10
1-1-77—Southern Cal 14, Michigan 6
1-2-78—Washington 27, Michigan 20
1-1-79—Southern Cal 17, Michigan 10
1-1-80—Southern Cal 17, Ohio St. 16
1-1-81—Michigan 23, Washington 6
1-1-82—Washington 28, Iowa 0
1-1-83—UCLA 24, Michigan 14
1-2-84—UCLA 45, Illinois 9
1-1-85—Southern Cal 20, Ohio St. 17
1-1-86—UCLA 45, Iowa 28
1-1-87—Arizona St. 22, Michigan 15
1-1-88—Michigan St. 20, Southern Cal 17
1-2-89—Michigan 22, Southern Cal 14
1-1-90—Southern Cal 17, Michigan 10
1-1-91—Washington 46, Iowa 34
1-1-92—Washington 34, Michigan 14

ORANGE BOWL

Present Site: Miami, Fla.
Stadium (Capacity): Orange Bowl (74,244)
Playing Surface: Grass
Playing Sites: Orange Bowl (since 1935)

1-1-35—Bucknell 26, Miami (Fla.) 0
1-1-36—Catholic 20, Mississippi 19
1-1-37—Duquesne 13, Mississippi St. 12
1-1-38—Auburn 6, Michigan St. 0
1-2-39—Tennessee 17, Oklahoma 0
1-1-40—Georgia Tech 21, Missouri 7
1-1-41—Mississippi St. 14, Georgetown 7
1-1-42—Georgia 40, Texas Christian 26
1-1-43—Alabama 37, Boston College 21
1-1-44—Louisiana St. 19, Texas A&M 14
1-1-45—Tulsa 26, Georgia Tech 12
1-1-46—Miami (Fla.) 13, Holy Cross 6
1-1-47—Rice 8, Tennessee 0
1-1-48—Georgia Tech 20, Kansas 14
1-1-49—Texas 41, Georgia 28

1-2-50—Santa Clara 21, Kentucky 13
1-1-51—Clemson 15, Miami (Fla.) 14
1-1-52—Georgia Tech 17, Baylor 14
1-1-53—Alabama 61, Syracuse 6
1-1-54—Oklahoma 7, Maryland 0
1-1-55—Duke 34, Nebraska 7
1-2-56—Oklahoma 20, Maryland 6
1-1-57—Colorado 27, Clemson 21
1-1-58—Oklahoma 48, Duke 21
1-1-59—Oklahoma 21, Syracuse 6
1-1-60—Georgia 14, Missouri 0
1-2-61—Missouri 21, Navy 14
1-1-62—Louisiana St. 25, Colorado 7
1-1-63—Alabama 17, Oklahoma 0
1-1-64—Nebraska 13, Auburn 7

1-1-65 — Texas 21, Alabama 17
1-1-66 — Alabama 39, Nebraska 28
1-2-67 — Florida 27, Georgia Tech 12
1-1-68 — Oklahoma 26, Tennessee 24
1-1-69 — Penn St. 15, Kansas 14

1-1-70 — Penn St. 10, Missouri 3
1-1-71 — Nebraska 17, Louisiana St. 12
1-1-72 — Nebraska 38, Alabama 6
1-1-73 — Nebraska 40, Notre Dame 6
1-1-74 — Penn St. 16, Louisiana St. 9

1-1-75 — Notre Dame 13, Alabama 11
1-1-76 — Oklahoma 14, Michigan 6
1-1-77 — Ohio St. 27, Colorado 10
1-2-78 — Arkansas 31, Oklahoma 6
1-1-79 — Oklahoma 31, Nebraska 24

1-1-80 — Oklahoma 24, Florida St. 7
1-1-81 — Oklahoma 18, Florida St. 17
1-1-82 — Clemson 22, Nebraska 15
1-1-83 — Nebraska 21, Louisiana St. 20
1-2-84 — Miami (Fla.) 31, Nebraska 30

1-1-85 — Washington 28, Oklahoma 17
1-1-86 — Oklahoma 25, Penn St. 10
1-1-87 — Oklahoma 42, Arkansas 8
1-1-88 — Miami (Fla.) 20, Oklahoma 14
1-2-89 — Miami (Fla.) 23, Nebraska 3

1-1-90 — Notre Dame 21, Colorado 6
1-1-91 — Colorado 10, Notre Dame 9
1-1-92 — Miami (Fla.) 22, Nebraska 0

COTTON BOWL

Present Site: Dallas, Tex.
Stadium (Capacity): Cotton Bowl (72,032)
Playing Surface: AstroTurf
Playing Sites: Fair Park Stadium, Dallas (1937); Cotton Bowl (since 1938)

1-1-37 — Texas Christian 16, Marquette 6
1-1-38 — Rice 28, Colorado 14
1-2-39 — St. Mary's (Cal.) 20, Texas Tech 13
1-1-40 — Clemson 6, Boston College 3
1-1-41 — Texas A&M 13, Fordham 12

1-1-42 — Alabama 29, Texas A&M 21
1-1-43 — Texas 14, Georgia Tech 7
1-1-44 — Texas 7, Randolph Field 7
1-1-45 — Oklahoma St. 34, Texas Christian 0
1-1-46 — Texas 40, Missouri 27

1-1-47 — Arkansas 0, Louisiana St. 0
1-1-48 — Southern Methodist 13, Penn St. 13
1-1-49 — Southern Methodist 21, Oregon 13
1-2-50 — Rice 27, North Caro. 13
1-1-51 — Tennessee 20, Texas 14

1-1-52 — Kentucky 20, Texas Christian 7
1-1-53 — Texas 16, Tennessee 0
1-1-54 — Rice 28, Alabama 6
1-1-55 — Georgia Tech 14, Arkansas 6
1-2-56 — Mississippi 14, Texas Christian 13

1-1-57 — Texas Christian 28, Syracuse 27
1-1-58 — Navy 20, Rice 7
1-1-59 — Texas Christian 0, Air Force 0
1-1-60 — Syracuse 23, Texas 14
1-2-61 — Duke 7, Arkansas 6

1-1-62 — Texas 12, Mississippi 7
1-1-63 — Louisiana St. 13, Texas 0
1-1-64 — Texas 28, Navy 6
1-1-65 — Arkansas 10, Nebraska 7
1-1-66 — Louisiana St. 14, Arkansas 7

12-31-66 — Georgia 24, Southern Methodist 9
1-1-68 — Texas A&M 20, Alabama 16
1-1-69 — Texas 36, Tennessee 13
1-1-70 — Texas 21, Notre Dame 17
1-1-71 — Notre Dame 24, Texas 11

1-1-72 — Penn St. 30, Texas 6
1-1-73 — Texas 17, Alabama 13
1-1-74 — Nebraska 19, Texas 3
1-1-75 — Penn St. 41, Baylor 20
1-1-76 — Arkansas 31, Georgia 10

1-1-77 — Houston 30, Maryland 21
1-2-78 — Notre Dame 38, Texas 10
1-1-79 — Notre Dame 35, Houston 34
1-1-80 — Houston 17, Nebraska 14
1-1-81 — Alabama 30, Baylor 2

1-1-82 — Texas 14, Alabama 12
1-1-83 — Southern Methodist 7, Pittsburgh 3
1-2-84 — Georgia 10, Texas 9
1-1-85 — Boston College 45, Houston 28
1-1-86 — Texas A&M 36, Auburn 16

1-1-87 — Ohio St. 28, Texas A&M 12
1-1-88 — Texas A&M 35, Notre Dame 10
1-2-89 — UCLA 17, Arkansas 3
1-1-90 — Tennessee 31, Arkansas 27
1-1-91 — Miami (Fla.) 46, Texas 3

1-1-92 — Florida St. 10, Texas A&M 2

SUGAR BOWL

Present Site: New Orleans, La.
Stadium (Capacity): Louisiana Superdome (72,704)
Playing Surface: AstroTurf
Playing Sites: Tulane Stadium, New Orleans (1935-74); Louisiana Superdome (since 1975)

1-1-35 — Tulane 20, Temple 14
1-1-36 — Texas Christian 3, Louisiana St. 2
1-1-37 — Santa Clara 21, Louisiana St. 14
1-1-38 — Santa Clara 6, Louisiana St. 0
1-2-39 — Texas Christian 15, Carnegie Tech 7

1-1-40 — Texas A&M 14, Tulane 13
1-1-41 — Boston College 19, Tennessee 13
1-1-42 — Fordham 2, Missouri 0
1-1-43 — Tennessee 14, Tulsa 7
1-1-44 — Georgia Tech 20, Tulsa 18

1-1-45 — Duke 29, Alabama 26
1-1-46 — Oklahoma St. 33, St. Mary's (Cal.) 13
1-1-47 — Georgia 20, North Caro. 10
1-1-48 — Texas 27, Alabama 7
1-1-49 — Oklahoma 14, North Caro. 6

1-2-50 — Oklahoma 35, Louisiana St. 0
1-1-51 — Kentucky 13, Oklahoma 7
1-1-52 — Maryland 28, Tennessee 13
1-1-53 — Georgia Tech 24, Mississippi 7
1-1-54 — Georgia Tech 42, West Va. 19

1-1-55—Navy 21, Mississippi 0
1-2-56—Georgia Tech 7, Pittsburgh 0
1-1-57—Baylor 13, Tennessee 7
1-1-58—Mississippi 39, Texas 7
1-1-59—Louisiana St. 7, Clemson 0

1-1-60—Mississippi 21, Louisiana St. 0
1-2-61—Mississippi 14, Rice 6
1-1-62—Alabama 10, Arkansas 3
1-1-63—Mississippi 17, Arkansas 13
1-1-64—Alabama 12, Mississippi 7

1-1-65—Louisiana St. 13, Syracuse 10
1-1-66—Missouri 20, Florida 18
1-2-67—Alabama 34, Nebraska 7
1-1-68—Louisiana St. 20, Wyoming 13
1-1-69—Arkansas 16, Georgia 2

1-1-70—Mississippi 27, Arkansas 22
1-1-71—Tennessee 34, Air Force 13
1-1-72—Oklahoma 40, Auburn 22
12-31-72—Oklahoma 14, Penn St. 0
12-31-73—Notre Dame 24, Alabama 23

12-31-74—Nebraska 13, Florida 10
12-31-75—Alabama 13, Penn St. 6
1-1-77—Pittsburgh 27, Georgia 3
1-2-78—Alabama 35, Ohio St. 6
1-1-79—Alabama 14, Penn St. 7

1-1-80—Alabama 24, Arkansas 9
1-1-81—Georgia 17, Notre Dame 10
1-1-82—Pittsburgh 24, Georgia 20
1-1-83—Penn St. 27, Georgia 23
1-2-84—Auburn 9, Michigan 7

1-1-85—Nebraska 28, Louisiana St. 10
1-1-86—Tennessee 35, Miami (Fla.) 7
1-1-87—Nebraska 30, Louisiana St. 15
1-1-88—Syracuse 16, Auburn 16
1-2-89—Florida St. 13, Auburn 7

1-1-90—Miami (Fla.) 33, Alabama 25
1-1-91—Tennessee 23, Virginia 22
1-1-92—Notre Dame 39, Florida 28

JOHN HANCOCK BOWL

Present Site: El Paso, Tex.
Stadium (Capacity): Sun Bowl (52,000)
Playing Surface: AstroTurf
Name Changes: Sun Bowl (1936-86); John Hancock Sun Bowl (1987-88); John Hancock Bowl (since 1989)
Playing Sites: Kidd Field, UTEP, El Paso (1936-62); Sun Bowl Stadium (since 1963)

1-1-36—Hardin-Simmons 14, New Mexico St. 14
1-1-37—Hardin-Simmons 34, UTEP 6
1-1-38—West Va. 7, Texas Tech 6
1-2-39—Utah 26, New Mexico 0
1-1-40—Catholic 0, Arizona St. 0

1-1-41—Case Reserve 26, Arizona St. 13
1-1-42—Tulsa 6, Texas Tech 0
1-1-43—Second Air Force 13, Hardin-Simmons 7
1-1-44—Southwestern (Tex.) 7, New Mexico 0
1-1-45—Southwestern (Tex.) 35, U. Mexico 0

1-1-46—New Mexico 34, Denver 24
1-1-47—Cincinnati 18, Virginia Tech 6
1-1-48—Miami (Ohio) 13, Texas Tech 12
1-1-49—West Va. 21, UTEP 12
1-2-50—UTEP 33, Georgetown 20

1-1-51—West Tex. St. 14, Cincinnati 13
1-1-52—Texas Tech 25, Pacific (Cal.) 14
1-1-53—Pacific (Cal.) 26, Southern Miss. 7
1-1-54—UTEP 37, Southern Miss. 14
1-1-55—UTEP 47, Florida St. 20

1-2-56—Wyoming 21, Texas Tech 14
1-1-57—Geo. Washington 13, UTEP 0
1-1-58—Louisville 34, Drake 20
12-31-58—Wyoming 14, Hardin-Simmons 6
12-31-59—New Mexico St. 28, North Texas 8

12-31-60—New Mexico St. 20, Utah St. 13
12-30-61—Villanova 17, Wichita St. 9
12-31-62—West Tex. St. 15, Ohio 14
12-31-63—Oregon 21, Southern Methodist 14
12-26-64—Georgia 7, Texas Tech 0

12-31-65—UTEP 13, Texas Christian 12
12-24-66—Wyoming 28, Florida St. 20
12-30-67—UTEP 14, Mississippi 7
12-28-68—Auburn 34, Arizona 10
12-20-69—Nebraska 45, Georgia 6

12-19-70—Georgia Tech 17, Texas Tech 9
12-18-71—Louisiana St. 33, Iowa St. 15
12-30-72—North Caro. 32, Texas Tech 28
12-29-73—Missouri 34, Auburn 17
12-28-74—Mississippi St. 26, North Caro. 24

12-26-75—Pittsburgh 33, Kansas 19
1-2-77—Texas A&M 37, Florida 14
12-31-77—Stanford 24, Louisiana St. 14
12-23-78—Texas 42, Maryland 0
12-22-79—Washington 14, Texas 7

12-27-80—Nebraska 31, Mississippi St. 17
12-26-81—Oklahoma 40, Houston 14
12-25-82—North Caro. 26, Texas 10
12-24-83—Alabama 28, Southern Methodist 7
12-22-84—Maryland 28, Tennessee 27

12-28-85—Georgia 13, Arizona 13
12-25-86—Alabama 28, Washington 6
12-25-87—Oklahoma St. 35, West Va. 33
12-24-88—Alabama 29, Army 28
12-30-89—Pittsburgh 31, Texas A&M 28

12-31-90—Michigan St. 17, Southern Cal 16
12-31-91—UCLA 6, Illinois 3

GATOR BOWL

Present Site: Jacksonville, Fla.
Stadium (Capacity): Gator Bowl (80,129)
Playing Surface: Grass
Playing Sites: Gator Bowl (since 1946)

1-1-46—Wake Forest 26, South Caro. 14
1-1-47—Oklahoma 34, North Caro. St. 13
1-1-48—Maryland 20, Georgia 20
1-1-49—Clemson 24, Missouri 23
1-2-50—Maryland 20, Missouri 7

1-1-51—Wyoming 20, Wash. & Lee 7
1-1-52—Miami (Fla.) 14, Clemson 0
1-1-53—Florida 14, Tulsa 13
1-1-54—Texas Tech 35, Auburn 13
12-31-54—Auburn 33, Baylor 13

12-31-55—Vanderbilt 25, Auburn 13
12-29-56—Georgia Tech 21, Pittsburgh 14
12-28-57—Tennessee 3, Texas A&M 0
12-27-58—Mississippi 7, Florida 3
1-2-60—Arkansas 14, Georgia Tech 7

12-31-60—Florida 13, Baylor 12
12-30-61—Penn St. 30, Georgia Tech 15
12-29-62—Florida 17, Penn St. 7
12-28-63—North Caro. 35, Air Force 0
1-2-65—Florida St. 36, Oklahoma 19

12-31-65—Georgia Tech 31, Texas Tech 21
12-31-66—Tennessee 18, Syracuse 12
12-30-67—Penn St. 17, Florida St. 17
12-28-68—Missouri 35, Alabama 10
12-27-69—Florida 14, Tennessee 13

1-2-71—Auburn 35, Mississippi 28
12-31-71—Georgia 7, North Caro. 3
12-30-72—Auburn 24, Colorado 3
12-29-73—Texas Tech 28, Tennessee 19
12-30-74—Auburn 27, Texas 3

12-29-75—Maryland 13, Florida 0
12-27-76—Notre Dame 20, Penn St. 9
12-30-77—Pittsburgh 34, Clemson 3
12-29-78—Clemson 17, Ohio St. 15
12-28-79—North Caro. 17, Michigan 15

12-29-80—Pittsburgh 37, South Caro. 9
12-28-81—North Caro. 31, Arkansas 27
12-30-82—Florida St. 31, West Va. 12
12-30-83—Florida 14, Iowa 6
12-28-84—Oklahoma St. 21, South Caro. 14

12-30-85—Florida St. 34, Oklahoma St. 23
12-27-86—Clemson 27, Stanford 21
12-31-87—Louisiana St. 30, South Caro. 13
1-1-89—Georgia 34, Michigan St. 27
12-30-89—Clemson 27, West Va. 7

1-1-91—Michigan 35, Mississippi 3
12-29-91—Oklahoma 48, Virginia 14

FLORIDA CITRUS BOWL

Present Site: Orlando, Fla.
Stadium (Capacity): Florida Citrus Bowl-Orange County (70,000)
Playing Surface: Grass
Name Changes: Tangerine Bowl (1947-82); Florida Citrus Bowl (since 1983)
Playing Sites: Tangerine Bowl, Orlando (1947-72); Florida Field, Gainesville (1973); Tangerine Bowl (now Florida Citrus Bowl) (1974-82); Orlando Stadium (now Florida Citrus Bowl) (1983-85); Florida Citrus Bowl-Orange County (since 1986)

1-1-47—Catawba 31, Maryville (Tenn.) 6
1-1-48—Catawba 7, Marshall 0
1-1-49—Murray St. 21, Sul Ross St. 21
1-2-50—St. Vincent 7, Emory & Henry 6
1-1-51—Morris Harvey 35, Emory & Henry 14

1-1-52—Stetson 35, Arkansas St. 20
1-1-53—East Tex. St. 33, Tennessee Tech 0
1-1-54—East Tex. St. 7, Arkansas St. 7
1-1-55—Nebraska-Omaha 7, Eastern Ky. 6
1-2-56—Juniata 6, Missouri Valley 6

1-1-57—West Tex. St. 20, Southern Miss. 13
1-1-58—East Tex. St. 10, Southern Miss. 9
12-27-58—East Tex. St. 26, Missouri Valley 7
1-1-60—Middle Tenn. St. 21, Presbyterian 12
12-30-60—Citadel 27, Tennessee Tech 0

12-29-61—Lamar 21, Middle Tenn. St. 14
12-22-62—Houston 49, Miami (Ohio) 21
12-28-63—Western Ky. 27, Coast Guard 0
12-12-64—East Caro. 14, Massachusetts 13
12-11-65—East Caro. 31, Maine 0

12-10-66—Morgan St. 14, West Chester 6
12-16-67—Tenn.-Martin 25, West Chester 8
12-27-68—Richmond 49, Ohio 42
12-26-69—Toledo 56, Davidson 33
12-28-70—Toledo 40, William & Mary 12

12-28-71—Toledo 28, Richmond 3
12-29-72—Tampa 21, Kent 18
12-22-73—Miami (Ohio) 16, Florida 7
12-21-74—Miami (Ohio) 21, Georgia 10
12-20-75—Miami (Ohio) 20, South Caro. 7

12-18-76—Oklahoma St. 49, Brigham Young 21
12-23-77—Florida St. 40, Texas Tech 17
12-23-78—North Caro. St. 30, Pittsburgh 17
12-22-79—Louisiana St. 34, Wake Forest 10
12-20-80—Florida 35, Maryland 20

12-19-81—Missouri 19, Southern Miss. 17
12-18-82—Auburn 33, Boston College 26
12-17-83—Tennessee 30, Maryland 23
12-22-84—Georgia 17, Florida St. 17
12-28-85—Ohio St. 10, Brigham Young 7

1-1-87—Auburn 16, Southern Cal 7
1-1-88—Clemson 35, Penn St. 10
1-2-89—Clemson 13, Oklahoma 6
1-1-90—Illinois 31, Virginia 21
1-1-91—Georgia Tech 45, Nebraska 21

1-1-92—California 37, Clemson 13

Note: No classified major teams participated in games from January 1, 1947, through December 30, 1960, or in 1961 and 1963 through 1967.

LIBERTY BOWL

Present Site: Memphis, Tenn.
Stadium (Capacity): Liberty Bowl Memorial (62,425)
Playing Surface: Grass
Playing Sites: Municipal Stadium, Philadelphia (1959-63); Convention Hall, Atlantic City, N.J. (1964); Liberty Bowl Memorial (since 1965)

12-19-59—Penn St. 7, Alabama 0
12-17-60—Penn St. 41, Oregon 12
12-16-61—Syracuse 15, Miami (Fla.) 14
12-15-62—Oregon St. 6, Villanova 0
12-21-63—Mississippi St. 16, North Caro. St. 12

12-19-64—Utah 32, West Va. 6
12-18-65—Mississippi 13, Auburn 7
12-10-66—Miami (Fla.) 14, Virginia Tech 7
12-16-67—North Caro. St. 14, Georgia 7
12-14-68—Mississippi 34, Virginia Tech 17

12-13-69—Colorado 47, Alabama 33
12-12-70—Tulane 17, Colorado 3
12-20-71—Tennessee 14, Arkansas 13
12-18-72—Georgia Tech 31, Iowa St. 30
12-17-73—North Caro. St. 31, Kansas 18
12-16-74—Tennessee 7, Maryland 3
12-22-75—Southern Cal 20, Texas A&M 0
12-20-76—Alabama 36, UCLA 6
12-19-77—Nebraska 21, North Caro. 17
12-23-78—Missouri 20, Louisiana St. 15
12-22-79—Penn St. 9, Tulane 6
12-27-80—Purdue 28, Missouri 25
12-30-81—Ohio St. 31, Navy 28
12-29-82—Alabama 21, Illinois 15
12-29-83—Notre Dame 19, Boston College 18

12-27-84—Auburn 21, Arkansas 15
12-27-85—Baylor 21, Louisiana St. 7
12-29-86—Tennessee 21, Minnesota 14
12-29-87—Georgia 20, Arkansas 17
12-28-88—Indiana 34, South Caro. 10
12-28-89—Mississippi 42, Air Force 29
12-27-90—Air Force 23, Ohio St. 11
12-29-91—Air Force 38, Mississippi St. 15

PEACH BOWL

Present Site: Atlanta, Ga.
Stadium (Capacity): Georgia Dome (70,500)
Playing Surface: Turf
Playing Sites: Grant Field, Atlanta (1968-70); Atlanta/Fulton County (1971-92); Georgia Dome (since 1993)

12-30-68—Louisiana St. 31, Florida St. 27
12-30-69—West Va. 14, South Caro. 3
12-30-70—Arizona St. 48, North Caro. 26
12-30-71—Mississippi 41, Georgia Tech 18
12-29-72—North Caro. St. 49, West Va. 13
12-28-73—Georgia 17, Maryland 16
12-28-74—Vanderbilt 6, Texas Tech 6
12-31-75—West Va. 13, North Caro. St. 10
12-31-76—Kentucky 21, North Caro. 0
12-31-77—North Caro. St. 24, Iowa St. 14
12-25-78—Purdue 41, Georgia Tech 21
12-31-79—Baylor 24, Clemson 18
1-2-81—Miami (Fla.) 20, Virginia Tech 10
12-31-81—West Va. 26, Florida 6
12-31-82—Iowa 28, Tennessee 22

12-30-83—Florida St. 28, North Caro. 3
12-31-84—Virginia 27, Purdue 24
12-31-85—Army 31, Illinois 29
12-31-86—Virginia Tech 25, North Caro. St. 24
1-2-88—Tennessee 27, Indiana 22
12-31-88—North Caro. St. 28, Iowa 23
12-30-89—Syracuse 19, Georgia 18
12-29-90—Auburn 27, Indiana 23
1-1-92—East Caro. 37, North Caro. St. 34

FIESTA BOWL

Present Site: Tempe, Ariz.
Stadium (Capacity): Sun Devil (74,783)
Playing Surface: Grass
Playing Sites: Sun Devil Stadium (since 1971)

12-27-71—Arizona St. 45, Florida St. 38
12-23-72—Arizona St. 49, Missouri 35
12-21-73—Arizona St. 28, Pittsburgh 7
12-28-74—Oklahoma St. 16, Brigham Young 6
12-26-75—Arizona St. 17, Nebraska 14
12-25-76—Oklahoma 41, Wyoming 7
12-25-77—Penn St. 42, Arizona St. 30
12-25-78—Arkansas 10, UCLA 10
12-25-79—Pittsburgh 16, Arizona 10
12-26-80—Penn St. 31, Ohio St. 19
1-1-82—Penn St. 26, Southern Cal 10
1-1-83—Arizona St. 32, Oklahoma 21
1-2-84—Ohio St. 28, Pittsburgh 23
1-1-85—UCLA 39, Miami (Fla.) 37
1-1-86—Michigan 27, Nebraska 23

1-2-87—Penn St. 14, Miami (Fla.) 10
1-1-88—Florida St. 31, Nebraska 28
1-2-89—Notre Dame 34, West Va. 21
1-1-90—Florida St. 41, Nebraska 17
1-1-91—Louisville 34, Alabama 7
1-1-92—Penn St. 42, Tennessee 17

INDEPENDENCE BOWL

Present Site: Shreveport, La.
Stadium (Capacity): Independence (50,459)
Playing Surface: Grass
Playing Sites: Independence Stadium (since 1976)

12-13-76—McNeese St. 20, Tulsa 16
12-17-77—Louisiana Tech 24, Louisville 14
12-16-78—East Caro. 35, Louisiana Tech 13
12-15-79—Syracuse 31, McNeese St. 7
12-13-80—Southern Miss. 16, McNeese St. 14

12-12-81—Texas A&M 33, Oklahoma St. 16
12-11-82—Wisconsin 14, Kansas St. 3
12-10-83—Air Force 9, Mississippi 3
12-15-84—Air Force 23, Virginia Tech 7
12-21-85—Minnesota 20, Clemson 13

350   *1992 NCAA FOOTBALL*

12-20-86—Mississippi 20, Texas Tech 17
12-19-87—Washington 24, Tulane 12
12-23-88—Southern Miss. 38, UTEP 18
12-16-89—Oregon 27, Tulsa 24
12-15-90—Louisiana Tech 34, Maryland 34
12-29-91—Georgia 24, Arkansas 15

HOLIDAY BOWL

Present Site: San Diego, Cal.
Stadium (Capacity): San Diego Jack Murphy (62,809)
Playing Surface: Grass
Playing Sites: San Diego Jack Murphy Stadium (since 1978)

12-22-78—Navy 23, Brigham Young 16
12-21-79—Indiana 38, Brigham Young 37
12-19-80—Brigham Young 46, Southern Methodist 45
12-18-81—Brigham Young 38, Washington St. 36
12-17-82—Ohio St. 47, Brigham Young 17
12-23-83—Brigham Young 21, Missouri 17
12-21-84—Brigham Young 24, Michigan 17
12-22-85—Arkansas 18, Arizona St. 17
12-30-86—Iowa 39, San Diego St. 38
12-30-87—Iowa 20, Wyoming 19

12-30-88—Oklahoma St. 62, Wyoming 14
12-29-89—Penn St. 50, Brigham Young 39
12-29-90—Texas A&M 65, Brigham Young 14
12-30-91—Iowa 13, Brigham Young 13

CALIFORNIA BOWL

Present Site: Fresno, Cal.
Stadium (Capacity): FSU Bulldog (40,513)
Playing Surface: Grass
Playing Sites: FSU Bulldog Stadium (since 1981)

12-19-81—Toledo 27, San Jose St. 25
12-18-82—Fresno St. 29, Bowling Green 28
12-17-83—Northern Ill. 20, Cal St. Fullerton 13
12-15-84—Nevada-Las Vegas 30, *Toledo 13
12-14-85—Fresno St. 51, Bowling Green 7

12-13-86—San Jose St. 37, Miami (Ohio) 7
12-12-87—Eastern Mich. 30, San Jose St. 27
12-10-88—Fresno St. 35, Western Mich. 30
12-9-89—Fresno St. 27, Ball St. 6
12-8-90—San Jose St. 48, Central Mich. 24
12-14-91—Bowling Green 28, Fresno St. 21

* *Won by forfeit.*

ALOHA BOWL

Present Site: Honolulu, Hawaii
Stadium (Capacity): Aloha (50,000)
Playing Surface: AstroTurf
Playing Sites: Aloha Stadium (since 1982)

12-25-82—Washington 21, Maryland 20
12-26-83—Penn St. 13, Washington 10
12-29-84—Southern Methodist 27, Notre Dame 20
12-28-85—Alabama 24, Southern Cal 3
12-27-86—Arizona 30, North Caro. 21

12-25-87—UCLA 20, Florida 16
12-25-88—Washington St. 24, Houston 22
12-25-89—Michigan St. 33, Hawaii 13
12-25-90—Syracuse 28, Arizona 0
12-25-91—Georgia Tech 18, Stanford 17

FREEDOM BOWL

Present Site: Anaheim, Cal.
Stadium (Capacity): Anaheim (70,962)
Playing Surface: Grass
Playing Sites: Anaheim Stadium (since 1984)

12-26-84—Iowa 55, Texas 17
12-30-85—Washington 20, Colorado 17
12-30-86—UCLA 31, Brigham Young 10
12-30-87—Arizona St. 33, Air Force 28
12-29-88—Brigham Young 20, Colorado 17

12-30-89—Washington 34, Florida 7
12-29-90—Colorado St. 32, Oregon 31
12-30-91—Tulsa 28, San Diego St. 17

Results of Major Bowl Games

351

HALL OF FAME BOWL

Present Site: Tampa, Fla.
Stadium (Capacity): Tampa (74,350)
Playing Surface: Grass
Playing Sites: Tampa Stadium (since 1986)

12-23-86—Boston College 27, Georgia 24
1-2-88—Michigan 28, Alabama 24
1-2-89—Syracuse 23, Louisiana St. 10
1-1-90—Auburn 31, Ohio St. 14
1-1-91—Clemson 30, Illinois 0
1-1-92—Syracuse 24, Ohio St. 17

COPPER BOWL

Present Site: Tucson, Ariz.
Stadium (Capacity): Arizona Wildcats (56,167)
Playing Surface: Grass
Playing Sites: Arizona Wildcats Stadium (since 1989)

12-31-89—Arizona 17, North Caro. St. 10
12-31-90—California 17, Wyoming 15
12-31-91—Indiana 24, Baylor 0

BLOCKBUSTER BOWL

Present Site: Miami, Fla.
Stadium (Capacity): Joe Robbie (73,000)
Playing Surface: Grass
Playing Sites: Joe Robbie Stadium (since 1990)

12-28-90—Florida St. 24, Penn St. 17
12-28-91—Alabama 30, Colorado 25

UNDEFEATED, UNTIED TEAM MATCHUPS IN BOWL GAMES

Bowl	Date	Winner (record going in, coach)	Loser (record going in, coach)
Rose	1-1-21	California 28 (8-0, Andy Smith)	Ohio St. 0 (7-0, John Wilce)
Rose	1-2-22	0-0 tie: California (9-0, Andy Smith) Wash. & Jeff. (10-0, Earle "Greasy" Neale)	
Rose	1-1-27	7-7 tie: Stanford (10-0, Glenn "Pop" Warner) Alabama (9-0, Wallace Wade)	
Rose	1-1-31	Alabama 24 (9-0, Wallace Wade)	Washington St. 0 (9-0, Orin "Babe" Hollingbery)
Orange	1-2-39	Tennessee 17 (10-0, Bob Neyland)	Oklahoma 0 (10-0, Tom Stidham)
Sugar	1-1-41	Boston College 19 (10-0, Frank Leahy)	Tennessee 13 (10-0, Bob Neyland)
Sugar	1-1-52	Maryland 28 (9-0, Jim Tatum)	Tennessee 13 (10-0, Bob Neyland)
Orange	1-2-56	Oklahoma 20 (10-0, Bud Wilkinson)	Maryland 6 (10-0, Jim Tatum)
Orange	1-1-72	Nebraska 38 (12-0, Bob Devaney)	Alabama 6 (11-0, Paul "Bear" Bryant)
Sugar	12-31-73	Notre Dame 24 (10-0, Ara Parseghian)	Alabama 23 (11-0, Paul "Bear" Bryant)
Fiesta	1-2-87	Penn St. 14 (11-0, Joe Paterno)	Miami (Fla.) 10 (11-0, Jimmy Johnson)
Orange	1-1-88	Miami (Fla.) 20 (11-0, Jimmy Johnson)	Oklahoma 14 (11-0, Barry Switzer)
Fiesta	1-2-89	Notre Dame 34 (11-0, Lou Holtz)	West Va. 21 (11-0, Don Nehlen)

UNDEFEATED TEAM MATCHUPS IN BOWL GAMES
(Both teams were undefeated but one or both was tied one or more times)

Bowl	Date	Winner (record going in, coach)	Loser (record going in, coach)
Rose	1-1-25	Notre Dame 27 (9-0, Knute Rockne)	Stanford 10 (7-0-1, Glenn "Pop" Warner)
Rose	1-1-26	Alabama 20 (9-0, Wallace Wade)	Washington 19 (10-0-1, Enoch Bagshaw)
Rose	1-2-33	Southern Cal 35 (9-0, Howard Jones)	Pittsburgh 0 (8-0-2, Jock Sutherland)
Rose	1-1-35	Alabama 29 (9-0, Frank Thomas)	Stanford 13 (9-0-1, Claude "Tiny" Thornhill)
Rose	1-1-38	California 13 (9-0-1, Leonard "Stub" Allison)	Alabama 0 (9-0, Frank Thomas)
Rose	1-1-40	Southern Cal 14 (7-0-2, Howard Jones)	Tennessee 0 (10-0, Bob Neyland)
Sugar	1-1-40	Texas A&M 14 (10-0, Homer Norton)	Tulane 13 (8-0-1, Lowell "Red" Dawson)
Rose	1-1-45	Southern Cal 25 (7-0-2, Jeff Cravath)	Tennessee 0 (7-0-1, John Barnhill)
Cotton	1-1-48	13-13 tie: Southern Methodist (9-0-1, Matty Bell) Penn St. (9-0, Bob Higgins)	
Orange	1-1-51	Clemson 15 (8-0-1, Frank Howard)	Miami (Fla.) 14 (9-0-1, Andy Gustafson)
Sugar	1-1-53	Georgia Tech 24 (11-0, Bobby Dodd)	Mississippi 7 (8-0-2, John Vaught)
Rose	1-1-69	Ohio St. 27 (9-0, Woody Hayes)	Southern Cal 16 (9-0-1, John McKay)
Rose	1-1-80	Southern Cal 17 (10-0-1, John Robinson)	Ohio St. 16 (11-0, Earle Bruce)
California	12-14-85	Fresno St. 51 (10-0-1, Jim Sweeney)	Bowling Green 7 (11-0, Denny Stolz)

REGULAR-SEASON MAJOR-BOWL GAME REMATCHES

Date	Regular Season	Date	Bowl Game Rematch
10-6-56	Iowa 14, Oregon St. 13	1-1-57	(Rose) Iowa 35, Oregon St. 19
10-31-59	Louisiana St. 7, Mississippi 3	1-1-60	(Sugar) Mississippi 21, Louisiana St. 0
9-18-65	Michigan St. 13, UCLA 3	1-1-66	(Rose) UCLA 14, Michigan St. 12
10-4-75	Ohio St. 41, UCLA 20	1-1-76	(Rose) UCLA 23, Ohio St. 10
11-11-78	Nebraska 17, Oklahoma 14	1-1-79	(Orange) Oklahoma 31, Nebraska 24
9-25-82	UCLA 31, Michigan 27	1-1-83	(Rose) UCLA 24, Michigan 14
9-7-87	Michigan St. 27, Southern Cal 13	1-1-88	(Rose) Michigan St. 20, Southern Cal 17

MOST CONSECUTIVE SEASONS WITH BOWL-GAME VICTORIES
Bowl, Opponent, Score

7 Florida St.—85 Gator, Oklahoma St. 34-23; 86 All-American, Indiana 27-13; 87 Fiesta, Nebraska 31-28; 88 Sugar, Auburn 13-7; 89 Fiesta, Nebraska 41-17; 90 Blockbuster, Penn St. 24-17; 92 Cotton, Texas A&M 10-2. Coach: Bobby Bowden.

7 UCLA—83 Rose, Michigan 24-14; 84 Rose, Illinois 45-9; 85 Fiesta, Miami (Fla.) 39-37; 86 Rose, Iowa 45-28; 86 Freedom, Brigham Young 31-10; 87 Aloha, Florida 20-16; 89 Cotton, Arkansas, 17-3. Coach: Terry Donahue.

6 Alabama—75 Sugar, Penn St. 13-6; 76 Liberty, UCLA 36-6; 78 Sugar, Ohio St. 35-6; 79 Sugar, Penn St. 14-7; 80 Sugar, Arkansas 24-9; 81 Cotton, Baylor 30-2. Coach: Paul "Bear" Bryant.

6 Nebraska—69 Sun, Georgia 45-6; 71 Orange, Louisiana St. 17-12; 72 Orange, Alabama 38-6; 73 Orange, Notre Dame 40-6; 74 Cotton, Texas 19-3; 74 Sugar, Florida 13-10. Coaches: Bob Devaney first 4 games, Tom Osborne last 2.

6 Georgia Tech—52 Orange, Baylor 17-14; 53 Sugar, Mississippi 24-7; 54 Sugar, West Va. 42-19; 55 Cotton, Arkansas 14-6; 56 Sugar, Pittsburgh 7-0; 56 Gator, Pittsburgh 21-14. Coach: Bobby Dodd.

MOST CONSECUTIVE BOWL-GAME VICTORIES

9 Southern Cal—23 Rose, Penn St. 14-3; 24 Los Angeles Christmas Festival, Missouri 20-7; 30 Rose, Pittsburgh 47-14; 32 Rose, Tulane 21-12; 33 Rose, Pittsburgh 35-0; 39 Rose, Duke 7-3; 40 Rose, Tennessee 14-0; 44 Rose, Washington 29-0; 45 Rose, Tennessee 25-0. Coaches: Elmer "Gus" Henderson first 2 games, Howard Jones next 5, Jeff Cravath last 2.

ALL-TIME BOWL-GAME RECORDS

This list includes all bowls played by a current major team, providing its opponent was classified major that season or it was a major team then. The list excludes games in which a home team served as a predetermined, preseason host regardless of its record and/or games scheduled before the season, thus eliminating the old Pineapple, Glass and Palm Festival. Following is the alphabetical list showing the record of each current major team in all major bowls and its record in the traditional "Big Four"—Rose, Orange, Sugar and Cotton:

	All Bowls W	L	T	Big Four W	L	T		All Bowls W	L	T	Big Four W	L	T
Air Force	6	4	1	0	1	1	Navy	3	4	1	2	2	1
Alabama	24	17	3	17	12	1	Nebraska	14	16	0	9	11	0
Arizona	2	5	1	—	—	—	Nevada	1	1	0	—	—	—
Arizona St.	9	5	1	1	0	0	Nevada-Las Vegas	#1	0	0	—	—	—
Arkansas	9	15	3	4	10	1	New Mexico	2	2	1	—	—	—
Army	2	1	0	—	—	—	New Mexico St.	2	0	1	—	—	—
Auburn	12	9	2	2	4	1	North Caro.	6	10	0	0	3	0
Ball St.	0	1	0	—	—	—	North Caro. St.	7	6	1	—	—	—
Baylor	7	7	0	1	3	0	Northern Ill.	1	0	0	—	—	—
Boston College	3	4	0	2	2	0	Northwestern	1	0	0	1	0	0
Bowling Green	1	3	0	—	—	—	Notre Dame	11	6	0	9	5	0
Brigham Young	5	10	1	—	—	—	Ohio	0	2	0	—	—	—
Cal St. Fullerton	0	1	0	—	—	—	Ohio St.	11	13	0	7	8	0
California	4	6	1	2	5	1	Oklahoma	19	10	1	15	6	0
Central Mich.	0	1	0	—	—	—	Oklahoma St.	9	3	0	2	0	0
Cincinnati	1	1	0	—	—	—	Oregon	3	5	0	1	3	0
Clemson	11	7	0	3	2	0	Oregon St.	2	2	0	1	2	0
Colorado	5	11	0	2	4	0	Pacific (Cal.)	2	1	0	—	—	—
Colorado St.	1	1	0	—	—	—	Penn St.	17	9	2	6	5	1
Duke	3	4	0	3	3	0	Pittsburgh	8	10	0	3	5	0
East Caro.	2	0	0	—	—	—	Purdue	4	1	0	1	0	0
Eastern Mich.	1	0	0	—	—	—	Rice	4	3	0	4	2	0
Florida	8	11	0	1	3	0	Rutgers	0	1	0	—	—	—
Florida St.	11	7	2	2	2	0	San Diego St.	1	3	0	—	—	—
Fresno St.	5	2	0	—	—	—	San Jose St.	4	3	0	—	—	—
Georgia	14	13	3	7	6	0	South Caro.	0	8	0	—	—	—
Georgia Tech	17	8	0	9	3	0	Southern Cal	22	12	0	19	8	0
Hawaii	0	1	0	—	—	—	Southern Methodist	4	6	1	2	2	1
Houston	7	5	1	2	2	0	Southern Miss.	2	4	0	—	—	—
Illinois	4	6	0	3	1	0	Stanford	7	7	1	5	5	1
Indiana	3	4	0	0	1	0	Syracuse	7	6	1	1	4	1
Iowa	6	5	1	2	3	0	Temple	1	1	0	0	1	0
Iowa St.	0	4	0	—	—	—	Tennessee	17	15	0	7	9	0
Kansas	1	5	0	0	2	0	Texas	16	16	2	12	10	1
Kansas St.	0	1	0	—	—	—	Texas A&M	11	8	0	5	4	0
Kent	0	1	0	—	—	—	Texas Christian	4	9	1	4	4	1
Kentucky	5	2	0	2	1	0	Texas Tech	4	13	1	0	1	0
Louisiana St.	11	16	1	7	10	1	Toledo	4	1	0	—	—	—
Louisiana Tech	0	0	1	—	—	—	Tulane	2	6	0	1	2	0
Louisville	2	1	1	—	—	—	Tulsa	4	7	0	1	2	0
Maryland	6	9	2	1	3	0	UCLA	10	7	1	6	5	0
Memphis St.	1	0	0	—	—	—	Utah	2	0	0	—	—	—
Miami (Fla.)	10	8	0	7	3	0	Utah St.	0	3	0	—	—	—
Miami (Ohio)	5	2	0	—	—	—	UTEP	5	4	0	—	—	—
Michigan	10	13	0	6	11	0	Vanderbilt	1	1	1	—	—	—
Michigan St.	5	5	0	3	2	0	Virginia	2	3	0	0	1	0
Minnesota	2	3	0	1	1	0	Virginia Tech	1	5	0	—	—	—
Mississippi	13	11	0	6	5	0	Wake Forest	1	2	0	—	—	—
Mississippi St.	4	3	0	1	1	0	Washington	12	7	1	7	5	1
Missouri	8	11	0	2	5	0	Washington St.	2	2	0	1	1	0

1992 NCAA FOOTBALL

	All Bowls			Big Four		
	W	L	T	W	L	T
West Va.	8	7	0	0	1	0
Western Mich.	0	2	0	—	—	—
Wisconsin	1	5	0	0	3	0
Wyoming	4	5	0	0	1	0

Later lost game by forfeit.

The following current Division I-A teams have not played in a major bowl game: Akron and Southwestern La. Nevada and Arkansas St. are new I-A members.

MAJOR BOWL-GAME RECORDS OF
NON-DIVISION I-A TEAMS
(Big Four record is in parentheses.)

Boston U. 0-1-0; Brown 0-1-0 (0-1-0); Bucknell 1-0-0 (1-0-0); Cal St. Northridge 0-1-0; Carnegie Mellon 0-1-0 (0-1-0); Case Reserve 1-0-0; Catholic 1-0-1 (1-0-0); Centenary 0-0-1; Centre 2-1-0; Citadel 1-0-0; Columbia 1-0-0 (1-0-0); Davidson 0-1-0; Dayton 0-1-0; Denver 0-2-0; Drake 2-1-0; Duquesne 1-0-0 (1-0-0); Fordham 1-1-0 (1-1-0); Geo. Washington 1-0-0; Georgetown 0-2-0 (0-1-0); Gonzaga 0-1-0; Hardin-Simmons 5-2-1; Harvard 1-0-0 (1-0-0); Holy Cross 0-1-0 (0-1-0); Long Beach St. (0-0-1); Marquette 0-1-0 (0-1-0); McNeese St. 1-2-0; University of Mexico 0-1-0; Montana St. 0-0-1; North Texas 0-2-0; Occidental 1-0-0; Ouachita 0-1-0; Pennsylvania 0-1-0 (0-1-0); Randolph Field 0-0-1 (0-0-1); Richmond 1-1-0; Santa Clara 3-0-0 (3-0-0); Second Air Force 1-0-0; Southwestern (Tex.) 2-0-0; St. Mary's (Cal.) 1-2-0 (1-1-0); Tampa 1-0-0; Tennessee Tech 0-1-0; Villanova 2-2-1; Wash. & Jeff. 0-0-1 (0-0-1); Wash. & Lee 0-1-0; West Tex. St. 3-0-0; West Va. Wesleyan 1-0-0; Wichita St. 0-3-0; William & Mary 1-2-0; Xavier (Ohio) 1-0-0. **TOTALS: 38-38-7 (10-8-2)**

25 FORMER MAJOR BOWL GAMES
(Games in which at least one team was classified major that season.)

Alamo (San Antonio, Tex.): 1-4-47—Hardin-Simmons 20, Denver 0

All-American (Birmingham, Ala.): 12-22-77—Maryland 17, Minnesota 17; 12-20-78—Texas A&M 28, Iowa St. 12; 12-29-79—Missouri 24, South Caro. 14; 12-27-80—Arkansas 34, Tulane 15; 12-31-81—Mississippi St. 10, Kansas 0; 12-31-82—Air Force 36, Vanderbilt 28; 12-22-83—West Va. 20, Kentucky 16; 12-29-84—Kentucky 20, Wisconsin 19; 12-31-85—Georgia Tech 17, Michigan St. 14; 12-31-86—Florida St. 27, Indiana 13; 12-22-87—Virginia 22, Brigham Young 16; 12-29-88—Florida 14, Illinois 10; 12-28-89—Texas Tech 49, Duke 21; 12-28-90—North Caro. St. 31, Southern Miss. 27

Aviation (Dayton, Ohio): 12-9-61—New Mexico 28, Western Mich. 12

Bacardi (Cuban National Sports Festival at Havana): 1-1-37—Auburn 7, Villanova 7

Bluebonnet (Houston, Tex.): 12-19-59—Clemson 23, Texas Christian 7; 12-17-60—Texas 3, Alabama 3; 12-16-61—Kansas 33, Rice 7; 12-22-62—Missouri 14, Georgia Tech 10; 12-21-63—Baylor 14, Louisiana St. 7; 12-19-64—Tulsa 14, Mississippi 7; 12-18-65—Tennessee 27, Tulsa 6; 12-17-66—Texas 19, Mississippi 0; 12-23-67—Colorado 31, Miami (Fla.) 21; 12-31-68—Southern Methodist 28, Oklahoma 27; 12-31-69—Houston 36, Auburn 7; 12-31-70—Alabama 24, Oklahoma 24; 12-31-71—Colorado 29, Houston 17; 12-31-72—Tennessee 24, Louisiana St. 17; 12-29-73—Houston 47, Tulane 7; 12-23-74—North Caro. St. 31, Houston 31; 12-27-75—Texas 38, Colorado 21; 12-31-76—Nebraska 27, Texas Tech 24; 12-31-77—Southern Cal 47, Texas A&M 28; 12-31-78—Stanford 25, Georgia 22; 12-31-79—Purdue 27, Tennessee 22; 12-31-80—North Caro. 16, Texas 7; 12-31-81—Michigan 33, UCLA 14; 12-31-82—Arkansas 28, Florida 24; 12-31-83—Oklahoma St. 24, Baylor 14; 12-31-84—West Va. 31, Texas Christian 14; 12-31-85—Air Force 24, Texas 16; 12-31-86—Baylor 21, Colorado 9; 12-31-87—Texas 32, Pittsburgh 27

Bluegrass (Louisville, Ky.): 12-13-58—Oklahoma St. 15, Florida St. 6

Camellia (Lafayette, La.): 12-30-48—Hardin-Simmons 49, Wichita St. 12

Cherry (Pontiac, Mich.): 12-22-84—Army 10, Michigan St. 6; 12-21-85—Maryland 35, Syracuse 18

Delta (Memphis, Tenn.): 1-1-48—Mississippi 13, Texas Christian 9; 1-1-49—William & Mary 20, Oklahoma St. 0

Dixie (Birmingham, Ala.): 1-1-48—Arkansas 21, William & Mary 19; 1-1-49—Baylor 20, Wake Forest 7

Dixie Classic (Dallas, Tex.): 1-2-22—Texas A&M 22, Centre 14; 1-1-25—West Va. Wesleyan 9, Southern Methodist 7; 1-1-34—Arkansas 7, Centenary 7

Fort Worth Classic (Fort Worth, Tex.): 1-1-21—Centre 63, Texas Christian 7

Garden State (East Rutherford, N.J.): 12-16-78—Arizona St. 34, Rutgers 18; 12-15-79—Temple 28, California 17; 12-14-80—Houston 35, Navy 0

Gotham (New York, N.Y.): 12-9-61—Baylor 24, Utah St. 9; 12-15-62—Nebraska 36, Miami (Fla.) 34

Great Lakes (Cleveland, Ohio): 12-6-47—Kentucky 24, Villanova 14

Harbor (San Diego, Cal.): 1-1-47—New Mexico 13, Montana St. 13; 1-1-48—Hardin-Simmons 53, San Diego St. 0; 1-1-49—Villanova 27, Nevada 7

Los Angeles Christmas Festival (Los Angeles, Cal.): 12-25-24—Southern Cal 20, Missouri 7

Mercy (Los Angeles, Cal.): 11-23-61—Fresno St. 36, Bowling Green 6

Oil (Houston, Tex.): 1-1-46—Georgia 20, Tulsa 6; 1-1-47—Georgia Tech 41, St. Mary's (Cal.) 19

Pasadena (called Junior Rose in 1967) (Pasadena, Cal.): 12-2-67—West Tex. St. 35, Cal St. Northridge 13; 12-6-69—San Diego St. 28, Boston U. 7; 12-19-70—Louisville 24, Long Beach St. 24; 12-18-71—Memphis St. 28, San Jose St. 9

Presidential Cup (College Park, Md.): 12-9-50—Texas A&M 40, Georgia 20
Raisin (Fresno, Cal.): 1-1-46—Drake 13, Fresno St. 12; 1-1-47—San Jose St. 20, Utah St. 0; 1-1-48—Pacific (Cal.) 26, Wichita St. 14; 1-1-49—Occidental 21, Colorado St. 20; 12-31-49—San Jose St. 20, Texas Tech 13
Salad (Phoenix, Ariz.): 1-1-48—Nevada 13, North Texas 6; 1-1-49—Drake 14, Arizona 13; 1-1-50—Xavier (Ohio) 33, Arizona St. 21; 1-1-51—Miami (Ohio) 34, Arizona St. 21; 1-1-52—Houston 26, Dayton 21
San Diego East-West Christmas Classic (San Diego, Cal.): 12-26-21—Centre 38, Arizona 0; 12-25-22—West Va. 21, Gonzaga 13
Shrine (Little Rock, Ark.): 12-18-48—Hardin-Simmons 40, Ouachita Baptist 12

OTHER MAJOR POSTSEASON GAMES

There was a proliferation of postseason benefit games specially scheduled at the conclusion of the regular season during the Great Depression (principally in 1931) to raise money for relief of the unemployed in response to the President's Committee on Mobilization of Relief Resources and for other charitable causes.

The exact number of these games is unknown, but it is estimated that more than 100 college games were played nationwide during this period, often irrespective of the competing teams' records. Proceeds went to the benefit of the emergency relief for unemployment and numerous charities.

Most notable among these postseason games were the Tennessee-New York U. game of 1931 and the Army-Navy contests of 1930 and 1931 (the two academies had severed athletics relations during the 1928-31 period and did not meet in regular-season play). All three games were played before huge crowds in New York City's Yankee Stadium.

Following is a list of the principal postseason benefit and charity games involving at least one major college. Not included (nor included in all-time team won-lost records) are several special feature, same-day double-header tournaments in 1931 in which four participating teams were paired to play halves or modified quarters.

Date	Site	Opposing Teams
12-6-30	New York	Colgate 7, New York U. 0
12-13-30	New York	Army 6, Navy 0
11-28-31	Kansas City	Temple 38, Missouri 6
11-28-31	Chicago	Purdue 7, Northwestern 0
11-28-31	Minneapolis	Minnesota 19, Ohio St. 7
11-28-31	Ann Arbor	Michigan 16, Wisconsin 0
11-28-31	Philadelphia	Penn St. 31, Lehigh 0
12-2-31	Chattanooga	Alabama 49, Tenn.-Chatt. 0
12-3-31	Brooklyn	Manhattan 7, Rutgers 6
12-5-31	Denver	Nebraska 20, Colorado St. 7
12-5-31	Pittsburgh	Carnegie Tech 0, Duquesne 0
12-5-31	New York	Tennessee 13, New York U. 0
12-5-31	St. Louis	St. Louis 31, Missouri 6
12-5-31	Topeka	Kansas 6, Washburn 0
12-5-31	Wichita	Kansas St. 20, Wichita St. 6
12-5-31	Columbia	Centre 9, South Caro. 7
12-5-31	Norman	Oklahoma City 6, Oklahoma 0
12-12-31	New York	Army 17, Navy 7
12-12-31	Tulsa	Oklahoma 20, Tulsa 7
1-2-33	El Paso	Southern Methodist 26, UTEP 0
12-8-34	St. Louis	Southern Methodist 7, Washington (Mo.) 0

COACHES WITH MOST BOWL VICTORIES

	Wins	Record		Wins	Record
Paul "Bear" Bryant	15	15-12-2	Darrell Royal	8	8-7-1
*Joe Paterno	14	14-7-1	Vince Dooley	8	8-10-2
*Bobby Bowden	11	11-3-1	*Tom Osborne	8	8-11
*Don James	10	10-4	Bob Devaney	7	7-3
John Vaught	10	10-8	Dan Devine	7	7-3
Bobby Dodd	9	9-4	Charlie McClendon	7	7-6
*Johnny Majors	9	9-7			
*Terry Donahue	8	8-2-1			
Barry Switzer	8	8-5			
*Lou Holtz	8	8-6-2			

* *Active coach.*

ALL-TIME MAJOR BOWL-GAME COACHING HISTORY

A total of 390 coaches have head-coached in history's 616 major bowl games (the term "major bowl" is defined above the alphabetical list of team bowl records). Below is an alphabetical list of all 390 bowl coaches, with their alma mater and year, their birth date, and their game-by-game bowl records, with name and date of each bowl, opponent, final score (own score first) and opposing coach (in parentheses). A handful coached service teams or colleges never in the major category but are included because they coached against a major team in a major bowl.

JIM AIKEN, 0-1-0   (Wash. & Jeff. '22)   b 5-26-99
Oregon	Cotton 1-1-49	Southern Methodist 12-21 (Matty Bell)

FRED AKERS, 2-8-0   (Arkansas '60)   b 3-17-38
Wyoming	Fiesta 12-19-76	Oklahoma 7-41 (Barry Switzer)
Texas	Cotton 1-2-78	Notre Dame 10-38 (Dan Devine)
Texas	Sun 12-23-78	Maryland 42-0 (Jerry Claiborne)
Texas	Sun 12-22-79	Washington 7-14 (Don James)
Texas	Bluebonnet 12-31-80	North Caro. 7-16 (Dick Crum)
Texas	Cotton 1-1-82	Alabama 14-12 (Paul "Bear" Bryant)
Texas	Sun 12-25-82	North Caro. 10-26 (Dick Crum)
Texas	Cotton 1-2-84	Georgia 9-10 (Vince Dooley)
Texas	Freedom 12-26-84	Iowa 17-55 (Hayden Fry)
Texas	Bluebonnet 12-31-85	Air Force 16-24 (Fisher DeBerry)

BILL ALEXANDER, 3-2-0   (Georgia Tech '12)   b 6-6-89
Georgia Tech	Rose 1-1-29	California 8-7 (Clarence "Nibs" Price)
Georgia Tech	Orange 1-1-40	Missouri 21-7 (Don Faurot)
Georgia Tech	Cotton 1-1-43	Texas 7-14 (Dana Bible)
Georgia Tech	Sugar 1-1-44	Tulsa 20-18 (Henry Frnka)
Georgia Tech	Orange 1-1-45	Tulsa 12-26 (Henry Frnka)

LEONARD "STUB" ALLISON, 1-0-0   (Carleton '17)   b 1892
California	Rose 1-1-38	Alabama 13-0 (Frank Thomas)

MIKE ARCHER, 1-1-0   (Miami, Fla. '75)   b 7-26-53
Louisiana St.	Gator 12-31-87	South Caro. 30-13 (Joe Morrison)
Louisiana St.	Hall of Fame 1-2-89	Syracuse 10-23 (Dick MacPherson)

IKE ARMSTRONG, 1-0-0   (Drake '23)   b 6-8-95
Utah	Sun 1-2-39	New Mexico 16-0 (Ted Shipkey)

BILL ARNSPARGER, 0-3-0   (Miami, Ohio '50)   b 12-16-26
Louisiana St.	Sugar 1-1-85	Nebraska 10-28 (Tom Osborne)
Louisiana St.	Liberty 12-27-85	Baylor 7-21 (Grant Teaff)
Louisiana St.	Sugar 1-1-87	Nebraska 15-30 (Tom Osborne)

CHARLEY BACHMAN, 0-1-0   (Notre Dame '17)   b 12-1-92
Michigan St.	Orange 1-1-38	Auburn 0-6 (Jack Meagher)

ENOCH BAGSHAW, 0-1-1   (Washington '08)   b 1884
Washington	Rose 1-1-24	Navy 14-14 (Bob Folwell)
Washington	Rose 1-1-26	Alabama 19-20 (Wallace Wade)

GEORGE BARCLAY, 0-1-0   (North Caro. '35)   b 5-14-11
Wash. & Lee	Gator 1-1-51	Wyoming 7-20 (Bowden Wyatt)

BILL BARNES, 0-1-0   (Tennessee '41)   b 10-20-17
UCLA	Rose 1-1-62	Minnesota 3-21 (Murray Warmath)

WILLIS BARNES, 1-1-1   (Nebraska)   b 10-22-00
New Mexico	Sun 1-1-44	Southwestern (Tex.) 0-7 (R.M. Medley)
New Mexico	Sun 1-1-46	Denver 34-24 (Clyde "Cac" Hubbard)
New Mexico	Harbor 1-1-47	Montana St. 13-13 (Clyde Carpenter)

JOHN BARNHILL, 2-1-1   (Tennessee '28)   b 2-21-03
Tennessee	Sugar 1-1-43	Tulsa 14-7 (Henry Frnka)
Tennessee	Rose 1-1-45	Southern Cal 0-25 (Jeff Cravath)
Arkansas	Cotton 1-1-47	Louisiana St. 0-0 (Bernie Moore)
Arkansas	Dixie 1-1-48	William & Mary 21-19 (Rube McCray)

BILL BATTLE, 4-1-0   (Alabama '63)   b 12-8-41
Tennessee	Sugar 1-1-71	Air Force 34-13 (Ben Martin)
Tennessee	Liberty 12-20-71	Arkansas 14-13 (Frank Broyles)
Tennessee	Bluebonnet 12-30-72	Louisiana St. 24-17 (Charlie McClendon)
Tennessee	Gator 12-29-73	Texas Tech 19-28 (Jim Carlen)
Tennessee	Liberty 12-16-74	Maryland 7-3 (Jerry Claiborne)

SAMMY BAUGH, 0-1-0   (Texas Christian '37)   b 3-17-14
Hardin-Simmons	Sun 12-31-58	Wyoming 6-14 (Bob Devaney)

ALEX BELL, 1-1-0   (Villanova '38)   b 8-12-15
Villanova	Sun 12-20-61	Wichita St. 17-9 (Hank Foldberg)
Villanova	Liberty 12-15-62	Oregon St. 0-6 (Tommy Prothro)

MATTY BELL, 1-1-1   (Centre '20)   b 2-22-99
Southern Methodist . .	Rose 1-1-36	Stanford 0-7 (Claude "Tiny" Thornhill)

Southern Methodist ..	Cotton 1-1-48	Penn St. 13-13 (Bob Higgins)
Southern Methodist ..	Cotton 1-1-49	Oregon 21-13 (Jim Aiken)

EMORY BELLARD, 2-3-0 (Southwest Tex. St. '49) b 12-17-27

Texas A&M...........	Liberty 12-22-75	Southern Cal 0-20 (John McKay)
Texas A&M...........	Sun 1-2-77	Florida 37-14 (Doug Dickey)
Texas A&M...........	Bluebonnet 12-31-77	Southern Cal 28-47 (John Robinson)
Mississippi St........	Sun 12-27-80	Nebraska 17-31 (Tom Osborne)
Mississippi St........	Hall of Fame 12-31-81	Kansas 10-0 (Don Fambrough)

ARTHUR "DUTCH" BERGMAN, 1-0-1 (Notre Dame '20) b 2-23-95

Catholic..............	Orange 1-1-36	Mississippi 20-19 (Ed Walker)
Catholic..............	Sun 1-1-40	Arizona St. 0-0 (Millard "Dixie" Howell)

HUGO BEZDEK, 1-1-0 (Chicago '06) b 4-1-84

Oregon	Rose 1-1-17	Pennsylvania 14-0 (Bob Folwell)
Penn St..............	Rose 1-1-23	Southern Cal 3-14 (Elmer "Gus" Henderson)

DANA BIBLE, 3-0-1 (Carson-Newman '12) b 10-8-91

Texas A&M...........	Dixie Classic 1-2-22	Centre 22-14 (Charley Moran)
Texas	Cotton 1-1-43	Georgia Tech 14-7 (Bill Alexander)
Texas	Cotton 1-1-44	Randolph Field 7-7 (Frank Tritico)
Texas	Cotton 1-1-46	Missouri 40-27 (Chauncey Simpson)

JACK BICKNELL, 2-2-0 (Montclair St. '60) b 2-20-38

Boston College	Tangerine 12-18-82	Auburn 26-33 (Pat Dye)
Boston College	Liberty 12-29-83	Notre Dame 18-19 (Gerry Faust)
Boston College	Cotton 1-1-85	Houston 45-28 (Bill Yeoman)
Boston College	Hall of Fame 12-23-86	Georgia 27-24 (Vince Dooley)

BERNIE BIERMAN, 0-1-0 (Minnesota '16) b 3-11-94

Tulane................	Rose 1-1-32	Southern Cal 12-21 (Howard Jones)

GARY BLACKNEY, 1-0-0 (Connecticut '67) b 12-10-55

Bowling Green	California Raisin 12-14-91	Fresno St. 28-21 (Jim Sweeney)

BOBBY BOWDEN, 11-3-1 (Samford '53) b 11-8-29

West Va...............	Peach 12-29-72	North Caro. St. 13-49 (Lou Holtz)
West Va...............	Peach 12-31-75	North Caro. St. 13-10 (Lou Holtz)
Florida St.	Tangerine 12-23-77	Texas Tech 40-17 (Steve Sloan)
Florida St.	Orange 1-1-80	Oklahoma 7-24 (Barry Switzer)
Florida St.	Orange 1-1-81	Oklahoma 17-18 (Barry Switzer)
Florida St.	Gator 12-30-82	West Va. 31-12 (Don Nehlen)
Florida St.	Peach 12-30-83	North Caro. 28-3 (Dick Crum)
Florida St.	Fla. Citrus 12-22-84	Georgia 17-17 (Vince Dooley)
Florida St.	Gator 12-30-85	Oklahoma St. 34-23 (Pat Jones)
Florida St.	All-American 12-31-86	Indiana 27-13 (Bill Mallory)
Florida St.	Fiesta 1-1-88	Nebraska 31-28 (Tom Osborne)
Florida St.	Sugar 1-2-89	Auburn 13-7 (Pat Dye)
Florida St.	Fiesta 1-1-90	Nebraska 41-17 (Tom Osborne)
Florida St.	Blockbuster 12-28-90	Penn St. 24-17 (Joe Paterno)
Florida St.	Cotton 1-1-92	Texas A&M 10-2 (R.C. Slocum)

JEFF BOWER, 0-1-0 (Southern Miss. '76) b 5-28-53

Southern Miss........	All-American 12-28-90	North Caro. St. 27-31 (Dick Sheridan)

SAM BOYD, 1-0-0 (Baylor '38) b 8-12-15

Baylor................	Sugar 1-1-57	Tennessee 13-7 (Bowden Wyatt)

WESLEY BRADSHAW, 0-1-0 (Baylor '23) b 11-26-98

Ouachita Baptist	Shrine 12-18-48	Hardin-Simmons 12-40 (Warren Woodson)

BILLY BREWER, 2-2-0 (Mississippi '61) b 10-8-35

Mississippi	Independence 12-10-83	Air Force 3-9 (Ken Hatfield)
Mississippi	Independence 12-20-86	Texas Tech 20-17 (Spike Dykes)
Mississippi	All-American 12-29-89	Air Force 42-29 (Fisher DeBerry)
Mississippi	Gator 1-1-91	Michigan 3-35 (Gary Moeller)

JOHN BRIDGERS, 2-1-0 (Auburn '47) b 1-13-22

Baylor................	Gator 12-31-60	Florida 12-13 (Ray Graves)
Baylor................	Gotham 12-9-61	Utah St. 24-9 (John Ralston)
Baylor................	Bluebonnet 12-21-63	Louisiana St. 14-7 (Charlie McClendon)

RICH BROOKS, 1-1-0 (Oregon St. '63) b 8-20-41

Oregon	Independence 12-16-89	Tulsa 27-24 (Dave Rader)
Oregon	Freedom 12-29-90	Colorado St. 31-32 (Earle Bruce)

J. O. "BUDDY" BROTHERS, 0-1-0 (Texas Tech '31) b 5-29-09

Tulsa	Gator 1-1-53	Florida 13-14 (Bob Woodruff)

MACK BROWN, 0-1-0 (Florida St. '74) b 8-27-51

Tulane................	Independence 12-19-87	Washington 12-24 (Don James)

FRANK BROYLES, 4-6-0 (Georgia Tech '47) b 12-26-24

Arkansas	Gator 1-2-60	Georgia Tech 14-7 (Bobby Dodd)
Arkansas	Cotton 1-2-61	Duke 6-7 (Bill Murray)
Arkansas	Sugar 1-1-62	Alabama 3-10 (Paul "Bear" Bryant)

Arkansas	Sugar 1-1-63	Mississippi 13-17 (John Vaught)
Arkansas	Cotton 1-1-65	Nebraska 10-7 (Bob Devaney)
Arkansas	Cotton 1-1-66	Louisiana St. 7-14 (Charlie McClendon)
Arkansas	Sugar 1-1-69	Georgia 16-2 (Vince Dooley)
Arkansas	Sugar 1-1-70	Mississippi 22-27 (John Vaught)
Arkansas	Liberty 12-20-71	Tennessee 13-14 (Bill Battle)
Arkansas	Cotton 1-1-76	Georgia 31-10 (Vince Dooley)

EARLE BRUCE, 7-5-0   (Ohio St. '53)   b 3-8-31

Tampa	Tangerine 12-29-72	Kent 21-18 (Don James)
Iowa St.	Peach 12-31-77	North Caro. St. 14-24 (Bo Rein)
Iowa St.	Hall of Fame 12-20-78	Texas A&M 12-28 (Tom Wilson)
Ohio St.	Rose 1-1-80	Southern Cal 16-17 (John Robinson)
Ohio St.	Fiesta 12-26-80	Penn St. 19-31 (Joe Paterno)
Ohio St.	Liberty 12-30-81	Navy 31-28 (George Welsh)
Ohio St.	Holiday 12-17-82	Brigham Young 47-17 (LaVell Edwards)
Ohio St.	Fiesta 1-2-84	Pittsburgh 28-23 (Foge Fazio)
Ohio St.	Rose 1-1-85	Southern Cal 17-20 (Ted Tollner)
Ohio St.	Fla. Citrus 12-28-85	Brigham Young 10-7 (LaVell Edwards)
Ohio St.	Cotton 1-1-87	Texas A&M 28-12 (Jackie Sherrill)
Colorado St.	Freedom 12-29-90	Oregon 32-31 (Rich Brooks)

MILT BRUHN, 0-2-0   (Minnesota '35)   b 7-28-12

Wisconsin	Rose 1-1-60	Washington 8-44 (Jim Owens)
Wisconsin	Rose 1-2-63	Southern Cal 37-42 (John McKay)

MIKE BRUMBELOW, 2-1-0   (Texas Christian '30)   b 7-13-06

UTEP	Sun 1-1-54	Southern Miss. 37-14 (Thad "Pie" Vann)
UTEP	Sun 1-1-55	Florida St. 47-20 (Tom Nugent)
UTEP	Sun 1-1-57	Geo. Washington 0-13 (Eugene "Bo" Sherman)

PAUL "BEAR" BRYANT, 15-12-2   (Alabama '36)   b 9-11-13

Kentucky	Great Lakes 12-6-47	Villanova 24-14 (Jordan Oliver)
Kentucky	Orange 1-2-50	Santa Clara 13-21 (Len Casanova)
Kentucky	Sugar 1-1-51	Oklahoma 13-7 (Bud Wilkinson)
Kentucky	Cotton 1-1-52	Texas Christian 20-7 (Leo "Dutch" Meyer)
Texas A&M	Gator 12-28-57	Tennessee 0-3 (Bowden Wyatt)
Alabama	Liberty 12-19-59	Penn St. 0-7 (Charles "Rip" Engle)
Alabama	Bluebonnet 12-17-60	Texas 3-3 (Darrell Royal)
Alabama	Sugar 1-1-62	Arkansas 10-3 (Frank Broyles)
Alabama	Orange 1-1-63	Oklahoma 17-0 (Bud Wilkinson)
Alabama	Sugar 1-1-64	Mississippi 12-7 (John Vaught)
Alabama	Orange 1-1-65	Texas 17-21 (Darrell Royal)
Alabama	Orange 1-1-66	Nebraska 39-28 (Bob Devaney)
Alabama	Sugar 1-2-67	Nebraska 34-7 (Bob Devaney)
Alabama	Cotton 1-1-68	Texas A&M 16-20 (Gene Stallings)
Alabama	Gator 12-28-68	Missouri 10-35 (Dan Devine)
Alabama	Liberty 12-13-69	Colorado 33-47 (Eddie Crowder)
Alabama	Bluebonnet 12-31-70	Oklahoma 24-24 (Chuck Fairbanks)
Alabama	Orange 1-1-72	Nebraska 6-38 (Bob Devaney)
Alabama	Cotton 1-1-73	Texas 13-17 (Darrell Royal)
Alabama	Sugar 12-31-73	Notre Dame 23-24 (Ara Parseghian)
Alabama	Orange 1-1-75	Notre Dame 11-13 (Ara Parseghian)
Alabama	Sugar 12-31-75	Penn St. 13-6 (Joe Paterno)
Alabama	Liberty 12-20-76	UCLA 36-6 (Terry Donahue)
Alabama	Sugar 1-2-78	Ohio St. 35-6 (Woody Hayes)
Alabama	Sugar 1-1-79	Penn St. 14-7 (Joe Paterno)
Alabama	Sugar 1-1-80	Arkansas 24-9 (Lou Holtz)
Alabama	Cotton 1-1-81	Baylor 30-2 (Grant Teaff)
Alabama	Cotton 1-1-82	Texas 12-14 (Fred Akers)
Alabama	Liberty 12-29-82	Illinois 21-15 (Mike White)

FRANK BURNS, 0-1-0   (Rutgers '49)   b 3-16-28

Rutgers	Garden State 12-16-78	Arizona St. 18-34 (Frank Kush)

LEON BURTNETT, 0-1-0   (Southwestern, Kan. '65)   b 5-30-43

Purdue	Peach 12-31-84	Virginia 24-27 (George Welsh)

WALLY BUTTS, 5-2-1   (Mercer '28)   b 2-7-05

Georgia	Orange 1-1-42	Texas Christian 40-26 (Leo "Dutch" Meyer)
Georgia	Rose 1-1-43	UCLA 9-0 (Edwin "Babe" Horrell)
Georgia	Oil 1-1-46	Tulsa 20-6 (Henry Frnka)
Georgia	Sugar 1-1-47	North Caro. 20-10 (Carl Snavely)
Georgia	Gator 1-1-48	Maryland 20-20 (Jim Tatum)
Georgia	Orange 1-1-49	Texas 28-41 (Blair Cherry)
Georgia	Presidential Cup 12-9-50	Texas A&M 20-40 (Harry Stiteler)
Georgia	Orange 1-1-60	Missouri 14-0 (Dan Devine)

EDDIE CAMERON, 1-0-0   (Wash. & Lee '24)   b 4-22-02

Duke	Sugar 1-1-45	Alabama 29-26 (Frank Thomas)

FRANK CAMP, 1-0-0   (Transylvania '30)   b 12-23-05
Louisville . . . .   Sun 1-1-58   Drake 34-20 (Warren Gaer)

JIM CARLEN, 2-5-1   (Georgia Tech '55)   b 7-11-33
West Va. . . . .   Peach 12-30-69   South Caro. 14-3 (Paul Dietzel)
Texas Tech . . . .   Sun 12-19-70   Georgia Tech 9-17 (Bud Carson)
Texas Tech . . . .   Sun 12-30-72   North Caro. 28-32 (Bill Dooley)
Texas Tech . . . .   Gator 12-29-73   Tennessee 28-19 (Bill Battle)
Texas Tech . . . .   Peach 12-28-74   Vanderbilt 6-6 (Steve Sloan)
South Caro. . . . .   Tangerine 12-20-75   Miami (Ohio) 7-20 (Dick Crum)
South Caro. . . . .   Hall of Fame 12-29-79   Missouri 14-24 (Warren Powers)
South Caro. . . . .   Gator 12-29-80   Pittsburgh 8-37 (Jackie Sherrill)

CLYDE CARPENTER, 0-0-1   (Montana '32)   b 4-17-08
Montana St. . . . .   Harbor 1-1-47   New Mexico 13-13 (Willis Barnes)

BUD CARSON, 1-1-0   (North Caro. '52)   b 4-28-30
Georgia Tech . . . .   Sun 12-19-70   Texas Tech 17-9 (Jim Carlen)
Georgia Tech . . . .   Peach 12-30-71   Mississippi 18-41 (Billy Kinard)

LEN CASANOVA, 2-2-0   (Santa Clara '27)   b 6-12-05
Santa Clara . . . .   Orange 1-2-50   Kentucky 21-13 (Paul "Bear" Bryant)
Oregon . . . .   Rose 1-1-58   Ohio St. 7-10 (Woody Hayes)
Oregon . . . .   Liberty 12-17-60   Penn St. 12-41 (Charles "Rip" Engle)
Oregon . . . .   Sun 12-31-63   Southern Methodist 21-14 (Hayden Fry)

MILES CASTEEL, 0-1-0   (Kalamazoo '25)   b 12-30-96
Arizona . . . .   Salad 1-1-49   Drake 13-14 (Al Kawal)

PETE CAWTHON, 0-2-0   (Southwestern, Tex. '20)   b 8-24-98
Texas Tech . . . .   Sun 1-1-38   West Va. 6-7 (Marshall "Little Sleepy" Glenn)
Texas Tech . . . .   Cotton 1-2-39   St. Mary's (Cal.) 13-20 (Edward "Slip" Madigan)

BLAIR CHERRY, 2-1-0   (Texas Christian '24)   b 9-7-01
Texas . . . .   Sugar 1-1-48   Alabama 27-7 (Harold "Red" Drew)
Texas . . . .   Orange 1-1-49   Georgia 41-28 (Wally Butts)
Texas . . . .   Cotton 1-1-51   Tennessee 14-20 (Bob Neyland)

JERRY CLAIBORNE, 3-8-0   (Kentucky '50)   b 8-26-28
Virginia Tech . . . .   Liberty 12-10-66   Miami (Fla.) 7-14 (Charlie Tate)
Virginia Tech . . . .   Liberty 12-14-68   Mississippi 17-34 (John Vaught)
Maryland . . . .   Peach 12-28-73   Georgia 16-17 (Vince Dooley)
Maryland . . . .   Liberty 12-16-74   Tennessee 3-7 (Bill Battle)
Maryland . . . .   Gator 12-29-75   Florida 13-0 (Doug Dickey)
Maryland . . . .   Cotton 1-1-77   Houston 21-30 (Bill Yeoman)
Maryland . . . .   Hall of Fame 12-22-77   Minnesota 17-7 (Cal Stoll)
Maryland . . . .   Sun 12-23-78   Texas 0-42 (Fred Akers)
Maryland . . . .   Tangerine 12-20-80   Florida 20-35 (Charley Pell)
Kentucky . . . .   Hall of Fame 12-22-83   West Va. 16-20 (Don Nehlen)
Kentucky . . . .   Hall of Fame 12-29-84   Wisconsin 20-19 (Dave McClain)

CECIL COLEMAN, 1-0-0   (Arizona St. '50)   b 4-12-26
Fresno St. . . . .   Mercy 11-23-61   Bowling Green 36-6 (Doyt Perry)

BOBBY COLLINS, 3-2-0   (Mississippi St. '55)   b 10-25-33
Southern Miss. . . . .   Independence 12-13-70   McNeese St. 16-14 (Ernie Duplechin)
Southern Miss. . . . .   Tangerine 12-19-81   Missouri 17-19 (Warren Powers)
Southern Methodist . .   Cotton 1-1-83   Pittsburgh 7-3 (Foge Fazio)
Southern Methodist . .   Sun 12-24-83   Alabama 7-28 (Ray Perkins)
Southern Methodist . .   Aloha 12-29-84   Notre Dame 27-20 (Gerry Faust)

JOHN COOPER, 2-4-0   (Iowa St. '62)   b 7-2-37
Arizona St. . . . .   Holiday 12-22-85   Arkansas 17-18 (Ken Hatfield)
Arizona St. . . . .   Rose 1-1-87   Michigan 22-15 (Glenn "Bo" Schembechler)
Arizona St. . . . .   Freedom 12-30-87   Air Force 33-28 (Fisher DeBerry)
Ohio St. . . . .   Hall of Fame 1-1-90   Auburn 14-31 (Pat Dye)
Ohio St. . . . .   Liberty 12-27-90   Air Force 11-23 (Fisher DeBerry)
Ohio St. . . . .   Hall of Fame 1-1-92   Syracuse 17-24 (Paul Pasqualoni)

LEE CORSO, 1-0-1   (Florida St. '57)   b 8-7-35
Louisville . . . .   Pasadena 12-19-70   Long Beach St. 24-24 (Jim Stangeland)
Indiana . . . .   Holiday 12-21-79   Brigham Young 38-37 (LaVell Edwards)

GENE CORUM, 0-1-0   (West Va. '48)   b 5-29-21
West Va. . . . .   Liberty 12-19-64   Utah 6-32 (Ray Nagel)

DON CORYELL, 1-0-0   (Washington '50)   b 10-17-24
San Diego St. . . . .   Pasadena 12-6-69   Boston U. 28-7 (Larry Naviaux)

TED COX, 1-0-0   (Minnesota '26)   b 6-30-03
Tulane . . . .   Sugar 1-1-35   Temple 20-14 (Glenn "Pop" Warner)

JEFF CRAVATH, 2-2-0   (Southern Cal '27)   b 2-5-05
Southern Cal . . . .   Rose 1-1-44   Washington 29-0 (Ralph "Pest" Welch)
Southern Cal . . . .   Rose 1-1-45   Tennessee 25-0 (John Barnhill)
Southern Cal . . . .   Rose 1-1-46   Alabama 14-34 (Frank Thomas)

Southern Cal .... Rose 1-1-48   Michigan 0-49 (H. O. "Fritz" Crisler)
H. O. "FRITZ" CRISLER, 1-0-0   (Chicago '22)   b 1-2-99
Michigan .... Rose 1-1-48   Southern Cal 49-0 (Jeff Cravath)
EDDIE CROWDER, 3-2-0   (Oklahoma '55)   b 8-26-31
Colorado .... Bluebonnet 12-23-67   Miami (Fla.) 31-21 (Charlie Tate)
Colorado .... Liberty 12-13-69   Alabama 47-33 (Paul "Bear" Bryant)
Colorado .... Liberty 12-12-70   Tulane 3-17 (Jim Pittman)
Colorado .... Bluebonnet 12-31-71   Houston 29-17 (Bill Yeoman)
Colorado .... Gator 12-20-72   Auburn 3-24 (Ralph "Shug" Jordan)
JACK CROWE, 0-1-0   (Ala.-Birmingham '70)   b 4-6-48
Arkansas .... Independence 12-29-91   Georgia 15-24 (Ray Goff)
JIM CROWLEY, 1-1-0   (Notre Dame '25)   b 9-10-02
Fordham .... Cotton 1-1-41   Texas A&M 12-13 (Homer Norton)
Fordham .... Sugar 1-1-42   Missouri 2-0 (Don Faurot)
DICK CRUM, 6-2-0   (Mount Union '57)   b 4-29-34
Miami (Ohio) .... Tangerine 12-21-74   Georgia 21-10 (Vince Dooley)
Miami (Ohio) .... Tangerine 12-20-75   South Caro. 20-7 (Jim Carlen)
North Caro. .... Gator 12-28-79   Michigan 17-15 (Glenn "Bo" Schembechler)
North Caro. .... Bluebonnet 12-31-80   Texas 16-7 (Fred Akers)
North Caro. .... Gator 12-28-81   Arkansas 31-27 (Lou Holtz)
North Caro. .... Sun 12-25-82   Texas 26-10 (Fred Akers)
North Caro. .... Peach 12-30-83   Florida St. 3-28 (Bobby Bowden)
North Caro. .... Aloha 12-27-86   Arizona 21-30 (Larry Smith)
FRAN CURCI, 1-0-0   (Miami, Fla. '60)   b 6-11-38
Kentucky .... Peach 12-31-76   North Caro. 21-0 (Bill Dooley)
BILL CURRY, 2-2-0   (Georgia Tech '65)   b 10-21-42
Georgia Tech .... All-American 12-31-85   Michigan St. 17-14 (George Perles)
Alabama .... Hall of Fame 1-2-88   Michigan 24-28 (Glenn "Bo" Schembechler)
Alabama .... Sun 12-24-88   Army 29-28 (Jim Young)
Alabama .... Sugar 1-1-90   Miami (Fla.) 25-33 (Dennis Erickson)
JACK "CACTUS JACK" CURTICE, 1-1-0   (Transylvania '30)   b 5-24-07
UTEP .... Sun 1-1-49   West Va. 12-21 (Dud DeGroot)
UTEP .... Sun 1-2-50   Georgetown 33-20 (Bob Margarita)
JOHN "OX" Da GROSA, 0-1-0   (Colgate '26)   b 2-17-02
Holy Cross .... Orange 1-1-46   Miami (Fla.) 6-13 (Jack Harding)
GARY DARNELL, 0-1-0   (Oklahoma St. '71)   b 10-15-48
Florida .... Freedom 12-29-89   Washington 7-34 (Don James)
DUFFY DAUGHERTY, 1-1-0   (Syracuse '40)   b 9-8-15
Michigan St. .... Rose 1-2-56   UCLA 17-14 (Henry "Red" Sanders)
Michigan St. .... Rose 1-1-66   UCLA 12-14 (Tommy Prothro)
BOB DAVIS, 0-1-0   (Utah '30)   b 2-13-08
Colorado St. .... Raisin 1-1-49   Occidental 20-21 (Roy Dennis)
PAUL DAVIS, 1-0-0   (Mississippi '47)   b 2-3-22
Mississippi St. .... Liberty 12-21-63   North Caro St. 16-12 (Earle Edwards)
LOWELL "RED" DAWSON, 0-1-0   (Tulane '30)   b 12-26-06
Tulane .... Sugar 1-1-40   Texas A&M 13-14 (Homer Norton)
FISHER DeBERRY, 4-2-0   (Wofford '60)   b 9-9-38
Air Force .... Independence 12-15-84   Virginia Tech 23-7 (Bill Dooley)
Air Force .... Bluebonnet 12-31-85   Texas 24-16 (Fred Akers)
Air Force .... Freedom 12-30-87   Arizona St. 28-33 (John Cooper)
Air Force .... Liberty 12-29-89   Mississippi 29-42 (Billy Brewer)
Air Force .... Liberty 12-27-90   Ohio St. 23-11 (John Cooper)
Air Force .... Liberty 12-29-91   Mississippi St. 38-15 (Jackie Sherrill)
DUD DeGROOT, 1-0-0   (Stanford '24)   b 11-20-95
West Va. .... Sun 1-1-49   UTEP 21-12 (Jack "Cactus Jack" Curtice)
ROY DENNIS, 1-0-0   (Occidental '33)   b 5-13-05
Occidental .... Raisin 1-1-49   Colorado St. 21-20 (Bob Davis)
HERB DEROMEDI, 0-1-0   (Michigan '60)   b 5-26-39
Central Mich. .... California Raisin 12-8-90 San Jose St. 24-48 (Terry Shea)
BOB DEVANEY, 7-3-0   (Alma '39)   b 4-2-15
Wyoming .... Sun 12-31-58   Hardin-Simmons 14-6 (Sammy Baugh)
Nebraska .... Gotham 12-15-62   Miami (Fla.) 36-34 (Andy Gustafson)
Nebraska .... Orange 1-1-64   Auburn 13-7 (Ralph "Shug" Jordan)
Nebraska .... Cotton 1-1-65   Arkansas 7-10 (Frank Broyles)
Nebraska .... Orange 1-1-66   Alabama 28-39 (Paul "Bear" Bryant)
Nebraska .... Sugar 1-2-67   Alabama 7-34 (Paul "Bear" Bryant)
Nebraska .... Sun 12-20-69   Georgia 45-6 (Vince Dooley)
Nebraska .... Orange 1-1-71   Louisiana St. 17-12 (Charlie McClendon)
Nebraska .... Orange 1-1-72   Alabama 38-6 (Paul "Bear" Bryant)
Nebraska .... Orange 1-1-73   Notre Dame 40-6 (Ara Parseghian)

DAN DEVINE, 7-3-0 (Minn.-Duluth '48) b 12-23-24
Missouri	Orange 1-1-60	Georgia 0-14 (Wally Butts)
Missouri	Orange 1-2-61	Navy 21-14 (Wayne Hardin)
Missouri	Bluebonnet 12-22-62	Georgia Tech 14-10 (Bobby Dodd)
Missouri	Sugar 1-1-66	Florida 20-18 (Ray Graves)
Missouri	Gator 12-28-68	Alabama 35-10 (Paul "Bear" Bryant)
Missouri	Orange 1-1-70	Penn St. 3-10 (Joe Paterno)
Notre Dame	Gator 12-27-76	Penn St. 20-9 (Joe Paterno)
Notre Dame	Cotton 1-2-78	Texas 38-10 (Fred Akers)
Notre Dame	Cotton 1-1-79	Houston 35-34 (Bill Yeoman)
Notre Dame	Sugar 1-1-81	Georgia 10-17 (Vince Dooley)

PHIL DICKENS, 1-0-0 (Tennessee '37) b 6-29-14
Wyoming	Sun 1-2-56	Texas Tech 21-14 (DeWitt Weaver)

DOUG DICKEY, 2-7-0 (Florida '54) b 6-24-32
Tennessee	Bluebonnet 12-18-65	Tulsa 27-6 (Glenn Dobbs)
Tennessee	Gator 12-31-66	Syracuse 18-12 (Ben Schwartzwalder)
Tennessee	Orange 1-1-68	Oklahoma 24-26 (Chuck Fairbanks)
Tennessee	Cotton 1-1-69	Texas 13-35 (Darrell Royal)
Tennessee	Gator 12-27-69	Florida 13-14 (Ray Graves)
Florida	Tangerine 12-22-73	Miami (Ohio) 7-16 (Bill Mallory)
Florida	Sugar 12-31-74	Nebraska 10-13 (Tom Osborne)
Florida	Gator 12-29-75	Maryland 0-13 (Jerry Claiborne)
Florida	Sun 1-2-77	Texas A&M 14-37 (Emory Bellard)

JIM DICKEY, 0-1-0 (Houston '56) b 3-22-34
Kansas St.	Independence 12-11-82	Wisconsin 3-14 (Dave McClain)

BILL "LONE STAR" DIETZ, 1-0-0 (Carlisle '12) b 8-15-85
Washington St.	Rose 1-1-16	Brown 14-0 (Ed Robinson)

PAUL DIETZEL, 2-2-0 (Miami, Ohio '48) b 9-5-24
Louisiana St.	Sugar 1-1-59	Clemson 7-0 (Frank Howard)
Louisiana St.	Sugar 1-1-60	Mississippi 0-21 (John Vaught)
Louisiana St.	Orange 1-1-62	Colorado 25-7 (Sonny Grandelius)
South Caro.	Peach 12-20-69	West Va. 3-14 (Jim Carlen)

BOBBY DOBBS, 2-0-0 (Army '46) b 10-13-22
UTEP	Sun 12-31-65	Texas Christian 13-12 (Abe Martin)
UTEP	Sun 12-30-67	Mississippi 14-7 (John Vaught)

GLENN DOBBS, 1-1-0 (Tulsa '43) b 7-12-20
Tulsa	Bluebonnet 12-19-64	Mississippi 14-7 (John Vaught)
Tulsa	Bluebonnet 12-18-65	Tennessee 6-27 (Doug Dickey)

BOBBY DODD, 9-4-0 (Tennessee '31) b 11-11-08
Georgia Tech	Oil 1-1-47	St. Mary's (Cal.) 41-19 (Jimmy Phelan)
Georgia Tech	Orange 1-1-48	Kansas 20-14 (George Sauer)
Georgia Tech	Orange 1-1-52	Baylor 17-14 (George Sauer)
Georgia Tech	Sugar 1-1-53	Mississippi 24-7 (John Vaught)
Georgia Tech	Sugar 1-1-54	West Va. 42-19 (Art Lewis)
Georgia Tech	Cotton 1-1-55	Arkansas 14-6 (Bowden Wyatt)
Georgia Tech	Sugar 1-2-56	Pittsburgh 7-0 (John Michelosen)
Georgia Tech	Gator 12-29-56	Pittsburgh 21-14 (John Michelosen)
Georgia Tech	Gator 1-2-60	Arkansas 7-14 (Frank Broyles)
Georgia Tech	Gator 12-30-61	Penn St. 15-30 (Charles "Rip" Engle)
Georgia Tech	Bluebonnet 12-22-62	Missouri 10-14 (Dan Devine)
Georgia Tech	Gator 12-31-65	Texas Tech 31-21 (J.T. King)
Georgia Tech	Orange 1-2-67	Florida 12-27 (Ray Graves)

ED DOHERTY, 0-2-0 (Boston College '44) b 7-25-18
Arizona St.	Salad 1-1-50	Xavier (Ohio) 21-33 (Ed Kluska)
Arizona St.	Salad 1-1-51	Miami (Ohio) 21-34 (Woody Hayes)

JACK DOLAND, 1-0-0 (Tulane '50) b 3-3-28
McNeese St.	Independence 12-13-76	Tulsa 20-16 (F. A. Dry)

TERRY DONAHUE, 8-2-1 (UCLA '67) b 6-24-44
UCLA	Liberty 12-30-76	Alabama 6-36 (Paul "Bear" Bryant)
UCLA	Fiesta 12-25-78	Arkansas 10-10 (Lou Holtz)
UCLA	Bluebonnet 12-31-81	Michigan 14-33 (Glenn "Bo" Schembechler)
UCLA	Rose 1-1-83	Michigan 24-14 (Glenn "Bo" Schembechler)
UCLA	Rose 1-2-84	Illinois 45-9 (Mike White)
UCLA	Fiesta 1-1-85	Miami (Fla.) 39-37 (Jimmy Johnson)
UCLA	Rose 1-1-86	Iowa 45-28 (Hayden Fry)
UCLA	Freedom 12-30-86	Brigham Young 31-10 (LaVell Edwards)
UCLA	Aloha 12-25-87	Florida 20-16 (Galen Hall)
UCLA	Cotton 1-2-89	Arkansas 17-3 (Ken Hatfield)
UCLA	John Hancock 12-31-91	Illinois 6-3 (Lou Tepper)

BILL DOOLEY, 2-7-0 (Mississippi St. '56) b 5-19-34
North Caro.	Peach 12-30-70	Arizona St. 26-48 (Frank Kush)

North Caro.	Gator 12-31-71	Georgia 3-7 (Vince Dooley)
North Caro.	Sun 12-30-72	Texas Tech 32-28 (Jim Carlen)
North Caro.	Sun 12-28-74	Mississippi St. 24-26 (Bob Tyler)
North Caro.	Peach 12-31-76	Kentucky 0-21 (Fran Curci)
North Caro.	Liberty 12-19-77	Nebraska 17-21 (Tom Osborne)
Virginia Tech	Peach 1-2-81	Miami (Fla.) 10-20 (Howard Schnellenberger)
Virginia Tech	Independence 12-15-84	Air Force 7-23 (Fisher DeBerry)
Virginia Tech	Peach 12-31-86	North Caro. St. 25-24 (Dick Sheridan)

VINCE DOOLEY, 8-10-2 (Auburn '54) b 9-4-32

Georgia	Sun 12-26-64	Texas Tech 7-0 (J. T. King)
Georgia	Cotton 12-31-66	Southern Methodist 24-9 (Hayden Fry)
Georgia	Liberty 12-16-67	North Caro. St. 7-14 (Earle Edwards)
Georgia	Sugar 1-1-69	Arkansas 2-16 (Frank Broyles)
Georgia	Sun 12-20-69	Nebraska 6-45 (Bob Devaney)
Georgia	Gator 12-31-71	North Caro. 7-3 (Bill Dooley)
Georgia	Peach 12-28-73	Maryland 17-16 (Jerry Claiborne)
Georgia	Tangerine 12-21-74	Miami (Ohio) 10-21 (Dick Crum)
Georgia	Cotton 1-1-76	Arkansas 10-31 (Frank Broyles)
Georgia	Sugar 1-1-77	Pittsburgh 3-27 (Johnny Majors)
Georgia	Bluebonnet 12-31-78	Stanford 22-25 (Bill Walsh)
Georgia	Sugar 1-1-81	Notre Dame 17-10 (Dan Devine)
Georgia	Sugar 1-1-82	Pittsburgh 20-24 (Jackie Sherrill)
Georgia	Sugar 1-1-83	Penn St. 23-27 (Joe Paterno)
Georgia	Cotton 1-2-84	Texas 10-9 (Fred Akers)
Georgia	Fla. Citrus 12-22-84	Florida St. 17-17 (Bobby Bowden)
Georgia	Sun 12-28-85	Arizona 13-13 (Larry Smith)
Georgia	Hall of Fame 12-23-86	Boston College 24-27 (Jack Bicknell)
Georgia	Liberty 12-29-87	Arkansas 20-17 (Ken Hatfield)
Georgia	Gator 1-1-89	Michigan St. 34-27 (George Perles)

CHARLES "GUS" DORAIS, 0-1-0 (Notre Dame '14) b 7-21-91

Gonzaga	San Diego East-West Christmas Classic 12-25-22	West Va. 13-21 (Clarence "Doc" Spears)

HAROLD "RED" DREW, 1-2-0 (Bates '16) b 11-9-94

Alabama	Sugar 1-1-48	Texas 7-27 (Blair Cherry)
Alabama	Orange 1-1-53	Syracuse 61-6 (Ben Schwartzwalder)
Alabama	Cotton 1-1-54	Rice 6-28 (Jess Neely)

BILL DRIVER, 0-1-0 (Missouri '09) b 11-7-83

Texas Christian	Fort Worth Classic 1-1-21	Centre 7-63 (Charley Moran)

F. A. DRY, 0-1-0 (Oklahoma St. '53) b 9-2-31

Tulsa	Independence 12-13-76	McNeese St. 16-20 (Jack Doland)

ERNIE DUPLECHIN, 0-2-0 (Louisiana Col. '55) b 7-19-32

McNeese St.	Independence 12-15-79	Syracuse 7-31 (Frank Maloney)
McNeese St.	Independence 12-13-80	Southern Miss. 14-16 (Bobby Collins)

PAT DYE, 7-2-1 (Georgia '62) b 11-6-39

East Caro.	Independence 12-16-78	Louisiana Tech 35-13 (Maxie Lambright)
Auburn	Tangerine 12-18-82	Boston College 33-26 (Jack Bicknell)
Auburn	Sugar 1-2-84	Michigan 9-7 (Glenn "Bo" Schembechler)
Auburn	Liberty 12-27-84	Arkansas 21-15 (Ken Hatfield)
Auburn	Cotton 1-1-86	Texas A&M 16-36 (Jackie Sherrill)
Auburn	Fla. Citrus 1-1-87	Southern Cal 16-7 (Ted Tollner)
Auburn	Sugar 1-1-88	Syracuse 16-16 (Dick MacPherson)
Auburn	Sugar 1-2-89	Florida St. 7-13 (Bobby Bowden)
Auburn	Hall of Fame 1-1-90	Ohio St. 31-14 (John Cooper)
Auburn	Peach 12-29-90	Indiana 27-23 (Bill Mallory)

SPIKE DYKES, 1-1-0 (Stephen F. Austin '59) b 4-15-38

Texas Tech	Independence 12-20-86	Mississippi 17-20 (Billy Brewer)
Texas Tech	All-American 12-28-89	Duke 49-21 (Steve Spurrier)

LLOYD EATON, 1-1-0 (Black Hills St. '40) b 3-23-18

Wyoming.............	Sun 12-24-66	Florida St. 28-20 (Bill Peterson)
Wyoming.............	Sugar 1-1-68	Louisiana St. 13-20 (Charlie McClendon)

BILL EDWARDS, 1-0-0 (Wittenberg '31) b 6-21-05

Case Reserve	Sun 1-1-41	Arizona St. 26-13 (Millard "Dixie" Howell)

EARLE EDWARDS, 1-1-0 (Penn St. '31) b 11-10-08

North Caro. St.	Liberty 12-21-63	Mississippi St. 12-16 (Paul Davis)
North Caro. St.	Liberty 12-16-67	Georgia 14-7 (Vince Dooley)

LaVELL EDWARDS, 5-10-1 (Utah St. '52) b 10-11-30

Brigham Young	Fiesta 12-28-74	Oklahoma St. 6-16 (Jim Stanley)
Brigham Young	Tangerine 12-18-76	Oklahoma St. 21-49 (Jim Stanley)
Brigham Young	Holiday 12-22-78	Navy 16-23 (George Welsh)
Brigham Young	Holiday 12-21-79	Indiana 37-38 (Lee Corso)

Brigham Young coach LaVell Edwards has led his Cougars to 16 bowl games in the past 18 seasons, including the last 14 years in a row. Only six coaches in history have more bowl appearances than Edwards.

Brigham Young	Holiday 12-19-80	Southern Methodist 46-45 (Ron Meyer)
Brigham Young	Holiday 12-18-81	Washington St. 38-36 (Jim Walden)
Brigham Young	Holiday 12-17-82	Ohio St. 17-47 (Earle Bruce)
Brigham Young	Holiday 12-23-83	Missouri 21-17 (Warren Powers)
Brigham Young	Holiday 12-21-84	Michigan 24-17 (Glenn "Bo" Schembechler)
Brigham Young	Fla. Citrus 12-28-85	Ohio St. 7-10 (Earle Bruce)
Brigham Young	Freedom 12-30-86	UCLA 10-31 (Terry Donahue)
Brigham Young	All-American 12-22-87	Virginia 16-22 (George Welsh)
Brigham Young	Freedom 12-29-88	Colorado 20-17 (Bill McCartney)
Brigham Young	Holiday 12-29-89	Penn St. 39-50 (Joe Paterno)
Brigham Young	Holiday 12-29-90	Texas A&M 14-65 (R. C. Slocum)
Brigham Young	Holiday 12-30-91	Iowa 13-13 (Hayden Fry)

RAY ELIOT, 2-0-0 (Illinois '32) b 6-13-05

Illinois...............	Rose 1-1-47	UCLA 45-14 (Bert LaBrucherie)
Illinois...............	Rose 1-1-52	Stanford 40-7 (Chuck Taylor)

BENNIE ELLENDER, 0-1-0 (Tulane '48) b 3-2-25

Tulane...............	Bluebonnet 12-29-73	Houston 7-47 (Bill Yeoman)

CHALMERS "BUMP" ELLIOTT, 1-0-0 (Michigan '48) b 1-30-25

Michigan............	Rose 1-1-65	Oregon St. 34-7 (Tommy Prothro)

PETE ELLIOTT, 1-1-0 (Michigan '49) b 9-29-26

California	Rose 1-1-59	Iowa 12-38 (Forest Evashevski)
Illinois...............	Rose 1-1-64	Washington 17-7 (Jim Owens)

JACK ELWAY, 0-2-0 (Washington St. '53) b 5-30-31

San Jose St.	California 12-19-81	Toledo 25-27 (Chuck Stobart)
Stanford	Gator 12-27-86	Clemson 21-27 (Danny Ford)

CHARLES "RIP" ENGLE, 3-1-0 (Western Md. '30) b 3-26-06

Penn St...............	Liberty 12-19-53	Alabama 7-0 (Paul "Bear" Bryant)

Penn St.	Liberty 12-17-60	Oregon 41-12 (Len Casanova)
Penn St.	Gator 12-30-61	Georgia Tech 30-15 (Bobby Dodd)
Penn St.	Gator 12-29-62	Florida 7-17 (Ray Graves)

EDDIE ERDELATZ, 2-0-0 (St. Mary's, Cal. '36) b 4-21-13

Navy	Sugar 1-1-55	Mississippi 21-0 (John Vaught)
Navy	Cotton 1-1-58	Rice 20-7 (Jess Neely)

DENNIS ERICKSON, 4-0-0 (Montana St. '70) b 3-24-47

Washington St.	Aloha 12-25-88	Houston 24-22 (Jack Pardee)
Miami (Fla.)	Sugar 1-1-90	Alabama 33-25 (Bill Curry)
Miami (Fla.)	Cotton 1-1-91	Texas 46-3 (David McWilliams)
Miami (Fla.)	Orange 1-1-92	Nebraska 22-0 (Tom Osborne)

FOREST EVASHEVSKI, 2-0-0 (Michigan '41) b 2-19-18

Iowa	Rose 1-1-57	Oregon St. 35-19 (Tommy Prothro)
Iowa	Rose 1-1-59	California 38-12 (Pete Elliott)

CHUCK FAIRBANKS, 3-1-1 (Michigan St. '55) b 6-10-33

Oklahoma	Orange 1-1-68	Tennessee 26-24 (Doug Dickey)
Oklahoma	Bluebonnet 12-31-68	Southern Methodist 27-28 (Hayden Fry)
Oklahoma	Bluebonnet 12-31-70	Alabama 24-24 (Paul "Bear" Bryant)
Oklahoma	Sugar 1-1-72	Auburn 40-22 (Ralph "Shug" Jordan)
Oklahoma	Sugar 12-31-72	Penn St. 14-0 (Joe Paterno)

DON FAMBROUGH, 0-2-0 (Kansas '48) b 10-19-22

Kansas	Liberty 12-17-73	North Caro. St. 18-31 (Lou Holtz)
Kansas	Hall of Fame 12-31-81	Mississippi St. 0-10 (Emory Bellard)

DON FAUROT, 0-4-0 (Missouri '25) b 6-23-02

Missouri	Orange 1-1-40	Georgia Tech 7-21 (Bill Alexander)
Missouri	Sugar 1-1-42	Fordham 0-2 (Jim Crowley)
Missouri	Gator 1-1-49	Clemson 23-24 (Frank Howard)
Missouri	Gator 1-2-50	Maryland 7-21 (Jim Tatum)

GERRY FAUST, 1-1-0 (Dayton '58) b 5-21-35

Notre Dame	Liberty 12-29-83	Boston College 19-18 (Jack Bicknell)
Notre Dame	Aloha 12-29-84	Southern Methodist 20-27 (Bobby Collins)

FOGE FAZIO, 0-2-0 (Pittsburgh '60) b 2-28-39

Pittsburgh	Cotton 1-1-83	Southern Methodist 3-7 (Bobby Collins)
Pittsburgh	Fiesta 1-2-84	Ohio St. 23-28 (Earle Bruce)

BEATTIE FEATHERS, 0-1-0 (Tennessee '34) b 6-1-12

North Caro. St.	Gator 1-1-47	Oklahoma 13-34 (Jim Tatum)

WES FESLER, 1-0-0 (Ohio St. '32) b 6-29-08

Ohio St.	Rose 1-2-50	California 17-14 (Lynn "Pappy" Waldorf)

CHARLIE FICKERT, 0-1-0 (Stanford '98) b 2-23-73

Stanford	Rose 1-1-02	Michigan 0-49 (Fielding "Hurry Up" Yost)

ROBERT FISHER, 1-0-0 (Harvard '12) b 12-3-88

Harvard	Rose 1-1-20	Oregon 7-6 (Charles "Shy" Huntington)

HANK FOLDBERG, 0-1-0 (Army '48) b 3-12-23

Wichita St.	Sun 12-30-61	Villanova 9-17 (Alex Bell)

BOB FOLWELL, 0-1-1 (Pennsylvania '08) b 1885

Pennsylvania	Rose 1-1-17	Oregon 0-14 (Hugo Bezdek)
Navy	Rose 1-1-24	Washington 14-14 (Enoch Bagshaw)

DANNY FORD, 6-2-0 (Alabama '70) b 4-2-48

Clemson	Gator 12-29-78	Ohio St. 17-15 (Woody Hayes)
Clemson	Peach 12-31-79	Baylor 18-24 (Grant Teaff)
Clemson	Orange 1-1-82	Nebraska 22-15 (Tom Osborne)
Clemson	Independence 12-21-85	Minnesota 13-20 (John Gutekunst)
Clemson	Gator 12-27-86	Stanford 27-21 (Jack Elway)
Clemson	Fla. Citrus 1-1-88	Penn St. 35-10 (Joe Paterno)
Clemson	Fla. Citrus 1-2-89	Oklahoma 23-6 (Barry Switzer)
Clemson	Gator 12-30-89	West Va. 27-7 (Don Nehlen)

HENRY FRNKA, 2-3-0 (Austin '26) b 3-16-03

Tulsa	Sun 1-1-42	Texas Tech 6-0 (Dell Morgan)
Tulsa	Sugar 1-1-43	Tennessee 7-14 (John Barnhill)
Tulsa	Sugar 1-1-44	Georgia Tech 18-20 (Bill Alexander)
Tulsa	Orange 1-1-45	Georgia Tech 26-12 (Bill Alexander)
Tulsa	Oil 1-1-46	Georgia 6-20 (Wally Butts)

HAYDEN FRY, 5-7-1 (Baylor '51) b 2-28-29

Southern Methodist . .	Sun 12-31-63	Oregon 13-21 (Len Casanova)
Southern Methodist . .	Cotton 12-31-66	Georgia 9-24 (Vince Dooley)
Southern Methodist . .	Bluebonnet 12-31-68	Oklahoma 28-27 (Chuck Fairbanks)
Iowa	Rose 1-1-82	Washington 0-28 (Don James)
Iowa	Peach 12-31-82	Tennessee 28-22 (Johnny Majors)
Iowa	Gator 12-30-83	Florida 6-14 (Charley Pell)
Iowa	Freedom 12-26-84	Texas 55-17 (Fred Akers)

Iowa	Rose 1-1-86	UCLA 28-45 (Terry Donahue)
Iowa	Holiday 12-30-86	San Diego St. 39-38 (Denny Stolz)
Iowa	Holiday 12-30-87	Wyoming 20-19 (Paul Roach)
Iowa	Peach 12-31-88	North Caro. St. 23-29 (Dick Sheridan)
Iowa	Rose 1-1-91	Washington 34-46 (Don James)
Iowa	Holiday 12-30-91	Brigham Young 13-13 (LaVell Edwards)

BILL FULCHER, 1-0-0   (Georgia Tech '57)   b 2-9-34
Georgia Tech ....   Liberty 12-18-72   Iowa St. 31-30 (Johnny Majors)

WARREN GAER, 0-1-0   (Drake '35)   b 2-7-12
Drake ....   Sun 1-1-58   Louisville 20-34 (Frank Camp)

JOE GAVIN, 0-1-0   (Notre Dame '31)   b 3-20-08
Dayton ....   Salad 1-1-52   Houston 21-26 (Clyde Lee)

GARY GIBBS, 1-0-0   (Oklahoma '75)   b 8-13-52
Oklahoma ....   Gator 12-29-91   Virginia 48-14 (George Welsh)

VINCE GIBSON, 0-2-0   (Florida St. '55)   b 3-27-33
Louisville ....   Independence 12-17-77   Louisiana Tech 14-24 (Maxie Lambright)
Tulane ....   Hall of Fame 12-27-80   Arkansas 15-34 (Lou Holtz)

CLAUDE GILBERT, 1-1-0   (San Jose St. '59)   b 7-10-32
San Jose St. ....   California 12-13-86   Miami (Ohio) 37-7 (Tim Rose)
San Jose St. ....   California 12-12-87   Eastern Mich. 27-30 (Jim Harkema)

SID GILLMAN, 1-1-0   (Ohio St. '34)   b 10-26-11
Miami (Ohio) ....   Sun 1-1-48   Texas Tech 13-12 (Dell Morgan)
Cincinnati ....   Sun 1-1-51   West Tex. St. 13-14 (Frank Kimbrough)

BILL GLASSFORD, 0-1-0   (Pittsburgh '37)   b 3-8-14
Nebraska ....   Orange 1-1-55   Duke 7-34 (Bill Murray)

MARSHALL "LITTLE SLEEPY" GLENN, 1-0-0   (West Va. '31)   b 4-22-08
West Va. ....   Sun 1-1-38   Texas Tech 7-6 (Pete Cawthon)

RAY GOFF, 1-1-0   (Georgia '78)   b 7-10-55
Georgia ....   Peach 12-30-89   Syracuse 18-19 (Dick MacPherson)
Georgia ....   Independence 12-29-91   Arkansas 24-15 (Jack Crowe)

MIKE GOTTFRIED, 0-1-0   (Morehead St. '66)   b 12-17-44
Pittsburgh ....   Bluebonnet 12-31-87   Texas 27-32 (David McWilliams)

RALPH GRAHAM, 0-1-0   (Kansas St. '34)   b 8-16-10
Wichita St. ....   Raisin 1-1-48   Pacific (Cal.) 14-26 (Larry Siemering)

SONNY GRANDELIUS, 0-1-0   (Michigan St. '51)   b 4-16-29
Colorado ....   Orange 1-1-62   Louisiana St. 7-25 (Paul Dietzel)

RAY GRAVES, 4-1-0   (Tennessee '43)   b 12-31-18
Florida ....   Gator 12-31-60   Baylor 13-12 (John Bridgers)
Florida ....   Gator 12-29-62   Penn St. 17-7 (Charles "Rip" Engle)
Florida ....   Sugar 1-1-66   Missouri 18-20 (Dan Devine)
Florida ....   Orange 1-2-67   Georgia Tech 27-12 (Bobby Dodd)
Florida ....   Gator 12-27-69   Tennessee 14-13 (Doug Dickey)

DENNIS GREEN, 0-1-0   (Iowa '71)   b 2-17-49
Stanford ....   Aloha 12-25-91   Georgia Tech 17-18 (Bobby Ross)

VEE GREEN, 1-0-0   (Illinois '24)   b 10-9-00
Drake ....   Raisin 1-1-46   Fresno St. 13-12 (Alvin "Pix" Pierson)

ART GUEPE, 1-0-0   (Marquette '37)   b 1-28-15
Vanderbilt ....   Gator 12-31-55   Auburn 25-13 (Ralph "Shug" Jordan)

ANDY GUSTAFSON, 1-3-0   (Pittsburgh '26)   b 4-3-03
Miami (Fla.) ....   Orange 1-1-51   Clemson 14-15 (Frank Howard)
Miami (Fla.) ....   Gator 1-1-52   Clemson 14-0 (Frank Howard)
Miami (Fla.) ....   Liberty 12-16-61   Syracuse 14-15 (Ben Schwartzwalder)
Miami (Fla.) ....   Gotham 12-15-62   Nebraska 34-36 (Bob Devaney)

JOHN GUTEKUNST, 1-1-0   (Duke '66)   b 4-13-44
Minnesota ....   Independence 12-21-85   Clemson 20-13 (Danny Ford)
Minnesota ....   Liberty 12-29-86   Tennessee 14-21 (Johnny Majors)

PAUL HACKETT, 1-0-0   (UC Davis '69)   b 6-5-47
Pittsburgh ....   John Hancock 12-30-89   Texas A&M 31-28 (R. C. Slocum)

JACK HAGERTY, 0-1-0   (Georgetown '26)   b 7-3-03
Georgetown ....   Orange 1-1-41   Mississippi St. 7-14 (Alvin McKeen)

GALEN HALL, 1-1-0   (Penn St. '62)   b 8-14-40
Florida ....   Aloha 12-25-87   UCLA 16-20 (Terry Donahue)
Florida ....   All-American 12-29-88   Illinois 14-10 (John Mackovic)

CURLEY HALLMAN, 1-0-0   (Texas A&M '70)   b 9-3-47
Southern Miss. ....   Independence 12-23-88   UTEP 38-18 (Bob Stull)

WAYNE HARDIN, 1-2-0   (Pacific, Cal. '50)   b 3-23-27
Navy ....   Orange 1-2-61   Missouri 14-21 (Dan Devine)
Navy ....   Cotton 1-1-64   Texas 6-28 (Darrell Royal)

| Temple . . . . | Garden State 12-15-79 | California 28-17 (Roger Theder) |

JACK HARDING, 1-0-0 (Pittsburgh '26) b 1-5-98
Miami (Fla.) . . . . Orange 1-1-48   Holy Cross 13-6 (John "Ox" Da Grosa)

JIM HARKEMA, 1-0-0 (Kalamazoo '64) b 6-25-42
Eastern Mich. . . . . California 12-12-87   San Jose St. 30-27 (Claude Gilbert)

KEN HATFIELD, 4-6-0 (Arkansas '65) b 6-8-43
Air Force . . . . Hall of Fame 12-31-82   Vanderbilt 36-28 (George MacIntyre)
Air Force . . . . Independence 12-10-83   Mississippi 9-3 (Billy Brewer)
Arkansas . . . . Liberty 12-27-84   Auburn 15-21 (Pat Dye)
Arkansas . . . . Holiday 12-22-85   Arizona St. 18-17 (John Cooper)
Arkansas . . . . Orange 1-1-87   Oklahoma 8-42 (Barry Switzer)
Arkansas . . . . Liberty 12-29-87   Georgia 17-20 (Vince Dooley)
Arkansas . . . . Cotton 1-2-89   UCLA 3-17 (Terry Donahue)
Arkansas . . . . Cotton 1-1-90   Tennessee 27-31 (Johnny Majors)
Clemson . . . . Hall of Fame 1-1-91   Illinois 30-0 (John Mackovic)
Clemson . . . . Fla. Citrus 1-1-92   California 13-37 (Bruce Snyder)

WOODY HAYES, 6-6-0 (Denison '35) b 2-14-13
Miami (Ohio) . . . . Salad 1-1-51   Arizona St. 34-21 (Ed Doherty)
Ohio St. . . . . Rose 1-1-55   Southern Cal 20-7 (Jess Hill)
Ohio St. . . . . Rose 1-1-58   Oregon 10-7 (Len Casanova)
Ohio St. . . . . Rose 1-1-69   Southern Cal 27-16 (John McKay)
Ohio St. . . . . Rose 1-1-71   Stanford 17-27 (John Ralston)
Ohio St. . . . . Rose 1-1-73   Southern Cal 17-42 (John McKay)
Ohio St. . . . . Rose 1-1-74   Southern Cal 42-21 (John McKay)
Ohio St. . . . . Rose 1-1-75   Southern Cal 17-18 (John McKay)
Ohio St. . . . . Rose 1-1-76   UCLA 10-23 (Dick Vermeil)
Ohio St. . . . . Orange 1-1-77   Colorado 27-10 (Bill Mallory)
Ohio St. . . . . Sugar 1-2-78   Alabama 6-35 (Paul "Bear" Bryant)
Ohio St. . . . . Gator 12-29-78   Clemson 15-17 (Danny Ford)

ELMER "GUS" HENDERSON, 2-0-0 (Oberlin '12) b 3-10-89
Southern Cal . . . . Rose 1-1-23   Penn St. 14-3 (Hugo Bezdek)
Southern Cal . . . . L.A. Christmas Festival   Missouri 20-7 (Gwinn Henry)
    12-25-24

GWINN HENRY, 0-1-0 (Howard Payne '17) b 8-5-87
Missouri . . . . L.A. Christmas Festival   Southern Cal 7-20 (Elmer "Gus" Henderson)
    12-25-24

BILL HESS, 0-2-0 (Ohio '47) b 2-5-23
Ohio . . . . Sun 12-31-62   West Tex. St. 14-15 (Joe Kerbel)
Ohio . . . . Tangerine 12-27-68   Richmond 42-49 (Frank Jones)

JIM HICKEY, 1-0-0 (William & Mary '42) b 1-22-20
North Caro. . . . . Gator 12-28-63   Air Force 35-0 (Ben Martin)

BOB HIGGINS, 1-0-1 (Penn St. '20) b 12-24-93
West Va. Wesleyan . . . Dixie Classic 1-1-25   Southern Methodist 9-7 (Ray Morrison)
Penn St. . . . . Cotton 1-1-48   Southern Methodist 13-13 (Matty Bell)

JESS HILL, 1-1-0 (Southern Cal '30) b 1-20-07
Southern Cal . . . . Rose 1-1-53   Wisconsin 7-0 (Ivy Williamson)
Southern Cal . . . . Rose 1-1-55   Ohio St. 7-20 (Woody Hayes)

JERRY HINES, 0-0-1 (New Mexico St. '26) b 10-11-03
New Mexico St. . . . . . . Sun 1-1-36   Hardin-Simmons 14-14 (Frank Kimbrough)

BERNARD A. HOBAN, 0-1-0 (Dartmouth '12) b 4-21-90
U. of Mexico . . . . Sun 1-1-45   Southwestern (Tex.) 0-35 (Randolph R. M. Medley)

ORIN "BABE" HOLLINGBERRY, 0-1-0 (No college) b 7-15-93
Washington St. . . . . Rose 1-1-31   Alabama 0-24 (Wallace Wade)

LOU HOLTZ, 8-6-2 (Kent '59) b 1-6-37
William & Mary . . . . . . Tangerine 12-28-70   Toledo 12-40 (Frank Lauterbur)
North Caro. St. . . . . Peach 12-29-72   West Va. 49-13 (Bobby Bowden)
North Caro. St. . . . . Liberty 12-17-73   Kansas 31-18 (Don Fambrough)
North Caro. St. . . . . Bluebonnet 12-23-74   Houston 31-31 (Bill Yeoman)
North Caro. St. . . . . Peach 12-31-75   West Va. 10-13 (Bobby Bowden)
Arkansas . . . . Orange 1-2-78   Oklahoma 31-6 (Barry Switzer)
Arkansas . . . . Fiesta 12-25-78   UCLA 10-10 (Terry Donahue)
Arkansas . . . . Sugar 1-1-80   Alabama 9-24 (Paul "Bear" Bryant)
Arkansas . . . . Hall of Fame 12-27-80   Tulane 34-15 (Vince Gibson)
Arkansas . . . . Gator 12-28-81   North Caro. 27-31 (Dick Crum)
Arkansas . . . . Bluebonnet 12-31-82   Florida 28-24 (Charley Pell)
Notre Dame . . . . Cotton 1-1-88   Texas A&M 10-35 (Jackie Sherrill)
Notre Dame . . . . Fiesta 1-2-89   West Va. 34-21 (Don Nehlen)
Notre Dame . . . . Orange 1-1-90   Colorado 21-6 (Bill McCartney)
Notre Dame . . . . Orange 1-1-91   Colorado 9-10 (Bill McCartney)
Notre Dame . . . . Sugar 1-1-92   Florida 39-28 (Steve Spurrier)

EDWIN "BABE" HORRELL, 0-1-0   (California '26)   b 9-29-02
UCLA ....   Rose 1-1-43   Georgia 0-9 (Wally Butts)

FRANK HOWARD, 3-3-0   (Alabama '31)   b 3-25-09
Clemson ....   Gator 1-1-49   Missouri 24-23 (Don Faurot)
Clemson ....   Orange 1-1-51   Miami (Fla.) 15-14 (Andy Gustafson)
Clemson ....   Gator 1-1-52   Miami (Fla.) 0-14 (Andy Gustafson)
Clemson ....   Orange 1-1-57   Colorado 21-27 (Dallas Ward)
Clemson ....   Sugar 1-1-59   Louisiana St. 0-7 (Paul Dietzel)
Clemson ....   Bluebonnet 12-19-59   Texas Christian 23-7 (Abe Martin)

MILLARD "DIXIE" HOWELL, 0-1-1   (Alabama '35)   b 11-24-12
Arizona St. ....   Sun 1-1-40   Catholic 0-0 (Arthur "Dutch" Bergman)
Arizona St. ....   Sun 1-1-41   Case Reserve 13-26 (Bill Edwards)

BILL HUBBARD, 2-0-0   (Stanford '30)   b 2-5-07
San Jose St. ....   Raisin 1-1-47   Utah St. 20-0 (E. L. "Dick" Romney)
San Jose St. ....   Raisin 12-31-49   Texas Tech 20-13 (Dell Morgan)

CLYDE "CAC" HUBBARD, 0-2-0   (Oregon St. '21)   b 9-13-97
Denver ....   Sun 1-1-46   New Mexico 24-34 (Willis Barnes)
Denver ....   Alamo 1-4-47   Hardin-Simmons 0-20 (Warren Woodson)

CHARLES "SHY" HUNTINGTON, 0-1-0   (Oregon)   b 7-7-91
Oregon ....   Rose 1-1-20   Harvard 6-7 (Robert Fisher)

HARVEY HYDE, 1-0-0   (Redlands '62)   b 7-13-39
Nevada-Las Vegas ...   California 12-15-84   Toledo 30-13 (Dan Simrell)

DON JAMES, 10-4-0   (Miami, Fla. '54)   b 12-31-32
Kent.................   Tangerine 12-29-72   Tampa 18-21 (Earle Bruce)
Washington ....   Rose 1-2-78   Michigan 27-20 (Glenn "Bo" Schembechler)
Washington ....   Sun 12-22-79   Texas 14-7 (Fred Akers)
Washington ....   Rose 1-1-81   Michigan 6-23 (Glenn "Bo" Schembechler)
Washington ....   Rose 1-1-82   Iowa 28-0 (Hayden Fry)
Washington ....   Aloha 12-25-82   Maryland 21-20 (Bobby Ross)
Washington ....   Aloha 12-26-83   Penn St. 10-13 (Joe Paterno)
Washington ....   Orange 1-1-85   Oklahoma 28-17 (Barry Switzer)
Washington ....   Freedom 12-30-85   Colorado 20-17 (Bill McCartney)
Washington ....   Sun 12-25-86   Alabama 6-28 (Ray Perkins)
Washington ....   Independence 12-18-87   Tulane 24-12 (Mack Brown)
Washington ....   Freedom 12-29-89   Florida 34-7 (Gary Darnell)
Washington ....   Rose 1-1-91   Iowa 46-34 (Hayden Fry)
Washington ....   Rose 1-1-92   Michigan 34-14 (Gary Moeller)

JIMMY JOHNSON, 3-4-0   (Arkansas '65)   b 7-16-43
Oklahoma St. ....   Independence 12-12-81   Texas A&M 16-33 (Tom Wilson)
Oklahoma St. ....   Bluebonnet 12-31-83   Baylor 24-14 (Grant Teaff)
Miami (Fla.) ....   Fiesta 1-1-85   UCLA 37-39 (Terry Donahue)
Miami (Fla.) ....   Sugar 1-1-86   Tennessee 7-35 (Johnny Majors)
Miami (Fla.) ....   Fiesta 1-2-87   Penn St. 10-14 (Joe Paterno)
Miami (Fla.) ....   Orange 1-1-88   Oklahoma 20-14 (Barry Switzer)
Miami (Fla.) ....   Orange 1-2-89   Nebraska 23-3 (Tom Osborne)

FRANK JONES, 1-1-0   (North Caro. '48)   b 8-30-21
Richmond ....   Tangerine 12-27-68   Ohio 49-42 (Bill Hess)
Richmond ....   Tangerine 12-28-71   Toledo 3-28 (John Murphy)

GOMER JONES, 0-1-0   (Ohio St. '36)   b 2-26-14
Oklahoma ....   Gator 1-2-65   Florida St. 19-36 (Bill Peterson)

HOWARD JONES, 5-0-0   (Yale '08)   b 8-23-85
Southern Cal ....   Rose 1-1-30   Pittsburgh 47-14 (Jock Sutherland)
Southern Cal ....   Rose 1-1-32   Tulane 21-12 (Bernie Bierman)
Southern Cal ....   Rose 1-2-33   Pittsburgh 35-0 (Jock Sutherland)
Southern Cal ....   Rose 1-2-39   Duke 7-3 (Wallace Wade)
Southern Cal ....   Rose 1-1-40   Tennessee 14-0 (Bob Neyland)

LARRY JONES, 0-1-0   (Louisiana St. '54)   b 12-18-33
Florida St. ....   Fiesta 12-27-71   Arizona St. 38-45 (Frank Kush)

LAWRENCE McC. "BIFF" JONES, 0-1-0   (Army '17)   b 10-8-95
Nebraska............   Rose 1-1-41   Stanford 13-21 (Clark Shaughnessy)

PAT JONES, 3-1-0   (Arkansas '69)   b 11-4-47
Oklahoma St. ....   Gator 12-28-84   South Caro. 21-14 (Joe Morrrison)
Oklahoma St. ....   Gator 12-30-85   Florida St. 23-34 (Bobby Bowden)
Oklahoma St. ....   Sun 12-25-87   West Va. 35-33 (Don Nehlen)
Oklahoma St. ....   Holiday 12-30-88   Wyoming 62-14 (Paul Roach)

RALPH "SHUG" JORDAN, 5-7-0   (Auburn '32)   b 9-25-10
Auburn...............   Gator 1-1-54   Texas Tech 13-35 (DeWitt Weaver)
Auburn...............   Gator 12-31-54   Baylor 33-13 (George Sauer)
Auburn...............   Gator 12-31-55   Vanderbilt 13-25 (Art Gueppe)
Auburn...............   Orange 1-1-64   Nebraska 7-13 (Bob Devaney)
Auburn...............   Liberty 12-18-65   Mississippi 7-13 (John Vaught)

1992 NCAA FOOTBALL

Auburn	Sun 12-28-68	Arizona 34-10 (Darrell Mudra)
Auburn	Bluebonnet 12-31-69	Houston 7-36 (Bill Yeoman)
Auburn	Gator 1-2-71	Mississippi 35-28 (John Vaught)
Auburn	Sugar 1-1-72	Oklahoma 22-40 (Chuck Fairbanks)
Auburn	Gator 12-30-72	Colorado 24-3 (Eddie Crowder)
Auburn	Sun 12-29-73	Missouri 17-34 (Al Onofrio)
Auburn	Gator 12-30-74	Texas 27-3 (Darrell Royal)

ERNIE JORGE, 1-1-0   (St. Mary's, Cal. '36)   b 10-7-14
Pacific (Cal.)	Sun 1-1-52	Texas Tech 14-25 (DeWitt Weaver)
Pacific (Cal.)	Sun 1-1-53	Southern Miss. 26-7 (Thad "Pie" Vann)

AL KAWAL, 1-0-0   (Northwestern '35)   b 7-4-12
Drake	Salad 1-1-49	Arizona 14-13 (Miles Casteel)

JOE KERBEL, 2-0-0   (Oklahoma '47)   b 5-3-21
West Tex. St.	Sun 12-21-62	Ohio 15-14 (Bill Hess)
West Tex. St.	Pasadena 12-2-67	Cal St. Northridge 35-13 (Sam Winningham)

BILL KERN, 0-1-0   (Pittsburgh '28)   b 9-2-06
Carnegie Mellon	Sugar 1-2-39	Texas Christian 7-15 (Leo "Dutch" Meyer)

FRANK KIMBROUGH, 2-0-1   (Hardin-Simmons '26)   b 6-24-04
Hardin-Simmons	Sun 1-1-36	New Mexico St. 14-14 (Jerry Hines)
Hardin-Simmons	Sun 1-1-37	UTEP 34-6 (Max Saxon)
West Tex. St.	Sun 1-1-51	Cincinnati 14-13 (Sid Gillman)

BILLY KINARD, 1-0-0   (Mississippi '56)   b 12-16-33
Mississippi	Peach 12-30-71	Georgia Tech 41-18 (Bud Carson)

DEWEY KING, 0-1-0   (North Dak. '50)   b 10-1-25
San Jose St.	Pasadena 12-18-71	Memphis St. 9-28 (Billy Murphy)

J. T. KING, 0-2-0   (Texas '38)   b 10-22-12
Texas Tech	Sun 12-26-64	Georgia 0-7 (Vince Dooley)
Texas Tech	Gator 12-31-65	Georgia Tech 21-31 (Bobby Dodd)

JIMMY KITTS, 1-1-0   (Southern Methodist)   b 6-14-00
Rice	Cotton 1-1-38	Colorado 28-14 (Bernard "Bunnie" Oakes)
Virginia Tech	Sun 1-1-47	Cincinnati 6-18 (Ray Nolting)

ED KLUSKA, 1-0-0   (Xavier, Ohio '40)   b 5-21-18
Xavier (Ohio)	Salad 1-1-50	Arizona St. 33-21 (Ed Doherty)

JOE KRIVAK, 0-0-0   (Syracuse '57)   b 3-20-35
Maryland	Independence 12-15-90	Louisiana Tech 34-34 (Joe Raymond Peace)

FRANK KUSH, 6-1-0   (Michigan St. '53)   b 1-20-29
Arizona St.	Peach 12-30-70	North Caro. 48-26 (Bill Dooley)
Arizona St.	Fiesta 12-27-71	Florida St. 45-38 (Larry Jones)
Arizona St.	Fiesta 12-23-72	Missouri 49-35 (Al Onofrio)
Arizona St.	Fiesta 12-21-73	Pittsburgh 28-7 (Johnny Majors)
Arizona St.	Fiesta 12-26-75	Nebraska 17-14 (Tom Osborne)
Arizona St.	Fiesta 12-25-77	Penn St. 30-42 (Joe Paterno)
Arizona St.	Garden State 12-16-78	Rutgers 34-18 (Frank Burns)

BERT LaBRUCHERIE, 0-1-0   (UCLA '29)   b 1-19-05
UCLA	Rose 1-1-47	Illinois 14-45 (Ray Eliot)

MAXIE LAMBRIGHT, 1-1-0   (Southern Miss. '49)   b 6-3-24
Louisiana Tech	Independence 12-17-77	Louisville 24-14 (Vince Gibson)
Louisiana Tech	Independence 12-16-78	East Caro. 13-35 (Pat Dye)

FRANK LAUTERBUR, 2-0-0   (Mount Union '49)   b 8-8-25
Toledo	Tangerine 12-26-69	Davidson 56-33 (Homer Smith)
Toledo	Tangerine 12-28-70	William & Mary 40-12 (Lou Holtz)

FRANK LEAHY, 1-1-0   (Notre Dame '31)   b 8-27-08
Boston College	Cotton 1-1-40	Clemson 3-6 (Jess Neely)
Boston College	Sugar 1-1-41	Tennessee 19-13 (Bob Neyland)

CLYDE LEE, 1-0-0   (Centenary '32)   b 2-11-08
Houston	Salad 1-1-52	Dayton 26-21 (Joe Gavin)

ART LEWIS, 0-1-0   (Ohio '36)   b 2-18-11
West Va.	Sugar 1-1-54	Georgia Tech 19-42 (Bobby Dodd)

BILL LEWIS, 1-0-0   (East Stroudsburg '63)   b 8-5-41
East Caro.	Peach 1-1-92	North Caro. St. 37-34 (Dick Sheridan)

LOU LITTLE, 1-0-0   (Pennsylvania '20)   12-6-93
Columbia	Rose 1-1-34	Stanford 7-0 (Claude "Tiny" Thornhill)

JIM LOOKABAUGH, 2-1-0   (Oklahoma St. '25)   b 6-15-02
Oklahoma St.	Cotton 1-1-45	Texas Christian 34-0 (Leo "Dutch" Meyer)
Oklahoma St.	Sugar 1-1-46	St. Mary's (Cal.) 33-13 (Jimmy Phelan)
Oklahoma St.	Delta 1-1-49	William & Mary 0-20 (Rube McCray)

AL LUGINBILL, 0-1-0   (Cal Poly Pomona '67)   b 11-3-46
San Diego St.	Freedom 12-30-91	Tulsa 17-28 (Dave Rader)

GEORGE MacINTYRE, 0-1-0 (Miami, Fla. '61) b 4-30-39
Vanderbilt . . . . Hall of Fame 12-31-82 Air Force 28-36 (Ken Hatfield)
JOHN MACKOVIC, 1-3-0 (Wake Forest '65) b 10-1-43
Wake Forest . . . . Tangerine 12-22-79 Louisiana St. 10-34 (Charlie McClendon)
Illinois . . . . All-American 12-29-88 Florida 10-14 (Galen Hall)
Illinois . . . . Fla. Citrus 1-1-90 Virginia 31-21 (George Welsh)
Illinois . . . . Hall of Fame 1-1-91 Clemson 0-30 (Ken Hatfield)
DICK MacPHERSON, 3-1-1 (Springfield '58) b 11-4-30
Syracuse . . . . Cherry 12-21-85 Maryland 18-35 (Bobby Ross)
Syracuse . . . . Sugar 1-1-88 Auburn 16-16 (Pat Dye)
Syracuse . . . . Hall of Fame 1-2-89 Louisiana St. 23-10 (Mike Archer)
Syracuse . . . . Peach 12-30-89 Georgia 19-18 (Ray Goff)
Syracuse . . . . Aloha 12-25-90 Arizona 28-0 (Dick Tomey)
EDWARD "SLIP" MADIGAN, 1-0-0 (Notre Dame '20) b 11-18-95
St. Mary's (Cal.) . . . . . . Cotton 1-2-39 Texas Tech 20-13 (Pete Cawthon)
JOHNNY MAJORS, 9-7-0 (Tennessee '57) b 5-21-35
Iowa St. . . . . Sun 12-18-71 Louisiana St. 15-33 (Charlie McClendon)
Iowa St. . . . . Liberty 12-18-72 Georgia Tech 30-31 (Bill Fulcher)
Pittsburgh . . . . Fiesta 12-21-73 Arizona St. 7-28 (Frank Kush)
Pittsburgh . . . . Sun 12-26-75 Kansas 33-19 (Bud Moore)
Pittsburgh . . . . Sugar 1-1-77 Georgia 27-3 (Vince Dooley)
Tennessee . . . . Bluebonnet 12-31-79 Purdue 22-27 (Jim Young)
Tennessee . . . . Garden State 12-13-81 Wisconsin 28-21 (Dave McClain)
Tennessee . . . . Peach 12-31-82 Iowa 22-28 (Hayden Fry)
Tennessee . . . . Fla. Citrus 12-17-83 Maryland 30-23 (Bobby Ross)
Tennessee . . . . Sun 12-24-84 Maryland 26-27 (Bobby Ross)
Tennessee . . . . Sugar 1-1-86 Miami (Fla.) 35-7 (Jimmy Johnson)
Tennessee . . . . Liberty 12-29-86 Minnesota 21-14 (John Gutekunst)
Tennessee . . . . Peach 1-2-88 Indiana 27-22 (Bill Mallory)
Tennessee . . . . Cotton 1-1-90 Arkansas 31-27 (Ken Hatfield)
Tennessee . . . . Sugar 1-1-91 Virginia 23-22 (George Welsh)
Tennessee . . . . Fiesta 1-1-92 Penn St. 17-42 (Joe Paterno)
BILL MALLORY, 4-5-0 (Miami, Ohio '57) b 5-30-35
Miami (Ohio) . . . . Tangerine 12-22-73 Florida 16-7 (Doug Dickey)
Colorado . . . . Bluebonnet 12-27-75 Texas 21-38 (Darrell Royal)
Colorado . . . . Orange 1-1-77 Ohio St. 10-27 (Woody Hayes)
Northern Ill. . . . . California 12-17-83 Cal St. Fullerton 20-13 (Gene Murphy)
Indiana . . . . All-American 12-31-86 Florida St. 13-27 (Bobby Bowden)
Indiana . . . . Peach 1-2-88 Tennessee 22-27 (Johnny Majors)
Indiana . . . . Liberty 12-28-88 South Caro. 34-10 (Joe Morrison)
Indiana . . . . Peach 12-29-90 Auburn 23-27 (Pat Dye)
Indiana . . . . Copper 12-31-91 Baylor 24-0 (Grant Teaff)
FRANK MALONEY, 1-0-0 (Michigan '62) b 9-26-40
Syracuse . . . . Independence 12-15-79 McNeese St. 31-7 (Ernie Duplechin)
BOB MARGARITA, 0-1-0 (Brown '44) b 11-3-20
Georgetown . . . . Sun 1-2-50 UTEP 20-33 (Jack "Cactus Jack" Curtice)
ABE MARTIN, 1-3-1 (Texas Christian '32) b 10-8-08
Texas Christian . . . . . . Cotton 1-2-56 Mississippi 13-14 (John Vaught)
Texas Christian . . . . . . Cotton 1-1-57 Syracuse 28-27 (Ben Schwartzwalder)
Texas Christian . . . . . . Cotton 1-1-59 Air Force 0-0 (Ben Martin)
Texas Christian . . . . . . Bluebonnet 12-19-59 Clemson 7-23 (Frank Howard)
Texas Christian . . . . . . Sun 12-31-65 UTEP 12-13 (Bobby Dobbs)
BEN MARTIN, 0-2-1 (Navy '46) b 6-28-21
Air Force . . . . Cotton 1-1-59 Texas Christian 0-0 (Abe Martin)
Air Force . . . . Gator 12-28-63 North Caro. 0-35 (Jim Hickey)
Air Force . . . . Sugar 1-1-71 Tennessee 13-34 (Bill Battle)
TONY MASON, 0-1-0 (Clarion '50) b 3-2-30
Arizona . . . . Fiesta 12-25-79 Pittsburgh 10-16 (Jackie Sherrill)
TOM McCANN, 0-1-0 (Illinois '24) b 11-7-98
Miami (Fla.) . . . . Orange 1-1-35 Bucknell 0-26 (Edward "Hook" Mylin)
BILL McCARTNEY, 1-5-0 (Missouri '62) b 8-22-40
Colorado . . . . Freedom 12-30-85 Washington 17-20 (Don James)
Colorado . . . . Bluebonnet 12-31-86 Baylor 9-21 (Grant Teaff)
Colorado . . . . Freedom 12-29-88 Brigham Young 17-20 (LaVell Edwards)
Colorado . . . . Orange 1-1-90 Notre Dame 6-21 (Lou Holtz)
Colorado . . . . Orange 1-1-91 Notre Dame 10-9 (Lou Holtz)
Colorado . . . . Blockbuster 12-28-91 Alabama 25-30 (Gene Stallings)
DAVE McCLAIN, 1-2-0 (Bowling Green '60) b 1-28-38
Wisconsin . . . . Garden State 12-13-81 Tennessee 21-28 (Johnny Majors)
Wisconsin . . . . Independence 12-11-82 Kansas St. 14-3 (Jim Dickey)
Wisconsin . . . . Hall of Fame 12-22-83 Kentucky 19-20 (Jerry Claiborne)

CHARLIE McCLENDON, 7-6-0 (Kentucky '50) b 10-17-22
Louisiana St.	Cotton 1-1-63	Texas 13-0 (Darrell Royal)
Louisiana St.	Bluebonnet 12-21-63	Baylor 7-14 (John Bridgers)
Louisiana St.	Sugar 1-1-65	Syracuse 13-10 (Ben Schwartzwalder)
Louisiana St.	Cotton 1-1-66	Arkansas 14-7 (Frank Broyles)
Louisiana St.	Sugar 1-1-68	Wyoming 20-13 (Lloyd Eaton)
Louisiana St.	Peach 12-30-68	Florida St. 31-27 (Bill Peterson)
Louisiana St.	Orange 1-1-71	Nebraska 12-17 (Bob Devaney)
Louisiana St.	Sun 12-18-71	Iowa St. 33-15 (Johnny Majors)
Louisiana St.	Bluebonnet 12-30-72	Tennessee 17-24 (Bill Battle)
Louisiana St.	Orange 1-1-74	Penn St. 9-16 (Joe Paterno)
Louisiana St.	Sun 12-31-77	Stanford 14-24 (Bill Walsh)
Louisiana St.	Liberty 12-23-78	Missouri 15-20 (Warren Powers)
Louisiana St.	Tangerine 12-22-79	Wake Forest 34-10 (John Mackovic)

RUBE McCRAY, 1-1-0 (Ky. Wesleyan '30) b 6-13-05
| William & Mary .... | Dixie 1-1-48 | Arkansas 19-21 (John Barnhill) |
| William & Mary .... | Delta 1-1-49 | Oklahoma St. 20-0 (Jim Lookabaugh) |

H. F. "POP" McKALE, 0-1-0 (Albion '10) b 6-12-87
| Arizona .... | San Diego East-West Christmas Classic 12-26-21 | Centre 0-38 (Charley Moran) |

JOHN McKAY, 6-3-0 (Oregon St. '50) b 7-5-23
Southern Cal.........	Rose 1-2-63	Wisconsin 42-37 (Milt Bruhn)
Southern Cal.........	Rose 1-2-67	Purdue 13-14 (Jack Mollenkopf)
Southern Cal.........	Rose 1-1-68	Indiana 14-3 (John Pont)
Southern Cal.........	Rose 1-1-69	Ohio St. 16-27 (Woody Hayes)
Southern Cal.........	Rose 1-1-70	Michigan 10-3 (Glenn "Bo" Schembechler)
Southern Cal.........	Rose 1-1-73	Ohio St. 42-17 (Woody Hayes)
Southern Cal.........	Rose 1-1-74	Ohio St. 21-42 (Woody Hayes)
Southern Cal.........	Rose 1-1-75	Ohio St. 18-17 (Woody Hayes)
Southern Cal.........	Liberty 12-22-75	Texas A&M 20-0 (Emory Bellard)

ALLYN McKEEN, 1-0-0 (Tennessee '29) b 1-26-05
| Mississippi St......... | Orange 1-1-41 | Georgetown 14-7 (Jack Hagerty) |

JOHNNIE McMILLAN, 0-1-0 (South Caro. '41) b 1-27-19
| South Caro. .... | Gator 1-1-46 | Wake Forest 14-26 (D. C. "Peahead" Walker) |

DAVID McWILLIAMS, 1-1-0 (Texas '64) b 4-18-42
| Texas .... | Bluebonnet 12-31-87 | Pittsburgh 32-27 (Mike Gottfried) |
| Texas .... | Cotton 1-1-91 | Miami (Fla.) 3-46 (Dennis Erickson) |

JACK MEAGHER, 1-0-1 (Notre Dame '17) b 7-4-94
| Auburn............... | Bacardi 1-1-37 | Villanova 7-7 (Maurice "Clipper" Smith) |
| Auburn............... | Orange 1-1-38 | Michigan St. 6-0 (Charlie Bachman) |

RANDOLPH R.M. MEDLEY, 2-0-0 (Mo. Wesleyan '21) b 9-22-98
| Southwestern (Tex.).. | Sun 1-1-44 | New Mexico 7-0 (Willis Barnes) |
| Southwestern (Tex.).. | Sun 1-1-45 | U. of Mexico 35-0 (Bernard A. Hoban) |

LEO "DUTCH" MEYER, 3-4-0 (Texas Christian '22) b 1-15-98
Texas Christian	Sugar 1-1-36	Louisiana St. 3-2 (Bernie Moore)
Texas Christian	Cotton 1-1-37	Marquette 16-6 (Frank Murray)
Texas Christian	Sugar 1-2-39	Carnegie Mellon 15-7 (Bill Kern)
Texas Christian	Orange 1-1-42	Georgia 26-40 (Wally Butts)
Texas Christian	Cotton 1-1-45	Oklahoma St. 0-34 (Jim Lookabaugh)
Texas Christian	Delta 1-1-48	Mississippi 9-13 (John Vaught)
Texas Christian	Cotton 1-1-52	Kentucky 7-20 (Paul "Bear" Bryant)

RON MEYER, 0-1-0 (Purdue '63) b 2-17-41
| Southern Methodist .. | Holiday 12-19-80 | Brigham Young 45-46 (LaVell Edwards) |

JOHN MICHELOSEN, 0-2-0 (Pittsburgh '38) b 2-13-16
| Pittsburgh............ | Sugar 1-2-56 | Georgia Tech 0-7 (Bobby Dodd) |
| Pittsburgh............ | Gator 12-29-56 | Georgia Tech 14-21 (Bobby Dodd) |

JACK MITCHELL, 1-0-0 (Oklahoma '49) b 12-3-24
| Kansas .... | Bluebonnet 12-16-61 | Rice 33-7 (Jess Neely) |

ODUS MITCHELL, 0-2-0 (West Tex. St. '25) b 6-29-99
| North Texas .... | Salad 1-1-48 | Nevada 6-13 (Joe Sheeketski) |
| North Texas .... | Sun 12-31-59 | New Mexico St. 8-28 (Warren Woodson) |

GARY MOELLER, 1-1-0 (Ohio St. '63) b 1-26-41
| Michigan .... | Gator 1-1-91 | Mississippi 35-3 (Billy Brewer) |
| Michigan .... | Rose 1-1-92 | Washington 14-34 (Don James) |

AL MOLDE, 0-1-0 (Gust. Adolphus '66) b 11-15-43
| Western Mich......... | California 12-10-88 | Fresno St. 30-35 (Jim Sweeney) |

JACK MOLLENKOPF, 1-0-0 (Bowling Green '31) b 11-24-05
| Purdue .... | Rose 1-2-67 | Southern Cal 14-13 (John McKay) |

BERNIE MOORE, 1-3-1 (Carson-Newman '17) b 4-30-95
Louisiana St. . . . . Sugar 1-1-36 Texas Christian 2-3 (Leo "Dutch" Meyer)
Louisiana St. . . . . Sugar 1-1-37 Santa Clara 14-21 (Lawrence "Buck" Shaw)
Louisiana St. . . . . Sugar 1-1-38 Santa Clara 0-6 (Lawrence "Buck" Shaw)
Louisiana St. . . . . Orange 1-1-44 Texas A&M 19-14 (Homer Norton)
Louisiana St. . . . . Cotton 1-1-47 Arkansas 0-0 (John Barnhill)

BUD MOORE, 0-1-0 (Alabama '61) b 10-16-39
Kansas . . . . Sun 12-26-75 Pittsburgh 19-33 (Johnny Majors)

CHARLEY MORAN, 2-1-0 (Tennessee '98) b 2-22-78
Centre . . . . Fort Worth Classic Texas Christian 63-7 (Bill Driver)
                                1-1-21
Centre . . . . San Diego East-West Arizona 38-0 (J. F. "Pop" McKale)
                                Christmas Classic
                                12-26-21
Centre . . . . Dixie Classic 1-2-22 Texas A&M 14-22 (Dana Bible)

DELL MORGAN, 0-3-0 (Austin '25) b 2-14-02
Texas Tech . . . . Sun 1-1-42 Tulsa 0-6 (Henry Frnka)
Texas Tech . . . . Sun 1-1-48 Miami (Ohio) 12-13 (Sid Gillman)
Texas Tech . . . . Raisin 12-31-49 San Jose St. 13-20 (Bill Hubbard)

JOE MORRISON, 0-3-0 (Cincinnati '59) b 8-21-37
South Caro. . . . . Gator 12-28-84 Oklahoma St. 14-21 (Pat Jones)
South Caro. . . . . Gator 12-31-87 Louisiana St. 13-30 (Mike Archer)
South Caro. . . . . Liberty 12-28-88 Indiana 10-34 (Bill Mallory)

RAY MORRISON, 0-1-0 (Vanderbilt '12) b 2-28-85
Southern Methodist . . Dixie Classic 1-1-25 West Va. Wesleyan 7-9 (Bob Higgins)

DARRELL MUDRA, 0-1-0 (Peru St. '51) b 1-4-29
Arizona . . . . Sun 12-28-68 Auburn 10-34 (Ralph "Shug" Jordan)

CLARENCE "BIGGIE" MUNN, 1-0-0 (Minnesota '32) b 9-11-08
Michigan St. . . . . Rose 1-1-54 UCLA 28-20 (Henry "Red" Sanders)

BILLY MURPHY, 1-0-0 (Mississippi St. '47) b 1-13-21
Memphis St. . . . . Pasadena 12-18-71 San Jose St. 28-9 (Dewey King)

GENE MURPHY, 0-1-0 (North Dak. '62) b 8-6-39
Cal St. Fullerton . . . . . California 12-17-83 Northern Ill. 13-20 (Bill Mallory)

JACK MURPHY, 1-0-0 (Heidelberg '54) b 8-6-32
Toledo . . . . Tangerine 12-28-71 Richmond 28-3 (Frank Jones)

BILL MURRAY, 2-1-0 (Duke '31) b 9-9-08
Duke . . . . Orange 1-1-55 Nebraska 34-7 (Bill Glassford)
Duke . . . . Orange 1-1-58 Oklahoma 21-48 (Bud Wilkinson)
Duke . . . . Cotton 1-2-61 Arkansas 7-6 (Frank Broyles)

FRANK MURRAY, 0-1-0 (Tufts '08) b 2-12-85
Marquette . . . . Cotton 1-1-37 Texas Christian 6-16 (Leo "Dutch" Meyer)

DENNY MYERS, 0-1-0 (Iowa '30) b 11-10-05
Boston College . . . . . Orange 1-1-43 Alabama 21-37 (Frank Thomas)

EDWARD "HOOK" MYLIN, 1-0-0 (Frank. & Marsh.) b 10-23-97
Bucknell . . . . Orange 1-1-35 Miami (Fla.) 26-0 (Tom McCann)

RAY NAGEL, 1-0-0 (UCLA '50) b 5-18-27
Utah . . . . Liberty 12-19-64 West Va. 32-6 (Gene Corum)

LARRY NAVIAUX, 0-1-0 (Nebraska '59) b 12-17-36
Boston U. . . . . Pasadena 12-6-69 San Diego St. 7-28 (Don Coryell)

EARLE "GREASY" NEALE, 0-0-1 (West Va. Wesleyan '14) b 11-5-91
Wash. & Jeff. . . . . Rose 1-2-22 California 0-0 (Andy Smith)

JESS NEELY, 4-3-0 (Vanderbilt '23) b 1-4-98
Clemson . . . . Cotton 1-1-40 Boston College 6-3 (Frank Leahy)
Rice . . . . Orange 1-1-47 Tennessee 8-0 (Bob Neyland)
Rice . . . . Cotton 1-2-50 North Caro. 27-13 (Carl Snavely)
Rice . . . . Cotton 1-1-54 Alabama 28-6 (Harold "Red" Drew)
Rice . . . . Cotton 1-1-58 Navy 7-20 (Eddie Erdelatz)
Rice . . . . Sugar 1-2-61 Mississippi 6-14 (John Vaught)
Rice . . . . Bluebonnet 12-16-61 Kansas 7-33 (Jack Mitchell)

DON NEHLEN, 3-4-0 (Bowling Green '58) b 1-1-36
West Va. . . . . Peach 12-31-81 Florida 26-6 (Charley Pell)
West Va. . . . . Gator 12-30-82 Florida St. 12-31 (Bobby Bowden)
West Va. . . . . Hall of Fame 12-22-83 Kentucky 20-16 (Jerry Claiborne)
West Va. . . . . Bluebonnet 12-31-84 Texas Christian 31-14 (Jim Wacker)
West Va. . . . . Sun 12-25-87 Oklahoma St. 33-35 (Pat Jones)
West Va. . . . . Fiesta 1-2-89 Notre Dame 21-34 (Lou Holtz)
West Va. . . . . Gator 12-30-89 Clemson 7-27 (Danny Ford)

BOB NEYLAND, 2-5-0 (Army '16) b 2-17-92
Tennessee . . . . Orange 1-2-39 Oklahoma 17-0 (Tom Stidham)

Tennessee	Rose 1-1-40	Southern Cal 0-14 (Howard Jones)
Tennessee	Sugar 1-1-41	Boston College 13-19 (Frank Leahy)
Tennessee	Orange 1-1-47	Rice 0-8 (Jess Neely)
Tennessee	Cotton 1-1-51	Texas 20-14 (Blair Cherry)
Tennessee	Sugar 1-1-52	Maryland 13-28 (Jim Tatum)
Tennessee	Cotton 1-1-53	Texas 0-16 (Ed Price)

RAY NOLTING, 1-0-0   (Cincinnati '36)   b 11-8-13

Cincinnati	Sun 1-1-47	Virginia Tech 18-6 (Jimmy Kitts)

HOMER NORTON, 2-2-1   (Birmingham Southern '16)   b 12-30-96

Centenary............	Dixie Classic 1-1-34	Arkansas 7-7 (Fred Thomsen)
Texas A&M..........	Sugar 1-1-40	Tulane 14-13 (Lowell "Red" Dawson)
Texas A&M..........	Cotton 1-1-41	Fordham 13-12 (Jim Crowley)
Texas A&M..........	Cotton 1-1-42	Alabama 21-29 (Frank Thomas)
Texas A&M..........	Orange 1-1-44	Louisiana St. 14-19 (Bernie Moore)

TOM NUGENT, 0-2-0   (Ithaca '36)   b 2-24-16

Florida St.	Sun 1-1-55	UTEP 20-47 (Mike Brumbelow)
Florida St.	Bluegrass 12-13-58	Oklahoma St. 6-15 (Cliff Speegle)

BERNARD "BUNNIE" OAKES, 0-1-0   (Illinois '24)   b 9-15-98

Colorado	Cotton 1-1-38	Rice 14-28 (Jimmy Kitts)

JORDAN OLIVAR, 1-1-0   (Villanova '38)   b 1-30-15

Villanova	Great Lakes 12-6-47	Kentucky 14-24 (Paul "Bear" Bryant)
Villanova	Harbor 1-1-49	Nevada 27-7 (Joe Sheeketski)

AL ONOFRIO, 1-1-0   (Arizona St. '43)   b 3-15-21

Missouri..............	Fiesta 12-23-72	Arizona St. 35-49 (Frank Kush)
Missouri..............	Sun 12-29-73	Auburn 34-17 (Ralph "Shug" Jordan)

BENNIE OOSTERBAAN, 1-0-0   (Michigan '28)   b 2-24-06

Michigan	Rose 1-1-51	California 14-6 (Lynn "Pappy" Waldorf)

TOM OSBORNE, 8-11-0   (Hastings '59)   b 2-23-37

Nebraska.............	Cotton 1-1-74	Texas 19-3 (Darrell Royal)
Nebraska.............	Sugar 12-31-74	Florida 13-10 (Doug Dickey)
Nebraska.............	Fiesta 12-26-75	Arizona St. 14-17 (Frank Kush)
Nebraska.............	Bluebonnet 12-31-76	Texas Tech 27-24 (Steve Sloan)
Nebraska.............	Liberty 12-19-77	North Caro. 21-17 (Bill Dooley)
Nebraska.............	Orange 1-1-79	Oklahoma 24-31 (Barry Switzer)
Nebraska.............	Cotton 1-1-80	Houston 14-17 (Bill Yeoman)
Nebraska.............	Sun 12-27-80	Mississippi St. 31-17 (Emory Bellard)
Nebraska.............	Orange 1-1-82	Clemson 15-22 (Danny Ford)
Nebraska.............	Orange 1-1-83	Louisiana St. 21-20 (Jerry Stovall)
Nebraska.............	Orange 1-2-84	Miami (Fla.) 30-31 (Howard Schnellenberger)
Nebraska.............	Sugar 1-1-85	Louisiana St. 28-10 (Bill Arnsparger)
Nebraska.............	Fiesta 1-1-86	Michigan 23-27 (Glenn "Bo" Schembechler)
Nebraska.............	Sugar 1-1-87	Louisiana St. 30-15 (Bill Arnsparger)
Nebraska.............	Fiesta 1-1-88	Florida St. 28-31 (Bobby Bowden)
Nebraska.............	Orange 1-2-89	Miami (Fla.) 3-23 (Jimmy Johnson)
Nebraska.............	Fiesta 1-1-90	Florida St. 17-41 (Bobby Bowden)
Nebraska.............	Fla. Citrus 1-1-91	Georgia Tech 21-45 (Bobby Ross)
Nebraska.............	Orange 1-1-92	Miami (Fla.) 0-22 (Dennis Erickson)

JIM OWENS, 2-1-0   (Oklahoma '50)   b 3-6-27

Washington	Rose 1-1-60	Wisconsin 44-8 (Milt Bruhn)
Washington	Rose 1-2-61	Minnesota 17-7 (Murray Warmath)
Washington	Rose 1-1-64	Illinois 7-17 (Pete Elliott)

JACK PARDEE, 0-1-0   (Texas A&M '57)   b 4-9-36

Houston..............	Aloha 12-25-88	Washington St. 22-24 (Dennis Erickson)

ARA PARSEGHIAN, 3-2-0   (Miami, Ohio '49)   b 5-21-23

Notre Dame	Cotton 1-1-70	Texas 17-21 (Darrell Royal)
Notre Dame	Cotton 1-1-71	Texas 24-11 (Darrell Royal)
Notre Dame	Orange 1-1-73	Nebraska 6-40 (Bob Devaney)
Notre Dame	Sugar 12-31-73	Alabama 24-23 (Paul "Bear" Bryant)
Notre Dame	Orange 1-1-75	Alabama 13-11 (Paul "Bear" Bryant)

PAUL PASQUALONI, 1-0-0   (Penn St. '72)   b 8-16-49

Syracuse	Hall of Fame 1-1-92	Ohio St. 24-17 (John Cooper)

JOE PATERNO, 14-7-1   (Brown '50)   b 12-21-26

Penn St...............	Gator 12-30-67	Florida St. 17-17 (Bill Peterson)
Penn St...............	Orange 1-1-69	Kansas 15-14 (Pepper Rodgers)
Penn St...............	Orange 1-1-70	Missouri 10-3 (Dan Devine)
Penn St...............	Cotton 1-1-72	Texas 30-6 (Darrell Royal)
Penn St...............	Sugar 12-31-72	Oklahoma 0-14 (Chuck Fairbanks)
Penn St...............	Orange 1-1-74	Louisiana St. 16-9 (Charlie McClendon)
Penn St...............	Cotton 1-1-75	Baylor 41-20 (Grant Teaff)
Penn St...............	Sugar 12-31-75	Alabama 6-13 (Paul "Bear" Bryant)
Penn St...............	Gator 12-27-76	Notre Dame 9-20 (Dan Devine)

Penn St.	Fiesta 12-25-77	Arizona St. 42-30 (Frank Kush)
Penn St.	Sugar 1-1-79	Alabama 7-14 (Paul "Bear" Bryant)
Penn St.	Liberty 12-22-79	Tulane 9-6 (Larry Smith)
Penn St.	Fiesta 12-26-80	Ohio St. 31-19 (Earle Bruce)
Penn St.	Fiesta 1-1-82	Southern Cal 26-10 (John Robinson)
Penn St.	Sugar 1-1-83	Georgia 27-23 (Vince Dooley)
Penn St.	Aloha 12-26-83	Washington 13-10 (Don James)
Penn St.	Orange 1-1-86	Oklahoma 10-25 (Barry Switzer)
Penn St.	Fiesta 1-1-87	Miami (Fla.) 14-10 (Jimmy Johnson)
Penn St.	Fla. Citrus 1-1-88	Clemson 10-35 (Danny Ford)
Penn St.	Holiday 12-29-89	Brigham Young 50-39 (LaVell Edwards)
Penn St.	Blockbuster 12-28-90	Florida St. 17-24 (Bobby Bowden)
Penn St.	Fiesta 1-1-92	Tennessee 42-17 (Johnny Majors)

JOE RAYMOND PEACE, 0-0-0 (Louisiana Tech '68) b 6-5-45
Louisiana Tech	Independence 12-15-90	Maryland 34-34 (Joe Krivak)

CHARLEY PELL, 2-3-0 (Alabama '64) b 2-27-41
Clemson	Gator 12-30-77	Pittsburgh 3-34 (Jackie Sherrill)
Florida	Tangerine 12-20-80	Maryland 35-20 (Jerry Claiborne)
Florida	Peach 12-31-81	West Va. 6-26 (Don Nehlen)
Florida	Bluebonnet 12-31-82	Arkansas 24-28 (Lou Holtz)
Florida	Gator 12-30-83	Iowa 14-6 (Hayden Fry)

RAY PERKINS, 3-0-0 (Alabama '67) b 11-6-41
Alabama	Sun 12-24-83	Southern Methodist 28-7 (Bobby Collins)
Alabama	Aloha 12-28-85	Southern Cal 24-3 (Ted Tollner)
Alabama	Sun 12-26-86	Washington 28-6 (Don James)

GEORGE PERLES, 3-3-0 (Michigan St. '60) b 7-16-34
Michigan St.	Cherry 12-22-84	Army 6-10 (Jim Young)
Michigan St.	All-American 12-31-85	Georgia Tech 14-17 (Bill Curry)
Michigan St.	Rose 1-1-88	Southern Cal 20-17 (Larry Smith)
Michigan St.	Gator 1-1-89	Georgia 27-34 (Vince Dooley)
Michigan St.	Aloha 12-25-89	Hawaii 33-13 (Bob Wagner)
Michigan St.	John Hancock 12-31-90	Southern Cal 17-16 (Larry Smith)

DOYT PERRY, 0-1-0 (Bowling Green '32) b 1-6-10
Bowling Green	Mercy 11-23-61	Fresno St. 6-36 (Cecil Coleman)

BILL PETERSON, 1-2-1 (Ohio Northern '46) b 5-14-20
Florida St.	Gator 1-2-65	Oklahoma 36-19 (Gomer Jones)
Florida St.	Sun 12-24-66	Wyoming 20-28 (Lloyd Eaton)
Florida St.	Gator 12-30-67	Penn St. 17-17 (Joe Paterno)
Florida St.	Peach 12-30-68	Louisiana St. 27-31 (Charlie McClendon)

JIMMY PHELAN, 0-3-0 (Notre Dame '19) b 12-5-92
Washington	Rose 1-1-37	Pittsburgh 0-21 (Jock Sutherland)
St. Mary's (Cal.)	Sugar 1-1-46	Oklahoma St. 12-33 (Jim Lookabaugh)
St. Mary's (Cal.)	Oil 1-1-47	Georgia Tech 19-41 (Bobby Dodd)

ALVIN "PIX" PIERSON, 0-1-0 (Nevada '22) b 7-25-98
Fresno St.	Raisin 1-1-46	Drake 12-13 (Vee Green)

JIM PITTMAN, 1-0-0 (Mississippi St. '50) b 8-28-25
Tulane	Liberty 12-12-70	Colorado 17-3 (Eddie Crowder)

JOHN PONT, 0-2-0 (Miami, Ohio '52) b 11-13-27
Miami (Ohio)	Tangerine 12-22-52	Houston 21-49 (Bill Yeoman)
Indiana	Rose 1-1-68	Southern Cal 3-14 (John McKay)

WARREN POWERS, 3-2-0 (Nebraska '63) b 2-19-41
Missouri	Liberty 12-23-78	Louisiana St. 20-15 (Charlie McClendon)
Missouri	Hall of Fame 12-29-79	South Caro. 24-14 (Jim Carlen)
Missouri	Liberty 12-27-80	Purdue 25-28 (Jim Young)
Missouri	Tangerine 12-19-81	Southern Miss. 19-17 (Bobby Collins)
Missouri	Holiday 12-23-83	Brigham Young 17-21 (LaVell Edwards)

CLARENCE "NIBS" PRICE, 0-1-0 (California '14) b 1889
California	Rose 1-1-29	Georgia Tech 7-8 (Bill Alexander)

ED PRICE, 1-0-0 (Texas '33) b 1-12-09
Texas	Cotton 1-1-53	Tennessee 16-0 (Bob Neyland)

TOMMY PROTHRO, 2-2-0 (Duke '42) b 7-20-20
Oregon St.	Rose 1-1-57	Iowa 19-35 (Forest Evashevski)
Oregon St.	Liberty 12-15-62	Villanova 6-0 (Alex Bell)
Oregon St.	Rose 1-1-65	Michigan 7-34 (Chalmers "Bump" Elliott)
UCLA	Rose 1-1-66	Michigan St. 14-12 (Duffy Daugherty)

DAVE RADER, 1-1-0 (Tulsa '80) b 3-9-57
Tulsa	Independence 12-16-89	Oregon 24-27 (Rich Brooks)
Tulsa	Freedom 12-30-91	San Diego St. 28-17 (Al Luginbill)

JOHN RALSTON, 2-2-0 (California '54) b 4-25-27
Utah St.	Sun 12-31-60	New Mexico St. 13-20 (Warren Woodson)

Utah St.	Gotham 12-9-61	Baylor 9-24 (John Bridgers)
Stanford	Rose 1-1-71	Ohio St. 27-17 (Woody Hayes)
Stanford	Rose 1-1-72	Michigan 13-12 (Glenn "Bo" Schembechler)

RED REESE, 1-0-0 (Washington St. '25) b 3-2-99
Second Air Force	Sun 1-1-43	Hardin-Simmons 13-7 (Warren Woodson)

BO REIN, 2-0-0 (Ohio St. '58) b 7-20-45
North Caro. St.	Peach 12-31-77	Iowa St. 24-14 (Earle Bruce)
North Caro. St.	Tangerine 12-23-78	Pittsburgh 30-17 (Jackie Sherrill)

PAUL ROACH, 0-3-0 (Black Hills St. '52) b 10-24-27
Wyoming.............	Holiday 12-30-87	Iowa 19-20 (Hayden Fry)
Wyoming.............	Holiday 12-30-88	Oklahoma St. 14-62 (Pat Jones)
Wyoming.............	Copper 12-31-90	California 15-17 (Bruce Snyder)

ED ROBINSON, 0-1-0 (Brown '96) b 10-15-73
Brown...............	Rose 1-1-16	Washington St. 0-14 (Bill "Lone Star" Dietz)

JOHN ROBINSON, 4-1-0 (Oregon '58) b 7-25-35
Southern Cal........	Rose 1-1-77	Michigan 14-6 (Glenn "Bo" Schembechler)
Southern Cal........	Bluebonnet 12-31-77	Texas A&M 47-28 (Emory Bellard)
Southern Cal........	Rose 1-1-79	Michigan 17-10 (Glenn "Bo" Schembechler)
Southern Cal........	Rose 1-1-80	Ohio St. 17-16 (Earle Bruce)
Southern Cal........	Fiesta 1-1-82	Penn St. 10-26 (Joe Paterno)

KNUTE ROCKNE, 1-0-0 (Notre Dame '14) b 3-4-88
Notre Dame.........	Rose 1-1-25	Stanford 27-10 (Glenn "Pop" Warner)

PEPPER RODGERS, 0-2-0 (Georgia Tech '55) b 10-8-31
Kansas..............	Orange 1-1-69	Penn St. 14-15 (Joe Paterno)
Georgia Tech	Peach 12-25-78	Purdue 21-41 (Jim Young)

DARRYL ROGERS, 1-0-0 (Fresno St. '57) b 5-28-34
Arizona St.	Fiesta 1-1-83	Oklahoma 32-21 (Barry Switzer)

E. L. "DICK" ROMNEY, 0-1-0 (Utah '17) b 2-12-95
Utah St.	Raisin 1-1-47	San Jose St. 0-20 (Bill Hubbard)

TIM ROSE, 0-1-0 (Xavier, Ohio '62) b 10-14-41
Miami (Ohio)	California 12-13-86	San Jose St. 7-37 (Claude Gilbert)

BOBBY ROSS, 4-2-0 (Va. Military '59) 12-23-36
Maryland............	Aloha 12-25-82	Washington 20-21 (Don James)
Maryland............	Fla. Citrus 12-17-83	Tennessee 23-30 (Johnny Majors)
Maryland............	Sun 12-22-84	Tennessee 27-26 (Johnny Majors)
Maryland............	Cherry 12-21-85	Syracuse 35-18 (Dick MacPherson)
Georgia Tech	Fla. Citrus 1-1-91	Nebraska 45-21 (Tom Osborne)
Georgia Tech	Aloha 12-25-91	Stanford 18-17 (Dennis Green)

DARRELL ROYAL, 8-7-1 (Oklahoma '50) b 7-6-24
Texas	Sugar 1-1-58	Mississippi 7-39 (John Vaught)
Texas	Cotton 1-1-60	Syracuse 14-23 (Ben Schwartzwalder)
Texas	Bluebonnet 12-17-60	Alabama 3-3 (Paul "Bear" Bryant)
Texas	Cotton 1-1-62	Mississippi 12-7 (John Vaught)
Texas	Cotton 1-1-63	Louisiana St. 0-13 (Charlie McClendon)
Texas	Cotton 1-1-64	Navy 28-6 (Wayne Hardin)
Texas	Orange 1-1-65	Alabama 21-17 (Paul "Bear" Bryant)
Texas	Bluebonnet 12-17-66	Mississippi 19-0 (John Vaught)
Texas	Cotton 1-1-69	Tennessee 36-13 (Doug Dickey)
Texas	Cotton 1-1-70	Notre Dame 21-17 (Ara Parseghian)
Texas	Cotton 1-1-71	Notre Dame 11-24 (Ara Parseghian)
Texas	Cotton 1-1-72	Penn St. 6-30 (Joe Paterno)
Texas	Cotton 1-1-73	Alabama 17-13 (Paul "Bear" Bryant)
Texas	Cotton 1-1-74	Nebraska 3-19 (Tom Osborne)
Texas	Gator 12-30-74	Auburn 3-27 (Ralph "Shug" Jordan)
Texas	Bluebonnet 12-27-75	Colorado 38-21 (Bill Mallory)

HENRY "RED" SANDERS, 0-2-0 (Vanderbilt '27) b 3-7-05
UCLA	Rose 1-1-54	Michigan St. 20-28 (Clarence "Biggie" Munn)
UCLA	Rose 1-2-56	Michigan St. 14-17 (Duffy Daugherty)

RALPH SASSE, 0-1-0 (Army '10) b 7-19-89
Mississippi St.	Orange 1-1-37	Duquesne 12-13 (John Smith)

GEORGE SAUER, 0-3-0 (Nebraska '34) b 12-11-10
Kansas..............	Orange 1-1-48	Georgia Tech 14-20 (Bobby Dodd)
Baylor..............	Orange 1-1-52	Georgia Tech 14-17 (Bobby Dodd)
Baylor..............	Gator 12-31-54	Auburn 13-33 (Ralph "Shug" Jordan)

MACK SAXON, 0-1-0 (Texas) b 1901
UTEP	Sun 1-1-37	Hardin-Simmons 6-34 (Frank Kimbrough)

GLENN "BO" SCHEMBECHLER, 5-12-0 (Miami, Ohio '51) b 4-1-29
Michigan	Rose 1-1-70	Southern Cal 3-10 (John McKay)
Michigan	Rose 1-1-72	Stanford 12-13 (John Ralston)
Michigan	Orange 1-1-76	Oklahoma 6-14 (Barry Switzer)

Michigan	Rose 1-1-77	Southern Cal 6-14 (John Robinson)
Michigan	Rose 1-2-78	Washington 20-27 (Don James)
Michigan	Rose 1-1-79	Southern Cal 10-17 (John Robinson)
Michigan	Gator 12-28-79	North Caro. 15-17 (Dick Crum)
Michigan	Rose 1-1-81	Washington 23-6 (Don James)
Michigan	Bluebonnet 12-31-81	UCLA 33-14 (Terry Donahue)
Michigan	Rose 1-1-83	UCLA 14-24 (Terry Donahue)
Michigan	Sugar 1-2-84	Auburn 7-9 (Pat Dye)
Michigan	Holiday 12-21-84	Brigham Young 17-24 (LaVell Edwards)
Michigan	Fiesta 1-1-86	Nebraska 27-23 (Tom Osborne)
Michigan	Rose 1-1-87	Arizona St. 15-22 (John Cooper)
Michigan	Hall of Fame 1-2-88	Alabama 28-24 (Bill Curry)
Michigan	Rose 1-2-89	Southern Cal 22-14 (Larry Smith)
Michigan	Rose 1-1-90	Southern Cal 10-17 (Larry Smith)

MERLE SCHLOSSER, 0-1-0   (Illinois '50)   b 10-14-27
| Western Mich. .... | Aviation 12-9-61 | New Mexico 12-28 (Bill Weeks) |

HOWARD SCHNELLENBERGER, 3-0-0   (Kentucky '56)   b 3-16-34
Miami (Fla.)	Peach 1-2-81	Virginia Tech 20-10 (Bill Dooley)
Miami (Fla.)	Orange 1-2-84	Nebraska 31-30 (Tom Osborne)
Louisville	Fiesta 1-1-91	Alabama 34-7 (Gene Stallings)

PAUL SCHUDEL, 0-1-0   (Miami, Ohio '66)   b 7-2-44
| Ball St. .... | California 12-9-89 | Fresno St. 6-27 (Jim Sweeney) |

BILL SCHUTTE, 0-1-0   (Idaho '33)   b 5-7-10
| San Diego St. .... | Harbor 1-1-48 | Hardin-Simmons 0-53 (Warren Woodson) |

BEN SCHWARTZWALDER, 2-5-0   (West Va. '35)   b 6-2-09
Syracuse	Orange 1-1-53	Alabama 6-61 (Harold "Red" Drew)
Syracuse	Cotton 1-1-57	Texas Christian 27-28 (Abe Martin)
Syracuse	Orange 1-1-59	Oklahoma 6-21 (Bud Wilkinson)
Syracuse	Cotton 1-1-60	Texas 23-14 (Darrell Royal)
Syracuse	Liberty 12-16-61	Miami (Fla.) 15-14 (Andy Gustafson)
Syracuse	Sugar 1-1-65	Louisiana St. 10-13 (Charlie McClendon)
Syracuse	Gator 12-31-66	Tennessee 12-18 (Doug Dickey)

CLARK SHAUGHNESSY, 1-0-0   (Minnesota '14)   b 3-6-92
| Stanford .... | Rose 1-1-41 | Nebraska 21-13 (Lawrence McC. "Biff" Jones) |

LAWRENCE "BUCK" SHAW, 2-0-0   (Notre Dame '22)   b 3-28-99
| Santa Clara .... | Sugar 1-1-37 | Louisiana St. 21-14 (Bernie Moore) |
| Santa Clara .... | Sugar 1-1-38 | Louisiana St. 6-0 (Bernie Moore) |

TERRY SHEA, 1-0-0   (Oregon '68)   b 6-12-46
| San Jose St. .... | California Raisin 12-8-90 | Central Mich. 48-24 (Herb Deromedi) |

JOE SHEEKETSKI, 1-1-0   (Notre Dame '33)   b 4-15-09
| Nevada .... | Salad 1-1-48 | North Texas 13-6 (Odus Mitchell) |
| Nevada .... | Harbor 1-1-49 | Villanova 7-27 (Jordan Olivar) |

DICK SHERIDAN, 2-3-0   (South Caro. '64)   b 8-9-41
North Caro. St.	Peach 12-31-86	Virginia Tech 24-25 (Bill Dooley)
North Caro. St.	Peach 12-31-88	Iowa 28-23 (Hayden Fry)
North Caro. St.	Copper 12-31-89	Arizona 10-17 (Dick Tomey)
North Caro. St.	All-American 12-28-90	Southern Miss. 31-27 (Jeff Bower)
North Caro. St.	Peach 1-1-92	East Caro. 34-37 (Bill Lewis)

EUGENE "BO" SHERMAN, 1-0-0   (Henderson St. '30)   b 7-5-08
| Geo. Washington .... | Sun 1-1-57 | UTEP 13-0 (Mike Brumbelow) |

JACKIE SHERRILL, 6-3-0   (Alabama '66)   b 11-28-43
Pittsburgh	Gator 12-30-77	Clemson 34-3 (Charley Pell)
Pittsburgh	Tangerine 12-23-78	North Caro. St. 17-30 (Bo Rein)
Pittsburgh	Fiesta 12-25-79	Arizona 16-10 (Tony Mason)
Pittsburgh	Gator 12-29-80	South Caro. 37-9 (Jim Carlen)
Pittsburgh	Sugar 1-1-82	Georgia 24-20 (Vince Dooley)
Texas A&M	Cotton 1-1-86	Auburn 36-16 (Pat Dye)
Texas A&M	Cotton 1-1-87	Ohio St. 12-28 (Earle Bruce)
Texas A&M	Cotton 1-1-88	Notre Dame 35-10 (Lou Holtz)
Mississippi St.	Liberty 12-29-91	Air Force 15-38 (Fisher DeBerry)

TED SHIPKEY, 0-1-0   (Stanford '27)   b 9-28-04
| New Mexico .... | Sun 1-2-39 | Utah 0-28 (Ike Armstrong) |

LARRY SIEMERING, 1-0-0   (San Francisco '35)   b 11-24-10
| Pacific (Cal.) .... | Raisin 1-1-48 | Wichita St. 26-14 (Ralph Graham) |

CHAUNCEY SIMPSON, 0-1-0   (Missouri '25)   b 12-21-02
| Missouri .... | Cotton 1-1-46 | Texas 27-40 (Dana Bible) |

DAN SIMRELL, 0-1-0   (Toledo '65)   b 4-9-43
| Toledo .... | California 12-15-84 | Nevada-Las Vegas 13-30 (Harvey Hyde) |

STEVE SLOAN, 0-2-1   (Alabama '66)   b 8-19-44
| Vanderbilt .... | Peach 12-28-74 | Texas Tech 6-6 (Jim Carlen) |

Texas Tech	Bluebonnet 12-31-76	Nebraska 24-27 (Tom Osborne)
Texas Tech	Tangerine 12-23-77	Florida St. 17-40 (Bobby Bowden)

R. C. SLOCUM, 1-2-0   (McNeese St. '67)   b 11-7-44

Texas A&M..........	John Hancock 12-30-89	Pittsburgh 28-31 (Paul Hackett)
Texas A&M..........	Holiday 12-29-90	Brigham Young 65-14 (LaVell Edwards)
Texas A&M..........	Cotton 1-1-92	Florida St. 2-10 (Bobby Bowden)

ANDY SMITH, 1-0-1   (Pennsylvania '06)   b 9-10-83

California	Rose 1-1-21	Ohio St. 28-0 (John Wilce)
California	Rose 1-2-22	Wash. & Jeff. 0-0 (Earle "Greasy" Neale)

HOMER SMITH, 0-1-0   (Princeton '54)   b 10-9-31

Davidson	Tangerine 12-26-69	Toledo 33-56 (Frank Lauterbur)

JOHN "LITTLE CLIPPER" SMITH, 1-0-0   (Notre Dame '29)   b 12-12-04

Duquesne	Orange 1-1-37	Mississippi St. 13-12 (Ralph Sasse)

LARRY SMITH, 2-4-1   (Bowling Green '62)   b 9-12-39

Tulane...............	Liberty 12-22-79	Penn St. 6-9 (Joe Paterno)
Arizona	Sun 12-28-85	Georgia 13-13 (Vince Dooley)
Arizona	Aloha 12-27-86	North Caro. 30-21 (Dick Crum)
Southern Cal........	Rose 1-1-88	Michigan St. 17-20 (George Perles)
Southern Cal........	Rose 1-2-89	Michigan 14-22 (Glenn "Bo" Schembechler)
Southern Cal........	Rose 1-1-90	Michigan 17-10 (Glenn "Bo" Schembechler)
Southern Cal........	John Hancock 12-31-90	Michigan St. 16-17 (George Perles)

MAURICE "CLIPPER" SMITH, 0-0-1   (Notre Dame '21)   b 10-15-98

Villanova	Bacardi 1-1-37	Auburn 7-7 (Jack Meagher)

CARL SNAVELY, 0-3-0   (Lebanon Valley '15)   b 7-30-94

North Caro.	Sugar 1-1-47	Georgia 10-20 (Wally Butts)
North Caro.	Sugar 1-1-49	Oklahoma 6-14 (Bud Wilkinson)
North Caro.	Cotton 1-2-50	Rice 13-27 (Jess Neely)

BRUCE SNYDER, 2-0-0   (Oregon '62)   b 3-14-40

California	Copper 12-31-90	Wyoming 17-15 (Paul Roach)
California	Fla. Citrus 1-1-92	Clemson 37-13 (Ken Hatfield)

CLARENCE "DOC" SPEARS, 1-0-0   (Dartmouth '16)   b 7-24-94

West Va...............	San Diego East-West Christmas Classic 12-25-22	Gonzaga 21-13 (Charles "Gus" Dorais)

CLIFF SPEEGLE, 1-0-0   (Oklahoma '41)   b 11-4-17

Oklahoma St.	Bluegrass 12-13-58	Florida St. 15-6 (Tom Nugent)

STEVE SPURRIER, 0-2-0   (Florida '67)   b 4-20-45

Duke	All-American 12-28-89	Texas Tech 21-49 (Spike Dykes)
Florida	Sugar 1-1-92	Notre Dame 28-39 (Lou Holtz)

GENE STALLINGS, 2-1-0   (Texas A&M '57)   b 3-2-35

Texas A&M..........	Cotton 1-1-68	Alabama 20-16 (Paul "Bear" Bryant)
Alabama	Fiesta 1-1-91	Louisville 7-34 (Howard Schnellenberger)
Alabama	Blockbuster 12-28-91	Colorado 30-25 (Bill McCartney)

JIM STANGELAND, 0-0-1   (Arizona St. '48)   b 12-21-21

Long Beach St.	Pasadena 12-19-70	Louisville 24-24 (Lee Corso)

JIM STANLEY, 2-0-0   (Texas A&M '59)   b 5-22-35

Oklahoma St.	Fiesta 12-28-74	Brigham Young 16-6 (LaVell Edwards)
Oklahoma St.	Tangerine 12-18-76	Brigham Young 49-12 (LaVell Edwards)

TOM STIDHAM, 0-1-0   (Haskell '27)   b 3-27-04

Oklahoma............	Orange 1-2-39	Tennessee 0-17 (Bob Neyland)

LON STINER, 1-0-0   (Nebraska '27)   b 6-20-03

Oregon St.	Rose 1-1-42	Duke 20-16 (Wallace Wade)

HARRY STITELER, 1-0-0   (Texas A&M '31)   b 9-17-09

Texas A&M..........	Presidential Cup 12-9-50	Georgia 40-20 (Wally Butts)

CHUCK STOBART, 1-0-0   (Ohio '59)   b 10-27-34

Toledo	California 12-19-81	San Jose St. 27-25 (Jack Elway)

CAL STOLL, 0-1-0   (Minnesota '50)   b 12-12-23

Minnesota............	Hall of Fame 12-22-77	Maryland 7-17 (Jerry Claiborne)

DENNY STOLZ, 0-3-0   (Alma '55)   b 9-12-34

Bowling Green	California 12-18-82	Fresno St. 28-29 (Jim Sweeney)
Bowling Green	California 12-14-85	Fresno St. 7-51 (Jim Sweeney)
San Diego St.	Holiday 12-30-86	Iowa 38-39 (Hayden Fry)

JERRY STOVALL, 0-1-0   (Louisiana St. '63)   b 4-30-41

Louisiana St.	Orange 1-1-83	Nebraska 20-21 (Tom Osborne)

BOB STULL, 0-1-0   (Kansas St. '68)   b 11-21-45

UTEP	Independence 12-23-88	Southern Miss. 18-38 (Curley Hallman)

JOCK SUTHERLAND, 1-3-0   (Pittsburgh '18)   b 3-21-89

Pittsburgh............	Rose 1-1-28	Stanford 6-7 (Glenn "Pop" Warner)

Pittsburgh.............	Rose 1-1-30	Southern Cal 14-47 (Howard Jones)
Pittsburgh.............	Rose 1-2-33	Southern Cal 0-35 (Howard Jones)
Pittsburgh.............	Rose 1-1-37	Washington 21-0 (Jimmy Phelan)

JIM SWEENEY, 4-1-0   (Portland '51)   b 9-1-29
Fresno St..............	California 12-18-82	Bowling Green 29-28 (Denny Stolz)
Fresno St..............	California 12-14-85	Bowling Green 51-7 (Denny Stolz)
Fresno St..............	California 12-10-88	Western Mich. 35-30 (Al Molde)
Fresno St..............	California 12-9-89	Ball St. 27-8 (Paul Schudel)
Fresno St..............	California 12-13-91	Bowling Green 21-28 (Gary Blackney)

BARRY SWITZER, 8-5-0   (Arkansas '60)   b 10-5-37
Oklahoma.............	Orange 1-1-76	Michigan 14-6 (Glenn "Bo" Schembechler)
Oklahoma.............	Fiesta 12-25-76	Wyoming 41-7 (Fred Akers)
Oklahoma.............	Orange 1-2-78	Arkansas 6-31 (Lou Holtz)
Oklahoma.............	Orange 1-1-79	Nebraska 31-24 (Tom Osborne)
Oklahoma.............	Orange 1-1-80	Florida St. 24-7 (Bobby Bowden)
Oklahoma.............	Orange 1-1-81	Florida St. 18-17 (Bobby Bowden)
Oklahoma.............	Sun 12-26-81	Houston 40-14 (Bill Yeoman)
Oklahoma.............	Fiesta 1-1-83	Arizona St. 21-32 (Darryl Rogers)
Oklahoma.............	Orange 1-1-85	Washington 17-28 (Don James)
Oklahoma.............	Orange 1-1-86	Penn St. 25-10 (Joe Paterno)
Oklahoma.............	Orange 1-1-87	Arkansas 42-8 (Ken Hatfield)
Oklahoma.............	Orange 1-1-88	Miami (Fla.) 14-20 (Jimmy Johnson)
Oklahoma.............	Fla. Citrus 1-2-89	Clemson 6-13 (Danny Ford)

CHARLIE TATE, 1-1-0   (Florida '42)   b 2-20-21
| Miami (Fla.)......... | Liberty 12-10-66 | Virginia Tech 14-7 (Jerry Claiborne) |
| Miami (Fla.)......... | Bluebonnet 12-23-67 | Colorado 21-31 (Eddie Crowder) |

JIM TATUM, 3-2-1   (North Caro. '35)   b 7-22-13
Oklahoma.............	Gator 1-1-47	North Caro. St. 34-13 (Beattie Feathers)
Maryland.............	Gator 1-1-48	Georgia 20-20 (Wally Butts)
Maryland.............	Gator 1-2-50	Missouri 20-7 (Don Faurot)
Maryland.............	Sugar 1-1-52	Tennessee 28-13 (Bob Neyland)
Maryland.............	Orange 1-1-54	Oklahoma 0-7 (Bud Wilkinson)
Maryland.............	Orange 1-2-56	Oklahoma 6-20 (Bud Wilkinson)

CHUCK TAYLOR, 0-1-0   (Stanford '43)   b 1-24-20
| Stanford .... | Rose 1-1-52 | Illinois 7-40 (Ray Eliot) |

GRANT TEAFF, 3-4-0   (McMurry '56)   b 11-12-33
Baylor................	Cotton 1-1-75	Penn St. 20-41 (Joe Paterno)
Baylor................	Peach 12-31-79	Clemson 24-18 (Danny Ford)
Baylor................	Cotton 1-1-81	Alabama 2-30 (Paul "Bear" Bryant)
Baylor................	Bluebonnet 12-31-83	Oklahoma St. 14-24 (Jimmy Johnson)
Baylor................	Liberty 12-27-85	Louisiana St. 21-7 (Bill Arnsparger)
Baylor................	Bluebonnet 12-31-86	Colorado 21-9 (Bill McCartney)
Baylor................	Copper 12-31-91	Indiana 0-24 (Bill Mallory)

EDDIE TEAGUE, 1-0-0   (North Caro. '44)   b 12-14-21
| Citadel.............. | Tangerine 12-30-60 | Tennessee Tech 27-0 (Wilburn Tucker) |

LOU TEPPER, 0-1-0   (Rutgers '67)   b 7-21-45
| Illinois............... | John Hancock 12-31-91 | UCLA 3-6 (Terry Donahue) |

ROBERT THEDER, 0-1-0   (Western Mich. '63)   b 9-22-39
| California .... | Garden State 12-15-79 | Temple 17-28 (Wayne Hardin) |

FRANK THOMAS, 4-2-0   (Notre Dame '23)   b 11-14-98
Alabama	Rose 1-1-35	Stanford 29-13 (Claude "Tiny" Thornhill)
Alabama	Rose 1-1-38	California 0-13 (Leonard "Stub" Allison)
Alabama	Cotton 1-1-42	Texas A&M 29-21 (Homer Norton)
Alabama	Orange 1-1-43	Boston College 37-21 (Denny Myers)
Alabama	Sugar 1-1-45	Duke 26-29 (Eddie Cameron)
Alabama	Rose 1-1-46	Southern Cal 34-14 (Jeff Cravath)

FRED THOMSEN, 0-0-1   (Nebraska '25)   b 4-25-97
| Arkansas .... | Dixie Classic 1-1-34 | Centenary 7-7 (Homer Norton) |

CLAUDE "TINY" THORNHILL, 1-2-0   (Pittsburgh '17)   b 4-14-93
Stanford	Rose 1-1-34	Columbia 0-7 (Lou Little)
Stanford	Rose 1-1-35	Alabama 13-29 (Frank Thomas)
Stanford	Rose 1-1-36	Southern Methodist 7-0 (Matty Bell)

GAYNELL TINSLEY, 0-1-0   (Louisiana St. '37)   b 2-1-15
| Louisiana St......... | Sugar 1-2-50 | Oklahoma 0-35 (Bud Wilkinson) |

TED TOLLNER, 1-2-0   (Cal Poly SLO '62)   b 5-29-40
Southern Cal........	Rose 1-1-85	Ohio St. 20-17 (Earle Bruce)
Southern Cal........	Aloha 12-28-85	Alabama 3-24 (Ray Perkins)
Southern Cal........	Fla. Citrus 1-1-87	Auburn 7-16 (Pat Dye)

DICK TOMEY, 1-1-0   (DePauw '61)   b 6-20-38
| Arizona .... | Copper 12-30-89 | North Caro. St. 17-10 (Dick Sheridan) |
| Arizona .... | Aloha 12-28-90 | Syracuse 0-28 (Dick MacPherson) |

JIM TRIMBLE, 0-1-0 (Indiana '42) b 5-29-18
Wichita St. . . . .   Camellia 12-30-48   Hardin-Simmons 12-49 (Warren Woodson)
FRANK TRITICO, 0-0-1 (Southwestern La. '34) b 3-25-09
Randolph Field . . . . . .   Cotton 1-1-44   Texas 7-7 (Dana Bible)
WILBURN TUCKER, 0-1-0 (Tennessee Tech '43) b 8-11-20
Tennessee Tech . . . . . .   Tangerine 12-30-60   Citadel 0-27 (Eddie Teague)
BOB TYLER, 1-0-0 (Mississippi '58) b 7-4-32
Mississippi St. . . . .   Sun 12-28-74   North Caro. 26-24 (Bill Dooley)
THAD "PIE" VANN, 0-2-0 (Mississippi '28) b 9-22-07
Southern Miss. . . . .   Sun 1-1-53   Pacific (Cal.) 7-26 (Ernie Jorge)
Southern Miss. . . . .   Sun 1-1-54   UTEP 14-37 (Mike Brumbelow)
JOHN VAUGHT, 10-8-0 (Texas Christian '33) b 5-6-08
Mississippi . . . .   Delta 1-1-48   Texas Christian 13-9 (Leo "Dutch" Meyer)
Mississippi . . . .   Sugar 1-1-53   Georgia Tech 7-24 (Bobby Dodd)
Mississippi . . . .   Sugar 1-1-55   Navy 0-21 (Eddie Erdelatz)
Mississippi . . . .   Cotton 1-2-56   Texas Christian 14-13 (Abe Martin)
Mississippi . . . .   Sugar 1-1-58   Texas 39-7 (Darrell Royal)
Mississippi . . . .   Gator 12-27-58   Florida 7-3 (Bob Woodruff)
Mississippi . . . .   Sugar 1-1-60   Louisiana St. 21-0 (Paul Dietzel)
Mississippi . . . .   Sugar 1-2-61   Rice 14-6 (Jess Neely)
Mississippi . . . .   Cotton 1-1-62   Texas 7-12 (Darrell Royal)
Mississippi . . . .   Sugar 1-1-63   Arkansas 17-13 (Frank Broyles)
Mississippi . . . .   Sugar 1-1-64   Alabama 7-12 (Paul "Bear" Bryant)
Mississippi . . . .   Bluebonnet 12-19-64   Tulsa 7-14 (Glenn Dobbs)
Mississippi . . . .   Liberty 12-18-65   Auburn 13-7 (Ralph "Shug" Jordan)
Mississippi . . . .   Bluebonnet 12-17-66   Texas 0-19 (Darrell Royal)
Mississippi . . . .   Sun 12-30-67   UTEP 7-14 (Bobby Dobbs)
Mississippi . . . .   Liberty 12-14-68   Virginia Tech 34-17 (Jerry Claiborne)
Mississippi . . . .   Sugar 1-1-70   Arkansas 27-22 (Frank Broyles)
Mississippi . . . .   Gator 1-2-71   Auburn 28-35 (Ralph "Shug" Jordan)
DICK VERMEIL, 1-0-0 (San Jose St. '58) b 10-30-36
UCLA . . . .   Rose 1-1-76   Ohio St. 23-10 (Woody Hayes)
BOB VOIGTS, 1-0-0 (Northwestern '39) b 3-29-16
Northwestern . . . .   Rose 1-1-49   California 20-14 (Lynn "Pappy" Waldorf)
JIM WACKER, 0-1-0 (Valparaiso '60) b 4-28-37
Texas Christian . . . . . .   Bluebonnet 12-31-84   West Va. 14-31 (Don Nehlen)
WALLACE WADE, 2-2-1 (Brown '17) b 6-15-92
Alabama . . . .   Rose 1-1-26   Washington 20-19 (Enoch Bagshaw)
Alabama . . . .   Rose 1-1-27   Stanford 7-7 (Glenn "Pop" Warner)
Alabama . . . .   Rose 1-1-31   Washington St. 24-0 (Orin "Babe" Hollingbery)
Duke . . . .   Rose 1-2-39   Southern Cal 3-7 (Howard Jones)
Duke . . . .   Rose 1-1-42   Oregon St. 16-20 (Lon Stiner)
BOB WAGNER, 0-1-0 (Wittenberg '69) b 5-16-47
Hawaii . . . .   Aloha 12-25-89   Michigan St. 13-33 (George Perles)
JIM WALDEN, 0-1-0 (Wyoming '60) b 4-10-38
Washington St. . . . .   Holiday 12-18-81   Brigham Young 36-38 (LaVell Edwards)
LYNN "PAPPY" WALDORF, 0-3-0 (Syracuse '25) b 10-3-02
California . . . .   Rose 1-2-49   Northwestern 14-20 (Bob Voigts)
California . . . .   Rose 1-2-50   Ohio St. 14-17 (Wes Fesler)
California . . . .   Rose 1-1-51   Michigan 6-14 (Bennie Oosterbaan)
D. C. "PEAHEAD" WALKER, 1-1-0 (Samford '22) b 2-17-00
Wake Forest . . . .   Gator 1-1-46   South Caro. 26-14 (Johnnie McMillan)
Wake Forest . . . .   Dixie 1-1-49   Baylor 7-20 (Bob Woodruff)
ED WALKER, 0-1-0 (Stanford '27) b 3-25-01
Mississippi . . . .   Orange 1-1-36   Catholic 19-20 (Arthur "Dutch" Bergman)
BILL WALSH, 2-0-0 (San Jose St. '54) b 11-30-31
Stanford . . . .   Sun 12-31-77   Louisiana St. 24-14 (Charlie McClendon)
Stanford . . . .   Bluebonnet 12-31-78   Georgia 25-22 (Vince Dooley)
DALLAS WARD, 1-0-0 (Oregon St. '27) b 8-11-06
Colorado . . . .   Orange 1-1-57   Clemson 27-21 (Frank Howard)
MURRAY WARMATH, 1-1-0 (Tennessee '35) b 12-26-13
Minnesota . . . .   Rose 1-2-61   Washington 7-17 (Jim Owens)
Minnesota . . . .   Rose 1-1-62   UCLA 21-3 (Bill Barnes)
GLENN "POP" WARNER, 1-2-1 (Cornell '95) b 4-5-71
Stanford . . . .   Rose 1-1-25   Notre Dame 10-27 (Knute Rockne)
Stanford . . . .   Rose 1-1-27   Alabama 7-7 (Wallace Wade)
Stanford . . . .   Rose 1-2-28   Pittsburgh 7-6 (Jock Sutherland)
Temple . . . .   Sugar 1-1-35   Tulane 14-20 (Ted Cox)
DeWITT WEAVER, 2-1-0 (Tennessee '37) b 5-11-12
Texas Tech . . . .   Sun 1-1-52   Pacific (Cal.) 25-14 (Ernie Jorge)

| Texas Tech | Gator 1-1-54 | Auburn 35-13 (Ralph "Shug" Jordan) |

Texas Tech .... Gator 1-1-54   Auburn 35-13 (Ralph "Shug" Jordan)
Texas Tech .... Sun 1-2-56   Wyoming 14-21 (Phil Dickens)

BILL WEEKS, 1-0-0   (Iowa St. '51)   b 10-20-29
New Mexico.......... Aviation 12-9-61   Western Mich. 28-12 (Merle Schlosser)

RALPH "PEST" WELCH, 0-1-0   (Purdue '30)   b 8-11-07
Washington .... Rose 1-1-44   Southern Cal 0-29 (Jeff Cravath)

GEORGE WELSH, 3-5-0   (Navy '56)   b 8-26-33
Navy .... Holiday 12-22-78   Brigham Young 23-16 (LaVell Edwards)
Navy .... Garden State 12-14-80   Houston 0-35 (Bill Yeoman)
Navy .... Liberty 12-30-81   Ohio St. 28-31 (Earle Bruce)
Virginia .... Peach 12-31-84   Purdue 27-24 (Leon Burtnett)
Virginia .... All-American 12-22-87   Brigham Young 22-16 (LaVell Edwards)
Virginia .... Fla. Citrus 1-1-90   Illinois 21-31 (John Mackovic)
Virginia .... Sugar 1-1-91   Tennessee 22-23 (Johnny Majors)
Virginia .... Gator 12-29-91   Oklahoma 14-48 (Gary Gibbs)

MIKE WHITE, 0-3-0   (California '58)   b 1-3-36
Illinois .... Liberty 12-29-82   Alabama 15-21 (Paul "Bear" Bryant)
Illinois .... Rose 1-2-84   UCLA 9-45 (Terry Donahue)
Illinois .... Peach 12-31-85   Army 29-31 (Jim Young)

JOHN WILCE, 0-1-0   (Wisconsin '10)   b 5-12-88
Ohio St. .... Rose 1-1-21   California 0-28 (Andy Smith)

BUD WILKINSON, 6-2-0   (Minnesota '37)   b 4-12-16
Oklahoma .... Sugar 1-1-49   North Caro. 14-6 (Carl Snavely)
Oklahoma .... Sugar 1-2-50   Louisiana St. 35-0 (Gaynell Tinsley)
Oklahoma .... Sugar 1-1-51   Kentucky 7-13 (Paul "Bear" Bryant)
Oklahoma .... Orange 1-1-54   Maryland 7-0 (Jim Tatum)
Oklahoma .... Orange 1-2-56   Maryland 20-6 (Jim Tatum)
Oklahoma .... Orange 1-1-58   Duke 48-21 (Bill Murray)
Oklahoma .... Orange 1-1-59   Syracuse 21-6 (Ben Schwartzwalder)
Oklahoma .... Orange 1-1-63   Alabama 0-17 (Paul "Bear" Bryant)

IVY WILLIAMSON, 0-1-0   (Michigan '33)   b 2-4-11
Wisconsin .... Rose 1-1-53   Southern Cal 0-7 (Jess Hill)

TOM WILSON, 2-0-0   (Texas Tech '66)   b 2-24-44
Texas A&M .... Hall of Fame 12-20-78   Iowa St. 28-18 (Earle Bruce)
Texas A&M .... Independence 12-12-81   Oklahoma St. 33-16 (Jimmy Johnson)

SAM WINNINGHAM, 0-1-0   (Colorado '50)   b 10-11-26
Cal St. Northridge .. Pasadena 12-2-67   West Tex. St. 13-35 (Joe Kerbel)

BOB WOODRUFF, 2-1-0   (Tennessee '39)   b 3-14-16
Baylor............... Dixie 1-1-49   Wake Forest 20-7 (D. C. "Peahead" Walker)
Florida .... Gator 1-1-53   Tulsa 14-13 (J. O. "Buddy" Brothers)
Florida .... Gator 12-27-58   Mississippi 3-7 (John Vaught)

WARREN WOODSON, 6-1-0   (Baylor '24)   b 2-24-03
Hardin-Simmons ..... Sun 1-1-43   Second Air Force 7-13 (Red Reese)
Hardin-Simmons ..... Alamo 1-4-47   Denver 20-6 (Clyde "Cac" Hubbard)
Hardin-Simmons ..... Harbor 1-1-48   San Diego St. 53-0 (Bill Schutte)
Hardin-Simmons ..... Shrine 12-18-48   Ouachita Baptist 40-12 (Wesley Bradshaw)
Hardin-Simmons ..... Camellia 12-30-48   Wichita St. 49-12 (Jim Trimble)
New Mexico St. ...... Sun 12-31-59   North Texas 28-8 (Odus Mitchell)
New Mexico St. ...... Sun 12-31-60   Utah St. 20-13 (John Ralston)

BOWDEN WYATT, 2-2-0   (Tennessee '39)   b 11-3-17
Wyoming .... Gator 1-1-51   Wash. & Lee 20-7 (George Barclay)
Arkansas .... Cotton 1-1-55   Georgia Tech 6-14 (Bobby Dodd)
Tennessee .... Sugar 1-1-57   Baylor 7-13 (Sam Boyd)
Tennessee .... Gator 12-26-57   Texas A&M 3-0 (Paul "Bear" Bryant)

BILL YEOMAN, 6-4-1   (Army '50)   b 12-26-27
Houston.............. Tangerine 12-22-62   Miami (Ohio) 49-21 (John Pont)
Houston.............. Bluebonnet 12-31-69   Auburn 36-7 (Ralph "Shug" Jordan)
Houston.............. Bluebonnet 12-31-71   Colorado 17-29 (Eddie Crowder)
Houston.............. Bluebonnet 12-29-73   Tulane 47-7 (Bennie Ellender)
Houston.............. Bluebonnet 12-23-74   North Caro. St. 31-31 (Lou Holtz)
Houston.............. Cotton 1-1-77   Maryland 30-21 (Jerry Claiborne)
Houston.............. Cotton 1-1-79   Notre Dame 34-35 (Dan Devine)
Houston.............. Cotton 1-1-80   Nebraska 17-14 (Tom Osborne)
Houston.............. Garden State 12-14-80   Navy 35-0 (George Welsh)
Houston.............. Sun 12-26-81   Oklahoma 14-40 (Barry Switzer)
Houston.............. Cotton 1-1-85   Boston College 28-45 (Jack Bicknell)

FIELDING "HURRY UP" YOST, 1-0-0   (Lafayette '97)   b 4-30-71
Michigan .... Rose 1-1-02   Stanford 49-0 (Charlie Fickert)

JIM YOUNG, 5-1-0   (Bowling Green '57)   b 4-21-35
Purdue .... Peach 12-25-78   Georgia Tech 41-21 (Pepper Rodgers)

Strong defensive plays such as this were not enough to help Nebraska defeat Houston in the 1980 Cotton Bowl. Bill Yeoman's Cougars won, 17-14, in their third Cotton Bowl appearance in four years.

Purdue	Bluebonnet 12-31-79	Tennessee 27-22 (Johnny Majors)
Purdue	Liberty 12-27-80	Missouri 28-25 (Warren Powers)
Army	Cherry 12-22-84	Michigan St. 10-6 (George Perles)
Army	Peach 12-31-85	Illinois 31-29 (Mike White)
Army	Sun 12-24-88	Alabama 28-29 (Bill Curry)

TEAM-BY-TEAM ALL-TIME MAJOR BOWL SCORES
WITH COACH OF EACH BOWL TEAM EACH YEAR

Listed below are the 103 I-A teams that have participated in history's 616 major bowl games (the term "major bowl" is defined above the alphabetical list of team bowl records). The teams are listed alphabetically, with each coach listed along with the bowl participated in, date played, opponent, score and team's all-time bowl-game record. The Big Four reference is that team's record in the traditional Big Four bowls—Rose, Orange, Sugar and Cotton. Following the I-A list is a group of 48 teams that played in a major bowl game or games but are no longer classified as I-A.

AIR FORCE	Bowl	Date	Opponent	Score
Ben Martin	Cotton	1-1-59	Texas Christian	0-0
Ben Martin	Gator	12-28-63	North Caro.	0-35
Ben Martin	Sugar	1-1-71	Tennessee	13-34
Ken Hatfield.......................	Hall of Fame	12-31-82	Vanderbilt	36-28
Ken Hatfield.......................	Independence	12-10-83	Mississippi	9-3
Fisher DeBerry	Independence	12-15-84	Virginia Tech	23-7
Fisher DeBerry	Bluebonnet	12-31-85	Texas	24-16
Fisher DeBerry	Freedom	12-30-87	Arizona St.	28-33
Fisher DeBerry	Liberty	12-28-89	Mississippi	29-42
Fisher DeBerry	Liberty	12-27-90	Ohio St.	23-11
Fisher DeBerry	Liberty	12-29-91	Mississippi St.	38-15

All bowls 6-4-1; Big four 0-1-1

ALABAMA	Bowl	Date	Opponent	Score
Wallace Wade	Rose	1-1-26	Washington	20-19
Wallace Wade	Rose	1-1-27	Stanford	7-7
Wallace Wade	Rose	1-1-31	Washington St.	24-0

Coach	Bowl	Date	Opponent	Score
Frank Thomas	Rose	1-1-35	Stanford	29-13
Frank Thomas	Rose	1-1-38	California	0-13
Frank Thomas	Cotton	1-1-42	Texas A&M	29-21
Frank Thomas	Orange	1-1-43	Boston College	37-21
Frank Thomas	Sugar	1-1-45	Duke	26-29
Frank Thomas	Rose	1-1-46	Southern Cal	34-14
Harold "Red" Drew	Sugar	1-1-48	Texas	7-27
Harold "Red" Drew	Orange	1-1-53	Syracuse	61-6
Harold "Red" Drew	Cotton	1-1-54	Rice	6-28
Paul "Bear" Bryant	Liberty	12-19-59	Penn St.	0-7
Paul "Bear" Bryant	Bluebonnet	12-17-60	Texas	3-3
Paul "Bear" Bryant	Sugar	1-1-62	Arkansas	10-3
Paul "Bear" Bryant	Orange	1-1-63	Oklahoma	17-0
Paul "Bear" Bryant	Sugar	1-1-64	Mississippi	12-7
Paul "Bear" Bryant	Orange	1-1-65	Texas	17-21
Paul "Bear" Bryant	Orange	1-1-66	Nebraska	39-28
Paul "Bear" Bryant	Sugar	1-2-67	Nebraska	34-7
Paul "Bear" Bryant	Cotton	1-1-68	Texas A&M	16-20
Paul "Bear" Bryant	Gator	12-28-68	Missouri	10-35
Paul "Bear" Bryant	Liberty	12-13-69	Colorado	33-47
Paul "Bear" Bryant	Bluebonnet	12-31-70	Oklahoma	24-24
Paul "Bear" Bryant	Orange	1-1-72	Nebraska	6-38
Paul "Bear" Bryant	Cotton	1-1-73	Texas	13-17
Paul "Bear" Bryant	Sugar	12-31-73	Notre Dame	23-24
Paul "Bear" Bryant	Orange	1-1-75	Notre Dame	11-13
Paul "Bear" Bryant	Sugar	12-31-75	Penn St.	13-6
Paul "Bear" Bryant	Liberty	12-20-76	UCLA	36-6
Paul "Bear" Bryant	Sugar	1-2-78	Ohio St.	35-6
Paul "Bear" Bryant	Sugar	1-1-79	Penn St.	14-7
Paul "Bear" Bryant	Sugar	1-1-80	Arkansas	24-9
Paul "Bear" Bryant	Cotton	1-1-81	Baylor	30-2
Paul "Bear" Bryant	Cotton	1-1-82	Texas	12-14
Paul "Bear" Bryant	Liberty	12-29-82	Illinois	21-15
Ray Perkins	Sun	12-24-83	Southern Methodist	28-7
Ray Perkins	Aloha	12-28-85	Southern Cal	24-3
Ray Perkins	Sun	12-25-86	Washington	28-6
Bill Curry	Hall of Fame	1-2-88	Michigan	24-28
Bill Curry	Sun	12-24-88	Army	29-28
Bill Curry	Sugar	1-1-90	Miami (Fla.)	25-33
Gene Stallings	Fiesta	1-1-91	Louisville	7-34
Gene Stallings	Blockbuster	12-28-91	Colorado	30-25

All bowls 24-17-3; Big four 17-12-1

ARIZONA

Coach	Bowl	Date	Opponent	Score
J. F. "Pop" McKale	San Diego E-W Christmas Classic	12-26-21	Centre	0-38
Miles Casteel	Salad	1-1-49	Drake	13-14
Darrell Mudra	Sun	12-28-68	Auburn	10-34
Tony Mason	Fiesta	12-25-79	Pittsburgh	10-16
Larry Smith	Sun	12-28-85	Georgia	13-13
Larry Smith	Aloha	12-27-86	North Caro.	30-21
Dick Tomey	Copper	12-31-89	North Caro. St.	17-10
Dick Tomey	Aloha	12-25-90	Syracuse	0-28

All bowls 2-5-1; Big four 0-0-0

ARIZONA ST.

Coach	Bowl	Date	Opponent	Score
Millard "Dixie" Howell	Sun	1-1-40	Catholic	0-0
Millard "Dixie" Howell	Sun	1-1-41	Case Reserve	13-26
Ed Doherty	Salad	1-1-50	Xavier (Ohio)	21-33
Ed Doherty	Salad	1-1-51	Miami (Ohio)	21-34
Frank Kush	Peach	12-30-70	North Caro.	48-26
Frank Kush	Fiesta	12-27-71	Florida St.	45-38
Frank Kush	Fiesta	12-23-72	Missouri	49-35
Frank Kush	Fiesta	12-21-73	Pittsburgh	28-7
Frank Kush	Fiesta	12-26-75	Nebraska	17-14
Frank Kush	Fiesta	12-25-77	Penn St.	30-42
Frank Kush	Garden State	12-16-78	Rutgers	34-18
Darryl Rogers	Fiesta	1-1-83	Oklahoma	32-21
John Cooper	Holiday	12-22-85	Arkansas	17-18
John Cooper	Rose	1-1-87	Michigan	22-15
John Cooper	Freedom	12-30-87	Air Force	33-28

All bowls 9-5-1; Big four 1-0-0

ARKANSAS	Bowl	Date	Opponent	Score
Fred Thomsen	Dixie Classic	1-1-34	Centenary	7-7
John Barnhill	Cotton	1-1-47	Louisiana St.	0-0
John Barnhill	Dixie	1-1-48	William & Mary	21-19
Bowden Wyatt	Cotton	1-1-55	Georgia Tech	6-14
Frank Broyles	Gator	1-2-60	Georgia Tech	14-7
Frank Broyles	Cotton	1-2-61	Duke	6-7
Frank Broyles	Sugar	1-1-62	Alabama	3-10
Frank Broyles	Sugar	1-1-63	Mississippi	13-17
Frank Broyles	Cotton	1-1-65	Nebraska	10-7
Frank Broyles	Cotton	1-1-66	Louisiana St.	7-14
Frank Broyles	Sugar	1-1-69	Georgia	16-2
Frank Broyles	Sugar	1-1-70	Mississippi	22-27
Frank Broyles	Liberty	12-20-71	Tennessee	13-14
Frank Broyles	Cotton	1-1-76	Georgia	31-10
Lou Holtz	Orange	1-2-78	Oklahoma	31-6
Lou Holtz	Fiesta	12-25-78	UCLA	10-10
Lou Holtz	Sugar	1-1-80	Alabama	9-24
Lou Holtz	Hall of Fame	12-27-80	Tulane	34-15
Lou Holtz	Gator	12-28-81	North Caro.	27-31
Lou Holtz	Bluebonnet	12-31-82	Florida	28-24
Ken Hatfield	Liberty	12-27-84	Auburn	15-21
Ken Hatfield	Holiday	12-22-85	Arizona St.	18-17
Ken Hatfield	Orange	1-1-87	Oklahoma	8-42
Ken Hatfield	Liberty	12-29-87	Georgia	17-20
Ken Hatfield	Cotton	1-2-89	UCLA	3-17
Ken Hatfield	Cotton	1-1-90	Tennessee	27-31
Jack Crowe	Independence	12-29-91	Georgia	15-24

All bowls 9-15-3; Big four 4-10-1

ARMY	Bowl	Date	Opponent	Score
Jim Young	Cherry	12-22-84	Michigan St.	10-6
Jim Young	Peach	12-31-85	Illinois	31-29
Jim Young	Sun	12-24-88	Alabama	28-29

All bowls 2-1-0; Big four 0-0-0

AUBURN	Bowl	Date	Opponent	Score
Jack Meagher	Bacardi, Cuba	1-1-37	Villanova	7-7
Jack Meagher	Orange	1-1-38	Michigan St.	6-0
Ralph "Shug" Jordan	Gator	1-1-54	Texas Tech	13-35
Ralph "Shug" Jordan	Gator	12-31-54	Baylor	33-13
Ralph "Shug" Jordan	Gator	12-31-55	Vanderbilt	13-25
Ralph "Shug" Jordan	Orange	1-1-64	Nebraska	7-13
Ralph "Shug" Jordan	Liberty	12-18-65	Mississippi	7-13
Ralph "Shug" Jordan	Sun	12-28-68	Arizona	34-10
Ralph "Shug" Jordan	Bluebonnet	12-31-69	Houston	7-36
Ralph "Shug" Jordan	Gator	1-2-71	Mississippi	35-28
Ralph "Shug" Jordan	Sugar	1-1-72	Oklahoma	22-40
Ralph "Shug" Jordan	Gator	12-30-72	Colorado	24-3
Ralph "Shug" Jordan	Sun	12-29-73	Missouri	17-34
Ralph "Shug" Jordan	Gator	12-30-74	Texas	27-3
Pat Dye	Tangerine	12-18-82	Boston College	33-26
Pat Dye	Sugar	1-2-84	Michigan	9-7
Pat Dye	Liberty	12-27-84	Arkansas	21-15
Pat Dye	Cotton	1-1-86	Texas A&M	16-36
Pat Dye	Florida Citrus	1-1-87	Southern Cal	16-7
Pat Dye	Sugar	1-1-88	Syracuse	16-16
Pat Dye	Sugar	1-2-89	Florida St.	7-13
Pat Dye	Hall of Fame	1-1-90	Ohio St.	31-24
Pat Dye	Peach	12-29-90	Indiana	27-23

All bowls 12-9-2; Big four 2-4-1

BALL ST.	Bowl	Date	Opponent	Score
Paul Schudel	California	12-9-89	Fresno St.	6-27

All bowls 0-1-0; Big four 0-0-0

BAYLOR	Bowl	Date	Opponent	Score
Bob Woodruff	Dixie	1-1-49	Wake Forest	20-7
George Sauer	Orange	1-1-52	Georgia Tech	14-17
George Sauer	Gator	12-31-54	Auburn	13-33
Sam Boyd	Sugar	1-1-57	Tennessee	13-7
John Bridgers	Gator	12-31-60	Florida	12-13
John Bridgers	Gotham	12-9-61	Utah St.	24-9
John Bridgers	Bluebonnet	12-21-63	Louisiana St.	14-7

Coach	Bowl	Date	Opponent	Score
Grant Teaff	Cotton	1-1-75	Penn St.	20-41
Grant Teaff	Peach	12-31-79	Clemson	24-18
Grant Teaff	Cotton	1-1-81	Alabama	2-30
Grant Teaff	Bluebonnet	12-31-83	Oklahoma St.	14-24
Grant Teaff	Liberty	12-27-85	Louisiana St.	21-7
Grant Teaff	Bluebonnet	12-31-86	Colorado	21-9
Grant Teaff	Copper	12-31-91	Indiana	0-24

All bowls 7-7-0; Big four 1-3-0

BOSTON COLLEGE
Coach	Bowl	Date	Opponent	Score
Frank Leahy	Cotton	1-1-40	Clemson	3-6
Frank Leahy	Sugar	1-1-41	Tennessee	19-13
Denny Myers	Orange	1-1-43	Alabama	21-37
Jack Bicknell	Tangerine	12-18-82	Auburn	26-33
Jack Bicknell	Liberty	12-29-83	Notre Dame	18-19
Jack Bicknell	Cotton	1-1-85	Houston	45-28
Jack Bicknell	Hall of Fame	12-23-86	Georgia	27-24

All bowls 3-4-0; Big four 2-2-0

BOWLING GREEN
Coach	Bowl	Date	Opponent	Score
Doyt Perry	Mercy	11-23-61	Fresno St.	6-36
Denny Stolz	California	12-18-82	Fresno St.	28-29
Denny Stolz	California	12-14-85	Fresno St.	7-51
Gary Blackney	California	12-14-91	Fresno St.	28-21

All bowls 1-3-0; Big four 0-0-0

BRIGHAM YOUNG
Coach	Bowl	Date	Opponent	Score
LaVell Edwards	Fiesta	12-28-74	Oklahoma St.	6-16
LaVell Edwards	Tangerine	12-18-76	Oklahoma St.	21-49
LaVell Edwards	Holiday	12-22-78	Navy	16-23
LaVell Edwards	Holiday	12-21-79	Indiana	37-38
LaVell Edwards	Holiday	12-19-80	Southern Methodist	46-45
LaVell Edwards	Holiday	12-18-81	Washington St.	38-36
LaVell Edwards	Holiday	12-17-82	Ohio St.	17-47
LaVell Edwards	Holiday	12-23-83	Missouri	21-17
LaVell Edwards	Holiday	12-21-84	Michigan	24-17
LaVell Edwards	Florida Citrus	12-28-85	Ohio St.	7-10
LaVell Edwards	Freedom	12-30-86	UCLA	10-31
LaVell Edwards	All-American	12-22-87	Virginia	16-22
LaVell Edwards	Freedom	12-29-88	Colorado	20-17
LaVell Edwards	Holiday	12-29-89	Penn St.	39-50
LaVell Edwards	Holiday	12-29-90	Texas A&M	14-65
LaVell Edwards	Holiday	12-30-91	Iowa	13-13

All bowls 5-10-1; Big four 0-0-0

CAL ST. FULLERTON
Coach	Bowl	Date	Opponent	Score
Gene Murphy	California	12-17-83	Northern Ill.	13-20

All bowls 0-1-0; Big four 0-0-0

CALIFORNIA
Coach	Bowl	Date	Opponent	Score
Andy Smith	Rose	1-1-21	Ohio St.	28-0
Andy Smith	Rose	1-2-22	Wash. & Jeff.	0-0
Clarence "Nibs" Price	Rose	1-1-29	Georgia Tech	7-8
Leonard "Stub" Allison	Rose	1-1-38	Alabama	13-0
Lynn "Pappy" Waldorf	Rose	1-1-49	Northwestern	14-20
Lynn "Pappy" Waldorf	Rose	1-2-50	Ohio St.	14-17
Lynn "Pappy" Waldorf	Rose	1-1-51	Michigan	6-14
Pete Elliott	Rose	1-1-59	Iowa	12-38
Roger Theder	Garden State	12-15-79	Temple	17-28
Bruce Snyder	Copper	12-31-90	Wyoming	17-15
Bruce Snyder	Florida Citrus	1-1-92	Clemson	37-13

All bowls 4-6-1; Big four 2-5-1

CENTRAL MICH.
Coach	Bowl	Date	Opponent	Score
Herb Deromedi	California	12-8-90	San Jose St.	24-48

All bowls 0-1-0; Big four 0-0-0

CINCINNATI
Coach	Bowl	Date	Opponent	Score
Ray Nolting	Sun	1-1-47	Virginia Tech	18-6
Sid Gillman	Sun	1-1-51	West Tex. St.	13-14

All bowls 1-1-0; Big four 0-0-0

CLEMSON
Coach	Bowl	Date	Opponent	Score
Jess Neely	Cotton	1-1-40	Boston College	6-3
Frank Howard	Gator	1-1-49	Missouri	24-23
Frank Howard	Orange	1-1-51	Miami (Fla.)	15-14

Frank Howard	Gator	1-1-52	Miami (Fla.)	0-14
Frank Howard	Orange	1-1-57	Colorado	21-27
Frank Howard	Sugar	1-1-59	Louisiana St.	0-7
Frank Howard	Bluebonnet	12-19-59	Texas Christian	23-7
Charley Pell	Gator	12-30-77	Pittsburgh	3-34
Danny Ford	Gator	12-29-78	Ohio St.	17-15
Danny Ford	Peach	12-31-79	Baylor	18-24
Danny Ford	Orange	1-1-82	Nebraska	22-15
Danny Ford	Independence	12-21-85	Minnesota	13-20
Danny Ford	Gator	12-27-86	Stanford	27-21
Danny Ford	Florida Citrus	1-1-88	Penn St.	35-10
Danny Ford	Florida Citrus	1-2-89	Oklahoma	23-6
Danny Ford	Gator	12-30-89	West Va.	27-7
Ken Hatfield	Hall of Fame	1-1-91	Illinois	30-0
Ken Hatfield	Florida Citrus	1-1-92	California	13-37

All bowls 11-7-0; Big four 3-2-0

COLORADO

	Bowl	Date	Opponent	Score
Bernard "Bunnie" Oaks	Cotton	1-1-38	Rice	14-28
Dallas Ward	Orange	1-1-57	Clemson	27-21
Sonny Grandelius	Orange	1-1-62	Louisiana St.	7-25
Eddie Crowder	Bluebonnet	12-23-67	Miami (Fla.)	31-21
Eddie Crowder	Liberty	12-13-69	Alabama	47-33
Eddie Crowder	Liberty	12-12-70	Tulane	3-17
Eddie Crowder	Bluebonnet	12-31-71	Houston	29-17
Eddie Crowder	Gator	12-30-72	Auburn	3-24
Bill Mallory	Bluebonnet	12-27-75	Texas	21-38
Bill Mallory	Orange	1-1-77	Ohio St.	10-27
Bill McCartney	Freedom	12-30-85	Washington	17-20
Bill McCartney	Bluebonnet	12-31-86	Baylor	9-21
Bill McCartney	Freedom	12-29-88	Brigham Young	17-20
Bill McCartney	Orange	1-1-90	Notre Dame	6-21
Bill McCartney	Orange	1-1-91	Notre Dame	10-9
Bill McCartney	Blockbuster	12-28-91	Alabama	25-30

All bowls 5-11-0; Big four 2-4-0

COLORADO ST.

	Bowl	Date	Opponent	Score
Bob Davis	Raisin	1-1-49	Occidental	20-21
Earle Bruce	Freedom	12-24-90	Oregon	32-31

All bowls 1-1-0; Big four 0-0-0

DUKE

	Bowl	Date	Opponent	Score
Wallace Wade	Rose	1-2-39	Southern Cal	3-7
Wallace Wade	Rose	1-1-42	Oregon St.	16-20
Eddie Cameron	Sugar	1-1-45	Alabama	29-26
Bill Murray	Orange	1-1-55	Nebraska	34-7
Bill Murray	Orange	1-1-58	Oklahoma	21-48
Bill Murray	Cotton	1-2-61	Arkansas	7-6
Steve Spurrier	All-American	12-28-89	Texas Tech	21-49

All bowls 3-4-0; Big four 3-3-0

EAST CARO.

	Bowl	Date	Opponent	Score
Pat Dye	Independence	12-16-78	Louisiana Tech	35-13
Bill Lewis	Peach	1-1-92	North Caro. St.	37-34

All bowls 2-0-0; Big four 0-0-0

EASTERN MICH.

	Bowl	Date	Opponent	Score
Jim Harkema	California	12-12-87	San Jose St.	30-27

All bowls 1-0-0; Big four 0-0-0

FLORIDA

	Bowl	Date	Opponent	Score
Bob Woodruff	Gator	1-1-53	Tulsa	14-13
Bob Woodruff	Gator	12-27-58	Mississippi	3-7
Ray Graves	Gator	12-31-60	Baylor	13-12
Ray Graves	Gator	12-29-62	Penn St.	17-7
Ray Graves	Sugar	1-1-66	Missouri	18-20
Ray Graves	Orange	1-2-67	Georgia Tech	27-12
Ray Graves	Gator	12-27-69	Tennessee	14-13
Doug Dickey	Tangerine	12-22-73	Miami (Ohio)	7-16
Doug Dickey	Sugar	12-31-74	Nebraska	10-13
Doug Dickey	Gator	12-29-75	Maryland	0-13
Doug Dickey	Sun	1-2-77	Texas A&M	14-37
Charley Pell	Tangerine	12-20-80	Maryland	35-20
Charley Pell	Peach	12-31-81	West Va.	6-26
Charley Pell	Bluebonnet	12-31-82	Arkansas	24-28

Charley Pell	Gator	12-30-83	Iowa	14-6
Galen Hall	Aloha	12-25-87	UCLA	16-20
Galen Hall	All-American	12-29-88	Illinois	14-10
Gary Darnell	Freedom	12-30-89	Washington	7-34
Steve Spurrier.....................	Sugar	1-1-92	Notre Dame	28-39

All bowls 8-11-0; Big four 1-3-0

FLORIDA ST.

	Bowl	Date	Opponent	Score
Tom Nugent.......................	Sun	1-1-55	UTEP	20-47
Tom Nugent.......................	Bluegrass	12-13-58	Oklahoma St.	6-15
Bill Peterson	Gator	1-2-65	Oklahoma	36-19
Bill Peterson	Sun	12-24-66	Wyoming	20-28
Bill Peterson	Gator	12-30-67	Penn St.	17-17
Bill Peterson	Peach	12-30-68	Louisiana St.	27-31
Larry Jones	Fiesta	12-27-71	Arizona St.	38-45
Bobby Bowden	Tangerine	12-23-77	Texas Tech	40-17
Bobby Bowden	Orange	1-1-80	Oklahoma	7-24
Bobby Bowden	Orange	1-1-81	Oklahoma	17-18
Bobby Bowden	Gator	12-30-82	West Va.	31-12
Bobby Bowden	Peach	12-30-83	North Caro.	28-3
Bobby Bowden	Florida Citrus	12-22-84	Georgia	17-17
Bobby Bowden	Gator	12-30-85	Oklahoma St.	34-23
Bobby Bowden	All-American	12-31-86	Indiana	27-13
Bobby Bowden	Fiesta	1-1-88	Nebraska	31-28
Bobby Bowden	Sugar	1-2-89	Auburn	13-7
Bobby Bowden	Fiesta	1-1-90	Nebraska	41-17
Bobby Bowden	Blockbuster	12-28-90	Penn St.	24-17
Bobby Bowden	Cotton	1-1-92	Texas A&M	10-2

All bowls 11-7-2; Big four 2-2-0

FRESNO ST.

	Bowl	Date	Opponent	Score
Alvin "Pix" Pierson	Raisin	1-1-46	Drake	12-13
Cecil Coleman	Mercy	11-23-61	Bowling Green	36-6
Jim Sweeney......................	California	12-18-82	Bowling Green	29-28
Jim Sweeney......................	California	12-14-85	Bowling Green	51-7
Jim Sweeney......................	California	12-10-88	Western Mich.	35-30
Jim Sweeney......................	California	12-9-89	Ball St.	27-6
Jim Sweeney......................	California	12-14-91	Bowling Green	21-28

All bowls 5-2-0; Big four 0-0-0

GEORGIA

	Bowl	Date	Opponent	Score
Wally Butts.......................	Orange	1-1-42	Texas Christian	40-26
Wally Butts.......................	Rose	1-1-43	UCLA	9-0
Wally Butts.......................	Oil	1-1-46	Tulsa	20-6
Wally Butts.......................	Sugar	1-1-47	North Caro.	20-10
Wally Butts.......................	Gator	1-1-48	Maryland	20-20
Wally Butts.......................	Orange	1-1-49	Texas	28-41
Wally Butts.......................	Presidential	12-9-50	Texas A&M	20-40
Wally Butts.......................	Orange	1-1-60	Missouri	14-0
Vince Dooley......................	Sun	12-26-64	Texas Tech	7-0
Vince Dooley......................	Cotton	12-31-66	Southern Methodist	24-9
Vince Dooley......................	Liberty	12-16-67	North Caro. St.	7-14
Vince Dooley......................	Sugar	1-1-69	Arkansas	2-16
Vince Dooley......................	Sun	12-20-69	Nebraska	6-45
Vince Dooley......................	Gator	12-31-71	North Caro.	7-3
Vince Dooley......................	Peach	12-28-73	Maryland	17-16
Vince Dooley......................	Tangerine	12-21-74	Miami (Ohio)	10-21
Vince Dooley......................	Cotton	1-1-76	Arkansas	10-31
Vince Dooley......................	Sugar	1-1-77	Pittsburgh	3-27
Vince Dooley......................	Bluebonnet	12-31-78	Stanford	22-25
Vince Dooley......................	Sugar	1-1-81	Notre Dame	17-10
Vince Dooley......................	Sugar	1-1-82	Pittsburgh	20-24
Vince Dooley......................	Sugar	1-1-83	Penn St.	23-27
Vince Dooley......................	Cotton	1-2-84	Texas	10-9
Vince Dooley......................	Florida Citrus	12-22-84	Florida St.	17-17
Vince Dooley......................	Sun	12-28-85	Arizona	13-13
Vince Dooley......................	Hall of Fame	12-23-86	Boston College	24-27
Vince Dooley......................	Liberty	12-29-87	Arkansas	20-17
Vince Dooley......................	Gator	1-1-89	Michigan St.	34-27
Ray Goff	Peach	12-30-89	Syracuse	18-19
Ray Goff	Independence	12-29-91	Arkansas	24-15

All bowls 14-13-3; Big four 7-6-0

GEORGIA TECH	Bowl	Date	Opponent	Score
Bill Alexander	Rose	1-1-29	California	8-7
Bill Alexander	Orange	1-1-40	Missouri	21-7
Bill Alexander	Cotton	1-1-43	Texas	7-14
Bill Alexander	Sugar	1-1-44	Tulsa	20-18
Bill Alexander	Orange	1-1-45	Tulsa	12-26
Bobby Dodd	Oil	1-1-47	St. Mary's (Cal.)	41-19
Bobby Dodd	Orange	1-1-48	Kansas	20-14
Bobby Dodd	Orange	1-1-52	Baylor	17-14
Bobby Dodd	Sugar	1-1-53	Mississippi	24-7
Bobby Dodd	Sugar	1-1-54	West Va.	42-19
Bobby Dodd	Cotton	1-1-55	Arkansas	14-6
Bobby Dodd	Sugar	1-2-56	Pittsburgh	7-0
Bobby Dodd	Gator	12-29-56	Pittsburgh	21-14
Bobby Dodd	Gator	1-2-60	Arkansas	7-14
Bobby Dodd	Gator	12-30-61	Penn St.	15-30
Bobby Dodd	Bluebonnet	12-22-62	Missouri	10-14
Bobby Dodd	Gator	12-31-65	Texas Tech	31-21
Bobby Dodd	Orange	1-2-67	Florida	12-27
Bud Carson	Sun	12-19-70	Texas Tech	17-9
Bud Carson	Peach	12-30-71	Mississippi	18-41
Bill Fulcher	Liberty	12-18-72	Iowa St.	31-30
Pepper Rodgers	Peach	12-25-78	Purdue	21-41
Bill Curry	All-American	12-31-85	Michigan St.	17-14
Bobby Ross	Florida Citrus	1-1-91	Nebraska	45-21
Bobby Ross	Aloha	12-25-91	Stanford	18-17

All bowls 17-8-0; Big four 9-3-0

HAWAII	Bowl	Date	Opponent	Score
Bob Wagner	Aloha	12-25-89	Michigan St.	13-33

All bowls 0-1-0; Big four 0-0-0

HOUSTON	Bowl	Date	Opponent	Score
Clyde Lee	Salad	1-1-52	Dayton	26-21
Bill Yeoman	Tangerine	12-22-62	Miami (Ohio)	49-21
Bill Yeoman	Bluebonnet	12-31-69	Auburn	36-7
Bill Yeoman	Bluebonnet	12-31-71	Colorado	17-29
Bill Yeoman	Bluebonnet	12-29-73	Tulane	47-7
Bill Yeoman	Bluebonnet	12-23-74	North Caro. St.	31-31
Bill Yeoman	Cotton	1-1-77	Maryland	30-21
Bill Yeoman	Cotton	1-1-79	Notre Dame	34-35
Bill Yeoman	Cotton	1-1-80	Nebraska	17-14
Bill Yeoman	Garden State	12-14-80	Navy	35-0
Bill Yeoman	Sun	12-26-81	Oklahoma	14-40
Bill Yeoman	Cotton	1-1-85	Boston College	28-45
Jack Pardee	Aloha	12-25-88	Washington St.	22-24

All bowls 7-5-1; Big four 2-2-0

ILLINOIS	Bowl	Date	Opponent	Score
Ray Eliot	Rose	1-1-47	UCLA	45-14
Ray Eliot	Rose	1-1-52	Stanford	40-7
Pete Elliott	Rose	1-1-64	Washington	17-7
Mike White	Liberty	12-29-82	Alabama	15-21
Mike White	Rose	1-2-84	UCLA	9-45
Mike White	Peach	12-31-85	Army	29-31
John Mackovic	All-American	12-29-88	Florida	10-14
John Mackovic	Florida Citrus	1-1-90	Virginia	31-21
John Mackovic	Hall of Fame	1-1-91	Clemson	0-30
Lou Tepper	John Hancock	12-31-91	UCLA	3-6

All bowls 4-6-0; Big four 3-1-0

INDIANA	Bowl	Date	Opponent	Score
John Pont	Rose	1-1-68	Southern Cal	3-14
Lee Corso	Holiday	12-21-79	Brigham Young	38-37
Bill Mallory	All-American	12-31-86	Florida St.	13-27
Bill Mallory	Peach	1-2-88	Tennessee	22-27
Bill Mallory	Liberty	12-28-88	South Caro.	34-10
Bill Mallory	Peach	12-29-90	Auburn	23-27
Bill Mallory	Copper	12-31-91	Baylor	24-0

All bowls 3-4-0; Big four 0-1-0

IOWA	Bowl	Date	Opponent	Score
Forest Evashevski	Rose	1-1-57	Oregon St.	35-19
Forest Evashevski	Rose	1-1-59	California	38-12

Hayden Fry	Rose	1-1-82	Washington	0-28
Hayden Fry	Peach	12-31-82	Tennessee	28-22
Hayden Fry	Gator	12-30-83	Florida	6-14
Hayden Fry	Freedom	12-26-84	Texas	55-17
Hayden Fry	Rose	1-1-86	UCLA	28-45
Hayden Fry	Holiday	12-30-86	San Diego St.	39-38
Hayden Fry	Holiday	12-30-87	Wyoming	20-19
Hayden Fry	Peach	12-31-88	North Caro. St.	23-28
Hayden Fry	Rose	1-1-91	Washington	34-46
Hayden Fry	Holiday	12-30-91	Brigham Young	13-13

All bowls 6-5-1; Big four 2-3-0

IOWA ST.	Bowl	Date	Opponent	Score
Johnny Majors	Sun	12-18-71	Louisiana St.	15-33
Johnny Majors	Liberty	12-18-72	Georgia Tech	30-31
Earle Bruce	Peach	12-31-77	North Caro. St.	14-24
Earle Bruce	Hall of Fame	12-20-78	Texas A&M	12-28

All bowls 0-4-0; Big four 0-0-0

KANSAS	Bowl	Date	Opponent	Score
George Sauer	Orange	1-1-48	Georgia Tech	14-20
Jack Mitchell	Bluebonnet	12-16-61	Rice	33-7
Pepper Rodgers	Orange	1-1-69	Penn St.	14-15
Don Fambrough	Liberty	12-17-73	North Caro. St.	18-31
Bud Moore	Sun	12-26-75	Pittsburgh	19-33
Don Fambrough	Hall of Fame	12-31-81	Mississippi St.	0-10

All bowls 1-5-0; Big four 0-2-0

KANSAS ST.	Bowl	Date	Opponent	Score
Jim Dickey	Independence	12-11-82	Wisconsin	3-14

All bowls 0-1-0; Big four 0-0-0

KENT	Bowl	Date	Opponent	Score
Don James	Tangerine	12-29-72	Tampa	18-21

All bowls 0-1-0; Big four 0-0-0

KENTUCKY	Bowl	Date	Opponent	Score
Paul "Bear" Bryant	Great Lakes	12- 6-47	Villanova	24-14
Paul "Bear" Bryant	Orange	1-2-50	Santa Clara	13-21
Paul "Bear" Bryant	Sugar	1-1-51	Oklahoma	13-7
Paul "Bear" Bryant	Cotton	1-1-52	Texas Christian	20-7
Fran Curci	Peach	12-31-76	North Caro.	21-0
Jerry Claiborne	Hall of Fame	12-22-83	West Va.	16-20
Jerry Claiborne	Hall of Fame	12-29-84	Wisconsin	20-19

All bowls 5-2-0; Big four 2-1-0

LOUISIANA ST.	Bowl	Date	Opponent	Score
Bernie Moore	Sugar	1-1-36	Texas Christian	2-3
Bernie Moore	Sugar	1-1-37	Santa Clara	14-21
Bernie Moore	Sugar	1-1-38	Santa Clara	0-6
Bernie Moore	Orange	1-1-44	Texas A&M	19-14
Bernie Moore	Cotton	1-1-47	Arkansas	0-0
Gaynell Tinsley	Sugar	1-2-50	Oklahoma	0-35
Paul Dietzel	Sugar	1-1-59	Clemson	7-0
Paul Dietzel	Sugar	1-1-60	Mississippi	0-21
Paul Dietzel	Orange	1-1-62	Colorado	25-7
Charlie McClendon	Cotton	1-1-63	Texas	13-0
Charlie McClendon	Bluebonnet	12-21-63	Baylor	7-14
Charlie McClendon	Sugar	1-1-65	Syracuse	13-10
Charlie McClendon	Cotton	1-1-66	Arkansas	14-7
Charlie McClendon	Sugar	1-1-68	Wyoming	20-13
Charlie McClendon	Peach	12-30-68	Florida St.	31-27
Charlie McClendon	Orange	1-1-71	Nebraska	12-17
Charlie McClendon	Sun	12-18-71	Iowa St.	33-15
Charlie McClendon	Bluebonnet	12-30-72	Tennessee	17-24
Charlie McClendon	Orange	1-1-74	Penn St.	9-16
Charlie McClendon	Sun	12-31-77	Stanford	14-24
Charlie McClendon	Liberty	12-23-78	Missouri	15-20
Charlie McClendon	Tangerine	12-22-79	Wake Forest	34-10
Jerry Stovall	Orange	1-1-83	Nebraska	20-21
Bill Arnsparger	Sugar	1-1-85	Nebraska	10-28
Bill Arnsparger	Liberty	12-27-85	Baylor	7-21

Bill Arnsparger	Sugar	1-1-87	Nebraska	15-30
Mike Archer.......................	Gator	12-31-87	South Caro.	30-13
Mike Archer.......................	Hall of Fame	1-2-89	Syracuse	10-23

All bowls 11-16-1; Big four 7-10-1

LOUISIANA TECH	**Bowl**	**Date**	**Opponent**	**Score**
Maxie Lambright	Independence	12-17-77	Louisville	24-14
Maxie Lambright	Independence	12-16-78	East Caro.	13-35
Joe Raymond Peace	Independence	12-15-90	Maryland	34-34

All bowls 1-1-1; Big four 0-0-0

LOUISVILLE	**Bowl**	**Date**	**Opponent**	**Score**
Frank Camp.......................	Sun	1-1-58	Drake	34-20
Lee Corso........................	Pasadena	12-19-70	Long Beach St.	24-24
Vince Gibson	Independence	12-17-77	Louisiana Tech	14-24
Howard Schnellenberger	Fiesta	1-1-91	Alabama	34-7

All bowls 2-1-1; Big four 0-0-0

MARYLAND	**Bowl**	**Date**	**Opponent**	**Score**
Jim Tatum........................	Gator	1-1-48	Georgia	20-20
Jim Tatum........................	Gator	1-2-50	Missouri	20-7
Jim Tatum........................	Sugar	1-1-52	Tennessee	28-13
Jim Tatum........................	Orange	1-1-54	Oklahoma	0-7
Jim Tatum........................	Orange	1-2-56	Oklahoma	6-20
Jerry Claiborne	Peach	12-28-73	Georgia	16-17
Jerry Claiborne	Liberty	12-16-74	Tennessee	3-7
Jerry Claiborne	Gator	12-29-75	Florida	13-0
Jerry Claiborne	Cotton	1-1-77	Houston	21-30
Jerry Claiborne	Hall of Fame	12-22-77	Minnesota	17-7
Jerry Claiborne	Sun	12-23-78	Texas	0-42
Jerry Claiborne	Tangerine	12-20-80	Florida	20-35
Bobby Ross	Aloha	12-25-82	Washington	20-21
Bobby Ross	Florida Citrus	12-17-83	Tennessee	23-30
Bobby Ross	Sun	12-22-84	Tennessee	27-26
Bobby Ross	Cherry	12-21-85	Syracuse	35-18
Joe Krivak	Independence	12-15-90	Louisiana Tech	34-34

All bowls 6-9-2; Big four 1-3-0

MEMPHIS ST.	**Bowl**	**Date**	**Opponent**	**Score**
Billy Murphy	Pasadena	12-18-71	San Jose St.	28-9

All bowls 1-0-0; Big four 0-0-0

MIAMI (FLA.)	**Bowl**	**Date**	**Opponent**	**Score**
Tom McCann	Orange	1-1-35	Bucknell	0-26
Jack Harding.....................	Orange	1-1-46	Holy Cross	13-6
Andy Gustafson..................	Orange	1-1-51	Clemson	14-15
Andy Gustafson..................	Gator	1-1-52	Clemson	14-0
Andy Gustafson..................	Liberty	12-16-61	Syracuse	14-15
Andy Gustafson..................	Gotham	12-15-62	Nebraska	34-36
Charlie Tate	Liberty	12-10-66	Virginia Tech	14-7
Charlie Tate	Bluebonnet	12-31-67	Colorado	21-31
Howard Schnellenberger	Peach	1-2-81	Virginia Tech	20-10
Howard Schnellenberger	Orange	1-2-84	Nebraska	31-30
Jimmy Johnson	Fiesta	1-1-85	UCLA	37-39
Jimmy Johnson	Sugar	1-1-86	Tennessee	7-35
Jimmy Johnson	Fiesta	1-2-87	Penn St.	10-14
Jimmy Johnson	Orange	1-1-88	Oklahoma	20-14
Jimmy Johnson	Orange	1-2-89	Nebraska	23-3
Dennis Erickson	Sugar	1-1-90	Alabama	33-25
Dennis Erickson	Cotton	1-1-91	Texas	46-3
Dennis Erickson	Orange	1-1-92	Nebraska	22-0

All bowls 10-8-0; Big four 7-3-0

MIAMI (OHIO)	**Bowl**	**Date**	**Opponent**	**Score**
Sid Gillman	Sun	1-1-48	Texas Tech	13-12
Woody Hayes	Salad	1-1-51	Arizona St.	34-21
John Pont........................	Tangerine	12-22-62	Houston	21-49
Bill Mallory	Tangerine	12-22-73	Florida	16-7
Dick Crum	Tangerine	12-21-74	Georgia	21-10
Dick Crum	Tangerine	12-20-75	South Caro.	20-7
Tim Rose........................	California	12-13-86	San Jose St.	7-37

All bowls 5-2-0; Big four 0-0-0

MICHIGAN	**Bowl**	**Date**	**Opponent**	**Score**
Fielding "Hurry Up" Yost	Rose	1-1-02	Stanford	49-0
H.O. "Fritz" Crisler	Rose	1-1-48	Southern Cal	49-0

Bennie Oosterbaan	Rose	1-1-51	California	14-6
Chalmers "Bump" Elliott	Rose	1-1-65	Oregon St.	34-7
Glenn "Bo" Schembechler	Rose	1-1-70	Southern Cal	3-10
Glenn "Bo" Schembechler	Rose	1-1-72	Stanford	12-13
Glenn "Bo" Schembechler	Orange	1-1-76	Oklahoma	6-14
Glenn "Bo" Schembechler	Rose	1-1-77	Southern Cal	6-14
Glenn "Bo" Schembechler	Rose	1-2-78	Washington	20-27
Glenn "Bo" Schembechler	Rose	1-1-79	Southern Cal	10-17
Glenn "Bo" Schembechler	Gator	12-28-79	North Caro.	15-17
Glenn "Bo" Schembechler	Rose	1-1-81	Washington	23-6
Glenn "Bo" Schembechler	Bluebonnet	12-31-81	UCLA	33-14
Glenn "Bo" Schembechler	Rose	1-1-83	UCLA	14-24
Glenn "Bo" Schembechler	Sugar	1-2-84	Auburn	7-9
Glenn "Bo" Schembechler	Holiday	12-21-84	Brigham Young	17-24
Glenn "Bo" Schembechler	Fiesta	1-1-86	Nebraska	27-23
Glenn "Bo" Schembechler	Rose	1-1-87	Arizona St.	15-22
Glenn "Bo" Schembechler	Hall of Fame	1-2-88	Alabama	28-24
Glenn "Bo" Schembechler	Rose	1-2-89	Southern Cal	22-14
Glenn "Bo" Schembechler	Rose	1-1-90	Southern Cal	10-17
Gary Moeller	Gator	1-1-91	Mississippi	35-3
Gary Moeller	Rose	1-1-92	Washington	14-34

All bowls 10-13-0; Big four 6-11-0

MICHIGAN ST.	**Bowl**	**Date**	**Opponent**	**Score**
Charlie Bachman	Orange	1-1-38	Auburn	0-6
Clarence "Biggie" Munn	Rose	1-1-54	UCLA	28-20
Duffy Daugherty	Rose	1-2-56	UCLA	17-14
Duffy Daugherty	Rose	1-1-66	UCLA	12-14
George Perles....................	Cherry	12-22-84	Army	6-10
George Perles....................	All-American	12-31-85	Georgia Tech	14-17
George Perles....................	Rose	1-1-88	Southern Cal	20-17
George Perles....................	Gator	1-1-89	Georgia	27-34
George Perles....................	Aloha	12-25-89	Hawaii	33-13
George Perles....................	John Hancock	12-31-90	Southern Cal	17-6

All bowls 5-5-0; Big four 3-2-0

MINNESOTA	**Bowl**	**Date**	**Opponent**	**Score**
Murray Warmath	Rose	1-2-61	Washington	7-17
Murray Warmath	Rose	1-1-62	UCLA	21-3
Cal Stoll.........................	Hall of Fame	12-22-77	Maryland	7-17
John Gutekunst...................	Independence	12-21-85	Clemson	20-13
John Gutekunst...................	Liberty	12-29-86	Tennessee	14-21

All bowls 2-3-0; Big four 1-1-0

MISSISSIPPI	**Bowl**	**Date**	**Opponent**	**Score**
Ed Walker........................	Orange	1-1-36	Catholic	19-20
John Vaught	Delta	1-1-48	Texas Christian	13-9
John Vaught	Sugar	1-1-53	Georgia Tech	7-24
John Vaught	Sugar	1-1-55	Navy	0-21
John Vaught	Cotton	1-2-56	Texas Christian	14-13
John Vaught	Sugar	1-1-58	Texas	39-7
John Vaught	Gator	12-27-58	Florida	7-3
John Vaught	Sugar	1-1-60	Louisiana St.	21-0
John Vaught	Sugar	1-2-61	Rice	14-6
John Vaught	Cotton	1-1-62	Texas	7-12
John Vaught	Sugar	1-1-63	Arkansas	17-13
John Vaught	Sugar	1-1-64	Alabama	7-12
John Vaught	Bluebonnet	12-19-64	Tulsa	7-14
John Vaught	Liberty	12-18-65	Auburn	13-7
John Vaught	Bluebonnet	12-17-66	Texas	0-19
John Vaught	Sun	12-30-67	UTEP	7-14
John Vaught	Liberty	12-14-68	Virginia Tech	34-17
John Vaught	Sugar	1-1-70	Arkansas	27-22
John Vaught	Gator	1-2-71	Auburn	28-35
Billy Kinard	Peach	12-30-71	Georgia Tech	41-18
Billy Brewer.....................	Independence	12-10-83	Air Force	3-9
Billy Brewer.....................	Independence	12-20-86	Texas Tech	20-17
Billy Brewer.....................	Liberty	12-28-89	Air Force	42-29
Billy Brewer.....................	Gator	1-1-91	Michigan	3-35

All bowls 13-11-0; Big four 6-5-0

MISSISSIPPI ST.	**Bowl**	**Date**	**Opponent**	**Score**
Ralph Sasse......................	Orange	1-1-37	Duquesne	12-13
Allyn McKeen	Orange	1-1-41	Georgetown	14-7

390

Paul Davis........................	Liberty	12-21-63	North Caro. St.	16-12
Bob Tyler	Sun	12-28-74	North Caro.	26-24
Emory Bellard....................	Sun	12-27-80	Nebraska	17-31
Emory Bellard....................	Hall of Fame	12-31-81	Kansas	10-0
Jackie Sherrill	Liberty	12-29-91	Air Force	15-38

All bowls 4-3-0; Big four 1-1-0

MISSOURI

	Bowl	Date	Opponent	Score
Gwinn Henry.....................	Los Angeles Christmas Festival	12-25-24	Southern Cal	7-20
Don Faurot........................	Orange	1-1-40	Georgia Tech	7-21
Don Faurot........................	Sugar	1-1-42	Fordham	0-2
Chauncey Simpson	Cotton	1-1-46	Texas	27-40
Don Faurot........................	Gator	1-1-49	Clemson	23-24
Don Faurot........................	Gator	1-2-50	Maryland	7-20
Dan Devine	Orange	1-1-60	Georgia	0-40
Dan Devine	Orange	1-2-61	Navy	21-14
Dan Devine	Bluebonnet	12-22-62	Georgia Tech	14-10
Dan Devine	Sugar	1-1-66	Florida	20-18
Dan Devine	Gator	12-28-68	Alabama	35-10
Dan Devine	Orange	1-1-70	Penn St.	3-10
Al Onofrio........................	Fiesta	12-23-72	Arizona St.	35-49
Al Onofrio........................	Sun	12-29-73	Auburn	34-17
Warren Powers...................	Liberty	12-23-78	Louisiana St.	20-15
Warren Powers...................	Hall of Fame	12-29-79	South Caro.	24-14
Warren Powers...................	Liberty	12-27-80	Purdue	25-28
Warren Powers...................	Tangerine	12-19-81	Southern Miss.	19-17
Warren Powers...................	Holiday	12-23-83	Brigham Young	17-21

All bowls 8-11-0; Big four 2-5-0

NAVY

	Bowl	Date	Opponent	Score
Bob Folwell	Rose	1-1-24	Washington	14-14
Eddie Erdelatz	Sugar	1-1-55	Mississippi	21-0
Eddie Erdelatz	Cotton	1-1-58	Rice	20-7
Wayne Hardin....................	Orange	1-1-61	Missouri	14-21
Wayne Hardin....................	Cotton	1-1-64	Texas	6-28
George Welsh.....................	Holiday	12-22-78	Brigham Young	23-16
George Welsh.....................	Garden State	12-14-80	Houston	0-35
George Welsh.....................	Liberty	12-30-81	Ohio St.	28-31

All bowls 3-4-1; Big four 2-2-1

NEBRASKA

	Bowl	Date	Opponent	Score
Lawrence McC. "Biff" Jones	Rose	1-1-41	Stanford	13-21
Bill Glassford	Orange	1-1-55	Duke	7-34
Bob Devaney	Gotham	12-15-62	Miami (Fla.)	36-34
Bob Devaney	Orange	1-1-64	Auburn	13-7
Bob Devaney	Cotton	1-1-65	Arkansas	7-10
Bob Devaney	Orange	1-1-66	Alabama	28-39
Bob Devaney	Sugar	1-2-67	Alabama	7-34
Bob Devaney	Sun	12-20-69	Georgia	45-6
Bob Devaney	Orange	1-1-71	Louisiana St.	17-12
Bob Devaney	Orange	1-1-72	Alabama	38-6
Bob Devaney	Orange	1-1-73	Notre Dame	40-6
Tom Osborne	Cotton	1-1-74	Texas	19-3
Tom Osborne	Sugar	12-31-74	Florida	13-10
Tom Osborne	Fiesta	12-26-75	Arizona St.	14-17
Tom Osborne	Bluebonnet	12-31-76	Texas Tech	27-24
Tom Osborne	Liberty	12-19-77	North Caro.	21-17
Tom Osborne	Orange	1-1-79	Oklahoma	24-31
Tom Osborne	Cotton	1-1-80	Houston	14-17
Tom Osborne	Sun	12-27-80	Mississippi St.	31-17
Tom Osborne	Orange	1-1-82	Clemson	15-22
Tom Osborne	Orange	1-1-83	Louisiana St.	21-20
Tom Osborne	Orange	1-2-84	Miami (Fla.)	30-31
Tom Osborne	Sugar	1-1-85	Louisiana St.	28-10
Tom Osborne	Fiesta	1-1-86	Michigan	23-27
Tom Osborne	Sugar	1-1-87	Louisiana St.	30-15
Tom Osborne	Fiesta	1-1-88	Florida St.	28-31
Tom Osborne	Orange	1-2-89	Miami (Fla.)	3-23
Tom Osborne	Fiesta	1-1-90	Florida St.	17-41

Team-by-Team Bowl Results

| Tom Osborne . . . . | Florida Citrus | 1-1-91 | Georgia Tech | 21-45 |
| Tom Osborne . . . . | Orange | 1-1-92 | Miami (Fla.) | 0-22 |

All bowls 14-16-0; Big four 9-11-0

NEVADA

	Bowl	Date	Opponent	Score
Joe Sheeketski	Salad	1-1-48	North Texas	13-6
Joe Sheeketski	Harbor	1-1-49	Villanova	7-27

All bowls 1-1-0; Big four 0-0-0

NEVADA-LAS VEGAS

	Bowl	Date	Opponent	Score
Harvey Hyde	California	12-15-84	Toledo	30-13

All bowls 1-0-0; Big four 0-0-0

NEW MEXICO

	Bowl	Date	Opponent	Score
Ted Shipkey	Sun	1-2-39	Utah	0-26
Willis Barnes	Sun	1-1-44	Southwestern (Tex.)	0-7
Willis Barnes	Sun	1-1-46	Denver	34-24
Willis Barnes	Harbor	1-1-47	Montana St.	13-13
Bill Weeks	Aviation	12-9-61	Western Mich.	28-12

All bowls 2-2-1; Big four 0-0-0

NEW MEXICO ST.

	Bowl	Date	Bowl	Date
Jerry Hines	Sun	1-1-36	Hardin-Simmons	14-14
Warren Woodson	Sun	12-31-59	North Texas	28-8
Warren Woodson	Sun	12-31-60	Utah St.	20-13

All bowls 2-0-1; Big four 0-0-0

NORTH CARO.

	Bowl	Date	Opponent	Score
Carl Snavely	Sugar	1-1-47	Georgia	10-20
Carl Snavely	Sugar	1-1-49	Oklahoma	6-14
Carl Snavely	Cotton	1-2-50	Rice	13-27
Jim Hickey	Gator	12-28-63	Air Force	35-0
Bill Dooley	Peach	12-30-70	Arizona St.	26-48
Bill Dooley	Gator	12-31-71	Georgia	3-7
Bill Dooley	Sun	12-30-72	Texas Tech	32-28
Bill Dooley	Sun	12-28-74	Mississippi St.	24-26
Bill Dooley	Peach	12-31-76	Kentucky	0-21
Bill Dooley	Liberty	12-19-77	Nebraska	17-21
Dick Crum	Gator	12-28-79	Michigan	17-15
Dick Crum	Bluebonnet	12-31-80	Texas	16-7
Dick Crum	Gator	12-28-81	Arkansas	31-27
Dick Crum	Sun	12-25-82	Texas	26-10
Dick Crum	Peach	12-30-83	Florida St.	3-28
Dick Crum	Aloha	12-27-86	Arizona	21-30

All bowls 6-10-0; Big four 0-3-0

NORTH CARO. ST.

	Bowl	Date	Opponent	Score
Beattie Feathers	Gator	1-1-47	Oklahoma	13-34
Earle Edwards	Liberty	12-21-63	Mississippi St.	12-16
Earle Edwards	Liberty	12-16-67	Georgia	14-7
Lou Holtz	Peach	12-29-72	West Va.	49-13
Lou Holtz	Liberty	12-17-73	Kansas	31-18
Lou Holtz	Bluebonnet	12-23-74	Houston	31-31
Lou Holtz	Peach	12-31-75	West Va.	10-13
Bo Rein	Peach	12-31-77	Iowa St.	24-14
Bo Rein	Tangerine	12-23-78	Pittsburgh	30-17
Dick Sheridan	Peach	12-31-86	Virginia Tech	24-25
Dick Sheridan	Peach	12-31-88	Iowa	28-23
Dick Sheridan	Copper	12-31-89	Arizona	10-17
Dick Sheridan	All-American	12-28-90	Southern Miss.	31-27
Dick Sheridan	Peach	1-1-92	East Caro.	34-37

All bowls 7-6-1; Big four 0-0-0

NORTHERN ILL.

	Bowl	Date	Opponent	Score
Bill Mallory	California	12-17-83	Cal St. Fullerton	20-13

All bowls 1-0-0; Big four 0-0-0

NORTHWESTERN

	Bowl	Date	Opponent	Score
Bob Voigts	Rose	1-1-49	California	20-14

All bowls 1-0-0; Big four 1-0-0

NOTRE DAME

	Bowl	Date	Opponent	Score
Knute Rockne	Rose	1-1-25	Stanford	27-10
Ara Parseghian	Cotton	1-1-70	Texas	17-21
Ara Parseghian	Cotton	1-1-71	Texas	24-11
Ara Parseghian	Orange	1-1-73	Nebraska	6-40
Ara Parseghian	Sugar	12-31-73	Alabama	24-23

Ara Parseghian....................	Orange	1-1-75	Alabama	13-11
Dan Devine	Gator	12-27-76	Penn St.	20-9
Dan Devine	Cotton	1-2-78	Texas	38-10
Dan Devine	Cotton	1-1-79	Houston	35-34
Dan Devine	Sugar	1-1-81	Georgia	10-17
Gerry Faust	Liberty	12-29-83	Boston College	19-18
Gerry Faust	Aloha	12-29-84	Southern Methodist	20-27
Lou Holtz	Cotton	1-1-88	Texas A&M	10-35
Lou Holtz	Fiesta	1-2-89	West Va.	34-21
Lou Holtz	Orange	1-1-90	Colorado	21-6
Lou Holtz	Orange	1-1-91	Colorado	9-10
Lou Holtz	Sugar	1-1-92	Florida	39-28

All bowls 11-6-0; Big four 8-5-0

OHIO	Bowl	Date	Opponent	Score
Bill Hess	Sun	12-31-62	West Tex. St.	14-15
Bill Hess	Tangerine	12-27-68	Richmond	42-49

All bowls 0-2-0; Big four 0-0-0

OHIO ST.	Bowl	Date	Opponent	Score
John Wilce	Rose	1-1-21	California	0-28
Wes Fesler	Rose	1-2-50	California	17-14
Woody Hayes	Rose	1-1-55	Southern Cal	20-7
Woody Hayes	Rose	1-1-58	Oregon	10-7
Woody Hayes	Rose	1-1-69	Southern Cal	27-16
Woody Hayes	Rose	1-1-71	Stanford	17-27
Woody Hayes	Rose	1-1-73	Southern Cal	17-42
Woody Hayes	Rose	1-1-74	Southern Cal	42-21
Woody Hayes	Rose	1-1-75	Southern Cal	17-18
Woody Hayes	Rose	1-1-76	UCLA	10-23
Woody Hayes	Orange	1-1-77	Colorado	27-10
Woody Hayes	Sugar	1-2-78	Alabama	6-35
Woody Hayes	Gator	12-29-78	Clemson	15-17
Earle Bruce	Rose	1-1-80	Southern Cal	16-17
Earle Bruce	Fiesta	12-26-80	Penn St.	19-31
Earle Bruce	Liberty	12-30-81	Navy	31-28
Earle Bruce	Holiday	12-17-82	Brigham Young	47-17
Earle Bruce	Fiesta	1-2-84	Pittsburgh	28-23
Earle Bruce	Rose	1-1-85	Southern Cal	17-20
Earle Bruce	Florida Citrus	12-28-85	Brigham Young	10-7
Earle Bruce	Cotton	1-1-87	Texas A&M	28-12
John Cooper.....................	Hall of Fame	1-1-90	Auburn	14-31
John Cooper.....................	Liberty	12-27-90	Air Force	11-23
John Cooper.....................	Hall of Fame	1-1-92	Syracuse	17-24

All bowls 11-13-0; Big four 7-8-0

OKLAHOMA	Bowl	Date	Opponent	Score
Tom Stidham.....................	Orange	1-2-39	Tennessee	0-17
Jim Tatum.......................	Gator	1-1-47	North Caro. St.	34-13
Bud Wilkinson	Sugar	1-1-49	North Caro.	14-6
Bud Wilkinson	Sugar	1-2-50	Louisiana St.	35-0
Bud Wilkinson	Sugar	1-1-51	Kentucky	7-13
Bud Wilkinson	Orange	1-1-54	Maryland	7-0
Bud Wilkinson	Orange	1-2-56	Maryland	20-6
Bud Wilkinson	Orange	1-1-58	Duke	48-21
Bud Wilkinson	Orange	1-1-59	Syracuse	21-6
Bud Wilkinson	Orange	1-1-63	Alabama	0-17
Gomer Jones	Gator	1-2-65	Florida St.	19-36
Chuck Fairbanks.................	Orange	1-1-68	Tennessee	26-24
Chuck Fairbanks.................	Bluebonnet	12-31-68	Southern Methodist	27-28
Chuck Fairbanks.................	Bluebonnet	12-31-70	Alabama	24-24
Chuck Fairbanks.................	Sugar	1-1-72	Auburn	40-22
Chuck Fairbanks.................	Sugar	12-31-72	Penn St.	14-0
Barry Switzer	Orange	1-1-76	Michigan	14-6
Barry Switzer	Fiesta	12-25-76	Wyoming	41-7
Barry Switzer	Orange	1-2-78	Arkansas	6-31
Barry Switzer	Orange	1-1-79	Nebraska	31-24
Barry Switzer	Orange	1-1-80	Florida St.	24-7
Barry Switzer	Orange	1-1-81	Florida St.	18-17
Barry Switzer	Sun	12-26-81	Houston	40-14
Barry Switzer	Fiesta	1-1-83	Arizona St.	21-32
Barry Switzer	Orange	1-1-85	Washington	17-28
Barry Switzer	Orange	1-1-86	Penn St.	25-10

	Bowl	Date	Opponent	Score
Barry Switzer	Orange	1-1-87	Arkansas	42-8
Barry Switzer	Orange	1-1-88	Miami (Fla.)	14-20
Barry Switzer	Florida Citrus	1-2-89	Clemson	6-13
Gary Gibbs	Gator	12-29-91	Virginia	48-14

All bowls 19-10-1; Big four 15-6-0

OKLAHOMA ST.

	Bowl	Date	Opponent	Score
Jim Lookabaugh	Cotton	1-1-45	Texas Christian	34-0
Jim Lookabaugh	Sugar	1-1-46	St. Mary's (Cal.)	33-13
Jim Lookabaugh	Delta	1-1-49	William & Mary	0-20
Cliff Speegle	Bluegrass	12-13-58	Florida St.	15-6
Jim Stanley	Fiesta	12-28-74	Brigham Young	16-6
Jim Stanley	Tangerine	12-18-76	Brigham Young	49-12
Jimmy Johnson	Independence	12-12-81	Texas A&M	16-33
Jimmy Johnson	Bluebonnet	12-31-83	Baylor	24-14
Pat Jones	Gator	12-28-84	South Caro.	21-14
Pat Jones	Gator	12-30-85	Florida St.	23-34
Pat Jones	Sun	12-25-87	West Va.	35-33
Pat Jones	Holiday	12-30-88	Wyoming	62-14

All bowls 9-3-0; Big four 2-0-0

OREGON

	Bowl	Date	Opponent	Score
Hugo Bezdek	Rose	1-1-17	Pennsylvania	14-0
Charles "Shy" Huntington.........	Rose	1-1-20	Harvard	6-7
Jim Aiken	Cotton	1-1-49	Southern Methodist	13-21
Len Casanova....................	Rose	1-1-58	Ohio St.	7-10
Len Casanova....................	Liberty	12-17-60	Penn St.	12-41
Len Casanova....................	Sun	12-31-63	Southern Methodist	21-14
Rich Brooks......................	Independence	12-16-89	Tulsa	27-24
Rich Brooks......................	Freedom	12-29-90	Colorado St.	31-32

All bowls 3-5-0; Big four 1-3-0

OREGON ST.

	Bowl	Date	Opponent	Score
Don Stiner	Rose	1-1-42	Duke	20-16
Tommy Prothro	Rose	1-1-57	Iowa	19-35
Tommy Prothro	Liberty	12-15-62	Villanova	6-0
Tommy Prothro	Rose	1-1-65	Michigan	7-34

All bowls 2-2-0; Big four 1-2-0

PACIFIC (CAL.)

	Bowl	Date	Opponent	Score
Larry Siemering..................	Raisin	1-1-48	Wichita St.	26-14
Ernie Jorge	Sun	1-1-52	Texas Tech	14-25
Ernie Jorge	Sun	1-1-53	Southern Miss.	26-7

All bowls 2-1-0; Big four 0-0-0

PENN ST.

	Bowl	Date	Opponent	Score
Hugo Bezdek	Rose	1-1-23	Southern Cal	3-14
Bob Higgins	Cotton	1-1-48	Southern Methodist	13-13
Charles "Rip" Engle	Liberty	12-19-59	Alabama	7-0
Charles "Rip" Engle	Liberty	12-17-60	Oregon	41-12
Charles "Rip" Engle	Gator	12-30-61	Georgia Tech	30-15
Charles "Rip" Engle	Gator	12-29-62	Florida	7-17
Joe Paterno	Gator	12-30-67	Florida St.	17-17
Joe Paterno	Orange	1-1-69	Kansas	15-14
Joe Paterno	Orange	1-1-70	Missouri	10-3
Joe Paterno	Cotton	1-1-72	Texas	30-6
Joe Paterno	Sugar	12-31-72	Oklahoma	0-14
Joe Paterno	Orange	1-1-74	Louisiana St.	16-9
Joe Paterno	Cotton	1-1-75	Baylor	41-20
Joe Paterno	Sugar	12-31-75	Alabama	6-13
Joe Paterno	Gator	12-27-76	Notre Dame	9-20
Joe Paterno	Fiesta	12-25-77	Arizona St.	42-30
Joe Paterno	Sugar	1-1-79	Alabama	7-14
Joe Paterno	Liberty	12-22-79	Tulane	9-6
Joe Paterno	Fiesta	12-26-80	Ohio St.	31-19
Joe Paterno	Fiesta	1-1-82	Southern Cal	26-10
Joe Paterno	Sugar	1-1-83	Georgia	27-23
Joe Paterno	Aloha	12-26-83	Washington	13-10
Joe Paterno	Orange	1-1-86	Oklahoma	10-25
Joe Paterno	Fiesta	1-2-87	Miami (Fla.)	14-10
Joe Paterno	Florida Citrus	1-1-88	Clemson	10-35

Joe Paterno	Holiday	12-29-89	Brigham Young	50-39
Joe Paterno	Blockbuster	12-28-90	Florida St.	17-24
Joe Paterno	Fiesta	1-1-92	Tennessee	42-17

All bowls 17-9-2; Big four 6-5-1

PITTSBURGH	Bowl	Date	Opponent	Score
Jock Sutherland	Rose	1-2-28	Stanford	6-7
Jock Sutherland	Rose	1-1-30	Southern Cal	14-47
Jock Sutherland	Rose	1-2-33	Southern Cal	0-35
Jock Sutherland	Rose	1-1-37	Washington	21-0
John Michelosen	Sugar	1-2-56	Georgia Tech	0-7
John Michelosen	Gator	12-29-56	Georgia Tech	14-21
Johnny Majors	Fiesta	12-21-73	Arizona St.	7-28
Johnny Majors	Sun	12-26-75	Kansas	33-19
Johnny Majors	Sugar	1-1-77	Georgia	27-3
Jackie Sherrill	Gator	12-30-77	Clemson	34-3
Jackie Sherrill	Tangerine	12-23-78	North Caro. St.	17-30
Jackie Sherrill	Fiesta	12-25-79	Arizona	16-10
Jackie Sherrill	Gator	12-29-80	South Caro.	37-9
Jackie Sherrill	Sugar	1-1-82	Georgia	24-20
Foge Fazio	Cotton	1-1-83	Southern Methodist	3-7
Foge Fazio	Fiesta	1-2-84	Ohio St.	23-28
Mike Gottfried	Bluebonnet	12-31-87	Texas	27-32
Paul Hackett	John Hancock	12-30-89	Texas A&M	31-28

All bowls 8-10-0; Big four 3-5-0

PURDUE	Bowl	Date	Opponent	Score
Jack Mollenkopf	Rose	1-2-67	Southern Cal	14-13
Jim Young	Peach	12-25-78	Georgia Tech	41-21
Jim Young	Bluebonnet	12-31-79	Tennessee	27-22
Jim Young	Liberty	12-27-80	Missouri	28-25
Leon Burtnett	Peach	12-31-84	Virginia	24-27

All bowls 4-1-0; Big four 1-0-0

RICE	Bowl	Date	Opponent	Score
Jimmy Kitts	Cotton	1-1-38	Colorado	28-14
Jess Neely	Orange	1-1-47	Tennessee	8-0
Jess Neely	Cotton	1-2-50	North Caro.	27-13
Jess Neely	Cotton	1-1-54	Alabama	28-6
Jess Neely	Cotton	1-1-58	Navy	7-20
Jess Neely	Sugar	1-2-61	Mississippi	6-14
Jess Neely	Bluebonnet	12-16-61	Kansas	7-33

All bowls 4-3-0; Big four 4-2-0

RUTGERS	Bowl	Date	Opponent	Score
Frank Burns	Garden State	12-16-78	Arizona St.	18-34

All bowls 0-1-0; Big four 0-0-0

SAN DIEGO ST.	Bowl	Date	Opponent	Score
Bill Schutte	Harbor	1-1-48	Hardin-Simmons	0-53
Don Coryell	Pasadena	12-6-69	Boston U.	28-7
Denny Stolz	Holiday	12-30-86	Iowa	38-39
Al Luginbill	Freedom	12-30-91	Tulsa	17-28

All bowls 1-3-0; Big four 0-0-0

SAN JOSE ST.	Bowl	Date	Opponent	Score
Bill Hubbard	Raisin	1-1-47	Utah St.	20-0
Bill Hubbard	Raisin	12-31-49	Texas Tech	20-13
Dewey King	Pasadena	12-18-71	Memphis St.	9-28
Jack Elway	California	12-19-81	Toledo	25-27
Claude Gilbert	California	12-31-86	Miami (Ohio)	37-7
Claude Gilbert	California	12-12-87	Eastern Mich.	27-30
Terry Shea	California	12-8-90	Central Mich.	48-24

All bowls 4-3-0; Big four 0-0-0

SOUTH CARO.	Bowl	Date	Opponent	Score
Johnny McMillan	Gator	1-1-46	Wake Forest	14-26
Paul Dietzel	Peach	12-30-69	West Va.	3-14
Jim Carlen	Tangerine	12-20-75	Miami (Ohio)	7-20
Jim Carlen	Hall of Fame	12-29-79	Missouri	14-24
Jim Carlen	Gator	12-29-80	Pittsburgh	9-37
Joe Morrison	Gator	12-28-84	Oklahoma St.	14-21
Joe Morrison	Gator	12-31-87	Louisiana St.	13-30
Joe Morrison	Liberty	12-28-88	Indiana	10-34

All bowls 0-8-0; Big four 0-0-0

Team-by-Team Bowl Results

After making just three bowl appearances in its first 85 seasons of football, South Carolina went to back-to-back bowls in 1979 and 1980 behind the running of George Rogers. In 1980, Rogers rushed for 1,781 yards and won the Heisman Trophy.

SOUTHERN CAL	Bowl	Date	Opponent	Score
Elmer "Gus" Henderson...........	Rose	1-1-23	Penn St.	14-3
Elmer "Gus" Henderson...........	Los Angeles Christmas Festival	12-25-24	Missouri	20-7
Howard Jones	Rose	1-1-30	Pittsburgh	47-14
Howard Jones	Rose	1-1-32	Tulane	21-12
Howard Jones	Rose	1-2-33	Pittsburgh	35-0
Howard Jones	Rose	1-2-39	Duke	7-3
Howard Jones	Rose	1-1-40	Tennessee	14-0
Jeff Cravath......................	Rose	1-1-44	Washington	29-0
Jeff Cravath......................	Rose	1-1-45	Tennessee	25-0
Jeff Cravath......................	Rose	1-1-46	Alabama	14-34
Jeff Cravath......................	Rose	1-1-48	Michigan	0-49
Jess Hill.........................	Rose	1-1-53	Wisconsin	7-0
Jess Hill.........................	Rose	1-1-55	Ohio St.	7-20
John McKay	Rose	1-1-63	Wisconsin	42-37
John McKay	Rose	1-2-67	Purdue	13-14
John McKay	Rose	1-1-68	Indiana	14-3
John McKay	Rose	1-1-69	Ohio St.	16-27
John McKay	Rose	1-1-70	Michigan	10-3
John McKay	Rose	1-1-73	Ohio St.	42-17
John McKay	Rose	1-1-74	Ohio St.	21-42
John McKay	Rose	1-1-75	Ohio St.	18-17
John McKay	Liberty	12-22-75	Texas A&M	20-0
John Robinson....................	Rose	1-1-77	Michigan	14-6
John Robinson....................	Bluebonnet	12-31-77	Texas A&M	47-28
John Robinson....................	Rose	1-1-79	Michigan	17-10
John Robinson....................	Rose	1-1-80	Ohio St.	17-16
John Robinson....................	Fiesta	1-1-82	Penn St.	10-26
Ted Tollner......................	Rose	1-1-85	Ohio St.	20-17
Ted Tollner......................	Aloha	12-28-85	Alabama	3-24
Ted Tollner......................	Florida Citrus	1-1-87	Auburn	7-16
Larry Smith	Rose	1-1-88	Michigan St.	17-20
Larry Smith	Rose	1-2-89	Michigan	14-22
Larry Smith	Rose	1-1-90	Michigan	17-10
Larry Smith	John Hancock	12-31-90	Michigan St.	16-17
All bowls 22-12-0; Big four 19-8-0				
SOUTHERN METHODIST	**Bowl**	**Date**	**Opponent**	**Score**
Ray Morrison	Dixie Classic	1-1-25	West Va. Wesleyan	7-9

	Rose	1-1-36	Stanford	0-7
Matty Bell	Rose	1-1-36	Stanford	0-7
Matty Bell	Cotton	1-1-48	Penn St.	13-13
Matty Bell	Cotton	1-1-49	Oregon	21-13
Hayden Fry	Sun	12-31-63	Oregon	14-21
Hayden Fry	Cotton	12-31-66	Georgia	9-24
Hayden Fry	Bluebonnet	12-31-68	Oklahoma	28-27
Ron Meyer	Holiday	12-19-80	Brigham Young	45-46
Bobby Collins	Cotton	1-1-83	Pittsburgh	7-3
Bobby Collins	Sun	12-24-83	Alabama	7-28
Bobby Collins	Aloha	12-29-84	Notre Dame	27-20

All bowls 4-6-1; Big four 2-2-1

SOUTHERN MISS.	Bowl	Date	Opponent	Score
Thad "Pie" Vann	Sun	1-1-53	Pacific (Cal.)	7-26
Thad "Pie" Vann	Sun	1-1-54	UTEP	14-37
Bobby Collins	Independence	12-13-80	McNeese St.	16-14
Bobby Collins	Tangerine	12-19-81	Missouri	17-19
Curley Hallman	Independence	12-23-88	UTEP	38-18
Jeff Bower	All-American	12-28-90	North Caro. St.	27-31

All bowls 2-4-0; Big four 0-0-0

STANFORD	Bowl	Date	Opponent	Score
Charlie Fickert	Rose	1-1-02	Michigan	0-49
Glenn "Pop" Warner	Rose	1-1-25	Notre Dame	10-27
Glenn "Pop" Warner	Rose	1-1-27	Alabama	7-7
Glenn "Pop" Warner	Rose	1-2-28	Pittsburgh	7-6
Claude "Tiny" Thornhill	Rose	1-1-34	Columbia	0-7
Claude "Tiny" Thornhill	Rose	1-1-35	Alabama	13-29
Claude "Tiny" Thornhill	Rose	1-1-36	Southern Methodist	7-0
Clark Shaughnessy	Rose	1-1-41	Nebraska	21-13
Chuck Taylor	Rose	1-1-52	Illinois	7-40
John Ralston	Rose	1-1-71	Ohio St.	27-17
John Ralston	Rose	1-1-72	Michigan	13-12
Bill Walsh	Sun	12-31-77	Louisiana St.	24-14
Bill Walsh	Bluebonnet	12-31-78	Georgia	25-22
Jack Elway	Gator	12-27-86	Clemson	21-27
Dennis Green	Aloha	12-25-91	Georgia Tech	17-18

All bowls 7-7-1; Big four 5-5-1

SYRACUSE	Bowl	Date	Opponent	Score
Ben Schwartzwalder	Orange	1-1-53	Alabama	6-61
Ben Schwartzwalder	Cotton	1-1-57	Texas Christian	27-28
Ben Schwartzwalder	Orange	1-1-59	Oklahoma	6-21
Ben Schwartzwalder	Cotton	1-1-60	Texas	23-14
Ben Schwartzwalder	Liberty	12-16-61	Miami (Fla.)	15-14
Ben Schwartzwalder	Sugar	1-1-65	Louisiana St.	10-13
Ben Schwartzwalder	Gator	12-31-66	Tennessee	12-18
Frank Maloney	Independence	12-15-79	McNeese St.	31-7
Dick MacPherson	Cherry	12-21-85	Maryland	18-35
Dick MacPherson	Sugar	1-1-88	Auburn	16-16
Dick MacPherson	Hall of Fame	1-2-89	Louisiana St.	23-10
Dick MacPherson	Peach	12-30-89	Georgia	19-18
Dick MacPherson	Aloha	12-25-90	Arizona	28-0
Paul Pasqualoni	Hall of Fame	1-1-92	Ohio St.	24-17

All bowls 7-6-1; Big four 1-4-1

TEMPLE	Bowl	Date	Opponent	Score
Glenn "Pop" Warner	Sugar	1-1-35	Tulane	14-20
Wayne Hardin	Garden State	12-15-79	California	28-17

All bowls 1-1-0; Big four 0-1-0

TENNESSEE	Bowl	Date	Opponent	Score
Bob Neyland	Orange	1-2-39	Oklahoma	17-0
Bob Neyland	Rose	1-1-40	Southern Cal	0-14
Bob Neyland	Sugar	1-1-41	Boston College	13-19
John Barnhill	Sugar	1-1-43	Tulsa	14-7
John Barnhill	Rose	1-1-45	Southern Cal	0-25
Bob Neyland	Orange	1-1-47	Rice	0-8
Bob Neyland	Cotton	1-1-51	Texas	20-14
Bob Neyland	Sugar	1-1-52	Baylor	7-13
Bob Neyland	Cotton	1-1-53	Texas	0-16
Bowden Wyatt	Sugar	1-1-57	Maryland	13-28
Bowden Wyatt	Gator	12-28-57	Texas A&M	3-0
Doug Dickey	Bluebonnet	12-18-65	Tulsa	27-6

Doug Dickey	Gator	12-31-66	Syracuse	18-12
Doug Dickey	Orange	1-1-68	Oklahoma	24-26
Doug Dickey	Cotton	1-1-69	Texas	13-36
Doug Dickey	Gator	12-27-69	Florida	13-14
Bill Battle	Sugar	1-1-71	Air Force	34-13
Bill Battle	Liberty	12-20-71	Arkansas	14-13
Bill Battle	Bluebonnet	12-30-72	Louisiana St.	24-17
Bill Battle	Gator	12-29-73	Texas Tech	19-28
Bill Battle	Liberty	12-16-74	Maryland	7-3
Johnny Majors	Bluebonnet	12-31-79	Purdue	22-27
Johnny Majors	Garden State	12-13-81	Wisconsin	28-21
Johnny Majors	Peach	12-31-82	Iowa	22-28
Johnny Majors	Florida Citrus	12-17-83	Maryland	30-23
Johnny Majors	Sun	12-24-84	Maryland	26-27
Johnny Majors	Sugar	1-1-86	Miami (Fla.)	35-7
Johnny Majors	Liberty	12-29-86	Minnesota	21-14
Johnny Majors	Peach	1-2-88	Indiana	27-22
Johnny Majors	Cotton	1-1-90	Arkansas	31-27
Johnny Majors	Sugar	1-1-91	Virginia	23-22
Johnny Majors	Fiesta	1-1-92	Penn St.	17-42

All bowls 17-15-0; Big four 7-9-0

TEXAS

	Bowl	Date	Opponent	Score
Dana Bible	Cotton	1-1-43	Georgia Tech	14-7
Dana Bible	Cotton	1-1-44	Randolph Field	7-7
Dana Bible	Cotton	1-1-46	Missouri	40-27
Blair Cherry	Sugar	1-1-48	Alabama	27-7
Blair Cherry	Orange	1-1-49	Georgia	41-28
Blair Cherry	Cotton	1-1-51	Tennessee	14-20
Ed Price	Cotton	1-1-53	Tennessee	16-0
Darrell Royal	Sugar	1-1-58	Mississippi	7-39
Darrell Royal	Cotton	1-1-60	Syracuse	14-23
Darrell Royal	Bluebonnet	12-17-60	Alabama	3-3
Darrell Royal	Cotton	1-1-62	Mississippi	12-7
Darrell Royal	Cotton	1-1-63	Louisiana St.	0-13
Darrell Royal	Cotton	1-1-64	Navy	28-6
Darrell Royal	Orange	1-1-65	Alabama	21-17
Darrell Royal	Bluebonnet	12-17-66	Mississippi	19-0
Darrell Royal	Cotton	1-1-69	Tennessee	36-13
Darrell Royal	Cotton	1-1-70	Notre Dame	21-17
Darrell Royal	Cotton	1-1-71	Notre Dame	11-24
Darrell Royal	Cotton	1-1-72	Penn St.	6-30
Darrell Royal	Cotton	1-1-73	Alabama	17-13
Darrell Royal	Cotton	1-1-74	Nebraska	3-19
Darrell Royal	Gator	12-30-74	Auburn	3-27
Darrell Royal	Bluebonnet	12-27-75	Colorado	38-21
Fred Akers	Cotton	1-2-78	Notre Dame	10-38
Fred Akers	Sun	12-23-78	Maryland	42-0
Fred Akers	Sun	12-22-79	Washington	7-14
Fred Akers	Bluebonnet	12-31-80	North Caro.	7-16
Fred Akers	Cotton	1-1-82	Alabama	14-12
Fred Akers	Sun	12-25-82	North Caro.	10-26
Fred Akers	Cotton	1-2-84	Georgia	9-10
Fred Akers	Freedom	12-26-84	Iowa	17-55
Fred Akers	Bluebonnet	12-31-85	Air Force	16-24
David McWilliams	Bluebonnet	12-31-87	Pittsburgh	32-27
David McWilliams	Cotton	1-1-91	Miami (Fla.)	3-46

All bowls 16-16-2; Big four 12-10-1

TEXAS A&M

	Bowl	Date	Opponent	Score
Dana Bible	Dixie Classic	1-2-22	Centre	22-14
Homer Norton	Sugar	1-1-40	Tulane	14-13
Homer Norton	Cotton	1-1-41	Fordham	13-12
Homer Norton	Cotton	1-1-42	Alabama	21-29
Homer Norton	Orange	1-1-44	Louisiana St.	14-19
Harry Stiteler	Presidential	12-9-50	Georgia	40-20
Paul "Bear" Bryant	Gator	12-28-57	Tennessee	0-3
Gene Stallings	Cotton	1-1-68	Alabama	20-16
Emory Bellard	Liberty	12-22-75	Southern Cal	0-20
Emory Bellard	Sun	1-2-77	Florida	37-14
Emory Bellard	Bluebonnet	12-31-77	Southern Cal	28-47
Tom Wilson	Hall of Fame	12-20-78	Iowa St.	28-12

Tom Wilson	Independence	12-12-81	Oklahoma St.	33-16
Jackie Sherrill	Cotton	1-1-86	Auburn	36-16
Jackie Sherrill	Cotton	1-1-87	Ohio St.	12-28
Jackie Sherrill	Cotton	1-1-88	Notre Dame	35-10
R. C. Slocum	John Hancock	12-30-89	Pittsburgh	28-31
R. C. Slocum	Holiday	12-29-90	Brigham Young	65-14
R. C. Slocum	Cotton	1-1-92	Florida St.	2-10

All bowls 11-8-0; Big four 5-4-0

TEXAS CHRISTIAN

Coach	Bowl	Date	Opponent	Score
Bill Driver	Fort Worth Classic	1-1-21	Centre	7-63
Leo "Dutch" Meyer	Sugar	1-1-36	Louisiana St.	3-2
Leo "Dutch" Meyer	Cotton	1-1-37	Marquette	16-6
Leo "Dutch" Meyer	Sugar	1-2-39	Carnegie Tech	15-7
Leo "Dutch" Meyer	Orange	1-1-42	Georgia	26-40
Leo "Dutch" Meyer	Cotton	1-1-45	Oklahoma St.	0-34
Leo "Dutch" Meyer	Delta	1-1-48	Mississippi	9-13
Leo "Dutch" Meyer	Cotton	1-1-52	Kentucky	7-20
Abe Martin	Cotton	1-2-56	Mississippi	13-14
Abe Martin	Cotton	1-1-57	Syracuse	28-27
Abe Martin	Cotton	1-1-59	Air Force	0-0
Abe Martin	Bluebonnet	12-19-59	Clemson	7-23
Abe Martin	Sun	12-31-65	UTEP	12-13
Jim Wacker	Bluebonnet	12-31-84	West Va.	14-31

All bowls 4-9-1; Big four 4-4-1

TEXAS TECH

Coach	Bowl	Date	Opponent	Score
Pete Cawthon	Sun	1-1-38	West Va.	6-7
Pete Cawthon	Cotton	1-2-39	St. Mary's (Cal.)	13-20
Dell Morgan	Sun	1-1-42	Tulsa	0-6
Dell Morgan	Sun	1-1-48	Miami (Ohio)	12-13
Dell Morgan	Raisin	12-31-49	San Jose St.	13-20
DeWitt Weaver	Sun	1-1-52	Pacific (Cal.)	25-14
DeWitt Weaver	Gator	1-1-54	Auburn	35-13
DeWitt Weaver	Sun	1-2-56	Wyoming	14-21
J. T. King	Sun	12-26-64	Georgia	0-7
J. T. King	Gator	12-31-65	Georgia Tech	21-31
Jim Carlen	Sun	12-19-70	Georgia Tech	9-17
Jim Carlen	Sun	12-30-72	North Caro.	28-32
Jim Carlen	Gator	12-29-73	Tennessee	28-19
Jim Carlen	Peach	12-28-74	Vanderbilt	6-6
Steve Sloan	Bluebonnet	12-31-76	Nebraska	24-27
Steve Sloan	Tangerine	12-23-77	Florida St.	17-40
Spike Dykes	Independence	12-20-86	Mississippi	17-20
Spike Dykes	All-American	12-28-89	Duke	49-21

All bowls 4-13-1; Big four 0-1-0

TOLEDO

Coach	Bowl	Date	Opponent	Score
Frank Lauterbur	Tangerine	12-26-69	Davidson	56-33
Frank Lauterbur	Tangerine	12-28-70	William & Mary	40-12
Jack Murphy	Tangerine	12-28-71	Richmond	28-3
Chuck Stobart	California	12-19-81	San Jose St.	27-25
Dan Simrell	California	12-15-84	Nevada-Las Vegas	13-30

All bowls 4-1-0; Big four 0-0-0

TULANE

Coach	Bowl	Date	Opponent	Score
Bernie Bierman	Rose	1-1-32	Southern Cal	12-21
Ted Cox	Sugar	1-1-35	Temple	20-14
Lowell "Red" Dawson	Sugar	1-1-40	Texas A&M	13-14
Jim Pittman	Liberty	12-12-70	Colorado	17-3
Bennie Ellender	Bluebonnet	12-29-73	Houston	7-47
Larry Smith	Liberty	12-22-79	Penn St.	6-9
Vince Gibson	Hall of Fame	12-27-80	Arkansas	15-34
Mack Brown	Independence	12-19-87	Washington	12-24

All bowls 2-6-0; Big four 1-2-0

TULSA

Coach	Bowl	Date	Opponent	Score
Henry Frnka	Sun	1-1-42	Texas Tech	6-0
Henry Frnka	Sugar	1-1-43	Tennessee	7-14
Henry Frnka	Sugar	1-1-44	Georgia Tech	18-20
Henry Frnka	Orange	1-1-45	Georgia Tech	26-12
Henry Frnka	Oil	1-1-46	Georgia	6-20
J. O. "Buddy" Brothers	Gator	1-1-53	Florida	13-14
Glenn Dobbs	Bluebonnet	12-19-64	Mississippi	14-7

	Bowl	Date	Opponent	Score
Glenn Dobbs	Bluebonnet	12-18-65	Tennessee	6-27
F. A. Dry	Independence	12-13-76	McNeese St.	16-20
Dave Rader	Independence	12-16-89	Oregon	24-27
Dave Rader	Freedom	12-30-91	San Diego St.	28-17

All bowls 4-7-0; Big four 1-2-0

UCLA

	Bowl	Date	Opponent	Score
Edwin "Babe" Horrell	Rose	1-1-43	Georgia	0-9
Bert LaBrucherie	Rose	1-1-47	Illinois	14-45
Henry "Red" Sanders	Rose	1-1-54	Michigan St.	20-28
Henry "Red" Sanders	Rose	1-2-56	Michigan St.	14-17
Bill Barnes	Rose	1-1-62	Minnesota	3-21
Tommy Prothro	Rose	1-1-66	Michigan St.	14-12
Dick Vermeil	Rose	1-1-76	Ohio St.	23-10
Terry Donahue	Liberty	12-20-76	Alabama	6-36
Terry Donahue	Fiesta	12-25-78	Arkansas	10-10
Terry Donahue	Bluebonnet	12-31-81	Michigan	14-33
Terry Donahue	Rose	1-1-83	Michigan	24-14
Terry Donahue	Rose	1-2-84	Illinois	45-9
Terry Donahue	Fiesta	1-1-85	Miami (Fla.)	39-37
Terry Donahue	Rose	1-1-86	Iowa	45-28
Terry Donahue	Freedom	12-30-86	Brigham Young	31-10
Terry Donahue	Aloha	12-25-87	Florida	20-16
Terry Donahue	Cotton	1-1-89	Arkansas	17-3
Terry Donahue	John Hancock	12-31-91	Illinois	6-3

All bowls 10-7-1; Big four 6-5-0

UTAH

	Bowl	Date	Opponent	Score
Ike Armstrong	Sun	1-2-39	New Mexico	26-0
Ray Nagel	Liberty	12-19-64	West Va.	32-6

All bowls 2-0-0; Big four 0-0-0

UTAH ST.

	Bowl	Date	Opponent	Score
E. L. "Dick" Romney	Raisin	1-1-47	San Jose St.	0-20
John Ralston	Sun	12-31-60	New Mexico St.	13-20
John Ralston	Gotham	12-9-61	Baylor	9-24

All bowls 0-3-0; Big four 0-0-0

UTEP

	Bowl	Date	Opponent	Score
Mack Saxon	Sun	1-1-37	Hardin-Simmons	6-34
Jack "Cactus Jack" Curtice	Sun	1-1-49	West Va.	12-21
Jack "Cactus Jack" Curtice	Sun	1-2-50	Georgetown	33-20
Mike Brumbelow	Sun	1-1-54	Southern Miss.	37-14
Mike Brumbelow	Sun	1-1-55	Florida St.	47-20
Mike Brumbelow	Sun	1-1-57	Geo. Washington	0-13
Bobby Dobbs	Sun	12-31-65	Texas Christian	13-12
Bobby Dobbs	Sun	12-30-67	Mississippi	14-7
Bob Stull	Independence	12-23-88	Southern Miss.	18-38

All bowls 5-4-0; Big four 0-0-0

VANDERBILT

	Bowl	Date	Opponent	Score
Art Guepe	Gator	12-31-55	Auburn	25-13
Steve Sloan	Peach	12-28-74	Texas Tech	6-6
George MacIntyre	Hall of Fame	12-31-82	Air Force	28-36

All bowls 1-1-1; Big four 0-0-0

VIRGINIA

	Bowl	Date	Opponent	Score
George Welsh	Peach	12-31-84	Purdue	27-24
George Welsh	All-American	12-22-87	Brigham Young	22-16
George Welsh	Florida Citrus	1-1-90	Illinois	21-31
George Welsh	Sugar	1-1-91	Tennessee	22-23
George Welsh	Gator	12-29-91	Oklahoma	14-48

All bowls 2-3-0; Big four 0-1-0

VIRGINIA TECH

	Bowl	Date	Opponent	Score
Jimmy Kitts	Sun	1-1-47	Cincinnati	6-18
Jerry Claiborne	Liberty	12-10-66	Miami (Fla.)	7-14
Jerry Claiborne	Liberty	12-14-68	Mississippi	17-34
Bill Dooley	Peach	1-2-81	Miami (Fla.)	10-20
Bill Dooley	Independence	12-15-84	Air Force	7-23
Bill Dooley	Peach	12-31-86	North Caro. St.	25-24

All bowls 1-5-0; Big four 0-0-0

WAKE FOREST

	Bowl	Date	Opponent	Score
D. C. "Peahead" Walker	Gator	1-1-46	South Caro.	26-14
D. C. "Peahead" Walker	Dixie	1-1-49	Baylor	7-20

John Mackovic	Tangerine	12-22-79	Louisiana St.	10-34

All bowls 1-2-0; Big four 0-0-0

WASHINGTON	**Bowl**	**Date**	**Opponent**	**Score**
Enoch Bagshaw	Rose	1-1-24	Navy	14-14
Enoch Bagshaw	Rose	1-1-26	Alabama	19-20
Jimmy Phelan	Rose	1-1-37	Pittsburgh	0-21
Ralph "Pest" Welch	Rose	1-1-44	Southern Cal	0-29
Jim Owens	Rose	1-1-60	Wisconsin	44-8
Jim Owens	Rose	1-2-61	Minnesota	17-7
Jim Owens	Rose	1-1-64	Illinois	7-17
Don James	Rose	1-2-78	Michigan	27-20
Don James	Sun	12-22-79	Texas	14-7
Don James	Rose	1-1-81	Michigan	6-23
Don James	Rose	1-1-82	Iowa	28-0
Don James	Aloha	12-25-82	Maryland	21-20
Don James	Aloha	12-26-83	Penn St.	10-13
Don James	Orange	1-1-85	Oklahoma	28-17
Don James	Freedom	12-30-85	Colorado	20-17
Don James	Sun	12-25-86	Alabama	6-28
Don James	Independence	12-19-87	Tulane	24-12
Don James	Freedom	12-30-89	Florida	34-7
Don James	Rose	1-1-91	Iowa	46-34
Don James	Rose	1-1-92	Michigan	34-14

All bowls 12-7-1; Big four 7-5-1

WASHINGTON ST.	**Bowl**	**Date**	**Opponent**	**Score**
Bill "Lone Star" Dietz	Rose	1-1-16	Brown	14-0
Orin "Babe" Hollingbery	Rose	1-1-31	Alabama	0-24
Jim Walden	Holiday	12-18-81	Brigham Young	36-38
Dennis Erickson	Aloha	12-25-88	Houston	24-22

All bowls 2-2-0; Big four 1-1-0

WEST VA.	**Bowl**	**Date**	**Opponent**	**Score**
Clarence "Doc" Spears	San Diego E-W Christmas Classic	12-25-22	Gonzaga	21-13
Marshall "Little Sleepy" Glen	Sun	1-1-38	Texas Tech	7-6
Dud DeGroot	Sun	1-1-49	UTEP	21-12
Art Lewis	Sugar	1-1-54	Georgia Tech	19-42
Gene Corum	Liberty	12-19-64	Utah	6-32
Jim Carlen	Peach	12-30-69	South Caro.	14-3
Bobby Bowden	Peach	12-29-72	North Caro. St.	13-49
Bobby Bowden	Peach	12-31-75	North Caro. St.	13-10
Don Nehlen	Peach	12-31-81	Florida	26-6
Don Nehlen	Gator	12-30-82	Florida St.	12-31
Don Nehlen	Hall of Fame	12-22-83	Kentucky	20-16
Don Nehlen	Bluebonnet	12-31-84	Texas Christian	31-14
Don Nehlen	Sun	12-25-87	Oklahoma St.	33-35
Don Nehlen	Fiesta	1-2-89	Notre Dame	21-34
Don Nehlen	Gator	12-30-89	Clemson	7-27

All bowls 8-7-0; Big four 0-1-0

WESTERN MICH.	**Bowl**	**Date**	**Opponent**	**Score**
Merle Schlosser	Aviation	12-9-61	New Mexico	12-28
Al Molde	California	12-10-88	Fresno St.	30-35

All bowls 0-2-0; Big four 0-0-0

WISCONSIN	**Bowl**	**Date**	**Opponent**	**Score**
Ivy Williamson	Rose	1-1-53	Southern Cal	0-7
Milt Bruhn	Rose	1-1-60	Washington	8-44
Milt Bruhn	Rose	1-2-63	Southern Cal	37-42
Dave McClain	Garden State	12-13-81	Tennessee	21-28
Dave McClain	Independence	12-11-82	Kansas St.	14-3
Dave McClain	Hall of Fame	12-22-83	Kentucky	19-20

All bowls 1-5-0; Big four 0-3-0

WYOMING	**Bowl**	**Date**	**Opponent**	**Score**
Bowden Wyatt	Gator	1-1-51	Wash. & Lee	20-7
Phil Dickens	Sun	1-2-56	Texas Tech	21-14
Bob Devaney	Sun	12-31-58	Hardin-Simmons	14-6
Lloyd Eaton	Sun	12-24-66	Florida St.	28-20
Lloyd Eaton	Sugar	1-1-68	Louisiana St.	13-20
Fred Akers	Fiesta	12-25-76	Oklahoma	7-41
Paul Roach	Holiday	12-30-87	Iowa	19-20

Paul Roach	Holiday	12-30-88	Oklahoma St.	14-62
Paul Roach	Copper	12-31-90	California	15-17

All bowls 4-5-0; Big four 0-1-0

PLAYED IN MAJOR BOWL—NO LONGER I-A

BOSTON U.

	Bowl	Date	Opponent	Score
Larry Naviaux	Pasadena	12-6-69	San Diego St.	7-28

All bowls 0-1-0; Big four 0-0-0

BROWN

	Bowl	Date	Opponent	Score
Ed Robinson	Rose	1-1-16	Washington St.	0-14

All bowls 0-1-0; Big four 0-1-0

BUCKNELL

	Bowl	Date	Opponent	Score
Edward "Hook" Mylin	Orange	1-1-35	Miami (Fla.)	26-0

All bowls 1-0-0; Big four 1-0-0

CAL ST. NORTHRIDGE

	Bowl	Date	Opponent	Score
Sam Winningham	Pasadena	12-2-67	West Tex. St.	13-35

All bowls 0-1-0; Big four 0-0-0

CARNEGIE MELLON

	Bowl	Date	Opponent	Score
Bill Kern	Sugar	1-2-39	Texas Christian	7-15

All bowls 0-1-0; Big four 0-1-0

CASE RESERVE

	Bowl	Date	Opponent	Score
Bill Edwards	Sun	1-1-41	Arizona St.	26-13

All bowls 1-0-0; Big four 0-0-0

CATHOLIC

	Bowl	Date	Opponent	Score
Arthur "Dutch" Bergman	Orange	1-1-36	Mississippi	20-19
Arthur "Dutch" Bergman	Sun	1-1-40	Arizona St.	0-0

All bowls 1-0-1; Big four 1-0-0

CENTENARY

	Bowl	Date	Opponent	Score
Homer Norton	Dixie Classic	1-1-34	Arkansas	7-7

All bowls 0-0-1; Big four 0-0-0

CENTRE

	Bowl	Date	Opponent	Score
Charley Moran	Fort Worth Classic	1-1-21	Texas Christian	63-7
Charley Moran	San Diego E-W Christmas Classic	12-26-21	Arizona	38-0
Charley Moran	Dixie Classic	1-2-22	Texas A&M	14-22

All bowls 2-1-0; Big four 0-0-0

CITADEL

	Bowl	Date	Opponent	Score
Eddie Teague	Tangerine	12-30-60	Tennessee Tech	27-0

All bowls 1-0-0; Big four 0-0-0

COLUMBIA

	Bowl	Date	Opponent	Score
Lou Little.....................	Rose	1-1-34	Stanford	7-0

All bowls 1-0-0; Big four 1-0-0

DAVIDSON

	Bowl	Date	Opponent	Score
Homer Smith.....................	Tangerine	12-26-69	Toledo	33-56

All bowls 0-1-0; Big four 0-0-0

DAYTON

	Bowl	Date	Opponent	Score
Joe Gavin	Salad	1-1-52	Houston	21-26

All bowls 0-1-0; Big four 0-0-0

DENVER

	Bowl	Date	Opponent	Score
Clyde "Cac" Hubbard	Sun	1-1-46	New Mexico	24-34
Clyde "Cac" Hubbard	Alamo	1-4-47	Hardin-Simmons	0-20

All bowls 0-2-0; Big four 0-0-0

DRAKE

	Bowl	Date	Opponent	Score
Vee Green.......................	Raisin	1-1-46	Fresno St.	13-12
Al Kawal	Salad	1-1-49	Arizona	14-13
Warren Gaer	Sun	1-1-58	Louisville	20-34

All bowls 2-1-0; Big four 0-0-0

DUQUESNE

	Bowl	Date	Opponent	Score
John "Little Clipper" Smith........	Orange	1-1-37	Mississippi St.	13-12

All bowls 1-0-0; Big four 0-0-0

FORDHAM

	Bowl	Date	Opponent	Score
Jim Crowley	Cotton	1-1-41	Texas A&M	12-13
Jim Crowley	Sugar	1-1-42	Missouri	2-0

All bowls 1-1-0; Big four 1-1-0

GEO. WASHINGTON	Bowl	Date	Opponent	Score
Eugene "Bo" Sherman	Sun	1-1-57	UTEP	13-0
All bowls 1-0-0; Big four 0-0-0				

GEORGETOWN	Bowl	Date	Opponent	Score
Jack Hagerty	Orange	1-1-41	Mississippi St.	7-14
Bob Margarita	Sun	1-2-50	UTEP	20-33
All bowls 0-2-0; Big four 0-1-0				

GONZAGA	Bowl	Date	Opponent	Score
Charles "Gus" Dorais	San Diego E-W Christmas Classic	12-15-22	West Va.	13-21
All bowls 0-1-0; Big four 0-0-0				

HARDIN-SIMMONS	Bowl	Date	Opponent	Score
Frank Kimbrough	Sun	1-1-36	New Mexico St.	14-14
Frank Kimbrough	Sun	1-1-37	UTEP	34-6
Warren Woodson	Sun	1-1-43	Second Air Force	7-13
Warren Woodson	Alamo	1-4-47	Denver	20-6
Warren Woodson	Harbor	1-1-48	San Diego St.	53-0
Warren Woodson	Shrine	12-18-48	Ouachita Baptist	40-12
Warren Woodson	Camellia	12-30-48	Wichita St.	29-12
Sammy Baugh	Sun	12-31-58	Wyoming	6-14
All bowls 5-2-1; Big four 0-0-0				

HARVARD	Bowl	Date	Opponent	Score
Robert Fisher	Rose	1-1-20	Oregon	7-6
All bowls 1-0-0; Big four 1-0-0				

HOLY CROSS	Bowl	Date	Opponent	Score
John "Ox" Da Grosa	Orange	1-1-46	Miami (Fla.)	6-13
All bowls 0-1-0; Big four 0-1-0				

LONG BEACH ST.	Bowl	Date	Opponent	Score
Jim Stangeland	Pasadena	12-19-70	Louisville	24-24
All bowls 0-0-1; Big four 0-0-0				

MARQUETTE	Bowl	Date	Opponent	Score
Frank Marshall	Cotton	1-1-37	Texas Christian	6-16
All bowls 0-1-0; Big four 0-1-0				

McNEESE ST.	Bowl	Date	Opponent	Score
Jack Doland	Independence	12-13-76	Tulsa	20-16
Ernie Duplechin	Independence	12-15-79	Syracuse	7-31
Ernie Duplechin	Independence	12-13-80	Southern Miss.	14-16
All bowls 1-2-0; Big four 0-0-0				

MONTANA ST.	Bowl	Date	Opponent	Score
Clyde Carpenter	Harbor	1-1-47	New Mexico	13-13
All bowls 0-0-1; Big four 0-0-0				

NORTH TEXAS	Bowl	Date	Opponent	Score
Odus Mitchell	Salad	1-1-48	Nevada	6-13
Odus Mitchell	Sun	12-31-59	New Mexico St.	8-28
All bowls 0-2-0; Big four 0-0-0				

OCCIDENTAL	Bowl	Date	Opponent	Score
Roy Dennis	Raisin	1-1-49	Colorado St.	21-20
All bowls 1-0-0; Big four 0-0-0				

OUACHITA BAPTIST	Bowl	Date	Opponent	Score
Wesley Bradshaw	Shrine	12-18-48	Hardin-Simmons	12-40
All bowls 0-1-0; Big four 0-0-0				

PENNSYLVANIA	Bowl	Date	Opponent	Score
Bob Folwell	Rose	1-1-17	Oregon	0-14
All bowls 0-1-0; Big four 0-1-0				

RANDOLPH FIELD	Bowl	Date	Opponent	Score
Frank Tritico	Cotton	1-1-44	Texas	7-7
All bowls 0-0-1; Big four 0-0-1				

RICHMOND	Bowl	Date	Opponent	Score
Frank Jones	Tangerine	12-27-68	Ohio	49-42
Frank Jones	Tangerine	12-28-71	Toledo	3-28
All bowls 1-1-0; Big four 0-0-0				

SANTA CLARA	Bowl	Date	Bowl	Date
Lawrence "Buck" Shaw	Sugar	1-1-37	Louisiana St.	21-14
Lawrence "Buck" Shaw	Sugar	1-1-38	Louisiana St.	6-0
Len Casanova	Orange	1-2-50	Kentucky	21-13
All bowls 3-0-0; Big four 3-0-0				

SECOND AIR FORCE	Bowl	Date	Opponent	Score
Red Reese	Sun	1-1-43	Hardin-Simmons	13-7
All bowls 1-0-0; Big four 0-0-0				

Team-by-Team Bowl Results

SOUTHWESTERN (TEX.)	Bowl	Date	Opponent	Score
Randolph R. M. Medley	Sun	1-1-44	New Mexico	7-0
Randolph R. M. Medley	Sun	1-1-45	U. of Mexico	35-0
All bowls 2-0-0; Big four 0-0-0				

ST. MARY'S (CAL.)	Bowl	Date	Opponent	Score
Edward "Slip" Madigan	Cotton	1-2-39	Texas Tech	20-13
Jimmy Phelan	Sugar	1-1-46	Oklahoma St.	13-33
Jimmy Phelan	Oil	1-1-47	Georgia Tech	19-41
All bowls 1-2-0; Big four 1-1-0				

TAMPA	Bowl	Date	Opponent	Score
Earle Bruce	Tangerine	12-29-72	Kent	21-18
All bowls 1-0-0; Big four 0-0-0				

TENNESSEE TECH	Bowl	Date	Opponent	Score
Wilburn Tucker	Tangerine	12-30-60	Citadel	0-27
All bowls 0-1-0; Big four 0-0-0				

U. OF MEXICO	Bowl	Date	Opponent	Score
Bernard A. Hoban.................	Sun	1-1-45	Southwestern (Tex.)	0-35
All bowls 0-1-0; Big four 0-0-0				

VILLANOVA	Bowl	Date	Opponent	Score
Maurice "Clipper" Smith	Bacardi	1-1-37	Auburn	7-7
Jordan Olivar	Great Lakes	12-6-47	Kentucky	14-24
Jordan Olivar	Harbor	1-1-49	Nevada	27-7
Alex Bell	Sun	12-30-61	Wichita St.	17-9
Alex Bell	Liberty	12-15-62	Oregon St.	0-6
All bowls 2-2-1; Big four 0-0-0				

WASH. & JEFF.	Bowl	Date	Opponent	Score
Earle "Greasy" Neale.............	Rose	1-2-22	California	0-0
All bowls 0-0-1; Big four 0-0-1				

WASH. & LEE	Bowl	Date	Opponent	Score
George Barclay	Gator	1-1-51	Wyoming	7-20
All bowls 0-1-0; Big four 0-0-0				

WEST TEX. ST.	Bowl	Date	Opponent	Score
Frank Kimbrough	Sun	1-1-51	Cincinnati	14-13
Joe Kerbel	Sun	12-31-62	Ohio	15-14
Joe Kerbel	Pasadena	12-2-67	Cal St. Northridge	35-13
All bowls 3-0-0; Big four 0-0-0				

WEST VA. WESLEYAN	Bowl	Date	Opponent	Score
Bob Higgins	Dixie Classic	1-1-25	Southern Methodist	9-7
All bowls 1-0-0; Big four 0-0-0				

WICHITA ST.	Bowl	Date	Opponent	Score
Ralph Graham	Raisin	1-1-48	Pacific (Cal.)	14-26
Jim Trimble	Camellia	12-30-48	Hardin-Simmons	12-49
Hank Foldberg	Sun	12-30-61	Villanova	9-17
All bowls 0-3-0; Big four 0-0-0				

WILLIAM & MARY	Bowl	Date	Opponent	Score
Rube McCray	Dixie	1-1-48	Arkansas	19-21
Rube McCray	Delta	1-1-49	Oklahoma St.	20-0
Lou Holtz	Tangerine	12-28-70	Toledo	12-40
All bowls 1-2-0; Big four 0-0-0				

XAVIER (OHIO)	Bowl	Date	Opponent	Score
Ed Kluska	Salad	1-1-50	Arizona St.	33-21
All bowls 1-0-0; Big four 0-0-0				

POSTSEASON BOWL INVOLVING NON-I-A TEAMS

ALAMO HERITAGE BOWL

Site: Miami, Fla.
Stadium (Capacity): Joe Robbie (73,000)
Playing Surface: Grass

Date	Score
12-21-91	Alabama St. 36, North Caro. A&T 13

NCAA-CERTIFIED POSTSEASON ALL-STAR GAMES

EAST-WEST SHRINE CLASSIC

Present Site: Palo Alto, Cal.
Stadium (Capacity): Stanford (85,500)
Playing Surface: Grass
Playing Sites: Ewing Field, San Francisco (1925); Kezar Stadium, San Francisco (1927-41); Sugar Bowl, New Orleans (1942); Kezar Stadium, San Francisco (1943-66); Candlestick Park, San Francisco (1967-68); Stanford Stadium, Palo Alto (1969); Oakland Coliseum (1971); Candlestick Park, San Francisco (1971-73); Stanford Stadium, Palo Alto (since 1974)

Date	Score (Attendance)	Date	Score (Attendance)	Date	Score (Attendance)
12-26-25	West 6-0 (20,000)	12-30-50	West 16-7 (60,000)	1-3-76	West 21-14 (75,000)
1-1-27	West 7-3 (15,000)	12-29-51	East 15-14 (60,000)	1-2-77	West 30-14 (45,000)
12-26-27	West 16-6 (27,500)	12-27-52	East 21-20 (60,000)	12-31-77	West 23-3 (65,000)
12-29-28	East 20-0 (55,000)	1-2-54	West 31-7 (60,000)	1-6-79	East 56-17 (72,000)
1-1-30	East 19-7 (58,000)	1-1-55	East 13-12 (60,000)	1-5-80	West 20-10 (75,000)
12-27-30	West 3-0 (40,000)	12-31-55	East 29-6 (60,000)	1-10-81	East 21-3 (76,000)
1-1-32	East 6-0 (45,000)	12-29-56	West 7-6 (60,000)	1-9-82	West 20-13 (75,000)
1-2-33	West 21-13 (45,000)	12-28-57	West 27-13 (60,000)	1-15-83	East 26-25 (72,999)
1-1-34	West 12-0 (35,000)	12-27-58	East 26-14 (60,000)	1-7-84	East 27-19 (77,000)
1-1-35	West 19-13 (52,000)	1-2-60	West 21-14 (60,000)	1-5-85	West 21-10 (72,000)
1-1-36	East 19-3 (55,000)	12-31-60	East 7-0 (60,000)	1-11-86	East 18-7 (77,000)
1-1-37	East 3-0 (38,000)	12-30-61	West 21-8 (60,000)	1-10-87	West 24-21 (74,000)
1-1-38	Tie 0-0 (55,000)	12-29-62	East 25-19 (60,000)	1-16-88	West 16-13 (62,000)
1-2-39	West 14-0 (60,000)	12-28-63	Tie 6-6 (60,000)	1-16-89	East 24-6 (76,000)
1-1-40	West 28-11 (50,000)	1-2-65	West 11-7 (60,000)	1-21-90	West 22-21 (78,000)
1-1-41	West 20-14 (60,000)	12-31-65	West 22-7 (47,000)	1-24-91	West 24-21 (70,000)
1-3-42	Tie 6-6 (35,000)	12-31-66	East 45-22 (46,000)	1-19-92	West 14-6 (83,000)
1-1-43	East 13-12 (57,000)	12-30-67	East 16-14 (29,000)		
1-1-44	Tie 13-13 (55,000)	12-28-68	West 18-7 (29,000)		
1-1-45	West 13-7 (60,000)	12-27-69	West 15-0 (70,000)		
1-1-46	Tie 7-7 (60,000)	1-2-71	West 17-13 (50,000)		
1-1-47	West 13-9 (60,000)	12-31-71	West 17-13 (35,000)		
1-1-48	East 40-9 (60,000)	12-30-72	East 9-3 (37,000)		
1-1-49	East 14-12 (60,000)	12-29-73	East 35-7 (30,000)		
12-31-49	East 28-6 (60,000)	12-28-74	East 16-14 (35,000)		

Series record: West won 35, East 27, 5 ties.

BLUE-GRAY ALL-STAR CLASSIC

Present Site: Montgomery, Ala.
Stadium (Capacity): Cramton Bowl (24,600)
Playing Surface: Grass
Playing Sites: Cramton Bowl, Montgomery (since 1939)

Date	Score (Attendance)	Date	Score (Attendance)	Date	Score (Attendance)
1-2-39	Blue 7-0 (8,000)	12-27-58	Blue 16-0 (16,000)	12-29-78	Gray 28-24 (18,380)
12-30-39	Gray 33-20 (10,000)	12-26-59	Blue 20-8 (20,000)	12-25-79	Blue 22-13 (18,312)
12-28-40	Blue 14-12 (14,000)	12-31-60	Blue 35-7 (18,000)	12-25-80	Blue 24-23 (25,000)
12-27-41	Gray 16-0 (15,571)	12-30-61	Gray 9-7 (18,000)	12-25-81	Blue 21-9 (19,000)
12-26-42	Gray 24-0 (16,000)	12-29-62	Blue 10-6 (20,000)	12-25-82	Gray 20-10 (21,000)
1943	No Game	12-28-63	Gray 21-14 (20,000)	12-25-83	Gray 17-13 (2,000)
12-30-44	Gray 24-7 (16,000)	12-26-64	Blue 10-6 (16,000)	12-25-84	Gray 33-6 (24,080)
12-29-45	Blue 26-0 (20,000)	12-25-65	Gray 23-19 (18,000)	12-25-85	Blue 27-20 (18,500)
12-28-46	Gray 20-13 (22,500)	12-24-66	Blue 14-9 (18,000)	12-25-86	Blue 31-7 (18,500)
12-27-47	Gray 33-6 (22,500)	12-30-67	Blue 22-16 (23,350)	12-25-87	Gray 12-10 (20,300)
12-25-48	Blue 19-13 (15,000)	12-28-68	Gray 28-7 (18,000)	12-25-88	Blue 22-21 (20,000)
12-31-49	Gray 27-13 (21,500)	12-27-69	Tie 6-6 (21,500)	12-25-89	Gray 28-10 (16,000)
12-30-50	Gray 31-6 (21,000)	12-28-70	Gray 38-7 (23,000)	12-25-90	Blue 17-14 (17,500)
12-29-51	Gray 20-14 (22,000)	12-28-71	Gray 9-0 (24,000)	12-25-91	Gray 20-12 (21,000)
12-27-52	Gray 28-7 (22,000)	12-27-72	Gray 27-15 (20,000)		
12-26-53	Gray 40-20 (18,500)	12-18-73	Blue 20-14 (21,000)		
12-25-54	Blue 14-7 (18,000)	12-17-74	Blue 29-24 (12,000)		
12-31-55	Gray 20-19 (19,000)	12-19-75	Blue 14-13 (10,000)		
12-29-56	Blue 14-0 (21,000)	12-24-76	Gray 31-10 (16,000)		
12-28-57	Gray 21-20 (16,000)	12-30-77	Blue 20-16 (5,000)		

Series record: Gray won 28, Blue 24, 1 tie.

HULA BOWL

Present Site: Honolulu, Hawaii
Stadium (Capacity): Aloha (50,000)
Playing Surface: AstroTurf
Format: From 1947 through 1950, the College All-Stars played the Hawaii All-Stars. Beginning in 1951, the Hawaiian team was augmented by players from the National Football League. This format, however, was changed to an all-collegiate contest—first between the East and West, then between North and South (in 1963), and then back to East and West in 1974. The results reflect the all-collegiate format only.
Playing Sites: Honolulu Stadium (1960-74); Aloha Stadium (since 1975)

Date	Score (Attendance)	Date	Score (Attendance)	Date	Score (Attendance)
1-10-60	East 34-8 (23,000)	1-4-75	East 34-25 (22,000)	1-13-90	West 21-13 (28,742)
1-8-61	East 14-7 (17,017)	1-10-76	East 16-0 (45,458)	1-19-91	East 23-10 (21,926)
1-7-62	Tie 7-7 (20,598)	1-8-77	West 20-17 (45,579)	1-11-92	West 27-20 (23,112)
1-6-63	North 20-13 (20,000)	1-7-78	West 42-22 (48,197)		
1-4-64	North 20-13 (18,177)	1-6-79	East 29-24 (49,132)		
1-9-65	South 16-14 (22,100)	1-5-80	East 17-10 (47,096)		
1-8-66	North 27-26 (25,000)	1-10-81	West 24-17 (39,010)		
1-7-67	North 28-27 (23,500)	1-9-82	West 26-23 (43,002)		
1-6-68	North 50-6 (21,000)	1-15-83	East 30-14 (39,456)		
1-4-69	North 13-7 (23,000)	1-7-84	West 21-16 (34,216)		
1-10-70	South 35-13 (25,000)	1-5-85	East 34-14 (30,767)		
1-9-71	North 42-32 (23,500)	1-11-86	West 23-10 (29,564)		
1-8-72	North 24-7 (23,000)	1-10-87	West 16-14 (17,775)		
1-6-73	South 17-3 (23,000)	1-16-88	West 20-18 (26,737)		
1-5-74	East 24-14 (23,000)	1-7-89	East 21-10 (25,000)		

Series records: North-South (1963-73)—North won 8, South 3. East-West (1960-62 and 1974 to date)—East won 11, West 10, 1 tie.

JAPAN BOWL

Present Site: Yokohama, Japan
Stadium (Capacity): Yokohama (30,000)
Playing Surface: Grass
Playing Sites: Tokyo Stadium (1976-79); Yokohama Stadium (since 1980)

Date	Score (Attendance)	Date	Score (Attendance)	Date	Score (Attendance)
1-18-76	West 27-18 (68,000)	1-11-86	East 31-14 (30,000)	1-12-91	West 20-14 (30,000)
1-16-77	West 21-10 (58,000)	1-11-87	West 24-17 (30,000)	1-11-92	East 14-13 (50,000)
1-15-78	East 26-10 (32,500)	1-10-88	West 17-3 (30,000)		
1-14-79	East 33-14 (55,000)	1-15-89	East 30-7 (29,000)		
1-13-80	West 28-17 (27,000)	1-13-90	East 24-10 (27,000)		
1-17-81	West 25-13 (30,000)				
1-16-82	West 28-17 (28,000)				
1-23-83	West 30-21 (30,000)				
1-15-84	West 26-21 (26,000)				
1-13-85	West 28-14 (30,000)				

Series record: West won 11, East 6.

CHICAGO COLLEGE ALL-STAR FOOTBALL GAME
(Discontinued after 1976 game.)

An all-star team composed of the top senior collegiate players would meet the National Football League champions (1933-66) or the Super Bowl champions (1967-75) from the previous season, beginning in 1934. The only times the all-stars did not play the league champions were in 1935 and 1946. All games were played at Soldier Field, Chicago, Ill.

Date	Score (Attendance)
8-31-34	(Tie) Chicago Bears 0-0 (79,432)
8-29-35	Chicago Bears 5, All-Stars 0 (77,450)
9-3-36	(Tie) Detroit 7-7 (76,000)
9-1-37	All-Stars 6, Green Bay 0 (84,560)
8-31-38	All-Stars 28, Washington 16 (74,250)
8-30-39	New York Giants 9, All-Stars 0 (81,456)
8-29-40	Green Bay 45, All-Stars 28 (84,567)
8-28-41	Chicago Bears 37, All-Stars 13 (98,203)
8-28-42	Chicago Bears 21, All-Stars 0 (101,100)
8-25-43	All-Stars 27, Washington 7 (48,471)
8-30-44	Chicago Bears 24, All-Stars 21 (48,769)
8-30-45	Green Bay 19, All-Stars 7 (92,753)
8-23-46	All-Stars 16, Los Angeles 0 (97,380)

Date	Score (Attendance)
8-22-47	All-Stars 16, Chicago Bears 0 (105,840)
8-20-48	Chicago Cardinals 28, All-Stars 0 (101,220)
8-12-49	Philadelphia 38, All-Stars 0 (93,780)
8-11-50	All-Stars 17, Philadelphia 7 (88,885)
8-17-51	Cleveland 33, All-Stars 0 (92,180)
8-15-52	Los Angeles 10, All-Stars 7 (88,316)
8-14-53	Detroit 24, All-Stars 10 (93,818)
8-13-54	Detroit 31, All-Stars 6 (93,470)
8-12-55	All-Stars 30, Cleveland 27 (75,000)
8-10-56	Cleveland 26, All-Stars 0 (75,000)
8-9-57	New York Giants 22, All-Stars 12 (75,000)
8-15-58	All-Stars 35, Detroit 19 (70,000)
8-14-59	Baltimore 29, All-Stars 0 (70,000)
8-12-60	Baltimore 32, All-Stars 7 (70,000)
8-4-61	Philadelphia 28, All-Stars 14 (66,000)
8-3-62	Green Bay 42, All-Stars 20 (65,000)
8-2-63	All-Stars 20, Green Bay 17 (65,000)
8-7-64	Chicago Bears 28, All-Stars 17 (65,000)
8-6-65	Cleveland 24, All-Stars 16 (68,000)
8-5-66	Green Bay 38, All-Stars 0 (72,000)
8-4-67	Green Bay 27, All-Stars 0 (70,934)
8-2-68	Green Bay 34, All-Stars 17 (69,917)
8-1-69	New York Jets 26, All-Stars 24 (74,208)
7-31-70	Kansas City 24, All-Stars 3 (69,940)
7-30-71	Baltimore 24, All-Stars 17 (52,289)
7-28-72	Dallas 20, All-Stars 7 (54,162)
7-27-73	Miami 14, All-Stars 3 (54,103)
1974	No game played
8-1-75	Pittsburgh 21, All-Stars 14 (54,103)
7-23-76	*Pittsburgh 24, All-Stars 0 (52,895)

* *Game was not completed due to thunderstorms.*

SPECIAL REGULAR-SEASON GAMES
KICKOFF CLASSIC

Present Site: East Rutherford, N.J.
Stadium (Capacity): Giants (76,000)
Playing Surface: AstroTurf
Sponsor: National Association of Collegiate Directors of Athletics (NACDA). It is a permitted 12th regular-season game.
Playing Sites: Giants Stadium (since 1983)

Date	Teams, Score (Attendance)
8-29-83	Nebraska 44, Penn St. 6 (71,123)
8-27-84	Miami (Fla.) 20, Auburn 18 (51,131)
8-29-85	Brigham Young 28, Boston Collge 14 (51,227)
8-27-86	Alabama 16, Ohio St. 10 (68,296)
8-30-87	Tennessee 23, Iowa 22 (54,681)
8-27-88	Nebraska 23, Texas A&M 14 (58,172)
8-31-89	Notre Dame 36, Virginia 13 (77,323)
8-31-90	Southern Cal 34, Syracuse 16 (57,293)
8-28-91	Penn St. 34, Georgia Tech 22 (77,409)
8-29-92	Iowa vs. North Caro. St.

PIGSKIN CLASSIC

Present Site: Anaheim, Cal.
Stadium (Capacity): Anaheim (70,962)
Playing Surface: Grass
Sponsor: Disneyland. It is a permitted 12th regular-season game.
Playing Sites: Anaheim Stadium (since 1990)

Date	Teams, Score (Attendance)
8-26-90	Tennessee 31, Colorado 31 (33,458)
8-29-91	Florida St. 44, Brigham Young 28 (38,363)
8-26-92	Texas A&M vs. Stanford

REGULAR-SEASON GAMES PLAYED IN FOREIGN COUNTRIES

TOKYO, JAPAN

(Called Mirage Bowl 1976-85, Coca-Cola Classic from 1986. Played at Tokyo Olympic Memorial Stadium 1976-87, Tokyo Dome from 1988.)

Date	Teams, Score (Attendance)
9-4-76	Grambling 42, Morgan St. 16 (50,000)
12-11-77	Grambling 35, Temple 32 (50,000)
12-10-78	Temple 28, Boston College 24 (55,000)
11-24-79	Notre Dame 40, Miami (Fla.) 15 (62,574)
11-30-80	UCLA 34, Oregon St. 3 (86,000)
11-28-81	Air Force 21, San Diego St. 16 (80,000)
11-27-82	Clemson 21, Wake Forest 17 (64,700)
11-26-83	Southern Methodist 34, Houston 12 (70,000)
11-17-84	Army 45, Montana 31 (60,000)
11-30-85	Southern Cal 20, Oregon 6 (65,000)
11-30-86	Stanford 29, Arizona 24 (55,000)
11-28-87	California 17, Washington St. 17 (45,000)
12-3-88	Oklahoma St. 45, Texas Tech 42 (56,000)
12-4-89	Syracuse 24, Louisville 13 (50,000)
12-2-90	Houston 62, Arizona St. 45 (50,000)
11-30-91	Clemson 33, Duke 21 (50,000)
12-6-92	Nebraska vs. Kansas St.

MELBOURNE, AUSTRALIA

Date	Teams, Score (Attendance)
12-6-85*	Wyoming 24, UTEP 21 (22,000)
12-4-87†	Brigham Young 30, Colorado St. 26 (76,652)

* *Played at V.F.L. Park.*   † *Played at Princes Park.*

YOKOHAMA, JAPAN

Date	Teams, Score (Attendance)
12-2-78	Brigham Young 28, Nevada-Las Vegas 24 (27,500)

OSAKA, JAPAN

Date	Teams, Score (Attendance)
9-3-78	Utah St. 10, Idaho St. 0 (15,000)

DUBLIN, IRELAND

(Called Emerald Isle Classic. Played at Lansdowne Road Stadium.)

Date	Teams, Score (Attendance)
11-19-88	Boston College 38, Army 24 (45,525)
12-2-89	Pittsburgh 46, Rutgers 29 (19,800)

LONDON, ENGLAND

Date	Teams, Score (Attendance)
10-16-88	Richmond 20, Boston U. 17 (6,000)

MILAN, ITALY

(Played at The Arena.)

Date	Teams, Score (Attendance)
10-28-89	Villanova 28, Rhode Island 25 (5,000)

LIMERICK, IRELAND

(Wild Geese Classic. Played at Limerick Gaelic Grounds.)

Date	Teams, Score (Attendance)
11-16-91	Holy Cross 24, Fordham 19 (17,411)

FRANKFURT, GERMANY

(Played at Wald Stadium.)

Date	Teams
9-19-92	Otterbein vs. Heidelberg

COLLEGE FOOTBALL TROPHY GAMES

Following is a list of the current college football trophy games. The games are listed alphabetically by the trophy-object name. The date refers to the season the trophy was first exchanged and is not necessarily the start of competition between the participants. A game involving interdivision teams is listed in the higher-division classification.

DIVISION I-A

Trophy	Date	Colleges
Anniversary Award	1985	Bowling Green-Kent
Apple Cup	1962	Washington-Washington St.
Axe	1933	California-Stanford
Bayou Bucket	1974	Houston-Rice
Beehive Boot	1971	Brigham Young, Utah, Weber St.
Beer Barrel	1925	Kentucky-Tennessee
Bell	1927	Missouri-Nebraska
Bell Clapper	1931	Oklahoma-Oklahoma St.
Big Game	1953	Arizona-Arizona St.
Blue Key Victory Bell	1940	Ball St.-Indiana St.
Bourbon Barrel	1967	Indiana-Kentucky
Brass Spittoon	1950	Indiana-Michigan St.
Brass Spittoon	1981	New Mexico St.-UTEP
Bronze Boot	1968	Colorado St.-Wyoming
Cannon	1943	Illinois-Purdue
Commander In Chief's	1972	Air Force, Army, Navy
Cy-Hawk	1977	Iowa-Iowa St.
Floyd of Rosedale	1935	Iowa-Minnesota
Foy-O.D.K.	1948	Alabama-Auburn
Fremont Cannon	1970	Nevada—Nevada-Las Vegas
Golden Egg	1927	Mississippi-Mississippi St.
Golden Hat	1941	Oklahoma-Texas
Governor's	1969	Kansas-Kansas St.
Governor's Cup	1958	Florida-Florida St.
Governor's Cup	1983	Colorado-Colorado St.
Illibuck	1925	Illinois-Ohio St.
Indian War Drum	1935	Kansas-Missouri
Iron Bowl	1983	Alabama-Auburn
Keg of Nails	1950	Cincinnati-Louisville
Kit Carson Rifle	1938	Arizona-New Mexico
Little Brown Jug	1909	Michigan-Minnesota
Megaphone	1949	Michigan St.-Notre Dame
Old Oaken Bucket	1925	Indiana-Purdue
Old Wagon Wheel	1948	Brigham Young-Utah St.
Paniolo Trophy	1979	Hawaii-Wyoming
Paul Bunyan Axe	1948	Minnesota-Wisconsin
Paul Bunyan-Governor of Michigan	1953	Michigan-Michigan St.
Peace Pipe	1929	Missouri-Oklahoma
Peace Pipe	1955	Miami (Ohio)-Western Mich.
Peace Pipe	1980	Bowling Green-Toledo
Ram-Falcon	1980	Air Force-Colorado St.
Sabine Shoe	1937	Lamar-Southwestern La.
Shillelagh	1952	Notre Dame-Southern Cal
Shillelagh	1958	Notre Dame-Purdue
Silver Spade	1955	New Mexico St.-UTEP
Steel Tire	1976	Akron-Youngstown St.
Telephone	1960	Iowa St.-Missouri
Textile Bowl	1981	Clemson-North Caro. St.
Tomahawk	1945	Illinois-Northwestern
Victory Bell	1942	Southern Cal-UCLA
Victory Bell	1948	Cincinnati-Miami (Ohio)
Victory Bell	1948	Duke-North Caro.
Victory Bell	1972	Cal St. Fullerton-Long Beach St.
Wagon Wheel	1946	Akron-Kent

DIVISION I-AA

Trophy	Date	Colleges
Bill Knight	1986	Massachusetts-New Hampshire
Brice-Colwell Musket	1946	Maine-New Hampshire
Chief Caddo	1962	Northwestern (La.)-Stephen F. Austin
Gem State	1978	Boise St., Idaho, Idaho St.
Governor's Cup	1972	Brown-Rhode Island
Governor's Cup	1975	Dartmouth-Princeton
Governor's Cup	1984	Eastern Wash.-Idaho
Harvey—Shin-A-Ninny Totem Pole	1961	Middle Tenn. St.-Tennessee Tech

Trophy	Date	Colleges
Little Brown Stein	1938	Idaho-Montana
Mare's	1987	Murray St.—Tenn.-Martin
Mayor's Cup	1981	Bethune-Cookman—Central Fla.
Ol' Mountain Jug	1937	Appalachian St.-Western Caro.
Painting Grizzly-Bobcat	1984	Montana-Montana St.
Red Belt	1978	Murray St.-Western Ky.
Ron Rogerson Memorial	1988	Maine-Rhode Island
Silver Shako	1976	Citadel-Va. Military
Team of Game's MVP	1960	Lafayette-Lehigh

DIVISION II

Trophy	Date	Colleges
Axe	1946	Cal St. Chico-Humboldt St.
Axe Bowl	1975	Northwood-Saginaw Valley
Backyard Bowl	1987	Cheyney-West Chester
Battle Axe	1948	Bemidji St.-Moorhead St.
Bell (Little Big Game)	1947	Santa Clara-St. Mary's (Cal.)
Bishop's	1970	Lenoir-Rhyne—Newberry
Board of Trustees	1987	Central Conn. St.-Western Conn. St.
Bronze Derby	1946	Newberry-Presbyterian
East Meets West	1987	Chadron St.-Peru St.
Elm City	1983	New Haven-Southern Conn. St.
Governor's	1979	Central Conn. St.-Southern Conn. St.
Heritage Bell	1979	Delta St.-Mississippi Col.
Miner's Bowl	1986	Mo. Southern St.-Pittsburg St.
Nickel	1938	North Dak.-North Dak.
Ol' School Bell	1988	Jacksonville St.-Troy St.
Old Hickory Stick	1931	Northeast Mo. St.-Northwest Mo. St.
Old Settler's Musket	1975	Adams St.-Fort Lewis St.
Sitting Bull	1953	North Dak.-South Dak.
Springfield Mayor's	1941	American Int'l-Springfield
Textile	1960	Clark Atlanta-Fort Valley St.
Top Dog	1971	Butler-Indianapolis
Traveling	1976	Ashland-Hillsdale
Victory Carriage	1960	Cal St. Sacramento-UC Davis
Wagon Wheel	1986	Eastern N. Mex.-West Tex. St.
Wooden Shoes	1977	Grand Valley St.-Wayne St. (Mich.)

DIVISION III

Trophy	Date	Colleges
Academic Bowl	1986	Carnegie Mellon-Case Reserve
Admiral's Cup	1980	Maine Maritime-Mass. Maritime
Baird Bros. Golden Stringer	1984	Case Reserve-Wooster
Bronze Turkey	1929	Knox-Monmouth (Ill.)
CBB	1966	Bates, Bowdoin, Colby
Conestoga Wagon	1963	Dickinson-Frank. & Marsh.
Cortaca Jug	1959	Cortland St.-Ithaca
Cranberry Bowl	1979	Bri'water (Mass.)-Mass. Maritime
Doehling-Heselton Helmet	1988	Lawrence-Ripon
Drum	1940	Occidental—Pomona-Pitzer
Dutchman's Shoes	1950	Rensselaer-Union (N.Y.)
Edmund Orgill	1954	Rhodes-Sewanee
Field Cup	1983	Evansville-Ky. Wesleyan
Founder's	1987	Chicago-Washington (Mo.)
Goal Post	1953	Juniata-Susquehanna
Goat	1931	Carleton-St. Olaf
Golden Circle	1988	Drake-Simpson
John Wesley	1984	Ky. Wesleyan-Union (Ky.)
Keystone Cup	1981	Delaware Valley-Widener
Little Brass Bell	1947	North Central-Wheaton (Ill.)
Little Brown Bucket	1938	Dickinson-Gettysburg
Little Three	1971	Amherst, Wesleyan, Williams
Mercer County Cup	1984	Grove City-Thiel
Monon Bell	1932	DePauw-Wabash
Mug	1931	Coast Guard-Norwich
Old Goal Post	1953	Juniata-Susquehanna
Old Musket	1964	Carroll (Wis.)-Carthage
Old Rocking Chair	1980	Hamilton-Middlebury
Old Tin Cup	1954	Gettysburg-Muhlenberg
Old Water Bucket	1989	Maranatha-N'western Col. (Wis.)
Paint Bucket	1965	Hamline-Macalester
President's Cup	1971	Case Reserve-John Carroll
Secretary's Cup	1981	Coast Guard-Merchant Marine

Trophy	Date	Colleges
Shoes	1946	Occidental-Whittier
Shot Glass	1938	Coast Guard-Rensselaer
Skull	1929	Ohio Wesleyan-Wittenberg
Steve Dean Memorial	1976	Catholic-Georgetown
Transit	1980	Rensselaer-Worcester Tech
Victory Bell	1946	Loras-St. Thomas (Minn.)
Victory Bell	1949	Upper Iowa-Wartburg
Wadsworth	1977	Middlebury-Norwich
Wagon Wheel	1957	Lewis & Clark-Willamette
Wilson Brothers Cup	1986	Hamline-St. Thomas (Minn.)
Wooden Shoes	1946	Hope-Kalamazoo

NON-NCAA MEMBERS

Trophy	Date	Colleges
Baptist Bible Bowl	1982	Maranatha-Pillsbury
Battle of the Ravine	1976	Henderson St.-Ouachita Baptist
Bell	*1931	Franklin-Hanover
Eagle-Rock	1980	Black Hills St.-Chadron St.
Home Stake-Gold Mine	1950	Black Hills St.-South Dak. Tech
KTEN Savage-Tiger	1979	East Central Okla.-Southeastern Okla.
Paint Bucket	1961	Jamestown-Valley City St.

* *Was reinstated in 1988 after a 17-year lapse.*

BLACK COLLEGE NATIONAL CHAMPIONS

Selected by the Pittsburgh Courier, 1920-1980, and compiled by Collie Nicholson, former Grambling sports information director; William Nunn Jr., Pittsburgh Courier sports editor, and Eric "Ric" Roberts, Pittsburgh Courier sports writer and noted black college sports historian. Selected from 1981 by the Sheridan Broadcasting Network, 411 Seventh Ave., Suite 1500, Pittsburgh, Pa. 15219-1905. Records include postseason games.

Year	Team	Won	Lost	Tied	Coach
1920	Howard	7	0	0	Edward Morrison
	Talladega	5	0	1	Jubie Bragg
1921	Talladega	6	0	1	Jubie Bragg
	Wiley	7	0	1	Jason Grant
1922	Hampton	6	1	0	Gideon Smith
1923	Virginia Union	6	0	1	Harold Martin
1924	Tuskegee	9	0	1	Cleve Abbott
	Wiley	8	0	1	Fred Long
1925	Tuskegee	8	0	1	Cleve Abbott
	Howard	6	0	2	Louis Watson
1926	Tuskegee	10	0	0	Cleve Abbott
	Howard	7	0	0	Louis Watson
1927	Tuskegee	9	0	1	Cleve Abbott
	Bluefield St. (Va.)	8	0	1	Harry Jefferson
1928	Bluefield St. (Va.)	8	0	1	Harry Jefferson
	Wiley	8	0	1	Fred Long
1929	Tuskegee	10	0	0	Cleve Abbott
1930	Tuskegee	11	0	1	Cleve Abbott
1931	Wilberforce	9	0	0	Harry Graves
1932	Wiley	9	0	0	Fred Long
1933	Morgan St.	9	0	0	Edward Hurt
1934	Kentucky St.	9	0	0	Henry Kean
1935	Texas College	9	0	0	Arnett Mumford
1936	West Va. St.	8	0	0	Adolph Hamblin
	Virginia St.	7	0	2	Harry Jefferson
1937	Morgan St.	7	0	0	Edward Hurt
1938	Florida A&M	8	0	0	Bill Bell
1939	Langston	9	0	0	Felton "Zip" Gayles
1940	Morris Brown	9	1	0	Artis Graves
1941	Morris Brown	8	1	0	William Nicks
1942	Florida A&M	9	0	0	Bill Bell
1943	Morgan St.	5	0	0	Edward Hurt
1944	Morgan St.	6	1	0	Edward Hurt
1945	Wiley	10	0	0	Fred Long
1946	Tennessee St.	10	1	0	Henry Kean
	Morgan St.	8	0	0	Edward Hurt
1947	Tennessee St.	10	0	0	Henry Kean
	Shaw	10	0	0	Brutus Wilson
1948	Southern-B.R.	12	0	0	Arnett Mumford
1949	Southern-B.R.	10	0	1	Arnett Mumford
	Morgan St.	8	0	0	Edward Hurt

Year	Team	Won	Lost	Tied	Coach
1950	Southern-B.R.	10	0	1	Arnett Mumford
	Florida A&M	8	1	1	Alonzo "Jake" Gaither
1951	Morris Brown	10	1	0	Edward "Ox" Clemons
1952	Florida A&M	8	2	0	Alonzo "Jake" Gaither
	Texas Southern	10	0	1	Alexander Durley
	Lincoln (Mo.)	8	0	1	Dwight Reed
	Virginia St.	8	1	0	Sylvester "Sal" Hall
1953	Prairie View	12	0	0	William Nicks
1954	Tennessee St.	10	1	0	Henry Kean
	Southern-B.R.	10	1	0	Arnett Mumford
	Florida A&M	8	1	0	Alonzo "Jake" Gaither
	Prairie View	10	1	0	William Nicks
1955	Grambling	10	0	0	Eddie Robinson
1956	Tennessee St.	10	0	0	Howard Gentry
1957	Florida A&M	9	0	0	Alonzo "Jake" Gaither
1958	Prairie View	10	0	1	William Nicks
1959	Florida A&M	10	0	0	Alonzo "Jake" Gaither
1960	Southern-B.R.	9	1	0	Arnett Mumford
1961	Florida A&M	10	0	0	Alonzo "Jake" Gaither
1962	Jackson St.	10	1	0	John Merritt
1963	Prairie View	10	1	0	William Nicks
1964	Prairie View	9	0	0	William Nicks
1965	Tennessee St.	9	0	1	John Merritt
1966	Tennessee St.	10	0	0	John Merritt
1967	Morgan St.	8	0	0	Earl Banks
	Grambling	9	1	0	Eddie Robinson
1968	Alcorn St.	9	1	0	Marino Casem
	North Caro. A&T	8	1	0	Hornsby Howell
1969	Alcorn St.	8	0	1	Marino Casem
1970	Tennessee St.	11	0	0	John Merritt
1971	Tennessee St.	9	1	0	John Merritt
1972	Grambling	11	2	0	Eddie Robinson
1973	Tennessee St.	10	0	0	John Merritt
1974	Grambling	11	1	0	Eddie Robinson
	Alcorn St.	9	2	0	Marino Casem
1975	Grambling	10	2	0	Eddie Robinson
1976	South Caro. St.	10	1	0	Willie Jeffries
1977	South Caro. St.	9	1	1	Willie Jeffries
	Grambling	10	1	0	Eddie Robinson
	Florida A&M	11	0	0	Rudy Hubbard
1978	Florida A&M	12	1	0	Rudy Hubbard
1979	Tennessee St.	8	3	0	John Merritt
1980	Grambling	10	2	0	Eddie Robinson
1981	South Caro. St.	10	3	0	Bill Davis
1982	Tennessee St.	*9	0	1	John Merritt
1983	Grambling	8	1	2	Eddie Robinson
1984	Alcorn St.	9	1	0	Marino Casem
1985	Jackson St.	8	3	0	W. C. Gorden
1986	Central St. (Ohio)	10	1	1	Billy Joe
1987	Central St. (Ohio)	10	1	1	Billy Joe
1988	Central St. (Ohio)	11	2	0	Billy Joe
1989	Central St. (Ohio)	10	2	0	Billy Joe
1990	#Central St. (Ohio)	11	1	0	Billy Joe
1991	¢Alabama St.	11	0	1	Houston Markham

* *Tennessee State's participation in the 1982 Division I-AA championship (1-1 record) voided. # NAIA Division I national champion. ¢ Alabama St. defeated North Caro. A&T, 36-13, in the inaugural Alamo Heritage Bowl, the first bowl game for the historically black schools.*

COACHES' RECORDS

Why is this man smiling? Perhaps because he has the highest winning percentage of any coach in history with at least 10 seasons of college coaching experience. Bob Reade's career mark of 125-16-1 (.884) in 13 seasons at Augustana (Illinois) places him ahead of legends Knute Rockne and Frank Leahy, both of whom also coached for 13 years.

WINNINGEST ALL-TIME DIVISION I-A COACHES
(By Percentage)

Minimum 10 years as head coach at Division I institutions; record at four-year colleges only; bowl games included; ties computed as half won, half lost. Active coaches indicated by (*). Hall of Fame members indicated by (†).

Coach (Alma Mater, Colleges Coached, Tenure)	Years	Won	Lost	Tied	Pct.
Knute K. Rockne (Notre Dame '14)†	13	105	12	5	.881
(Notre Dame 1918-30)					
Frank W. Leahy (Notre Dame '31)†	13	107	13	9	.864
(Boston College 1939-40; Notre Dame 1941-43, 1946-53)					
George W. Woodruff (Yale '89)†	12	142	25	2	.846
(Pennsylvania 1892-01; Illinois 1903; Carlisle 1905)					
Barry Switzer (Arkansas '60)	16	157	29	4	.837
(Oklahoma 1973-88)					
Percy D. Haughton (Harvard '99)†	13	96	17	6	.832
(Cornell 1899-00; Harvard 1908-16; Columbia 1923-24)					
Robert R. "Bob" Neyland (Army '16)†	21	173	31	12	.829
(Tennessee 1926-34, 1936-40, 1946-52)					
Fielding H. "Hurry Up" Yost (Lafayette '97)†	29	196	36	12	.828
(Ohio Wesleyan 1897; Nebraska 1898; Kansas 1899; Stanford 1900; Michigan 1901-23, 1925-26)					
Charles "Bud" Wilkinson (Minnesota '37)†	17	145	29	4	.826
(Oklahoma 1947-63)					
John B. "Jock" Sutherland (Pittsburgh '18)†	20	144	28	14	.812
(Lafayette 1919-23; Pittsburgh 1924-38)					
*Thomas W. "Tom" Osborne (Hastings '59)	19	186	43	3	.808
(Nebraska 1973—)					
Robert S. "Bob" Devaney (Alma '39)†	16	136	30	7	.806
(Wyoming 1957-61; Nebraska 1962-72)					
Frank W. Thomas (Notre Dame '23)†	19	141	33	9	.795
(Chattanooga 1925-28; Alabama 1931-42, 1944-46)					
*Joseph V. "Joe" Paterno (Brown '50)	26	240	62	3	.792
(Penn St. 1966—)					
Henry L. Williams (Yale '91)†	23	141	34	12	.786
(Army 1891; Minnesota 1900-21)					
Gilmour "Gloomy Gil" Dobie (Minnesota '02)†	33	180	45	15	.781
(North Dak. St. 1906-07; Washington 1908-16; Navy 1917-19; Cornell 1920-35; Boston College 1936-38)					
Paul W. "Bear" Bryant (Alabama '36)†	38	323	85	17	.780
(Maryland 1945; Kentucky 1946-53; Texas A&M 1954-57; Alabama 1958-82)					
Fred Folsom (Dartmouth '95)	19	106	28	6	.779
(Colorado 1895-99, 1901-02; Dartmouth 1903-06; Colorado 1908-15)					
Glenn "Bo" Schembechler (Miami, Ohio, '51)	27	234	65	8	.775
(Miami, Ohio 1963-68; Michigan 1969-89)					
Herbert O. "Fritz" Crisler (Chicago '22)†	18	116	32	9	.768
(Minnesota 1930-31; Princeton 1932-37; Michigan 1938-47)					
Charles B. "Charley" Moran (Tennessee '98)	18	122	33	12	.766
(Texas A&M 1909-14; Centre 1919-23; Bucknell 1924-26; Catawba 1930-33)					
William Wallace Wade (Brown '17)†	24	171	49	10	.765
(Alabama 1923-30; Duke 1931-41, 1946-50)					
Frank Kush (Michigan St. '53)	22	176	54	1	.764
(Arizona St. 1958-1979)					
Daniel E. "Dan" McGugin (Michigan '04)†	30	197	55	19	.762
(Vanderbilt 1904-17, 1919-34)					
James "Jimmy" Crowley (Notre Dame '25)	13	78	21	10	.761
(Michigan St. 1929-32; Fordham 1933-41)					
Andrew L. "Andy" Smith (Penn St., Pennsylvania '05)†	17	116	32	13	.761
(Pennsylvania 1909-12; Purdue 1913-15; California 1916-25)					
Danny L. Ford (Alabama '70)	‡12	96	29	4	.760
(Clemson 1978-89)					
Wayne Woodrow "Woody" Hayes (Denison '35)†	33	238	72	10	.759
(Denison 1946-48; Miami, Ohio, 1949-50; Ohio St. 1951-78)					
Earl H. "Red" Blaik (Miami, Ohio, '18; Army '20)†	25	166	48	14	.759
(Dartmouth 1934-40; Army 1941-58)					
Darrell Royal (Oklahoma '50)†	23	184	60	5	.749
(Mississippi St. 1954-55; Washington 1956; Texas 1957-76)					
John McKay (Oregon '50)†	16	127	40	8	.749
(Southern Cal 1960-75)					

Coach (Alma Mater, Colleges Coached, Tenure)	Years	Won	Lost	Tied	Pct.
John H. Vaught (Texas Christian '33)† .... (Mississippi 1947-70, 1973)	25	190	61	12	.745
*LaVell Edwards (Utah St. '52) .... (Brigham Young 1972—)	20	183	62	3	.744
Daniel J. "Dan" Devine (Minn.-Duluth '48)† .... (Arizona St. 1955-57; Missouri 1958-70; Notre Dame 1975-80)	22	172	57	9	.742
Elmer C. "Gus" Henderson (Oberlin '12) .... (Southern Cal 1919-24; Tulsa 1925-35; Occidental 1940-42)	20	126	42	7	.740
Ara Parseghian (Miami, Ohio, '49)† .... (Miami, Ohio, 1951-55; Northwestern 1956-63; Notre Dame 1964-74)	24	170	58	6	.739
*Robert "Bobby" Bowden (Samford '53)✓ .... (Samford 1959-62; West Va. 1970-75; Florida St. 1976—)	26	216	76	3	.737
Elmer F. Layden (Notre Dame '25) .... (Loras 1925-26; Duquesne 1927-33; Notre Dame 1934-40)	16	103	34	11	.733
Howard H. Jones (Yale '08)† .... (Syracuse 1908; Yale 1909; Ohio St. 1910; Yale 1913; Iowa 1916-23; Duke 1924; Southern Cal 1925-40)	29	194	64	21	.733
Frank W. Cavanaugh (Dartmouth '97)†.......................... (Cincinnati 1898; Holy Cross 1903-05; Dartmouth 1911-16; Boston College 1919-26; Fordham 1927-32)	24	145	48	17	.731
Glenn S. "Pop" Warner (Cornell '95)† .... (Georgia 1895-96; Cornell 1897-98; Carlisle 1899-1903; Cornell 1904-06; Carlisle 1907-14; Pittsburgh 1915-23; Stanford 1924-32; Temple 1933-38)	44	313	106	32	.729
James M. "Jim" Tatum (North Caro. '35)† .... (North Caro. 1942; Oklahoma 1946; Maryland 1947-55; North Caro. 1956-58)	14	100	35	7	.729
William W. "Bill" Roper (Princeton '03)† .... (Va. Military 1903-04; Princeton 1906-08; Missouri 1909; Princeton 1910-11; Swarthmore 1919; Princeton 1919-30)	22	112	37	19	.723
Francis A. Schmidt (Nebraska '14)†........................... (Tulsa 1919-21; Arkansas 1922-28; Texas Christian 1929-33; Ohio St. 1934-40; Idaho 1941-42)	24	158	57	11	.723
Albert R. "Doc" Kennedy (Kansas & Pennsylvania '03) .... (Kansas 1904-10; Haskell 1911-16)	13	85	31	7	.720
T. A. Dwight "Tad" Jones (Yale '08)† .... (Syracuse 1909-10; Yale 1916, 1920-27)	11	66	24	6	.719
*Patrick F. "Pat" Dye (Georgia '62) .... (East Caro. 1974-79; Wyoming 1980; Auburn 1981—)	18	148	57	4	.718
Vincent J. "Vince" Dooley (Auburn '54) .... (Georgia 1964-88)	25	201	77	10	.715
Dana X. Bible (Carson-Newman '12)† .... (Mississippi Col. 1913-15; Louisiana St. 1916; Texas A&M 1917, 1919-28; Nebraska 1929-36; Texas 1937-46)	33	198	72	23	.715
Robert L. "Bobby" Dodd (Tennessee '31) .... (Georgia Tech 1945-66)	22	165	64	8	.713
John W. Heisman (Brown '90, Pennsylvania '92)† .... (Oberlin 1892; Akron 1893; Oberlin 1894; Auburn 1895-99; Clemson 1900-03; Georgia Tech 1904-19; Pennsylvania 1920-22; Wash. & Jeff. 1923; Rice 1924-27)	36	185	70	17	.711
Ewald O. "Jumbo" Stiehm (Wisconsin '09) .... (Ripon 1910; Nebraska 1911-15; Indiana 1916-21)	12	59	23	4	.709
Henry R. "Red" Sanders (Vanderbilt '27) .... (Vanderbilt 1940-42, 1946-48; UCLA 1949-57)	15	102	41	3	.709
John F. "Chick" Meehan (Syracuse '18) .... (Syracuse 1920-24; New York U. 1925-31; Manhattan 1932-37)	18	115	44	14	.705
John J. McEwan (Army '17)..................................... (Army 1923-25; Oregon 1926-29; Holy Cross 1930-32)	10	59	23	6	.705
Benjamin G. "Bennie" Owen (Kansas '00)† .... (Washburn 1900; Bethany, Kan., 1901-04; Oklahoma 1905-26)	27	155	60	19	.703
Ike J. Armstrong (Drake '23)† .... (Utah 1925-49)	25	140	55	15	.702
Frank Broyles (Georgia Tech '47)† .... (Missouri 1957; Arkansas 1958-76)	20	149	62	6	.700
Lawrence McC. "Biff" Jones (Army '17)†........................ (Army 1926-29; Louisiana St. 1932-34; Oklahoma 1935-36; Nebraska 1937-41)	14	87	33	15	.700

‡ Last game of 1978 season counted as full season.   ✓ Includes games forfeited, team and/or individual statistics abrogated, and coaching records changed by action of the NCAA Council under the restitution provisions of Bylaw 19.6 of the Official Procedure Governing the NCAA Enforcement Program (adopted

ALL-TIME DIVISION I-A COACHING VICTORIES

Minimum 10 years as head coach at Division I institutions; record at four-year colleges only; bowl games included. After each coach's name is his alma mater, year graduated, total years coached, won-lost record and percentage, tenure at each college coached, and won-lost record there. Active coaches are denoted by an asterisk (*).

(Minimum 150 Victories)

323   Paul "Bear" Bryant (Born 9-11-13 Moro Bottoms, Ark.; Died 1-26-83)
     Alabama 1936 (38: 323-85-17 .780)
     Maryland 1945 (6-2-1); Kentucky 1946-53 (60-23-5); Texas A&M 1954-57 (25-14-2); Alabama 1958-82 (232-46-9)

314   Amos Alonzo Stagg (Born 8-16-1862 West Orange, N.J.; Died 3-17-65)
     Yale 1888 (57: 314-199-35 .605)
     Springfield 1890-91 (10-11-1); Chicago 1892-1932 (244-111-27); Pacific (Cal.) 1933-46 (60-77-7)

313   Glenn "Pop" Warner (Born 4-5-1871 Springville, N.Y.; Died 9-7-54)
     Cornell 1895 (44: 313-106-32 .729)
     Georgia 1895-96 (7-4-0); Cornell 1897-98, 1904-06 (36-13-3); Carlisle 1899-1903, 1907-13 (109-42-8); Pittsburgh 1915-23 (59-12-4); Stanford 1924-32 (71-17-8); Temple 1933-38 (31-18-9)

240   *Joe Paterno (Born 12-21-26 Brooklyn, N.Y.)
     Brown 1951 (26: 240-62-3 .792)
     Penn St. 1966-91 (240-62-3)

238   Wayne Woodrow "Woody" Hayes (Born 2-13-14 Clifton, Ohio; Died 3-12-87)
     Denison 1935 (33: 238-72-10 .759)
     Denison 1946-48 (19-6-0); Miami (Ohio) 1949-50 (14-5-0); Ohio St. 1951-78 (205-61-10)

234   Glenn "Bo" Schembechler (Born 9-1-29 Barberton, Ohio)
     Miami (Ohio) 1951 (27: 234-65-8 .775)
     Miami (Ohio) 1963-68 (40-17-3); Michigan 1969-89 (194-48-5)

216   *Bobby Bowden (Born 11-8-29 Birmingham, Ala.)
     Samford 1953 (✓26: 216-76-3 .737)
     Samford 1959-62 (31-6-0); West Va. 1970-75 (✓42-26-0); Florida St. 1976-91 (143-44-3)

207   Jess Neely (Born 1-4-1898 Smyrna, Tenn.; Died 4-9-83)
     Vanderbilt 1924 (40: 207-176-19 .539)
     Rhodes 1924-27 (20-17-2); Clemson 1931-39 (43-35-7); Rice 1940-66 (144-124-10)

203   Warren Woodson (Born 2-24-03 Fort Worth, Tex.)
     Baylor 1924 (31: 203-95-14 .673)
     Central Ark. 1935-39 (40-8-3); Hardin-Simmons 1941-42, 1946-51 (58-24-6); Arizona 1952-56 (26-22-2); New Mexico St. 1958-67 (63-36-3); Trinity (Tex.) 1972-73 (16-5-0)

201   Vince Dooley (Born 9-4-32 Mobile, Ala.)
     Auburn 1954 (25: 201-77-10 .715)
     Georgia 1964-88 (201-77-10)

201   Eddie Anderson (Born 11-13-1900 Mason City, Iowa; Died 4-26-74)
     Notre Dame 1922 (39: 201-128-15 .606)
     Loras 1922-24 (16-6-2); DePaul 1925-31 (21-22-3); Holy Cross 1933-38, 1950-64 (129-67-8); Iowa 1939-42, 1946-49 (35-33-2)

198   Dana Bible (Born 10-8-1891 Jefferson City, Tenn.; Died 1-19-80)
     Carson-Newman 1912 (33: 198-72-23 .715)
     Mississippi Col. 1913-15 (12-7-2); Louisiana St. 1916 (1-0-2); Texas A&M 1917, 1919-28 (72-19-9); Nebraska 1929-36 (50-15-7); Texas 1937-46 (63-31-3)

197   Dan McGugin (Born 7-29-1879 Tingley, Iowa; Died 1-19-36)
     Michigan 1904 (30: 197-55-19 .762)
     Vanderbilt 1904-17, 1919-34 (197-55-19)

196   Fielding "Hurry Up" Yost (Born 4-30-1871 Fairview, W. Va.; Died 8-20-46)
     Lafayette 1897 (29: 196-36-12 .828)
     Ohio Wesleyan 1897 (7-1-1); Nebraska 1898 (7-4-0); Kansas 1899 (10-0-0); Stanford 1900 (7-2-1); Michigan 1901-23, 1925-26 (165-29-10)

194   Howard Jones (Born 8-23-1885 Excello, Ohio; Died 7-27-41)
     Yale 1908 (29: 194-64-21 .733)
     Syracuse 1908 (6-3-1); Yale 1909, 1913 (15-2-3); Ohio St. 1910 (6-1-3); Iowa 1916-23 (42-17-1); Duke 1924 (4-5-0); Southern Cal 1925-40 (121-36-13)

190   John Vaught (Born 5-6-08 Olney, Tex.)
     Texas Christian 1933 (25: 190-61-12 .745)
     Mississippi 1947-70, 1973 (190-61-12)

189   *Hayden Fry (Born 2-28-29 Odessa, Tex.)
     Baylor 1951 (✓30: 189-140-9 .572)
     Southern Methodist 1962-72 (49-66-1); North Texas 1973-78 (✓40-23-3); Iowa 1979-90 (100-51-5)

186   *Tom Osborne (Born 2-23-37 Hastings, Neb.)
        Hastings 1959 (19: 186-43-3 .808)
        Nebraska 1973-91 (186-43-3)
185   John Heisman (Born 10-23-1869 Cleveland, Ohio; Died 10-3-36)
        Brown 1890 (36: 185-70-17 .711)
        Oberlin 1892, 1894 (11-3-1); Akron 1893 (5-2-0); Auburn 1895-99 (12-4-2); Clemson 1900-03
        (19-3-2); Georgia Tech 1904-19 (102-29-6); Pennsylvania 1920-22 (16-10-2); Wash. & Jeff.
        1923 (6-1-1); Rice 1924-27 (14-18-3)
184   Darrell Royal (Born 7-6-24 Hollis, Okla.)
        Oklahoma 1950 (23: 184-60-5 .749)
        Mississippi St. 1954-55 (12-8-0); Washington 1956 (5-5-0); Texas 1957-76 (167-47-5)
183   *LaVell Edwards (Born 10-11-30 Provo, Utah)
        Utah St. 1952 (20: 183-62-3 .744)
        Brigham Young 1972-91 (183-62-3)
180   Gil Dobie (Born 1-31-1879 Hastings, Minn.; Died 12-24-48)
        Minnesota 1902 (33: 180-45-15 .781)
        North Dak. St. 1906-07 (7-0-0); Washington 1908-16 (58-0-3); Navy 1917-19 (17-3-0); Cornell
        1920-35 (82-36-7); Boston College 1936-38 (16-6-5)
180   Carl Snavely (Born 7-30-1894 Omaha, Neb.; Died 7-12-75)
        Lebanon Valley 1915 (32: 180-96-16 .644)
        Bucknell 1927-33 (42-16-8); North Caro. 1934-35 (15-2-1); Cornell 1936-44 (46-26-3); North
        Caro. 1945-52 (44-33-4); Washington (Mo.) 1953-58 (33-19-0)
179   Jerry Claiborne (Born 8-26-28 Hopkinsville, Ky.)
        Kentucky 1950 (28: 179-122-8 .592)
        Virginia Tech 1961-70 (61-39-2); Maryland 1972-81 (77-37-3); Kentucky 1982-89 (36-40-3)
178   Ben Schwartzwalder (Born 6-2-09 Point Pleasant, W. Va.)
        West Va. 1933 (28: 178-96-3 .648)
        Muhlenberg 1946-48 (25-5-0); Syracuse 1949-73 (153-91-3)

176   Frank Kush (Born 1-20-29 Windber, Pa.)
        Michigan St. 1953 (22: 176-54-1 .764)
        Arizona St. 1958-79 (176-54-1)
176   Ralph Jordan (Born 9-25-10 Selma, Ala.; Died 7-17-80)
        Auburn 1932 (✓25: 176-83-6 .675)
        Auburn 1951-75 (✓176-83-6)
174   Lynn "Pappy" Waldorf (Born 10-3-02 Clifton Springs, N.Y.; Died 8-15-81)
        Syracuse 1925 (31: 174-100-22 .625)
        Oklahoma City 1925-27 (17-11-3); Oklahoma St. 1929-33 (34-10-7); Kansas St. 1934 (7-2-1);
        Northwestern 1935-46 (49-45-7); California 1947-56 (67-32-4)
173   Bob Neyland (Born 2-17-92 Greenville, Tex.; Died 3-28-62)
        Army 1916 (21: 173-31-12 .829)
        Tennessee 1926-34, 1936-40, 1946-52 (173-31-12)
172   Dan Devine (Born 12-23-24 Augusta, Wis.)
        Minn.-Duluth 1948 (22: 172-57-9 .742)
        Arizona St. 1955-57 (27-3-1); Missouri 1958-70 (92-38-7); Notre Dame 1975-80 (53-16-1)

172   *Lou Holtz (Born 1-6-37 Follansbee, W. Va.)
        Kent 1959 (22: 172-82-5 .674)
        William & Mary 1969-71 (13-20-0); North Caro. St. 1972-75 (33-12-3); Arkansas 1977-83 (60-
        21-2); Minnesota 1984-85 (10-12-0); Notre Dame 1986-91 (56-17-0)
171   Wallace Wade (Born 6-15-1892 Trenton, Tenn.; Died 10-7-86)
        Brown 1917 (24: 171-49-10 .765)
        Alabama 1923-30 (61-13-3); Duke 1931-41, 1946-50 (110-36-7)
170   Ara Parseghian (Born 5-21-23 Akron, Ohio)
        Miami (Ohio) 1949 (24: 170-58-6 .739)
        Miami (Ohio) 1951-55 (39-6-1); Northwestern 1956-63 (36-35-1); Notre Dame 1964-74 (95-17-
        4)
169   *Jim Sweeney (Born 9-1-29 Butte, Mont.)
        Portland 1951 (27: 169-125-3 .574)
        Montana St. 1963-67 (31-20-0); Washington St. 1968-75 (26-59-1); Fresno St. 1976-91 (112-
        46-2)
168   *Johnny Majors (Born 5-21-35 Lynchburg, Tenn.)
        Tennessee 1957 (24: 168-102-10 .618)
        Iowa St. 1968-72 (24-30-1); Pittsburgh 1973-76 (33-13-1); Tennessee 1977-91 (111-59-8)

168   Bob Blackman (Born 7-7-18 De Soto, Iowa)
        Southern Cal 1941 (30: 168-112-7 .598)
        Denver 1953-54 (12-6-2); Dartmouth 1955-70 (104-37-3); Illinois 1971-76 (29-36-1); Cornell
        1977-82 (23-33-1)
167   *Don James (Born 12-31-32 Massillon, Ohio)
        Miami (Fla.) 1954 (21: 167-75-3 .688)
        Kent 1971-74 (25-19-1); Washington 1975-91 (142-56-2)
166   Earl "Red" Blaik (Born 2-17-1897 Detroit, Mich.; Died 5-6-89)
        Miami (Ohio) 1918; Army 1920 (25: 166-48-14 .759)
        Dartmouth 1934-40 (45-15-4); Army 1941-58 (121-33-10)

165   Bobby Dodd (Born 11-11-08 Galax, Va.; Died 6-21-88)
        Tennessee 1931 (22: 165-64-8 .713)
        Georgia Tech 1945-66 (165-64-8)
165   Frank Howard (Born 3-25-09 Barlow Ben, Ala.)
        Alabama 1931 (30: 165-118-12 .580)
        Clemson 1940-69 (165-118-12)
163   Don Faurot (Born 6-23-02 Mountain Grove, Mo.)
        Missouri 1925 (28: 163-93-13 .630)
        Northeast Mo. St. 1926-34 (63-13-3); Missouri 1935-42, 1946-56 (100-80-10)
163   *Grant Teaff (Born 11-12-33 Hermleigh, Tex.)
        McMurry 1956 (29: 163-146-8 .527)
        McMurry 1960-65 (23-35-2); Angelo St. 1969-71 (19-11-0); Baylor 1972-91 (121-100-6)
162   Ossie Solem (Born 12-13-1891 Minneapolis, Minn.; Died 10-26-70)
        Minnesota 1915 (37: 162-117-20 .575)
        Luther 1920 (5-1-1); Drake 1921-31 (54-35-2); Iowa 1932-36 (15-21-4); Syracuse 1937-45 (30-
        27-6); Springfield 1946-57 (58-33-7)
160   Bill Yeoman (Born 12-26-27 Elnora, Ind.)
        Army 1949 (25: 160-108-8 .595)
        Houston 1962-86 (160-108-8)
158   Francis Schmidt (Born 12-3-1885 Downs, Kan.; Died 9-19-44)
        Nebraska 1914 (24: 158-57-11 .723)
        Tulsa 1919-21 (24-3-2); Arkansas 1922-28 (42-20-3); Texas Christian 1929-33 (46-6-5); Ohio
        St. 1934-40 (39-16-1); Idaho 1941-42 (7-12-0)
157   Barry Switzer (Born 10-5-37 Crossett, Ark.)
        Arkansas 1960 (16: 157-29-4 .837)
        Oklahoma 1973-88 (157-29-4)
157   Edward Robinson (Born 10-15-1873 Lynn, Miss.; Died 3-10-45)
        Brown 1896 (27: 157-88-13 .632)
        Nebraska 1896-97 (11-4-1); Brown 1898-1901 (24-17-3); Maine 1902 (6-2-0); Brown 1904-07,
        1910-25 (116-65-9)
155   Bennie Owen (Born 7-24-1875 Chicago, Ill.; Died 2-9-70)
        Kansas 1900 (27: 155-60-19 .703)
        Washburn 1900 (6-2-0); Bethany (Kan.) 1901-04 (27-4-3); Oklahoma 1905-26 (122-54-16)
155   Ray Morrison (Born 2-28-1885 Switzerland Co., Ind.; Died 11-19-82)
        Vanderbilt 1912 (34: 155-130-33 .539)
        Southern Methodist 1915-16 (2-13-2); Vanderbilt 1918 (4-2-0); Southern Methodist 1922-34
        (82-31-20); Vanderbilt 1935-39 (25-20-2); Temple 1940-48 (31-38-9); Austin 1949-52 (11-26-0)
153   Morley Jennings (Born 1-23-1885 Holland, Mich.; Died 5-13-85)
        Mississippi St. 1912 (29: 153-75-18 .658)
        Ouachita Baptist 1912-25 (70-15-12); Baylor 1926-40 (83-60-6)
153   Matty Bell (Born 2-22-1899 Baylor Co., Tex.; Died 6-30-83)
        Centre 1920 (26: 153-87-16 .630)
        Haskell 1920-21 (13-6-0); Carroll (Wis.) 1922 (4-3-0); Texas Christian 1923-28 (33-17-5); Texas
        A&M 1929-33 (24-21-3); Southern Methodist 1935-41, 1945-49 (79-40-8)
153   *Bill Dooley (Born 5-19-34 Mobile, Ala.)
        Mississippi St. 1956 (25: 153-123-5 .553)
        North Caro. 1967-77 (69-53-2); Virginia Tech 1978-86 (64-37-1); Wake Forest 1987-91 (21-32-
        2)
151   Lou Little (Born 12-6-1893 Leominster, Pa.; Died 5-28-79)
        Pennsylvania 1920 (33: 151-128-13 .539)
        Georgetown 1924-29 (41-12-3); Columbia 1930-56 (110-116-10)

✓ Includes games forfeited, team and/or individual statistics abrogated, and coaching records changed
by action of the NCAA Council under the restitution provisions of Bylaw 19.6 of the Official Procedure
Governing the NCAA Enforcement Program (adopted by the NCAA membership at the 69th annual
Convention in January 1975). The restitution provisions may be applied by the Council when a student-
athlete has been permitted to participate while ineligible as a result of a court order against his institution
or the NCAA, if the court order subsequently is overturned.

COACHES WITH 200 OR MORE CAREER VICTORIES

This list includes all coaches in NCAA history who have won at least 200 games at four-year colleges
(regardless of whether the college was an NCAA member at the time).

Coach (Alma Mater, Colleges Coached, Tenure)	Years	Won	Lost	Tied	Pct.
#Eddie Robinson (Leland '41).................................	†49	371	134	15	.728
(Grambling 1941-42, 1945—)					
Paul "Bear" Bryant (Alabama '36)	38	323	85	17	.780
(Maryland 1945; Kentucky 1946-53; Texas A&M 1954-57; Alabama 1958-82)					
Amos Alonzo Stagg (Yale '88)................................	57	314	199	35	.605
(Springfield 1890-91; Chicago 1892-1932; Pacific, Cal., 1933-46)					

Coach (Alma Mater, Colleges Coached, Tenure)	Years	Won	Lost	Tied	Pct.
Glenn S. "Pop" Warner (Cornell '95) .... (Georgia 1895-96; Cornell 1897-98; Carlisle 1899-1903; Cornell 1904-06; Carlisle 1907-14; Pittsburgh 1915-23; Stanford 1924-32; Temple 1933-38)	44	313	106	32	.729
#John Gagliardi (Colorado Col. '49) .... (Carroll, Mont. 1949-52; St. John's, Minn. 1953—)	†43	286	94	9	.747
#Ron Schipper (Hope '52) .... (Central, Iowa 1961—)	†31	242	60	3	.798
#Joe Paterno (Brown '50) .... (Penn St. 1966—)	26	240	62	3	.792
Wayne Woodrow "Woody" Hayes (Denison '35)......... (Denison 1946-48; Miami, Ohio 1949-50; Ohio St. 1951-78)	33	238	72	10	.759
Glenn "Bo" Schembechler (Miami, Ohio '51)............ (Miami, Ohio 1963-68; Michigan 1969-89)	27	234	65	8	.775
Arnett Mumford (Wilberforce '24)............. (Jarvis 1924-26; Bishop 1927-29; Texas College 1931-35; Southern-B.R. 1936-42, 1944-61)	†36	233	85	23	.717
††John Merritt (Kentucky St. '50)............ (Jackson St. 1953-62; Tennessee St. 1963-83)	†31	232	65	11	.771
#Roy Kidd (Eastern Ky. '54)............ (Eastern Ky. 1964—)	†28	230	81	8	.734
Fred Long (Millikin '18)............. (Paul Quinn 1921-22; Wiley 1923-47; Prairie View 1948; Texas College 1949-55; Wiley 1956-65)	†45	227	151	31	.593
#Jim Malosky (Minnesota '51)............. (Minn.-Duluth 1958—)	†34	218	99	11	.681
#Bobby Bowden (Samford '53)............. (Samford 1959-62; West Va. 1970-75; Florida St. 1976—)	26	216	76	3	.737
#Tubby Raymond (Michigan '50)............ (Delaware 1966—)	†26	212	85	2	.712
Jess Neely (Vanderbilt '24)............. (Southwestern, Tenn. 1924-27; Clemson 1931-39; Rice 1940-66)	40	207	176	19	.539
Jake Gaither (Knoxville '27)............. (Florida A&M 1945-69)	†25	203	36	4	.844
Warren Woodson (Baylor '24)............. (Conway St. 1935-40; Hardin-Simmons 1941-42, 1946-51; Arizona 1952-56; New Mexico St. 1958-67; Trinity, Tex. 1972-73)	31	203	95	14	.673
Vince Dooley (Auburn '54)............. (Georgia 1964-88)	25	201	77	10	.715
Eddie Anderson (Notre Dame '22) .... (Loras 1922-24; DePaul 1925-31; Holy Cross 1933-38; Iowa 1939-42, 1946-49; Holy Cross 1950-64)	39	201	128	15	.606
Darrell Mudra (Peru St. '51) .... (Adams St. 1959-62; North Dak. St. 1963-65; Arizona 1967-68; Western Ill. 1969-73; Florida St. 1974-75; Eastern Ill. 1978-82; Northern Iowa 1983-87)	†26	200	81	4	.709
#Fred Martinelli (Otterbein '51)............. (Ashland 1959—)	†33	200	114	12	.632

† Zero to nine years in Division I-A.   †† Tennessee State's participation in 1981 and 1982 Division I-AA championships (1-2 record) voided.   # Active coach.

COACHES WITH 200 OR MORE VICTORIES AT ONE COLLEGE

Coach (College, Tenure)	Years	Won	Lost	Tied	Pct.
#Eddie Robinson (Grambling 1941-42, 1945—)	†49	371	134	15	.728
#John Gagliardi (St. John's, Minn. 1953—)	†39	261	88	8	.742
Amos Alonzo Stagg (Chicago 1892-1932)	41	244	111	27	.674
#Ron Schipper (Central, Iowa 1961—)...............	†31	242	60	3	.798
#Joe Paterno (Penn St. 1966—)	26	240	62	3	.792
Paul "Bear" Bryant (Alabama 1958-82)	25	232	46	9	.824
#Roy Kidd (Eastern Ky. 1964—)	†28	230	81	8	.734
#Jim Malosky (Minn.-Duluth 1958—)	†34	218	99	11	.681
#Tubby Raymond (Delaware 1966—)	†26	212	85	2	.712
Wayne Woodrow "Woody" Hayes (Ohio St. 1951-78)	28	205	61	10	.761
Jake Gaither (Florida A&M 1945-69)	†25	203	36	4	.844
Vince Dooley (Georgia 1964-88)	25	201	77	10	.715
#Fred Martinelli (Ashland 1959—)	†33	200	114	12	.632

† Zero to nine years in Division I-A.   # Active coach.

MATCH-UPS OF COACHES EACH WITH 200 VICTORIES

Date	Coaches, Team (Victories Going In)	Winner (Score)
11-11-61	Arnett Mumford, Southern-B.R. (232)	
	Fred Long, Wiley (215)	Wiley (21-19)
1-1-78	Paul "Bear" Bryant, Alabama (272)	Alabama (35-6)
Sugar Bowl	"Woody" Hayes, Ohio St. (231)	
10-11-80	Eddie Robinson, Grambling (284)	Grambling (52-27)
	John Merritt, Tennessee St. (200)	
10-10-81	Eddie Robinson, Grambling (294)	
	John Merritt, Tennessee St. (209)	Tennessee St. (14-10)
10-9-82	Eddie Robinson, Grambling (301)	
	John Merritt, Tennessee St. (218)	Tennessee St. (22-8)
10-8-83	Eddie Robinson, Grambling (308)	Tie (7-7)
	John Merritt, Tennessee St. (228)	
11-28-87	John Gagliardi, St. John's (Minn.) (251)	
	Ron Schipper, Central (Iowa) (202)	Central (Iowa) (13-3)
11-25-89	John Gagliardi, St. John's (Minn.) (268)	St. John's (Minn.) (27-24)
	Ron Schipper, Central (Iowa) (224)	
12-28-90	Joe Paterno, Penn St. (229)	
Blockbuster	Bobby Bowden, Florida St. (204)	Florida St. (24-17)
Bowl		

COACHES WITH CAREER WINNING PERCENTAGE OF .800 OR BETTER

This list includes all coaches in history with a winning percentage of at least .800 over a career of at least 10 seasons at four-year colleges (regardless of division or association).

Coach (Alma Mater, Colleges Coached, Tenure)	Years	Won	Lost	Tied	Pct.
#Bob Reade (Cornell College '54)	†13	125	16	1	.884
(Augustana, Ill. 1979—)					
Knute Rockne (Notre Dame '14)	13	105	12	5	.881
(Notre Dame 1918-30)					
Frank Leahy (Notre Dame '31)	13	107	13	9	.864
(Boston College 1939-40; Notre Dame 1941-43, 1946-53)					
Doyt Perry (Bowling Green '32)	†10	77	11	5	.855
(Bowling Green 1955-64)					
George Woodruff (Yale '89)	12	142	25	2	.846
(Pennsylvania 1892-1901; Illinois 1903; Carlisle 1905)					
Jake Gaither (Knoxville '27)	†25	203	36	4	.844
(Florida A&M 1945-69)					
Dave Maurer (Denison '54)	†15	129	23	3	.842
(Wittenberg 1969-83)					
Paul Hoereman (Heidelberg '38)	†14	102	18	4	.839
(Heidelberg 1946-59)					
Barry Switzer (Arkansas '60)	16	157	29	4	.837
(Oklahoma 1973-88)					
#Mike Kelly (Manchester '70)	†11	109	21	1	.836
(Dayton 1981—)					
Don Coryell (Washington '50)	†15	127	24	3	.834
(Whittier 1957-59; San Diego St. 1961-72)					
Percy Haughton (Harvard '99)	13	96	17	6	.832
(Cornell 1899-1900; Harvard 1908-16; Columbia 1923-24)					
Robert "Bob" Neyland (Army '16)	21	173	31	12	.829
(Tennessee 1926-34, 1936-40, 1946-52)					
Fielding "Hurry Up" Yost (Lafayette '97)	29	196	36	12	:828
(Ohio Wesleyan 1897; Nebraska 1898; Kansas 1899; Stanford 1900; Michigan 1901-23, 1925-26)					
Charles "Bud" Wilkinson (Minnesota '37)	17	145	29	4	.826
(Oklahoma 1947-63)					
Charles "Chuck" Klausing (Slippery Rock '48)	†16	123	26	2	.821
(Indiana, Pa. 1964-69; Carnegie Mellon 1976-85)					
Vernon McCain (Langston '31)	†16	102	21	5	.816
(Md.-East. Shore 1948-63)					
John "Jock" Sutherland (Pittsburgh '18)	20	144	28	14	.812
(Lafayette 1919-23; Pittsburgh 1924-38)					
#Tom Osborne (Hastings '59)	19	186	43	3	.808
(Nebraska 1973—)					
Bob Devaney (Alma '39)	16	136	30	7	.806
(Wyoming 1957-61; Nebraska 1962-72)					

1992 NCAA FOOTBALL

Coach (Alma Mater, Colleges Coached, Tenure)	Years	Won	Lost	Tied	Pct.
Sid Gillman (Ohio St. '34)	†10	81	19	2	.804

(Miami, Ohio 1944-47; Cincinnati 1949-54)

†*Zero to nine years in Division I-A.*   #*Active coach.*

MAJOR-COLLEGE BROTHER VS. BROTHER COACHING MATCHUPS
(Each brother's victories in parentheses)

Bump Elliott, Michigan (6), vs. Pete, Illinois (1), 1960-66
Howard Jones, Yale 1909 and Iowa 1922 (2), vs. Tad, Syracuse 1909 and Yale 1922 (0)
Mack Brown, Tulane (2), vs. Watson, Vanderbilt (0), 1986-87
Vince Dooley, Georgia (1), vs. Bill, North Caro. (0), 1971 Gator Bowl

COACH OF THE YEAR AWARD
(Selected by the American Football Coaches Association and the Football Writers Association of America)
AFCA

1935	Lynn Waldorf, Northwestern
1936	Dick Harlow, Harvard
1937	Edward Mylin, Lafayette
1938	Bill Kern, Carnegie Tech
1939	Eddie Anderson, Iowa
1940	Clark Shaughnessy, Stanford
1941	Frank Leahy, Notre Dame
1942	Bill Alexander, Georgia Tech
1943	Amos Alonzo Stagg, Pacific (Cal.)
1944	Carroll Widdoes, Ohio St.
1945	Bo McMillin, Indiana
1946	Earl "Red" Blaik, Army
1947	Fritz Crisler, Michigan
1948	Bennie Oosterbaan, Michigan
1949	Bud Wilkinson, Oklahoma
1950	Charlie Caldwell, Princeton
1951	Chuck Taylor, Stanford
1952	Biggie Munn, Michigan St.
1953	Jim Tatum, Maryland
1954	Henry "Red" Sanders, UCLA
1955	Duffy Daugherty, Michigan St.
1956	Bowden Wyatt, Tennessee

	AFCA	FWAA
1957	"Woody" Hayes, Ohio St.	"Woody" Hayes, Ohio St.
1958	Paul Dietzel, Louisiana St.	Paul Dietzel, Louisiana St.
1959	Ben Schwartzwalder, Syracuse	Ben Schwartzwalder, Syracuse
1960	Murray Warmath, Minnesota	Murray Warmath, Minnesota
1961	Paul "Bear" Bryant, Alabama	Darrell Royal, Texas
1962	John McKay, Southern Cal	John McKay, Southern Cal
1963	Darrell Royal, Texas	Darrell Royal, Texas
1964	Frank Broyles, Arkansas, and Ara Parseghian, Notre Dame	Ara Parseghian, Notre Dame
1965	Tommy Prothro, UCLA	Duffy Daugherty, Michigan St.
1966	Tom Cahill, Army	Tom Cahill, Army
1967	John Pont, Indiana	John Pont, Indiana
1968	Joe Paterno, Penn St.	"Woody" Hayes, Ohio St.
1969	"Bo" Schembechler, Michigan	"Bo" Schembechler, Michigan
1970	Charles McClendon, Louisiana St., and Darrell Royal, Texas	Alex Agase, Northwestern
1971	Paul "Bear" Bryant, Alabama	Bob Devaney, Nebraska
1972	John McKay, Southern Cal	John McKay, Southern Cal
1973	Paul "Bear" Bryant, Alabama	Johnny Majors, Pittsburgh
1974	Grant Teaff, Baylor	Grant Teaff, Baylor
1975	Frank Kush, Arizona St.	"Woody" Hayes, Ohio St.
1976	Johnny Majors, Pittsburgh	Johnny Majors, Pittsburgh
1977	Don James, Washington	Lou Holtz, Arkansas
1978	Joe Paterno, Penn St.	Joe Paterno, Penn St.
1979	Earle Bruce, Ohio St.	Earle Bruce, Ohio St.
1980	Vince Dooley, Georgia	Vince Dooley, Georgia
1981	Danny Ford, Clemson	Danny Ford, Clemson
1982	Joe Paterno, Penn St.	Joe Paterno, Penn St.
1983	Ken Hatfield, Air Force	Howard Schnellenberger, Miami (Fla.)
1984	LaVell Edwards, Brigham Young	LaVell Edwards, Brigham Young
1985	Fisher DeBerry, Air Force	Fisher DeBerry, Air Force
1986	Joe Paterno, Penn St.	Joe Paterno, Penn St.

Coaches' Records

	AFCA	FWAA
1987	Dick MacPherson, Syracuse	Dick MacPherson, Syracuse
1988	Don Nehlen, West Va.	Lou Holtz, Notre Dame
1989	Bill McCartney, Colorado	Bill McCartney, Colorado
1990	Bobby Ross, Georgia Tech	Bobby Ross, Georgia Tech
1991	Don James, Washington	Don James, Washington

Outstanding offensive linemen such as two-time Outland Trophy winner Dave Rimington (left) have led a ground-oriented attack that has enabled Nebraska's Tom Osborne (right) to gain the highest winning percentage (.808) among active coaches with five or more years of Division I-A coaching experience.

WINNINGEST ACTIVE DIVISION I-A COACHES

Minimum five years as Division I-A head coach; record at four-year colleges only.

BY PERCENTAGE

Coach, College	Years	Won	Lost	Tied	*Pct.	BOWLS W	L	T
Tom Osborne, Nebraska	19	186	43	3	.808	8	11	0
Joe Paterno, Penn St.	26	240	62	3	.792	14	7	1
LaVell Edwards, Brigham Young	20	183	62	3	.744	5	10	1
Bobby Bowden, Florida St.	26	216	76	3	.737	11	3	1
Pat Dye, Auburn	18	148	57	4	.718	7	2	1
Dennis Erickson, Miami (Fla.)	10	83	34	1	.708	%5	2	0
Steve Spurrier, Florida	5	39	17	1	.693	0	2	0
Dick Sheridan, North Caro. St.	14	112	49	4	.691	%5	6	0
Terry Donahue, UCLA	16	125	54	8	.690	8	2	1
Jackie Sherrill, Mississippi St.	14	112	50	2	.689	6	3	0
Don James, Washington	21	167	75	3	.688	10	4	0
Herb Deromedi, Central Mich.	14	100	43	10	.686	0	1	0
Lou Holtz, Notre Dame	22	172	82	5	.674	8	6	2
Fisher DeBerry, Air Force	8	65	33	1	.662	4	2	0
Ken Hatfield, Clemson	13	100	53	3	.651	4	6	0

Coach, College	Years	Won	Lost	Tied	*Pct.	BOWLS W	L	T
Earle Bruce, Colorado St.	20	149	83	2	.641	7	5	0
John Cooper, Ohio St.	15	108	59	4	.640	2	4	0
Al Molde, Western Mich.	21	138	81	6	.627	%3	6	0
Johnny Majors, Tennessee	24	168	102	10	.618	9	7	0
Don Nehlen, West Va.	21	140	86	6	.616	3	4	0
Jim Wacker, Minnesota	21	144	91	3	.609	%13	2	0
Bill Mallory, Indiana	22	143	98	4	.592	4	5	0
Larry Smith, Southern Cal	16	104	75	5	.579	2	4	1
Jim Sweeney, Fresno St.	27	169	125	3	.574	4	1	0
Bob Wagner, Hawaii	5	34	25	2	.574	0	1	0
Hayden Fry, Iowa	30	189	140	9	.572	5	7	1
Pat Jones, Oklahoma St.	8	52	39	1	.571	3	1	0
Jim Harkema, Eastern Mich.	19	109	82	6	.568	%2	1	0
Bill McCartney, Colorado	10	65	49	3	.568	1	5	0
Dick Tomey, Arizona	15	93	70	6	.568	1	1	0
George Welsh, Virginia	19	121	93	4	.564	3	5	0
Howard Schnellenberger, Louisville	12	75	58	2	.563	3	0	0
George Perles, Michigan St.	9	57	44	4	.562	3	3	0
Billy Brewer, Mississippi	18	110	86	6	.559	%3	3	0
Bill Dooley, Wake Forest	25	153	123	5	.553	2	7	0
Paul Schudel, Ball St.	7	42	34	2	.551	0	1	0
John Mackovic, Texas	7	44	36	1	.549	1	3	0
Frank Beamer, Virginia Tech	11	64	55	3	.537	%0	1	0
✓Spike Dykes, Texas Tech	6	30	26	1	.535	1	1	0
Grant Teaff, Baylor	29	163	146	8	.527	3	4	0
Bruce Snyder, Arizona St.	12	66	62	6	.515	2	0	0
Bill Lewis, Georgia Tech	6	34	33	2	.507	1	0	0
Gerry Faust, Akron	11	60	60	3	.500	1	1	0
Nelson Stokley, Southwestern La.	6	32	33	1	.492	0	0	0
Bill Curry, Kentucky	12	64	68	4	.485	2	2	0
Gene Stallings, Alabama	9	45	51	1	.469	2	1	0
Gary Moeller, Michigan	5	25	29	3	.465	1	1	0
Gene Murphy, Cal St. Fullerton	14	72	87	1	.453	%0	2	0
Jerry Pettibone, Oregon St.	7	34	42	1	.448	0	0	0
Bob Stull, Missouri	8	40	50	1	.445	0	1	0
Rich Brooks, Oregon	15	71	93	4	.435	1	1	0
Chuck Stobart, Memphis St.	11	51	69	3	.427	1	0	0
Jim Walden, Iowa St.	14	62	87	6	.419	0	1	0
Jerry Berndt, Temple	13	54	77	3	.414	0	0	0
Chuck Shelton, Pacific (Cal.)	15	66	98	1	.403	0	0	0
Glen Mason, Kansas	6	26	39	1	.402	0	0	0
Tim Murphy, Cincinnati	5	21	34	1	.384	0	0	0
Mack Brown, North Caro.	8	32	56	1	.365	0	1	0
Jim Colletto, Purdue	6	21	45	1	.321	0	0	0

Less Than 5 Years in Division I-A
(Includes record at all four-year colleges)

Coach, College	Years	Won	Lost	Tied	*Pct.	BOWLS W	L	T
Mark Duffner, Maryland	6	60	5	1	.917	0	0	0
Dennis Franchione, New Mexico	9	80	19	2	.802	%6	5	0
Paul Pasqualoni, Syracuse	6	44	19	0	.698	%1	1	0
Jim Hess, New Mexico St.	17	115	72	5	.612	%5	3	0
Sparky Woods, South Caro.	8	53	34	5	.603	%2	2	0
George Chaump, Navy	10	62	49	2	.558	4	2	0
Buddy Teevens, Tulane	7	39	31	2	.556	0	0	0
Mike Price, Washington St.	11	59	64	0	.480	%1	1	0
Tom Lichtenberg, Ohio	5	21	31	3	.409	%0	1	0

* Ties computed as half won and half lost; bowl games included. % Includes record in NCAA and/or NAIA championships. ✓ Loss in Independence Bowl in first game.

BY VICTORIES
(Minimum 100 victories)

Coach, College, Winning Percentage	Won	Coach, College, Winning Percentage	Won
Joe Paterno, Penn St. .792	240	Don James, Washington .688	167
Bobby Bowden, Florida St. .737	216	Grant Teaff, Baylor .527	163
Hayden Fry, Iowa .572	189		
Tom Osborne, Nebraska .808	186	Bill Dooley, Wake Forest .553	153
LaVell Edwards, Brigham Young .744	183	Earle Bruce, Colorado St. .641	149
Lou Holtz, Notre Dame .674	172	Pat Dye, Auburn .718	148
Jim Sweeney, Fresno St. .574	169	Jim Wacker, Minnesota .609	144
Johnny Majors, Tennessee .618	168	Bill Mallory, Indiana .592	143

Coach, College, Winning Percentage	Won
Don Nehlen, West Va. .616	140
Al Molde, Western Mich. .627	138
Terry Donahue, UCLA .690	125
George Welsh, Virginia .564	121
Dick Sheridan, North Caro. St. .691	112
Jackie Sherrill, Mississippi St. .689	112
Billy Brewer, Mississippi .559	110
Jim Harkema, Eastern Mich. .568	109
John Cooper, Ohio St. .640	108
Larry Smith, Southern Cal .579	104

Coach, College, Winning Percentage	Won
Herb Deromedi, Central Mich. .686	100
Ken Hatfield, Clemson .651	100

Less Than 5 Years in Division I-A
(Includes record at all four-year colleges)

	Won
Jim Hess, New Mexico St. .612	115

ANNUAL DIVISION I-A HEAD-COACHING CHANGES

Year	Changes	Teams	Pct.	Year	Changes	Teams	Pct.
1947	27	125	.216	1972	17	121	.140
1948	24	121	.198	1973	36	126	†.286
1949	22	114	.193	1974	28	128	.219
1950	23	119	.193	1975	18	134	.134
1951	23	115	.200	1976	23	137	.168
1952	15	113	.133	1977	27	144	.188
1953	18	111	.162	1978	27	139	.194
1954	14	103	.136	1979	26	139	.187
1955	23	103	.223	1980	27	139	.194
1956	19	105	.181	1981	17	137	.123
1957	22	108	.204	1982	17	97	.175
1958	18	109	.165	1983	22	105	.210
1959	18	110	.164	1984	16	105	.152
1960	18	114	.158	1985	15	105	.143
1961	11	112	.098	1986	22	105	.210
1962	20	119	.168	1987	24	104	.231
1963	12	118	.102	1988	9	104	*.087
1964	14	116	.121	1989	19	106	.179
1965	16	114	.140	1990	20	106	.189
1966	16	116	.138	1991	16	106	.151
1967	21	114	.184	1992	16	107	.150
1968	14	114	.123				
1969	22	118	.186				
1970	13	118	.110				
1971	27	119	.227				

Record low.   †Record high.

RECORDS OF DIVISION I-A FIRST-YEAR HEAD COACHES

(Coaches with no previous head-coaching experience at a four-year college.)

Year	No.	Won	Lost	Tied	Pct.	Bowls	Team's Previous Season Record Won	Lost	Tied	Pct.	Bowls
1948	14	56	68	7	.454	0-1	76	52	8	.588	2-1
1949	8	26	49	3	.353	0-1	35	41	4	.463	0-0
1950	10	37	56	4	.402	0-0	49	42	6	.536	2-0
1951	13	60	67	4	.473	1-2	39	88	7	.317	1-1
1952	8	31	42	3	.428	0-0	38	40	0	.487	0-0
1953	8	29	45	5	.399	0-0	48	28	7	.620	1-2
1954	8	31	43	4	.423	0-0	40	33	7	.543	1-0
1955	9	36	50	4	.422	0-1	36	52	1	.410	0-0
1956	14	47	80	11	.380	1-0	61	68	6	.474	0-1
1957	9	32	50	6	.398	0-0	44	42	2	.511	0-0
1958	7	26	44	0	.371	0-0	37	31	2	.543	0-0
1959	8	34	43	2	.443	0-0	41	35	2	.538	0-1
1960	14	54	80	5	.406	1-0	57	78	2	.423	0-0
1961	8	26	50	0	.342	0-0	38	38	2	.500	0-0
1962	12	40	74	4	.356	2-0	52	66	2	.442	1-1
1963	8	23	49	6	.333	0-0	32	46	1	.411	0-1
1964	12	45	67	7	.408	1-1	42	71	4	.376	0-0
1965	8	28	47	2	.377	0-0	36	42	1	.462	0-0
1966	10	46	50	3	.480	0-0	38	56	5	.409	0-0
1967	18	58	114	5	.342	1-0	60	116	4	.344	0-1

Year	No.	Won	Lost	Tied	Pct.	Bowls	Team's Previous Season Record Won	Lost	Tied	Pct.	Bowls
1968	6	19	40	1	.325	0-0	20	38	2	.350	0-0
1969	15	49	90	1	.353	0-0	62	85	3	.423	0-1
1970	10	45	61	1	.425	1-0	46	54	0	.460	0-2
1971	12	57	72	0	.442	1-1	64	61	0	.512	0-1
1972	11	57	64	1	.471	1-0	53	64	2	.454	1-0
1973	14	84	63	8	.568	1-0	83	71	2	.538	3-0
1974	17	63	116	5	.356	1-0	78	105	1	.427	1-0
1975	10	38	72	0	.345	0-1	43	67	0	.391	0-0
1976	15	57	109	2	.345	3-1	72	91	5	.443	3-1
1977	14	55	94	5	.373	1-0	66	88	3	.430	0-2
1978	16	68	104	3	.397	0-0	77	96	3	.446	0-1
1979	11	53	66	3	.447	0-0	66	57	1	.536	2-2
1980	12	54	75	2	.420	0-0	60	68	3	.469	1-0
1981	6	25	40	0	.385	0-0	31	35	1	.470	0-1
1982	10	51	59	1	.464	0-1	58	57	2	.504	2-2
1983	12	51	82	2	.385	1-0	60	73	1	.451	1-1
1984	7	47	28	1	*.625	2-1	45	35	1	.562	3-0
1985	5	19	37	0	.339	0-0	20	32	4	.393	0-0
1986	12	53	81	0	.396	0-1	56	76	3	.426	1-1
1987	9	51	49	3	.510	1-1	52	50	1	.510	0-2
1988	4	25	20	0	.556	1-0	22	23	1	.489	1-1
1989	7	32	49	1	.396	0-2	39	43	0	.476	1-2
1990	9	46	42	2	.522	1-1	41	48	1	.461	0-1
1991	10	38	72	1	.347	1-0	46	64	2	.420	0-2

* Record percentage for first-year coaches. 1984 coaches and their records, with bowl game indicated by an asterisk (*): Pat Jones, Oklahoma St. (*10-2-0); Galen Hall, Florida (8-0-0, took over from Charley Pell after three games); Bill Arnsparger, Louisiana St. (8-*3-1); Fisher DeBerry, Air Force (*8-4-0); Dick Anderson, Rutgers (7-3-0); Mike Sheppard, Long Beach St. (4-7-0); Ron Chismar, Wichita St. (2-9-0).

MOST VICTORIES BY FIRST-YEAR HEAD COACHES

Coach, College, Year	W	L	T
Gary Blackney, Bowling Green, 1991	*11	1	0
John Robinson, Southern Cal, 1976	*11	1	0
Bill Battle, Tennessee, 1970	*11	1	0
Dick Crum, Miami (Ohio), 1974	*10	0	1
Barry Switzer, Oklahoma, 1973	10	0	1
John Jenkins, Houston, 1990	10	1	0
Dwight Wallace, Ball St., 1978	10	1	0
Chuck Fairbanks, Oklahoma, 1967	*10	1	0
Mike Archer, Louisiana St., 1987	*10	1	1
Curley Hallman, Southern Miss., 1988	*10	2	0
Pat Jones, Oklahoma St., 1984	*10	2	0
Earle Bruce, Tampa, 1972	*10	2	0
Billy Kinard, Mississippi, 1971	*10	2	0

* Bowl game victory included.
Only first-year coach to win a national championship: Bennie Oosterbaan, Michigan, 1948 (9-0-0).

WINNINGEST ACTIVE DIVISION I-AA COACHES

Minimum five years as a Division I-A and/or Division I-AA head coach; record at four-year colleges only.

BY PERCENTAGE

Coach, College	Years	Won	Lost	Tied	Pct.*	PLAYOFFS# W	L	T
Jimmy Satterfield, Furman	6	55	19	2	.743	7	3	0
Houston Markham, Alabama St.	5	39	13	3	.736	1	0	0
Roy Kidd, Eastern Ky.	28	230	81	8	.734	16	11	0
Eddie Robinson, Grambling	49	371	134	15	.728	9	7	0
†Chris Ault, Nevada	16	138	53	1	.721	9	7	0
Tubby Raymond, Delaware	26	212	85	2	.712	14	9	0
William Collick, Delaware St.	7	50	24	0	.676	0	0	0
Andy Talley, Villanova	12	75	39	2	.655	1	3	0
Bill Hayes, North Caro. A&T	16	114	60	2	.653	1	4	0
Carmen Cozza, Yale	27	162	86	5	.650	0	0	0
James Donnelly, Middle Tenn. St.	15	109	61	1	.640	5	5	0
Bill Bowes, New Hampshire	20	131	73	4	.639	1	3	0
Marino Casem, Southern-B.R.	25	154	87	8	.635	1	2	0
Skip Hall, Boise St.	5	37	22	0	.627	2	2	0
Jim Tressel, Youngstown St.	6	46	28	0	.622	5	3	0

Coach, College	Years	Won	Lost	Tied	Pct.*	PLAYOFFS# W	L	T
Steve Tosches, Princeton	5	30	19	1	.610	0	0	0
Ron Randleman, Sam Houston St.	23	145	95	4	.602	3	5	1
Willie Jeffries, South Caro. St.	19	117	84	6	.580	2	3	0
Jesse Branch, Southwest Mo. St.	6	38	28	1	.575	1	2	0
Joe Restic, Harvard	21	111	83	6	.570	0	0	0
Hank Small, Lehigh	6	37	28	1	.568	0	0	0
Ken Riley, Florida A&M	6	36	28	2	.561	0	0	0
Charlie Taaffe, Citadel	5	31	25	1	.553	0	2	0
Jim Reid, Massachusetts	6	36	29	2	.552	0	2	0
Bill Russo, Lafayette	14	81	66	1	.551	0	1	0
Dick Zornes, Eastern Wash.	13	72	59	2	.549	1	1	0
Jimmye Laycock, William & Mary	12	72	62	2	.537	1	3	0
Tom Jackson, Connecticut	9	51	46	0	.526	0	0	0
Sam Goodwin, Northwestern (La.)	11	59	59	4	.500	1	1	0
Dave Roberts, Northeast La.	8	44	44	3	.500	1	3	0
Don Read, Montana	22	114	115	1	.498	2	2	0
Bob Spoo, Eastern Ill.	5	28	29	0	.491	1	1	0
Buddy Nix, Tenn.-Chatt.	8	42	45	1	.483	0	1	0
Dennis Raetz, Indiana St.	12	64	69	1	.481	1	2	0
Phil Greco, Nicholls St.	5	25	29	1	.464	0	0	0
Bob Griffin, Rhode Island	29	99	117	1	.459	2	3	0
Jerry Moore, Appalachian St.	10	50	60	2	.455	0	2	0
Jack Harbaugh, Western Ky.	8	36	48	3	.431	0	0	0
Mike Mahoney, Murray St.	5	21	32	1	.398	0	0	0
Jim Ragland, Tennessee Tech	6	18	46	0	.281	0	0	0

Less Than 5 Years as Division I-A and/or Division I-AA Head Coach
(Includes record at all four-year colleges)

Coach, College	Years	Won	Lost	Tied	Pct.*	W	L	T
Al Bagnoli, Pennsylvania	10	85	19	0	.817	7	6	0
Terry Bowden, Samford	8	56	33	1	.628	2	1	0
Mike Cavan, East Tenn. St.	6	37	22	2	.623	0	0	0
Mickey Kwiatkowski, Brown	11	71	44	0	.617	0	5	0
Gene McDowell, Central Fla.	7	48	33	0	.593	3	2	0
Larry Glueck, Fordham	6	28	32	1	.467	1	2	0
Bob Smith, Southern Ill.	7	28	48	1	.370	0	0	0
Ray Tellier, Columbia	8	24	53	1	.314	0	1	0

† Nevada moves to Division I-A in 1992.   * Ties computed as half won and half lost.   # Playoffs includes all divisional championships as well as bowl games and NAIA playoffs.

BY VICTORIES
(Minimum 100 victories)

Coach, College, Winning Percentage	Won
Eddie Robinson, Grambling .728	371
Roy Kidd, Eastern Ky. .734	230
Tubby Raymond, Delaware .712	212
Carmen Cozza, Yale .650	162
Marino Casem, Southern-B.R. .635	154
Ron Randleman, Sam Houston St. .602	145
†Chris Ault, Nevada .721	138

† Nevada moves to I-A in 1992.

Coach, College, Winning Percentage	Won
Bill Bowes, New Hampshire .639	131
Willie Jeffries, South Caro. St. .580	117
Bill Hayes, North Caro. A&T .653	114
Don Read, Montana .498	114
Joe Restic, Harvard .570	111
James Donnelly, Middle Tenn. St. .640	109

ANNUAL DIVISION I-AA HEAD-COACHING CHANGES
(From the 1982 reorganization of the division for parallel comparisons)

Year	Changes	Teams	Pct.	Year	Changes	Teams	Pct.
1982	7	92	.076	1987	13	87	.149
1983	17	84	.202	1988	12	88	.136
1984	14	87	.161	1989	21	89	†.236
1985	11	87	.126	1990	16	89	.180
1986	18	86	.209	1991	6	87	*.069
				1992	14	89	.157

* Record low.   † Record high.

DIVISION I-AA COACH OF THE YEAR AWARD

(Selected by the American Football Coaches Association)

1983	Rey Dempsey, Southern Ill.	1988	Jimmy Satterfield, Furman
1984	Dave Arnold, Montana St.	1989	Erk Russell, Ga. Southern
1985	Dick Sheridan, Furman	1990	Tim Stowers, Ga. Southern
1986	Erk Russell, Ga. Southern	1991	Mark Duffner, Holy Cross
1987	Mark Duffner, Holy Cross		

DIVISION I-AA CHAMPIONSHIP COACHES

All coaches who have coached teams in the Division I-AA championship playoffs since 1978 are listed below with their playoff record, alma mater and year graduated, team, year coached, opponent, and score.

Terry Allen (1-2) (Northern Iowa '79)
Northern Iowa	90	Boise St. 3-20
Northern Iowa	91	Weber St. 38-21
Northern Iowa	91	Marshall 13-41

Dave Arnold (3-0) (Drake '67)
Montana St.	84	Arkansas St. 31-24
Montana St.	84	Rhode Island 32-20
Montana St.	84*	Louisiana Tech 19-6

Dave Arslanian (0-1) (Weber St. '72)
Weber St.	91	Northern Iowa 21-38

Chris Ault (9-7) (Nevada '68)
Nevada	78	Massachusetts 21-44
Nevada	79	Eastern Ky. 30-33
Nevada	83	Idaho St. 27-20
Nevada	83	North Texas 20-17 (OT)
Nevada	83	Southern Ill. 7-23
Nevada	85	Arkansas St. 24-23
Nevada	85	Furman 12-35
Nevada	86	Idaho 27-7
Nevada	86	Tennessee St. 33-6
Nevada	86	Ga. Southern 38-48
Nevada	90	Northeast La. 27-14
Nevada	90	Furman 42-35 (3 OT)
Nevada	90	Boise St. 59-52 (3 OT)
Nevada	90	Ga. Southern 13-36
Nevada	91	McNeese St. 22-16
Nevada	91	Youngstown St. 28-30

Randy Ball (0-1) (Northeast Mo. St. '73)
Western Ill.	91	Marshall 17-20 (OT)

Frank Beamer (0-1) (Virginia Tech '69)
Murray St.	86	Eastern Ill. 21-28

Terry Bowden (2-1) (West Va. '78)
Samford	91	New Hampshire 29-13
Samford	91	James Madison 24-21
Samford	91	Youngstown St. 0-10

Bill Bowes (0-1) (Penn St. '65)
New Hampshire	91	Samford 13-29

Jesse Branch (1-2) (Arkansas '64)
Southwest Mo. St.	89	Maine 38-35
Southwest Mo. St.	89	Stephen F. Austin 25-55
Southwest Mo. St.	90	Idaho 35-41

Billy Brewer (1-1) (Mississippi '61)
Louisiana Tech	82	South Caro. St. 38-3
Louisiana Tech	82	Delaware 0-17

Rick Carter (0-1) (Earlham '65)
Holy Cross	83	Western Caro. 21-28

Marino Casem (0-1) (Xavier, La. '56)
Alcorn St.	84	Louisiana Tech 21-44

George Chaump (4-2) (Bloomsburg '58)
Marshall	87	James Madison 41-12
Marshall	87	Weber St. 51-23
Marshall	87	Appalachian St. 24-10

Marshall . . . . 87 Northeast La. 42-43
Marshall . . . . 88 North Texas 7-0
Marshall . . . . 88 Furman 9-13

Pat Collins (4-0) (Louisiana Tech '63)
Northeast La. . . . . 87 North Texas 30-9
Northeast La. . . . . 87 Eastern Ky. 33-32
Northeast La. . . . . 87 Northern Iowa 44-41 (OT)
Northeast La. . . . . 87* Marshall 43-42

Archie Cooley (0-1) (Jackson St. '62)
Mississippi Val. . . . . 84 Louisiana Tech 19-66

Bruce Craddock (0-1) (Northeast Mo. St. '66)
Western Ill. . . . . 88 Western Ky. 32-35

Jim Criner (3-1) (Cal Poly Pomona '61)
Boise St. . . . . 80 Grambling 14-9
Boise St. . . . . 80* Eastern Ky. 31-29
Boise St. . . . . 81 Jackson St. 19-7
Boise St. . . . . 81 Eastern Ky. 17-23

Bill Davis (2-2) (Johnson Smith '65)
South Caro. St. . . . . 81 Tennessee St. 26-25
South Caro. St. . . . . 81 Idaho St. 12-41
South Caro. St. . . . . 82 Furman 17-0
South Caro. St. . . . . 82 Louisiana Tech 3-38

Rey Dempsey (3-0) (Geneva '58)
Southern Ill. . . . . 83 Indiana St. 23-7
Southern Ill. . . . . 83 Nevada 23-7
Southern Ill. . . . . 83* Western Caro. 43-7

Jim Dennison (0-1) (Wooster '60)
Akron . . . . 85 Rhode Island 27-35

Jim Donnan (3-1) (North Caro. St. '67)
Marshall . . . . 91 Western Ill. 20-17 (OT)
Marshall . . . . 91 Northern Iowa 41-13
Marshall . . . . 91 Eastern Ky. 14-7
Marshall . . . . 91 Youngstown St. 17-25

James "Boots" Donnelly (5-5) (Middle Tenn. St. '65)
Middle Tenn. St. . . . . 84 Eastern Ky. 27-10
Middle Tenn. St. . . . . 84 Indiana St. 42-41 (3 OT)
Middle Tenn. St. . . . . 84 Louisiana Tech 13-21
Middle Tenn. St. . . . . 85 Ga. Southern 21-28
Middle Tenn. St. . . . . 89 Appalachian St. 24-21

Middle Tenn. St. . . . . 89 Ga. Southern 3-45
Middle Tenn. St. . . . . 90 Jackson St. 28-7
Middle Tenn. St. . . . . 90 Boise St. 13-20
Middle Tenn. St. . . . . 91 Sam Houston St. 20-19 (OT)
Middle Tenn. St. . . . . 91 Eastern Ky. 13-23

Larry Donovan (0-1) (Nebraska '64)
Montana . . . . 82 Idaho 7-21

Fred Dunlap (1-2) (Colgate '50)
Colgate . . . . 82 Boston U. 21-7
Colgate . . . . 82 Delaware 13-20
Colgate . . . . 83 Western Caro. 23-24

Dennis Erickson (1-2) (Montana St. '70)
Idaho . . . . 82 Montana 21-7
Idaho . . . . 82 Eastern Ky. 30-38
Idaho . . . . 85 Eastern Wash. 38-42

Maurice "Mo" Forte (0-1) (Minnesota '71)
North Caro. A&T . . . . 86 Ga. Southern 21-52

Keith Gilbertson (2-3) (Central Wash. '71)
Idaho . . . . 86 Nevada 7-27
Idaho . . . . 87 Weber St. 30-59
Idaho . . . . 88 Montana 38-19
Idaho . . . . 88 Northwestern (La.) 38-30
Idaho . . . . 88 Furman 7-38

Sam Goodwin (1-1) (Henderson St. '66)
Northwestern (La.) . . . . 88 Boise St. 22-13
Northwestern (La.) . . . . 88 Idaho 30-38

W. C. Gorden (0-9) (Tennessee St. '52)
Jackson St. . . . . 78 Florida A&M 10-15
Jackson St. . . . . 81 Boise St. 7-19
Jackson St. . . . . 82 Eastern Ill. 13-16 (OT)
Jackson St. . . . . 85 Ga. Southern 0-27

Jackson St. 86	Tennessee St. 23-32	
Jackson St. 87	Arkansas St. 32-35	
Jackson St. 88	Stephen F. Austin 0-24	
Jackson St. 89	Montana 7-48	
Jackson St. 90	Middle Tenn. St. 7-28	

Mike Gottfried (0-1) (Morehead St. '66)
Murray St. 79   Lehigh 9-28

Lynn Graves (3-1) %(Stephen F. Austin '65)
Stephen F. Austin 89%	Grambling 59-56
Stephen F. Austin 89%	Southwest Mo. St. 55-25
Stephen F. Austin 89%	Furman 21-19
Stephen F. Austin 89%	Ga. Southern 34-37

Bob Griffin (2-3) (Southern Conn. St. '63)
Rhode Island 81	Idaho St. 0-51
Rhode Island 84	Richmond 23-17
Rhode Island 84	Montana St. 20-32
Rhode Island 85	Akron 35-27
Rhode Island 85	Furman 15-59

Skip Hall (2-2) (Concordia-M'head '66)
Boise St. 88	Northwestern (La.) 13-22
Boise St. 90	Northern Iowa 20-3
Boise St. 90	Middle Tenn. St. 20-13
Boise St. 90	Nevada 52-59 (3 OT)

Jim Hess (1-1) (Southeastern Okla. '59)
Stephen F. Austin 88	Jackson St. 24-0
Stephen F. Austin 88	Ga. Southern 6-27

Rudy Hubbard (2-0) (Ohio St. '68)
Florida A&M 78	Jackson St. 15-10
Florida A&M 78*	Massachusetts 35-28

Sonny Jackson (1-1) (Nicholls St. '63)
Nicholls St. 86	Appalachian St. 28-26
Nicholls St. 86	Ga. Southern 31-55

Roy Kidd (15-10) (Eastern Ky. '54)
Eastern Ky. 79	Nevada 33-30
Eastern Ky. 79*	Lehigh 30-7
Eastern Ky. 80	Lehigh 23-20
Eastern Ky. 80	Boise St. 29-31
Eastern Ky. 81	Delaware 35-28
Eastern Ky. 81	Boise St. 23-17
Eastern Ky. 81	Idaho St. 23-34
Eastern Ky. 82	Idaho St. 38-30
Eastern Ky. 82	Tennessee St. 13-7
Eastern Ky. 82*	Delaware 17-14
Eastern Ky. 83	Boston U. 20-24
Eastern Ky. 84	Middle Tenn. St. 10-27
Eastern Ky. 86	Furman 23-10
Eastern Ky. 86	Eastern Ill. 24-22
Eastern Ky. 86	Arkansas St. 10-24
Eastern Ky. 87	Western Ky. 40-17
Eastern Ky. 87	Northeast La. 32-33
Eastern Ky. 88	Massachusetts 28-17
Eastern Ky. 88	Western Ky. 41-24
Eastern Ky. 88	Ga. Southern 17-21
Eastern Ky. 89	Youngstown St. 24-28
Eastern Ky. 90	Furman 17-45
Eastern Ky. 91	Appalachian St. 14-3
Eastern Ky. 91	Middle Tenn. St. 23-13
Eastern Ky. 91	Marshall 7-14

Jim Koetter (0-1) (Idaho St. '61)
Idaho St. 83   Nevada 20-27

Dave Kragthorpe (3-0) (Utah St. '55)
Idaho St. 81	Rhode Island 51-0
Idaho St. 81	South Caro. St. 41-12
Idaho St. 81*	Eastern Ky. 34-23

Larry Lacewell (6-4) (Ark.-Monticello '55)
Arkansas St. 84	Tenn.-Chatt. 37-10
Arkansas St. 84	Montana St. 14-31
Arkansas St. 85	Grambling 10-7
Arkansas St. 85	Nevada 23-24
Arkansas St. 86	Sam Houston St. 48-7

Arkansas St. 86   Delaware 55-14
Arkansas St. 86   Eastern Ky. 24-10
Arkansas St. 86   Ga. Southern 21-48
Arkansas St. 87   Jackson St. 35-32
Arkansas St. 87   Northern Iowa 28-49

Jimmye Laycock (1-3) (William & Mary '70)
William & Mary 86   Delaware 17-51
William & Mary 89   Furman 10-24
William & Mary 90   Massachusetts 38-0
William & Mary 90   Central Fla. 38-52

Tom Lichtenberg (0-1) (Louisville '62)
Maine 89   Southwest Mo. St. 35-38

Gene McDowell (2-1) (Florida St. '63)
Central Fla. 90   Youngstown St. 20-17
Central Fla. 90   William & Mary 52-38
Central Fla. 90   Ga. Southern 7-44

John Merritt (1-2)† (Kentucky St. '50)
Tennessee St. ....81†   South Caro. St. 25-26 (OT)
Tennessee St. ....82†   Eastern Ill. 20-19
Tennessee St. ....82†   Eastern Ky. 7-13

Al Molde (1-2) (Gust. Adolphus '66)
Eastern Ill. 83   Indiana St. 13-16 (2 OT)
Eastern Ill. 86   Murray St. 28-21
Eastern Ill. 86   Eastern Ky. 22-24

Jerry Moore (0-1) (Baylor '61)
Appalachian St. 89   Middle Tenn. St. 21-24

Darrell Mudra (4-3) (Peru St. '51)
Eastern Ill. 82   Jackson St. 16-13 (OT)
Eastern Ill. 82   Tennessee St. 19-20
Northern Iowa 85   Eastern Wash. 17-14
Northern Iowa 85   Ga. Southern 33-40
Northern Iowa 87   Youngstown St. 31-28
Northern Iowa 87   Arkansas St. 49-28
Northern Iowa 87   Northeast La. 41-44 (OT)

Tim Murphy (0-1) (Springfield '78)
Maine 87   Ga. Southern 28-31 (OT)

Corky Nelson (0-3) (Southwest Tex. St. '64)
North Texas 83   Nevada 17-20 (OT)
North Texas 87   Northeast La. 9-30
North Texas 88   Marshall 0-7

Buddy Nix (0-1) (Livingston '61)
Tenn.-Chatt. 84   Arkansas St. 10-37

Bob Pickett (1-1) (Maine '59)
Massachusetts 78   Nevada 44-21
Massachusetts 78   Florida A&M 28-35

Mike Price (1-1) (Puget Sound '69)
Weber St. 87   Idaho 59-30
Weber St. 87   Marshall 23-51

Joe Purzycki (0-1) (Delaware '71)
James Madison 87   Marshall 12-41

Dennis Raetz (1-2) (Nebraska '68)
Indiana St. 83   Eastern Ill. 16-13 (2 OT)
Indiana St. 83   Southern Ill. 7-23
Indiana St. 84   Middle Tenn. St. 41-42 (3 OT)

Ron Randleman (0-2) (William Penn '64)
Sam Houston St. 86   Arkansas St. 7-48
Sam Houston St. 91   Middle Tenn. St. 19-20 (OT)

Harold "Tubby" Raymond (3-5) (Michigan '50)
Delaware 81   Eastern Ky. 28-35
Delaware 82   Colgate 20-13
Delaware 82   Louisiana Tech 17-0
Delaware 82   Eastern Ky. 14-17
Delaware 86   William & Mary 51-17
Delaware 86   Arkansas St. 14-55
Delaware 88   Furman 7-21
Delaware 91   James Madison 35-42 (2 OT)

Don Read (2-2) (Cal St. Sacramento '59)
Montana 88   Idaho 19-38
Montana 89   Jackson St. 48-7

Montana	89	Eastern Ill. 25-19
Montana	89	Ga. Southern 15-45

Jim Reid (0-2) (Maine '73)

Massachusetts	88	Eastern Ky. 17-28
Massachusetts	90	William & Mary 0-38

Dave Roberts (1-3) (Western Caro. '68)

Western Ky.	87	Eastern Ky. 17-40
Western Ky.	88	Western Ill. 35-32
Western Ky.	88	Eastern Ky. 24-41
Northeast La.	90	Nevada 14-27

Eddie Robinson (0-3) (Leland '41)

Grambling	80	Boise St. 9-14
Grambling	85	Arkansas St. 7-10
Grambling	89	Stephen F. Austin 56-59

Erk Russell (16-2) (Auburn '49)

Ga. Southern	85	Jackson St. 27-0
Ga. Southern	85	Middle Tenn. St. 28-21
Ga. Southern	85	Northern Iowa 40-33
Ga. Southern	85*	Furman 44-42
Ga. Southern	86	North Caro. A&T 52-21
Ga. Southern	86	Nicholls St. 55-31
Ga. Southern	86	Nevada 48-38
Ga. Southern	86*	Arkansas St. 48-21
Ga. Southern	87	Maine 31-28 (OT)
Ga. Southern	87	Appalachian St. 0-19
Ga. Southern	88	Citadel 38-20
Ga. Southern	88	Stephen F. Austin 27-6
Ga. Southern	88	Eastern Ky. 21-17
Ga. Southern	88	Furman 12-17
Ga. Southern	89	Villanova 52-36
Ga. Southern	89	Middle Tenn. St. 45-3
Ga. Southern	89	Montana 45-15
Ga. Southern	89*	Stephen F. Austin 37-34

Jimmy Satterfield (7-3) (South Caro. '62)

Furman	86	Eastern Ky. 10-23
Furman	88	Delaware 21-7
Furman	88	Marshall 13-9
Furman	88	Idaho 38-7
Furman	88*	Ga. Southern 17-12
Furman	89	William & Mary 24-10
Furman	89	Youngstown St. 42-23
Furman	89	Stephen F. Austin 19-21
Furman	90	Eastern Ky. 45-17
Furman	90	Nevada 35-42 (3 OT)

Rip Scherer (1-1) (William & Mary '74)

James Madison	91	Delaware 42-35 (2 OT)
James Madison	91	Samford 21-24

Dal Shealy (1-2) (Carson-Newman '60)

Richmond	84	Boston U. 35-33
Richmond	84	Rhode Island 17-23
Richmond	87	Appalachian St. 3-20

Dick Sheridan (3-3) (South Caro. '64)

Furman	82	South Caro. St. 0-17
Furman	83	Boston U. 35-16
Furman	83	Western Caro. 7-14
Furman	85	Rhode Island 59-15
Furman	85	Nevada 35-12
Furman	85	Ga. Southern 42-44

John L. Smith (1-2) (Weber St. '71)

Idaho	89	Eastern Ill. 21-38
Idaho	90	Southwest Mo. St. 41-35
Idaho	90	Ga. Southern 27-28

Bob Spoo (1-1) (Purdue '60)

Eastern Ill.	89	Idaho 38-21
Eastern Ill.	89	Montana 19-25

Tim Stowers (4-0) (Auburn '79)

Ga. Southern	90	Citadel 31-0
Ga. Southern	90	Idaho 28-27
Ga. Southern	90	Central Fla. 44-7
Ga. Southern	90*	Nevada 36-13

Charlie Taaffe (0-2) (Siena '73)
Citadel .88   Ga. Southern 20-38
Citadel .90   Ga. Southern 0-31

Andy Talley (0-2) (Southern Conn. St. '67)
Villanova 89   Ga. Southern 36-52
Villanova 91   Youngstown St. 16-17

Rick Taylor (1-3) (Gettysburg '64)
Boston U. 82   Colgate 7-21
Boston U. 83   Eastern Ky. 24-20
Boston U. 83   Furman 16-35
Boston U. 84   Richmond 33-35

Bill Thomas (1-1) (Tennessee St. '71)
Tennessee St. 86   Jackson St. 32-23
Tennessee St. 86   Nevada 6-33

Jim Tressel (5-3) (Baldwin-Wallace '75)
Youngstown St. 87   Northern Iowa 28-31
Youngstown St. 89   Eastern Ky. 28-24
Youngstown St. 89   Furman 23-42
Youngstown St. 90   Central Fla. 17-20
Youngstown St. 91   Villanova 17-16
Youngstown St. 91   Nevada 30-28
Youngstown St. 91   Samford 10-0
Youngstown St. . . . . .91*   Marshall 25-17

Bob Waters (3-1) (Presbyterian '60)
Western Caro. 83   Colgate 24-23
Western Caro. 83   Holy Cross 28-21
Western Caro. 83   Furman 14-7
Western Caro. 83   Southern Ill. 7-43

John Whitehead (1-2) (East Stroudsburg '50)
Lehigh .79   Murray St. 28-9
Lehigh .79   Eastern Ky. 7-30
Lehigh .80   Eastern Ky. 20-23

A. L. Williams (3-1) (Louisiana Tech '67)
Louisiana Tech 84   Mississippi Val. 66-19
Louisiana Tech 84   Alcorn St. 44-21
Louisiana Tech 84   Middle Tenn. St. 21-13
Louisiana Tech 84   Montana St. 6-19

Sparky Woods (2-2) (Carson-Newman '76)
Appalachian St. 86   Nicholls St. 26-28
Appalachian St. 87   Richmond 20-3
Appalachian St. 87   Ga. Southern 19-0
Appalachian St. 87   Marshall 10-24

Dick Zornes (1-1) (Eastern Wash. '68)
Eastern Wash. 85   Idaho 42-38
Eastern Wash. 85   Northern Iowa 14-17

† *Tennessee State's participation voided.* % *Stephen F. Austin's participation voided.* * *National championship.*

WINNINGEST ACTIVE DIVISION II COACHES
Minimum five years as a college head coach; record at four-year colleges only.
BY PERCENTAGE

Coach, College	Years	Won	Lost	Tied	Pct.*
Rocky Hager, North Dak. St.	5	49	10	1	.825
Bob Cortese, Fort Hays St.	12	100	29	3	.769
Ken Sparks, Carson-Newman	12	111	34	1	.764
Bill Burgess, Jacksonville St.	7	57	21	3	.722
Pokey Allen, Portland St.	6	54	22	2	.705
Dick Lowry, Hillsdale	18	136	57	2	.703
Willard Bailey, Norfolk St.	21	155	65	5	.700
Gene Carpenter, Millersville	23	152	66	5	.693
Jim Malosky, Minn.-Duluth	34	218	99	11	.681
Rocky Rees, Shippensburg	7	51	24	1	.678
Tom Hollman, Edinboro	8	53	25	2	.675
Joe Taylor, Hampton	9	61	29	3	.672
Frank Cignetti, Indiana (Pa.)	10	79	39	0	.669
Bill Davis, Savannah St.	13	92	47	1	.661
Jerry Vandergriff, Angelo St.	10	72	37	1	.659
Jon Lantz, Mo. Southern St.	6	39	21	2	.645
Fred Martinelli, Ashland	33	200	114	12	.632

Coach, College	Years	Won	Lost	Tied	Pct.*
Ron Harms, Texas A&I	23	147	85	4	.631
Claire Boroff, Neb.-Kearney	20	122	71	4	.629
Jeff Geiser, Adams St.	8	50	30	1	.623
Carl Iverson, Western St.	8	53	33	1	.615
Dennis Creehan, South Dak.	7	43	27	1	.613
Dennis Douds, East Stroudsburg	18	109	72	2	.601
Stan McGarvey, Mo. Western St.	7	44	29	2	.600
Douglas Porter, Fort Valley St.	22	128	85	4	.599
Joe Glenn, Northern Colo.	7	42	29	1	.590
Jack Bishop, Southern Utah	11	65	46	3	.583
Brad Smith, Chadron St.	5	28	20	1	.582
Lyle Setenich, Cal Poly SLO	9	55	40	1	.578
Bob Burt, Cal St. Northridge	7	43	32	0	.573
Terry Malley, Santa Clara	7	43	32	1	.572
Bill Bless, Indianapolis	20	111	82	8	.572
George Ihler, Saginaw Valley	9	51	40	1	.560
Monte Cater, Shepherd	11	58	46	2	.557
Pete Adrian, Bloomsburg	6	35	28	1	.555
Hampton Smith, Albany St. (Ga.)	16	87	70	3	.553
Gary Howard, Central Okla.	15	82	66	5	.552
Alex Rotsko, American Int'l	9	48	40	3	.544
Jim Paronto, Mesa St.	6	33	28	0	.541
Noel Martin, St. Cloud St.	9	53	45	0	.541
Gene Sobolewski, Clarion	9	49	42	0	.533
Woody Fish, Gardner-Webb	8	46	41	1	.528
Bud Elliott, Northwest Mo. St.	24	128	117	7	.522
Mike DeLong, Springfield	10	49	45	2	.521
Terry Noland, Central Mo. St.	9	50	46	1	.521
James Martin, Tuskegee	8	40	37	1	.519
Mike Ayers, Wofford	7	40	37	1	.519
Bob Mattos, Cal St. Sacramento	14	76	71	2	.517
Larry Kramer, Emporia St.	23	106	99	8	.516
Eddie Vowell, East Tex. St.	6	34	34	1	.500

* Ties computed as half won, half lost; bowl and postseason games included.

BY VICTORIES
(Minimum 80 victories)

Coach, College, Winning Percentage	Won
Jim Malosky, Minn.-Duluth .681	218
Fred Martinelli, Ashland .632	200
Willard Bailey, Norfolk St. .700	155
Gene Carpenter, Millersville .693	152
Ron Harms, Texas A&I .631	147
Dick Lowry, Hillsdale .703	136
Douglas Porter, Fort Valley St. .599	128
Bud Elliott, Northwest Mo. St. .522	128
Claire Boroff, Neb.-Kearney .629	122
Ken Sparks, Carson-Newman .764	111

Coach, College, Winning Percentage	Won
Bill Bless, Indianapolis .572	111
Dennis Douds, East Stroudsburg .601	109
Larry Kramer, Emporia St. .516	106
Bob Cortese, Fort Hays St. .769	100
Bill Davis, Savannah St. .661	92
Hampton Smith, Albany St. (Ga.) .553	87
Gary Howard, Central Okla. .552	82

DIVISION II CHAMPIONSHIP COACHES

All coaches who have coached teams in the Division II championship playoffs since 1973 are listed below with their playoff record, alma mater and year graduated, team, year coached, opponent, and score.

Phil Albert (1-3) (Arizona '66)

Towson St.	83	North Dak. St. 17-24
Towson St.	84	Norfolk St. 31-21
Towson St.	84	Troy St. 3-45
Towson St.	86	Central St. (Ohio) 0-31

Pokey Allen (8-4) (Utah '65)

Portland St.	87	Mankato St. 27-21
Portland St.	87	Northern Mich. 13-7
Portland St.	87	Troy St. 17-31
Portland St.	88	Bowie St. 34-17
Portland St.	88	Jacksonville St. 20-13
Portland St.	88	Texas A&I 35-27
Portland St.	88	North Dak. St. 21-35
Portland St.	89	West Chester 56-50 (3 OT)

Portland St.	89	Indiana (Pa.) 0-17
Portland St.	91	Northern Colo. 28-24
Portland St.	91	Mankato St. 37-27
Portland St.	91	Pittsburg St. 21-53

Mike Ayers (0-2) (Georgetown, Ky. '74)

Wofford	90	Mississippi Col. 19-70
Wofford	91	Mississippi Col. 15-28

Willard Bailey (0-6) (Norfolk St. '84)

Virginia Union	79	Delaware 28-58
Virginia Union	80	North Ala. 8-17
Virginia Union	81	Shippensburg 27-40
Virginia Union	82	North Dak. St. 20-21
Virginia Union	83	North Ala. 14-16
Norfolk St.	84	Towson St. 21-31

Bob Bartolomeo (0-1) (Butler '77)

Butler	91	Pittsburg St. 16-26

Tom Beck (0-2) (Northern Ill. '61)

Grand Valley St.	89	Indiana (Pa.) 24-34
Grand Valley St.	90	East Tex. St. 14-20

Bob Blasi (0-1) (Colorado St. '53)

Northern Colo.	80	Eastern Ill. 14-21

Bill Bowes (1-2) (Penn St. '65)

New Hampshire	75	Lehigh 35-21
New Hampshire	75	Western Ky. 3-14
New Hampshire	76	Montana St. 16-17

Chuck Broyles (6-1) (Pittsburg St. '70)

Pittsburg St.	90	Northeast Mo. St. 59-3
Pittsburg St.	90	East Tex. St. 60-28
Pittsburg St.	90	North Dak. St. 29-39
Pittsburg St.	91	Butler 26-16
Pittsburg St.	91	East Tex. St. 38-28
Pittsburg St.	91	Portland St. 53-21
Pittsburg St.	91*	Jacksonville St. 23-6

Sandy Buda (1-2) (Kansas '67)

Nebraska-Omaha	78	Youngstown St. 14-21
Nebraska-Omaha	84	Northwest Mo. St. 28-15
Nebraska-Omaha	84	North Dak. St. 14-25

Bill Burgess (8-4) (Auburn '63)

Jacksonville St.	88	West Chester 63-24
Jacksonville St.	88	Portland St. 13-20
Jacksonville St.	89	Alabama A&M 33-9
Jacksonville St.	89	North Dak. St. 21-17
Jacksonville St.	89	Angelo St. 34-16
Jacksonville St.	89	Mississippi Col. 0-3
Jacksonville St.	90	North Ala. 38-14
Jacksonville St.	90	Mississippi Col. 7-14
Jacksonville St.	91	Winston-Salem 49-24
Jacksonville St.	91	Mississippi Col. 35-7
Jacksonville St.	91	Indiana (Pa.) 27-20
Jacksonville St.	91	Pittsburg St. 6-23

Bob Burt (0-1) (Cal St. Los Angeles '62)

Cal St. Northridge	90	Cal Poly SLO 7-14

Gene Carpenter (1-1) (Huron '63)

Millersville	88	Indiana (Pa.) 27-24
Millersville	88	North Dak. St. 26-36

Marino Casem (0-1) (Xavier, La. '56)

Alcorn St.	74	Nevada-Las Vegas 22-35

Frank Cignetti (7-5) (Indiana, Pa. '60)

Indiana (Pa.)	87	Central Fla. 10-12
Indiana (Pa.)	88	Millersville 24-27
Indiana (Pa.)	89	Grand Valley St. 34-24
Indiana (Pa.)	89	Portland St. 17-0
Indiana (Pa.)	89	Mississippi Col. 14-26
Indiana (Pa.)	90	Winston-Salem 48-0
Indiana (Pa.)	90	Edinboro 14-7
Indiana (Pa.)	90	Mississippi Col. 27-8
Indiana (Pa.)	90	North Dak. St. 11-51
Indiana (Pa.)	91	Virginia Union 56-7

Indiana (Pa.) 91   Shippensburg 52-7
Indiana (Pa.) 91   Jacksonville St. 20-27

Bruce Craddock (0-1) (Northeast Mo. St. '66)
Northeast Mo. St. 82   Jacksonville St. 21-34

Rick Daniels (0-1) (West Chester '75)
West Chester................89   Portland St. 50-56 (3 OT)

Rey Dempsey (0-1) (Geneva '58)
Youngstown St. 74   Delaware 14-35

Jim Dennison (2-1) (Wooster 60)
Akron 76   Nevada-Las Vegas 26-6
Akron 76   Northern Mich. 29-26
Akron 76   Montana St. 13-24

Dennis Douds (0-1) (Slippery Rock '63)
East Stroudsburg 91   Shippensburg 33-34

Fred Dunlap (3-2) (Colgate '50)
Lehigh 73   Western Ky. 16-25
Lehigh 75   New Hampshire 21-35
Lehigh 77   Massachusetts 30-23
Lehigh 77   UC Davis 39-30
Lehigh ....77*   Jacksonville St. 33-0

Bud Elliott (0-1) (Baker '53)
Northwest Mo. St. 89   Pittsburg St. 7-28

Jimmy Feix (4-2) (Western Ky. '53)
Western Ky. 73   Lehigh 25-16
Western Ky. 73   Grambling 28-20
Western Ky. 73   Louisiana Tech 0-34
Western Ky. 75   Northern Iowa 14-12
Western Ky. 75   New Hampshire 14-3
Western Ky. 75   Northern Mich. 14-16

Bob Foster (0-1) (UC Davis '62)
UC Davis....................89   Angelo St. 23-28

Dennis Franchione (1-1) (Pittsburg St. '73)
Pittsburg St.................89   Northwest Mo. St. 28-7
Pittsburg St.................89   Angelo St. 21-24

Fred Freeman (0-1) (Mississippi Val. '66)
Hampton 85   Bloomsburg 28-38

Jim Fuller (3-5) (Alabama '67)
Jacksonville St. 77   Northern Ariz. 35-0
Jacksonville St. 77   North Dak. St. 31-7
Jacksonville St. 77   Lehigh 0-33
Jacksonville St. 78   Delaware 27-42
Jacksonville St. 80   Cal Poly SLO 0-15
Jacksonville St. 81   Southwest Tex. St. 22-38
Jacksonville St. 82   Northeast Mo. St. 34-21
Jacksonville St. 82   Southwest Tex. St. 14-19

Chan Gailey (3-0) (Florida '74)
Troy St. 84   Central St. (Ohio) 31-21
Troy St. 84   Towson St. 45-3
Troy St. ....84*   North Dak. St. 18-17

Joe Glenn (0-2) (South Dak. '71)
Northern Colo...............90   North Dak. St. 7-17
Northern Colo...............91   Portland St. 24-28

Ray Greene (1-1) (Akron '63)
Alabama A&M 79   Morgan St. 27-7
Alabama A&M 79   Youngstown St. 0-52

John Gregory (0-1) (Northern Iowa '61)
South Dak. St. 79   Youngstown St. 7-50

Herb Grenke (1-1) (Wis.-Milwaukee '63)
Northern Mich...............87   Angelo St. 23-20 (OT)
Northern Mich...............87   Portland St. 7-13

Wayne Grubb (4-3) (Tennessee '61)
North Ala...................80   Virginia Union 17-8
North Ala...................80   Eastern Ill. 31-56
North Ala...................83   Virginia Union 16-14
North Ala...................83   Central St. (Ohio) 24-27
North Ala...................85   Fort Valley St. 14-7
North Ala...................85   Bloomsburg 34-0
North Ala...................85   North Dak. St. 7-35

Coaches' Records   435

North Dakota State coach Rocky Hager has the highest winning percentage (.825) among active Division II coaches with five or more years of experience, and he has more Division II playoff victories (nine) than any other coach.

Rocky Hager (9-2) (North Dak. St. '74)
North Dak. St.	88	Augustana (S.D.) 49-7
North Dak. St.	88	Millersville 36-26
North Dak. St.	88	Cal St. Sacramento 42-20
North Dak. St.	88*	Portland St. 35-21
North Dak. St.	89	Edinboro 45-32
North Dak. St.	89	Jacksonville St. 17-21
North Dak. St.	90	Northern Colo. 17-7
North Dak. St.	90	Cal Poly SLO 47-0
North Dak. St.	90	Pittsburg St. 39-29
North Dak. St.	90*	Indiana (Pa.) 51-11
North Dak. St.	91	Mankato St. 7-27

Danny Hale (0-1) (West Chester '68)
West Chester	88	Jacksonville St. 24-63

Ron Harms (2-2) (Valparaiso '59)
Texas A&I	88	Mississippi Col. 39-15
Texas A&I	88	Tenn.-Martin 34-0
Texas A&I	88	Portland St. 27-35
Texas A&I	89	Mississippi Col. 19-34

Joe Harper (3-1) (UCLA '59)
Cal Poly SLO	78	Winston-Salem 0-17
Cal Poly SLO	80	Jacksonville St. 15-0
Cal Poly SLO	80	Santa Clara 38-14
Cal Poly SLO	80*	Eastern Ill. 21-13

Bill Hayes (1-2) (N. C. Central '64)
Winston-Salem	78	Cal Poly SLO 17-0
Winston-Salem	78	Delaware 0-41
Winston-Salem	87	Troy St. 14-45

Jim Heinitz (0-2) (South Dak. St. '72)
Augustana (S. D.)	88	North Dak. St. 7-49
Augustana (S. D.)	89	St. Cloud St. 20-27

Andy Hinson (0-1) (Bethune-Cookman '53)
Bethune-Cookman	77	UC Davis 16-34

Sonny Holland (3-0) (Montana St. '60)
Montana St.	76	New Hampshire 17-16
Montana St.	76	North Dak. St. 10-3
Montana St.	76*	Akron 24-13

Tom Hollman (1-2) (Ohio Northern '68)
Edinboro	89	North Dak. St. 32-45
Edinboro	90	Virginia Union 38-14
Edinboro	90	Indiana (Pa.) 7-14

Eric Holm (0-1) (Northeast Mo. St. '81)
Northeast Mo. St.	90	Pittsburg St. 3-59

Billy Joe (3-4) (Cheyney '70)
Central St. (Ohio)	83	Southwest Tex. St. 24-16
Central St. (Ohio)	83	North Ala. 27-24
Central St. (Ohio)	83	North Dak. St. 21-41
Central St. (Ohio)	84	Troy St. 21-31
Central St. (Ohio)	85	South Dak. 10-13 (2 OT)
Central St. (Ohio)	86	Towson St. 31-0
Central St. (Ohio)	86	North Dak. St. 12-35

Brian Kelly (0-1) (Assumption '83)
Grand Valley St.	91	East Tex. St. 15-36

Roy Kidd (0-1) (Eastern Ky. '54)
Eastern Ky.	76	North Dak. St. 7-10

Jim King (1-1)
Livingston	75	North Dak. 34-14
Livingston	75	Northern Mich. 26-28

Tony Knap (1-4) (Idaho '39)
Boise St.	73	South Dak. 53-10
Boise St.	73	Louisiana Tech 34-38
Boise St.	74	Central Mich. 6-20
Boise St.	75	Northern Mich. 21-24
Nevada-Las Vegas	76	Akron 6-26

Roy Kramer (3-0) (Maryville, Tenn. '53)
Central Mich.	74	Boise St. 20-6
Central Mich.	74	Louisiana Tech 35-14
Central Mich.	74*	Delaware 54-14

Gil Krueger (4-2) (Marquette '52)
Northern Mich.	75	Boise St. 24-21
Northern Mich.	75	Livingston 28-26
Northern Mich.	75*	Western Ky. 16-14
Northern Mich.	76	Delaware 28-17
Northern Mich.	76	Akron 26-29
Northern Mich.	77	North Dak. St. 6-20

Maxie Lambright (4-1) (Southern Miss. '49)
Louisiana Tech	73	Western Ill. 18-13
Louisiana Tech	73	Boise St. 38-34
Louisiana Tech	73*	Western Ky. 34-0
Louisiana Tech	74	Western Caro. 10-7
Louisiana Tech	74	Central Mich. 14-35

George Landis (1-1) (Penn St. '71)
Bloomsburg	85	Hampton 38-28
Bloomsburg	85	North Ala. 0-34

Henry Lattimore (1-1) (Jackson St. '57)
N. C. Central	88	Winston-Salem 31-16
N. C. Central	88	Cal St. Sacramento 7-56

Bill Lynch (0-1) (Butler '77)
Butler	88	Tenn.-Martin 6-23

Dick MacPherson (0-1) (Springfield '58)
Massachusetts	77	Lehigh 23-30

Pat Malley (1-1) (Santa Clara '53)
Santa Clara	80	Northern Mich. 27-26
Santa Clara	80	Cal Poly SLO 14-38

Noel Martin (1-1) (Nebraska '63)
St. Cloud St.	89	Augustana (S.D.) 27-20
St. Cloud St.	89	Mississippi Col. 24-55

Fred Martinelli (0-1) (Otterbein '51)
Ashland	86	North Dak. St. 0-50

Bob Mattos (2-1) (Cal St. Sacramento '64)
Cal St. Sacramento	88	UC Davis 35-14
Cal St. Sacramento	88	N. C. Central 56-7

Cal St. Sacramento 88   North Dak. St. 20-42

Gene McDowell (1-1) (Florida St. '65)
Central Fla. 87   Indiana (Pa.) 12-10
Central Fla. 87   Troy St. 10-31

Don McLeary (1-1) (Tennessee '70)
Tenn.-Martin 88   Butler 23-6
Tenn.-Martin 88   Texas A&I 0-34

Terry McMillan (1-1) (Southern Miss. '69)
Mississippi Col. 91   Wofford 28-15
Mississippi Col. 91   Jacksonville St. 7-35

Ron Meyer (1-1) (Purdue '63)
Nevada-Las Vegas 74   Alcorn St. 35-22
Nevada-Las Vegas 74   Delaware 11-49

Don Morton (8-3) (Augustana, Ill. '69)
North Dak. St...............81   Puget Sound 24-10
North Dak. St...............81   Shippensburg 18-6
North Dak. St...............81   Southwest Tex. St. 13-42
North Dak. St...............82   Virginia Union 21-20
North Dak. St...............82   UC Davis 14-19
North Dak. St...............83   Towson St. 24-17
North Dak. St...............83   UC Davis 26-17
North Dak. St...............83*   Central St. (Ohio) 41-21
North Dak. St...............84   UC Davis 31-23
North Dak. St...............84   Nebraska-Omaha 25-14
North Dak. St...............84   Troy St. 17-18

Darrell Mudra (5-2) (Peru St. '51)
Western Ill. 73   Louisiana Tech 13-18
Eastern Ill...................78   UC Davis 35-31
Eastern Ill...................78   Youngstown St. 26-22
Eastern Ill...................78*   Delaware 10-9
Eastern Ill...................80   Northern Colo. 21-14
Eastern Ill...................80   North Ala. 56-31
Eastern Ill...................80   Cal Poly SLO 13-21

Gene Murphy (0-1) (North Dak. '62)
North Dak. 79   Mississippi Col. 15-35

Bill Narduzzi (3-2) (Miami, Ohio '59)
Youngstown St. 78   Nebraska-Omaha 21-14
Youngstown St. 78   Eastern Ill. 22-26
Youngstown St. 79   South Dak. St. 50-7
Youngstown St. 79   Alabama A&M 52-0
Youngstown St. 79   Delaware 21-38

John O'Hara (0-1) (Panhandle St. '67)
Southwest Tex. St. 83   Central St. (Ohio) 16-24

Jerry Olson (0-1) (Valley City St. '55)
North Dak. 75   Livingston 14-34

Doug Porter (0-1) (Xavier, La. '52)
Fort Valley St. 82   Southwest Tex. St. 6-27

George Pugh (0-1) (Alabama '76)
Alabama A&M 89   Jacksonville St. 9-33

Bill Rademacher (1-3) (Northern Mich. '63)
Northern Mich...............80   Santa Clara 26-27
Northern Mich...............81   Elizabeth City St. 55-6
Northern Mich...............81   Southwest Tex. St. 0-62
Northern Mich...............82   UC Davis 21-42

Vito Ragazzo (1-1) (William & Mary '51)
Shippensburg 81   Virginia Union 40-27
Shippensburg 81   North Dak. St. 6-18

Tubby Raymond (7-4) (Michigan '50)
Delaware 73   Grambling 8-17
Delaware 74   Youngstown St. 35-14
Delaware 74   Nevada-Las Vegas 49-11
Delaware 74   Central Mich. 14-54
Delaware 76   Northern Mich. 17-28
Delaware 78   Jacksonville St. 42-27
Delaware 78   Winston-Salem 41-0
Delaware 78   Eastern Ill. 9-10
Delaware 79   Virginia Union 58-28
Delaware 79   Mississippi Col. 60-10
Delaware ....79*   Youngstown St. 38-21

Rocky Rees (1-1) (West Chester '71)
Shippensburg 91   East Stroudsburg 34-33
Shippensburg 91   Indiana (Pa.) 7-52

Rick Rhodes (4-1)
Troy St. 86   Virginia Union 31-7
Troy St. 86   South Dak. 28-42
Troy St. 87   Winston-Salem 45-14
Troy St. 87   Central Fla. 31-10
Troy St. .... 87*   Portland St. 31-17

Pete Richardson (0-3) (Dayton '68)
Winston-Salem 88   N. C. Central 16-31
Winston-Salem 90   Indiana (Pa.) 0-48
Winston-Salem 91   Jacksonville St. 24-49

Eddie Robinson (1-1) (Leland '41)
Grambling 73   Delaware 17-8
Grambling 73   Western Ky. 20-28

Dan Runkle (1-2) (Illinois Col. '68)
Mankato St. 87   Portland St. 21-27
Mankato St. 91   North Dak. St. 27-7
Mankato St. 91   Portland St. 27-37

Joe Salem (0-2) (Minnesota '61)
South Dak. 73   Boise St. 10-53
Northern Ariz. 77   Jacksonville St. 0-35

Lyle Setencich (1-1) (Fresno St. '68)
Cal Poly SLO 90   Cal St. Northridge 14-7
Cal Poly SLO 90   North Dak. St. 0-47

Stan Sheriff (0-1) (Cal Poly SLO '54)
Northern Iowa 75   Western Ky. 12-14

Sanders Shiver (0-1) (Carson-Newman '76)
Bowie St. 88   Portland St. 17-34

Ron Simonson (0-1) (Portland St. '65)
Puget Sound 81   North Dak. St. 10-24

Jim Sochor (4-8) (San Fran. St. '60)
UC Davis 77   Bethune-Cookman 34-16
UC Davis 77   Lehigh 30-39
UC Davis 78   Eastern Ill. 31-35
UC Davis 82   Northern Mich. 42-21
UC Davis 82   North Dak. St. 19-14

UC Davis 82   Southwest Tex. St. 9-34
UC Davis 83   Butler 25-6
UC Davis 83   North Dak. St. 17-26
UC Davis 84   North Dak. St. 23-31
UC Davis 85   North Dak. St. 12-31

UC Davis 86   South Dak. 23-26
UC Davis 88   Cal St. Sacramento 14-35

Earle Solomonson (6-0) (Augsburg '69)
North Dak. St. 85   UC Davis 31-12
North Dak. St. 85   South Dak. 16-7
North Dak. St. .... 85*   North Ala. 35-7
North Dak. St. 86   Ashland 50-0
North Dak. St. 86   Central St. (Ohio) 35-12

North Dak. St. .... 86*   South Dak. 27-7

Bill Sylvester (0-1) (Butler '50)
Butler 83   UC Davis 6-25

Joe Taylor (0-3) (Western Ill. '72)
Virginia Union 86   Troy St. 7-31
Virginia Union 90   Edinboro 14-38
Virginia Union 91   Indiana (Pa.) 7-56

Clarence Thomas (0-1)
Morgan St. 79   Alabama A&M 7-27

Vern Thomsen (0-1) (Peru St. '61)
Northwest Mo. St. 84   Nebraska-Omaha 15-28

Dave Triplett (3-2) (Iowa '72)
South Dak. 85   Central St. (Ohio) 13-10 (2 OT)
South Dak. 85   North Dak. St. 7-16
South Dak. 86   UC Davis 26-23
South Dak. 86   Troy St. 42-28
South Dak. 86   North Dak. St. 7-27

Coaches' Records   439

Jerry Vandergriff (2-2) (Corpus Christi '65)

Angelo St.	87	Northern Mich. 20-23 (OT)
Angelo St.	89	UC Davis 28-23
Angelo St.	89	Pittsburg St. 24-21
Angelo St.	89	Jacksonville St. 16-34

Eddie Vowell (2-2) (Southwestern Okla. '69)

East Tex. St.	90	Grand Valley St. 20-14
East Tex. St.	90	Pittsburg St. 28-60
East Tex. St.	91	Grand Valley St. 36-15
East Tex. St.	91	Pittsburg St. 28-38

Jim Wacker (8-2) (Valparaiso '60)

North Dak. St.	76	Eastern Ky. 10-7
North Dak. St.	76	Montana St. 3-10
North Dak. St.	77	Northern Mich. 20-6
North Dak. St.	77	Jacksonville St. 7-31
Southwest Tex. St.	81	Jacksonville St. 38-22
Southwest Tex. St.	81	Northern Mich. 62-0
Southwest Tex. St.	81*	North Dak. St. 42-13
Southwest Tex. St.	82	Fort Valley St. 27-6
Southwest Tex. St.	82	Jacksonville St. 19-14
Southwest Tex. St.	82*	UC Davis 34-9

Gerald Walker (0-1) (Lincoln, Mo. '62)

Elizabeth City St.	85	North Ala. 7-14

Bobby Wallace (0-1) (Mississippi St. '76)

North Ala.	90	Jacksonville St. 14-38

Johnnie Walton (0-1) (Elizabeth City St. '69)

Elizabeth City St.	81	Northern Mich. 6-55

Bob Waters (0-1) (Presbyterian '60)

Western Caro.	74	Louisiana Tech 7-10

John Williams (7-3) (Mississippi Col. '57)

Mississippi Col.	79	North Dak. 35-15
Mississippi Col.	79	Delaware 10-60
Mississippi Col.	88	Texas A&I 15-39
Mississippi Col.	89	Texas A&I 34-19
Mississippi Col.	89	St. Cloud St. 55-24
Mississippi Col.	89	Indiana (Pa.) 26-14
Mississippi Col.	89*	Jacksonville St. 3-0
Mississippi Col.	90	Wofford 70-19
Mississippi Col.	90	Jacksonville St. 14-7
Mississippi Col.	90	Indiana (Pa.) 8-27

* National championship.

WINNINGEST ACTIVE DIVISION III COACHES

Minimum five years as a college head coach; record at four-year colleges only.

BY PERCENTAGE

Coach, College	Years	Won	Lost	Tied	Pct.*
Bob Reade, Augustana (Ill.)	13	125	16	1	.884
Dick Farley, Williams	5	33	6	1	.838
Mike Kelly, Dayton	11	109	21	1	.836
Lou Desloges, Plymouth St.	6	51	10	2	.825
Ron Schipper, Central (Iowa)	31	242	60	3	.798
Larry Kehres, Mount Union	6	48	12	3	.786
Bill Manlove, Delaware Valley	23	182	53	1	.773
Bob Packard, Baldwin-Wallace	11	85	25	2	.768
John Luckhardt, Wash. & Jeff.	10	75	22	2	.768
Roger Harring, Wis.-La Crosse	23	184	58	6	.754
Mike Clary, Rhodes	8	53	16	4	.753
Rich Lackner, Carnegie Mellon	6	44	14	2	.750
Rick Giancola, Montclair St.	9	71	23	2	.750
Jim Svoboda, Neb. Wesleyan	5	39	13	0	.750
Walt Hameline, Wagner	11	86	28	2	.750
John Gagliardi, St. John's (Minn.)	43	286	94	9	.747
Jim Butterfield, Ithaca	25	191	65	1	.745
Frank Girardi, Lycoming	20	142	50	4	.735
Carl Poelker, Millikin	10	67	24	1	.734
Dennis Scannell, Mass.-Lowell	6	41	15	0	.732
Tom Gilburg, Frank. & Marsh.	17	117	44	2	.724
Ron Roberts, Lawrence	19	119	47	1	.716
Tony DeCarlo, John Carroll	5	34	13	2	.714

Coach, College	Years	Won	Lost	Tied	Pct.*
Scot Dapp, Moravian	5	37	15	0	.712
Hank Norton, Ferrum	7	54	22	1	.708
Dale Widolff, Occidental	10	66	27	2	.705
Jim Christopherson, Concordia-M'head	23	162	67	5	.703
Pete Schmidt, Albion	9	56	23	4	.699
Nick Mourouzis, DePauw	11	75	32	2	.697
Jim Chapman, Mercyhurst	6	43	19	1	.690
Ed Sweeney, Dickinson	7	48	21	2	.690
Greg Carlson, Wabash	9	57	26	1	.685
Ray Smith, Hope	22	132	59	8	.683
Don Miller, Trinity (Conn.)	25	134	61	5	.683
Scott Duncan, Rose-Hulman	6	40	19	1	.675
C. Wayne Perry, Hanover	10	65	31	2	.673
Lou Wacker, Emory & Henry	10	71	35	0	.670
D. J. LeRoy, Coe	9	65	32	2	.667
Kelly Kane, Monmouth (Ill.)	8	50	25	0	.667
Jim Moretti, Alfred	7	46	23	2	.662
Eric Hamilton, Trenton St.	15	95	50	4	.651
Vic Wallace, St. Thomas (Minn.)	11	74	39	4	.650
Duane Ford, Tufts	7	35	19	2	.643
Jim Williams, Simpson	6	39	22	0	.639
Bob Berezowitz, Wis.-Whitewater	7	44	25	4	.630
Dennis Riccio, St. Lawrence	5	31	19	0	.620
Bob Ricca, St. John's (N.Y.)	14	86	54	1	.613
Mike McClinchey, Frostburg St.	10	61	38	4	.612
Craig Rundle, Colorado Col.	6	36	23	0	.610
Jim Scott, Aurora	6	30	19	1	.610
J. R. Bishop, Wheaton (Ill.)	10	54	35	1	.606
John Huard, Maine Maritime	10	53	35	0	.602
Joe Harper, Cal Lutheran	19	115	76	3	.601
Bob Bierie, Loras	12	73	48	4	.600
Thomas Bell, Coast Guard	17	89	59	6	.597
Don Canfield, St. Olaf	19	104	73	1	.587
Dick Tressel, Hamline	14	79	56	2	.584
Keith Piper, Denison	38	196	138	17	.583
Don La Violette, St. Norbert	9	49	35	1	.582
Barry Streeter, Gettysburg	14	81	58	4	.580
Steve Frank, Hamilton	7	32	23	1	.580
Rob Ash, Drake	12	68	49	3	.579
Joe McDaniel, Centre	26	135	98	4	.578
Joe Bush, Hampden-Sydney	7	39	29	1	.572
Jeff Heacock, Muskingum	11	60	45	2	.570
Don Ruggeri, Mass. Maritime	19	95	72	1	.568
Norm Eash, Ill. Wesleyan	5	25	19	1	.567
Sam Sanders, Buffalo	10	54	42	2	.561
George Chryst, Wis.-Platteville	13	73	57	2	.561
Mickey Heinecken, Middlebury	19	84	66	2	.559
Brien Cullen, Worcester St.	7	34	27	0	.557
Robert Ford, Albany (N.Y.)	23	120	96	1	.555
Bob Naslund, Luther	14	72	59	0	.550

* Ties computed as half won, half lost; bowl and postseason games included.

BY VICTORIES
(Minimum 100 victories)

Coach, College, Winning Percentage	Won	Coach, College, Winning Percentage	Won
John Gagliardi, St. John's (Minn.) .747	286	Ray Smith, Hope .683	132
Ron Schipper, Central (Iowa) .798	242	Bob Reade, Augustana (Ill.) .884	125
Keith Piper, Denison .583	196	Peter Mazzaferro, Bri'water (Mass.) .522	125
Jim Butterfield, Ithaca .745	191	Robert Ford, Albany (N.Y.) .555	120
Roger Harring, Wis.-La Crosse .754	184	Ron Roberts, Lawrence .716	119
Bill Manlove, Delaware Valley .773	182	Tom Gilburg, Frank. & Marsh. .724	117
Jim Christopherson, Con.-M'head .703	162	Joe Harper, Cal Lutheran .601	115
Frank Girardi, Lycoming .735	142	Mike Kelly, Dayton .836	109
Joe McDaniel, Centre .578	135	Don Canfield, St. Olaf .587	104
Don Miller, Trinity (Conn.) .683	134		

DIVISION III CHAMPIONSHIP COACHES

All coaches who have coached teams in the Division III championship playoffs since 1973 are listed below with their playoff record, alma mater and year graduated, team, year coached, opponent, and score.

Phil Albert (2-1) (Arizona '66)
Towson St.	76	LIU-C. W. Post 14-10
Towson St.	76	St. Lawrence 38-36
Towson St.	76	St. John's (Minn.) 28-31

Dom Anile (0-1) (LIU-C. W. Post '59)
LIU-C. W. Post	76	Towson St. 10-14

Don Ault (0-1) (West Liberty St. '52)
Bethany (W. Va.)	80	Widener 12-43

Al Bagnoli (7-6) (Central Conn. St. '74)
Union (N. Y.)	83	Hofstra 51-19
Union (N. Y.)	83	Salisbury St. 23-21
Union (N. Y.)	83	Augustana (Ill.) 17-21
Union (N. Y.)	84	Plymouth St. 26-14
Union (N. Y.)	84	Augustana (Ill.) 6-23
Union (N. Y.)	85	Ithaca 12-13
Union (N. Y.)	86	Ithaca 17-24 (OT)
Union (N. Y.)	89	Cortland St. 42-14
Union (N. Y.)	89	Montclair St. 45-6
Union (N. Y.)	89	Ferrum 37-21
Union (N. Y.)	89	Dayton 7-17
Union (N. Y.)	91	Mass.-Lowell 55-16
Union (N. Y.)	91	Ithaca 23-35

Bob Berezowitz (1-2) (Wis.-Whitewater '67)
Wis.-Whitewater	88	Simpson 29-27
Wis.-Whitewater	88	Central (Iowa) 13-16
Wis.-Whitewater	90	St. Thomas (Minn.) 23-24

Don Birmingham (0-2) (Westmar '62)
Dubuque	79	Ithaca 7-27
Dubuque	80	Minn.-Morris 35-41

Jim Blackburn (0-1) (Virginia '71)
Randolph-Macon	84	Wash. & Jeff. 21-22

Bill Bless (0-1) (Indianapolis '63)
Indianapolis	75	Wittenberg 13-17

Steve Briggs (2-1) (Springfield '84)
Susquehanna	91	Dickinson 21-20
Susquehanna	91	Lycoming 31-24
Susquehanna	91	Ithaca 13-49

John Bunting (0-1) (North Caro. '72)
Glassboro St.	91	Ithaca 10-31

Jim Butterfield (21-7) (Maine '53)
Ithaca	74	Slippery Rock 27-14
Ithaca	74	Central (Iowa) 8-10
Ithaca	75	Fort Valley St. 41-12
Ithaca	75	Widener 23-14
Ithaca	75	Wittenberg 0-28
Ithaca	78	Wittenberg 3-6
Ithaca	79	Dubuque 27-7
Ithaca	79	Carnegie Mellon 15-6
Ithaca	79*	Wittenberg 14-10
Ithaca	80	Wagner 41-13
Ithaca	80	Minn.-Morris 36-0
Ithaca	80	Dayton 0-63
Ithaca	85	Union (N. Y.) 13-12
Ithaca	85	Montclair St. 50-28
Ithaca	85	Gettysburg 34-0
Ithaca	85	Augustana (Ill.) 7-20
Ithaca	86	Union (N. Y.) 24-17 (OT)
Ithaca	86	Montclair St. 29-15
Ithaca	86	Salisbury St. 40-44
Ithaca	88	Wagner 34-31 (OT)
Ithaca	88	Cortland St. 24-17
Ithaca	88	Ferrum 62-28
Ithaca	88*	Central (Iowa) 39-24
Ithaca	90	Trenton St. 14-24
Ithaca	91	Glassboro St. 31-10

Ithaca 91	Union (N. Y.) 35-23
Ithaca 91	Susquehanna 49-13
Ithaca 91*	Dayton 34-20

Jim Byers (0-1) (Michigan '59)
| Evansville .... 74 | Central (Iowa) 16-17 |

Don Canfield (0-1)
| Wartburg .... 82 | Bishop 7-32 |

Jerry Carle (0-1) (Northwestern '48)
| Colorado Col. .... 75 | Millsaps 21-28 |

Gene Carpenter (0-1) (Huron '63)
| Millersville.................. 79 | Wittenberg 14-21 |

Rick Carter (3-1) (Earlham '65)
Dayton 78	Carnegie Mellon 21-24
Dayton 80	Baldwin-Wallace 34-0
Dayton 80	Widener 28-24
Dayton 80*	Ithaca 63-0

Don Charlton (0-1) (Lock Haven '65)
| Hiram .... 87 | Augustana (Ill.) 0-53 |

Jim Christopherson (2-2) (Concordia-M'head '60)
Concordia-M'head 86	Wis.-Stevens Point 24-15
Concordia-M'head 86	Central (Iowa) 17-14
Concordia-M'head 86	Augustana (Ill.) 7-41
Concordia-M'head 88	Central (Iowa) 0-7

Mike Clary (0-1) (Rhodes '77)
| Rhodes .... 88 | Ferrum 10-35 |

Jay Cottone (0-1) (Norwich '71)
| Plymouth St. .... 84 | Union (N. Y.) 14-26 |

Scot Dapp (1-1) (West Chester '73)
| Moravian .... 88 | Widener 17-7 |
| Moravian .... 88 | Ferrum 28-49 |

Harper Davis (1-1) (Mississippi St. '49)
| Millsaps .... 75 | Colorado Col. 28-21 |
| Millsaps .... 75 | Wittenberg 22-55 |

Tony DeCarlo (0-1) (Kent '62)
| John Carroll .... 89 | Dayton 10-35 |

Bob Di Spirito (0-1) (Rhode Island '53)
| Slippery Rock .... 74 | Ithaca 14-27 |

Ed Farrell (0-1) (Rutgers '56)
| Bridgeport .... 73 | Juniata 14-35 |

Bob Ford (1-1) (Springfield '59)
| Albany (N. Y.) .... 77 | Hampden-Sydney 51-45 |
| Albany (N. Y.) .... 77 | Widener 15-33 |

Stokeley Fulton (0-1) (Hampden-Sydney '55)
| Hampden-Sydney .... 77 | Albany (N. Y.) 45-51 |

John Gagliardi (8-5) (Colorado Col. '49)
St. John's (Minn.) 76	Augustana (Ill.) 46-7
St. John's (Minn.) 76	Buena Vista 61-0
St. John's (Minn.) 76*	Towson St. 31-28
St. John's (Minn.) 77	Wabash 9-20
St. John's (Minn.) 85	Occidental 10-28
St. John's (Minn.) 87	Gust. Adolphus 7-3
St. John's (Minn.) 87	Central (Iowa) 3-13
St. John's (Minn.) 89	Simpson 42-35
St. John's (Minn.) 89	Central (Iowa) 27-24
St. John's (Minn.) 89	Dayton 0-28
St. John's (Minn.) 91	Coe 75-2
St. John's (Minn.) 91	Wis.-La Crosse 29-10
St. John's (Minn.) 91	Dayton 7-19

Joe Gardi (2-1) (Maryland '60)
Hofstra 90	Cortland St. 35-9
Hofstra 90	Trenton St. 38-3
Hofstra 90	Lycoming 10-20

Rick Giancola (3-3) (Glassboro St. '68)
Montclair St. 85	Western Conn. St. 28-0
Montclair St. 85	Ithaca 28-50
Montclair St. 86	Hofstra 24-21
Montclair St. 86	Ithaca 15-29
Montclair St. 89	Hofstra 23-6
Montclair St. 89	Union (N. Y.) 6-45

Frank Girardi (5-4) (West Chester '61)
Lycoming	85	Gettysburg 10-14
Lycoming	89	Dickinson 21-0
Lycoming	89	Ferrum 24-49
Lycoming	90	Carnegie Mellon 17-7
Lycoming	90	Wash. & Jeff. 24-0
Lycoming	90	Hofstra 20-10
Lycoming	90	Allegheny 14-21 (OT)
Lycoming	91	Wash. & Jeff. 18-16
Lycoming	91	Susquehanna 24-31

Larry Glueck (1-1) (Villanova '63)
Fordham	87	Hofstra 41-6
Fordham	87	Wagner 0-21

Eric Hamilton (1-1) (Trenton St. '75)
Trenton St.	90	Ithaca 24-14
Trenton St.	90	Hofstra 3-38

Walt Hameline (4-2) (Brockport St. '75)
Wagner	82	St. Lawrence 34-43
Wagner	87	Rochester 38-14
Wagner	87	Fordham 21-0
Wagner	87	Emory & Henry 20-15
Wagner	87*	Dayton 19-3
Wagner	88	Ithaca 31-34 (OT)

Roger Harring (2-2) (Wis.-La Crosse '58)
Wis.-La Crosse	83	Occidental 43-42
Wis.-La Crosse	83	Augustana (Ill.) 15-21
Wis.-La Crosse	91	Simpson 28-13
Wis.-La Crosse	91	St. John's (Minn.) 10-29

Jim Hershberger (1-2) (Northern Iowa '57)
Buena Vista	76	Carroll (Wis.) 20-14 (OT)
Buena Vista	76	St. John's (Minn.) 0-61
Buena Vista	86	Central (Iowa) 0-37

Fred Hill (1-1) (Upsala '57)
Montclair St.	81	Alfred 13-12
Montclair St.	81	Widener 12-23

James Jones (1-1) (Bishop '49)
Bishop	82	Wartburg 32-7
Bishop	82	West Ga. 6-27

Frank Joranko (0-1) (Albion '52)
Albion	77	Minn.-Morris 10-13

Dennis Kayser (1-2) (Ithaca '74)
Cortland St.	88	Hofstra 32-27
Cortland St.	88	Ithaca 17-24
Cortland St.	89	Union (N. Y.) 14-42

Larry Kehres (1-2) (Mount Union '71)
Mount Union	86	Dayton 42-36
Mount Union	86	Augustana (Ill.) 7-16
Mount Union	90	Allegheny 15-26

Mike Kelly (13-7) (Manchester '70)
Dayton	81	Augustana (Ill.) 19-7
Dayton	81	Lawrence 38-0
Dayton	81	Widener 10-17
Dayton	84	Augustana (Ill.) 13-14
Dayton	86	Mount Union 36-42
Dayton	87	Capital 52-28
Dayton	87	Augustana (Ill.) 38-36
Dayton	87	Central (Iowa) 34-0
Dayton	87	Wagner 3-19
Dayton	88	Wittenberg 28-35 (2 OT)
Dayton	89	John Carroll 35-10
Dayton	89	Millikin 28-16
Dayton	89	St. John's (Minn.) 28-0
Dayton	89*	Union (N. Y.) 17-7
Dayton	90	Augustana (Ill.) 24-14
Dayton	90	Allegheny 23-31
Dayton	91	Baldwin-Wallace 27-10
Dayton	91	Allegheny 28-25 (OT)
Dayton	91	St. John's (Minn.) 19-7
Dayton	91	Ithaca 20-34

Chuck Klausing (2-4) (Slippery Rock '48)

Carnegie Mellon	78	Dayton 24-21
Carnegie Mellon	78	Baldwin-Wallace 6-31
Carnegie Mellon	79	Minn.-Morris 31-25
Carnegie Mellon	79	Ithaca 6-15
Carnegie Mellon	83	Salisbury St. 14-16
Carnegie Mellon	85	Salisbury St. 22-35

Mickey Kwiatkowski (0-5) (Delaware '70)

Hofstra	83	Union (N. Y.) 19-51
Hofstra	86	Montclair St. 21-24
Hofstra	87	Fordham 6-41
Hofstra	88	Cortland St. 27-32
Hofstra	89	Montclair St. 6-23

Ron Labadie (0-2) (Adrian '71)

Adrian	83	Augustana (Ill.) 21-22
Adrian	88	Augustana (Ill.) 7-25

Rich Lackner (0-1) (Carnegie Mellon '79)

Carnegie Mellon	90	Lycoming 7-17

Don LaViolette (0-1) (St. Norbert '54)

St. Norbert	89	Central (Iowa) 7-55

D. J. LeRoy (0-2)

Wis.-Stevens Point	86	Concordia-M'head 15-24
Coe	91	St. John's (Minn.) 2-75

Leon Lomax (0-1) (Fort Valley St. '43)

Fort Valley St.	75	Ithaca 12-41

John Luckhardt (3-6) (Purdue '67)

Wash. & Jeff.	84	Randolph-Macon 22-21
Wash. & Jeff.	84	Central (Iowa) 0-20
Wash. & Jeff.	86	Susquehanna 20-28
Wash. & Jeff.	87	Allegheny 23-17 (OT)
Wash. & Jeff.	87	Emory & Henry 16-23
Wash. & Jeff.	89	Ferrum 7-41
Wash. & Jeff.	90	Ferrum 10-7
Wash. & Jeff.	90	Lycoming 0-24
Wash. & Jeff.	91	Lycoming 16-18

Bill Manlove (9-5) (Temple '58)

Widener	75	Albright 14-6
Widener	75	Ithaca 14-23
Widener	77	Central (Iowa) 19-0
Widener	77	Albany (N. Y.) 33-15
Widener	77*	Wabash 39-36
Widener	79	Baldwin-Wallace 29-8
Widener	79	Wittenberg 14-17
Widener	80	Bethany (W. Va.) 43-12
Widener	80	Dayton 24-28
Widener	81	West Ga. 10-3
Widener	81	Montclair St. 23-12
Widener	81*	Dayton 17-10
Widener	82	West Ga. 24-31 (3 OT)
Widener	88	Moravian 7-17

Dave Maurer (9-2) (Denison '54)

Wittenberg	73	San Diego 21-14
Wittenberg	73*	Juniata 41-0
Wittenberg	75	Indianapolis 17-13
Wittenberg	75	Millsaps 55-22
Wittenberg	75*	Ithaca 28-0
Wittenberg	78	Ithaca 6-3
Wittenberg	78	Minn.-Morris 35-14
Wittenberg	78	Baldwin-Wallace 10-24
Wittenberg	79	Millersville 21-14
Wittenberg	79	Widener 17-14
Wittenberg	79	Ithaca 10-14

Mike Maynard (0-1) (Ill. Wesleyan '80)

Redlands	90	Central (Iowa) 14-24

Mike McGlinchey (5-3)

Salisbury St.	83	Carnegie Mellon 16-14
Salisbury St.	83	Union (N. Y.) 21-23
Salisbury St.	85	Carnegie Mellon 35-22
Salisbury St.	85	Gettysburg 6-22
Salisbury St.	86	Emory & Henry 34-20

Salisbury St. 86   Susquehanna 31-17
Salisbury St. 86   Ithaca 44-40
Salisbury St. 86   Augustana (III.) 3-31

Steve Miller (0-1) (Cornell College '65)
Carroll (Wis.) 76   Buena Vista 14-20 (OT)

Al Molde (2-3) (Gust. Adolphus '66)
Minn.-Morris 77   Albion 13-10
Minn.-Morris 77   Wabash 21-37
Minn.-Morris 78   St. Olaf 23-10
Minn.-Morris 78   Wittenberg 14-35
Minn.-Morris 79   Carnegie Mellon 25-31

Ron Murphy (1-1)
Wittenberg 88   Dayton 35-28 (2 OT)
Wittenberg 88   Augustana (III.) 14-28

Dave Murray (0-1) (Springfield '81)
Cortland St. 90   Hofstra 9-35

Walt Nadzak (1-1) (Denison '57)
Juniata 73   Bridgeport 35-14
Juniata 73   Wittenberg 0-41

Frank Navarro (2-1)
Wabash 77   St. John's (Minn.) 20-9
Wabash 77   Minn.-Morris 37-21
Wabash 77   Widener 36-39

Ben Newcomb (0-1)
Augustana (III.) 76   St. John's (Minn.) 7-46

Hank Norton (4-4) (Lynchburg '51)
Ferrum 87   Emory & Henry 7-49
Ferrum 88   Rhodes 35-10
Ferrum 88   Moravian 49-28
Ferrum 88   Ithaca 28-62
Ferrum 89   Wash. & Jeff. 41-7
Ferrum 89   Lycoming 49-24
Ferrum 89   Union (N. Y.) 21-37
Ferrum 90   Wash. & Jeff. 7-10

Ken O'Keefe (5-1) (John Carroll '75)
Allegheny 90   Mount Union 26-15
Allegheny 90   Dayton 31-23
Allegheny 90   Central (Iowa) 24-7
Allegheny . . . . 90*   Lycoming 21-14 (OT)
Allegheny 91   Albion 24-21 (OT)
Allegheny 91   Dayton 25-28 (OT)

Bob Packard (0-2) (Baldwin-Wallace '65)
Baldwin-Wallace 82   Augustana (III.) 22-28
Baldwin-Wallace 91   Dayton 10-27

Paul Pasqualoni (0-1) (Penn St. '72)
Western Conn. St. 85   Montclair St. 0-28

Bobby Pate (3-1) (Georgia '63)
West Ga. 81   Widener 3-10
West Ga. 82   Widener 31-24 (3 OT)
West Ga. 82   Bishop 27-6
West Ga. . . . . 82*   Augustana (III.) 14-0

Keith Piper (0-1) (Baldwin-Wallace '48)
Denison 85   Mount Union 3-35

Carl Poelker (1-1) (Millikin '68)
Millikin 89   Augustana (III.) 21-12
Millikin 89   Dayton 16-28

Tom Porter (0-1) (St. Olaf '51)
St. Olaf 78   Minn.-Morris 10-23

John Potsklan (0-2) (Penn St. '49)
Albright 75   Widener 6-14
Albright 76   St. Lawrence 7-26

Steve Raarup (0-1) (Gust. Adolphus '53)
Gust. Adolphus 87   St. John's (Minn.) 3-7

Bob Reade (19-6) (Cornell College '54)
Augustana (III.) 81   Dayton 7-19
Augustana (III.) 82   Baldwin-Wallace 28-22
Augustana (III.) 82   St. Lawrence 14-0
Augustana (III.) 82   West Ga. 0-14
Augustana (III.) 83   Adrian 22-21

Augustana (Ill.). . . . . .83 Wis.-La Crosse 21-15
Augustana (Ill.). . . . . .83* Union (N. Y.) 21-17
Augustana (Ill.). . . . . .84 Dayton 14-13
Augustana (Ill.). . . . . .84 Union (N. Y.) 23-6
Augustana (Ill.). . . . . .84* Central (Iowa) 21-12
Augustana (Ill.). . . . . .85 Albion 26-10
Augustana (Ill.). . . . . .85 Mount Union 21-14
Augustana (Ill.). . . . . .85 Central (Iowa) 14-7
Augustana (Ill.). . . . . .85* Ithaca 20-7
Augustana (Ill.). . . . . .86 Hope 34-10
Augustana (Ill.). . . . . .86 Mount Union 16-7
Augustana (Ill.). . . . . .86 Concordia-M'head 41-7
Augustana (Ill.). . . . . .86* Salisbury St. 31-3
Augustana (Ill.). . . . . .87 Hiram 53-0
Augustana (Ill.). . . . . .87 Dayton 36-38
Augustana (Ill.). . . . . .88 Adrian 25-7
Augustana (Ill.). . . . . .88 Wittenberg 28-14
Augustana (Ill.). . . . . .88 Central (Iowa) 17-23 (2 OT)
Augustana (Ill.). . . . . .89 Millikin 12-21
Augustana (Ill.). . . . . .90 Dayton 14-24

Rocky Rees (1-1) (West Chester '71)
Susquehanna . . . . .86 Wash. & Jeff. 28-20
Susquehanna . . . . .86 Salisbury St. 17-31

Ron Roberts (1-1) (Wisconsin '54)
Lawrence . . . . .81 Minn.-Morris 21-14 (OT)
Lawrence . . . . .81 Dayton 0-38

Bill Russo (0-1)
Wagner . . . . .80 Ithaca 13-41

Sam Sanders (0-1) (Buffalo '60)
Alfred .81 Montclair St. 12-13

Dennis Scannell (0-1) (Villanova '74)
Mass.-Lowell . . . . .91 Union (N. Y.) 16-55

Ron Schipper (15-8) (Hope '52)
Central (Iowa). . . . . .74 Evansville 17-16
Central (Iowa). . . . . .74* Ithaca 10-8
Central (Iowa). . . . . .77 Widener 0-19
Central (Iowa). . . . . .84 Occidental 23-22
Central (Iowa). . . . . .84 Wash. & Jeff. 20-0
Central (Iowa). . . . . .84 Augustana (Ill.) 12-21
Central (Iowa). . . . . .85 Coe 27-7
Central (Iowa). . . . . .85 Occidental 71-0
Central (Iowa). . . . . .85 Augustana (Ill.) 7-14
Central (Iowa). . . . . .86 Buena Vista 37-0
Central (Iowa). . . . . .86 Concordia-M'head 14-17
Central (Iowa). . . . . .87 Menlo 17-0
Central (Iowa). . . . . .87 St. John's (Minn.) 13-3
Central (Iowa). . . . . .87 Dayton 0-34
Central (Iowa). . . . . .88 Concordia-M'head 7-0
Central (Iowa). . . . . .88 Wis.-Whitewater 16-13
Central (Iowa). . . . . .88 Augustana (Ill.) 23-17 (2 OT)
Central (Iowa). . . . . .88 Ithaca 24-39
Central (Iowa). . . . . .89 St. Norbert 55-7
Central (Iowa). . . . . .89 St. John's (Minn.) 24-27
Central (Iowa). . . . . .90 Redlands 24-14
Central (Iowa). . . . . .90 St. Thomas (Minn.) 33-32
Central (Iowa). . . . . .90 Allegheny 7-24

Pete Schmidt (0-2) (Alma '70)
Albion .85 Augustana (Ill.) 10-26
Albion .91 Allegheny 21-24 (OT)

Dick Smith (1-2) (Coe '68)
Minn.-Morris . . . . .80 Dubuque 41-35
Minn.-Morris . . . . .80 Ithaca 0-36
Minn.-Morris . . . . .81 Lawrence 14-21 (OT)

Ray Smith (0-1) (UCLA '61)
Hope . . . . .86 Augustana (Ill.) 10-34

Ray Solari (0-1) (California '51)
Menlo .87 Central (Iowa) 0-17

Ted Stratford (1-2) (St. Lawrence '57)
St. Lawrence . . . . .76 Albright 26-7
St. Lawrence . . . . .76 Towson St. 36-38

St. Lawrence 78   Baldwin-Wallace 7-71

Barry Streeter (2-1) (Lebanon Valley '71)
Gettysburg 85   Lycoming 14-10
Gettysburg 85   Salisbury St. 22-6
Gettysburg 85   Ithaca 0-34

Ed Sweeney (0-2) (LIU-C. W. Post '71)
Dickinson 89   Lycoming 0-21
Dickinson 91   Susquehanna 20-21

Andy Talley (1-1) (Southern Conn. St. '67)
St. Lawrence 82   Wagner 43-34
St. Lawrence 82   Augustana (Ill.) 0-14

Ray Tellier (0-1) (Connecticut '73)
Rochester 87   Wagner 14-38

Bob Thurness (0-1) (Coe '62)
Coe 85   Central (Iowa) 7-27

Lee Tressel (3-2) (Baldwin-Wallace '48)
Baldwin-Wallace 78   St. Lawrence 71-7
Baldwin-Wallace 78   Carnegie Mellon 31-6
Baldwin-Wallace . . . . 78*   Wittenberg 24-10
Baldwin-Wallace 79   Widener 8-29
Baldwin-Wallace 80   Dayton 0-34

Peter Vaas (0-1) (Holy Cross '74)
Allegheny 87   Wash. & Jeff. 17-23 (OT)

Andy Vinci (0-1) (Cal St. Los Angeles '63)
San Diego 73   Wittenberg 14-21

Ken Wable (1-1) (Muskingum '52)
Mount Union 85   Denison 35-3
Mount Union 85   Augustana (Ill.) 14-21

Lou Wacker (2-2) (Richmond '56)
Emory & Henry 86   Salisbury St. 20-34
Emory & Henry 87   Ferrum 49-7
Emory & Henry 87   Wash. & Jeff. 23-16
Emory & Henry 87   Wagner 15-20

Vic Wallace (1-1) (Cornell College '65)
St. Thomas (Minn.) 90   Wis.-Whitewater 24-23
St. Thomas (Minn.) 90   Central (Iowa) 32-33

Roger Welsh (0-1) (Muskingum '64)
Capital 87   Dayton 28-52

Dale Widolff (1-3) (Indiana Central '75)
Occidental 83   Wis.-La Crosse 42-43
Occidental 84   Central (Iowa) 22-23
Occidental 85   St. John's (Minn.) 28-10
Occidental 85   Central (Iowa) 0-71

Jim Williams (0-3) (Northern Iowa '60)
Simpson 88   Wis.-Whitewater 27-29
Simpson 89   St. John's (Minn.) 35-42
Simpson 91   Wis.-La Crosse 13-28

* *National championship.*

COACH OF THE YEAR AWARDS
(Selected by the American Football Coaches Association)
COLLEGE DIVISION

1960	Warren Woodson, New Mexico St.	1972	Harold "Tubby" Raymond, Delaware
1961	Jake Gaither, Florida A&M	1973	Dave Maurer, Wittenberg
1962	Bill Edwards, Wittenberg	1974	Roy Kramer, Central Mich.
1963	Bill Edwards, Wittenberg	1975	Dave Maurer, Wittenberg
1964	Clarence Stasavich, East Caro.	1976	Jim Dennison, Akron
1965	Jack Curtice, UC Santa Barb.	1977	Bill Manlove, Widener
1966	Dan Jessee, Trinity (Conn.)	1978	Lee Tressel, Baldwin-Wallace
1967	A. C. "Scrappy" Moore, Tenn.-Chatt.	1979	Bill Narduzzi, Youngstown St.
1968	Jim Root, New Hampshire	1980	Rick Carter, Dayton
1969	Larry Naviaux, Boston U.	1981	Vito Ragazzo, Shippensburg
1970	Bennie Ellender, Arkansas St.	1982	Jim Wacker, Southwest Tex. St.
1971	Harold "Tubby" Raymond, Delaware		

COLLEGE DIVISION I
(NCAA Division II and NAIA Division I)

1983	Don Morton, North Dak. St.
1984	Chan Gailey, Troy St.
1985	George Landis, Bloomsburg
1986	Earle Solomonson, North Dak. St.
1987	Rick Rhoades, Troy St.
1988	Rocky Hager, North Dak. St.
1989	John Williams, Mississippi Col.
1990	Rocky Hager, North Dak. St.
1991	Frank Cignetti, Indiana (Pa.)

COLLEGE DIVISION II
(NCAA Division III and NAIA Division II)

1983	Bob Reade, Augustana (Ill.)
1984	Bob Reade, Augustana (Ill.)
1985	Bob Reade, Augustana (Ill.)
1986	Bob Reade, Augustana (Ill.)
1987	Walt Hameline, Wagner
1988	Jim Butterfield, Ithaca
1989	Mike Kelly, Dayton
1990	Ken O'Keefe, Allegheny
1991	Mike Kelly, Dayton

ADDED OR RESUMED PROGRAMS

Behind a swarming defense that allowed the fewest points in Division I-AA (12 per game) and was second in total defense (241.2 yards per game), Villanova advanced to the Division I-AA playoffs in 1991 for the second time since the school resumed its football program in 1985.

NATIONALLY PROMINENT TEAMS THAT PERMANENTLY DROPPED FOOTBALL

Listed alphabetically below are the all-time records of teams formerly classified as major college that permanently discontinued football. Also included are those teams that, retroactively, are considered to have been major college (before the advent of official classification in 1937) by virtue of their schedules (i.e., at least half of their games versus other major-college opponents).

All schools listed were classified as major college, or considered to have been, for a minimum of 10 consecutive seasons.

Team	Inclusive Seasons	Years	Won	Lost	Tied	Pct.†
Carlisle Indian School	1893-1917	25	167	88	13	.647
Centenary	1894-1947	36	148	100	21	.589
Creighton	1900-1942	43	183	139	27	.563
Denver	1885-1960	73	273	262	40	.510
Detroit Mercy	1896-1964	64	305	200	25	.599
Geo. Washington	1890-1966	58	209	240	34	.468
Gonzaga	1892-1941	39	130	99	20	.562
Haskell Institute	1896-1938	43	199	166	18	.543
Lamar	1951-1989	39	171	225	9	.433
Long Beach St.	1955-1991	37	199	183	4	.521
Manhattan	1923-1942	20	77	75	11	.506
Marquette	1892-1960	68	273	220	38	.550
New York U.	1873-1952	66	201	231	32	.468
San Francisco	*1924-1951; 1959-1971	38	133	169	20	.444
St. Louis	1899-1949	49	235	179	33	.563
Texas-Arlington	1859-1985	27	129	150	2	.463
Wichita St.	1897-1986	89	375	402	47	.484
Xavier (Ohio)	1900-1973	61	302	223	21	.572

† *Ties computed as half won and half lost.*

* *Discontinued football during 1952 after having been classified major college. Resumed at the Division II level during 1959-71, when it was discontinued again.*

SENIOR COLLEGES THAT HAVE ADDED OR RESUMED VARSITY FOOTBALL SINCE 1968

NCAA MEMBER COLLEGES

1968 (4)
Boise St.; *Chicago; Jersey City St.; Nevada-Las Vegas.

1969 (2)
*Adelphi; Towson St.

1970 (6)
Cal St. Fullerton; *Fordham; *Georgetown; Plattsburgh St. (dropped 1979); Plymouth St.; *St. Mary's (Cal.).

1971 (6)
Boston St. (dropped 1982); D.C. Teachers; Federal City; *New England Col. (dropped 1973); Rochester Tech; St. Peter's (suspended after one game 1984, resumed 1985).

1972 (6)
Kean; *Lake Forest; Nicholls St.; Salisbury St.; *San Diego; Wm. Paterson.

1973 (7)
Albany St. (N.Y.); *Benedictine; Bowie St.; James Madison; New Haven; New York Tech (dropped 1984); Seton Hall (dropped 1982).

1974 (2)
FDU-Madison; Framingham St.

1975 (2)
*Brooklyn (dropped 1991); *Canisius.

1976 (1)
Oswego St. (dropped 1977).

1977 (2)
*Catholic; *Mankato St.

1978 (7)
*Buffalo; Dist. Columbia; Iona; Marist; Pace; *St. Francis (Pa.); *St. John's (N.Y.).

1979 (2)
Central Fla.; *Duquesne.

1980 (5)
*Loras; Lowell; *Miles; Ramapo; *Sonoma St.

1981 (4)
Buffalo St.; Mercyhurst; *West Ga.; Western New Eng.

1982 (2)
Valdosta St.; Westfield St.

1983 (2)
*Ky. Wesleyan; Stony Brook.

1984 (3)
Fitchburg St.; *Ga. Southern; *Samford.

1985 (6)
Ferrum; MacMurray; N.Y. Maritime; *St. Peter's; *Villanova; Worcester St.

1986 (4)
Menlo; *Quincy; *UC Santa Barb.; Wesley.

1987 (5)
*Aurora; *Drake; *N.Y. Maritime; *Quincy; St. John Fisher.

1988 (7)
Assumption; Bentley; Mass.-Boston; *MIT (last team was in 1901); Siena; Southeastern Mass.; Stonehill.

1989 (5)
*Gannon; Merrimack; Methodist; *Southern Methodist; *St. Peter's.

1990 (3)
*Hardin-Simmons; *Miles; Thomas More.
* *Previously dropped football.*

1991 (3)
Ala.-Birmingham; Charleston So.; Sacred Heart.

1992 (1)
*West Tex. St.

NON-NCAA COLLEGES

1968 (1)
Southwest St. (Minn.).

1969 (None)

1970 (1)
Mo. Western St.

1971 (4)
Concordia-St. Paul (Minn.); Gardner-Webb; Grand Valley St.; Mo. Southern St.

1972 (5)
Dr. Martin Luther; Mars Hill; Northwestern (Minn.); Pillsbury; Western Conn.

1973 (2)
Liberty; Mass. Maritime.

1974 (3)
*N.M. Highlands; Northeastern Ill. (dropped 1988); Saginaw Valley.

1975 (None)

1976 (2)
Maranatha; Mesa St.

1977 (2)
Evangel; Olivet Nazarene.

1978 (3)
*Baptist Christian (dropped 1983); *St. Ambrose; *Yankton (dropped 1984).

1979 (2)
Fort Lauderdale (dropped 1982); Lubbock Christian (dropped 1983).

1980 (1)
Mid-America Nazarene.

1981 (None)

1982 (None)

1983 (2)
Ga. Southwestern; Loras.

1984 (3)
Southwest Baptist; St. Paul Bible; *Union (Ky.).

1985 (4)
*Cumberland (Ky.); *Lambuth; *Tenn. Wesleyan; Tiffin.

1986 (3)
Trinity Bible (N.D.); Urbana; Wingate.

1987 (1)
Greenville.

1988 (5)
Campbellsville; Mary; Midwestern St.; Trinity (Ill.); *Western Mont.

1989 (None)

1990 (1)
Mt. St. Joseph (Ohio).

1991 (None)
* *Previously dropped football.*

SENIOR COLLEGES THAT DISCONTINUED FOOTBALL SINCE 1950

(Includes NCAA member colleges and nonmember colleges; also colleges that closed or merged with other institutions.)

1950 (9)
Alliance; Canisius (resumed 1975); Huntington; Oklahoma City; *Portland; Rio Grande; Rollins; *St. Louis; Steubenville.

1951 (38)
Arkansas Col.; Atlantic Christian; Canterbury; Catholic (resumed 1977); CCNY; Corpus Christi (resumed 1954, dropped 1967); Daniel Baker; Detroit Tech; *Duquesne; East Tex. Baptist; Gannon; *Georgetown (resumed 1970); Glassboro St. (resumed 1964); Hartwick; High Point; LeMoyne-Owen; Lowell Textile; Lycoming (resumed 1954); McKendree; Milligan; Mt. St. Mary's (Md.); Nevada (resumed 1952); New Bedford Textile; New England Col. (resumed 1971, dropped 1973); Niagara; Northern Idaho; Panzer; Shurtleff (resumed 1953, dropped 1954); Southern Idaho; Southwestern (Tenn.) (resumed 1952—name changed to Rhodes in 1986); Southwestern (Tex.); St. Mary's (Cal.) (resumed 1970); St. Michael's (N.M.); Tillotson; Tusculum; Washington (Md.); West Va. Wesleyan (resumed 1953); William Penn (resumed 1953).

1952 (13)
Aquinas; Clarkson; Erskine; Louisville Municipal; *Loyola (Cal.); Nebraska Central; Rider; Samuel Huston; *San Francisco (resumed 1959, dropped 1972); Shaw (resumed 1953, dropped 1979); St. Bonaventure; St. Martin's; Westmar (resumed 1953).

1953 (10)
Arnold; Aurora; Bethel (Tenn.); Cedarville; Champlain; Davis & Elkins (resumed 1955, dropped 1962); Georgetown (Ky.) (resumed 1955); *New York U.; *Santa Clara (resumed 1959); Union (Tenn.).

1954 (8)
Adelphi (resumed 1969, dropped 1972); Case Tech (resumed 1955); Quincy (resumed 1986); Shurtleff; St. Francis (Pa.) (resumed 1978); St. Michael's (Vt.); *Wash. & Lee (resumed 1955); York (Neb.).

1955 (2)
*Fordham (resumed 1970); St. Mary's (Minn.).

1956 (4)
Brooklyn (resumed 1975, dropped 1991); Hendrix (resumed 1957, dropped 1961); William Carey; Wisconsin Extension.

1957 (4)
Lewis; Midwestern (Iowa) (resumed 1966); Morris Harvey; Stetson.

1958 (None)

1959 (2)
Florida N&I; West Ga. (resumed 1981).

1960 (5)
Brandeis; Leland; Loras (resumed 1980); St. Ambrose (resumed 1978); Xavier (La.).

1961 (9)
*Denver; Hawaii (resumed 1962); Hendrix; Lincoln (Pa.); *Marquette; Paul Quinn; Scranton; Texas College; Tougaloo.

1962 (5)
Azusa (resumed 1965); Davis & Elkins; San Diego (resumed 1972); Southern Cal Col.; Westminster (Utah) (resumed 1965, dropped 1979).

1963 (3)
Benedictine (resumed 1973); *Hardin-Simmons (resumed 1990); St. Vincent's (Pa.).

1964 (2)
King's (Pa.); Paine.

1965 (7)
Claflin; *Detroit Mercy; Dillard; Miss. Industrial; Morris; Philander Smith; Rust.

1966 (1)
St. Augustine's.

1967 (6)
Benedict; Col. of Ozarks; Corpus Christi; *Geo. Washington; Jarvis Christian; South Caro. Trade.

1968 (2)
Edward Waters; Frederick.

1969 (7)
Allen; Case Tech and Western Reserve merged to form Case Western Reserve; George Fox; Louisiana Col.; UC San Diego; Wiley.

1970 (None)

1971 (5)
Bradley; *Buffalo (resumed 1978); Hiram Scott; Lake Forest (resumed 1972); Parsons.

1972 (8)
Adelphi; Haverford; North Dak.-Ellendale; Northern Montana; Northwood (Tex.); San Francisco; Sonoma St. (resumed 1980); UC Santa Barb. (resumed 1986).

1973 (2)
New England Col.; N.M. Highlands (resumed 1974).

1974 (6)
Col. of Emporia; D.C. Teachers; Drexel; Ill.-Chicago; Samford (resumed 1984); *Xavier (Ohio).

1975 (6)
Baptist Christian (resumed 1978, dropped 1983); Bridgeport; Federal City; *Tampa; Vermont; Wis.-Milwaukee.

1976 (3)
Mankato St. (resumed 1977); Northland; UC Riverside.

1977 (4)
Cal Tech; Oswego St.; Whitman; Yankton (resumed 1978, dropped 1984).

1978 (3)
Cal St. Los Angeles; Col. of Idaho; Rochester Tech.

1979 (5)
Eastern Montana; Miles (resumed 1980); Plattsburgh St.; Shaw; Westminster (Utah).

1980 (3)
†Gallaudet; Md.-East. Shore; U.S. Int'l.

1981 (2)
Bluefield St.; *Villanova (resumed 1985).

1982 (4)
Boston St.; Fort Lauderdale; Milton; Seton Hall.

1983 (3)
Baptist Christian; Cal Poly Pomona; Lubbock Christian.

1984 (5)
Fisk; New York Tech; So. Dak.-Springfield; St. Peter's (suspended after one game, resumed 1985); Yankton.

1985 (1)
Southern Colo.

1986 (4)
Drake (resumed 1987); N.Y. Maritime (resumed 1987, dropped 1989); Southeastern La.; *Texas-Arlington.

1987 (4)
Bishop; *Southern Methodist (resumed 1989); Western Mont. (resumed 1988); *Wichita St.

1988 (4)
Northeastern Ill.; St. Paul's; St. Peter's (resumed 1989); Texas Lutheran.

1989 (3)
Ga. Southwestern; Miles (resumed 1990); N.Y. Maritime.

1990 (1)
*Lamar.

1991 (2)
Brooklyn; West Tex. St. (resumed 1992).

1992 (1)
Long Beach St.

* Classified major college previous year.
† Did not play a 7-game varsity schedule, 1980-86.

Youngstown State nose tackle Pat Danko shows off the 1991 Division I-AA Football Championship trophy after the Penguins defeated Marshall, 25-17, to claim their first title in four playoff appearances.

1991 DIVISION I-AA CHAMPIONSHIP

PAULSON STADIUM, STATESBORO, GEORGIA; DECEMBER 21, 1991

	Youngstown St.	Marshall
First Downs	16	22
Rushes-Net Yardage	50-121	30-49
Passing Yardage	198	363
Return Yardage (Punts, Int. & Fum.)	36	8
Passes (Comp.-Att.-Int.)	9-15-0	30-43-2
Punts (Number-Average)	3-31.3	2-13.5
Fumbles (Number-Lost)	2-1	3-1
Penalties (Number-Yards)	5-30	7-61

Youngstown St.	0	3	3	19—25
Marshall	0	0	17	0—17

Game Conditions: Temperature, 65 degrees; Wind, 10-12 variable; Weather, Partly cloudy becoming sunny. Attendance: 12,667.

Second Quarter
Youngstown St.—Jeff Wilkins 23 field goal (32 yards in 7 plays, 5:20 left)

Third Quarter
Marshall—Troy Brown 13 pass from Michael Payton (Dewey Klein kick) (49 yards in 7 plays, 10:14 left)
Marshall—Ricardo Clark 18 pass from Payton (Klein kick) (60 yards in 8 plays, 5:08 left)
Youngstown St.—Wilkins 37 field goal (33 yards in 7 plays, 2:04 left)
Marshall—Klein 42 field goal (39 yards in 6 plays, 0:00 left)

Fourth Quarter
Youngstown St.—Herb Williams 33 pass from Ray Isaac (pass failed) (65 yards in 4 plays, 13:38 left)
Youngstown St.—Ryan Wood 3 run (run failed) (80 yards in 8 plays, 7:09 left)
Youngstown St.—Tamron Smith 5 run (Wilkins kick) (14 yards in 3 plays, 5:42 left)

Individual Leaders
Rushing—Youngstown St.: Smith, 88 yards on 30 carries; Marshall: Glenn Pedro, 50 yards on 13 carries.
Passing—Youngstown St.: Isaac, 9 of 15 for 198 yards; Marshall: Payton, 30 of 43 for 363 yards.
Receiving—Youngstown St.: Andre Ballinger, 4 catches for 89 yards; Marshall: Clark, 8 catches for 154 yards.

DIVISION I-AA ALL-TIME CHAMPIONSHIP RESULTS

Year	Champion	Coach	Score	Runner-Up	Site
1978	Florida A&M	Rudy Hubbard	35-28	Massachusetts	Wichita Falls, Tex.
1979	Eastern Ky.	Roy Kidd	30-7	Lehigh	Orlando, Fla.
1980	Boise St.	Jim Criner	31-29	Eastern Ky.	Sacramento, Cal.
1981	Idaho St.	Dave Kragthorpe	34-23	Eastern Ky.	Wichita Falls, Tex.
1982	Eastern Ky.	Roy Kidd	17-14	Delaware	Wichita Falls, Tex.
1983	Southern Ill.	Rey Dempsey	43-7	Western Caro.	Charleston, S.C.
1984	Montana St.	Dave Arnold	19-6	Louisiana Tech	Charleston, S.C.
1985	Ga. Southern	Erk Russell	44-42	Furman	Tacoma, Wash.
1986	Ga. Southern	Erk Russell	48-21	Arkansas St.	Tacoma, Wash.
1987	Northeast La.	Pat Collins	43-42	Marshall	Pocatello, Idaho
1988	Furman	Jimmy Satterfield	17-12	Ga. Southern	Pocatello, Idaho
1989	Ga. Southern	Erk Russell	37-34	Vacated	Statesboro, Ga.
1990	Ga. Southern	Tim Stowers	36-13	Nevada	Statesboro, Ga.
1991	Youngstown St.	Jim Tressel	25-17	Marshall	Statesboro, Ga.

1991 DIVISION I-AA CHAMPIONSHIP RESULTS

First Round
Nevada 22, McNeese St. 16
Youngstown St. 17, Villanova 16
James Madison 42, Delaware 35 (2 OT)
Samford 29, New Hampshire 13
Eastern Ky. 14, Appalachian St. 3
Middle Tenn. St. 20, Sam Houston St. 19 (OT)
Northern Iowa 38, Weber St. 21
Marshall 20, Western Ill. 17 (OT)

Quarterfinals
Youngstown St. 30, Nevada 28
Samford 24, James Madison 21
Eastern Ky. 23, Middle Tenn. St. 13
Marshall 41, Northern Iowa 13

Semifinals
Youngstown St. 10, Samford 0
Marshall 14, Eastern Ky. 7

Championship
Youngstown St. 25, Marshall 17

1991 DIVISION I-AA GAME SUMMARIES

FIRST-ROUND GAMES

Nevada 22, McNeese St. 16

McNeese St.	0	3	0	13—16
Nevada	6	9	7	0—22

N—Washington 2 run (kick failed)
N—Reeves 48 pass from Gatlin (Lester kick)
N—Safety, Neck runs out of end zone
M—Roberts 32 field goal
N—Singleton 48 pass from Gatlin (Lester kick)
M—Henry 18 pass from Acheson (Roberts kick)
M—Fontenette 10 pass from Acheson (pass failed)
A—15,962

Youngstown St. 17, Villanova 16

Villanova	7	9	0	0—16
Youngstown St.	0	7	7	3—17

V—Hart 42 pass from Colombo (Hoffman kick)
YS—Roberts 28 pass from Isaac (Wilkins kick)
V—Kennedy 3 run (kick failed)
V—Hoffman 28 field goal
YS—Hawkins 1 run (Wilkins kick)
YS—Wilkins 33 field goal
A—9,556

James Madison 42, Delaware 35 (2 OT)

James Madison	7	14	7	7	0	7—42
Delaware	7	0	14	14	0	0—35

D—Brown 1 run (Drozic kick)
JM—Sims 9 run (Weis kick)
JM—Brown 2 pass from Williams (Weis kick)
JM—Sims 9 run (Weis kick)
D—Malloy 33 pass from Vergantino (Drozic kick)
JM—Williams 24 run (Weis kick)
D—Brown 2 run (Drozic kick)
JM—Thurman 9 run (Weis kick)
D—Malloy 37 run (Drozic kick)
D—Johnson 48 run (Drozic kick)
JM—Sims 25 run (Weis kick) (2nd OT)
A—14,905

Samford 29, New Hampshire 13

Samford	7	0	7	15—29
New Hampshire	3	10	0	0—13

S—Edwards 10 run (O'Neal kick)
NH—Hjelte 23 field goal
NH—Hjelte 22 field goal
NH—Perry 3 pass from Griffin (Hjelte kick)
S—Edwards 1 run (O'Neal kick)
S—Safety, punt blocked out of end zone
S—O'Neal 27 field goal
S—O'Neal 44 field goal
S—Rory 5 run (O'Neal kick)
A—6,034

Eastern Ky. 14, Appalachian St. 3

Appalachian St.	3	0	0	0— 3
Eastern Ky.	0	7	0	7—14

AS—Millson 22 field goal
EK—Thomas 72 run (Duffy kick)
EK—Lester 15 run (Duffy kick)
A—2,750

Middle Tenn. St. 20, Sam Houston St. 19 (OT)

Sam Houston St.	6	7	0	0	6—19
Middle Tenn. St.	0	3	3	7	7—20

SH—Thomas 5 run (kick failed)
MT—Petrilli 42 field goal
SH—Thomas 2 run (Klein kick)
MT—Petrilli 33 field goal
MT—Campbell 2 run (Petrilli kick)
SH—Thomas 1 run (kick failed) (OT)
MT—Campbell 10 run (Petrilli kick) (OT)
A—2,000

Northern Iowa 38, Weber St. 21

Weber St.	0	7	14	0—21
Northern Iowa	14	10	7	7—38

NI—Schulte 15 pass from Johnson (Mitchell kick)
NI—Lister 8 run (Mitchell kick)
WS—Stilson 19 pass from Martin (Schmidle kick)
NI—Shedd 31 pass from Johnson (Mitchell kick)
NI—Mitchell 47 field goal
WS—Mitchell 4 run (Schmidle kick)

NI—Schulte 7 run (Mitchell kick)
WS—Ethridge 2 run (Schmidle kick)
NI—Schulte 7 pass from Johnson (Mitchell kick)
A—8,723

Marshall 20, Western Ill. 17 (OT)

Western Ill.	0	0	6	11	0—17
Marshall	14	0	3	0	3—20

M—Hatchett 3 run (Klein kick)
M—Brown 20 pass from Payton (Klein kick)
WI—Simmons 15 run (kick failed)
M—Klein 31 field goal
WI—Seman 42 field goal
WI—Earl 24 pass from Simmons (Carlson pass from Simmons)
M—Klein 28 field goal (OT)
A—16,840

QUARTERFINAL GAMES

Youngstown St. 30, Nevada 28

Youngstown St.	3	14	0	13—30	
Nevada	0	3	7	18—28	

YS—Wilkins 49 field goal
YS—Hawkins 2 run (Wilkins kick)
N—Schwendinger 38 field goal
YS—Isaac 6 run (Wilkins kick)
N—Senior 1 pass from Vargas (Schwendinger kick)
YS—Smith 1 run (kick failed)
N—Reeves 33 pass from Vargas (Schwendinger kick)
N—Schwendinger 35 field goal
YS—Isaac 1 run (Wilkins kick)
N—Senior 2 pass from Vargas (kick failed)
N—Safety, Bucciarelli runs out of end zone
A—13,476

Samford 24, James Madison 21

Samford	7	0	17	0—24	
James Madison	7	7	0	7—21	

S—Edwards 71 run (O'Neal kick)
JM—Brown 2 run (Weis kick)
JM—Williams 11 run (Weis kick)
S—Fisher 12 pass from Wiggins (O'Neal kick)
S—Primus 67 punt return (O'Neal kick)
S—O'Neal 38 field goal
JM—Foxx 9 pass from Williams (Weis kick)
A—9,028

Eastern Ky. 23, Middle Tenn. St. 13

Middle Tenn. St.	0	0	0	13—13	
Eastern Ky.	6	7	10	0—23	

EK—Thomas 57 pass from Crenshaw (kick failed)
EK—McCollum 38 pass from Ware (Duffy kick)
EK—Duffy 22 field goal
EK—Lester 5 run (Duffy kick)
MT—Dark 19 pass from Holcomb (run failed)
MT—Watkins 4 pass from Holcomb (Petrilli kick)
A—3,650

Marshall 41, Northern Iowa 13

Northern Iowa	10	3	0	0—13	
Marshall	21	14	3	3—41	

M—Dowler 49 pass from Payton (Klein kick)
NI—Mitchell 28 field goal
M—Pedro 4 run (Klein kick)
NI—Shedd 48 pass from Johnson (Mitchell kick)
M—Dowler 60 pass from Payton (Klein kick)
NI—Mitchell 35 field goal
M—Hatchett 7 run (Klein kick)
M—Dowler 20 pass from Payton (Klein kick)
M—Klein 28 field goal
M—Klein 40 field goal
A—16,889

SEMIFINAL GAMES

Youngstown St. 10, Samford 0

Samford	0	0	0	0—0	
Youngstown St.	7	0	3	0—10	

YS—Vecchione 6 fumble return (Wilkins kick)
YS—Wilkins 28 field goal
A—17,003

Marshall 14, Eastern Ky. 7

Eastern Ky.	0	0	0	7—	7
Marshall	7	0	7	0—	14

M—Payton 11 run (Klein kick)
M—Brown 36 pass from Payton (Klein kick)
EK—Lester 2 run (Duffy kick)
A—21,084

CHAMPIONSHIP RECORDS
INDIVIDUAL: SINGLE GAME

Net Yards Rushing
246—Tamron Smith, Youngstown St. (10) vs. Samford (0), 12-14-91.

Rushes Attempted
46—Tamron Smith, Youngstown St. (10) vs. Samford (0), 12-14-91.

Touchdowns by Rushing
6—Sean Sanders, Weber St. (59) vs. Idaho (30), 11-28-87.

Net Yards Passing
517—Todd Hammel, Stephen F. Austin (59) vs. Grambling (56), 11-25-89.

Passes Attempted
78—Tom Ehrhardt, Rhode Island (15) vs. Furman (59), 12-7-85.

Passes Completed
44—Willie Totten, Mississippi Val. (19) vs. Louisiana Tech (66), 11-24-84.

Passes Had Intercepted
7—Jeff Gilbert, Western Caro. (7) vs. Southern Ill. (43), 12-17-83.

Touchdown Passes Completed
6—Mike Smith, Northern Iowa (41) vs. Northeast La. (44), 12-12-87; Clemente Gordon, Grambling (56) vs. Stephen F. Austin (59), 11-25-89.

Completion Percentage (min. 15 attempts)
.792—Bill Vergantino, Delaware (35) vs. James Madison (42), 2 OT, 11-30-91 (19 of 24).

Net Yards Rushing and Passing
539—Todd Hammel, Stephen F. Austin (59) vs. Grambling (56), 11-25-89 (517 passing, 22 rushing).

Number of Rushing and Passing Plays
80—Willie Totten, Mississippi Val. (19) vs. Louisiana Tech (66), 11-24-84; Tom Ehrhardt, Rhode Island (15) vs. Furman (59), 12-7-85.

Punting Average (min. 3 punts)
50.3—Steve Rowe, Eastern Ky. (38) vs. Idaho (30), 12-4-82.

Number of Punts
14—Fred McRae, Jackson St. (0) vs. Stephen F. Austin (24), 11-26-88.

Passes Caught
18—Brian Forster, Rhode Island (23) vs. Richmond (17), 12-1-84.

Net Yards Receiving
264—Winky White, Boise St. (52) vs. Nevada (59), 3OT, 12-8-90 (11 catches).

Touchdown Passes Caught
4—Tony DiMaggio, Rhode Island (35) vs. Akron (27), 11-30-85.

Passes Intercepted
4—Greg Shipp, Southern Ill. (43) vs. Western Caro. (7), 12-17-83.

Yards Gained on Interception Returns
117—Kevin Sullivan, Massachusetts (44) vs. Nevada (21), 12-9-78.

Yards Gained on Punt Returns
84—Rob Friese, Eastern Wash. (14) vs. Northern Iowa (17), 12-7-85, TD.

Yards Gained on Kickoff Returns
232—Mike Cadore, Eastern Ky. (32) vs. Northeast La. (33), 12-5-87, 6 returns, 1 for 99-yard TD.

Points
36—Sean Sanders, Weber St. (59) vs. Idaho (30), 11-28-87.

Touchdowns
6—Sean Sanders, Weber St. (59) vs. Idaho (30), 11-28-87.

Extra Points
9—George Benyola, Louisiana Tech (66) vs. Mississippi Val. (19), 11-24-84.

INDIVIDUAL: TOURNAMENT

Net Yards Rushing
661—Tracy Ham, Ga. Southern, 1986 (128 vs. North Caro. A&T, 191 vs. Nicholls St., 162 vs. Nevada, 180 vs. Arkansas St.).

Rushes Attempted
123—Paul Whalen, Nevada, 1990 (21 vs. Northeast La., 34 vs. Furman, 44 vs. Boise St., 24 vs. Ga. Southern).

Net Yards Passing
1,449—Todd Hammel, Stephen F. Austin, 1989 (517 vs. Grambling, 405 vs. Southwest Mo. St., 224 vs. Furman, 303 vs. Ga. Southern).

Passes Attempted
177—Jeff Gilbert, Western Caro., 1983 (47 vs. Colgate, 52 vs. Holy Cross, 45 vs. Furman, 33 vs. Southern Ill.).

Passes Completed
94—Stan Humphries, Northeast La., 1987 (19 vs. North Texas, 33 vs. Eastern Ky., 16 vs. Northern Iowa, 26 vs. Marshall).

Touchdown Passes Completed
14—Todd Hammel, Stephen F. Austin, 1989 (5 vs. Grambling, 4 vs. Southwest Mo. St., 2 vs. Furman, 3 vs. Ga. Southern).

Completion Percentage (min. 2 games)
.667—Steve Nolan, Idaho, 1990, 56 of 84 (24-41 vs. Southwest Mo. St., 32-43 vs. Ga. Southern).

Passes Had Intercepted
11—Todd Hammel, Stephen F. Austin, 1989 (0 vs. Grambling, 4 vs. Southwest Mo. St., 2 vs. Furman, 5 vs. Ga. Southern).

Passes Caught
  36—Ross Ortega, Nevada, 1990 (1 vs. Northeast La., 15 vs. Furman, 10 vs. Boise St., 10 vs. Ga. Southern).
Net Yards Receiving
  520—Mike Barber, Marshall, 1987 (91 vs. James Madison, 146 vs. Weber St., 88 vs. Appalachian St., 195 vs. Northeast La.).
Touchdown Passes Caught
  6—Keith Baxter, Marshall, 1987 (1 vs. James Madison, 3 vs. Weber St., 0 vs. Appalachian St., 2 vs. Northeast La.).
Points
  66—Gerald Harris, Ga. Southern, 1986 (30 vs. North Caro. A&T, 18 vs. Nicholls St., 12 vs. Nevada, 6 vs. Arkansas St.).
Touchdowns
  11—Gerald Harris, Ga. Southern, 1986 (5 vs. North Caro. A&T, 3 vs. Nicholls St., 2 vs. Nevada, 1 vs. Arkansas St.).

INDIVIDUAL: LONGEST PLAYS

Longest Rush
  80—Vince Hall, Middle Tenn. St. (42) vs. Indiana St. (41), 12-1-84; David Green, Louisiana Tech (21) vs. Middle Tenn. St. (13), 12-8-84.
Longest Pass (including run)
  90—Paul Singer 22 pass to Derek Swanson and 68 fumble recovery advancement by Steve Williams, Western Ill. (32) vs. Western Ky. (35), 11-26-88.
Longest Field Goal
  56—Tony Zendejas, Nevada (27) vs. Idaho St. (20), 11-26-83.

Longest Punt
  88—Mike Cassidy, Rhode Island (20) vs. Montana St. (32), 12-8-84.
Longest Punt Return
  84—Rob Friese, Eastern Wash. (14) vs. Northern Iowa (17), 12-7-85, TD.
Longest Kickoff Return
  99—Mike Cadore, Eastern Ky. (32) vs. Northeast La. (33), 12-5-87, TD.
Longest Interception Return
  99—Dwayne Hans, Montana (19) vs. Idaho (38), 11-26-88, TD.

TEAM: SINGLE GAME

First Downs
  35—Northern Iowa (41) vs. Northeast La. (44), 12-12-87.
First Downs by Rushing
  20—Ga. Southern (48) vs. Nevada (38), 12-13-86; Eastern Ky. (28) vs. Massachusetts (17), 11-26-88.
First Downs by Passing
  28—Rhode Island (35) vs. Akron (27), 11-30-85.
Net Yards Rushing
  518—Arkansas St. (55) vs. Delaware (14), 12-6-86.
Rushes Attempted
  81—Youngstown St. (10) vs. Samford (0), 12-14-91.
Net Yards Passing
  532—Rhode Island (15) vs. Furman (59), 12-7-85.
Passes Attempted
  90—Rhode Island (15) vs. Furman (59), 12-7-85.
Passes Completed
  45—Mississippi Val. (19) vs. Louisiana Tech (66), 11-24-84; Rhode Island (15) vs. Furman (59), 12-7-85.
Completion Percentage (min. 10 attempts)
  .792—Delaware (35) vs. James Madison (42), 2 OT, 11-30-91 (19 of 24).
Passes Had Intercepted
  7—Western Caro. (7) vs. Southern Ill. (43), 12-17-83; Rhode Island (15) vs. Furman (59), 12-7-85; Weber St. (23) vs. Marshall (51), 12-5-87.
Net Yards Rushing and Passing
  703—Louisiana Tech (66) vs. Mississippi Val. (19), 11-24-84.
Rushing and Passing Plays
  114—Nevada (42) vs. Furman (35), 3OT, 12-1-90 (47 rushing, 67 passing).

Punting Average
  50.2—Montana St. (32) vs. Rhode Island (20), 12-8-84.
Number of Punts
  14—Jackson St. (0) vs. Stephen F. Austin (24), 11-26-88.
Punts Had Blocked
  2—Florida A&M (35) vs. Massachusetts (28), 12-16-78; Boise St. (14) vs. Grambling (9), 12-13-80.

Youngstown State running back Tamron Smith rushed for 536 yards in four playoff games, including a tournament-record 246 against Samford in the semifinals, to lead the Penguins to the 1991 Division I-AA championship.

Yards Gained on Punt Returns
93—Eastern Wash. (14) vs. Northern Iowa (17), 12-7-85.

Yards Gained on Kickoff Returns
232—Eastern Ky. (32) vs. Northeast La. (33), 12-5-87.

Yards Gained on Interception Returns
164—Marshall (51) vs. Weber St. (23), 12-5-87.

Yards Penalized
172—Tennessee St. (32) vs. Jackson St. (23), 11-29-86.

Fumbles Lost
6—South Caro. St. (12) vs. Idaho St. (41), 12-12-81; Idaho (38) vs. Eastern Wash. (42), 11-30-85.

Points
66—Louisiana Tech vs. Mississippi Val. (19), 11-24-84.

TEAM: TOURNAMENT

First Downs
105—Northeast La., 1987 (22 vs. North Texas, 31 vs. Eastern Ky., 24 vs. Northern Iowa, 28 vs. Marshall).

Net Yards Rushing
1,522—Ga. Southern, 1986 (442 vs. North Caro. A&T, 317 vs. Nicholls St., 466 vs. Nevada, 297 vs. Arkansas St.).

Net Yards Passing
1,449—Stephen F. Austin, 1989 (517 vs. Grambling, 405 vs. Southwest Mo. St., 224 vs. Furman, 303 vs. Ga. Southern).

Net Yards Rushing and Passing
2,241—Ga. Southern, 1986 (541 vs. North Caro. A&T, 484 vs. Nicholls St., 613 vs. Nevada, 603 vs. Arkansas St.).

Passes Attempted
185—Nevada, 1990 (29 vs. Northeast La., 67 vs. Furman, 36 vs. Boise St., 53 vs. Ga. Southern).

Passes Completed
98—Nevada, 1990 (12 vs. Northeast La., 39 vs. Furman, 20 vs. Boise St., 27 vs. Ga. Southern).

Passes Had Intercepted
11—Stephen F. Austin, 1989 (0 vs. Grambling, 4 vs. Southwest Mo. St., 2 vs. Furman, 5 vs. Ga. Southern).

Number of Punts
25—Furman, 1988 (8 vs. Delaware, 8 vs. Marshall, 4 vs. Idaho, 5 vs. Ga. Southern).

Yards Penalized
350—Ga. Southern, 1986 (106 vs. North Caro. A&T, 104 vs. Nicholls St., 75 vs. Nevada, 65 vs. Arkansas St.).

Fumbles Lost
9—Nevada, 1983 (3 vs. Idaho St., 4 vs. North Texas, 2 vs. Southern Ill.); Youngstown St., 1991 (3 vs. Villanova, 1 vs. Nevada, 4 vs. Samford, 1 vs. Marshall).

Points
203—Ga. Southern, 1986 (52 vs. North Caro. A&T, 55 vs. Nicholls St., 48 vs. Nevada, 48 vs. Arkansas St.).

INDIVIDUAL: CHAMPIONSHIP GAME

Net Yards Rushing
207—Mike Solomon, Florida A&M (35) vs. Massachusetts (28), 1978 (27 carries).

Rushes Attempted
31—Joe Ross, Ga. Southern (37) vs. Stephen F. Austin (34), 1989 (152 yards); Raymond Gross, Ga. Southern (36) vs. Nevada (13), 1990 (145 yards).

Touchdowns by Rushing
4—John Bagwell, Furman (42) vs. Ga. Southern (44), 1985.

Net Yards Passing
474—Tony Peterson, Marshall (42) vs. Northeast La. (43), 1987 (28 of 54).

Passes Attempted
57—Kelly Bradley, Montana St. (19) vs. Louisiana Tech (6), 1984 (32 completions).

Passes Completed
32—Kelly Bradley, Montana St. (19) vs. Louisiana Tech (6), 1984 (57 attempts).

Passes Had Intercepted
7—Jeff Gilbert, Western Caro. (7) vs. Southern Ill. (43), 1983.

Touchdown Passes Completed
4—Tracy Ham, Ga. Southern (44) vs. Furman (42), 1985; Tony Peterson, Marshall (42) vs. Northeast La. (43), 1987.

Completion Percentage (min. 8 attempts)
.760—Rick Johnson, Southern Ill. (43) vs. Western Caro. (7), 1983 (19 of 25).

Net Yards Rushing and Passing
509—Tracy Ham, Ga. Southern (44) vs. Furman (42), 1985 (56 plays).

Number of Rushing and Passing Plays
65—Kelly Bradley, Montana St. (19) vs. Louisiana Tech (6), 1984 (309 yards).

Punting Average (min. 3 punts)
48.3—Todd Fugate, Marshall (42) vs. Northeast La. (43), 1987 (3 punts).

Number of Punts
10—Rick Titus, Delaware (14) vs. Eastern Ky. (17), 1982 (41.6 average).

Passes Caught
11—David Booze, Eastern Ky. (29) vs. Boise St. (31), 1980 (212 yards).

Net Yards Receiving
212—David Booze, Eastern Ky. (29) vs. Boise St. (31), 1980 (11 catches).

Touchdown Passes Caught
2—Steve Bird, Eastern Ky. (23) vs. Idaho St. (34), 1981; Joseph Bignell, Montana St. (19) vs. Louisiana Tech (6), 1984; Frank Johnson, Ga. Southern (44) vs. Furman (42), 1985; Keith Baxter, Marshall (42) vs. Northeast La. (43), 1987; Larry Centers, Stephen F. Austin (34) vs. Ga. Southern (37), 1989.

Passes Intercepted
4—Greg Shipp, Southern Ill. (43) vs. Western Caro. (7), 1983.

Yards Gained on Interception Returns
49—Greg Shipp, Southern Ill. (43) vs. Western Caro. (7), 1983 (4 interceptions).

Yards Gained on Punt Returns
67—Rodney Oglesby, Ga. Southern (36) vs. Nevada (13), 1990 (6 returns).

Yards Gained on Kickoff Returns
207—Eric Rasheed, Western Caro. (7) vs. Southern Ill. (43), 1983 (6 returns).

Points
24—John Bagwell, Furman (42) vs. Ga. Southern (44), 1985.

Touchdowns
4—John Bagwell, Furman (42) vs. Ga. Southern (44), 1985.

Extra Points
6—Keven Esval, Furman (42) vs. Ga. Southern (44), 1985.

Field Goals
4—Tim Foley, Ga. Southern (48) vs. Arkansas St. (21), 1986.

Longest Rush
58—Dale Patton, Eastern Ky. (30) vs. Lehigh (7), 1979.

Longest Pass Completion
79—Tracy Ham to Ricky Harris, Ga. Southern (48) vs. Arkansas St. (21), 1986.

Longest Field Goal
55—David Cool, Ga. Southern (12) vs. Furman (17), 1988.

Longest Punt
72—Rick Titus, Delaware (14) vs. Eastern Ky. (17), 1982.

TEAM: CHAMPIONSHIP GAME

First Downs
28—Furman (42) vs. Ga. Southern (44), 1985; Ga. Southern (48) vs. Arkansas St. (21), 1986; Northeast La. (43) vs. Marshall (42), 1987.

First Downs by Rushing
19—Florida A&M (35) vs. Massachusetts (28), 1978.

First Downs by Passing
19—Marshall (42) vs. Northeast La. (43), 1987.

First Downs by Penalty
3—Eastern Ky. (23) vs. Idaho St. (34), 1981; Furman (42) vs. Ga. Southern (44), 1985; Northeast La. (43) vs. Marshall (42), 1987.

Net Yards Rushing
470—Florida A&M (35) vs. Massachusetts (28), 1978 (76 attempts).

Rushes Attempted
76—Florida A&M (35) vs. Massachusetts (28), 1978 (470 yards).

Net Yards Passing
474—Marshall (42) vs. Northeast La. (43), 1987 (28 of 54).

Passes Attempted
57—Montana St. (19) vs. Louisiana Tech (6), 1984 (32 completions).

Passes Completed
32—Montana St. (19) vs. Louisiana Tech (6), 1984 (57 attempts).

Completion Percentage (min. 10 attempts)
.760—Southern Ill. (43) vs. Western Caro. (7), 1983 (19 of 25).

Passes Had Intercepted
7—Western Caro. (7) vs. Southern Ill. (43), 1983.

Net Yards Rushing and Passing
640—Ga. Southern (44) vs. Furman (42), 1985 (77 plays).

Rushing and Passing Plays
86—Boise St. (31) vs. Eastern Ky. (29), 1980 (510 yards); Nevada (13) vs. Ga. Southern (36), 1990 (321 yards).

Punting Average (min. 3 punts)
48.3—Marshall (42) vs. Northeast La. (43), 1987 (3 punts).

Number of Punts
10—Delaware (14) vs. Eastern Ky. (17), 1982 (41.6 average).

Yards Gained on Punt Returns
67—Ga. Southern (36) vs. Nevada (13), 1990 (6 returns).

Yards Gained on Kickoff Returns
229—Western Caro. (7) vs. Southern Ill. (43), 1983 (8 returns).

Yards Gained on Interception Returns
48—Southern Ill. (43) vs. Western Caro. (7), 1983 (7 interceptions).

Yards Penalized
162—Idaho St. (34) vs. Eastern Ky. (23), 1981 (12 penalties).

Fumbles
5—Eastern Ky. (17) vs. Delaware (14), 1982; Western Caro. (7) vs. Southern Ill. (43), 1983; Louisiana Tech (6) vs. Montana St. (19), 1984; Northeast La. (43) vs. Marshall (42), 1987; Ga. Southern (12) vs. Furman (17), 1988; Ga. Southern (36) vs. Nevada (13), 1990.

Fumbles Lost
4—Northeast La. (43) vs. Marshall (42), 1987; Ga. Southern (36) vs. Nevada (13), 1990.

Points
48—Ga. Southern vs. Arkansas St. (21), 1986.

Attendance
25,725—Allen E. Paulson Stadium, Statesboro, Ga., 1989.

YEAR-BY-YEAR DIVISION I-AA CHAMPIONSHIP RESULTS

Year (Number of Teams)	Coach	Record	Result
1978 (4)			
Florida A&M	Rudy Hubbard	2-0	Champion
Massachusetts	Bob Pickett	1-1	Second
Jackson St.	W. C. Gorden	0-1	Lost 1st Round
Nevada	Chris Ault	0-1	Lost 1st Round
1979 (4)			
Eastern Ky.	Roy Kidd	2-0	Champion
Lehigh	John Whitehead	1-1	Second
Murray St.	Mike Gottfried	0-1	Lost 1st Round
Nevada	Chris Ault	0-1	Lost 1st Round

Year (Number of Teams)	Coach	Record	Result
1980 (4)			
Boise St.	Jim Criner	2-0	Champion
Eastern Ky.	Roy Kidd	1-1	Second
Grambling	Eddie Robinson	0-1	Lost 1st Round
Lehigh	John Whitehead	0-1	Lost 1st Round
1981 (8)			
Idaho St.	Dave Kragthorpe	3-0	Champion
Eastern Ky.	Roy Kidd	2-1	Second
Boise St.	Jim Criner	1-1	Semifinalist
South Caro. St.	Bill Davis	1-1	Semifinalist
Delaware	Tubby Raymond	0-1	Lost 1st Round
Jackson St.	W. C. Gorden	0-1	Lost 1st Round
Rhode Island	Bob Griffin	0-1	Lost 1st Round
*Tennessee St.	John Merritt	0-1	Vacated
1982 (12)			
Eastern Ky.	Roy Kidd	3-0	Champion
Delaware	Tubby Raymond	2-1	Second
Louisiana Tech	Billy Brewer	1-1	Semifinalist
*Tennessee St.	John Merritt	1-1	Vacated
Colgate	Fred Dunlap	1-1	Quarterfinalist
Eastern Ill.	Darrell Mudra	1-1	Quarterfinalist
Idaho	Dennis Erickson	1-1	Quarterfinalist
South Caro. St.	Bill Davis	1-1	Quarterfinalist
Boston U.	Rick Taylor	0-1	Lost 1st Round
Furman	Dick Sheridan	0-1	Lost 1st Round
Jackson St.	W. C. Gorden	0-1	Lost 1st Round
Montana	Larry Donovan	0-1	Lost 1st Round
1983 (12)			
Southern Ill.	Rey Dempsey	3-0	Champion
Western Caro.	Bob Waters	3-1	Second
Furman	Dick Sheridan	1-1	Semifinalist
Nevada	Chris Ault	2-1	Semifinalist
Boston U.	Rick Taylor	1-1	Quarterfinalist
Holy Cross	Rick Carter	0-1	Quarterfinalist
Indiana St.	Dennis Raetz	1-1	Quarterfinalist
North Texas	Corky Nelson	0-1	Quarterfinalist
Colgate	Fred Dunlap	0-1	Lost 1st Round
Eastern Ill.	Al Molde	0-1	Lost 1st Round
Eastern Ky.	Roy Kidd	0-1	Lost 1st Round
Idaho St.	Jim Koetter	0-1	Lost 1st Round
1984 (12)			
Montana St.	Dave Arnold	3-0	Champion
Louisiana Tech	A. L. Williams	3-1	Second
Middle Tenn. St.	James Donnelly	2-1	Semifinalist
Rhode Island	Bob Griffin	1-1	Semifinalist
Alcorn St.	Marino Casem	0-1	Quarterfinalist
Arkansas St.	Larry Lacewell	1-1	Quarterfinalist
Indiana St.	Dennis Raetz	0-1	Quarterfinalist
Richmond	Dal Shealy	1-1	Quarterfinalist
Boston U.	Rick Taylor	0-1	Lost 1st Round
Eastern Ky.	Roy Kidd	0-1	Lost 1st Round
Mississippi Val.	Archie Cooley Jr.	0-1	Lost 1st Round
Tenn.-Chatt.	Buddy Nix	0-1	Lost 1st Round
1985 (12)			
Ga. Southern	Erk Russell	4-0	Champion
Furman	Dick Sheridan	2-1	Second
Nevada	Chris Ault	1-1	Semifinalist
Northern Iowa	Darrell Mudra	1-1	Semifinalist
Arkansas St.	Larry Lacewell	1-1	Quarterfinalist
Eastern Wash.	Dick Zornes	1-1	Quarterfinalist
Middle Tenn. St.	James Donnelly	0-1	Quarterfinalist
Rhode Island	Bob Griffin	1-1	Quarterfinalist
Akron	Jim Dennison	0-1	Lost 1st Round
Grambling	Eddie Robinson	0-1	Lost 1st Round
Idaho	Dennis Erickson	0-1	Lost 1st Round
Jackson St.	W. C. Gorden	0-1	Lost 1st Round
1986 (16)			
Ga. Southern	Erk Russell	4-0	Champion
Arkansas St.	Larry Lacewell	3-1	Second

Year (Number of Teams)	Coach	Record	Result
Eastern Ky.	Roy Kidd	2-1	Semifinalist
Nevada	Chris Ault	2-1	Semifinalist
Delaware	Tubby Raymond	1-1	Quarterfinalist
Eastern Ill.	Al Molde	1-1	Quarterfinalist
Nicholls St.	Sonny Jackson	1-1	Quarterfinalist
Tennessee St.	William Thomas	1-1	Quarterfinalist
Appalachian St.	Sparky Woods	0-1	Lost 1st Round
Furman	Jimmy Satterfield	0-1	Lost 1st Round
Idaho	Keith Gilbertson	0-1	Lost 1st Round
Jackson St.	W. C. Gorden	0-1	Lost 1st Round
Murray St.	Frank Beamer	0-1	Lost 1st Round
North Caro. A&T	Maurice Forte	0-1	Lost 1st Round
Sam Houston St.	Ron Randleman	0-1	Lost 1st Round
William & Mary	Jimmye Laycock	0-1	Lost 1st Round
1987 (16)			
Northeast La.	Pat Collins	4-0	Champion
Marshall	George Chaump	3-1	Second
Appalachian St.	Sparky Woods	2-1	Semifinalist
Northern Iowa	Darrell Mudra	2-1	Semifinalist
Arkansas St.	Larry Lacewell	1-1	Quarterfinalist
Eastern Ky.	Roy Kidd	1-1	Quarterfinalist
Ga. Southern	Erk Russell	1-1	Quarterfinalist
Weber St.	Mike Price	1-1	Quarterfinalist
Idaho	Keith Gilbertson	0-1	Lost 1st Round
Jackson St.	W. C. Gorden	0-1	Lost 1st Round
James Madison	Joe Purzycki	0-1	Lost 1st Round
Maine	Tim Murphy	0-1	Lost 1st Round
North Texas	Corky Nelson	0-1	Lost 1st Round
Richmond	Dal Shealy	0-1	Lost 1st Round
Western Ky.	Dave Roberts	0-1	Lost 1st Round
Youngstown St.	Jim Tressel	0-1	Lost 1st Round
1988 (16)			
Furman	Jimmy Satterfield	4-0	Champion
Ga. Southern	Erk Russell	3-1	Second
Eastern Ky.	Roy Kidd	2-1	Semifinalist
Idaho	Keith Gilbertson	2-1	Semifinalist
Marshall	George Chaump	1-1	Quarterfinalist
Northwestern (La.)	Sam Goodwin	1-1	Quarterfinalist
Stephen F. Austin	Jim Hess	1-1	Quarterfinalist
Western Ky.	Dave Roberts	1-1	Quarterfinalist
Boise St.	Skip Hall	0-1	Lost 1st Round
Citadel	Charlie Taaffe	0-1	Lost 1st Round
Delaware	Tubby Raymond	0-1	Lost 1st Round
Jackson St.	W. C. Gorden	0-1	Lost 1st Round
Massachusetts	Jim Reid	0-1	Lost 1st Round
Montana	Don Read	0-1	Lost 1st Round
North Texas	Corky Nelson	0-1	Lost 1st Round
Western Ill.	Bruce Craddock	0-1	Lost 1st Round
1989 (16)			
Ga. Southern	Erk Russell	4-0	Champion
*Stephen F. Austin	Lynn Graves	3-1	Vacated
Furman	Jimmy Satterfield	2-1	Semifinalist
Montana	Don Read	2-1	Semifinalist
Eastern Ill.	Bob Spoo	1-1	Quarterfinalist
Middle Tenn. St.	James Donnelly	1-1	Quarterfinalist
Southwest Mo. St.	Jesse Branch	1-1	Quarterfinalist
Youngstown St.	Jim Tressel	1-1	Quarterfinalist
Appalachian St.	Jerry Moore	0-1	Lost 1st Round
Eastern Ky.	Roy Kidd	0-1	Lost 1st Round
Grambling	Eddie Robinson	0-1	Lost 1st Round
Idaho	John L. Smith	0-1	Lost 1st Round
Jackson St.	W. C. Gorden	0-1	Lost 1st Round
Maine	Tom Lichtenberg	0-1	Lost 1st Round
Villanova	Andy Talley	0-1	Lost 1st Round
William & Mary	Jimmye Laycock	0-1	Lost 1st Round
1990 (16)			
Ga. Southern	Tim Stowers	4-0	Champion
Nevada	Chris Ault	3-1	Second
Boise St.	Skip Hall	2-1	Semifinalist

Year (Number of Teams)	Coach	Record	Result
Central Fla.	Gene McDowell	2-1	Semifinalist
Furman	Jimmy Satterfield	1-1	Quarterfinalist
Idaho	John L. Smith	1-1	Quarterfinalist
Middle Tenn. St.	James Donnelly	1-1	Quarterfinalist
William & Mary	Jimmye Laycock	1-1	Quarterfinalist
Citadel	Charlie Taaffe	0-1	Lost 1st Round
Eastern Ky.	Roy Kidd	0-1	Lost 1st Round
Jackson St.	W. C. Gorden	0-1	Lost 1st Round
Massachusetts	Jim Reid	0-1	Lost 1st Round
Northeast La.	Dave Roberts	0-1	Lost 1st Round
Northern Iowa	Terry Allen	0-1	Lost 1st Round
Southwest Mo. St.	Jesse Branch	0-1	Lost 1st Round
Youngstown St.	Jim Tressel	0-1	Lost 1st Round
1991 (16)			
Youngstown St.	Jim Tressel	4-0	Champion
Marshall	Jim Donnan	3-1	Second
Eastern Ky.	Roy Kidd	2-1	Semifinalist
Samford	Terry Bowden	2-1	Semifinalist
James Madison	Rip Scherer	1-1	Quarterfinalist
Middle Tenn. St.	James Donnelly	1-1	Quarterfinalist
Nevada	Chris Ault	1-1	Quarterfinalist
Northern Iowa	Terry Allen	1-1	Quarterfinalist
Appalachian St.	Jerry Moore	0-1	Lost 1st Round
Delaware	Tubby Raymond	0-1	Lost 1st Round
McNeese St.	Bobby Keasler	0-1	Lost 1st Round
New Hampshire	Bill Bowes	0-1	Lost 1st Round
Sam Houston St.	Ron Randleman	0-1	Lost 1st Round
Villanova	Andy Talley	0-1	Lost 1st Round
Weber St.	Dave Arslanian	0-1	Lost 1st Round
Western Ill.	Randy Ball	0-1	Lost 1st Round

* *Competition in championship vacated by the NCAA.*

DIVISION I-AA CHAMPIONSHIP
ALL-TIME RECORD OF EACH COLLEGE
COACH-BY-COACH, 1978-91 (59 Colleges)

	Yrs	Won	Lost	CH	2D
AKRON					
Jim Dennison (Wooster '60) 85	1	0	1	0	0
ALCORN ST.					
Marino Casem (Xavier, La. '56) 84	1	0	1	0	0
APPALACHIAN ST.					
Sparky Woods (Carson-Newman '76) 86, 87	2	2	2	0	0
Jerry Moore (Baylor '61) 89, 91	2	0	2	0	0
TOTAL	4	2	4	0	0
ARKANSAS ST.					
Larry Lacewell (Ark.-Monticello '59) 84, 85, 86-2D, 87	4	6	4	0	1
BOISE ST.					
Jim Criner (Cal Poly Pomona '61) 80-CH, 81	2	3	1	1	0
Skip Hall (Concordia, Minn. '66) 88, 90	2	2	2	0	0
TOTAL	4	5	3	1	0
BOSTON U.					
Rick Taylor (Gettysburg '64) 82, 83, 84	3	1	3	0	0
CENTRAL FLA.					
Gene McDowell (Florida St. '63) 90	1	2	1	0	0
CITADEL					
Charlie Taaffe (Siena '73) 88, 90	2	0	2	0	0
COLGATE					
Fred Dunlap (Colgate '50) 82, 83	2	1	2	0	0
DELAWARE					
Tubby Raymond (Michigan '50) 81, 82-2D, 86, 87, 91 .	5	3	5	0	1
EASTERN ILL.					
Darrell Mudra (Peru St. '51) 82	1	1	1	0	0
Al Molde (Gust. Adolphus '66) 83, 86	2	1	2	0	0
Bob Spoo (Purdue '60) 89	1	1	1	0	0
TOTAL	4	3	4	0	0

	Yrs	Won	Lost	CH	2D
EASTERN KY.					
Roy Kidd (Eastern Ky. '54) 79-CH, 80-2D, 81-2D, 82-CH, 83, 84, 86, 87, 88, 89, 90, 91	12	15	10	2	2
EASTERN WASH.					
Dick Zornes (Eastern Wash. '68) 85	1	1	1	0	0
FLORIDA A&M					
Rudy Hubbard (Ohio St. '68) 78-CH	1	2	0	1	0
FURMAN					
Dick Sheridan (South Caro. '64) 82, 83, 85-2D	3	3	3	0	1
Jimmy Satterfield (South Caro. '62) 86, 88-CH, 89, 90	4	7	3	1	0
TOTAL	7	10	6	1	1
GA. SOUTHERN					
Erk Russell (Auburn '49) 85-CH, 86-CH, 87, 88-2D, 89-CH	5	16	2	3	1
Tim Stowers (Auburn '79) 90-CH	1	4	0	1	0
TOTAL	6	20	2	4	1
GRAMBLING					
Eddie Robinson (Leland '41) 80, 85, 89	3	0	3	0	0
HOLY CROSS					
Rick Carter (Earlham '65) 83	1	0	1	0	0
IDAHO					
Dennis Erickson (Montana St. '70) 82, 85	2	1	2	0	0
Keith Gilbertson (Central Wash. '71) 86, 87, 88.......	3	2	3	0	0
John L. Smith (Weber St. '71) 89, 90...............	2	1	2	0	0
TOTAL	7	4	7	0	0
IDAHO ST.					
Dave Kragthorpe (Utah St. '55) 81-CH	1	3	0	1	0
Jim Koetter (Idaho St. '61) 83	1	0	1	0	0
TOTAL	2	3	1	1	0
INDIANA ST.					
Dennis Raetz (Nebraska '68) 83, 84	2	1	2	0	0
JACKSON ST.					
W. C. Gorden (Tennessee St. '52) 78, 81, 82, 85, 86, 87, 88, 89, 90	9	0	9	0	0
JAMES MADISON					
Joe Purzycki (Delaware '71) 87	1	0	1	0	0
Rip Scherer (William & Mary '74) 91	1	1	1	0	0
TOTAL	2	1	2	0	0
LEHIGH					
John Whitehead (East Stroudsburg '50) 79-2D, 80 ...	2	1	2	0	1
LOUISIANA TECH					
Billy Brewer (Mississippi '61) 82	1	1	1	0	0
A. L. Williams (Louisiana Tech '57) 84-2D	1	3	1	0	1
TOTAL	2	4	2	0	1
MAINE					
Tim Murphy (Springfield '78) 87	1	0	1	0	0
Tom Lichtenberg (Louisville '62) 89	1	0	1	0	0
TOTAL	2	0	2	0	0
MARSHALL					
George Chaump (Bloomsburg '58) 87-2D, 88	2	4	2	0	1
Jim Donnan (North Caro. St. '67) 91-2D	1	3	1	0	1
TOTAL	3	7	3	0	2
MASSACHUSETTS					
Bob Pickett (Maine '59) 78-2D	1	1	1	0	1
Jim Reid (Maine '73) 88, 90	2	0	2	0	0
TOTAL	3	1	3	0	1
McNEESE ST.					
Bobby Keasler (Northeast La. '70) 91	1	0	1	0	0
MIDDLE TENN. ST.					
James Donnelly (Middle Tenn. St. '65) 84, 85, 89, 90, 91	5	5	5	0	0
MISSISSIPPI VAL.					
Archie Cooley Jr. (Jackson St. '62) 84	1	0	1	0	0

     1992 NCAA FOOTBALL

	Yrs	Won	Lost	CH	2D
MONTANA					
Larry Donovan (Nebraska '64) 82	1	0	1	0	0
Don Read (Cal St. Sacramento '59) 88, 89	2	2	2	0	0
TOTAL	3	2	3	0	0
MONTANA ST.					
Dave Arnold (Drake '67) 84-CH	1	3	0	1	0
MURRAY ST.					
Mike Gottfried (Morehead St. '66) 79	1	0	1	0	0
Frank Beamer (Virginia Tech '69) 86	1	0	1	0	0
TOTAL	2	0	2	0	0
NEVADA					
Chris Ault (Nevada '58) 78, 79, 83, 85, 86, 90-2D, 91 ..	7	9	7	0	1
NEW HAMPSHIRE					
Bill Bowes (Penn St. '65) 91	1	0	1	0	0
NICHOLLS ST.					
Sonny Jackson (Nicholls St. '63) 86	1	1	1	0	0
NORTH CARO. A&T					
Maurice Forte (Minnesota '71) 86	1	0	1	0	0
NORTH TEXAS					
Corky Nelson (Southwest Tex. St. '64) 83, 87, 88	3	0	3	0	0
NORTHEAST LA.					
Pat Collins (Louisiana Tech '63) 87-CH	1	4	0	1	0
Dave Roberts (Western Caro. '68) 90	1	0	1	0	0
TOTAL	2	4	1	1	0
NORTHERN IOWA					
Darrell Mudra (Peru St. '51) 85, 87	2	3	2	0	0
Terry Allen (Northern Iowa '79) 90, 91	2	1	2	0	0
TOTAL	4	4	4	0	0
NORTHWESTERN (LA.)					
Sam Goodwin (Henderson St. '68) 88	1	1	1	0	0
RHODE ISLAND					
Bob Griffin (Southern Conn. St. '63) 81, 84, 85	3	2	3	0	0
RICHMOND					
Dal Shealy (Carson-Newman '60) 84, 87	2	1	2	0	0
SAM HOUSTON ST.					
Ron Randleman (William Penn '64) 86, 91	2	0	2	0	0
SAMFORD					
Terry Bowden (West Va. '78) 91	1	2	1	0	0
SOUTH CARO. ST.					
Bill Davis (Johnson Smith '65) 81, 82	2	2	2	0	0
SOUTHERN ILL.					
Rey Dempsey (Geneva '58) 83-CH	1	3	0	1	0
SOUTHWEST MO. ST.					
Jesse Branch (Arkansas '64) 89, 90	2	1	2	0	0
STEPHEN F. AUSTIN¢					
Jim Hess (Southeast Okla. '59) 88	1	1	1	0	0
Lynn Graves (Stephen F. Austin '65) 89-2D	1	3	1	0	1
TOTAL	2	4	2	0	1
TENN.-CHATT.					
Buddy Nix (Livingston '61) 84	1	0	1	0	0
TENNESSEE ST.*					
John Merritt (Kentucky St. '50) 81, 82	2	1	2	0	0
William Thomas (Tennessee St. '71) 86	1	1	1	0	0
TOTAL	3	2	3	0	0
VILLANOVA					
Andy Talley (Southern Conn. St. '67) 89, 91	2	0	2	0	0
WEBER ST.					
Mike Price (Puget Sound '69) 87	1	1	1	0	0
Dave Arslanian (Weber St. '72) 91	1	0	1	0	0
TOTAL	2	1	2	0	0
WESTERN CARO.					
Bob Waters (Presbyterian '60) 83-2D	1	3	1	0	1

	Yrs	Won	Lost	CH	2D
WESTERN ILL.					
Bruce Craddock (Northeast Mo. St. '66) 88	1	0	1	0	0
Randy Ball (Northeast Mo. St. '73) 91	1	0	1	0	0
TOTAL	2	0	2	0	0
WESTERN KY.					
Dave Roberts (Western Caro. '68) 87, 88	2	1	2	0	0
WILLIAM & MARY					
Jimmye Laycock (William & Mary '70) 86, 89, 90	3	1	3	0	0
YOUNGSTOWN ST.					
Jim Tressel (Baldwin-Wallace '75) 87, 89, 90, 91-CH ..	4	5	3	1	0

* *Tennessee State's competition in the 1981 and 1982 Division I-AA championships was vacated by the NCAA (official record is 1-1).* ¢ *Stephen F. Austin's competition in the 1989 Division I-AA championship was vacated by the NCAA (official record is 1-1).*

ALL-TIME RESULTS

1978 First Round: Florida A&M 15, Jackson St. 10; Massachusetts 44, Nevada 21. **Championship:** Florida A&M 35, Massachusetts 28.

1979 First Round: Lehigh 28, Murray St. 9; Eastern Ky. 33, Nevada 30 (2 OT). **Championship:** Eastern Ky. 30, Lehigh 7.

1980 First Round: Eastern Ky. 23, Lehigh 20; Boise St. 14, Grambling 9. **Championship:** Boise St. 31, Eastern Ky. 29.

1981 First Round: Eastern Ky. 35, Delaware 28; Boise St. 19, Jackson St. 7; Idaho St. 51, Rhode Island 0; South Caro. St. 26, *Tennessee St. 25 (OT). **Semifinals:** Eastern Ky. 23, Boise St. 17; Idaho St. 41, South Caro. St. 12. **Championship:** Idaho St. 34, Eastern Ky. 23.

* *Tennessee State's participation in 1981 playoff vacated.*

1982 First Round: Idaho 21, Montana 7; Eastern Ill. 16, Jackson St. 13 (OT); South Caro. St. 17, Furman 0; Colgate 21, Boston U. 7. **Quarterfinals:** Eastern Ky. 38, Idaho 30; *Tennessee St. 20, Eastern Ill. 19; Louisiana Tech 38, South Caro. St. 3; Delaware 20, Colgate 13. **Semifinals:** Eastern Ky. 13, *Tennessee St. 7; Delaware 17, Louisiana Tech 0. **Championship:** Eastern Ky. 17, Delaware 14.

* *Tennessee State's participation in 1982 playoff vacated.*

1983 First Round: Indiana St. 16, Eastern Ill. 13 (2 OT); Nevada 27, Idaho St. 20; Western Caro. 24, Colgate 23; Boston U. 24, Eastern Ky. 20. **Quarterfinals:** Southern Ill. 23, Indiana St. 7; Nevada 20, North Texas 17 (OT); Western Caro. 28, Holy Cross 21; Furman 35, Boston U. 16. **Semifinals:** Southern Ill. 23, Nevada 7; Western Caro. 14, Furman 7. **Championship:** Southern Ill. 43, Western Caro. 7.

1984 First Round: Louisiana Tech 66, Mississippi Val. 19; Middle Tenn. St. 27, Eastern Ky. 10; Richmond 35, Boston U. 33; Arkansas St. 37, Tenn.-Chatt. 10. **Quarterfinals:** Louisiana Tech 44, Alcorn St. 21; Middle Tenn. St. 42, Indiana St. 41 (3 OT); Rhode Island 23, Richmond 17; Montana St. 31, Arkansas St. 14. **Semifinals:** Louisiana Tech 21, Middle Tenn. St. 13; Montana St. 32, Rhode Island 20. **Championship:** Montana St. 19, Louisiana Tech 6.

1985 First Round: Ga. Southern 27, Jackson St. 0; Eastern Wash. 42, Idaho 38; Rhode Island 35, Akron 27; Arkansas St. 10, Grambling 7. **Quarterfinals:** Ga. Southern 28, Middle Tenn. St. 21; Northern Iowa 17, Eastern Wash. 14; Furman 59, Rhode Island 15; Nevada 24, Arkansas St. 23. **Semifinals:** Ga. Southern 40, Northern Iowa 33; Furman 35, Nevada 12. **Championship:** Ga. South-

ern 44, Furman 42.

1986 First Round: Nevada 27, Idaho 7; Tennessee St. 32, Jackson St. 23; Ga. Southern 52, North Caro. A&T 21; Nicholls St. 28, Appalachian St. 26; Arkansas St. 48, Sam Houston St. 7; Delaware 51, William & Mary 17; Eastern Ill. 28, Murray St. 21; Eastern Ky. 23, Furman 10. **Quarterfinals:** Nevada 33, Tennessee St. 6; Ga. Southern 55, Nicholls St. 31; Arkansas St. 55, Delaware 14; Eastern Ky. 24, Eastern Ill. 22. **Semifinals:** Ga. Southern 48, Nevada 38; Arkansas St. 24, Eastern Ky. 10. **Championship:** Ga. Southern 48, Arkansas St. 21.

1987 First Round: Appalachian St. 20, Richmond 3; Ga. Southern 31, Maine 28 (OT); Weber St. 59, Idaho 30; Marshall 41, James Madison 12; Northeast La. 30, North Texas 9; Eastern Ky. 40, Western Ky. 17; Northern Iowa 31, Youngstown St. 28; Arkansas St. 35, Jackson St. 32. **Quarterfinals:** Appalachian St. 19, Ga. Southern 0; Marshall 51, Weber St. 23; Northeast La. 33, Eastern Ky. 32; Northern Iowa 49, Arkansas St. 28. **Semifinals:** Marshall 24, Appalachian St. 10; Northeast La. 44, Northern Iowa 41 (2 OT). **Championship:** Northeast La. 43, Marshall 42.

1988 First Round: Idaho 38, Montana 19; Northwestern (La.) 22, Boise St. 13; Furman 21, Delaware 7; Marshall 7, North Texas 0; Ga. Southern 38, Citadel 20; Stephen F. Austin 24, Jackson St. 0; Western Ky. 35, Western Ill. 32; Eastern Ky. 28, Massachusetts 17. **Quarterfinals:** Idaho 38, Northwestern (La.) 30; Furman 13, Marshall 9; Ga. Southern 27, Stephen F. Austin 6; Eastern Ky. 41, Western Ky. 24. **Semifinals:** Furman 38, Idaho 7; Ga. Southern 21, Eastern Ky. 17. **Championship:** Furman 17, Ga. Southern 12.

1989 First Round: Ga. Southern 52, Villanova 36; Middle Tenn. St. 24, Appalachian St. 21; Eastern Ill. 38, Idaho 21; Montana 48, Jackson St. 7; Furman 24, William & Mary 10; Youngstown St. 28, Eastern Ky. 24; ¢Stephen F. Austin 59, Grambling 56; Southwest Mo. St. 38, Maine 35. **Quarterfinals:** Ga. Southern 45, Middle Tenn. St. 3; Montana 25, Eastern Ill. 19; Furman 42, Youngstown St. 23; ¢Stephen F. Austin 55, Southwest Mo. St. 25. **Semifinals:** Ga. Southern 45, Montana 15; ¢Stephen F. Austin 21, Furman 19. **Championship:** Ga. Southern 37, ¢Stephen F. Austin 34.

¢ *Stephen F. Austin's participation in 1989 playoff vacated.*

1990 First Round: Middle Tenn. St. 28, Jackson St. 7; Boise St. 20, Northern Iowa 3; Nevada 29, Northeast La. 14; Furman 45, Eastern Ky. 17; Central Fla. 20, Youngstown St. 17; William & Mary 38, Massachusetts 0; Ga. Southern 31, Citadel 0; Idaho 41, Southwest Mo. St. 35. **Quarterfinals: Boise St. 20, Middle Tenn. St. 13; Nevada 42, Furman 35 (3 OT); Central Fla. 52, William & Mary 38; Ga. Southern 28, Idaho 27. **Semifinals:** Nevada 59, Boise St. 52 (3 OT); Ga. Southern 44, Central Fla. 7. **Championship:** Ga. Southern 36, Nevada 13.

1991 First Round: Nevada 22, McNeese St. 16; Youngstown St. 17, Villanova 16; James Madison 42, Delaware 35 (2 OT); Samford 29, New Hamp-shire 13; Eastern Ky. 14, Appalachian St. 3; Middle Tenn. St. 20, Sam Houston St. 19 (OT); Northern Iowa 38, Weber St. 21; Marshall 20, Western Ill. 17 (OT). **Quarterfinals:** Youngstown St. 30, Nevada 28; Samford 24, James Madison 21; Eastern Ky. 23, Middle Tenn. St. 13; Marshall 41, Northern Iowa 13. **Semifinals:** Youngstown St. 10, Samford 0; Marshall 14, Eastern Ky. 7. **Championship:** Youngstown St. 25, Marshall 17.

1991 DIVISION II CHAMPIONSHIP

BRALY MUNICIPAL STADIUM,
FLORENCE, ALABAMA; DECEMBER 14, 1991

	Pittsburg St.	Jacksonville St.
First Downs	18	16
Rushing Yardage	195	152
Passing Yardage	159	81
Return Yardage	13	20
Passes (Comp.-Att.-Int.)	10-14-0	8-12-1
Punts (Number-Average)	4-39.8	4-29.8
Fumbles (Number-Lost)	1-0	4-1
Penalties (Number-Yards)	3-18	2-30

Pittsburg St.	7	6	7	3—23
Jacksonville St.	0	6	0	0— 6

First Quarter
Pittsburg St.—Ronnie West 17 pass from Brian Hutchins (James Jenkins kick) (58 yards in 10 plays, 1:33 left)

Second Quarter
Jacksonville St.—Terence Bowens 3 run (kick failed) (70 yards in 15 plays, 9:34 left)
Pittsburg St.—Hutchins 13 run (kick failed) (76 yards in 6 plays, 0:16 left)

Third Quarter
Pittsburg St.—Darren Dawson 10 run (Jenkins kick) (66 yards in 12 plays, 3:12 left)

Fourth Quarter
Pittsburg St.—Jenkins 22 field goal (52 yards in 12 plays, 9:15 left)

Individual Leaders
Rushing—Pittsburg St.: Dawson, 95 yards on 23 carries; Jacksonville St.: Nickey Edmondson, 54 yards on 14 carries.
Passing—Pittsburg St.: Hutchins, 10 of 14 for 159 yards; Jacksonville St.: Edmondson, 5 of 8 for 49 yards.
Receiving—Pittsburg St.: West, 8 catches for 129 yards; Jacksonville St.: Henry Ray, 3 catches for 41 yards.

DIVISION II ALL-TIME CHAMPIONSHIP RESULTS

Year	Champion	Coach	Score	Runner-Up	Site
1973	Louisiana Tech	Maxie Lambright	34-0	Western Ky.	Sacramento, Cal.
1974	Central Mich.	Roy Kramer	54-14	Delaware	Sacramento, Cal.
1975	Northern Mich.	Gil Krueger	16-14	Western Ky.	Sacramento, Cal.
1976	Montana St.	Sonny Holland	24-13	Akron	Wichita Falls, Tex.
1977	Lehigh	John Whitehead	33-0	Jacksonville St.	Wichita Falls, Tex.
1978	Eastern Ill.	Darrell Mudra	10-9	Delaware	Longview, Tex.
1979	Delaware	Tubby Raymond	38-21	Youngstown St.	Albuquerque, N. M.
1980	Cal Poly SLO	Joe Harper	21-13	Eastern Ill.	Albuquerque, N. M.
1981	Southwest Tex. St.	Jim Wacker	42-13	North Dak. St.	McAllen, Tex.
1982	Southwest Tex. St.	Jim Wacker	34-9	UC Davis	McAllen, Tex.
1983	North Dak. St.	Don Morton	41-21	Central St. (Ohio)	McAllen, Tex.
1984	Troy St.	Chan Gailey	18-17	North Dak. St.	McAllen, Tex.
1985	North Dak. St.	Earle Solomonson	35-7	North Ala.	McAllen, Tex.
1986	North Dak. St.	Earle Solomonson	27-7	South Dak.	Florence, Ala.
1987	Troy St.	Rick Rhoades	31-17	Portland St.	Florence, Ala.
1988	North Dak. St.	Rocky Hager	35-21	Portland St.	Florence, Ala.
1989	Mississippi Col.	John Williams	3-0	Jacksonville St.	Florence, Ala.
1990	North Dak. St.	Rocky Hager	51-11	Indiana (Pa.)	Florence, Ala.
1991	Pittsburg St.	Chuck Broyles	23-6	Jacksonville St.	Florence, Ala.

REGIONAL CHAMPIONSHIP RESULTS

Before 1973, there was no Division II Football Championship. Instead, four regional bowl games were played in order to provide postseason action for what then were called NCAA College Division member institutions. Following are the results of those bowl games:

EAST (Tangerine Bowl)

Year	Champion	Coach	Score	Runner-Up	Site
1964	East Caro.	Clarence Stasavich	14-13	Massachusetts	Orlando, Fla.
1965	East Caro.	Clarence Stasavich	31-0	Maine	Orlando, Fla.
1966	Morgan St.	Earl Banks	14-6	West Chester	Orlando, Fla.
1967	Tenn.-Martin	Robert Carroll	25-8	West Chester	Orlando, Fla.

EAST (Boardwalk Bowl)

Year	Champion	Coach	Score	Runner-Up	Site
1968	Delaware	Tubby Raymond	31-24	Indiana (Pa.)	Atlantic City, N. J.
1969	Delaware	Tubby Raymond	31-13	N. C. Central	Atlantic City, N. J.
1970	Delaware	Tubby Raymond	38-23	Morgan St.	Atlantic City, N. J.
1971	Delaware	Tubby Raymond	72-22	LIU-C. W. Post	Atlantic City, N. J.
1972	Massachusetts	Dick MacPherson	35-14	UC Davis	Atlantic City, N. J.

MIDEAST (Grantland Rice Bowl)

Year	Champion	Coach	Score	Runner-Up	Site
1964	Middle Tenn. St.	Charles Murphy	20-0	Muskingum	Murfreesboro, Tenn.
1965	Ball St.	Ray Louthen	14-14	—	Murfreesboro, Tenn.
	Tennessee St.	John Merritt			
1966	Tennessee St.	John Merritt	34-7	Muskingum	Murfreesboro, Tenn.
1967	Eastern Ky.	Roy Kidd	27-13	Ball St.	Murfreesboro, Tenn.
1968	Louisiana Tech	Maxie Lambright	33-13	Akron	Murfreesboro, Tenn.
1969	East Tenn. St.	John Bell	34-14	Louisiana Tech	Baton Rouge, La.
1970	Tennessee St.	John Merritt	26-25	Southwestern La.	Baton Rouge, La.
1971	Tennessee St.	John Merritt	26-23	McNeese St.	Baton Rouge, La.
1972	Louisiana Tech	Maxie Lambright	35-0	Tennessee Tech	Baton Rouge, La.

MIDWEST (Pecan Bowl)

Year	Champion	Coach	Score	Runner-Up	Site
1964	Northern Iowa	Stan Sheriff	19-17	Lamar	Abilene, Tex.
1965	North Dak. St.	Darrell Mudra	20-7	Grambling	Abilene, Tex.
1966	North Dak.	Marv Helling	42-24	Parsons	Abilene, Tex.
1967	Texas-Arlington	Burley Bearden	13-0	North Dak. St.	Abilene, Tex.
1968	North Dak. St.	Ron Erhardt	23-14	Arkansas St.	Arlington, Tex.
1969	Arkansas St.	Bennie Ellender	29-21	Drake	Arlington, Tex.
1970	Arkansas St.	Bennie Ellender	38-21	Central Mo. St.	Arlington, Tex.

MIDWEST (Pioneer Bowl)

Year	Champion	Coach	Score	Runner-Up	Site
1971	Louisiana Tech	Maxie Lambright	14-3	Eastern Mich.	Wichita Falls, Tex.
1972	Tennessee St.	John Merritt	29-7	Drake	Wichita Falls, Tex.

WEST (Camellia Bowl)

Year	Champion	Coach	Score	Runner-Up	Site
1964	Montana St.	Jim Sweeney	28-7	Cal St. Sacramento	Sacramento, Cal.
1965	Cal St. Los Angeles	Homer Beatty	18-10	UC Santa Barb.	Sacramento, Cal.
1966	San Diego St.	Don Coryell	28-7	Montana St.	Sacramento, Cal.
1967	San Diego St.	Don Coryell	27-6	San Fran. St.	Sacramento, Cal.
1968	Humboldt St.	Frank VanDeren	29-14	Fresno St.	Sacramento, Cal.
1969	North Dak. St.	Ron Erhardt	30-3	Montana	Sacramento, Cal.
1970	North Dak. St.	Ron Erhardt	31-16	Montana	Sacramento, Cal.
1971	Boise St.	Tony Knap	32-28	Cal St. Chico	Sacramento, Cal.
1972	North Dak.	Jerry Olson	38-21	Cal Poly SLO	Sacramento, Cal.

1991 DIVISION II CHAMPIONSHIP RESULTS

First Round
Pittsburg St. 26, Butler 16
East Tex. St. 36, Grand Valley St. 15
Portland St. 28, Northern Colo. 24
Mankato St. 27, North Dak. St. 7
Jacksonville St. 49, Winston-Salem 24
Mississippi Col. 28, Wofford 15
Indiana (Pa.) 56, Virginia Union 7
Shippensburg 34, East Stroudsburg 33 (OT)

Quarterfinals
Pittsburg St. 38, East Tex. St. 28
Portland St. 37, Mankato St. 27
Jacksonville St. 35, Mississippi Col. 7
Indiana (Pa.) 52, Shippensburg 7

Semifinals
Pittsburg St. 53, Portland St. 21
Jacksonville St. 27, Indiana (Pa.) 20

Championship
Pittsburg St. 23, Jacksonville St. 6

CHAMPIONSHIP RECORDS
INDIVIDUAL: SINGLE GAME

Net Yards Rushing
243—Eddie Brundidge, Troy St. (31) vs. Virginia Union (7), 11-29-86.

Rushes Attempted
51—Terry Morrow, Central St. (Ohio) (31) vs. Towson St. (0), 11-28-86.

Touchdowns by Rushing
   4—Dick Dunham, Central Mich. (54) vs. Delaware (14), 12-14-74; Robby Robson, Youngstown St. (50) vs. South Dak. St. (7), 11-24-79; Heath Sherman, Texas A&I (34) vs. Tenn.-Martin (0), 11-26-88; Darren Dawson, Pittsburg St. (60) vs. East Tex. St. (28), 11-24-90.

Net Yards Passing
   443—Tom Bertoldi, Northern Mich. (55) vs. Elizabeth City St. (6), 11-28-81.

Passes Attempted
   59—Bob Biggs, UC Davis (14) vs. Massachusetts (35), 12-9-72.

Passes Completed
   32—Darren Del'Andrae, Portland St. (56) vs. West Chester (50), 3 OT, 11-18-89.

Passes Had Intercepted
   7—George Coussan, Southwestern La. (25) vs. Tennessee St. (26), 12-12-70.

Touchdown Passes Completed
   6—Darren Del'Andrae, Portland St. (56) vs. West Chester (50), 3 OT, 11-18-89.

Completion Percentage (min. 8 attempts)
   .833—Tony Aliucci, Indiana (Pa.) (56) vs. Virginia Union (7), 11-23-91 (10 of 12).

Net Yards Rushing and Passing
   444—Tom Bertoldi, Northern Mich. (55) vs. Elizabeth City St. (6), 11-28-81.

Number of Rushing and Passing Plays
   63—Bob Biggs, UC Davis (14) vs. Massachusetts (35), 12-9-72.

Punting Average (min. 3 punts)
   53.7—Chris Humes, UC Davis (23) vs. Angelo St. (28), 11-18-89.

Number of Punts
   12—Dan Gentry, Tennessee Tech (0) vs. Louisiana Tech (35), 12-9-72.

Passes Caught
   14—Don Hutt, Boise St. (34) vs. Louisiana Tech (38), 12-8-73.

Net Yards Receiving
   220—Steve Hansley, Northwest Mo. St. (15) vs. Nebraska-Omaha (28), 11-24-84.

Touchdown Passes Caught
   4—Steve Kreider, Lehigh (30) vs. Massachusetts (23), 11-26-77; Scott Asman, West Chester (50) vs. Portland St. (56), 3 OT, 11-18-89.

Passes Intercepted
   5—Don Pinson, Tennessee St. (26) vs. Southwestern La. (25), 12-12-70.

Yards Gained on Interception Returns
   113—Darren Ryals, Millersville (27) vs. Indiana (Pa.) (24), 2 returns for 53- and 60-yard TDs, 11-19-88.

Yards Gained on Punt Returns
   138—Rick Caswell, Western Ky. (14) vs. New Hampshire (3), 12-6-75.

Yards Gained on Kickoff Returns
   182—Larry Anderson, LIU-C. W. Post (22) vs. Delaware (72), 12-11-71.

Points
   24—Six times. Most recent: Darren Dawson, Pittsburg St. (60) vs. East Tex. St. (28), 11-24-90.

Touchdowns
   4—Six times. Most recent: Darren Dawson, Pittsburg St. (60) vs. East Tex. St. (28), 11-24-90.

Extra Points
   10—Larry Washington, Delaware (72) vs. LIU-C. W. Post (22), 12-11-71.

Field Goals
   4—Mario Ferretti, Northern Mich. (55) vs. Elizabeth City St. (6), 11-28-81; Ken Kubisz, North Dak. St. (26) vs. UC Davis (17), 12-3-83.

INDIVIDUAL: TOURNAMENT

Net Yards Rushing
   619—Tony Satter, North Dak. St., 1990 (160 vs. Northern Colo., 109 vs. Cal Poly SLO, 176 vs. Pittsburg St., 174 vs. Indiana, Pa.).

Rushes Attempted
   96—Lawrence Jefferson, Western Ky., 1975 (33 vs. Northern Iowa, 29 vs. New Hampshire, 34 vs. Northern Mich.).

Net Yards Passing
   1,226—Chris Crawford, Portland St., 1988 (248 vs. Bowie St., 375 vs. Jacksonville St., 270 vs. Texas A&I, 333 vs. North Dak. St.).

Passes Attempted
   139—Chris Crawford, Portland St., 1988 (31 vs. Bowie St., 41 vs. Jacksonville St., 32 vs. Texas A&I, 35 vs. North Dak. St.).

Passes Completed
   94—Chris Crawford, Portland St., 1988 (20 vs. Bowie St., 27 vs. Jacksonville St., 25 vs. Texas A&I, 22 vs. North Dak. St.).

Touchdown Passes Completed
   10—Chris Crawford, Portland St., 1988 (2 vs. Bowie St., 2 vs. Jacksonville St., 3 vs. Texas A&I, 3 vs. North Dak. St.).

Completion Percentage (min. 2 games)
   .824—Mike Turk, Troy St., 1984, 14 of 17 (4-5 vs. Central St., Ohio, 5-5 vs. Towson St., 5-7 vs. North Dak. St.).

Passes Had Intercepted
   9—Dennis Tomek, Western Ky., 1973 (0 vs. Lehigh, 6 vs. Grambling, 3 vs. Louisiana Tech).

Passes Caught
   27—Don Hutt, Boise St., 1973 (13 vs. South Dak., 14 vs. Louisiana Tech).

Net Yards Receiving
   452—Henry Newson, Portland St., 1991 (94 vs. Northern Colo., 209 vs. Mankato St., 149 vs. Pittsburg St.).

Touchdown Passes Caught
   7—Steve Kreider, Lehigh, 1977 (4 vs. Massachusetts, 1 vs. UC Davis, 2 vs. Jacksonville St.).

Points
   54—Chris Simdorn, North Dak. St., 1988 (6 vs. Augustana, S.D., 18 vs. Millersville, 18 vs. Cal St. Sacramento, 12 vs. Portland St.).

Touchdowns
   9—Chris Simdorn, North Dak. St., 1988 (1 vs. Augustana, S.D., 3 vs. Millersville, 3 vs. Jacksonville St., 2 vs. Portland St.).

INDIVIDUAL: LONGEST PLAYS

Longest Rush
84—Dick Kelley, Delaware (38) vs. Morgan St. (23), 12-12-70, TD.

Longest Pass Completion
91—Ken O'Brien to Allen Fleming, UC Davis (42) vs. Northern Mich. (21), 11-27-82, TD.

Longest Field Goal
50—Ted Clem, Troy St. (18) vs. North Dak. St. (17), 12-8-84.

Longest Punt
76—Chris Humes, UC Davis (23) vs. Angelo St. (28), 11-18-89.

Longest Punt Return
91—Winford Wilborn, Louisiana Tech (14) vs. Eastern Mich. (3), 12-11-71, TD.

Longest Kickoff Return
100—Ken Bowles, Nevada-Las Vegas (6) vs. Akron (26), 11-26-76, TD.

Longest Interception Return
100—Charles Harris, Jacksonville St. (34) vs. Northeast Mo. St. (21), 11-27-82, TD.

Longest Fumble Return
93—Ray Neal, Middle Tenn. St. (20) vs. Muskingum (0), 12-12-64, TD.

TEAM: SINGLE GAME

First Downs
34—Delaware (72) vs. LIU-C. W. Post (22), 12-11-71; Delaware (60) vs. Mississippi Col. (10), 12-1-79; Cal St. Sacramento (56) vs. N. C. Central (7), 11-26-88.

First Downs by Rushing
27—Delaware (72) vs. LIU-C. W. Post (22), 12-11-71.

First Downs by Passing
23—Central Fla. (10) vs. Troy St. (31), 12-5-87; Portland St. (56) vs. West Chester (50), 3 OT, 11-18-89.

Net Yards Rushing
566—Jacksonville St. (63) vs. West Chester (24), 11-19-88.

Rushes Attempted
84—Southwest Tex. St. (34) vs. UC Davis (9), 12-11-82.

Net Yards Passing
464—Northern Mich. (55) vs. Elizabeth City St. (6), 11-28-81.

Passes Attempted
60—San Fran. St. (6) vs. San Diego St. (27), 12-9-67; Central Fla. (10) vs. Troy St. (31), 12-5-87.

Passes Completed
36—Central Fla. (10) vs. Troy St. (31), 12-5-87.

Completion Percentage (min. 10 attempts)
.813—Delaware (60) vs. Mississippi Col. (10), 12-1-79 (13 of 16).

Passes Had Intercepted
8—Southwestern La. (25) vs. Tennessee St. (26), 12-12-70.

Net Yards Rushing and Passing
695—Northern Mich. (55) vs. Elizabeth City St. (6), 11-28-81.

Rushing and Passing Plays
98—Northern Mich. (55) vs. Elizabeth City St. (6), 11-28-81.

Punting Average
53.7—UC Davis (23) vs. Angelo St. (28), 11-18-89.

Number of Punts
12—Tennessee Tech (0) vs. Louisiana Tech (35), 12-9-72; Delaware (8) vs. Grambling (17), 12-1-73; Western Ky. (0) vs. Louisiana Tech (34), 12-15-73.

Punts Had Blocked
2—Delaware (31) vs. Indiana (Pa.) (24), 12-14-68; Humboldt St. (29) vs. Fresno St. (14), 12-14-68; Northeast Mo. St. (21) vs. Jacksonville St. (34), 11-27-82.

Yards Gained on Punt Returns
140—Southwest Tex. St. (62) vs. Northern Mich. (0), 12-5-81.

Yards Gained on Kickoff Returns
251—LIU-C. W. Post (22) vs. Delaware (72), 12-11-71.

Yards Gained on Interception Returns
131—Millersville (27) vs. Indiana (Pa.) (24), 11-19-88.

Yards Penalized
166—San Diego St. (27) vs. San Fran. St. (6), 12-9-67.

Number of Penalties
21—San Diego St. (27) vs. San Fran. St. (6), 12-9-67.

Fumbles
10—Winston-Salem (0) vs. Delaware (41), 12-2-78.

Fumbles Lost
7—Louisiana Tech (10) vs. Western Caro. (7), 11-30-74.

Points
72—Delaware vs. LIU-C. W. Post (22), 12-11-72.

TEAM: TOURNAMENT

First Downs
98—North Dak. St., 1990 (27 vs. Northern Colo., 23 vs. Cal Poly SLO, 25 vs. Pittsburg St., 23 vs. Indiana, Pa.).

Net Yards Rushing
1,660—North Dak. St., 1988 (474 vs. Augustana, S.D., 434 vs. Millersville, 413 vs. Cal St. Sacramento, 339 vs. Portland St.).

Net Yards Passing
1,226—Portland St., 1988 (248 vs. Bowie St., 375 vs. Jacksonville St., 270 vs. Texas A&I, 333 vs. North Dak. St.).

Net Yards Rushing and Passing
1,969—North Dak. St., 1990 (455 vs. Northern Colo., 463 vs. Cal Poly SLO, 424 vs. Pittsburg St., 627 vs. Indiana, Pa.).

Passes Attempted
139—Portland St., 1988 (31 vs. Bowie St., 41 vs. Jacksonville St., 32 vs. Texas A&I, 35 vs. North Dak. St.).

Passes Completed
94—Portland St., 1988 (20 vs. Bowie St., 27 vs. Jacksonville St., 25 vs. Texas A&I, 22 vs. North Dak. St.).

Passes Had Intercepted
10—Western Ky., 1973 (0 vs. Lehigh, 6 vs. Grambling, 4 vs. Louisiana Tech).

Number of Punts
29—Western Ky., 1973 (6 vs. Lehigh, 11 vs. Grambling, 12 vs. Louisiana Tech).

Yards Penalized
292—Eastern Ill., 1980 (92 vs. Northern Colo.,

60 vs. North Ala., 140 vs. Cal Poly SLO).

Fumbles
16—Delaware, 1978 (8 vs. Jacksonville St., 2 vs. Winston-Salem, 6 vs. Eastern Ill.).

Fumbles Lost
12—Delaware, 1978 (6 vs. Jacksonville St., 2 vs. Winston-Salem, 4 vs. Eastern Ill.).

Points
162—North Dak. St., 1988 (49 vs. Augustana, S.D., 36 vs. Millersville, 42 vs. Cal St. Sacramento, 35 vs. Portland St.).

Ronald Moore of Pittsburg State looks for tough yardage in the Gorillas' 23-6 victory over Jacksonville State in the 1991 Division II title game. Moore and teammate Darren Dawson were the tournament's top two rushers with 536 and 522 yards, respectively.

YEAR-BY-YEAR DIVISION II CHAMPIONSHIP RESULTS

Year (Number of Teams)	Coach	Record	Result
1973 (8)			
Louisiana Tech	Maxie Lambright	3-0	Champion
Western Ky.	Jimmy Feix	2-1	Second
Boise St.	Tony Knap	1-1	Semifinalist
Grambling	Eddie Robinson	1-1	Semifinalist
Delaware	Tubby Raymond	0-1	Lost 1st Round
Lehigh	Fred Dunlap	0-1	Lost 1st Round
South Dak.	Joe Salem	0-1	Lost 1st Round
Western Ill.	Darrell Mudra	0-1	Lost 1st Round
1974 (8)			
Central Mich.	Roy Kramer	3-0	Champion
Delaware	Tubby Raymond	2-1	Second
Louisiana Tech	Maxie Lambright	1-1	Semifinalist

Year (Number of Teams)	Coach	Record	Result
Nevada-Las Vegas	Ron Meyer	1-1	Semifinalist
Alcorn St.	Marino Casem	0-1	Lost 1st Round
Boise St.	Tony Knap	0-1	Lost 1st Round
Western Caro...................	Bob Waters	0-1	Lost 1st Round
Youngstown St.	Rey Dempsey	0-1	Lost 1st Round
1975 (8)			
Northern Mich.................	Gil Krueger	3-0	Champion
Western Ky.	Jimmy Feix	2-1	Second
Livingston	Jim King	1-1	Semifinalist
New Hampshire	Bill Bowes	1-1	Semifinalist
Boise St.	Tony Knap	0-1	Lost 1st Round
Lehigh	Fred Dunlap	0-1	Lost 1st Round
North Dak.....................	Jerry Olson	0-1	Lost 1st Round
Northern Iowa	Stan Sheriff	0-1	Lost 1st Round
1976 (8)			
Montana St....................	Sonny Holland	3-0	Champion
Akron	Jim Dennison	2-1	Second
North Dak. St.................	Jim Wacker	1-1	Semifinalist
Northern Mich.................	Gil Krueger	1-1	Semifinalist
Delaware	Tubby Raymond	0-1	Lost 1st Round
Eastern Ky.	Roy Kidd	0-1	Lost 1st Round
Nevada-Las Vegas	Tony Knap	0-1	Lost 1st Round
New Hampshire	Bill Bowes	0-1	Lost 1st Round
1977 (8)			
Lehigh	John Whitehead	3-0	Champion
Jacksonville St................	Jim Fuller	2-1	Second
North Dak. St.................	Jim Wacker	1-1	Semifinalist
UC Davis	Jim Sochor	1-1	Semifinalist
Bethune-Cookman	Andy Hinson	0-1	Lost 1st Round
Massachusetts	Dick MacPherson	0-1	Lost 1st Round
Northern Ariz..................	Joe Salem	0-1	Lost 1st Round
Northern Mich.................	Gil Krueger	0-1	Lost 1st Round
1978 (8)			
Eastern Ill.	Darrell Mudra	3-0	Champion
Delaware	Tubby Raymond	2-1	Second
Winston-Salem	Bill Hayes	1-1	Semifinalist
Youngstown St.	Bill Narduzzi	1-1	Semifinalist
Cal Poly SLO	Joe Harper	0-1	Lost 1st Round
Jacksonville St................	Jim Fuller	0-1	Lost 1st Round
Nebraska-Omaha...............	Sandy Buda	0-1	Lost 1st Round
UC Davis	Jim Sochor	0-1	Lost 1st Round
1979 (8)			
Delaware	Tubby Raymond	3-0	Champion
Youngstown St.	Bill Narduzzi	2-1	Second
Alabama A&M	Ray Greene	1-1	Semifinalist
Mississippi Col.	John Williams	1-1	Semifinalist
Morgan St.	Clarence Thomas	0-1	Lost 1st Round
North Dak.....................	Gene Murphy	0-1	Lost 1st Round
South Dak. St.	John Gregory	0-1	Lost 1st Round
Virginia Union.................	Willard Bailey	0-1	Lost 1st Round
1980 (8)			
Cal Poly SLO	Joe Harper	3-0	Champion
Eastern Ill.	Darrell Mudra	2-1	Second
North Ala.	Wayne Grubb	1-1	Semifinalist
Santa Clara	Pat Malley	1-1	Semifinalist
Jacksonville St................	Jim Fuller	0-1	Lost 1st Round
Northern Colo.	Bob Blasi	0-1	Lost 1st Round
Northern Mich.................	Bill Rademacher	0-1	Lost 1st Round
Virginia Union.................	Willard Bailey	0-1	Lost 1st Round
1981 (8)			
Southwest Tex. St.	Jim Wacker	3-0	Champion
North Dak. St.................	Don Morton	2-1	Second
Northern Mich.................	Bill Rademacher	1-1	Semifinalist
Shippensburg	Vito Ragazzo	1-1	Semifinalist
Elizabeth City St.	Johnnie Walton	0-1	Lost 1st Round
Jacksonville St................	Jim Fuller	0-1	Lost 1st Round
Puget Sound	Ron Simonson	0-1	Lost 1st Round
Virginia Union.................	Willard Bailey	0-1	Lost 1st Round
1982 (8)			
Southwest Tex. St.	Jim Wacker	3-0	Champion

Year (Number of Teams)	Coach	Record	Result
UC Davis	Jim Sochor	2-1	Second
Jacksonville St.	Jim Fuller	1-1	Semifinalist
North Dak. St.	Don Morton	1-1	Semifinalist
Fort Valley St.	Doug Porter	0-1	Lost 1st Round
Northeast Mo. St.	Bruce Craddock	0-1	Lost 1st Round
Northern Mich.	Bill Rademacher	0-1	Lost 1st Round
Virginia Union	Willard Bailey	0-1	Lost 1st Round
1983 (8)			
North Dak. St.	Don Morton	3-0	Champion
Central St. (Ohio)	Billy Joe	2-1	Second
North Ala.	Wayne Grubb	1-1	Semifinalist
UC Davis	Jim Sochor	1-1	Semifinalist
Butler	Bill Sylvester	0-1	Lost 1st Round
Southwest Tex. St.	John O'Hara	0-1	Lost 1st Round
Towson St.	Phil Albert	0-1	Lost 1st Round
Virginia Union	Willard Bailey	0-1	Lost 1st Round
1984 (8)			
Troy St.	Chan Gailey	3-0	Champion
North Dak. St.	Don Morton	2-1	Second
Nebraska-Omaha	Sandy Buda	1-1	Semifinalist
Towson St.	Phil Albert	1-1	Semifinalist
Central St. (Ohio)	Billy Joe	0-1	Lost 1st Round
Norfolk St.	Willard Bailey	0-1	Lost 1st Round
Northwest Mo. St.	Vern Thomsen	0-1	Lost 1st Round
UC Davis	Jim Sochor	0-1	Lost 1st Round
1985 (8)			
North Dak. St.	Earle Solomonson	3-0	Champion
North Ala.	Wayne Grubb	2-1	Second
Bloomsburg	George Landis	1-1	Semifinalist
South Dak.	Dave Triplett	1-1	Semifinalist
Central St. (Ohio)	Billy Joe	0-1	Lost 1st Round
Fort Valley St.	Gerald Walker	0-1	Lost 1st Round
Hampton	Fred Freeman	0-1	Lost 1st Round
UC Davis	Jim Sochor	0-1	Lost 1st Round
1986 (8)			
North Dak. St.	Earle Solomonson	3-0	Champion
South Dak.	Dave Triplett	2-1	Second
Central St. (Ohio)	Billy Joe	1-1	Semifinalist
Troy St.	Rick Rhodes	1-1	Semifinalist
Ashland	Fred Martinelli	0-1	Lost 1st Round
Towson St.	Phil Albert	0-1	Lost 1st Round
UC Davis	Jim Sochor	0-1	Lost 1st Round
Virginia Union	Joe Taylor	0-1	Lost 1st Round
1987 (8)			
Troy St.	Rick Rhodes	3-0	Champion
Portland St.	Pokey Allen	2-1	Second
Central Fla.	Gene McDowell	1-1	Semifinalist
Northern Mich.	Herb Grenke	1-1	Semifinalist
Angelo St.	Jerry Vandergriff	0-1	Lost 1st Round
Indiana (Pa.)	Frank Cignetti	0-1	Lost 1st Round
Mankato St.	Dan Runkle	0-1	Lost 1st Round
Winston-Salem	Bill Hayes	0-1	Lost 1st Round
1988 (16)			
North Dak. St.	Rocky Hager	4-0	Champion
Portland St.	Pokey Allen	3-1	Second
Cal St. Sacramento	Bob Mattos	2-1	Semifinalist
Texas A&I	Ron Harms	2-1	Semifinalist
Jacksonville St.	Bill Burgess	1-1	Quarterfinalist
Millersville	Gene Carpenter	1-1	Quarterfinalist
N. C. Central	Henry Lattimore	1-1	Quarterfinalist
Tenn.-Martin	Don McLeary	1-1	Quarterfinalist
Augustana (S. D.)	Jim Heinitz	0-1	Lost 1st Round
Bowie St.	Sanders Shiver	0-1	Lost 1st Round
Butler	Bill Lynch	0-1	Lost 1st Round
Indiana (Pa.)	Frank Cignetti	0-1	Lost 1st Round
Mississippi Col.	John Williams	0-1	Lost 1st Round
UC Davis	Jim Sochor	0-1	Lost 1st Round
West Chester	Danny Hale	0-1	Lost 1st Round
Winston-Salem	Pete Richardson	0-1	Lost 1st Round

Year (Number of Teams)	Coach	Record	Result
1989 (16)			
Mississippi Col.	John Williams	4-0	Champion
Jacksonville St...................	Bill Burgess	3-1	Second
Angelo St.	Jerry Vandergriff	2-1	Semifinalist
Indiana (Pa.)	Frank Cignetti	2-1	Semifinalist
North Dak. St.	Rocky Hager	1-1	Quarterfinalist
Pittsburg St.	Dennis Franchione	1-1	Quarterfinalist
Portland St.	Pokey Allen	1-1	Quarterfinalist
St. Cloud St.	Noel Martin	1-1	Quarterfinalist
Alabama A&M	George Pugh	0-1	Lost 1st Round
Augustana (S. D.)	Jim Heinitz	0-1	Lost 1st Round
Edinboro	Tom Hollman	0-1	Lost 1st Round
Grand Valley St.	Tom Beck	0-1	Lost 1st Round
Northwest Mo. St.	Bud Elliott	0-1	Lost 1st Round
Texas A&I	Ron Harms	0-1	Lost 1st Round
UC Davis	Bob Foster	0-1	Lost 1st Round
West Chester	Rick Daniels	0-1	Lost 1st Round
1990 (16)			
North Dak. St...................	Rocky Hager	4-0	Champion
Indiana (Pa.)	Frank Cignetti	3-1	Second
Mississippi Col.	John Williams	2-1	Semifinalist
Pittsburg St.	Chuck Broyles	2-1	Semifinalist
Cal Poly SLO	Lyle Setencich	1-1	Quarterfinalist
East Tex. St.	Eddie Vowell	1-1	Quarterfinalist
Edinboro	Tom Hollman	1-1	Quarterfinalist
Jacksonville St...................	Bill Burgess	1-1	Quarterfinalist
Cal St. Northridge	Bob Burt	0-1	Lost 1st Round
Grand Valley St.	Tom Beck	0-1	Lost 1st Round
North Ala.	Bobby Wallace	0-1	Lost 1st Round
Northeast Mo. St.	Eric Holm	0-1	Lost 1st Round
Northern Colo.	Joe Glenn	0-1	Lost 1st Round
Virginia Union..................	Joe Taylor	0-1	Lost 1st Round
Winston-Salem	Pete Richardson	0-1	Lost 1st Round
Wofford	Mike Ayers	0-1	Lost 1st Round
1991 (16)			
Pittsburg St.	Chuck Broyles	4-0	Champion
Jacksonville St...................	Bill Burgess	3-1	Second
Indiana (Pa.)	Frank Cignetti	2-1	Semifinalist
Portland St.	Pokey Allen	2-1	Semifinalist
East Tex. St.	Eddie Vowell	1-1	Quarterfinalist
Mankato St.....................	Dan Runkle	1-1	Quarterfinalist
Mississippi Col.	Terry McMillan	1-1	Quarterfinalist
Shippensburg	Rocky Rees	1-1	Quarterfinalist
Butler	Bob Bartolomeo	0-1	Lost 1st Round
East Stroudsburg	Dennis Douds	0-1	Lost 1st Round
Grand Valley St.	Brian Kelly	0-1	Lost 1st Round
Northern Colo.	Joe Glenn	0-1	Lost 1st Round
North Dak. St...................	Rocky Hager	0-1	Lost 1st Round
Virginia Union..................	Joe Taylor	0-1	Lost 1st Round
Winston-Salem	Pete Richardson	0-1	Lost 1st Round
Wofford	Mike Ayers	0-1	Lost 1st Round

DIVISION II CHAMPIONSHIP
ALL-TIME RECORD OF EACH COLLEGE
COACH-BY-COACH, 1973-91 (75 Colleges)

	Yrs	Won	Lost	CH	2D
AKRON					
Jim Dennison (Wooster '60) 76-2D	1	2	1	0	1
ALABAMA A&M					
Ray Greene (Akron '63) 79	1	1	1	0	0
George Pugh (Alabama '76) 89	1	0	1	0	0
TOTAL	2	1	2	0	0
ALCORN ST.					
Marino Casem (Xavier, La. '56) 74	1	0	1	0	0
ANGELO ST.					
Jerry Vandergriff (Corpus Christi '65) 87, 89	2	2	2	0	0
ASHLAND					
Fred Martinelli (Otterbein '51) 86..................	1	0	1	0	0

	Yrs	Won	Lost	CH	2D
AUGUSTANA (S. D.)					
Jim Heinitz (South Dak. St. '72) 88, 89	2	0	2	0	0
BETHUNE-COOKMAN					
Andy Hinson (Bethune-Cookman '53) 77	1	0	1	0	0
BLOOMSBURG					
George Landis (Penn St. '71) 85	1	1	1	0	0
BOISE ST.					
Tony Knap (Idaho '39) 73, 74, 75	3	1	3	0	0
BOWIE ST.					
Sanders Shiver (Carson-Newman '76) 88	1	0	1	0	0
BUTLER					
Bill Sylvester (Butler '50) 83	1	0	1	0	0
Bill Lynch (Butler '77) 88	1	0	1	0	0
Bob Bartolomeo (Butler '77) 91	1	0	1	0	0
TOTAL	3	0	3	0	0
CAL POLY SLO					
Joe Harper (UCLA '59) 78, 80-CH..................	2	3	1	1	0
Lyle Setencich (Fresno St. '68) 90..................	1	1	1	0	0
TOTAL	3	4	2	1	0
CAL ST. NORTHRIDGE					
Bob Burt (Cal St. Los Angeles '62) 90	1	0	1	0	0
CAL ST. SACRAMENTO					
Bob Mattos (Cal St. Sacramento '64) 88	1	2	1	0	0
CENTRAL FLA.					
Gene McDowell (Florida St. '65) 87	1	1	1	0	0
CENTRAL MICH.					
Roy Kramer (Maryville, Tenn. '53) 74-CH............	1	3	0	1	0
CENTRAL ST. (OHIO)					
Billy Joe (Cheyney '70) 83-2D, 84, 85, 86	4	3	4	0	1
DELAWARE					
Tubby Raymond (Michigan '50) 73, 74-2D, 76, 78-2D, 79-CH..	5	7	4	1	2
EAST STROUDSBURG					
Dennis Douds (Slippery Rock '63) 91...............	1	0	1	0	0
EAST TEX. ST.					
Eddie Vowell (Southwestern Okla. '69) 90, 91	2	2	2	0	0
EASTERN ILL.					
Darrell Mudra (Peru St. '51) 78-CH, 80-2D	2	5	1	1	1
EASTERN KY.					
Roy Kidd (Eastern Ky. '54) 76	1	0	1	0	0
EDINBORO					
Tom Hollman (Ohio Northern '68) 89, 90	2	1	2	0	0
ELIZABETH CITY ST.					
Johnnie Walton (Elizabeth City St. '69) 81	1	0	1	0	0
FORT VALLEY ST.					
Doug Porter (Xavier, La. '52) 82	1	0	1	0	0
Gerald Walker (Lincoln, Mo. '62) 85	1	0	1	0	0
TOTAL	2	0	2	0	0
GRAMBLING					
Eddie Robinson (Leland '41) 73.....................	1	1	1	0	0
GRAND VALLEY ST.					
Tom Beck (Northern Ill. '61) 89, 90	2	0	2	0	0
Brian Kelly (Assumption '83) 91	1	0	1	0	0
TOTAL	3	0	3	0	0
HAMPTON					
Fred Freeman (Mississippi Val. '66) 85	1	0	1	0	0
INDIANA (PA.)					
Frank Cignetti (Indiana, Pa. '60) 87, 88, 89, 90-2D, 91 .	5	7	5	0	1
JACKSONVILLE ST.					
Jim Fuller (Alabama '67) 77-2D, 78, 80, 81, 82	5	3	5	0	1
Bill Burgess (Auburn '63) 88, 89-2D, 90, 91-2D.......	4	8	4	0	2
TOTAL	9	11	9	0	3

Division II Championship Results, Records

477

	Yrs	Won	Lost	CH	2D
LEHIGH					
Fred Dunlap (Colgate '50) 73, 75	2	0	2	0	0
John Whitehead (East Stroudsburg '50) 77-CH	1	3	0	1	0
TOTAL	3	3	2	1	0
LIVINGSTON					
Jim King '75	1	1	1	0	0
LOUISIANA TECH					
Maxie Lambright (Southern Miss. '49) 73-CH, 74	2	4	1	1	0
MANKATO ST.					
Dan Runkle (Illinois Col. '68) 87, 91	2	1	2	0	0
MASSACHUSETTS					
Dick MacPherson (Springfield '58) 77	1	0	1	0	0
MILLERSVILLE					
Gene Carpenter (Huron '63) 88	1	1	1	0	0
MISSISSIPPI COL.					
John Williams (Mississippi Col. '57) 79, 88, 89-CH, 90	4	7	3	1	0
Terry McMillan (Southern Miss. '69) 91	1	1	1	0	0
TOTAL	5	8	4	1	0
MONTANA ST.					
Sonny Holland (Montana St. '60) 76-CH	1	3	0	1	0
MORGAN ST.					
Clarence Thomas 79	1	0	1	0	0
N. C. CENTRAL					
Henry Lattimore (Jackson St. '57) 88	1	1	1	0	0
NEBRASKA-OMAHA					
Sandy Buda (Kansas '67) 78, 84	2	1	2	0	0
NEVADA-LAS VEGAS					
Ron Meyer (Purdue '63) 74.	1	1	1	0	0
Tony Knap (Idaho '39) 76	1	0	1	0	0
TOTAL	2	1	2	0	0
NEW HAMPSHIRE					
Bill Bowes (Penn St. '65) 75, 76	2	1	2	0	0
NORFOLK ST.					
Willard Bailey (Norfolk St. '62) 84	1	0	1	0	0
NORTH ALA.					
Wayne Grubb (Tennessee '61) 80, 83, 85-2D	3	4	3	0	1
Bobby Wallace (Mississippi St. '76) 90	1	0	1	0	0
TOTAL	4	4	4	0	1
NORTH DAK.					
Jerry Olson (Valley City St. '55) 75	1	0	1	0	0
Gene Murphy (North Dak. '62) 79	1	0	1	0	0
TOTAL	2	0	2	0	0
NORTH DAK. ST.					
Jim Wacker (Valparaiso '60) 76, 77	2	2	2	0	0
Don Morton (Augustana, Ill. '69) 81-2D, 82, 83-CH, 84-2D	4	8	3	1	2
Earle Solomonson (Augsburg '69) 85-CH, 86-CH	2	6	0	2	0
Rocky Hager (North Dak. St. '74) 88-CH, 89, 90-CH, 91	4	9	2	2	0
TOTAL	12	25	7	5	2
NORTHEAST MO. ST.					
Bruce Craddock (Northeast Mo. St. '66) 82	1	0	1	0	0
Eric Holm (Northeast Mo. St. '81) 90	1	0	1	0	0
TOTAL	2	0	2	0	0
NORTHERN ARIZ.					
Joe Salem (Minnesota '61) 77	1	0	1	0	0
NORTHERN COLO.					
Bob Blasi (Colorado St. '53) 80	1	0	1	0	0
Joe Glenn (South Dak. '71) 90, 91.	2	0	2	0	0
TOTAL	3	0	3	0	0
NORTHERN IOWA					
Stan Sheriff (Cal Poly SLO '54) 75	1	0	1	0	0

1992 NCAA FOOTBALL

	Yrs	Won	Lost	CH	2D
NORTHERN MICH.					
Gil Krueger (Marquette '52) 75-CH, 76, 77	3	4	2	1	0
Bill Rademacher (Northern Mich. '63) 80, 81, 82	3	1	3	0	0
Herb Grenke (Wis.-Milwaukee '63) 87	1	1	1	0	0
TOTAL	7	6	6	1	0
NORTHWEST MO. ST.					
Vern Thomsen (Peru St. '61) 84	1	0	1	0	0
Bud Elliott (Baker '53) 89	1	0	1	0	0
TOTAL	2	0	2	0	0
PITTSBURG ST.					
Dennis Franchione (Pittsburg St. '73) 89	1	1	1	0	0
Chuck Broyles (Pittsburg St. '70) 90, 91-CH	2	6	1	1	0
TOTAL	3	7	2	1	0
PORTLAND ST.					
Pokey Allen (Utah '65) 87-2D, 88-2D, 89, 91	4	8	4	0	2
PUGET SOUND					
Ron Simonson (Portland St. '65) 81	1	0	1	0	0
SANTA CLARA					
Pat Malley (Santa Clara '53) 80	1	1	1	0	0
SHIPPENSBURG					
Vito Ragazzo (William & Mary '51) 81	1	1	1	0	0
Rocky Rees (West Chester '71) 91	1	1	1	0	0
TOTAL	2	2	2	0	0
SOUTH DAK.					
Joe Salem (Minnesota '61) 73	1	0	1	0	0
Dave Triplett (Iowa '72) 85, 86-2D	2	3	2	0	1
TOTAL	3	3	3	0	1
SOUTH DAK. ST.					
John Gregory (Northern Iowa '61) 79	1	0	1	0	0
SOUTHWEST TEX. ST.					
Jim Wacker (Valparaiso '60) 81-CH, 82-CH	2	6	0	2	0
John O'Hara (Panhandle St. '67) 83	1	0	1	0	0
TOTAL	3	6	1	2	0
ST. CLOUD ST.					
Noel Martin (Nebraska '63) 89	1	1	1	0	0
TEXAS A&I					
Ron Harms (Valparaiso '59) 88, 89	2	2	2	0	0
TENN.-MARTIN					
Don McLeary (Tennessee '70) 88	1	1	1	0	0
TOWSON ST.					
Phil Albert (Arizona '66) 83, 84, 86	3	1	3	0	0
TROY ST.					
Chan Gailey (Florida '74) 84-CH	1	3	0	1	0
Rick Rhodes 86, 87-CH	2	4	1	1	0
TOTAL	3	7	1	2	0
UC DAVIS					
Jim Sochor (San Fran. St. '60) 77, 78, 82-2D, 83,					
84, 85, 86, 88	8	4	8	0	1
Bob Foster (UC Davis '62) 89	1	0	1	0	0
TOTAL	9	4	9	0	1
VIRGINIA UNION					
Willard Bailey (Norfolk St. '62) 79, 80, 81, 82, 83	5	0	5	0	0
Joe Taylor (Western Ill. '72) 86, 90, 91	3	0	3	0	0
TOTAL	8	0	8	0	0
WEST CHESTER					
Danny Hale (West Chester '68) 88	1	0	1	0	0
Rick Daniels (West Chester '75) 89	1	0	1	0	0
TOTAL	2	0	2	0	0
WESTERN CARO.					
Bob Waters (Presbyterian '60) 74	1	0	1	0	0
WESTERN ILL.					
Darrell Mudra (Peru St. '51) 73	1	0	1	0	0
WESTERN KY.					
Jimmy Feix (Western Ky. '53) 73-2D, 75-2D	2	4	2	0	2

Division II Championship Results, Records   479

	Yrs	Won	Lost	CH	2D
WINSTON-SALEM					
Bill Hayes (N. C. Central '64) 78, 87	2	1	2	0	0
Pete Richardson (Dayton '68) 88, 90, 91	3	0	3	0	0
TOTAL	5	1	5	0	0
WOFFORD					
Mike Ayers (Georgetown, Ky. '74) 90, 91	2	0	2	0	0
YOUNGSTOWN ST.					
Rey Dempsey (Geneva '58) 74......................	1	0	1	0	0
Bill Narduzzi (Miami, Ohio '59) 78, 79-2D	2	3	2	0	1
TOTAL	3	3	3	0	1

ALL-TIME RESULTS

1973 First Round: Grambling 17, Delaware 8; Western Ky. 25, Lehigh 16; Louisiana Tech 18, Western Ill. 13; Boise St. 53, South Dak. 10. **Semifinals:** Western Ky. 28, Grambling 20; Louisiana Tech 38, Boise St. 34. **Championship:** Louisiana Tech 34, Western Ky. 0.

1974 First Round: Central Mich. 20, Boise St. 6; Louisiana Tech 10, Western Caro. 7; Nevada-Las Vegas 35, Alcorn St. 22; Delaware 35, Youngstown St. 14. **Semifinals:** Central Mich. 35, Louisiana Tech 14; Delaware 49, Nevada-Las Vegas 11. **Championship:** Central Mich. 54, Delaware 14.

1975 First Round: Northern Mich. 24, Boise St. 21; Livingston 34, North Dak. 14; Western Ky. 14, Northern Iowa 12; New Hampshire 35, Lehigh 21. **Semifinals:** Northern Mich. 28, Livingston 26; Western Ky. 14, New Hampshire 3. **Championship:** Northern Mich. 16, Western Ky. 14.

1976 First Round: Akron 26, Nevada-Las Vegas 6; Northern Mich. 28, Delaware 17; North Dak. St. 10, Eastern Ky. 7; Montana St. 17, New Hampshire 16. **Semifinals:** Akron 29, Northern Mich. 26; Montana St. 10, North Dak. St. 3. **Championship:** Montana St. 24, Akron 13.

1977 First Round: UC Davis 34, Bethune-Cookman 16; Lehigh 30, Massachusetts 23; North Dak. St. 20, Northern Mich. 6; Jacksonville St. 35, Northern Ariz. 0. **Semifinals:** Lehigh 39, UC Davis 30; Jacksonville St. 31, North Dak. St. 7. **Championship:** Lehigh 33, Jacksonville St. 0.

1978 First Round: Winston-Salem 17, Cal Poly SLO 0; Delaware 42, Jacksonville St. 27; Youngstown St. 21, Nebraska-Omaha 14; Eastern Ill. 35, UC Davis 31. **Semifinals:** Delaware 41, Winston-Salem 0; Eastern Ill. 26, Youngstown St. 22. **Championship:** Eastern Ill. 10, Delaware 9.

1979 First Round: Delaware 58, Virginia Union 28; Mississippi Col. 35, North Dak. 15; Youngstown St. 50, South Dak. St. 7; Alabama A&M 27, Morgan St. 7. **Semifinals:** Delaware 60, Mississippi Col. 10; Youngstown St. 52, Alabama A&M 0. **Championship:** Delaware 38, Youngstown St. 21.

1980 First Round: Eastern Ill. 21, Northern Colo. 14; North Ala. 17, Virginia Union 8; Santa Clara 27, Northern Mich. 26; Cal Poly SLO 15, Jacksonville St. 0. **Semifinals:** Eastern Ill. 56, North Ala. 31; Cal Poly SLO 38, Santa Clara 14. **Championship:** Cal Poly SLO 21, Eastern Ill. 13.

1981 First Round: Northern Mich. 55, Elizabeth City St. 6; Southwest Tex. St. 38, Jacksonville St. 22; North Dak. St. 24, Puget Sound 10; Shippensburg 40, Virginia Union 27. **Semifinals:** Southwest Tex. St. 62, Northern Mich. 0; North Dak. St. 18, Shippensburg 6. **Championship:** Southwest Tex. St. 42, North Dak. St. 13.

1982 First Round: Southwest Tex. St. 27, Fort Valley St. 6; Jacksonville St. 34, Northeast Mo. St. 21; North Dak. St. 21, Virginia Union 20; UC Davis 42, Northern Mich. 21. **Semifinals:** Southwes Tex. St. 19, Jacksonville St. 14; UC Davis 19 North Dak. St. 14. **Championship:** Southwes Tex. St. 34, UC Davis 9.

1983 First Round: UC Davis 25, Butler 6; North Dak. St. 24, Towson St. 17; North Ala. 16, Virginia Union 14; Central St. (Ohio) 24, Southwest Tex. St. 16. **Semifinals:** North Dak. St. 26, UC Davis 17; Central St. (Ohio) 27, North Ala. 24. **Championship:** North Dak. St. 41, Central St. (Ohio) 21.

1984 First Round: North Dak. St. 31, UC Davis 23; Nebraska-Omaha 28, Northwest Mo. St. 15; Troy St. 31, Central St. (Ohio) 21; Towson St. 31, Norfolk St. 21. **Semifinals:** North Dak. St. 25, Nebraska-Omaha 14; Troy St. 45, Towson St. 3. **Championship:** Troy St. 18, North Dak. St. 17.

1985 First Round: North Dak. St. 31, UC Davis 12; South Dak. 13, Central St. (Ohio) 10 (2 OT); Bloomsburg 38, Hampton 28; North Ala. 14, Fort Valley St. 7. **Semifinals:** North Dak. St. 16, South Dak. 7; North Ala. 34, Bloomsburg 0. **Championship:** North Dak. St. 35, North Ala. 7.

1986 First Round: North Dak. St. 50, Ashland 0; Central St. (Ohio) 31, Towson St. 0; Troy St. 31, Virginia Union 7; South Dak. 26, UC Davis 23. **Semifinals:** North Dak. St. 35, Central St. (Ohio) 12; South Dak. 42, Troy St. 28. **Championship:** North Dak. St. 27, South Dak. 7.

1987 First Round: Portland St. 27, Mankato St. 21; Northern Mich. 23, Angelo St. 20 (OT); Central Fla. 12, Indiana (Pa.) 10; Troy St. 45, Winston-Salem 14. **Semifinals:** Portland St. 13, Northern Mich. 7; Troy St. 31, Central Fla. 10. **Championship:** Troy St. 31, Portland St. 17.

1988 First Round: North Dak. St. 49, Augustana (S.D.) 7; Millersville 27, Indiana (Pa.) 24; Cal St. Sacramento 35, UC Davis 14; N.C. Central 31, Winston-Salem 16; Texas A&I 39, Mississippi Col. 15; Tenn.-Martin 23, Butler 6; Portland St. 34, Bowie St. 17; Jacksonville St. 63, West Chester 24. **Quarterfinals:** North Dak. St. 36, Millersville 24; Cal St. Sacramento 56, N.C. Central 7; Texas A&I 34, Tenn.-Martin 0; Portland St. 20, Jacksonville St. 13. **Semifinals:** North Dak. St. 42, Cal St. Sacramento 20; Portland St. 35, Texas A&I 27. **Championship:** North Dak. St. 35, Portland St. 21.

1989 First Round: Mississippi Col. 34, Texas A&I 19; St. Cloud St. 27, Augustana (S.D.) 20; Portland St. 56, West Chester 50 (3 OT); Indiana (Pa.) 34, Grand Valley St. 24; Pittsburg St. 28, Northwest Mo. St. 7; Angelo St. 28, UC Davis 23; North Dak. St. 45, Edinboro 32; Jacksonville St. 33, Alabama A&M 9. **Quarterfinals:** Mississippi Col. 55, St. Cloud St. 24; Indiana (Pa.) 17, Portland St. 0; Angelo St. 24, Pittsburg St. 21; Jacksonville St. 21, North Dak. St. 17. **Semifinals:** Mississippi Col. 26, Indiana (Pa.) 14; Jacksonville St. 34, Angelo St. 16. **Championship:** Mississippi Col. 3, Jacksonville

St. 0.

1990 First Round: Mississippi Col. 70, Wofford 19; Jacksonville St. 38, North Ala. 14; Indiana (Pa.) 48, Winston-Salem 0; Edinboro 38, Virginia Union 14; North Dak. St. 17, Northern Colo. 7; Cal Poly SLO 14, Cal St. Northridge 7; Pittsburg St. 59, Northeast Mo. St. 3; East Tex. St. 20, Grand Valley St. 14. **Quarterfinals:** Mississippi Col. 14, Jacksonville St. 7; Indiana (Pa.) 14, Edinboro 7; North Dak. St. 47, Cal Poly SLO 0; Pittsburg St. 60, East Tex. St. 28. **Semifinals:** Indiana (Pa.) 27, Mississippi Col. 8; North Dak. St. 39, Pittsburg St. 29. **Championship:** North Dak. St. 51, Indiana (Pa.) 11.

1991 First Round: Pittsburg St. 26, Butler 16; East Tex. St. 36, Grand Valley St. 15; Portland St. 28, Northern Colo. 24; Mankato St. 27, North Dak. St. 7; Jacksonville St. 49, Winston-Salem 24; Mississippi Col. 28, Wofford 15; Indiana (Pa.) 56, Virginia Union 7; Shippensburg 34, East Stroudsburg 33 (OT). **Quarterfinals:** Pittsburg St. 38, East Tex. St. 28; Portland St. 37, Mankato St. 27; Jacksonville St. 35, Mississippi Col. 7; Indiana (Pa.) 52, Shippensburg 7. **Semifinals:** Pittsburg St. 53, Portland St. 21; Jacksonville St. 27, Indiana (Pa.) 20. **Championship:** Pittsburg St. 23, Jacksonville St. 6.

1991 DIVISION III CHAMPIONSHIP

AMOS ALONZO STAGG BOWL, HAWKINS STADIUM, BRADENTON, FLORIDA; DECEMBER 14, 1991

	Ithaca	Dayton
First Downs	29	11
Rushing Yardage	296	135
Passing Yardage	262	79
Return Yardage	1	28
Passes (Comp.-Att.-Int.)	15-26-1	10-21-2
Punts (Number-Average)	3-37.7	7-38.7
Fumbles (Number-Lost)	5-3	2-1
Penalties (Number-Yards)	2-22	3-38

Ithaca	6	14	0	14	—34
Dayton	10	7	0	3	—20

First Quarter
Dayton—Pat Hofacre 17 pass from Steve Keller (Brad Burns kick) (66 yards in 6 plays, 9:26 left)
Ithaca—Jeff Wittman 1 run (kick failed) (87 yards in 10 plays, 4:50 left)
Dayton—Burns 30 field goal (4 yards in 4 plays, 0:18 left)

Second Quarter
Dayton—Scot Alexander 9 run (Burns kick) (64 yards in 7 plays, 11:32 left)
Ithaca—Nick Ismailoff 42 pass from Todd Wilkowski (Matt Sullivan kick) (78 yards in 3 plays, 10:31 left)
Ithaca—Wittman 3 run (Sullivan kick) (65 yards in 8 plays, 3:25 left)

Fourth Quarter
Ithaca—Wittman 6 run (Sullivan kick) (56 yards in 6 plays, 14:02 left)
Dayton—Burns 24 field goal (7 yards in 4 plays, 11:01 left)
Ithaca—Ismailoff 32 pass from Wilkowski (Sullivan kick) (80 yards in 9 plays, 6:43 left)

Individual Leaders
Rushing—Ithaca: Wittman, 159 yards on 30 carries; Dayton: Keith Miller, 55 yards on 11 carries.
Passing—Ithaca: Wilkowski, 15 of 25 for 262 yards; Dayton: Keller, 9 of 16 for 71 yards.
Receiving—Ithaca: Ismailoff, 10 catches for 193 yards; Dayton: Bill Franks, 3 catches for 24 yards.

DIVISION III ALL-TIME CHAMPIONSHIP RESULTS

Year	Champion	Coach	Score	Runner-Up	Site
1973	Wittenberg	Dave Maurer	41-0	Juniata	Phenix City, Ala.
1974	Central (Iowa)	Ron Schipper	10-8	Ithaca	Phenix City, Ala.
1975	Wittenberg	Dave Maurer	28-0	Ithaca	Phenix City, Ala.
1976	St. John's (Minn.)	John Gagliardi	31-28	Towson St.	Phenix City, Ala.
1977	Widener	Bill Manlove	39-36	Wabash	Phenix City, Ala.
1978	Baldwin-Wallace	Lee Tressel	24-10	Wittenberg	Phenix City, Ala.
1979	Ithaca	Jim Butterfield	14-10	Wittenberg	Phenix City, Ala.
1980	Dayton	Rick Carter	63-0	Ithaca	Phenix City, Ala.
1981	Widener	Bill Manlove	17-10	Dayton	Phenix City, Ala.
1982	West Ga.	Bobby Pate	14-0	Augustana (Ill.)	Phenix City, Ala.
1983	Augustana (Ill.)	Bob Reade	21-17	Union (N. Y.)	Kings Island, Ohio
1984	Augustana (Ill.)	Bob Reade	21-12	Central (Iowa)	Kings Island, Ohio
1985	Augustana (Ill.)	Bob Reade	20-7	Ithaca	Phenix City, Ala.
1986	Augustana (Ill.)	Bob Reade	31-3	Salisbury St.	Phenix City, Ala.
1987	Wagner	Walt Hameline	19-3	Dayton	Phenix City, Ala.
1988	Ithaca	Jim Butterfield	39-24	Central (Iowa)	Phenix City, Ala.
1989	Dayton	Mike Kelly	17-7	Union (N. Y.)	Phenix City, Ala.
1990	Allegheny	Ken O'Keefe	21-14 (OT)	Lycoming	Bradenton, Fla.
1991	Ithaca	Jim Butterfield	34-20	Dayton	Bradenton, Fla.

REGIONAL CHAMPIONSHIP RESULTS
(Before Division III Championship)

EAST (Knute Rockne Bowl)

Year	Champion	Coach	Score	Runner-Up	Site
1969	Randolph-Macon	Ted Keller	47-28	Bridgeport	Bridgeport, Conn.
1970	Montclair St.	Clary Anderson	7-6	Hampden-Sydney	Atlantic City, N. J.
1971	Bridgeport	Ed Farrell	17-12	Hampden-Sydney	Atlantic City, N. J.
1972	Bridgeport	Ed Farrell	27-22	Slippery Rock	Atlantic City, N. J.

WEST (Amos Alonzo Stagg Bowl)

Year	Champion	Coach	Score	Runner-Up	Site
1969	Wittenberg	Dave Maurer	27-21	William Jewell	Springfield, Ohio
1970	Capital	Gene Slaughter	34-21	Luther	Columbus, Ohio
1971	Vacated		20-10	Ohio Wesleyan	Phenix City, Ala.
1972	Heidelberg	Pete Riesen	28-16	Fort Valley St.	Phenix City, Ala.

1991 DIVISION III CHAMPIONSHIP RESULTS

Regionals
St. John's (Minn.) 75, Coe 2
Wis.-La Crosse 28, Simpson 13
Allegheny 24, Albion 21 (OT)
Dayton 27, Baldwin-Wallace 10
Ithaca 31, Glassboro St. 10
Union (N. Y.) 55, Mass.-Lowell 16
Lycoming 18, Wash. & Jeff. 16
Susquehanna 21, Dickinson 20

Quarterfinals
St. John's (Minn.) 29, Wis.-La Crosse 10
Dayton 28, Allegheny 25 (OT)
Ithaca 35, Union (N. Y.) 23
Susquehanna 31, Lycoming 24

Semifinals
Dayton 19, St. John's (Minn.) 7
Ithaca 49, Susquehanna 13

Championship
Ithaca 34, Dayton 20

CHAMPIONSHIP RECORDS

INDIVIDUAL: SINGLE GAME

Net Yards Rushing
389—Ricky Gales, Simpson (35) vs. St. John's (Minn.) (42), 11-18-89.

Rushes Attempted
51—Ricky Gales, Simpson (35) vs. St. John's (Minn.) (42), 11-18-89.

Touchdowns by Rushing
5—Jeff Norman, St. John's (Minn.) (46) vs. Augustana (Ill.) (7), 11-20-76; Mike Coppa, Salisbury St. (44) vs. Ithaca (40), 12-6-86; Paul Parker, Ithaca (62) vs. Ferrum (28), 12-3-88; Kevin Hofacre, Dayton (35) vs. John Carroll (10), 11-18-89.

Net Yards Passing
405—Ed Hesson, Glassboro St. (10) vs. Ithaca (31), 11-23-91.

Passes Attempted
53—Walter Briggs, Montclair St. (28) vs. Ithaca (50), 11-30-85.

Passes Completed
32—Tim Lynch, Hofstra (10) vs. Lycoming (20), 12-1-90.

Passes Had Intercepted
7—Rick Steil, Dubuque (7) vs. Ithaca (27), 11-17-79.

Touchdown Passes Completed
5—Pat Mayew, St. John's (Minn.) (75) vs. Coe (2), 11-23-91.

Completion Percentage (min. 8 attempts)
.900—Robb Disbennett, Salisbury St. (16) vs. Carnegie Mellon (14), 11-19-83 (18 of 20).

Net Yards Rushing and Passing
432—Mike Hensel, Carnegie Mellon (22) vs. Salisbury St. (35), 11-23-85.

Number of Rushing and Passing Plays
66—Steve Thompson, Carroll (Wis.) (14) vs. Buena Vista (20), 11-20-76.

Punting Average (min. 3 punts)
48.5—Phil Macken, Minn.-Morris (25) vs. Carnegie Mellon (31), 11-17-79.

Number of Punts
14—Tim Flynn, Gettysburg (14) vs. Lycoming (10), 11-23-85.

Passes Caught
13—Keith Willike, Capital (28) vs. Dayton (52), 11-21-87.

Net Yards Receiving
253—Eric Welgat, Augustana (Ill.) (36) vs. Dayton (38), 11-28-87.

Touchdown Passes Caught
3—Ed Sellers, Albany (N.Y.) (51) vs. Hampden-Sydney (45), 11-19-77; Jose Tirado, Baldwin-Wallace (31) vs. Carnegie Mellon (6), 11-25-78; David Parker, Bishop (32) vs. Wartburg (7), 11-20-82; Vince Boddy, Mount Union (35) vs. Denison (3), 11-23-85; Tom McDonald, Central (Iowa) (37) vs. Buena Vista (0), 11-22-86; Keith Willike, Capital (28) vs. Dayton (52), 11-21-87; Eric Welgat, Augustana (Ill.) (36) vs. Dayton (38), 11-28-87.

Passes Intercepted
3—John Brunelli, Montclair St. (7) vs. Hampden-Sydney (6), 11-28-70; John Bertino, Ithaca (27) vs. Dubuque (7), 11-17-79; Troy Westerman, Augustana (Ill.) (23) vs.

Union (N.Y.) (6), 11-24-84; Mike Gray, Augustana (III.) (23) vs. Union (N.Y.) (6), 11-24-84; Rich Samuelson, Union (N.Y.) (17) vs. Ithaca (24), OT, 11-22-86; Mike Gray, Augustana (III.) (31) vs. Salisbury St. (3), 12-13-86; Tom Knapp, Ithaca (39) vs. Central (Iowa) (24), 12-10-88.

Yards Gained on Interception Returns
100—Jay Zunic, Ithaca (31) vs. Glassboro St. (10), 11-23-91 (2 interceptions, 1 for 100-yard TD).

Yards Gained on Punt Returns
98—Leroy Horn, Montclair St. (28) vs. Western Conn. St. (0), 11-23-85.

Yards Gained on Kickoff Returns
190—George Day, Susquehanna (31) vs. Lycoming (24), 11-30-91.

Points
36—Mike Coppa, Salisbury St. (44) vs. Ithaca (40), 12-6-86.

Touchdowns
6—Mike Coppa, Salisbury St. (44) vs. Ithaca (40), 12-6-86.

Extra Points
9—Tim Robinson, Baldwin-Wallace (71) vs. St. Lawrence (7), 11-18-78.

INDIVIDUAL: TOURNAMENT

Net Yards Rushing
671—Mike Coppa, Salisbury St., 1986 (223 vs. Emory & Henry, 129 vs. Susquehanna, 271 vs. Ithaca, 48 vs. Augustana, III.).

Rushes Attempted
119—Terry Underwood, Wagner, 1987 (39 vs. Rochester, 29 vs. Fordham, 34 vs. Emory & Henry, 17 vs. Dayton).

Net Yards Passing
932—Ed Dougherty, Lycoming, 1990 (261 vs. Carnegie Mellon, 286 vs. Wash. & Jeff., 220 vs. Hofstra, 165 vs. Allegheny).

Passes Attempted
141—Brett Russ, Union (N.Y.), 1989 (23 vs. Cortland St., 37 vs. Montclair St., 38 vs. Ferrum, 43 vs. Dayton).

Passes Completed
80—Brett Russ, Union (N.Y.), 1989 (13 vs. Cortland St., 22 vs. Montclair St., 23 vs. Ferrum, 22 vs. Dayton).

Touchdown Passes Completed
8—Brett Russ, Union (N.Y.), 1989 (3 vs. Cortland St., 3 vs. Montclair St., 2 vs. Ferrum, 0 vs. Dayton).

Completion Percentage (min. 2 games)
.667—Greg Thomas, Central (Iowa), 1989, 10 of 15 (5-7 vs. St. Norbert, 5-8 vs. St. John's, Minn.)

Passes Had Intercepted
9—Rollie Wiebers, Buena Vista, 1976 (4 vs. Carroll, Wis., 5 vs. St. John's, Minn.).

Passes Caught
39—Nick Ismailoff, Ithaca, 1991 (12 vs. Glassboro St., 6 vs. Union, N.Y., 11 vs. Susquehanna, 10 vs. Dayton).

Net Yards Receiving
599—Nick Ismailoff, Ithaca, 1991 (179 vs. Glassboro St., 122 vs. Union, N.Y., 105 vs. Susquehanna, 193 vs. Dayton).

Touchdown Passes Caught
5—Nick Ismailoff, Ithaca, 1991 (1 vs. Glassboro St., 1 vs. Union, N.Y., 1 vs. Susquehanna, 2 vs. Dayton).

Points
60—Jeff Norman, St. John's (Minn.), 1976 (34 vs. Augustana, III., 13 vs. Buena Vista, 13 vs. Towson St.); Brad Price, Augustana (III.), 1986 (24 vs. Hope, 6 vs. Mount Union, 12 vs. Concordia-M'head, 18 vs. Salisbury St.); Mike Coppa, Salisbury St., 1986 (6 vs. Emory & Henry, 18 vs. Susquehanna, 36 vs. Ithaca, 0 vs. Augustana, III.).

Touchdowns
10—Brad Price, Augustana (III.), 1986 (4 vs. Hope, 1 vs. Mount Union, 2 vs. Concordia-M'head, 3 vs. Salisbury St.); Mike Coppa, Salisbury St., 1986 (1 vs. Emory & Henry, 3 vs. Susquehanna, 6 vs. Ithaca, 0 vs. Augustana, III.).

INDIVIDUAL: LONGEST PLAYS

Longest Rush
93—Rick Papke, Augustana (III.) (17) vs. Central (Iowa) (23), 12-3-88, TD.

Longest Pass Completion
96—Mark Blom to Tom McDonald, Central (Iowa) (37) vs. Buena Vista (0), 11-22-86, TD.

Longest Field Goal
52—Rod Vesling, St. Lawrence (43) vs. Wagner (34), 11-20-82.

Longest Punt
79—Tom Hansen, Ithaca (3) vs. Wittenberg (6), 11-18-78.

Longest Punt Return
78—Pete Minturn, Ithaca (34) vs. Gettysburg (0), 12-7-85, TD.

Longest Kickoff Return
100—Tom Deery, Widener (23) vs. Montclair St. (12), 11-30-81, TD.

Division III Championship Results, Records   483

Longest Interception Return
100—Jay Zunic, Ithaca (31) vs. Glassboro St. (10), 11-23-91, TD.

TEAM: SINGLE GAME

First Downs
35—Central (Iowa) (71) vs. Occidental (0), 12-7-85.

First Downs by Rushing
30—Central (Iowa) (71) vs. Occidental (0), 12-7-85.

First Downs by Passing
20—Glassboro St. (10) vs. Ithaca (31), 11-23-91.

Net Yards Rushing
530—St. John's (Minn.) (46) vs. Augustana (Ill.) (7), 11-20-76.

Rushes Attempted
83—Capital (34) vs. Luther (21), 11-28-70; Baldwin-Wallace (31) vs. Carnegie Mellon (6), 11-25-78.

Net Yards Passing
429—Hofstra (38) vs. Trenton St. (3), 11-24-90.

Passes Attempted
59—Montclair St. (28) vs. Ithaca (50), 11-30-85.

Passes Completed
32—Hofstra (10) vs. Lycoming (20), 12-1-90.

Completion Percentage (min. 10 attempts)
.857—Salisbury St. (16) vs. Carnegie Mellon (14), 11-19-83 (18 of 21).

Passes Had Intercepted
9—Dubuque (7) vs. Ithaca (27), 11-17-79.

Net Yards Rushing and Passing
607—Ferrum (49) vs. Moravian (28), 11-26-88.

Rushing and Passing Plays
101—Union (N.Y.) (45) vs. Montclair St. (6), 11-25-89.

Punting Average
48.5—Minn.-Morris (25) vs. Carnegie Mellon (31), 11-17-79.

Number of Punts
14—Gettysburg (14) vs. Lycoming (10), 11-23-85.

Yards Gained on Punt Returns
100—Gettysburg (22) vs. Salisbury St. (6), 11-30-85.

Yards Gained on Kickoff Returns
234—Ithaca (40) vs. Salisbury St. (44), 12-6-86.

Yards Gained on Interception Returns
176—Augustana (Ill.) (14) vs. St. Lawrence (0), 11-27-82.

Yards Penalized
166—Ferrum (49) vs. Moravian (28), 11-26-88.

Fumbles Lost
6—Albright (7) vs. St. Lawrence (26), 11-20-76; St. John's (Minn.) (7) vs. Dayton (19), 12-7-91.

Points
75—St. John's (Minn.) vs. Coe (2), 11-23-91.

TEAM: TOURNAMENT

First Downs
94—Ithaca, 1991 (22 vs. Glassboro St., 15 vs. Union, N.Y., 28 vs. Susquehanna, 29 vs. Dayton).

Net Yards Rushing
1,377—Ithaca, 1988 (251 vs. Wagner, 293 vs. Cortland St., 425 vs. Ferrum, 408 vs. Central, Iowa).

Net Yards Passing
1,068—Hofstra, 1990 (300 vs. Cortland St., 429 vs. Trenton St., 339 vs. Lycoming).

Net Yards Rushing and Passing
1,867—Ithaca, 1991 (486 vs. Glassboro St., 350 vs. Union, N.Y., 473 vs. Susquehanna, 558 vs. Dayton).

Passes Attempted
150—Hofstra, 1990 (51 vs. Cortland St., 50 vs. Trenton St., 49 vs. Lycoming).

Passes Completed
87—Hofstra, 1990 (31 vs. Cortland St., 24 vs. Trenton St., 32 vs. Lycoming).

Passes Had Intercepted
11—Hofstra, 1990 (5 vs. Cortland St., 3 vs. Trenton St., 3 vs. Lycoming).

Number of Punts
30—Central (Iowa), 1988 (12 vs. Concordia-M'head, 8 vs. Wis.-Whitewater, 5 vs. Augustana, Ill., 5 vs. Ithaca).

Yards Penalized
331—Wagner, 1987 (61 vs. Rochester, 80 vs. Fordham, 87 vs. Emory & Henry, 103 vs. Dayton).

Fumbles Lost
10—Wittenberg, 1978 (4 vs. Ithaca, 2 vs. Minn.-Morris, 4 vs. Baldwin-Wallace).

Points
159—Ithaca, 1988 (34 vs. Wagner, 24 vs. Cortland St., 62 vs. Ferrum, 39 vs. Central, Iowa).

YEAR-BY-YEAR DIVISION III CHAMPIONSHIP RESULTS

Year (Number of Teams)	Coach	Record	Result
1973 (4)			
Wittenberg	Dave Maurer	2-0	Champion
Juniata	Walt Nadzak	1-1	Second
Bridgeport	Ed Farrell	0-1	Semifinalist
San Diego	Andy Vinci	0-1	Semifinalist
1974 (4)			
Central (Iowa)	Ron Schipper	2-0	Champion
Ithaca	Jim Butterfield	1-1	Second
Evansville	Jim Byers	0-1	Semifinalist
Slippery Rock	Bob Di Spirito	0-1	Semifinalist

Year (Number of Teams)	Coach	Record	Result
1975 (8)			
Wittenberg......................	Dave Maurer	3-0	Champion
Ithaca..........................	Jim Butterfield	2-1	Second
Millsaps........................	Harper Davis	1-1	Semifinalist
Widener........................	Bill Manlove	1-1	Semifinalist
Albright........................	John Potsklan	0-1	Lost 1st Round
Colorado Col...................	Jerry Carle	0-1	Lost 1st Round
Fort Valley St..................	Leon Lomax	0-1	Lost 1st Round
Indianapolis	Bill Bless	0-1	Lost 1st Round
1976 (8)			
St. John's (Minn.)...............	John Gagliardi	3-0	Champion
Towson St.	Phil Albert	2-1	Second
Buena Vista.....................	Jim Hershberger	1-1	Semifinalist
St. Lawrence...................	Ted Stratford	1-1	Semifinalist
Albright........................	John Potsklan	0-1	Lost 1st Round
Augustana (Ill.).................	Ben Newcomb	0-1	Lost 1st Round
Carroll (Wis.)..................	Steve Miller	0-1	Lost 1st Round
LIU-C. W. Post	Dom Anile	0-1	Lost 1st Round
1977 (8)			
Widener........................	Bill Manlove	3-0	Champion
Wabash	Frank Navarro	2-1	Second
Albany (N.Y.)...................	Bob Ford	1-1	Semifinalist
Minn.-Morris	Al Molde	1-1	Semifinalist
Albion	Frank Joranko	0-1	Lost 1st Round
Central (Iowa).................	Ron Schipper	0-1	Lost 1st Round
Hampden-Sydney	Stokeley Fulton	0-1	Lost 1st Round
St. John's (Minn.)...............	John Gagliardi	0-1	Lost 1st Round
1978 (8)			
Baldwin-Wallace	Lee Tressel	3-0	Champion
Wittenberg......................	Dave Maurer	2-1	Second
Carnegie Mellon...............	Chuck Klausing	1-1	Semifinalist
Minn.-Morris	Al Molde	1-1	Semifinalist
Dayton	Rick Carter	0-1	Lost 1st Round
Ithaca..........................	Jim Butterfield	0-1	Lost 1st Round
St. Lawrence...................	Ted Stratford	0-1	Lost 1st Round
St. Olaf........................	Tom Porter	0-1	Lost 1st Round
1979 (8)			
Ithaca..........................	Jim Butterfield	3-0	Champion
Wittenberg......................	Dave Maurer	2-1	Second
Carnegie Mellon...............	Chuck Klausing	1-1	Semifinalist
Widener........................	Bill Manlove	1-1	Semifinalist
Baldwin-Wallace	Lee Tressel	0-1	Lost 1st Round
Dubuque	Don Birmingham	0-1	Lost 1st Round
Millersville	Gene Carpenter	0-1	Lost 1st Round
Minn.-Morris	Al Molde	0-1	Lost 1st Round
1980 (8)			
Dayton	Rick Carter	3-0	Champion
Ithaca..........................	Jim Butterfield	2-1	Second
Minn.-Morris	Dick Smith	1-1	Semifinalist
Widener........................	Bill Manlove	1-1	Semifinalist
Baldwin-Wallace	Lee Tressel	0-1	Lost 1st Round
Bethany (W. Va.)................	Don Ault	0-1	Lost 1st Round
Dubuque	Don Birmingham	0-1	Lost 1st Round
Wagner	Bill Russo	0-1	Lost 1st Round
1981 (8)			
Widener........................	Bill Manlove	3-0	Champion
Dayton	Mike Kelly	2-1	Second
Lawrence.......................	Ron Roberts	1-1	Semifinalist
Montclair St.	Fred Hill	1-1	Semifinalist
Alfred	Sam Sanders	0-1	Lost 1st Round
Augustana (Ill.).................	Bob Reade	0-1	Lost 1st Round
Minn.-Morris	Dick Smith	0-1	Lost 1st Round
West Ga.	Bobby Pate	0-1	Lost 1st Round
1982 (8)			
West Ga.	Bobby Pate	3-0	Champion
Augustana (Ill.).................	Bob Reade	2-1	Second
Bishop	James Jones	1-1	Semifinalist
St. Lawrence...................	Andy Talley	1-1	Semifinalist
Baldwin-Wallace	Bob Packard	0-1	Lost 1st Round
Wagner	Walt Hameline	0-1	Lost 1st Round

Year (Number of Teams)	Coach	Record	Result
Wartburg	Don Canfield	0-1	Lost 1st Round
Widener	Bill Manlove	0-1	Lost 1st Round
1983 (8)			
Augustana (Ill.)	Bob Reade	3-0	Champion
Union (N. Y.)	Al Bagnoli	2-1	Second
Salisbury St.	Mike McGlinchey	1-1	Semifinalist
Wis.-La Crosse	Roger Harring	1-1	Semifinalist
Adrian	Ron Labadie	0-1	Lost 1st Round
Carnegie Mellon	Chuck Klausing	0-1	Lost 1st Round
Hofstra	Mickey Kwiatkowski	0-1	Lost 1st Round
Occidental	Dale Widolff	0-1	Lost 1st Round
1984 (8)			
Augustana (Ill.)	Bob Reade	3-0	Champion
Central (Iowa)	Ron Schipper	2-1	Second
Union (N.Y.)	Al Bagnoli	1-1	Semifinalist
Wash. & Jeff.	John Luckhardt	1-1	Semifinalist
Dayton	Mike Kelly	0-1	Lost 1st Round
Occidental	Dale Widolff	0-1	Lost 1st Round
Plymouth St.	Jay Cottone	0-1	Lost 1st Round
Randolph-Macon	Jim Blackburn	0-1	Lost 1st Round
1985 (16)			
Augustana (Ill.)	Bob Reade	4-0	Champion
Ithaca	Jim Butterfield	3-1	Second
Central (Iowa)	Ron Schipper	2-1	Semifinalist
Gettysburg	Barry Streeter	2-1	Semifinalist
Montclair St.	Rick Giancola	1-1	Quarterfinalist
Mount Union	Ken Wable	1-1	Quarterfinalist
Occidental	Dale Widolff	1-1	Quarterfinalist
Salisbury St.	Mike McGlinchey	1-1	Quarterfinalist
Albion	Pete Schmidt	0-1	Lost 1st Round
Carnegie Mellon	Chuck Klausing	0-1	Lost 1st Round
Coe	Bob Thurness	0-1	Lost 1st Round
Denison	Keith Piper	0-1	Lost 1st Round
Lycoming	Frank Girardi	0-1	Lost 1st Round
St. John's (Minn.)	John Gagliardi	0-1	Lost 1st Round
Union (N.Y.)	Al Bagnoli	0-1	Lost 1st Round
Western Conn. St.	Paul Pasqualoni	0-1	Lost 1st Round
1986 (16)			
Augustana (Ill.)	Bob Reade	4-0	Champion
Salisbury St.	Mike McGlinchey	3-1	Second
Concordia-M'head	Jim Christopherson	2-1	Semifinalist
Ithaca	Jim Butterfield	2-1	Semifinalist
Central (Iowa)	Ron Schipper	1-1	Quarterfinalist
Montclair St.	Rick Giancola	1-1	Quarterfinalist
Mount Union	Larry Kehres	1-1	Quarterfinalist
Susquehanna	Rocky Rees	1-1	Quarterfinalist
Buena Vista	Jim Hershberger	0-1	Lost 1st Round
Dayton	Mike Kelly	0-1	Lost 1st Round
Emory & Henry	Lou Wacker	0-1	Lost 1st Round
Hofstra	Mickey Kwiatkowski	0-1	Lost 1st Round
Hope	Ray Smith	0-1	Lost 1st Round
Union (N.Y.)	Al Bagnoli	0-1	Lost 1st Round
Wash. & Jeff.	John Luckhardt	0-1	Lost 1st Round
Wis.-Stevens Point	D. J. LeRoy	0-1	Lost 1st Round
1987 (16)			
Wagner	Walt Hameline	4-0	Champion
Dayton	Mike Kelly	3-1	Second
Central (Iowa)	Ron Schipper	2-1	Semifinalist
Emory & Henry	Lou Wacker	2-1	Semifinalist
Augustana (Ill.)	Bob Reade	1-1	Quarterfinalist
Fordham	Larry Glueck	1-1	Quarterfinalist
St. John's (Minn.)	John Gagliardi	1-1	Quarterfinalist
Wash. & Jeff.	John Luckhardt	1-1	Quarterfinalist
Allegheny	Peter Vaas	0-1	Lost 1st Round
Capital	Roger Welsh	0-1	Lost 1st Round
Ferrum	Hank Norton	0-1	Lost 1st Round
Gust. Adolphus	Steve Raarup	0-1	Lost 1st Round
Hiram	Don Charlton	0-1	Lost 1st Round
Hofstra	Mickey Kwiatkowski	0-1	Lost 1st Round
Menlo	Ray Solari	0-1	Lost 1st Round

Year (Number of Teams)	Coach	Record	Result
Rochester	Ray Tellier	0-1	Lost 1st Round
1988 (16)			
Ithaca	Jim Butterfield	4-0	Champion
Central (Iowa).................	Ron Schipper	3-1	Second
Augustana (Ill.)	Bob Reade	2-1	Semifinalist
Ferrum	Hank Norton	2-1	Semifinalist
Cortland St.	Dennis Kayser	1-1	Quarterfinalist
Moravian	Scot Dapp	1-1	Quarterfinalist
Wis.-Whitewater	Bob Berezowitz	1-1	Quarterfinalist
Wittenberg....................	Ron Murphy	1-1	Quarterfinalist
Adrian	Ron Labadie	0-1	Lost Regionals
Concordia-M'head	Jim Christopherson	0-1	Lost Regionals
Dayton	Mike Kelly	0-1	Lost Regionals
Hofstra	Mickey Kwiatkowski	0-1	Lost Regionals
Rhodes	Mike Clary	0-1	Lost Regionals
Simpson	Jim Williams	0-1	Lost Regionals
Wagner	Walt Hameline	0-1	Lost Regionals
Widener	Bill Manlove	0-1	Lost Regionals
1989 (16)			
Dayton	Mike Kelly	4-0	Champion
Union (N.Y.)	Al Bagnoli	3-1	Second
Ferrum	Hank Norton	2-1	Semifinalist
St. John's (Minn.)	John Gagliardi	2-1	Semifinalist
Central (Iowa).................	Ron Schipper	1-1	Quarterfinalist
Lycoming	Frank Girardi	1-1	Quarterfinalist
Millikin	Carl Poelker	1-1	Quarterfinalist
Montclair St.	Rick Giancola	1-1	Quarterfinalist
Augustana (Ill.)	Bob Reade	0-1	Lost Regionals
Cortland St.	Dennis Kayser	0-1	Lost Regionals
Dickinson	Ed Sweeney	0-1	Lost Regionals
Hofstra	Mickey Kwiatkowski	0-1	Lost Regionals
John Carroll	Tony DeCarlo	0-1	Lost Regionals
Simpson	Jim Williams	0-1	Lost Regionals
St. Norbert....................	Don LaViolette	0-1	Lost Regionals
Wash. & Jeff..................	John Luckhardt	0-1	Lost Regionals
1990 (16)			
Allegheny	Ken O'Keefe	4-0	Champion
Lycoming	Frank Girardi	3-1	Second
Central (Iowa).................	Ron Schipper	2-1	Semifinalist
Hofstra	Joe Gardi	2-1	Semifinalist
Dayton	Mike Kelly	1-1	Quarterfinalist
St. Thomas (Minn.)	Vic Wallace	1-1	Quarterfinalist
Trenton St.....................	Eric Hamilton	1-1	Quarterfinalist
Wash. & Jeff..................	John Luckhardt	1-1	Quarterfinalist
Augustana (Ill.)	Bob Reade	0-1	Lost Regionals
Carnegie Mellon...............	Rich Lackner	0-1	Lost Regionals
Cortland St.	Dave Murray	0-1	Lost Regionals
Ferrum	Hank Norton	0-1	Lost Regionals
Ithaca	Jim Butterfield	0-1	Lost Regionals
Mount Union...................	Larry Kehres	0-1	Lost Regionals
Redlands	Mike Maynard	0-1	Lost Regionals
Wis.-Whitewater	Bob Berezowitz	0-1	Lost Regionals
1991 (16)			
Ithaca	Jim Butterfield	4-0	Champion
Dayton	Mike Kelly	3-1	Second
St. John's (Minn.)	John Gagliardi	2-1	Semifinalist
Susquehanna	Steve Briggs	2-1	Semifinalist
Allegheny	Ken O'Keefe	1-1	Quarterfinalist
Lycoming	Frank Girardi	1-1	Quarterfinalist
Union (N. Y.)	Al Bagnoli	1-1	Quarterfinalist
Wis.-La Crosse	Roger Harring	1-1	Quarterfinalist
Albion	Pete Schmidt	0-1	Lost Regionals
Baldwin-Wallace	Bob Packard	0-1	Lost Regionals
Coe..........................	D. J. LeRoy	0-1	Lost Regionals
Dickinson	Ed Sweeney	0-1	Lost Regionals
Glassboro St.	John Bunting	0-1	Lost Regionals
Mass.-Lowell..................	Dennis Scannell	0-1	Lost Regionals
Simpson	Jim Williams	0-1	Lost Regionals
Wash. & Jeff..................	John Luckhardt	0-1	Lost Regionals

DIVISION III CHAMPIONSHIP
ALL-TIME RECORD OF EACH COLLEGE
COACH-BY-COACH, 1973-91 (82 Colleges)

	Yrs	Won	Lost	CH	2D
ADRIAN					
Ron Labadie (Adrian '71) 83, 88	2	0	2	0	0
ALBANY (N.Y.)					
Bob Ford (Springfield '59) 77	1	1	1	0	0
ALBION					
Frank Joranko (Albion '52) 77	1	0	1	0	0
Pete Schmidt (Alma '70) 85, 91	2	0	2	0	0
TOTAL	3	0	3	0	0
ALBRIGHT					
John Potsklan (Penn St. '49) 75, 76................	2	0	2	0	0
ALFRED					
Sam Sanders (Buffalo '60) 81......................	1	0	1	0	0
ALLEGHENY					
Peter Vaas (Holy Cross '74) 87.....................	1	0	1	0	0
Ken O'Keefe (John Carroll '75) 90-CH, 91	2	5	1	1	0
TOTAL	3	5	2	1	0
AUGUSTANA (ILL.)					
Ben Newcomb 76	1	0	1	0	0
Bob Reade (Cornell College '54) 81, 82-2D, 83-CH, 84-CH, 85-CH, 86-CH, 87, 88, 89, 90..............	10	19	6	4	1
TOTAL	11	19	7	4	1
BALDWIN-WALLACE					
Lee Tressel (Baldwin-Wallace '48) 78-CH, 79, 80	3	3	2	1	0
Bob Packard (Baldwin-Wallace '65) 82, 91	2	0	2	0	0
TOTAL	5	3	4	1	0
BETHANY (W. VA.)					
Don Ault (West Liberty St. '52) 80	1	0	1	0	0
BISHOP					
James Jones (Bishop '49) 82	1	1	1	0	0
BRIDGEPORT					
Ed Farrell (Rutgers '56) 73	1	0	1	0	0
BUENA VISTA					
Jim Hershberger (Northern Iowa '57) 76, 86	2	1	2	0	0
CAPITAL					
Roger Welsh (Muskingum '64) 87	1	0	1	0	0
CARNEGIE MELLON					
Chuck Klausing (Slippery Rock '48) 78, 79, 83, 85	4	2	4	0	0
Rich Lackner (Carnegie Mellon '79) 90	1	0	1	0	0
TOTAL	5	2	5	0	0
CARROLL (WIS.)					
Steve Miller (Cornell College '65) 76................	1	0	1	0	0
CENTRAL (IOWA)					
Ron Schipper (Hope '52) 74-CH, 77, 84-2D, 85, 86, 87, 88-2D, 89, 90...............................	9	15	8	1	2
COE					
Bob Thurness (Coe '62) 85.........................	1	0	1	0	0
D. J. LeRoy 91	1	0	1	0	0
TOTAL	2	0	2	0	0
COLORADO COL.					
Jerry Carle (Northwestern '48) 75	1	0	1	0	0
CONCORDIA-M'HEAD					
Jim Christopherson (Concordia-M'head '60) 86, 88	2	2	2	0	0
CORTLAND ST.					
Dennis Kayser (Ithaca '74) 88, 89	2	1	2	0	0
Dave Murray (Springfield '81) 90...................	1	0	1	0	0
TOTAL	3	1	3	0	0

	Yrs	Won	Lost	CH	2D
DAYTON					
Rick Carter (Earlham '65) 78, 80-CH	2	3	1	1	0
Mike Kelly (Manchester '70) 81-2D, 84, 86, 87-2D,					
88, 89-CH, 90, 91-2D	8	13	7	1	3
TOTAL	10	16	8	2	3
DENISON					
Keith Piper (Baldwin-Wallace '48) 85	1	0	1	0	0
DICKINSON					
Ed Sweeney (LIU-C. W. Post '71) 89, 91	2	0	2	0	0
DUBUQUE					
Don Birmingham (Westmar '62) 79, 80..............	2	0	2	0	0
EMORY & HENRY					
Lou Wacker (Richmond '56) 86, 87	2	2	2	0	0
EVANSVILLE					
Jim Byers (Michigan '59) 74........................	1	0	1	0	0
FERRUM					
Hank Norton (Lynchburg '51) 87, 88, 89, 90	4	4	4	0	0
FORDHAM					
Larry Glueck (Villanova '63) 87	1	1	1	0	0
FORT VALLEY ST.					
Leon Lomax (Fort Valley St. '43) 75	1	0	1	0	0
GETTYSBURG					
Barry Streeter (Lebanon Valley '71) 85	1	2	1	0	0
GLASSBORO ST.					
John Bunting (North Caro. '72) 91	1	0	1	0	0
GUST. ADOLPHUS					
Steve Raarup (Gust. Adolphus '53) 87	1	0	1	0	0
HAMPDEN-SYDNEY					
Stokeley Fulton (Hampden-Sydney '55) 77	1	0	1	0	0
HIRAM					
Don Charlton (Lock Haven '65) 87	1	0	1	0	0
HOFSTRA					
Mickey Kwiatkowski (Delaware '70) 83, 86, 87, 88,					
89	5	0	5	0	0
Joe Gardi (Maryland '60) 90.......................	1	2	1	0	0
TOTAL	6	2	6	0	0
HOPE					
Ray Smith (UCLA '61) 86	1	0	1	0	0
INDIANAPOLIS					
Bill Bless (Indianapolis '63) 75	1	0	1	0	0
ITHACA					
Jim Butterfield (Maine '53) 74-2D, 75-2D, 78, 79-CH,					
80-2D, 85-2D, 86, 88-CH, 90, 91-CH	10	21	7	3	4
JOHN CARROLL					
Tony DeCarlo (Kent '62) 89	1	0	1	0	0
JUNIATA					
Walt Nadzak (Denison '57) 73-2D	1	1	1	0	1
LAWRENCE					
Ron Roberts (Wisconsin '54) 81	1	1	1	0	0
LIU-C. W. POST					
Dom Anile (LIU-C. W. Post '59) 76	1	0	1	0	0
LYCOMING					
Frank Girardi (West Chester '61) 85, 89, 90-2D, 91 ...	4	5	4	0	1
MASS.-LOWELL					
Dennis Scannell (Villanova '74) 91	1	0	1	0	0
MENLO					
Ray Solari (California '51) 87	1	0	1	0	0
MILLERSVILLE					
Gene Carpenter (Huron '63) 79	1	0	1	0	0
MILLIKIN					
Carl Poelker (Millikin '68) 89	1	1	1	0	0
MILLSAPS					
Harper Davis (Mississippi St. '49) 75...............	1	1	1	0	0

	Yrs	Won	Lost	CH	2D
MINN.-MORRIS					
Al Molde (Gust. Adolphus '66) 77, 78, 79	3	2	3	0	0
Dick Smith (Coe '68) 80, 81	2	1	2	0	0
TOTAL	5	3	5	0	0
MONTCLAIR AT.					
Fred Hill (Upsala '57) 81	1	1	1	0	0
Rick Giancola (Glassboro St. '68) 85, 86, 89	3	3	3	0	0
TOTAL	4	4	4	0	0
MORAVIAN					
Scot Dapp (West Chester '73) 88	1	1	1	0	0
MOUNT UNION					
Ken Wable (Muskingum '52) 85	1	1	1	0	0
Larry Kehres (Mount Union '71) 86, 90	2	1	2	0	0
TOTAL	3	2	3	0	0
OCCIDENTAL					
Dale Widolff (Indiana Central '75) 83, 84, 85	3	1	3	0	0
PLYMOUTH ST.					
Jay Cottone (Norwich '71) 84	1	0	1	0	0
RANDOLPH-MACON					
Jim Blackburn (Virginia '71) 84	1	0	1	0	0
REDLANDS					
Mike Maynard (Ill. Wesleyan '80) 90	1	0	1	0	0
RHODES					
Mike Clary (Rhodes '77) 88	1	0	1	0	0
ROCHESTER					
Ray Tellier (Connecticut '73) 87	1	0	1	0	0
ST. JOHN'S (MINN.)					
John Gagliardi (Colorado Col. '49) 76-CH, 77, 85,					
87, 89, 91	6	8	5	1	0
ST. LAWRENCE					
Ted Stratford (St. Lawrence '57) 76, 78	2	1	2	0	0
Andy Talley (Southern Conn. St. '67) 82	1	1	1	0	0
TOTAL	3	2	3	0	0
ST. NORBERT					
Don LaViolette (St. Norbert '54) 89	1	0	1	0	0
ST. OLAF					
Tom Porter (St. Olaf '51) 78	1	0	1	0	0
ST. THOMAS (MINN.)					
Vic Wallace (Cornell College '65) 90	1	1	1	0	0
SALISBURY ST.					
Mike McGlinchey 83, 85, 86-2D	3	5	3	0	1
SAN DIEGO					
Andy Vinci (Cal St. Los Angeles '63) 73	1	0	1	0	0
SIMPSON					
Jim Williams (Northern Iowa '60) 88, 89, 91	3	0	3	0	0
SLIPPERY ROCK					
Bob Di Spirito (Rhode Island '53) 74	1	0	1	0	0
SUSQUEHANNA					
Rocky Rees (West Chester '71) 86	1	1	1	0	0
Steve Briggs (Springfield '84) 91	1	2	1	0	0
TOTAL	2	3	2	0	0
TOWSON ST.					
Phil Albert (Arizona '66) 76-2D	1	2	1	0	1
TRENTON ST.					
Eric Hamilton (Trenton St. '75) 90	1	1	1	0	0
UNION (N.Y.)					
Al Bagnoli (Central Conn. St. '74) 83-2D, 84, 85,					
86, 89-2D, 91	6	7	6	0	2
WABASH					
Frank Navarro 77-2D	1	2	1	0	1
WAGNER					
Bill Russo 80	1	0	1	0	0
Walt Hameline (Brockport St. '75) 82, 87-CH, 88	3	4	2	1	0
TOTAL	4	4	3	1	0

	Yrs	Won	Lost	CH	2D
WARTBURG					
Don Canfield 82	1	0	1	0	0
WASH. & JEFF.					
John Luckhardt (Purdue '67) 84, 86, 87, 89, 90, 91....	6	3	6	0	0
WESTERN CONN. ST.					
Paul Pasqualoni (Penn St. '72) 85	1	0	1	0	0
WEST GA.					
Bobby Pate (Georgia '63) 81, 82-CH	2	3	1	1	0
WIDENER					
Bill Manlove (Temple '58) 75, 77-CH, 79, 80, 81-CH, 82, 88	7	9	5	2	0
WIS.-LA CROSSE					
Roger Harring (Wis.-La Crosse '58) 83, 91...........	2	2	2	0	0
WIS.-STEVENS POINT					
D. J. LeRoy 86	1	0	1	0	0
WIS.-WHITEWATER					
Bob Berezowitz (Wis.-Whitewater '67) 88, 90	2	1	2	0	0
WITTENBERG					
Dave Maurer (Denison '54) 73-CH, 75-CH, 78-2D, 79-2D	4	9	2	2	2
Ron Murphy 88..................................	1	1	1	0	0
TOTAL	5	10	3	2	2

ALL-TIME RESULTS

1973 Semifinals: Juniata 35, Bridgeport 14; Wittenberg 21, San Diego 14. **Championship:** Wittenberg 41, Juniata 0.

1974 Semifinals: Central (Iowa) 17, Evansville 16; Ithaca 27, Slippery Rock 14. **Championship:** Central (Iowa) 10, Ithaca 8.

1975 First Round: Widener 14, Albright 6; Ithaca 41, Fort Valley St. 12; Wittenberg 17, Indianapolis 13; Millsaps 28, Colorado Col. 21. **Semifinals:** Ithaca 23, Widener 14; Wittenberg 55, Millsaps 22. **Championship:** Wittenberg 28, Ithaca 0.

1976 First Round: St. John's (Minn.) 46, Augustana (Ill.) 7; Buena Vista 20, Carroll (Wis.) 14 (OT); St. Lawrence 26, Albright 7; Towson St. 14, LIU-C.W. Post 10. **Semifinals:** St. John's (Minn.) 61, Buena Vista 0; Towson St. 38, St. Lawrence 36. **Championship:** St. John's (Minn.) 31, Towson St. 28.

1977 First Round: Minn.-Morris 13, Albion 10; Wabash 20, St. John's (Minn.) 9; Widener 19, Central (Iowa) 0; Albany (N.Y.) 51, Hampden-Sydney 45. **Semifinals:** Wabash 37, Minn.-Morris 21; Widener 33, Albany (N.Y.) 15. **Championship:** Widener 39, Wabash 36.

1978 First Round: Minn.-Morris 23, St. Olaf 10; Wittenberg 6, Ithaca 3; Carnegie Mellon 24, Dayton 21; Baldwin-Wallace 71, St. Lawrence 7. **Semifinals:** Wittenberg 35, Minn.-Morris 14; Baldwin-Wallace 31, Carnegie Mellon 6. **Championship:** Baldwin-Wallace 24, Wittenberg 10.

1979 First Round: Wittenberg 21, Millersville 14; Widener 29, Baldwin-Wallace 8; Carnegie Mellon 31, Minn.-Morris 25; Ithaca 27, Dubuque 7. **Semifinals:** Wittenberg 17, Widener 14; Ithaca 15, Carnegie Mellon 6. **Championship:** Ithaca 14, Wittenberg 10.

1980 First Round: Ithaca 41, Wagner 13; Minn.-Morris 41, Dubuque 35; Dayton 34, Baldwin-Wallace 0; Widener 43, Bethany (W. Va.) 12. **Semifinals:** Ithaca 36, Minn.-Morris 0; Dayton 28, Widener 24. **Championship:** Dayton 63, Ithaca 0.

1981 First Round: Dayton 19, Augustana (Ill.) 7; Lawrence 21, Minn.-Morris 14 (OT); Montclair St. 13, Alfred 12; Widener 10, West Ga. 3. **Semifinals:** Dayton 38, Lawrence 0; Widener 23, Montclair St.

12. **Championship:** Widener 17, Dayton 10.

1982 First Round: Augustana (Ill.) 28, Baldwin-Wallace 22; St. Lawrence 43, Wagner 34; Bishop 32, Wartburg 7; West Ga. 31, Widener 24 (3 OT). **Semifinals:** Augustana (Ill.) 14, St. Lawrence 0; West Ga. 27, Bishop 6. **Championship:** West Ga. 14, Augustana (Ill.) 0.

Dayton's Dan Rosenbaum is tripped up during a kickoff return in Dayton's 34-20 loss to Ithaca in the 1991 Amos Alonzo Stagg Bowl, the Division III title game. It was the Flyers' fifth trip to the championship finals and their second in three years.

1983 First Round: Union (N.Y.) 51, Hofstra 19; Salisbury St. 16, Carnegie Mellon 14; Augustana (Ill.) 22, Adrian 21; Wis.-La Crosse 43, Occidental 42. **Semifinals:** Union (N.Y.) 23, Salisbury St. 21; Augustana (Ill.) 21, Wis.-La Crosse 15. **Championship:** Augustana (Ill.) 21, Union (N.Y.) 17.

1984 First Round: Union (N.Y.) 26, Plymouth St. 14; Augustana (Ill.) 14, Dayton 13; Wash. & Jeff. 22, Randolph-Macon 21; Central (Iowa) 23, Occidental 22. **Semifinals:** Augustana (Ill.) 23, Union (N.Y.) 6; Central (Iowa) 20, Wash. & Jeff. 0. **Championship:** Augustana (Ill.) 21, Central (Iowa) 12.

1985 First Round: Ithaca 13, Union (N.Y.) 12; Montclair St. 28, Western Conn. St. 0; Salisbury St. 35, Carnegie Mellon 22; Gettysburg 14, Lycoming 10; Augustana (Ill.) 26, Albion 10; Mount Union 35, Denison 3; Central (Iowa) 27, Coe 7; Occidental 28, St. John's (Minn.) 10. **Quarterfinals:** Ithaca 50, Montclair St. 28; Gettysburg 22, Salisbury St. 6; Augustana (Ill.) 21, Mount Union 14; Central (Iowa) 71, Occidental 0. **Semifinals:** Ithaca 34, Gettysburg 0; Augustana (Ill.) 14, Central (Iowa) 7. **Championship:** Augustana (Ill.) 20, Ithaca 7.

1986 First Round: Ithaca 24, Union (N.Y.) 17 (OT); Montclair St. 24, Hofstra 21; Susquehanna 28, Wash. & Jeff. 20; Salisbury St. 34, Emory & Henry 20; Mount Union 42, Dayton 36; Augustana (Ill.) 34, Hope 10; Central (Iowa) 37, Buena Vista 0; Concordia-M'head 24, Wis.-Stevens Point 15. **Quarterfinals:** Ithaca 29, Montclair St. 15; Salisbury St. 31, Susquehanna 17; Augustana (Ill.) 16, Mount Union 7; Concordia-M'head 17, Central (Iowa) 14. **Semifinals:** Salisbury St. 44, Ithaca 40; Augustana (Ill.) 41, Concordia-M'head 7. **Championship:** Augustana (Ill.) 31, Salisbury St. 3.

1987 First Round: Wagner 38, Rochester 14; Fordham 41, Hofstra 6; Wash. & Jeff. 23, Allegheny 17 (OT); Emory & Henry 49, Ferrum 7; Dayton 52, Capital 28; Augustana (Ill.) 53, Hiram 0; St. John's (Minn.) 7, Gust. Adolphus 3; Central (Iowa) 17, Menlo 0. **Quarterfinals:** Wagner 21, Fordham 0; Emory & Henry 23, Wash. & Jeff. 16; Dayton 38, Augustana (Ill.) 36; Central (Iowa) 13, St. John's (Minn.) 3. **Semifinals:** Wagner 20, Emory & Henry

15; Dayton 34, Central (Iowa) 0. **Championship:** Wagner 19, Dayton 3.

1988 Regionals: Cortland St. 32, Hofstra 27; Ithaca 34, Wagner 31 (OT); Ferrum 35, Rhodes 12; Moravian 17, Widener 7; Wittenberg 35, Dayton 28 (2 OT); Augustana (Ill.) 25, Adrian 7; Central (Iowa) 7, Concordia-M'head 0; Wis.-Whitewater 29, Simpson 27. **Quarterfinals:** Ithaca 24, Cortland St. 17; Ferrum 49, Moravian 28; Augustana (Ill.) 28, Wittenberg 14; Central (Iowa) 16, Wis.-Whitewater 13. **Semifinals:** Ithaca 62, Ferrum 28; Central (Iowa) 23, Augustana 17 (2 OT). **Championship:** Ithaca 39, Central (Iowa) 24.

1989 Regionals: Union (N.Y.) 42, Cortland St. 14; Ithaca 23, Hofstra 6; Lycoming 21, Dickinson 0; Ferrum 41, Wash. & Jeff. 7; Dayton 35, John Carroll 10; Millikin 21, Augustana (Ill.) 12; Central (Iowa) 55, St. Norbert 7; St. John's (Minn.) 42, Simpson 35. **Quarterfinals:** Union (N.Y.) 45, Montclair St. 6; Ferrum 49, Lycoming 24; Dayton 28, Millikin 16; St. John's (Minn.) 27, Central (Iowa) 24. **Semifinals:** Union (N.Y.) 37, Ferrum 21; Dayton 28, St. John's (Minn.) 0. **Championship:** Dayton 17, Union (N.Y.) 7.

1990 Regionals: Hofstra 35, Cortland St. 9; Trenton St. 24, Ithaca 14; Wash. & Jeff. 10, Ferrum 7; Lycoming 17, Carnegie Mellon 7; Dayton 24, Augustana (Ill.) 14; Allegheny 26, Mount Union 15; St. Thomas (Minn.) 24, Wis.-Whitewater 23; Central (Iowa) 24, Redlands 3. **Quarterfinals:** Hofstra 38, Trenton St. 3; Lycoming 24, Wash. & Jeff. 0; Allegheny 31, Dayton 23; Central (Iowa) 33, St. Thomas (Minn.) 32. **Semifinals:** Lycoming 20, Hofstra 10; Allegheny 24, Central (Iowa) 7. **Championship:** Allegheny 21, Lycoming 14 (OT).

1991 Regionals: St. John's (Minn.) 75, Coe 2; Wis.-La Crosse 28, Simpson 13; Allegheny 24, Albion 21 (OT); Dayton 27, Baldwin-Wallace 10; Ithaca 31, Glassboro St. 10; Union (N.Y.) 55, Mass.-Lowell 16; Lycoming 18, Wash. & Jeff. 16; Susquehanna 21, Dickinson 20. **Quarterfinals:** St. John's (Minn.) 29, Wis.-La Crosse 3; Dayton 28, Allegheny 25 (OT); Ithaca 35, Union (N.Y.) 23; Susquehanna 31, Lycoming 24. **Semifinals:** Dayton 19, St. John's (Minn.) 7; Ithaca 49, Susquehanna 13. **Championship:** Ithaca 34, Dayton 20.

COLLEGE FOOTBALL ATTENDANCE RECORDS

Total attendance at college football games topped 36 million in 1991 for the third year in a row and the ninth time in the past 10 years. Average attendance at Division I-A games increased by more than 500 fans, but total attendance at all college games was down slightly from 1990.

ALL-TIME COLLEGE ATTENDANCE

	No. Teams	Games	Total Attendance	Avg.	Yearly Change Total	Percent
1948	685	—	19,134,159	—	—	—
1949	682	—	19,651,995	—	Up 517,836	2.71
1950	674	—	18,961,688	—	Down 690,307	3.51
1951	635	—	17,480,533	—	Down 1,481,155	7.81
1952	625	—	17,288,062	—	Down 192,471	1.10
1953	618	—	16,681,731	—	Down 606,331	3.51
1954	614	—	17,048,603	—	Up 366,872	2.20
1955	621	—	17,266,556	—	Up 217,953	1.28
1956	618	—	18,031,805	—	Up 765,249	4.43
1957	618	2,586	18,290,724	7,073	Up 258,919	1.44
1958	618	2,673	19,280,709	7,213	Up 989,985	5.41
1959	623	2,695	19,615,344	7,278	Up 334,635	1.74
1960	620	2,711	20,403,409	7,526	Up 788,065	4.02
1961	616	2,697	20,677,604	7,667	Up 274,195	1.34
1962	610	2,679	21,227,162	7,924	Up 549,558	2.66
1963	616	2,686	22,237,094	8,279	Up 1,009,932	4.76
1964	622	2,745	23,354,477	8,508	Up 1,117,383	5.02
1965	616	2,749	24,682,572	8,979	Up 1,328,095	5.69
1966	616	2,768	25,275,899	9,131	Up 593,327	2.40
1967	610	2,764	26,430,639	9,562	Up 1,154,740	4.57
1968	612	2,786	27,025,846	9,701	Up 595,207	2.25
1969	615	2,820	27,626,160	9,797	Up 600,314	2.22
1970	617	2,895	29,465,604	10,178	*Up 1,839,444	*6.66
1971	618	2,955	30,455,442	10,306	Up 989,838	3.36
1972	620	2,997	30,828,802	10,287	Up 373,360	1.23
1973	630	3,062	31,282,540	10,216	Up 453,738	1.47
1974	634	3,101	31,234,855	10,073	Down 47,685	0.15
1975	634	3,089	31,687,847	10,258	Up 452,992	1.45
1976	637	3,108	32,012,008	10,299	Up 324,161	1.02
1977	638	3,145	32,905,178	10,463	Up 893,170	2.79
1978	643	3,163	34,251,606	10,829	Up 1,346,428	4.09
1979	643	3,174	35,020,284	11,033	Up 768,678	2.24
1980	642	3,196	35,540,975	11,120	Up 520,691	1.49
1981	648	3,217	35,807,040	11,131	Up 266,065	0.75
1982	649	3,224	36,538,637	*11,333	Up 731,597	2.04
1983	651	3,250	36,301,877	11,170	Down 236,760	0.65
1984	654	3,270	*36,652,179	11,209	Up 350,302	0.96
1985	661	3,309	36,312,022	10,974	Down 340,157	0.93
1986	666	3,339	36,387,905	10,898	Up 75,883	0.21
1987	667	3,353	36,462,671	10,875	Up 74,766	0.21
1988	680	3,360	35,581,790	10,590	Down 880,881	2.42
1989	673	3,360	36,406,297	10,790	Up 824,507	2.32
1990	673	3,374	36,626,547	10,846	Up 220,250	0.60
1991	681	3,378	36,565,880	10,825	Down 60,667	0.17

* Record

The 10 largest regular-season college-football crowds in the 44 seasons that official national attendance records have been maintained:

Crowd	Date	Home	Visitor
106,255	11-17-79	Michigan 15,	Ohio St. 18
106,208	10-8-88	Michigan 17,	Michigan St. 3
106,188	10-13-90	Michigan 27,	Michigan St. 28
106,156	11-23-91	Michigan 31,	Ohio St. 3
106,145	9-28-91	Michigan 31,	Florida St. 51
106,141	10-11-86	Michigan 27,	Michigan St. 6
106,138	9-14-91	Michigan 24,	Notre Dame 14
106,137	11-25-89	Michigan 28,	Ohio St. 18
106,115	11-19-83	Michigan 24,	Ohio St. 21
106,113	10-9-82	Michigan 31,	Michigan St. 17

Highest Weeks of the Weekly Top-10 Attended Games:

Total	Date
833,285	10-22-83
827,232	9-16-89
825,455	9-22-84
820,668	11-18-89
819,980	10-18-86
816,954	9-14-91
816,618	9-28-91
816,458	10-13-84
815,853	11-10-90
815,423	11-5-88

The 20 largest regular-season college-football crowds for games not played at Michigan:

Attendance	Date	Score (Home Team in Boldface)	Site
97,731	9-28-91	**Tennessee** 30, Auburn 21	Knoxville, Tenn.
97,372	11-30-85	**Tennessee** 30, Vanderbilt 0	Knoxville, Tenn.

494

Attendance	Date	Score (Home Team in Boldface)	Site
97,123	11-11-90	Notre Dame 34, **Tennessee** 29	Knoxville, Tenn.
97,117	9-14-91	**Tennessee** 30, UCLA 16	Knoxville, Tenn.
96,874	10-13-90	**Tennessee** 45, Florida 3	Knoxville, Tenn.
96,748	10-18-80	Alabama 27, **Tennessee** 0	Knoxville, Tenn.
96,732	10-20-90	Alabama 9, **Tennessee** 6	Knoxville, Tenn.
96,672	11-16-91	**Penn St.** 35, Notre Dame 13	University Park, Pa.
96,664	11-2-91	**Tennessee** 52, Memphis St. 24	Knoxville, Tenn.
96,445	10-26-91	**Penn St.** 51, West Va. 6	University Park, Pa.
96,304	9-21-91	**Penn St.** 33, Brigham Young 7	University Park, Pa.
96,058	10-7-89	**Tennessee** 17, Georgia 14	Knoxville, Tenn.
95,974	9-21-91	**Tennessee** 26, Mississippi St. 24	Knoxville, Tenn.
95,937	11-16-91	**Tennessee** 36, Mississippi 25	Knoxville, Tenn.
95,927	9-28-91	**Penn St.** 28, Boston College 21	University Park, Pa.
95,824	9-3-83	Pittsburgh 13, **Tennessee** 3	Knoxville, Tenn.
95,729	10-19-91	**Penn St.** 37, Rutgers 17	University Park, Pa.
95,585	11-12-83	Mississippi 13, **Tennessee** 10	Knoxville, Tenn.
95,422	10-20-84	**Tennessee** 28, Alabama 27	Knoxville, Tenn.
95,357	11-2-91	Iowa 16, **Ohio St.** 9	Columbus, Ohio

ANNUAL DIVISION I-A ATTENDANCE

Year	Teams	Games	Attendance	Avg.	Year	Teams	Games	Attendance	Avg.
1976	137	796	23,917,522	30,047	1986	105	611	25,692,095	42,049
1977	144	799	24,613,285	30,805	1987	104	607	25,471,744	41,963
1978	139	772	25,017,915	32,407	1988	104	605	25,079,490	41,454
1979	139	774	25,862,801	33,414	1989	106	603	25,307,915	41,970
1980	139	776	26,499,022	34,148	1990	106	615	25,513,098	41,485
1981	137	768	*26,588,688	34,621	1991	106	610	25,646,067	42,043
1982	97	567	24,771,855	*43,689					
1983	105	602	25,381,761	42,162					
1984	105	606	25,783,807	42,548					
1985	105	605	25,434,412	42,040					

Record.

ANNUAL DIVISION I-AA ATTENDANCE

Year	Teams	Games	Attendance	Avg.	Year	Teams	Games	Attendance	Avg.
1978	38	201	2,032,766	10,113	1985	87	471	5,143,077	10,919
1979	39	211	2,073,890	9,829	1986	86	456	5,044,992	11,064
1980	46	251	2,617,932	10,430	1987	87	460	5,129,250	11,151
1981	50	270	2,950,156	10,927	1988	88	465	4,801,637	10,326
1982	92	483	*5,655,519	*11,709	1989	89	471	5,278,520	11,020
1983	84	450	4,879,709	10,844	1990	87	473	5,328,477	11,265
1984	87	465	5,061,480	10,885	1991	89	490	5,386,425	10,993

Record.

ANNUAL DIVISION II ATTENDANCE

Year	Teams	Games	Attendance	Avg.	Year	Teams	Games	Attendance	Avg.
1978	103	518	*2,871,683	*5,544	1985	114	569	2,475,325	4,350
1979	105	526	2,775,569	5,277	1986	111	551	2,404,852	4,365
1980	111	546	2,584,765	4,734	1987	107	541	2,424,041	4,481
1981	121	589	2,726,537	4,629	1988	117	580	2,570,964	4,493
1982	126	618	2,745,964	4,443	1989	116	579	2,572,496	4,428
1983	122	611	2,705,892	4,429	1990	120	580	2,472,811	4,263
1984	114	568	2,413,947	4,250	1991	128	622	2,490,929	4,005

Record.

ANNUAL DIVISION III ATTENDANCE

Year	Teams	Games	Attendance	Avg.	Year	Teams	Games	Attendance	Avg.
1978	204	931	*2,447,366	*2,629	1985	203	954	1,898,734	1,990
1979	195	870	2,162,495	2,486	1986	208	987	1,888,963	1,914
1980	189	878	2,006,053	2,285	1987	209	981	1,982,506	2,021
1981	189	878	1,965,090	2,238	1988	215	994	1,871,751	1,883
1982	195	901	2,002,857	2,223	1989	213	977	1,957,257	1,948
1983	194	894	1,849,902	2,069	1990	220	1,036	2,015,560	1,946
1984	195	903	1,951,842	2,162	1991	225	1,054	2,004,799	1,902

Record.

ANNUAL NON-NCAA ATTENDANCE

Year	Teams	Games	Attendance	Avg.	Year	Teams	Games	Attendance	Avg.
1978	159	741	1,881,876	2,540	1985	152	710	1,360,474	1,916
1979	165	793	*2,145,529	*2,706	1986	156	734	1,357,003	1,849
1980	157	745	1,833,203	2,461	1987	160	764	1,455,130	1,905
1981	151	712	1,576,569	2,214	1988	156	716	1,257,948	1,757
1982	139	655	1,362,442	2,080	1989	149	723	1,333,328	1,899
1983	146	693	1,484,613	2,142	1990	140	673	1,296,601	1,927
1984	153	728	1,441,103	1,980	1991	133	602	1,037,660	1,724

* Record.

†PRE-1948 REGULAR-SEASON AND NON-MICHIGAN CROWDS IN EXCESS OF 100,000

Crowd	Date	Site	Opponents, Score
120,000*	11-26-27	Soldier Field, Chicago	Notre Dame 7, Southern Cal 6
120,000*	10-13-28	Soldier Field, Chicago	Notre Dame 7, Navy 0
112,912	11-16-29	Soldier Field, Chicago	Notre Dame 13, Southern Cal 12
110,000*	11-27-26	Soldier Field, Chicago	Army 21, Navy 21
110,000*	11-29-30	Soldier Field, Chicago	Notre Dame 7, Army 6
104,953	12-6-47	Los Angeles	Notre Dame 38, Southern Cal 7
101,799	11-30-68	Philadelphia	Army 21, Navy 14
100,428	12-2-67	Philadelphia	Navy 19, Army 14

* Estimated attendance, others are audited figures.

† Since 1956, when Michigan Stadium's capacity was increased to 101,000, there have been 121 100,000-plus crowds at Michigan. The 10 largest crowds are listed on page 494. Therefore, there has been a total of 129 regular-season crowds in excess of 100,000.

ADDITIONAL RECORDS

Highest Average Attendance Per Home Game: 105,588, Michigan, 1985 (633,530 in 6)
Highest Total Home Attendance: 731,281, Michigan, 1987 (7 games)
Highest Total Attendance, Home and Away: 1,005,195, Michigan, 1986 (12 games)
Highest Bowl Game Attendance: 106,869, 1973 Rose Bowl (Southern Cal 42, Ohio St. 17)
Most Consecutive Home Sellout Crowds: 181, Nebraska (current, from Nov. 3, 1962)
Most Consecutive 100,000-Plus Crowds: 103, Michigan (current, from Nov. 8, 1975)

1991 ATTENDANCE

LEADING DIVISION I-A TEAMS IN 1991 HOME ATTENDANCE

	G	Attend.	Avg.	Change			G	Attend.	Avg.	Change	
1. Michigan	6	632,024	105,337	Up	829	31. UCLA	5	245,760	49,152	Down	5,451
2. Tennessee	6	578,389	96,398	Down	11,235	32. West Va.	6	292,103	48,684	Down	7,539
3. Penn St.	6	575,077	95,846	Up	10,642	33. Georgia Tech	7	333,370	47,624	Up	5,610
4. Ohio St.	7	620,845	88,692	Up	3,343	34. Indiana	5	236,482	47,296	Up	1,700
5. Florida	6	506,729	84,455	Up	9,194	35. North Caro.	7	324,500	46,357	Up	714
6. Georgia	7	577,922	82,560	Up	2,387	36. Arkansas	7	322,998	46,143	Down	3,356
7. Auburn	7	552,155	78,879	Down	2,546	37. Arizona	6	272,588	45,431	Down	8,667
8. Nebraska	7	533,715	76,245	Up	6	38. Air Force	6	264,734	44,122	Up	1,626
9. Alabama	6	453,094	75,516	Up	3,553	39. Virginia Tech	6	262,126	43,688	Up	1,167
10. Clemson	7	513,915	73,416	Down	5,780	40. Syracuse	6	260,993	43,499	Down	3,474
11. Washington	6	433,703	72,284	Up	1,298	41. North Caro. St.	7	304,473	43,496	Down	171
12. Michigan St.	6	421,231	70,205	Down	3,674	42. Hawaii	7	304,148	43,450	Up	2,070
13. Iowa	6	420,424	70,071	Up	9,057	43. Iowa St.	6	254,007	42,335	Up	6,339
14. Texas	6	414,563	69,094	Down	6,913	44. Maryland	5	210,789	42,158	Up	10,494
15. Oklahoma	7	483,394	69,056	Down	399	45. Virginia	7	291,100	41,586	Down	2,431
16. Louisiana St.	6	412,476	68,746	Down	2,782	46. Oregon	5	207,569	41,514	Up	4,160
17. South Caro.	7	456,952	65,279	Down	236	47. Mississippi St.	7	282,347	40,335	Up	9,672
18. Southern Cal	6	385,226	64,204	Down	4,141	48. Army	8	320,841	40,105	Up	2,130
19. Texas A&M	6	379,906	63,318	Up	9,066	49. Missouri	6	238,879	39,813	Up	1,096
20. Brigham Young	7	433,341	61,906	Down	4,096	50. Purdue	6	235,029	39,172	Down	2,907
21. Florida St.	6	367,833	61,306	Up	77	51. Mississippi	5	193,800	38,760	Up	1,101
22. Notre Dame	6	354,450	59,075	None	—	52. Baylor	5	190,100	38,020	Up	667
23. Miami (Fla.)	6	347,785	57,964	Down	4,132	53. Texas Tech	6	226,822	37,804	Down	5,037
24. Arizona St.	6	334,287	55,715	Down	4,979	54. Pittsburgh	6	219,074	36,512	Down	1,696
25. Illinois	6	333,642	55,607	Down	5,213	55. Louisville	6	218,974	36,496	Down	4,482
26. Kentucky	6	327,250	54,542	Down	931	56. Minnesota	6	218,219	36,370	Down	4,022
27. Stanford	7	367,044	52,435	Up	11,438	57. Vanderbilt	5	179,028	35,806	Up	3,236
28. Colorado	6	311,458	51,910	Up	181	58. Northwestern	6	209,023	34,837	Up	6,775
29. Wisconsin	7	347,735	49,676	Down	1,351	59. Fresno St.	6	203,394	33,899	Up	1,018
30. California	7	346,500	49,500	Down	1,032	60. San Diego St.	7	232,020	33,146	Up	11,087

	G	Attend.	Avg.	Change			G	Attend.	Avg.	Change	
61. Houston	5	165,395	33,079	Up	3,145	66. Kansas	5	149,662	29,932	Down	843
62. East Caro.	5	160,208	32,042	Up	3,385	67. Duke	6	177,727	29,621	Up	4,009
63. Memphis St.	6	191,896	31,983	Up	8,381	68. UTEP	6	176,155	29,359	Up	7,132
64. Tulsa	7	218,652	31,236	Up	8,371	69. Kansas St.	6	174,367	29,061	Up	7,968
65. Rice	4	121,700	30,425	Up	8,554	70. Boston College.	6	172,033	28,672	Up	4,389

Designated home team at off-campus neutral sites (total included in averages above): Georgia 1g Jacksonville 81,679 (avg. 82,707 six home games); Texas 1g Dallas 75,587; Brigham Young 1g Anaheim 38,363 (avg. 65,830 six home—17th); Georgia Tech 1g East Rutherford 77,409; Arkansas 4g Little Rock avg. 47,895; Virginia Tech 1g Orlando 58,991; Maryland 1g Baltimore 57,416; Mississippi St. 1g Orlando 69,328; Army 1g Philadelphia 67,858; Mississippi 2g Jackson avg. 48,750; Northwestern 1g Cleveland 73,830; Duke 1g Tokyo 50,000.

OTHER TEAM LEADERS IN 1991 HOME ATTENDANCE

Division I-AA

	G	Attend.	Avg.	Change			G	Attend.	Avg.	Change	
1. Grambling	8	217,444	27,181	Down	2,971	16. Harvard	5	79,146	15,829	Down	271
2. Florida A&M	7	176,448	25,207	Up	5,779	17. Northeast La.	5	77,846	15,569	Down	515
3. Jackson St.	7	162,162	23,166	Down	1,374	18. Appalachian St.	5	77,811	15,562	Down	1,529
4. Howard	6	134,845	22,474	Up	4,227	19. Eastern Ky.	6	91,000	15,167	Up	600
5. Alabama St.	6	134,572	22,429	Up	2,215	20. Southern-B.R.	6	90,963	15,161	Down	11,028
6. Marshall	7	153,726	21,961	Up	6,560	21. Central Fla.	6	89,927	14,988	Down	79
7. Nevada	7	151,019	21,574	Up	5,017	22. North Caro. A&T	5	71,775	14,355	Down	143
8. Yale	5	102,850	20,570	Up	6,233	23. South Caro. St.	6	85,602	14,267	Up	1,732
9. Delaware	5	98,999	19,800	Up	2,350	24. Furman	6	85,173	14,196	Down	1,012
10. Boise St.	7	138,396	19,771	Down	1,398	25. Holy Cross	5	67,695	13,539	Down	103
11. Citadel	5	92,476	18,495	Up	2,207	26. McNeese St.	6	78,012	13,004	Down	1,421
12. Mississippi Val.	6	107,979	17,997	Up	10,436	27. Middle Tenn. St.	4	51,500	12,875	Up	708
13. Arkansas St.	6	103,191	17,199	Up	1,880	28. William & Mary	5	63,918	12,784	Up	270
14. Pennsylvania	5	84,371	16,874	Down	1,174	29. Southern Ill.	4	48,900	12,225	Up	3,225
15. Ga. Southern	5	83,519	16,704	Down	1,174	30. Idaho	7	85,500	12,214	Up	2,274

Division II

	G	Attend.	Avg.	Change			G	Attend.	Avg.	Change	
1. Norfolk St.	6	100,675	16,779	Up	1,875	9. Morehouse	4	33,314	8,329	Up	1,379
2. Jacksonville St.	5	71,400	14,280	Down	595	10. Morris Brown	4	31,000	7,750	Down	1,490
3. Winston-Salem .	5	63,257	12,651	Up	5,830	11. Alabama A&M	3	21,450	7,150	Down	1,100
4. North Dak. St.	5	59,515	11,903	Up	853	12. Angelo St.	5	35,200	7,040	Down	760
5. Tuskegee	4	42,837	10,709	Down	2,021	13. Cal St.					
6. Portland St.	6	60,973	10,162	Down	1,819	Sacramento .	4	26,576	6,644	Up	4,108
7. Texas A&I	5	48,300	9,660	Up	1,180	14. Troy St.	4	24,500	6,125	Up	475
8. Indiana (Pa.)	5	41,900	8,380	Up	608	15. Shippensburg	5	30,100	6,020	Up	1,503

Division III

	G	Attend.	Avg.	Change			G	Attend.	Avg.	Change	
1. Dayton	6	45,942	7,657	Up	1,472	6. Ithaca	5	24,521	4,904	Up	2,450
2. Baldwin-						7. Emory & Henry	5	23,119	4,624	Up	754
Wallace	5	30,086	6,017	Up	2,617	8. Union (N.Y.)	4	17,700	4,425	Up	645
3. Williams	4	23,716	5,929	Up	169	9. Ala.-					
4. Hofstra	4	21,072	5,268	Up	660	Birmingham .	6	25,468	4,245	Up	4,245
5. St. John's						10. Wesleyan	4	16,450	4,113	Up	1,900
(Minn.)	5	25,500	5,100	Up	760						

Non-NCAA

	G	Attend.	Avg.	Change			G	Attend.	Avg.	Change	
1. Central Ark.	5	29,512	5,902	Down	70	3. Northeastern					
2. West Va. St.	6	28,800	4,800	Up	3,025	Okla.	5	22,500	4,500	None	—

Designated home team at off-campus neutral sites (total included in averages above): Grambling 1g Shreveport 41,258, 1g East Rutherford 30,750, 1g Dallas 42,670, 1g New Orleans 62,891; Florida A&M 1g Miami 20,503, 1g Atlanta 49,767, 1g Tampa 40,249; Jackson St. 1g Mobile 9,200, 1g Atlanta 32,857, 1g Birmingham 17,581 (avg. 25,564 four home—2nd); Howard 1g Indianapolis 62,007; Alabama St. 1g Mobile 32,000; Mississippi Val. 1g Memphis 25,891; South Caro. St. 1g Columbia 46,000; Holy Cross 1g Limerick, Ireland 17,411; Middle Tenn. St. 1g Nashville 20,000.

LEADING CONFERENCES AND INDEPENDENT GROUPS
BELOW DIVISION I-AA

	Total Teams	Games	1991 Attendance	Avg. PG	Change+ In Avg.		Change+ In Total	
Central Intercollegiate	11	53	349,962	6,603	Up	122	Up	32,371
Southern Intercollegiate	9	33	210,372	6,375	Down	592	Down	54,369
Western Football	6	29	158,954	5,481	Down	530	Down	27,391
Gulf South#	7	36	192,826	5,356	Down	864	Down	6,202
North Central	10	50	234,684	4,694	None		Down	14,210
Lone Star	8	36	153,883	4,275	Down	78	Down	15,902
Pennsylvania	14	67	282,701	4,219	Up	99	Up	6,666
Arkansas Intercollegiate	7	35	118,290	3,380	Down	195	Down	3,246
Old Dominion Athletic	6	31	101,774	3,283	Up	309	Up	15,536
Missouri Intercollegiate#	10	52	170,504	3,279	Down	223	Up	2,414
Midwest Intercollegiate	11	57	182,136	3,195	Up	172	Up	9,823
South Atlantic	8	41	126,004	3,073	Up	230	Up	9,428
Oklahoma Intercollegiate#	6	29	86,800	2,993	Down	307	Down	5,600
New England Small College	10	40	118,328	2,958	Up	225	Up	9,004
Div. II Independents#	15	68	191,197	2,812	Down	301	Down	29,794

	Total Teams	Games	1991 Attendance	Avg. PG	Change+ In Avg.		Change+ In Total	
West Va. Intercollegiate#	8	41	111,431	2,718	Up	983	Up	45,500
Empire#	3	14	37,793	2,700	Up	1,020	Up	14,275
Middle Atlantic	9	43	110,035	2,559	Down	56	Down	5,010
Minnesota Intercollegiate.......	10	46	116,967	2,543	Up	327	Up	12,796
Texas Intercollegiate#	6	33	83,318	2,525	Up	928	Up	36,995
Ohio Athletic.................	10	49	121,704	2,484	Up	46	Up	2,620
Rocky Mountain#.............	8	41	101,061	2,465	Up	503	Up	24,532

DIVISIONS I-A AND I-AA CONFERENCES AND INDEPENDENT GROUPS

	Total Teams	Games	1991 Attendance	Avg. PG	Change+ In Avg.		Change+ In Total	
Southeastern (I-A)	10	61	4,063,190	*66,610	Up	2,740	Down	152,210
Big Ten (I-A)	10	61	3,674,654	60,240	Up	1,348	Up	141,150
Pacific-10 (I-A)	10	59	2,851,991	48,339	Down	1,181	Down	20,182
Big Eight (I-A)	8	49	2,308,238	47,107	Up	1,029	Up	50,413
Atlantic Coast (I-A)	8	51	*2,257,413	*44,263	Up	1,949	Up	268,632
Southwest (I-A)	9	50	2,062,309	41,246	Up	1,864	Down	24,939
Big East (I-A)@	8	47	1,788,611	38,056	Down	2,865	Down	93,744
I-A Independents#	17	95	3,576,983	37,652	Up	854	Up	81,146
Western Athletic (I-A)	9	55	1,883,861	34,252	Up	1,801	Up	99,054
Southwestern (I-AA)#	8	47	*856,491	18,223	Down	2,481	Up	28,322
Big West (I-A)	8	37	570,332	15,414	Down	459	Down	80,468
Mid-Eastern (I-AA)	7	40	*578,412	*14,460	Up	1,240	Up	102,503
Mid-American (I-A)	9	45	608,485	13,522	Down	3,020	Down	135,883
Southern (I-AA)	8	46	*574,059	*12,480	Up	1,065	Up	71,811
Ivy Group (I-AA)	8	39	466,928	11,973	Up	479	Down	4,317
Big Sky (I-AA)	9	56	*623,326	11,131	Up	510	Up	92,266
Southland (I-AA)#	8	41	392,513	9,573	Down	1,108	Down	77,463
I-AA Independents#	11	61	582,782	9,554	Down	350	Down	41,144
Yankee (I-AA)	9	48	431,522	8,990	Jp	348	Up	8,063
Gateway (I-AA)	7	38	332,482	8,750	Up	44	Up	19,073
Ohio Valley (I-AA)#	8	42	316,755	7,542	Down	3,552	Down	182,458
Patriot League (I-AA)	6	32	231,155	7,224	Down	239	Up	7,262
DIVISION I-A	106	610	25,646,067	42,043	Up	558	Up	132,969
DIVISION I-AA#...............	89	490	5,386,425	10,993	Down	226	Up	23,918
I-A & I-AA Combined#	195	1,100	31,032,492	28,211	Down	37	Up	156,887
NCAA DIVISION II#	128	622	2,490,929	4,005	Down	113	Down	62,139
NCAA DIVISION III#...........	225	1,054	2,004,799	1,902	Down	35	Down	19,330
ALL NON-NCAA#	133	602	1,037,660	1,724	Down	172	Down	136,085
ALL VARSITY TEAMS	681	3,378	36,565,880	10,825	Down	21	Down	60,667

By Percentage of Capacity: Div. I-A 78.4 percent—Southeastern 95.5, Atlantic Coast 89.3, Big Ten 83.1, Big Eight 81.6, I-A Independents 79.8, Western Athletic 73.0, Southwest Athletic 72.8, Pacific-10 70.4, Big East 69.7, Mid-American 54.9, Big West 53.4; Div. I-AA 53.6 percent—Southern 75.0, Big Sky 67.3, Mid-Eastern 62.1, Yankee 58.5, Southland 56.4, Gateway 54.5, Southwestern 53.6, Ohio Valley 51.4, Patriot 48.2, I-AA Independents 45.7, Ivy 31.8.

* Record high for this conference. + The 1991 figures used for comparison reflect changes in conference, division and association lineups to provide parallel, valid comparisons (i.e., 1991 lineups vs. same teams in 1990, whether members or not); conferences and independent groups and divisions marked (#) did not have the same lineups in 1991 as in 1990. @ New conference.

ANNUAL LEADING DIVISION I-A TEAMS IN PER-GAME HOME ATTENDANCE

Team	G	Attendance	Average	Team	G	Attendance	Average
1949				**1952**			
Michigan...............6		563,363	93,894	Ohio St.................6		453,911	75,652
Ohio St.................5		382,146	76,429	Michigan...............6		395,907	65,985
Southern Methodist....8		484,000	60,500	Texas ....#5		311,160	62,232
1950				**1953**			
Michigan...............6		493,924	82,321	Ohio St.................5		397,998	79,600
Ohio St.................5		368,021	73,604	Southern Cal 6		413,617	68,936
Southern Methodist....5		309,000	61,800	Michigan...............6		353,860	58,977
1951				**1954**			
Ohio St.................6		455,737	75,956	Ohio St.................6		479,840	79,973
Michigan...............6		445,635	74,273	Michigan...............6		409,454	68,242
Illinois 4		237,035	59,259	UCLA 5		318,371	63,674

Team	G	Attendance	Average
1955			
Michigan	7	544,838	77,834
Ohio St.	7	493,178	70,454
Southern Cal	7	467,085	66,726
1956			
Ohio St.	6	494,575	82,429
Michigan	7	566,145	80,878
Minnesota	6	375,407	62,568
1957			
Michigan	6	504,954	84,159
Ohio St.	6	484,118	80,686
Minnesota	5	319,942	63,988
1958			
Ohio St.	6	499,352	82,225
Michigan	6	405,115	67,519
Louisiana St.	5	296,576	59,315
1959			
Ohio St.	6	495,536	82,589
Michigan	6	456,385	76,064
Louisiana St.	7	408,727	58,390
1960			
Ohio St.	5	413,583	82,717
Michigan St.	4	274,367	68,592
Michigan	6	374,682	62,447
1961			
Ohio St.	5	414,712	82,942
Michigan	7	514,924	73,561
Louisiana St.	6	381,409	63,651
1962			
Ohio St.	6	497,644	82,941
Michigan St.	4	272,568	68,142
Louisiana St.	6	397,701	66,284
1963			
Ohio St.	5	416,023	83,205
Louisiana St.	6	396,846	66,141
Michigan St.	5	326,597	65,319
1964			
Ohio St.	7	583,740	83,391
Michigan St.	4	284,933	71,233
Michigan	6	388,829	64,805
1965			
Ohio St.	5	416,282	83,256
Michigan	6	480,487	80,081
Michigan St.	5	346,296	69,259
1966			
Ohio St.	6	488,399	81,400
Michigan St.	6	426,750	71,125
Michigan	6	413,599	68,933
1967			
Ohio St.	5	383,502	76,700
Michigan	6	447,289	74,548
Michigan St.	6	411,916	68,653
1968			
Ohio St.	6	482,564	80,427
Southern Cal	5	354,945	70,989
Michigan St.	6	414,177	69,030
1969			
Ohio St.	5	431,175	86,235
Michigan	6	428,780	71,463
Michigan St.	5	352,123	70,425
1970			
Ohio St.	5	432,451	86,490
Michigan	6	476,164	79,361
Purdue	5	340,090	68,018
1971			
Ohio St.	6	506,699	84,450
Michigan	7	564,376	80,625
Wisconsin	6	408,885	68,148

Team	G	Attendance	Average
1972			
Michigan	6	513,398	85,566
Ohio St.	6	509,420	84,903
Nebraska	6	456,859	76,143
1973			
Ohio St.	6	523,369	87,228
Michigan	7	595,171	85,024
Nebraska	6	456,726	76,121
1974			
Michigan	6	562,105	93,684
Ohio St.	6	525,314	87,552
Nebraska	7	534,388	76,341
1975			
Michigan	7	689,146	98,449
Ohio St.	6	527,141	87,856
Nebraska	7	533,368	76,195
1976			
Michigan	7	722,113	103,159
Ohio St.	6	526,216	87,702
Tennessee	7	564,922	80,703
1977			
Michigan	7	729,418	104,203
Ohio St.	6	525,535	87,589
Tennessee	7	582,979	83,283
1978			
Michigan	6	629,690	104,948
Ohio St.	7	614,881	87,840
Tennessee	†8	627,381	78,422
1979			
Michigan	7	730,315	104,331
Ohio St.	7	611,794	87,399
Tennessee	6	512,139	85,357
1980			
Michigan	6	625,750	104,292
Tennessee	†8	709,193	88,649
Ohio St.	7	615,476	87,925
1981			
Michigan	6	632,990	105,498
Tennessee	6	558,996	93,166
Ohio St.	6	521,760	86,960
1982			
Michigan	6	631,743	105,291
Tennessee	6	561,102	93,517
Ohio St.	7	623,152	89,022
1983			
Michigan	6	626,916	104,486
Ohio St.	6	534,110	89,018
Tennessee	†8	679,420	84,928
1984			
Michigan	7	726,734	103,819
Tennessee	7	654,602	93,515
Ohio St.	6	536,691	89,449
1985			
Michigan	6	633,530	*105,588
Tennessee	7	658,690	94,099
Ohio St.	6	535,284	89,214
1986			
Michigan	6	631,261	105,210
Tennessee	7	643,317	91,902
Ohio St.	6	536,210	89,368
1987			
Michigan	7	*731,281	104,469
Tennessee	‡8	705,434	88,179
Ohio St.	6	511,772	85,295
1988			
Michigan	6	628,807	104,801
Tennessee	6	551,677	91,946
Ohio St.	6	516,972	86,162

Team	G	Attendance	Average
1989			
Michigan	6	632,136	105,356
Tennessee	6	563,502	93,917
Ohio St.	6	511,812	85,302
1990			
Michigan	6	627,046	104,508
Tennessee	7	666,540	95,220
Ohio St.	6	536,297	89,383
1991			
Michigan	6	632,024	105,337
Tennessee	6	578,389	96,398
Penn St.	6	575,077	95,846

* Record.   # Includes neutral-site game (Oklahoma) at Dallas counted as a home game (75,500).   † Includes neutral-site game at Memphis counted as a home game. Attendance: 1978 (40,879), 1980 (50,003), 1983 (20,135).   ‡ Includes neutral-site game at East Rutherford (54,681).

ANNUAL LEADING DIVISION I-AA TEAMS IN PER-GAME HOME ATTENDANCE

Year		Avg.	Year		Avg.
1978	Southern-B.R.	28,333	1986	Jackson St.	25,177
1979	Grambling	29,900	1987	Jackson St.	*32,734
1980	Southern-B.R.	29,708	1988	Jackson St.	26,500
1981	Grambling	30,835	1989	Jackson St.	32,269
1982	Southern-B.R.	32,265	1990	Grambling	30,152
1983	Jackson St.	29,117	1991	Grambling	27,181
1984	Jackson St.	29,215			
1985	Yale	29,347			

* Record.

ANNUAL LEADING DIVISION II TEAMS IN PER-GAME HOME ATTENDANCE

Year		Avg.	Year		Avg.
1958	Southern Miss.	11,998	1978	Delaware	18,981
1959	Southern Miss.	13,964	1979	Delaware	19,644
1960	Florida A&M	12,083	1980	Alabama A&M	15,820
1961	Akron	12,988	1981	Norfolk St.	19,750
1962	Mississippi Col.	13,125	1982	Norfolk St.	16,183
1963	San Diego St.	14,200	1983	Norfolk St.	15,417
1964	Southern-B.R.	12,633	1984	Norfolk St.	18,500
1965	San Diego St.	15,227	1985	Norfolk St.	18,430
1966	San Diego St.	15,972	1986	Norfolk St.	13,836
1967	San Diego St.	*41,030	1987	North Dak. St.	14,120
1968	San Diego St.	36,969	1988	Central Fla.	21,905
1969	Grambling	27,680	1989	North Dak. St.	16,833
1970	Tampa	24,204	1990	Norfolk St.	14,904
1971	Grambling	29,341	1991	Norfolk St.	16,779
1972	Grambling	22,663			
1973	Morgan St.	22,371			
1974	Southern-B.R.	33,563			
1975	Texas Southern	22,800			
1976	Southern-B.R.	25,864			
1977	Florida A&M	21,376			

* Record.

ANNUAL LEADING DIVISION III TEAMS IN PER-GAME HOME ATTENDANCE

Year		Avg.	Year		Avg.
1974	Albany St. (Ga.)	9,380	1984	Dayton	8,332
1975	Wittenberg	7,000	1985	Villanova	11,740
1976	Morehouse	11,600	1986	Villanova	*11,883
1977	Dayton	10,315	1987	Trinity (Conn.)	6,254
1978	Dayton	9,827	1988	St. John's (Minn.)	5,788
1979	Central Fla.	11,240	1989	Dayton	5,962
1980	Central Fla.	10,450	1990	Dayton	6,185
1981	Dayton	10,025	1991	Dayton	7,657
1982	Dayton	7,906			
1983	Dayton	6,542			

* Record.

ANNUAL LEADING NON-NCAA TEAMS IN PER-GAME HOME ATTENDANCE

Year		Avg.	Year		Avg.
1974	Texas A&I	12,000	1984	Elon	6,100
1975	Texas A&I	11,000	1985	Emporia St.	5,120
1976	Texas A&I	12,000	1986	Elon	5,833
1977	Texas A&I	*14,400	1987	Ark.-Pine Bluff	9,172
1978	Angelo St.	12,391	1988	Ark.-Pine Bluff	7,214
1979	Texas A&I	11,667	1989	Ark.-Pine Bluff	13,920
1980	Angelo St.	8,099	1990	Ark.-Pine Bluff	12,356
1981	Presbyterian	8,000	1991	Central Ark.	5,902
1982	Lenoir-Rhyne	6,040			
1983	Northeastern Okla.	7,575			

* Record.

MAJOR BOWL GAME ATTENDANCE (CURRENT SITE)

(For participating teams, refer to pages 346-352)

ROSE BOWL

(Rose Bowl Stadium, Pasadena, Cal.; Capacity: 99,563)

Date		Date		Date		Date	
1-1-02	8,000	1-1-37	87,196	1-1-57	97,126	1-1-77	106,182
1-1-16	7,000	1-1-38	90,000	1-1-58	98,202	1-2-78	105,312
1-1-17	26,000	1-2-39	89,452	1-1-59	98,297	1-1-79	105,629
1-1-20	30,000	1-1-40	92,200	1-1-60	100,809	1-1-80	105,526
1-1-21	42,000	1-1-41	91,500	1-2-61	97,314	1-1-81	104,863
1-2-22	40,000	1-1-42#	56,000	1-1-62	98,214	1-1-82	105,611
1-1-23	43,000	1-1-43	93,000	1-1-63	98,698	1-1-83	104,991
1-1-24	40,000	1-1-44	68,000	1-1-64	96,957	1-2-84	103,217
1-1-25	53,000	1-1-45	91,000	1-1-65	100,423	1-1-85	102,594
1-1-26	50,000	1-1-46	93,000	1-1-66	100,087	1-1-86	103,292
1-1-27	57,417	1-1-47	90,000	1-2-67	100,807	1-1-87	103,168
1-2-28	65,000	1-1-48	93,000	1-1-68	102,946	1-1-88	103,847
1-1-29	66,604	1-1-49	93,000	1-1-69	102,063	1-2-89	101,688
1-1-30	72,000	1-2-50	100,963	1-1-70	103,878	1-1-90	103,450
1-1-31	60,000	1-1-51	98,939	1-1-71	103,839	1-1-91	101,273
1-1-32	75,562	1-1-52	96,825	1-1-72	103,154	1-1-92	103,566
1-2-33	78,874	1-1-53	101,500	1-1-73	*106,869		
1-1-34	35,000	1-1-54	101,000	1-1-74	105,267		
1-1-35	84,474	1-1-55	89,191	1-1-75	106,721		
1-1-36	84,474	1-2-56	100,809	1-1-76	105,464		

* Record attendance.   # Game held at Duke, Durham, N.C., due to war-time West Coast restrictions.

ORANGE BOWL

(Orange Bowl Stadium, Miami, Fla.; Capacity: 74,244)

Date		Date		Date		Date	
1-1-35	5,134	1-2-50	64,816	1-1-65	72,647	1-1-80	66,714
1-1-36	6,568	1-1-51	65,181	1-1-66	72,214	1-1-81	71,043
1-1-37	9,210	1-1-52	65,839	1-2-67	72,426	1-1-82	72,748
1-1-38	18,972	1-1-53	66,280	1-1-68	77,993	1-1-83	68,713
1-2-39	32,191	1-1-54	68,640	1-1-69	77,719	1-2-84	72,549
1-1-40	29,278	1-1-55	68,750	1-1-70	77,282	1-1-85	56,294
1-1-41	29,554	1-2-56	76,561	1-1-71	80,699	1-1-86	74,178
1-1-42	35,786	1-1-57	73,280	1-1-72	78,151	1-1-87	52,717
1-1-43	25,166	1-1-58	76,561	1-1-73	80,010	1-1-88	74,760
1-1-44	25,203	1-1-59	75,281	1-1-74	60,477	1-2-89	79,480
1-1-45	23,279	1-1-60	72,186	1-1-75	71,801	1-1-90	*81,190
1-1-46	35,709	1-2-61	72,212	1-1-76	76,799	1-1-91	77,062
1-1-47	36,152	1-1-62	68,150	1-1-77	65,537	1-1-92	77,747
1-1-48	59,578	1-1-63	72,880	1-2-78	60,987		
1-1-49	60,523	1-1-64	72,647	1-1-79	66,365		

* Record attendance.

SUGAR BOWL

(Louisiana Superdome, New Orleans, La.; Capacity: 72,704)

Date		Date		Date		Date	
1-1-35	22,026	1-2-50	82,470	1-1-65	65,000	1-1-80	77,486
1-1-36	35,000	1-1-51	82,000	1-1-66	67,421	1-1-81	77,895
1-1-37	41,000	1-1-52	82,000	1-2-67	82,000	1-1-82	77,224
1-1-38	45,000	1-1-53	82,000	1-1-68	78,963	1-1-83	78,124
1-2-39	50,000	1-1-54	76,000	1-1-69	82,113	1-2-84	77,893
1-1-40	73,000	1-1-55	82,000	1-1-70	82,500	1-1-85	75,608
1-1-41	73,181	1-2-56	80,175	1-1-71	78,655	1-1-86	77,432
1-1-42	72,000	1-1-57	81,000	1-1-72	84,031	1-1-87	76,234
1-1-43	70,000	1-1-58	82,000	12-31-72	80,123	1-1-88	75,495
1-1-44	69,000	1-1-59	82,000	12-31-73	*85,161	1-2-89	61,934
1-1-45	72,000	1-1-60	83,000	12-31-74	67,890	1-1-90	77,452
1-1-46	75,000	1-2-61	82,851	12-31-75	75,212	1-1-91	75,132
1-1-47	73,300	1-1-62	82,910	1-1-77	76,117	1-1-92	76,447
1-1-48	72,000	1-1-63	82,900	1-2-78	76,811		
1-1-49	82,000	1-1-64	80,785	1-1-79	76,824		

* Record attendance.

COTTON BOWL

(Cotton Bowl Stadium, Dallas, Tex.; Capacity: 72,032)

Date		Date		Date		Date	
1-1-37	17,000	1-1-52	75,347	12-31-66	75,400	1-1-82	73,243
1-1-38	37,000	1-1-53	75,504	1-1-68	75,504	1-1-83	60,359
1-2-39	40,000	1-1-54	75,504	1-1-69	72,000	1-2-84	67,891
1-1-40	20,000	1-1-55	75,504	1-1-70	73,000	1-1-85	56,522
1-1-41	45,500	1-2-56	75,504	1-1-71	72,000	1-1-86	73,137
1-1-42	38,000	1-1-57	68,000	1-1-72	72,000	1-1-87	74,188
1-1-43	36,000	1-1-58	75,504	1-1-73	72,000	1-1-88	73,006
1-1-44	15,000	1-1-59	75,504	1-1-74	67,500	1-2-89	74,304
1-1-45	37,000	1-1-60	75,504	1-1-75	67,500	1-1-90	74,358
1-1-46	45,000	1-2-61	74,000	1-1-76	74,500	1-1-91	73,521
1-1-47	38,000	1-1-62	75,504	1-1-77	54,500	1-1-92	73,728
1-1-48	43,000	1-1-63	75,504	1-2-78	*76,601		
1-1-49	69,000	1-1-64	75,504	1-1-79	32,500		
1-2-50	75,347	1-1-65	75,504	1-1-80	72,032		
1-1-51	75,349	1-1-66	76,200	1-1-81	74,281		

* Record attendance.

JOHN HANCOCK BOWL#

(Sun Bowl Stadium, El Paso, Tex.; Capacity: 51,270)

Date		Date		Date		Date	
1-1-36	11,000	1-1-51	16,000	12-31-65	27,450	12-27-80	34,723
1-1-37	10,000	1-1-52	17,000	12-24-66	24,381	12-26-81	33,816
1-1-38	12,000	1-1-53	11,000	12-30-67	34,685	12-25-82	31,359
1-2-39	13,000	1-1-54	9,500	12-28-68	32,307	12-24-83	41,412
1-1-40	12,000	1-1-55	14,000	12-20-69	29,723	12-22-84	50,126
1-1-41	14,000	1-2-56	14,500	12-19-70	30,512	12-28-85	*52,203
1-1-42	14,000	1-1-57	13,500	12-18-71	33,503	12-25-86	48,722
1-1-43	16,000	1-1-58	12,000	12-30-72	31,312	12-25-87	43,240
1-1-44	18,000	12-31-58	13,000	12-29-73	30,127	12-24-88	48,719
1-1-45	13,000	12-31-59	14,000	12-28-74	30,131	12-30-89	44,887
1-1-46	15,000	12-31-60	16,000	12-26-75	33,240	12-31-90	50,562
1-1-47	10,000	12-30-61	15,000	1-2-77	33,252	12-31-91	42,821
1-1-48	18,000	12-31-62	16,000	12-31-77	31,318		
1-1-49	13,000	12-31-63	26,500	12-23-78	33,122		
1-2-50	15,000	12-26-64	28,500	12-22-79	33,412		

* Record attendance.   # Named Sun Bowl before 1989.

GATOR BOWL

(Gator Bowl Stadium, Jacksonville, Fla.; Capacity: 80,129)

Date		Date		Date		Date	
1-2-46	7,362	12-31-60	50,112	12-29-75	64,012	12-30-85	79,417
1-1-47	10,134	12-30-61	50,202	12-27-76	67,827	12-27-86	80,104
1-1-48	16,666	12-29-62	50,026	12-30-77	72,289	12-31-87	82,119
1-1-49	32,939	12-28-63	50,018	12-29-78	72,011	1-1-89	76,236
1-2-50	18,409	1-2-65	50,408	12-28-79	70,407	12-30-89	*82,911
1-1-51	19,834	12-31-65	60,127	12-29-80	72,297	1-1-91	68,927
1-1-52	34,577	12-31-66	60,312	12-28-81	71,009	12-29-91	62,003
1-1-53	30,015	12-30-67	68,019	12-30-82	80,913		
1-1-54	28,641	12-28-68	68,011	12-30-83	81,293		
12-31-54	28,426	12-27-69	72,248	12-28-84	82,138		
12-31-55	32,174	1-2-71	71,136				
12-29-56	36,256	12-31-71	71,208				
12-28-57	41,160	12-30-72	71,114				
12-27-58	41,312	12-29-73	62,109				
1-2-60	45,104	12-30-74	63,811				

Record attendance.

LIBERTY BOWL †

(Liberty Bowl Memorial Stadium, Memphis, Tenn.; Capacity: 62,425)

Date		Date		Date		Date	
12-19-59	36,211	12-13-69	50,042	12-22-79	50,021	12-28-89	60,128
12-17-60	16,624	12-12-70	44,640	12-27-80	53,667	12-27-90	13,144
12-16-61	15,712	12-20-71	51,410	12-30-81	43,216	12-29-91	*61,497
12-15-62	17,048	12-18-72	50,021	12-29-82	54,123		
12-31-63	8,309	12-17-73	50,011	12-29-83	38,229		
12-19-64	6,059	12-16-74	51,284	12-27-84	50,108		
12-18-65	38,607	12-22-75	52,129	12-27-85	40,186		
12-10-66	39,101	12-20-76	52,736	12-29-86	51,327		
12-16-67	35,045	12-19-77	49,456	12-29-87	53,249		
12-14-68	46,206	12-23-78	53,064	12-28-88	39,210		

Record attendance. † *Played at Philadelphia, 1959-63; Atlantic City, 1964; Memphis, from 1965.*

FLORIDA CITRUS BOWL

(Florida Citrus Bowl—Orange County Stadium, Orlando, Fla.; Capacity: 70,000)

Date		Date		Date		Date	
12-30-60	13,000	12-18-76	37,812	12-19-81	50,045	1-1-87	51,113
12-22-62	7,500	12-23-77	44,502	12-18-82	51,296	1-1-88	53,152
12-27-68	16,114	12-23-78	31,356	12-17-83	50,183	1-2-89	53,571
12-26-69	16,311	12-22-79	38,666	12-22-84	51,821	1-1-90	60,016
12-28-70	15,164	12-20-80	52,541	12-28-85	50,920	1-1-91	*72,328
12-28-71	16,750					1-1-92	64,192
12-29-72	20,062						
12-22-73	@37,234						
12-21-74	20,246						
12-20-75	20,247						

Record attendance. # Named Tangerine Bowl before 1982. The first 14 games in the Tangerine Bowl, through 1-1-60, are not listed because no major teams were involved. The same is true for those games played in December 1961, 1963, 1964, 1965, 1966 and 1967. @ Played at Gainesville, Fla.

PEACH BOWL

(Georgia Dome, Atlanta, Ga.; Capacity: 70,500)

Date		Date		Date		Date	
12-30-68	35,545	12-25-78	20,277	12-30-83	25,648	12-31-88	44,635
12-30-69	48,452	12-31-79	57,971	12-31-84	41,107	12-30-89	44,991
12-30-70	52,126	1-2-81	45,384	12-31-85	29,857	12-29-90	38,912
12-30-71	36,771	12-31-81	37,582	12-31-86	53,668	1-1-92	*59,322
12-29-72	52,671	12-31-82	50,134	1-2-88	58,737		
12-28-73	38,107						
12-28-74	31,695						
12-31-75	45,134						
12-31-76	54,132						
12-31-77	36,733						

Record attendance.

FIESTA BOWL
(Sun Devil Stadium, Tempe, Ariz.; Capacity: 74,783)

Date		Date		Date		Date	
12-27-71	51,089	12-25-76	48,174	1-1-82	71,053	1-2-87	73,098
12-23-72	51,318	12-25-77	57,727	1-1-83	70,533	1-1-88	72,112
12-21-73	50,878	12-25-78	55,227	1-2-84	66,484	1-2-89	*74,911
12-28-74	50,878	12-25-79	55,347	1-1-85	60,310	1-1-90	73,953
12-26-75	51,396	12-26-80	66,738	1-1-86	72,454	1-1-91	69,098
						1-1-92	71,133

* Record attendance.

INDEPENDENCE BOWL
(Independence Stadium, Shreveport, La.; Capacity: 50,459)

Date		Date		Date		Date	
12-13-76	15,542	12-12-81	47,300	12-20-86	46,369	12-29-91	46,932
12-17-77	18,500	12-11-82	*49,503	12-19-87	41,683		
12-16-78	18,200	12-10-83	41,274	12-23-88	20,242		
12-15-79	27,234	12-15-84	41,000	12-16-89	30,333		
12-13-80	45,000	12-21-85	42,800	12-15-90	48,325		

* Record attendance.

HOLIDAY BOWL
(San Diego Jack Murphy Stadium, San Diego, Cal.; Capacity: 62,809)

Date		Date		Date		Date	
12-28-78	52,500	12-17-82	52,533	12-30-86	59,473	12-29-90	61,441
12-21-79	52,200	12-23-83	51,480	12-30-87	*61,892	12-30-91	60,646
12-19-80	50,214	12-21-84	61,243	12-30-88	60,718		
12-18-81	52,419	12-22-85	42,324	12-29-89	61,113		

* Record attendance.

CALIFORNIA BOWL
(FSU Bulldog Stadium, Fresno, Cal.; Capacity: 40,000)

Date		Date		Date		Date	
12-19-81	15,565	12-15-84	21,741	12-12-87	24,000	12-8-90	25,431
12-18-82	30,000	12-14-85	32,554	12-10-88	31,272	12-14-91	*34,825
12-17-83	20,464	12-13-86	10,743	12-9-89	31,610		

* Record attendance.

ALOHA BOWL
(Aloha Stadium, Honolulu, Hawaii; Capacity: 50,000)

Date		Date		Date		Date	
12-25-82	30,055	12-28-85	35,183	12-25-88	35,132	12-25-91	34,433
12-26-83	37,212	12-27-86	26,743	12-25-89	*50,000		
12-29-84	41,777	12-25-87	24,839	12-25-90	14,185		

* Record attendance.

FREEDOM BOWL
(Anaheim Stadium, Anaheim, Cal.; Capacity: 70,962)

Date		Date		Date		Date	
12-26-84	24,093	12-30-86	*55,422	12-29-88	35,941	12-29-90	41,450
12-30-85	30,961	12-30-87	33,261	12-30-89	33,858	12-30-91	34,217

* Record attendance.

HALL OF FAME BOWL
(Tampa Stadium, Tampa, Fla.; Capacity: 74,350)

Date		Date		Date		Date	
12-23-86	25,368	1-2-89	51,112	1-1-91	*63,154	1-1-92	57,789
1-2-88	60,156	1-1-90	52,535				

* Record attendance.

1992 NCAA FOOTBALL

COPPER BOWL
(Arizona Wildcats Stadium, Tucson, Ariz.; Capacity: 56,167)

Date	Date	Date
12-31-89 . . . . . .*37,237	12-31-90 36,340	12-31-91 35,752

* Record attendance.

BLOCKBUSTER BOWL
(Joe Robbie Stadium, Miami, Fla.; Capacity: 73,000)

Date	Date
12-28-90 . . . . . .*74,021	12-28-91 52,644

* Record attendance.

FORMER MAJOR BOWL GAMES

ALAMO (San Antonio, Tex.): 1-4-47 (3,730)

ALL-AMERICAN (Birmingham, Ala., named Hall of Fame Classic until 1985 and then discontinued after 1990 game; played at Legion Field, capacity 75,952) 12-22-77 (47,000); 12-20-78 (41,500); 12-29-79 (62,785); 12-27-80 (30,000); 12-31-81 (41,672); 12-31-82 (75,000); 12-22-83 (42,000); 12-29-84 (47,300); 12-31-85 (45,000); 12-31-86 (30,000); 12-22-87 (37,000); 12-29-88 (48,218); 12-28-89 (47,750); 12-28-90 (44,000)

AVIATION (Dayton, Ohio): 12-9-61 (3,694)

BACARDI (Havana, Cuba): 1-1-37 (12,000)

BLUEBONNET (Houston, Tex., played at Rice Stadium 1959-67 and 1985, Astrodome 1968-84 and from 1986; Astrodome capacity 60,000): 12-19-59 (55,000); 12-17-60 (68,000); 12-16-61 (52,000); 12-22-62 (55,000); 12-21-63 (50,000); 12-19-64 (50,000); 12-18-65 (40,000); 12-17-66 (67,000); 12-23-67 (30,156); 12-31-68 (53,543); 12-31-69 (55,203); 12-31-70 (53,829); 12-31-71 (54,720); 12-30-72 (52,961); 12-29-73 (44,358); 12-23-74 (35,122); 12-27-75 (52,748); 12-31-76 (48,618); 12-31-77 (52,842); 12-31-78 (34,084); 12-31-79 (40,542); 12-31-80 (36,667); 12-31-81 (40,309); 12-31-82 (31,557); 12-31-83 (50,090); 12-31-84 (43,260); 12-31-85 (42,000); 12-31-86 (40,476); 12-31-87 (23,282)

BLUEGRASS (Louisville, Ky.): 12-23-58 (7,000)

CAMELLIA (Lafayette, La.): 12-30-48 (4,500)

CHERRY (Pontiac, Mich.): 12-22-84 (70,332); 12-21-85 (51,858)

DELTA (Memphis, Tenn.): 1-1-48 (28,120); 1-1-49 (15,069)

DIXIE BOWL (Birmingham, Ala.): 1-1-48 (22,000); 1-1-49 (20,000)

DIXIE CLASSIC (Dallas, Tex.): 1-2-22 (12,000); 1-1-25 (7,000); 1-1-34 (12,000)

FORT WORTH CLASSIC (Fort Worth, Tex.): 1-1-21 (9,000)

GARDEN STATE (East Rutherford, N.J.): 12-16-78 (33,402); 12-15-79 (55,493); 12-14-80 (41,417); 12-13-81 (38,782)

GOTHAM (New York City): 12-9-61 (15,123); 12-15-62 (6,166)

GREAT LAKES (Cleveland, Ohio): 12-6-47 (14,908)

HARBOR (San Diego, Cal.): 1-1-47 (7,000); 1-1-48 (12,000); 1-1-49 (20,000)

LOS ANGELES CHRISTMAS FESTIVAL (Los Angeles, Cal.): 12-25-24 (47,000)

MERCY (Los Angeles, Cal.): 11-23-61 (33,145)

OIL (Houston, Tex.): 1-1-46 (27,000); 1-1-47 (23,000)

PASADENA (Pasadena, Cal.): 12-2-67 (28,802); 12-6-69 (41,276); 12-19-70 (20,472); 12-18-71 (15,244)

PRESIDENTIAL CUP (College Park, Md.): 12-9-50 (12,245)

RAISIN (Fresno, Cal.): 1-1-46 (10,000); 1-1-47 (13,000); 1-1-48 (13,000); 1-1-49 (10,000); 12-31-49 (9,000)

SALAD (Phoenix, Ariz.): 1-1-48 (12,500); 1-1-49 (17,500); 1-1-50 (18,500); 1-1-51 (23,000); 1-1-52 (17,000)

SAN DIEGO EAST-WEST CHRISTMAS CLASSIC (San Diego, Cal.): 12-26-21 (5,000); 12-25-22 (5,000)

SHRINE (Little Rock, Ark.): 12-18-48 (5,000)

1991 STATISTICAL LEADERS

Dan Eichloff of Kansas was the only person to finish among the Division I-A top 20 in both punting and field goals in 1991. Eichloff finished second in field-goal kicking with 1.64 per game, and his punting average

RUSHING

	1991 Class	Games	Car.	Yards	Avg.	TD	Yds.PG
Marshall Faulk, San Diego St.	Fr	9	201	1429	7.1	21	158.78
Vaughn Dunbar, Indiana	Sr	11	336	1699	5.1	11	154.45
Trevor Cobb, Rice	Jr	11	360	1692	4.7	14	153.82
Jason Davis, Louisiana Tech	Jr	10	244	1351	5.5	14	135.10
Chris Hughley, Tulsa	Jr	10	267	1326	5.0	8	132.60
Ryan Benjamin, Pacific (Cal.)	Jr	12	226	1581	7.0	13	131.75
Tony Sands, Kansas	Sr	11	273	1442	5.3	9	131.09
Billy Smith, Central Mich.	Sr	11	374	1440	3.9	6	130.91
Derek Brown, Nebraska	So	11	230	1313	5.7	14	119.36
Mike Gaddis, Oklahoma	Sr	11	221	1240	5.6	14	112.73
Tony Smith, Southern Miss.	Sr	9	194	998	5.1	8	110.89
Greg Hill, Texas A&M	Fr	11	240	1216	5.1	12	110.55
Tico Duckett, Michigan St.	Jr	11	272	1204	4.4	5	109.45
Kevin Williams, UCLA	Jr	10	168	1089	6.5	8	108.90
Ricky Powers, Michigan	So	11	230	1187	5.2	9	107.91
Russell White, California	Jr	11	241	1177	4.9	14	107.00
Natrone Means, North Caro.	So	10	201	1030	5.1	11	103.00
Brian Copeland, Colorado St.	Sr	10	190	1028	5.4	5	102.80
Errict Rhett, Florida	So	11	224	1109	5.0	10	100.82
Reggie Yarbrough, Cal St. Fullerton	Sr	9	195	905	4.6	3	100.56
Corey Harris, Vanderbilt	Sr	11	229	1103	4.8	4	100.27
Eric Gallon, Kansas St.	Jr	11	224	1102	4.9	9	100.18
Timothy Curtis, Ohio	So	11	271	1085	4.0	10	98.64
Tommy Vardell, Stanford	Sr	11	226	1084	4.8	20	98.55
Ron Rivers, Fresno St.	So	10	134	984	7.3	5	98.40
Rob Perez, Air Force	Sr	12	233	1157	5.0	10	96.42
Corey Croom, Ball St.	Jr	11	291	1053	3.6	8	95.73
Roger Grant, Utah St.	Sr	11	218	1017	4.7	4	92.45
Lamont Warren, Colorado	Fr	9	157	830	5.3	7	92.22
David Small, Cincinnati	Fr	11	198	1004	5.1	4	91.27

PASSING EFFICIENCY

(Min. 15 att. per game)	1991 Class	Gms.	Att.	Cmp.	Cmp. Pct.	Int.	Int. Pct.	Yards	Yds./Att.	TD	TD Pct.	Rating Points
Elvis Grbac, Michigan	Jr	11	228	152	66.67	5	2.19	1955	8.57	24	10.53	169.0
Ty Detmer, Brigham Young	Sr	12	403	249	61.79	12	2.98	4031	10.00	35	8.68	168.5
Jeff Garcia, San Jose St.	So	9	160	99	61.87	5	3.13	1519	9.49	12	7.50	160.1
Matt Blundin, Virginia	Sr	9	224	135	60.27	0	.00	1902	8.49	19	8.48	159.6
Troy Kopp, Pacific (Cal.)	Jr	12	449	275	61.25	16	3.56	3767	8.39	37	8.24	151.8
Steve Stenstrom, Stanford	So	9	197	119	60.41	7	3.55	1683	8.54	15	7.61	150.2
Tony Sacca, Penn St.	Sr	12	292	169	57.88	5	1.71	2488	8.52	21	7.19	149.8
Rick Mirer, Notre Dame	Jr	12	234	132	56.41	10	4.27	2116	9.04	18	7.69	149.2
Shane Matthews, Florida	Jr	11	361	218	60.39	18	4.99	3130	8.67	28	7.76	148.8
Keithen McCant, Nebraska	Sr	11	168	97	57.74	8	4.76	1454	8.65	13	7.74	146.5
Casey Weldon, Florida St.	Sr	11	313	189	60.38	8	2.56	2527	8.07	22	7.03	146.3
Billy Joe Hobert, Washington	So	11	285	173	60.70	10	3.51	2271	7.97	22	7.72	146.1
Jeff Blake, East Caro.	Sr	11	368	203	55.16	8	2.17	3073	8.35	28	7.61	146.1
Matt Rodgers, Iowa	Sr	9	255	166	65.10	10	3.92	2054	8.05	14	5.49	143.0
Mike Pawlawski, California	Sr	11	316	191	60.44	13	4.11	2517	7.97	21	6.65	141.1
Kevin Verdugo, Colorado St.	Sr	11	265	159	60.00	11	4.15	2138	8.07	17	6.42	140.6
T. J. Rubley, Tulsa	Sr	11	260	148	56.92	9	3.46	2054	7.90	18	6.92	139.2
Gino Torretta, Miami (Fla.)	Jr	11	371	205	55.26	8	2.16	3095	8.34	20	5.39	138.8
David Lowery, San Diego St.	So	12	311	176	56.59	12	3.86	2575	8.28	19	6.11	138.6
Marvin Graves, Syracuse	So	11	221	131	59.28	11	4.98	1912	8.65	10	4.52	136.9
Len Williams, Northwestern	Jr	11	212	131	61.79	6	2.83	1630	7.69	10	4.72	136.3
Tom Corontzos, Wyoming	Sr	11	363	203	55.92	8	2.20	2868	7.90	19	5.23	135.2
Bucky Richardson, Texas A&M	Sr	10	156	79	50.64	10	6.41	1492	9.56	8	5.13	135.1
Tommy Maddox, UCLA	So	11	315	192	60.95	15	4.76	2505	7.95	16	5.08	135.0
William Robinson, Mississippi St.	Jr	9	141	77	54.61	7	4.96	1167	8.28	8	5.67	132.9
Andy Kelly, Tennessee	Sr	11	361	228	63.16	15	4.16	2759	7.64	15	4.16	132.8
Frank Dolce, Utah	Jr	11	314	177	56.37	10	3.18	2444	7.78	16	5.10	132.2
J. J. Joe, Baylor	So	11	206	109	52.91	8	3.88	1853	9.00	7	3.40	131.9
Bobby Fuller, South Caro.	Sr	11	340	202	59.41	8	2.35	2524	7.42	15	4.41	131.6
Matt Veatch, San Jose St.	Sr	9	206	110	53.40	8	3.88	1752	8.50	9	4.37	131.5

TOTAL OFFENSE

	RUSHING			PASSING		TOTAL OFFENSE				
	Car.	Gain	Loss	Net	Att.	Yards	Plays	Yards	Avg.	TDR*	Yds.PG
Ty Detmer, Brigham Young	75	272	302	-30	403	4031	478	4001	8.37	39	333.42
David Klingler, Houston	92	212	374	-162	497	3388	589	3226	5.48	30	322.60
Troy Kopp, Pacific (Cal.)	47	114	195	-81	449	3767	496	3686	7.43	38	307.17
Jeff Blake, East Caro.	77	286	177	109	368	3073	445	3182	7.15	31	289.27
Gino Torretta, Miami (Fla.)	49	174	114	60	371	3095	420	3155	7.51	22	286.82

	RUSHING				PASSING		TOTAL OFFENSE				
	Car.	Gain	Loss	Net	Att.	Yards	Plays	Yards	Avg.	TDR*	Yds.PG
Shane Matthews, Florida	50	149	139	10	361	3130	411	3140	7.64	29	285.45
Dave Brown, Duke	90	334	277	57	437	2794	527	2851	5.41	25	259.18
Andy Kelly, Tennessee	57	170	110	60	361	2759	418	2819	6.74	18	256.27
Jason Verduzco, Illinois	47	137	181	-44	382	2825	429	2781	6.48	15	252.82
Alex Van Pelt, Pittsburgh	26	55	74	-19	398	2796	424	2777	6.55	16	252.45
Tom Corontzos, Wyoming	86	174	313	-139	363	2868	449	2729	6.08	22	248.09
Matt Rodgers, Iowa	61	270	117	153	255	2054	316	2207	6.98	18	245.22
Trent Green, Indiana	102	400	199	201	318	2462	420	2663	6.34	23	242.09
Drew Bledsoe, Washington St.	104	258	352	-94	358	2741	462	2647	5.73	19	240.64
Casey Weldon, Florida St.	38	99	129	-30	313	2527	351	2497	7.11	22	227.00
Tommy Maddox, UCLA	72	176	209	-33	315	2505	387	2472	6.39	18	224.73
Frank Dolce, Utah	77	226	213	13	314	2444	391	2457	6.28	20	223.36
Mike Pawlawski, California	37	60	126	-66	316	2517	353	2451	6.94	22	222.82
Shawn Jones, Georgia Tech	114	538	177	361	339	2288	453	2649	5.85	18	220.75
David Lowery, San Diego St.	59	147	132	15	311	2575	370	2590	7.00	22	215.83
Bobby Fuller, South Caro.	49	57	218	-161	340	2524	389	2363	6.07	15	214.82
Paul Watson, Kansas St.	110	350	308	42	304	2312	414	2354	5.69	15	214.00
Matt Blundin, Virginia	30	69	59	10	224	1902	254	1912	7.53	20	212.44
Billy Joe Hobert, Washington	33	117	61	56	285	2271	318	2327	7.32	27	211.55
Erik White, Bowling Green	57	154	71	83	323	2204	380	2287	6.02	18	207.91
Robert Hall, Texas Tech	91	468	190	278	220	1788	311	2066	6.64	16	206.60
Will Furrer, Virginia Tech	23	85	56	29	257	1820	280	1849	6.60	15	205.44
Tony Sacca, Penn St.	84	242	303	-61	292	2488	376	2427	6.45	25	202.25
Rick Mirer, Notre Dame	75	377	71	306	234	2116	309	2422	7.84	27	201.83
Kevin Meger, Toledo	94	511	104	407	276	1787	370	2194	5.93	11	199.45

*Touchdowns responsible for are players' TDs scored and passed for.

RECEPTIONS PER GAME

	1991 Class	Games	Catches	Yards	TD	Ct.PG
Fred Gilbert, Houston	Jr	11	106	957	7	9.64
Aaron Turner, Pacific (Cal.)	Jr	11	92	1604	18	8.36
Marcus Grant, Houston	Jr	11	78	1262	10	7.09
Wilbert Ursin, Tulane	So	11	70	969	9	6.36
Carl Winston, New Mexico	So	12	76	1177	7	6.33
Sean LaChapelle, UCLA	Jr	11	68	987	11	6.18
Greg Primus, Colorado St.	Jr	11	67	1081	8	6.09
Chris Walsh, Stanford	Sr	11	66	934	6	6.00
Mark Szlachcic, Bowling Green	Jr	11	65	943	8	5.91
Kelly Blackwell, Texas Christian	Sr	11	64	762	6	5.82
Robert Rivers, Wyoming	Sr	10	57	742	7	5.70
Mario Bailey, Washington	Sr	11	62	1037	17	5.64
James Guarantano, Rutgers	Sr	11	62	740	2	5.64
Desmond Howard, Michigan	Jr	11	61	950	19	5.55
Rod Moore, Utah St.	Sr	11	60	944	10	5.45
Kameno Bell, Illinois	Sr	11	60	484	0	5.45
Jason Wolf, Southern Methodist	Jr	11	59	565	4	5.36
Patrick Rowe, San Diego St.	Sr	11	57	822	5	5.18
Daryl Hobbs, Pacific (Cal.)	Sr	12	62	772	12	5.17

RECEIVING YARDS PER GAME

	1991 Class	Games	Catches	Yards	TD	Yds.PG
Aaron Turner, Pacific (Cal.)	Jr	11	92	1604	18	145.82
Marcus Grant, Houston	Jr	11	78	1262	10	114.73
Greg Primus, Colorado St.	Jr	11	67	1081	8	98.27
Ryan Yarborough, Wyoming	So	11	53	1081	13	98.27
Carl Winston, New Mexico	So	12	76	1177	7	98.08
Mario Bailey, Washington	Sr	11	62	1037	17	94.27
Sean LaChapelle, UCLA	Jr	11	68	987	11	89.73
Wilbert Ursin, Tulane	So	11	70	969	9	88.09
Fred Gilbert, Houston	Jr	11	106	957	7	87.00
Desmond Howard, Michigan	Jr	11	61	950	19	86.36
Rod Moore, Utah St.	Sr	11	60	944	10	85.82
Mark Szlachcic, Bowling Green	Jr	11	65	943	8	85.73
Chris Walsh, Stanford	Sr	11	66	934	6	84.91
Eric Drage, Brigham Young	So	12	46	1018	10	84.83
Bryan Rowley, Utah	Jr	12	60	1011	11	84.25
Hunter Gallimore, East Caro.	Sr	11	49	881	8	80.09
Carl Pickens, Tennessee	Jr	11	49	877	5	79.73
Richard Hill, Ohio	Sr	11	49	863	3	78.45
Todd Kinchen, Louisiana St.	Sr	11	53	855	5	77.73
Melvin Bonner, Baylor	Jr	11	34	836	4	76.00
Mark Benson, Northwestern	Sr	11	45	831	7	75.55
Patrick Rowe, San Diego St.	Sr	11	57	822	5	74.73

INTERCEPTIONS

	1991 Class	Games	Int.	Yards	TD	Int.PG
Terrell Buckley, Florida St.	Jr	12	12	238	2	1.00
Carlton Gray, UCLA	Jr	11	10	119	1	.91
Willie Clay, Georgia Tech	Sr	12	9	66	1	.75
Ray Buchanan, Louisville	Jr	11	8	89	0	.73
Tracy Saul, Texas Tech	Jr	11	8	79	0	.73
Richard Palmer, Eastern Mich.	So	11	7	219	1	.64
Ron Carpenter, Miami (Ohio)	Jr	11	7	197	1	.64
Ron Edwards, Utah St.	Sr	11	7	146	2	.64
Walter Bailey, Washington	Jr	11	7	114	2	.64
Willie Lindsey, Northwestern	Jr	11	7	52	0	.64
Darrius Watson, Cal St. Fullerton	So	10	6	17	0	.60
Steve Israel, Pittsburgh	Sr	11	6	127	1	.55
George Teague, Alabama	Jr	11	6	96	0	.55
Scott Harmon, Oklahoma St.	So	11	6	90	0	.55
George Chatlos, Navy	Jr	11	6	90	1	.55
Jimmy Young, Purdue	So	11	6	29	1	.55
Michael McFarland, Baylor	Jr	11	6	15	0	.55

SCORING

	1991 Class	Games	TD	XP	FG	Points	Pts.PG
Marshall Faulk, San Diego St.	Fr	9	23	2	0	140	15.56
Desmond Howard, Michigan	Jr	11	23	0	0	138	12.55
Tommy Vardell, Stanford	Sr	11	20	0	0	120	10.91
Jerome Bettis, Notre Dame	So	12	20	0	0	120	10.00
Aaron Turner, Pacific (Cal.)	Jr	11	18	0	0	108	9.82
Mario Bailey, Washington	Sr	11	17	0	0	102	9.27
Russell White, California	Jr	11	16	2	0	98	8.91
Doug Brien, California	So	11	0	41	19	98	8.91
Derek Mahoney, Fresno St.	So	11	0	63	11	96	8.73
Jason Davis, Louisiana Tech	Jr	10	14	0	0	84	8.40
Calvin Jones, Nebraska	Fr	10	14	0	0	84	8.40
Ryan Benjamin, Pacific (Cal.)	Jr	12	16	2	0	98	8.17
Michael Carter, Hawaii	So	12	16	0	0	96	8.00
Carlos Huerta, Miami (Fla.)	Sr	11	0	37	17	88	8.00
Terry Venetoulias, Texas A&M	So	11	0	49	13	88	8.00
Craig Fayak, Penn St.	So	12	0	42	17	93	7.75
Lin Elliott, Texas Tech	Sr	11	0	34	17	85	7.73
Dan Eichloff, Kansas	So	11	0	31	18	85	7.73
John Biskup, Syracuse	Jr	11	0	34	17	85	7.73
Derek Brown, Nebraska	So	11	14	0	0	84	7.64
Chip Hilleary, Kansas	Jr	11	14	0	0	84	7.64
Mike Gaddis, Oklahoma	Sr	11	14	0	0	84	7.64
Trevor Cobb, Rice	Jr	11	14	0	0	84	7.64
Marcus Wilson, Vanderbilt	Jr	9	11	2	0	68	7.56
Anthony Brenner, East Caro.	So	11	0	40	14	82	7.45

ALL-PURPOSE RUNNERS

	1991 Class	Games	Rush	Rec.	PR	KOR	Yards	Total Yds.PG
Ryan Benjamin, Pacific (Cal.)	Jr	12	1581	612	4	798	2995	249.58
Vaughn Dunbar, Indiana	Sr	11	1699	252	0	262	2213	201.18
Marshall Faulk, San Diego St.	Fr	9	1429	201	0	33	1663	184.78
Trevor Cobb, Rice	Jr	11	1692	136	0	16	1844	167.64
Corey Harris, Vanderbilt	Sr	11	1103	283	0	445	1831	166.45
Tony Smith, Southern Miss.	Sr	9	998	97	115	271	1481	164.56
Desmond Howard, Michigan	Jr	11	165	950	261	373	1749	159.00
Chris Hughley, Tulsa	Jr	10	1326	74	0	190	1590	159.00
Russell White, California	Jr	11	1177	139	0	408	1724	156.73
Dion Johnson, East Caro.	Sr	11	255	743	162	513	1673	152.09
Charles Levy, Arizona	Fr	10	505	289	0	682	1476	147.60
Jason Davis, Louisiana Tech	Jr	10	1351	110	0	14	1475	147.50
Aaron Turner, Pacific (Cal.)	Jr	11	0	1604	0	0	1604	145.82
Harold Robinson, Akron	Sr	11	48	779	0	771	1598	145.27
Billy Smith, Central Mich.	Sr	11	1440	79	0	17	1536	139.64
Glyn Milburn, Stanford	Jr	11	598	454	186	276	1514	137.64
Errict Rhett, Florida	So	11	1109	361	0	0	1470	133.64
Tony Sands, Kansas	Sr	11	1442	7	0	0	1449	131.73
Derek Brown, Nebraska	So	11	1313	86	0	24	1423	129.36
Brad Smith, Kent	Sr	9	645	202	0	292	1139	126.56

PUNT RETURNS

(Min. 1.2 per game)	1991 Class	No.	Yds.	TD	Avg.
Bo Campbell, Virginia Tech...	Jr	15	273	0	18.20
Desmond Howard, Michigan .	Jr	15	261	1	17.40
David Palmer, Alabama	Fr	24	386	3	16.08
Kevin Williams, Miami (Fla.) .	So	36	560	3	15.56
James McMillion, Iowa St. ...	So	17	251	0	14.76
Kevin Smith, Texas A&M	Sr	19	275	2	14.47
Michael James, Arkansas ...	Sr	19	272	1	14.32
Darnell Stephens, Clemson...	Fr	25	352	1	14.08
Brad Clark, Brigham Young ..	Jr	20	269	1	13.45
Marshall Roberts, Rutgers ...	Sr	34	454	0	13.35
Eric Blount, North Caro.	Sr	31	394	1	12.71
Jeff Burris, Notre Dame	So	18	227	0	12.61
Thomas Bailey, Auburn	Fr	42	528	1	12.57
Tracy Saul, Texas Tech	Jr	16	200	0	12.50
George Coghill, Wake Forest .	Jr	25	312	1	12.48
V. Brownlee, Mississippi.....	Sr	28	341	1	12.18
Matt Gay, Kansas ...	Jr	15	182	0	12.13
Eric Guliford, Arizona St.	Jr	15	178	1	11.87
Darian Hagan, Colorado	Sr	25	287	0	11.48
Terry Vaughn, Arizona	So	24	269	1	11.21

KICKOFF RETURNS

(Min. 1.2 per game)	1991 Class	No.	Yds.	TD	Avg.
F. Montgomery, New Mex. St .	Jr	25	734	1	29.36
Ronald Rice, Eastern Mich. ...	Fr	11	319	0	29.00
Jeff Sydner, Hawaii	Jr	18	495	0	27.50
C. Hawkins, Michigan St.	Sr	20	548	0	27.40
Eric Blount, North Caro.......	Sr	25	679	1	27.16
Andre Hastings, Georgia	So	14	380	0	27.14
Floyd Foreman, Utah St.	Sr	27	730	0	27.04
Gary Melton, Rutgers	Sr	17	435	1	25.59
Charles Levy, Arizona	Fr	27	682	0	25.26
Donovan Moore, Oregon	Jr	13	327	0	25.15
Qadry Ismail, Syracuse	Jr	19	475	1	25.00

PUNTING

(Min. 3.6 per game)	1991 Class	No.	Avg.
Mark Bounds, Texas Tech	Sr	53	46.81
Jason Christ, Air Force	Sr	50	45.66
Pete Raether, Arkansas	So	65	43.63
Shayne Edge, Florida	Fr	46	43.28
Charles Langston, Houston	Sr	52	43.19
Eric Bruun, Purdue	Sr	59	43.19
Garret Henson, New Mexico St.	Sr	54	43.07
Rusty Clark, Utah St.	Sr	56	43.04
Ray Magana, Long Beach St.	Sr	57	42.91
David Lawrence, Vanderbilt........	Jr	54	42.74
Ed Bunn, UTEP	Jr	63	42.46
Dan Eichloff, Kansas	So	54	42.33
Pat O'Neill, Syracuse	So	45	42.20
John Jett, East Caro.	Sr	48	42.19
Jeff Buffaloe, Memphis St.	Jr	50	42.06
Mike Stigge, Nebraska............	Jr	39	42.03
Ed Garno, Virginia	Sr	47	42.02
Brian Parvin, Nevada-Las Vegas....	Jr	48	41.94
Scot Armstrong, Georgia	So	40	41.90
Bill Hawk, Kentucky..............	Sr	54	41.76

FIELD GOALS

	1991 Class	Games	FGA	FG	Pct.	FGPG
Doug Brien, California	So	11	28	19	.679	1.73
Dan Eichloff, Kansas	So	11	24	18	.750	1.64
Jason Elam, Hawaii	Jr	12	24	19	.792	1.58
Carlos Huerta, Miami (Fla.)	Sr	11	21	17	.810	1.55
John Biskup, Syracuse	Jr	11	22	17	.773	1.55
Nelson Welch, Clemson	Fr	11	26	17	.654	1.55
Lin Elliott, Texas Tech	Sr	11	26	17	.654	1.55
Eric Lange, Tulsa	Jr	11	18	16	.889	1.45
Joe Wood, Air Force	Sr	12	22	17	.773	1.42
Craig Fayak, Penn St.	So	12	26	17	.654	1.42
Chuck Selinger, Central Mich.	So	11	24	15	.625	1.36
Jim Von Wyl, Auburn	Sr	11	26	15	.577	1.36
Pedro Suarez, Louisiana St.	Jr	10	19	13	.684	1.30
Mike Green, Wake Forest	So	11	19	14	.737	1.27
Anthony Brenner, East Caro.	So	11	22	14	.636	1.27
Jeff Jacke, Missouri	Jr	9	14	11	.786	1.22
Daron Alcorn, Akron	Jr	11	17	13	.765	1.18
Terry Venetoulias, Texas A&M	So	11	18	13	.722	1.18
Louis Perez, UCLA	Jr	11	18	13	.722	1.18
Brian Lee, Mississippi	Jr	11	19	13	.684	1.18

1991 DIVISION I-A TEAM LEADERS

TOTAL OFFENSE

	Games	Plays	Yds.	Avg.	TD*	Yds.PG		Games	Plays	Yds.	Avg.	TD*	Yds.PG
Fresno St.	11	922	5961	6.5	62	541.91	Notre Dame	12	831	5466	6.6	55	455.50
Pacific (Cal.)	12	871	6135	7.0	61	511.25	Florida St.	12	897	5401	6.0	53	450.08
Nebraska	11	800	5571	7.0	60	506.45	Houston	11	877	4909	5.6	44	446.27
San Jose St. . .	11	813	5279	6.5	47	479.91	California	11	845	4907	5.8	47	446.09
Brigham Young . .	12	837	5754	6.9	54	479.50	Miami (Fla.)	11	768	4854	6.3	41	441.27
San Diego St.	12	955	5739	6.0	52	478.25	Michigan	11	769	4831	6.3	50	439.18
Washington	11	861	5191	6.0	60	471.91	East Caro.	11	794	4808	6.1	43	437.09
Tennessee	11	878	5145	5.9	36	467.73	Texas A&M	11	847	4804	5.7	47	436.73
Florida	11	787	5028	6.4	45	457.09	Wyoming	11	842	4737	5.6	38	430.64
UCLA	11	831	5019	6.0	39	456.27	Indiana	11	835	4709	5.6	35	428.09

*Touchdowns scored by rushing-passing only

TOTAL DEFENSE

	Games	Plays	Yds.	Avg.	TD*	Yds.PG		Games	Plays	Yds.	Avg.	TD*	Yds.PG
Texas A&M	11	683	2446	3.6	19	222.4	Ball St.	11	752	3118	4.1	14	283.5
Washington	11	730	2608	3.6	12	237.1	Oklahoma	11	731	3144	4.3	15	285.8
Texas	11	769	2848	3.7	15	258.9	Tennessee	11	679	3154	4.6	24	286.7
Clemson	11	718	2895	4.0	17	263.2	Miami (Fla.)	11	790	3176	4.0	9	288.7
Miami (Ohio)	11	747	2980	4.0	15	270.9	Tulsa	11	715	3231	4.5	26	293.7
Iowa	11	712	2987	4.2	20	271.5	Alabama	11	714	3303	4.6	13	300.3
Central Mich.	11	741	3001	4.0	16	272.8	North Caro. St. . . .	11	710	3346	4.7	22	304.2
Georgia Tech	12	831	3333	4.0	22	277.8	Indiana	11	672	3349	5.0	26	304.5
Penn St.	12	805	3366	4.2	22	280.5	Fresno St.	11	685	3379	4.9	25	307.2
Florida St.	12	776	3375	4.3	22	281.3	Florida	11	742	3383	4.6	16	307.5

*Touchdowns scored by rushing-passing only

RUSHING OFFENSE

	Games	Car.	Yds.	Avg.	TD	Yds.PG		Games	Car.	Yds.	Avg.	TD	Yds.PG
Nebraska	11	595	3885	6.5	45	353.2	Michigan	11	510	2709	5.3	26	246.3
Air Force	12	760	4057	5.3	34	338.1	Kansas	11	614	2698	4.4	30	245.3
Fresno St.	11	613	3303	5.4	42	300.3	Louisiana Tech . . .	11	521	2671	5.1	23	242.8
Army	11	701	3222	4.6	23	292.9	Baylor	11	595	2604	4.4	29	236.7
Hawaii	12	626	3416	5.5	32	284.7	Vanderbilt	11	611	2597	4.3	19	236.1
Notre Dame	12	584	3229	5.5	37	269.1	Mississippi St. . . .	11	529	2589	4.9	24	235.4
Texas A&M	11	633	2850	4.5	34	259.1	Washington	11	524	2551	4.9	34	231.9
Clemson	11	614	2813	4.6	28	255.7	Ohio St.	11	584	2522	4.3	27	229.3
Alabama	11	557	2772	5.0	24	252.0	Colorado	11	554	2499	4.5	23	227.2
Oklahoma	11	606	2752	4.5	33	250.2	Akron	11	515	2373	4.6	20	215.7

RUSHING DEFENSE

	Games	Car.	Yds.	Avg.	TD	Yds.PG		Games	Car.	Yds.	Avg.	TD	Yds.PG
Clemson	11	360	587	1.6	5	53.4	Syracuse	11	400	1186	3.0	9	107.8
Washington	11	390	738	1.9	6	67.1	Central Mich.	11	439	1202	2.7	8	109.3
Florida St.	12	398	994	2.5	9	82.8	Miami (Ohio)	11	447	1209	2.7	2	109.9
Texas A&M	11	393	946	2.4	13	86.0	Georgia Tech	12	462	1344	2.9	10	112.0
Penn St.	12	408	1120	2.7	9	93.3	Baylor	11	423	1236	2.9	13	112.4
Florida	11	399	1103	2.8	7	100.3	Ohio St.	11	390	1250	3.2	8	113.6
Louisiana Tech . . .	11	386	1105	2.9	8	100.5	Texas	11	465	1335	2.9	8	121.4
UCLA	11	403	1110	2.8	13	100.9	North Caro. St. . . .	11	381	1349	3.5	12	122.6
Oklahoma	11	403	1140	2.8	5	103.6	North Caro.	11	437	1352	3.1	7	122.9
Michigan	11	397	1142	2.9	7	103.8	Iowa	11	450	1384	3.1	9	125.8

SCORING OFFENSE

	Games	Pts.	Avg.		Games	Pts.	Avg.
Fresno St.	11	486	44.2	Brigham Young	12	420	35.0
Washington	11	461	41.9	East Caro.	11	372	33.8
Nebraska	11	454	41.3	San Jose St.	11	372	33.8
California	11	406	36.9	San Diego St.	12	403	33.6
Michigan	11	406	36.9	Miami (Fla.)	11	364	33.1
Florida St.	12	439	36.6	Florida	11	361	32.8
Texas A&M	11	402	36.5	Houston	11	353	32.1
Pacific (Cal.)	12	435	36.3	Stanford	11	351	31.9
Penn St.	12	432	36.0	Oklahoma	11	335	30.5
Notre Dame	12	426	35.5	Tennessee	11	335	30.5

SCORING DEFENSE

	Games	Pts.	Avg.		Games	Pts.	Avg.
Miami (Fla.)	11	100	9.1	Colorado	11	150	13.6
Washington	11	101	9.2	Ball St.	11	150	13.6
Alabama	11	118	10.7	Florida	11	152	13.8
Virginia	11	119	10.8	Penn St.	12	167	13.9
Miami (Ohio)	11	140	12.7	Mississippi St.	11	156	14.2
Oklahoma	11	143	13.0	Central Mich.	11	157	14.3
Texas A&M	11	144	13.1	Ohio St.	11	163	14.8
Texas	11	145	13.2	Iowa	11	166	15.1
Bowling Green	11	147	13.4	Michigan	11	169	15.4
Clemson	11	148	13.5				

PASSING OFFENSE

	Games	Att.	Cmp.	Int.	Pct.	Yards	Yds./Att.	TD	Yds.PG
Houston	11	591	330	24	55.8	4101	6.9	33	372.8
Brigham Young	12	420	257	14	61.2	4125	9.8	35	343.8
Pacific (Cal.)	12	500	300	18	60.0	4114	8.2	42	342.8
Florida	11	390	235	19	60.3	3393	8.7	32	308.5
East Caro.	11	414	229	10	55.3	3379	8.2	30	307.2
San Jose St.	11	374	211	14	56.4	3338	8.9	21	303.5
New Mexico	12	518	246	24	47.5	3584	6.9	20	298.7
Wyoming	11	400	227	10	56.7	3264	8.2	24	296.7
Miami (Fla.)	11	396	223	11	56.3	3244	8.2	20	294.9
Washington St.	11	395	218	16	55.2	3028	7.7	19	275.3
San Diego St.	12	434	228	15	52.5	3263	7.5	22	271.9
Duke	11	450	236	16	52.4	2887	6.4	20	262.5
Illinois	11	392	240	11	61.2	2877	7.3	16	261.5
Florida St.	12	390	234	11	60.0	3114	8.0	28	259.5
Texas Christian	11	445	239	19	53.7	2840	6.4	17	258.2
Tennessee	11	366	231	15	63.1	2813	7.7	16	255.7
Pittsburgh	11	401	229	14	57.1	2809	7.0	15	255.4
UCLA	11	332	203	15	61.1	2710	8.2	17	246.4
South Caro.	11	367	217	8	59.1	2703	7.4	15	245.7
Missouri	11	406	218	15	53.7	2661	6.6	18	241.9

PASS EFFICIENCY DEFENSE

	Games	Att.	Cmp.	Cmp. Pct.	Int.	Int. Pct.	Yards	Yds./Att.	TD	TD Pct.	Rating Points
Texas	11	304	115	37.83	15	4.93	1513	4.98	7	2.30	77.37
Texas A&M	11	290	129	44.48	14	4.83	1500	5.17	6	2.07	85.10
Washington	11	340	156	45.88	21	6.18	1870	5.50	6	1.76	85.55
Miami (Fla.)	11	346	175	50.58	19	5.49	1724	4.98	7	2.02	88.13
Penn St.	12	397	172	43.32	26	6.55	2246	5.66	13	3.27	88.56
Virginia	11	267	137	51.31	12	4.49	1512	5.66	1	.37	91.13
Arizona St.	11	290	143	49.31	23	7.93	1676	5.78	9	3.10	92.24
Tulsa	11	275	129	46.91	18	6.55	1586	5.77	10	3.64	94.26
Georgia Tech	12	369	178	48.24	18	4.88	1989	5.39	12	3.25	94.49
Oklahoma	11	328	161	49.09	25	7.62	2004	6.11	10	3.05	95.22
Fresno St.	11	269	109	40.52	13	4.83	1697	6.31	10	3.72	96.11
Alabama	11	289	136	47.06	20	6.92	1851	6.40	9	3.11	97.30
Miami (Ohio)	11	300	143	47.67	21	7.00	1771	5.90	13	4.33	97.55
Wisconsin	11	258	132	51.16	15	5.81	1470	5.70	10	3.88	100.19
Eastern Mich.	11	290	147	50.69	18	6.21	1785	6.16	9	3.10	100.22
Ball St.	11	252	122	48.41	12	4.76	1607	6.38	6	2.38	100.31
Florida St.	12	378	192	50.79	25	6.61	2381	6.30	13	3.44	101.83
Central Mich.	11	302	160	52.98	14	4.64	1799	5.96	8	2.65	102.49
Colorado	11	286	141	49.30	13	4.55	1886	6.59	6	2.10	102.53
North Caro. St.	11	329	175	53.19	18	5.47	1997	6.07	10	3.04	103.27

LONGEST PLAYS OF THE 1991 SEASON

DIVISION I-A

RUSHING

Player, Team (Opponent)	Yards
Chris Anderson, Alabama (Temple)	96
Deon Strother, Southern Cal (California)	92
Brandon Bennett, South Caro. (East Tenn. St.)	89
Tico Duckett, Michigan St. (Minnesota)	88
Danny Woodson, Alabama (Temple)	85
Chris Gray, Air Force (New Mexico)	85
Michael Carter, Hawaii (Air Force)	85
Jay Barry, Washington (Nebraska)	81
Edrian Oliver, Army (Harvard)	81
Tony Smith, Southern Miss. (Tulane)	81

PASSING

Passer-Receiver, Team (Opponent)	Yards
Gino Torretta-Horace Copeland, Miami, Fla. (Arkansas)	99
Matt Veatch-Byron Jackson, San Jose St. (Minnesota)	95
Matt Blundin-Tyrone Davis, Virginia (North Caro. St.)	*91
Tony Lowery-Lee Deramus, Wisconsin (Eastern Mich.)	89
Andy Kelly-Carl Pickens, Tennessee (Auburn)	87
Jeff Brothers-Clarence Sevillian, Vanderbilt (Duke)	86
George Malauulu-David Lockhart, Arizona (Stanford)	85
Rick Mirer-Tony Smith, Notre Dame (Air Force)	83
Shawn Jones-Keenan Walker, Georgia Tech (Maryland)	82

*Did not score.

INTERCEPTIONS

Player, Team (Opponent)	Yards
Sebastian Savage, North Caro. St. (North Caro.)	99
Mark McMillian, Alabama (Tenn.-Chatt.)	98
Rodney Mazion, Nevada-Las Vegas (New Mexico)	96
Kirk Alexander, Virginia Tech (Cincinnati)	95
Chris Hobbs, Memphis St. (Tennessee)	95
Greg Grandison, East Caro. (Virginia Tech)	95

PUNT RETURNS

Player, Team (Opponent)	Yards
Craig Thompson, Eastern Mich. (Western Mich.)	96
Desmond Howard, Michigan (Ohio St.)	93
Kevin Williams, Miami, Fla. (Penn St.)	91
Troy Vincent, Wisconsin (Western Ill.)	90
David Palmer, Alabama (Louisiana St.)	90
Jerrod Washington, Virginia (Virginia Tech)	90

KICKOFF RETURNS

Player, Team (Opponent)	Yards
Anthony Prior, Washington St. (Southern Cal)	100
Fred Montgomery, New Mexico St. (Long Beach St.)	100
Darrick Branch, Hawaii (New Mexico)	98
Harold Robinson, Akron (Arkansas St.)	97
Gary Melton, Rutgers (Northwestern)	96
Qadry Ismail, Syracuse (Florida St.)	95

FIELD GOALS

Player, Team (Opponent)	Yards
Jason Hanson, Washington St. (Nevada-Las Vegas)	62
Jeff Ireland, Baylor (Rice)	58
Joe Wood, Air Force (Notre Dame)	58
Jason Elam, Hawaii (Wyoming)	55
Jason Hanson, Washington St. (Fresno St.)	54
Chris Bonoil, Louisiana Tech (Eastern Mich.)	54
Chris Yergenson, Utah (Colorado St.)	54

PUNTS

Player, Team (Opponent)	Yards
Ed Bunn, UTEP (New Mexico)	83
Pete Raether, Arkansas (Southwestern La.)	83
Mark Bounds, Texas Tech (Texas)	78
Dennis Nicholl, Central Mich. (Ball St.)	75
Bill Hawk, Kentucky (Tennessee)	75
Rusty Carlsen, Utah St. (Pacific, Cal.)	75

RUSHING

	1991 Class	Games	Car.	Yards	Avg.	TD	Yds.PG
Al Rosier, Dartmouth	Sr	10	258	1432	5.6	12	143.20
Jerome Bledsoe, Massachusetts	Sr	11	264	1545	5.9	11	140.45
Derrick Franklin, Indiana St.	Sr	11	318	1505	4.7	12	136.82
Jerome Fuller, Holy Cross	Sr	11	266	1465	5.5	12	133.18
Jamie Jones, Eastern Ill.	Sr	11	233	1403	6.0	4	127.55
Markus Thomas, Eastern Ky.	Jr	11	178	1353	7.6	10	123.00
Willie English, Central Fla.	Jr	11	236	1338	5.7	13	121.64
Toby Davis, Illinois St.	Jr	10	253	1169	4.6	7	116.90
Chris Kouri, Yale	Sr	10	209	1101	5.3	8	110.10
Michael Murray, Delaware St.	Sr	11	226	1200	5.3	9	109.09
Kenny Sims, James Madison	Jr	11	191	1199	6.3	9	109.00
Geoff Mitchell, Weber St.	Sr	11	239	1170	4.9	24	106.36
Jack Douglas, Citadel	Sr	11	266	1152	4.3	13	104.73
Carl Tremble, Furman	Jr	9	159	927	5.8	11	103.00
Barry Bourassa, New Hampshire	Jr	11	230	1130	4.9	15	102.73
Nick Crawford, Yale	Sr	10	210	1024	4.9	8	102.40
Joe Campbell, Middle Tenn. St.	Sr	11	198	1121	5.7	14	101.91
Eric Gant, Grambling	Fr	11	194	1111	5.7	5	101.00
Tamron Smith, Youngstown St.	So	10	181	1009	5.6	8	100.90
John McNiff, Cornell	Sr	8	204	806	4.0	8	100.75

PASSING EFFICIENCY

(Min. 15 att. per game)	1991 Class	Gms.	Att.	Cmp.	Cmp. Pct.	Int.	Int. Pct.	Yards	Yds./ Att.	TD	TD Pct.	Rating Points
Michael Payton, Marshall	Jr	9	216	143	66.20	5	2.31	2333	10.80	19	8.80	181.3
Eriq Williams, James Madison	Jr	11	192	107	55.73	7	3.65	1914	9.97	19	9.90	164.8
Hugh Swilling, Furman	So	9	153	85	55.56	5	3.27	1422	9.29	14	9.15	157.3
Chris Vargas, Nevada	So	9	153	91	59.48	4	2.61	1386	9.06	10	6.54	151.9
Jeff Thorne, Eastern Ill.	So	11	246	151	61.38	6	2.44	1920	7.80	21	8.54	150.2
Connell Maynor, North Caro. A&T	Sr	10	192	110	57.29	5	2.60	1527	7.95	18	9.38	149.8
Jay Johnson, Northern Iowa	Jr	11	222	125	56.31	6	2.70	1950	8.78	16	7.21	148.5
Doug Nussmeier, Idaho	So	11	384	230	59.90	11	2.86	3300	8.59	25	6.51	147.8
Jamie Martin, Weber St.	Jr	11	500	310	62.00	17	3.40	4125	8.25	35	7.00	147.6
Chris Hakel, William & Mary	Sr	11	357	232	64.99	9	2.52	2974	8.33	18	5.04	146.6
Ricky Jones, Alabama St.	Sr	10	240	126	52.50	7	2.92	2041	8.50	19	7.92	144.2
Steve McNair, Alcorn St.	Fr	10	337	189	56.08	15	4.45	2895	8.59	24	7.12	142.8
Kenyon Earl, Tenn.-Chatt.	Fr	11	181	93	51.38	8	4.42	1643	9.08	13	7.18	142.5
Chad Roghair, Princeton	Sr	10	239	147	61.51	8	3.35	1886	7.89	14	5.86	140.4
Glenn Kempa, Lehigh	Sr	11	474	286	60.34	15	3.16	3565	7.52	31	6.54	138.8
Tom Ciaccio, Holy Cross	Sr	11	385	232	60.26	18	4.68	3010	7.82	25	6.49	138.0
Kelly Holcomb, Middle Tenn. St.	Fr	11	209	130	62.20	4	1.91	1763	8.44	5	2.39	137.1
James Wade, Tennessee St.	Jr	10	243	132	54.32	11	4.53	2020	8.31	15	6.17	135.5
Tom Colombo, Villanova	Jr	11	342	214	62.57	16	4.68	2540	7.43	20	5.85	134.9
Antoine Ezell, Florida A&M	Sr	10	258	139	53.88	11	4.26	2156	8.36	14	5.43	133.5

TOTAL OFFENSE

	RUSHING				PASSING			TOTAL OFFENSE			
	Car.	Gain	Loss	Net	Att.	Yards	Plays	Yards	Avg.	TDR*	Yds.PG
Jamie Martin, Weber St.	91	440	228	212	500	4125	591	4337	7.34	37	394.27
Glenn Kempa, Lehigh	39	80	134	-54	474	3565	513	3511	6.84	31	319.18
Doug Nussmeier, Idaho	88	318	158	160	384	3300	472	3460	7.33	26	314.55
Steve McNair, Alcorn St.	57	329	87	242	337	2895	394	3137	7.96	30	313.70
Tom Ciaccio, Holy Cross	62	254	132	122	385	3010	447	3132	7.01	27	284.73
Brad Lebo, Montana	104	146	413	-267	457	3380	561	3113	5.55	21	283.00
Cornelius Benton, Connecticut	66	228	171	57	376	2701	442	2758	6.24	19	275.80
Robbie Justino, Liberty	59	91	234	-143	427	3176	486	3033	6.24	19	275.73
Chris Hakel, William & Mary	53	112	136	-24	357	2974	410	2950	7.20	24	268.18
Jermaine Hall, Bethune-Cookman	67	223	244	-21	427	2666	494	2645	5.35	22	264.50
Michael Payton, Marshall	50	180	134	46	216	2333	266	2379	8.94	20	264.33
John Bonds, Northern Ariz.	75	227	263	-36	352	2679	427	2643	6.19	13	264.30
Matt Griffin, New Hampshire	70	198	98	100	311	2469	381	2569	6.74	25	256.90
Fred Gatlin, Nevada	71	384	106	278	279	2192	350	2470	7.06	23	247.00
Ricky Jones, Alabama St.	76	546	129	417	240	2041	316	2458	7.78	24	245.80
Jim Russell, Colgate	147	754	289	465	296	2166	443	2631	5.94	15	239.18
Roy Johnson, Arkansas St.	170	984	202	782	263	1747	433	2529	5.84	19	229.91
Tom Colombo, Villanova	40	91	116	-25	342	2540	382	2515	6.58	20	228.64
Mark Tenneson, Eastern Wash.	66	197	142	55	338	2399	404	2454	6.07	22	223.09
Trevor Cavanaugh, Idaho St.	111	438	189	249	311	2169	422	2418	5.73	18	219.82

*Touchdowns responsible for are players' TDs scored and passed for.

RECEPTIONS PER GAME

	1991 Class	Games	Catches	Yards	TD	CLPG
Alfred Pupunu, Weber St.	Sr	11	93	1204	12	8.45
Mark Didio, Connecticut	Sr	11	88	1354	8	8.00
Kasey Dunn, Idaho	Sr	11	85	1263	6	7.73
Pat Nelson, Liberty	Sr	11	81	1075	4	7.36
Horace Hamm, Lehigh	Sr	11	75	1044	13	6.82
Alex Davis, Connecticut	Jr	11	74	909	7	6.73
Jeff Parker, Bethune-Cookman	Sr	10	67	828	6	6.70
Dave Hall, Weber St.	Sr	11	73	1043	10	6.64
Bryan Reeves, Nevada	So	10	62	931	5	6.20
Cedric Tillman, Alcorn St.	Sr	10	58	790	11	5.80
Torrance Small, Alcorn St.	Sr	10	55	1068	7	5.50
Mike Bobo, Dartmouth	Sr	10	55	725	10	5.50
Darrell Philon, Southeast Mo. St.	Sr	11	60	815	4	5.45
Tom Garlick, Fordham	Jr	9	47	692	8	5.22
Alan Williams, William & Mary	Sr	11	57	598	5	5.18
Hendricks Johnson, Northern Ariz.	Sr	10	51	859	6	5.10
Nate Singleton, Grambling	Sr	11	55	1047	11	5.00
Ches Salyer, Southeast Mo. St.	Sr	11	54	690	5	4.91
Marvin Turk, Montana	Sr	11	53	1047	13	4.82
Darren Rizzi, Rhode Island	Jr	11	53	782	5	4.82

RECEIVING YARDS PER GAME

	1991 Class	Games	Catches	Yards	TD	Yds.PG
Mark Didio, Connecticut	Sr	11	88	1354	8	123.09
Kasey Dunn, Idaho	Sr	11	85	1263	6	114.82
Alfred Pupunu, Weber St.	Sr	11	93	1204	12	109.45
Torrance Small, Alcorn St.	Sr	10	55	1068	7	106.80
Pat Nelson, Liberty	Sr	11	81	1075	4	97.73
Nate Singleton, Grambling	Sr	11	55	1047	11	95.18
Marvin Turk, Montana	Sr	11	53	1047	13	95.18
Horace Hamm, Lehigh	Sr	11	75	1044	13	94.91
Dave Hall, Weber St.	Sr	11	73	1043	10	94.82
Bryan Reeves, Nevada	So	10	62	931	5	93.10
Michael Lerch, Princeton	Jr	10	47	886	6	88.60
Brian Dowler, Marshall	Sr	11	48	946	10	86.00
Hendricks Johnson, Northern Ariz.	Sr	10	51	859	6	85.90
Mark Roman, Holy Cross	Sr	11	50	937	11	85.18
Jeff Parker, Bethune-Cookman	Sr	10	67	828	6	82.80
Alex Davis, Connecticut	Jr	11	74	909	7	82.64
Chris Singleton, Nevada	So	11	43	893	8	81.18
Jimmy Smith, Jackson St.	Sr	10	43	804	4	80.40
Cedric Tillman, Alcorn St.	Sr	10	58	790	11	79.00
Carl Gibbons, Bethune-Cookman	Sr	10	48	790	9	79.00

INTERCEPTIONS

	1991 Class	Games	Int.	Yards	TD	Int.PG
Warren McIntire, Delaware	Jr	11	9	208	2	.82
Isaac Morehouse, Jackson St.	Sr	10	8	84	1	.80
William Carroll, Florida A&M	Jr	11	8	150	0	.73
Morgan Ryan, Montana St.	So	11	8	108	0	.73
Frank Robinson, Boise St.	Sr	11	8	101	2	.73
Darryl Pounds, Nicholls St.	Fr	11	8	40	0	.73
Alonza Barnett, North Caro. A&T	Jr	10	7	45	1	.70
Ricky Hill, South Caro. St.	Sr	11	7	129	1	.64
Marcus Durgin, Samford	So	11	7	97	1	.64
Adrion Smith, Southwest Mo. St	So	11	7	75	1	.64

SCORING

	1991 Class	Games	TD	XP	FG	Points	Pts.PG
Geoff Mitchell, Weber St.	Sr	11	28	2	0	170	15.45
Barry Bourassa, New Hampshire	Jr	11	21	0	0	126	11.45
Pat Kennedy, Villanova	Sr	9	15	0	0	90	10.00
Mark Lookenbill, Lehigh	Jr	11	18	0	0	108	9.82
Nate Singleton, Grambling	Sr	11	17	0	0	102	9.27
Brian Mitchell, Northern Iowa	Sr	11	0	40	19	97	8.82
Mike Giardi, Harvard	So	9	13	0	0	78	8.67
Robert Green, William & Mary	Sr	9	13	0	0	78	8.67
Rick Schwendinger, Nevada	Sr	11	0	57	12	93	8.45
Al Rosier, Dartmouth	Sr	10	13	2	0	80	8.00
Keith Elias, Princeton	So	10	13	2	0	80	8.00
Andrew Burr, Furman	Sr	11	0	45	14	87	7.91
Jerome Fuller, Holy Cross	Sr	11	14	0	0	84	7.64
Tim Lester, Eastern Ky.	Sr	11	14	0	0	84	7.64
Joe Campbell, Middle Tenn. St.	Sr	11	14	0	0	84	7.64

	1991 Class	Games	TD	XP	FG	Points	Pts.PG
Walter Dunson, Middle Tenn. St.	Jr	11	14	0	0	84	7.64
Horace Hamm, Lehigh	Sr	11	14	0	0	84	7.64
Mike Black, Boise St.	Sr	11	0	36	15	81	7.36
Carl Tremble, Furman	Jr	9	11	0	0	66	7.33
Dewey Klein, Marshall	Sr	11	0	50	10	80	7.27

ALL-PURPOSE RUNNERS

	1991 Class	Games	Rush	Rec.	PR	KOR	Total Yards	Yds.PG
Barry Bourassa, New Hampshire	Jr	11	1130	426	0	596	2152	195.64
Al Rosier, Dartmouth	Sr	10	1432	113	0	290	1835	183.50
Jerome Bledsoe, Massachusetts	Sr	11	1545	178	0	293	2016	183.27
Jamie Jones, Eastern Ill.	Sr	11	1403	299	0	305	2007	182.45
Brett Brown, Brown	Jr	10	821	191	0	657	1669	166.90
Jerome Fuller, Holy Cross	Sr	11	1465	249	86	0	1800	163.64
Bryan Reeves, Nevada	So	10	1	931	329	268	1529	152.90
Michael Lerch, Princeton	Jr	10	63	886	6	546	1501	150.10
Toby Davis, Illinois St.	Jr	10	1169	309	0	0	1478	147.80
Marcus Dowdell, Tennessee St.	Sr	9	-1	355	0	915	1269	141.00
Geoff Mitchell, Weber St.	Sr	11	1170	160	0	196	1526	138.73
Brian James, Samford	Sr	11	48	861	0	611	1520	138.18
Derrick Franklin, Indiana St.	Sr	11	1505	14	0	0	1519	138.09
Willie English, Central Fla.	Jr	11	1338	164	0	0	1502	136.55
Laurence Arico, Lehigh	Sr	9	849	292	0	47	1188	132.00
Markus Thomas, Eastern Ky.	Jr	11	1353	20	0	57	1430	130.00
Horace Hamm, Lehigh	Sr	11	6	1044	0	371	1421	129.18
Troy Brown, Marshall	Jr	11	-14	607	354	468	1415	128.64
Harold Wright, Eastern Wash.	So	11	910	309	0	189	1408	128.00
Torrance Small, Alcorn St.	Sr	10	-9	1068	221	0	1280	128.00

PUNT RETURNS

(Min. 1.2 per game)	1991 Class	No.	Yds.	TD	Avg.	(Min. 1.2 per game)	1991 Class	No.	Yds.	TD	Avg.
Ashley Ambrose, Miss. Val.	Sr	28	514	3	18.36	Marcus Durgin, Samford	So	15	169	0	11.27
Troy Brown, Marshall	Jr	24	354	1	14.75	A. Archer, James Madison	Jr	31	345	1	11.13
T. Armstead, Grambling	Sr	23	317	1	13.78	Tyrone Davis, Florida A&M	Sr	22	243	0	11.05
D. Caparotti, Massachusetts	Jr	26	355	1	13.65	Bryan Reeves, Nevada	So	30	329	0	10.97
Mike Dickinson, Central Fla.	Jr	31	387	3	12.48	Kerry Lawyer, Boise St.	Fr	24	261	0	10.88
J. Seymore, Arkansas St.	Fr	16	188	1	11.75	Horace Brooks, Alabama St.	Jr	16	174	0	10.88
Kerry Hayes, Western Caro.	Fr	19	222	1	11.68	L. G. Parrish, Liberty	Sr	15	161	0	10.73
J. Parker, Bethune-Cookman	Sr	15	173	0	11.53	Kenny Shedd, Northern Iowa	Jr	29	300	2	10.34
Bill Cobb, Pennsylvania	So	15	170	1	11.33	G. Hoffmeister, Dartmouth	Jr	25	257	1	10.28
Sean Hill, Montana St.	So	22	248	1	11.27	Jerry Avery, Northern Ariz.	So	24	245	0	10.21

KICKOFF RETURNS

(Min. 1.2 per game)	1991 Class	No.	Yds.	TD	Avg.	(Min. 1.2 per game)	1991 Class	No.	Yds.	TD	Avg.
Paul Ashby, Alabama St.	Jr	17	520	2	30.59	Rob Tesch, Montana St.	Jr	16	443	0	27.69
David Lucas, Florida A&M	Sr	21	596	3	28.38	Torrance Forney, Citadel	Jr	16	443	0	27.69
B. Bourassa, New Hampshire	Jr	21	596	1	28.38	C. Johnson, Southern-B.R.	Jr	24	655	0	27.29
Jerry Ellison, Tenn.-Chatt.	So	13	368	1	28.31	Leon Brown, Eastern Ky.	Jr	19	507	0	26.68
Kerry Lawyer, Boise St.	Fr	16	448	0	28.00	Bryan Herrien, Alcorn St.	Sr	21	552	1	26.29
						Chris Pierce, Rhode Island	Jr	18	473	2	26.28

PUNTING

(Min. 3.6 per game)	1991 Class	No.	Avg.	(Min. 3.6 per game)	1991 Class	No.	Avg.
Harold Alexander, Appalachian St.	Jr	64	47.02	Don Norton, Ga. Southern	Sr	73	40.82
Pumpy Tudors, Tenn.-Chatt.	Sr	53	45.55	Jeff Meader, Holy Cross	So	46	40.59
Tom Sugg, Idaho	Jr	53	44.74	Rob Sims, Pennsylvania	Jr	53	40.47
Terry Belden, Northern Ariz.	So	43	44.37	Darrell Schneider, Eastern Wash.	Jr	50	40.16
Leo Araguz, Stephen F. Austin	Jr	72	42.61	Chad McCarty, Northeast La.	Jr	56	40.00
Gene Vadas, Delaware	Sr	40	42.50	Eric Willingham, Citadel	Sr	41	39.85
Brian Dowler, Marshall	Sr	50	41.76	Gerald Dasbach, Sam Houston St.	Sr	67	39.79
Pat Neck, McNeese St.	So	83	41.60	Tim Mosley, Northern Iowa	So	52	39.23
Colin Godfrey, Tennessee St.	Jr	63	41.44	Rick Schwendinger, Nevada	Sr	54	39.17
Jeff Bolser, Towson St.	Sr	67	41.30	Chuck Poplos, Delaware St.	Fr	56	38.93

FIELD GOALS

	1991 Class	Games	FGA	FG	Pct.	FGPG
Brian Mitchell, Northern Iowa	Sr	11	24	19	.792	1.73
Eric Roberts, McNeese St.	Sr	11	22	16	.727	1.45
Mike Black, Boise St.	Sr	11	19	15	.789	1.36
Alex Lacson, Eastern Wash.	Fr	11	22	15	.682	1.36
David Cool, Ga. Southern	Sr	11	17	14	.824	1.27
Andrew Burr, Furman	Sr	11	18	14	.778	1.27
Mark Klein, Sam Houston St.	Sr	11	24	14	.583	1.27
Daniel Gipson, Tennessee Tech	So	11	18	13	.722	1.18
Michael O'Neal, Samford	Jr	11	19	13	.684	1.18
Franco Grilla, Central Fla.	Jr	11	21	13	.619	1.18
Cameron Bair, Illinois St.	Jr	11	22	13	.591	1.18
Daniel Whitehead, Liberty	Fr	11	17	12	.706	1.09
Gilad Landau, Grambling	Fr	11	17	12	.706	1.09
Skip Shelton, Nicholls St.	Jr	11	19	12	.632	1.09
Rick Schwendinger, Nevada	Sr	11	20	12	.600	1.09
Jason McLaughlin, Lafayette	Fr	11	21	12	.571	1.09
Robert Avriett, Citadel	So	9	13	9	.692	1.00
Tom Boccafola, Columbia	Sr	10	15	10	.667	1.00
Jeff Wilkins, Youngstown St.	So	11	17	11	.647	1.00
Jay Millson, Appalachian St.	Jr	11	24	11	.458	1.00

1991 DIVISION I-AA TEAM LEADERS

TOTAL OFFENSE

	Games	Plays	Yds.	Avg.	TD*	Yds.PG		Games	Plays	Yds.	Avg.	TD*	Yds.PG
Weber St.	11	986	6395	6.5	69	581.36	New Hampshire	11	786	4695	6.0	48	426.82
Nevada	11	900	5606	6.2	60	509.64	Grambling	11	786	4684	6.0	39	425.82
Idaho	11	833	5306	6.4	46	482.36	Connecticut	11	836	4659	5.6	30	423.55
Holy Cross	11	818	5138	6.3	48	467.09	North Caro. A&T	11	787	4625	5.9	51	420.45
Lehigh	11	850	5133	6.0	46	466.64	James Madison	11	739	4552	6.2	46	413.82
Alcorn St.	10	695	4666	6.7	51	466.60	Northern Ariz.	11	808	4539	5.6	34	412.64
William & Mary	11	805	5082	6.3	47	462.00	Middle Tenn. St.	11	705	4517	6.4	38	410.64
Villanova	11	878	5034	5.7	53	457.64	Furman	11	759	4399	5.8	42	399.91
Alabama St.	11	765	4715	6.2	58	428.64	Delaware	11	760	4391	5.8	43	399.18
Marshall	11	709	4705	6.6	50	427.73	Central Fla.	11	780	4345	5.6	31	395.00

*Touchdowns scored by rushing-passing only

TOTAL DEFENSE

	Games	Plays	Yds.	Avg.	TD*	Yds.PG		Games	Plays	Yds.	Avg.	TD*	Yds.PG
South Caro. St.	11	682	2298	3.4	18	208.9	N'western (La.)	11	736	3145	4.3	19	285.9
Villanova	11	689	2653	3.9	17	241.2	Southwest Tex. St.	11	700	3179	4.5	22	289.0
McNeese St.	11	751	2666	3.5	12	242.4	Princeton	10	712	2895	4.1	22	289.5
Northern Iowa	11	739	2680	3.6	20	243.6	Alcorn St.	10	709	2976	4.2	25	297.6
Sam Houston St.	11	755	2878	3.8	14	261.6	Alabama St.	11	718	3274	4.6	23	297.6
Western Ill.	11	693	2930	4.2	18	266.4	Illinois St.	11	754	3284	4.4	22	298.5
Mississippi Val.	11	674	3017	4.5	24	274.3	Nicholls St.	11	714	3305	4.6	23	300.5
Eastern Ky.	11	709	3027	4.3	19	275.2	Northeast La.	11	768	3344	4.4	19	304.0
North Caro. A&T	11	698	3032	4.3	20	275.6	Youngstown St.	11	742	3362	4.5	23	305.6
Ga. Southern	11	732	3112	4.3	17	282.9	Southwest Mo. St.	11	752	3424	4.6	25	311.3

*Touchdowns scored by rushing-passing only

RUSHING OFFENSE

	Games	Car.	Yds.	Avg.	TD	Yds.PG		Games	Car.	Yds.	Avg.	TD	Yds.PG
Va. Military	11	703	3486	5.0	29	316.9	Dartmouth	10	545	2457	4.5	21	245.7
Delaware St.	11	628	3277	5.2	28	297.9	Massachusetts	11	580	2660	4.6	19	241.8
Yale	10	572	2950	5.2	24	295.0	Middle Tenn. St.	11	477	2641	5.5	32	240.1
Southwest Tex. St.	11	653	3166	4.8	33	287.8	Youngstown St.	11	593	2615	4.4	32	237.7
Citadel	11	678	3081	4.5	28	280.1	Southwest Mo. St.	11	556	2606	4.7	33	236.9
Delaware	11	575	3013	5.2	31	273.9	James Madison	11	525	2573	4.9	26	233.9
North Caro. A&T	11	566	3012	5.3	31	273.8	Harvard	10	533	2258	4.2	20	225.8
Eastern Ky.	11	572	2902	5.1	38	263.8	Austin Peay	11	593	2466	4.2	17	224.2
Western Ky.	11	585	2860	4.9	25	260.0	Alabama St.	11	496	2438	4.9	33	221.6
Furman	11	569	2728	4.8	28	248.0	Indiana St.	11	547	2378	4.3	20	216.2

RUSHING DEFENSE

	Games	Car.	Yds.	Avg.	TD	Yds.PG		Games	Car.	Yds.	Avg.	TD	Yds.PG
Boise St.	11	356	928	2.6	10	84.4	North Caro. A&T	11	434	1270	2.9	14	115.5
South Caro. St.	11	404	938	2.3	10	85.3	Nevada	11	408	1293	3.2	12	117.5
Delaware St.	11	423	1079	2.6	17	98.1	Southwest Tex. St.	11	397	1313	3.3	11	119.4
McNeese St.	11	449	1089	2.4	9	99.0	Alcorn St.	10	401	1266	3.2	14	126.6
Villanova	11	402	1122	2.8	8	102.0	Princeton	10	437	1297	3.0	13	129.7
Sam Houston St.	11	456	1165	2.6	7	105.9	New Hampshire	11	443	1444	3.3	13	131.3
Alabama St.	11	365	1170	3.2	8	106.4	Texas Southern	11	414	1457	3.5	10	132.5
Northern Iowa	11	448	1241	2.8	10	112.8	Liberty	11	409	1475	3.6	14	134.1
Delaware	11	396	1246	3.1	13	113.3	Southern-B.R.	11	486	1501	3.1	16	136.5
Eastern Ky.	11	424	1266	3.0	6	115.1	Massachusetts	11	409	1507	3.7	11	137.0

SCORING OFFENSE

	Games	Pts.	Avg.		Games	Pts.	Avg.
Nevada	11	496	45.1	Furman	11	363	33.0
Weber St.	11	495	45.0	Lehigh	11	363	33.0
Alabama St.	11	453	41.2	Delaware	11	358	32.5
Marshall	11	414	37.6	New Hampshire	11	356	32.4
Villanova	11	397	36.1	Boise St.	11	355	32.3
Alcorn St.	10	357	35.7	James Madison	11	351	31.9
North Caro. A&T	11	381	34.6	William & Mary	11	343	31.2
Idaho	11	375	34.1	Eastern Ky.	11	333	30.3
Holy Cross	11	372	33.8	Samford	11	332	30.2
Northern Iowa	11	366	33.3	Youngstown St.	11	331	30.1

SCORING DEFENSE

	Games	Pts.	Avg.		Games	Pts.	Avg.
Villanova	11	132	12.0	Western Ill.	11	167	15.2
McNeese St.	11	134	12.2	Northwestern (La.)	11	169	15.4
Sam Houston St.	11	145	13.2	Alabama St.	11	170	15.5
Eastern Ky.	11	147	13.4	Holy Cross	11	174	15.8
Middle Tenn. St.	11	151	13.7	Northeast La.	11	175	15.9
Samford	11	154	14.0	Illinois St.	11	176	16.0
South Caro. St.	11	157	14.3	Southwest Tex. St.	11	179	16.3
Northern Iowa	11	158	14.4	Mississippi Val.	11	182	16.5
Ga. Southern	11	160	14.5				
North Caro. A&T	11	163	14.8				

PASSING OFFENSE

	Games	Att.	Cmp.	Int.	Pct.	Yards	Yds./Att.	TD	Yds.PG
Weber St.	11	516	320	17	62.0	4280	8.3	36	389.1
Idaho	11	424	251	12	59.2	3699	8.7	26	336.3
Alcorn St.	10	371	205	19	55.3	3299	8.9	28	329.9
Montana	11	487	262	14	53.8	3624	7.4	24	329.5
Nevada	11	432	245	18	56.7	3578	8.3	27	325.3
Lehigh	11	479	287	16	59.9	3566	7.4	31	324.2
Connecticut	11	465	269	19	57.8	3316	7.1	21	301.5
Liberty	11	436	262	22	60.1	3257	7.5	19	296.1
Holy Cross	11	403	239	20	59.3	3211	8.0	26	291.9
William & Mary	11	368	238	9	64.7	3099	8.4	20	281.7
Bethune-Cookman	10	445	221	18	49.7	2774	6.2	21	277.4
Marshall	11	298	186	8	62.4	3032	10.2	28	275.6
Northern Ariz.	11	396	216	23	54.5	2978	7.5	13	270.7
New Hampshire	11	350	181	21	51.7	2765	7.9	26	251.4
Florida A&M	11	323	170	14	52.6	2764	8.6	20	251.3
Samford	11	429	224	14	52.2	2731	6.4	19	248.3
Villanova	11	377	232	18	61.5	2715	7.2	21	246.8
Boston U.	11	403	230	19	57.1	2710	6.7	18	246.4
Southeast Mo. St.	11	423	244	22	57.7	2653	6.3	17	241.2
Idaho St.	11	360	202	17	56.1	2645	7.3	24	240.5

PASS EFFICIENCY DEFENSE

	Games	Att.	Cmp.	Cmp. Pct.	Int.	Int. Pct.	Yards	Yds./ Att.	TD	TD Pct.	Rating Points
South Caro. St.	11	278	96	34.53	21	7.55	1360	4.89	8	2.88	70.01
Mississippi Val.	11	254	112	44.09	24	9.45	1343	5.29	7	2.76	78.71
McNeese St.	11	302	145	48.01	20	6.62	1577	5.22	3	.99	81.91
Ga. Southern	11	230	105	45.65	21	9.13	1341	5.83	6	2.61	84.98
Western Ill.	11	246	113	45.93	12	4.88	1338	5.44	5	2.03	88.57
Northeast La.	11	260	124	47.69	11	4.23	1252	4.82	8	3.08	89.83
Alcorn St.	10	308	125	40.58	14	4.55	1710	5.55	11	3.57	89.92
Villanova	11	287	142	49.48	21	7.32	1531	5.33	9	3.14	90.00
Jackson St.	10	244	97	39.75	25	10.25	1516	6.21	14	5.74	90.39
North Caro. A&T	11	264	118	44.70	22	8.33	1762	6.67	6	2.27	91.59
Northern Iowa	11	291	139	47.77	13	4.47	1439	4.95	10	3.44	91.71
Sam Houston St.	11	299	140	46.82	16	5.35	1713	5.73	7	2.34	91.97
Samford	11	341	177	51.91	23	6.74	1874	5.50	9	2.64	93.29
Appalachian St.	11	251	118	47.01	16	6.37	1543	6.15	6	2.39	93.79
Northwestern (La.)	11	269	129	47.96	20	7.43	1559	5.80	10	3.72	94.04
Boise St.	11	427	209	48.95	28	6.56	2500	5.85	13	3.04	95.06
Princeton	10	275	129	46.91	15	5.45	1598	5.81	9	3.27	95.61
Holy Cross	11	367	180	49.05	21	5.72	2029	5.53	13	3.54	95.73
Stephen F. Austin	11	222	100	45.05	10	4.50	1266	5.70	8	3.60	95.83
Alabama St.	11	353	157	44.48	21	5.95	2104	5.96	15	4.25	96.67

LONGEST PLAYS OF THE 1991 SEASON

DIVISION I-AA

RUSHING

Player, Team (Opponent)	Yards
Barry Bourassa, New Hampshire (Boston U.)	97
Steve Eaton, Southwest Tex. St. (Prairie View)	90
Markus Thomas, Eastern Ky. (Murray St.)	90
Chris Kouri, Yale (Princeton)	90
John Newson, Rhode Island (Richmond)	89
Carl Smith, Maine (Rutgers)	89

PASSING

Passer-Receiver, Team (Opponent)	Yards
Todd Donnan-Troy Brown, Marshall (Va. Military)	99
Tom Ciaccio-Mark Roman, Holy Cross (Bucknell)	95
Chad Roghair-Michael Lerch, Princeton (Brown)	90
Mark Tenneson-Harold Wright, Eastern Wash. (Idaho St.)	85
Robert Hemby-Quincy Miller, South Caro. St. (Morgan St.)	85
Tremaine Lewis-Vreeland Mosby, Murray St. (Tenn.-Martin)	85

INTERCEPTIONS

Player, Team (Opponent)	Yards
Derek Grier, Marshall (East Tenn. St.)	100
Sherriden May, Idaho (Sonoma St.)	98
Sean Roundtree, Northern Ariz. (N. M. Highlands)	97
Sean Wallace, Southern-B. R. (Grambling)	96

PUNT RETURNS

Player, Team (Opponent)	Yards
Kerry Hayes, Western Caro. (Tenn.-Chatt.)	95
Orlando Crenshaw, Middle Tenn. St. (Southeast Mo. St.)	87
Troy Brown, Marshall (Morehead St.)	86
Sean Hill, Montana St. (Northern Ariz.)	85
Greg Hoffmeister, Dartmouth (Cornell)	85

KICKOFF RETURNS

Player, Team (Opponent)	Yards
Tim Mitchell, Eastern Wash. (Boise St.)	99
David Lucas, Florida A&M (North Caro. A&T)	99
Bill Whitley, Furman (Western Caro.)	98
Paul Ashby, Alabama St. (Grambling)	97
Billy Marsh, East Tenn. St. (Western Caro.)	96
Len Rainey, Northern Ariz. (Eastern Wash.)	96

FIELD GOALS

Player, Team (Opponent)	Yards
Chuck Rawlinson, Stephen F. Austin (Sam Houston St.)	58
Brian Mitchell, Northern Iowa (Illinois St.)	57
Eric Roberts, McNeese St. (Northern Iowa)	54
Steve Leo, Delaware (Richmond)	53
David Cool, Ga. Southern (Western Caro.)	53
Skip Shelton, Nicholls St. (Sam Houston St.)	53

PUNTS

Player, Team (Opponent)	Yards
Darren Svendsen, Montana St. (Minn.-Duluth)	78
Harold Alexander, Appalachian St. (Marshall)	77
Jim Kantowski, East Tenn. St. (Va. Military)	73
Jed Wallace, Fordham (Colgate)	73
Tim Mosley, Northern Iowa (Augustana, S.D.)	71

1991 DIVISION II INDIVIDUAL LEADERS

RUSHING

	1991 Class	Games	Car.	Yards	TD	Yds.PG
Quincy Tillmon, Emporia St.	So	9	259	1544	17	171.6
Troy Mills, Cal St. Sacramento	Sr	10	223	1668	17	166.8
Zed Robinson, Southern Utah	Jr	11	254	1828	18	166.2
Shannon Burnell, North Dak.	So	9	272	1461	14	162.3
Nelson Edmonds, Northern Mich.	Jr	10	328	1517	10	151.7
Chad Guthrie, Northeast Mo. St.	Jr	11	302	1649	17	149.9
Rob Clodfelter, Livingstone	So	10	283	1379	14	137.9
Bill Adams, Shepherd	So	10	301	1332	9	133.2
Howard Rodman, Tuskegee	So	10	205	1265	11	126.5
Brian Barton, Mesa St.	Sr	9	237	1120	5	124.4
Shawn Graves, Wofford	Jr	11	178	1331	20	121.0
Kevin Kimble, Butler	Jr	10	307	1175	10	117.5
Scott Schulte, Hillsdale	So	10	245	1144	14	114.4
Gaynor Blackmon, Northern Colo.	Fr	9	243	1027	13	114.1
Jeremy Monroe, Michigan Tech	So	10	163	1133	14	113.3
Aron Wise, Santa Clara	Jr	10	206	1127	12	112.7
Richard Parker, San Fran. St.	Jr	10	203	1093	5	109.3
Everette Norwood, Winston-Salem	Sr	10	182	1070	13	107.0
Darren Dawson, Pittsburg St.	Sr	11	196	1176	14	106.9
Patrick Gamble, Morehouse	Sr	10	168	1056	8	105.6
Michael Mann, Indiana (Pa.)	So	10	156	1054	11	105.4
Alfredo Hylton, Fort Hays St.	Sr	11	173	1135	10	103.2
Revis Davis, Delta St.	Sr	10	184	1029	8	102.9
Rodney Clemente, Portland St.	Jr	10	198	1018	10	101.8
Landrum Hale, Eastern N. Mex.	Jr	11	232	1108	7	100.7
Bill Pettyjohn, Shippensburg	Sr	11	225	1101	16	100.1

PASSING EFFICIENCY

(Min. 15 att. per game)	1991 Class	Games	Att.	Cmp.	Pct.	Int.	Yards	TD	Rating Points
Jayson Merrill, Western St.	Sr	10	309	195	63.1	11	3484	35	187.9
John Charles, Portland St.	Jr	11	247	147	59.5	7	2619	32	185.5
James Armendariz, Southern Utah	Sr	11	184	109	59.2	5	1839	17	168.0
Tony Aliucci, Indiana (Pa.)	Sr	10	190	122	64.2	6	1885	13	163.6
Jack Hull, Grand Valley St.	Sr	10	179	109	60.8	6	1709	15	162.0
Matt Cook, Mo. Southern St.	Jr	11	275	141	51.2	7	2637	25	156.7
Trevor Spradley, Southwest Baptist	Jr	11	256	168	65.6	10	2492	13	156.1
Andy Breault, Kutztown	Jr	10	360	225	62.5	20	2927	37	153.4
Joe Stochmal, Southern Conn. St.	Jr	9	191	105	54.9	12	1839	17	152.5
Maurice Heard, Tuskegee	Sr	10	332	190	57.2	13	2614	30	145.2
Scott Wood, St. Mary's (Cal.)	Sr	11	357	206	57.7	9	3006	22	143.6
Paul Romanowski, Butler	Sr	10	265	157	59.2	11	2214	18	143.4
V. J. Lechman, Northern Colo.	Jr	10	203	119	58.6	5	1706	11	141.9
Bobby Fresques, Cal St. Sacramento	Sr	10	154	89	57.7	2	1280	8	142.0
Chris Livingstone, Northeast Mo. St.	So	11	268	158	58.9	7	2126	17	141.1
Steward Perez, Chadron St.	Sr	11	314	179	57.0	18	2643	22	139.3
Chris Teal, West Ga.	So	10	301	176	58.4	13	2311	20	136.1
Carl Wright, Virginia Union	Sr	10	329	173	52.5	18	2634	26	134.8
Bob Bounds, East Tex. St.	Sr	11	196	104	53.0	9	1825	7	133.7
Mark Ramstack, Mo. Western St.	Jr	10	224	117	52.2	6	1770	14	133.7

Emporia State tailback Quincy Tillmon led Division II in rushing (171.6 yards per game) and scoring (12.7 points per game) as a sophomore in 1991.

TOTAL OFFENSE

	1991 Class	Games	Plays	Yards	Yds.PG
Jayson Merrill, Western St.	Sr	10	337	3400	340.0
Andy Breault, Kutztown	Jr	10	407	2850	285.0
Troy Mott, Wayne St. (Neb.)	Jr	10	514	2822	282.2
Leonard Williams, Tenn.-Martin	Sr	10	348	2787	278.7
Carl Wright, Virginia Union	Sr	10	377	2683	268.3
Maurice Heard, Tuskegee	Sr	10	372	2666	266.6
Rob Tomlinson, Cal St. Chico	Sr	9	395	2393	265.9
Scott Wood, St. Mary's (Cal.)	Sr	11	411	2846	258.7
John St. Jacques, Santa Clara	Jr	11	405	2834	257.6
Matt Cook, Mo. Southern St.	Jr	11	347	2768	251.6
Steward Perez, Chadron St.	Sr	11	371	2628	238.9
Joe Stochmal, Southern Conn. St.	Jr	9	303	2144	238.2
Mike Quinn, UC Davis	Sr	10	407	2378	237.8
Charles Parks, Clark Atlanta	Sr	10	207	2356	235.6
Jimmy Broadway, Lock Haven	Sr	10	519	2314	231.4
Bill Bair, Mansfield	Jr	11	429	2544	231.3
Ken Suhl, New Haven	Jr	10	356	2302	230.2
Chris Teal, West Ga.	So	10	328	2255	225.5
Vernon Buck, Wingate	Fr	10	388	2244	224.4
John Charles, Portland St.	Jr	11	283	2456	223.3
Trevor Spradley, Southwest Baptist	Jr	11	332	2422	220.2
Tim Myers, Clarion	Jr	10	350	2133	213.3
Chris Fagan, Millersville	Jr	10	401	2077	207.7
John Spear, Sonoma St.	Sr	11	359	2267	206.1
Jack Hull, Grand Valley St.	Sr	10	287	2059	205.9

RECEPTIONS PER GAME

	1991 Class	Games	Catches	Yards	TD	Ct.PG
Jesse Lopez, Cal St. Hayward	Sr	10	86	861	4	8.6
Brian Fleming, UC Santa Barb.	Sr	8	61	705	8	7.6
Marlon Goolsby, Wayne St. (Neb.)	Sr	10	75	827	7	7.5
Carl Bruere, N.M. Highlands	Sr	10	72	963	8	7.2
Remus James, Virginia St.	So	10	69	1190	6	6.9

	1991 Class	Games	Catches	Yards	TD	Ct.PG
Amahl Thomas, UC Santa Barb.	Sr	8	55	791	9	6.9
Mike Ragin, Wingate	So	10	68	893	5	6.8
Khevin Pratt, Cal St. Chico	Jr	9	58	1016	6	6.4
Joseph Washington, Tuskegee	Jr	10	63	1050	12	6.3
David Jackson, St. Mary's (Cal.)	Sr	11	66	1086	9	6.0
Tony Willis, New Haven	So	10	59	986	12	5.9
Reggie Alexander, Western St.	Jr	10	58	951	15	5.8
Felix Lewis, Clark Atlanta	Sr	10	58	916	8	5.8
Lee Harper, Wayne St. (Neb.)	Sr	10	58	848	6	5.8
David Pignone, Central Conn. St.	Sr	10	58	676	3	5.8
Wade Leduc, Emporia St.	Jr	10	58	773	4	5.8
Fontaine Walker, Northeast Mo. St.	Jr	11	62	641	6	5.6

RECEIVING YARDS PER GAME

	1991 Class	Games	Catches	Yards	TD	Yds.PG
Rod Smith, Mo. Southern St.	Jr	11	60	1439	15	130.8
Remus James, Virginia St.	So	10	69	1190	6	119.0
Khevin Pratt, Cal St. Chico	Jr	9	58	1016	6	112.9
Terren Adams, Mo. Western St.	Jr	11	61	1232	12	112.0
Joseph Washington, Tuskegee	Jr	10	63	1050	12	105.0
Tyrone Johnson, Western St.	So	10	32	1039	12	103.9
Rodney Hounshell, Virginia Union	Jr	10	51	1034	8	103.4
Amahl Thomas, UC Santa Barb.	Sr	8	55	791	9	98.9
David Jackson, St. Mary's (Cal.)	Sr	11	66	1086	9	98.7
Tony Willis, New Haven	So	10	59	986	12	98.6
Chris Thomas, Cal Poly SLO	Jr	9	48	877	5	97.4
Carl Bruere, N.M. Highlands	Sr	10	72	963	8	96.3
Reggie Alexander, Western St.	Jr	10	58	951	15	95.1
Ronnie West, Pittsburg St.	Sr	11	50	1044	12	94.9
Jay Rhoades, Chadron St.	Sr	11	52	1016	13	92.4
Johnny Cox, Fort Lewis	Jr	10	52	919	11	91.9
Felix Lewis, Clark Atlanta	Sr	10	58	916	8	91.6
Wade Hopkins, Southwest Baptist	Sr	10	46	907	3	90.7
Leo Mendenhall, West Ga.	Sr	10	55	906	9	90.6
Mike Ragin, Wingate	So	10	68	893	5	89.3
Brian Fleming, UC Santa Barb.	Sr	8	61	705	8	88.1
Christopher Holder, Tuskegee	Sr	10	52	874	14	87.4
Jesse Lopez, Cal St. Hayward	Sr	10	86	861	4	86.1
Johnnie Barnes, Hampton	Sr	11	50	934	7	84.9
Lee Harper, Wayne St. (Neb.)	Sr	10	58	848	6	84.8

SCORING

	1991 Class	Games	TD	XP	FG	Points	Pts.PG
Quincy Tillmon, Emporia St.	So	9	19	0	0	114	12.7
Troy Mills, Cal St. Sacramento	Sr	10	21	0	0	126	12.6
Shawn Graves, Wofford	Jr	11	20	2	0	122	11.1
Chad Guthrie, Northeast Mo. St.	Jr	11	20	0	0	120	10.9
Zed Robinson, Southern Utah	Jr	11	18	4	0	112	10.2
Christopher Holder, Tuskegee	Sr	10	16	4	0	100	10.0
Aron Wise, Santa Clara	Jr	10	16	0	0	96	9.6
Gaynor Blackmon, Northern Colo.	Fr	9	14	0	0	84	9.3
Shannon Burnell, North Dak.	So	9	14	0	0	84	9.3
Eric Rajala, Minn.-Duluth	Sr	10	15	0	0	90	9.0
Tony Evans, Colorado Mines	So	10	15	0	0	90	9.0
Scott Schulte, Hillsdale	So	10	15	0	0	90	9.0
Reggie Alexander, Western St.	Jr	10	15	0	0	90	9.0
Mark Steinmeyer, Kutztown	Sr	10	15	0	0	90	9.0
Jeremy Monroe, Michigan Tech	So	10	15	0	0	90	9.0
Rob Clodfelter, Livingstone	So	10	14	4	0	88	8.8
Ronald Meadows, Johnson Smith	Sr	10	13	10	0	88	8.8
Bill Pettyjohn, Shippensburg	Sr	11	16	0	0	96	8.7
Rodney Clemente, Portland St.	Jr	10	14	2	0	86	8.6
Everette Norwood, Winston-Salem	Sr	10	14	0	0	84	8.4
David McCartney, Chadron St.	So	10	14	0	0	84	8.4
Rod Smith, Mo. Southern St.	Jr	11	15	2	0	92	8.4
Ronald Moore, Pittsburg St.	Jr	11	14	4	0	88	8.0
Floyd Mathis, Carson-Newman	So	10	13	0	0	78	7.8
Michael Mann, Indiana (Pa.)	So	10	13	0	0	78	7.8

FIELD GOALS

	1991 Class	Games	FGA	FG	Pct.	FGPG
Billy Watkins, East Tex. St.	So	11	24	15	62.5	1.36
Jim Crouch, Cal St. Sacramento	Sr	10	16	13	81.3	1.30
Don Kelly, Valdosta St.	Jr	10	19	12	63.2	1.20
Matt Stone, Troy St.	Sr	11	18	13	72.2	1.18
Jason Monday, Lenoir-Rhyne	Jr	11	21	13	61.9	1.18
Tim Hatcher, Sonoma St.	Jr	11	23	13	56.5	1.18
Matt Stehman, Mansfield	Jr	11	18	13	72.2	1.18
Ed Detwiler, East Stroudsburg	Jr	11	21	13	61.9	1.18
Jorge Diaz, Morningside	Sr	10	12	10	83.3	1.00
Jason Norton, Catawba	Fr	10	14	10	71.4	1.00
Brad Heim, Millersville	So	10	16	10	62.5	1.00
Andre Kwasnick, Gardner-Webb	So	11	20	11	55.0	1.00
Howie Guarini, Shippensburg	Sr	11	18	10	55.6	.91
John Duke, Shepherd	Sr	10	13	9	69.2	.90

PUNT RETURNS

(Min. 1.2 per game)	1991 Class	Ret.	Yds.	Avg.	(Min. 1.2 per game)	1991 Class	Ret.	Yds.	Avg.
Douglas Grant, Savannah St.	So	19	331	17.4	Mike Gillock, Indianapolis	So	12	137	11.4
Ross Giles, Western St.	Jr	14	239	17.1	Chad Ziegler, San Fran. St.	Jr	17	193	11.4
Danny Lee, Jacksonville St.	Jr	20	339	17.0	Joe Brown, Cameron	Jr	14	156	11.1
Miguel Callier, Mississippi Col.	Fr	29	479	16.5	Marise Houston, Alabama A&M	Sr	14	151	10.8
Brian Lukas, Michigan Tech	Jr	13	185	14.2	Mark Steinmeyer, Kutztown	Sr	16	170	10.6
Dedric Smith, Savannah St.	So	16	215	13.4	Antonio Hill, Valdosta St.	Fr	27	276	10.2
Marlon Worthy, Clarion	Fr	12	160	13.3	Bobby Beaudoin, Mesa St.	Jr	17	171	10.1
Joe Genasci, UC Davis	Sr	25	330	13.2	Tom Hagert, North Dak.	So	15	149	9.9
John Miller, Mansfield	Jr	18	237	13.2	Daniel Rederford, Southern Utah	So	17	167	9.8
Alan Boschma, Portland St.	Sr	22	281	12.8	David Boone, Morehouse	Sr	11	108	9.8

KICKOFF RETURNS

(Min. 1.2 per game)	1991 Class	Ret.	Yds.	Avg.	(Min. 1.2 per game)	1991 Class	Ret.	Yds.	Avg.
Winston Horshaw, Shippensburg	Jr	15	536	35.7	James Whitley, Mo. Western St.	So	22	608	27.6
Anthony Rivera, Western St.	Jr	18	635	35.3	Clayton Holmes, Carson-Newman	Sr	13	355	27.3
Joe Barsi, Cal Poly SLO	Sr	13	390	30.0	Derrick Johnson, St. Cloud St.	Jr	15	403	26.9
Joe Randolph, Elon	Jr	16	471	29.4	Matt Pericolosi, Central Conn. St.	So	21	564	26.9
Chip Lewis, Catawba	So	12	352	29.3	Freeman Baysinger, Humboldt St.	Sr	20	533	26.7
Chris Thomas, Cal Poly SLO	Jr	16	461	28.8	Brian Lukas, Michigan Tech	Jr	11	292	26.5
Brian Allred, Cal St. Sacramento	Sr	13	371	28.5	Dean Herrboldt, South Dak. St.	Fr	13	342	26.3
Philip O'Neal, Elizabeth City St.	Fr	10	284	28.4	John Raba, New Haven	Jr	25	653	26.1
Troy Mills, Cal St. Sacramento	Sr	14	393	28.1	Christopher Holder, Tuskegee	Sr	18	470	26.1
Karl Evans, Mo. Southern St.	Jr	14	388	27.7	Willie Mozeke, East Tex. St.	Sr	14	362	25.9

PUNTING

(Min. 3.6 per game)	1991 Class	No.	Avg.	(Min. 3.6 per game)	1991 Class	No.	Avg.
Doug O'Neill, Cal Poly SLO	Sr	42	45.1	Chris Afarian, Santa Clara	So	48	40.1
John Crittenden, North Ala.	Jr	49	43.2	Aaron Kanner, Catawba	Jr	63	40.1
John Plasky, Presbyterian	Jr	70	41.6	Andy Wilhoit, Cal St. Sacramento	Jr	49	40.1
James Morris, Angelo St.	Fr	56	41.5	John Scherwinski, Mankato St.	Jr	56	39.9
Jason Smith, Mississippi Col.	Sr	44	41.3	Scott Smith, New Haven	Jr	46	39.8
Ed Detwiler, East Stroudsburg	Jr	47	40.8	Lawrence Holmes, Norfolk St.	So	56	39.7
Mark Ambos, Ashland	Sr	63	40.7	Steve Kinsey, Adams St.	Sr	44	39.7
Paul Irland, Central Okla.	Jr	66	40.6	Larry Israel, UC Santa Barb.	So	47	39.6
Chris Hilliker, Livingston	Sr	70	40.3	Tobey Schneider, Northern Colo.	So	58	39.4
Richie Ambrose, Gardner-Webb	So	76	40.2	Doug Joyce, Millersville	Sr	54	39.4

INTERCEPTIONS

	1991 Class	G	No.	Yds.	Int.PG		1991 Class	G	No.	Yds.	Int.PG
Jeff Fickes, Shippensburg	Sr	11	12	154	1.1	Desmond Brown, Tuskegee	Jr	9	8	77	.9
Paul Deberry, Virginia Union	Sr	10	10	91	1.0	Tony Robinson, Slippery Rock	Jr	10	8	100	.8
Rodney Bradley, Neb.-Omaha	Jr	10	10	25	1.0	Shawn Jones, Kutztown	Sr	10	8	99	.8
Keith Sweeney, Springfield	So	10	10	81	1.0	C. Holmes, Carson-Newman	Sr	10	8	199	.8
Jonathan Wilson, Hampton	Sr	11	10	63	.9	Ian Brown, Shepherd	Sr	10	8	46	.8
Brian McGowan, Cent. Conn. St.	So	10	9	64	.9	Curtis Bunch, East Stroudsburg	Sr	11	8	156	.7
Jessie Chavis, Norfolk St.	Sr	10	9	179	.9	Shayne Mains, Shippensburg	Jr	11	8	95	.7

1991 DIVISION II TEAM LEADERS

TOTAL OFFENSE

	Games	Plays	Yds.	Yds.PG		Games	Plays	Yds.	Yds.PG
Western St.	10	721	5498	549.8	Indiana (Pa.)	10	705	4328	432.8
Tuskegee	10	706	4770	477.0	New Haven	10	732	4322	432.2
Virginia Union	10	772	4712	471.2	Savannah St.	11	766	4734	430.4
Mo. Southern St.	11	786	5064	460.4	Emporia St.	10	749	4288	428.8
North Dak. St.	9	651	4078	453.1	Kutztown	10	691	4236	423.6
East Tex. St.	11	778	4949	449.9	West Ga.	11	766	4637	421.5
Pittsburg St.	11	677	4927	447.9	Southern Conn. St.	9	599	3791	421.2
Cal St. Sacramento	10	703	4441	444.1	Santa Clara	11	781	4617	419.7
Southern Utah	11	768	4805	436.8	Portland St.	11	738	4607	418.8
Michigan Tech	10	660	4330	433.0	Chadron St.	11	740	4581	416.5

TOTAL DEFENSE

	Games	Plays	Yds.	Yds.PG		Games	Plays	Yds.	Yds.PG
Ashland	11	691	2150	195.5	Sonoma St.	11	746	2826	256.9
Indiana (Pa.)	10	600	2135	213.5	Virginia Union	10	676	2623	262.3
Elizabeth City St.	9	515	1984	220.4	Shepherd	10	644	2675	267.5
Butler	10	663	2236	223.6	Mankato St.	10	612	2676	267.6
Gardner-Webb	11	758	2529	229.9	Jacksonville St.	9	609	2409	267.7
Texas A&I	10	712	2380	238.0	North Dak. St.	9	548	2411	267.9
Carson-Newman	10	662	2385	238.5	Nebraska-Omaha	10	684	2695	269.5
Grand Valley St.	11	679	2658	241.6	Slippery Rock	10	655	2703	270.3
St. Cloud St.	9	569	2210	245.6	Ferris St.	11	715	2998	272.5
Angelo St.	10	689	2519	251.9	East Tex. St.	11	721	3073	279.4

RUSHING OFFENSE

	Games	Car.	Yds.	Yds.PG		Games	Plays	Yds.	Yds.PG
Wofford	11	638	3827	347.9	Fort Hays St.	11	580	2996	272.4
Jacksonville St.	9	489	2992	332.4	Southern Utah	11	563	2885	262.3
Winston-Salem	10	602	3254	325.4	Adams St.	10	563	2477	247.7
Carson-Newman	10	546	3209	320.9	Cal St. Sacramento	10	461	2405	240.5
Pittsburg St.	11	677	3527	320.6	Texas A&I	10	505	2392	239.2
Springfield	10	626	3149	314.9	Minn.-Duluth	10	566	2378	237.8
North Dak. St.	9	522	2654	294.9	Grand Valley St.	11	547	2583	234.8
Michigan Tech	10	520	2895	289.5	Savannah St.	11	461	2567	233.4
Colorado Mines	10	536	2872	287.2	New Haven	10	425	2264	226.4
Northwest Mo. St.	11	594	3131	284.6	San Fran. St.	10	494	2253	225.3

RUSHING DEFENSE

	Games	Car.	Yds.	Yds.PG		Games	Car.	Yds.	Yds.PG
Sonoma St.	11	358	700	63.6	Butler	10	415	1016	101.6
Wayne St. (Neb.)	10	367	707	70.7	Minn.-Duluth	10	335	1045	104.5
Indiana (Pa.)	10	325	732	73.2	West Liberty St.	10	390	1048	104.8
Gardner-Webb	11	430	806	73.3	Angelo St.	10	388	1077	107.7
Elizabeth City St.	9	284	694	77.1	Mankato St.	10	381	1080	108.0
Carson-Newman	10	330	833	83.3	Shippensburg	11	399	1223	111.2
Ashland	11	434	956	86.9	Savannah St.	11	436	1231	111.9
St. Cloud St.	9	378	848	94.2	Virginia Union	10	364	1145	114.5
Bloomsburg	10	318	972	97.2	Eastern N. Mex.	11	395	1263	114.8
Shepherd	10	355	993	99.3	Northern Colo.	10	357	1164	116.4

SCORING OFFENSE

	Games	TD	XP	2XP	DXP	FG	Saf.	Pts.	Avg.
Western St.	10	67	48	4	0	1	0	461	46.1
Carson-Newman	10	57	53	0	0	7	1	418	41.8
Virginia Union	10	57	38	2	0	3	2	397	39.7
Savannah St.	11	61	48	1	0	3	0	425	38.6
Tuskegee	10	56	26	7	0	0	1	378	37.8
Pittsburg St.	11	59	39	5	0	4	0	415	37.7
Indiana (Pa.)	10	52	40	1	0	5	0	369	36.9
Cal St. Sacramento	10	48	36	2	0	13	0	367	36.7
Kutztown	10	49	43	4	0	5	0	360	36.0
Mo. Southern St.	11	55	43	1	0	4	0	387	35.2
Jacksonville St.	9	43	39	0	0	5	2	316	35.1
Portland St.	11	54	41	3	0	4	1	385	35.0
Winston-Salem	10	51	26	7	0	0	0	346	34.6
Michigan Tech	10	49	40	0	0	3	0	343	34.3
Southern Utah	11	53	34	6	0	2	1	372	33.8
Southern Conn. St.	9	42	39	1	0	3	0	302	33.6
West Ga.	11	49	44	2	0	7	0	363	33.0
St. Mary's (Cal.)	11	50	42	2	0	5	0	361	32.8
New Haven	10	44	38	0	0	6	0	320	32.0
East Tex. St.	11	44	38	2	0	15	0	351	31.9

SCORING DEFENSE

	Games	TD	XP	2XP	DXP	FG	Saf.	Pts.	Avg.
Butler	10	9	6	1	0	3	0	71	7.1
Indiana (Pa.)	10	10	6	2	0	3	0	79	7.9
Jacksonville St.	9	11	6	0	0	2	0	78	8.7
Ashland	11	15	12	1	0	2	0	110	10.0
Grand Valley St.	11	18	11	1	0	3	0	130	11.8
Northern Colo.	10	18	7	2	0	3	0	128	12.8
Texas A&I	10	18	12	1	0	4	0	134	13.4
Angelo St.	10	14	12	1	0	12	0	134	13.4
North Dak. St.	9	17	9	1	0	3	0	122	13.6
Hillsdale	11	19	10	1	0	8	0	150	13.6
Pittsburg St.	11	20	14	3	0	5	0	155	14.1
North Dak.	9	18	13	2	0	2	0	131	14.6
Elizabeth City St.	9	19	11	1	0	0	3	133	14.8
Nebraska-Omaha	10	19	14	1	0	6	0	148	14.8
Mississippi Col.	10	18	17	0	0	8	0	149	14.9
Mankato St.	10	20	15	2	0	5	0	154	15.4
Saginaw Valley	11	23	17	2	0	3	1	170	15.5
Carson-Newman	10	19	13	2	0	8	0	155	15.5
Michigan Tech	10	22	13	3	0	2	0	157	15.7
Catawba	10	24	2	3	0	2	0	158	15.8
East Tex. St.	11	23	10	5	0	4	2	174	15.8

PASSING OFFENSE

	Games	Att.	Cmp.	Pct.	Int.	Yards	Yds.PG
Western St.	10	330	203	61.5	12	3574	357.4
St. Mary's (Cal.)	11	394	228	57.9	10	3354	304.9
Tuskegee	10	376	214	56.9	14	3017	301.7
Kutztown	10	370	228	61.6	22	3001	300.1
East Tex. St.	11	319	169	53.0	14	3123	283.9
Cal St. Chico	9	326	186	57.1	12	2527	280.8
UC Santa Barb.	8	339	171	50.4	13	2217	277.1
Portland St.	11	309	175	56.6	10	3034	275.8
Santa Clara	11	371	199	53.6	16	2992	272.0
Tenn.-Martin	11	404	196	48.5	15	2960	269.1
Wayne St. (Neb.)	10	417	237	56.8	18	2687	268.7
Mo. Southern St.	11	298	153	51.3	7	2951	268.3
Southwest Baptist	11	335	202	60.3	14	2928	266.2
UC Davis	10	387	214	55.3	16	2651	265.1
N.M. Highlands	10	445	210	47.2	27	2644	264.4
Virginia Union	10	332	173	52.1	18	2634	263.4
Sonoma St.	11	360	196	54.4	19	2894	263.1
Mo. Western St.	11	358	187	52.2	14	2866	260.5
Chadron St.	11	331	186	56.2	18	2728	248.0
Wingate	10	384	206	53.6	19	2473	247.3

PASS EFFICIENCY DEFENSE

	Games	Att.	Cmp.	Pct.	Int.	Yards	TD	Rating Points
Carson-Newman	10	332	128	38.5	31	1552	6	64.9
Virginia Union	10	312	108	34.6	27	1478	9	66.6
Texas A&I	10	276	108	39.1	19	1174	6	68.1
Butler	10	248	103	41.5	19	1220	3	71.3
Indiana (Pa.)	10	275	135	49.0	29	1403	4	75.5
Angelo St.	10	301	125	41.5	17	1442	5	75.8
Elizabeth City St.	9	232	87	37.5	20	1266	9	78.8
Jacksonville St.	9	228	101	44.3	16	1142	5	79.4
Slippery Rock	10	260	110	42.3	20	1444	6	81.1
Shepherd	10	289	127	43.9	25	1682	7	83.4
Michigan Tech	10	245	113	46.1	11	1287	2	83.9
Ashland	11	257	120	46.6	12	1194	6	83.9
Springfield	10	255	115	45.1	26	1511	8	84.8
Norfolk St.	10	265	93	35.0	25	1736	11	84.9
Nebraska-Omaha	10	267	134	50.1	22	1311	9	86.0
Hillsdale	11	229	107	46.7	22	1374	6	86.4
North Dak. St.	9	166	74	44.5	12	927	5	86.8
Grand Valley St.	11	225	97	43.1	13	1213	7	86.9
Sonoma St.	11	388	176	45.3	23	2126	9	87.0
Gardner-Webb	11	328	141	42.9	19	1723	13	88.4

LONGEST PLAYS OF THE 1991 SEASON

DIVISION II

RUSHING

Player, Team (Opponent)	Yards
Lester Frye, Edinboro (Calif., Pa.)	99
Tom Shiban, Ashland (Northern Mich.)	94
Michael Mann, Indiana, Pa. (Shippensburg)	93
Baldomar Cortez, Cal Poly SLO (Neb.-Kearney)	92
Troy Ausmus, Minn.-Duluth (St. Francis, Ill.)	91
Ramsey Selanders, Western St. (N.M. Highlands)	90
Allen Moore, Washburn (Northeast Mo. St.)	89
Reggie Brown, Carson-Newman (St. Francis, Ill.)	88
Mike Wise, Missouri-Rolla (Washburn)	88
Lucius Cole, Savannah St. (Cheyney)	86

PASSING

Passer-Receiver, Team (Opponent)	Yards
Matt Cook-Rod Smith, Mo. Southern St. (Mo. Western St.)	98
Kyle Morris-Alvin Fortenberry, Mississippi Col. (Central Ark.)	97
Marty Follis-Chad Postal, Bemidji St. (Northern St.)	96
Jeff McDonald-Omar Rogers, Neb.-Kearney (Adams St.)	96
Oscar Cedillos-Randy Montoya, N.M. Highlands (Langston)	95
Brad Widhalm-Mark Krasovich, Adams St. (Colorado Mines)	94
Jayson Merrill-Tyrone Johnson, Western St. (Fort Lewis)	94
Maurice Heard-Chris Holder, Tuskegee (Alabama A&M)	92
David Lafferty-Chris Thomas, Cal Poly SLO (Cal St. Sacramento)	89
Todd Lacey-Carlton Liggins, Eastern N. Mex. (Western N. Mex.)	89

INTERCEPTIONS

Player, Team (Opponent)	Yards
Tyrone English, Alabama A&M (Central St., Ohio)	100
Gary Boehler, Colorado Mines (Fort Hays St.)	100
Roosevelt Brooks, Elon (Mars Hill)	100
Marcus Clifton, Virginia St. (Norfolk St.)	96
Frank Andrews, Clarion (Indiana, Pa.)	95
McGrue Booker, Elizabeth City St. (Virginia St.)	93
Jesse Chavis, Norfolk St. (Elizabeth City St.)	90
Ulysses Smith, Savannah St. (Cheyney)	90
Joe Brookins, East Tex. St. (Livingston)	85

PUNT RETURNS

Player, Team (Opponent)	Yards
Paul Peters, Cal St. Northridge (Santa Clara)	96
Joe Genasci, UC Davis (Cal St. Northridge)	94
Ross Giles, Western St. (Menlo)	89
Doug Grant, Savannah St. (Albany St., Ga.)	85
Chip Lewis, Catawba (Wingate)	82
Alan Boschma, Portland St. (Cal St. Sacramento)	81

KICKOFF RETURNS

Player, Team (Opponent)	Yards
Winston Horshaw, Shippensburg (Edinboro)	99
Matt Pericolosi, Central Conn. St. (Hofstra)	98
Keith Higdon, Cheyney (Central St., Ohio)	98
Joe Randolph, Elon (Mars Hill)	98
Ozzie Young, Valparaiso (Hillsdale)	97
Paul Peters, Cal St. Northridge (Portland St.)	95
Shawn Jones, Kutztown (Mansfield)	95
John Raba, New Haven (Wofford)	95
Joe Barsi, Cal Poly SLO (UC Davis)	94

FIELD GOALS

Player, Team (Opponent)	Yards
Billy Watkins, East Tex. St. (Angelo St.)	53
Ozden Karakurt, Delta St. (Valdosta St.)	51
Billy Watkins, East Tex. St. (Pittsburg St.)	51
Jason Norton, Catawba (Elon)	50
Ozden Karakurt, Delta St. (Tenn.-Martin)	50

PUNTS

Player, Team (Opponent)	Yards
John Crittenden, North Ala. (Central Mo. St.)	80
John Plasky, Presbyterian (Lenoir-Rhyne)	78
Ed Detwiler, East Stroudsburg (Millersville)	75
Ed Detwiler, East Stroudsburg (Bloomsburg)	75
Andy Wilhoit, Cal St. Sacramento (Abilene Christian)	74
Barry Reese, Abilene Christian (Texas A&I)	72
Mark Ambos, Ashland (Ferris St.)	72
Alan Kaniper, Washburn (Pittsburg St.)	71
Adam Valencia, Wayne St., Neb. (Wis.-Stevens Point)	71
Ken Hagle, Michigan Tech (Moorhead St.)	70

1991 DIVISION III INDIVIDUAL LEADERS

RUSHING

	1991 Class	Games	Car.	Yards	TD	Yds.PG
Hank Wineman, Albion	Sr	9	307	1629	14	181.0
Eric Grey, Hamilton	Jr	8	217	1439	13	179.9
Anthony Russo, St. John's (N.Y.)	So	10	287	1685	18	168.5
Chris Babirad, Wash. & Jeff.	Jr	9	224	1508	18	167.6
Eric Frees, Western Md.	Sr	10	304	1545	15	154.5
Wes Stearns, Merchant Marine	Jr	8	216	1219	7	152.4
Kevin Piecewicz, Mass. Maritime	So	9	230	1289	13	143.2
Heath Butler, N'western Col. (Wis.)	So	8	212	1138	7	142.3
Alex Plomaritis, Dickinson	Jr	9	217	1238	11	137.6
Stanley Drayton, Allegheny	Jr	10	245	1375	27	137.5
Willie Beers, John Carroll	Jr	10	292	1362	14	136.2
Sean Rorke, Williams	Jr	6	136	808	4	134.7
Buddy Bass, Millsaps	Sr	9	266	1209	11	134.3
Don D'Aiuto, Marist	So	10	235	1321	10	132.1
Jason Wooley, Worcester Tech	So	9	205	1176	16	130.7
Carl Cravens, Sewanee	So	9	252	1166	9	129.6
Vlad Telemaque, Union (N.Y.)	Sr	9	178	1166	14	129.6
Chris Humbles, Ill. Wesleyan	Sr	8	152	1012	11	126.5
Brian Grandison, Wooster	Sr	10	259	1236	11	123.6
Mark Guerrettaz, Rose-Hulman	Sr	10	240	1204	6	120.4
Steve Dixon, Beloit	So	10	236	1183	12	118.3
Frank Baker, Chicago	Jr	10	269	1180	8	118.0
Chris Harper, Carthage	So	8	178	939	12	117.4
Devin Leftwich, Wheaton (Ill.)	Jr	9	204	1047	11	116.3
Jon MacSwan, Alfred	Sr	10	244	1150	13	115.0
Bobby Wright, Neb. Wesleyan	Sr	10	231	1138	8	113.8
Jon Zimmerman, Luther	So	9	200	1018	10	113.1

PASSING EFFICIENCY

(Min. 15 att. per game)	1991 Class	Games	Att.	Cmp.	Pct.	Int.	Yards	TD	Rating Points
Pat Mayew, St. John's (Minn.)	Sr	9	247	154	62.3	4	2408	30	181.0
Gary Urwiler, Eureka	Sr	10	171	103	60.2	5	1656	18	170.3
John Koz, Baldwin-Wallace	So	10	239	153	64.0	4	2014	21	160.4
Rick Renshaw, Wesley	Sr	11	263	159	60.4	12	2379	26	159.8
Willie Reyna, La Verne	Jr	8	267	170	63.6	6	2543	16	158.8
Jim Ballard, Mount Union	So	10	278	159	57.1	8	2310	27	153.1
Tom Monken, Ill. Wesleyan	Jr	9	203	114	56.1	6	1654	20	151.1
Aaron Keen, Washington (Mo.)	So	10	176	106	60.2	5	1487	13	149.8
Jim Weigel, Buffalo St.	Jr	9	154	82	53.2	10	1330	16	147.0
Ben Cammarano, Allegheny	Sr	10	176	93	52.8	3	1598	11	146.3
Dwayne Bowyer, Hampden-Sydney	Jr	10	204	116	56.8	12	1812	14	142.2
James Lane, Trinity (Conn.)	Sr	8	225	135	60.0	9	1736	17	141.7
Steve Keller, Dayton	Jr	10	207	116	56.0	3	1753	10	140.1
Brett Russ, Union (N.Y.)	Sr	9	224	145	64.7	2	1587	11	138.6
Tim Tully, Wheaton (Ill.)	Jr	8	124	60	48.3	2	1050	8	137.4

(Min. 15 att. per game)	1991 Class	Games	Att.	Cmp.	Pct.	Int.	Yards	TD	Rating Points
Dick Puccio, Cortland St.	Sr	9	226	140	61.9	12	1817	12	136.2
Brian Harmon, Redlands	Jr	9	184	109	59.2	7	1453	9	134.1
Ed Dougherty, Lycoming	Sr	9	304	186	61.1	13	2203	18	132.9
Dave Ceppetelli, Worcester Tech	Jr	9	239	142	59.4	16	1944	13	132.2
Dave Robinson, Maine Maritime	Sr	8	252	138	54.7	7	1849	16	131.7
Dennis Goettl, Wis.-La Crosse	Sr	10	291	167	57.3	15	2362	13	130.0

TOTAL OFFENSE

	1991 Class	Games	Plays	Yards	Yds.PG
Willie Reyna, La Verne	Jr	8	220	2633	329.1
Pat Mayew, St. John's (Minn.)	Sr	9	338	2601	289.0
Bill Hyland, Iona	Jr	10	433	2574	257.4
Jordan Poznick, Principia	So	8	414	2051	256.4
Brad Hensley, Kenyon	Fr	10	441	2554	255.4
Ed Dougherty, Lycoming	Sr	9	354	2259	251.0
John Guglielmo, Johns Hopkins	Jr	10	404	2426	242.6
Dennis Goettl, Wis.-La Crosse	Sr	10	364	2399	239.9
Andy Pickering, William Penn	Sr	10	606	2398	239.8
Jim Ballard, Mount Union	So	10	333	2371	237.1
Kevin Wesoloski, Westfield St.	Jr	10	390	2328	232.8
Rick Renshaw, Wesley	Sr	11	332	2439	221.7
Bill Meekings, Frank. & Marsh.	So	10	403	2213	221.3
Dave Robinson, Maine Maritime	Sr	8	302	1768	221.0
Chad Hohne, Evansville	Jr	10	405	2206	220.6
James Lane, Trinity (Conn.)	Sr	8	279	1744	218.0
Bob Sheffield, Concordia (Ill.)	Jr	8	405	1733	216.6
Stefan Bergan, Gallaudet	Fr	9	368	1946	216.2
Luke Hanks, Otterbein	So	10	428	2127	212.7
Dan Dwyer, Williams	Sr	8	282	1697	212.1
Steve Rohrscheib, Wis.-Eau Claire	Sr	10	449	2089	208.9
Dave Ceppetelli, Worcester Tech	Jr	9	260	1879	208.8
Tim Tully, Wheaton (Ill.)	Jr	8	261	1657	207.1
Jack Lamb, Elmhurst	Jr	9	346	1860	206.7
Tom Stallings, St. Thomas (Minn.)	Jr	9	126	1839	204.3
Terry O'Hare, Wagner	So	8	275	1634	204.3
Dennis Bogacz, Wis.-Whitewater	Sr	10	333	2012	201.2

RECEPTIONS PER GAME

	1991 Class	Games	Catches	Yards	TD	Ct.PG
Ron Severance, Otterbein	Sr	10	85	929	4	8.5
Rick Sems, Grove City	Jr	9	73	1023	7	8.1
Rod Zerbel, La Verne	Sr	9	70	785	4	7.8
Matt Newton, Principia	So	9	69	863	5	7.7
Chris Bisaillon, Ill. Wesleyan	Jr	9	65	1068	17	7.2
Chris Murphy, Georgetown	Jr	10	72	1034	7	7.2
John Guss, Maine Maritime	Sr	8	57	819	8	7.1
Mike Muraca, Wesleyan	Jr	8	55	631	1	6.9
Matt Shell, Cortland St.	Sr	9	61	719	3	6.8
Kevin Fayette, Juniata	Sr	9	61	865	2	6.8
Barry Rose, Wis.-Stevens Point	Sr	10	63	1107	10	6.3
Chris Morkert, Concordia (Ill.)	Sr	8	50	671	3	6.3
Rodd Patten, Framingham St.	So	8	49	956	13	6.1
Jim Bradford, Carleton	Sr	9	55	878	9	6.1
Sean McCabe, Kenyon	Sr	10	61	755	5	6.1
Dan Fichter, Brockport St.	Sr	10	61	947	11	6.1
Ed Bubonics, Mount Union	Jr	10	61	1081	13	6.1

RECEIVING YARDS PER GAME

	1991 Class	Games	Catches	Yards	TD	Yds.PG
Rodd Patten, Framingham St.	So	8	49	956	13	119.5
Chris Bisaillon, Ill. Wesleyan	Jr	9	65	1068	17	118.7
Rick Sems, Grove City	Jr	9	73	1023	7	113.7
Tim Peters, Westfield St.	So	10	53	1116	9	111.6
Barry Rose, Wis.-Stevens Point	Sr	10	63	1107	10	110.7
Ed Bubonics, Mount Union	Jr	10	61	1081	13	108.1
John O'Neill, St. Thomas (Minn.)	So	9	40	931	9	103.4
Chris Murphy, Georgetown	Jr	10	72	1034	7	103.4
John Guss, Maine Maritime	Sr	8	57	819	8	102.4
Joe Richards, Johns Hopkins	So	10	53	1023	6	102.3
Brian Mylott, Worcester Tech	Jr	9	49	899	8	99.9
Fran Naselli, Wesley	Jr	11	57	1079	14	98.1
Jim Bradford, Carleton	Sr	9	55	878	9	97.6
Kevin Fayette, Juniata	Sr	9	61	865	2	96.1
Matt Newton, Principia	So	9	69	863	5	95.9

	1991 Class	Games	Catches	Yards	TD	Yds.PG
Anthony Talton, Wis.-Whitewater	Sr	10	41	952	10	95.2
Dan Fichter, Brockport St.	Sr	10	61	947	11	94.7
Ron Severance, Otterbein	Sr	10	85	929	4	92.9
Nick Ismailoff, Ithaca	Sr	9	54	836	5	92.9
David Morales, La Verne	Jr	9	47	833	5	92.6
Zac Kraft, Frank. & Marsh.	So	10	53	890	6	89.0
Brian Sarver, William Penn	Jr	10	60	888	8	88.8
Darren Stohlmann, Neb. Wesleyan	Sr	10	60	877	9	87.7
Rod Zerbel, La Verne	Sr	9	70	785	4	87.2
Hanz Hoag, Evansville	Fr	10	58	859	4	85.9

SCORING

	1991 Class	Games	TD	XP	FG	Points	Pts.PG
Stanley Drayton, Allegheny	Jr	10	28	0	0	168	16.8
Chris Babirad, Wash. & Jeff.	Jr	9	22	2	0	134	14.9
Chris Bisaillon, Ill. Wesleyan	Jr	9	18	4	0	112	12.4
Al White, Wm. Paterson	So	10	20	4	0	124	12.4
Erik Orndorff, Lebanon Valley	Jr	10	20	0	0	120	12.0
Pat Hofacre, Dayton	So	10	19	0	0	114	11.4
Scott Berent, Cortland St.	Sr	9	17	0	0	102	11.3
Phelan Piestrup, La Verne	Fr	9	16	6	0	102	11.3
Eric Grey, Hamilton	Jr	8	15	0	0	90	11.3
Jason Wooley, Worcester Tech	So	9	16	2	0	98	10.9
Derrick Jett, Thomas More	Fr	10	18	0	0	108	10.8
Anthony Russo, St. John's (N.Y.)	So	10	18	0	0	108	10.8
Curt Landreth, Redlands	Sr	9	16	0	0	96	10.7
Hank Wineman, Albion	Sr	9	16	0	0	96	10.7
Tony McClain, Millikin	Sr	7	12	0	0	72	10.3
Vlad Telemaque, Union (N.Y.)	Sr	9	15	0	0	90	10.0
Eric Frees, Western Md.	Sr	10	16	2	0	98	9.8
Kevin Piecewicz, Mass. Maritime	So	9	14	4	0	88	9.8
Jay Conzemius, St. John's (Minn.)	Sr	9	14	4	0	88	9.8
Rodd Patten, Framingham St.	So	8	13	0	0	78	9.8
Trent Nauholz, Simpson	Jr	10	16	0	0	96	9.6
Jon Thorpe, Albright	Sr	10	16	0	0	96	9.6
Rory McTigue, Frostburg St.	Sr	9	14	0	0	84	9.3
Bill Johnson, Mass.-Dartmouth	So	9	14	0	0	84	9.3
Alex Plomaritis, Dickinson	Sr	9	12	9	1	84	9.3

FIELD GOALS

	1991 Class	Games	FGA	FG	Pct.	FGPG
Greg Harrison, Union (N.Y.)	So	9	16	12	75.0	1.33
Michael Cass, Pomona-Pitzer	Sr	8	16	9	56.3	1.13
Walter Lopez, Wagner	Sr	10	20	11	55.0	1.10
Jay Chabot, Plymouth St.	Sr	9	12	9	75.0	1.00
Brian Reising, Wabash	Sr	9	12	9	75.0	1.00
Chris Wild, Tufts	Sr	8	12	8	66.7	1.00
Matt Seagreaves, Susquehanna	Fr	10	19	10	52.6	1.00
Keith Woulfe, Western Conn. St.	Sr	10	13	9	69.2	.90
Erick Renshaw, Loras	Fr	10	20	9	45.0	.90
Michael Duffy, Randolph-Macon	Jr	10	13	9	69.2	.90
Anthony DeGuzman, Georgetown	Sr	10	15	9	60.0	.90
Dave Bergmann, San Diego	Sr	10	17	9	52.9	.90
James Cowper, Iona	So	9	16	8	50.0	.89
Rick Phelps, Western New Eng.	Jr	8	13	7	53.8	.88

PUNT RETURNS

(Min. 1.2 per game)	1991 Class	Ret.	Yds.	Avg.	(Min. 1.2 per game)	1991 Class	Ret.	Yds.	Avg.
Jordan Nixon, Augustana (Ill.)	Sr	27	473	17.5	Shane Stadler, Beloit	Sr	16	204	12.8
Matt Tyler, Quincy	Fr	11	192	17.5	Clarence Inscore, Guilford	Jr	16	201	12.6
Marcus Teague, Denison	Sr	13	214	16.5	James Williams, Ferrum	So	13	161	12.4
Bill Kaikis, Capital	Sr	14	222	15.9	Troy Young, Sacred Heart	Fr	16	195	12.2
Mike Naslund, Luther	Sr	18	274	15.2	Rod Zerbel, La Verne	Sr	13	157	12.1
Doug Smith, MIT	Jr	10	145	14.5	Jeff Hartung, Simpson	Sr	29	346	11.9
Derrick McCoy, Montclair St.	Sr	18	255	14.2	Fran Naselli, Wesley	Jr	17	201	11.8
Rich Callahan, Bentley	Jr	23	309	13.4	Remondo Williams, Waynesburg	Fr	14	164	11.7
Ryan Reynolds, Thomas More	Fr	13	172	13.2	Pierre Copes, Salisbury St.	Sr	20	230	11.5
Terry Dickey, DePauw	Sr	17	224	13.2					

KICKOFF RETURNS

(Min. 1.2 per game)	1991 Class	Ret.	Yds.	Avg.
Tom Reason, Albion	So	13	423	32.5
Fran Naselli, Wesley	Jr	16	506	31.6
Ed Bubonics, Mount Union	Jr	14	387	27.6
Chad Klunder, Wartburg	Fr	17	466	27.4
Steve Hayko, Widener	Jr	13	355	27.3
Michael Boone, Glassboro St.	So	15	407	27.1
Bill Sedgwick, Ursinus	So	23	623	27.1
Petie Davis, Wesley	So	12	323	26.9
Darin Zielsdorf, Gust. Adolphus	Sr	13	348	26.8
Criss Maple, Heidelberg	Sr	20	530	26.5

(Min. 1.2 per game)	1991 Class	Ret.	Yds.	Avg.
Jerrett Gordon, Wilmington (Ohio)	So	26	686	26.4
Steve Harris, Carroll (Wis.)	Jr	11	288	26.2
Jeff Schleusner, Ripon	Jr	14	366	26.1
M. Lundstrom, Concordia-M'head	Sr	19	486	25.6
Rich Callahan, Bentley	Jr	23	579	25.2
Jon Bilitz, N'western Col. (Wis.)	Sr	12	301	25.1
Mike Muraca, Wesleyan	Jr	27	677	25.1
Alden Smith, Davidson	So	21	525	25.0
Eric LaPlaca, Bowdoin	Jr	26	647	24.9

PUNTING

(Min. 3.6 per game)	1991 Class	No.	Avg.
Jeff Stolte, Chicago	So	54	42.5
R. C. Freedman, Mercyhurst	Jr	43	41.6
Tom Smith, Bethany (W. Va.)	Fr	43	40.6
John Hardy, Wesley	So	44	40.2
Michael Manzella, LIU-C.W. Post	Jr	65	39.4
Sean McQuown, Claremont-M-S	Sr	72	39.3
Steve Schott, Denison	Sr	44	38.7
Mike Helmly, Ky. Wesleyan	So	79	38.7
Marc Elmore, Sewanee	So	59	38.6
John Paul Case, Thomas More	Jr	36	38.6

(Min. 3.6 per game)	1991 Class	No.	Avg.
Adam Chatterton, Nichols	Fr	32	38.6
Drew Fassett, Davidson	So	44	38.6
Bryan Wiggins, Waynesburg	Sr	35	38.5
Andy Mahle, Otterbein	So	56	38.4
Jeff Shooks, Albion	Fr	34	38.4
Bob Ehert, Wash. & Lee	Sr	83	38.4
Paul McCord, Western Md.	So	45	38.3
Pete Pistone, Cal Lutheran	So	65	38.2
Curtis Fox, Neb. Wesleyan	Sr	58	38.1

INTERCEPTIONS

	1991 Class	G	No.	Yds.	Int.PG
Murray Meadows, Millsaps	Sr	9	11	46	1.2
Shaughn White, Dickinson	Sr	9	10	90	1.1
Howie North, Fitchburg St.	Fr	9	9	23	1.0
Tim Keane, Loras	Sr	10	9	67	.9
Jim Badgley, Canisius	Sr	8	7	33	.9
Scott Mahle, St. Peter's	So	8	7	87	.9
Richard Matthews, Coe	Jr	10	8	88	.8

	1991 Class	G	No.	Yds.	Int.PG
Neil Crowley, Bri'water (Mass.)	Sr	10	8	86	.8
Marlo Hollingshed, MacMurray	Jr	10	8	0	.8
Dennis Mrugalski, Buffalo St.	Jr	10	8	19	.8
Jim Chorney, Thiel	Sr	9	7	41	.8
Craig Garritano, FDU-Madison	Jr	9	7	78	.8
Rob Ferraro, Mass.-Boston	Jr	9	7	25	.8
Ken Morrell, Mass.-Dartmouth	Fr	9	7	104	.8

1991 DIVISION III TEAM LEADERS

TOTAL OFFENSE

	Games	Plays	Yds.	Yds.PG
St. John's (Minn.)	9	651	4534	503.8
Union (N.Y.)	9	691	4417	490.8
Ferrum	9	604	4285	476.1
Ill. Wesleyan	9	663	4135	459.4
Allegheny	10	658	4464	446.4
Worcester Tech	9	670	3973	441.4
Wheaton (Ill.)	9	666	3938	437.6
Dayton	10	789	4368	436.8
Cortland St.	10	770	4301	430.1
Redlands	9	624	3850	427.8

	Games	Plays	Yds.	Yds.PG
Lycoming	9	715	3847	427.4
Williams	8	615	3405	425.6
Trinity (Conn.)	8	622	3364	420.5
Albion	9	664	3752	416.9
Carleton	9	679	3742	415.8
Wis.-La Crosse	10	742	4147	414.7
Coe	10	730	4125	412.5
Wash. & Jeff.	9	649	3654	406.0
Carnegie Mellon	10	703	4056	405.6
Ill. Benedictine	10	623	4016	401.6

TOTAL DEFENSE

	Games	Plays	Yds.	Yds.PG
Wash. & Jeff.	9	537	1287	143.0
Mass.-Lowell	10	602	1769	176.9
Lycoming	9	530	1615	179.4
Simpson	10	652	1835	183.5
Plymouth St.	10	592	1918	191.8
Millsaps	9	574	1739	193.2
Augustana (Ill.)	9	568	1742	193.6
Eureka	10	633	1956	195.6
Ohio Wesleyan	10	642	1994	199.4
Aurora	9	512	1887	209.7

	Games	Plays	Yds.	Yds.PG
Ramapo	10	569	2124	212.4
Coe	10	715	2216	221.6
Dayton	10	621	2217	221.7
Marist	10	629	2220	222.0
Defiance	10	629	2225	222.5
Millikin	9	614	2063	229.2
Waynesburg	9	512	2084	231.6
Union (N.Y.)	9	599	2088	232.0
St. Francis (Pa.)	9	584	2102	233.6
Wis.-La Crosse	10	650	2339	233.9

RUSHING OFFENSE

	Games	Car.	Yds.	Yds.PG		Games	Car.	Yds.	Yds.PG
Ferrum	9	492	3253	361.4	San Diego	10	478	2741	274.1
Wheaton (Ill.)	9	533	2800	311.1	Ill. Wesleyan	9	443	2445	271.7
Augustana (Ill.)	9	612	2749	305.4	Simpson	10	617	2692	269.2
Carnegie Mellon	10	587	3006	300.6	Albion	9	462	2416	268.4
Dickinson	9	517	2694	299.3	Wm. Paterson	10	551	2674	267.4
Frostburg St.	10	540	2886	288.6	Redlands	9	438	2380	264.4
Union (N.Y.)	9	438	2561	284.6	Dayton	10	572	2579	257.9
Thomas More	10	591	2837	283.7	Susquehanna	10	563	2526	252.6
Allegheny	10	471	2753	275.3	Williams	8	406	2017	252.1
Millikin	9	514	2476	275.1	Mass.-Dartmouth	9	502	2239	248.8

RUSHING DEFENSE

	Games	Car.	Yds.	Yds.PG		Games	Car.	Yds.	Yds.PG
Wash. & Jeff.	9	317	581	64.6	Eureka	10	357	766	76.6
Lycoming	9	310	605	67.2	Ramapo	10	346	768	76.8
Ohio Wesleyan	10	355	674	67.4	Cal Lutheran	10	337	784	78.4
Mass.-Lowell	10	340	679	67.9	Marist	10	358	840	84.0
Dayton	10	336	698	69.8	Ohio Northern	10	418	868	86.8
Susquehanna	10	327	715	71.5	Augustana (Ill.)	9	340	794	88.2
Dickinson	9	313	650	72.2	St. John's (N.Y.)	10	374	883	88.3
Simpson	10	392	731	73.1	Frank. & Marsh.	10	380	894	89.4
Millsaps	9	336	663	73.7	Wis.-La Crosse	10	366	901	90.1
Plymouth St.	10	342	759	75.9	Coe	10	415	909	90.9

SCORING OFFENSE

	Games	TD	XP	2XP	DXP	FG	Saf.	Pts.	Avg.
Union (N.Y.)	9	54	50	1	0	13	0	415	46.1
St. John's (Minn.)	9	55	39	5	0	4	0	391	43.4
Allegheny	10	52	43	0	1	6	0	375	37.5
Ill. Wesleyan	9	45	34	5	0	7	0	335	37.2
Eureka	10	50	42	0	2	4	3	364	36.4
Coe	10	51	36	4	0	3	0	359	35.9
Ferrum	9	44	39	0	0	5	1	320	35.6
Cortland St.	10	48	40	3	0	7	0	355	35.5
Redlands	9	46	35	0	0	2	0	317	35.2
Worcester Tech	9	46	33	1	0	1	1	316	35.1
Augustana (Ill.)	9	45	31	3	0	3	0	316	35.1
Wesley	11	54	38	1	0	5	2	383	34.8
Hampden-Sydney	10	49	41	4	0	1	1	348	34.8
Ithaca	9	42	35	2	0	6	2	313	34.8
Wheaton (Ill.)	9	43	32	3	0	5	0	311	34.6
Trinity (Conn.)	8	38	30	2	0	3	0	271	33.9
Lycoming	9	41	37	0	0	5	1	300	33.3
Wash. & Jeff.	9	41	35	1	0	4	1	297	33.0
Dayton	10	44	39	1	0	7	0	326	32.6
Simpson	10	46	28	5	0	4	0	326	32.6

SCORING DEFENSE

	Games	TD	XP	2XP	DXP	FG	Saf.	Pts.	Avg.
Mass.-Lowell	10	8	3	0	0	1	0	54	5.4
Wash. & Jeff.	9	9	4	0	0	1	0	61	6.8
Dayton	10	11	6	0	0	0	0	72	7.2
Millsaps	9	9	5	1	0	2	0	67	7.4
Eureka	10	10	5	2	0	5	0	84	8.4
Kalamazoo	9	10	7	0	0	3	0	76	8.4
Simpson	10	12	7	1	0	2	0	87	8.7
Lycoming	9	10	6	2	0	3	0	79	8.8
Emory & Henry	10	11	10	1	0	4	0	90	9.0
Allegheny	10	13	8	0	0	2	1	94	9.4
St. John's (Minn.)	9	12	5	2	0	2	0	87	9.7
Redlands	9	12	6	1	0	3	0	89	9.9
Beloit	10	15	7	1	0	0	0	99	9.9
Williams	8	11	7	1	0	2	0	81	10.1
Plymouth St.	10	14	8	2	0	2	0	102	10.2
Union (N.Y.)	9	12	9	1	0	3	0	92	10.2
Ithaca	9	13	10	2	0	1	0	95	10.6
Augustana (Ill.)	9	13	9	2	0	2	0	97	10.8
Central (Iowa)	9	15	4	1	0	1	0	99	11.0
Albion	9	13	6	2	0	3	1	99	11.0

PASSING OFFENSE

	Games	Att.	Cmp.	Pct.	Int.	Yards	Yds.PG
St. John's (Minn.)	9	275	171	62.2	7	2725	302.8
La Verne	9	296	184	62.2	10	2669	296.6
Georgetown	10	428	217	50.7	24	2868	286.8
Iona	10	370	180	48.6	19	2713	271.3
Lycoming	9	339	201	59.3	15	2384	264.9
Carleton	9	293	142	48.5	20	2359	262.1
Kenyon	10	394	203	51.5	18	2563	256.3
Johns Hopkins	10	337	187	55.5	12	2562	256.2
Wis.-La Crosse	10	298	172	57.7	15	2518	251.8
William Penn	10	457	212	46.4	31	2502	250.2
Principia	9	399	183	45.9	24	2230	247.8
Maine Maritime	8	254	140	55.1	7	1933	241.6
Wesleyan	8	367	170	46.3	37	1931	241.4
Mount Union	10	295	166	56.3	8	2403	240.3
Framingham St.	8	269	131	48.7	17	1918	239.8
Cortland St.	10	326	195	59.8	17	2373	237.3
Evansville	10	348	179	51.4	13	2365	236.5
Elmhurst	9	325	140	43.1	12	2096	232.9
Worcester Tech	9	256	151	59.0	17	2059	228.8
Coe	10	285	124	43.5	19	2259	225.9

PASS EFFICIENCY DEFENSE

	Games	Att.	Cmp.	Pct.	Int.	Yards	TD	Rating Points
Wash. & Jeff.	9	220	72	32.7	15	706	3	50.3
Eureka	10	276	101	36.5	20	1096	2	57.7
Mass.-Lowell	10	262	97	37.0	26	1090	6	59.5
Millsaps	9	238	91	38.2	22	1076	2	60.4
Coe	10	300	113	37.6	28	1307	7	63.1
Simpson	10	260	96	36.9	20	1104	5	63.5
Augustana (Ill.)	9	228	90	39.4	13	948	2	65.9
Western New Eng.	8	170	66	38.8	16	805	6	71.3
Lycoming	9	220	98	44.5	15	1010	3	73.8
Emory & Henry	10	219	89	40.6	14	1097	3	74.4
Plymouth St.	10	250	99	39.6	18	1159	8	74.6
Kalamazoo	9	183	83	45.3	18	950	4	76.4
Aurora	9	201	78	38.8	11	893	7	76.5
Waynesburg	9	189	79	41.8	16	980	5	77.1
Allegheny	10	308	147	47.7	20	1358	6	78.1
St. John's (Minn.)	9	222	95	42.7	22	1226	6	78.1
Centre	10	237	103	43.4	23	1266	7	78.6
Williams	8	244	108	44.2	15	1138	6	79.2
Cornell College	9	214	87	40.6	13	1051	7	80.3
Frostburg St.	10	209	91	43.5	15	1083	5	80.4

LONGEST PLAYS OF THE 1991 SEASON

DIVISION III

RUSHING

Player, Team (Opponent)	Yards
Shaun Trejo, Redlands (Menlo)	97
Bruce Saban, John Carroll (Otterbein)	96
Chad Blunt, Case Reserve (Ohio Wesleyan)	95
Oliver Bridges, Stony Brook (Pace)	95
Rory McTigue, Frostburg St. (Catholic)	93
Matt Whitcomb, Middlebury (Bates)	93
Leon Williams, Ohio Northern (Otterbein)	93

PASSING

Passer-Receiver, Team (Opponent)	Yards
Carlos Nazario-Ray Marshall, St. Peter's (Georgetown)	99
Ted Kluender-Jeff Scherer, Carleton (Macalester)	98
Erik Orndorff-Bob Schwenk, Lebanon Valley (Western Md.)	98
Brad Hensley-Gavin Pearlman, Kenyon (Earlham)	91
Willie Reyna-Bill Battin, La Verne (Azusa Pacific)	90

INTERCEPTIONS

Player, Team (Opponent)	Yards
Randy Asche, Loras (Quincy)	100
Bruce Harris, Marist (St. John's, N.Y.)	97
Jeff Eckler, La Verne (Claremont-M-S)	94
Curtis Turner, Hampden-Sydney (Bridgewater, Va.)	93
Matt Harrison, Sacred Heart (Western New Eng.)	85

PUNT RETURNS

Player, Team (Opponent)	Yards
Rob Allard, Nichols (Curry)	97
Thomas Stephens, Maryville, Tenn. (Methodist)	91
Chris Adams, Gannon (Thiel)	87
Bill Zagger, Stony Brook (Bentley)	87
Nick Ismailoff, Ithaca (St. Lawrence)	86

KICKOFF RETURNS

Player, Team (Opponent)	Yards
Mark Cox, Hofstra (New Hampshire)	97
Brian Lazear, Wheaton, Ill. (Ill. Wesleyan)	95
Bill Sedgwick, Ursinus (Frank. & Marsh.)	95
Nate Thompson, Dubuque (Wartburg)	95
Warren Tweedy, Frostburg St. (Bridgewater, Va.)	95
Darin Zielsdorf, Gust. Adolphus (Central, Iowa)	95

FIELD GOALS

Player, Team (Opponent)	Yards
Anthony DeGuzman, Georgetown (Frank. & Marsh.)	55
Anthony DeGuzman, Georgetown (St. Peter's)	54
Dave Bergmann, UC San Diego (Whittier)	53
Mike Malvin, Albany, N.Y. (St. Lawrence)	53
Nick Mystrom, Colorado Col. (St. Mary of the Plains)	50

PUNTS

Player, Team (Opponent)	Yards
Sean McQuown, Claremont-M-S (Pomona-Pitzer)	79
Chuck Thall, Case Reserve (Carnegie Mellon)	77
Bob Ehert, Wash. & Lee (Hampden-Sydney)	76
Mike Gabrielson, Wartburg (Simpson)	75
Sean McQuown, Claremont-M-S (La Verne)	73

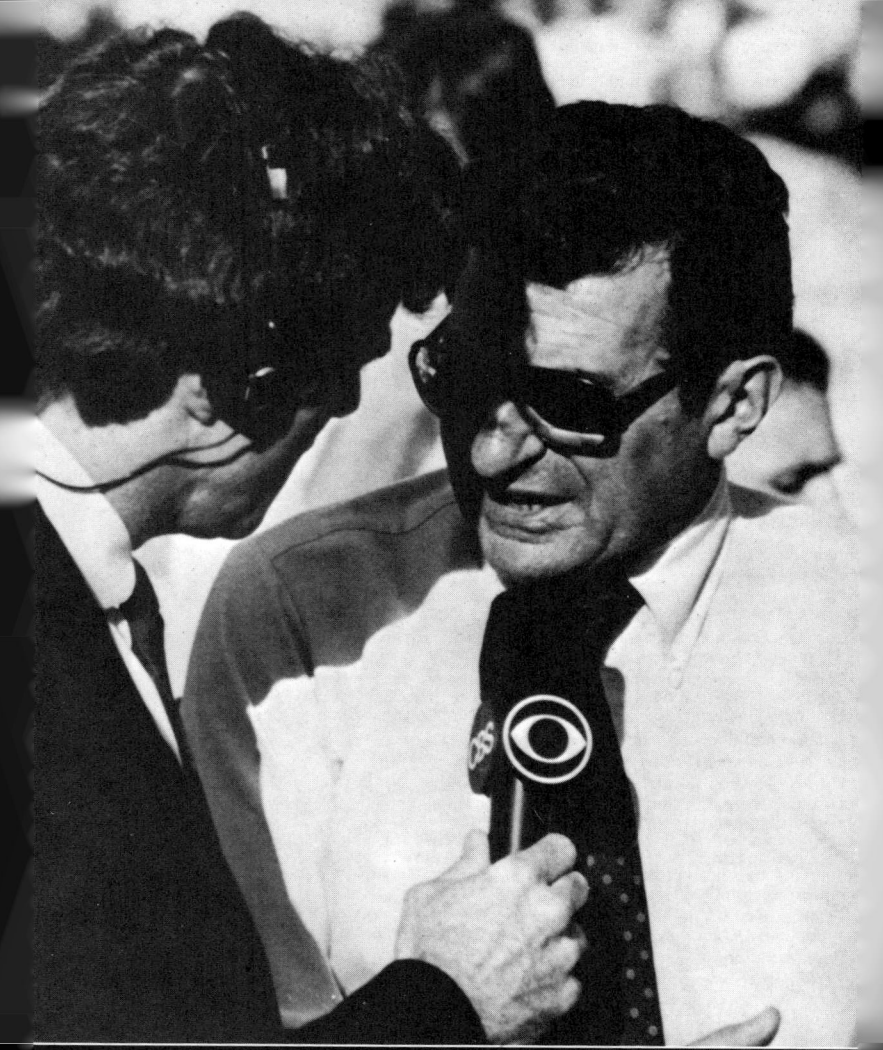

Penn State coach Joe Paterno is just one bowl win away from tying Paul "Bear" Bryant for the most head-coaching victories in major bowl games. Paterno leads active coaches in major-bowl wins (14) and

NATIONAL CHAMPIONSHIP COACHES OF THE 20th CENTURY, ALL-TIME MAJOR BOWL COACHING LEADERS, MATCHUPS, ALMA MATERS

By James M. Van Valkenburg
Director of Statistics

Howard Jones ties Paul "Bear" Bryant with six titles each atop the list of coaches whose teams have won or shared national championships in major-college football in the 20th century. Knute Rockne and Bernie Bierman are equal with Woody Hayes and Frank Leahy, all with five. Bob Zuppke and Bill Roper are alongside John McKay and Bob Neyland, all at four. Legends like Amos Alonzo Stagg and Glenn "Pop" Warner are added to the list.

This is what happens when we add the rating system leaders and other published national title lists since 1900 to the current system, which started with The Associated Press national poll in 1936. This takes us back to Fielding "Hurry Up" Yost's Michigan "Point-A-Minute" teams (one played in the first Rose Bowl, January 1, 1902). That was before the forward pass was legalized in 1906 by the newly organized NCAA, a group of rules reformers.

It is true that college football dates back to 1869, but we would argue that it was not a national game until the turn of the century. It also is true that early rating systems and national title lists were not perfect, but the current poll-bowl system certainly is not perfect, either. So what? It is all we have. Rest assured, all the teams sharing national championships were outstanding teams. Most had perfect records. Most won bowl games. It easily could be argued, for instance, that Miami (Florida) and Washington, coached by Dennis Erickson and Don James, respectively, both deserved the national title they shared in 1991.

Later in this section, we will look at the all-time leading bowl coaches, both for all bowls and for the traditional Big Four; coaches who have taken two, three and four different colleges to a bowl, and the top coaching matchups of all time among history's 616 major bowl games. Top current coaches like Penn State's Joe Paterno, Florida State's Bobby Bowden and Nebraska's Tom Osborne are prominent in this list.

Then we will look at the alma maters of history's 390 major bowl coaches. This will show Notre Dame on top with 15 alums who head-coached a college to a major bowl—Rockne and 14 of his players. Rather amazing when you consider that Rockne died 61 years ago in a plane crash after a relatively short coaching career (1918-30). Tennessee (13) and Alabama (10) follow. In the bowl section of this book, we have added game-by-game bowl results for all 390 coaches, including the opposing coach that day.

Jones won it at three colleges

Remarkably, Jones won or shared his six national crowns at three different colleges—the first at Yale in 1909, the second at Iowa in 1921 and the last four at Southern California, where he was 5-0 in the Rose Bowl. His last title was in 1939, 30 years after his first.

Just as remarkably, Bierman won all five of his titles in an eight-year span at Minnesota ending with 1941. He was stopped only by World War II.

Jones is the only multiple-college coach among the leaders. Bryant won all of his in a 19-year span at Alabama, Rockne and Leahy won all of theirs at Notre Dame, Hayes all of his at Ohio State, McKay at Southern California, Neyland at Tennessee, Zuppke at Illinois and Roper at Princeton.

Paterno and Erickson lead active coaches with two each. Five have won one each.

Paterno leads near misses

Paterno leads the list in national championship near misses. Three times—in 1968, 1969 and 1973—his teams were undefeated and untied, then won a major bowl game, yet were not rated or voted a piece of the title by anyone. The same thing happened twice to Frank Kush at Arizona State (1970 and 1976) and to several others, like Bobby Dodd (1952 season at Georgia Tech), Bud Wilkinson (1949 at Oklahoma) and Wally Butts (1946 at Georgia). In the era when the bowls came after the polls, Wilkinson did win the 1950 title before losing to Bryant's Kentucky team in the Sugar Bowl, and Butts' 1942 team was rated on top by one of the rating systems.

Paterno also took perfect-record teams to bowls after the 1978 and 1985 seasons, only to lose games that doubtless would have earned Penn State at least a share of the championship.

Notable additions

Adding the rating systems to the first part of the poll-bowl era produces a limited but outstanding group of additions to the national-titlist group, topped by Clark Shaughnessy's perfect-record Stanford team of 1940 that beat Nebraska in the Rose Bowl on January 1, 1941. Shaughnessy began the modern T-formation era, installed Frankie Albert at quarterback and transformed a team that was 1-7-1 in 1939. It was the biggest one-season turnaround to that point (and still is tied for first).

Another major addition is Neyland's perfect-record 1938 Tennessee team that beat Oklahoma in the Orange Bowl. Still another is H.O. "Fritz" Crisler's perfect-record 1947 Michigan team that beat Southern California in the Rose Bowl. Also Jim Tatum's unbeaten-untied 1951 Maryland team that beat Tennessee in the Sugar Bowl and Neyland's 11-1 1950 Tennessee team that beat Texas in the Cotton Bowl. Remember, the 1950 and 1951 poll champions lost in bowls.

The current system

The current poll-bowl system for choosing national champions, recorded earlier in this book, began with the first Associated Press national poll in 1936 and the first Cotton Bowl after that season, on January 1, 1937 (last of the Big Four). The United Press International poll was added in 1950, the Football Writers Association of America award was added in 1954, and the National Football Foundation and Hall of Fame Award entered the picture in 1959. Last year, the USA Today/CNN poll was added and UPI combined with NFFHF for one award, so that we still have four national championship awards.

The polls were conducted before the bowl games by AP in 1936-64 and 1966-67, by UPI in 1950-73, by the FWAA in 1954 and by the NFFHF in 1959-70. UPI was the last to make the change, doing so after its winner, Alabama, lost to AP winner Notre Dame in the Sugar Bowl on New Year's Eve, 1973. Since then, we have had fewer shared championships than in any other period since UPI joined AP in the poll business in 1950. Oklahoma won the AP title in 1974 but was on probation and thus not eligible for the others. Alabama and Southern California shared the 1978 crown. Every other season until 1990—11 years in a row and 14 times in a 15-year span—one team swept all four national championship awards.

Adding the early years

Stagg, Warner, Rockne, Jones, Zuppke, Roper, Yost, Crisler, Shaughnessy and other great coaches like Jock Sutherland, John Heisman, Wallace Wade, Gil Dobie, Frank Thomas and Matty Bell enter the national championship picture by adding the rating systems and national title lists published before the first AP poll, started by Alan Gould in 1936.

Stagg was one of the game's coaching pioneers, a disciple of Walter Camp at Yale. Camp had invented the line of scrimmage in 1881, with 11 players on a side, downs and yards to go, thus revolutionizing a game that started as a form of soccer. Camp, known as the father of American football, helped choose the first all-America team in 1889. Stagg, a divinity student, was chosen as an end on that team. By the dawn of the 20th century, Stagg had started the ninth year of his long career at Chicago, and 250 colleges were playing football.

In 1907, the Jones boys, Howard and quarterback Tad, helped Yale to a third straight unbeaten season. Two years later, at age 24, Howard coached his first of six national title teams, also at Yale. Meanwhile, an even more famous pair—Warner and his halfback acclaimed the world's greatest athlete, Jim Thorpe—was making history at Carlisle (Pennsylvania) School for Indians.

The forward pass had been legalized in 1906, but it was not popularized until 1913, when little-known Notre Dame, with Rockne at end and Gus Dorais throwing, shocked Army in New York, 35-13, completing 13 of 17 for 243 yards. Rockne's first two national title teams were his perfect-record 1919 and 1920 teams led by George Gipp. Zuppke and gifted Harold "Red" Grange were on top in 1923.

The South entered the scene with Wade's Alabama teams sharing crowns in 1925 (Rose Bowl winners after that season) and 1926 (after a Rose Bowl tie with Warner's Stanford team). Thomas, a Notre Dame graduate, coached Alabama's 1934 champions to a perfect record, including a memorable 29-13 victory over Stanford in the Rose Bowl on January 1, 1935. Millard "Dixie" Howell was the passer and end Don Hutson made six brilliant catches. That very season, the ball had become more bullet-shaped and passers like Sammy Baugh came on the scene. The "other end" on that Alabama team was Bryant, who later coached six national champions.

Michigan's Crisler, who had shared his first national title at Princeton in 1935, headed the NCAA Football Rules Committee. One of his players, David Nelson (after inventing the Winged-T at Delaware), served on the committee for three decades and led the way to greater safety and a more effective passing game before his death in 1991. Stagg ended his incredible 57-year coaching career in 1946 while at Pacific (California) and lived to be 102. It had started in 1891 at Springfield College, where one of his players was James Naismith, inventor of basketball and also credited with inventing the football helmet.

We used the Athletic Foundation national championship list, researched and compiled by Bill Schroeder and first published in 1941, from 1900 through 1949, a year before the first UPI poll. Also, for 1900 through 1923 we used the Parke Davis national title list first published in the Spaulding Football Guide of 1934. From 1924, its inception, through its last year, 1940, we used the Dickinson System. From 1934 through 1935 (a year before the FWAA award began), we used both the Dunkel System and the Litkenhous System. We did not use the ratings devised by Paul Williamson (a member of the Sugar Bowl committee) and others, in order to limit the number of teams used. All the rating systems used are in the national championship section in this book. Here is the complete 20th century coaching list:

NATIONAL CHAMPIONSHIP COACHES OF THE 20TH CENTURY

Coach	Nat'l Titles	Team, Nat'l Champ. Seasons
Paul "Bear" Bryant	6	Alabama +*61, >*64, +65, >*73, +78, +*79
Howard Jones	6	Yale *09; Iowa *21; Southern Cal t28, +31, +*32, +tt39
Woody Hayes	5	Ohio St. +*54, +57, t61, +*68, >*70
Bernie Bierman	5	Minnesota *34, *35, ✓36, *40, *41
Frank Leahy	5	Notre Dame ✓43, t46, *47, *49, t53
Knute Rockne	5	Notre Dame *19, *20, +*24, *29, *30
John McKay	4	Southern Cal +*62, +67, +*72, +74
Bob Neyland	4	Tennessee +*38, >*40, +50, >*51
Bob Zuppke	4	Illinois *14, ✓19, *23, t27
Bill Roper##	4	Princeton t06, tt11, t20, *22
Barry Switzer	3	Oklahoma *74, +75, +85
Ara Parseghian	3	Notre Dame ✓64, t66, +*73

Coach	Nat'l Titles	Team, Nat'l Champ. Seasons
Darrell Royal	3	Texas +*63, +*69, >*70
Bud Wilkinson	3	Oklahoma >*50, +*55, *56
Earl "Red" Blaik	3	Army *44, *45, t46
Glenn "Pop" Warner	3	Pittsburgh *16, ✓18; Stanford t*26
Percy Haughton..............	3	Harvard t10, *12, *13
Dennis Erickson#	2	Miami (Fla.) +89, +*91
Joe Paterno#.................	2	Penn St. +82, +*86
Bob Devaney	2	Nebraska +t70, +*71
Duffy Daugherty	2	Michigan St. >*65, t66
Jim Tatum....................	2	Maryland +*51, >*53
H.O. "Fritz" Crisler	2	Princeton *35; Michigan +*47
John "Jock" Sutherland	2	Lafayette *21, Pittsburgh t37
Harry Kipke	2	Michigan *32, t33
Wallace Wade	2	Alabama +*25, t*26
Gil Dobie.....................	2	Cornell *21, *22
Charles Daly	2	Army *14, *16
Amos Alonzo Stagg	2	Chicago *05, *13
Fielding "Hurry Up" Yost	2	Michigan +*01, *02
Don James#	1	Washington +*91
Bobby Ross	1	Georgia Tech +t90
Bill McCartney#	1	Colorado +90
Lou Holtz#	1	Notre Dame +*88
Jimmy Johnson	1	Miami (Fla.) +*87
LaVell Edwards#	1	Brigham Young +*84
Howard Schnellenberger#	1	Miami (Fla.) +83
Danny Ford	1	Clemson +*81
Vince Dooley.................	1	Georgia +*80
John Robinson...............	1	Southern Cal +78
Dan Devine	1	Notre Dame +77
Johnny Majors#..............	1	Pittsburgh +*76
Frank Broyles	1	Arkansas >*64
John Vaught	1	Mississippi +t60
Murray Warmath	1	Minnesota >60
Ben Schwartzwalder	1	Syracuse +*59
Paul Dietzel	1	Louisiana St. +*58
Forest Evashevski	1	Iowa +58
Ralph "Shug" Jordan	1	Auburn *57
Henry "Red" Sanders	1	UCLA *54
Clarence "Biggie" Munn	1	Michigan St. *52
Bennie Oosterbaan	1	Michigan *49
Wally Butts	1	Georgia +42
Paul Brown	1	Ohio St. ✓42
Harry Stuhldreher	1	Wisconsin ✓42
Clark Shaughnessy	1	Stanford +*40
Homer Norton	1	Texas A&M +*39
Carl Snavely	1	Cornell *39
Leo "Dutch" Meyer...........	1	Texas Christian +*38
Elmer Layden	1	Notre Dame ✓38
Leonard "Stub" Allison	1	California +37
Matty Bell	1	Southern Methodist >*35
Frank Thomas	1	Alabama +*34
Bill Alexander	1	Georgia Tech +*28
J. B. Hawley	1	Dartmouth *25
Andy Smith	1	California +*20
Robert Fisher	1	Harvard t19
John Heisman	1	Georgia Tech *17
Albert H. Sharpe	1	Cornell *15
Sol Metzger	1	Pennsylvania t08
William Knox.................	1	Yale t07
Foster Rockwell	1	Yale t06
J. E. Owsley.................	1	Yale *05
Carl S. Williams	1	Pennsylvania *04
A.R.T. Hillebrand	1	Princeton *03
Joseph Swan	1	Yale t02
William Reid	1	Harvard *01
Malcolm McBride	1	Yale *00

* Undefeated-untied in that regular season, did not play in a bowl game.   +* Undefeated-untied that regular season, also won bowl game after that season (note: bowl may have January date in following year).   >* Undefeated-untied that regular season, then lost in bowl game after that season.   t* Undefeated-untied that regular season, then tied in bowl game after that season.   t Unbeaten

but once tied that regular season, did not play in a bowl game.   +t Unbeaten but once tied that regular season, then won in a bowl game.   +tt Unbeaten but twice tied that regular season, then won in a bowl game.   ✓ Lost once that regular season, did not play in a bowl game.   + Lost once that regular season, then won in a bowl game.   > Lost once that regular season, then lost in a bowl game.   # Active in 1992.   ## Athletic Foundation lists as volunteer alumni coach, 06 and 11.

Polls and rating systems used: Athletic Foundation 1900-49, Davis 1900-23, Dickinson 1924-40, Litkenhous and Dunkel 1934-53, Associated Press 1936-91, United Press International 1950-90, Football Writers Association 1954-91, National Football Foundation and Hall of Fame 1959-90, NFFHF/UPI 1991, USA Today/CNN 1991.

All-time major bowl coaching leaders

Bryant remains on top of the major-bowl coaching lists, but he no longer dominates: Paterno is just one victory behind, with Bowden third and James tied for fourth. As a reminder, we are using the definition of "major bowl" above the list of all-time team records in major bowls in this book: All bowl games played by a current Division I-A team if its opponent was classified major (later University Division, then Division I) then or it was major then (excluding games in which a home team served as a predetermined host and/or games scheduled before the season). We start with most bowl games (# active in 1992):

HEAD COACH, MOST MAJOR BOWL GAMES

Name	Games	W-L-T	Name	Games	W-L-T
Paul "Bear" Bryant	29	(15-12-2)	Charlie McClendon	13	(7-6)
Joe Paterno	22	(14-7-1)	Hayden Fry#	13	(5-7-1)
Vince Dooley	20	(8-10-2)	Earle Bruce#	12	(7-5)
Tom Osborne#	19	(8-11)	Woody Hayes	12	(6-6)
John Vaught	18	(10-8)	Ralph "Shug" Jordan	12	(5-7)
Glenn "Bo" Schembechler	17	(5-12)	Terry Donahue#	11	(8-2-1)
Johnny Majors#	16	(9-7)	Bill Yeoman	11	(6-4-1)
Lou Holtz#	16	(8-6-2)	Jerry Claiborne	11	(3-8)
Darrell Royal#	16	(8-7-1)	Pat Dye#	10	(7-2-1)
LaVell Edwards#	16	(5-10-1)	Bob Devaney	10	(7-3)
Bobby Bowden#	15	(11-3-1)	Dan Devine	10	(7-3)
Don James#	14	(10-4)	Frank Broyles	10	(4-6)
Bobby Dodd	13	(9-4)	Ken Hatfield#	10	(4-6)
Barry Switzer	13	(8-5)	Fred Akers	10	(2-8)

MOST HEAD-COACHING VICTORIES IN MAJOR BOWL GAMES

Name	Games	W-L-T	Name	Games	W-L-T
Paul "Bear" Bryant	15	(15-12-2)	Charlie McClendon	7	(7-6)
Joe Paterno#	14	(14-7-1)	Frank Kush	6	(6-1)
Bobby Bowden#	11	(11-3-1)	Warren Woodson	6	(6-1)
Don James#	10	(10-4)	Bud Wilkinson	6	(6-2)
John Vaught	10	(10-8)	Dick Crum	6	(6-2)
Bobby Dodd	9	(9-4)	Danny Ford	6	(6-2)
Johnny Majors#	9	(9-7)	John McKay	6	(6-3)
Terry Donahue#	8	(8-2-1)	Jackie Sherrill#	6	(6-3)
Barry Switzer	8	(8-5)	Bill Yeoman	6	(6-4-1)
Lou Holtz#	8	(8-6-2)	Woody Hayes	6	(6-6)
Darrell Royal	8	(8-7-1)	Howard Jones	5	(5-0)
Vince Dooley	8	(8-10-2)	Jim Young	5	(5-1)
Tom Osborne#	8	(8-11)	Wally Butts	5	(5-2-1)
Pat Dye#	7	(7-2-1)	Ralph "Shug" Jordan	5	(5-7)
Bob Devaney	7	(7-3)	Hayden Fry#	5	(5-7-1)
Dan Devine	7	(7-3)	LaVell Edwards#	5	(5-10-1)
Earle Bruce#	7	(7-5)	Glenn "Bo" Schembechler	5	(5-12)

We started with most bowl games on the theory that just getting there is most important. Most wins certainly is close, and winning percentage should be added in the interest of fairness. After all, there were far fewer bowls in the early years, the Big Ten Conference had a no-bowl policy until after World War II, and Notre Dame did not play in bowls until 1970 (except for Rockne's trip with his Four Horsemen to play Warner's Ernie Nevers-led Stanford team after the 1924 season). And no-repeat pacts in the Orange and Rose kept some great coaches from adding to their totals, Wilkinson being the foremost example. That is why we also list games involving only the traditional Big Four—Rose, Orange, Sugar and Cotton. This presents a little different picture, brings oldtimers into focus (note Bryant and Dodd did better in the Big Four), and provides some new angles on current coaches (look at Johnny Majors and Terry Donahue in percentage):

HIGHEST WINNING PERCENTAGE, HEAD-COACHING IN MAJOR BOWLS

(Minimum three major bowl wins and .600 percentage)

Name	Record	@Pct.	Name	Record	@Pct.
Howard Jones	5-0	1.000	Danny Ford	6-2	.750
Dennis Erickson#	4-0	1.000	Charles "Rip" Engle	3-1	.750
Howard Schnellenberger#	3-0	1.000	Pat Jones#	3-1	.750
Ray Perkins#	3-0	1.000	Don James#	10-4	.714
Dana Bible	3-0-1	.875	Bob Devaney	7-3	.700
Frank Kush	6-1	.857	Dan Devine	7-3	.700
Warren Woodson	6-1	.857	Dick MacPherson	3-1-1	.700
Jim Young	5-1	.833	Chuck Fairbanks	3-1-1	.700
John Robinson	4-1	.800	Bobby Dodd	9-4	.692
Ray Graves	4-1	.800	Wally Butts	5-2-1	.688
Bill Battle	4-1	.800	John McKay	6-3	.667
Jim Sweeney#	4-1	.800	Jackie Sherrill#	6-3	.667
Terry Donahue#	8-2-1	.773	Bobby Ross	4-2	.667
Bobby Bowden#	11-3-1	.767	Fisher DeBerry#	4-2	.667
Pat Dye#	7-2-1	.750	Frank Thomas	4-2	.667
Bud Wilkinson	6-2	.750	Joe Paterno#	14-7-1	.659
Dick Crum	6-2	.750	Barry Switzer	8-5	.615

@ Ties computed as half won, half lost.   # Active in 1992.

HEAD COACH, MOST TRADITIONAL BIG FOUR BOWL GAMES

Name	Games	W-L-T	Name	Games	W-L-T
Paul "Bear" Bryant	20	(12-8)	Bud Wilkinson	8	(6-2)
Darrell Royal	12	(6-6)	John McKay	8	(5-3)
Glenn "Bo" Schembechler	12	(2-10)	Frank Broyles	8	(3-5)
Tom Osborne#	11	(4-7)	Vince Dooley	8	(3-5)
Joe Paterno#	10	(6-4)	Bobby Dodd	7	(6-1)
John Vaught	10	(6-4)	Bob Devaney	7	(4-3)
Woody Hayes	10	(5-5)	Dan Devine	7	(4-3)
Barry Switzer	9	(6-3)	Bob Neyland	7	(2-5)

Active in 1992.

MOST HEAD-COACHING VICTORIES IN TRADITIONAL BIG FOUR BOWL GAMES

Name	Wins	W-L-T	Name	Wins	W-L-T
Paul "Bear" Bryant	12	(12-8)	Woody Hayes	5	(5-5)
Bobby Dodd	6	(6-1)	Terry Donahue#	4	(4-0)
Bud Wilkinson	6	(6-2)	Johnny Majors#	4	(4-0)
Barry Switzer	6	(6-3)	Wally Butts	4	(4-1)
Joe Paterno#	6	(6-4)	Frank Thomas	4	(4-2)
John Vaught	6	(6-4)	Jess Neely	4	(4-2)
Darrell Royal	6	(6-6)	Charlie McClendon	4	(4-2)
Howard Jones	5	(5-0)	Bob Devaney	4	(4-3)
Don James#	5	(5-1)	Dan Devine	4	(4-3)
John McKay	5	(5-3)	Tom Osborne#	4	(4-7)

Active in 1992.

HIGHEST WINNING PERCENTAGE, HEAD-COACHING IN TRADITIONAL BIG FOUR BOWL GAMES

(Minimum three wins and over .500 percentage)

Name	Record	@Pct.	Name	Record	@Pct.
Howard Jones	5-0	1.000	Charlie McClendon	4-2	.667
Johnny Majors#	4-0	1.000	Jess Neely	4-2	.667
Terry Donahue#	4-0	1.000	Frank Thomas	4-2	.667
John Robinson	3-0	1.000	John McKay	5-3	.625
Dennis Erickson#	3-0	1.000	Paul "Bear" Bryant	12-8	.600
Chuck Fairbanks	3-0	1.000	Joe Paterno#	6-4	.600
Bobby Dodd	6-1	.857	John Vaught	6-4	.600
Don James#	5-1	.833	Ara Parseghian	3-2	.600
Wally Butts	4-1	.800	Bill Alexander	3-2	.600
Bud Wilkinson	6-2	.750	Bob Devaney	4-3	.571
Jackie Sherrill#	3-1	.750	Dan Devine	4-3	.571
Barry Switzer	6-3	.667			

@ Ties computed as half won, half lost.   # Active in 1992.

In the bowl section of this book is a detailed list of the leaders in most consecutive seasons with bowl-game victories. Bowden's seventh straight last season (over Texas A&M in the Cotton Bowl) tied the record set by Donahue. Bryant and Dobbs each won six in six seasons. It might be fun, though, to find those coaches who made all six of the above lists, plus the list of national championships won or shared in the 20th century. It would be a short list.

Only three men, all current coaches, have taken four different colleges to major bowls—Lou Holtz, Earle Bruce and Bill Mallory. Just seven, including current coaches Ken Hatfield, Johnny Majors, Jackie Sherrill and Larry Smith, have taken three different colleges, and 13 current coaches are among the 55 who have taken two differnt teams (# active in 1992):

UCLA's Terry Donahue is one of only six coaches with perfect records in the traditional "Big Four" bowl games–Rose, Sugar, Cotton and Orange. Donahue's Bruins are undefeated in three trips to the Rose Bowl and one Cotton Bowl appearance.

COACHES WHO HAVE TAKEN FOUR DIFFERENT COLLEGES TO MAJOR BOWL GAMES

Name	First	Second	Third	Fourth
Lou Holtz#	William & Mary	North Caro. St.	Arkansas	Notre Dame
Earle Bruce#	Tampa	Iowa St.	Ohio St.	Colorado St.
Bill Mallory#	Miami (Ohio)	Colorado	Northern Ill.	Indiana

COACHES WHO HAVE TAKEN THREE DIFFERENT COLLEGES TO MAJOR BOWL GAMES

Name	First	Second	Third
Paul "Bear" Bryant	Kentucky	Texas A&M	Alabama
Jim Carlen	West Va.	Texas Tech	South Caro.
Jerry Claiborne	Virginia Tech	Maryland	Kentucky
Ken Hatfield#	Air Force	Arkansas	Clemson
Johnny Majors#	Iowa St.	Pittsburgh	Tennessee
Jackie Sherrill#	Pittsburgh	Texas A&M	Mississippi St.
Larry Smith#	Tulane	Arizona	Southern Cal
Bowden Wyatt	Wyoming	Arkansas	Tennessee

COACHES WHO HAVE TAKEN TWO DIFFERENT COLLEGES TO MAJOR BOWL GAMES

Name	First	Second
Fred Akers	Wyoming	Texas
John Barnhill	Tennessee	Arkansas
Emory Bellard...................................	Texas A&M	Mississippi St.
Hugo Bezdek	Oregon	Penn St.
Dana Bible	Texas A&M	Texas

Name	First	Second
Bobby Bowden#	West Va.	Florida St.
Len Casanova	Santa Clara	Oregon
Bobby Collins	Southern Miss.	Southern Methodist
John Cooper#	Arizona St.	Ohio St.
Lee Corso	Louisville	Indiana
Dick Crum	Miami (Ohio)	North Caro.
Bill Curry#	Georgia Tech	Alabama
Bob Devaney	Wyoming	Nebraska
Dan Devine	Missouri	Notre Dame
Doug Dickey	Tennessee	Florida
Paul Dietzel	Louisiana St.	South Caro.
Bill Dooley#	North Caro.	Virginia Tech
Pat Dye#	East Caro.	Auburn
Pete Elliott	California	Illinois
Jack Elway	San Jose St.	Stanford
Dennis Erickson#	Washington St.	Miami (Fla.)
Bob Folwell	Pennsylvania	Navy
Hayden Fry#	Southern Methodist	Iowa
Vince Gibson	Louisville	Tulane
Sid Gillman	Miami (Ohio)	Cincinnati
Wayne Hardin	Navy	Temple
Woody Hayes	Miami (Ohio)	Ohio St.
Bob Higgins	West Va. Wesleyan	Penn St.
Don James#	Kent	Washington
Jimmy Johnson	Oklahoma St.	Miami (Fla.)
Frank Kimbrough	Hardin-Simmons	West Tex. St.
Jimmy Kitts	Rice	Virginia Tech
John Mackovic#	Wake Forest	Illinois
Jess Neely	Clemson	Rice
Homer Norton	Centenary	Texas A&M
Charley Pell	Clemson	Florida
Jimmy Phelan	Washington	St. Mary's (Cal.)
John Pont	Miami (Ohio)	Indiana
Tommy Prothro	Oregon St.	UCLA
John Ralston	Utah St.	Stanford
Pepper Rodgers	Kansas	Georgia Tech
Bobby Ross	Maryland	Georgia Tech
George Sauer	Kansas	Baylor
Howard Schnellenberger#	Miami (Fla.)	Louisville
Steve Sloan	Vanderbilt	Texas Tech
Steve Spurrier#	Duke	Florida
Gene Stallings#	Texas A&M	Alabama
Denny Stolz	Bowling Green	San Diego St.
Jim Tatum	Oklahoma	Maryland
Wallace Wade	Alabama	Duke
Glenn "Pop" Warner	Stanford	Temple
George Welsh#	Navy	Virginia
Bob Woodruff	Baylor	Florida
Warren Woodson	Hardin-Simmons	New Mexico St.
Jim Young	Purdue	Army

Active in 1992.

Great bowl coaching matchups

We define a great bowl coaching matchup as one in which each coach had won at least 100 games going into the bowl and each had a career winning percentage of at least .700. There have been only 29 such games in bowl history.

The first and the one with possibly the most dramatic ending came in the Rose Bowl, January 2, 1939, when Wallace Wade's undefeated, untied and—believe it or not—unscored upon Duke team was beaten by Howard Jones' Southern California team, 7-3. The winning play was a 21-yard touchdown pass with 40 seconds to go from fourth-string quarterback Doyle Nave to second-string end Al Kueger. It is one of the all-time classics.

Only one of the great 29 coaching matchups found both coaches above the career 80-percent level and 100 wins. That came in the January 1, 1986, Orange Bowl when Barry Switzer and Oklahoma defeated Joe Paterno and Penn State, 25-10, to win the 1985 national title. Paterno's team went in undefeated and untied, while Switzer's was 10-1, with only a major upset loss to Kansas. Penn State was the 13th team to enter these special 29 matchups with a perfect record and the ninth to lose. Only Paul "Bear" Bryant (nine) head-coached in more of these 29 than Paterno (seven); next are Bobby Bowden and Ara Parseghian, five each.

Switzer was the eighth coach in this special 29 to emerge with a national championship. The others were Brigham Young's LaVell Edwards (1984 season), Paterno (1982), Bryant (1978), Southern California's John McKay (1974), Parseghian (1973), Nebraska's Bob Devaney (1971) and Texas' Darrell Royal (1969; remember, most of the games have January dates the following years). Most of the teams in these matchups had a logical shot for at least a share of the national title. Here are all 29, ranked by combined winning percentage:

Pct.	Comb. Record	Coach	Record Entering Bowl	Teams-Records	Score
.818	(312-67-6)	Barry Switzer	125-24-4 .830	Oklahoma (10-1)	25
	Orange 1-1-86	Joe Paterno#	187-43-2 .810	Penn St. (11-0)	10
.791	(406-101-17)	Paul "Bear" Bryant	283-77-16 .774	Alabama (10-1)	14
	Sugar 1-1-79	Joe Paterno#	123-24-1 .834	Penn St. (11-0)	7
.791	(275-72-2)	Joe Paterno#	111-24-1 .820	Penn St. (10-1)	42
	Fiesta 12-25-77	Frank Kush	164-48-1 .772	Arizona St. (9-2)	30
.787	(322-84-9)	"Bo" Schembechler	195-55-7 .772	Michigan (9-1-1)	27
	Fiesta 1-1-86	Tom Osborne#	127-29-2 .810	Nebraska (9-2)	23
.785	(299-72-27)	Howard Jones	190-60-19 .742	Southern Cal (7-0-2)	14
	Rose 1-1-40	Bob Neyland	109-12-8 .876	Tennessee (10-0)	0
.772	(384-112-4)	Paul "Bear" Bryant	219-57-3 .790	Penn St. (7-3-1)	50
	Holiday 12-29-89	LaVell Edwards#	165-55-1 .749	Brigham Young (10-2)	39
.772	(268-73-17)	Paul "Bear" Bryant	131-47-13 .720	Alabama (9-1)	17
	Orange 1-1-63	Bud Wilkinson	137-26-4 .832	Oklahoma (8-2)	0
.768	(503-143-25)	Paul "Bear" Bryant	272-76-16 .769	Alabama (10-1)	35
	Sugar 1-1-78	Woody Hayes	231-67-9 .767	Ohio St. (9-2)	6
.768	(336-94-22)	Bob Devaney	126-28-6 .806	Nebraska (12-0)	38
	Orange 1-1-72	Paul "Bear" Bryant	210-66-16 .747	Alabama (11-0)	6
.768	(312-92-7)	Joe Paterno#	161-34-1 .824	Penn St. (10-1)	27
	Sugar 1-1-83	Vince Dooley	151-58-6 .716	Georgia (11-0)	23
.766	(303-90-7)	LaVell Edwards#	117-37-1 .758	Brigham Young (12-0)	24
	Holiday 12-21-84	"Bo" Schembechler	186-53-6 .771	Michigan (8-2)	17
.766	(236-69-9)	Dan Devine	135-47-8 .732	Notre Dame (8-3)	20
	Gator 12-27-76	Joe Paterno#	101-22-1 .819	Penn St. (7-4)	9
.765	(361-109-5)	Bobby Bowden#	193-72-3 .726	Florida St. (9-2)	41
	Fiesta 1-1-90	Tom Osborne#	168-37-2 .816	Nebraska (10-1)	17
.762	(433-133-6)	Bobby Bowden#	204-74-3 .731	Florida St. (9-2)	24
	Block'er 12-28-90	Joe Paterno#	229-59-3 .792	Penn St. (9-2)	17
.762	(304-87-23)	Howard Jones	182-60-17 .736	Southern Cal (8-2)	7
	Rose 1-2-39	Wallace Wade	122-27-6 .806	Duke (9-0)	3
.760	(284-85-13)	Bob Devaney	135-30-7 .805	Nebraska (8-2-1)	40
	Orange 1-1-73	Ara Parseghian	149-55-6 .724	Notre Dame (8-2)	6
.760	(277-80-22)	Paul "Bear" Bryant	140-49-13 .725	Alabama (8-2)	12
	Sugar 1-1-64	John Vaught	137-31-9 .799	Mississippi (7-0-2)	7
.758	(320-97-16)	John McKay	118-36-8 .753	Southern Cal (9-1-1)	18
	Rose 1-1-75	Woody Hayes	202-61-8 .760	Ohio St. (10-0-1)	17
.755	(320-102-5)	Bobby Bowden#	173-69-3 .712	Florida St. (10-1)	31
	Fiesta 1-1-88	Tom Osborne#	147-33-2 .813	Nebraska (10-1)	28
.755	(372-114-20)	Darrell Royal	152-46-4 .762	Texas (9-1)	17
	Cotton 1-1-73	Paul "Bear" Bryant	220-68-16 .750	Alabama (10-1)	13
.752	(291-88-23)	Dan Devine	104-33-8 .745	Missouri (7-3)	35
	Gator 12-28-68	Paul "Bear" Bryant	187-55-15 .757	Alabama (8-2)	10
.752	(411-128-22)	Ara Parseghian	169-58-6 .738	Notre Dame (9-2)	13
	Orange 1-1-75	Paul "Bear" Bryant	242-70-16 .762	Alabama (11-0)	11
.752	(300-94-15)	Woody Hayes	191-60-8 .753	Ohio St. (9-0-1)	42
	Rose 1-1-74	John McKay	109-34-7 .750	Southern Cal (9-1-1)	21
.747	(277-89-14)	John Vaught	177-54-12 .753	Mississippi (7-3)	27
	Sugar 1-1-70	Frank Broyles	100-35-2 .737	Arkansas (9-1)	22
.747	(390-125-22)	Ara Parseghian	159-56-6 .733	Notre Dame (10-0)	24
	Sugar 12-31-73	Paul "Bear" Bryant	231-69-16 .756	Alabama (11-0)	23
.737	(267-92-10)	Ara Parseghian	132-51-6 .714	Notre Dame (9-1)	24
	Cotton 1-1-71	Darrell Royal	135-41-4 .761	Texas (10-0)	11
.726	(247-90-10)	Darrell Royal	124-41-4 .746	Texas (9-1)	21
	Cotton 1-1-70	Ara Parseghian	123-49-6 .708	Notre Dame (10-0)	17
.726	(309-115-6)	Bobby Bowden#	184-70-3 .722	Florida St. (10-1)	13
	Sugar 1-2-89	Pat Dye#	125-45-3 .731	Auburn (10-1)	7
.712	(315-125-8)	Vince Dooley	168-64-7 .718	Georgia (7-4)	17
	Fla. Cit. 12-22-84	Bobby Bowden#	147-61-1 .706	Fla. State (7-3-1)	17

Active in 1992.

In terms of total combined victories, the awesome 503 by Bryant and Woody Hayes in the January 1, 1978, Sugar Bowl leads the list, followed by 433 for Paterno and Bowden in the December 28, 1990, Blockbuster Bowl; 411 for Bryant-Parseghian in the January 1, 1975, Orange, and 406 for Bryant and Paterno in the January 1, 1979, Sugar. The Sugar Bowl had seven of the special 29, the Orange five, Rose and Fiesta four each, Cotton three, Gator and Holiday two each, and Blockbuster and Florida Citrus one each.

Other great ones

There were five matchups in bowl history in which both coaches were above .800 in career winning percentage, or one was close to .900 and the other was over .700, but one or both came in with fewer than 100 but more than 50 career wins. Heading that list is the Bud Wilkinson vs. Jim Tatum matchup of two perfect-record teams in the January 2, 1956, Orange Bowl, one of three Orange matchups on the list.

Pct.	Comb. Record	Coach	Record Entering Bowl	Teams-Records	Score
.846	(169-27-9)	Bud Wilkinson	83-8-3 .899	Oklahoma (10-0)	20
	Orange 1-2-56	Jim Tatum	86-19-6 .802	Maryland (10-0)	6
.837	(116-21-4)	Barry Switzer	61-6-2 .899	Oklahoma (10-1)	31
	Orange 1-1-79	Tom Osborne#	55-15-2 .778	Nebraska (9-2)	24
.825	(209-43-3)	Joe Paterno#	150-33-1 .818	Penn St. (9-2)	26
	Fiesta 1-1-82	John Robinson	59-10-2 .845	Southern Cal (9-2)	10
.806	(198-43-12)	Bud Wilkinson	103-9-3 .909	Oklahoma (9-1)	48
	Orange 1-1-58	Bill Murray	95-34-9 .721	Duke (6-2-2)	21
.771	(275-75-19)	Knute Rockne	57-4-3 .914	Notre Dame (9-0)	27
	Rose 1-1-25	"Pop" Warner	218-71-16 .741	Stanford (7-0-1)	10

Active in 1992.

That was Rockne's only bowl trip, as mentioned. He had two more national title teams before his death in 1931. There were many more close-to-.900 vs. over-.700 (or both over .800) matchups in bowl history. Using a minimum of at least 25 career wins by each, here are the top four:

Pct.	Comb. Record	Coach	Record Entering Bowl	Teams-Records	Score
.870	(78-10-4)	Cecil Coleman	25-4-0 .862	Fresno St. (9-0)	36
	Mercy 11-23-61	Doyt Perry	53-6-4 .873	Bowling Green (8-1)	6
.826	(137-26-7)	Barry Switzer	31-1-1 .955	Oklahoma (10-1)	14
	Orange 1-1-76	"Bo" Schembechler	106-25-6 .796	Michigan (8-1-2)	6
.810	(83-18-4)	Paul "Bear" Bryant	45-15-3 .738	Kentucky (10-1)	13
	Sugar 1-1-51	Bud Wilkinson	38-3-1 .917	Oklahoma (10-0)	7
.809	(166-37-6)	John Robinson	30-6-0 .833	Southern Cal (11-1)	17
	Rose 1-1-79	"Bo" Schembechler	136-31-6 .803	Michigan (10-1)	10

The four games above involved three national championships: Robinson's team and Switzer's were voted No. 1 after they won, while Wilkinson's team had been voted No. 1 before the bowl loss to Bryant and Kentucky.

As for the top team matchups, without regard to career coaching records, all of those are in this book in the bowl section. There were 13 matchups of two undefeated, untied teams in bowls, the last one Notre Dame over West Virginia in the January 2, 1989, Fiesta. There were 14 more bowl games in which both teams were undefeated but at least one team had been tied one or more times. The last one was Fresno State over Bowling Green in the December 14, 1985, California.

Notre Dame leads alma mater list

Knute Rockne and his boys, you might call them, put Notre Dame on top with 15 graduates who head-coached a team to a major bowl game. Tennessee, where West Point graduate Bob Neyland was a big influence, is next with 13, followed by Alabama at 10.

Miami (Ohio), known as the Cradle of Coaches, is tied for fifth with seven behind Pittsburgh's eight. Other colleges with seven graduates who took teams to major bowls are Michigan, Minnesota and Oklahoma. Those that produced six bowl coaches are Army, Bowling Green, Georgia Tech, Nebraska, Ohio State, Stanford and Texas Christian.

Rockne, the all-time major-college leader with an .881 winning percentage, head-coached Notre Dame from 1918 through 1930 before a plane crash in Kansas in March 1931 ended his life. Before 1918, he was an assistant coach, instructor, and a player who helped popularize the forward pass. An end, he teamed with passer Gus Dorais in a shocking 1913 upset over Army, as mentioned. Notre Dame's no-bowl policy, which did not end until 1970, kept all but one of his teams (the 1924 Four Horsemen) out of bowls. A 1931 Notre Dame graduate, Frank Leahy, second in all-time percentage at .864, could not take his Notre Dame teams to bowls but twice took Boston College.

The other 13 Notre Dame graduates, all associated with Rockne as teammates or under him as players in his years as assistant or head coach, are Charlie Bachman ('17), Arthur "Dutch" Bergman ('20), Jim Crowley ('25), Dorais ('14), Joe Gavin ('31), Edward "Slip" Madigan ('20), Jack Meagher ('17), Jimmy Phelan ('19), Lawrence "Buck" Shaw ('22), Joe Sheeketski ('33), John "Clipper" Smith ('29), Maurice "Little Clipper" Smith ('21) and Frank Thomas ('23). Their teams and bowl records are in the bowl section.

1992 NCAA FOOTBALL

Current Tennessee head coach Johnny Majors is among the 13 Tennessee graduates, and Ray Perkins of Arkansas State and Jackie Sherrill of Mississippi State are among the 10 Alabama graduates, headed by Paul "Bear" Bryant. Alabama's graduates took their teams to 71 bowl games. Tennessee's are second with 57. Rockne, Majors, Bryant and Perkins are among 81 coaches (just under 21 percent of the total) who took their alma mater to a major bowl.

Rockne, Neyland and Bryant are just three of the national championship coaches of the 20th century who had immense influence on the development of bowl coaches. By checking the various lists, including the alma mater list that follows, you can find endless coach-player connections (and there are many more involving head coach-assistant we do not have).

The state of Ohio could be called the Cradle of Bowl Coaches. It has produced 37 coaches from 15 colleges who have head-coached teams to a leading 146 bowl games. The state of Texas is second with 32 bowl coaches (also from 15 colleges; 108 bowl games). Next on the state list are California, 29; Pennsylvania, 24; Indiana, 20; Tennessee, 19; Michigan, 17; Alabama, 17 (their graduates went to 129 bowl games—second place); New York, 12, and Oklahoma, 12.

History's 390 bowl coaches came from 171 colleges located in 45 states and the District of Columbia. Sixty-six are head-coaching in Division I-A (107 teams). Here is the list by alma maters with year graduated, if available:

Alabama
Bill Battle '63
*Paul "Bear" Bryant '36
Danny Ford '70
Frank Howard '31
Millard "Dixie" Howell '35
Bud Moore '61
Charley Pell '64
*Ray Perkins '67#
Jackie Sherrill '66#
Steve Sloan '66
Ala.-Birmingham
Jack Crowe '70#
Albion
H.F. "Pop" McKale '10
Alma
Bob Devaney '39
Denny Stolz '55
Arizona St.
Cecil Coleman '50
Al Onofrio '43
Jim Stangeland '48
Arkansas
Fred Akers '60
*Ken Hatfield '65#
Jimmy Johnson '65
Pat Jones '69#
Barry Switzer '60
Army
Bobby Dobbs '46
Hank Foldberg '48
Lawrence McC. "Biff" Jones '17
Bob Neyland '16
Ralph Sasse '10
Bill Yeoman '50
Auburn
John Bridgers '47
Vince Dooley '54
Ralph "Shug" Jordan '32
Austin
Henry Frnka '26
Dell Morgan '25
Bates
Harold "Red" Drew '16
Baylor
*Sam Boyd '38
Wesley Bradshaw '23
Hayden Fry '51#
Warren Woodson '24
Birmingham-Southern
Homer Norton '16

Black Hills St.
Lloyd Eaton '40
Paul Roach '52
Boston College
Ed Doherty '44
Bowling Green
Dave McClain '60
Jack Mollenkopf '31
Don Nehlen '58#
*Doyt Perry '32
Larry Smith '62#
Jim Young '57
Brown
Bob Margarita '44
Joe Paterno '50#
*Ed Robinson '96
Wallace Wade '17
California
Edwin "Babe" Horrell '26
*Clarence "Nibs" Price '14
John Ralston '54
Mike White '58
UC Davis
Paul Hackett '47#
Cal Poly Pomona
Al Luginbill '67#
Cal Poly SLO
Ted Tollner '62
Carleton
Leonard "Stub" Allison '17
Carlisle
Bill "Lone Star" Dietz '12
Carson-Newman
Dana Bible '12
Bernie Moore '17
Centenary
Clyde Lee '32
Centre
Matty Bell '20
Chicago
Hugo Bezdek '06
H.O. "Fritz" Crisler '22
Cincinnati
Joe Morrison '59
*Ray Nolting '36
Clarion
Tony Mason '50
Colgate
John "Ox" Da Grosa '26

Colorado
Sam Winningham '50
Connecticut
Gary Blackney '67#
Cornell
Glenn "Pop" Warner '95
Dartmouth
Bernard A. Hoban '12
Clarence "Doc" Spears '16
Dayton
Gerry Faust '58#
Denison
Woody Hayes '35
DePauw
Dick Tomey '61#
Drake
Ike Armstrong '23
*Warren Gaer '35
Duke
John Gutekunst '66
*Bill Murray '31
Tommy Prothro '42
East Stroudsburg
Bill Lewis '63#
Florida
*Doug Dickey '54
*Steve Spurrier '67#
Charley Tate '42
Florida St.
Mack Brown '74#
Lee Corso '57
Vince Gibson '55
Frank. & Marsh.
Edward "Hook" Mylin
Fresno St.
Darryl Rogers '57
Georgetown
*Jack Hagerty '26
Georgia
Pat Dye '62#
*Ray Goff '78#
Georgia Tech
*Bill Alexander '12
Frank Broyles '47
Jim Carlen '55
*Bill Curry '65#
*Bill Fulcher '57
*Pepper Rodgers '55

Gust. Adolphus
Al Molde '66#
Hardin-Simmons
*Frank Kimbrough '26
Harvard
*Robert Fisher '12
Haskell
Tom Stidham '27
Hastings
Tom Osborne '59#
Heidelberg
Jack Murphy '54
Henderson St.
Eugene "Bo" Sherman '30
Houston
Jim Dickey '56
Howard Payne
Gwinn Henry '17
Idaho
Bill Schutte '33
Illinois
*Ray Eliot '32
Vee Green '24
Tom McCann '24
Bernard "Bunnie" Oakes '24
Merle Schlosser '50
Indiana
Jim Trimble '42
Iowa
Dennis Green '71
Denny Myers '30
Iowa St.
John Cooper '62#
Bill Weeks '51
Ithaca
Tom Nugent '36
Kalamazoo
Miles Casteel '25
Jim Harkema '64#
Kansas
*Don Fambrough '48
Kansas St.
Ralph Graham '34
Bob Stull '68#
Kent
Lou Holtz '59#
Kentucky
*Jerry Claiborne '50
Charlie McClendon '50
Howard Schnellenberger '56#
Ky. Wesleyan
Rube McCray '30
Lafayette
Fielding "Hurry Up" Yost '97
Lebanon Valley
Carl Snavely '25
Louisiana Col.
Ernie Duplechin '55
Louisiana St.
Larry Jones '54
*Jerry Stovall '63
*Gaynell Tinsley '37
Louisiana Tech
*Joe Raymond Peace '68#
Marquette
Art Guepe '37

McMurry
Grant Teaff '56#
McNeese St.
R.C. Slocum '67#
Mercer
Wally Butts '28
Miami (Fla.)
Mike Archer '75
Fran Curci '60
Don James '54#
George MacIntyre '61
Miami (Ohio)
Bill Arnsparger '50
Paul Dietzel '48
*Bill Mallory '57#
Ara Parseghian '49
*John Pont '52
Glenn "Bo" Schembechler '51
Paul Schudel '66#

Michigan
Herb Deromedi '60#
*Chalmers "Bump" Elliott '48
Pete Elliott '49
Forest Evashevski '41
Frank Maloney '62
*Bennie Oosterbaan '28
Ivy Williamson '33
Michigan St.
Chuck Fairbanks '55
Sonny Grandelius '51
Frank Kush '53
*George Perles '60#
Minnesota
Bernie Bierman '16
Milt Bruhn '35
Ted Cox '26
Clarence "Biggie" Munn '32
Clark Shaughnessy '14
*Cal Stoll '50
Bud Wilkinson '37

Minn.-Duluth
Dan Devine '48
Mississippi
*Billy Brewer '61#
Paul Davis '47
*Billy Kinard '36
Bob Tyler '58
Thad "Pie" Vann '28
Mississippi St.
Bobby Collins '55
Bill Dooley '56#
Billy Murphy '47
Jim Pittman '50
Missouri
Bill Driver '09
*Don Faurot '48
Bill McCartney '62#
*Chancey Simpson '25
Mo. Wesleyan
Randolph R.M. Medley '21
Montclair St.
Jack Bicknell '60
Montana
Clyde Carpenter '32
Montana St.
Dennis Erickson '70#
Morehead St.
Mike Gottfried '66

Mount Union
Dick Crum '57
Frank Lauterbur '49
Navy
Ben Martin '46
*George Welsh '56#
Nebraska
Willie Barnes
Larry Naviaux '59
Warren Powers '63
George Sauer '34
Lon Stiner '27
Fred Thomsen '25
Nevada
Alvin "Pix" Pierson '22
New Mexico St.
Jerry Hines '26
North Caro.
George Barclay '35
Bud Carson '52
Frank Jones '48
Jim Tatum '35
Eddie Teague '44
North Dak.
Dewey King '50
Gene Murphy '62#
Northwestern
Al Kawal '35
*Bob Voigts '39
Notre Dame
Charlie Bachman '17
Arthur "Dutch" Bergman '20
Jim Crowley '25
Gus Dorais '14
Joe Gavin '31
Frank Leahy '31
Edward "Slip" Madigan '20
Jack Meagher '17
Jimmy Phelan '19
*Knute Rockne '14
Lawrence "Buck" Shaw '22
Joe Sheeketski '33
John "Little Clipper" Smith '29
Maurice "Clipper" Smith '21
Frank Thomas '23
Oberlin
Elmer "Gus" Henderson '12
Occidental
*Roy Dennis '33
Ohio
*Bill Hess '47
Art Lewis '36
Chuck Stobart '59#
Ohio Northern
Bill Peterson '46
Ohio St.
*Earle Bruce '53#
*Wes Fesler '32
Sid Gillman '34
Gomer Jones '36
Gary Moeller '63#
Bo Rein '58
Oklahoma
Eddie Crowder '55
*Gary Gibbs '75#
Joe Kerbel '47
Jack Mitchell '49
Jim Owens '50
Darrell Royal '50
Cliff Speegle '41

Oklahoma St.
Gary Darnell '71
F. A. Dry '53
*Jim Lookabaugh '25

Oregon
*Charles "Shy" Huntington
John Robinson '58
Terry Shea '68
Bruce Snyder '62#

Oregon St.
Rich Brooks '63#
Clyde "Cac" Hubbard '21
John McKay '50
Dallas Ward '27

Pacific (Cal.)
Wayne Hardin '50

Pennsylvania
*Bob Folwell '08
Lou Little '20
Andy Smith '06

Penn St.
Earle Edwards '31
Galen Hall '62
*Bob Higgins '20
Paul Pasqualoni '72#

Peru St.
Darrell Mudra '52

Pittsburgh
*Foge Fazio '60
Bill Glassford '37
Andy Gustafson '26
Jack Harding '26
Joe Kern '28
*John Michelosen '38
*Jock Sutherland '16
Claude "Tiny" Thornhill '17

Portland
Jim Sweeney '51#

Princeton
Homer Smith '54

Purdue
Ron Meyer '63
Ralph "Pest" Welch '30

Redlands
Harvey Hyde '62

Rutgers
*Frank Burns '49
Lou Tepper '67#

St. Mary's (Cal.)
Eddie Erdelatz '36
Ernie Jorge '36

Samford
Bobby Bowden '63#
D. C. "Peahead" Walker '22

San Francisco
Larry Siemering '35

San Jose St.
*Claude Gilbert '59
Dick Vermeil '58
Bill Walsh '54#

Santa Clara
*Len Casanova '27

South Caro.
*Johnny McMillian '41
Dick Sheridan '64#

Southern Cal
*Jeff Cravath '27
*Jess Hill '30

Southern Methodist
Jimmy Kitts

Southern Miss.
*Jeff Bower '76#
Maxie Lambright '49

Southwest Tex. St.
Emory Bellard '49

Southwestern (Kan.)
Leon Burtnett '65

Southwestern (Tex.)
Pete Cawthon '20

Southwestern La.
Frank Tritico '34

Springfield
Dick MacPherson '58

Stanford
Dud DeGroot '24
*Charlie Fickert '98
Bill Hubbard '30
Ted Shipkey '27
*Chuck Taylor '43
Ed Walker '27

Stephen F. Austin
Spike Dykes '59#

Syracuse
Duffy Daugherty '40
Joe Krivak '57
Lynn "Pappy" Waldorf '25

Tennessee
Bill Barnes '41
*John Barnhill '28
Phil Dickens '32
Bobby Dodd '31
Beattie Feathers '34
Ray Graves '43
*Johnny Majors '57#
Allyn McKeen '29
Charley Moran '98
Murray Warmath '35
DeWitt Weaver '37
Bob Woodruff '39
*Bowden Wyatt '39

Tennessee Tech
*Wilburn Tucker '43

Texas
J. T. King '38
*David McWilliams '64
*Ed Price '33
Mack Saxon

Texas A&M
Curley Hallman '70#
Jack Pardee '57
*Gene Stallings '57#
Jim Stanley '59
*Harry Stiteler '31

Texas Christian
Sammy Baugh '37
Mike Brumbelow '50
Blair Cherry '24
*Abe Martin '32
*Leo "Dutch" Meyer '22
John Vaught '33

Texas Tech
J. O. "Buddy" Brothers '31
Tom Wilson '66

Toledo
*Dan Simrell '65

Transylvania
Frank Camp '30
Jack "Cactus Jack" Curtice '30

Tufts
Frank Murray '08

Tulane
*Lowell "Red" Dawson '30
Jack Doland '50
*Bennie Ellender '48

Tulsa
*Glenn Dobbs '43
*Dave Rader '80#

UCLA
*Terry Donahue '67#
*Bert LaBrucherie '29
Ray Nagel '50

Utah
Bob Davis '30
E. L. "Dick" Romney '17

Utah St.
LaVell Edwards '52#

Valparaiso
Jim Wacker '60#

Vanderbilt
Ray Morrison '12
Jess Neely '23
Henry "Red" Sanders '27

Villanova
*Alex Bell '38
*Jordan Olivar '38

Va. Military
Bobby Ross '59

Wake Forest
*John Mackovic '65#

Washington
*Enoch Bagshaw '08
Don Coryell '50

Washington St.
Jack Elway '53
Red Reese '25

Wash. & Lee
Eddie Cameron '24

Wash. & Jeff.
Jim Aiken '22

West Tex. St.
Odus Mitchell '25

West Va.
*Gene Corum '49
*Marshall "Little Sleepy" Glenn '31
Ben Schwartzwalder '35

West Va. Wesleyan
Earle "Greasy" Neale '14

Western Md.
Charles "Rip" Engle '30

Western Mich.
Robert Theder '63

William & Mary
Jim Hickey '42

Wisconsin
John Wilce '10

Wittenberg
Bill Edwards '31
Bob Wagner '69#

Wofford
Fisher DeBerry '60#

Wyoming
Jim Walden '60#

Xavier (Ohio)
*Ed Kluska '40
Tim Rose '62

Preview/Review

Yale
Howard Jones '08
No College
Orin "Babe" Hollingbery
* Took his alma mater to a bowl.

Active in 1992.

1991 CONFERENCE STANDINGS

Chris Hughley rushed for 1,326 yards in 1991 to help Tulsa to a 9-2 record after a 3-8 campaign in 1990. Only nine major-college teams have experienced bigger single-season turnarounds. The Golden Hurricane had the fourth-best winning percentage among Division I-A independ-

1991 CONFERENCE STANDINGS

DIVISION I-A

ATLANTIC COAST CONFERENCE

Team	CONFERENCE					FULL SEASON				
	W	L	T	Pts.	OP	W	L	T	Pts.	OP
Clemson	6	0	1	180	90	9	1	1	304	148
North Caro. St..	5	2	0	163	150	9	2	0	270	185
Georgia Tech ..	5	2	0	165	91	7	5	0	265	197
Virginia	4	2	1	185	90	8	2	1	313	119
North Caro. ..	3	4	0	131	118	7	4	0	282	199
Maryland	2	5	0	87	163	2	9	0	138	302
Duke	1	6	0	106	207	4	6	1	231	280
Wake Forest ...	1	6	0	86	194	3	8	0	195	300

Bowl Games (1-3-0): Clemson (lost to California, 37-13, in Florida Citrus); North Caro. St. (lost to East Caro., 37-34, in Peach); Georgia Tech (beat Stanford, 18-17, in Aloha); Virginia (lost to Oklahoma, 48-14, in Gator)

BIG EAST CONFERENCE

Team	CONFERENCE					FULL SEASON				
	W	L	T	Pts.	OP	W	L	T	Pts.	OP
Miami (Fla.) ...	0	0	0	0	0	11	0	0	364	100
Syracuse	0	0	0	0	0	9	2	0	297	183
Pittsburgh	0	0	0	0	0	6	5	0	244	241
Rutgers	0	0	0	0	0	6	5	0	217	217
West Va........	0	0	0	0	0	6	5	0	187	224
Virginia Tech ..	0	0	0	0	0	5	6	0	275	229
Boston College.	0	0	0	0	0	4	7	0	247	246
Temple	0	0	0	0	0	2	9	0	145	290

Note: *Because teams play an unequal number of games, the league standings are not kept. The team with the highest ranking in the USA Today/CNN Coaches' Poll was declared champion.*

Bowl Games (2-0-0): Miami (Fla.) (beat Nebraska, 22-0, in Orange); Syracuse (beat Ohio St., 24-17, in Hall of Fame)

BIG EIGHT CONFERENCE

Team	CONFERENCE					FULL SEASON				
	W	L	T	Pts.	OP	W	L	T	Pts.	OP
Nebraska†	6	0	1	285	121	9	1	1	454	208
Colorado†	6	0	1	181	93	8	2	1	304	150
Oklahoma	5	2	0	206	93	8	3	0	335	143
Kansas St.	4	3	0	159	121	7	4	0	263	226
Kansas	3	4	0	187	175	6	5	0	313	244
Iowa St.	1	5	1	71	190	3	7	1	157	266
Missouri	1	6	0	121	289	3	7	1	223	403
Oklahoma St. ..	0	6	1	72	200	0	10	1	106	307

† *Nebraska and Colorado tied, 19-19, on November 2 and shared the title.*

Bowl Games (1-2-0): Nebraska (lost to Miami, Fla., 22-0, in Orange); Colorado (lost to Alabama, 30-25, in Blockbuster); Oklahoma (beat Virginia, 48-14, in Gator)

BIG TEN CONFERENCE

Team	CONFERENCE					FULL SEASON				
	W	L	T	Pts.	OP	W	L	T	Pts.	OP
Michigan......	8	0	0	316	91	10	1	0	406	169
Iowa	7	1	0	190	139	10	1	0	330	166
Ohio St.	5	3	0	166	115	8	3	0	260	163
Indiana	5	3	0	214	138	6	4	1	281	224
Illinois	4	4	0	153	118	6	5	0	261	182
Purdue	3	5	0	132	182	4	7	0	219	272
Michigan St. ...	3	5	0	142	189	3	8	0	162	272
Wisconsin.....	2	6	0	113	169	5	6	0	172	194
Northwestern ..	2	6	0	94	234	3	8	0	160	306
Minnesota	1	7	0	65	210	2	9	0	104	302

Bowl Games (1-3-1): Michigan (lost to Washington, 34-14, in Rose); Iowa (tied Brigham Young, 13-13, in Holiday); Ohio St. (lost to Syracuse, 24-17, in Hall of Fame); Indiana (beat Baylor, 24-0, in Copper); Illinois (lost to UCLA, 6-3, in John Hancock)

BIG WEST CONFERENCE

Team	CONFERENCE					FULL SEASON				
	W	L	T	Pts.	OP	W	L	T	Pts.	OP
Fresno St.†	6	1	0	279	133	10	1	0	486	207
San Jose St. ...	6	1	0	276	137	6	4	1	372	298
Utah St.	5	2	0	153	101	5	6	0	219	265
Pacific (Cal.) ...	4	3	0	253	239	5	7	0	435	481
Nev.-Las Vegas.	2	5	0	153	239	4	7	0	220	360
Long Beach St.*	2	5	0	159	215	2	9	0	207	412
New Mexico St.	2	5	0	173	228	2	9	0	224	350
Cal St. Fullerton	1	6	0	97	251	2	9	0	138	376

† *Fresno St. beat San Jose St., 31-28, on November 23.* * *Long Beach St. dropped its football program effective with 1992 season.*

Bowl Games (0-1-0): Fresno St. (lost to Bowling Green, 28-21, in California)

MID-AMERICAN ATHLETIC CONFERENCE

Team	CONFERENCE					FULL SEASON				
	W	L	T	Pts.	OP	W	L	T	Pts.	OP
Bowling Green .	8	0	0	192	88	10	1	0	251	147
Central Mich. ..	3	1	4	127	101	6	1	4	205	157
Miami (Ohio) ..	4	3	1	145	94	6	4	1	214	140
Toledo	4	3	1	138	110	5	5	1	187	209
Ball St.	4	4	0	96	108	6	5	0	159	150
Western Mich. .	4	4	0	161	173	6	5	0	218	253
Eastern Mich. ..	3	4	1	121	145	3	7	1	144	232
Ohio	1	6	1	114	211	2	8	1	176	308
Kent	1	7	0	134	198	1	10	0	159	307

Bowl Games (1-0-0): Bowling Green (beat Fresno St., 28-21, in California)

PACIFIC-10 CONFERENCE

Team	CONFERENCE					FULL SEASON				
	W	L	T	Pts.	OP	W	L	T	Pts.	OP
Washington ...	8	0	0	321	77	11	0	0	461	101
California	6	2	0	237	164	9	2	0	406	226
Stanford	6	2	0	241	159	8	3	0	351	228
UCLA	6	2	0	237	122	8	3	0	317	187
Arizona St.	4	4	0	158	174	6	5	0	218	210
Arizona	3	5	0	180	266	4	7	0	248	361
Washington St.	3	5	0	191	260	4	7	0	280	340
Southern Cal ..	2	6	0	178	218	3	8	0	229	276
Oregon	1	7	0	112	205	3	8	0	186	248
Oregon St.	1	7	0	86	296	1	10	0	125	365

Bowl Games (3-1-0): Washington (beat Michigan, 34-14, in Rose); California (beat Clemson, 37-13, in Florida Citrus); Stanford (lost to Georgia Tech, 18-17, in Aloha); UCLA (beat Illinois, 6-3, in John Hancock)

SOUTHEASTERN CONFERENCE

Team	CONFERENCE					FULL SEASON				
	W	L	T	Pts.	OP	W	L	T	Pts.	OP
Florida	7	0	0	226	74	10	1	0	361	152
Alabama	6	1	0	128	101	10	1	0	294	118
Tennessee	5	2	0	190	136	9	2	0	335	221
Georgia	4	3	0	192	163	8	3	0	312	204
Mississippi St..	4	3	0	145	119	7	4	0	276	156
Louisiana St. ..	3	4	0	116	157	5	6	0	248	263
Vanderbilt	3	4	0	127	192	5	6	0	205	267
Auburn	2	5	0	128	170	5	6	0	233	214
Mississippi	1	6	0	148	189	5	6	0	242	223
Kentucky	0	7	0	113	212	3	8	0	190	268

Bowl Games (2-3-0): Florida (lost to Notre Dame, 39-28, in Sugar); Alabama (beat Colorado, 30-25, in Blockbuster); Tennessee (lost to Penn St., 42-17, in Fiesta); Georgia (beat Arkansas, 24-15, in Independence); Mississippi St. (lost to Air Force, 38-15, in Liberty)

SOUTHWEST ATHLETIC CONFERENCE

Team	CONFERENCE					FULL SEASON			
	W	L	T	Pts.	OP	W	L	T	Pts.	OP
Texas A&M	8	0	0	289	95	10	1	0	402	144
Baylor	5	3	0	192	138	8	3	0	282	180
Arkansas	5	3	0	131	117	6	5	0	160	179
Texas Tech . . .	5	3	0	244	215	6	5	0	315	272
Texas Christian.	4	4	0	173	223	7	4	0	279	267
Texas	4	4	0	169	111	5	6	0	195	145
Houston	3	5	0	260	250	4	7	0	353	344
Rice	2	6	0	148	233	4	7	0	239	287
Southern Meth. .	0	8	0	73	297	1	10	0	141	359

Bowl Games (0-3-0): Texas A&M (lost to Florida St., 10-2, in Cotton); Baylor (lost to Indiana, 24-0, in Copper); Arkansas (lost to Georgia, 24-15, in Independence)

WESTERN ATHLETIC CONFERENCE

Team	CONFERENCE					FULL SEASON			
	W	L	T	Pts.	OP	W	L	T	Pts.	OP
Brigham Young . .	7	0	1	324	194	8	3	1	420	308
San Diego St. . .	6	1	1	275	214	8	3	1	403	337
Air Force	6	2	0	210	183	9	3	0	344	248
Utah	4	4	0	203	222	7	5	0	276	277
Hawaii	3	5	0	218	231	4	7	1	335	388
Wyoming	2	5	1	242	295	4	6	1	305	357
UTEP	2	5	1	194	183	4	7	1	254	252
Colorado St. . . .	2	6	0	206	241	3	8	0	265	375
New Mexico . . .	2	6	0	177	286	3	9	0	240	473

Bowl Games (1-1-1): Brigham Young (tied Iowa, 13-13, in Holiday); San Diego St. (lost to Tulsa, 28-17, in Freedom); Air Force (beat Mississippi St., 38-15, in Liberty)

DIVISION I-A INDEPENDENTS

Team	FULL SEASON				SCORING	
	W	L	T	Pct.	For	Agst.
East Caro.	10	1	0	.909	372	243
Florida St.	10	2	0	.833	439	186
Penn St.	10	2	0	.833	432	167
Louisiana Tech . . .	8	1	2	.818	280	194
Tulsa	9	2	0	.818	305	208
Notre Dame	9	3	0	.750	426	261
Akron	5	6	0	.455	257	308
Memphis St.	5	6	0	.455	228	229
Army	4	7	0	.364	196	226
Cincinnati	4	7	0	.364	201	323
Southern Miss. . . .	4	7	0	.364	212	225
South Caro.	3	6	2	.364	250	268
Southwestern La. . .	2	8	1	.227	148	269
Louisville	2	9	0	.182	135	335
Northern Ill.	2	9	0	.182	143	364
Navy	1	10	0	.091	160	321
Tulane	1	10	0	.091	146	384

Bowl Games (5-0-0): East Caro. (beat North Caro. St., 37-34, in Peach); Florida St. (beat Texas A&M, 10-2, in Cotton); Penn St. (beat Tennessee, 42-17, in Fiesta); Tulsa (beat San Diego St., 28-17, in Freedom); Notre Dame (beat Florida, 39-28, in Sugar)

> Two Division I-A teams – Miami (Fla.) and Washington – finished the 1991 regular season with perfect records. Both were 11-0.

DIVISION I-AA

BIG SKY CONFERENCE

Team	CONFERENCE					FULL SEASON			
	W	L	T	Pts.	OP	W	L	T	Pts.	OP
Nevada*	8	0	0	329	177	11	0	0	496	198
Weber St.	6	2	0	369	314	8	3	0	495	383
Montana	6	2	0	222	183	7	4	0	274	241
Boise St.	4	4	0	234	162	7	4	0	355	197
Idaho	4	4	0	271	232	6	5	0	375	313
Eastern Wash. . .	4	4	0	246	286	5	6	0	301	364
Idaho St.	2	6	0	207	275	3	7	1	286	358
Northern Ariz. . .	1	7	0	193	328	3	8	0	294	404
Montana St.	1	7	0	127	241	2	9	0	197	300

* *Will move to Division I-A in 1992.*

Division I-AA Playoffs (1-2-0): Nevada (1-1, lost in quarterfinals to Youngstown St., 30-28); Weber St. (0-1, lost in first round to Northern Iowa, 38-21)

GATEWAY COLLEGIATE ATHLETIC CONFERENCE

Team	CONFERENCE					FULL SEASON			
	W	L	T	Pts.	OP	W	L	T	Pts.	OP
Northern Iowa .	5	1	0	150	90	10	1	0	366	158
Southern Ill. . . .	4	2	0	129	122	7	4	0	238	271
Western Ill.	4	2	0	108	99	7	3	1	255	167
SW Mo. St.	3	3	0	156	121	6	4	1	295	199
Indiana St.	2	4	0	89	174	5	6	0	229	242
Eastern Ill.	2	4	0	149	138	4	7	0	307	264
Illinois St.	1	5	0	77	114	5	6	0	218	176

Division I-AA Playoffs (1-2-0): Northern Iowa (1-1, lost in quarterfinals to Marshall, 41-13); Western Ill. (0-1, lost in first round to Marshall, 20-17, in overtime)

IVY GROUP

Team	CONFERENCE					FULL SEASON			
	W	L	T	Pts.	OP	W	L	T	Pts.	OP
Dartmouth	6	0	1	215	140	7	2	1	283	209
Princeton	5	2	0	172	126	8	2	0	253	171
Harvard	4	2	1	163	160	4	5	1	203	223
Yale	4	3	0	172	135	6	4	0	241	190
Cornell	4	3	0	139	124	5	5	0	181	218
Pennsylvania . .	2	5	0	113	143	2	8	0	142	236
Brown	1	6	0	163	246	1	9	0	227	372
Columbia	1	6	0	114	177	1	9	0	154	249

Ivy Group teams do not participate in postseason games.

MID-EASTERN ATHLETIC CONFERENCE

Team	CONFERENCE					FULL SEASON			
	W	L	T	Pts.	OP	W	L	T	Pts.	OP
No. Caro. A&T .	5	1	0	207	111	9	2	0	381	163
Delaware St. . . .	4	2	0	162	110	8	3	0	300	220
Beth.-Cookman .	4	2	0	162	146	5	5	0	264	256
South Caro. St. .	3	3	0	108	110	7	4	0	234	157
Florida A&M . . .	3	3	0	168	134	6	5	0	325	238
Howard	1	5	0	96	171	2	9	0	208	319
Morgan St.	1	5	0	73	194	1	10	0	128	425

Postseason Game (0-1-0): North Caro. A&T (lost to Alabama St., 36-13, in Alamo Heritage Bowl)

OHIO VALLEY CONFERENCE

Team	CONFERENCE					FULL SEASON			
	W	L	T	Pts.	OP	W	L	T	Pts.	OP
Eastern Ky. . . .	7	0	0	216	74	10	1	0	333	147
Middle Tenn. St.	6	1	0	218	47	8	3	0	312	151
Morehead St.† .	3	3	0	103	133	4	7	0	189	345
Austin Peay . . .	3	4	0	111	156	5	6	0	191	231
SE Mo. St.	3	4	0	126	220	3	8	0	213	374
Tennessee St.† .	2	4	0	119	154	3	8	0	206	286
Tennessee Tech .	2	5	0	161	130	2	9	0	221	244
Murray St.	1	6	0	67	207	3	8	0	162	313

† *Morehead St. and Tennessee St. did not meet in 1991.*

Division I-AA Playoffs (3-2-0): Eastern Ky. (2-1, lost in semifinals to Marshall, 14-7); Middle Tenn. St. (1-1, lost in quarterfinals to Eastern Ky., 23-13)

PATRIOT LEAGUE

Team	CONFERENCE					FULL SEASON			
	W	L	T	Pts.	OP	W	L	T	Pts.	OP
Holy Cross	5	0	0	185	84	11	0	0	372	174
Lehigh	3	2	0	172	103	9	2	0	363	235
Lafayette	3	2	0	133	138	6	5	0	277	312
Colgate	3	2	0	119	115	4	7	0	224	311
Bucknell	1	4	0	62	155	1	9	0	99	326
Fordham	0	5	0	59	135	2	8	0	149	242

Patriot League teams do not participate in postseason games.

SOUTHERN CONFERENCE

Team	CONFERENCE				FULL SEASON			
	W	L	T	Pts.	OP	W	L	T	Pts.	OP
Appalachian St.	6	1	0	156	97	8	3	0	212	188
Marshall	5	2	0	260	146	8	3	0	414	195
Citadel	5	2	0	156	120	7	4	0	238	183
Furman	4	3	0	228	160	7	4	0	363	217
Tenn.-Chatt.	4	3	0	216	190	7	4	0	305	293
Va. Military	2	5	0	137	243	4	7	0	243	373
Western Caro.	2	5	0	146	197	2	9	0	179	345
East Tenn. St.	0	7	0	114	260	1	10	0	183	396

Division I-AA Playoffs (3-2-0): Marshall (3-1, lost to Youngstown St. in championship game, 25-17); Appalachian St. (0-1, lost in first round to Eastern Ky., 14-3)

SOUTHLAND CONFERENCE

Team	CONFERENCE				FULL SEASON			
	W	L	T	Pts.	OP	W	L	T	Pts.	OP
McNeese St.†	4	1	2	120	78	6	3	2	176	134
Sam Hous. St.	5	2	0	122	89	8	2	1	222	145
Northeast La.	4	2	1	168	110	7	3	1	237	175
SW Tex. St.	4	3	0	150	89	7	4	0	307	179
N'western (La.)	4	3	0	124	84	6	5	0	192	169
Nicholls St.	2	5	0	102	118	4	7	0	157	189
North Texas	2	5	0	90	192	3	7	1	137	325
S. F. Austin	1	5	1	69	185	2	8	1	151	279

†*McNeese St. defeated Sam Houston St., 19-17, on November 16.*

Division I-AA Playoffs (0-2-0): Sam Houston St. (0-1, lost in first round to Middle Tenn. St., 20-19, in overtime); McNeese St. (0-1, lost in first round to Nevada, 22-16)

SOUTHWESTERN ATHLETIC CONFERENCE

Team	CONFERENCE				FULL SEASON			
	W	L	T	Pts.	OP	W	L	T	Pts.	OP
Alabama St.	6	0	1	279	104	10	0	1	453	170
Alcorn St.	4	2	1	206	139	7	2	1	357	190
Southern-B.R.	4	3	0	191	178	4	7	0	255	286
Mississippi Val.	3	3	1	176	159	3	7	1	307	182
Texas Southern	3	3	1	164	130	5	5	1	270	208
Grambling	3	4	0	232	221	5	6	0	330	338
Jackson St.	2	4	0	124	124	5	5	0	247	202
Prairie View	0	6	0	33	350	0	11	0	48	617

Postseason Game (1-0-0): Alabama St. (beat North Caro. A&T, 36-13, in Alamo Heritage Bowl)

YANKEE CONFERENCE

Team	CONFERENCE				FULL SEASON			
	W	L	T	Pts.	OP	W	L	T	Pts.	OP
Delaware	7	1	0	273	153	10	1	0	358	199
Villanova	7	1	0	308	102	10	1	0	397	132
New Hampshire	7	1	0	267	186	9	2	0	356	252
Rhode Island	3	5	0	155	249	6	5	0	266	330
Boston U.	3	5	0	177	209	4	7	0	232	292
Massachusetts	3	5	0	151	150	4	7	0	205	208
Connecticut	2	6	0	164	250	3	8	0	241	340
Maine	2	6	0	130	244	3	8	0	210	333
Richmond	2	6	0	134	216	2	9	0	210	350

Division I-AA Playoffs (0-3-0): Delaware (0-1, lost in first round to James Madison, 42-35, in double overtime); Villanova (0-1, lost in first round to Youngstown St., 17-16); New Hampshire (0-1, lost in first round to Samford, 29-13)

DIVISION I-AA INDEPENDENTS

Team	FULL SEASON				SCORING	
	W	L	T	Pct.	For	Agst.
Samford	10	1	0	.909	332	154
James Madison	8	3	0	.727	351	284
Youngstown St.	8	3	0	.727	331	195
Ga. Southern	7	4	0	.636	257	160
Central Fla.	6	5	0	.545	278	230
William & Mary	5	6	0	.455	343	320
Liberty	4	7	0	.364	233	248
Northeastern	4	7	0	.364	239	277
Western Ky.	3	8	0	.273	235	301
Arkansas St.*	1	10	0	.091	189	361
Towson St.	1	10	0	.091	212	378

* *Will move to Division I-A in 1992.*

Division I-AA Playoffs (7-2-0): James Madison (1-1, lost in quarterfinals to Samford, 24-21); Samford (2-1, lost in semifinals to Youngstown St., 10-0); Youngstown St. (4-0, beat Marshall in championship game, 25-17)

> **Nevada (11-0) and Holy Cross (11-0) were the only Division I-AA teams with perfect regular-season records in 1991. Alabama State had no losses but tied one of its 11 games.**

DIVISION II

CENTRAL INTERCOLLEGIATE ATHLETIC ASSN.

Team	CONFERENCE				FULL SEASON			
	W	L	T	Pts.	OP	W	L	T	Pts.	OP
Winston-Salem	6	0	0	242	105	9	2	0	370	226
Virginia Union	5	1	0	235	74	8	3	0	404	220
Eliz. City St.	5	1	0	155	98	7	2	0	211	133
Norfolk St.	5	1	0	148	103	7	3	0	233	210
Livingstone	3	3	0	119	151	5	5	0	197	228
N. C. Central	3	3	0	133	187	4	6	0	195	324
Johnson Smith	2	4	0	118	132	2	7	1	140	291
Bowie St.	1	5	0	63	152	4	5	0	174	222
Virginia St.	1	5	0	93	160	3	7	0	173	229
Hampton	1	5	0	114	178	2	9	0	228	359
Fayetteville St.	0	6	0	44	159	0	10	0	72	317

Division II Playoffs (0-2-0): Virginia Union (0-1, lost in first round to Indiana, Pa., 56-7); Winston-Salem (0-1, lost in first round to Jacksonville St., 49-24)

GULF SOUTH CONFERENCE

Team	CONFERENCE				FULL SEASON			
	W	L	T	Pts.	OP	W	L	T	Pts.	OP
Jacksonville St.	6	0	0	179	46	9	0	0	316	78
Mississippi Col.	4	1	1	148	75	6	3	1	254	149
Valdosta St.	4	1	1	139	122	6	3	1	219	167
Livingston	2	4	0	78	129	6	5	0	164	217
West Ga.	2	4	0	151	210	6	5	0	363	301
Delta St.	1	5	0	101	121	3	7	0	195	209
North Ala.	1	5	0	79	172	3	7	0	160	251

Division II Playoffs (4-2-0): Jacksonville St. (3-1, lost in championship game to Pittsburg St., 23-6); Mississippi Col. (1-1, lost in quarterfinals to Jacksonville St., 35-7)

LONE STAR CONFERENCE

Team	CONFERENCE				FULL SEASON			
	W	L	T	Pts.	OP	W	L	T	Pts.	OP
Eastern N. Mex.	5	1	0	123	110	7	3	1	246	180
East Tex. St.	4	1	1	204	109	7	3	1	351	184
Angelo St.	4	1	1	183	88	6	3	1	285	134
Texas A&I	4	2	0	148	85	7	3	0	245	134
Cameron	1	5	0	62	150	3	7	0	172	217
Central Okla.	1	5	0	87	182	3	7	0	148	256
Abilene Christ.	1	5	0	59	142	1	9	0	73	259

Division II Playoffs (1-1-0): East Tex. St. (1-1, lost in quarterfinals to Pittsburg St., 38-28)

MIDWEST INTERCOLLEGIATE FOOTBALL CONFERENCE

Team	CONFERENCE				FULL SEASON			
	W	L	T	Pts.	OP	W	L	T	Pts.	OP
Butler	9	1	0	243	71	9	1	0	243	71
Grand Valley St.	8	2	0	277	113	9	2	0	298	130
Ashland	8	2	0	239	100	9	2	0	290	110
Ferris St.	5	5	0	161	185	5	6	0	174	218
Hillsdale	5	5	0	203	144	6	5	0	203	150
Saginaw Valley	5	5	0	181	163	6	5	0	191	170
Wayne St. (Mich.)	4	6	0	177	271	4	6	0	177	271
St. Joseph's (Ind.)	4	6	0	143	211	4	6	0	143	211
Northern Mich.	3	6	1	130	245	3	6	1	130	245
Indianapolis	2	8	0	129	211	2	8	0	129	211
Valparaiso	1	8	1	104	273	1	8	1	104	273

Division II Playoffs (0-2-0): Butler (0-1, lost in first round to Pittsburg St., 26-16); Grand Valley St. (0-1, lost in first round to East Tex. St., 36-15)

MISSOURI INTERCOLLEGIATE ATHLETIC ASSN.

Team	CONFERENCE W	L	T	Pts.	OP	FULL SEASON W	L	T	Pts.	OP
Pittsburg St.	8	0	1	343	128	9	1	1	415	155
Mo. Southern St.	7	2	0	315	157	8	3	0	387	229
SW Baptist	5	4	0	232	224	7	4	0	300	252
Central Mo. St. ..	5	4	0	182	225	5	6	0	195	288
NE Mo. St.	5	4	0	276	286	5	6	0	318	361
Emporia St.* ...	4	5	0	280	323	5	5	0	308	350
N'west Mo. St. .	4	5	0	219	233	5	6	0	292	300
Missouri-Rolla .	3	5	1	151	179	4	6	1	192	221
Mo. Western St.	2	7	0	228	321	4	7	0	309	368
Washburn	1	8	0	84	234	1	10	0	94	304

* Emporia St. not eligible for championship but games counted in standings.

Division II Playoffs (4-0-0): Pittsburg St. (4-0, beat Jacksonville St. in championship game, 23-6)

ROCKY MOUNTAIN ATHLETIC CONFERENCE

Team	CONFERENCE W	L	T	Pts.	OP	FULL SEASON W	L	T	Pts.	OP
Western St.† ...	6	0	0	280	138	9	1	0	461	227
Fort Hays St. ...	4	2	0	143	140	8	3	0	312	217
Colorado Mines	3	3	0	195	199	6	4	0	317	299
Chadron St. ...	3	3	0	165	141	5	5	1	343	289
Mesa St.	3	3	0	124	142	3	7	0	169	296
Adams St......	2	4	0	100	121	6	4	0	230	183
Fort Lewis	0	6	0	122	248	2	8	0	203	356
N.M. Highlands*	—	—	—	—	—	1	9	0	142	401

† Western St. (1-1, lost in semifinals of NAIA Division I playoffs to Central St., Ohio, 20-13). * N.M. Highlands not eligible for championship.

NORTH CENTRAL INTERCOLLEGIATE ATHLETIC CONFERENCE

Team	CONFERENCE W	L	T	Pts.	OP	FULL SEASON W	L	T	Pts.	OP
North Dak. St. ...	7	1	0	269	101	7	2	0	286	122
Northern Colo. .	6	2	0	204	109	8	2	0	271	128
North Dak.	6	2	0	207	117	7	2	0	228	131
Mankato St.	5	3	0	153	112	7	3	0	216	154
South Dak. St. .	5	3	0	127	175	7	3	0	162	195
St. Cloud St. ...	5	3	0	175	138	6	3	0	192	152
Neb.-Omaha ...	4	4	0	117	134	6	4	0	185	148
Morningside ...	1	7	0	127	214	2	8	0	147	237
South Dak.	1	7	0	97	242	1	8	0	104	261
Augustana (S.D.)	0	8	0	113	247	0	10	0	145	320

Division II Playoffs (1-3-0): North Dak. St. (0-1, lost in first round to Mankato St., 27-7); Northern Colo. (0-1, lost in first round to Portland St., 28-24); Mankato St. (1-1, lost in quarterfinals to Portland St., 37-27)

SOUTH ATLANTIC CONFERENCE

Team	CONFERENCE W	L	T	Pts.	OP	FULL SEASON W	L	T	Pts.	OP
Carson-Newman† ...	7	0	0	299	114	10	0	0	439	193
Catawba	5	2	0	159	116	7	3	0	229	158
Lenoir-Rhyne .	4	3	0	163	169	6	5	0	240	238
Wingate	3	4	0	179	234	5	5	0	244	277
Elon	3	4	0	174	139	6	5	0	295	181
Gardner-Webb .	3	4	0	140	162	6	5	0	234	186
Presbyterian..	3	4	0	126	188	4	7	0	199	332
Mars Hill......	1	6	0	142	260	3	7	0	229	299

† Carson-Newman (0-1, lost in quarterfinals of NAIA Division I playoffs to Western St., 38-21). Record does not count three forfeited games in regular seson.

NORTHERN CALIFORNIA ATHLETIC CONFERENCE

Team	CONFERENCE W	L	T	Pts.	OP	FULL SEASON W	L	T	Pts.	OP
Sonoma St.....	5	0	0	142	65	9	2	0	265	175
UC Davis	3	2	0	116	86	7	3	0	238	215
Humboldt St.†*	2	3	0	85	125	5	5	0	188	217
Cal St. Chico† .	2	3	0	105	129	4	6	0	243	301
San Fran. St.† .	2	3	0	122	126	3	7	0	257	288
Cal St. Hayward	1	4	0	67	106	3	7	0	186	254

† Humboldt St., Cal St. Chico and San Fran. St. all tied for third place with no advantage given to head-to-head competition. * Does not include 35-30 Humboldt St. victory over British Columbia.

SOUTHERN INTERCOLLEGIATE ATHLETIC CONFERENCE

Team	CONFERENCE W	L	T	Pts.	OP	FULL SEASON W	L	T	Pts.	OP
Fort Valley St.†	5	2	0	216	154	7	3	0	250	184
Clark Atlanta† .	5	2	0	178	124	6	3	1	255	196
Tuskegee†	5	2	0	287	131	6	4	0	378	234
Morehouse† ...	5	2	0	136	109	6	4	0	213	178
Alabama A&M† .	5	2	0	142	161	5	6	0	196	333
Savannah St...	4	3	0	289	170	7	4	0	425	253
Albany St. (Ga.)	2	6	0	127	221	3	7	0	178	268
Morris Brown..	1	5	0	76	158	4	6	0	164	272
Miles	0	8	0	64	287	1	10	0	135	392

† All five teams declared cochampions.

PENNSYLVANIA STATE ATHLETIC CONFERENCE

Team	CONFERENCE W	L	T	Pts.	OP	FULL SEASON W	L	T	Pts.	OP
Western Division										
Indiana (Pa.) ...	6	0	0	193	58	10	0	0	369	79
Shippensburg..	4	2	0	167	108	9	2	0	346	246
Slippery Rock .	4	2	0	123	108	6	4	0	216	195
Edinboro	3	3	0	114	103	7	4	0	228	199
Clarion	2	4	0	150	153	5	5	0	277	263
Lock Haven ...	2	4	0	70	165	4	7	0	120	305
Calif. (Pa.).....	0	6	0	34	156	1	9	0	100	288
Eastern Division										
E. Stroudsburg .	5	0	1	140	78	8	2	1	286	226
Kutztown	4	2	0	239	124	6	4	0	360	233
Bloomsburg ..	4	2	0	162	154	5	5	0	250	222
West Chester ..	3	3	0	109	130	6	5	0	220	218
Millersville	2	3	1	154	152	4	5	1	224	287
Mansfield	2	4	0	137	163	5	5	1	268	266
Cheyney	0	6	0	80	220	0	11	0	118	475

Division II Playoffs (3-3-0): Indiana (Pa.) (2-1, lost in semifinals to Jacksonville St., 27-20); East Stroudsburg (0-1, lost in first round to Shippensburg, 34-33); Shippensburg (1-1, lost in quarterfinals to Indiana, Pa., 52-7)

WESTERN FOOTBALL CONFERENCE

Team	CONFERENCE W	L	T	Pts.	OP	FULL SEASON W	L	T	Pts.	OP
Portland St. ...	5	0	0	181	115	9	2	0	385	255
Southern Utah .	4	1	0	178	132	7	3	1	372	279
Cal St. Sac.....	3	2	0	147	121	8	2	0	367	224
Cal Poly SLO ..	2	3	0	119	135	4	6	0	271	272
Cal St. N'ridge .	1	4	0	114	204	3	7	0	175	287
Santa Clara ...	0	5	0	118	150	5	6	0	309	281

Division II Playoffs (2-1-0): Portland St. (2-1, lost in semifinals to Pittsburg St., 53-21)

DIVISION II INDEPENDENTS

Team	W	L	T	Pct.	For	Agst.
Wofford	9	2	0	.818	347	243
Shepherd†	8	2	0	.800	271	172
Springfield	7	3	0	.700	271	192
South. Conn. St.	6	3	0	.667	302	277
Michigan Tech	6	4	0	.600	343	157
Minn.-Duluth	6	4	0	.600	258	192
UC Santa Barb.	5	3	0	.625	217	221
St. Mary's (Cal.)	6	5	0	.545	361	195
Tenn.-Martin*	5	6	0	.455	280	330
Troy St.*	5	6	0	.455	230	200
American Int'l	4	5	1	.450	222	198
West Liberty St.	4	5	1	.450	170	222
Neb.-Kearney	4	6	1	.409	192	272
New Haven	3	7	0	.300	320	378
Wayne St. (Neb.)	3	7	0	.300	238	324
Bemidji St.	2	7	0	.222	152	308
Kentucky St.	2	9	0	.182	103	330
Central Conn. St.	1	8	1	.150	206	325
Winona St.	1	9	0	.100	141	355
Newberry	1	10	0	.091	133	335

†Shepherd (0-1, lost in quarterfinals of NAIA Division I playoffs to Central St., Ohio, 34-22). * Will move to Division I-AA in 1992.

Division II Playoffs [0-1-0]: Wofford (0-1, lost in first round to Mississippi Col., 28-15)

> Carson-Newman (10-0), Indiana (Pa.) (10-0) and Jacksonville State (9-0) were the only Division II teams with perfect regular-season records in 1991.

DIVISION III

ASSOCIATION OF MIDEAST COLLEGES

Team	W	L	T	Pts.	OP	W	L	T	Pts.	OP
Thomas More	3	0	0	93	40	10	0	0	293	129
Defiance	2	1	0	76	27	8	2	0	268	120
Wilmington (Ohio)	1	2	0	45	68	1	9	0	136	312
Bluffton	0	3	0	15	94	1	8	0	113	281

ATLANTIC COLLEGIATE FOOTBALL CONFERENCE

Team	W	L	T	Pts.	OP	W	L	T	Pts.	OP
St. Francis (Pa.)	3	0	0	63	28	6	3	0	140	107
Marist	2	1	0	81	40	6	4	0	239	143
Gallaudet	1	2	0	42	83	1	7	1	119	263
St. John Fisher	0	3	0	13	48	0	9	0	41	269

CENTENNIAL FOOTBALL CONFERENCE

Team	W	L	T	Pts.	OP	W	L	T	Pts.	OP
Dickinson	7	0	0	218	79	9	0	0	278	114
Frank. & Marsh.	5	2	0	136	99	6	4	0	191	144
Western Md.	4	3	0	158	108	5	5	0	211	151
Johns Hopkins	3	4	0	145	116	5	4	1	227	155
Ursinus	3	4	0	85	125	5	5	0	114	154
Muhlenberg	3	4	0	90	139	3	7	0	128	246
Gettysburg	2	5	0	60	127	2	7	0	73	211
Swarthmore	1	6	0	95	194	2	7	0	124	238

Division III Playoffs [0-1-0]: Dickinson (0-1, lost in first round of South Region to Susquehanna, 21-20)

COLLEGE CONFERENCE OF ILLINOIS AND WISCONSIN

Team	W	L	T	Pts.	OP	W	L	T	Pts.	OP
Augustana (Ill.)	7	1	0	275	89	8	1	0	316	97
Ill. Wesleyan†	6	1	1	295	140	7	1	1	335	176
Wheaton (Ill.)†	6	1	1	284	117	7	1	1	311	130
Millikin	5	3	0	213	105	6	3	0	236	119
Carroll (Wis.)@	4	4	0	141	155	5	4	0	177	155
North Central	3	5	0	109	217	4	5	0	151	252
Elmhurst	2	6	0	155	297	2	7	0	171	340
Carthage	2	6	0	142	208	3	6	0	183	243
North Park	0	8	0	47	333	0	9	0	61	368

† Ill. Wesleyan and Wheaton (Ill.) tied, 24-24, September 21. @ Carroll (Wis.) will move to Midwest Collegiate Athletic Conference, North Division, in 1992.

EASTERN COLLEGIATE FOOTBALL CONFERENCE

Team	W	L	T	Pts.	OP	W	L	T	Pts.	OP
Stonehill	5	0	0	120	37	5	4	0	148	140
Bentley	4	1	0	106	39	5	4	0	168	134
Siena	2	3	0	60	67	3	5	0	87	145
West. New Eng.	2	3	0	62	86	3	5	0	81	130
Assumption	1	4	0	67	125	1	8	0	91	249
MIT	1	4	0	70	131	1	7	0	83	215

IOWA INTERCOLLEGIATE ATHLETIC CONFERENCE

Team	W	L	T	Pts.	OP	W	L	T	Pts.	OP
Simpson	8	0	0	261	73	10	0	0	326	87
Central (Iowa)	7	1	0	234	74	8	1	0	260	99
Loras	5	3	0	186	139	7	3	0	241	157
Wartburg	5	3	0	254	132	6	4	0	305	166
Luther	5	3	0	170	126	5	4	0	191	148
Upper Iowa	2	6	0	131	229	2	8	0	173	302
William Penn	2	6	0	160	342	2	8	0	166	373
Dubuque	1	7	0	76	255	1	8	0	88	278
Buena Vista	1	7	0	121	223	1	9	0	142	295

Division III Playoffs [0-1-0]: Simpson (0-1, lost in first round of West Region to Wis.-La Crosse, 28-13)

LIBERTY FOOTBALL CONFERENCE

Team	W	L	T	Pts.	OP	W	L	T	Pts.	OP
St. John's (N.Y.)	4	1	0	186	120	6	4	0	280	210
Iona	3	1	1	150	100	7	2	1	283	171
LIU-C.W. Post	3	2	0	129	95	4	6	0	201	260
Stony Brook	2	3	0	71	118	4	5	0	161	151
Merch. Marine	1	3	1	92	114	2	6	1	159	181
Pace	1	4	0	85	166	2	8	0	179	302

MICHIGAN INTERCOLLEGIATE ATHLETIC ASSN.

	CONFERENCE				FULL SEASON			
Team	W	L	T	Pts.	OP	W	L	T	Pts.	OP
Albion†	4	0	1	133	62	8	0	1	258	99
Olivet†	4	0	1	91	62	7	1	1	196	152
Hope	2	3	0	63	83	5	4	0	143	142
Kalamazoo	2	3	0	63	40	5	4	0	162	76
Adrian	1	4	0	40	112	4	5	0	104	142
Alma	1	4	0	46	77	4	5	0	127	172

† Cochampions Albion and Olivet tied, 14-14, on October 26.

Division III Playoffs (0-1-0): Albion (0-1, lost in first round of North Region to Allegheny, 24-21, in overtime)

MIDDLE ATLANTIC STATES COLLEGIATE ATHLETIC CONFERENCE

	CONFERENCE				FULL SEASON			
Team	W	L	T	Pts.	OP	W	L	T	Pts.	OP
Lycoming	8	0	0	263	79	9	0	0	300	79
Susquehanna	7	1	0	206	120	9	1	0	267	139
Moravian	5	3	0	162	127	7	3	0	197	160
Lebanon Valley	5	3	0	190	166	6	3	1	224	198
Albright	3	5	0	142	194	5	5	0	177	227
Delaware Valley	3	5	0	151	204	3	7	0	195	293
Juniata	3	5	0	102	152	3	7	0	124	191
Widener	2	6	0	95	172	3	7	0	122	185
Wilkes	0	8	0	89	186	1	9	0	116	268

Division III Playoffs (3-2-0): Lycoming (1-1, lost in quarterfinals to Susquehanna, 31-24); Susquehanna (2-1, lost in semifinals to Ithaca, 49-13)

MIDWEST COLLEGIATE ATHLETIC CONFERENCE

	CONFERENCE				FULL SEASON			
Team	W	L	T	Pts.	OP	W	L	T	Pts.	OP
North Division										
Beloit†	4	0	0	93	39	9	1	0	222	99
Ripon	2	2	0	53	74	5	4	0	128	160
St. Norbert	2	2	0	59	47	4	5	0	114	117
Lawrence	2	2	0	70	61	3	6	0	139	219
Lake Forest	0	4	0	56	110	2	7	0	135	234
South Division										
Coe†	5	0	0	233	61	9	1	0	359	157
Cornell College	4	1	0	124	103	7	2	0	205	136
Monmouth (Ill.)	3	2	0	121	80	4	5	0	202	183
Knox	2	3	0	87	121	3	6	0	146	240
Grinnell	1	4	0	108	208	2	7	0	162	326
Illinois Col.	0	5	0	23	123	2	7	0	81	189

† Coe defeated Beloit, 26-10, in championship playoff.

Division III Playoffs (0-1-0): Coe (0-1, lost in first round of West Region to St. John's, Minn., 75-2)

MINNESOTA INTERCOLLEGIATE ATHLETIC CONFERENCE#

	CONFERENCE				FULL SEASON			
Team	W	L	T	Pts.	OP	W	L	T	Pts.	OP
St. John's (Minn.)	8	0	0	362	87	9	0	0	391	87
St. Olaf	6	2	0	222	175	7	2	0	244	196
Bethel (Minn.)	5	3	0	178	141	6	3	0	213	147
St. Thomas (Minn.)	5	3	0	185	170	6	3	0	200	176
Gust. Adolphus	5	3	0	226	154	5	4	0	251	180
Hamline	4	4	0	183	163	5	4	0	213	170
Carleton	3	5	0	237	209	3	6	0	259	239
Concordia-M'head	3	5	0	179	141	3	6	0	195	162
Augsburg	1	7	0	67	301	2	7	0	91	315
Macalester	0	8	0	21	319	1	8	0	41	333

The November 2 games were not played because of snowstorms. Those games were: St. John's (Minn.) at Bethel (Minn.), Augsburg at Gust. Adolphus, Concordia-M'head at St. Thomas (Minn.), Hamline at Macalester, Carleton at St. Olaf.

Division III Playoffs (2-1-0): St. John's (Minn.) (2-1, lost in semifinals to Dayton, 19-7)

NEW ENGLAND FOOTBALL CONFERENCE

	CONFERENCE				FULL SEASON			
Team	W	L	T	Pts.	OP	W	L	T	Pts.	OP
Northern Division										
Mass.-Lowell	5	0	0	113	28	10	0	0	228	54
Maine Maritime	3	2	0	87	58	5	3	0	182	140
Plymouth St.\$	3	2	0	127	34	6	2	1	236	81
Mass.-Boston	2	3	0	68	96	4	5	0	122	145
Nichols	2	3	0	53	74	4	5	0	133	113
Curry	0	5	0	18	176	0	9	0	34	304

\$ Does not include 21-6 loss to Cortland St. in ECAC playoff game.

	CONFERENCE				FULL SEASON			
Team	W	L	T	Pts.	OP	W	L	T	Pts.	OP
Southern Division										
Bri'water (Mass.)	6	0	0	169	89	8	2	0	246	133
Mass.-Dartmouth	4	2	0	196	115	6	3	0	231	156
Mass. Maritime	4	2	0	179	145	6	3	0	260	222
Westfield St.†	3	3	0	161	168	4	6	0	236	270
Framingham St.	1	5	0	149	171	2	6	0	176	221
Worcester St.†	1	5	0	80	202	2	8	0	119	302
Fitchburg St.	1	5	0	47	91	2	7	0	74	154

† Does not include Westfield St. forfeit to Worcester St. for ineligible player.

Division III Playoffs (0-1-0): Mass.-Lowell (0-1, lost in first round of East Region to Union, N. Y., 55-16)

NEW ENGLAND SMALL COLLEGE ATHLETIC CONFERENCE

	CONFERENCE				FULL SEASON			
Team	W	L	T	Pts.	OP	W	L	T	Pts.	OP
Williams	7	0	0	222	81	7	1	0	222	81
Trinity (Conn.)	6	0	1	257	118	6	1	1	271	139
Tufts	5	3	0	147	151	5	3	0	147	151
Colby	5	3	0	200	137	5	3	0	200	137
Hamilton	4	2	1	168	116	4	3	1	185	167
Bowdoin	4	3	0	155	161	4	4	0	169	209
Wesleyan	2	5	0	95	167	3	5	0	111	180
Middlebury	2	5	0	133	134	2	6	0	158	167
Amherst	0	6	1	80	236	0	7	1	87	269
Bates	0	7	1	95	251	0	7	1	95	251

NEW JERSEY ATHLETIC CONFERENCE

	CONFERENCE				FULL SEASON			
Team	W	L	T	Pts.	OP	W	L	T	Pts.	OP
Glassboro St.	5	1	0	141	84	9	1	0	267	139
Wm. Paterson	4	1	1	160	106	8	1	1	296	144
Ramapo†	4	2	0	151	91	6	3	0	208	128
Trenton St.	3	2	1	104	121	5	3	1	184	159
Montclair St.	3	3	0	128	93	5	5	0	197	157
Kean	1	5	0	109	114	3	7	0	160	189
Jersey City St.	0	6	0	46	230	0	9	1	68	307

† Does not include 35-21 loss to Wesley in ECAC Southwest Bowl.

Division III Playoffs (0-1-0): Glassboro St. (0-1, lost in first round of East Region to Ithaca, 31-10)

NORTH COAST ATHLETIC CONFERENCE#

	CONFERENCE				FULL SEASON			
Team	W	L	T	Pts.	OP	W	L	T	Pts.	OP
Allegheny	7	0	0	298	72	10	0	0	375	94
Case Reserve	5	1	0	167	81	7	3	0	212	174
Ohio Wesleyan	6	2	0	250	120	8	2	0	309	135
Wittenberg	5	3	0	196	77	5	5	0	229	157
Kenyon	3	4	0	141	168	5	5	0	214	218
Denison	3	4	0	142	154	3	7	0	174	215
Wooster	3	5	0	142	227	3	7	0	164	306
Earlham	1	6	0	90	283	1	8	0	128	369
Oberlin	0	8	0	21	265	0	9	0	21	293

North Coast Athletic Conference teams do not all play the same number of conference games. Standings are determined by winning percentage (there are no designated conference games).

Division III Playoffs (1-1-0): Allegheny (1-1, lost in quarterfinals to Dayton, 28-25, in overtime)

OHIO ATHLETIC CONFERENCE

Team	CONFERENCE					FULL SEASON				
	W	L	T	Pts.	OP	W	L	T	Pts.	OP
Baldwin-Wallace	9	0	0	275	102	10	0	0	320	118
Mount Union ..	7	1	1	266	130	8	1	1	290	138
Muskingum ...	6	3	0	228	193	7	3	0	238	196
John Carroll ...	5	2	2	213	114	5	3	2	220	138
Capital	5	3	1	191	136	6	3	1	232	150
Heidelberg	4	4	1	274	168	4	5	1	274	182
Ohio Northern..	3	5	1	172	139	3	6	1	198	168
Otterbein	2	7	0	137	229	2	8	0	155	249
Hiram	1	8	0	97	367	1	9	0	97	405
Marietta	0	9	0	88	363	0	10	0	95	384

Division III Playoffs (0-1-0): Baldwin-Wallace (0-1, lost in first round of North Region to Dayton, 27-10)

OLD DOMINION ATHLETIC CONFERENCE

Team	CONFERENCE					FULL SEASON				
	W	L	T	Pts.	OP	W	L	T	Pts.	OP
Guilford†	4	1	0	97	70	8	2	0	225	140
Emory & Henry	4	1	0	88	27	8	2	0	216	90
Hampden-Sydney	3	2	0	111	103	7	2	1	348	234
Randolph-Macon......	3	2	0	119	74	4	6	0	202	192
Bri'water (Va.) .	1	4	0	65	108	2	8	0	133	282
Wash. & Lee ...	0	5	0	21	119	1	9	0	103	226

† Guilford defeated Emory & Henry, 17-16, on October 26.

PRESIDENTS' ATHLETIC CONFERENCE

Team	CONFERENCE					FULL SEASON				
	W	L	T	Pts.	OP	W	L	T	Pts.	OP
Wash. & Jeff..	4	0	0	138	34	8	1	0	297	61
Waynesburg...	3	1	0	109	66	6	3	0	199	121
Thiel	2	2	0	55	105	5	4	0	159	176
Grove City.....	1	3	0	53	100	3	6	0	180	261
Beth. (W. Va.) .	0	4	0	69	119	2	7	0	189	300

Division III Playoffs (0-1-0): Wash. & Jeff. (0-1, lost in first round of South Region to Lycoming, 18-16)

SOUTHERN CALIFORNIA INTERCOLLEGIATE ATHLETIC CONFERENCE

Team	CONFERENCE					FULL SEASON				
	W	L	T	Pts.	OP	W	L	T	Pts.	OP
Redlands......	5	0	0	205	51	7	2	0	317	89
La Verne	4	1	0	143	83	7	2	0	263	146
Occidental.....	3	2	0	109	109	5	4	0	164	179
Whittier......	2	3	0	97	105	3	6	0	135	181
Pomona-Pitzer .	1	4	0	64	166	2	6	0	136	254
Claremont-M-S.	0	5	0	42	146	0	9	0	62	241

SOUTHERN COLLEGIATE ATHLETIC CONFERENCE

Team	CONFERENCE					FULL SEASON				
	W	L	T	Pts.	OP	W	L	T	Pts.	OP
Millsaps	3	1	0	68	30	7	2	0	167	67
Sewanee†	2	1	1	55	43	7	1	1	180	101
Rhodes†	2	1	1	60	39	6	2	1	203	96
Centre	2	2	0	40	44	5	5	0	138	160
Trinity (Tex.) ..	0	4	0	27	94	1	9	0	91	194

† Sewanee and Rhodes tied, 14-14, on October 12.

UNIVERSITY ATHLETIC ASSOCIATION

Team	CONFERENCE					FULL SEASON				
	W	L	T	Pts.	OP	W	L	T	Pts.	OP
Carnegie Mellon	4	0	0	118	26	9	1	0	301	122
Rochester	3	1	0	72	41	7	3	0	159	118
Case Reserve ..	2	2	0	45	93	7	3	0	212	174
Wash. (Mo.) ...	1	3	0	67	65	6	4	0	193	160
Chicago.......	0	4	0	29	106	0	10	0	87	195

WISCONSIN STATE UNIVERSITY CONFERENCE

Team	CONFERENCE					FULL SEASON				
	W	L	T	Pts.	OP	W	L	T	Pts.	OP
Wis.-La Crosse.	7	1	0	217	110	9	1	0	290	131
Wis.-Stevens Pt.	6	2	0	199	99	6	3	1	216	121
Wis.-Whitewater..	6	2	0	169	90	6	4	0	213	147
Wis.-Platteville.	4	3	1	148	128	6	3	1	217	150
Wis.-Oshkosh ..	4	4	0	135	135	5	5	0	151	166
Wis.-Stout	3	5	0	123	192	5	5	0	179	211
Wis.-River Falls	2	5	1	146	169	4	5	1	185	191
Wis.-Superior ..	1	6	1	102	249	2	6	1	126	256
Wis.-Eau Claire	1	6	1	164	231	2	7	1	184	255

Division III Playoffs (1-1-0): Wis.-La Crosse (1-1, lost in quarterfinals to St. John's, Minn., 29-10)

DIVISION III INDEPENDENTS

Team	FULL SEASON				SCORING	
	W	L	T	Pct.	For	Agst.
Dayton	10	0	0	1.000	326	72
Eureka#	10	0	0	1.000	364	84
Union (N.Y.)	9	0	0	1.000	413	92
Ithaca	8	1	0	.889	313	93
Buffalo St.	8	2	0	.800	242	186
Hofstra	8	2	0	.800	380	224
Neb. Wesleyan# ..	8	2	0	.800	310	235
Wesley@	8	2	0	.800	348	168
Ferrum	7	2	0	.778	320	136
Worcester Tech .	7	2	0	.778	316	152
Wabash.........	7	2	0	.778	204	132
Alfred	7	3	0	.700	230	159
Cortland St.	7	3	0	.700	355	155
Frostburg St.	7	3	0	.700	307	166
Maryville (Tenn.) .	7	3	0	.700	206	135
San Diego	7	3	0	.700	287	170
Coast Guard	6	3	0	.667	201	174
MacMurray......	6	3	1	.650	203	244
Aurora	5	3	1	.611	184	135
DePauw	6	4	0	.600	208	154
Georgetown	6	4	0	.600	225	194
St. Lawrence	6	4	0	.600	231	176
Upsala	6	4	0	.600	197	182
Ala.-Birmingham .	4	3	2	.556	170	196
Mercyhurst......	5	4	0	.556	191	189
Sacred Heart	5	4	0	.556	131	135
Albany (N.Y.)	5	5	0	.500	206	223
Brockport St.	5	5	0	.500	222	252
Cal Lutheran* ...	5	5	0	.500	163	183
Catholic	5	5	0	.500	167	188
Evansville.......	5	5	0	.500	199	220
Wagner	5	5	0	.500	235	234
N'western (Wis.) .	4	4	0	.500	135	161
St. Peter's	4	4	0	.500	123	151
Davidson	4	5	0	.444	179	204
Rensselaer	4	5	0	.444	143	168
Drake	4	6	0	.400	200	162
Charleston So....	3	6	0	.333	119	209
Colorado Col.....	3	6	0	.333	157	204
Buffalo	3	7	0	.300	231	304
Gannon	3	7	0	.300	155	229
Hobart	3	7	0	.300	154	271
Quincy..........	3	7	0	.300	181	244
Rose-Hulman	3	7	0	.300	217	256
Concordia (Ill.) ...	2	6	0	.250	140	212
Canisius	2	7	0	.222	131	231
FDU-Madison	2	7	0	.222	88	222
Menlo	2	7	0	.222	71	278
Principia	2	7	0	.222	154	285
III. Benedictine ..	2	8	0	.200	173	321
Ky. Wesleyan ...	2	8	0	.200	119	229
Methodist	2	8	0	.200	98	325
Norwich	2	8	0	.200	149	319
Salisbury St.	1	9	0	.100	157	276
Western Conn. St..	1	9	0	.100	102	253
Blackburn	0	9	0	.000	58	379
Duquesne	0	9	0	.000	100	314

#Eureka (0-1, lost in first round of NAIA Division II championship to Georgetown, Ky., 42-14); Neb. Wesleyan (0-1, lost in first round of NAIA Division II championship to Peru St., Neb., 41-20). @ Does not count 35-21 victory over Ramapo in ECAC Southwest Bowl. * Will join Southern California Intercollegiate Athletic Conference in 1992.

Division III Playoffs [8-2-0]: Ithaca (4-0, won national championship over Dayton, 34-20); Dayton (3-1, lost in championship game to Ithaca, 34-20); Union (N. Y.) (1-1, lost in quarterfinals to Ithaca, 35-23)

Eleven Division III teams had perfect records in the 1991 regular season.

1992 SCHEDULES
1991 RESULTS

Michigan's Elvis Grbac, who led Division I-A in passing efficiency (169.0 rating) as a junior in 1991, returns this season to quarterback the Wolverines against a Big Ten schedule featuring four conference teams

SCHEDULE OF 1992-93 BOWL GAMES

The following 17 postseason football bowl games have been recommended for recertification by the Postseason Football Subcommittee of the NCAA Special Events Committee for 1992-93.

All starting times are *Eastern Standard Time.*

BLOCKBUSTER BOWL—January 1, 1993, 1:30 p.m.
Joe Robbie Stadium (73,000), Miami, Florida
Televising Network: CBS

FEDERAL EXPRESS ORANGE BOWL—January 1, 1993, 8 p.m.
Orange Bowl Stadium (74,244), Miami, Florida
Televising Network: NBC

FIESTA BOWL—January 1, 1993, 4:30 p.m.
Sun Devil Stadium (74,783), Tempe, Arizona
Televising Network: NBC

FLORIDA CITRUS BOWL—January 1, 1993, 1 or 1:30 p.m.
Florida Citrus Bowl-Orange County Stadium (70,000), Orlando, Florida
Televising Network: ABC

FREEDOM BOWL—December 29, 1992, 9 p.m.
Anaheim Stadium (70,962), Anaheim, California
Televising Network: Raycom

GATOR BOWL—December 31, 1992, 6 p.m.
Gator Bowl (80,129), Jacksonville, Florida
Televising Network: TBS (Tentative)

HALL OF FAME BOWL—January 1, 1993, 11 a.m.
Tampa Stadium (74,350), Tampa, Florida
Televising Network: ESPN

JEEP EAGLE ALOHA BOWL—December 25, 1992, 3:30 p.m.
Aloha Stadium (50,000), Honolulu, Hawaii
Televising Network: ABC

JOHN HANCOCK BOWL—December 31, 1992, 2:30 p.m.
Sun Bowl Stadium (52,000), El Paso, Texas
Televising Network: CBS

LAS VEGAS SILVER BOWL—December 18, 1992, 8 p.m.
Sam Boyd Silver Bowl (32,000), Las Vegas, Nevada
Televising Network: ESPN

LIBERTY BOWL—December 31, 1992, 8 p.m.
Liberty Bowl Stadium (62,425), Memphis, Tennessee
Televising Network: ESPN

MOBIL COTTON BOWL—January 1, 1993, 1 p.m.
Cotton Bowl (72,032), Dallas, Texas
Televising Network: NBC

PEACH BOWL—January 2, 1993, 8 p.m.
Georgia Dome (70,500), Atlanta, Georgia
Televising Network: ESPN

POULAN/WEED EATER INDEPENDENCE BOWL—December 31, 1992, 12:30 p.m.
Independence Stadium (50,459), Shreveport, Louisiana
Televising Network: ESPN

ROSE BOWL—January 1, 1993, 5 p.m.
Rose Bowl (99,563), Pasadena, California
Televising Network: ABC

1992 NCAA FOOTBALL

THRIFTY CAR RENTAL HOLIDAY BOWL—December 30, 1992, 8 p.m.
San Diego Jack Murphy Stadium (62,809), San Diego, California
Televising Network: ESPN

USF&G SUGAR BOWL—January 1, 1993, 8:30 p.m.
Louisiana Superdome (72,704), New Orleans, Louisiana
Televising Network: ABC

1992 DIVISIONS I-A & I-AA SCHEDULES

Listed alphabetically in this section are 1992 schedules and 1991 records of all teams classified Division I-A and Division I-AA in football. The division designation for each school is indicated to the right of the school name.

Coaching records (below head coaches' names) are for all seasons as the head coach at any four-year collegiate institution.

Game date and starting time are subject to change.

AIR FORCE . . . Air Force Academy, Colo. 80840   I-A

Coach: Fisher DeBerry, Wofford '60
Record: 8 yrs., W-65, L-33, T-1

1992 SCHEDULE

Rice ■	Sep 5
Hawaii ■	Sep 12
Wyoming ■	Sep 19
New Mexico ■	Sep 26
UTEP	Oct 3*
Navy ■	Oct 10
Colorado St. ■	Oct 17
San Diego St.	Oct 24*
Utah ■	Oct 31
Army	Nov 7
Brigham Young ■	Nov 14

1991 RECORD

48	Weber St.	31	
31	Colorado St.	26	
24	Utah	21	
21	San Diego St.	20	
7	Brigham Young	21	
51	Wyoming	28	
46	Navy	6	
15	Notre Dame	28	
20	UTEP	13
32	New Mexico	34
25	Army	0
24	Hawaii	20
344	(9-3-0)	248
	Liberty Bowl	
38	Mississippi St.	15

Conference: Western Athl. Conf.   Enrollment: 4,400.   Colors: Blue & Silver.
Nickname: Falcons.   Stadium: Falcon (1962), 53,533 capacity.   Natural turf.
1991 home attendance: 264,734 in 6 games.
Director of Athletics: Col. Ken Schweitzer.
Sports Info. Director: Dave Kellogg   303-472-2313

AKRON . . . Akron, Ohio 44325   I-A

Coach: Gerry Faust, Dayton '58
Record: 11 yrs., W-60, L-60, T-3

1992 SCHEDULE

Eastern Mich.	Sep 5*
Toledo ■	Sep 12*
Western Mich.	Sep 19
Ohio	Oct 3
Kent	Oct 10
Ball St.	Oct 17
Bowling Green ■	Oct 24
Central Mich. ■	Oct 31
Temple ■	Nov 7
Youngstown St. ■	Nov 14
Cincinnati	Nov 21

1991 RECORD

12	Western Mich.	35	
3	Illinois St.	25	
29	Central Mich.	31	
49	Northern Ariz.	14	
20	East Caro.	56	
38	Youngstown St.	24	
28	Arkansas St.	23	
17	Northern Ill.	7	
24	Virginia Tech	42
0	Army	19
37	Temple	32
257	(5-6-0)	308

Conference: Mid-American Conf.   Enrollment: 30,232.   Colors: Blue & Gold.
Nickname: Zips.   Stadium: Rubber Bowl (1940), 35,482 capacity.   Artificial turf.
1991 home attendance: 69,744 in 5 games.
Director of Athletics: Jim Dennison.
Sports Info. Director: Mac Yates   216-972-7468

ALABAMA . . . University, Ala. 35486   I-A

Coach: Gene Stallings, Texas A&M '57
Record: 9 yrs., W-45, L-51, T-1

1992 SCHEDULE

Vanderbilt ■	Sep 5
Southern Miss. [Birmingham, Ala.]	Sep 12
Arkansas [Little Rock, Ark.]	Sep 19*
Louisiana Tech ■	Sep 26
South Caro. ■	Oct 3
Tulane	Oct 10*
Tennessee	Oct 17
Mississippi ■	Oct 24
Louisiana St.	Nov 7*
Mississippi St.	Nov 14
Auburn ■	Nov 26

1991 RECORD

41	Temple	3	
0	Florida	35	
10	Georgia	0	
48	Vanderbilt	17	
53	Tenn.-Chatt.	7	
62	Tulane	0	
24	Tennessee	19	
13	Mississippi St.	7	
20	Louisiana St.	17
10	Memphis St.	7
13	Auburn	6
294	(10-1-0)	118
	Blockbuster Bowl	
30	Colorado	25

Conference: Southeastern Conf.   Enrollment: 20,000.   Colors: Crimson & White.
Nickname: Crimson Tide.   Stadium: Bryant-Denny (1929), 70,123 capacity.   Natural turf.
1991 home attendance: 453,094 in 6 games.
Director of Athletics: Hootie Ingram.
Sports Info. Director: Larry White   205-348-6084

ALABAMA STATE . . . Montgomery, Ala. 36195   I-AA

Coach: Houston Markham, Alcorn St. '65
Record: 5 yrs., W-39, L-13, T-3

1992 SCHEDULE

Southern-B.R.	Sep 12*
Alcorn St.	Sep 19
Troy St.	Sep 26*
Central St. (Ohio) [Indianapolis, Ind.]	Oct 3
Jackson St. ■	Oct 10*
Texas Southern [Mobile, Ala.]	Oct 17*
Prairie View ■	Oct 24*
Alabama A&M [Birmingham, Ala.]	Oct 31
Grambling	Nov 7
Mississippi Val. ■	Nov 14

1991 RECORD

28	Jackson St.	27	
19	Southern-B.R.	16	
18	Alcorn St.	13	
22	Troy St.	19	
14	Texas Southern	14	
31	Samford	28	
92	Prairie View	0	
59	Alabama A&M	13	
60	Grambling	14
48	Mississippi Val.	20
62	Johnson Smith	6
453	(10-0-1)	170
	Alamo Heritage Bowl	
36	North Caro. A&T	13

Conference: Southwestern.   Enrollment: 4,200.   Colors: Black & Gold.
Nickname: Hornets.   Stadium: Cramton, 24,600 capacity.   Natural turf.
1991 home attendance: 134,572 in 6 games.
Director of Athletics: Arthur Barnett.
Sports Info. Director: Jack Jeffery   205-240-6857

■ Home games on each schedule [neutral sites shown in brackets].   *Night Games.

ALCORN STATE . . . Lorman, Miss. 39096　　　　I-AA

Coach: Cardell Jones, Alcorn St. '65
Record: 1 yr., W-7, L-2, T-1

1992 SCHEDULE

Grambling [Shreveport, La.] ....Sep 5*
Alabama St. ■ ....Sep 19
Howard ....Sep 26
Sam Houston St. ....Oct 3*
Texas Southern ■ ....Oct 10
Prairie View ....Oct 17
Southern-B.R. ■ ....Oct 24
Jacksonville St. ....Oct 31
Mississippi Val. ....Nov 7
Jackson St. ■ ....Nov 21

1991 RECORD

27	Grambling	22
38	Alabama A&M	10
13	Alabama St.	18
67	Hampton	14
46	Howard	27
7	Texas Southern	26
61	Prairie View	0
52	Southern-B.R.	29

28	Mississippi Val.	28
18	Jackson St.	16
357	(7-2-1)	190

Conference: Southwestern.　Enrollment: 3,100.　Colors: Purple & Gold.
Nickname: Braves.　Stadium: Alcorn State (1930), 25,000 capacity.　Natural turf.
1991 home attendance: 47,211 in 4 games.
Director of Athletics: Cardell Jones.
Sports Info. Director: Gus Howard　601-877-6466

APPALACHIAN STATE . . . Boone, N.C. 28608　　　　I-AA

Coach: Jerry Moore, Baylor '61
Record: 10 yrs., W-50, L-60, T-2

1992 SCHEDULE

North Caro. St. ....Sep 5
Wake Forest ....Sep 12*
East Tenn. St. ■ ....Sep 26
Citadel ■ ....Oct 3
James Madison ....Oct 10
Va. Military ....Oct 17
Furman ■ ....Oct 24
Tenn.-Chatt. ....Oct 31*
Marshall ....Nov 7
North Caro. A&T ■ ....Nov 14
Western Caro. ■ ....Nov 21

1991 RECORD

9	Marshall	3
0	Clemson	34
24	Va. Military	19
8	James Madison	31
42	Tenn.-Chatt.	7
17	Wake Forest	3
21	East Tenn. St.	14
26	Furman	23

10	Citadel	17
31	Mississippi Col.	23
24	Western Caro.	14
212		188
	I-AA Championship	
3	Eastern Ky.	14

Conference: Southern Conf.　Enrollment: 11,501.　Colors: Black & Gold.
Nickname: Mountaineers.　Stadium: Kidd Brewer (1962), 18,000 capacity.　Artificial turf.
1991 home attendance: 77,811 in 5 games.
Director of Athletics: Roachel Laney.
Sports Info. Director: Rick Covington　704-262-3080

ARIZONA . . . Tucson, Ariz. 85721　　　　I-A

Coach: Dick Tomey, DePauw '61
Record: 15 yrs., W-93, L-70, T-6

1992 SCHEDULE

Utah St. ■ ....Sep 5*
Washington St. ■ ....Sep 12*
Oregon St. ....Sep 19
Miami (Fla.) ....Sep 26
UCLA ■ ....Oct 3*
Stanford ....Oct 17
California ....Oct 24
New Mexico St. ■ ....Oct 31*
Washington ■ ....Nov 7
Southern Cal ....Nov 14
Arizona St. ■ ....Nov 21*

1991 RECORD

14	Ohio St.	38
28	Stanford	23
21	California	23
45	Long Beach St.	21
0	Washington	54
14	UCLA	54
9	Miami (Fla.)	36
45	Oregon St.	21

27	Washington St.	40
31	Southern Cal	14
14	Arizona St.	37
248	(4-7-0)	361

Conference: Pacific-10.　Enrollment: 35,647.　Colors: Cardinal & Navy.
Nickname: Wildcats.　Stadium: Arizona (1928), 56,167 capacity.　Natural turf.
1991 home attendance: 272,588 in 6 games.
Director of Athletics: Cedric Dempsey.
Sports Info. Director: Butch Henry　602-621-4163

ARIZONA STATE . . . Tempe, Ariz. 85287　　　　I-A

Coach: Bruce Snyder, Oregon '63
Record: 12 yrs., W-66, L-62, T-6

1992 SCHEDULE

Washington ■ ....Sep 5*
Louisville ■ ....Sep 19*
Nebraska ....Sep 26
Oregon ....Oct 3
Pacific (Cal.) ■ ....Oct 10*
Oregon St. ■ ....Oct 17*
UCLA ....Oct 24
Southern Cal ■ ....Oct 31*
Washington St. ....Nov 7
California ■ ....Nov 14*
Arizona ....Nov 21*

1991 RECORD

30	Oklahoma St.	3
32	Southern Cal	25
9	Nebraska	18
21	Utah	15
24	Oregon St.	7
3	Washington St.	17
16	UCLA	21
16	Washington	44

24	Oregon	21
6	California	25
37	Arizona	14
218	(6-5-0)	210

Conference: Pacific-10.　Enrollment: 43,426.　Colors: Maroon & Gold.
Nickname: Sun Devils.　Stadium: Sun Devil (1958), 74,865 capacity.　Natural turf.
1991 home attendance: 334,287 in 6 games.
Director of Athletics: Charles S. Harris.
Sports Info. Director: Mark Brand　602-965-6592

ARKANSAS . . . Fayetteville, Ark. 72701　　　　I-A

Coach: Jack Crowe, Ala.-Birmingham '70
Record: 4 yrs., W-14, L-29, T-0

1992 SCHEDULE

Citadel ■ ....Sep 5
South Caro. ....Sep 12*
Alabama [Little Rock, Ark.] ....Sep 19*
Memphis St. ■ ....Sep 26*
Georgia ■ ....Oct 3
Tennessee ....Oct 10
Mississippi [Little Rock, Ark.] ......Oct 17*
Auburn ....Oct 31
Mississippi St. ....Nov 7
Southern Methodist [Little Rock, Ark.] ...Nov 21
Louisiana St. ■ ....Nov 28

1991 RECORD

3	Miami (Fla.)	31
17	Southern Methodist	6
9	Southwestern La.	7
17	Mississippi	24
22	Texas Christian	21
29	Houston	17
14	Texas	13
5	Baylor	9

21	Texas Tech	38
3	Texas A&M	13
20	Rice	0
160	(6-5-0)	179
	Poulan Independence Bowl	
15	Georgia	24

Conference: Southeastern Conf.　Enrollment: 14,000.　Colors: Cardinal & White.
Nickname: Razorbacks.　Stadium: Razorback (1938), 52,860 capacity.　Artificial turf.
1991 home attendance: 322,998 in 7 games.
Director of Athletics: Frank Broyles.
Sports Info. Director: Rick Schaeffer　501-575-2751

■ Home games on each schedule [neutral sites shown in brackets].　*Night Games.

ARKANSAS STATE . . . State University, Ark.   72467   I-A

Coach: Ray Perkins, Alabama '67
Record: 4 yrs., W-32, L-17, T-1
1992 SCHEDULE

Toledo	Sep 5*
Oklahoma	Sep 12
Northern Ill. ■	Sep 19
Southern Ill. ■	Sep 26
Northwestern (La.) ■	Oct 3
Troy St. ■	Oct 10
Memphis St.	Oct 17*
Mississippi St.	Oct 24
Louisiana Tech	Oct 31*
East Caro.	Nov 14
Southwestern La.	Nov 21*

1991 RECORD

24	Colorado St.	38	20	Southwest Mo. St.	37
3	Northwestern (La.)	28	20	Troy St.	17
21	Northern Ill.	22	13	Southwestern La.	17
21	Memphis St.	31			
10	Louisiana Tech	42	189	(1-10-0)	361
20	Central Fla.	31			
14	Louisiana St.	70			
23	Akron	28			

Conference: I-A Independents.   Enrollment: 9,800.   Colors: Scarlet & Black.
Nickname: Indians.   Stadium: Indian (1974), 33,410 capacity.   Natural turf.
1991 home attendance: 103,191 in 6 games.
Director of Athletics: Charles Thornton.
Sports Info. Director: Jerry Schaeffer   501-972-2541

ARMY . . . West Point, N.Y.   10996   I-A

Coach: Bob Sutton, Eastern Mich. '74
Record: 1 yr., W-4, L-7, T-0
1992 SCHEDULE

Holy Cross ■	Sep 12
North Caro.	Sep 19*
Citadel ■	Sep 26
Lafayette ■	Oct 10
Rutgers [East Rutherford, N.J.]	Oct 17
Wake Forest	Oct 24
Eastern Mich. ■	Oct 31
Air Force ■	Nov 7
Northern Ill. ■	Nov 14
Boston College ■	Nov 21
Navy [Philadelphia, Pa.]	Dec 5

1991 RECORD

51	Colgate	22	0	Air Force	25
12	North Caro.	20	19	Akron	0
21	Harvard	20	3	Navy	24
12	Rutgers	14			
14	Citadel	20	196	(4-7-0)	226
37	Louisville	12			
17	Boston College	28			
10	Vanderbilt	41			

Conference: I-A Independents.   Enrollment: 4,300.   Colors: Black, Gold, Gray.
Nickname: Cadets, Black Knights.   Stadium: Michie (1924), 39,929 capacity.   Artificial turf.
1991 home attendance: 320,841 in 8 games.
Director of Athletics: Al Vanderbush.
Sports Info. Director: Robert Kinney   914-938-3303

AUBURN . . . Auburn, Ala.   36830   I-A

Coach: Pat Dye, Georgia '62
Record: 18 yrs., W-148, L-57, T-4
1992 SCHEDULE

Mississippi	Sep 5*
Samford ■	Sep 12*
Louisiana St. ■	Sep 19*
Southern Miss. ■	Sep 26
Vanderbilt ■	Oct 3
Mississippi St.	Oct 10*
Florida	Oct 17
Southwestern La. ■	Oct 24
Arkansas ■	Oct 31
Georgia ■	Nov 14
Alabama	Nov 26

1991 RECORD

32	Ga. Southern	17	50	Southwestern La.	7
23	Mississippi	13	27	Georgia	37
14	Texas	10	6	Alabama	13
21	Tennessee	30			
9	Southern Miss.	10	233	(5-6-0)	214
24	Vanderbilt	22			
17	Mississippi St.	24			
10	Florida	31			

Conference: Southeastern Conf.   Enrollment: 19,700.   Colors: Burnt Orange & Navy Blue.
Nickname: Tigers.   Stadium: Jordan Hare (1939), 85,214 capacity.   Natural turf.
1991 home attendance: 552,155 in 7 games.
Director of Athletics: Milo R. Lude.
Sports Info. Director: David Housel   205-844-4750

AUSTIN PEAY STATE . . . Clarksville, Tenn.   37044   I-AA

Coach: Roy Gregory, Tenn.-Chatt. '68
Record: 1 yr., W-5, L-6, T-0
1992 SCHEDULE

Eastern Ill. ■	Sep 5*
Knoxville ■	Sep 12*
Southern Ill.	Sep 19
Southeast Mo. St.	Sep 26*
Murray St.	Oct 3
Middle Tenn. St.	Oct 10
Tennessee Tech ■	Oct 17
Tennessee St.	Oct 24
Morehead St. ■	Oct 31
Eastern Ky. ■	Nov 14
Tenn.-Martin ■	Nov 21

1991 RECORD

18	Western Ky.	14	28	Tenn.-Martin	34
17	Southern Ill.	21	0	Eastern Ky.	21
17	Kentucky St.	6	27	Murray St.	9
24	Southeast Mo. St.	21			
8	Middle Tenn. St.	23	191	(5-6-0)	231
7	Tennessee Tech	32			
31	Tennessee St.	17			
14	Morehead St.	33			

Conference: Ohio Valley Conf.   Enrollment: 7,400.   Colors: Red & White.
Nickname: Governors.   Stadium: Municipal (1946), 10,000 capacity.   Artificial turf.
1991 home attendance: 34,659 in 7 games.
Director of Athletics: Tim Weiser.
Sports Info. Director: Brad Kirtley   615-648-7561

BALL STATE . . . Muncie, Ind.   47306   I-A

Coach: Paul Schudel, Miami (Ohio) '66
Record: 7 yrs., W-42, L-34, T-2
1992 SCHEDULE

Clemson	Sep 5
Kansas	Sep 12
Kent	Sep 19
Miami (Ohio) ■	Sep 26
Western Mich. ■	Oct 3
Eastern Mich. ■	Oct 10
Akron	Oct 17
Central Mich. ■	Oct 24
Ohio	Oct 31
Toledo ■	Nov 7
Bowling Green	Nov 14

1991 RECORD

7	Miami (Ohio)	15	10	Ohio	6
33	Navy	10	9	Toledo	3
16	Texas Christian	22	13	Bowling Green	14
28	Kent	27			
14	Indiana St.	10	159	(6-5-0)	150
16	Western Mich.	25			
10	Eastern Mich.	8			
3	Central Mich.	10			

Conference: Mid-American Conf.   Enrollment: 19,000.   Colors: Cardinal & White.
Nickname: Cardinals.   Stadium: Ball State (1967), 16,319 capacity.   Natural turf.
1991 home attendance: 46,181 in 4 games.
Director of Athletics: Don Purvis.
Sports Info. Director: Joe Hernandez   317-285-8242

■ Home games on each schedule [neutral sites shown in brackets].   *Night Games.

BAYLOR . . . Waco, Tex. 76706   I-A

Coach: Grant Teaff, McMurry '56
Record: 29 yrs., W-163, L-146, T-8

1992 SCHEDULE

Louisiana Tech ■	Sep 5*
Colorado ■	Sep 12*
Utah St. ■	Sep 19*
Texas Tech	Sep 26*
Southern Methodist ■	Oct 3
Texas Christian	Oct 10*
Houston	Oct 17
Texas A&M	Oct 24
Georgia Tech ■	Nov 7
Rice	Nov 14
Texas ■	Nov 21

1991 RECORD

27	UTEP	7	
16	Colorado	14	
47	Missouri	21	
45	Southern Methodist	7	
38	Houston	21	
17	Rice	20	
12	Texas A&M	34	
26	Texas Christian	9	
9	Arkansas	5	
24	Texas Tech	31	
21	Texas	11	

282   (8-3-0)   180

Domino's Copper Bowl

0 Indiana 24

Conference: Southwest Conf. Enrollment: 12,000. Colors: Green & Gold.
Nickname: Bears. Stadium: Floyd Casey (1950), 48,500 capacity. Artificial turf.
1991 home attendance: 190,100 in 5 games.
Director of Athletics: Grant Teaff.
Sports Info. Director: Maxey Parrish 817-755-1234

BETHUNE-COOKMAN . . . Daytona Beach, Fla. 32015   I-AA

Coach: Sylvester Collins, Jackson St. '72
Record: First year as head coach

1992 SCHEDULE

Savannah St. [Jacksonville, Fla.]	Sep 5*
Central Fla.	Sep 12*
Delaware St. [Ft. Lauderdale, Fla.]	Sep 19
Samford ■	Sep 26
Howard	Oct 10
South Caro. St.	Oct 17
Albany St. (Ga.) ■	Oct 24
North Caro. A&T	Oct 31
Norfolk St. ■	Nov 14
Morgan St.	Nov 21
Florida A&M [Tampa, Fla.]	Nov 28

1991 RECORD

20	Savannah St.	35	
28	Delaware St.	20	
38	Morgan St.	6	
6	Central Fla.	32	
20	Howard	14	
24	South Caro. St.	21	
25	Albany St. (Ga.)	30	
24	North Caro. A&T	39	
51	Morris Brown	13	
28	Florida A&M	46	

264   (5-5-0)   256

Conference: Mid-Eastern. Enrollment: 1,700. Colors: Maroon & Gold.
Nickname: Wildcats. Stadium: Memorial, 10,000 capacity. Natural turf.
1991 home attendance: 41,994 in 5 games.
Director of Athletics: Lynn Thompson.
Sports Info. Director: Johnny Randolph 904-255-1401

BOISE STATE . . . Boise, Ida. 83725   I-AA

Coach: Skip Hall, Concordia (Minn.) '66
Record: 5 yrs., W-37, L-22, T-0

1992 SCHEDULE

Tenn.-Chatt. ■	Sep 5*
Idaho St.	Sep 12*
Pacific (Cal.) ■	Sep 19*
Stephen F. Austin	Sep 26*
Montana ■	Oct 3*
Northern Ariz.	Oct 10*
Weber St. ■	Oct 17*
Portland St. ■	Oct 24*
Montana St.	Oct 31
Eastern Wash.	Nov 14
Idaho ■	Nov 21

1991 RECORD

35	Liberty	14	
48	Long Beach St.	14	
31	Eastern Wash.	17	
38	Stephen F. Austin	7	
7	Montana	21	
57	Northern Ariz.	14	
14	Nevada	17	
38	Idaho St.	16	
31	Montana St.	14	
32	Weber St.	35	
24	Idaho	28	

355   (7-4-0)   197

Conference: Big Sky Conf. Enrollment: 14,254. Colors: Orange & Blue.
Nickname: Broncos. Stadium: Bronco (1970), 22,600 capacity. Artificial turf.
1991 home attendance: 138,396 in 7 games.
Director of Athletics: Gene Bleymaier.
Sports Info. Director: Max Corbet 208-385-1515

BOSTON COLLEGE . . . Chestnut Hill, Mass. 02167   I-A

Coach: Tom Coughlin, Syracuse '68
Record: 3 yrs., W-11, L-17, T-1

1992 SCHEDULE

Rutgers ■	Sep 5
Northwestern ■	Sep 12
Navy ■	Sep 19
Michigan St. ■	Sep 26
West Va.	Oct 3
Penn St.	Oct 17
Tulane	Oct 24*
Temple ■	Oct 31
Notre Dame	Nov 7
Syracuse ■	Nov 14
Army	Nov 21

1991 RECORD

13	Rutgers	20	
13	Michigan	35	
14	Georgia Tech	30	
21	Penn St.	28	
33	Louisville	3	
24	West Va.	31	
28	Army	17	
38	Pittsburgh	12	
33	Temple	13	
16	Syracuse	38	
14	Miami (Fla.)	19	

247   (4-7-0)   246

Conference: Big East Conference. Enrollment: 8,574. Colors: Maroon & Gold.
Nickname: Eagles. Stadium: Alumni (1957), 32,000 capacity. Artificial turf.
1991 home attendance: 172,033 in 6 games.
Director of Athletics: Chet Gladchuk.
Sports Info. Director: Reid Oslin 617-552-3004

BOSTON U. . . . Boston, Mass. 02215   I-AA

Coach: Dan Allen, Hanover '78
Record: 2 yrs., W-9, L-13, T-0

1992 SCHEDULE

Temple	Sep 5
William & Mary	Sep 19
Massachusetts	Sep 26
Villanova ■	Oct 3
Delaware	Oct 10
Richmond ■	Oct 17
Rhode Island	Oct 24
New Hampshire ■	Oct 31
Maine	Nov 7
Connecticut ■	Nov 14
Northeastern ■	Nov 21

1991 RECORD

22	William & Mary	48	
10	Towson St.	8	
23	Holy Cross	27	
7	Massachusetts	15	
6	Villanova	56	
21	Delaware	35	
18	Richmond	32	
43	Rhode Island	0	
26	New Hampshire	45	
27	Maine	0	
29	Connecticut	26	

232   (4-7-0)   292

Conference: Yankee. Enrollment: 13,848. Colors: Scarlet & White.
Nickname: Terriers. Stadium: Nickerson Field (1930), 17,369 capacity. Artificial turf.
1991 home attendance: 23,777 in 6 games.
Director of Athletics: Gary Strickler.
Sports Info. Director: Ed Carpenter 617-353-2872

■ Home games on each schedule [neutral sites shown in brackets]. *Night Games.

BOWLING GREEN . . . Bowling Green, Ohio   43403   I-A

Coach: Gary Blackney, Connecticut '67
Record: 1 yr., W-11, L-1, T-0
1992 SCHEDULE

Western Mich. ■ ....Sep 5
Ohio St. ....Sep 12
Wisconsin ....Sep 19
East Caro. ■ ....Sep 26
Central Mich. ....Oct 3
Ohio ■ ....Oct 10
Toledo ....Oct 17*
Akron ....Oct 24
Miami (Ohio) ■ ....Oct 31
Kent ....Nov 7
Ball St. ■ ....Nov 14

1991 RECORD

17	Eastern Mich.	6	17	Miami (Ohio)	7
17	West Va.	24	35	Kent	7
20	Cincinnati	16	14	Ball St.	13
22	Navy	19			
17	Central Mich.	10	251	(10-1-0)	147
45	Ohio	14		**California Raisin Bowl**	
24	Toledo	21	28	Fresno St.	21
23	Western Mich.	10			

Conference: Mid-American Conf.   Enrollment: 18,000.   Colors: Orange & Brown.
Nickname: Falcons.   Stadium: Doyt Perry Field (1966), 30,599 capacity.   Natural turf.
1991 home attendance: 69,900 in 5 games.
Director of Athletics: Jack Gregory.
Sports Info. Director: Steve Barr   419-372-7076

BRIGHAM YOUNG . . . Provo, Utah   84602   I-A

Coach: LaVell Edwards, Utah St. '52
Record: 20 yrs., W-183, L-62, T-3
1992 SCHEDULE

UTEP ....Sep 5*
San Diego St. ■ ....Sep 10*
UCLA ■ ....Sep 19
Hawaii ....Sep 26*
Utah St. ■ ....Oct 2*
Fresno St. ■ ....Oct 10
Wyoming ....Oct 17
Notre Dame ....Oct 24
Penn St. ■ ....Oct 31
New Mexico ■ ....Nov 7
Air Force ....Nov 14
Utah ....Nov 21

1991 RECORD

28	Florida St.	44	40	Colorado St.	17
23	UCLA	27	56	Wyoming	31
7	Penn St.	33	52	San Diego St.	52
21	Air Force	7	48	Utah	17
38	Utah St.	10			
31	UTEP	29	420	(8-3-1)	308
35	Hawaii	18		**Thrifty Holiday Bowl**	
41	New Mexico	23	13	Iowa	13

Conference: Western Athl. Conf.   Enrollment: 27,000.   Colors: Royal Blue & White.
Nickname: Cougars.   Stadium: B Y U (1964), 65,000 capacity.   Natural turf.
1991 home attendance: 433,341 in 7 games.
Director of Athletics: Glen Tuckett.
Sports Info. Director: Ralph Zobell   801-378-4911

BROWN . . . Providence, R.I.   02912   I-AA

Coach: Mickey Kwiatkowski, Delaware '70
Record: 11 yrs., W-71, L-44, T-0
1992 SCHEDULE

Yale ■ ....Sep 19
Bucknell ....Sep 26
William & Mary ....Oct 3
Princeton ....Oct 10
Lehigh ■ ....Oct 17
Pennsylvania ■ ....Oct 24
Cornell ....Oct 31
Harvard ....Nov 7
Dartmouth ■ ....Nov 14
Columbia ....Nov 21

1991 RECORD

20	Yale	36	13	Dartmouth	45
0	Marshall	46	28	Columbia	23
36	Rhode Island	38			
37	Princeton	59	227	(1-9-0)	372
28	Holy Cross	42			
19	Pennsylvania	28			
17	Cornell	20			
29	Harvard	35			

Conference: Ivy League.   Enrollment: 5,519.   Colors: Brown, Cardinal & White.
Nickname: Bears.   Stadium: Brown (1925), 20,000 capacity.   Natural turf.
1991 home attendance: 35,600 in 5 games.
Director of Athletics: David Roach.
Sports Info. Director: Christopher Humm   401-863-2219

BUCKNELL . . . Lewisburg, Pa.   17837   I-AA

Coach: Lou Maranzana, Dartmouth '70
Record: 3 yrs., W-13, L-18, T-0
1992 SCHEDULE

Bloomsburg ■ ....Sep 5
Villanova ....Sep 12
Towson St. ....Sep 19*
Brown ■ ....Sep 26
Dartmouth ....Oct 3
Columbia ....Oct 10
Holy Cross ....Oct 24
Fordham ■ ....Oct 31
Lehigh ....Nov 7
Lafayette ■ ....Nov 14
Colgate ■ ....Nov 21

1991 RECORD

7	Hofstra	43	6	Holy Cross	42
0	Villanova	40	13	Lehigh	41
21	Fordham	14			
16	Dartmouth	34	99	(1-9-0)	326
7	Cornell	23			
16	Lafayette	20			
7	Princeton	31			
6	Colgate	38			

Conference: Patriot League.   Enrollment: 3,400.   Colors: Orange & Blue.
Nickname: Bison.   Stadium: Christy Mathewson (1924), 13,100 capacity.   Natural turf.
1991 home attendance: 20,293 in 4 games.
Director of Athletics: Rick Hartzell.
Sports Info. Director: Bo Smolka   717-524-1227

CAL STATE FULLERTON . . . Fullerton, Cal.   92634   I-A

Coach: Gene Murphy, North Dak. '62
Record: 14 yrs., W-72, L-87, T-1
1992 SCHEDULE

Cal St. Northridge ■ ....Sep 5*
UCLA ....Sep 12
Georgia ....Sep 19
Cal St. Sacramento ■ ....Sep 26*
Nevada ■ ....Oct 3*
San Jose St. ....Oct 10*
Southwestern La. ....Oct 17*
Utah St. ■ ....Oct 31*
Pacific (Cal.) ....Nov 7
New Mexico St. ....Nov 14
Nevada-Las Vegas ....Nov 28

1991 RECORD

3	Mississippi St.	47	7	San Jose St.	35
7	Texas Tech	41	7	Fresno St.	38
17	Cal St. Northridge	10	37	Long Beach St.	36
14	Georgia	27			
28	Pacific (Cal.)	56	138	(2-9-0)	376
3	Nevada-Las Vegas	25			
3	Utah St.	26			
12	New Mexico St.	35			

Conference: Big West.   Enrollment: 25,000.   Colors: Blue, Orange & White.
Nickname: Titans.   Stadium: Titan (1992), 10,000 capacity.   Natural turf.
1991 home attendance: 11,168 in 4 games.
Director of Athletics: Bill Shumard.
Sports Info. Director: Mel Franks   714-773-3970

■ Home games on each schedule [neutral sites shown in brackets].   *Night Games.

CALIFORNIA . . . Berkeley, Cal. 94720   I-A

Coach: Keith Gilbertson, Central Wash. '71
Record: 3 yrs., W-28, L-9, T-0
1992 SCHEDULE

San Jose St. ■ ....Sep 5
Purdue ....Sep 12
Kansas ....Sep 24*
Oregon St. ■ ....Oct 3
Washington ....Oct 10
Southern Cal ....Oct 17
Arizona ■ ....Oct 24
UCLA ■ ....Oct 31
Oregon ....Nov 7
Arizona St. ....Nov 14*
Stanford ■ ....Nov 21

1991 RECORD

86	Pacific (Cal.)	24	27 Oregon St.	14
42	Purdue	18	25 Arizona St.	6
23	Arizona	21	21 Stanford	38
27	UCLA	24		
45	Oregon	7	406	226
17	Washington	24	(9-2-0)	
41	San Jose St.	20	**Florida Citrus Bowl**	
52	Southern Cal	30	37 Clemson	13

Conference: Pacific-10. Enrollment: 32,000. . Colors: Blue & Gold.
Nickname: Golden Bears. Stadium: Memorial (1923), 75,662 capacity. Artificial turf.
1991 home attendance: 346,500 in 7 games.
Director of Athletics: Robert L. Bockrath.
Sports Info. Director: Kevin Reneau 510-642-5363

CENTRAL FLORIDA . . . Orlando, Fla. 32816   I-AA

Coach: Gene McDowell, Florida St. '63
Record: 7 yrs., W-48, L-33, T-0
1992 SCHEDULE

Gardner-Webb ■ ....Sep 5*
Bethune-Cookman ■ ....Sep 12*
Troy St. ■ ....Sep 19*
Western Ill. ....Sep 26
Savannah St. ■ ....Oct 3*
Nicholls St. ■ ....Oct 17*
Western Ky. ....Oct 24
Liberty ....Oct 31
Buffalo ■ ....Nov 7
James Madison ■ ....Nov 14
Samford ....Nov 21

1991 RECORD

21	Troy St.	10	31 Savannah St.	33
31	James Madison	49	31 Liberty	26
12	Valdosta St.	0	52 Millersville	6
25	East Caro.	47		
32	Bethune-Cookman	6	278	230
31	Arkansas St.	20	(6-5-0)	
6	Samford	13		
6	Ga. Southern	20		

Conference: I-AA Independents. Enrollment: 20,000. Colors: Black & Gold.
Nickname: Knights. Stadium: Orlando (1936), 70,000 capacity. Natural turf.
1991 home attendance: 89,927 in 6 games.
Director of Athletics: Gene McDowell.
Sports Info. Director: Bob Cefalo 407-823-2464

CENTRAL MICHIGAN . . . Mt. Pleasant, Mich. 48859   I-A

Coach: Herb Deromedi, Michigan '60
Record: 14 yrs., W-100, L-43, T-10
1992 SCHEDULE

Kentucky ....Sep 5*
Michigan St. ....Sep 12
Ohio ■ ....Sep 19
Toledo ■ ....Sep 26
Bowling Green ■ ....Oct 3
Miami (Ohio) ....Oct 10
Kent ■ ....Oct 17
Ball St. ■ ....Oct 24
Akron ....Oct 31
Eastern Mich. ■ ....Nov 7
Western Mich. ....Nov 14

1991 RECORD

17	Ohio	17	10 Ball St.	3
27	Southwestern La.	24	14 Eastern Mich.	14
20	Michigan St.	3	27 Western Mich.	17
31	Akron	29		
16	Toledo	16	205	157
10	Bowling Green	17	(6-1-4)	
10	Miami (Ohio)	10		
23	Kent	7		

Conference: Mid-American Conf. Enrollment: 16,866. Colors: Maroon & Gold.
Nickname: Chippewas. Stadium: Kelly-Shorts (1972), 20,086 capacity. Artificial turf.
1991 home attendance: 100,134 in 5 games.
Director of Athletics: Dave Keilitz.
Sports Info. Director: Fred Stabley Jr. 517-774-3277

CINCINNATI . . . Cincinnati, Ohio 45221   I-A

Coach: Tim Murphy, Springfield '78
Record: 5 yrs., W-21, L-34, T-1
1992 SCHEDULE

Penn St. ■ ....Sep 5*
Miami (Ohio) ....Sep 19
Tennessee ....Sep 26
Kent ■ ....Oct 3*
Memphis St. ■ ....Oct 10*
East Caro. ....Oct 17
Southern Miss. ....Oct 24
Louisville ■ ....Oct 31*
Rutgers ■ ....Nov 7*
Kentucky ■ ....Nov 14
Akron ■ ....Nov 21

1991 RECORD

0	Penn St.	81	17 Kentucky	20
16	North Caro.	51	30 Middle Tenn. St.	10
16	Bowling Green	20	19 East Caro.	30
9	Miami (Ohio)	22		
30	Louisville	7	201	323
38	Kent	19	(4-7-0)	
9	Virginia Tech	56		
17	Southern Miss.	7		

Conference: I-A Independents. Enrollment: 36,000. Colors: Red & Black.
Nickname: Bearcats. Stadium: Nippert (1916), 35,000 capacity. Artificial turf.
1991 home attendance: 65,557 in 4 games.
Director of Athletics: Rick Taylor.
Sports Info. Director: Tom Hathaway 513-556-5191

CITADEL . . . Charleston, S.C. 29409   I-AA

Coach: Charlie Taaffe, Siena '73
Record: 5 yrs., W-31, L-25, T-1
1992 SCHEDULE

Arkansas ....Sep 5
Wofford ■ ....Sep 12*
East Tenn. St. ■ ....Sep 19*
Army ....Sep 26
Appalachian St. ....Oct 3
Tenn.-Chatt. ■ ....Oct 10*
Marshall ■ ....Oct 17
Western Caro. ....Oct 24
Newberry ■ ....Nov 7
Va. Military ■ ....Nov 14
Furman ....Nov 21

1991 RECORD

33	Presbyterian	10	31 Marshall	37
12	Wofford	15	17 East Tenn. St.	7
26	Tenn.-Chatt.	33	10 Furman	6
38	Western Caro.	13		
20	Army	14	238	183
17	William & Mary	24	(7-4-0)	
17	Va. Military	14		
17	Appalachian St.	10		

Conference: Southern Conf. Enrollment: 2,000. Colors: Blue & White.
Nickname: Bulldogs. Stadium: Johnson Hagood (1948), 22,500 capacity. Natural turf.
1991 home attendance: 92,476 in 5 games.
Director of Athletics: Walt Nadzak.
Sports Info. Director: Josh Baker 803-792-5120

■ Home games on each schedule [neutral sites shown in brackets].   *Night Games.

CLEMSON . . . Clemson, S.C. 29631   I-A

Coach: Ken Hatfield, Arkansas '65
Record: 13 yrs., W-100, L-53, T-2

1992 SCHEDULE

Ball St. ■	Sep 5
Florida St. ■	Sep 12
Georgia Tech	Sep 26
Tenn.-Chatt. ■	Oct 3
Virginia	Oct 10
Duke ■	Oct 17
North Caro. St.	Oct 24
Wake Forest	Oct 31
North Caro. ■	Nov 7
Maryland	Nov 14
South Caro. ■	Nov 21

1991 RECORD

34	Appalachian St.	0	40	Maryland	7
37	Temple	7	41	South Caro.	24
9	Georgia Tech	7	33	Duke	21
12	Georgia	27			
20	Virginia	20	304	(9-1-1)	148
29	North Caro. St.	19		**Florida Citrus Bowl**	
28	Wake Forest	10	13	California	37
21	North Caro.	6			

Conference: Atlantic Coast Conf. Enrollment: 17,295. Colors: Purple & Orange.
Nickname: Tigers. Stadium: Memorial (1942), 79,854 capacity. Natural turf.
1991 home attendance: 513,915 in 7 games.
Director of Athletics: Bobby Robinson.
Sports Info. Director: Tim Bourret 803-656-2114

COLGATE . . . Hamilton, N.Y. 13346   I-AA

Coach: Mike Foley, Colgate '78
Record: 4 yrs., W-17, L-27, T-0

1992 SCHEDULE

Rutgers	Sep 12*
Fordham	Sep 19
Pennsylvania	Sep 26
Columbia	Oct 3
Buffalo ■	Oct 10
Cornell ■	Oct 17
Lehigh	Oct 24
Lafayette ■	Oct 31
William & Mary ■	Nov 7
Holy Cross ■	Nov 14
Bucknell	Nov 21

1991 RECORD

10	Northeastern	35	22	Lehigh	21
22	Army	51	31	Lafayette	48
14	Duke	42	3	Holy Cross	28
31	Cornell	13			
21	Princeton	30	224	(4-7-0)	311
7	Yale	25			
25	Fordham	12			
38	Bucknell	6			

Conference: Patriot League. Enrollment: 2,700. Colors: Maroon.
Nickname: Red Raiders. Stadium: Andy Kerr (1937), 10,221 capacity. Natural turf.
1991 home attendance: 14,136 in 5 games.
Director of Athletics: Mark Murphy.
Sports Info. Director: Bob Cornell 315-824-7616

COLORADO . . . Boulder, Colo. 80309   I-A

Coach: Bill McCartney, Missouri '62
Record: 10 yrs., W-65, L-49, T-3

1992 SCHEDULE

Colorado St. ■	Sep 5
Baylor	Sep 12*
Minnesota	Sep 19*
Iowa ■	Sep 26
Missouri	Oct 3*
Oklahoma ■	Oct 17
Kansas St. ■	Oct 24
Nebraska	Oct 31
Oklahoma St. ■	Nov 7
Kansas	Nov 14
Iowa St. ■	Nov 21

1991 RECORD

30	Wyoming	13	16	Oklahoma St.	12
14	Baylor	16	30	Kansas	24
58	Minnesota	0	17	Iowa St.	14
21	Stanford	28			
55	Missouri	7	304	(8-2-1)	150
34	Oklahoma	17		**Blockbuster Bowl**	
10	Kansas St.	0	25	Alabama	30
19	Nebraska	19			

Conference: Big Eight Conf. Enrollment: 25,176. Colors: Silver, Gold & Black.
Nickname: Buffaloes. Stadium: Folsom (1924), 51,748 capacity. Artificial turf.
1991 home attendance: 311,458 in 6 games.
Director of Athletics: Bill Marolt.
Sports Info. Director: David Plati 303-492-5626

COLORADO STATE . . . Fort Collins, Colo. 80523   I-A

Coach: Earle Bruce, Ohio St. '53
Record: 20 yrs., W-149, L-83, T-2

1992 SCHEDULE

Colorado	Sep 5
Idaho ■	Sep 12
Fresno St.	Sep 19*
Louisiana St.	Sep 26*
Utah ■	Oct 3
UTEP ■	Oct 10
Air Force	Oct 17
Wyoming ■	Oct 24
San Diego St. ■	Oct 31
Hawaii	Nov 7*
Ohio ■	Nov 14
New Mexico	Nov 21

1991 RECORD

38	Arkansas St.	24	17	Brigham Young	40
26	Air Force	31	32	San Diego St.	42
14	Nebraska	71	36	New Mexico	38
7	Southern Miss.	39			
28	Hawaii	16	265	(3-8-0)	375
23	UTEP	18			
16	Utah	21			
28	Wyoming	35			

Conference: Western Athl. Conf. Enrollment: 20,600. Colors: Green & Gold.
Nickname: Rams. Stadium: Hughes (1968), 30,000 capacity. Natural turf.
1991 home attendance: 125,309 in 5 games.
Director of Athletics: Corey Johnson.
Sports Info. Director: Gary Ozzello. 303-491-5067

COLUMBIA . . . New York, N.Y. 10027   I-AA

Coach: Ray Tellier, Connecticut '73
Record: 8 yrs., W-24, L-53, T-1

1992 SCHEDULE

Harvard ■	Sep 19
Fordham	Sep 26
Colgate ■	Oct 3
Bucknell ■	Oct 10
Pennsylvania	Oct 17
Yale	Oct 24
Princeton ■	Oct 31
Dartmouth	Nov 7
Cornell ■	Nov 14
Brown ■	Nov 21

1991 RECORD

16	Harvard	21	21	Cornell	28
9	Lehigh	22	23	Brown	28
16	Fordham	20			
20	Pennsylvania	14	154	(1-9-0)	249
15	Lafayette	30			
9	Yale	36			
6	Princeton	22			
19	Dartmouth	22			

Conference: Ivy League. Enrollment: 3,300. Colors: Columbia Blue & White.
Nickname: Lions. Stadium: Lawrence A. Wien (1984), 17,000 capacity. Natural turf.
1991 home attendance: 29,030 in 5 games.
Director of Athletics: Dr. John Reeves.
Sports Info. Director: Bill Steinman 212-854-2534

■ Home games on each schedule [neutral sites shown in brackets]. *Night Games.

CONNECTICUT . . . Storrs, Conn. 06269 I-AA

Coach: Tom Jackson, Penn St. '70
Record: 9 yrs., W-51, L-46, T-0
1992 SCHEDULE

New Haven ■ .... Sep 5
New Hampshire .... Sep 12
Northeastern .... Sep 26
Yale ■ .... Oct 3
Villanova ■ .... Oct 10
Massachusetts .... Oct 17
Maine ■ .... Oct 24
Richmond ■ .... Oct 31
Delaware .... Nov 7
Boston U. .... Nov 14
Rhode Island ■ .... Nov 21

1991 RECORD

24	Furman	35	18	Delaware	49
16	New Hampshire	21	26	Boston U.	29
19	Lehigh	35	10	Rhode Island	20
13	Villanova	35			
34	Yale	20	241	(3-8-0)	340
26	Massachusetts	21			
20	Maine	41			
35	Richmond	34			

Conference: Yankee. Enrollment: 12,636. Colors: National Flag Blue & White.
Nickname: Huskies. Stadium: Memorial (1953), 16,200 capacity. Natural turf.
1991 home attendance: 43,129 in 5 games.
Director of Athletics: Lew Perkins.
Sports Info. Director: Tim Tolokan   203-486-3531

CORNELL . . . Ithaca, N.Y. 14853 I-AA

Coach: Jim Hofher, Cornell '79
Record: 2 yrs., W-12, L-8, T-0
1992 SCHEDULE

Princeton ■ .... Sep 19
Lehigh ■ .... Sep 26
Lafayette ■ .... Oct 3
Harvard .... Oct 10
Colgate .... Oct 17
Dartmouth ■ .... Oct 24
Brown ■ .... Oct 31
Yale .... Nov 7
Columbia .... Nov 14
Pennsylvania ■ .... Nov 21

1991 RECORD

0	Princeton	18	28	Columbia	21
13	Colgate	31	13	Pennsylvania	14
23	Bucknell	7			
6	Stanford	56	181	(5-5-0)	218
22	Harvard	17			
25	Dartmouth	31			
20	Brown	17			
31	Yale	6			

Conference: Ivy League. Enrollment: 12,900. Colors: Carnelian & White.
Nickname: Big Red. Stadium: Schoellkopf (1915), 27,000 capacity. Artificial turf.
1991 home attendance: 41,500 in 4 games.
Director of Athletics: Laing Kennedy
Sports Info. Director: Dave Wohlhueter   607-255-3752

DARTMOUTH . . . Hanover, N.H. 03755 I-AA

Coach: John Lyons, Pennsylvania '74
Record: First year as head coach
1992 SCHEDULE

Pennsylvania ■ .... Sep 19
New Hampshire .... Sep 26
Bucknell ■ .... Oct 3
Holy Cross .... Oct 10
Yale ■ .... Oct 17
Cornell .... Oct 24
Harvard .... Oct 31
Columbia ■ .... Nov 7
Brown .... Nov 14
Princeton .... Nov 21

1991 RECORD

21	Pennsylvania	15	45	Brown	13
34	Bucknell	16	31	Princeton	13
28	Lehigh	30			
6	Holy Cross	23	283	(7-2-1)	209
28	Yale	24			
31	Cornell	25			
31	Harvard	31			
28	Columbia	19			

Conference: Ivy League. Enrollment: 4,000. Colors: Dartmouth Green & White.
Nickname: Big Green. Stadium: Memorial Field (1923), 20,416 capacity. Natural turf.
1991 home attendance: 38,807 in 5 games.
Director of Athletics: Dick Jaeger.
Sports Info. Director: Kathy Slattery   603-646-2468

DELAWARE . . . Newark, Del. 19716 I-AA

Coach: Harold Raymond, Michigan '50
Record: 26 yrs., W-212, L-85, T-2
1992 SCHEDULE

Massachusetts ■ .... Sep 12
Rhode Island ■ .... Sep 19
West Chester ■ .... Sep 26
New Hampshire .... Oct 3
Boston U. ■ .... Oct 10
Villanova .... Oct 17
Navy .... Oct 24
Maine .... Oct 31
Connecticut ■ .... Nov 7
Richmond .... Nov 14
Towson St. ■ .... Nov 21

1991 RECORD

28	West Chester	0	34	Maine	10
24	Massachusetts	7	49	Connecticut	18
28	William & Mary	21	23	Richmond	17
42	Rhode Island	7			
28	New Hampshire	45	358	(10-1-0)	199
35	Boston U.	21		I-AA Championship	
38	Villanova	28	35	James Madison	42
29	Navy	25			

Conference: Yankee. Enrollment: 15,219. Colors: Blue & Gold.
Nickname: Fightin' Blue Hens. Stadium: Delaware (1952), 23,000 capacity. Natural turf.
1991 home attendance: 98,999 in 5 games.
Director of Athletics: Edgar Johnson.
Sports Info. Director: Benjamin M. Sherman   302-831-2186

DELAWARE STATE . . . Dover, Del. 19901 I-AA

Coach: William Collick, Delaware '74
Record: 7 yrs., W-50, L-24, T-0
1992 SCHEDULE

Cheyney [Wilmington, Del.] .... Sep 5
Youngstown St. .... Sep 12*
Bethune-Cookman [Ft. Lauderdale, Fla.] . Sep 19
Towson St. ■ .... Oct 10
Florida A&M ■ .... Oct 17
Morgan St. .... Oct 24
South Caro. St. ■ .... Oct 31
North Caro. A&T ■ .... Nov 7
Liberty .... Nov 14
Howard .... Nov 21

1991 RECORD

20	Bethune-Cookman	28	31	North Caro. A&T	26
33	Youngstown St.	29	46	Northeastern	20
13	Towson St.	7	56	Howard	12
37	Jackson St.	34			
9	Liberty	20	300	(8-3-0)	220
10	Florida A&M	20			
26	Morgan St.	10			
19	South Caro. St.	14			

Conference: Mid-Eastern. Enrollment: 2,600. Colors: Red & Blue.
Nickname: Hornets. Stadium: Alumni Field (1957), 5,000 capacity. Natural turf.
1991 home attendance: 30,904 in 6 games.
Director of Athletics: John Martin.
Sports Info. Director: Matt Santos   302-739-4926

■ Home games on each schedule [neutral sites shown in brackets].   *Night Games.

DUKE . . . Durham, N.C. 27706 — I-A

Coach: Barry Wilson, Georgia '65
Record: 2 yrs., W-8, L-13, T-1

1992 SCHEDULE

Florida St.	Sep 5*
Vanderbilt	Sep 12*
Rice ■	Sep 19
Virginia ■	Sep 26
East Caro. ■	Oct 10
Clemson	Oct 17
Maryland ■	Oct 24
Georgia Tech ■	Oct 31
Wake Forest ■	Nov 7
North Caro. St.	Nov 14
North Caro. ■	Nov 21

1991 RECORD

24	South Caro.	24	31	North Caro. St.	32
42	Rutgers	22	14	North Caro.	47
42	Colgate	14	21	Clemson	33
3	Virginia	34			
17	Vanderbilt	13	231	(4-6-1)	280
17	Maryland	13			
6	Georgia Tech	17			
14	Wake Forest	31			

Conference: Atlantic Coast Conf.   Enrollment: 6,300.   Colors: Royal Blue & White.
Nickname: Blue Devils.   Stadium: Wallace Wade (1929), 33,941 capacity.   Natural turf.
1991 home attendance: 177,727 in 6 games.
Director of Athletics: Tom Butters.
Sports Info. Director: Mike Cragg   919-684-2633

EAST CAROLINA . . . Greenville, N.C. 27834 — I-A

Coach: Steve Logan, Tulsa '75
Record: First year as head coach

1992 SCHEDULE

Syracuse ■	Sep 5*
Virginia Tech ■	Sep 12
South Caro.	Sep 19*
Bowling Green ■	Sep 26
Duke	Oct 10
Cincinnati ■	Oct 17
Pittsburgh	Oct 24
Southern Miss. ■	Oct 29*
West Va.	Nov 7
Arkansas St. ■	Nov 14
Memphis St.	Nov 21

1991 RECORD

31	Illinois	38	48	Southern Miss.	20
20	Memphis St.	13	24	Virginia Tech	17
47	Central Fla.	25	30	Cincinnati	19
31	South Caro.	20			
56	Akron	20	372	(10-1-0)	243
23	Syracuse	20		**Peach Bowl**	
24	Pittsburgh	23	37	North Caro. St.	34
38	Tulane	28			

Conference: I-A Independents.   Enrollment: 16,038.   Colors: Purple & Gold.
Nickname: Pirates.   Stadium: Ficklen (1963), 35,000 capacity.   Natural turf.
1991 home attendance: 160,208 in 5 games.
Director of Athletics: Dave Hart.
Sports Info. Director: Charles Bloom   919-757-4522

EAST TENNESSEE STATE . . . Johnson City, Tenn. 37614 — I-AA

Coach: Mike Cavan, Georgia '72
Record: 6 yrs., W-37, L-22, T-2

1992 SCHEDULE

Va. Military ■	Sep 5*
Mars Hill ■	Sep 12*
Citadel	Sep 19*
Appalachian St.	Sep 26
Morehead St. ■	Oct 3*
Charleston So. ■	Oct 10
Louisiana Tech	Oct 17
Furman ■	Oct 31
Tenn.-Chatt.	Nov 7*
Western Caro.	Nov 14
Marshall ■	Nov 21

1991 RECORD

20	Va. Military	35	26	Tenn.-Chatt.	43
6	Samford	31	7	Citadel	17
15	Western Caro.	29	9	Marshall	63
43	Newberry	12			
7	South Caro.	55	183	(1-10-0)	396
14	Appalachian St.	21			
13	North Caro. A&T	38			
23	Furman	52			

Conference: Southern Conf.   Enrollment: 12,000.   Colors: Blue & Gold.
Nickname: Buccaneers.   Stadium: Memorial (1977), 12,000 capacity.   Artificial turf.
1991 home attendance: 25,597 in 7 games.
Director of Athletics: Janice Shelton.
Sports Info. Director: John Cathey   615-929-4220

EASTERN ILLINOIS . . . Charleston, Ill. 61920 — I-AA

Coach: Bob Spoo, Purdue '60
Record: 5 yrs., W-28, L-29, T-0

1992 SCHEDULE

Austin Peay	Sep 5*
Marshall	Sep 12*
Murray St. ■	Sep 19*
Illinois St.	Sep 26
Southern Ill. ■	Oct 3*
Indiana St. ■	Oct 10
Western Ill.	Oct 17
Southwest Mo. St.	Oct 24
Youngstown St.	Oct 31
Northern Iowa ■	Nov 7
Western Ky. ■	Nov 14

1991 RECORD

62	Lock Haven	16	26	Western Ky.	28
13	Iowa St.	42	35	Southwest Mo. St.	29
30	Eastern Wash.	12	17	Northern Iowa	18
27	Murray St.	28			
15	Western Ill.	16	307	(4-7-0)	264
15	Indiana St.	16			
37	Illinois St.	28			
30	Southern Ill.	31			

Conference: Gateway.   Enrollment: 10,000.   Colors: Blue & Gray.
Nickname: Panthers.   Stadium: O'Brien (1970), 10,000 capacity.   Natural turf.
1991 home attendance: 31,600 in 5 games.
Director of Athletics: Mike Ryan.
Sports Info. Director: Dave Kidwell   217-581-6408

EASTERN KENTUCKY . . . Richmond, Ky. 40475 — I-AA

Coach: Roy Kidd, Eastern Ky. '54
Record: 28 yrs., W-230, L-81, T-8

1992 SCHEDULE

Western Ky.	Sep 5
Northeast La. ■	Sep 19*
Tennessee Tech ■	Sep 26*
Southeast Mo. St. ■	Oct 3
Samford	Oct 10*
Middle Tenn. St.	Oct 17
Tenn.-Martin	Oct 24
Tennessee St. ■	Oct 31
Murray St. ■	Nov 7
Austin Peay	Nov 14
Morehead St.	Nov 21

1991 RECORD

14	Louisville	24	21	Austin Peay	0
49	Southeast Mo. St.	7	41	Morehead St.	10
17	Middle Tenn. St.	7			
19	Tennessee Tech	13	333	(10-1-0)	147
10	Ga. Southern	6		**I-AA Championship**	
37	Western Ky.	22	14	Appalachian St.	3
56	Tenn.-Martin	21	23	Middle Tenn. St.	13
27	Tennessee St.	20	7	Marshall	14
42	Murray St.	17			

Conference: Ohio Valley Conf.   Enrollment: 16,500.   Colors: Maroon & White.
Nickname: Colonels.   Stadium: Roy Kidd (1969), 20,000 capacity.   Natural turf.
1991 home attendance: 91,000 in 6 games.
Director of Athletics: Roy Kidd.
Sports Info. Director: Karl Park   606-622-1253

■ Home games on each schedule [neutral sites shown in brackets].   *Night Games.

EASTERN MICHIGAN . . . Ypsilanti, Mich. 48197   I-A

Coach: Jim Harkema, Kalamazoo '64
Record: 19 yrs., W-109, L-82, T-6
1992 SCHEDULE

Akron ■	Sep 5*
Louisiana Tech	Sep 12*
Penn St.	Sep 19
Kent ■	Sep 26*
Miami (Ohio) ■	Oct 3*
Ball St.	Oct 10
Western Mich.	Oct 17
Ohio ■	Oct 24*
Army	Oct 31
Central Mich.	Nov 7
Toledo	Nov 14

1991 RECORD

6	Bowling Green	17	14 Central Mich.	14
3	Purdue	49	13 Ohio	10
3	Miami (Ohio)	29	14 Toledo	21
14	Louisiana Tech	17		
6	Wisconsin	21	144 (3-7-1)	232
21	Kent	20		
8	Ball St.	10		
42	Western Mich.	24		

Conference: Mid-American Conf. Enrollment: 25,000. Colors: Green & White.
Nickname: Eagles. Stadium: Rynearson (1969), 30,000 capacity. Artificial turf.
1991 home attendance: 29,690 in 5 games.
Director of Athletics: Gene Smith.
Sports Info. Director: Jim Streeter 313-487-0317

EASTERN WASHINGTON . . . Cheney, Wash. 99004   I-AA

Coach: Dick Zornes, Eastern Wash. '68
Record: 13 yrs., W-72, L-59, T-2
1992 SCHEDULE

Portland St. ■	Sep 12
Sonoma St. ■	Sep 19
Montana	Sep 26
Weber St. ■	Oct 3
Montana St. ■	Oct 10
Idaho ■	Oct 17
Northern Ariz.	Oct 24*
Idaho St.	Oct 31*
Northeast La.	Nov 7*
Boise St. ■	Nov 14

1991 RECORD

20	Cal St. Northridge	13	44 Northern Ariz.	29
12	Eastern Ill.	30	36 Idaho St.	43
17	Boise St.	31	22 Montana St.	21
59	Weber St.	63		
20	Montana	17	301 (5-6-0)	364
23	Portland St.	35		
14	Nevada	51		
34	Idaho	31		

Conference: Big Sky Conf. Enrollment: 8,000. Colors: Red & White.
Nickname: Eagles. Stadium: Woodward (1967), 6,000 capacity. Natural turf.
1991 home attendance: 23,508 in 6 games.
Director of Athletics: Dick Zornes.
Sports Info. Director: Dave Cook 509-359-6334

FLORIDA . . . Gainesville, Fla. 32604   I-A

Coach: Steve Spurrier, Florida '67
Record: 5 yrs., W-39, L-17, T-1
1992 SCHEDULE

Kentucky ■	Sep 12*
Tennessee	Sep 19
Mississippi St.	Oct 1*
Louisiana St. ■	Oct 10
Auburn ■	Oct 17
Louisville ■	Oct 24
Georgia [Jacksonville, Fla.]	Oct 31
Southern Miss. ■	Nov 7
South Caro. ■	Nov 14
Vanderbilt	Nov 21
Florida St.	Nov 28

1991 RECORD

59	San Jose St.	21	45 Georgia	13
35	Alabama	0	35 Kentucky	26
21	Syracuse	38	14 Florida St.	9
29	Mississippi St.	7		
16	Louisiana St.	0	361 (10-1-0)	152
35	Tennessee	18	USF&G Sugar Bowl	
41	Northern Ill.	10	28 Notre Dame	39
31	Auburn	10		

Conference: Southeastern Conf. Enrollment: 34,500. Colors: Orange & Blue.
Nickname: Gators. Stadium: Florida Field (1929), 83,000 capacity. Natural turf.
1991 home attendance: 506,729 in 6 games.
Director of Athletics: Jeremy Foley.
Sports Info. Director: John Humenik 904-375-4683

FLORIDA A&M . . . Tallahassee, Fla. 32307   I-AA

Coach: Ken Riley, Florida A&M '69
Record: 6 yrs., W-36, L-28, T-2
1992 SCHEDULE

Ga. Southern	Sep 5
South Caro. St. ■	Sep 12*
Miami (Fla.)	Sep 19
Tennessee St. [Atlanta, Ga.]	Sep 26
Howard ■	Oct 3*
North Caro. A&T [Orlando, Fla.]	Oct 10
Delaware St.	Oct 17
Morgan St. ■	Oct 31
Southern-B.R.	Nov 7*
Grambling	Nov 14
Bethune-Cookman [Tampa, Fla.]	Nov 28

1991 RECORD

47	Tuskegee	24	24 Southern-B.R.	20
21	Howard	28	22 Grambling	25
21	Ga. Southern	28	46 Bethune-Cookman	28
43	Tennessee St.	7		
19	North Caro. A&T	41	325 (6-5-0)	238
20	Delaware St.	10		
7	South Caro. St.	21		
55	Morgan St.	6		

Conference: Mid-Eastern. Enrollment: 8,300. Colors: Orange & Green.
Nickname: Rattlers. Stadium: Bragg Memorial (1957), 25,500 capacity. Natural turf.
1991 home attendance: 176,448 in 7 games.
Director of Athletics: Walter Reed.
Sports Info. Director: Alvin Hollins 904-599-3200

FLORIDA STATE . . . Tallahassee, Fla. 32306   I-A

Coach: Bobby Bowden, Samford '53
Record: 26 yrs., W-216, L-76, T-3
1992 SCHEDULE

Duke ■	Sep 5*
Clemson	Sep 12
North Caro. St.	Sep 19
Wake Forest ■	Sep 26*
Miami (Fla.)	Oct 3
North Caro. ■	Oct 10
Georgia Tech	Oct 17
Virginia	Oct 31
Maryland ■	Nov 7
Tulane ■	Nov 14
Florida ■	Nov 28

1991 RECORD

44	Brigham Young	28	40 Louisville	15
38	Tulane	11	38 South Caro.	10
58	Western Mich.	0	16 Miami (Fla.)	17
51	Michigan	31	9 Florida	14
46	Syracuse	14		
33	Virginia Tech	20	439 (10-2-0)	186
39	Middle Tenn. St.	10	Mobil Cotton Bowl	
27	Louisiana St.	16	10 Texas A&M	2

Conference: Atlantic Coast Conf. Enrollment: 28,077. Colors: Garnet & Gold.
Nickname: Seminoles. Stadium: Doak S. Campbell (1950), 60,519 capacity. Natural turf.
1991 home attendance: 367,833 in 6 games.
Director of Athletics: Bob Goin.
Sports Info. Director: Wayne Hogan 904-644-1403

■ Home games on each schedule [neutral sites shown in brackets]. *Night Games.

Divisions I-A & I-AA 1992 Schedules and 1991 Results

FORDHAM . . . New York, N.Y.   10458   I-AA

Coach: Larry Glueck, Villanova '63
Record: 6 yrs., W-28, L-32, T-1

1992 SCHEDULE

Lehigh	Sep 12
Colgate ■	Sep 19
Columbia ■	Sep 26
Pennsylvania ■	Oct 3
Yale	Oct 10
Hofstra	Oct 16*
Lafayette ■	Oct 24
Bucknell	Oct 31
Villanova	Nov 14
Holy Cross	Nov 21

1991 RECORD

7	Lehigh	32	7	Lafayette	33
14	Bucknell	21	19	Holy Cross	24
17	Princeton	20	9	Villanova	14
20	Columbia	16			
14	Harvard	7	149	(2-8-0)	242
30	Hofstra	50			
12	Colgate	25			

Conference: Patriot League.   Enrollment: 6,600.   Colors: Maroon & White.
Nickname: Rams.   Stadium: Jack Coffey Field (1930), 7,000 capacity.   Natural turf.
1991 home attendance: 25,051 in 6 games.
Director of Athletics: Frank McLaughlin.
Sports Info. Director: Joe Del Balso   212-579-2445

FRESNO STATE . . . Fresno, Cal.   93740   I-A

Coach: Jim Sweeney, Portland '51
Record: 27 yrs., W-169, L-125, T-3

1992 SCHEDULE

Pacific (Cal.)	Sep 5*
Oregon St.	Sep 12
Colorado St. ■	Sep 19*
Washington St. ■	Sep 26*
Louisiana Tech ■	Oct 3*
Brigham Young	Oct 10
Hawaii	Oct 17*
New Mexico ■	Oct 24*
Wyoming ■	Oct 31*
Utah ■	Nov 7*
San Diego St.	Nov 21*
UTEP	Nov 28*

1991 RECORD

55	Northern Ill.	7	59	Pacific (Cal.)	14
34	Washington St.	30	38	Cal St. Fullerton	7
24	Oregon St.	20	31	San Jose St.	28
94	New Mexico	17			
42	Long Beach St.	14	486	(10-1-0)	207
42	New Mexico St.	28		**California Raisin Bowl**	
48	Nevada-Las Vegas	22	21	Bowling Green	28
19	Utah St.	20			

Conference: Western Athl. Conf.   Enrollment: 19,586.   Colors: Cardinal & Blue.
Nickname: Bulldogs.   Stadium: Bulldog (1981), 40,953 capacity.   Natural turf.
1991 home attendance: 203,394 in 6 games.
Director of Athletics: Gary Cunningham.
Sports Info. Director: Scott Johnson   209-278-2509

FURMAN . . . Greenville, S.C.   29613   I-AA

Coach: Jimmy Satterfield, South Caro. '62
Record: 6 yrs., W-55, L-19, T-2

1992 SCHEDULE

Liberty ■	Sep 5*
North Caro.	Sep 12*
Presbyterian ■	Sep 19
Ga. Southern ■	Sep 26
Va. Military ■	Oct 3
Marshall	Oct 10*
Appalachian St.	Oct 24
East Tenn. St.	Oct 31
Western Caro. ■	Nov 7
Tenn.-Chatt.	Nov 14
Citadel ■	Nov 21

1991 RECORD

35	Connecticut	24	17	Georgia Tech	19
31	Liberty	7	24	Tenn.-Chatt.	21
52	Presbyterian	7	6	Citadel	10
42	Western Caro.	14			
46	Va. Military	28	363	(7-4-0)	217
35	Marshall	38			
23	Appalachian St.	26			
52	East Tenn. St.	23			

Conference: Southern Conf.   Enrollment: 2,500.   Colors: Purple & White.
Nickname: Paladins.   Stadium: Paladin (1981), 16,000 capacity.   Natural turf.
1991 home attendance: 85,173 in 6 games.
Director of Athletics: Ray Parlier.
Sports Info. Director: Hunter Reid   803-294-2061

GEORGIA . . . Athens, Ga.   30602   I-A

Coach: Ray Goff, Georgia '78
Record: 3 yrs., W-19, L-16, T-0

1992 SCHEDULE

South Caro.	Sep 5*
Tennessee ■	Sep 12
Cal St. Fullerton ■	Sep 19
Mississippi ■	Sep 26
Arkansas	Oct 3
Ga. Southern ■	Oct 10
Vanderbilt ■	Oct 17
Kentucky	Oct 24*
Florida [Jacksonville, Fla.]	Oct 31
Auburn	Nov 14
Georgia Tech ■	Nov 28

1991 RECORD

48	Western Caro.	0	13	Florida	45
31	Louisiana St.	10	37	Auburn	27
0	Alabama	10	18	Georgia Tech	15
27	Cal St. Fullerton	14			
27	Clemson	12	312	(8-3-0)	204
37	Mississippi	17		**Poulan Independence Bowl**	
25	Vanderbilt	27	24	Arkansas	15
49	Kentucky	27			

Conference: Southeastern Conf.   Enrollment: 28,341.   Colors: Red & Black.
Nickname: Bulldogs.   Stadium: Sanford (1929), 85,434 capacity.   Natural turf.
1991 home attendance: 577,922 in 7 games.
Director of Athletics: Vince Dooley.
Sports Info. Director: Claude Felton   404-542-1621

GEORGIA SOUTHERN . . . Statesboro, Ga.   30460   I-AA

Coach: Tim Stowers, Auburn '79
Record: 2 yrs., W-19, L-7, T-0

1992 SCHEDULE

Florida A&M	Sep 5
Valdosta St. ■	Sep 12
Savannah St. ■	Sep 19
Furman	Sep 26
Georgia	Oct 10
James Madison ■	Oct 17
Jacksonville St. ■	Oct 24
Middle Tenn. St. ■	Oct 31
Mississippi Col. ■	Nov 7
Troy St. ■	Nov 14
Youngstown St.	Nov 21

1991 RECORD

17	Auburn	32	17	Youngstown St.	19
29	Savannah St.	6	19	Troy St.	12
13	Northeast La.	21	40	Nicholls St.	6
28	Florida A&M	21			
6	Eastern Ky.	10	257	(7-4-0)	160
44	Western Caro.	6			
24	James Madison	21			
20	Central Fla.	6			

Conference: Southern Conf.   Enrollment: 13,500.   Colors: Blue & White.
Nickname: Eagles.   Stadium: Paulson (1984), 18,000 capacity.   Natural turf.
1991 home attendance: 83,519 in 5 games.
Director of Athletics: David Wagner.
Sports Info. Director: Matt Rogers   912-681-5239

■ Home games on each schedule [neutral sites shown in brackets].   *Night Games.

1992 NCAA FOOTBALL

GEORGIA TECH . . . Atlanta, Ga. 30332

Coach: Bill Lewis, East Stroudsburg '63
Record: 6 yrs., W-34, L-33, T-2

1992 SCHEDULE

Western Caro. ■	Sep 12*
Virginia	Sep 19
Clemson ■	Sep 26
North Caro. St. ■	Oct 3
Maryland	Oct 10
Florida St. ■	Oct 17
North Caro.	Oct 24
Duke ■	Oct 31
Baylor	Nov 7
Wake Forest ■	Nov 14
Georgia	Nov 28

1991 RECORD

22	Penn St.	34	17	Duke	6
30	Boston College	14	19	Furman	17
24	Virginia	21	27	Wake Forest	3
7	Clemson	9	15	Georgia	18
21	North Caro. St.	28			
34	Maryland	10	265	(7-5-0)	197
14	South Caro.	23		**Jeep Eagle Aloha Bowl**	
35	North Caro.	14	18	Stanford	17

Conference: Atlantic Coast Conf.   Enrollment: 11,900.   Colors: Old Gold & White.
Nickname: Yellow Jackets.   Stadium: Bobby Dodd/Grant Field (1914),
46,000 capacity.   Artificial turf.
1991 home attendance: 333,370 in 7 games.
Director of Athletics: Homer Rice.
Sports Info. Director: Mike Finn   404-894-5445

GRAMBLING . . . Grambling, La. 71245

Coach: Eddie Robinson, Leland '41
Record: 49 yrs., W-371, L-134, T-15

1992 SCHEDULE

Alcorn St. [Shreveport, La.]	Sep 5*
Virginia Union	Sep 12*
Tennessee St. ■	Sep 19*
Prairie View [Dallas, Tex.]	Oct 3*
Mississippi Val. [New Orleans, La.]	Oct 17
Jackson St. ■	Oct 24
Texas Southern	Oct 31*
Alabama St. ■	Nov 7
Florida A&M	Nov 14
Southern-B.R.	Nov 28

1991 RECORD

22	Alcorn St.	27	14	Alabama St.	60
37	Virginia Union	46	25	Virginia A&M	22
24	Tennessee St.	21	30	Southern-B.R.	31
12	North Caro. A&T	28			
77	Prairie View	7	330	(5-6-0)	338
37	Mississippi Val.	35			
22	Jackson St.	34			
30	Texas Southern	27			

Conference: Southwestern.   Enrollment: 7,030.   Colors: Black & Gold.
Nickname: Tigers.   Stadium: Robinson (1983), 22,000 capacity.   Natural turf.
1991 home attendance: 217,444 in 8 games.
Director of Athletics: Eddie Robinson.
Sports Info. Director: Stanley Lewis   318-274-2761

HARVARD . . . Cambridge, Mass. 02138

Coach: Joseph Restic, Villanova '52
Record: 21 yrs., W-111, L-83, T-6

1992 SCHEDULE

Columbia	Sep 19
William & Mary ■	Sep 26
Holy Cross	Oct 3
Cornell ■	Oct 10
Lafayette	Oct 17
Princeton	Oct 24
Dartmouth ■	Oct 31
Brown ■	Nov 7
Pennsylvania	Nov 14
Yale ■	Nov 21

1991 RECORD

21	Columbia	16	22	Pennsylvania	18
20	Army	21	13	Yale	23
13	Holy Cross	28			
7	Fordham	14	203	(4-5-1)	223
17	Cornell	22			
24	Princeton	21			
31	Dartmouth	31			
35	Brown	29			

Conference: Ivy League.   Enrollment: 6,592.   Colors: Crimson, Black & White.
Nickname: Crimson.   Stadium: Harvard (1903), 37,289 capacity.   Natural turf.
1991 home attendance: 79,146 in 5 games.
Director of Athletics: William Cleary Jr.
Sports Info. Director: John Veneziano   617-495-2206

HAWAII . . . Honolulu, Hawaii 96822

Coach: Bob Wagner, Wittenberg '69
Record: 5 yrs., W-34, L-25, T-2

1992 SCHEDULE

Oregon	Sep 5
Air Force	Sep 12
Brigham Young ■	Sep 26*
Utah	Oct 10
Fresno St. ■	Oct 17*
Nevada-Las Vegas ■	Oct 24*
UTEP	Oct 31*
Colorado St. ■	Nov 7*
San Diego St.	Nov 14*
Wyoming ■	Nov 21*
Tulsa ■	Nov 28*
Pittsburgh ■	Dec 5

1991 RECORD

32	Wyoming	17	24	UTEP	41
10	Iowa	53	35	San Jose St.	35
35	New Mexico	13	20	Air Force	24
30	Pacific (Cal.)	21	42	Notre Dame	48
16	Colorado St.	28			
21	San Diego St.	47	335	(4-7-1)	388
18	Brigham Young	35			
52	Utah	26			

Conference: Western Athl. Conf.   Enrollment: 18,874.   Colors: Green & White.
Nickname: Rainbow Warriors.   Stadium: Aloha (1975), 50,000 capacity.   Artificial turf.
1991 home attendance: 304,148 in 7 games.
Director of Athletics: Stan Sheriff.
Sports Info. Director: Eddie Inouye   808-956-7523

HOLY CROSS . . . Worcester, Mass. 01610

Coach: Peter Vaas, Holy Cross '74
Record: 4 yrs., W-29, L-11, T-1

1992 SCHEDULE

Army	Sep 12
Massachusetts ■	Sep 19
Yale	Sep 26
Harvard ■	Oct 3
Dartmouth ■	Oct 10
Princeton ■	Oct 17
Bucknell ■	Oct 24
Lehigh ■	Oct 31
Lafayette	Nov 7
Colgate	Nov 14
Fordham ■	Nov 21

1991 RECORD

22	Massachusetts	20	42	Bucknell	6
27	Boston U.	23	24	Fordham	19
45	Pennsylvania	0	28	Colgate	3
28	Harvard	13			
23	Dartmouth	6	372	(11-0-0)	174
42	Brown	28			
43	Lehigh	42			
48	Lafayette	14			

Conference: Patriot League.   Enrollment: 2,600.   Colors: Royal Purple.
Nickname: Crusaders.   Stadium: Fitton Field (1924), 23,500 capacity.   Natural turf.
1991 home attendance: 67,695 in 5 games.
Director of Athletics: Ron Perry.
Sports Info. Director: Jeff Nelson   508-793-2583

■ Home games on each schedule [neutral sites shown in brackets].   *Night Games.

HOUSTON . . . Houston, Tex.   77004   I-A

Coach: John Jenkins, Arkansas '73
Record: 2 yrs., W-14, L-8, T-0

1992 SCHEDULE

Tulsa .... Sep 5*
Illinois ■ .... Sep 19
Michigan .... Sep 26
Southwestern La. ■ .... Oct 3
Baylor .... Oct 17
Texas .... Oct 24
Texas Christian ■ .... Oct 31
Southern Methodist .... Nov 7
Texas A&M ■ .... Nov 12
Texas Tech .... Nov 21
Rice ■ .... Nov 28

1991 RECORD

73	Louisiana Tech	3	
10	Miami (Fla.)	40	
10	Illinois	51	
21	Baylor	38	
17	Arkansas	29	
49	Southern Methodist	20	
18	Texas A&M	27	
23	Texas	14	
41	Rice	21	
45	Texas Christian	49	
46	Texas Tech	52	
353	(4-7-0)	344	

Conference: Southwest Conf. Enrollment: 34,000. Colors: Scarlet & White.
Nickname: Cougars. Stadium: Astrodome (1965), 60,000 capacity. Artificial turf.
1991 home attendance: 165,395 in 5 games.
Director of Athletics: Rudy Davalos.
Sports Info. Director: Ted Nance 713-743-9404

HOWARD . . . Washington, D.C.   20059   I-AA

Coach: Steve Wilson, Howard '79
Record: 2 yrs., W-16, L-17, T-0

1992 SCHEDULE

Morehouse .... Sep 5
Alabama A&M [Los Angeles, Cal.] .. Sep 12*
Cheyney [Philadelphia, Pa.] ...... Sep 19
Alcorn St. ■ .... Sep 26
Florida A&M .... Oct 3*
Bethune-Cookman ■ .... Oct 10
North Caro. A&T ■ .... Oct 24
Bowie St. ■ .... Oct 31
South Caro. St. .... Nov 7
Morgan St. ■ .... Nov 14
Delaware St. ■ .... Nov 21

1991 RECORD

62	Fayetteville St.	0	
28	Florida A&M	21	
5	South Caro. St.	10	
0	Temple	40	
27	Alcorn St.	46	
14	Bethune-Cookman	20	
9	North Caro. A&T	26	
16	Central St. (Ohio)	49	
7	Towson St.	13	
28	Morgan St.	38	
12	Delaware St.	56	
208	(2-9-0)	319	

Conference: Mid-Eastern. Enrollment: 12,500. Colors: Blue & White.
Nickname: Bison. Stadium: Greene (1986), 7,500 capacity. Artificial turf.
1991 home attendance: 134,845 in 6 games.
Director of Athletics: David C. Simmons.
Sports Info. Director: Edward Hill 202-806-7182

IDAHO . . . Moscow, Ida.   83843   I-AA

Coach: John L. Smith, Weber St. '71
Record: 3 yrs., W-24, L-12, T-0

1992 SCHEDULE

St. Cloud St. ■ .... Sep 5*
Colorado St. .... Sep 12
Weber St. ■ .... Sep 19
Cal St. Northridge ■ .... Oct 3
Idaho St. ■ .... Oct 10
Eastern Wash. .... Oct 17
Northern Iowa .... Oct 24*
Northern Ariz. ■ .... Oct 31
Montana .... Nov 7
Montana St. ■ .... Nov 14
Boise St. .... Nov 21

1991 RECORD

49	Sonoma St.	7	
41	Southwest Tex. St.	38	
48	Montana St.	14	
14	Northern Iowa	36	
23	Nevada	31	
17	Weber St.	45	
46	Idaho St.	21	
31	Eastern Wash.	34	
44	Northern Ariz.	28	
34	Montana	35	
28	Boise St.	24	
375	(6-5-0)	313	

Conference: Big Sky Conf. Enrollment: 14,202. Colors: Silver & Gold.
Nickname: Vandals. Stadium: Kibbie (1975), 16,000 capacity. Artificial turf.
1991 home attendance: 85,500 in 7 games.
Director of Athletics: To be named.
Sports Info. Director: Rance Pugmire 208-885-0211

IDAHO STATE . . . Pocatello, Ida.   83209   I-AA

Coach: Brian McNeely, Wichita St. '79
Record: First year as head coach

1992 SCHEDULE

Mesa St. ■ .... Sep 5*
Boise St. ■ .... Sep 12*
Northern Iowa .... Sep 19
Northern Ariz. .... Sep 26*
Central Wash. ■ .... Oct 3*
Idaho .... Oct 10
Montana St. .... Oct 17
Weber St. .... Oct 24
Eastern Wash. ■ .... Oct 31*
Southern Utah ■ .... Nov 14*
Montana ■ .... Nov 21*

1991 RECORD

38	Mesa St.	7	
7	Kansas St.	41	
13	Montana	24	
45	Northern Ariz.	14	
20	Nevada	41	
21	Idaho	46	
7	Montana St.	16	
16	Boise St.	38	
43	Eastern Wash.	36	
35	Southern Utah	35	
41	Weber St.	60	
286	(3-7-1)	358	

Conference: Big Sky Conf. Enrollment: 11,037. Colors: Orange & Black.
Nickname: Bengals. Stadium: Holt Arena (1970), 12,000 capacity. Artificial turf.
1991 home attendance: 28,347 in 5 games.
Director of Athletics: Randy Hoffman.
Sports Info. Director: Glenn Alford 208-236-3651

ILLINOIS . . . Champaign, Ill.   61820   I-A

Coach: Lou Tepper, Rutgers '67
Record: 1 yr., W-0, L-1, T-0

1992 SCHEDULE

Northern Ill. ■ .... Sep 5
Missouri ■ .... Sep 12
Houston .... Sep 19
Minnesota .... Oct 3*
Ohio St. .... Oct 10
Iowa ■ .... Oct 17
Northwestern ■ .... Oct 24
Wisconsin .... Oct 31
Purdue ■ .... Nov 7
Michigan .... Nov 14
Michigan St. ■ .... Nov 21

1991 RECORD

38	East Caro.	31	
19	Missouri	23	
51	Houston	10	
24	Minnesota	3	
10	Ohio St.	7	
21	Iowa	24	
11	Northwestern	17	
22	Wisconsin	6	
41	Purdue	14	
0	Michigan	20	
24	Michigan St.	27	
261	(6-5-0)	182	
	John Hancock Bowl		
3	UCLA	6	

Conference: Big Ten Conf. Enrollment: 35,766. Colors: Orange & Blue.
Nickname: Fighting Illini. Stadium: Memorial (1923), 69,200 capacity. Artificial turf.
1991 home attendance: 333,642 in 6 games.
Director of Athletics: Ron Guenther.
Sports Info. Director: Mike Pearson 217-333-1390

■ Home games on each schedule [neutral sites shown in brackets].   *Night Games.

ILLINOIS STATE ... Normal, Ill. 61761 I-AA

Coach: Jim Heacock, Muskingum '70
Record: 4 yrs., W-16, L-28, T-0
1992 SCHEDULE

Southwest St. (Minn.) ■	Sep 5*
Northern Ill.	Sep 12*
Indiana St.	Sep 19*
Eastern Ill. ■	Sep 26
Northern Iowa	Oct 3
Youngstown St.	Oct 10*
Southwest Mo. St. ■	Oct 17
Southern Ill. ■	Oct 24
Western Ill.	Oct 31
Western Ky.	Nov 7
Southeast Mo. St.	Nov 14

1991 RECORD

19	St. Francis (Ill.)	17	6 Southwest Mo. St.	21
25	Akron	3	24 Northern Ill.	27
42	Southeast Mo. St.	7	31 Western Ky.	8
11	Southern Ill.	14		
6	Indiana St.	3	218 (5-6-0)	176
14	Northern Iowa	17		
28	Eastern Ill.	37		
12	Western Ill.	22		

Conference: Gateway. Enrollment: 22,000. Colors: Red & White.
Nickname: Redbirds. Stadium: Hancock (1963), 15,000 capacity. Artificial turf.
1991 home attendance: 53,952 in 6 games.
Director of Athletics: Ron Wellman.
Sports Info. Director: Kenny Mossman 309-438-3825

INDIANA ... Bloomington, Ind. 47405 I-A

Coach: Bill Mallory, Miami (Ohio) '57
Record: 22 yrs., W-143, L-98, T-4
1992 SCHEDULE

Miami (Ohio) ■	Sep 12
Kentucky	Sep 19*
Missouri ■	Sep 26
Michigan St.	Oct 3
Northwestern	Oct 10
Michigan ■	Oct 17
Wisconsin ■	Oct 24
Minnesota	Oct 31*
Iowa ■	Nov 7
Ohio St. ■	Nov 14
Purdue	Nov 21

1991 RECORD

27	Notre Dame	49	21 Iowa	38
13	Kentucky	10	16 Ohio St.	20
27	Missouri	27	24 Purdue	22
31	Michigan St.	0		
44	Northwestern	6	281 (6-4-1)	224
16	Michigan	24	**Domino's Copper Bowl**	
28	Wisconsin	20	24 Baylor	0
34	Minnesota	8		

Conference: Big Ten Conf. Enrollment: 34,500. Colors: Cream & Crimson.
Nickname: Fightin' Hoosiers. Stadium: Memorial (1960), 52,354 capacity. Artificial turf.
1991 home attendance: 236,602 in 5 games.
Director of Athletics: Clarence Doninger.
Sports Info. Director: Kit Klingelhoffer 812-855-2421

INDIANA STATE ... Terre Haute, Ind. 47809 I-AA

Coach: Dennis Raetz, Nebraska '68
Record: 12 yrs., W-64, L-69, T-1
1992 SCHEDULE

Oklahoma St.	Sep 5*
Western Ky.	Sep 12
Illinois St. ■	Sep 19*
Lock Haven ■	Sep 26*
Youngstown St. ■	Oct 3
Eastern Ill.	Oct 17
Glenville St. ■	Oct 17
Western Ill.	Oct 24
Northern Iowa ■	Oct 31
Southwest Mo. St. ■	Nov 14
Southern Ill.	Nov 21

1991 RECORD

25	Kansas St.	26	7 Western Ill.	6
35	Central Mo. St.	6	21 Northern Iowa	49
39	Concord	8	31 Western Ky.	14
10	Ball St.	14		
3	Illinois St.	6	229 (5-6-0)	242
16	Eastern Ill.	15		
19	Southwest Mo. St.	68		
23	Southern Ill.	30		

Conference: Gateway. Enrollment: 12,005. Colors: Blue & White.
Nickname: Sycamores. Stadium: Memorial (1970), 20,500 capacity. Artificial turf.
1991 home attendance: 35,984 in 7 games.
Director of Athletics: Brian Faison.
Sports Info. Director: Eric Ruden 812-237-4161

IOWA ... Iowa City, Iowa 52242 I-A

Coach: Hayden Fry, Baylor '51
Record: 30 yrs., W-189, L-140, T-9
1992 SCHEDULE

North Caro. St. [East Rutherford, N.J.]	Aug 29*
Miami (Fla.) ■	Sep 5*
Iowa St. ■	Sep 12
Colorado	Sep 26
Michigan	Oct 3
Wisconsin ■	Oct 10
Illinois	Oct 17
Purdue ■	Oct 24
Ohio St. ■	Oct 31
Indiana	Nov 7
Northwestern ■	Nov 14
Minnesota	Nov 21*

1991 RECORD

53	Hawaii	10	38 Indiana	21
29	Iowa St.	10	24 Northwestern	10
58	Northern Ill.	7	23 Minnesota	8
24	Michigan	43		
10	Wisconsin	6	330 (10-1-0)	166
24	Illinois	21	**Thrifty Holiday Bowl**	
31	Purdue	21	13 Brigham Young	13
16	Ohio St.	9		

Conference: Big Ten Conf. Enrollment: 28,000. Colors: Old Gold & Black.
Nickname: Hawkeyes. Stadium: Kinnick (1929), 70,311 capacity. Natural turf.
1991 home attendance: 420,424 in 6 games.
Director of Athletics: Bob Bowlsby.
Sports Info. Director: George Wine 319-335-9411

IOWA STATE ... Ames, Iowa 50011 I-A

Coach: Jim Walden, Wyoming '60
Record: 14 yrs., W-92, L-87, T-6
1992 SCHEDULE

Ohio ■	Sep 5
Iowa	Sep 12
Tulane ■	Sep 19
Northern Iowa ■	Sep 26
Oklahoma	Oct 3
Kansas ■	Oct 17
Oklahoma St.	Oct 24
Missouri ■	Oct 31
Kansas St.	Nov 7
Nebraska ■	Nov 14
Colorado	Nov 21

1991 RECORD

42	Eastern Ill.	13	7 Kansas St.	37
10	Iowa	29	13 Nebraska	38
6	Wisconsin	7	14 Colorado	17
28	Rice	27		
8	Oklahoma	29	157 (3-7-1)	266
0	Kansas	41		
6	Oklahoma St.	6		
23	Missouri	22		

Conference: Big Eight Conf. Enrollment: 25,707. Colors: Cardinal & Gold.
Nickname: Cyclones. Stadium: Cyclone-Jack Trice (1975), 50,000 capacity. Artificial turf.
1991 home attendance: 254,007 in 6 games.
Director of Athletics: Max Urick.
Sports Info. Director: Dave Starr 515-294-3372

■ Home games on each schedule [neutral sites shown in brackets]. *Night Games.

JACKSON STATE . . . Jackson, Miss. 39217 — I-AA

Coach: James Carson, Jackson St. '63
Record: First year as head coach

1992 SCHEDULE

Tuskegee ■ .... Sep 5*
Tennessee St. [Memphis, Tenn.] .... Sep 12*
Stephen F. Austin .... Sep 19*
Mississippi Val. ■ .... Sep 26*
South Caro. St. [Columbia, S.C.] .... Oct 3
Alabama St. .... Oct 10*
Southern-B.R. .... Oct 17*
Grambling .... Oct 24
Texas Southern ■ .... Nov 7*
Prairie View ■ .... Nov 14*
Alcorn St. .... Nov 21

1991 RECORD

27	Alabama St.	28	17	South Caro. St.	6
41	Tennessee St.	19	16	Alcorn St.	18
31	Stephen F. Austin	16			
14	Mississippi Val.	23	247	(5-5-0)	202
34	Delaware St.	37			
20	Southern-B.R.	21			
34	Grambling	22			
13	Texas Southern	12			

Conference: Southwestern. Enrollment: 6,699. Colors: Blue & White.
Nickname: Tigers. Stadium: Mississippi Memorial (1949), 62,512 capacity. Natural turf.
1991 home attendance: 162,162 in 7 games.
Director of Athletics: W. C. Gorden.
Sports Info. Director: Samuel Jefferson 601-968-2273

JAMES MADISON . . . Harrisonburg, Va. 22807 — I-AA

Coach: William "Rip" Scherer, William & Mary '74
Record: 1 yr., W-9, L-4, T-0

1992 SCHEDULE

Virginia Tech .... Sep 5*
Richmond .... Sep 12
Hofstra ■ .... Sep 19*
Youngstown St. .... Sep 26*
Northeastern ■ .... Oct 3
Appalachian St. ■ .... Oct 10
Ga. Southern .... Oct 17
Towson St. .... Oct 24
William & Mary ■ .... Oct 31
Liberty ■ .... Nov 7
Central Fla. .... Nov 14

1991 RECORD

12	Virginia Tech	41	35	Liberty	34
49	Central Fla.	31	21	Youngstown St.	28
31	Appalachian St.	8	27	Northeastern	10
29	William & Mary	28			
24	Massachusetts	7	351	(8-3-0)	284
55	Towson St.	31		**I-AA Championship**	
21	Ga. Southern	24	42	Delaware	35
47	Richmond	42	21	Samford	24

Conference: I-AA Independents. Enrollment: 11,000. Colors: Purple & Gold.
Nickname: Dukes. Stadium: Bridgeforth (1975), 15,000 capacity. Artificial turf.
1991 home attendance: 58,775 in 5 games.
Director of Athletics: Dean Ehlers.
Sports Info. Director: Gary Michael 703-568-6154

KANSAS . . . Lawrence, Kan. 66045 — I-A

Coach: Glen Mason, Ohio St. '72
Record: 6 yrs., W-26, L-39, T-1

1992 SCHEDULE

Oregon St. .... Sep 5
Ball St. ■ .... Sep 12
Tulsa .... Sep 19*
California ■ .... Sep 24*
Kansas St. ■ .... Oct 10
Iowa St. .... Oct 17
Oklahoma .... Oct 24
Oklahoma St. ■ .... Oct 31
Nebraska .... Nov 7
Colorado .... Nov 14
Missouri .... Nov 21

1991 RECORD

30	Toledo	7	23	Nebraska	59
23	Tulsa	17	24	Colorado	30
54	New Mexico St.	14	53	Missouri	29
19	Virginia	31			
12	Kansas St.	16	313	(6-5-0)	244
41	Iowa St.	0			
3	Oklahoma	41			
31	Oklahoma St.	0			

Conference: Big Eight Conf. Enrollment: 29,150. Colors: Crimson & Blue.
Nickname: Jayhawks. Stadium: Memorial (1921), 50,250 capacity. Artificial turf.
1991 home attendance: 149,662 in 5 games.
Director of Athletics: Bob Frederick.
Sports Info. Director: Doug Vance 913-864-3417

KANSAS STATE . . . Manhattan, Kan. 66506 — I-A

Coach: Bill Snyder, William Jewell '63
Record: 3 yrs., W-13, L-20, T-0

1992 SCHEDULE

Montana ■ .... Sep 19*
Temple ■ .... Sep 26*
New Mexico St. ■ .... Oct 3
Kansas .... Oct 10
Utah St. .... Oct 17
Colorado .... Oct 24
Oklahoma .... Oct 31
Iowa St. ■ .... Nov 7
Missouri .... Nov 14
Oklahoma St. .... Nov 21
Nebraska [Tokyo, Japan] .... Dec 6

1991 RECORD

26	Indiana St.	25	37	Iowa St.	7
41	Idaho St.	7	32	Missouri	0
34	Northern Ill.	17	36	Oklahoma St.	26
3	Washington	56			
16	Kansas	12	263	(7-4-0)	226
31	Nebraska	38			
0	Colorado	10			
7	Oklahoma	28			

Conference: Big Eight Conf. Enrollment: 21,902. Colors: Purple & White.
Nickname: Wildcats. Stadium: K S U (1968), 42,000 capacity. Artificial turf.
1991 home attendance: 174,367 in 6 games.
Director of Athletics: Milt Richards.
Sports Info. Director: Ben Boyle 913-532-6735

KENT . . . Kent, Ohio 44242 — I-A

Coach: Pete Cordelli, North Caro. St. '76
Record: 1 yr., W-1, L-10, T-0

1992 SCHEDULE

Pittsburgh .... Sep 5
Ohio ■ .... Sep 12
Ball St. ■ .... Sep 19
Eastern Mich. .... Sep 26*
Cincinnati .... Oct 3*
Akron ■ .... Oct 10
Central Mich. .... Oct 17
Western Mich. ■ .... Oct 24
Toledo .... Oct 31
Bowling Green ■ .... Nov 7
Miami (Ohio) .... Nov 14

1991 RECORD

10	Western Mich.	13	14	Toledo	13
0	North Caro. St.	47	7	Bowling Green	35
27	Ball St.	28	9	Miami (Ohio)	20
6	Kentucky	24			
20	Eastern Mich.	21	159	(1-10-0)	307
19	Cincinnati	38			
7	Central Mich.	23			
40	Ohio	45			

Conference: Mid-American Conf. Enrollment: 33,468. Colors: Navy Blue & Gold.
Nickname: Golden Flashes. Stadium: Dix (1969), 30,520 capacity. Natural turf.
1991 home attendance: 25,111 in 5 games.
Director of Athletics: Paul Amodio.
Sports Info. Director: John Wagner 216-672-2110

■ Home games on each schedule [neutral sites shown in brackets].   *Night Games.

1992 NCAA FOOTBALL

KENTUCKY . . . Lexington, Ky.   40506   I-A

Coach: Bill Curry, Georgia Tech '65
Record: 12 yrs., W-64, L-68, T-4

1992 SCHEDULE

Central Mich. ■	Sep 5*
Florida	Sep 12*
Indiana ■	Sep 19*
South Caro. ■	Sep 26*
Mississippi	Oct 3*
Louisiana St.	Oct 17*
Georgia	Oct 24*
Mississippi St. ■	Oct 31*
Vanderbilt	Nov 7
Cincinnati	Nov 14
Tennessee	Nov 21

1991 RECORD

23	Miami (Ohio)	20	7	Vanderbilt	17
10	Indiana	13	26	Florida	35
24	Kent	6	7	Tennessee	16
14	Mississippi	35			
6	Mississippi St.	31	190	(3-8-0)	268
26	Louisiana St.	29			
27	Georgia	49			
20	Cincinnati	17			

Conference: Southeastern Conf.   Enrollment: 23,000.   Colors: Blue & White.
Nickname: Wildcats.   Stadium: Commonwealth (1973), 58,000 capacity.   Natural turf.
1991 home attendance: 327,250 in 6 games.
Director of Athletics: C. M. Newton.
Sports Info. Director: Chris Cameron   606-257-3838

LAFAYETTE . . . Easton, Pa.   18042   I-AA

Coach: Bill Russo, Brown '69
Record: 14 yrs., W-81, L-66, T-1

1992 SCHEDULE

Hofstra ■	Sep 12
Buffalo ■	Sep 19
Princeton	Sep 26
Cornell	Oct 3
Army	Oct 10
Harvard ■	Oct 17
Fordham	Oct 24
Colgate	Oct 31
Holy Cross ■	Nov 7
Bucknell	Nov 14
Lehigh	Nov 21

1991 RECORD

42	Buffalo	21	33	Fordham	7
21	Va. Military	42	48	Colgate	31
14	Yale	24	18	Lehigh	36
20	Pennsylvania	12			
20	Bucknell	16	277	(6-5-0)	312
30	Columbia	15			
17	Hofstra	60			
14	Holy Cross	48			

Conference: Patriot League.   Enrollment: 2,050.   Colors: Maroon & White.
Nickname: Leopards.   Stadium: Fisher Field (1926), 13,750 capacity.   Natural turf.
1991 home attendance: 32,959 in 6 games.
Director of Athletics: Eve Atkinson.
Sports Info. Director: Steve Pulver   215-250-5122

LEHIGH . . . Bethlehem, Pa.   18015   I-AA

Coach: Hank Small, Gettysburg '69
Record: 6 yrs., W-37, L-28, T-1

1992 SCHEDULE

Fordham ■	Sep 12
New Hampshire ■	Sep 19
Cornell	Sep 26
Princeton ■	Oct 3
Northeastern	Oct 10
Brown	Oct 17
Colgate ■	Oct 24
Holy Cross	Oct 31
Bucknell ■	Nov 7
William & Mary	Nov 14
Lafayette	Nov 21

1991 RECORD

32	Fordham	7	21	Colgate	22
35	Connecticut	19	48	Bucknell	13
22	Columbia	9	36	Lafayette	18
30	Dartmouth	28			
35	Northeastern	22	363	(9-2-0)	235
28	Pennsylvania	17			
42	Holy Cross	43			
41	William & Mary	37			

Conference: Patriot League.   Enrollment: 4,500.   Colors: Brown & White.
Nickname: Engineers.   Stadium: Goodman (1988), 16,000 capacity.   Natural turf.
1991 home attendance: 71,021 in 6 games.
Director of Athletics: Joseph D. Sterrett.
Sports Info. Director: Glenn Hofmann   215-758-3174

LIBERTY . . . Lynchburg, Va.   24506   I-AA

Coach: Sam Rutigliano, Tulsa '56
Record: 3 yrs., W-18, L-14, T-0

1992 SCHEDULE

Furman	Sep 5*
Morgan St. ■	Sep 12
Concord ■	Sep 19*
North Caro. A&T	Sep 26
Towson St.	Oct 3*
Troy St.	Oct 17*
Northern Ill.	Oct 24
Central Fla. ■	Oct 31
James Madison	Nov 7
Delaware St. ■	Nov 14
Kutztown ■	Nov 21

1991 RECORD

14	Boise St.	35	26	Central Fla.	31
7	Furman	31	16	Kutztown	17
39	West Va. Tech	11	19	Samford	31
10	Morehead St.	12			
20	Delaware St.	9	233	(4-7-0)	248
10	Youngstown St.	8			
38	Towson St.	28			
34	James Madison	35			

Conference: I-AA Independents.   Enrollment: 10,000.   Colors: Red, White & Blue.
Nickname: Flames.   Stadium: Liberty (1989), 12,000 capacity.   Artificial turf.
1991 home attendance: 27,350 in 5 games.
Director of Athletics: Chuck Burch.
Sports Info. Director: Mitch Goodman   804-582-2292

LOUISIANA STATE . . . Baton Rouge, La.   70893   I-A

Coach: Curley Hallman, Texas A&M '70
Record: 4 yrs., W-28, L-17, T-0

1992 SCHEDULE

Texas A&M ■	Sep 5
Mississippi St. ■	Sep 12*
Auburn	Sep 19*
Colorado St. ■	Sep 26*
Tennessee ■	Oct 3*
Florida	Oct 10
Kentucky ■	Oct 17*
Mississippi [Jackson, Miss.]	Oct 31*
Alabama ■	Nov 7*
Tulane ■	Nov 21*
Arkansas	Nov 28

1991 RECORD

10	Georgia	31	17	Alabama	20
7	Texas A&M	45	19	Mississippi St.	28
16	Vanderbilt	14	39	Tulane	20
0	Florida	16			
70	Arkansas St.	14	248	(5-6-0)	263
29	Kentucky	26			
16	Florida St.	27			
25	Mississippi	22			

Conference: Southeastern Conf.   Enrollment: 25,977.   Colors: Purple & Gold.
Nickname: Fighting Tigers.   Stadium: Tiger (1924), 80,140 capacity.   Natural turf.
1991 home attendance: 412,476 in 6 games.
Director of Athletics: Joe Dean.
Sports Info. Director: Herb Vincent   504-388-8226

■ Home games on each schedule [neutral sites shown in brackets].   *Night Games.

LOUISIANA TECH ... Ruston, La. 71272 I-A

Coach: Joe Raymond Peace, Louisiana Tech '68
Record: 4 yrs., W-25, L-15, T-4

1992 SCHEDULE

Baylor	Sep 5*
Eastern Mich. ■	Sep 12*
Southern Miss.	Sep 19
Alabama	Sep 26
Fresno St.	Oct 3*
Southwestern La. ■	Oct 10*
East Tenn. St. ■	Oct 17
Arkansas St. ■	Oct 31*
South Caro.	Nov 7
Mississippi	Nov 14
West Va.	Nov 21

1991 RECORD

3	Houston	73	48	Southern Ill.	16
21	Montana	11	30	Southern Miss.	14
17	Eastern Mich.	14	21	UTEP	17
42	Arkansas St.	10			
37	Northern Ill.	3	280	(8-1-2)	194
12	South Caro.	12			
14	Southwestern La.	14			
35	Northeast La.	10			

Conference: I-A Independents. Enrollment: 10,200. Colors: Red & Blue.
Nickname: Bulldogs. Stadium: Joe Aillet (1968), 30,600 capacity. Natural turf.
1991 home attendance: 69,125 in 4 games.
Director of Athletics: Jerry Stovall.
Sports Info. Director: Keith Prince 318-257-3144

LOUISVILLE ... Louisville, Ky. 40292 I-A

Coach: Howard Schnellenberger, Kentucky '56
Record: 12 yrs., W-75, L-58, T-2

1992 SCHEDULE

Ohio St.	Sep 5
Memphis St. ■	Sep 12
Arizona St.	Sep 19*
Wyoming ■	Sep 26
Syracuse ■	Oct 3
Virginia Tech ■	Oct 10
Tulsa ■	Oct 17
Florida	Oct 24
Cincinnati	Oct 31*
Texas A&M	Nov 7
Pittsburgh	Nov 14

1991 RECORD

24	Eastern Ky.	14	15	Florida St.	40
11	Tennessee	28	7	Memphis St.	35
15	Ohio St.	23	0	Tulsa	40
28	Southern Miss.	14			
7	Cincinnati	30	135	(2-9-0)	335
3	Boston College	33			
12	Army	37			
13	Virginia Tech	41			

Conference: I-A Independents. Enrollment: 21,000. Colors: Red, Black & White.
Nickname: Cardinals. Stadium: Cardinal (1956), 35,500 capacity. Artificial turf.
1991 home attendance: 218,974 in 6 games.
Director of Athletics: William Olsen.
Sports Info. Director: Kenny Klein 502-588-6581

MAINE ... Orono, Me. 04469 I-AA

Coach: Kirk Ferentz, Connecticut '78
Record: 2 yrs., W-6, L-16, T-0

1992 SCHEDULE

New Hampshire ■	Sep 5
Kutztown ■	Sep 12
Northeastern ■	Sep 19
Richmond	Oct 3
Rhode Island ■	Oct 17
Connecticut	Oct 24
Delaware ■	Oct 31
Boston U. ■	Nov 7
Massachusetts	Nov 14
Villanova	Nov 21

1991 RECORD

7	Villanova	48	10	Delaware	34
14	Northeastern	15	0	Boston U.	27
3	Massachusetts	10	49	Towson St.	34
20	New Hampshire	38			
19	Richmond	15	210	(3-8-0)	333
17	Rutgers	40			
30	Rhode Island	52			
41	Connecticut	20			

Conference: Yankee. Enrollment: 13,200. Colors: Blue & White.
Nickname: Black Bears. Stadium: Alumni (1942), 10,000 capacity. Natural turf.
1991 home attendance: 46,054 in 6 games.
Director of Athletics: Michael Ploszek.
Sports Info. Director: Matt Bourque 207-581-1086

MARSHALL ... Huntington, W. Va. 25715 I-AA

Coach: Jim Donnan, North Caro. St. '67
Record: 2 yrs., W-17, L-9, T-0

1992 SCHEDULE

Morehead St. ■	Sep 5*
Eastern Ill. ■	Sep 12*
Va. Military	Sep 19
Missouri	Oct 3
Furman ■	Oct 10*
Citadel	Oct 17
Tenn.-Chatt. ■	Oct 24
Western Caro.	Oct 31
Appalachian St. ■	Nov 7
Tennessee Tech ■	Nov 14
East Tenn. St.	Nov 21

1991 RECORD

3	Appalachian St.	9	61	Va. Military	0
24	New Hampshire	23	63	East Tenn. St.	9
70	Morehead St.	11			
46	Brown	0	414	(8-3-0)	195
38	Furman	35		**I-AA Championship**	
14	North Caro. St.	15	20	Western Ill.	17
31	Tenn.-Chatt.	38	41	Northern Iowa	13
27	Western Caro.	24	14	Eastern Ky.	7
37	Citadel	31	17	Youngstown St.	25

Conference: Southern Conf. Enrollment: 12,000. Colors: Green & White.
Nickname: Thundering Herd. Stadium: Marshall University (1991),
28,000 capacity. Artificial turf.
1991 home attendance: 153,726 in 7 games.
Director of Athletics: William Lee Moon.
Sports Info. Director: Gary Richter 304-696-5275

MARYLAND ... College Park, Md. 20740 I-A

Coach: Mark Duffner, William & Mary '75
Record: 6 yrs., W-60, L-5, T-1

1992 SCHEDULE

Virginia	Sep 5
North Caro. St. ■	Sep 12
West Va.	Sep 19
Penn St.	Sep 26
Pittsburgh ■	Oct 3
Georgia Tech ■	Oct 10
Wake Forest ■	Oct 17
Duke	Oct 24
North Caro. ■	Oct 31
Florida St.	Nov 7
Clemson ■	Nov 14

1991 RECORD

17	Virginia	6	7	Penn St.	47
17	Syracuse	31	7	Clemson	40
7	West Va.	37	17	North Caro. St.	20
20	Pittsburgh	24			
10	Georgia Tech	34	138	(2-9-0)	302
23	Wake Forest	22			
13	Duke	17			
0	North Caro.	24			

Conference: Atlantic Coast Conf. Enrollment: 25,671. Colors: Red, White, Black & Gold.
Nickname: Terps. Stadium: Byrd (1950), 45,000 capacity. Natural turf.
1991 home attendance: 210,789 in 5 games.
Director of Athletics: Andy Geiger.
Sports Info. Director: Herb Hartnett 301-314-7064

■ Home games on each schedule [neutral sites shown in brackets]. *Night Games.

1992 NCAA FOOTBALL

MASSACHUSETTS . . . Amherst, Mass. 01003 I-AA

Coach: Mike Hodges, Maine '67
Record: First year as head coach

1992 SCHEDULE

Delaware	Sep 12
Holy Cross	Sep 19
Boston U. ■	Sep 26
Rhode Island	Oct 10
Connecticut ■	Oct 17
Villanova ■	Oct 24
Northeastern ■	Oct 31
Richmond	Nov 7
Maine ■	Nov 14
New Hampshire	Nov 21

1991 RECORD

7	Delaware	24	42	Richmond	14
20	Holy Cross	22	14	Villanova	24
10	Maine	3	28	New Hampshire	35
15	Boston U.	7			
7	James Madison	24	205	(4-7-0)	208
14	Rhode Island	17			
21	Connecticut	26			
27	Northeastern	12			

Conference: Yankee. Enrollment: 17,400. Colors: Maroon & White.
Nickname: Minutemen. Stadium: Warren McGuirk (1965), 16,000 capacity. Natural turf.
1991 home attendance: 41,069 in 5 games.
Director of Athletics: To be named.
Sports Info. Director: Howard Davis 413-545-2439

McNEESE STATE . . . Lake Charles, La. 70601 I-AA

Coach: Bobby Keasler, Northeast La. '70
Record: 2 yrs., W-11, L-10, T-2

1992 SCHEDULE

Southwest Mo. St. ■	Sep 5*
Northern Iowa ■	Sep 12*
Nevada	Sep 19
Nicholls St.	Sep 26*
Northeast La. ■	Oct 10*
Northwestern (La.) ■	Oct 17*
Southwest Tex. St.	Oct 24
North Texas	Oct 31*
Stephen F. Austin	Nov 7
Sam Houston St. ■	Nov 14*
Weber St.	Nov 21

1991 RECORD

5	Northern Iowa	30	7	Stephen F. Austin	7
3	Southwest Mo. St.	7	19	Sam Houston St.	17
31	Montana	3	17	Tenn.-Martin	16
21	Nicholls St.	3			
10	Northeast La.	10	176	(6-3-2)	134
3	Northwestern (La.)	20		I-AA Championship	
19	Southwest Tex. St.	18	16	Nevada	22
41	North Texas	3			

Conference: Southland Conf. Enrollment: 7,350. Colors: Blue & Gold.
Nickname: Cowboys. Stadium: Cowboy (1965), 20,000 capacity. Natural turf.
1991 home attendance: 78,021 in 6 games.
Director of Athletics: Bob Hayes.
Sports Info. Director: Louis Bonnette 318-475-5207

MEMPHIS STATE . . . Memphis, Tenn. 38152 I-A

Coach: Chuck Stobart, Ohio '59
Record: 11 yrs., W-51, L-69, T-3

1992 SCHEDULE

Southern Miss.	Sep 5
Louisville	Sep 12
Mississippi St. ■	Sep 19*
Arkansas ■	Sep 26*
Cincinnati ■	Oct 10*
Arkansas St. ■	Oct 17*
Tulsa	Oct 24
Tulane	Oct 31
Mississippi	Nov 7
Tennessee ■	Nov 14
East Caro. ■	Nov 21

1991 RECORD

24	Southern Cal	10	24	Tennessee	52
0	Mississippi	10	35	Louisville	7
13	East Caro.	20	7	Alabama	10
31	Arkansas St.	21			
21	Missouri	31	228	(5-6-0)	229
17	Southern Miss.	12			
28	Mississippi St.	23			
28	Tulsa	33			

Conference: I-A Independents. Enrollment: 21,500. Colors: Blue & Gray.
Nickname: Tigers. Stadium: Liberty Bowl (1965), 62,380 capacity. Natural turf.
1991 home attendance: 191,896 in 6 games.
Director of Athletics: Charles Cavagnaro.
Sports Info. Director: Bob Winn 901-678-2337

MIAMI (FLORIDA) . . . Coral Gables, Fla. 33124 I-A

Coach: Dennis Erickson, Montana St. '70
Record: 10 yrs., W-83, L-34, T-1

1992 SCHEDULE

Iowa	Sep 5*
Florida A&M ■	Sep 19
Arizona ■	Sep 26
Florida St. ■	Oct 3
Penn St.	Oct 10
Texas Christian ■	Oct 17
Virginia Tech	Oct 24
West Va. ■	Oct 31
Temple ■	Nov 14
Syracuse	Nov 21
San Diego St.	Nov 28*

1991 RECORD

31	Arkansas	3	17	Florida St.	16
40	Houston	10	19	Boston College	14
34	Tulsa	10	39	San Diego St.	12
40	Oklahoma St.	3			
26	Penn St.	20	364	(11-0-0)	100
55	Long Beach St.	0		Fed. Express Orange Bowl	
36	Arizona	9	22	Nebraska	0
27	West Va.	3			

Conference: Big East Conference. Enrollment: 13,153. Colors: Orange, Green, White.
Nickname: Hurricanes. Stadium: Orange Bowl (1935), 74,244 capacity. Natural turf.
1991 home attendance: 347,785 in 6 games.
Director of Athletics: Dave Maggard.
Sports Info. Director: Linda Venzon 305-284-3244

MIAMI (OHIO) . . . Oxford, Ohio 45056 I-A

Coach: Randy Walker, Miami (Ohio) '76
Record: 2 yrs., W-11, L-9, T-2

1992 SCHEDULE

West Va.	Sep 5
Indiana	Sep 12
Cincinnati ■	Sep 19
Ball St.	Sep 26
Eastern Mich.	Oct 3*
Central Mich. ■	Oct 10
Ohio	Oct 17
Toledo ■	Oct 24
Bowling Green	Oct 31
Western Mich. ■	Nov 7
Kent ■	Nov 14

1991 RECORD

15	Ball St.	7	7	Bowling Green	17
20	Kentucky	23	23	Western Mich.	24
29	Eastern Mich.	3	20	Kent	9
22	Cincinnati	9			
27	Southwestern La.	14	214	(6-4-1)	140
10	Central Mich.	10			
34	Ohio	0			
7	Toledo	24			

Conference: Mid-American Conf. Enrollment: 16,000. Colors: Red & White.
Nickname: Redskins. Stadium: Fred C. Yager (1983), 25,183 capacity. Natural turf.
1991 home attendance: 90,598 in 4 games.
Director of Athletics: R. C. Johnson.
Sports Info. Director: Brian Teter 513-529-4327

■ Home games on each schedule [neutral sites shown in brackets].   *Night Games.

MICHIGAN ... Ann Arbor, Mich.   48109   I-A

Coach: Gary Moeller, Ohio St. '63
Record: 5 yrs., W-25, L-29, T-3
1992 SCHEDULE

Notre Dame	Sep 12
Oklahoma St. ■	Sep 19
Houston ■	Sep 26
Iowa ■	Oct 3
Michigan St. ■	Oct 10
Indiana	Oct 17
Minnesota ■	Oct 24
Purdue	Oct 31
Northwestern	Nov 7
Illinois ■	Nov 14
Ohio St.	Nov 21

1991 RECORD

35	Boston College	13	59	Northwestern	14
24	Notre Dame	14	20	Illinois	0
31	Florida St.	51	31	Ohio St.	3
43	Iowa	24			
45	Michigan St.	28	406	(10-1-0)	169
24	Indiana	16		**Rose Bowl**	
52	Minnesota	6	14	Washington	34
42	Purdue	0			

Conference: Big Ten Conf.   Enrollment: 36,306.   Colors: Maize & Blue.
Nickname: Wolverines.   Stadium: Michigan (1927), 102,000 capacity.   Natural turf.
1991 home attendance: 632,024 in 6 games.
Director of Athletics: Jack Weidenbach.
Sports Info. Director: Bruce Madej 313-763-4423

MICHIGAN STATE ... East Lansing, Mich.   48824   I-A

Coach: George Perles, Michigan St. '60
Record: 9 yrs., W-57, L-44, T-4
1992 SCHEDULE

Central Mich. ■	Sep 12
Notre Dame ■	Sep 19
Boston College	Sep 26
Indiana ■	Oct 3
Michigan	Oct 10
Minnesota	Oct 17*
Ohio St. ■	Oct 24
Northwestern	Oct 31
Wisconsin ■	Nov 7
Purdue ■	Nov 14
Illinois	Nov 21

1991 RECORD

3	Central Mich.	20	20	Wisconsin	7
10	Notre Dame	49	17	Purdue	27
7	Rutgers	14	27	Illinois	24
0	Indiana	31			
28	Michigan	45	162	(3-8-0)	272
20	Minnesota	12			
17	Ohio St.	27			
13	Northwestern	16			

Conference: Big Ten Conf.   Enrollment: 42,695.   Colors: Green & White.
Nickname: Spartans.   Stadium: Spartan (1957), 76,000 capacity.   Artificial turf.
1991 home attendance: 421,231 in 6 games.
Director of Athletics: Merrily Dean Baker.
Sports Info. Director: Ken Hoffman 517-355-2271

MIDDLE TENNESSEE STATE ... Murfreesboro, Tenn.   37132   I-AA

Coach: Boots Donnelly, Middle Tenn. St. '65
Record: 15 yrs., W-109, L-61, T-1
1992 SCHEDULE

Tennessee St. [Nashville, Tenn.]	Sep 5*
Nebraska	Sep 12
Murray St.	Sep 26*
Northern Ill.	Oct 3*
Austin Peay ■	Oct 10
Eastern Ky. ■	Oct 17
Southeast Mo. St.	Oct 24
Ga. Southern	Oct 31
Tenn.-Martin	Nov 7
Morehead St. ■	Nov 14
Tennessee Tech ■	Nov 21

1991 RECORD

42	Tennessee St.	6	10	Cincinnati	30
7	Eastern Ky.	17	31	Morehead St.	3
35	Murray St.	3	28	Tennessee Tech	10
23	Western Ky.	21			
23	Austin Peay	8	312	(8-3-0)	151
10	Florida St.	39		**I-AA Championship**	
52	Southeast Mo. St.	0	20	Sam Houston St.	19
51	Tenn.-Martin	14	13	Eastern Ky.	23

Conference: Ohio Valley Conf.   Enrollment: 15,763.   Colors: Blue & White.
Nickname: Blue Raiders.   Stadium: Johnny Floyd (1969), 15,000 capacity.   Artificial turf.
1991 home attendance: 51,500 in 4 games.
Director of Athletics: John Stanford.
Sports Info. Director: Ed Given 615-898-2450

MINNESOTA ... Minneapolis, Minn.   55455   I-A

Coach: Jim Wacker, Valparaiso '60
Record: 21 yrs., W-144, L-91, T-3
1992 SCHEDULE

San Jose St. ■	Sep 12*
Colorado ■	Sep 19*
Pittsburgh	Sep 26
Illinois ■	Oct 3*
Purdue	Oct 10
Michigan St. ■	Oct 17*
Michigan	Oct 24
Indiana ■	Oct 31*
Ohio St.	Nov 7
Wisconsin	Nov 14
Iowa ■	Nov 21*

1991 RECORD

26	San Jose St.	20	6	Ohio St.	35
0	Colorado	58	16	Wisconsin	19
13	Pittsburgh	14	8	Iowa	23
3	Illinois	24			
6	Purdue	3	104	(2-9-0)	302
12	Michigan St.	20			
6	Michigan	52			
8	Indiana	34			

Conference: Big Ten Conf.   Enrollment: 47,000.   Colors: Maroon & Gold.
Nickname: Golden Gophers.   Stadium: Metrodome (1982), 62,345 capacity.   Artificial turf.
1991 home attendance: 218,219 in 6 games.
Director of Athletics: Rick Bay.
Sports Info. Director: Robert Peterson 612-625-4090

MISSISSIPPI ... University, Miss.   38677   I-A

Coach: Billy Brewer, Mississippi '61
Record: 18 yrs., W-110, L-86, T-6
1992 SCHEDULE

Auburn ■	Sep 5*
Tulane ■	Sep 12*
Vanderbilt	Sep 19*
Georgia	Sep 26
Kentucky ■	Oct 3*
Arkansas [Little Rock, Ark.]	Oct 17*
Alabama	Oct 24
Louisiana St. [Jackson, Miss.]	Oct 31*
Memphis St. ■	Nov 7
Louisiana Tech ■	Nov 14
Mississippi St. ■	Nov 28

1991 RECORD

22	Tulane	3	22	Louisiana St.	25
10	Memphis St.	0	25	Tennessee	36
13	Auburn	23	9	Mississippi St.	24
38	Ohio	14			
24	Arkansas	17	242	(5-6-0)	223
35	Kentucky	14			
17	Georgia	37			
27	Vanderbilt	30			

Conference: Southeastern Conf.   Enrollment: 11,033.   Colors: Cardinal Red & Navy Blue.
Nickname: Rebels.   Stadium: Vaught-Hemingway (1941), 42,577 capacity.   Natural turf.
1991 home attendance: 193,800 in 5 games.
Director of Athletics: Warner Alford.
Sports Info. Director: Langston Rogers 601-232-7522

■ Home games on each schedule [neutral sites shown in brackets].   *Night Games.

MISSISSIPPI STATE . . . Mississippi State, Miss.   39762   I-A

Coach: Jackie Sherrill, Alabama '66
Record: 14 yrs., W-112, L-50, T-2
1992 SCHEDULE

Texas	Sep 5*
Louisiana St.	Sep 12*
Memphis St.	Sep 19*
Florida ■	Oct 1*
Auburn ■	Oct 10*
South Caro.	Oct 17
Arkansas St. ■	Oct 24
Kentucky	Oct 31*
Arkansas ■	Nov 7
Alabama ■	Nov 14
Mississippi	Nov 28

1991 RECORD

47 Cal St. Fullerton	3	7 Alabama	13
13 Texas	6	28 Louisiana St.	19
48 Tulane	0	24 Mississippi	9
24 Tennessee	26		
7 Florida	29	276 (7-4-0)	156
31 Kentucky	6	**Liberty Bowl**	
23 Memphis St.	28	15 Air Force	38
24 Auburn	17		

Conference: Southeastern Conf. Enrollment: 13,741. Colors: Maroon & White.
Nickname: Bulldogs. Stadium: Scott Field (1935), 41,200 capacity. Natural turf.
1991 home attendance: 282,347 in 7 games.
Director of Athletics: Larry Templeton.
Sports Info. Director: Joe Dier   601-325-2703

MISSISSIPPI VALLEY . . . Itta Bena, Miss.   38941   I-AA

Coach: Larry Dorsey, Tennessee St. '76
Record: 2 yrs., W-12, L-9, T-1
1992 SCHEDULE

Lane ■	Sep 12*
Miles	Sep 19*
Jackson St.	Sep 26*
Southern-B.R.	Oct 3*
Knoxville	Oct 10
Grambling [Chicago, Ill.]	Oct 17
Texas Southern	Oct 24
Prairie View ■	Oct 31
Alcorn St.	Nov 7
Alabama St.	Nov 14

1991 RECORD

10 Tennessee St.	7	41 Prairie View	0
35 Central Ark.	3	28 Alcorn St.	28
30 Lane	13	20 Alabama St.	48
56 Miles	0		
23 Jackson St.	14	307 (7-3-1)	182
7 Southern-B.R.	0		
35 Grambling	37		
22 Texas Southern	32		

Conference: Southwestern. Enrollment: 2,340. Colors: Green & White.
Nickname: Delta Devils. Stadium: Magnolia (1958), 10,500 capacity. Natural turf.
1991 home attendance: 107,979 in 6 games.
Director of Athletics: Chuck Prophet.
Sports Info. Director: Chuck Prophet   601-254-9041

MISSOURI . . . Columbia, Mo.   65201   I-A

Coach: Bob Stull, Kansas St. '68
Record: 8 yrs., W-40, L-50, T-1
1992 SCHEDULE

Illinois	Sep 12
Texas A&M ■	Sep 19
Indiana	Sep 26
Marshall ■	Oct 3
Colorado ■	Oct 8*
Oklahoma St.	Oct 17
Nebraska ■	Oct 24
Iowa St.	Oct 31
Oklahoma	Nov 7
Kansas St. ■	Nov 14
Kansas ■	Nov 21

1991 RECORD

23 Illinois	19	16 Oklahoma	56
21 Baylor	47	0 Kansas St.	32
27 Indiana	27	29 Kansas	53
31 Memphis St.	25		
7 Colorado	55	223 (3-7-1)	403
41 Oklahoma St.	7		
6 Nebraska	63		
22 Iowa St.	23		

Conference: Big Eight Conf. Enrollment: 24,660. Colors: Old Gold & Black.
Nickname: Tigers. Stadium: Faurot Field (1926), 62,000 capacity. Artificial turf.
1991 home attendance: 238,879 in 6 games.
Director of Athletics: Dan Devine.
Sports Info. Director: Bob Brendel   314-882-6501

MONTANA . . . Missoula, Mont.   59812   I-AA

Coach: Don Read, Cal St. Sacramento'59
Record: 22 yrs., W-114, L-115, T-1
1992 SCHEDULE

Washington St.	Sep 5
Cal St. Chico ■	Sep 12
Kansas St.	Sep 19*
Eastern Wash. ■	Sep 26
Boise St.	Oct 3*
Weber St.	Oct 10*
Northern Ariz. ■	Oct 17
Montana St. ■	Oct 24
Idaho ■	Nov 7
Hofstra ■	Nov 14
Idaho St.	Nov 21*

1991 RECORD

38 Humboldt St.	6	16 Montana St.	9
11 Louisiana Tech	21	28 Nevada	35
3 McNeese St.	31	35 Idaho	34
24 Idaho St.	13		
17 Eastern Wash.	20	274 (7-4-0)	241
21 Boise St.	7		
47 Weber St.	38		
34 Northern Ariz.	27		

Conference: Big Sky Conf. Enrollment: 10,400. Colors: Copper, Silver & Gold.
Nickname: Grizzlies. Stadium: Washington-Grizzly (1986), 15,400 capacity. Natural turf.
1991 home attendance: 59,376 in 5 games.
Director of Athletics: Bill Moos.
Sports Info. Director: Dave Guffey   406-243-6899

MONTANA STATE . . . Bozeman, Mont.   59717   I-AA

Coach: Cliff Hysell, Montana St. '66
Record: First year as head coach
1992 SCHEDULE

Cal St. Sacramento	Sep 5*
Stephen F. Austin ■	Sep 12
Mesa St. ■	Sep 19
Weber St.	Sep 26*
Northern Ariz. ■	Oct 3
Eastern Wash.	Oct 10
Idaho St. ■	Oct 17
Montana	Oct 24
Boise St. ■	Oct 31
Idaho	Nov 14
Nevada-Las Vegas	Nov 21

1991 RECORD

30 Minn.-Duluth	14	9 Montana	16
23 Sam Houston St.	26	14 Boise St.	31
17 Cal St. Sacramento	19	21 Eastern Wash.	22
14 Idaho	48		
12 Nevada	54	197 (2-9-0)	300
25 Weber St.	36		
16 Northern Ariz.	27		
16 Idaho St.	7		

Conference: Big Sky Conf. Enrollment: 10,100. Colors: Blue & Gold.
Nickname: Bobcats. Stadium: Reno H. Sales (1973), 15,197 capacity. Natural turf.
1991 home attendance: 62,343 in 7 games.
Director of Athletics: Doug Fullerton.
Sports Info. Director: Bill Lamberty   406-994-5133

■ Home games on each schedule [neutral sites shown in brackets].   *Night Games.

MOREHEAD STATE . . . Morehead, Ky.   40351   I-AA

Coach: Cole Proctor, Morehead St. '68
Record: 2 yrs., W-9, L-13, T-0

1992 SCHEDULE

Marshall	Sep 5*
West Va. St. ■	Sep 12*
Tenn.-Martin	Sep 26*
East Tenn. St.	Oct 3*
Tennessee St. ■	Oct 10
Murray St. ■	Oct 17
Tennessee Tech	Oct 24
Austin Peay	Oct 31
Southeast Mo. St. ■	Nov 7
Middle Tenn. St.	Nov 14
Eastern Ky. ■	Nov 21

1991 RECORD

14	Samford	52	16	Southeast Mo. St.	17
11	Marshall	70	3	Middle Tenn. St.	31
21	Western Ky.	48	10	Eastern Ky.	41
28	Tenn.-Martin	32			
12	Liberty	10	189	(4-7-0)	345
20	Murray St.	10			
21	Tennessee Tech	20			
33	Austin Peay	14			

Conference: Ohio Valley Conf.   Enrollment: 8,516.   Colors: Blue & Gold.
Nickname: Eagles.   Stadium: Jayne (1964), 10,000 capacity.   Artificial turf.
1991 home attendance: 19,800 in 5 games.
Director of Athletics: Steve Hamilton.
Sports Info. Director: Randy Stacy   606-783-2500

MORGAN STATE . . . Baltimore, Md.   21239   I-AA

Coach: Ricky Diggs, Shippensburg '75
Record: 1 yr., W-1, L-10, T-0

1992 SCHEDULE

Liberty	Sep 12
North Caro. A&T	Sep 19
Johnson Smith ■	Sep 26
Buffalo	Oct 3
South Caro. St.	Oct 10
Central St. (Ohio) ■	Oct 17
Delaware St. ■	Oct 24
Florida A&M	Oct 31
Western Ill.	Nov 7
Howard	Nov 14
Bethune-Cookman ■	Nov 21

1991 RECORD

7	North Caro. A&T	26	6	Florida A&M	55
9	Norfolk St.	27	6	Western Ill.	44
6	Bethune-Cookman	38	38	Howard	28
22	Youngstown St.	57			
6	Northern Iowa	56	128	(1-10-0)	425
6	South Caro. St.	21			
12	Virginia Union	47			
10	Delaware St.	26			

Conference: Mid-Eastern.   Enrollment: 4,750.   Colors: Blue & Orange.
Nickname: Bears.   Stadium: Hughes, 10,000 capacity.   Natural turf.
1991 home attendance: 36,844 in 5 games.
Director of Athletics: Leonard Braxton.
Sports Info. Director: Joe McIver   301-319-3831

MURRAY STATE . . . Murray, Ky.   42071   I-AA

Coach: Mike Mahoney, Southern Conn. St. '74
Record: 5 yrs., W-21, L-32, T-1

1992 SCHEDULE

Southeast Mo. St. ■	Sep 3*
Eastern Ill. ■	Sep 19*
Middle Tenn. St. ■	Sep 26*
Austin Peay ■	Oct 3
Tenn.-Martin	Oct 10*
Morehead St.	Oct 17
Tennessee Tech ■	Oct 31*
Eastern Ky.	Nov 7
Tennessee St. ■	Nov 14
Western Ky. ■	Nov 21

1991 RECORD

27	Southern Ill.	31	17	Eastern Ky.	42
0	Western Ky.	14	14	Southeast Mo. St.	10
28	Eastern Ill.	27	9	Austin Peay	27
3	Middle Tenn. St.	35			
7	Tennessee St.	28	162	(3-8-0)	313
40	Tenn.-Martin	34			
10	Morehead St.	20			
7	Tennessee Tech	45			

Conference: Ohio Valley Conf.   Enrollment: 8,328.   Colors: Blue & Gold.
Nickname: Racers.   Stadium: Stewart (1973), 16,800 capacity.   Artificial turf.
1991 home attendance: 20,862 in 6 games.
Director of Athletics: Mike Strickland.
Sports Info. Director: Jimmy Wilder   502-762-4270

NAVY . . . Annapolis, Md.   21402   I-A

Coach: George Chaump, Bloomsburg '58
Record: 10 yrs., W-62, L-49, T-2

1992 SCHEDULE

Virginia ■	Sep 12*
Boston College	Sep 19
Rutgers ■	Sep 26
North Caro.	Oct 3
Air Force	Oct 10
Delaware ■	Oct 24
Notre Dame [East Rutherford, N.J.]	Oct 31
Tulane ■	Nov 7
Vanderbilt ■	Nov 14
Rice	Nov 21
Army [Philadelphia, Pa.]	Dec 5

1991 RECORD

10	Ball St.	33	7	Tulane	34
10	Virginia	17	24	Wake Forest	52
21	William & Mary	26	24	Army	3
19	Bowling Green	22			
6	Air Force	46	160	(1-10-0)	321
14	Temple	21			
25	Delaware	29			
0	Notre Dame	38			

Conference: I-A Independents.   Enrollment: 4,300.   Colors: Navy Blue & Gold.
Nickname: Midshipmen.   Stadium: Navy-Marine Corps Mem. (1959),
   30,000 capacity.   Natural turf.
1991 home attendance: 150,579 in 6 games.
Director of Athletics: Jack Lengyel.
Sports Info. Director: Tom Bates   301-268-6226

NEBRASKA . . . Lincoln, Neb.   68588   I-A

Coach: Tom Osborne, Hastings '59
Record: 19 yrs., W-186, L-43, T-3

1992 SCHEDULE

Utah ■	Sep 5
Middle Tenn. St. ■	Sep 12
Washington	Sep 19
Arizona St. ■	Sep 26
Oklahoma St. ■	Oct 10
Missouri	Oct 24
Colorado ■	Oct 31
Kansas ■	Nov 7
Iowa St.	Nov 14
Oklahoma	Nov 27
Kansas St. [Tokyo, Japan]	Dec 6

1991 RECORD

59	Utah St.	28	59	Kansas	23
71	Colorado St.	14	38	Iowa St.	13
21	Washington	36	19	Oklahoma	14
18	Arizona St.	9			
49	Oklahoma St.	15	454	(9-1-1)	208
38	Kansas St.	31		**Fed. Express Orange Bowl**	
63	Missouri	6	0	Miami (Fla.)	22
19	Colorado	19			

Conference: Big Eight Conf.   Enrollment: 24,000.   Colors: Scarlet & Cream.
Nickname: Cornhuskers.   Stadium: Memorial (1923), 73,650 capacity.   Artificial turf.
1991 home attendance: 533,715 in 7 games.
Director of Athletics: Bob Devaney.
Sports Info. Director: Don Bryant   402-472-5959

■ Home games on each schedule [neutral sites shown in brackets].   *Night Games.

NEVADA . . . Reno, Nev.　89557　　I-A

Coach: Chris Ault, Nevada '68
Record: 16 yrs., W-138, L-53, T-1

1992 SCHEDULE

Wyoming	Sep 5
Pacific (Cal.) ■	Sep 12
McNeese St. ■	Sep 19
Tulane	Sep 26*
Cal St. Fullerton	Oct 3*
Nevada-Las Vegas	Oct 17*
New Mexico St. ■	Oct 24
Weber St. ■	Oct 31
San Jose St.	Nov 7
Utah St. ■	Nov 14
Texas Southern ■	Nov 21

1991 RECORD

50	Nevada-Las Vegas	8	55	Weber St.	49
45	Northwestern (La.)	14	35	Montana	28
72	North Texas	0	45	Northern Ariz.	16
54	Montana St.	12			
31	Idaho	23	496	(11-0-0)	198
41	Idaho St.	20		**I-AA Championship**	
51	Eastern Wash.	14	22	McNeese St.	16
17	Boise St.	14	28	Youngstown St.	30

Conference: Big West.　Enrollment: 11,800.　Colors: Silver & Blue.
Nickname: Wolf Pack.　Stadium: Mackay (1965), 30,485 capacity.　Natural turf.
1991 home attendance: 151,019 in 7 games.
Director of Athletics: Chris Ault.
Sports Info. Director: Paul Stuart　702-784-4600

NEVADA-LAS VEGAS . . . Las Vegas, Nev.　89154　　I-A

Coach: Jim Strong, Mo. Southern St. '76
Record: 2 yrs., W-8, L-14, T-0

1992 SCHEDULE

UTEP ■	Sep 12*
Northern Ariz. ■	Sep 19*
Oregon	Sep 26
Pacific (Cal.)	Oct 3
New Mexico St.	Oct 10*
Nevada ■	Oct 17*
Hawaii	Oct 24*
San Jose St. ■	Oct 31
Utah St.	Nov 7
Montana St. ■	Nov 21
Cal St. Fullerton ■	Nov 28

1991 RECORD

8	Nevada	50	14	Utah St.	27
23	Oregon St.	9	38	New Mexico St.	28
23	New Mexico	22	23	Pacific (Cal.)	44
13	Washington St.	40			
19	Long Beach St.	34	220	(4-7-0)	360
25	Cal St. Fullerton	3			
22	Fresno St.	48			
12	San Jose St.	55			

Conference: Big West.　Enrollment: 19,561.　Colors: Scarlet & Gray.
Nickname: Rebels.　Stadium: Sam Boyd Silver Bowl (1971), 32,000 capacity.　Artificial turf.
1991 home attendance: 120,527 in 6 games.
Director of Athletics: Jim Weaver.
Sports Info. Director: Joe Hawk　702-739-3207

NEW HAMPSHIRE . . . Durham, N.H.　03824　　I-AA

Coach: Bill Bowes, Penn St. '65
Record: 20 yrs., W-131, L-73, T-4

1992 SCHEDULE

Maine	Sep 5
Connecticut ■	Sep 12
Lehigh	Sep 19
Dartmouth ■	Sep 26
Delaware ■	Oct 3
Richmond	Oct 10
Northeastern ■	Oct 24
Boston U.	Oct 31
Villanova ■	Nov 7
Rhode Island	Nov 14
Massachusetts ■	Nov 21

1991 RECORD

23	Marshall	24	7	Villanova	33
21	Connecticut	16	42	Rhode Island	35
48	Hofstra	28	35	Massachusetts	28
38	Maine	20			
45	Delaware	28	356		252
34	Richmond	0		**I-AA Championship**	
18	Northeastern	14	13	Samford	29
45	Boston U.	26			

Conference: Yankee.　Enrollment: 11,000.　Colors: Blue & White.
Nickname: Wildcats.　Stadium: Cowell (1936), 12,500 capacity.　Natural turf.
1991 home attendance: 49,352 in 6 games.
Director of Athletics: Gilbert Chapman.
Sports Info. Director: Eric McDowell　603-862-3907

NEW MEXICO . . . Albuquerque, N.M.　87131　　I-A

Coach: Dennis Franchione, Pittsburg St. '73
Record: 9 yrs., W-80, L-19, T-2

1992 SCHEDULE

Texas Christian ■	Sep 5*
New Mexico St. ■	Sep 12*
Southern Methodist ■	Sep 19*
Air Force	Sep 26
San Diego St. ■	Oct 3*
Wyoming	Oct 10
Utah ■	Oct 17*
Fresno St.	Oct 24*
Brigham Young	Nov 7
UTEP ■	Nov 14
Colorado St. ■	Nov 21

1991 RECORD

19	UTEP	35	23	Brigham Young	41
7	Texas Christian	60	34	Air Force	32
13	Hawaii	35	7	Utah	30
22	Nevada-Las Vegas	23	38	Colorado St.	36
17	New Mexico St.	10			
17	Fresno St.	94	240	(3-9-0)	473
24	San Diego St.	38			
19	Wyoming	39			

Conference: Western Athl. Conf.　Enrollment: 24,194.　Colors: Cherry & Silver.
Nickname: Lobos.　Stadium: University (1960), 30,646 capacity.　Natural turf.
1991 home attendance: 79,112 in 5 games.
Director of Athletics: Gary Ness.
Sports Info. Director: Greg Remington　505-277-2026

NEW MEXICO STATE . . . Las Cruces, N.M.　88003　　I-A

Coach: Jim Hess, Southeast Okla. '59
Record: 17 yrs., W-115, L-72, T-5

1992 SCHEDULE

Weber St. ■	Sep 5*
New Mexico ■	Sep 12*
UTEP	Sep 19*
Utah St.	Sep 26
Kansas St.	Oct 3
Nevada-Las Vegas ■	Oct 10*
Pacific (Cal.) ■	Oct 17
Nevada	Oct 24
Arizona	Oct 31*
Cal St. Fullerton ■	Nov 14
San Jose St.	Nov 21

1991 RECORD

21	UTEP	22	28	Long Beach St.	24
14	Kansas	54	28	Nevada-Las Vegas	38
10	New Mexico	17	21	Utah St.	46
6	Oregon	29			
13	San Jose St.	39	224	(2-9-0)	350
28	Fresno St.	42			
20	Pacific (Cal.)	27			
35	Cal St. Fullerton	12			

Conference: Big West.　Enrollment: 14,400.　Colors: Crimson & White.
Nickname: Aggies.　Stadium: Aggie Memorial (1978), 30,300 capacity.　Natural turf.
1991 home attendance: 69,968 in 5 games.
Director of Athletics: Al Gonzales.
Sports Info. Director: Steve Shutt　505-646-3929

■ Home games on each schedule [neutral sites shown in brackets].　*Night Games.

Divisions I-A & I-AA 1992 Schedules and 1991 Results　　583

NICHOLLS STATE ... Thibodaux, La. 70301   I-AA

Coach: Phil Greco, Tulane '70
Record: 5 yrs., W-25, L-29, T-1

1992 SCHEDULE

Northeast La. ■	Sep 5*
Texas A&I	Sep 12*
McNeese St. ■	Sep 26*
Southwest Tex. St.	Oct 3*
Sam Houston St. ■	Oct 10
Central Fla.	Oct 17*
Stephen F. Austin	Oct 24
Southern-B.R. ■	Oct 31
North Texas	Nov 7*
Northwestern (La.)	Nov 14*
Troy St. ■	Nov 21

1991 RECORD

3	Texas A&I	7	19	North Texas	24
15	Northeast La.	10	10	Northwestern (La.)	16
25	Troy St.	17	6	Ga. Southern	40
10	Southwest Tex. St.	19			
3	McNeese St.	21	155	(4-7-0)	189
19	Sam Houston St.	28			
24	Stephen F. Austin	0			
21	Southern-B.R.	7			

Conference: Southland Conf. Enrollment: 7,445. Colors: Red & Gray.
Nickname: Colonels. Stadium: John L. Guidry (1972), 12,800 capacity. Natural turf.
1991 home attendance: 10,662 in 5 games.
Director of Athletics: Phil Greco.
Sports Info. Director: Ron Mears 504-448-4282

NORTH CAROLINA ... Chapel Hill, N.C. 27514   I-A

Coach: Mack Brown, Florida St. '74
Record: 8 yrs., W-32, L-56, T-1

1992 SCHEDULE

Wake Forest	Sep 5
Furman ■	Sep 12*
Army ■	Sep 19*
North Caro. St. ■	Sep 26
Navy ■	Oct 3
Florida St.	Oct 10
Virginia ■	Oct 17
Georgia Tech ■	Oct 24
Maryland ■	Oct 31
Clemson	Nov 7
Duke	Nov 21

1991 RECORD

51	Cincinnati	16	6	Clemson	21
20	Army	12	21	South Caro.	17
7	North Caro. St.	24	47	Duke	14
59	William & Mary	36			
24	Wake Forest	10	282	(7-4-0)	199
9	Virginia	14			
14	Georgia Tech	35			
24	Maryland	0			

Conference: Atlantic Coast Conf. Enrollment: 21,757. Colors: Blue & White.
Nickname: Tar Heels. Stadium: Kenan (1927), 52,000 capacity. Natural turf.
1991 home attendance: 324,500 in 7 games.
Director of Athletics: John Swofford.
Sports Info. Director: Rick Brewer 919-962-2123

NORTH CAROLINA A&T ... Greensboro, N.C. 27411   I-AA

Coach: Bill Hayes, N.C. Central '64
Record: 16 yrs., W-114, L-60, T-2

1992 SCHEDULE

N.C. Central ■	Sep 5
Winston-Salem ■	Sep 12
Morgan St. ■	Sep 19
Liberty ■	Sep 26
Norfolk St.	Oct 3
Florida A&M [Orlando, Fla.]	Oct 10
Howard	Oct 24
Bethune-Cookman ■	Oct 31
Delaware St.	Nov 7
Appalachian St.	Nov 14
South Caro. St. ■	Nov 21

1991 RECORD

26	Morgan St.	7	39	Bethune-Cookman	24
48	N.C. Central	0	26	Delaware St.	31
10	Winston-Salem	13	49	South Caro. St.	21
28	Grambling	12			
50	Norfolk St.	14	381		163
41	Florida A&M	19		**Alamo Heritage Bowl**	
38	East Tenn. St.	13	13	Alabama St.	36
26	Howard	9			

Conference: Mid-Eastern. Enrollment: 6,500. Colors: Blue & Gold.
Nickname: Aggies. Stadium: Aggie (1981), 17,500 capacity. Natural turf.
1991 home attendance: 71,775 in 5 games.
Director of Athletics: Willie J. Burden.
Sports Info. Director: Charles Mooney 919-334-7582

NORTH CAROLINA STATE ... Raleigh, N.C. 27695   I-A

Coach: Dick Sheridan, South Caro. '64
Record: 14 yrs., W-112, L-49, T-4

1992 SCHEDULE

Iowa [East Rutherford, N.J.]	Aug 29*
Appalachian St. ■	Sep 5
Maryland ■	Sep 12
Florida St. ■	Sep 19
North Caro.	Sep 26
Georgia Tech	Oct 3
Texas Tech ■	Oct 10
Virginia Tech	Oct 17
Clemson ■	Oct 24
Virginia	Nov 7
Duke ■	Nov 14
Wake Forest ■	Nov 21

1991 RECORD

7	Virginia Tech	0	10	Virginia	42
47	Kent	0	32	Duke	31
30	Wake Forest	3	20	Maryland	17
24	North Caro.	7			
28	Georgia Tech	21	270	(9-2-0)	185
15	Marshall	14		**Peach Bowl**	
19	Clemson	29	34	East Caro.	37
38	South Caro.	21			

Conference: Atlantic Coast Conf. Enrollment: 26,683. Colors: Red & White.
Nickname: Wolfpack. Stadium: Carter-Finley (1966), 47,000 capacity. Natural turf.
1991 home attendance: 304,473 in 7 games.
Director of Athletics: Todd Turner.
Sports Info. Director: Mark Bockelman 919-515-2102

NORTH TEXAS ... Denton, Tex. 76203   I-AA

Coach: Dennis Parker, Southeast Okla.'72
Record: 1 yr., W-3, L-7, T-1

1992 SCHEDULE

Abilene Christian ■	Sep 5*
Southern Methodist	Sep 12
Southwest Mo. St.	Sep 19*
Texas	Sep 26*
Northwestern (La.) ■	Oct 10*
Stephen F. Austin	Oct 17
Sam Houston St.	Oct 24
McNeese St. ■	Oct 31*
Nicholls St. ■	Nov 7*
Southwest Tex. St.	Nov 14
Northeast La. ■	Nov 21

1991 RECORD

24	Abilene Christian	0	24	Nicholls St.	19
2	Oklahoma	40	8	Southwest Tex. St.	36
0	Nevada	72	21	Northeast La.	44
21	Southwest Mo. St.	21			
10	Northwestern (La.)	24	137	(3-7-1)	325
18	Stephen F. Austin	14			
6	Sam Houston St.	14			
3	McNeese St.	41			

Conference: Southland Conf. Enrollment: 27,108. Colors: Green & White.
Nickname: Mean Green, Eagles. Stadium: Fouts Field (1952), 20,000 capacity. Artificial turf.
1991 home attendance: 44,273 in 5 games.
Director of Athletics: Steve Sloan.
Sports Info. Director: Brian Briscoe 817-565-2664

■ Home games on each schedule [neutral sites shown in brackets].   *Night Games.

1992 NCAA FOOTBALL

NORTHEAST LOUISIANA . . . Monroe, La.   71209   I-AA

Coach: Dave Roberts, Western Caro. '68
Record: 8 yrs., W-44, L-44, T-3
1992 SCHEDULE

Nicholls St.	Sep 5*
Southwestern La.	Sep 12*
Eastern Ky.	Sep 19*
Southwest Tex. St. ■	Sep 26*
Delta St. ■	Oct 3*
McNeese St.	Oct 10*
Sam Houston St. ■	Oct 17*
Northwestern (La.)	Oct 24
Eastern Wash. ■	Nov 7*
Stephen F. Austin ■	Nov 14*
North Texas	Nov 21

1991 RECORD

21	Southwestern La.	10	10	Louisiana Tech	35
10	Nicholls St.	15	48	Stephen F. Austin	20
21	Ga. Southern	13	44	North Texas	21
17	Mississippi Col.	7			
17	Southwest Tex. St.	8	237	(7-3-1)	175
10	McNeese St.	10			
15	Sam Houston St.	27			
24	Northwestern (La.)	9			

Conference: Southland Conf.   Enrollment: 11,189.   Colors: Maroon & Gold.
Nickname: Indians.   Stadium: Malone (1978), 23,277 capacity.   Natural turf.
1991 home attendance: 77,846 in 5 games.
Director of Athletics: Benny Hollis.
Sports Info. Director: Bob Anderson   318-342-5460

NORTHEASTERN . . . Boston, Mass.   02115   I-AA

Coach: Barry Gallup, Boston College '69
Record: 1 yr., W-4, L-7, T-0
1992 SCHEDULE

Northern Ariz.	Sep 12*
Maine	Sep 19
Connecticut ■	Sep 26
James Madison	Oct 3
Lehigh ■	Oct 10
Youngstown St. ■	Oct 17
New Hampshire	Oct 24
Massachusetts	Oct 31
Rhode Island ■	Nov 7
Towson St. ■	Nov 14
Boston U.	Nov 21

1991 RECORD

35	Colgate	10	20	Rhode Island	28
15	Maine	14	20	Delaware St.	46
7	Youngstown St.	59	10	James Madison	27
34	Lock Haven	0			
22	Lehigh	35	239	(4-7-0)	277
50	Towson St.	13			
14	New Hampshire	18			
12	Massachusetts	27			

Conference: I-AA Independents.   Enrollment: 14,500.   Colors: Red & Black.
Nickname: Huskies.   Stadium: E.S. Parsons (1933), 7,000 capacity.   Artificial turf.
1991 home attendance: 24,926 in 6 games.
Director of Athletics: Irwin Cohen.
Sports Info. Director: Jack Grinold   617-437-2691

NORTHERN ARIZONA . . . Flagstaff, Ariz.   86011   I-AA

Coach: Steve Axman, LIU-C. W. Post '69
Record: 2 yrs., W-8, L-14, T-0
1992 SCHEDULE

Southern Utah ■	Sep 5*
Northeastern ■	Sep 12*
Nevada-Las Vegas	Sep 19*
Idaho St. ■	Sep 26*
Montana St.	Oct 3
Boise St. ■	Oct 10*
Montana	Oct 17
Eastern Wash. ■	Oct 24*
Idaho	Oct 31
Weber St.	Nov 7*
Minn.-Duluth ■	Nov 14*

1991 RECORD

22	Eastern N. Mex.	15	29	Eastern Wash.	44
65	N.M. Highlands	12	28	Idaho	44
38	Weber St.	43	16	Nevada	45
14	Akron	49			
14	Idaho St.	45	294	(3-8-0)	404
27	Montana St.	16			
14	Boise St.	57			
27	Montana	34			

Conference: Big Sky Conf.   Enrollment: 17,698.   Colors: Blue & Gold.
Nickname: Lumberjacks.   Stadium: Walkup Skydome (1977), 15,300 capacity.   Artificial turf.
1991 home attendance: 37,236 in 6 games.
Director of Athletics: Tom Jurich.
Sports Info. Director: Wylie Smith   602-523-6791

NORTHERN ILLINOIS . . . DeKalb, Ill.   60115   I-A

Coach: Charlie Sadler, Northeast Okla. '71
Record: 1 yr., W-2, L-9, T-0
1992 SCHEDULE

Illinois	Sep 5
Illinois St. ■	Sep 12*
Arkansas St.	Sep 19
Wisconsin	Sep 26
Middle Tenn. St. ■	Oct 3*
Southern Miss. ■	Oct 10
Liberty ■	Oct 24*
Western Mich.	Oct 31
Southwestern La.	Nov 7
Army	Nov 14
Toledo ■	Nov 21

1991 RECORD

7	Fresno St.	55	12	Southwestern La.	13
22	Arkansas St.	21	27	Illinois St.	24
17	Kansas St.	34	21	Toledo	42
7	Iowa	58			
3	Louisiana Tech	37	143	(2-9-0)	364
10	Western Mich.	22			
10	Florida	41			
7	Akron	17			

Conference: I-A Independents.   Enrollment: 24,895.   Colors: Cardinal & Black.
Nickname: Huskies.   Stadium: Huskie (1965), 30,998 capacity.   Artificial turf.
1991 home attendance: 55,523 in 5 games.
Director of Athletics: Gerald K. O'Dell.
Sports Info. Director: Mike Korcek   815-753-1706

NORTHERN IOWA . . . Cedar Falls, Iowa   50613   I-AA

Coach: Terry Allen, Northern Iowa '79
Record: 3 yrs., W-27, L-9, T-0
1992 SCHEDULE

McNeese St. ■	Sep 12*
Idaho St. ■	Sep 19
Iowa St.	Sep 26
Illinois St. ■	Oct 3
Western Ky. ■	Oct 10*
Southern Ill.	Oct 17
Idaho ■	Oct 24*
Indiana St.	Oct 31
Eastern Ill.	Nov 7
Western Ill. ■	Nov 14*
Southwest Mo. St. ■	Nov 21*

1991 RECORD

30	McNeese St.	5	49	Indiana St.	21
45	Augustana (S.D.)	22	24	Western Ill.	17
20	Southern Ill.	21	18	Eastern Ill.	17
36	Idaho	14			
56	Morgan St.	6	366	(10-1-0)	158
17	Illinois St.	14		**I-AA Championship**	
49	Western Ky.	21	38	Weber St.	21
22	Southwest Mo. St.	0	13	Marshall	41

Conference: Gateway.   Enrollment: 13,100.   Colors: Purple & Old Gold.
Nickname: Panthers.   Stadium: U.N.I.-Dome (1976), 16,400 capacity.   Artificial turf.
1991 home attendance: 55,183 in 5 games.
Director of Athletics: Christopher Ritrievi.
Sports Info. Director: Nancy Justis   319-273-6354

■ Home games on each schedule [neutral sites shown in brackets].   *Night Games.

NORTHWESTERN . . . Evanston, Ill. 60208   I-A

Coach: Gary Barnett, Missouri '69
Record: 2 yrs., W-8, L-11, T-1
1992 SCHEDULE

Notre Dame [Chicago, Ill.]	Sep 5
Boston College	Sep 12
Stanford	Sep 19
Purdue	Oct 3
Indiana ■	Oct 10
Ohio St.	Oct 17
Illinois	Oct 24
Michigan St. ■	Oct 31
Michigan ■	Nov 7
Iowa	Nov 14
Wisconsin ■	Nov 21

1991 RECORD

7	Rice	36	14	Michigan	59
18	Rutgers	22	10	Iowa	24
41	Wake Forest	14	14	Wisconsin	32
14	Purdue	17			
6	Indiana	44	160	(3-8-0)	306
3	Ohio St.	34			
17	Illinois	11			
16	Michigan St.	13			

Conference: Big Ten Conf. Enrollment: 7,400. Colors: Purple & White.
Nickname: Wildcats. Stadium: Dyche (1926), 49,256 capacity. Artificial turf.
1991 home attendance: 209,023 in 6 games.
Director of Athletics: Bruce A. Corrie.
Sports Info. Director: Tim Clodjeaux 708-491-7503

NORTHWESTERN STATE (LOUISIANA) . . . Natchitoches, La. 71497   I-AA

Coach: Sam Goodwin, Henderson St. '66
Record: 11 yrs., W-59, L-59, T-4
1992 SCHEDULE

Mississippi Col. ■	Sep 5*
Troy St.	Sep 12
East Tex. St. ■	Sep 26*
Arkansas St.	Oct 3
North Texas	Oct 10*
McNeese St.	Oct 17*
Northeast La. ■	Oct 24
Southwest Tex. St. ■	Oct 31*
Sam Houston St. ■	Nov 7*
Nicholls St. ■	Nov 14*
Stephen F. Austin	Nov 21

1991 RECORD

28	Arkansas St.	3	3	Sam Houston St.	13
14	Nevada	45	16	Nicholls St.	10
0	UTEP	14	52	Stephen F. Austin	0
26	East Tex. St.	23			
24	North Texas	10	192	(6-5-0)	169
20	McNeese St.	3			
9	Northeast La.	24			
0	Southwest Tex. St.	24			

Conference: Southland Conf. Enrollment: 7,703. Colors: Purple & White.
Nickname: Demons. Stadium: Turpin (1976), 16,522 capacity. Artificial turf.
1991 home attendance: 48,000 in 5 games.
Director of Athletics: Tynes Hildebrand.
Sports Info. Director: Doug Ireland 318-357-6467

NOTRE DAME . . . Notre Dame, Ind. 46556   I-A

Coach: Lou Holtz, Kent '59
Record: 22 yrs., W-172, L-82, T-5
1992 SCHEDULE

Northwestern [Chicago, Ill.]	Sep 5
Michigan ■	Sep 12
Michigan St. ■	Sep 19
Purdue ■	Sep 26
Stanford ■	Oct 3
Pittsburgh	Oct 10
Brigham Young ■	Oct 24
Navy [East Rutherford, N.J.]	Oct 31
Boston College ■	Nov 7
Penn St.	Nov 14
Southern Cal	Nov 28

1991 RECORD

49	Indiana	27	38	Navy	0
14	Michigan	24	34	Tennessee	35
49	Michigan St.	10	13	Penn St.	35
45	Purdue	20	48	Hawaii	42
42	Stanford	26			
42	Pittsburgh	7	426	(9-3-0)	261
28	Air Force	15		USF&G Sugar Bowl	
24	Southern Cal	20	39	Florida	28

Conference: I-A Independents. Enrollment: 9,500. Colors: Gold & Blue.
Nickname: Fighting Irish. Stadium: Notre Dame (1930), 59,075 capacity. Natural turf.
1991 home attendance: 354,450 in 6 games.
Director of Athletics: Dick Rosenthal.
Sports Info. Director: John Heisler 219-239-7516

OHIO . . . Athens, Ohio 45701   I-A

Coach: Tom Lichtenberg, Louisville '62
Record: 5 yrs., W-21, L-31, T-3
1992 SCHEDULE

Iowa St.	Sep 5
Kent	Sep 12
Central Mich. ■	Sep 19
Western Mich. ■	Sep 26
Akron ■	Oct 3
Bowling Green	Oct 10
Miami (Ohio) ■	Oct 17
Eastern Mich.	Oct 24*
Ball St.	Oct 31
Youngstown St. ■	Nov 7
Colorado St.	Nov 14

1991 RECORD

17	Central Mich.	17	6	Ball St.	10
35	Tennessee Tech	14	10	Eastern Mich.	13
14	Mississippi	38	13	Tulsa	45
9	Western Mich.	35			
13	Toledo	17	176	(2-8-1)	308
14	Bowling Green	45			
0	Miami (Ohio)	34			
45	Kent	40			

Conference: Mid-American Conf. Enrollment: 17,050. Colors: Kelly Green & White.
Nickname: Bobcats. Stadium: Peden (1929), 20,000 capacity. Natural turf.
1991 home attendance: 60,800 in 5 games.
Director of Athletics: Harold McElhaney.
Sports Info. Director: Frank Morgan 614-593-1299

OHIO STATE . . . Columbus, Ohio 43210   I-A

Coach: John Cooper, Iowa St. '62
Record: 15 yrs., W-108, L-59, T-4
1992 SCHEDULE

Louisville ■	Sep 5
Bowling Green ■	Sep 12
Syracuse	Sep 19*
Wisconsin	Oct 3
Illinois ■	Oct 10
Northwestern	Oct 17
Michigan St.	Oct 24
Iowa	Oct 31
Minnesota ■	Nov 7
Indiana	Nov 14
Michigan ■	Nov 21

1991 RECORD

38	Arizona	14	35	Minnesota	6
23	Louisville	15	20	Indiana	16
33	Washington St.	19	3	Michigan	31
31	Wisconsin	16			
7	Illinois	10	260	(8-3-0)	163
34	Northwestern	3		Hall of Fame Bowl	
27	Michigan St.	17	17	Syracuse	24
9	Iowa	16			

Conference: Big Ten Conf. Enrollment: 54,000. Colors: Scarlet & Gray.
Nickname: Buckeyes. Stadium: Ohio (1922), 91,470 capacity. Natural turf.
1991 home attendance: 620,845 in 7 games.
Director of Athletics: James L. Jones.
Sports Info. Director: Steve Snapp 614-292-6861

■ Home games on each schedule [neutral sites shown in brackets]. *Night Games.

OKLAHOMA . . . Norman, Okla.   73019   I-A

Coach: Gary Gibbs, Oklahoma '75
Record: 3 yrs., W-24, L-10, T-0
1992 SCHEDULE

Texas Tech .... Sep 3*
Arkansas St. ■ .... Sep 12
Southern Cal ■ .... Sep 19
Iowa St. ■ .... Oct 3
Texas [Dallas, Tex.] .... Oct 10
Colorado .... Oct 17
Kansas .... Oct 24
Kansas St. ■ .... Oct 31
Missouri ■ .... Nov 7
Oklahoma St. .... Nov 14
Nebraska ■ .... Nov 27

1991 RECORD

40	North Texas	2	56 Missouri	16
55	Utah St.	21	21 Oklahoma St.	6
27	Virginia Tech	17	14 Nebraska	19
29	Iowa St.	8		
7	Texas	10	335 (8-3-0) 143	
17	Colorado	34	**Mazda Gator Bowl**	
41	Kansas	3	48 Virginia	14
28	Kansas St.	7		

Conference: Big Eight Conf. Enrollment: 20,000. Colors: Crimson & Cream.
Nickname: Sooners. Stadium: Owen Field (1924), 75,004 capacity. Artificial turf.
1991 home attendance: 483,394 in 7 games.
Director of Athletics: Donnie Duncan.
Sports Info. Director: Mike Treps 405-325-8225

OKLAHOMA STATE . . . Stillwater, Okla.   74078   I-A

Coach: Pat Jones, Arkansas '69
Record: 8 yrs., W-52, L-39, T-1
1992 SCHEDULE

Indiana St. ■ .... Sep 5*
Michigan .... Sep 19
Tulsa ■ .... Sep 26*
Texas Christian .... Oct 3*
Nebraska .... Oct 10
Missouri ■ .... Oct 17
Iowa St. ■ .... Oct 24
Kansas .... Oct 31
Colorado .... Nov 7
Oklahoma ■ .... Nov 14
Kansas St. ■ .... Nov 21

1991 RECORD

7	Tulsa	13	12 Colorado	16
3	Arizona St.	30	6 Oklahoma	21
21	Texas Christian	24	26 Kansas St.	36
3	Miami (Fla.)	40		
15	Nebraska	49	106 (0-10-1) 307	
7	Missouri	41		
6	Iowa St.	6		
0	Kansas	31		

Conference: Big Eight Conf. Enrollment: 20,000. Colors: Orange & Black.
Nickname: Cowboys. Stadium: Lewis (1972), 50,440 capacity. Artificial turf.
1991 home attendance: 162,756 in 6 games.
Director of Athletics: Jim Garner.
Sports Info. Director: Steve Buzzard 405-744-5749

OREGON . . . Eugene, Ore.   97403   I-A

Coach: Rich Brooks, Oregon St. '63
Record: 15 yrs., W-71, L-93, T-4
1992 SCHEDULE

Hawaii ■ .... Sep 5
Stanford .... Sep 12
Texas Tech ■ .... Sep 19
Nevada-Las Vegas ■ .... Sep 26
Arizona St. ■ .... Oct 3
Southern Cal .... Oct 10
Washington ■ .... Oct 17
Washington St. .... Oct 31
California ■ .... Nov 7
UCLA ■ .... Nov 14
Oregon St. .... Nov 21

1991 RECORD

40	Washington St.	14	21 Arizona St.	24
28	Texas Tech	13	7 UCLA	16
17	Utah	24	3 Oregon St.	14
14	Southern Cal	30		
29	New Mexico St.	6	186 (3-8-0) 248	
7	California	45		
7	Washington	29		
13	Stanford	33		

Conference: Pacific-10. Enrollment: 17,000. Colors: Green & Yellow.
Nickname: Ducks. Stadium: Autzen (1967), 41,678 capacity. Artificial turf.
1991 home attendance: 207,569 in 5 games.
Director of Athletics: Bill Byrne.
Sports Info. Director: Steve Hellyer 503-346-5488

OREGON STATE . . . Corvallis, Ore.   97331   I-A

Coach: Jerry Pettibone, Oklahoma '63
Record: 7 yrs., W-34, L-42, T-1
1992 SCHEDULE

Kansas ■ .... Sep 5
Fresno St. ■ .... Sep 12
Arizona ■ .... Sep 19
Utah .... Sep 26*
California .... Oct 3
Washington St. ■ .... Oct 10
Arizona St. .... Oct 17*
Stanford ■ .... Oct 24
UCLA .... Nov 7
Washington .... Nov 14
Oregon ■ .... Nov 21

1991 RECORD

10	Utah	22	14 California	27
9	Nevada-Las Vegas	23	6 Washington	58
20	Fresno St.	24	14 Oregon	3
7	Washington St.	55		
7	Arizona St.	24	125 (1-10-0) 365	
7	UCLA	44		
10	Stanford	40		
21	Arizona	45		

Conference: Pacific-10. Enrollment: 16,100. Colors: Orange & Black.
Nickname: Beavers. Stadium: Parker (1953), 35,362 capacity. Artificial turf.
1991 home attendance: 149,812 in 6 games.
Director of Athletics: Dutch Baughman.
Sports Info. Director: Hal Cowan 503-737-3720

PACIFIC (CALIFORNIA) . . . Stockton, Cal.   95211   I-A

Coach: Walt Harris, Pacific (Cal.) '68
Record: 2 yrs., W-6, L-17, T-0
1992 SCHEDULE

Fresno St. ■ .... Sep 5*
Nevada .... Sep 12
Boise St. .... Sep 19*
Nevada-Las Vegas ■ .... Oct 3
Arizona St. .... Oct 10*
New Mexico St. .... Oct 17
Washington .... Oct 24
Cal St. Fullerton ■ .... Nov 7
San Jose St. .... Nov 14
Utah St. ■ .... Nov 21

1991 RECORD

40	Cal St. Sacramento	43	51 Long Beach St.	24
24	California	86	14 Fresno St.	59
34	San Diego St.	55	14 Utah St.	21
21	Hawaii	30	44 Nevada-Las Vegas	23
56	Cal St. Fullerton	28		
63	Cal Poly SLO	28	435 (5-7-0) 481	
47	San Jose St.	64		
27	New Mexico St.	20		

Conference: Big West. Enrollment: 3,800. Colors: Orange & Black.
Nickname: Tigers. Stadium: Amos Alonzo Stagg (1950), 30,163 capacity. Natural turf.
1991 home attendance: 51,093 in 5 games.
Director of Athletics: Ted Leland.
Sports Info. Director: Kevin Messenger 209-946-2479

■ Home games on each schedule [neutral sites shown in brackets].   *Night Games.

PENN STATE . . . University Park, Pa.　16802　　　I-A

Coach: Joe Paterno, Brown '50
Record: 26 yrs., W-240, L-62, T-3

1992 SCHEDULE

Cincinnati	Sep　5*
Temple ■	Sep 12
Eastern Mich. ■	Sep 19
Maryland ■	Sep 26
Rutgers [East Rutherford, N.J.]	Oct　3
Miami (Fla.) ■	Oct 10
Boston College ■	Oct 17
West Va.	Oct 24
Brigham Young	Oct 31
Notre Dame	Nov 14
Pittsburgh ■	Nov 21

1991 RECORD

34	Georgia Tech	22	51	West Va.	6
81	Cincinnati	0	47	Maryland	7
10	Southern Cal	21	35	Notre Dame	13
33	Brigham Young	7	32	Pittsburgh	20
28	Boston College	21			
24	Temple	7	432	(10-2-0)	167
20	Miami (Fla.)	26		**Fiesta Bowl**	
37	Rutgers	17	42	Tennessee	17

Conference: Big Ten Conf.　Enrollment: 30,500.　Colors: Blue & White.
Nickname: Nittany Lions.　Stadium: Beaver (1960), 93,000 capacity.　Natural turf.
1991 home attendance: 575,077 in 6 games.
Director of Athletics: Jim Tarman.
Sports Info. Director: Budd Thalman　814-865-1757

PENNSYLVANIA . . . Philadelphia, Pa.　19104　　　I-AA

Coach: Al Bagnoli, Central Conn. St. '74
Record: 10 yrs., W-85, L-19, T-0

1992 SCHEDULE

Dartmouth	Sep 19
Colgate ■	Sep 26
Fordham	Oct　3
William & Mary ■	Oct 10
Columbia ■	Oct 17
Brown	Oct 24
Yale ■	Oct 31
Princeton	Nov　7
Harvard ■	Nov 14
Cornell	Nov 21

1991 RECORD

15	Dartmouth	21	18	Harvard	22
0	Holy Cross	45	14	Cornell	13
12	Lafayette	20			
14	Columbia	20	142	(2-8-0)	236
17	Lehigh	28			
28	Brown	19			
12	Yale	31			
12	Princeton	17			

Conference: Ivy League.　Enrollment: 9,300.　Colors: Red & Blue.
Nickname: Red & Blue, Quakers.　Stadium: Franklin Field (1895),
60,546 capacity.　Artificial turf.
1991 home attendance: 84,371 in 5 games.
Director of Athletics: Paul Rubincam.
Sports Info. Director: To be named　215-898-6128

PITTSBURGH . . . Pittsburgh, Pa.　15213　　　I-A

Coach: Paul Hackett, UC Davis '69
Record: 3 yrs., W-10, L-12, T-1

1992 SCHEDULE

Kent ■	Sep　5
West Va. ■	Sep 12
Rutgers ■	Sep 17*
Minnesota ■	Sep 26
Maryland ■	Oct　3
Notre Dame ■	Oct 10
Temple	Oct 17
East Caro. ■	Oct 24
Syracuse	Oct 31
Louisville ■	Nov 14
Penn St.	Nov 21
Hawaii	Dec　5

1991 RECORD

34	West Va.	3	12	Boston College	38
35	Southern Miss.	14	22	Rutgers	17
26	Temple	7	20	Penn St.	32
14	Minnesota	13			
24	Maryland	20	244	(6-5-0)	241
7	Notre Dame	42			
27	Syracuse	31			
23	East Caro.	24			

Conference: Big East Conference.　Enrollment: 13,500.　Colors: Blue & Gold.
Nickname: Panthers.　Stadium: Pitt (1925), 56,500 capacity.　Artificial turf.
1991 home attendance: 219,074 in 6 games.
Director of Athletics: L. Oval Jaynes.
Sports Info. Director: Ron Wahl　412-648-8240

PRAIRIE VIEW A&M . . . Prairie View, Tex.　77445　　　I-AA

Coach: Ronald Beard, Eastern Mich. '74
Record: 1 yr., W-0, L-11, T-0

1992 SCHEDULE

Texas Southern [Houston, Tex.]	Sep　5*
Angelo St. ■	Sep 12*
Langston ■	Sep 19*
Grambling [Dallas, Tex.]	Oct　3*
West Tex. St.	Oct 10*
Alcorn St. ■	Oct 17
Alabama St.	Oct 24*
Mississippi Val.	Oct 31
Southwest Tex. St. ■	Nov　7
Jackson St.	Nov 14*
Southern-B.R. ■	Nov 21*

1991 RECORD

6	Texas Southern	23	0	Mississippi Val.	41
0	Angelo St.	55	6	Southwest Tex. St.	59
0	Southwest Mo. St.	61	20	Southern-B.R.	56
3	Texas A&I	41			
7	Grambling	77	48	(0-11-0)	617
6	Cameron	51			
0	Alcorn St.	61			
0	Alabama St.	92			

Conference: Southwestern.　Enrollment: 6,300.　Colors: Purple & Gold.
Nickname: Panthers.　Stadium: Blackshear (1960), 6,600 capacity.　Natural turf.
1991 home attendance: 19,660 in 3 games.
Director of Athletics: Barbara Jacket.
Sports Info. Director: Jacqueline Davis　409-857-2114

PRINCETON . . . Princeton, N.J.　08544　　　I-AA

Coach: Steve Tosches, Rhode Island '79
Record: 5 yrs., W-30, L-19, T-1

1992 SCHEDULE

Cornell	Sep 19
Lafayette ■	Sep 26
Lehigh	Oct　3
Brown ■	Oct 10
Holy Cross	Oct 17
Harvard ■	Oct 24
Columbia	Oct 31
Pennsylvania ■	Nov　7
Yale	Nov 14
Dartmouth ■	Nov 21

1991 RECORD

18	Cornell	0	22	Yale	16
20	Fordham	17	13	Dartmouth	31
30	Colgate	21			
59	Brown	37	253	(8-2-0)	171
31	Bucknell	7			
21	Harvard	24			
22	Columbia	6			
17	Pennsylvania	12			

Conference: Ivy League.　Enrollment: 4,500.　Colors: Orange & Black.
Nickname: Tigers.　Stadium: Palmer (1914), 45,725 capacity.　Natural turf.
1991 home attendance: 55,624 in 5 games.
Director of Athletics: Robert Myslik.
Sports Info. Director: Mark Panus　609-258-3568

■ Home games on each schedule [neutral sites shown in brackets].　　*Night Games.

1992 NCAA FOOTBALL

PURDUE . . . West Lafayette, Ind.   47907   I-A

Coach: Jim Colletto, UCLA '67
Record: 6 yrs., W-21, L-45, T-1
1992 SCHEDULE

California ■	Sep 12
Toledo ■	Sep 19
Notre Dame	Sep 26
Northwestern ■	Oct 3
Minnesota ■	Oct 10
Wisconsin	Oct 17
Iowa	Oct 24
Michigan ■	Oct 31
Illinois	Nov 7
Michigan St.	Nov 14
Indiana ■	Nov 21

1991 RECORD

49	Eastern Mich.	3	14	Illinois	41
18	California	42	27	Michigan St.	17
20	Notre Dame	45	22	Indiana	24
17	Northwestern	14			
3	Minnesota	6	219	(4-7-0)	272
28	Wisconsin	7			
21	Iowa	31			
0	Michigan	42			

Conference: Big Ten Conf.   Enrollment: 35,647.   Colors: Old Gold & Black.
Nickname: Boilermakers.   Stadium: Ross-Ade (1924), 67,861 capacity.   Natural turf.
1991 home attendance: 235,029 in 6 games.
Director of Athletics: John Hicks (Interim).
Sports Info. Director: Mark Adams   317-494-3200

RHODE ISLAND . . . Kingston, R.I.   02881   I-AA

Coach: Bob Griffin, Southern Conn. St. '63
Record: 20 yrs., W-99, L-117, T-1
1992 SCHEDULE

Towson St. ■	Sep 12
Delaware	Sep 19
Richmond ■	Sep 26
Hofstra	Oct 2*
Massachusetts ■	Oct 10
Maine	Oct 17
Boston U. ■	Oct 24
Villanova	Oct 31
Northeastern	Nov 7
New Hampshire ■	Nov 14
Connecticut	Nov 21

1991 RECORD

10	Richmond	19	28	Northeastern	20
7	Delaware	42	35	New Hampshire	42
45	Towson St.	25	20	Connecticut	10
38	Brown	36			
17	Massachusetts	14	266	(6-5-0)	330
52	Maine	30			
0	Boston U.	43			
14	Villanova	49			

Conference: Yankee.   Enrollment: 12,500.   Colors: Blue, White & Gold.
Nickname: Rams.   Stadium: Meade Stadium (1928), 10,000 capacity.   Natural turf.
1991 home attendance: 34,119 in 5 games.
Director of Athletics: Thomas R. Dougan.
Sports Info. Director: Jim Norman   401-792-2409

RICE . . . Houston, Tex.   77251   I-A

Coach: Fred Goldsmith, Florida '67
Record: 4 yrs., W-13, L-28, T-1
1992 SCHEDULE

Air Force	Sep 5
Duke	Sep 19
Sam Houston St. ■	Sep 26
Texas ■	Oct 3
Southern Methodist ■	Oct 10
Texas A&M	Oct 17
Texas Christian	Oct 24
Texas Tech ■	Nov 7
Baylor ■	Nov 14
Navy ■	Nov 21
Houston	Nov 28

1991 RECORD

36	Northwestern	7	31	Southern Methodist	10
28	Tulane	19	21	Houston	41
27	Iowa St.	28	0	Arkansas	20
7	Texas	28			
20	Baylor	17	239	(4-7-0)	287
28	Texas Christian	39			
20	Texas Tech	40			
21	Texas A&M	38			

Conference: Southwest Conf.   Enrollment: 2,600.   Colors: Blue & Gray.
Nickname: Owls.   Stadium: Rice (1950), 70,000 capacity.   Artificial turf.
1991 home attendance: 121,700 in 4 games.
Director of Athletics: J. R. "Bobby" May.
Sports Info. Director: Bill Cousins   713-527-4034

RICHMOND . . . Richmond, Va.   23173   I-AA

Coach: Jim Marshall, Tenn.-Martin '69
Record: 3 yrs., W-4, L-29, T-0
1992 SCHEDULE

James Madison ■	Sep 12
Villanova	Sep 19
Rhode Island	Sep 26
Maine ■	Oct 3
New Hampshire ■	Oct 10
Boston U.	Oct 17
Va. Military [Norfolk, Va.]	Oct 24
Connecticut	Oct 31
Massachusetts ■	Nov 7
Delaware ■	Nov 14
William & Mary ■	Nov 21

1991 RECORD

19	Rhode Island	10	14	Massachusetts	42
3	Villanova	35	17	Delaware	23
27	Va. Military	38	7	William & Mary	49
15	Maine	19			
0	New Hampshire	34	210	(2-9-0)	350
32	Boston U.	18			
42	James Madison	47			
34	Connecticut	35			

Conference: Yankee.   Enrollment: 2,800.   Colors: Red & Blue.
Nickname: Spiders.   Stadium: Richmond (1929), 22,611 capacity.   Artificial turf.
1991 home attendance: 49,504 in 5 games.
Director of Athletics: Chuck Boone.
Sports Info. Director: Chris Moore   804-289-8365

RUTGERS . . . New Brunswick, N.J.   08903   I-A

Coach: Doug Graber, Wayne St. (Mich.) '66
Record: 3 yrs., W-15, L-18, T-0
1992 SCHEDULE

Boston College	Sep 5
Colgate ■	Sep 12*
Pittsburgh ■	Sep 17*
Navy	Sep 26
Penn St. [East Rutherford, N.J.]	Oct 3
Syracuse	Oct 10
Army [East Rutherford, N.J.]	Oct 17
Virginia Tech ■	Oct 31
Cincinnati	Nov 7*
West Va. ■	Nov 14
Temple	Nov 21

1991 RECORD

20	Boston College	13	3	West Va.	28
22	Duke	42	17	Pittsburgh	22
22	Northwestern	18	41	Temple	0
14	Michigan St.	7			
14	Army	12	217	(6-5-0)	217
40	Maine	17			
17	Penn St.	37			
7	Syracuse	21			

Conference: Big East Conference.   Enrollment: 22,000.   Colors: Scarlet.
Nickname: Scarlet Knights.   Stadium: Rutgers (1938), 25,000 capacity.   Natural turf.
1991 home attendance: 131,236 in 6 games.
Director of Athletics: Fred E. Gruninger.
Sports Info. Director: Peter Kowalski   908-932-4200

■ Home games on each schedule [neutral sites shown in brackets].   *Night Games.

Divisions I-A & I-AA 1992 Schedules and 1991 Results   589

SAM HOUSTON STATE . . . Huntsville, Tex.   77341   I-AA

Coach: Ron Randleman, William Penn '64
Record: 23 yrs., W-145, L-95, T-4

1992 SCHEDULE

Western Ill. ■ .... Sep 12*
Angelo St. ■ .... Sep 19*
Rice .... Sep 26
Alcorn St. ■ .... Oct 3*
Nicholls St. .... Oct 10
Northeast La. .... Oct 17*
North Texas ■ .... Oct 24
Stephen F. Austin ■ .... Oct 31
Northwestern (La.) .... Nov 7*
McNeese St. .... Nov 14*
Southwest Tex. St. ■ .... Nov 21

1991 RECORD

26	Montana St.	23	13	Northwestern (La.)	3
37	Texas Southern	6	17	McNeese St.	19
16	Angelo St.	6	20	Southwest Tex. St.	14
21	Western Ill.	21			
28	Nicholls St.	19	222	(8-2-1)	145
27	Northeast La.	15		**I-AA Championship**	
14	North Texas	6	19	Middle Tenn. St.	20
3	Stephen F. Austin	13			

Conference: Southland Conf.   Enrollment: 13,252.   Colors: Orange & White with Blue Trim.
Nickname: Bearkats.   Stadium: Elliott T. Bowers (1986), 14,000 capacity.   Artificial turf.
1991 home attendance: 42,822 in 5 games.
Director of Athletics: Ronnie Choate.
Sports Info. Director: Paul Ridings Jr.   409-294-1764

SAMFORD . . . Birmingham, Ala.   35229   I-AA

Coach: Terry Bowden, West Va. '78
Record: 8 yrs., W-56, L-33, T-1

1992 SCHEDULE

West Ga. ■ .... Sep 5*
Auburn .... Sep 12*
Tennessee Tech .... Sep 19*
Bethune-Cookman .... Sep 26
Western Caro. ■ .... Oct 3*
Eastern Ky. ■ .... Oct 10*
Southeast Mo. St. ■ .... Oct 17
Ala.-Birmingham ■ .... Oct 31
Troy St. .... Nov 7
Tenn.-Martin .... Nov 14
Central Fla. ■ .... Nov 21

1991 RECORD

34	Harding	0	35	William & Mary	13
52	Morehead St.	14	31	Liberty	19
31	East Tenn. St.	6			
20	Tennessee Tech	16	332	(10-1-0)	154
48	Southeast Mo. St.	24		**I-AA Championship**	
13	Central Fla.	6	29	New Hampshire	13
28	Alabama St.	31	24	James Madison	21
16	Western Caro.	3	0	Youngstown St.	10
24	Troy St.	22			

Conference: I-AA Independents.   Enrollment: 4,164.   Colors: Crimson & Blue.
Nickname: Bulldogs.   Stadium: Seibert (1960), 6,700 capacity.   Natural turf.
1991 home attendance: 27,852 in 5 games.
Director of Athletics: Steve Allgood.
Sports Info. Director: Riley Adair   205-870-2799

SAN DIEGO STATE . . . San Diego, Cal.   92182   I-A

Coach: Al Luginbill, Cal Poly Pomona '67
Record: 3 yrs., W-20, L-14, T-2

1992 SCHEDULE

Southern Cal ■ .... Sep 5*
Brigham Young .... Sep 10*
UCLA ■ .... Sep 26
New Mexico .... Oct 3*
UTEP ■ .... Oct 17*
Air Force ■ .... Oct 24*
Colorado St. .... Oct 31
Wyoming .... Nov 7
Hawaii ■ .... Nov 14*
Fresno St. ■ .... Nov 21*
Miami (Fla.) ■ .... Nov 28*

1991 RECORD

49	Long Beach St.	13	24	Wyoming	22
55	Pacific (Cal.)	34	42	Colorado St.	32
20	Air Force	21	52	Brigham Young	52
12	UCLA	37	12	Miami (Fla.)	39
47	Hawaii	21			
38	New Mexico	24	403	(8-3-1)	337
28	UTEP	21		**Freedom Bowl**	
24	Utah	21	17	Tulsa	28

Conference: Western Athl. Conf.   Enrollment: 35,200.   Colors: Scarlet & Black.
Nickname: Aztecs.   Stadium: Jack Murphy (1967), 60,400 capacity.   Natural turf.
1991 home attendance: 232,020 in 7 games.
Director of Athletics: Fred Miller.
Sports Info. Director: John Rosenthal   619-594-5547

SAN JOSE STATE . . . San Jose, Cal.   95192   I-A

Coach: Ron Turner, Pacific (Cal.) '77
Record: First year as head coach

1992 SCHEDULE

California .... Sep 5
Minnesota .... Sep 12*
Southwestern La. ■ .... Sep 19*
Stanford .... Sep 26
Wyoming ■ .... Oct 3
Cal St. Fullerton ■ .... Oct 10*
Utah St. .... Oct 24
Nevada-Las Vegas .... Oct 31
Nevada ■ .... Nov 7
Pacific (Cal.) .... Nov 14
New Mexico St. ■ .... Nov 21

1991 RECORD

21	Florida	59	35	Cal St. Fullerton	7
20	Minnesota	26	35	Hawaii	35
32	Long Beach St.	20	28	Fresno St.	31
23	Utah St.	7			
39	New Mexico St.	13	372	(6-4-1)	298
64	Pacific (Cal.)	47			
20	California	41			
55	Nevada-Las Vegas	12			

Conference: Big West.   Enrollment: 30,000.   Colors: Gold, White & Blue.
Nickname: Spartans.   Stadium: Spartan (1932), 31,218 capacity.   Natural turf.
1991 home attendance: 63,163 in 4 games.
Director of Athletics: Thomas Brennan.
Sports Info. Director: Lawrence Fan   408-924-1217

SOUTH CAROLINA . . . Columbia, S.C.   29208   I-A

Coach: Sparky Woods, Carson-Newman '76
Record: 8 yrs., W-53, L-34, T-5

1992 SCHEDULE

Georgia ■ .... Sep 5*
Arkansas ■ .... Sep 12*
East Caro. ■ .... Sep 19*
Kentucky ■ .... Sep 26*
Alabama .... Oct 3
Mississippi St. ■ .... Oct 17
Vanderbilt .... Oct 24
Tennessee ■ .... Oct 31
Louisiana Tech ■ .... Nov 7
Florida .... Nov 14
Clemson .... Nov 21

1991 RECORD

24	Duke	24	10	Florida St.	38
16	West Va.	21	17	North Caro.	21
28	Virginia Tech	21	24	Clemson	41
20	East Caro.	31			
55	East Tenn. St.	7	250	(3-6-2)	268
12	Louisiana Tech	12			
23	Georgia Tech	14			
21	North Caro. St.	38			

Conference: Southeastern Conf.   Enrollment: 25,613.   Colors: Garnet & Black.
Nickname: Fighting Gamecocks.   Stadium: Williams-Brice (1934),
72,400 capacity.   Natural turf.
1991 home attendance: 456,952 in 7 games.
Director of Athletics: King Dixon.
Sports Info. Director: Kerry Tharp   803-777-5204

■ Home games on each schedule [neutral sites shown in brackets].   *Night Games.

1992 NCAA FOOTBALL

SOUTH CAROLINA STATE . . . Orangeburg, S.C. 29117   I-AA

Coach: Willie Jeffries, South Caro. St. '60
Record: 19 yrs., W-117, L-84, T-6

1992 SCHEDULE

Newberry	Sep 5
Florida A&M	Sep 12*
Southern-B.R. [Atlanta, Ga.]	Sep 19
Jackson St. [Columbia, S.C.]	Oct 3
Morgan St. ■	Oct 10
Bethune-Cookman ■	Oct 17
N.C. Central ■	Oct 24
Delaware St.	Oct 31
Howard ■	Nov 7
Charleston So. [Summerville, S.C.]	Nov 14
North Caro. A&T	Nov 21

1991 RECORD

28	Newberry	7	12	Charleston So.	0
10	Howard	5	6	Jackson St.	17
30	Southern-B.R.	23	21	North Caro. A&T	49
50	Johnson Smith	0			
21	Morgan St.	6	234	(7-4-0)	157
21	Bethune-Cookman	24			
21	Florida A&M	7			
14	Delaware St.	19			

Conference: Mid-Eastern. Enrollment: 5,000. Colors: Garnet & Blue.
Nickname: Bulldogs. Stadium: Dawson Bulldog (1955), 14,000 capacity. Natural turf.
1991 home attendance: 85,602 in 6 games.
Director of Athletics: Willie Jeffries.
Sports Info. Director: Bill Hamilton 803-536-7060

SOUTHEAST MISSOURI STATE . . . Cape Girardeau, Mo. 63701   I-AA

Coach: John Mumford, Pittsburg St. '79
Record: 2 yrs., W-10, L-11, T-0

1992 SCHEDULE

Murray St. ■	Sep 3*
Southern Ill.	Sep 12
Austin Peay ■	Sep 26*
Eastern Ky.	Oct 3
Tennessee Tech	Oct 10
Samford	Oct 17
Middle Tenn. St. ■	Oct 24
Tenn.-Martin ■	Oct 31
Morehead St.	Nov 7
Illinois St. ■	Nov 14
Tennessee St.	Nov 21

1991 RECORD

27	Southern Ill.	28	0	Middle Tenn. St.	52
29	Tenn.-Martin	36	17	Morehead St.	16
7	Eastern Ky.	49	10	Murray St.	14
7	Illinois St.	42			
21	Austin Peay	24	213	(3-8-0)	374
24	Samford	48			
34	Tennessee Tech	31			
37	Tennessee St.	34			

Conference: Ohio Valley Conf. Enrollment: 9,000. Colors: Red & Black.
Nickname: Indians. Stadium: Houck (1930), 10,000 capacity. Natural turf.
1991 home attendance: 37,383 in 6 games.
Director of Athletics: Richard McDuffie.
Sports Info. Director: Ron Hines 314-651-2294

SOUTHERN CALIFORNIA . . . Los Angeles, Cal. 90089   I-A

Coach: Larry Smith, Bowling Green '62
Record: 16 yrs., W-104, L-75, T-5

1992 SCHEDULE

San Diego St.	Sep 5*
Oklahoma	Sep 19
Washington	Oct 3
Oregon ■	Oct 10
California ■	Oct 17
Washington St. ■	Oct 24
Arizona St.	Oct 31*
Stanford	Nov 7
Arizona ■	Nov 14
UCLA	Nov 21
Notre Dame ■	Nov 28

1991 RECORD

10	Memphis St.	24	3	Washington	14
21	Penn St.	10	14	Arizona	31
25	Arizona St.	32	21	UCLA	24
30	Oregon	14			
34	Washington St.	27	229	(3-8-0)	276
21	Stanford	24			
20	Notre Dame	24			
30	California	52			

Conference: Pacific-10. Enrollment: 28,374. Colors: Cardinal & Gold.
Nickname: Trojans. Stadium: L.A. Coliseum (1923), 92,500 capacity. Natural turf.
1991 home attendance: 385,226 in 6 games.
Director of Athletics: Mike McGee.
Sports Info. Director: Tim Tessalone 213-740-8480

SOUTHERN ILLINOIS . . . Carbondale, Ill. 62901   I-AA

Coach: Bob Smith, Bradley '62
Record: 7 yrs., W-28, L-48, T-1

1992 SCHEDULE

Troy St. ■	Sep 5
Southeast Mo. St. ■	Sep 12
Austin Peay ■	Sep 19
Arkansas St.	Sep 26
Eastern Ill.	Oct 3*
Western Ill. ■	Oct 10
Northern Iowa ■	Oct 17
Illinois St.	Oct 24
Western Ky.	Oct 31
Southwest Mo. St.	Nov 7
Indiana St. ■	Nov 21

1991 RECORD

28	Southeast Mo. St.	27	30	Indiana St.	23
31	Murray St.	27	31	Eastern Ill.	30
21	Austin Peay	17	16	Louisiana Tech	48
21	Northern Iowa	20			
14	Illinois St.	11	238	(7-4-0)	271
13	Southwest Mo. St.	17			
13	Troy St.	30			
20	Western Ill.	21			

Conference: Gateway. Enrollment: 24,325. Colors: Maroon & White.
Nickname: Salukis. Stadium: McAndrew (1975), 17,324 capacity. Artificial turf.
1991 home attendance: 48,900 in 4 games.
Director of Athletics: Jim Hart.
Sports Info. Director: Fred Huff 618-453-7235

SOUTHERN METHODIST . . . Dallas, Tex. 75275   I-A

Coach: Tom Rossley, Cincinnati '69
Record: 1 yr., W-1, L-10, T-0

1992 SCHEDULE

Tulane ■	Sep 5*
North Texas ■	Sep 12
New Mexico ■	Sep 19*
Texas Christian ■	Sep 26*
Baylor	Oct 3
Rice	Oct 10
Texas Tech	Oct 24
Texas A&M ■	Oct 31
Houston ■	Nov 7
Texas	Nov 14
Arkansas [Little Rock, Ark.]	Nov 21

1991 RECORD

6	Arkansas	17	10	Rice	31
11	Vanderbilt	14	6	Texas A&M	65
7	Baylor	45	26	Tulsa	31
31	Tulane	17			
14	Texas Tech	38	141	(1-10-0)	359
20	Houston	49			
0	Texas	34			
10	Texas Christian	18			

Conference: Southwest Conf. Enrollment: 5,471. Colors: Red & Blue.
Nickname: Mustangs. Stadium: Ownby (1926), 23,783 capacity. Artificial turf.
1991 home attendance: 88,179 in 5 games.
Director of Athletics: Forrest Gregg.
Sports Info. Director: Ed Wisneski 214-692-2883

■ Home games on each schedule [neutral sites shown in brackets]. *Night Games.

SOUTHERN MISSISSIPPI . . . Hattiesburg, Miss. 39406 I-A

Coach: Jeff Bower, Southern Miss. '76
Record: 2 yrs., W-4, L-8, T-0
1992 SCHEDULE

Memphis St. ■	Sep 5
Alabama [Birmingham, Ala.]	Sep 12
Louisiana Tech ■	Sep 19
Auburn	Sep 26
Tulsa ■	Oct 3
Northern Ill.	Oct 10
Tulane	Oct 15*
Cincinnati ■	Oct 24
East Caro.	Oct 29*
Florida	Nov 7
Virginia Tech	Nov 14

1991 RECORD

25	Delta St.	7	10	Tulsa	13
14	Pittsburgh	35	20	East Caro.	48
39	Colorado St.	7	14	Louisiana Tech	30
14	Louisville	28			
10	Auburn	9	212	(4-7-0)	225
12	Memphis St.	17			
47	Tulane	14			
7	Cincinnati	17			

Conference: I-A Independents.   Enrollment: 13,500.   Colors: Black & Gold.
Nickname: Golden Eagles.   Stadium: Roberts (1976), 33,000 capacity.   Natural turf.
1991 home attendance: 68,778 in 4 games.
Director of Athletics: Bill McLellan.
Sports Info. Director: M.R. Napier   601-266-4503

SOUTHERN-BATON ROUGE . . . Baton Rouge, La. 70813 I-AA

Coach: Marino Casem, Xavier (La.) '56
Record: 25 yrs., W-154, L-87, T-8
1992 SCHEDULE

Alabama St. ■	Sep 12*
South Caro. St. [Atlanta, Ga.]	Sep 19
Mississippi Val.	Oct 3*
Winston-Salem [Shreveport, La.]	Oct 10
Jackson St. ■	Oct 17*
Alcorn St.	Oct 24
Nicholls St.	Oct 31
Florida A&M	Nov 7*
Texas Southern ■	Nov 14*
Prairie View	Nov 21*
Grambling [New Orleans, La.]	Nov 28

1991 RECORD

16	Alabama St.	19	14	Tennessee St.	33
38	Texas Southern	30	56	Prairie View	20
23	South Caro. St.	30	31	Grambling	30
0	Mississippi Val.	7			
21	Jackson St.	20	255	(4-7-0)	286
29	Alcorn St.	52			
7	Nicholls St.	21			
20	Florida A&M	24			

Conference: Southwestern.   Enrollment: 9,500.   Colors: Blue & Gold.
Nickname: Jaguars.   Stadium: A.W. Mumford (1928), 24,000 capacity.   Natural turf.
1991 home attendance: 90,963 in 6 games.
Director of Athletics: Marino Casem.
Sports Info. Director: Rodney Lockett   504-771-4142

SOUTHWEST MISSOURI STATE . . . Springfield, Mo. 65804 I-AA

Coach: Jesse Branch, Arkansas '64
Record: 6 yrs., W-38, L-28, T-1
1992 SCHEDULE

McNeese St.	Sep 5*
Washburn ■	Sep 12*
North Texas ■	Sep 19*
Western Ky.	Sep 26
Western Ill. ■	Oct 3
Tulsa	Oct 10
Illinois St.	Oct 17
Eastern Ill. ■	Oct 24
Southern Ill. ■	Nov 7
Indiana St.	Nov 14
Northern Iowa	Nov 21*

1991 RECORD

13	Tulsa	34	0	Northern Iowa	22
7	McNeese St.	3	21	Illinois St.	6
61	Prairie View	0	29	Eastern Ill.	35
21	North Texas	21			
17	Southern Ill.	13	295	(6-4-1)	199
21	Western Ill.	26			
68	Indiana St.	19			
37	Arkansas St.	20			

Conference: Gateway.   Enrollment: 20,672.   Colors: Maroon & White.
Nickname: Bears.   Stadium: Plaster Field (1941), 16,600 capacity.   Artificial turf.
1991 home attendance: 58,603 in 5 games.
Director of Athletics: Bill Rowe.
Sports Info. Director: Mark Stillwell   417-836-5402

SOUTHWEST TEXAS STATE . . . San Marcos, Tex. 78666 I-AA

Coach: Jim Bob Helduser, Texas Lutheran '79
Record: First year as head coach
1992 SCHEDULE

Texas A&I ■	Sep 5*
Texas Southern [San Antonio, Tex.]	Sep 12*
Youngstown St. ■	Sep 19*
Northeast La.	Sep 26*
Nicholls St. ■	Oct 3*
Stephen F. Austin ■	Oct 10*
McNeese St. ■	Oct 24
Northwestern (La.)	Oct 31*
Prairie View	Nov 7
North Texas ■	Nov 14
Sam Houston St.	Nov 21

1991 RECORD

29	Texas A&I	14	59	Prairie View	6
38	Idaho	41	36	North Texas	8
19	Nicholls St.	10	14	Sam Houston St.	20
8	Northeast La.	17			
31	Stephen F. Austin	15	307	(7-4-0)	179
31	Texas Southern	29			
18	McNeese St.	19			
24	Northwestern (La.)	0			

Conference: Southland Conf.   Enrollment: 20,214.   Colors: Maroon & Gold.
Nickname: Bobcats.   Stadium: Bobcat (1981), 14,104 capacity.   Natural turf.
1991 home attendance: 42,884 in 5 games.
Director of Athletics: Richard Hannan.
Sports Info. Director: Tony Brubaker   512-245-2966

SOUTHWESTERN LOUISIANA . . . Lafayette, La. 70506 I-A

Coach: Nelson Stokley, Louisiana St. '68
Record: 6 yrs., W-32, L-33, T-1
1992 SCHEDULE

Tennessee	Sep 5
Northeast La. ■	Sep 12*
San Jose St.	Sep 19*
Houston	Oct 3
Louisiana Tech	Oct 10*
Cal St. Fullerton ■	Oct 17*
Auburn	Oct 24
Tulsa	Oct 31
Northern Ill. ■	Nov 7
Arkansas St. ■	Nov 21*

1991 RECORD

10	Northeast La.	21	13	Northern Ill.	12
24	Central Mich.	27	7	Auburn	50
15	Wyoming	28	17	Arkansas St.	13
7	Arkansas	9			
7	Texas A&M	34	148	(2-8-1)	269
14	Miami (Ohio)	27			
20	Tulsa	34			
14	Louisiana Tech	14			

Conference: I-A Independents.   Enrollment: 17,000.   Colors: Vermilion & White.
Nickname: Ragin' Cajuns.   Stadium: Cajun Field (1971), 31,000 capacity.   Natural turf.
1991 home attendance: 80,294 in 4 games.
Director of Athletics: Nelson Stokley.
Sports Info. Director: Dan McDonald   318-231-6331

■ Home games on each schedule [neutral sites shown in brackets].   *Night Games.

STANFORD . . . Stanford, Cal. 94305 {I-A}

Coach: Bill Walsh, San Jose St. '59
Record: 2 yrs., W-17, L-7, T-0

1992 SCHEDULE

Texas A&M [Anaheim, Cal.]	Aug 26*
Oregon ■	Sep 12
Northwestern ■	Sep 19
San Jose St. ■	Sep 26
Notre Dame	Oct 3
UCLA	Oct 10
Arizona ■	Oct 17
Oregon St.	Oct 24
Washington	Oct 31
Southern Cal ■	Nov 7
Washington St. ■	Nov 14
California	Nov 21

1991 RECORD

7	Washington	42		27	UCLA	10
23	Arizona	28		49	Washington St.	14
28	Colorado	21		38	California	21
26	Notre Dame	42				
56	Cornell	6		351	(8-3-0)	228
24	Southern Cal	21			**Jeep Eagle Aloha Bowl**	
40	Oregon St.	10		17	Georgia Tech	18
33	Oregon	13				

Conference: Pacific-10.   Enrollment: 6,556.   Colors: Cardinal & White.
Nickname: Cardinal.   Stadium: Stanford (1921), 85,500 capacity.   Natural turf.
1991 home attendance: 367,044 in 7 games.
Director of Athletics: Ted Leland.
Sports Info. Director: Gary Migdol   415-723-4418

STEPHEN F. AUSTIN . . . Nacogdoches, Tex. 75962 {I-AA}

Coach: John Pearce, East Tex. St. '70
Record: First year as head coach

1992 SCHEDULE

Ark.-Monticello ■	Sep 5*
Montana St.	Sep 12
Jackson St. ■	Sep 19*
Boise St. ■	Sep 26*
Southwest Tex. St.	Oct 10*
North Texas ■	Oct 17
Nicholls St.	Oct 24
Sam Houston St.	Oct 31
McNeese St. ■	Nov 7
Northeast La.	Nov 14*
Northwestern (La.) ■	Nov 21

1991 RECORD

50	Ark.-Monticello	9		7	McNeese St.	7
16	Jackson St.	31		20	Northeast La.	48
7	Boise St.	38		0	Northwestern (La.)	52
9	Youngstown St.	16				
15	Southwest Tex. St.	31		151	(2-8-1)	277
14	North Texas	18				
0	Nicholls St.	24				
13	Sam Houston St.	3				

Conference: Southland Conf.   Enrollment: 12,800.   Colors: Purple & White.
Nickname: Lumberjacks.   Stadium: Homer Bryce (1973), 14,575 capacity.   Artificial turf.
1991 home attendance: 48,005 in 5 games.
Director of Athletics: Steve McCarty.
Sports Info. Director: Gregg Fort   409-568-2606

SYRACUSE . . . Syracuse, N.Y. 13244 {I-A}

Coach: Paul Pasqualoni, Penn St. '72
Record: 6 yrs., W-44, L-19, T-0

1992 SCHEDULE

East Caro.	Sep 5*
Texas ■	Sep 12
Ohio St. ■	Sep 19*
Louisville	Oct 3
Rutgers ■	Oct 10
West Va.	Oct 17
Temple	Oct 24
Pittsburgh ■	Oct 31
Virginia Tech ■	Nov 7
Boston College	Nov 14
Miami (Fla.) ■	Nov 21

1991 RECORD

37	Vanderbilt	10		27	Temple	6
31	Maryland	17		38	Boston College	16
38	Florida	21		16	West Va.	10
24	Tulane	0				
14	Florida St.	46		297	(9-2-0)	183
20	East Caro.	23			**Hall of Fame Bowl**	
31	Pittsburgh	27		24	Ohio St.	17
21	Rutgers	7				

Conference: Big East Conference.   Enrollment: 11,600.   Colors: Orange.
Nickname: Orangemen.   Stadium: Carrier Dome (1980), 50,000 capacity.   Artificial turf.
1991 home attendance: 260,993 in 6 games.
Director of Athletics: Jake Crouthamel.
Sports Info. Director: Larry Kimball   315-443-2608

TEMPLE . . . Philadelphia, Pa. 19122 {I-A}

Coach: Jerry Berndt, Bowling Green '62
Record: 13 yrs., W-54, L-77, T-3

1992 SCHEDULE

Boston U. ■	Sep 5
Penn St.	Sep 12
Virginia Tech ■	Sep 19
Kansas St.	Sep 26*
Washington St.	Oct 3
Pittsburgh ■	Oct 17
Syracuse ■	Oct 24
Boston College	Oct 31
Akron	Nov 7
Miami (Fla.)	Nov 14
Rutgers ■	Nov 21

1991 RECORD

3	Alabama	41		13	Boston College	33
7	Pittsburgh	26		0	Rutgers	41
7	Clemson	37		32	Akron	37
40	Howard	0				
7	Penn St.	24		145	(2-9-0)	290
9	West Va.	10				
21	Navy	14				
6	Syracuse	27				

Conference: Big East Conference.   Enrollment: 34,000.   Colors: Cherry & White.
Nickname: Owls.   Stadium: Veterans (1971), 60,540 capacity.   Artificial turf.
1991 home attendance: 103,261 in 5 games.
Director of Athletics: Charles Theokas.
Sports Info. Director: Al Shrier   215-787-7445

TENNESSEE . . . Knoxville, Tenn. 37996 {I-A}

Coach: John Majors, Tennessee '57
Record: 24 yrs., W-168, L-102, T-10

1992 SCHEDULE

Southwestern La. ■	Sep 5
Georgia	Sep 12
Florida ■	Sep 19
Cincinnati ■	Sep 26
Louisiana St.	Oct 3*
Arkansas ■	Oct 10
Alabama ■	Oct 17
South Caro.	Oct 31
Memphis St.	Nov 14
Kentucky ■	Nov 21
Vanderbilt	Nov 28

1991 RECORD

28	Louisville	11		36	Mississippi	25
30	UCLA	16		16	Kentucky	7
26	Mississippi St.	24		45	Vanderbilt	0
30	Auburn	21				
18	Florida	35		335	(9-2-0)	221
19	Alabama	24			**Fiesta Bowl**	
52	Memphis St.	24		17	Penn St.	42
35	Notre Dame	34				

Conference: Southeastern Conf.   Enrollment: 26,055.   Colors: Orange & White.
Nickname: Volunteers.   Stadium: Neyland (1921), 91,902 capacity.   Artificial turf.
1991 home attendance: 578,389 in 6 games.
Director of Athletics: Doug Dickey.
Sports Info. Director: Bud Ford   615-974-1212

■ Home games on each schedule [neutral sites shown in brackets].   *Night Games.

TENNESSEE-CHATTANOOGA . . . Chattanooga, Tenn.   37402   I-AA

Coach: Buddy Nix, Livingston '61
Record: 8 yrs., W-42, L-45, T-1
1992 SCHEDULE
Boise St. .... Sep 5*
Tenn.-Martin ■ .... Sep 12*
Central Ark. ■ .... Sep 26*
Clemson .... Oct 3
Citadel .... Oct 10*
Western Caro. ■ .... Oct 17*
Marshall .... Oct 24
Appalachian St. ■ .... Oct 31*
East Tenn. St. ■ .... Nov 7*
Furman ■ .... Nov 14
Va. Military .... Nov 21

1991 RECORD
21	Tenn.-Martin	14		43	East Tenn. St.	26
35	Tennessee Tech	14		21	Furman	24
33	Citadel	26		50	Va. Military	14
7	Appalachian St.	42				
7	Alabama	53		305	(7-4-0)	293
24	Western Caro.	27				
38	Marshall	31				
26	Western Ky.	22				

Conference: Southern Conf.   Enrollment: 6,717.   Colors: Navy Blue & Gold.
Nickname: Moccasins.   Stadium: Chamberlain Field (1947), 10,501 capacity.   Natural turf.
1991 home attendance: 46,719 in 6 games.
Director of Athletics: Ed Farrell.
Sports Info. Director: Neil Magnussen 615-755-4618

TENNESSEE-MARTIN . . . Martin, Tenn.   38238   I-AA

Coach: Don McLeary, Tennessee '70
Record: 8 yrs., W-40, L-46, T-0
1992 SCHEDULE
Delta St. ■ .... Sep 5*
Tenn.-Chatt. .... Sep 12*
Morehead St. ■ .... Sep 26*
Tennessee Tech .... Oct 3
Murray St. ■ .... Oct 10*
Tennessee St. .... Oct 17
Eastern Ky. ■ .... Oct 24
Southeast Mo. St. .... Oct 31
Middle Tenn. St. ■ .... Nov 7
Samford ■ .... Nov 14
Austin Peay .... Nov 21

1991 RECORD
14	Tenn.-Chatt.	21		14	Middle Tenn. St.	51
36	Southeast Mo. St.	29		34	Austin Peay	28
28	Washburn	7		16	McNeese St.	17
32	Morehead St.	28				
24	Tennessee Tech	16		280	(5-6-0)	330
34	Murray St.	40				
27	Delta St.	37				
21	Eastern Ky.	56				

Conference: Ohio Valley Conf.   Enrollment: 5,494.   Colors: Orange, White & Royal Blue.
Nickname: Pacers.   Stadium: Pacer (1964), 7,500 capacity.   Natural turf.
1991 home attendance: 23,671 in 4 games.
Director of Athletics: Don McLeary.
Sports Info. Director: Lee Wilmot 901-587-7630

TENNESSEE STATE . . . Nashville, Tenn.   37203   I-AA

Coach: To be named
1992 SCHEDULE
Middle Tenn. St. [Nashville, Tenn.] ...... Sep 5*
Jackson St. [Memphis, Tenn.] .... Sep 12*
Grambling .... Sep 19*
Florida A&M [Atlanta, Ga.] .... Sep 26
Morehead St. .... Oct 10
Tenn.-Martin ■ .... Oct 17
Austin Peay ■ .... Oct 24
Eastern Ky. .... Oct 31
Tennessee Tech .... Nov 7
Murray St. .... Nov 14
Southeast Mo. St. ■ .... Nov 21

1991 RECORD
7	Mississippi Val.	10		20	Eastern Ky.	27
6	Middle Tenn. St.	42		14	Tennessee Tech	10
19	Jackson St.	41		33	Southern-B.R.	14
21	Grambling	24				
7	Florida A&M	43		206	(3-8-0)	286
28	Murray St.	7				
34	Southeast Mo. St.	37				
17	Austin Peay	31				

Conference: Ohio Valley Conf.   Enrollment: 7,500.   Colors: Blue & White.
Nickname: Tigers.   Stadium: W.J. Hale (1953), 16,000 capacity.   Natural turf.
1991 home attendance: 34,511 in 4 games.
Director of Athletics: William A. Thomas.
Sports Info. Director: Johnny M. Franks 615-320-3596

TENNESSEE TECH . . . Cookeville, Tenn.   38505   I-AA

Coach: Jim Ragland, Tennessee Tech '64
Record: 6 yrs., W-18, L-46, T-0
1992 SCHEDULE
Lock Haven ■ .... Sep 12*
Samford ■ .... Sep 19*
Eastern Ky. ■ .... Sep 26*
Tenn.-Martin ■ .... Oct 3
Southeast Mo. St. ■ .... Oct 10
Austin Peay .... Oct 17
Morehead St. ■ .... Oct 24
Murray St. ■ .... Oct 31*
Tennessee St. ■ .... Nov 7
Marshall .... Nov 14
Middle Tenn. St. .... Nov 21

1991 RECORD
14	Tenn.-Chatt.	35		45	Murray St.	7
14	Ohio	35		10	Tennessee St.	14
16	Samford	20		10	Middle Tenn. St.	28
13	Eastern Ky.	19				
16	Tenn.-Martin	24		221	(2-9-0)	244
31	Southeast Mo. St.	34				
32	Austin Peay	7				
20	Morehead St.	21				

Conference: Ohio Valley Conf.   Enrollment: 8,140.   Colors: Purple & Gold.
Nickname: Golden Eagles.   Stadium: Tucker (1966), 16,500 capacity.   Artificial turf.
1991 home attendance: 27,040 in 4 games.
Director of Athletics: David Larimore.
Sports Info. Director: Rob Schabert 615-372-3088

TEXAS . . . Austin, Tex.   78712   I-A

Coach: John Mackovic, Wake Forest '65
Record: 7 yrs., W-44, L-36, T-1
1992 SCHEDULE
Mississippi St. ■ .... Sep 5*
Syracuse .... Sep 12
North Texas ■ .... Sep 26*
Rice .... Oct 3
Oklahoma [Dallas, Tex.] .... Oct 10
Houston ■ .... Oct 24
Texas Tech .... Oct 31
Texas Christian .... Nov 7
Southern Methodist ■ .... Nov 14
Baylor .... Nov 21
Texas A&M ■ .... Nov 26*

1991 RECORD
6	Mississippi St.	13		32	Texas Christian	0
10	Auburn	14		11	Baylor	21
28	Rice	7		14	Texas A&M	31
10	Oklahoma	7				
13	Arkansas	14		195	(5-6-0)	145
34	Southern Methodist	0				
23	Texas Tech	15				
14	Houston	23				

Conference: Southwest Conf.   Enrollment: 49,961.   Colors: Burnt Orange & White.
Nickname: Longhorns.   Stadium: Memorial (1924), 80,000 capacity.   Artificial turf.
1991 home attendance: 414,563 in 6 games.
Director of Athletics: Deloss Dodds.
Sports Info. Director: Bill Little 512-471-7437

■ Home games on each schedule [neutral sites shown in brackets].   *Night Games.

1992 NCAA FOOTBALL

TEXAS A&M . . . College Station, Tex.   77843   I-A

Coach: R. C. Slocum, McNeese St. '67
Record: 3 yrs., W-27, L-9, T-1
1992 SCHEDULE

1992 SCHEDULE	
Stanford [Anaheim, Cal.]	Aug 26*
Louisiana St.	Sep 5
Tulsa ■	Sep 12*
Missouri	Sep 19
Texas Tech ■	Oct 3
Rice ■	Oct 17
Baylor ■	Oct 24
Southern Methodist	Oct 31
Louisville ■	Nov 7
Houston	Nov 12
Texas Christian ■	Nov 21
Texas	Nov 26*

1991 RECORD

45	Louisiana St.	7	13	Arkansas	3
34	Tulsa	35	65	Southern Methodist	6
34	Southwestern La.	7	31	Texas	14
37	Texas Tech	14			
34	Baylor	12	402	(10-1-0)	144
27	Houston	18		**Mobil Cotton Bowl**	
38	Rice	21	2	Florida St.	10
44	Texas Christian	7			

Conference: Southwest Conf.   Enrollment: 40,000.   Colors: Maroon & White.
Nickname: Aggies.   Stadium: Kyle Field (1925), 70,210 capacity.   Artificial turf.
1991 home attendance: 379,906 in 6 games.
Director of Athletics: John David Crow.
Sports Info. Director: Alan Cannon   409-845-5725

TEXAS CHRISTIAN . . . Fort Worth, Tex.   76129   I-A

Coach: Pat Sullivan, Auburn '72
Record: First year as head coach
1992 SCHEDULE

1992 SCHEDULE	
New Mexico	Sep 5*
Western Mich. ■	Sep 12*
Southern Methodist	Sep 26*
Oklahoma St. ■	Oct 3*
Baylor ■	Oct 10*
Miami (Fla.)	Oct 17
Rice ■	Oct 24
Houston	Oct 31
Texas ■	Nov 7
Texas Tech ■	Nov 14
Texas A&M	Nov 21

1991 RECORD

60	New Mexico	7	7	Texas A&M	44
22	Ball St.	16	0	Texas	32
24	Oklahoma St.	21	49	Houston	45
30	Texas Tech	16			
21	Arkansas	22	279	(7-4-0)	267
39	Rice	28			
9	Baylor	26			
18	Southern Methodist	10			

Conference: Southwest Conf.   Enrollment: 6,900.   Colors: Purple & White.
Nickname: Horned Frogs.   Stadium: Amon G. Carter (1929), 46,000 capacity.   Artificial turf.
1991 home attendance: 152,646 in 6 games.
Director of Athletics: Frank Windegger.
Sports Info. Director: Glen Stone   817-921-7969

TEXAS SOUTHERN . . . Houston, Tex.   77004   I-AA

Coach: Walter Highsmith, Florida A&M '64
Record: 3 yrs., W-12, L-19, T-2
1992 SCHEDULE

1992 SCHEDULE	
Prairie View [Houston, Tex.]	Sep 5*
Southwest Tex. St. [San Antonio, Tex.]	Sep 12*
Central St. (Ohio)	Sep 26
Knoxville ■	Oct 3
Alcorn St.	Oct 10
Alabama St. [Mobile, Ala.]	Oct 17*
Mississippi Val. ■	Oct 24
Grambling ■	Oct 31*
Jackson St.	Nov 7*
Southern-B.R.	Nov 14*
Nevada	Nov 21

1991 RECORD

19	Central St. (Ohio)	10	32	Mississippi Val.	22
23	Prairie View	6	27	Grambling	30
6	Sam Houston St.	37	12	Jackson St.	13
30	Southern-B.R.	38			
52	Lane	0	270	(5-5-1)	208
14	Alabama St.	14			
26	Alcorn St.	7			
29	Southwest Tex. St.	31			

Conference: Southwestern.   Enrollment: 10,000.   Colors: Maroon & Gray.
Nickname: Tigers.   Stadium: Robertson (1965), 25,000 capacity.   Natural turf.
1991 home attendance: 76,500 in 7 games.
Director of Athletics: Curtis Williams.
Sports Info. Director: Andre Smith   713-527-7270

TEXAS TECH . . . Lubbock, Tex.   79409   I-A

Coach: Spike Dykes, Stephen F. Austin '59
Record: 6 yrs., W-30, L-26, T-1
1992 SCHEDULE

1992 SCHEDULE	
Oklahoma ■	Sep 3*
Wyoming ■	Sep 12*
Oregon	Sep 19
Baylor ■	Sep 26*
Texas A&M	Oct 3
North Caro. St.	Oct 10
Southern Methodist ■	Oct 24
Texas ■	Oct 31
Rice	Nov 7
Texas Christian	Nov 14
Houston ■	Nov 21

1991 RECORD

41	Cal St. Fullerton	7	38	Arkansas	21
13	Oregon	28	31	Baylor	24
17	Wyoming	22	52	Houston	46
16	Texas Christian	30			
14	Texas A&M	37	315	(6-5-0)	272
38	Southern Methodist	14			
40	Rice	20			
15	Texas	23			

Conference: Southwest Conf.   Enrollment: 25,099.   Colors: Scarlet & Black.
Nickname: Red Raiders.   Stadium: Jones (1947), 50,500 capacity.   Artificial turf.
1991 home attendance: 226,822 in 6 games.
Director of Athletics: T. Jones.
Sports Info. Director: Joe Hornaday   806-742-2770

TOLEDO . . . Toledo, Ohio   43606   I-A

Coach: Gary Pinkel, Kent '75
Record: 1 yr., W-5, L-5, T-1
1992 SCHEDULE

1992 SCHEDULE	
Arkansas St. ■	Sep 5*
Akron	Sep 12*
Purdue	Sep 19
Central Mich.	Sep 26
Western Mich. ■	Oct 10*
Bowling Green ■	Oct 17*
Miami (Ohio)	Oct 24
Kent ■	Oct 31
Ball St.	Nov 7
Eastern Mich. ■	Nov 14
Northern Ill.	Nov 21

1991 RECORD

7	Kansas	30	3	Ball St.	9
23	Western Mich.	13	21	Eastern Mich.	14
16	Central Mich.	16	42	Northern Ill.	21
17	Ohio	13			
0	Washington	48	187	(5-5-1)	209
21	Bowling Green	24			
24	Miami (Ohio)	7			
13	Kent	14			

Conference: Mid-American Conf.   Enrollment: 24,781.   Colors: Blue & Gold.
Nickname: Rockets.   Stadium: Glass Bowl (1937), 26,248 capacity.   Artificial turf.
1991 home attendance: 117,322 in 6 games.
Director of Athletics: Allen R. Bohl.
Sports Info. Director: Rod Brandt   419-537-3790

■ Home games on each schedule [neutral sites shown in brackets].   *Night Games.

TOWSON STATE . . . Towson, Md. 21204 I-AA

Coach: Gordy Combs, Towson St. '72
Record: First year as head coach

1992 SCHEDULE

Rhode Island	Sep 12
Bucknell ■	Sep 19*
Hofstra ■	Sep 26*
Liberty ■	Oct 3*
Delaware St.	Oct 10
William & Mary	Oct 17
James Madison ■	Oct 24
Indiana (Pa.)	Oct 31
Northeastern ■	Nov 14
Delaware	Nov 21

1991 RECORD

8	Boston U.	10	13	Howard	7
7	Delaware St.	13	34	Maine	49
25	Rhode Island	45	17	Youngstown St.	27
10	Indiana (Pa.)	54			
31	James Madison	55	212	(1-10-0)	378
13	Northeastern	50			
28	Liberty	38			
26	Hofstra	30			

Conference: I-AA Independents. Enrollment: 9,600. Colors: Gold & White.
Nickname: Tigers. Stadium: Minnegan Stadium, 5,000 capacity. Natural turf.
1991 home attendance: 18,425 in 6 games.
Director of Athletics: Bill Hunter.
Sports Info. Director: Peter Schlehr 301-830-2232

TULANE . . . New Orleans, La. 70118 I-A

Coach: Buddy Teevens, Dartmouth '79
Record: 7 yrs., W-39, L-31, T-2

1992 SCHEDULE

Southern Methodist	Sep 5*
Mississippi	Sep 12*
Iowa St.	Sep 19
Nevada ■	Sep 26*
Alabama ■	Oct 10*
Southern Miss. ■	Oct 15*
Boston College ■	Oct 24*
Memphis St. ■	Oct 31
Navy	Nov 7
Florida St.	Nov 14
Louisiana St.	Nov 21*

1991 RECORD

3	Mississippi	22	28	East Caro.	38
11	Florida St.	38	34	Navy	7
0	Mississippi St.	48	20	Louisiana St.	39
19	Rice	28			
0	Syracuse	24	146	(1-10-0)	384
17	Southern Methodist	31			
0	Alabama	62			
14	Southern Miss.	47			

Conference: I-A Independents. Enrollment: 11,049. Colors: Olive Green & Sky Blue.
Nickname: Green Wave. Stadium: Superdome (1975), 69,065 capacity. Artificial turf.
1991 home attendance: 152,500 in 6 games.
Director of Athletics: Kevin White.
Sports Info. Director: Lenny Vangilder 504-865-5506

TULSA . . . Tulsa, Okla. 74104 I-A

Coach: David Rader, Tulsa '80
Record: 4 yrs., W-23, L-23, T-0

1992 SCHEDULE

Houston ■	Sep 5*
Texas A&M	Sep 12*
Kansas ■	Sep 19*
Oklahoma ■	Sep 26*
Southern Miss.	Oct 3
Southwest Mo. St. ■	Oct 10
Louisville	Oct 17
Memphis St. ■	Oct 24
Southwestern La. ■	Oct 31
UTEP	Nov 7*
Hawaii	Nov 28*

1991 RECORD

34	Southwest Mo. St.	13	40	Louisville	0
13	Oklahoma St.	7	45	Ohio	13
17	Kansas	23	31	Southern Methodist	26
35	Texas A&M	34			
10	Miami (Fla.)	34	305	(9-2-0)	208
34	Southwestern La.	20		**Freedom Bowl**	
33	Memphis St.	28	28	San Diego St.	17
13	Southern Miss.	10			

Conference: I-A Independents. Enrollment: 4,500. Colors: Blue & Gold.
Nickname: Golden Hurricane. Stadium: Skelly (1930), 40,385 capacity. Artificial turf.
1991 home attendance: 218,652 in 7 games.
Director of Athletics: Rick Dickson.
Sports Info. Director: Don Tomkalski 918-631-2395

UCLA . . . Los Angeles, Cal. 90024 I-A

Coach: Terry Donahue, UCLA '67
Record: 16 yrs., W-125, L-54, T-8

1992 SCHEDULE

Cal St. Fullerton ■	Sep 12
Brigham Young	Sep 19
San Diego St. ■	Sep 26
Arizona	Oct 3*
Stanford ■	Oct 10
Washington St.	Oct 17
Arizona St. ■	Oct 24
California	Oct 31
Oregon St. ■	Nov 7
Oregon	Nov 14
Southern Cal ■	Nov 21

1991 RECORD

27	Brigham Young	23	10	Stanford	27
16	Tennessee	30	16	Oregon	7
37	San Diego St.	12	24	Southern Cal	21
24	California	27			
54	Arizona	14	317	(8-3-0)	187
44	Oregon St.	7		**John Hancock Bowl**	
21	Arizona St.	16	6	Illinois	3
44	Washington St.	3			

Conference: Pacific-10. Enrollment: 33,770. Colors: Blue & Gold.
Nickname: Bruins. Stadium: Rose Bowl (1922), 99,563 capacity. Natural turf.
1991 home attendance: 245,760 in 5 games.
Director of Athletics: Peter Dalis.
Sports Info. Director: Marc Dellins 213-206-6831

UTAH . . . Salt Lake City, Utah 84112 I-A

Coach: Ron McBride, San Jose St. '63
Record: 2 yrs., W-11, L-12, T-0

1992 SCHEDULE

Nebraska	Sep 5
Utah St.	Sep 12
Oregon St. ■	Sep 26*
Colorado St.	Oct 3
Hawaii ■	Oct 10
New Mexico	Oct 17*
UTEP ■	Oct 24
Air Force	Oct 31
Fresno St.	Nov 7*
Wyoming ■	Nov 14
Brigham Young ■	Nov 21

1991 RECORD

12	Utah St.	7	26	Hawaii	52
22	Oregon St.	10	30	New Mexico	7
21	Air Force	24	10	UTEP	9
24	Oregon	17	17	Brigham Young	48
15	Arizona St.	21			
57	Wyoming	42	276	(7-5-0)	277
21	Colorado St.	16			
21	San Diego St.	24			

Conference: Western Athl. Conf. Enrollment: 24,000. Colors: Crimson & White.
Nickname: Utes. Stadium: Robert Rice (1927), 35,000 capacity. Artificial turf.
1991 home attendance: 157,592 in 6 games.
Director of Athletics: Chris Hill.
Sports Info. Director: Bruce Woodbury 801-581-3510

■ Home games on each schedule [neutral sites shown in brackets]. *Night Games.

1992 NCAA FOOTBALL

UTAH STATE . . . Logan, Utah   84322   I-A

Coach: Charlie Weatherbie, Oklahoma St. '77
Record: First year as head coach

1992 SCHEDULE

Arizona	Sep 5*
Utah ■	Sep 12
Baylor	Sep 19*
New Mexico St. ■	Sep 26
Brigham Young	Oct 2*
Kansas St. ■	Oct 17
San Jose St. ■	Oct 24
Cal St. Fullerton	Oct 31*
Nevada-Las Vegas ■	Nov 7
Nevada	Nov 14
Pacific (Cal.)	Nov 21

1991 RECORD

7	Utah	12	27	Nevada-Las Vegas	14
28	Nebraska	59	21	Pacific (Cal.)	14
21	Oklahoma	55	46	New Mexico St.	21
7	San Jose St.	23			
10	Brigham Young	38	219	(5-6-0)	265
26	Cal St. Fullerton	3			
6	Long Beach St.	7			
20	Fresno St.	19			

Conference: Big West. Enrollment: 15,572. Colors: Navy Blue & White.
Nickname: Aggies. Stadium: E.L. Romney (1968), 30,257 capacity. Natural turf.
1991 home attendance: 39,341 in 4 games.
Director of Athletics: Rod Tueller.
Sports Info. Director: Craig Hislop 801-750-1361

UTEP . . . El Paso, Tex.   79968   I-A

Coach: David Lee, Vanderbilt '75
Record: 3 yrs., W-9, L-25, T-1

1992 SCHEDULE

Brigham Young ■	Sep 5*
Nevada-Las Vegas ■	Sep 12*
New Mexico St. ■	Sep 19*
Air Force ■	Oct 3*
Colorado St.	Oct 10
San Diego St.	Oct 17*
Utah	Oct 24
Hawaii ■	Oct 31*
Tulsa ■	Nov 7*
New Mexico	Nov 14
Fresno St. ■	Nov 28*

1991 RECORD

35	New Mexico	19	13	Air Force	20
7	Baylor	27	41	Hawaii	24
22	New Mexico St.	21	9	Utah	10
14	Northwestern (La.)	0	17	Louisiana Tech	21
28	Wyoming	28			
18	Colorado St.	23	254	(4-7-1)	252
29	Brigham Young	31			
21	San Diego St.	28			

Conference: Western Athl. Conf. Enrollment: 16,700. Colors: Orange, White & Blue.
Nickname: Miners. Stadium: Sun Bowl (1963), 52,000 capacity. Artificial turf.
1991 home attendance: 176,155 in 6 games.
Director of Athletics: Brad Hovious.
Sports Info. Director: Eddie Mullens 915-747-5330

VANDERBILT . . . Nashville, Tenn.   37212   I-A

Coach: Gerry DiNardo, Notre Dame '75
Record: 1 yr., W-5, L-6, T-0

1992 SCHEDULE

Alabama	Sep 5
Duke ■	Sep 12*
Mississippi ■	Sep 19*
Auburn	Oct 3
Wake Forest ■	Oct 10
Georgia	Oct 17
South Caro. ■	Oct 24
Kentucky	Nov 7
Navy	Nov 14
Florida ■	Nov 21
Tennessee ■	Nov 28

1991 RECORD

10	Syracuse	37	41	Army	10
14	Southern Methodist	11	17	Kentucky	7
14	Louisiana St.	16	0	Tennessee	45
17	Alabama	48			
13	Duke	17	205	(5-6-0)	267
22	Auburn	24			
27	Georgia	25			
30	Mississippi	27			

Conference: Southeastern Conf. Enrollment: 9,000. Colors: Black & Gold.
Nickname: Commodores. Stadium: Vanderbilt Stadium (1981),
   41,000 capacity. Artificial turf.
1991 home attendance: 179,028 in 5 games.
Director of Athletics: Paul Hoolahan.
Sports Info. Director: Lew Harris 615-322-4121

VILLANOVA . . . Villanova, Pa.   19085   I-AA

Coach: Andy Talley, Southern Conn. St. '67
Record: 12 yrs., W-75, L-39, T-2

1992 SCHEDULE

West Chester ■	Sep 4*
Bucknell ■	Sep 12
Richmond ■	Sep 19
Boston U.	Oct 3
Connecticut	Oct 10
Delaware ■	Oct 17
Massachusetts	Oct 24
Rhode Island ■	Oct 31
New Hampshire	Nov 7
Fordham	Nov 14
Maine ■	Nov 21

1991 RECORD

48	Maine	7	33	New Hampshire	7
40	Bucknell	0	24	Massachusetts	14
35	Richmond	3	14	Fordham	9
35	Connecticut	13			
56	Boston U.	6	397	(10-1-0)	132
28	Delaware	38		**I-AA Championship**	
35	William & Mary	21	16	Youngstown St.	17
49	Rhode Island	14			

Conference: Yankee. Enrollment: 6,500. Colors: Blue & White.
Nickname: Wildcats. Stadium: Villanova (1929), 12,000 capacity. Artificial turf.
1991 home attendance: 45,519 in 5 games.
Director of Athletics: Theodore Aceto.
Sports Info. Director: James H. DeLorenzo 215-645-4120

VIRGINIA . . . Charlottesville, Va.   22903   I-A

Coach: George Welsh, Navy '56
Record: 19 yrs., W-121, L-93, T-4

1992 SCHEDULE

Maryland ■	Sep 5
Navy	Sep 12*
Georgia Tech ■	Sep 19
Duke	Sep 26
Wake Forest	Oct 3
Clemson ■	Oct 10
North Caro.	Oct 17
William & Mary ■	Oct 24
Florida St.	Oct 31
North Caro. St. ■	Nov 7
Virginia Tech	Nov 21

1991 RECORD

6	Maryland	17	42	Va. Military	0
17	Navy	10	42	North Caro. St.	10
21	Georgia Tech	24	38	Virginia Tech	0
34	Duke	3			
31	Kansas	19	313	(8-2-1)	119
20	Clemson	20		**Mazda Gator Bowl**	
14	North Caro.	9	14	Oklahoma	48
48	Wake Forest	7			

Conference: Atlantic Coast Conf. Enrollment: 18,137. Colors: Orange & Blue.
Nickname: Cavaliers. Stadium: Scott (1931), 42,000 capacity. Artificial turf.
1991 home attendance: 291,100 in 7 games.
Director of Athletics: Jim Copeland.
Sports Info. Director: Rich Murray 804-982-5500

■ Home games on each schedule [neutral sites shown in brackets]. *Night Games.

VIRGINIA MILITARY . . . Lexington, Va.   24450   I-AA

Coach: Jim Shuck, Indiana '76
Record: 3 yrs., W-10, L-22, T-1

1992 SCHEDULE

East Tenn. St. ....Sep 5*
William & Mary ....Sep 12
Marshall ■ ....Sep 19
West Va. Tech ■ ....Sep 26
Furman ....Oct 3
Western Caro. ....Oct 10
Appalachian St. ■ ....Oct 17
Richmond [Norfolk, Va.] ....Oct 24
Wofford ■ ....Nov 7
Citadel ....Nov 14
Tenn.-Chatt. ■ ....Nov 21

1991 RECORD

35	East Tenn. St.	20	27	Western Caro.	25
19	Appalachian St.	24	0	Marshall	61
42	Lafayette	21	14	Tenn.-Chatt.	50
38	Richmond	27			
28	Furman	46	243	(4-7-0)	373
26	William & Mary	40			
14	Citadel	17			
0	Virginia	42			

Conference: Southern Conf. Enrollment: 1,300. Colors: Red, White & Yellow.
Nickname: Keydets. Stadium: Alumni Field (1962), 10,000 capacity. Natural turf.
1991 home attendance: 50,079 in 6 games.
Director of Athletics: Davis Babb.
Sports Info. Director: Wade Branner 703-464-7253

VIRGINIA TECH . . . Blacksburg, Va.   24061   I-A

Coach: Frank Beamer, Virginia Tech '69
Record: 11 yrs., W-64, L-55, T-3

1992 SCHEDULE

James Madison ■ ....Sep 5*
East Caro. ....Sep 12
Temple ....Sep 19
West Va. ■ ....Sep 26
Louisville ....Oct 10
North Caro. St. ■ ....Oct 17
Miami (Fla.) ■ ....Oct 24
Rutgers ....Oct 31
Syracuse ....Nov 7
Southern Miss. ■ ....Nov 14
Virginia ■ ....Nov 21

1991 RECORD

41	James Madison	12	42	Akron	24
0	North Caro. St.	7	17	East Caro.	24
21	South Caro.	28	0	Virginia	38
17	Oklahoma	27			
20	West Va.	14	275	(5-6-0)	229
20	Florida St.	33			
56	Cincinnati	9			
41	Louisville	13			

Conference: Big East Conference. Enrollment: 23,000. Colors: Orange & Maroon.
Nickname: Gobblers, Hokies. Stadium: Lane (1965), 51,000 capacity. Natural turf.
1991 home attendance: 262,126 in 6 games.
Director of Athletics: Dave Braine.
Sports Info. Director: Dave Smith 703-231-6726

WAKE FOREST . . . Winston-Salem, N.C.   27109   I-A

Coach: Bill Dooley, Mississippi St. '56
Record: 25 yrs., W-153, L-123, T-5

1992 SCHEDULE

North Caro. ■ ....Sep 5
Appalachian St. ■ ....Sep 12*
Florida St. ....Sep 26*
Virginia ■ ....Oct 3
Vanderbilt ....Oct 10
Maryland ....Oct 17
Army ■ ....Oct 24
Clemson ■ ....Oct 31
Duke ....Nov 7
Georgia Tech ....Nov 14
North Caro. St. ....Nov 21

1991 RECORD

40	Western Caro.	24	31	Duke	14
3	North Caro. St.	30	3	Georgia Tech	27
14	Northwestern	41	52	Navy	24
3	Appalachian St.	17			
10	North Caro.	24	195	(3-8-0)	300
22	Maryland	23			
7	Virginia	48			
10	Clemson	28			

Conference: Atlantic Coast Conf. Enrollment: 3,400. Colors: Old Gold & Black.
Nickname: Demon Deacons. Stadium: Groves (1968), 31,500 capacity. Natural turf.
1991 home attendance: 101,539 in 5 games.
Director of Athletics: Gene Hooks.
Sports Info. Director: John Justus 919-759-5640

WASHINGTON . . . Seattle, Wash.   98195   I-A

Coach: Don James, Miami (Fla.) '54
Record: 21 yrs., W-167, L-75, T-3

1992 SCHEDULE

Arizona St. ....Sep 5*
Wisconsin ■ ....Sep 12
Nebraska ■ ....Sep 19
Southern Cal ■ ....Oct 3
California ■ ....Oct 10
Oregon ....Oct 17
Pacific (Cal.) ■ ....Oct 24
Stanford ■ ....Oct 31
Arizona ....Nov 7*
Oregon St. ■ ....Nov 14
Washington St. ....Nov 21

1991 RECORD

42	Stanford	7	14	Southern Cal	3
36	Nebraska	21	58	Oregon St.	6
56	Kansas St.	3	56	Washington St.	21
54	Arizona	0			
48	Toledo	0	461	(11-0-0)	101
24	California	17		**Rose Bowl**	
29	Oregon	7	34	Michigan	14
44	Arizona St.	16			

Conference: Pacific-10. Enrollment: 34,000. Colors: Purple & Gold.
Nickname: Huskies. Stadium: Husky (1920), 72,500 capacity. Artificial turf.
1991 home attendance: 433,703 in 6 games.
Director of Athletics: Barbara Hedges.
Sports Info. Director: To be named 206-543-8333

WASHINGTON STATE . . . Pullman, Wash.   99164   I-A

Coach: Mike Price, Puget Sound '69
Record: 11 yrs., W-59, L-64, T-0

1992 SCHEDULE

Montana ■ ....Sep 5
Arizona ....Sep 12*
Fresno St. ....Sep 26*
Temple ■ ....Oct 3
Oregon St. ....Oct 10
UCLA ■ ....Oct 17
Southern Cal ....Oct 24
Oregon ■ ....Oct 31
Arizona St. ■ ....Nov 7
Stanford ....Nov 14
Washington ■ ....Nov 21

1991 RECORD

14	Oregon	40	40	Arizona	27
30	Fresno St.	34	14	Stanford	49
19	Ohio St.	33	21	Washington	56
40	Nevada-Las Vegas	13			
55	Oregon St.	7	280	(4-7-0)	340
27	Southern Cal	34			
17	Arizona St.	3			
3	UCLA	44			

Conference: Pacific-10. Enrollment: 17,500. Colors: Crimson & Gray.
Nickname: Cougars. Stadium: Clarence D. Martin (1972), 40,000 capacity. Artificial turf.
1991 home attendance: 109,502 in 5 games.
Director of Athletics: Jim Livengood.
Sports Info. Director: Rod Commons 509-335-0270

■ Home games on each schedule [neutral sites shown in brackets]. *Night Games.

WEBER STATE ... Ogden, Utah 84408   I-AA

Coach: Dave Arslanian, Weber St. '72
Record: 3 yrs., W-16, L-18, T-0

1992 SCHEDULE

New Mexico St.	Sep 5*
Southern Utah ■	Sep 12*
Idaho	Sep 19
Montana St. ■	Sep 26*
Eastern Wash.	Oct 3
Montana ■	Oct 10*
Boise St.	Oct 17*
Idaho St. ■	Oct 24
Nevada	Oct 31
Northern Ariz.	Nov 7*
McNeese St. ■	Nov 21

1991 RECORD

31	Air Force	48	
33	Southern Utah	14	
43	Northern Ariz.	38	
63	Eastern Wash.	59	
36	Montana St.	25	
45	Idaho	17	
38	Montana	47	
49	Nevada	55	
62	N.M. Highlands	7	
35	Boise St.	32	
60	Idaho St.	41	
495	(8-3-0)	**383**	
	I-AA Championship		
21	Northern Iowa	38	

Conference: Big Sky Conf. Enrollment: 14,500. Colors: Royal Purple & White.
Nickname: Wildcats. Stadium: Wildcat (1966), 17,500 capacity. Natural turf.
1991 home attendance: 37,601 in 6 games.
Director of Athletics: Tom Stewart.
Sports Info. Director: Brad Larsen   801-626-6010

WEST VIRGINIA ... Morgantown, W.Va. 26505   I-A

Coach: Don Nehlen, Bowling Green '58
Record: 21 yrs., W-140, L-86, T-6

1992 SCHEDULE

Miami (Ohio) ■	Sep 5
Pittsburgh	Sep 12
Maryland ■	Sep 19
Virginia Tech	Sep 26
Boston College ■	Oct 3
Syracuse ■	Oct 17
Penn St.	Oct 24
Miami (Fla.)	Oct 31
East Caro. ■	Nov 7
Rutgers	Nov 14
Louisiana Tech ■	Nov 21

1991 RECORD

3	Pittsburgh	34	
24	Bowling Green	17	
21	South Caro.	16	
37	Maryland	7	
14	Virginia Tech	20	
10	Temple	9	
31	Boston College	24	
6	Penn St.	51	
28	Rutgers	3	
3	Miami (Fla.)	27	
10	Syracuse	16	
187	(6-5-0)	**224**	

Conference: Big East Conference. Enrollment: 20,000. Colors: Old Gold & Blue.
Nickname: Mountaineers. Stadium: Mountaineer Field (1980),
63,500 capacity. Artificial turf.
1991 home attendance: 292,103 in 6 games.
Director of Athletics: Ed Pastilong.
Sports Info. Director: Shelly Poe 304-293-2821

WESTERN CAROLINA ... Cullowhee, N.C. 28723   I-AA

Coach: Steve Hodgin, North Caro. '71
Record: 2 yrs., W-5, L-17, T-0

1992 SCHEDULE

Mars Hill ■	Sep 5*
Georgia Tech	Sep 12*
Ferrum ■	Sep 26*
Samford ■	Oct 3*
Va. Military ■	Oct 10
Tenn.-Chatt.	Oct 17*
Citadel ■	Oct 24
Marshall ■	Oct 31
Furman	Nov 7
East Tenn. St. ■	Nov 14
Appalachian St.	Nov 21

1991 RECORD

0	Georgia	48	
24	Wake Forest	40	
29	East Tenn. St.	15	
14	Furman	42	
13	Citadel	38	
6	Ga. Southern	44	
27	Tenn.-Chatt.	24	
3	Samford	16	
24	Marshall	27	
25	Va. Military	27	
14	Appalachian St.	24	
179	(2-9-0)	**345**	

Conference: Southern Conf. Enrollment: 6,300. Colors: Purple & Gold.
Nickname: Catamounts. Stadium: E.J. Whitmire (1974), 12,000 capacity. Artificial turf.
1991 home attendance: 42,478 in 4 games.
Director of Athletics: Bobby N. Setzer.
Sports Info. Director: Steve White 704-227-7171

WESTERN ILLINOIS ... Macomb, Ill. 61455   I-AA

Coach: Randy Ball, Northeast Mo. St. '73
Record: 2 yrs., W-10, L-12, T-1

1992 SCHEDULE

Mo. Western St. ■	Sep 5*
Sam Houston St.	Sep 12*
Western Ky. ■	Sep 19*
Central Fla. ■	Sep 26
Southwest Mo. St.	Oct 3
Southern Ill.	Oct 10
Eastern Ill. ■	Oct 17
Indiana St.	Oct 24
Illinois St. ■	Oct 31
Morgan St. ■	Nov 7
Northern Iowa	Nov 14*

1991 RECORD

42	Washburn	3	
13	Wisconsin	31	
27	St. Ambrose	7	
21	Sam Houston St.	21	
16	Eastern Ill.	15	
26	Southwest Mo. St.	21	
21	Southern Ill.	20	
22	Illinois St.	12	
6	Indiana St.	7	
44	Morgan St.	6	
17	Northern Iowa	24	
255	(7-3-1)	**167**	
	I-AA Championship		
17	Marshall	20	

Conference: Gateway. Enrollment: 13,750. Colors: Purple & Gold.
Nickname: Leathernecks. Stadium: Hanson Field (1948), 15,000 capacity. Natural turf.
1991 home attendance: 48,260 in 6 games.
Director of Athletics: Helen Smiley.
Sports Info. Director: Larry Heimburger 309-298-1133

WESTERN KENTUCKY ... Bowling Green, Ky. 42101   I-AA

Coach: Jack Harbaugh, Bowling Green '61
Record: 8 yrs., W-36, L-48, T-3

1992 SCHEDULE

Eastern Ky. ■	Sep 5
Indiana St. ■	Sep 12
Western Ill.	Sep 19*
Southwest Mo. St. ■	Sep 26
Northern Iowa	Oct 10*
Troy St.	Oct 17
Central Fla. ■	Oct 24
Southern Ill.	Oct 31
Illinois St.	Nov 7
Eastern Ill.	Nov 14
Murray St.	Nov 21

1991 RECORD

14	Austin Peay	18	
14	Murray St.	0	
48	Morehead St.	21	
21	Middle Tenn. St.	23	
22	Eastern Ky.	37	
23	Troy St.	39	
21	Northern Iowa	49	
22	Tenn.-Chatt.	26	
28	Eastern Ill.	26	
14	Indiana St.	31	
8	Illinois St.	31	
235	(3-8-0)	**301**	

Conference: I-AA Independents. Enrollment: 15,720. Colors: Red & White.
Nickname: Hilltoppers. Stadium: L.T. Smith (1968), 17,500 capacity. Natural turf.
1991 home attendance: 46,802 in 6 games.
Director of Athletics: Lou Marciani.
Sports Info. Director: Paul Just 502-745-4298

■ Home games on each schedule [neutral sites shown in brackets].   *Night Games.

WESTERN MICHIGAN . . . Kalamazoo, Mich.   49008   I-A

Coach: Al Molde, Gust. Adolphus '66
Record: 21 yrs., W-138, L-81, T-6

1992 SCHEDULE

Bowling Green	Sep 5
Texas Christian	Sep 12*
Akron ■	Sep 19
Ohio	Sep 26
Ball St. ■	Oct 3
Toledo	Oct 10*
Eastern Mich. ■	Oct 17
Kent	Oct 24
Northern Ill. ■	Oct 31
Miami (Ohio)	Nov 7
Central Mich. ■	Nov 14

1991 RECORD

13	Kent	10	10	Bowling Green	23
35	Akron	12	24	Miami (Ohio)	23
0	Florida St.	58	17	Central Mich.	27
13	Toledo	23			
35	Ohio	9	218	(6-5-0)	253
25	Ball St.	16			
22	Northern Ill.	10			
24	Eastern Mich.	42			

Conference: Mid-American Conf.   Enrollment: 27,708.   Colors: Brown & Gold.
Nickname: Broncos.   Stadium: Waldo (1939), 30,000 capacity.   Natural turf.
1991 home attendance: 68,749 in 6 games.
Director of Athletics: Leland Byrd.
Sports Info. Director: John Beatty   616-387-4104

WILLIAM AND MARY . . . Williamsburg, Va.   23185   I-AA

Coach: Jimmye Laycock, William & Mary '70
Record: 12 yrs., W-72, L-62, T-2

1992 SCHEDULE

Va. Military ■	Sep 12
Boston U. ■	Sep 19
Harvard ■	Sep 26
Brown ■	Oct 3
Pennsylvania	Oct 10
Towson St. ■	Oct 17
Virginia	Oct 24
James Madison	Oct 31
Colgate	Nov 7
Lehigh ■	Nov 14
Richmond	Nov 21

1991 RECORD

48	Boston U.	22	37	Lehigh	41
21	Delaware	28	13	Samford	35
26	Navy	21	49	Richmond	7
28	James Madison	29			
36	North Caro.	59	343	(5-6-0)	320
40	Va. Military	26			
24	Citadel	17			
21	Villanova	35			

Conference: I-AA Independents.   Enrollment: 5,500.   Colors: Green & Gold.
Nickname: Indians, Tribe.   Stadium: Walter Zable (1935), 15,000 capacity.   Natural turf.
1991 home attendance: 63,918 in 5 games.
Director of Athletics: John Randolph.
Sports Info. Director: Jean Elliott   804-221-3368

WISCONSIN . . . Madison, Wis.   53711   I-A

Coach: Barry Alvarez, Nebraska '69
Record: 2 yrs., W-6, L-16, T-0

1992 SCHEDULE

Washington	Sep 12
Bowling Green ■	Sep 19
Northern Ill. ■	Sep 26
Ohio St. ■	Oct 3
Iowa	Oct 10
Purdue ■	Oct 17
Indiana	Oct 24
Illinois ■	Oct 31
Michigan St.	Nov 7
Minnesota ■	Nov 14
Northwestern	Nov 21

1991 RECORD

31	Western Ill.	13	7	Michigan St.	20
7	Iowa St.	6	19	Minnesota	16
21	Eastern Mich.	6	32	Northwestern	14
16	Ohio St.	31			
6	Iowa	10	172	(5-6-0)	194
7	Purdue	28			
20	Indiana	28			
6	Illinois	22			

Conference: Big Ten Conf.   Enrollment: 43,000.   Colors: Cardinal & White.
Nickname: Badgers.   Stadium: Camp Randall (1917), 77,745 capacity.   Artificial turf.
1991 home attendance: 347,735 in 7 games.
Director of Athletics: Pat Richter.
Sports Info. Director: Steve Malchow   608-262-1811

WYOMING . . . Laramie, Wyo.   82071   I-A

Coach: Joe Tiller, Montana St. '65
Record: 1 yr., W-4, L-6, T-1

1992 SCHEDULE

Nevada ■	Sep 5
Texas Tech	Sep 12*
Air Force ■	Sep 19
Louisville ■	Sep 26
San Jose St. ■	Oct 3
New Mexico ■	Oct 10
Brigham Young ■	Oct 17
Colorado St.	Oct 24
Fresno St.	Oct 31*
San Diego St. ■	Nov 7
Utah	Nov 14
Hawaii	Nov 21*

1991 RECORD

17	Hawaii	32	35	Colorado St.	28
13	Colorado	30	22	San Diego St.	24
28	Southwestern La.	15	31	Brigham Young	56
22	Texas Tech	17			
28	UTEP	28	305	(4-6-1)	357
28	Air Force	51			
42	Utah	57			
39	New Mexico	19			

Conference: Western Athl. Conf.   Enrollment: 10,000.   Colors: Brown & Yellow.
Nickname: Cowboys.   Stadium: War Memorial (1950), 33,500 capacity.   Natural turf.
1991 home attendance: 111,450 in 6 games.
Director of Athletics: Paul Roach.
Sports Info. Director: Kevin McKinney   307-766-2256

YALE . . . New Haven, Conn.   06520   I-AA

Coach: Carmen Cozza, Miami (Ohio) '52
Record: 27 yrs., W-162, L-86, T-5

1992 SCHEDULE

Brown	Sep 19
Holy Cross ■	Sep 26
Connecticut	Oct 3
Fordham ■	Oct 10
Dartmouth	Oct 17
Columbia ■	Oct 24
Pennsylvania	Oct 31
Cornell ■	Nov 7
Princeton ■	Nov 14
Harvard	Nov 21

1991 RECORD

36	Brown	20	16	Princeton	22
24	Lafayette	14	23	Harvard	13
20	Connecticut	34			
25	Colgate	7	241	(6-4-0)	190
24	Dartmouth	28			
36	Columbia	9			
31	Pennsylvania	12			
6	Cornell	31			

Conference: Ivy League.   Enrollment: 5,200.   Colors: Yale Blue and White.
Nickname: Elis, Bulldogs.   Stadium: Yale Bowl (1914), 70,896 capacity.   Natural turf.
1991 home attendance: 102,850 in 5 games.
Director of Athletics: Harold E. Woodsum Jr.
Sports Info. Director: Steve Ulrich   203-432-1456

■ Home games on each schedule [neutral sites shown in brackets].   *Night Games.

YOUNGSTOWN STATE ... Youngstown, Ohio 44555   I-AA

Coach: Jim Tressel, Baldwin-Wallace '75
Record: 6 yrs., W-46, L-28, T-0

1992 SCHEDULE

Clarion ■	Sep 5*
Delaware St. ■	Sep 12*
Southwest Tex. St.	Sep 19*
James Madison ■	Sep 26*
Indiana St.	Oct 3
Illinois St. ■	Oct 10*
Northeastern	Oct 17
Eastern Ill. ■	Oct 31
Ohio	Nov 7
Akron	Nov 14
Ga. Southern ■	Nov 21

1991 RECORD

24	Edinboro	0	40	Slippery Rock	21
29	Delaware St.	33	27	Towson St.	17
57	Morgan St.	22			
59	Northeastern	7	331	(8-3-0)	195
16	Stephen F. Austin	9		**I-AA Championship**	
24	Akron	38	17	Villanova	16
8	Liberty	10	30	Nevada	28
19	Ga. Southern	17	10	Samford	0
28	James Madison	21	25	Marshall	17

Conference: I-AA Independents.   Enrollment: 14,822.   Colors: Scarlet & White.
Nickname: Penguins.   Stadium: Arnold D. Stambaugh (1982), 16,000 capacity.   Artificial turf.
1991 home attendance: 38,097 in 6 games.
Director of Athletics: Joe Malmisur.
Sports Info. Director: Greg Gulas   216-742-3192

■ Home games on each schedule [neutral sites shown in brackets].   *Night Games.

1992 SCHEDULES BY DATES

This listing by dates includes all 1992-season games involving Divisions I-A and I-AA teams, as of printing deadline.

Neutral sites, indicated by footnote numbers, are listed at the end of each date. Asterisks (*) indicate night games.

Game date and starting time are subject to change.

HOME	OPPONENT
Wednesday	
August 26	
Texas A&M .... Stanford(1)*	
(1) Anaheim, Cal.	
Saturday	
August 29	
Iowa .... North Caro. St.(1)*	
(1) East Rutherford, N.J.	
Thursday	
September 3	
Southeast Mo. St. .... Murray St.*	
Texas Tech .... Oklahoma*	
Friday	
September 4	
Villanova .... West Chester*	
Saturday	
September 5	
Air Force .... Rice	
Alabama .... Vanderbilt	
Arizona .... Utah St.*	
Arizona St. .... Washington*	
Arkansas .... Citadel	
Austin Peay .... Eastern Ill.*	
Baylor .... Louisiana Tech*	
Bethune-Cookman ..... Savannah St.(1)*	
Boise St. .... Tenn.-Chatt.*	
Boston College .... Rutgers	
Bowling Green .... Western Mich.	
Bucknell .... Bloomsburg	
California .... San Jose St.	
Central Fla. .... Gardner-Webb*	
Cincinnati .... Penn St.*	
Clemson .... Ball St.	
Colorado .... Colorado St.	
Connecticut .... New Haven	
Delaware St. .... Cheyney(2)*	
East Caro. .... Syracuse*	
East Tenn. St. .... Va. Military*	
Eastern Mich. .... Akron*	
Florida St. .... Duke*	
Cal St. Fullerton ...... Cal St. Northridge*	
Furman .... Liberty*	
Ga. Southern .... Florida A&M	
Grambling .... Alcorn St.(3)*	
Idaho .... St. Cloud St.*	
Idaho St. .... Mesa St.*	
Illinois .... Northern Ill.	
Illinois St. .... Southwest St.(Minn.)*	
Iowa .... Miami (Fla.)*	
Iowa St. .... Ohio	
Jackson St. .... Tuskegee*	
Kentucky .... Central Mich.*	

HOME	OPPONENT
Louisiana St. .... Texas A&M	
Maine .... New Hampshire	
Marshall .... Morehead St.*	
McNeese St. .... Southwest Mo. St.*	
Mississippi .... Auburn*	
Nebraska .... Utah	
New Mexico .... Texas Christian*	
New Mexico St. .... Weber St.*	
Nicholls St. .... Northeast La.*	
North Caro. St. .... Appalachian St.	
North Texas .... Abilene Christian*	
Northern Ariz. .... Southern Utah*	
Northwestern .... Notre Dame(4)	
Northwestern (La.) ..... Mississippi Col.*	
Ohio St. .... Louisville	
Oklahoma St. .... Indiana St.	
Oregon .... Hawaii	
Oregon St. .... Kansas	
Pacific (Cal.) .... Fresno St.*	
Pittsburgh .... Kent	
Prairie View .... Texas Southern(5)*	
Samford .... West Ga.*	
San Diego St. .... Southern Cal*	
South Caro. .... Georgia*	
Southern Ill. .... Troy St.	
Southern Methodist .... Tulane*	
Southern Miss. .... Memphis St.	
Stephen F. Austin ..... Ark.-Monticello*	
Temple .... Boston U.	
Tennessee .... Southwestern La.	
Tenn.-Martin .... Delta St.*	
Tennessee St. ...... Middle Tenn. St.(6)*	
Texas .... Mississippi St.*	
UTEP .... Brigham Young*	
Toledo .... Arkansas St.*	
Tulsa .... Houston*	
Virginia .... Maryland	
Virginia Tech .... James Madison*	
Wake Forest .... North Caro.	
Washington St. .... Montana	
West Va. .... Miami (Ohio)	
Western Caro. .... Mars Hill*	
Western Ill. .... Mo. Western St.*	
Western Ky. .... Eastern Ky.	
Wyoming .... Nevada	
Youngstown St. .... Clarion*	
(1) Jacksonville, Fla.	
(2) Wilmington, Del.	
(3) Shreveport, La.	
(4) Chicago, Ill.	
(5) Houston, Tex.	
(6) Nashville, Tenn.	
Thursday	
September 10	
Brigham Young .... San Diego St.*	
Saturday	
September 12	
Air Force .... Hawaii	

HOME	OPPONENT
Akron .... Toledo*	
Alabama .... Southern Miss.(1)	
Arizona .... Washington St.*	
Army .... Holy Cross	
Auburn .... Samford*	
Austin Peay .... Knoxville*	
Baylor .... Colorado*	
Boston College .... Northwestern	
Central Fla. .... Bethune-Cookman*	
Citadel .... Wofford*	
Clemson .... Florida St.	
Colorado St. .... Idaho	
Delaware .... Massachusetts	
East Caro. .... Virginia Tech	
East Tenn. St. .... Mars Hill*	
Florida .... Kentucky*	
Florida A&M .... South Caro. St.*	
Georgia .... Tennessee	
Ga. Southern .... Valdosta St.	
Georgia Tech .... Western Caro.*	
Howard .... Alabama A&M(2)*	
Idaho St. .... Boise St.*	
Illinois .... Missouri	
Indiana .... Miami (Ohio)*	
Iowa .... Iowa St.	
Kansas .... Ball St.	
Kent .... Ohio	
Lafayette .... Hofstra	
Lehigh .... Fordham	
Liberty .... Morgan St.	
Louisiana St. .... Mississippi St.*	
Louisiana Tech .... Eastern Mich.*	
Louisville .... Memphis St.	
Maine .... Kutztown	
Marshall .... Eastern Ill.*	
Maryland .... North Caro. St.	
McNeese St. .... Northern Iowa*	
Michigan St. .... Central Mich.	
Minnesota .... San Jose St.*	
Mississippi .... Tulane*	
Mississippi Val. .... Lane*	
Montana .... Cal St. Chico	
Montana St. .... Stephen F. Austin	
Morehead St. .... West Va. St.*	
Navy .... Virginia*	
Nebraska .... Middle Tenn. St.	
Nevada-Las Vegas .... UTEP*	
Nevada .... Pacific (Cal.)	
New Hampshire .... Connecticut	
New Mexico St. .... New Mexico*	
North Caro. .... Furman*	
North Caro. A&T .... Winston-Salem	
Northern Ariz. .... Northeastern*	
Northern Ill. .... Illinois St.*	
Notre Dame .... Michigan	
Ohio St. .... Bowling Green	
Oklahoma .... Arkansas St.	
Oregon St. .... Fresno St.	
Penn St. .... Temple	
Pittsburgh .... West Va.	
Prairie View .... Angelo St.*	
Purdue .... California	
Rhode Island .... Towson St.	

HOME	OPPONENT
Richmond	James Madison
Rutgers	Colgate*
Sam Houston St.	Western Ill.*
South Caro.	Arkansas*
Southern Ill.	Southeast Mo. St.
Southern Methodist	North Texas
Southern-B.R.	Alabama St.*
Southwestern La.	Northeast La.*
Southwest Mo. St.	Washburn*
Southwest Tex. St.	Texas Southern(3)*
Stanford	Oregon
Syracuse	Texas
Tenn.-Chatt.	Tenn.-Martin*
Tennessee St.	Jackson St.(4)*
Tennessee Tech	Lock Haven*
Texas A&M	Tulsa*
Texas Christian	Western Mich.*
Texas Tech	Wyoming*
Troy St.	Northwestern (La.)
UCLA	Cal St. Fullerton
Utah St.	Utah
Vanderbilt	Duke*
Villanova	Bucknell
Wake Forest	Appalachian St.*
Washington	Wisconsin
Weber St.	Southern Utah*
Western Ky.	Indiana St.
William & Mary	Va. Military
Youngstown St.	Delaware St.*

(1) Birmingham, Ala.
(2) Los Angeles, Cal.
(3) San Antonio, Tex.
(4) Memphis, Tenn.

Thursday September 17

Rutgers	Pittsburgh*

Saturday September 19

Alcorn St.	Alabama St.
Arizona St.	Louisville*
Arkansas	Alabama(1)*
Arkansas St.	Northern Ill.
Auburn	Louisiana St.*
Baylor	Utah St.*
Bethune-Cookman	Delaware St.(2)
Boise St.	Pacific (Cal.)*
Boston College	Navy
Brigham Young	UCLA
Brown	Yale
Central Fla.	Troy St.*
Central Mich.	Ohio
Citadel	East Tenn. St.*
Columbia	Harvard
Cornell	Princeton
Dartmouth	Pennsylvania
Delaware	Rhode Island
Duke	Rice
Eastern Ill.	Murray St.*
Eastern Ky.	Northeast La.*
Eastern Wash.	Sonoma St.
Fordham	Colgate
Fresno St.	Colorado St.*
Furman	Presbyterian
Georgia	Cal St. Fullerton
Ga. Southern	Savannah St.
Grambling	Tennessee St.*
Holy Cross	Massachusetts
Houston	Illinois
Idaho	Weber St.
Indiana St.	Illinois St.*
Iowa St.	Tulane
James Madison	Hofstra*
Kansas St.	Montana*

HOME	OPPONENT
Kent	Ball St.
Kentucky	Indiana*
Lafayette	Buffalo
Lehigh	New Hampshire
Liberty	Concord*
Maine	Northeastern
Memphis St.	Mississippi St.*
Miami (Fla.)	Florida A&M
Miami (Ohio)	Cincinnati
Michigan	Oklahoma St.
Michigan St.	Notre Dame
Miles	Mississippi Val.*
Minnesota	Colorado*
Missouri	Texas A&M
Montana St.	Mesa St.
Nevada-Las Vegas	Northern Ariz.*
Nevada	McNeese St.
New Mexico	Southern Methodist*
North Caro.	Army*
North Caro. A&T	Morgan St.
North Caro. St.	Florida St.
Northern Iowa	Idaho St.
Oklahoma	Southern Cal
Oregon	Texas Tech
Oregon St.	Arizona
Penn St.	Eastern Mich.
Prairie View	Langston*
Purdue	Toledo
Sam Houston St.	Angelo St.
San Jose St.	Southwestern La.*
South Caro.	East Caro.
South Caro. St.	Southern-B.R.(3)
Southern Ill.	Austin Peay
Southern Miss.	Louisiana Tech
Southwest Mo. St.	North Texas*
Southwest Tex. St.	Youngstown St.*
Stanford	Northwestern
Stephen F. Austin	Jackson St.*
Syracuse	Ohio St.*
Temple	Virginia Tech
Tennessee	Florida
Tennessee Tech	Samford*
UTEP	New Mexico St.*
Towson St.	Bucknell*
Tulsa	Kansas*
Vanderbilt	Mississippi*
Villanova	Richmond
Virginia	Georgia Tech
Va. Military	Marshall
Washington	Nebraska
West Va.	Maryland
Western Ill.	Western Ky.*
Western Mich.	Akron
William & Mary	Boston U.
Wisconsin	Bowling Green
Wyoming	Air Force

(1) Little Rock, Ark.
(2) Ft. Lauderdale, Fla.
(3) Atlanta, Ga.

Thursday September 24

Kansas	California*

Saturday September 26

Air Force	New Mexico
Alabama	Louisiana Tech
Appalachian St.	East Tenn. St.
Arkansas St.	Southern Ill.
Army	Citadel
Auburn	Southern Miss.
Ball St.	Miami (Ohio)
Bethune-Cookman	Samford
Boston College	Michigan St.

HOME	OPPONENT
Bowling Green	East Caro.
Bucknell	Brown
Central Mich.	Toledo
Central St. (Ohio)	Texas Southern
Colorado	Iowa
Cornell	Lehigh
Delaware	West Chester
Duke	Virginia
Eastern Ky.	Tennessee Tech*
Eastern Mich.	Kent*
Florida St.	Wake Forest*
Fordham	Columbia
Fresno St.	Washington St.*
Cal St. Fullerton	Cal St. Sacramento*
Furman	Ga. Southern
Georgia	Mississippi
Georgia Tech	Clemson
Harvard	William & Mary
Hawaii	Brigham Young*
Howard	Alcorn St.
Illinois St.	Eastern Ill.
Indiana	Missouri
Indiana St.	Lock Haven*
Iowa St.	Northern Iowa
Jackson St.	Mississippi Val.*
Kansas St.	Temple*
Kentucky	South Caro.*
Louisiana St.	Colorado St.*
Louisville	Wyoming
Massachusetts	Boston U.
Memphis St.	Arkansas*
Miami (Fla.)	Arizona
Michigan	Houston
Montana	Eastern Wash.
Morgan St.	Johnson Smith
Murray St.	Middle Tenn. St.*
Navy	Rutgers
Nebraska	Arizona St.
New Hampshire	Dartmouth
Nicholls St.	McNeese St.*
North Caro.	North Caro. St.
North Caro. A&T	Liberty
Northeastern	Connecticut
Northeast La.	Southwest Tex. St.*
Northern Ariz.	Idaho St.*
Northwestern (La.)	East Tex. St.*
Notre Dame	Purdue
Ohio	Western Mich.
Oklahoma St.	Tulsa*
Oregon	Nevada-Las Vegas
Penn St.	Maryland
Pennsylvania	Colgate
Pittsburgh	Minnesota
Princeton	Lafayette
Rhode Island	Richmond
Rice	Sam Houston St.
Southeast Mo. St.	Austin Peay*
Southern Methodist	Texas Christian*
Stanford	San Jose St.
Stephen F. Austin	Boise St.*
Tennessee	Cincinnati
Tenn.-Chatt.	Central Ark.*
Tenn.-Martin	Morehead St.*
Tennessee St.	Florida A&M(1)
Texas	North Texas*
Texas Tech	Baylor*
Towson St.	Hofstra*
Troy St.	Alabama St.*
Tulane	Nevada*
UCLA	San Diego St.
Utah	Oregon St.*
Utah St.	New Mexico St.
Va. Military	West Va. Tech
Virginia Tech	West Va.
Weber St.	Montana St.*
Western Caro.	Ferrum*
Western Ill.	Central Fla.
Western Ky.	Southwest Mo. St.

HOME	OPPONENT
Wisconsin	Northern Ill.
Yale	Holy Cross
Youngstown St.	James Madison*
(1) Atlanta, Ga.	

Thursday
October 1

Mississippi St.	Florida*

Friday
October 2

Brigham Young	Utah St.*

Saturday
October 3

HOME	OPPONENT
Alabama	South Caro.
Alabama St.	Central St. (Ohio)(1)
Appalachian St.	Citadel
Arizona	UCLA*
Arkansas	Georgia
Arkansas St.	Northwestern (La.)
Auburn	Vanderbilt
Baylor	Southern Methodist
Boise St.	Montana*
Boston U.	Villanova
California	Oregon St.
Central Fla.	Savannah St.*
Central Mich.	Bowling Green
Cincinnati	Kent*
Clemson	Tenn.-Chatt.
Colorado St.	Utah
Columbia	Colgate
Connecticut	Yale
Cornell	Lafayette
Dartmouth	Bucknell
East Tenn. St.	Morehead St.*
Eastern Ill.	Southern Ill.*
Eastern Ky.	Southeast Mo. St.
Eastern Mich.	Miami (Ohio)*
Eastern Wash.	Weber St.
Florida A&M	Howard*
Fordham	Pennsylvania
Fresno St.	Louisiana Tech*
Cal St. Fullerton	Nevada*
Furman	Va. Military
Georgia Tech	North Caro. St.
Holy Cross	Harvard
Houston	Southwestern La.
Idaho	Cal St. Northridge
Idaho St.	Central Wash.*
Indiana St.	Youngstown St.
James Madison	Northeastern
Kansas St.	New Mexico St.
Lehigh	Princeton
Louisiana St.	Tennessee*
Louisville	Syracuse
Maryland	Pittsburgh
Miami (Fla.)	Florida St.
Michigan	Iowa
Michigan St.	Indiana
Minnesota	Illinois*
Mississippi	Kentucky*
Missouri	Marshall
Montana St.	Northern Ariz.
Murray St.	Austin Peay
New Hampshire	Delaware
New Mexico	San Diego St.*
North Caro.	Navy
Northeast La.	Delta St.*
Northern Ill.	Middle Tenn. St.*
Northern Iowa	Illinois St.
Notre Dame	Stanford
Ohio	Akron
Oklahoma	Iowa St.

HOME	OPPONENT
Oregon	Arizona St.
Pacific (Cal.)	Nevada-Las Vegas
Prairie View	Grambling(2)*
Purdue	Northwestern
Rice	Texas
Richmond	Maine
Rutgers	Penn St.(3)
Sam Houston St.	Alcorn St.*
Samford	Western Caro.*
South Caro. St.	Jackson St.(4)
Southern Miss.	Tulsa
Southern-B.R.	Mississippi Val.*
Southwest Mo. St.	Western Ill.
Southwest Tex. St.	Nicholls St.*
Tennessee Tech	Tenn.-Martin
UTEP	Air Force*
Texas A&M	Texas Tech
Texas Christian	Oklahoma St.*
Texas Southern	Knoxville
Towson St.	Liberty*
Wake Forest	Virginia
Washington	Southern Cal
Washington St.	Temple
West Va.	Boston College
Western Mich.	Ball St.
William & Mary	Brown
Wisconsin	Ohio St.
Wyoming	San Jose St.
(1) Indianapolis, Ind.	
(2) Dallas, Tex.	
(3) East Rutherford, N.J.	
(4) Columbia, S.C.	

Thursday
October 8

Missouri	Colorado*

Saturday
October 10

HOME	OPPONENT
Air Force	Navy
Alabama St.	Jackson St.*
Alcorn St.	Texas Southern
Arizona St.	Pacific (Cal.) *
Arkansas St.	Troy St.
Army	Lafayette
Ball St.	Eastern Mich.
Bowling Green	Ohio
Brigham Young	Fresno St.
Citadel	Tenn.-Chatt.*
Colgate	Buffalo
Colorado St.	UTEP
Columbia	Bucknell
Connecticut	Villanova
Delaware	Boston U.
Delaware St.	Towson St.
Duke	East Caro.
East Tenn. St.	Charleston So.
Eastern Ill.	Indiana St.
Eastern Wash.	Montana St.
Florida	Louisiana St.
Florida A&M	North Caro. A&T(1)
Florida St.	North Caro.
Georgia	Ga. Southern
Harvard	Cornell
Holy Cross	Dartmouth
Howard	Bethune-Cookman
Idaho	Idaho St.
Iowa	Wisconsin
James Madison	Appalachian St.
Kansas	Kansas St.
Kent	Akron
Knoxville	Mississippi Val.
Louisiana Tech	Southwestern La.*
Louisville	Virginia Tech
Marshall	Furman*

HOME	OPPONENT
Maryland	Georgia Tech
McNeese St.	Northeast La.*
Memphis St.	Cincinnati*
Miami (Ohio)	Central Mich.
Michigan	Michigan St.
Middle Tenn. St.	Austin Peay
Mississippi St.	Auburn*
Morehead St.	Tennessee St.
Nebraska	Oklahoma St.
New Mexico St.	Nevada-Las Vegas*
Nicholls St.	Sam Houston St.
North Caro. St.	Texas Tech
North Texas	Northwestern (La.) *
Northeastern	Lehigh
Northern Ariz.	Boise St.*
Northern Ill.	Southern Miss.
Northern Iowa	Western Ky.*
Northwestern	Indiana
Ohio St.	Illinois
Oklahoma	Texas(2)
Oregon St.	Washington St.
Penn St.	Miami (Fla.)
Pennsylvania	William & Mary
Pittsburgh	Notre Dame
Princeton	Brown
Purdue	Minnesota
Rhode Island	Massachusetts
Rice	Southern Methodist
Richmond	New Hampshire
Samford	Eastern Ky.*
San Jose St.	Cal St. Fullerton*
South Caro. St.	Morgan St.
Southern Cal	Oregon
Southern Ill.	Western Ill.
Southern-B.R.	Winston-Salem(3)
Southwest Tex. St.	Stephen F. Austin*
Syracuse	Rutgers
Tennessee	Arkansas
Tenn.-Martin	Murray St.*
Tennessee Tech	Southeast Mo. St.
Texas Christian	Baylor*
Toledo	Western Mich.*
Tulane	Alabama*
Tulsa	Southwest Mo. St.
UCLA	Stanford
Utah	Hawaii
Vanderbilt	Wake Forest
Virginia	Clemson
Washington	California
Weber St.	Montana*
West Tex. St.	Prairie View*
Western Caro.	Va. Military
Wyoming	New Mexico
Yale	Fordham
Youngstown St.	Illinois St.*
(1) Orlando, Fla.	
(2) Dallas, Tex.	
(3) Shreveport, La.	

Thursday
October 15

Tulane	Southern Miss.*

Saturday
October 17

HOME	OPPONENT
Air Force	Colorado St.
Alabama St.	Texas Southern(1)*
Arizona St.	Oregon St.*
Arkansas	Mississippi(2)*
Austin Peay	Tennessee Tech
Ball St.	Akron
Baylor	Houston
Boise St.	Weber St.*
Boston U.	Richmond
Brown	Lehigh

HOME	OPPONENT
Central Fla.	Nicholls St.*
Central Mich.	Kent
Citadel	Marshall
Clemson	Duke
Colgate	Cornell
Colorado	Oklahoma
Dartmouth	Yale
Delaware St.	Florida A&M
East Caro.	Cincinnati
Eastern Wash.	Idaho
Florida	Auburn
Georgia	Vanderbilt
Ga. Southern	James Madison
Georgia Tech	Florida St.
Hawaii	Fresno St.*
Holy Cross	Princeton
Illinois	Iowa
Illinois St.	Southwest Mo. St.
Indiana	Michigan
Indiana St.	Glenville St.
Iowa St.	Kansas
Lafayette	Harvard
Liberty	Troy St.*
Louisiana St.	Kentucky*
Louisiana Tech	East Tenn. St.
Louisville	Tulsa
Maine	Rhode Island
Maryland	Wake Forest
Massachusetts	Connecticut
McNeese St.	Northwestern (La.)*
Memphis St.	Arkansas St.*
Miami (Fla.)	Texas Christian
Middle Tenn. St.	Eastern Ky.
Minnesota	Michigan St.*
Mississippi Val.	Grambling(3)
Montana	Northern Ariz.
Montana St.	Idaho St.
Morehead St.	Murray St.
Morgan St.	Central St. (Ohio)
Nevada-Las Vegas	Nevada*
New Mexico	Utah*
New Mexico St.	Pacific (Cal.)
North Caro.	Virginia
Northeastern	Youngstown St.
Northeast La.	Sam Houston St.
Ohio	Miami (Ohio)
Ohio St.	Northwestern
Oklahoma St.	Missouri
Oregon	Washington
Penn St.	Boston College
Pennsylvania	Columbia
Prairie View	Alcorn St.
Rutgers	Army(4)
Samford	Southeast Mo. St.
San Diego St.	UTEP*
South Caro.	Mississippi St.
South Caro. St.	Bethune-Cookman
Southern Cal	California
Southern Ill.	Northern Iowa
Southern-B.R.	Jackson St.*
Southwestern La.	Cal St. Fullerton*
Stanford	Arizona
Stephen F. Austin	North Texas
Temple	Pittsburgh
Tennessee	Alabama
Tenn.-Chatt.	Western Caro.*
Tennessee St.	Tenn.-Martin
Texas A&M	Rice
Toledo	Bowling Green*
Troy St.	Western Ky.
Utah St.	Kansas St.
Villanova	Delaware
Va. Military	Appalachian St.
Virginia Tech	North Caro. St.
Washington St.	UCLA
West Va.	Syracuse
Western Ill.	Eastern Ill.
Western Mich.	Eastern Mich.

HOME	OPPONENT
William & Mary	Towson St.
Wisconsin	Purdue
Wyoming	Brigham Young
(1) Mobile, Ala.	
(2) Little Rock, Ark.	
(3) Chicago, Ill.	
(4) East Rutherford, N.J.	

Saturday
October 24

HOME	OPPONENT
Akron	Bowling Green
Alabama	Mississippi
Alabama St.	Prairie View*
Alcorn St.	Southern-B.R.
Appalachian St.	Furman
Auburn	Southwestern La.
Ball St.	Central Mich.
Bethune-Cookman	Albany St. (Ga.)
Boise St.	Portland St.*
Brown	Pennsylvania
California	Arizona
Colorado	Kansas St.
Colorado St.	Wyoming
Connecticut	Maine
Cornell	Dartmouth
Duke	Maryland
Eastern Mich.	Ohio*
Florida	Louisville
Fordham	Lafayette
Fresno St.	New Mexico*
Ga. Southern	Jacksonville St.
Grambling	Jackson St.
Hawaii	Nevada-Las Vegas*
Holy Cross	Bucknell
Howard	North Caro. A&T
Illinois	Northwestern
Illinois St.	Southern Ill.
Indiana	Wisconsin
Iowa	Purdue
Kansas	Oklahoma
Kent	Western Mich.
Kentucky	Georgia*
Lehigh	Colgate
Marshall	Tenn.-Chatt.
Massachusetts	Villanova
Miami (Ohio)	Toledo
Michigan	Minnesota
Michigan St.	Ohio St.
Mississippi St.	Arkansas St.
Missouri	Nebraska
Montana	Montana St.
Morgan St.	Delaware St.
Navy	Delaware
Nevada	New Mexico St.
New Hampshire	Northeastern
North Caro.	Georgia Tech
North Caro. St.	Clemson
Northern Ariz.	Eastern Wash.*
Northern Ill.	Liberty
Northern Iowa	Idaho*
Northwestern (La.)	Northeast La.
Notre Dame	Brigham Young
Oklahoma St.	Iowa St.
Oregon St.	Stanford
Pittsburgh	East Caro.
Princeton	Harvard
Rhode Island	Boston U.
Sam Houston St.	North Texas
San Diego St.	Air Force*
South Caro. St.	N.C. Central
Southeast Mo. St.	Middle Tenn. St.
Southern Cal	Washington St.
Southern Miss.	Cincinnati
Southwest Mo. St.	Eastern Ill.
Southwest Tex. St.	McNeese St.
Stephen F. Austin	Nicholls St.
Temple	Syracuse

HOME	OPPONENT
Tenn.-Martin	Eastern Ky.
Tennessee St.	Austin Peay
Tennessee Tech	Morehead St.
Texas	Houston
Texas A&M	Baylor
Texas Christian	Rice
Texas Southern	Mississippi Val.
Texas Tech	Southern Methodist
Towson St.	James Madison
Tulane	Boston College*
Tulsa	Memphis St.
UCLA	Arizona St.
Utah	UTEP
Utah St.	San Jose St.
Vanderbilt	South Caro.
Virginia	William & Mary
Va. Military	Richmond(1)
Virginia Tech	Miami (Fla.)
Wake Forest	Army
Washington	Pacific (Cal.)
Weber St.	Idaho St.
West Va.	Penn St.
Western Caro.	Citadel
Western Ill.	Indiana St.
Western Ky.	Central Fla.
Yale	Columbia
(1) Norfolk, Va.	

Thursday
October 29

HOME	OPPONENT
East Caro.	Southern Miss.*

Saturday
October 31

HOME	OPPONENT
Air Force	Utah
Akron	Central Mich.
Alabama St.	Alabama A&M(1)
Arizona	New Mexico St.*
Arizona St.	Southern Cal*
Army	Eastern Mich.
Auburn	Arkansas
Austin Peay	Morehead St.
Boston College	Temple
Boston U.	New Hampshire
Bowling Green	Miami (Ohio)
Brigham Young	Penn St.
Bucknell	Fordham
California	UCLA
Cincinnati	Louisville*
Colgate	Lafayette
Colorado St.	San Diego St.
Columbia	Princeton
Connecticut	Richmond
Cornell	Brown
Delaware St.	South Caro. St.
East Tenn. St.	Furman
Eastern Ky.	Tennessee St.
Florida	Georgia(2)
Florida A&M	Morgan St.
Fresno St.	Wyoming*
Cal St. Fullerton	Utah St.*
Ga. Southern	Middle Tenn. St.
Georgia Tech	Duke
Harvard	Dartmouth
Holy Cross	Lehigh
Houston	Texas Christian
Howard	Bowie St.
Idaho	Northern Ariz.
Idaho St.	Eastern Wash.*
Indiana St.	Northern Iowa
Iowa	Ohio St.
Iowa St.	Missouri
James Madison	William & Mary
Kansas	Oklahoma St.
Kentucky	Mississippi St.*

HOME	OPPONENT
Southern Cal	Arizona
Southern-B.R.	Texas Southern*
Southwest Tex. St.	North Texas
Stanford	Washington St.
Tenn.-Chatt.	Furman
Tenn.-Martin	Samford
Texas	Southern Methodist
Texas Christian	Texas Tech
Toledo	Eastern Mich.
Towson St.	Northeastern
Utah	Wyoming
Villanova	Fordham
Virginia Tech	Southern Miss.
Washington	Oregon St.
Western Caro.	East Tenn. St.
Western Mich.	Central Mich.
William & Mary	Lehigh
Wisconsin	Minnesota
Yale	Princeton

(1) Summerville, S. C.

Saturday
November 21

HOME	OPPONENT
Alcorn St.	Jackson St.
Appalachian St.	Western Caro.
Arizona	Arizona St.*
Arkansas	Southern Methodist(1)
Army	Boston College
Austin Peay	Tenn.-Martin
Baylor	Texas
Boise St.	Idaho
Boston U.	Northeastern
Bucknell	Colgate
California	Stanford
Cincinnati	Akron
Clemson	South Caro.
Colorado	Iowa St.
Columbia	Brown
Connecticut	Rhode Island
Cornell	Pennsylvania
Delaware	Towson St.
Duke	North Caro.
East Tenn. St.	Marshall
Furman	Citadel
Harvard	Yale
Hawaii	Wyoming*
Holy Cross	Fordham
Howard	Delaware St.
Idaho St.	Montana*
Illinois	Michigan St.

HOME	OPPONENT
Lafayette	Lehigh
Liberty	Kutztown
Louisiana St.	Tulane*
Memphis St.	East Caro.
Middle Tenn. St.	Tennessee Tech
Minnesota	Iowa*
Missouri	Kansas
Morehead St.	Eastern Ky.
Morgan St.	Bethune-Cookman
Murray St.	Western Ky.
Nevada-Las Vegas	Montana St.
Nevada	Texas Southern
New Hampshire	Massachusetts
New Mexico	Colorado St.
Nicholls St.	Troy St.
North Caro. A&T	South Caro. St.
North Caro. St.	Wake Forest
North Texas	Northeast La.
Northern Ill.	Toledo
Northern Iowa	Southwest Mo. St.*
Northwestern	Wisconsin
Ohio St.	Michigan
Oklahoma St.	Kansas St.
Oregon St.	Oregon
Pacific (Cal.)	Utah St.
Penn St.	Pittsburgh
Prairie View	Southern-B.R.*
Princeton	Dartmouth
Purdue	Indiana
Rice	Navy
Richmond	William & Mary
Sam Houston St.	Southwest Tex. St.
Samford	Central Fla.
San Diego St.	Fresno St.*
San Jose St.	New Mexico St.
Southern Ill.	Indiana St.
Southwestern La.	Arkansas St.*
Stephen F. Austin	Northwestern (La.)
Syracuse	Miami (Fla.)
Temple	Rutgers
Tennessee	Kentucky
Tennessee St.	Southeast Mo. St.
Texas A&M	Texas Christian
Texas Tech	Houston
UCLA	Southern Cal
Utah	Brigham Young
Vanderbilt	Florida
Villanova	Maine
Va. Military	Tenn.-Chatt.
Virginia Tech	Virginia
Washington St.	Washington

HOME	OPPONENT
Weber St.	McNeese St.
West Va.	Louisiana Tech
Youngstown St.	Ga. Southern

(1) Little Rock, Ark.

Thursday
November 26

HOME	OPPONENT
Alabama	Auburn
Texas	Texas A&M*

Friday
November 27

HOME	OPPONENT
Oklahoma	Nebraska

Saturday
November 28

HOME	OPPONENT
Arkansas	Louisiana St.
Florida A&M	Bethune-Cookman(1)
Florida St.	Florida
Georgia	Georgia Tech
Houston	Rice
Mississippi	Mississippi St.
Nevada-Las Vegas	Cal St. Fullerton
San Diego St.	Miami (Fla.)*
Southern Cal	Notre Dame
Southern-B.R.	Grambling(2)
UTEP	Fresno St.*
Vanderbilt	Tennessee

(1) Tampa, Fla.
(2) New Orleans, La.

Saturday
December 5

HOME	OPPONENT
Hawaii	Pittsburgh
Navy	Army(1)

(1) Philadelphia, Pa.

Sunday
December 6

HOME	OPPONENT
Kansas St.	Nebraska(1)

(1) Tokyo, Japan

1992 NCAA Divisions II & III Schedules

Below each school's name and location is the name of its 1992 head coach and his won-lost-tied record for all seasons as a college head coach. Schedules for 1992 are on the left, with 1991 records on the right.
Home games on each schedule are indicated by a square (■) and night games are indicated by an asterisk (*). Neutral sites are designated by symbol (†).
Game date and starting time are subject to change.

ABILENE CHRISTIAN . . . . Abilene, TX 79699
Ronnie Peacock (1 yr., 1-9-0)

1992		1991	
North Texas	S 5*	7	Angelo St. 28
Cal St. Sacramento	S19*	0	North Texas 24
Midwestern St. ■	S26*	0	Northern Colo. 20
Eastern N. Mex.	O 3	7	Cal St. Sacramento 45
Central Okla.	O10*	20	Eastern N. Mex. 32
Angelo St. ■	O17*	24	Central Okla. 7
Cameron	O24*	9	Angelo St. 36
East Tex. St. ■	O31	3	Cameron 10
Texas A&I	N 7*	3	East Tex. St. 37
		0	Texas A&I 20

Colors: Purple & White.   Nickname: Wildcats.   II

ADAMS STATE . . . . Alamosa, CO 81102
Jeff Geiser (8 yrs., 50-30-1)

1992		1991	
Northwestern Okla. ■	S 5	42	N.M. Highlands 13
Southwestern Okla.	S12*	16	Western St. 28
Western St.	S26	21	Neb.-Kearney 14
Chadron St. ■	O 3	35	Western N. Mex. 21
Colorado Mines	O10	32	Northwestern Okla. 13
Fort Hays St.	O17	32	Fort Lewis 21
Fort Lewis ■	O24	21	Colorado Mines 34
Mesa St.	O31*	11	Mesa St. 7
N.M. Highlands ■	N 7	20	Fort Hays St. 21
Western N. Mex.	N14	0	Chadron St. 10

Colors: Green & White.   Nickname: Indians.   II

ADRIAN . . . . Adrian, MI 49221
Jim Lyall (2 yrs., 8-9-1)

1992		1991	
Mount Union	S12	14	Heidelberg 0
Defiance ■	S19	26	Defiance 3
Ill. Wesleyan ■	S26	12	Northwood 7
Evansville	O 3	12	Carnegie Mellon 20
Olivet	O10	14	Olivet .25
Alma ■	O17	0	Alma .10
Hope	O24	6	Hope .20
Albion ■	O31	7	Albion 48
Kalamazoo	N 7	13	Kalamazoo 9

Colors: Gold & Black.   Nickname: Bulldogs.   III

ALABAMA A&M . . . . Normal, AL 35762
Raymond Bonner (1 yr., 2-3-0)

1992		1991	
Miles ■	A29*	23	Miles .13
Jacksonville St.†	S 5*	18	Jacksonville St. 44
Howard†	S12*	10	Alcorn St. 38
North Ala.	S19*	13	Central St. (Ohio) 31
Savannah St. ■	S26	27	Savannah St. 25
Morris Brown	O 3	12	Morris Brown 7
Morehouse	O10	25	Albany St. (Ga.) 20
Albany St. (Ga.) ■	O17	7	Fort Valley St. 35
Fort Valley St.	O24	13	Alabama St. 59
Alabama St.†	O31	28	Clark Atlanta 18
Clark Atlanta	N 7	20	Tuskegee 43

Colors: Maroon & White.   Nickname: Bulldogs.   II

ALABAMA-BIRMINGHAM . . . . . Birmingham, AL 35294
Jim Hilyer (1 yr., 4-3-2)

1992		1991	
Millsaps ■	S 5	14	Millsaps 28
Gallaudet ■	S12	10	Evangel 28
Wash. & Lee	S19	34	Wash. & Lee 21
Tenn. Wesleyan	S26	35	Hampden-Sydney 35
Miles ■	O 3	17	Lindenwood 17
Charleston So. ■	O17	33	Charleston So. 19
Ferrum	O24	7	Ferrum 35
Samford	O31	9	Hastings 7
Lindenwood	N 7	25	Clinch Valley 6
Clinch Valley	N14		

Colors: Green & Gold.   Nickname: Blazers.   III

ALBANY (NEW YORK) . . . . Albany, NY 12222
Robert Ford (23 yrs., 120-96-1)

1992		1991	
Ithaca ■	S12*	3	Springfield 21
Springfield	S18*	14	Alfred .17
Brockport St.	S26	7	Ithaca .38
Alfred ■	O 3*	7	Union (N.Y.) 47
Union (N.Y.) ■	O10*	45	Western Conn. St. 3
Cortland St.	O17	21	Cortland St. 34
Norwich	O24	21	Norwich 14
Salisbury St. ■	O31	20	Salisbury St. 18
Western Conn. St.	N 7	29	Wagner 19
St. Lawrence	N14	39	St. Lawrence 12

Colors: Purple & Gold.   Nickname: Great Danes.   III

ALBANY STATE (GEORGIA) . . . . Albany, GA 31705
Hampton Smith (16 yrs., 87-70-3)

1992		1991	
Miles ■	S12*	16	Miles .12
Livingston ■	S19	21	Livingston 22
Morehouse	S26	15	Morehouse 20
Tuskegee ■	O 3*	6	Tuskegee 56
Savannah St. ■	O10	16	Savannah St. 51
Alabama A&M	O17	20	Alabama A&M 25
Bethune-Cookman	O24	30	Bethune-Cookman 25
Clark Atlanta ■	O31	6	Clark Atlanta 14
Morris Brown	N 7	28	Morris Brown 22
Fort Valley St.	N14	20	Fort Valley St. 22

Colors: Blue & Gold.   Nickname: Golden Rams.   II

ALBION . . . . Albion, MI 49224
Pete Schmidt (9 yrs., 56-23-4)

1992		1991	
Thiel ■	S 5	35	Denison 14
Whittier ■	S12*	29	Wabash 10
Wabash	S19	20	Kenyon 13
DePauw ■	S26	41	Lawrence 6
Kalamazoo ■	O10	10	Kalamazoo 6
Hope	O17	35	Hope 5
Olivet ■	O24	14	Olivet .14
Adrian	O31	48	Adrian 7
Alma ■	N 7	26	Alma .16

III Championship

		21	Allegheny 24

Colors: Purple & Gold.   Nickname: Britons.   III

ALBRIGHT . . . . Reading, PA 19604
Jeff Sparagana (6 yrs., 16-44-0)

1992		1991	
Western Md. ■	S12*	14	Western Md. 13
Wilkes	S19	38	Wilkes .27
Lebanon Valley ■	S26*	10	Lebanon Valley 28
Delaware Valley	O 3	14	Delaware Valley 13
Merchant Marine	O10	21	Merchant Marine 20
Widener ■	O17	25	Widener 26
Juniata	O24	13	Juniata 26
Lycoming ■	O31	8	Lycoming 43
Moravian ■	N 7	20	Moravian 0
Susquehanna	N14	24	Susquehanna 31

Colors: Cardinal & White.   Nickname: Lions.   III

ALFRED . . . . Alfred, NY 14802
Jim Moretti (7 yrs., 46-23-2)

1992		1991	
St. John Fisher ■	S12*	38	Randolph-Macon 14
Brockport St. ■	S19	17	Albany (N.Y.) 14
Ithaca	S26	8	Ithaca .31
Albany (N.Y.)	O 3*	31	St. Lawrence 6
St. Lawrence	O10	30	Hobart 10
Hobart ■	O17	8	Susquehanna 31
Mercyhurst ■	O24	39	Ripon 6
Buffalo St.	O31	13	Buffalo St. 33
Canisius ■	N 7	22	Canisius 3
LIU-C.W. Post	N14	24	LIU-C.W. Post 11

Colors: Purple & Gold.   Nickname: Saxons.   III

■ Home games on each schedule.   *Night Games.

ALLEGHENY .... Meadville, PA 16335
Ken O'Keefe (2 yrs., 24-1-1)

Opponent	Date		Pts	Opponent	Opp
Westminster (Pa.)	S12		23	Carnegie Mellon	12
Wooster	S19		19	Juniata	10
Case Reserve ■	S26		37	Oberlin	2
Carnegie Mellon ■	O 3		63	Denison	20
Wittenberg	O10		75	Earlham	0
Kenyon ■	O17		34	Wooster	6
Oberlin	O24		22	Wittenberg	16
Denison ■	O31		43	Kenyon	21
Ohio Wesleyan	N 7		24	Ohio Wesleyan	7
Earlham ■	N14		35	Duquesne	0
				III Championship	
			24	Albion	21
			25	Dayton	28

Colors: Blue & Gold. Nickname: Gators. **III**

ALMA .... Alma, MI 48801
Jim Cole (1 yr., 4-5-0)

Opponent	Date		Pts	Opponent	Opp
John Carroll ■	S12		0	West Ga.	55
Franklin	S19		21	Marietta	7
Bluffton	S26		21	Franklin	19
Ill. Benedictine	O 3		39	Ill. Benedictine	14
Hope	O10		7	Hope	10
Adrian	O17		10	Adrian	0
Kalamazoo ■	O24		0	Kalamazoo	27
Olivet	O31		13	Olivet	14
Albion	N 7		16	Albion	26

Colors: Maroon & Cream. Nickname: Scots. **III**

AMERICAN INTERNATIONAL ... Springfield, MA 01109
Alex Rotsko (9 yrs., 48-40-3)

Opponent	Date		Pts	Opponent	Opp
Springfield	S11*		7	Plymouth St.	7
Millersville	S19*		13	West Chester	36
Central Conn. St. ■	S26		47	Springfield	31
Southern Conn. St.	O 2*		41	Southern Conn. St.	0
Ithaca ■	O10		20	Ithaca	23
New Haven	O17		35	New Haven	34
Valdosta St.	O24		17	Bowie St.	20
East Stroudsburg ■	O31		21	Central Conn. St.	18
Bowie St. ■	N 7		14	Findlay	17
Springfield ■	N14		7	Springfield	12

Colors: Gold & White. Nickname: Yellow Jackets. **II**

AMHERST .... Amherst, MA 01002
John McKechnie (1st yr. as head coach)

Opponent	Date		Pts	Opponent	Opp
Hamilton ■	S26		26	Bates	26
Bowdoin	O 3		0	Middlebury	35
Middlebury	O10		7	Worcester Tech	33
Colby ■	O17		15	Bowdoin	27
Wesleyan	O24		15	Wesleyan	32
Tufts ■	O31		17	Tufts	28
Trinity (Conn.)	N 7		7	Trinity (Conn.)	51
Williams	N14		0	Williams	37

Colors: Purple & White. Nickname: Lord Jeffs. **III**

ANDERSON .... Anderson, IN 46012
Mike Manley (9 yrs., 32-61-3)

Opponent	Date		Pts	Opponent	Opp
Aurora ■	S12		17	Defiance	20
Carthage	S19		7	Dayton	50
Geneva	S26		33	Bluffton	34
Franklin ■	O 3		36	Hanover	26
Hanover	O10		28	Manchester	20
Manchester	O17		23	Wabash	6
Wabash ■	O24		7	DePauw	12
DePauw	O31		20	Rose-Hulman	17
Rose-Hulman	N 7		40	Franklin	22
Taylor ■	N14		33	Taylor	16

Colors: Orange & Black. Nickname: Ravens. **III**

ANGELO STATE .... San Angelo, TX 76909
Jerry Vandergriff (10 yrs., 72-37-1)

Opponent	Date		Pts	Opponent	Opp
Henderson St. ■	S 5*		28	Abilene Christian	7
Prairie View	S12*		55	Prairie View	0
Sam Houston St.	S19*		6	Sam Houston St.	16
Southern Utah	S26*		13	Cal Poly SLO	2
Eastern N. Mex. ■	O10*		12	Eastern N. Mex.	13
Abilene Christian	O17*		36	Abilene Christian	9
Central Okla. ■	O24*		41	Central Okla.	10
Cameron ■	O31*		34	Cameron	7
East Tex. St.	N 7		39	East Tex. St.	0
Texas A&I ■	N14		21	Texas A&I	17

Colors: Blue & Gold. Nickname: Rams. **II**

ASHLAND .... Ashland, OH 44805
Fred Martinelli (33 yrs., 200-114-12)

Opponent	Date		Pts	Opponent	Opp
Valparaiso	S 5		30	Valparaiso	7
Ferris St. ■	S12		35	Ferris St.	7
Slippery Rock ■	S19		51	Calif. (Pa.)	10
Hillsdale	S 26*		29	Hillsdale	7
Wayne St. (Mich.) ■	O 3		21	Wayne St. (Mich.)	7
Saginaw Valley	O10		26	Saginaw Valley	6
St. Joseph's (Ind.) ■	O17		9	St. Joseph's (Ind.)	0
Grand Valley St.	O24		7	Grand Valley St.	38
Butler	O31		12	Butler	14
Indianapolis ■	N 7		21	Indianapolis	7
Northern Mich.	N14		49	Northern Mich.	7

Colors: Purple & Gold. Nickname: Eagles. **II**

ASSUMPTION .... Worcester, MA 01615
Bernie Gaughan (4 yrs., 8-24-1)

Opponent	Date		Pts	Opponent	Opp
St. Peter's	S12		27	MIT	21
MIT ■	S19		3	Stonehill	26
Stonehill	S26		0	Sacred Heart	13
Nichols ■	O 3		12	Bentley	22
Bentley	O10		15	Hobart	36
Western New Eng.	O17		9	Upsala	33
Curry ■	O24		19	Siena	20
Siena ■	O31		6	Western New Eng.	36
Mass.-Lowell ■	N 7		0	Marist	42
Sacred Heart ■	N14				

Colors: Royal Blue & White. Nickname: Greyhounds. **III**

AUGSBURG .... Minneapolis, MN 55454
Jack Osberg (1 yr., 2-7-0)

Opponent	Date		Pts	Opponent	Opp
Wis.-Superior ■	S12*		24	Concordia (St.P.)	14
St. John's (Minn.) ■	S19*		13	St. Olaf	35
Gust. Adolphus	S26		3	Bethel (Minn.)	32
Hamline ■	O 3		0	Concordia-M'head	55
Bethel (Minn.)	O10		0	St. John's (Minn.)	46
St. Thomas (Minn.) ■	O17		7	Carleton	20
Macalester	O24*		12	Hamline	33
Carleton ■	O31		3	St. Thomas (Minn.)	27
Concordia-M'head	N 7		29	Macalester	14
St. Olaf†	N13				

Colors: Maroon & Gray. Nickname: Auggies. **III**

AUGUSTANA (ILLINOIS) .... Rock Island, IL 61201
Bob Reade (13 yrs., 125-16-1)

Opponent	Date		Pts	Opponent	Opp
Loras ■	S12		41	North Central	0
Drake	S19		41	Minn.-Morris	8
North Park ■	O 3		62	Elmhurst	0
North Central	O10		41	North Park	0
Ill. Wesleyan	O17		17	Carroll (Wis.)	0
Elmhurst ■	O24		19	Wheaton (Ill.)	42
Millikin	O31		38	Ill. Wesleyan	35
Carthage ■	N 7		31	Carthage	12
Wheaton (Ill.) ■	N14		26	Millikin	0

Colors: Gold & Blue. Nickname: Vikings. **III**

AUGUSTANA (SOUTH DAKOTA) . Sioux Falls, SD 57102
Jim Heinitz (7 yrs., 29-46-1)

Opponent	Date		Pts	Opponent	Opp
Neb.-Kearney	S 3		10	Southwest St. (Minn.)	28
Gust. Adolphus ■	S12		22	Northern Iowa	45
North Dak. St. ■	S19		6	North Dak. St.	41
Nebraska-Omaha	S 26*		18	Nebraska-Omaha	26
Northern Colo. ■	O 3		6	Northern Colo.	51
North Dak.	O10		15	North Dak.	20
South Dak. ■	O17		14	South Dak.	27
South Dak. St.	O24		20	South Dak. St.	31
Morningside ■	O31		16	St. Cloud St.	23
St. Cloud St.	N 7		14	Mankato St.	28
Mankato St. ■	N14				

Colors: Blue & Yellow. Nickname: Vikings. **II**

AURORA .... Aurora, IL 60506
Jim Scott (6 yrs., 30-19-1)

Opponent	Date		Pts	Opponent	Opp
Anderson	S12		13	Wheaton (Ill.)	27
Trinity (Ill.)	S19		25	Concordia (Ill.)	13
Elmhurst ■	S26		0	Hope	12
Drake ■	O 3		14	Drake	7
Olivet Nazarene	O10		21	Olivet Nazarene	21
MacMurray	O17		35	North Park	14
Ill. Benedictine ■	O24		25	Ill. Benedictine	7
Chicago	O31		26	Trinity (Ill.)	7
Wartburg ■	N 7		25	Culver-Stockton	7

Colors: Royal Blue & White. Nickname: Spartans. **III**

■ Home games on each schedule.   *Night Games.

BALDWIN-WALLACE . . . . Berea, OH 44017
Bob Packard (11 yrs., 85-25-2)

Wittenberg	S12	45	Wittenberg	16
Hiram	S19	55	Hiram	6
Muskingum	S26*	21	Mount Union	18
Mount Union	O 3	50	Marietta	13
Otterbein ■	O10	10	Ohio Northern	6
Capital ■	O17	41	Muskingum	21
Marietta	O24	21	Capital	7
Heidelberg ■	O31	21	John Carroll	0
Ohio Northern ■	N 7	35	Otterbein	18
John Carroll ■	N14	21	Heidelberg	13
		10	Dayton	27

III Championship

Colors: Brown & Gold. Nickname: Yellow Jackets. III

BATES . . . . Lewiston, ME 04240
Rick Pardy (3 yrs., 17-11-2)

Trinity (Conn.)	S26	26	Amherst	26
Tufts ■	O 3	6	Wesleyan	26
Williams ■	O10	6	Middlebury	24
Wesleyan ■	O17	6	Williams	28
Middlebury	O24	25	Trinity (Conn.)	56
Colby ■	O31	7	Colby	41
Bowdoin	N 7	13	Bowdoin	34
Hamilton	N14	6	Tufts	16

Colors: Garnet. Nickname: Bobcats. III

BELOIT . . . . Beloit, WI 53511
Ed DeGeorge (15 yrs., 70-65-1)

Concordia (Wis.)	S12	17	Concordia (Wis.)	7
Cornell College ■	S19	35	Knox	7
Knox ■	S26	34	Grinnell	13
Coe	O 3	13	Cornell College	7
Ripon ■	O10	19	Ripon	14
Carroll (Wis.) ■	O17	20	Trinity (Ill.)	13
Lawrence	O24	26	Lawrence	12
St. Norbert	O31	7	St. Norbert	0
Lake Forest ■	N 7	41	Lake Forest	13
		10	Coe	26

Colors: Gold & Blue. Nickname: Buccaneers. III

BEMIDJI STATE . . . . Bemidji, MN 56601
Kris Diaz (3 yrs., 7-22-0)

St. John's (Minn.)	S12	0	St. John's (Minn.)	29
Wayne St. (Neb.) ■	S19	14	Mayville St.	10
Michigan Tech ■	S26	10	Northern St. (S.D.)	12
Minn.-Duluth	O 3	0	Michigan Tech	35
Southwest St. (Minn.)	O10	19	Minn.-Duluth	48
Moorhead St. ■	O17	28	Southwest St. (Minn.)	60
Winona St.	O24	7	Moorhead St.	42
Minn.-Morris ■	O31	28	Minn.-Morris	25
Northern St. (S.D.)	N 7	46	Southwest St. (Minn.)	47
Neb.-Kearney†	N14			

Colors: Kelly Green & White. Nickname: Beavers. II

BENTLEY . . . . Waltham, MA 02154
Peter Yetten (4 yrs., 19-11-1)

Curry ■	S11*	33	MIT	6
Stony Brook	S19	6	Stony Brook	24
Nichols ■	S25*	35	Curry	0
MIT ■	O 3	22	Assumption	12
Assumption ■	O10	19	Siena	7
Siena	O17	25	Western New Eng.	0
Western New Eng.	O24	7	Stonehill	14
Stonehill	O31	15	Worcester Tech	49
Upsala ■	N 7	6	St. John's (N.Y.)	22
St. John's (N.Y.) ■	N14			

Colors: Blue & Gold. Nickname: Falcons. III

BETHANY (WEST VIRGINIA) . . . . Bethany, WV 26032
Don Turner (20 yrs., 92-100-3)

Mercyhurst ■	S 5	16	Mercyhurst	27
Capital	S12	14	Capital	41
Duquesne ■	S19	58	Duquesne	40
Wash. & Jeff. ■	S26	21	Thiel	28
Thiel ■	O 3	23	Waynesburg	38
Grove City ■	O10	23	Gannon	19
Waynesburg	O17	9	Westminster (Pa.)	53
Gannon	O24	12	Wash. & Jeff.	27
Clinch Valley	O31	21	Grove City	27

Colors: Green & White. Nickname: Bison. III

BETHEL (MINNESOTA) . . . . St. Paul, MN 55112
Steve Johnson (4 yrs., 16-12-1)

Central (Iowa)	S12	35	Northwestern Minn.	6
Macalester	S19*	10	Hamline	7
Carleton ■	S26	32	Augsburg	3
Concordia-M'head	O 3	42	Gust. Adolphus	21
Augsburg ■	O10	13	Macalester	7
St. John's (Minn.)	O17	6	St. Olaf	17
Gust. Adolphus ■	O24	21	St. Thomas (Minn.)	28
Hamline	O31	3	Concordia-M'head	10
St. Olaf ■	N 7	51	Carleton	48
St. Thomas (Minn.) ■	N14			

Colors: Royal Blue & Gold. Nickname: Royals. III

BLACKBURN . . . . Carlinville, IL 62626
Don Flowers (1 yr., 0-9-0)

Chicago	S 5	0	Principia	26
Maranatha ■	S12	13	Illinois Col.	25
Illinois Col.	S19	12	Lakeland	47
North Park	S26	0	Concordia (Wis.)	43
Ky. Wesleyan ■	O 3	0	Eureka	46
Principia	O10	0	Greenville	77
MacMurray	O24	17	MacMurray	28
Crown (Ind.) ■	O31	7	Iowa Wesleyan	59
Concordia (Ill.) ■	N14	9	Concordia (Ill.)	28

Colors: Scarlet & Black. Nickname: Beavers. III

BLOOMSBURG . . . . Bloomsburg, PA 17815
Pete Adrian (6 yrs., 35-28-1)

Bucknell	S 5	21	Shippensburg	24
Shippensburg	S12	9	Lock Haven	14
Lock Haven ■	S19	21	Edinboro	23
East Stroudsburg†	S26	19	Kutztown	67
Millersville	O 3	37	Central Conn. St.	7
Clarion	O10	10	East Stroudsburg	20
Kutztown ■	O17	44	Cheyney	14
West Chester	O24	31	Mansfield	24
Cheyney	N 7	24	Millersville	17
Mansfield ■	N14	34	West Chester	12

Colors: Maroon & Gold. Nickname: Huskies. II

BLUFFTON . . . . Bluffton, OH 45817
Carlin Carpenter (13 yrs., 54-64-1)

Ohio Northern	S12	28	Hanover	56
Hanover ■	S19	3	Thomas More	34
Alma ■	S26	34	Anderson	33
Grove City	O 3	14	Olivet	26
Urbana	O17	3	Tiffin	39
Mt. St. Joseph	O24	12	Mt. St. Joseph	19
Wilmington (Ohio) ■	O31	12	Wilmington (Ohio)	14
Defiance ■	N 7	0	Defiance	46
Thomas More ■	N14	7	Urbana	14

Colors: Purple & White. Nickname: Beavers. III

BOWDOIN . . . . Brunswick, ME 04011
Howard Vandersea (16 yrs., 65-74-2)

Middlebury ■	S26	27	Middlebury	22
Amherst ■	O 3	14	Trinity (Conn.)	35
Hamilton	O17	19	Hamilton	35
Trinity (Conn.) ■	O24	27	Amherst	15
Wesleyan	O31	21	Tufts	13
Bates ■	N 7	14	Worcester Tech	48
Colby	N14	34	Bates	13
Tufts†	N29	13	Colby	28

Colors: White. Nickname: Polar Bears. III

BOWIE STATE . . . . Bowie, MD 20715
Sanders Shiver (3 yrs., 13-14-1)

Livingstone	S 5	3	Livingstone	19
Hampton	S12*	17	Hampton	14
N.C. Central ■	S19	49	N.C. Central	32
Virginia St. ■	S26	14	Virginia St.	19
Virginia Union ■	O 3	9	Virginia Union	41
Norfolk St. ■	O10	13	Norfolk St.	35
Elizabeth City St. ■	O17	7	Elizabeth City St.	24
Winston-Salem	O24*	20	American Int'l	17
Howard	O31	42	Central Conn. St.	21
American Int'l	N 7			
Wofford	N14			

Colors: Black & Gold. Nickname: Bulldogs. II

■ Home games on each schedule.   *Night Games.

1992 NCAA FOOTBALL

BRIDGEWATER (VIRGINIA) .... Bridgewater, VA 22812
Max Lowe (1st yr. as head coach)

1992 Schedule	Date	1991	Results	
Clinch Valley	S12	13	Ferrum	41
Emory & Henry	S19	0	Emory & Henry	16
Wesley ■	S26	0	Wesley	40
Hampden-Sydney ■	O 3	23	Hampden-Sydney	37
Methodist ■	O10	34	Methodist	0
Guilford	O17	6	Guilford	14
Frostburg St.	O24	14	Frostburg St.	63
Wash. & Lee ■	O31	29	Wash. & Lee	7
Randolph-Macon	N 7	7	Randolph-Macon	34
Davidson ■	N14	7	Davidson	30

Colors: Crimson & Gold. Nickname: Eagles.   III

BRIDGEWATER STATE (Mass.) Bridgewater, MA 02324
Peter Mazzaferro (28 yrs., 125-114-10)

1992 Schedule	Date	1991	Results	
Kean	S12	0	Mass.-Lowell	22
Maine Maritime	S19	30	St. John's (N.Y.)	12
Mass.-Boston ■	S26	22	Fitchburg St.	7
Fitchburg St.	O 3	26	Mass.-Dartmouth	25
Framingham St. ■	O10	45	Westfield St.	12
Westfield St.	O17	17	Worcester St.	13
Plymouth St.	O24	40	Curry	0
Worcester St. ■	O31	30	Framingham St.	19
Mass. Maritime	N 7	16	Mass. Maritime	13
Mass.-Dartmouth ■	N14	7	Mass.-Lowell	10

Colors: Red & White. Nickname: Bears.   III

BROCKPORT STATE .... Brockport, NY 14420
Ed Matejkovic (6 yrs., 22-37-0)

1992 Schedule	Date	1991	Results	
Denison	S 5	23	Tiffin	22
Jersey City St.	S12	41	Sacred Heart	0
Alfred	S19	13	Glassboro St.	36
Albany (N.Y.) ■	S26	30	Western Conn. St.	6
Buffalo St. ■	O 3	14	Buffalo St.	27
Cortland St. ■	O10	14	Cortland St.	52
Norwich ■	O17	35	Canisius	14
St. John Fisher	O24	30	Buffalo	30
Frostburg St. ■	O31	24	Mercyhurst	13
Mercyhurst ■	N 7	0	Ithaca	52

Colors: Green & Gold. Nickname: Golden Eagles.   III

BUENA VISTA .... Storm Lake, IA 50588
Kevin Twait (2 yrs., 2-18-0)

1992 Schedule	Date	1991	Results	
Cornell College	S12	14	Cornell College	23
Loras ■	S19	21	Upper Iowa	22
Simpson	S26	7	Central (Iowa)	28
Central (Iowa) ■	O 3	27	William Penn	28
Upper Iowa	O17	27	Dubuque	10
Wartburg ■	O24	21	Teikyo Westmar	57
William Penn	O31	14	Loras	50
Dubuque	N 7	19	Luther	29
Luther ■	N14	6	Wartburg	26
		0	Simpson	30

Colors: Navy Blue & Gold. Nickname: Beavers.   III

BUFFALO .... Buffalo, NY 14260
Jim Ward (1st yr. as head coach)

1992 Schedule	Date	1991	Results	
Edinboro	S 5	21	Lafayette	42
New Haven	S12	3	Montclair St.	7
Lafayette	S19	0	Westminster (Pa.)	38
Mansfield ■	S26	33	Hofstra	38
Morgan St. ■	O 3	49	Canisius	7
Colgate	O10	0	Ithaca	50
Hofstra ■	O24	30	Brockport St.	28
Central Conn. St.	O31	49	Duquesne	0
Central Fla.	N 7	21	Southern Conn. St.	49
		25	East Stroudsburg	45

Colors: Buffalo Blue, White & Red. Nickname: Bulls.   III

BUFFALO STATE .... Buffalo, NY 14222
Jerry Boyes (6 yrs., 19-36-0)

1992 Schedule	Date	1991	Results	
Mansfield ■	S12	34	Hobart	0
Canisius	S19*	24	Canisius	17
Cortland St. ■	S26	23	Geneva	6
Brockport St.	O 3	0	Cortland St.	35
Ithaca	O24	28	Brockport St.	14
Alfred ■	O31	28	Mercyhurst	21
Hobart ■	N 7	22	Gannon	13
Gannon ■	N14	23	Ithaca	41
		33	Alfred	13
		28	Grove City	26
		23	Worcester Tech	17

Colors: Orange & Black. Nickname: Bengals.   III

BUTLER .... Indianapolis, IN 46208
Ken LaRose (1st yr. as head coach)

1992 Schedule	Date	1991	Results	
Northern Mich. ■	S 5	28	Northern Mich.	0
St. Joseph's (Ind.) ■	S12	37	St. Joseph's (Ind.)	10
Grand Valley St.	S19	33	Grand Valley St.	0
Indianapolis ■	O 3	22	Indianapolis	3
Wayne St. (Mich.)	O10	12	Wayne St. (Mich.)	7
Valparaiso ■	O17	22	Valparaiso	2
Ferris St.	O24	6	Ferris St.	7
Ashland ■	O31	14	Ashland	12
Hillsdale ■	N 7	26	Hillsdale	20
Saginaw Valley	N14	13	Saginaw Valley	10
			II Championship	
		16	Pittsburg St.	26

Colors: Blue & White. Nickname: Bulldogs.   II

CAL LUTHERAN .... Thousand Oaks, CA 91360
Joe Harper (19 yrs., 115-76-3)

1992 Schedule	Date	1991	Results	
Pomona-Pitzer ■	S12	19	Azusa-Pacific	21
Azusa-Pacific ■	S26	0	Cal St. Hayward	27
San Diego	O 3	23	UC Santa Barb.	33
Claremont-M-S	O10	21	San Diego	20
Occidental ■	O17	0	Sonoma St.	28
Menlo ■	O24	6	La Verne	28
Redlands	O31*	12	Occidental	0
La Verne ■	N 7	33	Claremont-M-S	7
Whittier	N14*	28	Whittier	9
		21	Redlands	10

Colors: Purple & Gold. Nickname: Kingsmen.   III

CAL POLY SLO .... San Luis Obispo, CA 93407
Lyle Setencich (9 yrs., 55-40-1)

1992 Schedule	Date	1991	Results	
North Dak. St.	S12*	28	UC Chico	31
Cal St. Chico	S19	7	Sonoma St.	27
Sonoma St. ■	O 3*	23	Angelo St.	13
UC Davis	O10*	66	Neb.-Kearney	3
Cal St. Sacramento ■	O17*	28	Pacific (Cal.)	63
Cal St. Northridge	O24*	20	Cal St. Sacramento	21
Santa Clara	O31	28	Cal St. Northridge	16
Southern Utah ■	N 7*	15	Santa Clara	10
Portland St.	N14*	21	Southern Utah	33
		35	Portland St.	55

Colors: Green & Gold. Nickname: Mustangs.   II

CAL STATE CHICO .... Chico, CA 95929
Gary Houser (2 yrs., 10-10-0)

1992 Schedule	Date	1991	Results	
Santa Clara ■	S 5	26	Santa Clara	32
Montana	S12	0	Carroll (Mont.)	6
Cal Poly SLO ■	S19	52	UC Santa Barb.	31
St. Mary's (Cal.) ■	O 3	14	St. Mary's (Cal.)	38
Cal St. Sacramento	O10*	21	Cal St. Sacramento	63
Cal St. Hayward ■	O17*	17	San Fran. St.	34
San Fran. St.	O24	24	UC Davis	20
UC Davis	O31*	17	Sonoma St.	38
Sonoma St. ■	N 7*	17	Humboldt St.	29
Humboldt St.	N14*	30	Cal St. Hayward	8

Colors: Cardinal & White. Nickname: Wildcats.   II

CAL STATE HAYWARD .... Hayward, CA 94542
Tim Tierney (17 yrs., 69-98-5)

1992 Schedule	Date	1991	Results	
San Diego	S 5*	27	Cal Lutheran	0
St. Mary's (Cal.) ■	S12	19	St. Mary's (Cal.)	51
Azusa-Pacific ■	S19	21	Santa Clara	35
Redlands	O 3*	21	San Diego	20
Cal St. Chico	O17*	31	UC Santa Barb.	42
Sonoma St.	O24	13	Sonoma St.	22
San Fran. St. ■	O31	17	San Fran. St.	32
Humboldt St. ■	N 7*	6	Humboldt St.	6
UC Davis ■	N14	13	UC Davis	16
		8	Cal St. Chico	30

Colors: Red, Black & White. Nickname: Pioneers.   II

CAL STATE NORTHRIDGE .... Northridge, CA 91330
Bob Burt (7 yrs., 43-32-0)

1992 Schedule	Date	1991	Results	
Cal St. Fullerton ■	S 5*	13	Eastern Wash.	20
UC Davis ■	S12*	12	Eastern N. Mex.	10
San Fran. St. ■	S19*	10	Cal St. Fullerton	17
Central Okla. ■	S26*	9	Central Okla.	7
Idaho	O 3	17	UC Davis	29
Santa Clara	O17	45	Santa Clara	27
Cal Poly SLO ■	O24*	16	Cal Poly SLO	28
Southern Utah	O31	13	Southern Utah	56
Portland St.	N 7*	13	Portland St.	38
Cal St. Sacramento ■	N14*	12	Cal St. Sacramento	55

Colors: Red, White & Black. Nickname: Matadors.   II

■ Home games on each schedule.   *Night Games.

CAL STATE SACRAMENTO .... Sacramento, CA 95819
Bob Mattos (14 yrs., 76-71-2)

Montana St. ■ ....S 5*	43	Pacific (Cal.) 40
Abilene Christian ■ S19*	19	Montana St. 17
Cal St. Fullerton S26*	45	Abilene Christian 7
UC Davis ....O 3*	50	UC Davis 18
Cal St. Chico ■ O10*	63	Cal St. Chico 21
Cal Poly SLO O17*	21	Cal Poly SLO 20
Southern Utah O24	19	Southern Utah 22
Portland St. ■ O31*	19	Portland St. 35
Santa Clara ■ ....N 7*	33	Santa Clara 32
Cal St. Northridge N14*	55	Cal St. Northridge 12

Colors: Green & Gold.   Nickname: Hornets.   II

CALIFORNIA (PENNSYLVANIA) ... California, PA 15419
Jeff Petrucci (11 yrs., 51-59-2)

West Liberty St. ■ ......S 5	16	Kutztown 42
West Va. Wesleyan S12	7	New Haven 31
Fairmont St. S19	10	Ashland 51
Kutztown ■ S26	0	Shippensburg 45
East Stroudsburg ....O 3	33	Cheyney 8
Slippery Rock ■ O10	3	Slippery Rock 20
Indiana (Pa.) O17	8	Indiana (Pa.) 10
Edinboro ■ O24	10	Edinboro 45
Clarion O31	6	Clarion 26
Lock Haven ■ ....N 7	7	Lock Haven 10
Shippensburg N14		

Colors: Red & Black.   Nickname: Vulcans.   II

CAMERON ....Lawton, OK 73505
Frank Crosson (2 yrs., 5-15-0)

Mo. Southern St. ■ ....S 5*	16	Mo. Southern St. 34
Tarleton St. ■ S12*	24	Tarleton St. 7
East Central (Okla.) ■ S19*	19	East Central (Okla.) 20
West Tex. St. ■ S26*	7	Texas A&I 30
Texas A&I ....O 3*	51	Prairie View 6
Eastern N. Mex. O17*	16	Eastern N. Mex. 20
Abilene Christian ■ O24*	10	Abilene Christian 3
Angelo St. O31*	0	Angelo St. 34
Central Okla. ....N 7	22	Central Okla. 24
East Tex. St. ■ N14	7	East Tex. St. 39

Colors: Black & Gold.   Nickname: Aggies.   II

CANISIUS ....Buffalo, NY 14208
Barry Mynter (16 yrs., 75-78-2)

St. Francis (Pa.) S12	17	Buffalo St. 24
Buffalo St. ■ S19*	6	St. Lawrence 39
St. Lawrence ■ S26	21	St. John Fisher 0
Mercyhurst ....O 3	15	Mercyhurst 21
St. John Fisher O10	19	Buffalo 49
Frostburg St. ■ O17	14	Brockport St. 35
Hobart O24	34	Hobart 9
Duquesne ■ O31	14	Cortland St. 32
Alfred ....N 7	3	Alfred 22
Marist ■ N14		

Colors: Blue & Gold.   Nickname: Golden Griffins.   III

CAPITAL ....Columbus, OH 43209
Roger Welsh (5 yrs., 30-27-3)

Bethany (W.Va.) ■ S12	41	Bethany (W.Va.) 14
John Carroll ■ S19	16	Otterbein 7
Hiram S26	7	John Carroll 7
Marietta ....O 3	14	Mount Union 21
Heidelberg ■ O10	30	Hiram 2
Baldwin-Wallace O17	26	Ohio Northern 10
Muskingum O24	7	Baldwin-Wallace 21
Ohio Northern ■ O31	29	Heidelberg 48
Mount Union ....N 7	28	Muskingum 14
Otterbein ■ N14	34	Marietta 6

Colors: Purple & White.   Nickname: Crusaders.   III

CARLETON ....Northfield, MN 55057
Bob Sullivan (13 yrs., 68-56-0)

Northwestern Minn. ■ S12	22	Wis.-Platteville 30
Hamline ■ S19*	30	Concordia-M'head 20
Bethel (Minn.) S26	23	St. John's (Minn.) 56
St. Thomas (Minn.) ■ .....O 3	19	St. Thomas (Minn.) 28
Macalester O10	13	Hamline 19
St. Olaf O17	59	Augsburg 7
Concordia-M'head ■ O24	21	Gust. Adolphus 28
Augsburg O31	40	Macalester 0
St. John's (Minn.) ■ .....N 7	48	Bethel (Minn.) 51
Gust. Adolphus† N14*		

Colors: Maize & Blue.   Nickname: Knights.   III

CARNEGIE MELLON ....Pittsburgh, PA 15213
Rich Lackner (6 yrs., 44-14-2)

Juniata ■ ....S 5*	12	Allegheny 23
Washington (Mo.) S12*	20	Washington (Mo.) 12
Rochester ■ S19	37	Chicago 0
Allegheny ....O 3	28	Duquesne 14
Trinity (Tex.) O10*	20	Adrian 12
Chicago ■ O17	18	Rochester 14
Duquesne ■ O24	43	Grove City 14
Grove City ■ O31	55	Wooster 14
Catholic ....N 7	25	Coast Guard 19
Case Reserve N14	43	Case Reserve 0

Colors: Cardinal, White & Gray.   Nickname: Tartans.   III

CARROLL (WISCONSIN) ....Waukesha, WI 53186
Merle Masonholder (10 yrs., 36-53-0)

North Central ■ ....S 5	19	Ill. Wesleyan 49
Kalamazoo S19	20	Carthage 27
Illinois Col. S26	13	Millikin 7
Monmouth (Ill.) ■ ....O 3	27	North Central 6
Lawrence ■ O10	0	Augustana (Ill.) 17
Beloit O17	28	Elmhurst 20
Lake Forest ■ O24	19	North Park 8
Ripon O31	36	Ill. Benedictine 15
St. Norbert ■ ....N 7	15	Wheaton (Ill.) 21

Colors: Orange & White.   Nickname: Pioneers.   III

CARSON-NEWMAN ....Jefferson City, TN 37760
Ken Sparks (12 yrs., 111-34-1)

Fayetteville St. ■ ....S 5	44	Fayetteville St. 21
Howard Payne ■ S12	6	Central St. (Ohio) 3
Elon S19	52	Wingate 35
Catawba ....O 3	24	Elon 0
Wingate ■ O10	24	Catawba 3
Mars Hill O17	57	Mars Hill 15
Gardner-Webb ■ O24	52	Gardner-Webb 14
Lenoir-Rhyne O31*	42	Lenoir-Rhyne 25
New Haven ....N 7	69	St. Francis (Ill.) 17
Presbyterian ■ N14	48	Presbyterian 20
		NAIA Div. I Championship	
		21 Western St. 38

Colors: Orange & Blue.   Nickname: Eagles.   II

CARTHAGE ....Kenosha, WI 53140
Jack Synold (4 yrs., 12-24-0)

Anderson S19	55	North Park 6
Ill. Benedictine S26	21	Carroll (Wis.) 20
Elmhurst ....O 3	22	Wheaton (Ill.) 45
Millikin ■ O10	0	Ill. Wesleyan 28
Wheaton (Ill.) ■ O17	41	Ill. Benedictine 35
Ill. Wesleyan O24	10	Millikin 34
North Park O31	0	North Central 12
Augustana (Ill.) ■ ......N 7	12	Augustana (Ill.) 31
North Central N14	16	Elmhurst 32

Colors: Red & White.   Nickname: Redmen.   III

CASE RESERVE ....Cleveland, OH 44106
Ron Stuckey (5 yrs., 25-24-0)

Rochester S12	7	Rochester 14
Washington (Mo.) S19*	22	Washington (Mo.) 21
Allegheny S26	36	Earlham 15
Wittenberg ■ ....O 3	20	Wooster 23
Kenyon O10	14	Wittenberg 13
Oberlin ■ O17	16	Chicago 15
Denison O24	41	Ohio Wesleyan 16
Ohio Wesleyan ■ O31	15	Denison 14
Chicago ....N 7	41	Oberlin 0
Carnegie Mellon ■ N14	0	Carnegie Mellon 43

Colors: Blue, Gray & White.   Nickname: Spartans.   III

CATAWBA ....Salisbury, NC 28144
J. D. Haglan (1 yr., 7-3-0)

Lees-McRae ■ ....S 5	21	Lees-McRae 13
Mars Hill S19*	33	Mars Hill 6
Wofford ■ S26	16	Wofford 22
Carson-Newman ■ ....O 3	3	Carson-Newman 24
Presbyterian O10	13	Presbyterian 21
Gardner-Webb ■ O17	24	Gardner-Webb 21
Elon ■ O24	20	Elon 14
Newberry ■ O31	33	Newberry 7
Wingate ....N 7	46	Wingate 20
Lenoir-Rhyne ■ N14	20	Lenoir-Rhyne 10

Colors: Blue & White.   Nickname: Indians.   II

■ Home games on each schedule.   *Night Games.

CATHOLIC .... Washington, DC 20064
Rick Novak (2 yrs., 10-10-0)

1992 Opponent	Date	Pts	1991 Opponent	Pts
St. John Fisher	S 5	32	Gallaudet	24
Swarthmore ■	S12	7	Frostburg St.	29
Randolph-Macon ■	S19	10	Randolph-Macon	7
Iona	S26	19	Iona	24
Methodist	O 3	14	Wesley	41
Duquesne	O10*	17	Newport News App.	13
Gallaudet ■	O17	20	Methodist	0
Sacred Heart	O24	17	Georgetown	21
Georgetown ■	O31	21	Western Conn. St.	23
Carnegie Mellon ■	N 7	10	Chicago	6

Colors: Cardinal & Black.   Nickname: Cardinals.   III

CENTRE .... Danville, KY 40422
Joe McDaniel (26 yrs., 135-98-4)

1992 Opponent	Date	Pts	1991 Opponent	Pts
Hampden-Sydney	S12	26	Hampden-Sydney	42
Maryville (Tenn.) ■	S19	5	Maryville (Tenn.)	21
Wash. & Lee ■	S26	24	Wash. & Lee	7
Sewanee ■	O 3	3	Sewanee	10
Millsaps	O10	7	Millsaps	14
Trinity (Tex.) ■	O24	14	Mt. St. Joseph	13
Ky. Wesleyan ■	O31	14	Thomas More	20
Davidson	N 7	15	Ky. Wesleyan	13
Rhodes	N14	14	Trinity (Tex.)	8
		16	Rhodes	12

Colors: Gold & White.   Nickname: Colonels.   III

CENTRAL ARKANSAS .... Conway, AR 72032
Mike Isom (2 yrs., 17-6-2)

1992 Opponent	Date	Pts	1991 Opponent	Pts
East Tex. St. ■	S 5*	9	Mississippi Col.	34
Delta St.	S12*	3	Mississippi Val.	35
Fort Hays St.	S19*	30	Delta St.	15
Tenn.-Chatt.	S26*	17	Southwestern Okla.	17
Ouachita Bapt. ■	O 3*	21	Ouachita Bapt.	6
Harding	O10*	6	Harding	6
Ark.-Monticello ■	O17*	21	Ark.-Monticello	14
Henderson St.	O24*	21	Henderson St.	20
Southern Ark. ■	O31	21	Southern Ark.	20
Arkansas Tech	N 7	26	Arkansas Tech	14
		38	Moorhead St.	18
		19	Central St. (Ohio)	16
		NAIA Div. I Championship		
		30	Northeastern Okla.	14

Colors: Purple & Gray.   Nickname: Bears.   II

CHADRON STATE .... Chadron, NE 69337
Brad Smith (5 yrs., 28-20-1)

1992 Opponent	Date	Pts	1991 Opponent	Pts
South Dak. Tech	S12	35	Montana Tech	35
Black Hills St.	S19	47	South Dak. Tech	14
Peru St.†	S26	49	Black Hills St.	14
Adams St.	O 3	21	Fort Lewis	19
N.M. Highlands ■	O10	28	Mesa St.	33
Colorado Mines ■	O17	9	Fort Hays St.	10
Western St.	O24	48	Colorado Mines	28
Fort Hays St. ■	O31	49	Western St.	51
Fort Lewis	N 7	19	Neb.-Kearney	30
Mesa St. ■	N14	28	Wayne St. (Neb.)	55
		10	Adams St.	0

Colors: Cardinal & White.   Nickname: Eagles.   II

CENTRAL CONNECTICUT STATE. New Britain, CT 06050
To be named

1992 Opponent	Date	Pts	1991 Opponent	Pts
Hofstra	S 5*	35	Mansfield	35
Trenton St.	S11*	19	Hofstra	30
Glassboro St. ■	S19	14	West Chester	34
American Int'l	S26	34	New Haven	41
New Haven ■	O 3	7	Bloomsburg	37
Springfield ■	O16*	26	Springfield	23
Buffalo ■	O31	12	Lenoir-Rhyne	20
Southern Conn. St.	N 7	18	American Int'l	21
Wm. Paterson ■	N14	21	Bowie St.	42
		20	Southern Conn. St.	42

Colors: Blue & White.   Nickname: Blue Devils.   II

CHARLESTON SOUTHERN .... Charleston, SC 29411
David Dowd (1 yr., 3-7-0)

1992 Opponent	Date	Pts	1991 Opponent	Pts
Methodist ■	S 5	8	Methodist	18
Gardner-Webb	S12	0	Mars Hill	29
Newport News App. ■	S19	13	Newport News App.	9
Guilford ■	S26	6	Guilford	40
Newberry	O 3	19	Ala.-Birmingham	33
East Tenn. St.	O10	17	Davidson	23
Ala.-Birmingham	O17	35	Gallaudet	16
Davidson	O24	0	South Caro. St.	12
South Caro. St. ■	N14	14	Frostburg St.	19

Colors: Blue & Gold.   Nickname: Buccaneers.

CENTRAL (IOWA) .... Pella, IA 50219
Ron Schipper (31 yrs., 242-60-3)

1992 Opponent	Date	Pts	1991 Opponent	Pts
Bethel (Minn.) ■	S12	26	Gust. Adolphus	25
Dubuque	S19	12	Loras	3
Wartburg ■	S26	28	Buena Vista	7
Buena Vista	O 3	35	Dubuque	7
William Penn ■	O10	3	Simpson	12
Simpson	O17	83	William Penn	18
Loras	O24	41	Upper Iowa	0
Upper Iowa ■	O31	10	Wartburg	6
Luther	N 7	22	Luther	21

Colors: Red & White.   Nickname: Flying Dutchmen.   III

CHEYNEY .... Cheyney, PA 19319
Chris Roulhac (1st yr. as head coach)

1992 Opponent	Date	Pts	1991 Opponent	Pts
Delaware St.†	S 5	7	Central St. (Ohio)	87
Morris Brown ■	S12	14	Morris Brown	21
Howard†	S19	3	Savannah St.	62
West Chester ■	O 3	0	East Stroudsburg	28
East Stroudsburg	O10	8	Calif. (Pa.)	33
Slippery Rock ■	O17	6	Mansfield	41
Mansfield ■	O24	32	Millersville	42
Millersville	O31*	14	Bloomsburg	44
Bloomsburg ■	N 7	14	Kutztown	35
Kutztown	N14	14	West Chester	30
		6	Wofford	52

Colors: Blue & White.   Nickname: Wolves.   II

CENTRAL MISSOURI STATE.. Warrensburg, MO 64093
Terry Noland (9 yrs., 50-46-1)

1992 Opponent	Date	Pts	1991 Opponent	Pts
North Ala.	S 5*	14	North Ala.	28
Mo. Southern St. ■	S19*	6	Indiana St.	35
Southwest Baptist	S26	0	Mo. Southern St.	35
Emporia St.	O 3	24	Southwest Baptist	17
Northwest Mo. St.	O10	17	Emporia St.	44
Washburn	O17	30	Northwest Mo. St.	27
Northeast Mo. St. ■	O24	21	Washburn	0
Missouri-Rolla ■	O31	38	Northeast Mo. St.	37
Mo. Western St.	N 7	7	Missouri-Rolla	13
Pittsburg St.	N14	31	Mo. Western St.	24
		14	Pittsburg St.	28

Colors: Cardinal & Black.   Nickname: Mules.   II

CHICAGO .... Chicago, IL 60637
Greg Quick (3 yrs., 3-26-0)

1992 Opponent	Date	Pts	1991 Opponent	Pts
Blackburn ■	S 5	13	Concordia (Ill.)	17
Concordia (Ill.)	S12	0	Carnegie Mellon	37
Lawrence ■	S19	6	Kalamazoo	18
Kalamazoo	S26	7	Rochester	28
Rochester ■	O 3	12	Ky. Wesleyan	15
Drake	O10	15	Case Reserve	16
Carnegie Mellon	O17	0	Trinity (Tex.)	6
Washington (Mo.) ■	O24	21	Quincy	23
Aurora ■	O31	7	Washington (Mo.)	25
Case Reserve	N 7	6	Catholic	10

Colors: White & Maroon.   Nickname: Maroons.   III

CENTRAL OKLAHOMA .... Edmond, OK 73034
Gary Howard (15 yrs., 82-66-5)

1992 Opponent	Date	Pts	1991 Opponent	Pts
Northwest Mo. St.	S 5	14	Northwest Mo. St.	38
Fort Hays St.	S12*	24	Southern Utah	21
Southern Utah	S19*	7	Cal St. Northridge	9
Cal St. Northridge ■	S26*	21	East Tex. St.	51
East Tex. St.	O 3	7	Abilene Christian	24
Abilene Christian ■	O10*	13	Texas A&I	23
Texas A&I	O17*	10	Angelo St.	41
Angelo St. ■	O24*	9	Western N. Mex.	6
Cameron ■	N 7	24	Cameron	22
Eastern N. Mex.	N14	12	Eastern N. Mex.	21

Colors: Bronze & Blue.   Nickname: Bronchos.   II

CLAREMONT-MUDD-SCRIPPS... Claremont, CA 91711
John Zinda (23 yrs., 87-112-3)

1992 Opponent	Date	Pts	1991 Opponent	Pts
Rhodes ■	S12	3	Whittier	15
San Diego	S26*	5	Menlo	17
Menlo ■	O 3	3	Redlands	44
Cal Lutheran ■	O10	14	Occidental	17
Redlands	O17*	9	Pomona-Pitzer	22
Pomona-Pitzer	O24	2	San Diego	30
Whittier ■	O31	7	Cal Lutheran	33
Occidental	N 7*	10	La Verne	34
La Verne ■	N14	6	Whittier	29

Colors: Maroon, Gold & White.   Nickname: Stags.   III

■ Home games on each schedule.   *Night Games.

CLARION .... Clarion, PA 16214
Gene Sobolewski (9 yrs., 49-42-0)

Youngstown St. ....S 5*	24	Fairmont St. 21	
New Haven ....S 19	28	Westminster (Pa.) 14	
Westminster (Pa.) ■ ....S 26	42	New Haven 48	
Edinboro ....O 3	19	Indiana (Pa.) 41	
Bloomsburg O10	9	Edinboro 17	
Lock Haven O17	33	Kutztown 27	
Shippensburg O24	26	Lock Haven 27	
Calif. (Pa.) ■ ....O 31	34	Shippensburg 19	
Slippery Rock ....N 7	26	Calif. (Pa.) 6	
Indiana (Pa.) ■ N14	36	Slippery Rock 43	

Colors: Blue & Gold. Nickname: Golden Eagles. II

CLARK ATLANTA .... Atlanta, GA 30314
Willie Hunter (2 yrs., 10-9-1)

Morris Brown ....S 7	6	Morris Brown 29	
West Ga. ■ ....S 26	14	Livingstone 33	
Fort Valley St.† ....O 3*	16	Johnson Smith 16	
Tuskegee ■ O10	42	West Ga. 14	
Kentucky St. ■ O17	12	Fort Valley St. 14	
Miles O24	6	Miles 53	
Albany St. (Ga.) ....O 31	6	Albany St. (Ga.) 14	
Alabama A&M ....N 7	28	Alabama A&M 18	
Morehouse ■ N14	19	Morehouse 31	

Colors: Red, Black & Gray. Nickname: Panthers. II

COAST GUARD .... New London, CT 06320
Tom Bell (17 yrs., 89-59-6)

Mass.-Lowell S12*	14	Rensselaer 7	
Rensselaer ■ S19	46	Worcester Tech 34	
Stony Brook ■ S26	17	Norwich 7	
Norwich ....O 3	13	Wesleyan 16	
Western Conn. St. ■ O17	7	Union (N.Y.) 37	
Union (N.Y.) O24	21	Trinity (Conn.) 14	
Plymouth St. ■ ....O 31	19	Carnegie Mellon 25	
Worcester Tech ....N 7	39	Pace 14	
Merchant Marine N14	25	Merchant Marine 20	

Colors: Blue, White & Orange. Nickname: Cadets, Bears. III

COE .... Cedar Rapids, IA 52402
D. J. LeRoy (9 yrs., 65-32-2)

Wartburg S12	20	Wartburg 10	
William Penn ■ S19	7	Simpson 49	
Ripon S26	42	Lawrence 20	
Beloit ■ ....O 3	31	Upper Iowa 7	
Grinnell O10	77	Grinnell 26	
Illinois Col. O17	35	Illinois Col. 6	
Monmouth (Ill.) ■ O24	32	Monmouth (Ill.) 21	
Knox ....O 31	56	Knox 0	
Cornell College ■ ....N 7	33	Cornell College 8	
	26	Beloit 10	
III Championship			
	2	St. John's (Minn.) 75	

Colors: Crimson & Gold. Nickname: Kohawks. III

COLBY .... Waterville, ME 04901
Tom Austin (6 yrs., 17-31-0)

Williams ....S 26	6	Trinity (Conn.) 10	
Middlebury ■ ....O 3	21	Hamilton 17	
Wesleyan ■ O10	29	Tufts 42	
Amherst O17	30	Wesleyan 0	
Hamilton ■ O24	14	Williams 32	
Bates ....O 31	41	Bates 7	
Tufts ....N 7	31	Middlebury 16	
Bowdoin ■ N14	28	Bowdoin 13	

Colors: Blue & Gray. Nickname: White Mules. III

COLORADO COLLEGE .... Colorado Springs, CO 80903
Craig Rundle (5 yrs., 36-23-0)

Grinnell ■ S12	17	Pomona-Pitzer 13	
Pomona-Pitzer ■ S19	9	Millsaps 19	
Greenville IL ■ ....S 26	52	Tabor 0	
Austin ■ O10	6	St. Mary (Kan.) 26	
Trinity (Tex.) O17*	19	Sterling 28	
Millsaps O24	21	Trinity (Tex.) 14	
Hardin-Simmons ....O 31*	14	Hardin-Simmons 41	
Washington (Mo.) ■ ....N 7	19	Washington (Mo.) 23	
Hastings N14	0	Redlands 40	

Colors: Black & Gold. Nickname: Tigers. III

COLORADO SCHOOL OF MINES ..... Golden, CO 80401
Marvin Kay (23 yrs., 74-139-4)

Midland Lutheran ....S 5	19	Hastings 7	
Doane S12	49	Mesa St. 20	
Hastings ■ S19	24	Fort Hays St. 28	
Western St. ■ ....O 3	55	Midland Lutheran 13	
Adams St. ■ O10	18	Western St. 56	
Chadron St. O17	42	Fort Lewis 26	
Fort Hays St. O24	28	Chadron St. 48	
Fort Lewis ....O 31	34	Adams St. 21	
Mesa St. ....N 7	8	St. Mary's (Cal.) 49	
N.M. Highlands N14	40	Rocky Mountain 31	

Colors: Silver & Blue. Nickname: Orediggers. II

CONCORDIA (ILLINOIS) .... River Forest, IL 60305
Jim Braun (13 yrs., 49-63-3)

Chicago ■ S12	17	Chicago 13	
N'western Col. (Wis.) S19	13	Aurora 25	
Maranatha ■ S26	14	Lakeland 17	
Lakeland ....O 3	28	Eureka 42	
Eureka ■ O10	5	Concordia (Wis.) 24	
Concordia (Wis.) O17	7	Greenville 42	
Greenville ■ O24	28	MacMurray 40	
MacMurray ■ ....O 31	28	Blackburn 9	
Principia ....N 7			
Blackburn N14			

Colors: Maroon & Gold. Nickname: Cougars. III

CONCORDIA-MOORHEAD .... Moorhead, MN 56560
Jim Christopherson (23 yrs., 162-67-5)

Moorhead St. S12	16	Moorhead St. 21	
Gust. Adolphus ■ S19	20	Carleton 30	
Hamline S26	20	Hamline 30	
Bethel (Minn.) ■ ....O 3	55	Augsburg 0	
St. Thomas (Minn.) O10	20	Gust. Adolphus 30	
Macalester ■ O17	34	Macalester 0	
Carleton O24	13	St. Olaf 24	
St. Olaf ....O 31	10	Bethel (Minn.) 3	
Augsburg ■ ....N 7	7	St. John's (Minn.) 24	
St. John's (Minn.)† N14			

Colors: Maroon & Gold. Nickname: Cobbers. III

CORNELL COLLEGE .... Mt. Vernon, IA 52314
Steve Miller (13 yrs., 58-58-3)

Buena Vista ■ S12	23	Buena Vista 14	
Beloit S19	37	Concordia (St.P.) 0	
St. Norbert ■ S26	14	Ripon 6	
Lake Forest ....O 3	7	Beloit 13	
Knox ■ O10	29	Knox 12	
Monmouth (Ill.) O17	21	Monmouth (Ill.) 16	
Grinnell O24	38	Grinnell 35	
Illinois Col. ■ ....O 31	28	Illinois Col. 7	
Coe ....N 7	8	Coe 33	

Colors: Purple & White. Nickname: Rams. III

CORTLAND STATE .... Cortland, NY 13045
Dave Murray (2 yrs., 17-5-0)

Ferrum ■ ....S 5	71	St. John Fisher 0	
Montclair St. S12	67	Wilkes 6	
Mansfield S19	31	Mansfield 17	
Buffalo St. ....S 26	35	Buffalo St. 0	
Brockport St. O10	52	Brockport St. 14	
Albany (N.Y.) O17	34	Albany (N.Y.) 21	
Springfield O24	13	Springfield 20	
Wash. & Jeff. ....O 31	32	Canisius 14	
Ithaca ■ ....N 7	14	Ithaca 23	
Southern Conn. St. ■ N14	6	Hofstra 40	
	21	Plymouth St. 6	

Colors: Red & White. Nickname: Red Dragons. III

CURRY .... Milton, MA 02186
John Doherty (9 yrs., 41-38-0)

Bentley S11*	7	Framingham St. 27	
Western New Eng. ■ S19	9	Worcester St. 26	
Framingham St. ■ ....S 26	3	Mass.-Boston 8	
Stonehill ....O 3	0	Bentley 35	
Nichols ■ O10	0	Plymouth St. 58	
Assumption O24	6	Mass.-Lowell 42	
Hartwick ■ ....O 31	0	Bri'water (Mass.) 40	
MIT ....N 7	6	Nichols 41	
	3	Maine Maritime 27	

Colors: Purple & White. Nickname: Colonels. III

■ Home games on each schedule.   *Night Games.

DAVIDSON .... Davidson, NC 28036
Dave Fagg (6 yrs., 17-40-1)

Opponent	Date	Pts	1991 Result	Pts
Guilford ■	S 5	3	Guilford	21
Sewanee	S12	32	Clinch Valley	7
Rhodes	S19	9	Rhodes	13
Emory & Henry ■	S 26	14	Emory & Henry	39
Wash. & Lee ■	O10	16	Wash. & Lee	14
Methodist	O17	28	Methodist	30
Charleston So. ■	O24	33	Charleston So.	17
Hampden-Sydney	O31	14	Hampden-Sydney	56
Centre ■	N 7	30	Bridgewater (Va.)	7
Bridgewater (Va.)	N14			

Colors: Red & Black.   Nickname: Wildcats.   III

DAYTON .... Dayton, OH 45469
Mike Kelly (11 yrs., 109-21-1)

Opponent	Date	Pts	1991 Result	Pts
Wis.-Platteville ■	S12*	42	Urbana	0
Wheaton (Ill.)	S19	24	John Carroll	7
Urbana	S26	50	Anderson	7
Mt. St. Joseph ■	O 3*	48	Mercyhurst	21
Mercyhurst	O10	13	Drake	0
Drake	O17	21	Northwood	6
Thomas More ■	O24	35	Gannon	6
Evansville ■	O31	31	Ferrum	12
Hofstra	N 7	14	Hofstra	7
Mt. Senario ■	N14	48	Evansville	6
III Championship				
		27	Baldwin-Wallace	10
		28	Allegheny	25
		19	St. John's (Minn.)	7
		20	Ithaca	34

Colors: Red & Blue.   Nickname: Flyers.   III

DEFIANCE .... Defiance, OH 43512
Malen Luke (4 yrs., 19-19-0)

Opponent	Date	Pts	1991 Result	Pts
Hanover ■	S 5	30	Manchester	7
Adrian	S19	20	Anderson	17
Olivet	S26	3	Adrian	26
Kalamazoo ■	O 3	43	Olivet	14
Mt. St. Joseph ■	O10	14	Wilmington (Ohio)	10
Wilmington (Ohio) ■	O17	24	West Liberty St.	10
Urbana ■	O24	44	Urbana	6
Thomas More	O31	46	Bluffton	0
Bluffton	N 7	28	Mt. St. Joseph	13
Wooster ■	N14	16	Thomas More	17

Colors: Purple & Gold.   Nickname: Yellow Jackets.   III

DELAWARE VALLEY .... Doylestown, PA 18901
Bill Manlove (23 yrs., 182-53-1)

Opponent	Date	Pts	1991 Result	Pts
Wagner ■	S12	30	Wagner	40
Juniata ■	S19	28	Juniata	20
Lycoming	S26	10	Lycoming	41
Albright ■	O 3	13	Albright	14
Wilkes ■	O10	9	Susquehanna	31
Susquehanna	O17	35	Wilkes	24
Lebanon Valley ■	O24	20	Lebanon Valley	31
Moravian	O31	15	Moravian	35
Wesley	N 7	14	Wesley	45
Widener	N14	21	Widener	8

Colors: Green & Gold.   Nickname: Aggies.   III

DELTA STATE .... Cleveland, MS 38733
Don Skelton (4 yrs., 18-21-2)

Opponent	Date	Pts	1991 Result	Pts
Tenn.-Martin ■	S 5*	7	Southern Miss.	25
Central Ark. ■	S12*	35	Henderson St.	6
Henderson St.	S19*	15	Central Ark.	30
North Ala. ■	S26*	31	North Ala.	6
Northeast La.	O 3*	0	Jacksonville St.	9
Jacksonville St.	O10	37	Tenn.-Martin	27
Livingston ■	O24*	18	Livingston	25
West Ga.	O31	15	West Ga.	20
Valdosta St.	N 7	37	Valdosta St.	34
Mississippi Col.	N14	10	Mississippi Col.	27

Colors: Green & White.   Nickname: Statesmen.   II

DENISON .... Granville, OH 43023
Keith Piper (38 yrs., 196-138-17)

Opponent	Date	Pts	1991 Result	Pts
Brockport St. ■	S 5	14	Albion	35
Muskingum	S12	3	Muskingum	10
Oberlin ■	S19	15	Wabash	16
Ohio Wesleyan	O 3	20	Allegheny	63
Earlham ■	O10	21	Ohio Wesleyan	28
Wooster	O17	33	Kenyon	7
Case Reserve ■	O24	8	Oberlin	0
Allegheny	O31	14	Case Reserve	15
Wittenberg ■	N 7	7	Wittenberg	21
Kenyon	N14	21	Wooster	20

Colors: Red & White.   Nickname: Big Red.   III

DePAUW .... Greencastle, IN 46135
Nick Mourouzis (11 yrs., 75-32-2)

Opponent	Date	Pts	1991 Result	Pts
Hope	S12	14	Hope	23
Millsaps ■	S19	15	Ohio Wesleyan	21
Albion	S26	15	Millsaps	14
Hanover	O 3	36	Rose-Hulman	6
Rose-Hulman ■	O10	41	Taylor	13
Taylor	O17	17	Manchester	10
Manchester ■	O24	12	Anderson	7
Anderson ■	O31	9	Franklin	0
Franklin	N 7	21	Hanover	37
Wabash	N14	18	Wabash	23

Colors: Old Gold & Black.   Nickname: Tigers.   III

DICKINSON .... Carlisle, PA 17013
Ed Sweeney (7 yrs., 48-21-2)

Opponent	Date	Pts	1991 Result	Pts
Hobart	S12	24	St. Francis (Pa.)	2
Muhlenberg ■	S19	42	Muhlenberg	0
Georgetown	S26	36	Georgetown	30
Union (N.Y.) ■	O 3	22	Frank. & Marsh.	19
Frank. & Marsh. ■	O10	28	Western Md.	25
Western Md.	O17	40	Swarthmore	15
Swarthmore ■	O24	25	Johns Hopkins	6
Johns Hopkins	O31	26	Gettysburg	0
Gettysburg ■	N 7	35	Ursinus	14
Ursinus	N14		III Championship	
		20	Susquehanna	21

Colors: Red & White.   Nickname: Red Devils.   III

DRAKE .... Des Moines, IA 50311
Rob Ash (12 yrs., 68-49-3)

Opponent	Date	Pts	1991 Result	Pts
Simpson	S12	7	Simpson	16
Augustana (Ill.) ■	S19	21	Rose-Hulman	31
Millikin ■	S26	28	Hope	31
Aurora	O 3	21	Neb. Wesleyan	26
Chicago ■	O10	27	Aurora	14
Dayton	O17	0	Dayton	13
Quincy ■	O24	21	Wis.-Oshkosh	0
Ill. Benedictine	O31	14	Millikin	23
Olivet Nazarene ■	N 7	6	St. Norbert	0
Evansville	N14	55	Ill. Benedictine	8

Colors: Blue & White.   Nickname: Bulldogs.   III

DUBUQUE .... Dubuque, IA 52001
Mike Messer (2 yrs., 3-15-0)

Opponent	Date	Pts	1991 Result	Pts
Graceland ■	S12	12	Graceland	23
Central (Iowa) ■	S19	14	Wartburg	56
Eureka	S26	18	Upper Iowa	13
Luther	O 3	7	Central (Iowa)	35
Upper Iowa ■	O10	10	Buena Vista	27
Loras	O17	7	Loras	10
Simpson ■	O24	6	Luther	47
Wartburg	O31	0	Simpson	51
Buena Vista ■	N 7	14	William Penn	16
William Penn	N14			

Colors: Blue & White.   Nickname: Spartans.   III

DUQUESNE .... Pittsburgh, PA 15282
Dan McCann (9 yrs., 33-49-2)

Opponent	Date	Pts	1991 Result	Pts
Grove City	S12	0	Wash. & Jeff.	61
Bethany (W.Va.)	S19	27	Grove City	31
Thiel ■	S26*	40	Bethany (W.Va.)	58
Gannon ■	O 3*	14	Carnegie Mellon	28
Catholic ■	O10*	13	Gannon	20
St. John's (N.Y.)	O17	6	Waynesburg	20
Carnegie Mellon	O24	0	St. Francis (Pa.)	12
Canisius	O31	0	Buffalo	49
St. Francis (Pa.) ■	N 7	0	Allegheny	35
Wagner	N14			

Colors: Red & Blue.   Nickname: Dukes.   III

EARLHAM .... Richmond, IN 47374
Frank Carr (7 yrs., 9-56-0)

Opponent	Date	Pts	1991 Result	Pts
Manchester ■	S 5	22	Manchester	38
Otterbein ■	S12	15	Case Reserve	36
Wittenberg ■	S19	0	Allegheny	75
Kenyon	S26	16	Thomas More	48
Oberlin ■	O 3	10	Ohio Wesleyan	34
Denison	O10	0	Wittenberg	29
Ohio Wesleyan ■	O17	24	Oberlin	0
Principia ■	O24	20	Wooster	54
Wooster	O31	21	Kenyon	55
Allegheny	N14			

Colors: Maroon & White.   Nickname: Hustlin' Quakers.   III

■ Home games on each schedule.   *Night Games.

EAST STROUDSBURG .... East Stroudsburg, PA 18301
Dennis Douds (18 yrs., 109-72-2)

Opponent			Opponent	
Southern Conn. St. ■	.......S 12	34	Lenoir-Rhyne	17
Indiana (Pa.)	.............S 19	43	Southern Conn. St.	41
Bloomsburg†	.............S 26	0	Indiana (Pa.)	34
Calif. (Pa.) ■	...............O 3	28	Cheyney	0
Cheyney ■	.................O 10	26	Mansfield	10
Mansfield	..................O 17	17	Millersville	17
Millersville ■	...............O 24	20	Bloomsburg	10
American Int'l	..............O 31	21	Kutztown	20
Kutztown ■	.................N 7	28	West Chester	21
West Chester	..............N 14	24	Shippensburg	31
		45	Buffalo	25
			II Championship	
		33	Shippensburg	34

Colors: Red & Black.   Nickname: Warriors.   **II**

EAST TEXAS STATE............. Commerce, TX 75428
Eddie Vowell (6 yrs., 34-34-1)

Opponent			Opponent	
Central Ark.	.............S 5*	44	Livingston	6
Pittsburg St.	............S 12*	20	Pittsburg St.	13
Southern Ark. ■	..........S 19	6	Southern Ark.	14
Northwestern (La.)	.......S 26*	23	Northwestern (La.)	26
Central Okla.	.............O 3	51	Central Okla.	21
Texas A&I ■	..............O 10*	24	Texas A&I	22
Iowa Wesleyan ■	.........O 17	54	Wayne St. (Neb.)	16
Eastern N. Mex. ■	........O 24	14	Eastern N. Mex.	17
Abilene Christian	..........O 31	37	Abilene Christian	3
Angelo St. ■	..............N 7	39	Angelo St.	39
Cameron	.................N 14	29	Cameron	7
			II Championship	
		36	Grand Valley St.	15
		28	Pittsburg St.	38

Colors: Blue & Gold.   Nickname: Lions.   **II**

EASTERN NEW MEXICO.......... Portales, NM 88130
Howard Stearns (1st yr. as head coach)

Opponent			Opponent	
N.M. Highlands	...........S 5*	15	Northern Ariz.	22
Western N. Mex.	.........S 12	42	Western N. Mex.	10
Western N. Mex. ■	........S 19	10	Cal St. Northridge	12
Abilene Christian ■	.......O 3	36	N.M. Highlands	6
Angelo St.	...............O 10*	32	Abilene Christian	20
Cameron ■	...............O 17*	13	Angelo St.	12
East Tex. St.	..............O 24	20	Cameron	16
Texas A&I ■	..............O 31	17	East Tex. St.	14
West Tex. St.	..............N 7	20	Texas A&I	36
Central Okla. ■	.............N 14	20	Neb.-Kearney	12
		21	Central Okla.	12

Colors: Silver & Green.   Nickname: Greyhounds.   **II**

EDINBORO .... Edinboro, PA 16444
Tom Hollman (8 yrs., 53-25-2)

Opponent			Opponent	
Buffalo ■	..................S 5	0	Youngstown St.	24
Northwood ■	...............S 12	25	Northwood	14
Southern Conn. St. ■	.....S 19	35	Southern Conn. St.	16
Clarion ■	.................O 3	23	Bloomsburg	21
Lock Haven	...............O 10	17	Clarion	9
Shippensburg ■	...........O 17	28	Lock Haven	12
Calif. (Pa.) ■	..............O 24	7	Shippensburg	45
Slippery Rock ■	...........O 31	45	Calif. (Pa.)	10
Indiana (Pa.) ■	.............N 7	0	Slippery Rock	7
Millersville	................N 14	17	Indiana (Pa.)	20
		31	Fairmont St.	21

Colors: Red & White.   Nickname: Fighting Scots.   **II**

ELIZABETH CITY STATE ..... Elizabeth City, NC 27909
Alvin T. Kelley (1 yr., 7-2-0)

Opponent			Opponent	
Winston-Salem	............S 5	21	Fayetteville St.	6
Fayetteville St. ■	..........S 12*	17	Knoxville	8
Central St. (Ohio)†	........S 19*	21	Norfolk St.	26
Norfolk St.	................S 26*	40	N.C. Central	15
N.C. Central	..............O 3	24	Virginia Union	23
Virginia Union ■	..........O 10	24	Bowie St.	7
Bowie St. ■	...............O 17	23	Virginia St.	6
Virginia St. ■	..............O 24	23	Hampton	21
Hampton ■	................O 31	18	Kentucky St.	21
Kentucky St.	..............N 7			

Colors: Royal Blue & White.   Nickname: Vikings.   **II**

ELMHURST......................... Elmhurst, IL 60126
Charlie Goehl (3 yrs., 3-24-0)

Opponent			Opponent	
Ill. Benedictine ■	...........S 12	6	Millikin	33
Aurora	....................S 26	24	North Central	49
Carthage ■	................O 3	20	Augustana (Ill.)	62
North Park	................O 10	16	Ill. Benedictine	43
North Central ■	............O 17	41	North Park	13
Augustana (Ill.) ■	..........O 24	20	Carroll (Wis.)	28
Ill. Wesleyan ■	............O 31	20	Wheaton (Ill.)	55
Wheaton (Ill.)	..............N 7	12	Ill. Wesleyan	41
Millikin	...................N 14	32	Carthage	16

Colors: Blue & White.   Nickname: Bluejays.   **III**

ELON .... Elon College, NC 27244
Leon Hart (3 yrs., 12-20-0)

Opponent			Opponent	
Wofford ■	.................S 5*	14	Wofford	21
Carson-Newman ■	.........S 19	38	N.C. Central	14
Newberry ■	................S 26	31	Fayetteville St.	0
Lenoir-Rhyne	..............O 3*	0	Carson-Newman	24
Mars Hill	..................O 10	27	Lenoir-Rhyne	28
Presbyterian ■	.............O 17	54	Mars Hill	19
Catawba	..................O 24	38	Presbyterian	14
Gardner-Webb ■	...........O 31	14	Catawba	20
Lees-McRae ■	.............N 7	10	Gardner-Webb	13
Wingate	..................N 14	38	Newberry	7
		31	Wingate	21

Colors: Maroon & Gold.   Nickname: Fightin' Christians.   **II**

EMORY AND HENRY.............. Emory, VA 24327
Lou Wacker (10 yrs., 71-35-0)

Opponent			Opponent	
Cumberland (Ky.) ■	........S 5	14	Wash. & Lee	0
Wash. & Lee	..............S 12	16	Bridgewater (Va.)	0
Bridgewater (Va.) ■	........S 19	39	Davidson	0
Davidson	.................S 26	6	Millsaps	14
Millsaps ■	.................O 3	21	Hampden-Sydney	0
Hampden-Sydney	..........O 10	21	Randolph-Macon	10
Randolph-Macon ■	.........O 17	16	Guilford	7
Guilford	..................O 24	35	Wittenberg	17
Ferrum	...................N 7	28	Ferrum	10
Maryville (Tenn.) ■	.........N 14	20	Maryville (Tenn.)	8

Colors: Blue & Gold.   Nickname: Wasps.   **III**

EMPORIA STATE .... Emporia, KS 66801
Larry Kramer (23 yrs., 106-99-8)

Opponent			Opponent	
Fort Hays St. ■	.............S 5*	28	Fort Hays St.	27
Mo. Southern St. ■	........S 12*	23	Mo. Western St.	22
Mo. Western St. ■	.........S 19*	42	Northeast Mo. St.	41
Northeast Mo. St. ■	........S 26	44	Central Mo. St.	17
Central Mo. St.	............O 3	49	Washburn	18
Washburn	.................O 10*	21	Missouri-Rolla	27
Missouri-Rolla ■	...........O 17	20	Southwest Baptist	42
Southwest Baptist	.........O 24	36	Pittsburg St.	70
Pittsburg St. ■	.............O 31	36	Northwest Mo. St.	41
Northwest Mo. St.	.........N 7	9	Mo. Southern St.	45

Colors: Black & Gold.   Nickname: Hornets.   **II**

EUREKA............................ Eureka, IL 61530
John Tully (2 yrs., 15-6-0)

Opponent			Opponent	
MacMurray ■	...............S 5	35	N'western Col. (Wis.)	3
Monmouth (Ill.) ■	..........S 12	42	Knox	7
North Central	..............S 19*	37	Monmouth (Ill.)	3
Dubuque ■	................S 26	45	MacMurray	9
Quincy	....................O 3	46	Blackburn	0
Concordia (Ill.)	.............O 10	42	Concordia (Ill.)	28
Lakeland ■	................O 17	28	Lakeland	7
Ky. Wesleyan	..............O 24	13	Ky. Wesleyan	6
Concordia (Wis.)	..........O 31	55	Concordia (Wis.)	6
Greenville ■	...............N 7	22	Greenville	15
			NAIA Div. II Championship	
		14	Georgetown (Ky.)	42

Colors: Maroon & Gold.   Nickname: Red Devils.   **III**

EVANSVILLE...................... Evansville, IN 47722
Robin Cooper (4 yrs., 25-13-0)

Opponent			Opponent	
Franklin ■	.................S 12	12	Franklin	20
Ky. Wesleyan	..............S 19*	26	Ky. Wesleyan	0
Rose-Hulman ■	............S 26	14	Union (Ky.)	16
Adrian ■	..................O 3	10	Georgetown (Ky.)	56
Lambuth	..................O 10	17	Lambuth	10
Tusculum ■	...............O 17	44	Tusculum	19
Dayton	....................O 31	22	Campbellsville	37
Cumberland (Tenn.) ■	......N 7	18	Cumberland (Tenn.)	0
Drake ■	..................N 14	30	Cumberland (Ky.)	14
		6	Dayton	48

Colors: Purple & White.   Nickname: Purple Aces.   **III**

■ Home games on each schedule.   *Night Games.

FAIRLEIGH DICKINSON-MADISON . Madison, NJ 07940
Bill Klika (18 yrs., 41-112-1)

1992 Schedule		1991 Results	
Jersey City St. ■	S18*	28 Jersey City St.	8
Johns Hopkins	S25*	6 Johns Hopkins	23
St. John's (N.Y.) ■	O 2*	7 St. John's (N.Y.)	21
Trenton St. ■	O 9*	7 Trenton St. ■	34
Frank. & Marsh.	O17	7 Frank. & Marsh.	34
Ursinus ■	O24	17 Ursinus	10
Upsala	O31	3 Upsala	18
Marist	N 7	7 Marist	26
Iona ■	N13*	6 Iona	48

Colors: Columbia, Navy & White. Nickname: Jersey Devils. III

FAYETTEVILLE STATE .... Fayetteville, NC 28301
Ray McDougal (13 yrs., 55-69-3)

1992 Schedule		1991 Results	
Carson-Newman	S 5	21 Carson-Newman	44
Elizabeth City St.	S12*	6 Howard	62
Norfolk St.	S19*	6 Elizabeth City St.	21
Winston-Salem	S26	8 Elon	31
N.C. Central ■	O10*	8 Winston-Salem	28
Virginia St.	O17	0 N.C. Central	14
Johnson Smith	O24	14 Virginia St.	31
Livingstone ■	N 7	0 Johnson Smith	24
Newberry	N14	14 Norfolk St.	28
		9 Livingstone	34

Colors: White & Royal Blue. Nickname: Broncos. II

FERRIS STATE .... Big Rapids, MI 49307
Keith Otterbein (6 yrs., 30-34-1)

1992 Schedule		1991 Results	
Northwood†	S 5	13 Michigan Tech	33
Ashland	S12	7 Ashland	35
Hillsdale ■	S19*	23 Hillsdale	16
Wayne St. (Mich.)	S26	24 Wayne St. (Mich.)	27
Northern Mich.	O 3	17 Northern Mich.	27
Valparaiso	O10	28 Valparaiso	9
Grand Valley St.	O17	6 Grand Valley St.	28
Butler ■	O24	7 Butler	6
Indianapolis	O31	21 Indianapolis	6
Saginaw Valley ■	N 7	18 Saginaw Valley	15
St. Joseph's (Ind.) ■	N14	10 St. Joseph's (Ind.)	16

Colors: Crimson & Gold. Nickname: Bulldogs. II

FERRUM .... Ferrum, VA 24088
Hank Norton (7 yrs., 54-22-1)

1992 Schedule		1991 Results	
Cortland St.	S 5	41 Bridgewater (Va.)	13
Ramapo	S12	54 Stonehill	13
Western Caro.	S26*	14 Westminster (Pa.)	7
Westminster (Pa.) ■	O 3	61 Guilford	13
Guilford ■	O10	48 Newport News App.	21
Newport News App.	O17	35 Ala.-Birmingham	31
Ala.-Birmingham ■	O24	12 Dayton	31
Mansfield	O31	10 Emory & Henry	28
Emory & Henry ■	N 7	45 Methodist	3
Methodist	N21		

Colors: Black & Gold. Nickname: Panthers. III

FITCHBURG STATE .... Fitchburg, MA 01420
Vin Keough (2 yrs., 4-14-0)

1992 Schedule		1991 Results	
Western New Eng.	S12	0 Nichols	34
Framingham St. ■	S19	6 Maine Maritime	21
Westfield St. ■	S25*	7 Bri'water (Mass.)	22
Bri'water (Mass.) ■	O 3	9 Worcester St.	10
Worcester St.	O10	21 Mass.-Boston	8
Mass. Maritime ■	O17	9 Mass. Maritime	19
Mass.-Dartmouth	O24	16 Framingham St.	14
Maine Maritime	O31	0 Mass.-Dartmouth	14
Mass.-Boston	N 7	6 Westfield St.	12

Colors: Green, Gold & White. Nickname: Falcons. III

FORT HAYS STATE. .... Hays, KS 67601
Bob Cortese (12 yrs., 100-29-3)

1992 Schedule		1991 Results	
Emporia St.	S 5*	27 Emporia St.	28
Central Okla. ■	S12*	12 Arkansas Tech	9
Central Ark. ■	S19*	28 Colorado Mines	24
Neb.-Kearney	S26	14 Mesa St.	21
N.M. Highlands	O 3	28 Wayne St. (Neb.)	20
Mesa St.	O10*	10 Chadron St.	9
Adams St. ■	O17	21 Western St.	42
Colorado Mines ■	O24	43 Neb.-Kearney	20
Chadron St.	O31	49 Fort Lewis	24
Western St. ■	N 7	21 Adams St.	20
Fort Lewis	N14	59 Panhandle St.	0

Colors: Black & Gold. Nickname: Tigers. II

FORT LEWIS .... Durango, CO 81301
Kevin Donnalley (1st yr. as head coach)

1992 Schedule		1991 Results	
West Tex. St.	S12	0 Doane	27
Montana Tech ■	S19	13 Montana Tech	51
Western N. Mex.	S26	19 Chadron St.	21
Mesa St. ■	O 3	25 Western St.	70
Western St.	O10	26 Colorado Mines	42
N.M. Highlands	O17	21 Adams St.	32
Adams St.	O24	39 Panhandle St.	20
Colorado Mines	O31	24 Fort Hays St.	49
Chadron St. ■	N 7	7 Mesa St.	34
Fort Hays St.	N14	27 N.M. Highlands	12

Colors: Blue & Gold. Nickname: Raiders. II

FORT VALLEY STATE. .... Ft. Valley, GA 31030
Douglas Porter (22 yrs., 128-85-4)

1992 Schedule		1991 Results	
Central St. (Ohio)	S 5	45 Miles	6
Morehouse ■	S12	20 Morehouse	17
Valdosta St.†	S19*	0 Valdosta St.	7
Morris Brown†	S26*	26 Morris Brown	21
Clark Atlanta†	O 3*	12 Clark Atlanta	14
North Ala. ■	O10	34 North Ala.	23
Miles	O17	35 Alabama A&M	7
Alabama A&M ■	O24	22 Tuskegee	39
Tuskegee	O31	34 Savannah St.	30
Savannah St.	N 7	22 Albany St. (Ga.)	20
Albany St. (Ga.) ■	N14		

Colors: Royal Blue & Old Gold. Nickname: Wildcats. II

FRAMINGHAM STATE .... Framingham, MA 01701
Thomas Raeke (7 yrs., 23-39-0)

1992 Schedule		1991 Results	
Fitchburg St.	S19	27 Curry	7
Curry	S26	29 Mass. Maritime	32
Westfield St. ■	O 3	35 Westfield St.	44
Bri'water (Mass.)	O10	40 Worcester St.	22
Worcester St. ■	O17	0 Plymouth St.	43
Mass. Maritime	O24	14 Fitchburg St.	16
Mass.-Dartmouth ■	O31	19 Bri'water (Mass.)	30
Maine Maritime	N 7	12 Mass.-Dartmouth	27
Mass.-Boston ■	N14		

Colors: Black & Gold. Nickname: Rams. III

FRANKLIN .... Franklin, IN 46131
Mike McClure (3 yrs., 12-18-0)

1992 Schedule		1991 Results	
Evansville	S12	19 Alma	21
Alma	S19	5 Thomas More	14
Thomas More ■	S26	10 Wabash	44
Anderson	O 3	34 Rose-Hulman	39
Wabash	O10	17 Taylor	3
Rose-Hulman	O17	16 Manchester	20
Taylor	O24	0 DePauw	9
Manchester ■	O31	22 Anderson	40
DePauw ■	N 7	31 Hanover	34
Hanover	N14		

Colors: Old Gold & Navy Blue. Nickname: Grizzlies. III

FRANKLIN AND MARSHALL. ..... Lancaster, PA 17604
Tom Gilburg (17 yrs., 117-44-2)

1992 Schedule		1991 Results	
Moravian	S12	6 Moravian	7
Ursinus ■	S19	19 Ursinus	7
Muhlenberg	S26	25 Muhlenberg	21
Georgetown ■	O 3	15 Georgetown	31
Dickinson	O10	19 Dickinson	22
FDU-Madison ■	O17	34 FDU-Madison	7
Western Md. ■	O24	19 Western Md.	15
Swarthmore	O31	26 Swarthmore	12
Johns Hopkins ■	N 7	14 Johns Hopkins	16
Gettysburg	N14	14 Gettysburg	6

Colors: Blue & White. Nickname: Diplomats. III

FROSTBURG STATE .... Frostburg, MD 21532
Mike McClinchey (10 yrs., 61-38-4)

1992 Schedule		1991 Results	
Lycoming ■	S12	32 Grove City	37
Thiel	S19	29 Catholic	7
Salisbury St. ■	S26	35 Thiel	14
Wesley ■	O 3	39 Salisbury St.	14
Geneva	O10	33 Western Conn. St.	3
Canisius	O17	6 Mercyhurst	21
Bridgewater (Va.) ■	O24	63 Bridgewater (Va.)	14
Brockport St. ■	O31	30 Norwich	17
Waynesburg	N 7	22 Waynesburg	18
Methodist ■	N14	19 Charleston So.	21
		46 Wm. Paterson	16

Colors: Red, White & Black. Nickname: Bobcats. III

■ Home games on each schedule.   *Night Games.

GALLAUDET ....Washington, DC 20785
Richard Pelletier (3 yrs., 9-18-1)

Opponent	Date	Result	Opponent	Pts
Ala.-Birmingham	S12	24	Catholic	32
Georgetown ■	S19	7	Jersey City St.	7
Stevens Tech	S26	12	Georgetown	35
St. Francis (Pa.) ■	O 3	21	Marist	46
Wesley	O10	14	St. Francis (Pa.)	34
Catholic	O17	9	Wesley	52
St. Peter's	O24	7	St. John Fisher	3
Newport News App. ■	O31	9	St. Peter's	19
St. John Fisher ■	N 7	16	Charleston So.	35

Colors: Buff & Blue. Nickname: Bison.   III

GANNON ....Erie, PA 16541
Tom Herman (3 yrs., 9-17-0)

Opponent	Date	Result	Opponent	Pts
St. Francis (Pa.) ■	S 5	14	St. Francis (Pa.)	16
Waynesburg	S12	14	Mercyhurst	40
Mercyhurst	S19	31	Grove City	19
Duquesne	O 3*	20	Duquesne	13
LIU-C.W. Post ■	O10	19	Bethany (W.Va.)	23
Wash. & Jeff.	O17	13	Buffalo St.	22
Bethany (W.Va.) ■	O24	6	Dayton	35
Thiel ■	O31	14	Thomas More	34
Grove City	N 7	25	St. John Fisher	0
Buffalo St.	N14	6	Thiel	27

Colors: Maroon & Gold. Nickname: Golden Knights.   III

GARDNER-WEBB ....Boiling Springs, NC 28017
Woody Fish (8 yrs., 46-41-1)

Opponent	Date	Result	Opponent	Pts
Central Fla.	S 5*	31	Johnson Smith	0
Charleston So. ■	S12	7	Livingston	24
Newberry	S19	10	Newberry	0
Lees-McRae ■	S26	50	Lees-McRae	0
Wingate ■	O 3	34	Wingate	24
Lenoir-Rhyne	O10*	6	Lenoir-Rhyne	24
Catawba ■	O17	21	Catawba	24
Carson-Newman	O24	16	Carson-Newman	52
Elon ■	O31	13	Elon	10
Presbyterian	N 7	8	Presbyterian	10
Mars Hill ■	N14	42	Mars Hill	18

Colors: Scarlet, White & Black. Nickname: Bulldogs.   II

GEORGETOWN ....Washington, DC 20057
Scotty Glacken (22 yrs., 92-89-2)

Opponent	Date	Result	Opponent	Pts
Ursinus ■	S12	6	Ursinus	12
Gallaudet	S19	35	Gallaudet	12
Dickinson ■	S26	30	Dickinson	36
Frank. & Marsh.	O 3	31	Frank. & Marsh.	15
St. Peter's ■	O10	19	St. Peter's	14
Swarthmore	O17	31	Swarthmore	0
Johns Hopkins ■	O24	14	Johns Hopkins	40
Catholic	O31	21	Catholic	17
St. John's (N.Y.)	N 7	26	St. John's (N.Y.)	21
Wash. & Lee ■	N14	12	Wash. & Lee	27

Colors: Blue & Gray. Nickname: Hoyas.   III

GETTYSBURG ....Gettysburg, PA 17325
Barry Streeter (14 yrs., 81-58-4)

Opponent	Date	Result	Opponent	Pts
Widener ■	S12	6	Widener	27
Western Md.	S19	7	Western Md.	12
Swarthmore ■	S26	20	Swarthmore	8
Johns Hopkins	O 2*	20	Johns Hopkins	19
Stony Brook ■	O10	7	Muhlenberg	28
Ursinus ■	O17	0	Ursinus	20
Muhlenberg	O24	7	Union (N.Y.)	57
Union (N.Y.)	O31	0	Dickinson	26
Dickinson	N 7	6	Frank. & Marsh.	14
Frank. & Marsh. ■	N14			

Colors: Orange & Blue. Nickname: Bullets.   III

GLASSBORO STATE ....Glassboro, NJ 08028
John Bunting (4 yrs., 26-13-2)

Opponent	Date	Result	Opponent	Pts
Newport News App. ■	S12	28	Newport News App.	14
Central Conn. St.	S19	36	Brockport St.	13
Jersey City St. ■	S25*	42	Jersey City St.	14
Trenton St.	O 3	21	Trenton St.	0
Salisbury St.	O10	34	Salisbury St.	7
Ramapo ■	O17	17	Ramapo	14
Wagner ■	O23*	23	Wagner	21
Kean	O31	28	Kean	12
Wm. Paterson ■	N 7*	14	Wm. Paterson	28
Montclair St.	N14*	31	Montclair St.	16
		III Championship		
		10	Ithaca	31

Colors: Brown & Gold. Nickname: Profs.   III

GRAND VALLEY STATE..........Allendale, MI 49401
Brian Kelly (1 yr., 9-3-0)

Opponent	Date	Result	Opponent	Pts
St. Joseph's (Ind.)	S 5	31	St. Joseph's (Ind.)	3
Indiana (Pa.) ■	S12	21	North Dak. St.	17
Butler ■	S19	0	Butler	33
Indianapolis	S26	31	Indianapolis	13
Saginaw Valley ■	O 3	10	Saginaw Valley	14
Northern Mich.	O10	35	Northern Mich.	0
Ferris St. ■	O17	28	Ferris St.	6
Ashland ■	O24	38	Ashland	7
Hillsdale	O31	9	Hillsdale	6
Wayne St. (Mich.) ■	N 7	59	Wayne St. (Mich.)	28
Valparaiso	N14	36	Valparaiso	3
		II Championship		
		15	East Tex. St.	36

Colors: Blue, Black & White. Nickname: Lakers.   II

GRINNELL........................Grinnell, IA 50112
Greg Wallace (4 yrs., 7-27-1)

Opponent	Date	Result	Opponent	Pts
Colorado Col.	S12	13	Lake Forest	35
Principia ■	S19	27	Principia	20
Lake Forest ■	S26	0	Beloit	34
St. Norbert	O 3	14	Ripon	29
Coe ■	O10	26	Coe	77
Knox	O17	20	Knox	39
Cornell College ■	O24	35	Cornell College	38
Monmouth (Ill.) ■	O31	13	Monmouth (Ill.)	54
Illinois Col.	N 7	14	Illinois Col.	0

Colors: Scarlet & Black. Nickname: Pioneers.   III

GROVE CITY....................Grove City, PA 16127
Christopher Smith (8 yrs., 25-45-2)

Opponent	Date	Result	Opponent	Pts
Duquesne ■	S12	37	Frostburg St.	32
Waynesburg ■	S26	31	Duquesne	27
Bluffton ■	O 3	12	Waynesburg	20
Bethany (W.Va.) ■	O10	19	Gannon	31
Thiel ■	O17	3	Wash. & Jeff.	38
Wash. & Jeff. ■	O24	14	Carnegie Mellon	43
Carnegie Mellon	O31	12	Thiel	21
Gannon ■	N 7	26	Bethany (W.Va.)	21
Oberlin ■	N14	26	Buffalo St.	28

Colors: Crimson & White. Nickname: Wolverines.   III

GUILFORD....................Greensboro, NC 27410
Mike Ketchum (1 yr., 8-2-0)

Opponent	Date	Result	Opponent	Pts
Davidson ■	S 5	21	Davidson	3
Methodist	S12	34	Methodist	0
Hampden-Sydney	S19	24	Hampden-Sydney	21
Charleston So. ■	S26	40	Charleston So.	6
Salisbury St. ■	O 3	20	Salisbury St.	6
Ferrum	O10	13	Ferrum	61
Bridgewater (Va.) ■	O17	14	Bridgewater (Va.)	6
Emory & Henry ■	O24	17	Emory & Henry	16
Randolph-Macon	O31	17	Randolph-Macon	20
Wash. & Lee ■	N 7	25	Wash. & Lee	7

Colors: Crimson & Gray. Nickname: Quakers.   III

GUSTAVUS ADOLPHUS..........St. Peter, MN 56082
Steve Byrne (4 yrs., 21-18-0)

Opponent	Date	Result	Opponent	Pts
Augustana (S.D.)	S12	25	Central (Iowa)	26
Concordia-M'head	S19	63	Macalester	0
Augsburg ■	S26	28	St. Olaf	13
St. John's (Minn.)	O 3	21	Bethel (Minn.)	42
St. Olaf ■	O10	30	Concordia-M'head	20
Hamline ■	O17	14	St. John's (Minn.)	35
Bethel (Minn.) ■	O24	28	Carleton	21
St. Thomas (Minn.) ■	O31	14	Hamline	16
Macalester	N 7	28	St. Thomas (Minn.)	7
Carleton†	N14*			

Colors: Black & Gold. Nickname: Golden Gusties.   III

HAMILTON.......................Clinton, NY 13323
Steve Frank (7 yrs., 32-23-1)

Opponent	Date	Result	Opponent	Pts
Amherst	S26	0	Williams	15
Wesleyan	O 3	17	Colby	21
Trinity (Conn.) ■	O10	35	Bowdoin	19
Bowdoin ■	O17	28	Trinity (Conn.)	28
Colby	O24	24	Middlebury	6
Williams ■	O31	35	Wesleyan	12
Middlebury ■	N 7	29	Tufts	15
Bates	N14	17	Union (N.Y.)	51

Colors: Buff & Blue. Nickname: Continentals.   III

■ Home games on each schedule.   *Night Games.

HAMLINE ....St. Paul, MN 55104
Dick Tressel (14 yrs., 79-56-2)

Mt. Senario	S 12	30	Trinity (Tex.)	7
Carleton	S 19	7	Bethel (Minn.)	10
Concordia-M'head ■	S 26	30	Concordia-M'head	20
Augsburg	O 3	25	St. John's (Minn.)	35
St. John's (Minn.) ■	O 10	19	Central St. (Ohio)	13
Gust. Adolphus	O 17	30	St. Thomas (Minn.)	33
St. Olaf ■	O 24	33	Augsburg	12
Bethel (Minn.) ■	O 31	16	Gust. Adolphus	14
St. Thomas (Minn.)	N 7	23	St. Olaf	26
Macalester†	N 14			

Colors: Red & Gray.   Nickname: Pipers.   III

HAMPDEN-SYDNEY .....Hampden-Sydney, VA 23943
Joe Bush (7 yrs., 39-29-1)

Centre ■	S 12	42	Centre	26
Guilford ■	S 19	21	Guilford	24
Union (Ky.) ■	S 26	35	Ala.-Birmingham	35
Bridgewater (Va.)	O 3	37	Bridgewater (Va.)	23
Emory & Henry ■	O 10	0	Emory & Henry	21
Wash. & Lee	O 17	24	Wash. & Lee	7
Wesley	O 24	50	Wesley	49
Davidson ■	O 31	56	Davidson	14
Methodist	N 7	54	Methodist	7
Randolph-Macon ■	N 14	29	Randolph-Macon	28

Colors: Garnet & Gray.   Nickname: Tigers.   III

HAMPTON...................Hampton, VA 23668
Joe Taylor (9 yrs., 61-29-3)

Johnson Smith ■	S 5*	15	Johnson Smith	26
Bowie St. ■	S 12*	14	Bowie St.	17
Virginia Union	S 19*	13	Virginia Union	49
Morehouse ■	O 3	14	Alcorn St.	67
Virginia St.	O 10	17	Morehouse	20
Norfolk St. ■	O 17	39	Virginia St.	37
Tuskegee	O 24	12	Norfolk St.	26
Elizabeth City St.	O 31	33	Tuskegee	46
Winston-Salem	N 7*	21	Elizabeth City St.	23
N.C. Central ■	N 14	6	Winston-Salem	20
		44	N.C. Central	28

Colors: Royal Blue & White.   Nickname: Pirates.   II

HANOVER.....................Hanover, IN 47243
C. Wayne Perry (10 yrs., 65-31-2)

Defiance ■	S 5	56	Bluffton	28
Thomas More	S 12	37	Mt. St. Joseph	12
Bluffton	S 19	46	Georgetown (Ky.)	55
DePauw ■	O 3	26	Anderson	36
Anderson	O 10	14	Wabash	26
Wabash ■	O 17	36	Rose-Hulman	32
Rose-Hulman	O 24	17	Taylor	8
Taylor ■	O 31	35	Manchester	19
Manchester	N 7	37	DePauw	31
Franklin ■	N 14	34	Franklin	31

Colors: Red & Blue.   Nickname: Panthers.   III

HARDIN-SIMMONS.............Abilene, TX 79698
Jimmie Keeling (2 yrs., 8-11-0)

Panhandle St.	S 12*	12	Austin Peay	6
Sul Ross St. ■	S 19	17	Howard Payne	21
Millsaps	S 26	17	Lindenwood	35
Howard Payne	O 3	49	Taylor	14
McMurry ■	O 10	38	Austin Peay	22
Tarleton St. ■	O 17	17	McMurry	6
Sul Ross St.	O 24	0	Tarleton St.	35
Colorado Col. ■	O 31*	41	Colorado Col.	14
Midwestern St.	N 7*	35	Howard Payne	42
Austin ■	N 14	21	Midwestern St.	32

Colors: Purple & Gold.   Nickname: Cowboys.   III

HEIDELBERG......................Tiffin, OH 44883
Dick West (8 yrs., 36-43-1)

Olivet ■	S 12	0	Adrian	14
Otterbein†	S 19	21	Muskingum	28
John Carroll	S 26	48	Marietta	0
Muskingum	O 3	14	Ohio Northern	14
Capital	O 10	37	Otterbein	14
Mount Union	O 17	21	John Carroll	23
Hiram ■	O 24	23	Mount Union	32
Baldwin-Wallace	O 31	48	Capital	29
Marietta ■	N 7	49	Hiram	7
Ohio Northern ■	N 14	13	Baldwin-Wallace	21

Colors: Red, Orange & Black.   Nickname: Student Princes.   III

HENDERSON STATE..........Arkadelphia, AR 71923
Ken Turner (2 yrs., 9-9-2)

Angelo St.	S 5*	6	Delta St.	35
East Central (Okla.) ■	S 12*	17	East Central (Okla.)	17
Delta St. ■	S 19*	17	Mississippi Col.	24
Mississippi Col.	S 26*	21	Northeastern Okla.	24
Northeastern Okla.	O 3*	34	Southern Ark.	13
Southern Ark. ■	O 10	17	Arkansas Tech	14
Arkansas Tech	O 17	20	Central Ark.	21
Central Ark. ■	O 24*	21	Ouachita Bapt.	7
Ouachita Bapt.	O 31	13	Harding	16
Harding ■	N 7	30	Ark.-Monticello	20
Ark.-Monticello	N 12*			

Colors: Red & Gray.   Nickname: Reddies.   II

HILLSDALE ....Hillsdale, MI 49242
Dick Lowry (18 yrs., 136-57-2)

Saginaw Valley	S 5	14	Saginaw Valley	0
Valparaiso ■	S 12	49	Valparaiso	27
Ferris St.	S 19*	16	Ferris St.	23
Ashland ■	S 26*	7	Ashland	29
Northwood ■	O 3	0	Northwood	6
Indianapolis	O 10	35	Indianapolis	7
Northern Mich. ■	O 17	24	Northern Mich.	0
St. Joseph's (Ind.)	O 24	0	St. Joseph's (Ind.)	10
Grand Valley St. ■	O 31	6	Grand Valley St.	9
Butler	N 7	20	Butler	26
Wayne St. (Mich.) ■	N 14	32	Wayne St. (Mich.)	13

Colors: Royal Blue & White.   Nickname: Chargers.   II

HIRAM ....Hiram, OH 44234
Don Charlton (9 yrs., 34-46-4)

Wash. & Jeff.	S 12	0	Ohio Wesleyan	38
Baldwin-Wallace ■	S 19	6	Baldwin-Wallace	55
Capital ■	S 26	15	Ohio Northern	44
Otterbein	O 3*	13	Muskingum	39
Marietta	O 10	2	Capital	30
Ohio Northern ■	O 17	35	Marietta	29
Heidelberg	O 24	7	John Carroll	48
Muskingum ■	O 31	0	Otterbein	28
John Carroll	N 7	7	Heidelberg	49
Mount Union ■	N 14	12	Mount Union	45

Colors: Red & Blue.   Nickname: Terriers.   III

HOBART ....Geneva, NY 14456
William Maxwell (1 yr., 3-7-0)

Dickinson ■	S 12	0	Buffalo St.	34
St. John Fisher	S 19	13	Swarthmore	29
Union (N.Y.)	S 26	17	Union (N.Y.)	44
St. Lawrence ■	O 3	0	St. Lawrence	41
Rochester ■	O 10	10	Alfred	30
Alfred	O 17	36	Assumption	15
Canisius ■	O 24	9	Canisius	34
Pace	O 31	19	Pace	14
Buffalo St.	N 7	15	Rensselaer	16
Rensselaer ■	N 14	35	St. John Fisher	14

Colors: Orange & Purple.   Nickname: Statesmen.   III

HOFSTRA ....Hempstead, NY 11550
Joe Gardi (2 yrs., 20-3-0)

Central Conn. St. ■	S 5*	43	Bucknell	7
Lafayette	S 12	30	Central Conn. St.	19
James Madison	S 19*	28	New Hampshire	48
Towson St.	S 26*	54	LIU-C.W. Post	24
Rhode Island ■	O 2*	38	Buffalo	33
Southern Conn. St. ■	O 9*	50	Fordham	30
Fordham ■	O 16*	60	Lafayette	17
Buffalo	O 24	30	Towson St.	26
Dayton ■	N 7	7	Dayton	14
Montana	N 14	40	Cortland St.	6

Colors: Blue, Gold & White.   Nickname: Flying Dutchmen.   III

HOPE ....Holland, MI 49423
Ray Smith (22 yrs., 132-59-8)

DePauw ■	S 12	14	Findlay	17
Ill. Wesleyan ■	S 19	23	DePauw	14
Wabash ■	S 26	31	Drake	28
Trinity (Ill.)	O 3	12	Aurora	0
Alma	O 10	10	Alma	7
Albion ■	O 17	19	Albion	35
Adrian ■	O 24	20	Adrian	6
Kalamazoo	O 31	0	Kalamazoo	14
Olivet ■	N 7	14	Olivet	21

Colors: Orange & Blue.   Nickname: Flying Dutchmen.   III

■ Home games on each schedule.   *Night Games.

HUMBOLDT STATE.................Arcata, CA 95521
Fred Whitmire (1 yr., 5-5-0)

Azusa-Pacific	.............S 5	22	Rocky Mountain	12
Western Mont. ■	...........S12*	6	Montana	38
St. Mary's (Cal.)	........S19	17	St. Mary's (Cal.)	14
Southern Ore.	............S26	35	Azusa-Pacific	 0
Santa Clara ■	............O 3*	23	Santa Clara	28
Whitworth ■	..............O10*	6	UC Davis	44
San Fran. St.	............O17	0	Sonoma St.	35
UC Davis ■	................O24	6	Cal St. Hayward	16
Sonoma St. ■	..............O31	0	Cal St. Chico	17
Cal St. Hayward ■	.......N 7*	44	San Fran. St.	13
Cal St. Chico ■	...........N14*			

Colors: Green & Gold.   Nickname: Lumberjacks.   II

ILLINOIS BENEDICTINE ....Lisle, IL 60532
John Welty (2 yrs., 3-16-0)

Loras ■	..................S 5	12	Loras	23
Millikin ■	................S12	7	Kalamazoo	22
Elmhurst ■	...............S19	26	Rose-Hulman	16
Carthage ■	...............S26	6	Alma	39
Alma ■	...................O 3	43	Elmhurst	16
Quincy	...................O10	35	Carthage	41
Olivet Nazarene ■	........O17	19	Olivet Nazarene	48
Aurora	...................O24	7	Aurora	25
Drake ■	..................O31	0	Carroll (Wis.)	36
Trinity (Ill.)	.............N 7	8	Drake	55

Colors: Cardinal & White.   Nickname: Eagles.   III

ILLINOIS COLLEGE.............Jacksonville, IL 62650
Bill Anderson (14 yrs., 33-93-0)

Principia ■	...............S12	27	Principia	14
Blackburn ■	...............S19	25	Blackburn	13
Carroll (Wis.) ■	..........S26	6	Lake Forest	18
Lawrence	.................O 3	0	St. Norbert	21
Monmouth (Ill.)	...........O10	7	Monmouth (Ill.)	17
Coe ■	....................O17	6	Coe	35
Knox ■	...................O24	3	Knox	29
Cornell College ■	.........O31	7	Cornell College	28
Grinnell ■	................N 7	0	Grinnell	14

Colors: Royal Blue & White.   Nickname: Blueboys.   III

ILLINOIS WESLEYAN ....Bloomington, IL 61701
Norm Eash (5 yrs., 25-19-1)

Hope ■	...................S19	49	Carroll (Wis.)	19
Adrian ■	.................S26	24	Wheaton (Ill.)	24
North Central ■	...........O 3	40	Quincy	36
Wheaton (Ill.)	............O10	28	Carthage	 0
Augustana (Ill.) ■	........O17	27	Millikin	24
Carthage ■	...............O24	44	North Central	 9
Elmhurst	.................O31	35	Augustana (Ill.)	38
Millikin ■	................N 7	41	Elmhurst	12
North Park ■	..............N14	47	North Park	14

Colors: Green & White.   Nickname: Titans.   III

INDIANA (PENNSYLVANIA).........Indiana, PA 15705
Frank Cignetti (10 yrs., 79-39-0)

Grand Valley St.	..........S12	41	Northeast Mo. St.	11
East Stroudsburg ■	........S19	37	Lock Haven	14
Lock Haven ■	..............O 3	34	East Stroudsburg	 0
Shippensburg	.............O10	41	Clarion	19
Calif. (Pa.) ■	.............O17	54	Towson St.	10
Slippery Rock	............O24	47	Shippensburg	 0
Towson St. ■	..............O31	10	Calif. (Pa.)	 8
Edinboro ■	................N 7	38	Slippery Rock	 0
Clarion	...................N14	47	Millersville	 0
		20	Edinboro	17
			II Championship	
		56	Virginia Union	 7
		52	Shippensburg	 7
		20	Jacksonville St.	27

Colors: Crimson & Gray.   Nickname: Indians.   II

INDIANAPOLIS ....Indianapolis, IN 46227
Bill Bless (20 yrs., 111-82-8)

Wayne St. (Mich.) ■	.......S 5	35	Wayne St. (Mich.)	13
Northern Mich. ■	..........S12	20	Northern Mich.	31
St. Joseph's (Ind.)	.......S19	28	St. Joseph's (Ind.)	10
Grand Valley St. ■	........S26	13	Grand Valley St.	31
Butler ■	.................O 3	3	Butler	22
Hillsdale ■	...............O10	7	Hillsdale	35
Saginaw Valley ■	..........O17	7	Saginaw Valley	21
Valparaiso	...............O24	3	Valparaiso	 6
Ferris St. ■	..............O31	6	Ferris St.	21
Ashland	..................N 7	7	Ashland	21

Colors: Crimson & Gray.   Nickname: Greyhounds.   II

IONA ....New Rochelle, NY 10801
Harold Crocker (7 yrs., 28-41-1)

St. John's (N.Y.) ■	.......S12	20	Marist	16
Siena ■	..................S19	27	St. John's (N.Y.)	30
Catholic ■	................S26	26	Sacred Heart	 6
Marist	...................O 3	24	Catholic	19
Wagner ■	.................O10	37	Stony Brook	 6
LIU-C.W. Post	.............O17	15	Wagner	24
Pace	.....................O24	20	LIU-C.W. Post	19
Sacred Heart ■	............O31	38	Pace	17
Merchant Marine	...........N 7	28	Merchant Marine	28
FDU-Madison ■	..............N13*	48	FDU-Madison	 6

Colors: Maroon & Gold.   Nickname: Gaels.   III

ITHACA ....Ithaca, NY 14850
Jim Butterfield (25 yrs., 191-65-1)

Albany (N.Y.) ■	...........S12*	45	St. Lawrence	 7
Montclair St. ■	...........S19	38	Albany (N.Y.)	 7
Alfred ■	.................S26	31	Alfred	 8
Springfield ■	.............O 3	10	Springfield	14
American Int'l	............O10	23	American Int'l	20
St. Lawrence	..............O17	50	Buffalo	 0
Buffalo St. ■	.............O24	41	Buffalo St.	23
Mercyhurst ■	...............O31	23	Cortland St.	14
Cortland St.	..............N 7	52	Brockport St.	 0
Wash. & Jeff. ■	...........N14		**III Championship**	
		31	Glassboro St.	10
		35	Union (N.Y.)	23
		49	Susquehanna	13
		34	Dayton	20

Colors: Blue & Gold.   Nickname: Bombers.   III

JACKSONVILLE STATE........Jacksonville, AL 36265
Bill Burgess (7 yrs., 57-21-3)

Alabama A&M†	...............S 5*	44	Alabama A&M	18
West Ga.	..................S19*	50	West Ga.	24
Valdosta St. ■	............S26	24	Valdosta St.	 3
Mississippi Col.	..........O 3*	17	Mississippi Col.	 6
Delta St. ■	...............O10	9	Delta St.	 0
North Ala.	................O17*	48	North Ala.	13
Ga. Southern	..............O24	51	Wofford	 7
Alcorn St. ■	..............O31	31	Livingston	 0
Livingston ■	..............N 7	42	Kentucky St.	 7
Kentucky St. ■	............N14		**II Championship**	
		49	Winston-Salem	24
		35	Mississippi Col.	 7
		27	Indiana (Pa.)	20
		6	Pittsburg St.	23

Colors: Red & White.   Nickname: Gamecocks.   II

JERSEY CITY STATE............Jersey City, NJ 07305
Bill Olear (1st yr. as head coach)

Brockport St. ■	...........S12	7	Gallaudet	 7
FDU-Madison ■	..............S18*	8	FDU-Madison	28
Glassboro St. ■	...........S25*	14	Glassboro St.	40
Upsala ■	.................O 3	0	Upsala	25
Ramapo ■	.................O10	0	Ramapo	47
Kean ■	...................O17	10	Kean	43
Trenton St.	...............O24	7	Trenton St.	29
Wm. Paterson ■	.............O30*	7	Wm. Paterson	36
Montclair St. ■	...........N 7	8	Montclair St.	35
St. Peter's ■	.............N14	7	St. Peter's	17

Colors: Green & Gold.   Nickname: Gothic Knights.   III

JOHN CARROLL ....Cleveland, OH 44118
Tony DeCarlo (5 yrs., 34-13-2)

Alma	.....................S12	7	Dayton	24
Capital	...................S19	42	Marietta	 7
Heidelberg ■	..............S26	7	Capital	 7
Ohio Northern	.............O 3	39	Otterbein	 0
Mount Union ■	..............O10	20	Mount Union	20
Muskingum ■	...............O17	23	Heidelberg	21
Otterbein	................O24	48	Hiram	 7
Marietta ■	................O31	0	Baldwin-Wallace	21
Hiram ■	..................N 7	17	Ohio Northern	 7
Baldwin-Wallace	...........N14	17	Muskingum	24

Colors: Blue & Gold.   Nickname: Blue Streaks.   III

■ Home games on each schedule.   *Night Games.

JOHNS HOPKINS .... Baltimore, MD 21218
Jim Margraff (2 yrs., 10-8-2)

1992 Opponent	Date		Score	1991 Opponent	Score
Lebanon Valley	S12		19	Lebanon Valley	19
Swarthmore	S19		47	Swarthmore	19
FDU-Madison ■	S25*		23	FDU-Madison	6
Gettysburg ■	0 2*		19	Gettysburg	20
Ursinus	O10		28	Ursinus	0
Muhlenberg ■	O17*		8	Muhlenberg	14
Georgetown ■	O24		40	Georgetown	14
Dickinson ■	O31		6	Dickinson	25
Frank. & Marsh.	N 7		16	Frank. & Marsh.	14
Western Md. ■	N14		21	Western Md.	24

Colors: Blue & Black. Nickname: Blue Jays. III

KENTUCKY WESLEYAN .... Owensboro, KY 42301
Randy Awrey (2 yrs., 2-18-0)

1992 Opponent	Date		Score	1991 Opponent	Score
Mt. Senario	S 5		7	Washington (Mo.)	25
Tenn. Wesleyan	S12*		7	Thomas More	37
Evansville ■	S19*		0	Evansville	26
Rhodes ■	S26		7	Rhodes	43
Blackburn	0 3		0	Tenn. Wesleyan	20
Lakeland ■	O10		15	Chicago	12
Principia	O17		6	Eureka	13
Eureka ■	O24		13	Centre	15
Centre ■	O31		6	Sewanee	31
Sewanee ■	N14		47	Mt. Senario	7

Colors: Purple & White. Nickname: Panthers. III

JOHNSON C. SMITH .... Charlotte, NC 28216
Ray Lee (1st yr. as head coach)

1992 Opponent	Date		Score	1991 Opponent	Score
Hampton	S 5*		0	Gardner-Webb	31
Norfolk St. ■	S12		26	Hampton	15
Morehouse ■	S19		6	Norfolk St.	32
Morgan St.	S26		16	Clark Atlanta	16
Winston-Salem ■	0 3		0	South Caro. St.	50
Glenville St. ■	O10		14	Livingstone	17
Livingstone	O17		24	Fayetteville St.	0
Fayetteville St. ■	O24		32	Winston-Salem	40
Morris Brown	O31		16	N.C. Central	28
N.C. Central	N 7		6	Alabama St.	62

Colors: Blue & Gold. Nickname: Golden Bulls. II

KENYON .... Gambier, OH 43022
Jim Meyer (3 yrs., 16-13-1)

1992 Opponent	Date		Score	1991 Opponent	Score
Marietta	S12*		40	Wilmington (Ohio)	12
Ohio Wesleyan	S19		20	Otterbein	18
Earlham ■	S26		13	Albion	20
Wooster	0 3		0	Wittenberg	22
Case Reserve ■	O10		17	Oberlin	7
Allegheny	O17		7	Denison	33
Wittenberg ■	O24		21	Allegheny	43
Waynesburg ■	O31		23	Wooster	6
Oberlin ■	N 7		18	Ohio Wesleyan	36
Denison ■	N14		55	Earlham	21

Colors: Purple & White. Nickname: Lords. III

JUNIATA .... Huntingdon, PA 16652
Chris Coller (1st yr. as head coach)

1992 Opponent	Date		Score	1991 Opponent	Score
Carnegie Mellon	S 5*		10	Allegheny	19
Delaware Valley	S19		20	Delaware Valley	28
Randolph-Macon	S26		12	Randolph-Macon	20
Widener ■	0 3		13	Widener	0
Moravian	O10		6	Moravian	42
Lycoming	O17		7	Lycoming	28
Albright ■	O24		26	Albright	13
Susquehanna ■	O31		16	Susquehanna	34
Wilkes	N 7		14	Wilkes	0
Lebanon Valley ■	N14		0	Lebanon Valley	7

Colors: Yale Blue & Old Gold. Nickname: Indians. III

KNOX .... Galesburg, IL 61401
Randy Oberembt (7 yrs., 25-37-1)

1992 Opponent	Date		Score	1991 Opponent	Score
Rose-Hulman ■	S12		7	Eureka	41
Concordia (St.P.)	S19		7	Beloit	35
Beloit	S26		24	Principia	20
Ripon ■	0 3		21	Lawrence	23
Cornell College	O10		12	Cornell College	29
Grinnell ■	O17		39	Grinnell	20
Illinois Col.	O24		29	Illinois Col.	3
Coe ■	O31		0	Coe	56
Monmouth (Ill.)	N 7		7	Monmouth (Ill.)	13

Colors: Purple & Gold. Nickname: Siwash. III

KALAMAZOO .... Kalamazoo, MI 49007
Dave Warmack (2 yrs., 8-9-1)

1992 Opponent	Date		Score	1991 Opponent	Score
Wooster	S12		22	Ill. Benedictine	7
Carroll (Wis.) ■	S19		45	Lakeland	7
Chicago ■	S26		18	Chicago	6
Defiance	0 3		14	Trinity (Ill.)	16
Albion	O10		6	Albion	10
Olivet ■	O17		7	Olivet	17
Alma	O24		27	Alma	0
Hope ■	O31		14	Hope	0
Adrian ■	N 7		9	Adrian	13

Colors: Orange & Black. Nickname: Hornets. III

KUTZTOWN .... Kutztown, PA 19530
Barry Fetterman (4 yrs., 14-27-0)

1992 Opponent	Date		Score	1991 Opponent	Score
Maine	S12		42	Calif. (Pa.)	16
Shippensburg ■	S19		35	Shippensburg	44
Calif. (Pa.)	S26		36	Millersville	45
Mansfield	0 3		43	Bloomsburg	19
Millersville ■	O10		27	Clarion	33
Bloomsburg ■	O17		42	West Chester	3
Lock Haven ■	O24		20	East Stroudsburg	21
West Chester ■	O31		35	Cheyney	14
East Stroudsburg	N 7		39	Mansfield	22
Cheyney ■	N14		17	Liberty	16
Liberty	N21				

Colors: Maroon & Gold. Nickname: Golden Bears. II

KEAN .... Union, NJ 07083
Brian Carlson (1st yr. as head coach)

1992 Opponent	Date		Score	1991 Opponent	Score
Bri'water (Mass.) ■	S12		9	Lycoming	37
Upsala ■	S19		14	Upsala	0
Ramapo ■	S26		9	Ramapo	13
Wm. Paterson	0 3*		17	Wm. Paterson	26
Montclair St. ■	O10		14	Montclair St.	21
Jersey City St. ■	O17		43	Jersey City St.	10
Glassboro St. ■	O31		0	Mass.-Lowell	24
Trenton St.	N 7*		12	Glassboro St.	28
Salisbury St. ■	N14		14	Trenton St.	16
			37	Salisbury St.	14

Colors: Royal Blue & Silver. Nickname: Cougars. III

LA VERNE .... La Verne, CA 91750
Rex Huigens (1 yr., 7-2-0)

1992 Opponent	Date		Score	1991 Opponent	Score
San Diego ■	S12		20	Redlands	27
Whittier	S19*		12	Whittier	2
Pomona-Pitzer ■	0 3		38	Pomona-Pitzer	10
Azusa-Pacific	O10		27	Azusa-Pacific	12
Menlo ■	O17		28	Cal Lutheran	6
Redlands ■	O24		28	Menlo	7
Occidental	O31		37	San Diego	38
Cal Lutheran	N 7		34	Claremont-M-S	10
Claremont-M-S	N14		39	Occidental	34

Colors: Orange & Green. Nickname: Leopards. III

KENTUCKY STATE .... Frankfort, KY 40601
George James Jr. (10 yrs., 45-57-3)

1992 Opponent	Date		Score	1991 Opponent	Score
Findlay ■	S 5*		17	Morehouse	14
Wingate	S12*		9	Wingate	17
Knoxville	S19		17	Knoxville	29
N.C. Central ■	S26*		6	Austin Peay	17
Lane ■	0 3*		7	N.C. Central	22
Central St. (Ohio)	O10		6	Findlay	22
Clark Atlanta	O17		7	Winston-Salem	28
St. Francis (Ill.) ■	O24		0	Central St. (Ohio)	77
Norfolk St.	O31		6	St. Francis (Ill.)	46
Elizabeth City St. ■	N 7		21	Elizabeth City St.	18
Jacksonville St.	N14		7	Jacksonville St.	42

Colors: Green & Gold. Nickname: Thorobreds. II

LAKE FOREST .... Lake Forest, IL 60045
Maury Waugh (11 yrs., 36-62-2)

1992 Opponent	Date		Score	1991 Opponent	Score
Wheaton (Ill.)	S12		35	Grinnell	13
North Park ■	S19		6	Trinity (Ill.)	28
Grinnell	S26		18	Illinois Col.	6
Cornell College ■	0 3		6	Monmouth (Ill.)	36
St. Norbert ■	O10		7	St. Norbert	31
Ripon	O17		23	Ripon	24
Carroll (Wis.) ■	O24		14	Wartburg	41
Lawrence	O31		13	Lawrence	14
Beloit	N 7		13	Beloit	41

Colors: Red & Black. Nickname: Foresters. III

■ Home games on each schedule.   *Night Games.

LAWRENCE......Appleton, WI 54911
Ron Roberts (19 yrs., 119-47-1)

N'western Col. (Wis.) ■	S12	14 Macalester	20
Chicago	S19	12 Concordia (Wis.)	34
Monmouth (Ill.)	S26	20 Coe	42
Illinois Col. ■	O 3	23 Knox	21
Carroll (Wis.)	O10	0 Albion	41
St. Norbert ■	O17	18 St. Norbert	22
Beloit ■	O24	12 Beloit	26
Lake Forest	O31	14 Lake Forest	13
Ripon ■	N 7	26 Ripon	0

Colors: Navy & White. Nickname: Vikings. III

LEBANON VALLEY......Annville, PA 17003
James Monos (6 yrs., 23-35-2)

Johns Hopkins ■	S12	19 Johns Hopkins	19
Lycoming ■	S19	19 Lycoming	30
Albright	S26*	28 Albright	10
Susquehanna ■	O 3*	20 Susquehanna	21
Wilkes	O10	24 Wilkes	19
Moravian ■	O17	32 Moravian	42
Delaware Valley	O24	31 Delaware Valley	23
Western Md.	O31	15 Western Md.	13
Widener ■	N 7	28 Widener	24
Juniata	N14	7 Juniata	0

Colors: Royal Blue & White. Nickname: Flying Dutchmen. III

LENOIR-RHYNE......Hickory, NC 28603
Charles Forbes (16 yrs., 74-78-3)

Newberry ■	S12*	17 East Stroudsburg	34
Wofford	S19*	31 Newberry	10
Presbyterian	S26	9 Wofford	13
Elon ■	O 3*	24 Presbyterian	12
Gardner-Webb ■	O10*	28 Elon	27
Wingate	O17	24 Gardner-Webb	6
West Liberty St.	O24	38 Wingate	27
Carson-Newman ■	O31*	20 Central Conn. St.	12
Mars Hill ■	N 7	25 Carson-Newman	42
Catawba	N14	14 Mars Hill	35
		10 Catawba	20

Colors: Red & Black. Nickname: Bears. II

LIVINGSTON......Livingston, AL 35470
Lloyd Sisco (1 yr., 6-5-0)

Knoxville ■	S 5*	6 East Tex. St.	44
Ark.-Monticello ■	S12*	24 Gardner-Webb	7
Albany St. (Ga.)	S19	22 Albany St. (Ga.)	21
West Ga. ■	O 3*	24 Ark.-Monticello	16
Valdosta St.	O10*	32 West Ga.	21
Mississippi Col. ■	O17	7 Valdosta St.	20
Delta St.	O24*	14 Mississippi Col.	25
North Ala. ■	O31*	25 Delta St.	18
Jacksonville St.	N 7	0 North Ala.	14
		0 Jacksonville St.	31
		10 Knoxville	0

Colors: Red & White. Nickname: Tigers. II

LIVINGSTONE......Salisbury, NC 28144
Delano Tucker (2 yrs., 8-11-0)

Bowie St. ■	S 5	17 Virginia Union	49
Lees-McRae ■	S19	19 Bowie St.	3
Virginia St.	O 3	14 Clark Atlanta	33
Johnson Smith	O17	28 Lees-McRae	7
Savannah St.	O24	18 Winston-Salem	54
N.C. Central ■	O31	8 Virginia St.	6
Fayetteville St.	N 7	17 Johnson Smith	14
Winston-Salem	N14	28 Morris Brown	31
		14 N.C. Central	22
		34 Fayetteville St.	28

Colors: Blue & Black. Nickname: Fighting Bears. II

LOCK HAVEN......Lock Haven, PA 17745
Dennis Therrell (2 yrs., 5-17-0)

Mansfield ■	S 5	16 Eastern Ill.	62
Tennessee Tech	S12*	14 Indiana (Pa.)	37
Bloomsburg	S19	14 Bloomsburg	9
Indiana St.	S26*	7 Slippery Rock	33
Indiana (Pa.)	O 3	0 Northeastern	34
Edinboro ■	O10	12 Edinboro	28
Clarion	O17	27 Clarion	26
Kutztown	O24	13 West Chester	7
Shippensburg ■	O31	0 Shippensburg	34
Calif. (Pa.)	N 7	10 Calif. (Pa.)	7
Slippery Rock ■	N14	7 Mansfield	28

Colors: Crimson & White. Nickname: Bald Eagles. II

LONG ISLAND-C.W. POST......Brookville, NY 11548
Tom Marshall (9 yrs., 42-43-1)

Salisbury St.	S12	10 Salisbury St.	5
Ramapo ■	S19	28 Merchant Marine	6
Marist ■	S26	24 Hofstra	54
Pace	O 3	55 Pace	8
Gannon	O10	13 Stony Brook	7
Iona ■	O17	19 Iona	20
St. John's (N.Y.)	O23*	14 St. John's (N.Y.)	54
Wagner ■	O31	13 Wagner	26
Springfield	N 7	14 Springfield	56
Alfred ■	N14	11 Alfred	24

Colors: Green & Gold. Nickname: Pioneers. III

LORAS......Dubuque, IA 52001
Bob Bierie (12 yrs., 73-48-4)

Ill. Benedictine ■	S 5	23 Ill. Benedictine	12
Augustana (Ill.)	S12	3 Central (Iowa)	12
Buena Vista	S19	18 Luther	6
William Penn ■	S26	14 Simpson	31
Simpson	O10	33 Upper Iowa	13
Dubuque ■	O17	10 Dubuque	7
Central (Iowa)	O24	50 Buena Vista	14
Luther ■	O31	24 Wartburg	30
Upper Iowa	N 7	34 William Penn	26
Wartburg ■	N14	32 Quincy	6

Colors: Purple & Gold. Nickname: Duhawks. III

LUTHER......Decorah, IA 52101
Bob Naslund (14 yrs., 72-59-0)

St. Olaf ■	S12	13 St. Olaf	22
Simpson ■	S19	21 William Penn	18
Upper Iowa	S26	6 Loras	18
Dubuque ■	O 3	20 Wartburg	17
Wartburg	O10	13 Simpson	14
Trinity (Ill.) ■	O17	47 Dubuque	6
William Penn ■	O24	29 Buena Vista	19
Loras	O31	13 Upper Iowa	12
Central (Iowa) ■	N 7	21 Central (Iowa)	22
Buena Vista	N14		

Colors: Blue & White. Nickname: Norsemen, Norse. III

LYCOMING......Williamsport, PA 17701
Frank Girardi (20 yrs., 142-50-4)

Frostburg St.	S12	37 Kean	0
Lebanon Valley	S19	30 Lebanon Valley	20
Delaware Valley ■	S26	41 Delaware Valley	10
Widener	O10	31 Widener	0
Juniata ■	O17	28 Juniata	7
Moravian ■	O24	21 Moravian	3
Albright	O31	43 Albright	8
Susquehanna ■	N 7	35 Susquehanna	31
Wilkes	N14	34 Wilkes	0
		III Championship	
		18 Wash. & Jeff.	16
		24 Susquehanna	31

Colors: Blue & Gold. Nickname: Warriors. III

MACALESTER......St. Paul, MN 55105
Gary Etcheverry (2 yrs., 2-17-0)

Huron ■	S12	20 Lawrence	14
Bethel (Minn.) ■	S19*	0 Gust. Adolphus	63
St. Thomas (Minn.)	S26	0 St. Thomas (Minn.)	22
St. Olaf	O 3	0 St. Olaf	62
Carleton	O10	0 Bethel (Minn.)	13
Concordia-M'head	O17	0 Concordia-M'head	34
Augsburg ■	O24*	0 St. John's (Minn.)	56
St. John's (Minn.)	O31	0 Carleton	40
Gust. Adolphus ■	N 7	14 Augsburg	29
Hamline†	N14		

Colors: Orange & Blue. Nickname: Scots. III

MacMURRAY......Jacksonville, IL 62650
Michael Hensley (5 yrs., 19-30-1)

Eureka	S 5	24 Quincy	31
Manchester ■	S12	36 Monmouth (Ill.)	35
Monmouth (Ill.) ■	S19	12 Manchester	12
Quincy ■	S26	9 Eureka	45
Concordia (Wis.)	O 3	13 Concordia (Wis.)	11
Greenville ■	O10	27 Greenville	26
Aurora ■	O17	0 Iowa Wesleyan	31
Blackburn ■	O24	28 Blackburn	17
Concordia (Ill.)	O31	40 Concordia (Ill.)	28
Lakeland	N 7	14 Lakeland	8

Colors: Navy & Scarlet. Nickname: Fighting Highlanders. III

MAINE MARITIME ....Castine, ME 04420
John Huard (10 yrs., 53-35-0)

1992 Opponent	Date		1991	Opponent	
Bri'water (Mass.) ■	S19		40	Westfield St.	28
Worcester St.	S26		21	Fitchburg St.	6
Mass. Maritime ■	O 3		34	Mass. Maritime	48
Mass.-Dartmouth	O10		0	Nichols	6
Plymouth St.	O17		35	Mass.-Boston	28
Mass.-Boston ■	O24		18	Plymouth St.	8
Fitchburg St.	O31		7	Mass.-Lowell	13
Framingham St. ■	N 7		27	Curry	3
Westfield St.	N14				

Colors: Royal Blue & Gold. Nickname: Mariners. III

MANCHESTER ....North Manchester, IN 46962
Dale Liston (9 yrs., 35-47-0)

1992 Opponent	Date		1991	Opponent	
Earlham ■	S 5		7	Defiance	30
MacMurray	S12		12	MacMurray	12
Clinch Valley	S19		39	Earlham	22
Wabash	O 3		6	Taylor	26
Taylor ■	O10		20	Anderson	28
Anderson ■	O17		10	DePauw	17
DePauw	O24		20	Franklin	16
Franklin	O31		19	Hanover	35
Hanover ■	N 7		7	Wabash	28
Rose-Hulman ■	N14		27	Rose-Hulman	18

Colors: Black & Old Gold. Nickname: Spartans.

MANKATO STATE ....Mankato, MN 56001
Dan Runkle (11 yrs., 56-64-2)

1992 Opponent	Date		1991	Opponent	
St. Francis (Ill.)	S 5*		10	Portland St.	7
Northwest Mo. St.	S12		53	Northwest Mo. St.	35
Northern Colo. ■	S19		13	Northern Colo.	24
Morningside ■	S26*		24	Morningside	15
St. Cloud St.	O 3		14	St. Cloud St.	20
Nebraska-Omaha	O10*		17	Nebraska-Omaha	0
North Dak. St. ■	O17		13	North Dak. St.	21
North Dak.	O24		21	North Dak.	15
South Dak. ■	O31		23	South Dak. St.	0
South Dak. St.	N 7		28	Augustana (S.D.)	14
Augustana (S.D.)	N14			**II Championship**	
			27	North Dak. St.	7
			27	Portland St.	37

Colors: Purple & Gold. Nickname: Mavericks. II

MANSFIELD ....Mansfield, PA 16933
Tom Elsasser (9 yrs., 35-52-6)

1992 Opponent	Date		1991	Opponent	
Lock Haven	S 5		35	Central Conn. St.	35
Buffalo St.	S12		18	Montclair St.	7
Cortland St. ■	S19		17	Cortland St.	31
Buffalo	S26		9	West Chester	31
Kutztown ■	O 3		10	East Stroudsburg	26
West Chester	O 9*		41	Cheyney	6
East Stroudsburg ■	O17		33	Slippery Rock	23
Cheyney	O24		31	Millersville	30
Ferrum ■	O31		24	Bloomsburg	31
Millersville ■	N 7		22	Kutztown	39
Bloomsburg	N14		28	Lock Haven	7

Colors: Red & Black. Nickname: Mountaineers. II

MARIETTA ....Marietta, OH 45750
Gene Epley (5 yrs., 18-32-1)

1992 Opponent	Date		1991	Opponent	
Kenyon ■	S12*		7	Alma	21
Ohio Northern	S19		7	John Carroll	42
Mount Union	S26*		0	Heidelberg	48
Capital ■	O 3		13	Baldwin-Wallace	50
Hiram ■	O10		0	Muskingum	49
Otterbein	O17		29	Hiram	35
Baldwin-Wallace ■	O24		21	Otterbein	22
John Carroll	O31		6	Ohio Northern	40
Heidelberg ■	N 7		6	Mount Union	43
Muskingum	N14		6	Capital	34

Colors: Navy Blue & White. Nickname: Pioneers. III

MARIST ....Poughkeepsie, NY 12601
Jim Parady (1st yr. as head coach)

1992 Opponent	Date		1991	Opponent	
Siena	S12		16	Iona	20
Pace	S19		12	Siena	13
LIU-C.W. Post	S26		28	Pace	7
Iona ■	O 3		46	Gallaudet	21
St. Francis (Pa.) ■	O10		28	St. John Fisher	3
Wagner	O17		7	St. Francis (Pa.)	16
Rensselaer	O24		13	Rensselaer	38
St. John's (N.Y.) ■	O31		21	St. John's (N.Y.)	18
FDU-Madison ■	N 7		26	FDU-Madison	7
Canisius	N14		42	Assumption	0

Colors: Black, Red & White. Nickname: Red Foxes. III

MARS HILL ....Mars Hill, NC 28754
Felton Stephens (4 yrs., 18-24-0)

1992 Opponent	Date		1991	Opponent	
Western Caro.	S 5*		29	Charleston So.	0
East Tenn. St.	S12*		6	Catawba	33
Catawba ■	S19*		19	Wingate	25
Wingate	S26*		20	Concord	21
Concord	O 3		19	Elon	54
Elon ■	O10		15	Carson-Newman	57
Carson-Newman ■	O17		30	Presbyterian	35
Presbyterian ■	O24		38	Lees-McRae	18
Lees-McRae	O31		35	Lenoir-Rhyne	14
Lenoir-Rhyne	N 7		18	Gardner-Webb	42
Gardner-Webb	N14				

Colors: Blue & Gold. Nickname: Lions. II

MARYVILLE (TENNESSEE) ....Maryville, TN 37801
Phil Wilks (4 yrs., 18-21-0)

1992 Opponent	Date		1991	Opponent	
Tenn. Wesleyan ■	S 5		14	Tenn. Wesleyan	17
Lambuth	S12		13	Rhodes	7
Centre	S19		21	Centre	5
Sewanee ■	S26		21	Lambuth	11
Clinch Valley ■	O 3		26	Clinch Valley	16
Cumberland (Tenn.)	O10		7	Sewanee	28
Rhodes ■	O24		38	Cumberland (Tenn.)	6
Methodist ■	O31		27	Methodist	6
Tusculum	N 7		37	Tusculum	19
Emory & Henry	N14		8	Emory & Henry	20

Colors: Orange & Garnet. Nickname: Scots. III

MASS.-DARTMOUTH .....North Dartmouth, MA 02747
William Kavanaugh (2 yrs., 7-11-0)

1992 Opponent	Date		1991	Opponent	
Stonehill	S12		16	Stonehill	0
Worcester St. ■	S19		13	Nichols	7
Mass. Maritime	S26		6	Mass.-Lowell	34
Maine Maritime ■	O10		25	Bri'water (Mass.)	26
Mass.-Boston	O17		51	Mass. Maritime	30
Fitchburg St. ■	O24		24	Westfield St.	33
Framingham St.	O31		55	Fitchburg St.	14
Westfield St. ■	N 7		14	Framingham St.	0
Bri'water (Mass.)	N14				

Colors: Gold & Blue. Nickname: Corsairs. III

MASS. MARITIME ....Buzzards Bay, MA 02532
Don Ruggeri (19 yrs., 95-72-1)

1992 Opponent	Date		1991	Opponent	
Nichols ■	S12		18	Plymouth St.	35
Mass.-Dartmouth ■	S26		32	Framingham St.	29
Maine Maritime	O 3		48	Maine Maritime	34
Mass.-Boston ■	O10		15	Mass.-Boston	8
Fitchburg St.	O17		30	Mass.-Dartmouth	51
Framingham St. ■	O24		19	Fitchburg St.	9
Westfield St.	O30*		43	Westfield St.	34
Bri'water (Mass.) ■	N 7		42	Worcester St.	6
Worcester St.	N14		13	Bri'water (Mass.)	16

Colors: Blue & Gold. Nickname: Buccaneers. III

MASSACHUSETTS-BOSTON ....Boston, MA 02125
Jim Kent (4 yrs., 12-23-1)

1992 Opponent	Date		1991	Opponent	
Westfield St. ■	S19		18	Worcester St.	7
Bri'water (Mass.)	S26		6	Plymouth St.	21
Worcester St. ■	O 3		8	Curry	3
Mass. Maritime	O10		8	Mass. Maritime	15
Mass.-Dartmouth ■	O17		8	Fitchburg St.	21
Maine Maritime	O24		28	Maine Maritime	35
MIT ■	O31		14	Nichols	6
Fitchburg St. ■	N 7		20	MIT	6
Framingham St.	N14		12	Mass.-Lowell	31

Colors: Blue & White. Nickname: Beacons. III

MASSACHUSETTS-LOWELL ....Lowell, MA 01854
Dennis Scannell (6 yrs., 41-15-0)

1992 Opponent	Date		1991	Opponent	
Coast Guard ■	S12*		22	Bri'water (Mass.)	0
Norwich ■	S19*		25	Westfield St.	13
Worcester Tech ■	S26*		34	Mass.-Dartmouth	6
Plymouth St.	O 3		10	Plymouth St.	3
Sacred Heart	O10		17	Nichols	0
Susquehanna ■	O17		42	Curry	6
Western Conn. St. ■	O24		24	Kean	0
Assumption	N 7		13	Maine Maritime	7
Stonehill	N14		31	Mass.-Boston	12
			10	Bri'water (Mass.)	7
				III Championship	
			16	Union (N.Y.)	55

Colors: Red, White & Blue. Nickname: Chiefs. III

■ Home games on each schedule.   *Night Games.

MENLO .... Menlo Park, CA 94025
Ray Solari (6 yrs., 29-25-1)

Redlands ■	S12	3	San Diego	13
Occidental ■	S19	0	Western St.	42
Whittier ■	S26	17	Claremont-M-S	7
Claremont-M-S	O 3	14	Whittier	7
San Fran. St.	O10	0	Redlands	48
La Verne	O17	7	San Fran. St.	55
Cal Lutheran	O24	7	La Verne	28
San Diego ■	N 7	15	Azusa-Pacific	22
Azusa-Pacific ■	N14	9	St. Mary's (Cal.)	56

Colors: Blue & White.   Nickname: Oaks.   III

MERCHANT MARINE .... Kings Point, NY 11024
Charlie Pravata (1 yr., 2-6-1)

Norwich	S12	21	Norwich	14
Western Conn. St.	S19	21	LIU-C.W. Post	28
Pace ■	S26	21	Pace	22
Albright	O10	20	Albright	21
Worcester Tech ■	O17	14	St. John's (N.Y.)	29
Stony Brook	O24	23	Stony Brook	7
Muhlenberg ■	O31	28	Iona	28
Iona ■	N 7	6	Ursinus	7
Coast Guard ■	N14	20	Coast Guard	25

Colors: Blue & Gray.   Nickname: Mariners.   III

MERCYHURST .... Erie, PA 16546
Jim Chapman (6 yrs., 43-19-1)

Bethany (W.Va.)	S 5	27	Bethany (W.Va.)	16
Gannon ■	S19	40	Gannon	7
St. Francis (Pa.)	S26	21	Dayton	48
Canisius ■	O 3	21	Canisius	15
Dayton	O10	21	Buffalo St.	28
Wittenberg ■	O17	21	Frostburg St.	6
Alfred	O24	20	Geneva	17
Ithaca	O31	7	Wash. & Jeff.	28
Brockport St.	N 7	13	Brockport St.	24

Colors: Blue & Green.   Nickname: Lakers.   III

MESA STATE .... Grand Junction, CO 81501
Jim Paronto (6 yrs., 33-28-0)

Idaho St.	S 5*	7	Idaho St.	38
Northern Colo. ■	S12	20	Colorado Mines	49
Montana St.	S19	14	Southern Utah	49
N.M. Highlands	S26	21	Fort Hays St.	14
Fort Lewis	O 3	33	Chadron St.	28
Fort Hays St. ■	O10*	0	Western St.	33
Western St. ■	O17*	0	Neb.-Kearney	39
Neb.-Kearney	O24	24	Western N. Mex.	28
Adams St. ■	O31*	7	Adams St.	11
Colorado Mines ■	N 7	34	Fort Lewis	7
Chadron St.	N14			

Colors: Maroon, White & Gold.   Nickname: Mavericks.   II

METHODIST .... Fayetteville, NC 28311
John Crea (9 yrs., 30-59-1)

Charleston So.	S 5	18	Charleston So.	8
Guilford ■	S12	0	Guilford	34
Salisbury St. ■	S19	21	Salisbury St.	41
Catholic ■	O 3	13	Newport News App.	34
Bridgewater (Va.)	O10	0	Bridgewater (Va.)	34
Davidson ■	O17	30	Davidson	28
Maryville (Tenn.)	O31	0	Catholic	20
Hampden-Sydney ■	N 7	6	Maryville (Tenn.)	27
Frostburg St.	N14	7	Hampden-Sydney	54
Ferrum	N21	7	Ferrum	45

Colors: Green & Gold.   Nickname: Monarchs.   III

MICHIGAN TECH .... Houghton, MI 49931
Bernie Anderson (5 yrs., 21-27-0)

Wis.-Stevens Point ■	S 5	21	Missouri-Rolla	24
Northern St. (S.D.)	S12*	33	Ferris St.	13
Minn.-Morris	S19	41	St. Norbert	0
Bemidji St. ■	S26	58	Trinity (Ill.)	7
Winona St.	O 3	21	Moorhead St.	28
Minn.-Duluth ■	O10	35	Bemidji St.	0
Wayne St. (Neb.)	O31	42	Winona St.	9
Valparaiso†	N 7	21	Minn.-Duluth	28
Moorhead St.†	N14	46	Minn.-Morris	14
		25	Olivet Nazarene	34

Colors: Silver & Gold.   Nickname: Huskies.   II

MIDDLEBURY .... Middlebury, VT 05753
Mickey Heinecken (19 yrs., 84-66-2)

Bowdoin ■	S26	22	Bowdoin	27
Colby	O 3	35	Amherst	0
Amherst ■	O10	24	Bates	6
Williams	O17	16	Tufts	20
Bates ■	O24	6	Hamilton	24
Trinity (Conn.)	O31	14	Williams	26
Hamilton	N 7	16	Colby	31
Tufts ■	N14	25	Norwich	33

Colors: Blue & White.   Nickname: Panthers.   III

MILLERSVILLE .... Millersville, PA 17551
Gene Carpenter (23 yrs., 152-66-5)

Shepherd	S12	30	Shepherd	20
American Int'l ■	S19*	34	Norfolk St.	16
Shippensburg	S26	45	Kutztown	36
Bloomsburg ■	O 3	3	West Chester	12
Kutztown	O10	17	East Stroudsburg	17
West Chester ■	O17	42	Cheyney	32
East Stroudsburg	O24	30	Mansfield	31
Cheyney ■	O31*	0	Indiana (Pa.)	47
Mansfield	N 7	17	Bloomsburg	24
Edinboro ■	N14	6	Central Fla.	52

Colors: Black & Gold.   Nickname: Marauders.   II

MILLIKIN .... Decatur, IL 62522
Carl Poelker (10 yrs., 67-24-1)

Ill. Benedictine	S12	33	Elmhurst	6
Drake	S26	53	North Park	6
Wheaton (Ill.) ■	O 3	7	Carroll (Wis.)	13
Carthage	O10	17	Wheaton (Ill.)	15
North Park ■	O17	24	Ill. Wesleyan	27
North Central	O24	34	Carthage	10
Augustana (Ill.) ■	O31	23	Drake	14
Ill. Wesleyan ■	N 7	45	North Central	2
Elmhurst ■	N14	0	Augustana (Ill.)	26

Colors: Royal Blue & White.   Nickname: Big Blue.   III

MILLSAPS .... Jackson, MS 39210
Tommy Ranager (3 yrs., 16-10-1)

Ala.-Birmingham ■	S 5	28	Ala.-Birmingham	0
Greenville ■	S12	31	Trinity (Tex.)	7
DePauw	S19	19	Colorado Col.	9
Hardin-Simmons ■	S26	14	DePauw	15
Emory & Henry	O 3	14	Emory & Henry	6
Centre ■	O10	14	Centre	7
Colorado Col. ■	O24	14	Central Meth.	7
Sewanee	O31	20	Sewanee	6
Rhodes ■	N 7	3	Rhodes	10
Trinity (Tex.) ■	N14			

Colors: Purple & White.   Nickname: Majors.   III

MINNESOTA-DULUTH .... Duluth, MN 55812
James Malosky (34 yrs., 218-99-11)

Wis.-Eau Claire ■	S 5	14	Montana St.	30
St. Cloud St.	S12	21	Wis.-Eau Claire	7
St. Francis (Ill.)	S19	14	St. Cloud St.	17
Northern St. (S.D.) ■	S26	33	St. Francis (Ill.)	35
Bemidji St.	O 3	34	Minn.-Morris	0
Michigan Tech	O10	21	Northern St. (S.D.)	14
Southwest St. (Minn.) ■	O17	48	Bemidji St.	19
Moorhead St.	O24	28	Michigan Tech	21
Winona St. ■	O31	7	Southwest St. (Minn.)	43
Minn.-Morris	N 7	38	Winona St.	6
Northern Ariz.	N14*			

Colors: Maroon & Gold.   Nickname: Bulldogs.   II

MISSISSIPPI COLLEGE .... Clinton, MS 39058
Terry McMillan (1 yr., 7-4-1)

Northwestern (La.)	S 5*	34	Central Ark.	9
North Ala.	S12*	31	North Ala.	3
Henderson St. ■	S26*	42	Henderson St.	17
Jacksonville St. ■	O 3*	7	Northeast La.	17
West Ga. ■	O10*	6	Jacksonville St.	17
Livingston	O17	25	Livingston	14
Texas A&I ■	O24	49	West Ga.	21
Valdosta St.	O31*	10	Valdosta St.	10
Ga. Southern ■	N 7	23	Appalachian St.	31
Delta St. ■	N14	27	Delta St.	10

II Championship

		28	Wofford	15
		7	Jacksonville St.	35

Colors: Blue & Gold.   Nickname: Choctaws.   II

■ Home games on each schedule.   *Night Games.

MISSOURI-ROLLA................Rolla, MO 65401
Jim Anderson (1st yr. as head coach)

1992 Opponent	Date		1991 Opponent	
Iowa Wesleyan	S 5*	24	Michigan Tech	21
Northwest Mo. St.	S19	17	Iowa Wesleyan	21
Pittsburg St. ■	S26	20	Northwest Mo. St.	21
Mo. Western St.	O 3*	6	Pittsburg St.	6
Mo. Southern St. ■	O10	14	Mo. Western St.	26
Emporia St.	O17	6	Mo. Southern St.	42
Washburn ■	O24	27	Emporia St.	21
Central Mo. St.	O31	28	Washburn	13
Southwest Baptist	N 7	13	Central Mo. St.	7
Northeast Mo. St. ■	N14	21	Southwest Baptist	26
		16	Northeast Mo. St.	17

Colors: Silver & Gold.   Nickname: Miners.   II

MISSOURI SOUTHERN STATE.......Joplin, MO 64801
Jon Lantz (6 yrs., 39-21-2)

1992 Opponent	Date		1991 Opponent	
Cameron ■	S 5*	34	Cameron	16
Emporia St. ■	S12*	38	Portland St.	56
Central Mo. St.	S19*	35	Central Mo. St.	0
Mo. Western St. ■	S26*	37	Mo. Western St.	26
Washburn ■	O 3*	31	Washburn	6
Missouri-Rolla	O10	42	Missouri-Rolla	6
Southwest Baptist ■	O17*	42	Southwest Baptist	21
Pittsburg St.	O24*	21	Pittsburg St.	43
Northwest Mo. St. ■	O31	20	Northwest Mo. St.	3
Northeast Mo. St.	N 7	42	Northeast Mo. St.	43
		45	Emporia St.	9

Colors: Green & Gold.   Nickname: Lions.   II

MISSOURI WESTERN STATE....St. Joseph, MO 64507
Stan McGarvey (7 yrs., 44-29-2)

1992 Opponent	Date		1991 Opponent	
Western Ill.	S 5*	46	Wayne St. (Neb.)	27
Peru St. ■	S12*	35	Peru St.	20
Emporia St. ■	S19*	22	Emporia St.	23
Mo. Southern St.	S26*	26	Mo. Southern St.	37
Missouri-Rolla ■	O 3*	26	Missouri-Rolla	14
Southwest Baptist	O10	34	Southwest Baptist	43
Pittsburg St.	O17	14	Pittsburg St.	59
Northwest Mo. St.	O24	26	Northwest Mo. St.	49
Northeast Mo. St. ■	O31	21	Northeast Mo. St.	42
Central Mo. St. ■	N 7	24	Central Mo. St.	31
Washburn	N14	35	Washburn	23

Colors: Black & Gold.   Nickname: Griffons.   II

MIT............................Cambridge, MA 02139
Dwight Smith (4 yrs., 10-18-1)

1992 Opponent	Date		1991 Opponent	
Assumption	S19	6	Bentley	33
Western New Eng. ■	S26	21	Assumption	27
Bentley	O 3	22	Western New Eng.	7
Westfield St. ■	O10	6	Siena	27
Stonehill ■	O17	15	Stonehill	37
Nichols	O24	7	Sacred Heart	26
Mass.-Boston	O31	6	Mass.-Boston	20
Curry ■	N 7	0	Stony Brook	38

Colors: Cardinal & Gray.   Nickname: Beavers.   III

MONMOUTH (ILLINOIS).........Monmouth, IL 61462
Kelly Kane (8 yrs., 50-25-0)

1992 Opponent	Date		1991 Opponent	
Eureka	S12	35	MacMurray	36
MacMurray ■	S19	3	Eureka	37
Lawrence ■	S26	7	St. Norbert	24
Carroll (Wis.)	O 3	36	Lake Forest	6
Illinois Col. ■	O10	17	Illinois Col.	7
Cornell College ■	O17	16	Cornell College	21
Coe	O24	21	Coe	32
Grinnell	O31	54	Grinnell	13
Knox ■	N 7	13	Knox	7

Colors: Crimson & White.   Nickname: Fighting Scots.   III

MONTCLAIR STATE.......Upper Montclair, NJ 07043
Rick Giancola (9 yrs., 71-23-2)

1992 Opponent	Date		1991 Opponent	
Cortland St. ■	S12	7	Mansfield	18
Ithaca	S19	7	Buffalo	3
Ramapo	O 3	14	Wagner	26
Kean	O10	17	Ramapo	23
Wm. Paterson ■	O17*	21	Kean	14
Salisbury St.	O24	12	Wm. Paterson	27
Trenton St. ■	O31*	41	Salisbury St.	17
Jersey City St.	N 7	7	Trenton St.	0
Glassboro St. ■	N14*	35	Jersey City St.	8
		16	Glassboro St.	21

Colors: Scarlet & White.   Nickname: Red Hawks.   III

MORAVIAN.................Bethlehem, PA 18018
Scot Dapp (5 yrs., 37-15-0)

1992 Opponent	Date		1991 Opponent	
Frank. & Marsh. ■	S12	7	Frank. & Marsh.	6
Susquehanna ■	S19	0	Susquehanna	10
Widener	S26	17	Widener	13
Wilkes ■	O 3	23	Wilkes	10
Juniata ■	O10	42	Juniata	6
Lebanon Valley	O17	42	Lebanon Valley	32
Lycoming	O24	3	Lycoming	21
Delaware Valley ■	O31	35	Delaware Valley	15
Albright	N 7	0	Albright	20
Muhlenberg ■	N14	28	Muhlenberg	27

Colors: Blue & Gray.   Nickname: Greyhounds.   III

MOREHOUSE.................Atlanta, GA 30314
Craig Cason (1 yr., 6-4-0)

1992 Opponent	Date		1991 Opponent	
Howard ■	S 5	14	Kentucky St.	17
Fort Valley St.	S12	13	Winston-Salem	28
Johnson Smith	S19	17	Fort Valley St.	20
Albany St. (Ga.) ■	S26	20	Albany St. (Ga.)	15
Hampton	O 3	20	Hampton	17
Alabama A&M ■	O10	30	Lane	7
Tuskegee†	O17*	14	Tuskegee	9
Morris Brown ■	O24	42	Savannah St.	34
Savannah St.	O31	24	Miles	0
Miles	N 7	19	Clark Atlanta	31
Clark Atlanta	N14			

Colors: Maroon & White.   Nickname: Maroon Tigers/Tigers.   II

MORNINGSIDE.................Sioux City, IA 51106
Dave Dolch (6 yrs., 23-38-2)

1992 Opponent	Date		1991 Opponent	
Northeast Mo. St. ■	S 5	13	Northwestern (Iowa)	7
Wayne St. (Neb.) ■	S12	7	Wayne St. (Neb.)	16
South Dak.	S19	42	South Dak.	7
Mankato St.	S26*	15	Mankato St.	24
North Dak. ■	O 3	0	North Dak.	35
Northern Colo.	O10	7	Northern Colo.	10
South Dak. St. ■	O17	17	South Dak. St.	27
Nebraska-Omaha ■	O24	22	Nebraska-Omaha	27
Augustana (S.D.)	O31	10	North Dak. St.	56
North Dak. St.	N 7	14	St. Cloud St.	28
St. Cloud St. ■	N14			

Colors: Maroon & White.   Nickname: Chiefs.   II

MORRIS BROWN.................Atlanta, GA 30314
Greg Thompson (11 yrs., 45-55-4)

1992 Opponent	Date		1991 Opponent	
Clark Atlanta	S 7	6	Clark Atlanta	29
Cheyney	S12	21	Cheyney	14
Tuskegee	S19	23	Tuskegee	21
Fort Valley St.†	S26*	21	Fort Valley St.	26
Alabama A&M ■	O 3	7	Alabama A&M	12
Miles ■	O10	21	Miles	7
Savannah St. ■	O17	0	Savannah St.	56
Morehouse	O24	31	Livingstone	28
Johnson Smith	O31	21	Albany St. (Ga.)	28
Albany St. (Ga.) ■	N 7	13	Bethune-Cookman	51

Colors: Purple & Black.   Nickname: Wolverines.   II

MOUNT UNION.................Alliance, OH 44601
Larry Kehres (6 yrs., 48-12-3)

1992 Opponent	Date		1991 Opponent	
Adrian ■	S12	24	Wooster	8
Muskingum	S19*	13	Ohio Northern	10
Marietta ■	S26*	18	Baldwin-Wallace	21
Baldwin-Wallace ■	O 3	21	Capital	14
John Carroll	O10	20	John Carroll	3
Heidelberg ■	O17	21	Otterbein	18
Ohio Northern	O24	32	Heidelberg	23
Otterbein ■	O31	53	Muskingum	6
Capital ■	N 7	43	Marietta	6
Hiram	N14	45	Hiram	12

Colors: Purple & White.   Nickname: Purple Raiders.   III

MUHLENBERG.................Allentown, PA 18104
Fran Meagher (7 yrs., 22-46-0)

1992 Opponent	Date		1991 Opponent	
Susquehanna ■	S12	11	Susquehanna	30
Dickinson	S19	0	Dickinson	42
Frank. & Marsh. ■	S26	21	Frank. & Marsh.	25
Western Md.	O 3	6	Western Md.	34
Swarthmore ■	O10	12	Swarthmore	10
Johns Hopkins	O17*	14	Johns Hopkins	8
Gettysburg ■	O24	28	Gettysburg	7
Merchant Marine	O31	9	Ursinus	13
Ursinus	N 7	0	Wash. & Jeff.	49
Moravian	N14	27	Moravian	28

Colors: Cardinal & Gray.   Nickname: Mules.   III

■ Home games on each schedule.   *Night Games.

MUSKINGUM .... New Concord, OH 43762
Jeff Heacock (11 yrs., 60-45-2)

Opponent	Date	Pts	Opponent	Pts
Denison	S12	10	Denison	3
Mount Union ■	S19*	28	Heidelberg	21
Baldwin-Wallace	S26*	26	Otterbein	13
Heidelberg ■	O 3	39	Hiram	13
Ohio Northern ■	O10	49	Marietta	0
John Carroll	O17	21	Baldwin-Wallace	41
Capital ■	O24	21	Ohio Northern	7
Hiram	O31	6	Mount Union	53
Otterbein	N 7	14	Capital	28
Marietta ■	N14	24	John Carroll	17

Colors: Black & Magenta.   Nickname: Fighting Muskies.   III

NEBRASKA-KEARNEY .... Kearney, NE 68849
Claire Boroff (20 yrs., 122-71-4)

Opponent	Date	Pts	Opponent	Pts
Augustana (S.D.) ■	S 3	7	Northern St. (S.D.)	6
Nebraska-Omaha	S12*	13	South Dak. St.	16
Moorhead St.	S19	14	Nebraska-Omaha	40
Fort Hays St. ■	S26	7	Moorhead St.	24
Wayne St. (Neb.)	O 3	14	Adams St.	21
Portland St.	O10*	3	Cal Poly SLO	66
St. Francis (Ill.)	O17	25	Wayne St. (Neb.)	17
Mesa St. ■	O24	39	Mesa St.	0
Northern St. (S.D.)	O31	20	Fort Hays St.	43
Bemidji St.†	N14	30	Chadron St.	19
		20	Eastern N. Mex.	20

Colors: Royal Blue & Old Gold.   Nickname: Antelopes.   II

NEBRASKA-OMAHA .... Omaha, NE 68182
Tom Mueller (2 yrs., 8-13-0)

Opponent	Date	Pts	Opponent	Pts
Wayne St. (Neb.) ■	S 5*	28	Wayne St. (Neb.)	0
Neb.-Kearney ■	S12*	40	Neb.-Kearney	13
St. Cloud St.	S19	10	St. Cloud St.	14
Augustana (S.D.) ■	S26*	26	Augustana (S.D.)	18
South Dak. St.	O 3	13	South Dak. St.	21
Mankato St. ■	O10*	0	Mankato St.	17
Northern Colo.	O17	13	Northern Colo.	7
Morningside	O24	27	Morningside	22
North Dak. St. ■	O31*	13	North Dak.	28
North Dak.	N 7	15	South Dak.	7
South Dak. ■	N14			

Colors: Black & Crimson.   Nickname: Mavericks.   II

NEBRASKA WESLEYAN .... Lincoln, NE 68504
Jim Svoboda (5 yrs., 39-13-0)

Opponent	Date	Pts	Opponent	Pts
Austin ■	S 5	16	Dak. Wesleyan	10
Kan. Wesleyan	S12*	43	Northwestern (Iowa)	14
Northwestern (Iowa)	S26	21	Missouri Valley	14
Hastings ■	O 3	26	Drake	21
Dana	O10	20	Concordia (Neb.)	6
Doane	O24	16	Hastings	28
Midland Lutheran ■	O31	56	Midland Lutheran	49
Concordia (Neb.) ■	N 7	43	Doane	33
Peru St.	N14	27	St. Ambrose	34
		42	Dana	26

NAIA Div. II Championship

		20	Peru St.	41

Colors: Yellow & Brown.   Nickname: Plainsmen.   III

NEW HAVEN .... West Haven, CT 06516
Mark Whipple (4 yrs., 25-15-0)

Opponent	Date	Pts	Opponent	Pts
Connecticut	S 5	31	Calif. (Pa.)	7
Buffalo ■	S12	48	Clarion	42
Clarion	S19	14	Virginia Union	43
Virginia Union	S26	41	Central Conn. St.	34
Central Conn. St.	O 3	20	West Chester	34
American Int'l ■	O17	34	American Int'l	35
Southern Conn. St. ■	O24	60	Southern Conn. St.	64
Springfield	O31	21	Springfield	46
Carson-Newman ■	N 7	21	Wofford	42
Shepherd	N14	30	Shippensburg	31

Colors: Blue & Gold.   Nickname: Chargers.   II

NEW MEXICO HIGHLANDS ...... Las Vegas, NM 87701
Jim Ewan (1st yr. as head coach)

Opponent	Date	Pts	Opponent	Pts
Eastern N. Mex. ■	S 5*	12	Northern Ariz.	65
Western N. Mex.	S12	13	Adams St.	42
Northwestern Okla.	S19	6	Eastern N. Mex.	36
Mesa St. ■	S26	17	Southwestern Okla.	37
Fort Hays St. ■	O 3	13	Western N. Mex.	49
Chadron St.	O10	37	Langston	7
Fort Lewis	O17	6	Northwestern Okla.	23
West Tex. St. ■	O24	19	Western St.	53
Western St.	O31	7	Weber St.	62
Adams St.	N 7	12	Fort Lewis	27
Colorado Mines ■	N14			

Colors: Purple & White.   Nickname: Cowboys.   II

NEWBERRY .... Newberry, NC 29108
Brad Senter (1 yr., 1-10-0)

Opponent	Date	Pts	Opponent	Pts
South Caro. St. ■	S 5	7	South Caro. St.	28
Lenoir-Rhyne	S12*	7	Lenoir-Rhyne	31
Gardner-Webb ■	S19	0	Gardner-Webb	10
Elon ■	S26	12	East Tenn. St.	43
Charleston So.	O 3	7	North Ala.	21
Wofford ■	O17	41	Lees-McRae	19
Lees-McRae	O24	6	Wofford	49
Catawba	O31	19	Wingate	31
Citadel	N 7	7	Catawba	33
Fayetteville St. ■	N14	7	Elon	38
Presbyterian	N26	17	Presbyterian	32

Colors: Scarlet & Gray.   Nickname: Indians.   II

NICHOLS .... Dudley, MA 01570
Jack Charney (6 yrs., 27-27-0)

Opponent	Date	Pts	Opponent	Pts
Mass. Maritime	S12	34	Fitchburg St.	13
Stonehill ■	S19	7	Mass.-Dartmouth	13
Bentley	S25*	0	Plymouth St.	37
Assumption	O 3	6	Maine Maritime	0
Curry	O10	0	Mass.-Lowell	17
Sacred Heart ■	O17	13	Sacred Heart	20
MIT ■	O24	6	Mass.-Boston	14
Western New Eng. ■	O31	41	Curry	6
Worcester St.	N 7	26	Worcester St.	6

Colors: Black & Green.   Nickname: Bison.   III

NORFOLK STATE .... Norfolk, VA 23504
Willard Bailey (21 yrs., 155-65-5)

Opponent	Date	Pts	Opponent	Pts
Virginia St. ■	S 5*	18	Virginia St.	12
Johnson Smith	S12	27	Morgan St.	9
Fayetteville St. ■	S19*	32	Johnson Smith	6
Elizabeth City St. ■	S26*	16	Millersville	34
North Caro. A&T ■	O 3	26	Elizabeth City St.	21
Bowie St.	O10	14	North Caro. A&T	50
Hampton	O17	35	Bowie St.	13
Virginia Union ■	O24*	26	Hampton	12
Kentucky St.	O31	11	Virginia Union	39
Bethune-Cookman	N14	28	Fayetteville St.	14

Colors: Green & Gold.   Nickname: Spartans.   II

NORTH ALABAMA .... Florence, AL 35630
Bobby Wallace (4 yrs., 19-23-0)

Opponent	Date	Pts	Opponent	Pts
Central Mo. St. ■	S 5	28	Central Mo. St.	7
Mississippi Col. ■	S12*	3	Mississippi Col.	31
Alabama A&M ■	S19*	6	Delta St.	31
Delta St.	S26*	21	Newberry	7
Fort Valley St.	O10	23	Fort Valley St.	34
Jacksonville St. ■	O17*	13	Jacksonville St.	48
Troy St. ■	O24*	9	Troy St.	31
Livingston	O31*	14	Livingston	0
West Ga. ■	N 7*	26	West Ga.	28
Valdosta St.	N14*	17	Valdosta St.	34

Colors: Purple & Gold.   Nickname: Lions.   II

NORTH CAROLINA CENTRAL .... Durham, NC 27707
Bishop Harris (1 yr., 4-6-0)

Opponent	Date	Pts	Opponent	Pts
North Caro. A&T ■	S 5	0	North Caro. A&T	48
Virginia St. ■	S12*	14	Elon	38
Bowie St.	S19	32	Bowie St.	49
Kentucky St. ■	S26*	20	Kentucky St.	7
Elizabeth City St. ■	O 3	15	Elizabeth City St.	40
Fayetteville St. ■	O10*	14	Fayetteville St.	0
Winston-Salem	O17	22	Winston-Salem	68
South Caro. St.	O24	22	Livingstone	14
Livingstone	O31	28	Johnson Smith	16
Johnson Smith ■	N 7	28	Hampton	44
Hampton	N14			

Colors: Maroon & Gray.   Nickname: Eagles.   II

NORTH CENTRAL .... Naperville, IL 60540
Paul Connor (7 yrs., 27-35-1)

Opponent	Date	Pts	Opponent	Pts
Carroll (Wis.)	S 5	42	Upper Iowa	35
Eureka ■	S19*	0	Augustana (Ill.)	41
Ill. Wesleyan	O 3	49	Elmhurst	24
Augustana (Ill.) ■	O10	31	North Park	0
Elmhurst	O17	6	Carroll (Wis.)	27
Millikin	O24	0	Wheaton (Ill.)	36
Wheaton (Ill.)	O31	9	Ill. Wesleyan	44
North Park ■	N 7	12	Carthage	0
Carthage ■	N14	2	Millikin	45

Colors: Cardinal & White.   Nickname: Cardinals.   III

■ Home games on each schedule.   *Night Games.

NORTH DAKOTA .... Grand Forks, ND 58202
Roger Thomas (8 yrs., 34-44-1)

1992 Schedule	Date	Pts	1991 Results	Pts
South Dak. St.	S19	21	Moorhead St.	14
South Dak. ■	S26	36	South Dak. St.	10
Morningside	O 3	21	South Dak.	6
Augustana (S.D.) ■	O10	0	Morningside	0
St. Cloud St.	O17	20	Augustana (S.D.)	15
Mankato St. ■	O24	21	St. Cloud St.	17
Northern Colo.	O31	18	Mankato St.	21
Nebraska-Omaha ■	N 7	28	Nebraska-Omaha	13
North Dak. St.	N14	28	North Dak. St.	35

Colors: Green & White.   Nickname: Sioux.   II

NORTH DAKOTA STATE............. Fargo, ND 58105
Rocky Hager (5 yrs., 49-10-1)

1992 Schedule	Date	Pts	1991 Results	Pts
Cal Poly SLO ■	S12*	17	Grand Valley St.	21
Augustana (S.D.)	S19	41	Augustana (S.D.)	6
South Dak. St. ■	S26*	35	South Dak. St.	0
South Dak.	O 3	35	South Dak.	12
St. Cloud St. ■	O10	32	St. Cloud St.	9
Mankato St.	O17	21	Mankato St.	13
Northern Colo. ■	O24	14	Northern Colo.	23
Nebraska-Omaha ■	O31*	56	Morningside	10
Morningside	N 7	35	North Dak.	28
North Dak.	N14		II Championship	
		7	Mankato St.	27

Colors: Yellow & Green.   Nickname: Bison.   II

NORTH PARK .... Chicago, IL 60625
Tim Rucks (2 yrs., 1-17-0)

1992 Schedule	Date	Pts	1991 Results	Pts
Lake Forest	S19	6	Carthage	55
Blackburn ■	S26	6	Millikin	53
Augustana (Ill.)	O 3	0	North Central	31
Elmhurst ■	O10	0	Augustana (Ill.)	41
Millikin	O17	13	Elmhurst	41
Wheaton (Ill.) ■	O24	14	Aurora	35
Carthage	O31	8	Carroll (Wis.)	19
North Central ■	N 7	0	Wheaton (Ill.)	46
Ill. Wesleyan ■	N14	14	Ill. Wesleyan	47

Colors: Blue & Gold.   Nickname: Vikings.   III

NORTHEAST MISSOURI STATE... Kirksville, MO 63501
Eric Holm (2 yrs., 14-8-0)

1992 Schedule	Date	Pts	1991 Results	Pts
Morningside ■	S 5	31	Iowa Wesleyan	34
Iowa Wesleyan ■	S12*	11	Indiana (Pa.)	41
Washburn ■	S19	14	Washburn	7
Emporia St.	S26	41	Emporia St.	42
Southwest Baptist ■	O 3	25	Southwest Baptist	37
Pittsburg St.	O10	20	Pittsburg St.	55
Northwest Mo. St. ■	O17	37	Northwest Mo. St.	28
Central Mo. St.	O24	37	Central Mo. St.	38
Mo. Western St.	O31	42	Mo. Western St.	21
Mo. Southern St. ■	N 7	43	Mo. Southern St.	42
Missouri-Rolla	N14	17	Missouri-Rolla	16

Colors: Purple & White.   Nickname: Bulldogs.   II

NORTHERN COLORADO .... Greeley, CO 80639
Joe Glenn (7 yrs., 42-29-1)

1992 Schedule	Date	Pts	1991 Results	Pts
Western St. ■	S 5	47	Western St.	19
Mesa St.	S12	20	Abilene Christian	0
Mankato St.	S19	24	Mankato St.	13
St. Cloud St. ■	S26	31	St. Cloud St.	19
Augustana (S.D.)	O 3	51	Augustana (S.D.)	6
Morningside ■	O10	10	Morningside	7
Nebraska-Omaha ■	O17	7	Nebraska-Omaha	13
North Dak. St.	O24	23	North Dak. St.	14
North Dak. ■	O31	45	South Dak.	20
South Dak.	N 7	13	South Dak. St.	17
South Dak. St. ■	N14		II Championship	
		24	Portland St.	28

Colors: Navy & Gold.   Nickname: Bears.   II

NORTHERN MICHIGAN .... Marquette, MI 49855
Mark Marana (1 yr., 3-6-1)

1992 Schedule	Date	Pts	1991 Results	Pts
Butler ■	S 5	0	Butler	28
Indianapolis	S12	31	Indianapolis	20
Saginaw Valley ■	S19	7	Saginaw Valley	14
Valparaiso ■	S26	12	Valparaiso	17
Ferris St.	O 3	27	Ferris St.	17
Grand Valley St. ■	O10	0	Grand Valley St.	35
Hillsdale	O17	0	Hillsdale	24
Wayne St. (Mich.) ■	O24	20	Wayne St. (Mich.)	13
St. Joseph's (Ind.)	N 7	21	St. Joseph's (Ind.)	28
Ashland	N14	7	Ashland	49

Colors: Old Gold & Olive Green.   Nickname: Wildcats.   II

NORTHWEST MISSOURI STATE .. Maryville, MO 64468
Bud Elliott (24 yrs., 128-117-7)

1992 Schedule	Date	Pts	1991 Results	Pts
Central Okla. ■	S 5	38	Central Okla.	14
Mankato St.	S12	35	Mankato St.	53
Missouri-Rolla ■	S19	29	Missouri-Rolla	20
Washburn	S26*	29	Washburn	3
Pittsburg St. ■	O 3	0	Pittsburg St.	38
Central Mo. St. ■	O10	27	Central Mo. St.	30
Northeast Mo. St.	O17	28	Northeast Mo. St.	37
Mo. Western St. ■	O24	49	Mo. Western St.	26
Mo. Southern St.	O31	3	Mo. Southern St.	26
Emporia St.	N 7	41	Emporia St.	36
Southwest Baptist	N14	21	Southwest Baptist	23

Colors: Green & White.   Nickname: Bearcats.   II

NORTHWESTERN (WISCONSIN) . Watertown, WI 53094
Dennis Gorsline (21 yrs., 72-80-0)

1992 Schedule	Date	Pts	1991 Results	Pts
Lawrence	S12	3	Eureka	35
Concordia (Ill.) ■	S19	8	Maranatha	34
Principia ■	S26	28	Northwestern Minn.	18
Maranatha ■	O 3	14	Concordia (St.P.)	26
Concordia (St.P.)	O10	16	Principia	28
Northwestern Minn. ■	O17	40	Dr. Martin Luther	14
Dr. Martin Luther	O24	12	Mt. Senario	6
Mt. Senario	O31	14	Maranatha	0

Colors: Black & Red.   Nickname: Trojans.   III

NORTHWOOD..................... Midland, MI 48640
Tom Danna (7 yrs., 19-47-0)

1992 Schedule	Date	Pts	1991 Results	Pts
Ferris St.†	S 5	7	Slippery Rock	17
Edinboro	S12	14	Edinboro	25
Westminster (Pa.) ■	S19	7	Adrian	12
Hillsdale	O 3	6	Hillsdale	0
Wayne St. (Mich.) ■	O17	0	Findlay	10
Saginaw Valley	O24	6	Dayton	21
St. Francis (Ill.) ■	O31	7	Saginaw Valley	10
Findlay	N 7	5	St. Francis (Ill.)	3

Colors: Columbia Blue & White.   Nickname: Northmen.   II

NORWICH .... Northfield, VT 05663
Steve Hackett (1 yr., 2-8-0)

1992 Schedule	Date	Pts	1991 Results	Pts
Merchant Marine ■	S12	13	St. Lawrence	42
Mass.-Lowell	S19*	14	Merchant Marine	21
Plymouth St.	S26	24	Western Conn. St.	22
Coast Guard	O 3	7	Coast Guard	17
Worcester Tech ■	O10	0	Union (N.Y.)	66
Brockport St.	O17	20	Springfield	41
Albany (N.Y.) ■	O24	7	Worcester Tech	35
St. Lawrence	O31	14	Albany (N.Y.)	21
Western Conn. St.	N14	17	Frostburg St.	29
		33	Middlebury	25

Colors: Maroon & Gold.   Nickname: Cadets.   III

OBERLIN........................ Oberlin, OH 44074
Larry Story (2 yrs., 1-18-0)

1992 Schedule	Date	Pts	1991 Results	Pts
Thiel ■	S12	0	Thiel	28
Denison	S19	2	Allegheny	37
Ohio Wesleyan ■	S26	0	Wittenberg	50
Earlham	O 3	0	Ohio Wesleyan	43
Wooster ■	O10	7	Kenyon	17
Case Reserve	O17	12	Wooster	27
Allegheny ■	O24	0	Denison	26
Wittenberg	O31	0	Earlham	24
Kenyon ■	N 7	0	Case Reserve	41
Grove City	N14			

Colors: Crimson & Gold.   Nickname: Yeomen.   III

OCCIDENTAL.................. Los Angeles, CA 90041
Dale Widolff (10 yrs., 66-27-2)

1992 Schedule	Date	Pts	1991 Results	Pts
Menlo	S19	31	Pomona-Pitzer	9
Trinity (Tex.) ■	S26*	19	Azusa-Pacific	14
Whittier	O 3*	17	Claremont-M-S	14
Pomona-Pitzer ■	O10*	17	Trinity (Tex.)	16
Cal Lutheran	O17	0	Cal Lutheran	12
San Diego	O24*	20	Whittier	14
La Verne ■	O31	0	Redlands	33
Claremont-M-S ■	N 7*	34	La Verne	39
Redlands	N14*	19	San Diego	28

Colors: Orange & Black.   Nickname: Tigers.   III

■ Home games on each schedule.   *Night Games.

OHIO NORTHERN .... Ada, OH 45810
Tom Kaczkowski (6 yrs., 18-40-1)

Bluffton ■	S12	26 Olivet	29
Marietta ■	S19	10 Mount Union	13
Otterbein	S26*	44 Hiram	15
John Carroll ■	O 3	14 Heidelberg	14
Muskingum	O10	6 Baldwin-Wallace	10
Hiram	O17	10 Capital	26
Mount Union ■	O24	7 Muskingum	21
Capital	O31	40 Marietta	6
Baldwin-Wallace	N 7	7 John Carroll	17
Heidelberg ■	N14	34 Otterbein	17

Colors: Orange & Black. Nickname: Polar Bears.   III

OHIO WESLEYAN .... Delaware, OH 43015
Mike Hollway (9 yrs., 47-40-2)

Kenyon ■	S19	38 Hiram	0
Oberlin	S26	21 DePauw	15
Denison ■	O 3	58 Wooster	0
Wilmington (Ohio) ■	O10	43 Oberlin	0
Earlham	O17	28 Denison	21
Wooster ■	O24	34 Earlham	10
Case Reserve	O31	16 Case Reserve	41
Allegheny ■	N 7	7 Allegheny	24
Wittenberg	N14	36 Kenyon	18
		28 Wittenberg	6

Colors: Red & Black. Nickname: Battling Bishops.   III

OLIVET .... Olivet, MI 49076
Dominic Livedoti (4 yrs., 19-15-2)

Heidelberg ■	S12	29 Ohio Northern	26
Taylor	S19	36 Taylor	7
Defiance ■	S26	14 Defiance	43
Wilmington (Ohio) ■	O 3	26 Bluffton	14
Adrian ■	O10	25 Adrian	14
Kalamazoo	O17	17 Kalamazoo	7
Albion	O24	14 Albion	14
Alma ■	O31	14 Alma	13
Hope	N 7	21 Hope	14

Colors: Red & White. Nickname: Comets.   III

OTTERBEIN .... Westerville, OH 43081
John Hussey (1 yr., 2-8-0)

Earlham	S12	18 Kenyon	20
Heidelberg†	S19	7 Capital	16
Ohio Northern ■	S26*	13 Muskingum	26
Hiram	O 3*	0 John Carroll	39
Baldwin-Wallace	O10	14 Heidelberg	37
Marietta ■	O17	18 Mount Union	21
John Carroll ■	O24	22 Marietta	21
Mount Union	O31	28 Hiram	0
Muskingum ■	N 7	18 Baldwin-Wallace	35
Capital	N14	17 Ohio Northern	34

Colors: Tan & Cardinal. Nickname: Cardinals.   III

PACE .... Pleasantville, NY 10570
Douglas Bieling (1st yr. as head coach)

Stony Brook	S12	13 Wm. Paterson	27
Marist ■	S19	7 Marist	28
Merchant Marine	S26	22 Merchant Marine	21
LIU-C.W. Post ■	O 3	8 LIU-C.W. Post	55
St. John's (N.Y.)	O 9*	28 St. John's (N.Y.)	38
Upsala	O17	46 Upsala	24
Iona ■	O24	17 Iona	38
Hobart ■	O31	14 Hobart	19
Wagner	N 7	14 Coast Guard	39
Hartwick	N14	10 Stony Brook	14

Colors: Blue & Gold. Nickname: Setters.   III

PITTSBURG STATE .... Pittsburg, KS 66762
Chuck Broyles (2 yrs., 25-2-1)

Friends ■	S 5*	59 Friends	7
East Tex. St.	S12*	13 East Tex. St.	20
Southwest Baptist ■	S19*	23 Southwest Baptist	17
Missouri-Rolla	S26	6 Missouri-Rolla	6
Northwest Mo. St.	O 3	38 Northwest Mo. St.	0
Northeast Mo. St. ■	O10	55 Northeast Mo. St.	20
Mo. Western St.	O17	59 Mo. Western St.	14
Mo. Southern St. ■	O24*	43 Mo. Southern St.	21
Emporia St.	O31	70 Emporia St.	36
Washburn ■	N 7	21 Washburn	0
Central Mo. St.	N14	28 Central Mo. St.	14
		II Championship	
		26 Butler	16
		38 East Tex. St.	28
		53 Portland St.	21
		23 Jacksonville St.	6

Colors: Crimson & Gold. Nickname: Gorillas.   II

PLYMOUTH STATE .... Plymouth, NH 03264
Lou Desloges (6 yrs., 51-10-2)

Wilkes	S12	7 American Int'l	7
Norwich ■	S26	35 Mass. Maritime	18
Mass.-Lowell ■	O 3	21 Mass.-Boston	6
Western Conn. St.	O10	37 Nichols	0
Maine Maritime	O17	3 Mass.-Lowell	10
Bri'water (Mass.) ■	O24	58 Curry	0
Coast Guard	O31	43 Framingham St.	0
Stony Brook	N 7	8 Maine Maritime	18
Worcester Tech ■	N14	24 Westfield St.	22
		6 Cortland St.	21

Colors: Green & White. Nickname: Panthers.   III

POMONA-PITZER .... Claremont, CA 91711
Clarence Thomas (15 yrs., 46-85-3)

Cal Lutheran	S12	13 Colorado Col.	17
Colorado Col.	S19	9 Occidental	31
Redlands ■	S26	10 La Verne	38
La Verne	O 3	20 Whittier	34
Occidental	O10*	22 Claremont-M-S	9
Whittier ■	O17	56 Principia	15
Claremont-M-S ■	O24	3 Redlands	54
San Diego	O31	3 San Diego	56

Colors: Blue, White & Orange. Nickname: Sagehens.   III

PORTLAND STATE .... Portland, OR 97201
Pokey Allen (6 yrs., 54-22-2)

Eastern Wash.	S12	7 Mankato St.	10
Texas A&I ■	S19*	56 Mo. Southern St.	38
Sonoma St.	S26	14 Texas A&I	35
Southern Utah ■	O 3*	30 Sonoma St.	6
Neb.-Kearney ■	O10*	33 Southern Utah	30
Boise St.	O24*	35 Eastern Wash.	23
Cal St. Sacramento	O31*	62 St. Francis (Ill.)	28
Cal St. Northridge	N 7*	20 Santa Clara	18
Cal Poly SLO	N14*	35 Cal St. Sacramento	19
		38 Cal St. Northridge	13
		55 Cal Poly SLO	35
		II Championship	
		28 Northern Colo.	24
		37 Mankato St.	27
		21 Pittsburg St.	53

Colors: Green & White. Nickname: Vikings.   II

PRESBYTERIAN .... Clinton, SC 29325
John Perry (8 yrs., 39-49-0)

Fairmont St.	S 5	10 Citadel	33
Furman	S19	7 Furman	52
Lenoir-Rhyne ■	S26	12 Lenoir-Rhyne	24
Wofford	O 3*	24 Wofford	42
Catawba ■	O10	21 Catawba	13
Elon	O17	14 Elon	38
Mars Hill	O24	35 Mars Hill	30
Wingate ■	O31	14 Wingate	27
Gardner-Webb ■	N 7	10 Gardner-Webb	8
Carson-Newman	N14	20 Carson-Newman	48
Newberry	N26	32 Newberry	17

Colors: Garnet & Blue. Nickname: Blue Hose.   II

PRINCIPIA .... Elsah, IL 62028
Michael Barthelmess (2 yrs., 2-14-1)

Illinois Col. ■	S12	26 Blackburn	0
Grinnell	S19	14 Illinois Col.	27
N'western Col. (Wis.)	S26	20 Grinnell	27
Blackburn ■	O10	20 Knox	24
Ky. Wesleyan ■	O17	15 Maranatha	53
Earlham	O24	3 Central Meth.	49
Washington (Mo.)	O31	28 N'western Col. (Wis.)	16
Concordia (Ill.) ■	N 7	15 Pomona-Pitzer	56
		13 Washington (Mo.)	33

Colors: Navy Blue & Gold. Nickname: Panthers.   III

■ Home games on each schedule.   *Night Games.

QUINCY .... Quincy, IL 62301
Kevin Gundy (1 yr., 3-7-0)

Opponent	Date		Opponent	Score
Benedictine ■	S12	31	MacMurray	24
Central Meth.	S19	14	William Penn	0
MacMurray	S26	21	Doane	23
Eureka ■	O 3	10	Culver-Stockton	24
Ill. Benedictine ■	O10	36	Ill. Wesleyan	40
Greenville IL	O17	16	Benedictine	19
Drake	O24	17	Central Meth.	20
Lakeland ■	O31	7	Olivet Nazarene	41
Concordia (Wis.)	N 7	23	Chicago	21
Culver-Stockton ■	N14	6	Loras	32

Colors: Brown & White. Nickname: Hawks. III

RAMAPO .... Mahwah, NJ 07430
Jim Miceli (4 yrs., 28-8-0)

Opponent	Date		Opponent	Score
Ferrum ■	S12	12	Stony Brook	0
LIU-C.W. Post	S19	21	Wagner	9
Kean	S26	13	Kean	9
Montclair St.	O 3	23	Montclair St.	17
Jersey City St. ■	O10	47	Jersey City St.	0
Glassboro St.	O17	14	Glassboro St.	17
Wm. Paterson	O23*	29	Wm. Paterson	16
Southern Conn. St. ■	O31	24	Southern Conn. St.	28
Trenton St.	N14	25	Trenton St.	32
		20	Wesley	31

Colors: Red & Gold. Nickname: Roadrunners. III

RANDOLPH-MACON .... Ashland, VA 23005
Joe Riccio (1 yr., 4-6-0)

Opponent	Date		Opponent	Score
Wesley ■	S12	14	Alfred	38
Catholic	S19	28	Wesley	31
Juniata ■	S26	7	Catholic	10
Wash. & Lee	O 3	20	Juniata	12
Western Md. ■	O10	27	Wash. & Lee	0
Emory & Henry	O17	14	Western Md.	27
Worcester Tech	O24	10	Emory & Henry	21
Guilford ■	O31	20	Guilford	17
Bridgewater (Va.) ■	N 7	34	Bridgewater (Va.)	7
Hampden-Sydney	N14	28	Hampden-Sydney	29

Colors: Lemon & Black. Nickname: Yellow Jackets. III

REDLANDS .... Redlands, CA 92373
Mike Maynard (4 yrs., 24-13-0)

Opponent	Date		Opponent	Score
Menlo	S12	27	La Verne	20
San Diego	S19*	14	San Diego	17
Pomona-Pitzer	S26	44	Claremont-M-S	3
Cal St. Hayward ■	O 3*	48	Menlo	0
Claremont-M-S ■	O17*	47	Whittier	18
La Verne	O24	54	Pomona-Pitzer	3
Cal Lutheran ■	O31*	33	Occidental	7
Whittier	N 7	40	Colorado Col.	0
Occidental ■	N14*	10	Cal Lutheran	21

Colors: Maroon & Gray. Nickname: Bulldogs. III

RENSSELAER .... Troy, NY 12181
Joe King (3 yrs., 13-12-2)

Opponent	Date		Opponent	Score
Upsala ■	S19	7	Coast Guard	14
Worcester Tech ■	S26	24	Siena	14
Siena	O 3	14	Worcester Tech	26
Union (N.Y.)	O10	14	Stonehill	9
Marist	O17	10	Union (N.Y.)	35
Rochester	O24	38	Marist	13
St. Lawrence ■	O31	6	Rochester	21
Hobart	N 7	14	St. Lawrence	21
	N14	16	Hobart	15

Colors: Cherry & White. Nickname: Engineers. III

RHODES .... Memphis, TN 38112
Mike Clary (8 yrs., 53-16-4)

Opponent	Date		Opponent	Score
Claremont-M-S	S12	7	Maryville (Tenn.)	14
Davidson	S19	13	Davidson	9
Ky. Wesleyan ■	S26	43	Ky. Wesleyan	7
Lambuth ■	O 3	45	Lambuth	13
Washington (Mo.) ■	O10	14	Sewanee	14
Sewanee	O17	35	Washington (Mo.)	14
Maryville (Tenn.)	O24	24	Trinity (Tex.)	6
Trinity (Tex.)	O31*	10	Millsaps	3
Millsaps	N 7	12	Centre	16
Centre ■	N14			

Colors: Cardinal & Black. Nickname: Lynx. III

RIPON .... Ripon, WI 54971
Ron Ernst (1 yr., 5-4-0)

Opponent	Date		Opponent	Score
Lakeland ■	S12	21	Lakeland	9
Northwestern Minn.	S19	13	Minn.-Morris	10
Coe ■	S26	6	Cornell College	14
Knox	O 3	29	Grinnell	14
Beloit	O10	14	Beloit	19
Lake Forest ■	O17	24	Lake Forest	23
St. Norbert	O24	15	St. Norbert	6
Carroll (Wis.) ■	O31	6	Alfred	39
Lawrence	N 7	0	Lawrence	26

Colors: Crimson & White. Nickname: Redmen. III

ROCHESTER .... Rochester, NY 14627
Rich Parrinello (4 yrs., 23-16-0)

Opponent	Date		Opponent	Score
Case Reserve ■	S12	14	Case Reserve	7
Carnegie Mellon	S19	32	St. John Fisher	0
Washington (Mo.) ■	S26*	16	Washington (Mo.)	9
Chicago	O 3	28	Chicago	7
Hobart	O10	14	Carnegie Mellon	18
St. John Fisher ■	O17	20	Wash. & Jeff.	14
St. Lawrence	O24	21	Rensselaer	6
Rensselaer ■	O31	0	Worcester Tech	17
Union (N.Y.) ■	N 7	14	St. Lawrence	13
		0	Union (N.Y.)	27

Colors: Yellow & Blue. Nickname: Yellowjackets. III

ROSE-HULMAN .... Terre Haute, IN 47803
Scott Duncan (6 yrs., 40-19-1)

Opponent	Date		Opponent	Score
Washington (Mo.) ■	S 5	27	Mt. St. Joseph	32
Knox	S12	31	Drake	21
Evansville ■	S26	16	Ill. Benedictine	26
Taylor ■	O 3	6	DePauw	36
DePauw	O10	39	Franklin	34
Franklin	O17	32	Hanover	36
Hanover ■	O24	24	Wabash	0
Wabash	O31	17	Anderson	20
Anderson ■	N 7	7	Taylor	24
Manchester	N14	18	Manchester	27

Colors: Red & White. Nickname: Fightin' Engineers. III

SACRED HEART .... Fairfield, CT 06432
Gary Reho (1 yr., 5-4-0)

Opponent	Date		Opponent	Score
St. John's (N.Y.)	S19	0	Brockport St.	41
St. Peter's	S26	6	Iona	26
Stony Brook	O 3	6	St. Peter's	13
Mass.-Lowell ■	O10	13	Assumption	0
Nichols	O17	20	Nichols	13
Catholic ■	O24	26	MIT	7
Iona	O31	19	Western New Eng.	3
Stonehill ■	N 7	19	Stonehill	6
Assumption	N14	22	Upsala	26

Colors: Red & White. Nickname: Pioneers. III

SAGINAW VALLEY STATE University Center, MI 48710
George Ihler (9 yrs., 51-40-1)

Opponent	Date		Opponent	Score
Hillsdale ■	S 5	0	Hillsdale	14
Wayne St. (Mich.)	S12	9	Wayne St. (Mich.)	21
Northern Mich.	S19	14	Northern Mich.	7
St. Joseph's (Ind.) ■	S26	38	St. Joseph's (Ind.)	33
Grand Valley St.	O 3	14	Grand Valley St.	10
Ashland ■	O10	6	Ashland	26
Indianapolis	O17	21	Indianapolis	7
Northwood ■	O24	10	Northwood	7
Valparaiso ■	O31	54	Valparaiso	14
Ferris St.	N 7	15	Ferris St.	18
Butler ■	N14	10	Butler	13

Colors: Red, White & Blue. Nickname: Cardinals. II

SALISBURY STATE .... Salisbury, MD 21801
Joe Rotellini (2 yrs., 2-17-0)

Opponent	Date		Opponent	Score
LIU-C.W. Post ■	S12	5	LIU-C.W. Post	10
Methodist	S19	41	Methodist	21
Frostburg St. ■	S26	14	Frostburg St.	39
Guilford	O 3	0	Guilford	20
Glassboro St. ■	O10	7	Glassboro St.	34
Montclair St. ■	O24	31	Wagner	38
Albany (N.Y.)	O31	17	Montclair St.	41
Newport News App. ■	N 7	18	Albany (N.Y.)	20
Kean ■	N14	10	Newport News App.	16
		14	Kean	37

Colors: Maroon & Gold. Nickname: Sea Gulls. III

■ Home games on each schedule.   *Night Games.

Divisions II and III 1992 Schedules and 1991 Results

SAN DIEGO .... San Diego, CA 92110
Brian Fogarty (9 yrs., 43-39-2)

Cal St. Hayward ■	S 5*	13 Menlo	3
La Verne	S12	17 Redlands	14
Redlands ■	S19*	20 Cal Lutheran	21
Claremont-M-S ■	S26*	20 Cal St. Hayward	21
Cal Lutheran ■	O 3	31 Whittier	7
Whittier	O10*	30 Claremont-M-S	3
Azusa-Pacific	O17	38 La Verne	37
Occidental ■	O24*	56 Pomona-Pitzer	3
Pomona-Pitzer	O31	34 Azusa-Pacific	42
Menlo	N 7	28 Occidental	19

Colors: Columbia Blue, Navy & White.   Nickname: Toreros.   III

SAN FRANCISCO STATE ..... San Francisco, CA 94132
Harold Hamilton (1 yr., 3-7-0)

St. Mary's (Cal.)	S 5	13 St. Mary's (Cal.)	51
Cal St. Northridge	S19*	16 Santa Clara	31
Santa Clara	S26*	23 Southern Utah	42
Menlo	O10	27 UC Santa Barb.	31
Humboldt St. ■	O17	55 Menlo	7
Cal St. Chico	O24	34 Cal St. Chico	17
Cal St. Hayward	O31	32 Cal St. Hayward	17
UC Davis	N 7	21 UC Davis	24
Sonoma St.	N14	23 Sonoma St.	24
		13 Humboldt St.	44

Colors: Purple & Gold.   Nickname: Gators.   II

SANTA CLARA .... Santa Clara, CA 95053
Terry Malley (7 yrs., 43-32-1)

Cal St. Chico ■	S 5	32 Cal St. Chico	26
Sonoma St. ■	S12*	31 San Fran. St.	16
UC Davis ■	S19*	21 UC Davis	31
San Fran. St. ■	S26*	35 Cal St. Hayward	21
Humboldt St.	O 3*	28 Humboldt St.	23
Southern Utah ■	O10*	31 Southern Utah	14
Cal St. Northridge ■	O17	27 Cal St. Northridge	45
Cal Poly SLO ■	O31	18 Portland St.	20
Cal St. Sacramento	N 7*	10 Cal Poly SLO	15
St. Mary's (Cal.)	N14	32 Cal St. Sacramento	33
		44 St. Mary's (Cal.)	14

Colors: Bronco Red & White.   Nickname: Broncos.   II

SAVANNAH STATE .... Savannah, GA 31404
Bill Davis (13 yrs., 92-47-1)

Bethune-Cookman†	S 5*	35 Bethune-Cookman	20
Tuskegee†	S12	6 Ga. Southern	29
Ga. Southern	S19	43 Tuskegee	38
Alabama A&M	S26	62 Cheyney	3
Central Fla.	O 3*	25 Alabama A&M	27
Albany St. (Ga.)	O10	51 Albany St. (Ga.)	16
Morris Brown	O17	56 Morris Brown	0
Livingstone ■	O24*	34 Morehouse	42
Morehouse ■	O31	33 Central Fla.	31
Fort Valley St. ■	N 7	30 Fort Valley St.	34
Miles	N14	50 Miles	13

Colors: Blue & Orange.   Nickname: Tigers.   II

SEWANEE (UNIV. of the SOUTH) .. Sewanee, TN 37375
Bill Samko (5 yrs., 23-21-1)

Davidson ■	S12	35 Cumberland (Tenn.)	14
Tenn. Wesleyan	S19	10 Tenn. Wesleyan	7
Maryville (Tenn.)	S26	25 Trinity (Tex.)	6
Centre ■	O 3	10 Centre	3
Rhodes ■	O17	14 Rhodes	14
Wash. & Lee	O24	28 Maryville (Tenn.)	7
Millsaps ■	O31	21 Wash. & Lee	13
Trinity (Tex.)	N 7*	6 Millsaps	20
Ky. Wesleyan	N14	31 Ky. Wesleyan	17

Colors: Purple & White.   Nickname: Tigers.   III

SHEPHERD .... Shepherdstown, WV 25443
Monte Cater (11 yrs., 58-46-2)

Shippensburg	S 5	28 Shippensburg	49
Millersville ■	S12	20 Millersville	30
Glenville St.	S19	13 Glenville St.	10
West Liberty St.	S26	33 West Liberty St.	8
West Va. St. ■	O 3	26 West Va. St.	7
West Va. Wesleyan	O17	34 Georgetown (Ky.)	31
Concord ■	O24	21 West Va. Wesleyan	7
West Va. Tech	O31	32 Concord	7
Fairmont St. ■	N 7	31 West Va. Tech	7
New Haven ■	N14	33 Fairmont St.	16
		NAIA Div. I Championship	
		22 Central St. (Ohio)	34

Colors: Blue & Gold.   Nickname: Rams.   II

SHIPPENSBURG .... Shippensburg, PA 17257
Rocky Rees (7 yrs., 51-24-1)

Shepherd ■	S 5	49 Shepherd	28
Bloomsburg ■	S12	24 Bloomsburg	21
Kutztown	S19	44 Kutztown	35
Millersville ■	S26	45 Calif. (Pa.)	0
Slippery Rock	O 3	24 Slippery Rock	20
Indiana (Pa.) ■	O10	0 Indiana (Pa.)	47
Edinboro	O17	45 Edinboro	7
Clarion ■	O24	19 Clarion	34
Lock Haven	O31	34 Lock Haven	0
West Chester	N 7	31 East Stroudsburg	24
Calif. (Pa.) ■	N14	31 New Haven	30
		II Championship	
		34 East Stroudsburg	33
		7 Indiana (Pa.)	52

Colors: Red & Blue.   Nickname: Red Raiders.   II

SIENA .... Loudonville, NY 12211
Jack DuBois (5 yrs., 11-32-0)

Marist ■	S12	13 Marist	12
Iona	S19	14 Rensselaer	24
Hartwick	O 2*	0 Wm. Paterson	42
Rensselaer ■	O10	0 Western New Eng.	13
Bentley ■	O17	27 MIT	6
Stonehill	O24	7 Bentley	19
Assumption	O31	6 Stonehill	10
St. Peter's	N 7	20 Assumption	19
Western New Eng. ■	N14		

Colors: Green & Gold.   Nickname: Saints.   III

SIMPSON .... Indianola, IA 50125
Jim Williams (6 yrs., 39-22-0)

Drake ■	S12	16 Drake	7
Luther	S19	49 Coe	7
Buena Vista ■	S26	27 Wartburg	16
Wartburg	O 3	31 Loras	14
Loras ■	O10	12 Central (Iowa)	3
Central (Iowa) ■	O17	14 Luther	13
Dubuque	O24	56 William Penn	20
William Penn ■	N 7	51 Dubuque	0
Upper Iowa	N14	40 Upper Iowa	7
		30 Buena Vista	0
		III Championship	
		13 Wis.-La Crosse	28

Colors: Red & Gold.   Nickname: Redmen.   III

SLIPPERY ROCK .... Slippery Rock, PA 16057
George Mihalik (4 yrs., 19-18-4)

Fairmont St. ■	S12	17 Northwood	7
Ashland	S19	32 Fairmont St.	7
Shippensburg ■	O 3	33 Lock Haven	7
Calif. (Pa.)	O10	20 Shippensburg	24
Cheyney	O17	20 Calif. (Pa.)	3
Indiana (Pa.) ■	O24	23 Mansfield	33
Edinboro	O31	0 Indiana (Pa.)	38
Clarion ■	N 7	7 Edinboro	0
Lock Haven	N14	43 Clarion	36
		21 Youngstown St.	40

Colors: Green & White.   Nickname: Rockets, The Rock.   II

SONOMA STATE .... Rohnert Park, CA 94928
Tim Walsh (3 yrs., 20-11-0)

Santa Clara	S12*	7 Idaho	49
Eastern Wash.	S19	33 UC Santa Barb.	7
Portland St. ■	S26	27 Cal Poly SLO	7
Cal Poly SLO	O 3*	6 Portland St.	30
St. Mary's (Cal.)	O10	28 Cal Lutheran	0
UC Davis	O17*	22 St. Mary's (Cal.)	17
Cal St. Hayward ■	O24	22 Cal St. Hayward	13
Humboldt St. ■	O31	35 Humboldt St.	0
Cal St. Chico	N 7*	38 Cal St. Chico	17
San Fran. St. ■	N14	24 San Fran. St.	23
		23 UC Davis	12

Colors: Navy Blue & White.   Nickname: Cossacks.   II

SOUTH DAKOTA .... Vermillion, SD 57069
Dennis Creehan (7 yrs., 43-27-1)

Northern St. (S.D.) ■	S 5	7 South Dak. St.	19
South Dak. St.	S12	7 Morningside	42
Morningside ■	S19	6 North Dak.	21
North Dak.	S26	12 North Dak. St.	35
North Dak. St. ■	O 3	18 South Dak. St.	21
South Dak. St. ■	O10	27 Augustana (S.D.)	18
Augustana (S.D.)	O17	0 St. Cloud St.	45
St. Cloud St. ■	O24	20 Northern Colo.	45
Mankato St.	O31	7 Nebraska-Omaha	15
Northern Colo. ■	N 7		
Nebraska-Omaha	N14		

Colors: Red & White.   Nickname: Coyotes.   II

SOUTH DAKOTA STATE.........Brookings, SD 57007
Mike Daly (1 yr., 7-3-0)

Opponent	Date		Us	Opponent	Them
South Dak. ■	S12		16	Neb.-Kearney	13
North Dak. ■	S19		19	South Dak.	7
North Dak. St.	S26*		10	North Dak.	36
Nebraska-Omaha ■	O 3		0	North Dak. St.	35
South Dak.	O10		21	Nebraska-Omaha	13
Morningside	O17		21	South Dak.	18
Augustana (S.D.) ■	O24		27	Morningside	17
St. Cloud St.	O31		31	Augustana (S.D.)	20
Mankato St. ■	N 7		0	Mankato St.	23
Northern Colo.	N14		17	Northern Colo.	13

Colors: Yellow & Blue. Nickname: Jackrabbits.　II

SOUTHERN CONNECTICUT STATE . New Haven, CT 06515
Richard Cavanaugh (7 yrs., 28-42-0)

Opponent	Date		Us	Opponent	Them
East Stroudsburg ■	S12		41	East Stroudsburg	43
Edinboro ■	S19		16	Edinboro	35
Springfield	S25*		31	Springfield	7
American Int'l ■	O 2*		0	American Int'l	41
Hofstra	O 9*		31	Trenton St.	26
Trenton St. ■	O16*		64	New Haven	60
New Haven	O24		28	Ramapo	24
Ramapo	O31		49	Buffalo	21
Central Conn. St. ■	N 7		42	Central Conn. St.	20
Cortland St.	N14				

Colors: Blue & White. Nickname: Owls.　II

SOUTHERN UTAH...............Cedar City, UT 84720
Jack Bishop (11 yrs., 65-46-3)

Opponent	Date		Us	Opponent	Them
Northern Ariz.	S 5*		14	Weber St.	33
Weber St.	S12*		21	Central Okla.	24
Central Okla. ■	S19*		49	Mesa St.	14
Angelo St. ■	S26*		42	San Fran. St.	23
Portland St.	O 3*		30	Portland St.	33
Santa Clara	O10*		37	Santa Clara	31
St. Mary's (Cal.) ■	O17		33	St. Mary's (Cal.)	18
Cal St. Sacramento ■	O24		22	Cal St. Sacramento	19
Cal St. Northridge ■	O31		56	Cal St. Northridge	28
Cal Poly SLO	N 7*		33	Cal Poly SLO	21
Idaho St.	N14*		35	Idaho St.	35

Colors: Scarlet, Royal Blue & White. Nickname: Thunderbirds.　II

SOUTHWEST BAPTIST ....Bolivar, MO 65613
Jim Hall (4 yrs., 18-23-0)

Opponent	Date		Us	Opponent	Them
Ouachita Bapt.	S 5*		42	Olivet Nazarene	7
Pittsburg St.	S19*		26	Ouachita Bapt.	21
Central Mo. St. ■	S26		17	Pittsburg St.	23
Northeast Mo. St.	O 3		17	Central Mo. St.	24
Mo. Western St. ■	O10		37	Northeast Mo. St.	25
Mo. Southern St.	O17*		43	Mo. Western St.	34
Emporia St. ■	O24		21	Mo. Southern St.	42
Washburn	O31		42	Emporia St.	20
Missouri-Rolla ■	N 7		6	Washburn	21
Northwest Mo. St. ■	N14		26	Missouri-Rolla	21
			23	Northwest Mo. St.	21

Colors: Purple & White. Nickname: Bearcats.　II

SPRINGFIELD.................Springfield, MA 01109
Mike DeLong (10 yrs., 49-45-2)

Opponent	Date		Us	Opponent	Them
American Int'l ■	S11*		21	Albany (N.Y.)	3
Albany (N.Y.) ■	S18*		31	American Int'l	47
Southern Conn. St. ■	S25*		7	Southern Conn. St.	31
Ithaca	O 3		14	Ithaca	10
Central Conn. St.	O16*		41	Norwich	20
Cortland St.	O24		23	Central Conn. St.	26
New Haven	O31		20	Cortland St.	13
LIU-C.W. Post ■	N 7		14	New Haven	21
American Int'l	N14		56	LIU-C.W. Post	14
			12	American Int'l	7

Colors: Maroon & White. Nickname: Chiefs.　II

ST. CLOUD STATE ....St. Cloud, MN 56301
Noel Martin (9 yrs., 53-45-0)

Opponent	Date		Us	Opponent	Them
Idaho	S 5*		17	Minn.-Duluth	14
Minn.-Duluth	S12		14	Nebraska-Omaha	10
Nebraska-Omaha ■	S19		19	Northern Colo.	31
Northern Colo.	S26		20	Mankato St.	14
Mankato St. ■	O 3		9	North Dak. St.	32
North Dak. St.	O10		17	North Dak.	17
North Dak. ■	O17		45	South Dak.	0
South Dak.	O24		23	Augustana (S.D.)	16
South Dak. St. ■	O31		28	Morningside	14
Augustana (S.D.) ■	N 7				
Morningside	N14				

Colors: Cardinal & Black. Nickname: Huskies.　II

ST. FRANCIS (PENNSYLVANIA) .....Loretto, PA 15940
Frank Pergolizzi (3 yrs., 12-17-0)

Opponent	Date		Us	Opponent	Them
Gannon	S 5		16	Gannon	14
Canisius ■	S12		2	Dickinson	24
Wagner ■	S19		6	Wesley	14
Mercyhurst ■	S26		34	Gallaudet	14
Gallaudet	O 3		16	Marist	7
Marist	O10		34	St. Peter's	13
St. Peter's ■	O17		12	Duquesne	0
Hartwick	O24		13	St. John Fisher	7
St. John Fisher ■	O31		7	Thiel	14
Duquesne	N 7				

Colors: Red & White. Nickname: Red Flash.　III

ST. JOHN FISHER ....Rochester, NY 14618
Paul Vosburgh (1st yr. as head coach)

Opponent	Date		Us	Opponent	Them
Catholic ■	S 5		0	Cortland St.	71
Alfred	S12*		0	Rochester	32
Hobart ■	S19		0	Canisius	21
Hartwick ■	S26		3	Marist	28
Canisius ■	O10		14	St. Lawrence	37
Rochester	O17		3	Gallaudet	7
Brockport St. ■	O24		7	St. Francis (Pa.)	13
St. Francis (Pa.)	O31		0	Gannon	25
Gallaudet	N 7		14	Hobart	32
Stony Brook	N14				

Colors: Cardinal & Gold. Nickname: Cardinals.　III

ST. JOHN'S (MINNESOTA) ....Collegeville, MN 56321
John Gagliardi (43 yrs., 286-94-9)

Opponent	Date		Us	Opponent	Them
Bemidji St. ■	S12		29	Bemidji St.	0
Augsburg	S19*		43	St. Thomas (Minn.)	15
St. Olaf ■	S26		56	Carleton	7
Gust. Adolphus ■	O 3		35	Hamline	25
Hamline	O10		46	Augsburg	0
Bethel (Minn.) ■	O17		35	Gust. Adolphus	14
St. Thomas (Minn.)	O24		56	Macalester	0
Macalester ■	O31		67	St. Olaf	19
Carleton	N 7		24	Concordia-M'head	7
Concordia-M'head†	N14			**III Championship**	
			75	Coe	2
			29	Wis.-La Crosse	10
			7	Dayton	19

Colors: Red & White. Nickname: Johnnies.　III

ST. JOHN'S (NEW YORK).........Jamaica, NY 11439
Bob Ricca (14 yrs., 86-54-1)

Opponent	Date		Us	Opponent	Them
Iona	S12		30	Iona	27
Sacred Heart	S19		12	Bri'water (Mass.)	30
Wagner ■	S25*		35	Stony Brook	37
FDU-Madison	O 2*		21	FDU-Madison	7
Pace ■	O 9*		38	Pace	28
Duquesne ■	O17		29	Merchant Marine	14
LIU-C.W. Post ■	O23*		54	LIU-C.W. Post	14
Marist	O31		18	Marist	21
Georgetown ■	N 7		21	Georgetown	26
Bentley	N14		22	Bentley	6

Colors: Red & White. Nickname: Redmen.　III

ST. JOSEPH'S (INDIANA).......Rensselaer, IN 47978
Bill Reagan (7 yrs., 28-41-1)

Opponent	Date		Us	Opponent	Them
Grand Valley St. ■	S 5		3	Grand Valley St.	31
Butler	S12		10	Butler	37
Indianapolis ■	S19		10	Indianapolis	28
Saginaw Valley	S26		33	Saginaw Valley	38
Valparaiso ■	O 3		13	Valparaiso	10
Ashland	O17		0	Ashland	9
Hillsdale ■	O24		10	Hillsdale	0
Wayne St. (Mich.)	O31		20	Wayne St. (Mich.)	27
Northern Mich. ■	N 7		28	Northern Mich.	21
Ferris St.	N14		16	Ferris St.	10

Colors: Cardinal & Purple. Nickname: Pumas.　II

ST. LAWRENCE.....................Canton, NY 13617
Dennis Riccio (5 yrs., 31-19-0)

Opponent	Date		Us	Opponent	Them
Union (N.Y.)	S12		42	Norwich	14
Canisius	S26		7	Ithaca	45
Hobart	O 3		39	Canisius	6
Alfred ■	O10		41	Hobart	0
Ithaca ■	O17		6	Alfred	31
Rochester ■	O24		37	St. John Fisher	14
Norwich ■	O31		13	Western Conn. St.	0
Rensselaer	N 7		21	Rensselaer	14
Albany (N.Y.) ■	N14		13	Rochester	14
			12	Albany (N.Y.)	39

Colors: Scarlet & Brown. Nickname: Saints.　III

■ Home games on each schedule.　　　*Night Games.

ST. MARY'S (CALIFORNIA)........Moraga, CA 94575
Mike Rasmussen (2 yrs., 13-8-0)

Opponent	Date	Pts	Opponent	Pts
San Fran. St. ■	S 5	51	San Fran. St.	13
Cal St. Hayward	S12	14	Humboldt St.	17
Humboldt St. ■	S19	51	Cal St. Hayward	19
UC Davis	S 26*	12	UC Davis	13
Cal St. Chico	O 3	38	Cal St. Chico	14
Sonoma St. ■	O10	17	Sonoma St.	22
Southern Utah ■	O17	18	Southern Utah	33
Western N. Mex. ■	N 7	41	UC Santa Barb.	3
Santa Clara ■	N14	49	Colorado Mines	8
		56	Menlo	9
		14	Santa Clara	44

Colors: Red & Blue. Nickname: Gaels. II

ST. NORBERT.....................DePere, WI 54115
Don La Violette (9 yrs., 49-35-1)

Opponent	Date	Pts	Opponent	Pts
Wis.-Oshkosh	S12*	10	Wis.-Oshkosh	16
Concordia (Wis.) ■	S19*	0	Michigan Tech	41
Cornell College	S 26	24	Monmouth (Ill.)	7
Grinnell ■	O 3	0	Illinois Col.	0
Lake Forest	O10	31	Lake Forest	7
Lawrence	O17	0	Lawrence	15
Ripon ■	O24	6	Ripon	7
Beloit ■	O31	0	Beloit	7
Carroll (Wis.)	N 7	0	Drake	6

Colors: Green & Gold. Nickname: Green Knights. III

ST. OLAF........................Northfield, MN 55057
Don Canfield (19 yrs., 104-73-1)

Opponent	Date	Pts	Opponent	Pts
Luther	S12	22	Luther	21
St. Thomas (Minn.) ■	S19	35	Augsburg	13
St. John's (Minn.)	S 26	0	Gust. Adolphus	28
Macalester ■	O 3	62	Macalester	0
Gust. Adolphus	O10	26	St. Thomas (Minn.)	25
Carleton	O17	24	Bethel (Minn.)	6
Hamline	O24	24	Concordia-M'head	13
Concordia-M'head ■	O31	19	St. John's (Minn.)	67
Bethel (Minn.)	N 7	26	Hamline	23
Augsburg†	N13			

Colors: Black & Gold. Nickname: Oles. III

ST. PETER'S......................Jersey City, NJ 07306
Roy Miller (8 yrs., 31-46-0)

Opponent	Date	Pts	Opponent	Pts
Assumption ■	S12	13	Western New Eng.	3
Hartwick ■	S19	13	Sacred Heart	6
Sacred Heart ■	S 26	13	Georgetown	19
Western New Eng.	O 3	13	St. Francis (Pa.)	34
Georgetown	O10	19	Gallaudet	9
St. Francis (Pa.)	O17	20	Wesley	30
Gallaudet ■	O24	14	Upsala	43
Siena ■	N 7	17	Jersey City St.	7
Jersey City St.	N14			

Colors: Blue & White. Nickname: Peacocks. III

ST. THOMAS (MINNESOTA).......St. Paul, MN 55105
Vic Wallace (11 yrs., 74-39-4)

Opponent	Date	Pts	Opponent	Pts
Wis.-River Falls ■	S12	15	St. Ambrose	6
St. Olaf	S19	15	St. John's (Minn.)	43
Macalester ■	S 26	15	Macalester	2
Carleton	O 3	28	Carleton	19
Concordia-M'head ■	O10	25	St. Olaf	26
Augsburg	O17	33	Hamline	30
St. John's (Minn.) ■	O24	27	Bethel (Minn.)	21
Gust. Adolphus	O31	27	Augsburg	3
Hamline ■	N 7	7	Gust. Adolphus	28
Bethel (Minn.)	N14			

Colors: Purple & Gray. Nickname: Tommies. III

STONEHILL....................North Easton, MA 02356
David Swanton (2 yrs., 8-8-1)

Opponent	Date	Pts	Opponent	Pts
Mass.-Dartmouth ■	S 5	0	Mass.-Dartmouth	16
Nichols	S19	13	Ferrum	54
Assumption ■	S 26	26	Assumption	3
Curry ■	O 3	9	Rensselaer	14
Western New Eng.	O10	33	Western New Eng.	15
MIT	O17	37	MIT	4
Siena	O24	10	Siena	6
Bentley ■	O31	14	Bentley	7
Sacred Heart	N 7	6	Sacred Heart	19
Mass.-Lowell ■	N14			

Colors: Purple & White. Nickname: Chieftains. III

STONY BROOK................Stony Brook, NY 11794
Sam Kornhauser (8 yrs., 32-41-1)

Opponent	Date	Pts	Opponent	Pts
Pace ■	S12	0	Ramapo	12
Bentley ■	S19	24	Bentley	6
Coast Guard	S 26	37	St. John's (N.Y.)	35
Sacred Heart ■	O 3	6	Iona	37
Gettysburg	O10	7	LIU-C.W. Post	13
Wesley	O17	14	Wesley	6
Merchant Marine ■	O24	7	Merchant Marine	23
Western Conn. St.	O31	14	Western Conn. St.	9
Plymouth St. ■	N 7	38	MIT	0
St. John Fisher ■	N14	14	Pace	10

Colors: Scarlet & Gray. Nickname: Patriots. III

SUSQUEHANNA................Selinsgrove, PA 17870
Steve Briggs (2 yrs., 18-5-0)

Opponent	Date	Pts	Opponent	Pts
Muhlenberg	S12	30	Muhlenberg	11
Moravian	S19	10	Moravian	0
Wilkes ■	S 26	14	Wilkes	6
Lebanon Valley	O 3*	0	Lebanon Valley	20
Delaware Valley ■	O10	31	Delaware Valley	9
Mass.-Lowell	O17	31	Alfred	8
Widener ■	O24	34	Widener	10
Juniata	O31	31	Juniata	16
Lycoming	N 7	31	Lycoming	35
Albright ■	N14	31	Albright	24
III Championship				
		21	Dickinson	20
		31	Lycoming	24
		13	Ithaca	49

Colors: Orange & Maroon. Nickname: Crusaders. III

SWARTHMORE...................Swarthmore, PA 19081
Karl Miran (2 yrs., 9-10-0)

Opponent	Date	Pts	Opponent	Pts
Catholic	S12	29	Hobart	13
Johns Hopkins	S19	19	Johns Hopkins	47
Gettysburg ■	S 26	8	Gettysburg	20
Ursinus ■	O 3	7	Ursinus	28
Muhlenberg	O10	10	Muhlenberg	12
Georgetown ■	O17	0	Georgetown	31
Dickinson	O24	15	Dickinson	40
Frank. & Marsh. ■	O31	12	Frank. & Marsh.	26
Western Md.	N 7	24	Western Md.	21

Colors: Garnet & White. Nickname: Garnet. III

TEXAS A&I......................Kingsville, TX 78363
Ron Harms (23 yrs., 147-82-4)

Opponent	Date	Pts	Opponent	Pts
Southwest Tex. St. ■	S 5*	7	Nicholls St.	3
Nichols St. ■	S12*	14	Southwest Tex. St.	29
Portland St.	S19*	35	Portland St.	14
Cameron ■	O 3*	41	Prairie View	3
East Tex. St.	O10*	30	Cameron	7
Central Okla. ■	O17*	22	East Tex. St.	24
Mississippi Col.	O24	23	Central Okla.	13
Eastern N. Mex.	O31	36	Eastern N. Mex.	20
Abilene Christian ■	N 7*	20	Abilene Christian	0
Angelo St.	N14	17	Angelo St.	21

Colors: Blue & Gold. Nickname: Javelinas. II

THIEL..........................Greenville, PA 16125
Charles Giangrosso (3 yrs., 18-11-0)

Opponent	Date	Pts	Opponent	Pts
Albion ■	S 5	28	Oberlin	0
Oberlin	S12	14	Frostburg St.	35
Frostburg St. ■	S19	28	Bethany (W.Va.)	21
Duquesne	S 26*	0	Wash. & Jeff.	40
Bethany (W.Va.)	O 3	21	Clinch Valley	23
Wash. & Jeff. ■	O10	21	Grove City	12
Grove City	O17	6	Waynesburg	32
Waynesburg ■	O24	14	St. Francis (Pa.)	7
Gannon	O31	27	Gannon	6

Colors: Blue & Gold. Nickname: Tomcats. III

THOMAS MORE............Crestview Hills, KY 41017
Vic Clark (2 yrs., 13-6-0)

Opponent	Date	Pts	Opponent	Pts
Cumberland (Tenn.) ■	S 5	37	Ky. Wesleyan	7
Hanover ■	S12	34	Bluffton	3
Wilmington (Ohio)	S19	14	Franklin	7
Franklin	S 26	48	Earlham	16
Waynesburg	O10	42	Wilmington (Ohio)	21
Tenn. Wesleyan ■	O17	20	Centre	14
Dayton	O24	24	Mt. St. Joseph	14
Defiance ■	O31	19	Mt. St. Joseph	18
Mt. St. Joseph	N 7	17	Defiance	7
Bluffton ■	N14	28	Tenn. Wesleyan	13

Colors: Royal Blue & White. Nickname: Blue Rebels. III

■ Home games on each schedule.   *Night Games.

TRENTON STATE................Trenton, NJ 08650
Eric Hamilton (15 yrs., 95-50-4)

Opponent	Date	Score	Opponent	Score
Wesley	S 5	27	Wm. Paterson	27
Central Conn. St. ■	S11*	20	Upsala	0
Wm. Paterson ■	S18*	0	Glassboro St.	21
Glassboro St. ■	O 3	34	FDU-Madison	7
FDU-Madison	O 9*	26	Southern Conn. St.	31
Southern Conn. St. ■	O16*	29	Jersey City St.	7
Jersey City St. ■	O24	0	Montclair St.	27
Montclair St.	O31*	16	Kean	14
Kean ■	N 7*	32	Ramapo	25
Ramapo	N14			

Colors: Navy Blue & Gold. Nickname: Lions. III

UC DAVIS.....................Davis, CA 95616
Bob Foster (3 yrs., 22-9-0)

Opponent	Date	Score	Opponent	Score
Cal St. Northridge	S12*	31	Cal Poly SLO	28
Santa Clara	S19*	31	Santa Clara	21
St. Mary's (Cal.) ■	S26*	13	St. Mary's (Cal.)	12
Cal St. Sacramento ■	O 3*	18	Cal St. Sacramento	50
Cal Poly SLO ■	O10*	29	Cal St. Northridge	17
Sonoma St. ■	O17*	44	Humboldt St.	6
Humboldt St.	O24	20	Cal St. Chico	24
Cal St. Chico ■	O31*	24	San Fran. St.	21
San Fran. St.	N 7	16	Cal St. Hayward	13
Cal St. Hayward	N14	12	Sonoma St.	23

Colors: Blue & Gold. Nickname: Aggies. II

TRINITY (CONNECTICUT).........Hartford, CT 06106
Don Miller (25 yrs., 134-61-5)

Opponent	Date	Score	Opponent	Score
Bates ■	S26	10	Colby	6
Williams	O 3	35	Bowdoin	14
Hamilton	O10	30	Williams	27
Tufts ■	O17	28	Hamilton	28
Bowdoin	O24	56	Bates	25
Middlebury ■	O31	14	Coast Guard	21
Amherst ■	N 7	51	Amherst	7
Wesleyan	N14	47	Wesleyan	11

Colors: Blue & Gold. Nickname: Bantams. III

UC SANTA BARBARA.......Santa Barbara, CA 93106
Rick Candaele (2 yrs., 14-6-0)

(No team in 1992)

Score	Opponent	Score
7	Sonoma St.	33
33	Cal Lutheran	23
31	Cal St. Chico	52
31	San Fran. St.	27
42	Cal St. Hayward	31
28	Azusa-Pacific	7
3	St. Mary's (Cal.)	41
42	Azusa-Pacific	7

Colors: Blue & Gold. Nickname: Gauchos. II

TRINITY (TEXAS).............San Antonio, TX 78212
Steven Mohr (2 yrs., 2-18-0)

Opponent	Date	Score	Opponent	Score
Tabor ■	S12*	7	Hamline	30
Austin ■	S19*	7	Millsaps	31
Occidental	S26*	7	Austin	13
Washington (Mo.)	O 3*	6	Sewanee	25
Carnegie Mellon ■	O10*	14	Washington (Mo.)	19
Colorado Col. ■	O17*	16	Occidental	17
Centre	O24	14	Colorado Col.	21
Rhodes ■	O31*	6	Chicago	0
Sewanee ■	N 7*	6	Rhodes	24
Millsaps	N14	8	Centre	14

Colors: Maroon & White. Nickname: Tigers. III

UNION (NEW YORK).........Schenectady, NY 12308
John Audino (2 yrs., 9-13-0)

Opponent	Date	Score	Opponent	Score
St. Lawrence	S12	49	Worcester Tech	27
Worcester Tech	S19	44	Hobart	17
Hobart ■	S26	47	Albany (N.Y.)	7
Dickinson	O 3	66	Norwich	0
Albany (N.Y.) ■	O10*	35	Rensselaer	10
Rensselaer	O17	37	Coast Guard	7
Coast Guard ■	O24	57	Gettysburg	7
Gettysburg ■	O31	51	Hamilton	17
Rochester	N 7	27	Rochester	0

III Championship

Score	Opponent	Score
55	Mass.-Lowell	16
23	Ithaca	35

Colors: Garnet. Nickname: Dutchmen. III

TROY STATE ....Troy, AL 36081
Larry Blakeney (1 yr., 5-6-0)

Opponent	Date	Score	Opponent	Score
Southern Ill.	S 5	10	Central Fla.	21
Northwestern (La.) ■	S 12	13	West Ga.	10
Central Fla.	S19*	17	Nicholls St.	25
Alabama St. ■	S26*	19	Alabama St.	22
Valdosta St. ■	O 3*	20	Valdosta St.	14
Arkansas St.	O10	30	Southern Ill.	13
Liberty	O17*	39	Western Ky.	23
North Ala.	O24*	31	North Ala.	9
Samford ■	N 7	22	Samford	24
Ga. Southern	N14	17	Arkansas St.	20
Nicholls St.	N21	12	Ga. Southern	19

Colors: Cardinal, Gray & Black. Nickname: Trojans. II

UPPER IOWA ....Fayette, IA 52142
Paul Rudolph (4 yrs., 28-8-0)

Opponent	Date	Score	Opponent	Score
Wis.-Whitewater	S10*	35	North Central	42
Wartburg	S19	22	Buena Vista	21
Luther ■	S26	13	Dubuque	18
William Penn	O 3	7	Coe	31
Dubuque	O10	13	Loras	33
Buena Vista ■	O17	24	Wartburg	36
Mid-America Naz.	O24	0	Central (Iowa)	41
Central (Iowa)	O31	40	William Penn	27
Loras ■	N 7	12	Luther	13
Simpson ■	N14	7	Simpson	40

Colors: Blue & White. Nickname: Peacocks. III

TUFTS........................Medford, MA 02155
Duane Ford (7 yrs., 35-19-2)

Opponent	Date	Score	Opponent	Score
Wesleyan ■	S26	10	Wesleyan	0
Bates ■	O 3	3	Williams	33
Trinity (Conn.)	O17	42	Colby	29
Williams ■	O24	20	Middlebury	16
Amherst	O31	13	Bowdoin	21
Colby ■	N 7	28	Amherst	17
Middlebury	N14	15	Hamilton	29
Bowdoin†	N29	16	Bates	6

Colors: Blue & Brown. Nickname: Jumbos. III

UPSALA....................East Orange, NJ 07019
Mike Walsh (1 yr., 10-19-1)

Opponent	Date	Score	Opponent	Score
Western Conn. St. ■	S12	16	Western Conn. St.	8
Kean	S19	0	Kean	14
Rensselaer	S26	0	Trenton St.	20
Jersey City St.	O 3	25	Jersey City St.	0
Wm. Paterson	O10	12	Wm. Paterson	46
Pace ■	O17	24	Pace	46
Wilkes	O24	33	Assumption	9
FDU-Madison ■	O31	18	FDU-Madison	3
Bentley	N 7	43	St. Peter's	14
Wesley ■	N14	26	Sacred Heart	22

Colors: Blue & Gray. Nickname: Vikings. III

TUSKEGEE..................Tuskegee Inst., AL 36088
James Martin (8 yrs., 40-37-1)

Opponent	Date	Score	Opponent	Score
Jackson St.	S 5*	24	Florida A&M	47
Savannah St.†	S12	38	Savannah St.	43
Morris Brown ■	S19	21	Morris Brown	23
Albany St. (Ga.)	O 3*	55	Miles	7
Clark Atlanta	O10	56	Albany St. (Ga.)	6
Morehouse†	O17*	47	Clark Atlanta	19
Hampton	O24	9	Morehouse	14
Fort Valley St.	O31	46	Hampton	33
Miles ■	N 7	39	Fort Valley St.	22
		43	Alabama A&M	20

Colors: Old Gold & Crimson. Nickname: Golden Tigers. II

URSINUS ....Collegeville, PA 19426
Steve Gilbert (4 yrs., 17-22-0)

Opponent	Date	Score	Opponent	Score
Georgetown	S12	12	Georgetown	6
Frank. & Marsh.	S19	7	Frank. & Marsh.	19
Western Md. ■	S26	3	Western Md.	27
Swarthmore	O 3	28	Swarthmore	7
Johns Hopkins ■	O10	0	Johns Hopkins	28
Gettysburg	O17	20	Gettysburg	0
FDU-Madison	O24	7	FDU-Madison	17
Worcester Tech ■	O31	13	Muhlenberg	9
Muhlenberg	N 7	7	Merchant Marine	6
Dickinson ■	N14	14	Dickinson	35

Colors: Old Gold, Red & Black. Nickname: Bears. III

■ Home games on each schedule.   *Night Games.

VALDOSTA STATE .... Valdosta, GA 31698
Hal Mumme (2 yrs., 24-11-0)

Opponent	Date		Opponent	
Ga. Southern	S12	0	Central Fla.	12
Fort Valley St.†	S19*	7	Fort Valley St.	0
Jacksonville St.	S26	3	Jacksonville St.	24
Troy St.	O 3*	14	Troy St.	20
Livingston ■	O10*	20	Livingston	7
West Ga.	O17*	38	West Ga.	37
American Int'l ■	O24	59	Lees-McRae	13
Mississippi Col. ■	O31*	10	Mississippi Col.	10
Delta St.	N 7	34	Delta St.	27
North Ala. ■	N14*	34	North Ala.	17

Colors: Red & Black.   Nickname: Blazers.   II

VALPARAISO .... Valparaiso, IN 46383
Tom Horne (4 yrs., 19-40-2)

Opponent	Date		Opponent	
Ashland ■	S 5	7	Ashland	30
Hillsdale	S12	27	Hillsdale	49
Wayne St. (Mich.) ■	S19	9	Wayne St. (Mich.)	21
Northern Mich.	S26	17	Northern Mich.	17
St. Joseph's (Ind.)	O 3	10	St. Joseph's (Ind.)	13
Ferris St.	O10	9	Ferris St.	28
Butler	O17	2	Butler	22
Indianapolis ■	O24	6	Indianapolis	3
Saginaw Valley	O31	10	Saginaw Valley	54
Michigan Tech†	N 7	3	Grand Valley St.	36
Grand Valley St.	N14			

Colors: Brown & Gold.   Nickname: Crusaders.   II

VIRGINIA STATE .... Petersburg, VA 23803
Louis Anderson (1 yr., 3-7-0)

Opponent	Date		Opponent	
Norfolk St.	S 5*	12	Norfolk St.	18
N.C. Central	S12*	24	Knoxville	22
Winston-Salem ■	S19	19	West Va. St.	25
Bowie St.	S26	19	Winston-Salem	32
Livingstone ■	O 3	19	Bowie St.	14
Hampton ■	O10	6	Livingstone	8
Fayetteville St. ■	O17	37	Hampton	39
Elizabeth City St.	O24	31	Fayetteville St.	14
Virginia Union	O31	6	Elizabeth City St.	23
West Va. St. ■	N 7	0	Virginia Union	34

Colors: Orange & Navy Blue.   Nickname: Trojans.   II

VIRGINIA UNION .... Richmond, VA 23220
Mel Rose (4 yrs., 16-23-0)

Opponent	Date		Opponent	
Grambling ■	S12*	49	Livingstone	17
Hampton ■	S19*	46	Grambling	37
New Haven ■	S26	49	Hampton	13
Bowie St.	O 3	43	New Haven	14
Elizabeth City St.	O10	41	Bowie St.	9
Norfolk St.	O24*	23	Elizabeth City St.	24
Virginia St.	O31	47	Morgan St.	12
Central St. (Ohio)	N 7	39	Norfolk St.	11
		34	Virginia St.	0
		26	Central St. (Ohio)	27
II Championship				
		7	Indiana (Pa.)	56

Colors: Steel Gray & Maroon.   Nickname: Panthers.   II

WABASH .... Crawfordsville, IN 47933
Greg Carlson (9 yrs., 57-26-1)

Opponent	Date		Opponent	
Albion ■	S19	10	Albion	29
Hope	S26	16	Denison	15
Manchester ■	O 3	44	Franklin	10
Franklin ■	O10	26	Hanover	14
Hanover ■	O17	23	Anderson	6
Anderson	O24	0	Rose-Hulman	24
Rose-Hulman ■	O31	34	Taylor	9
Taylor	N 7	28	Manchester	7
DePauw ■	N14	27	DePauw	18

Colors: Scarlet & White.   Nickname: Little Giants.   III

WAGNER .... Staten Island, NY 10301
Walt Hameline (11 yrs., 86-28-2)

Opponent	Date		Opponent	
Delaware Valley	S12	40	Delaware Valley	30
St. Francis (Pa.)	S19	9	Ramapo	21
St. John's (N.Y.)	S25*	26	Montclair St.	14
Newport News App. ■	O 3	19	Newport News App.	32
Iona	O10	24	Iona	15
Marist ■	O17	38	Salisbury St.	31
Glassboro St.	O23*	21	Glassboro St.	28
LIU-C.W. Post	O31	26	LIU-C.W. Post	13
Pace ■	N 7	0	Albany (N.Y.)	29
Duquesne ■	N14	13	Wm. Paterson	21

Colors: Green & White.   Nickname: Seahawks.   III

WARTBURG .... Waverly, IA 50677
Bob Nielson (3 yrs., 15-12-1)

Opponent	Date		Opponent	
Coe ■	S12	12	Coe	20
Upper Iowa ■	S19	56	Dubuque	14
Central (Iowa)	S26	16	Simpson	27
Simpson ■	O 3	17	Luther	20
Luther ■	O10	67	William Penn	7
William Penn	O17	36	Upper Iowa	24
Buena Vista	O24	41	Lake Forest	14
Dubuque ■	O31	30	Loras	24
Aurora ■	N 7	16	Central (Iowa)	10
Loras	N14	26	Buena Vista	6

Colors: Orange & Black.   Nickname: Knights.   III

WASHBURN .... Topeka, KS 66621
Dennis Caryl (5 yrs., 21-31-0)

Opponent	Date		Opponent	
Southwest Mo. St.	S12*	3	Western Ill.	42
Northeast Mo. St.	S19	7	Tenn.-Martin	28
Northwest Mo. St. ■	S26*	7	Northeast Mo. St.	14
Mo. Southern St.	O 3*	3	Northwest Mo. St.	29
Emporia St. ■	O10*	6	Mo. Southern St.	31
Central Mo. St. ■	O17	18	Emporia St.	49
Missouri-Rolla	O24	0	Central Mo. St.	21
Southwest Baptist ■	O31	13	Missouri-Rolla	28
Pittsburg St.	N 7	14	Southwest Baptist	6
Mo. Western St. ■	N14	0	Pittsburg St.	21
		23	Mo. Western St.	35

Colors: Yale Blue & White.   Nickname: Ichabods.   II

WASHINGTON (MISSOURI) .... St. Louis, MO 63130
Larry Kindbom (9 yrs., 45-42-1)

Opponent	Date		Opponent	
Rose-Hulman	S 5	25	Ky. Wesleyan	7
Carnegie Mellon ■	S12*	12	Carnegie Mellon	20
Case Reserve ■	S19*	21	Case Reserve	22
Rochester	S26*	9	Rochester	16
Trinity (Tex.) ■	O 3*	19	Trinity (Tex.)	14
Rhodes	O10	12	Central Meth.	7
Central Meth. ■	O17*	14	Rhodes	35
Chicago	O24	33	Principia	13
Principia ■	O31	23	Colorado Col.	19
Colorado Col.	N 7	25	Chicago	7

Colors: Red & Green.   Nickname: Bears.   III

WASHINGTON AND JEFFERSON .. Washington, PA 15301
John Luckhardt (10 yrs., 75-22-2)

Opponent	Date		Opponent	
Hiram ■	S12	61	Duquesne	0
Widener	S19	7	Widener	0
Bethany (W.Va.) ■	S26	33	Waynesburg	19
Waynesburg	O 3	40	Thiel	0
Thiel ■	O10	38	Grove City	3
Gannon ■	O17	14	Rochester	20
Grove City ■	O24	27	Bethany (W.Va.)	12
Cortland St. ■	O31	28	Mercyhurst	0
Ithaca	N14	49	Muhlenberg	0
III Championship				
		16	Lycoming	18

Colors: Red & Black.   Nickname: Presidents.   III

WASHINGTON AND LEE .... Lexington, VA 24450
Gary Fallon (14 yrs., 64-69-1)

Opponent	Date		Opponent	
Emory & Henry ■	S12	0	Emory & Henry	14
Ala.-Birmingham	S19	21	Ala.-Birmingham	34
Centre	S26	7	Centre	24
Randolph-Macon ■	O 3	0	Randolph-Macon	27
Davidson	O10	14	Davidson	16
Hampden-Sydney ■	O17	7	Hampden-Sydney	21
Sewanee	O24	13	Sewanee	21
Bridgewater (Va.)	O31	7	Bridgewater (Va.)	8
Guilford	N 7	7	Guilford	25
Georgetown ■	N14	7	Georgetown	12

Colors: Royal Blue & White.   Nickname: Generals.   III

WAYNE STATE (MICHIGAN) .... Detroit, MI 48202
Brian VanGorder (1st yr. as head coach)

Opponent	Date		Opponent	
Indianapolis ■	S 5	13	Indianapolis	35
Saginaw Valley ■	S12	21	Saginaw Valley	9
Valparaiso	S19	21	Valparaiso	9
Ferris St. ■	S26	27	Ferris St.	24
Ashland	O 3	7	Ashland	21
Butler ■	O10	7	Butler	42
Northwood	O17	21	Northern Mich.	6
Northern Mich.	O24	27	St. Joseph's (Ind.)	20
St. Joseph's (Ind.) ■	O31	28	Grand Valley St.	59
Grand Valley St.	N 7	13	Hillsdale	32
Hillsdale	N14			

Colors: Green & Gold.   Nickname: Tartars.   II

■ Home games on each schedule.   *Night Games.

WAYNE STATE (NEBRASKA) .... Wayne, NE 68787
Dennis Wagner (3 yrs., 14-18-0)

Nebraska-Omaha	S 5*	27	Mo. Western St.	46
Morningside	S12	0	Nebraska-Omaha	28
Bemidji St.	S19	16	Morningside	7
Mayville St.	S26	22	Wis.-Stevens Point	17
Neb.-Kearney ■	O 3	20	Fort Hays St.	28
St. Francis (Ill.) ■	O10	17	Neb.-Kearney	25
Southwest St.(Minn.) ■	O24	16	East Tex. St.	54
Michigan Tech ■	O31	32	Iowa Wesleyan	56
Peru St.	N 7	55	Chadron St.	28
Iowa Wesleyan	N14	33	Northern St. (S.D.)	35

Colors: Black & Gold.   Nickname: Wildcats.   II

WAYNESBURG .... Waynesburg, PA 15370
Ty Clarke (5 yrs., 23-26-0)

Urbana	S 5	14	Geneva	0
Gannon ■	S12	20	Grove City	12
Grove City ■	S26	19	Wash. & Jeff.	33
Wash. & Jeff.	O 3	38	Bethany (W.Va.)	15
Thomas More ■	O10	20	Duquesne	6
Bethany (W.Va.) ■	O17	31	Urbana	6
Thiel	O24	7	Westminster (Pa.)	21
Kenyon	O31	32	Thiel	6
Frostburg St. ■	N 7	18	Frostburg St.	22

Colors: Orange & Black.   Nickname: Yellow Jackets.   III

WESLEY .... Dover, DE 19901
Tim Keating (4 yrs., 18-20-0)

Trenton St. ■	S 5	31	Randolph-Macon	28
Randolph-Macon	S12	14	St. Francis (Pa.)	6
Geneva ■	S19	40	Bridgewater (Va.)	0
Bridgewater (Va.) ■	S26	41	Catholic	14
Frostburg St.	O 3	52	Gallaudet	9
Gallaudet ■	O10	6	Stony Brook	14
Stony Brook ■	O17	49	Hampden-Sydney	50
Hampden-Sydney ■	O24	30	St. Peter's	20
Delaware Valley ■	N 7	45	Delaware Valley	14
Upsala	N14	40	Western Conn. St.	13
		31	Ramapo	20

Colors: Blue & White.   Nickname: Wolverines.   III

WESLEYAN .... Middletown, CT 06457
Frank Hauser (1st yr. as head coach)

Tufts	S26	0	Tufts	10
Hamilton ■	O 3	26	Bates	6
Colby	O10	16	Coast Guard	13
Bates	O17	0	Colby	30
Amherst ■	O24	32	Amherst	15
Bowdoin ■	O31	12	Hamilton	35
Williams	N 7	14	Williams	24
Trinity (Conn.) ■	N14	11	Trinity (Conn.)	47

Colors: Red & Black.   Nickname: Cardinals.   III

WEST CHESTER .... West Chester, PA 19383
Rick Daniels (3 yrs., 20-12-0)

Villanova	S 4*	0	Delaware	28
Wingate ■	S19	36	American Int'l	13
Delaware	S26	34	Central Conn. St.	14
Cheyney	O 3	31	Mansfield	9
Mansfield ■	O 9*	0	Millersville	3
Millersville	O17	34	New Haven	20
Bloomsburg ■	O24	3	Kutztown	42
Kutztown	O31	7	Lock Haven	13
Shippensburg ■	N 7	21	East Stroudsburg	28
East Stroudsburg ■	N14	30	Cheyney	14
		12	Bloomsburg	34

Colors: Purple & Gold.   Nickname: Golden Rams.   II

WEST GEORGIA .... Carrollton, GA 30118
Ron Jurney (2 yrs., 7-15-0)

Samford	S 5*	55	Alma	0
Jacksonville St. ■	S19*	10	Troy St.	13
Clark Atlanta	S26	24	Jacksonville St.	50
Livingston	O 3*	42	Clark Atlanta	28
Mississippi Col.	O10*	21	Livingston	32
Valdosta St. ■	O17*	49	Wofford	42
Knoxville ■	O24*	37	Valdosta St.	38
Delta St. ■	O31	21	Mississippi Col.	49
North Ala.	N 7*	20	Delta St.	15
Lane ■	N14	28	North Ala.	26
		56	Lane	8

Colors: Red & Blue.   Nickname: Braves.   II

WEST LIBERTY STATE .... West Liberty, WV 26074
Bob Eaton (2 yrs., 8-11-1)

Calif. (Pa.)	S 5	0	Concord	24
West Va. Tech	S19	35	West Va. Tech	7
Shepherd ■	S26	38	Tiffin	21
Glenville St. ■	O 3	7	Shepherd	33
West Va. St.	O10	35	Glenville St.	33
Tiffin ■	O17	7	West Va. St.	6
Lenoir-Rhyne ■	O24	10	Defiance	24
Concord	O31	10	Fairmont St.	10
West Va. Wesleyan ■	N 7	21	West Va. Wesleyan	50
Fairmont St.	N14	7	Geneva	14

Colors: Gold & Black.   Nickname: Hilltoppers.   II

WEST TEXAS STATE .... Canyon, TX 79016
Ron Steele (1st yr. as head coach)   (No team in 1991)

Southwestern Okla. ■	S 5*
Fort Lewis	S12
Cameron	S26*
Western N. Mex. ■	O 3*
Prairie View ■	O10*
Southeastern Okla. ■	O17
N.M. Highlands	O24
Tarleton St.	O31
Eastern N. Mex. ■	N 7
Panhandle St.	N14

Colors: Maroon & White.   Nickname: Buffaloes.   II

WESTERN CONNECTICUT STATE .. Danbury, CT 06810
To be named

Upsala	S12	8	Upsala	16
Merchant Marine ■	S19	22	Norwich	24
Wm. Paterson ■	S26	6	Brockport St.	30
Plymouth St. ■	O10	3	Frostburg St.	33
Coast Guard	O17	3	Albany (N.Y.)	45
Mass.-Lowell	O24	0	St. Lawrence	13
Stony Brook ■	O31	15	Wilkes	17
Albany (N.Y.) ■	N 7	9	Stony Brook	14
Norwich ■	N14	23	Catholic	21
		13	Wesley	40

Colors: Blue & White.   Nickname: Colonials.   III

WESTERN MARYLAND .... Westminster, MD 21157
Dale Sprague (7 yrs., 17-49-2)

Albright	S12*	13	Albright	14
Gettysburg ■	S19	12	Gettysburg	7
Ursinus	S26	27	Ursinus	3
Muhlenberg ■	O 3	34	Muhlenberg	6
Randolph-Macon	O10	27	Randolph-Macon	14
Dickinson ■	O17	25	Dickinson	28
Frank. & Marsh.	O24	15	Frank. & Marsh.	19
Lebanon Valley ■	O31	13	Lebanon Valley	15
Swarthmore ■	N 7	21	Swarthmore	24
Johns Hopkins	N14	24	Johns Hopkins	21

Colors: Green & Gold.   Nickname: Green Terrors.   III

WESTERN NEW ENGLAND ...... Springfield, MA 01119
Gerry Martin (1 yr., 3-5-0)

Fitchburg St. ■	S12	3	St. Peter's	13
Curry	S19	7	MIT	22
MIT ■	S26	13	Siena	0
St. Peter's ■	O 3	6	Stonehill	33
Stonehill ■	O10	0	Bentley	25
Assumption ■	O17	3	Sacred Heart	19
Bentley ■	O24	36	Assumption	6
Nichols	O31	13	Westfield St.	12
Hartwick	N 7			
Siena	N14			

Colors: Blue & Gold.   Nickname: Golden Bears.   III

WESTERN STATE .... Gunnison, CO 81231
Carl Iverson (8 yrs., 53-33-1)

Northern Colo.	S 5	19	Northern Colo.	47
Eastern N. Mex. ■	S12	42	Menlo	0
Western Mont. ■	S19	28	Adams St.	16
Adams St. ■	S26	70	Fort Lewis	25
Colorado Mines	O 3	56	Colorado Mines	18
Fort Lewis ■	O10	33	Mesa St.	9
Mesa St.	O17*	42	Fort Hays St.	21
Chadron St. ■	O24	51	Chadron St.	49
N.M. Highlands ■	O31	53	N.M. Highlands	19
Fort Hays St.	N 7	67	Western N. Mex.	23

NAIA Div. I Championship

		38	Carson-Newman	21
		13	Central St. (Ohio)	20

Colors: Crimson & Slate.   Nickname: Mountaineers.   II

■ Home games on each schedule.   *Night Games.

WESTFIELD STATE .... Westfield, MA 01085
Steve Marino (2 yrs., 7-13-0)

Opponent	Date		Opponent	
Mass.-Boston	S19	28	Maine Maritime	40
Fitchburg St. ■	S25*	13	Mass.-Lowell	25
Framingham St.	O 3	26	Worcester St.	15
MIT	O10	44	Framingham St.	35
Bri'water (Mass.) ■	O17	12	Bri'water (Mass.)	45
Worcester St.	O24	33	Mass.-Dartmouth	24
Mass. Maritime ■	O30*	34	Mass. Maritime	43
Mass.-Dartmouth	N 7	22	Plymouth St.	24
Maine Maritime ■	N14	12	Fitchburg St.	6
		12	Western New Eng.	13

Colors: Navy & White. Nickname: Owls. III

WHEATON (ILLINOIS) .... Wheaton, IL 60187
J. R. Bishop (10 yrs., 54-35-1)

Opponent	Date		Opponent	
Lake Forest ■	S12	27	Aurora	13
Dayton ■	S19	24	Ill. Wesleyan	24
Millikin	O 3	45	Carthage	22
Ill. Wesleyan ■	O10	15	Millikin	17
Carthage	O17	36	North Central	0
North Park	O24	42	Augustana (Ill.)	19
North Central ■	O31	55	Elmhurst	20
Elmhurst ■	N 7	46	North Park	0
Augustana (Ill.)	N14	21	Carroll (Wis.)	15

Colors: Orange & Blue. Nickname: Crusaders. III

WHITTIER .... Whittier, CA 90608
Ken Visser (1 yr., 3-6-0)

Opponent	Date		Opponent	
Albion ■	S12*	15	Claremont-M-S	3
La Verne ■	S19*	2	La Verne	12
Menlo	S26	7	Menlo	14
Occidental	O 3*	34	Pomona-Pitzer	20
San Diego ■	O10*	7	San Diego	31
Pomona-Pitzer	O17	18	Redlands	47
Azusa-Pacific ■	O24*	14	Occidental	20
Claremont-M-S	O31	9	Cal Lutheran	28
Redlands ■	N 7	29	Claremont-M-S	6
Cal Lutheran ■	N14*			

Colors: Purple & Gold. Nickname: Poets. III

WIDENER .... Chester, PA 19013
Bill Cubit (1st yr. as head coach)

Opponent	Date		Opponent	
Gettysburg	S12	27	Gettysburg	6
Wash. & Jeff. ■	S19	0	Wash. & Jeff.	7
Moravian ■	S26	13	Moravian	17
Juniata	O 3	0	Juniata	13
Lycoming ■	O10	0	Lycoming	31
Albright	O17	26	Albright	25
Susquehanna	O24	10	Susquehanna	34
Wilkes ■	O31	14	Wilkes	3
Lebanon Valley	N 7	24	Lebanon Valley	28
Delaware Valley ■	N14	8	Delaware Valley	21

Colors: Blue & Gold. Nickname: Pioneers. III

WILKES .... Wilkes-Barre, PA 18766
Joe DeMelfi (2 yrs., 2-18-0)

Opponent	Date		Opponent	
Plymouth St. ■	S12*	6	Cortland St.	67
Albright ■	S19	27	Albright	28
Susquehanna	S26	6	Susquehanna	14
Moravian	O 3	10	Moravian	23
Lebanon Valley ■	O10	19	Lebanon Valley	24
Delaware Valley	O17	28	Delaware Valley	35
Upsala ■	O24	17	Western Conn. St.	15
Widener	O31	3	Widener	14
Juniata ■	N 7	0	Juniata	14
Lycoming	N14	0	Lycoming	34

Colors: Navy & Gold. Nickname: Colonels. III

WILLIAM PATERSON .... Wayne, NJ 07470
Gerry Gallagher (6 yrs., 22-32-1)

Opponent	Date		Opponent	
Geneva ■	S 5	27	Pace	13
Trenton St.	S18*	27	Trenton St.	27
Western Conn. St.	S26	42	Siena	0
Kean ■	O 3*	26	Kean	17
Upsala ■	O10	46	Upsala	12
Montclair St.	O17*	27	Montclair St.	12
Ramapo ■	O23*	16	Ramapo	29
Jersey City St. ■	O30*	36	Jersey City St.	7
Glassboro St.	N 7*	28	Glassboro St.	14
Central Conn. St.	N14	21	Wagner	13
		16	Frostburg St.	46

Colors: Orange & Black. Nickname: Pioneers. III

WILLIAM PENN .... Oskaloosa, IA 52577
To be named

Opponent	Date		Opponent	
Coe	S19	0	Quincy	14
Loras	S26	18	Luther	21
Upper Iowa ■	O 3	6	Graceland	17
Central (Iowa)	O10	28	Buena Vista	27
Wartburg ■	O17	7	Wartburg	67
Luther	O24	18	Central (Iowa)	83
Buena Vista ■	O31	20	Simpson	56
Simpson	N 7	27	Upper Iowa	40
Dubuque ■	N14	20	Loras	34
		16	Dubuque	14

Colors: Navy Blue & Gold. Nickname: The Statesmen. III

WILLIAMS .... Williamstown, MA 01267
Dick Farley (5 yrs., 33-6-1)

Opponent	Date		Opponent	
Colby ■	S26	15	Hamilton	0
Trinity (Conn.) ■	O 3	33	Tufts	3
Bates	O10	27	Trinity (Conn.)	30
Middlebury ■	O17	28	Bates	6
Tufts	O24	32	Colby	14
Hamilton	O31	26	Middlebury	14
Wesleyan ■	N 7	24	Wesleyan	14
Amherst	N14	37	Amherst	0

Colors: Purple. Nickname: Ephs. III

WILMINGTON (OHIO) .... Wilmington, OH 45177
Mike Wallace (1 yr., 1-9-0)

Opponent	Date		Opponent	
Cumberland (Ky.)	S 5	12	Kenyon	40
Thomas More ■	S19	14	Campbellsville	29
Tiffin ■	S26	28	Tiffin	42
Olivet	O 3	10	Defiance	14
Ohio Wesleyan	O10	14	Tarleton St.	44
Defiance	O17	21	Thomas More	42
Geneva ■	O24	9	West Va. Tech	21
Bluffton	O31	14	Bluffton	12
Wooster ■	N 7	0	Geneva	46
Mt. St. Joseph ■	N14	14	Mt. St. Joseph	28

Colors: Green & White. Nickname: Quakers. III

WINGATE .... Wingate, NC 28174
Steve Wilt (6 yrs., 28-30-0)

Opponent	Date		Opponent	
Kentucky St. ■	S12*	17	Kentucky St.	9
West Chester	S19	35	Carson-Newman	52
Mars Hill ■	S26*	25	Mars Hill	19
Gardner-Webb	O 3	24	Gardner-Webb	34
Carson-Newman	O10	17	Glenville St.	15
Lenoir-Rhyne ■	O17	27	Lenoir-Rhyne	38
Wofford	O24*	31	Newberry	19
Presbyterian	O31	27	Presbyterian	14
Catawba ■	N 7	20	Catawba	46
Elon ■	N14	21	Elon	31

Colors: Navy Blue & Old Gold. Nickname: Bulldogs. II

WINONA STATE .... Winona, MN 55987
Tom Hosier (18 yrs., 66-106-3)

Opponent	Date		Opponent	
Wis.-La Crosse	S12	3	Wis.-Eau Claire	13
Wis.-Eau Claire	S19*	18	Wis.-La Crosse	34
Moorhead St.	S26	7	St. Francis (Ill.)	41
Michigan Tech ■	O 3	14	Southwest St. (Minn.)	47
Minn.-Morris	O10	3	Moorhead St.	41
Northern St. (S.D.)	O17	9	Michigan Tech	42
Bemidji St. ■	O24	29	Minn.-Morris	33
Minn.-Duluth	O31	10	Northern St. (S.D.)	47
Southwest St. (Minn.) ■	N 7	6	Minn.-Duluth	38
Northern St. (S.D.)†	N14	42	Teikyo Westmar	19

Colors: Purple & White. Nickname: Warriors. II

WINSTON-SALEM STATE .. Winston-Salem, NC 27102
Pete Richardson (4 yrs., 34-10-1)

Opponent	Date		Opponent	
Elizabeth City St. ■	S 5	28	Morehouse	13
North Caro. A&T	S12	13	North Caro. A&T	10
Virginia St.	S19	32	Virginia St.	19
Fayetteville St. ■	S26	54	Livingstone	18
Johnson Smith	O 3	28	Fayetteville St.	8
Southern-B.R.†	O10	28	Kentucky St.	7
N.C. Central	O17	68	N.C. Central	22
Bowie St. ■	O24*	35	Wofford	42
Wofford	O31*	40	Johnson Smith	32
Hampton ■	N 7*	20	Hampton	6
Livingstone ■	N14		II Championship	
		24	Jacksonville St.	49

Colors: Scarlet & White. Nickname: Rams. II

■ Home games on each schedule.   *Night Games.

WISCONSIN-EAU CLAIRE .... Eau Claire, WI 54702
Greg Polnasek (1st year as head coach)

Minn.-Duluth	S 5	13	Winona St.	3
Winona St. ■	S19*	7	Minn.-Duluth	21
Wis.-River Falls	S26	34	Wis.-River Falls	20
Wis.-Stout ■	O 3*	20	Wis.-Stout	40
Wis.-Superior	O10	26	Wis.-Superior	26
Wis.-Oshkosh ■	O17	14	Wis.-Oshkosh	31
Wis.-La Crosse	O24	29	Wis.-La Crosse	45
Wis.-Whitewater ■	O31	6	Wis.-Whitewater	26
Wis.-Stevens Point ■	N 7	7	Wis.-Stevens Point	14
Wis.-Platteville	N14	28	Wis.-Platteville	29

Colors: Navy Blue & Old Gold.   Nickname: Blugolds.   III

WISCONSIN-LA CROSSE .... La Crosse, WI 54601
Roger Harring (23 yrs., 184-58-6)

Winona St. ■	S12	34	Winona St.	18
Wis.-Stevens Point	S19	21	Wis.-Stevens Point	6
Wis.-Platteville ■	S26	14	Wis.-Platteville	12
Wis.-Superior ■	O 3	58	Wis.-Superior	7
St. Ambrose	O10	39	St. Ambrose	3
Wis.-River Falls	O17	14	Wis.-River Falls	10
Wis.-Eau Claire ■	O24	45	Wis.-Eau Claire	29
Wis.-Oshkosh	O31	14	Wis.-Oshkosh	6
Wis.-Whitewater	N 7	14	Wis.-Whitewater	25
Wis.-Stout ■	N14	37	Wis.-Stout	15

III Championship

	28	Simpson	13
	10	St. John's (Minn.)	29

Colors: Maroon & Gray.   Nickname: Eagles.   III

WISCONSIN-OSHKOSH .... Oshkosh, WI 54901
Ron Cardo (8 yrs., 33-44-4)

St. Norbert ■	S12*	16	St. Norbert	10
Wis.-River Falls ■	S19*	21	Wis.-River Falls	7
Wis.-Stout	S26	24	Wis.-Stout	11
Wis.-Platteville ■	O 3	7	Wis.-Platteville	13
Wis.-Stevens Point	O10	7	Wis.-Stevens Point	35
Wis.-Eau Claire	O17	31	Wis.-Eau Claire	14
St. Ambrose	O24	0	Drake	21
Wis.-La Crosse ■	O31	6	Wis.-La Crosse	14
Wis.-Superior	N 7	32	Wis.-Superior	13
Wis.-Whitewater ■	N14	7	Wis.-Whitewater	28

Colors: Gold, Black & White.   Nickname: Titans.   III

WISCONSIN-PLATTEVILLE .... Platteville, WI 53818
George Chryst (13 yrs., 73-57-2)

Dayton ■	S12*	30	Carleton	22
Wis.-Whitewater ■	S19*	6	Wis.-Whitewater	21
Wis.-La Crosse	S26	12	Wis.-La Crosse	14
Wis.-Oshkosh	O 3	13	Wis.-Oshkosh	7
Wis.-River Falls ■	O10	15	Wis.-River Falls	15
Wis.-Superior	O17	39	Wis.-Superior	10
Wis.-Stout ■	O24	8	Wis.-Stout	15
Wis.-Stevens Point	O31	26	Wis.-Stevens Point	18
St. Ambrose ■	N 7	39	St. Ambrose	0
Wis.-Eau Claire ■	N14	29	Wis.-Eau Claire	28

Colors: Orange & Blue.   Nickname: Pioneers.   III

WISCONSIN-RIVER FALLS .... River Falls, WI 54022
John O'Grady (3 yrs., 16-12-2)

Minn.-Morris ■	S 5	14	Minn.-Morris	0
St. Thomas (Minn.)	S12	7	Wis.-Oshkosh	21
Wis.-Oshkosh	S19*	20	Wis.-Eau Claire	34
Wis.-Eau Claire ■	S26	25	St. Ambrose	22
Wis.-Platteville	O10	15	Wis.-Platteville	15
Winston-Salem ■	O17	10	Wis.-La Crosse	14
Wis.-Whitewater	O24	7	Wis.-Whitewater	24
Wis.-Superior ■	O31	24	Wis.-Superior	20
Wis.-Stout	N 7	18	Wis.-Stevens Point	34
Wis.-Stevens Point	N14	45	Wis.-Stout	7

Colors: Red & White.   Nickname: Falcons.   III

WISCONSIN-STEVENS POINT Stevens Point, WI 54481
John Miech (4 yrs., 27-12-2)

Michigan Tech ■	S 5	0	Baker	0
Minn.-Morris ■	S12*	6	Wis.-La Crosse	21
Wis.-La Crosse ■	S19	17	Wayne St. (Neb.)	22
Wis.-Whitewater	O 3	16	Wis.-Whitewater	10
Wis.-Oshkosh ■	O10	35	Wis.-Oshkosh	7
Wis.-Stout	O17	37	Wis.-Stout	0
Wis.-Superior ■	O24	39	Wis.-Superior	10
Wis.-Platteville ■	O31	18	Wis.-Platteville	26
Wis.-Eau Claire ■	N 7	14	Wis.-Eau Claire	7
Wis.-River Falls	N14	34	Wis.-River Falls	18

Colors: Purple & Gold.   Nickname: Pointers.   III

WISCONSIN-STOUT .... Stout, WI 54751
Rich Lawrence (8 yrs., 38-45-1)

Mayville St.	S 5	36	Mt. Senario	0
Wis.-Superior	S19	17	Wis.-Superior	0
Wis.-Oshkosh ■	S26	11	Wis.-Oshkosh	24
Wis.-Eau Claire	O 3*	40	Wis.-Eau Claire	20
Wis.-Whitewater ■	O10	18	Wis.-Whitewater	21
Wis.-Stevens Point ■	O17	0	Wis.-Stevens Point	37
Wis.-Platteville	O24	15	Wis.-Platteville	8
St. Ambrose ■	O31	20	St. Ambrose	19
Wis.-River Falls ■	N 7	15	Wis.-La Crosse	37
Wis.-La Crosse	N14	7	Wis.-River Falls	45

Colors: Navy Blue & White.   Nickname: Blue Devils.   III

WISCONSIN-SUPERIOR .... Superior, WI 54880
Ted Thompson (2 yrs., 3-14-1)

Concordia (St.P.) ■	S 5	24	Mt. Senario	7
Augsburg	S12*	0	Wis.-Stout	17
Wis.-Stout ■	S19	16	Wis.-Whitewater	14
Wis.-Whitewater ■	S26	7	Wis.-La Crosse	58
Wis.-La Crosse	O 3	26	Wis.-Eau Claire	26
Wis.-Eau Claire ■	O10	10	Wis.-Platteville	39
Wis.-Platteville ■	O17	10	Wis.-Stevens Point	39
Wis.-Stevens Point	O24	20	Wis.-River Falls	24
Wis.-River Falls	O31	13	Wis.-Oshkosh	32
Wis.-Oshkosh ■	N 7			

Colors: Orange & Black.   Nickname: Yellowjackets.   III

WISCONSIN-WHITEWATER ..... Whitewater, WI 53190
Bob Berezowitz (7 yrs., 44-25-4)

Upper Iowa ■	S10*	17	St. Francis (Ill.)	28
Wis.-Platteville	S19*	21	Wis.-Platteville	6
Wis.-Superior ■	S26	14	Wis.-Superior	16
Wis.-Stevens Point ■	O 3	10	Wis.-Stevens Point	16
Wis.-Stout	O10	21	Wis.-Stout	18
St. Ambrose	O17	27	St. Ambrose	29
Wis.-River Falls ■	O24	24	Wis.-River Falls	7
Wis.-Eau Claire	O31	26	Wis.-Eau Claire	6
Wis.-La Crosse ■	N 7	25	Wis.-La Crosse	14
Wis.-Oshkosh	N14	28	Wis.-Oshkosh	7

Colors: Purple & White.   Nickname: Warhawks.   III

WITTENBERG .... Springfield, OH 45501
Doug Neibhur (3 yrs., 16-13-0)

Baldwin-Wallace ■	S12	16	Baldwin-Wallace	45
Earlham	S19	39	Wooster	6
Wooster ■	S26	50	Oberlin	0
Case Reserve	O 3	22	Kenyon	0
Allegheny ■	O10	13	Case Reserve	14
Mercyhurst	O17	16	Allegheny	22
Kenyon	O24	29	Earlham	0
Oberlin ■	O31	17	Emory & Henry	35
Denison	N 7	21	Denison	7
Ohio Wesleyan ■	N14	6	Ohio Wesleyan	28

Colors: Red & White.   Nickname: Tigers.   III

WOFFORD .... Spartanburg, SC 29303
Mike Ayers (7 yrs., 40-37-1)

Elon	S 5*	21	Elon	14
Citadel	S12*	15	Citadel	12
Lenoir-Rhyne ■	S19*	13	Lenoir-Rhyne	9
Catawba	S26	22	Catawba	16
Presbyterian ■	O 3*	42	Presbyterian	24
Lees-McRae ■	O10	42	West Ga.	49
Newberry	O17	49	Newberry	6
Wingate ■	O24*	42	Winston-Salem	35
Winston-Salem ■	O31*	7	Jacksonville St.	51
Va. Military ■	N 7	42	New Haven	21
Bowie St. ■	N14	52	Cheyney	6

II Championship

	15	Mississippi Col.	28

Colors: Old Gold & Black.   Nickname: Terriers.   II

WOOSTER .... Wooster, OH 44691
Bob Tucker (7 yrs., 23-44-0)

Kalamazoo ■	S12	8	Mount Union	24
Allegheny ■	S19	6	Wittenberg	39
Wittenberg ■	S26	0	Ohio Wesleyan	58
Kenyon ■	O 3	23	Case Reserve	20
Oberlin	O10	6	Allegheny	34
Denison ■	O17	27	Oberlin	12
Ohio Wesleyan	O24	14	Carnegie Mellon	55
Earlham ■	O31	6	Kenyon	23
Wilmington (Ohio)	N 7	54	Earlham	20
Defiance	N14	20	Denison	21

Colors: Black & Old Gold.   Nickname: Fighting Scots.   III

■ Home games on each schedule.   *Night Games.

Divisions II and III 1992 Schedules and 1991 Results

WORCESTER POLYTECHNIC .... Worcester, MA 01609
Jack Siedlecki (4 yrs., 27-8-1)

Worcester St. ■	S11*	47	Worcester St.	0
Union (N.Y.) ■	S19	27	Union (N.Y.)	49
Mass.-Lowell ■	S26*	34	Coast Guard	46
Rensselaer	O 3	26	Rensselaer	14
Norwich	O10	33	Amherst	7
Merchant Marine	O17	35	Norwich	7
Randolph-Macon ■	O24	48	Bowdoin	14
Ursinus	O31	17	Rochester	0
Coast Guard ■	N 7	49	Bentley	15
Plymouth St.	N14	17	Buffalo St.	23

Colors: Crimson & Gray.   Nickname: Engineers.   III

WORCESTER STATE .... Worcester, MA 01602
Brien Cullen (7 yrs., 34-27-0)

Worcester Tech	S11*	0	Worcester Tech	47
Mass.-Dartmouth	S19	7	Mass.-Boston	18
Maine Maritime ■	S26	26	Curry	9
Mass.-Boston ■	O 3	15	Westfield St.	26
Fitchburg St. ■	O10	10	Fitchburg St.	9
Framingham St.	O17	22	Framingham St.	40
Westfield St. ■	O24	13	Bri'water (Mass.)	30
Bri'water (Mass.)	O31	14	Mass.-Dartmouth	55
Nichols ■	N 7	6	Mass. Maritime	42
Mass. Maritime ■	N14	6	Nichols	26

Colors: Royal Blue & Gold.   Nickname: Lancers.   III

■ Home games on each schedule.   *Night Games.